WEST AFRICA

An early confrontation between Europe and Africa: reception of the Rev. H. Townsend and Mrs Townsend, and the Rev. A. Mann, by Atiba, King of Yoruba, at Oyo (Ago Are), on September 28th, 1853. (From *The Church Missionary Intelligence*, Vol. VII, 1856.)

WEST AFRICA

W. B. MORGAN, M.A., Ph.D.
Reader in Geography, University of London King's College
(formerly of University College, Ibadan)

J. C. PUGH, M.A., Ph.D., A.R.I.C.S.
Professor of Geography, University of London King's College
(formerly of University College, Ibadan)

METHUEN & CO LTD
11 NEW FETTER LANE LONDON EC4

First published 1969
© *1969 W. B. Morgan and J. C. Pugh*
Printed in Great Britain by
Butler & Tanner Ltd, Frome and London

SBN 416 26900 1

Distributed in the U.S.A. by Barnes & Noble Inc.

Contents

Preface

Jean Brunhes has defined regional geography as the crown of geographical study, and this eminence has perhaps been attained by some of the regional monographs of the French school. Many English-speaking geographers would agree with Brunhes' definition, but the position of regional studies in the English-speaking schools is variable and anomalous. In some university departments they are largely neglected. In others they occupy a large part of the Honours syllabus, but frequently possessing a character which Brunhes might fail to recognize. It is perhaps not without significance that in the entries for the United Kingdom in the World Directory of Geographers, only three university teachers listed general regional studies among their interests, although individual countries or areas were frequently specified.

This position arises largely from the difficulties of presenting a regional study as an integrated whole. A few writers have achieved some measure of success in co-ordinating the various aspects of the subject by the use of some common theme or by literary *tour de force*. Mackinder's *Britain and the British Seas* is probably still the outstanding example of such work in English. A major difficulty is the great variety of data which has to be included. A certain degree of sorting and grouping of material is inevitable, particularly in the teaching of regional geography or in its presentation in text books. Influenced by a body of opinion which has been largely environmentalist, geographers have tended to present the necessary factual information in ordered succession under the headings of Geology, Geomorphology, Climatology, Biogeography, Population, Settlement, Production and Communications. Historical and Political Geography are sometimes added in the later stages. The approach has been sufficiently criticized by Stevens and Wooldridge[1], and Hartshorne has shown that there is no reason to assume that there should be any standard order of importance.[2] Material split under these headings and in the order described presents a considerable problem of reunification in order to relate human activities and distribution to the nature of the physical environment in the way claimed by many geographers to be essential in regional work.

Nevertheless, for the beginner this customary succession has the great advantage of elasticity, new material being inserted into the appropriate place without difficulty. This advantage compensates the disadvantage of, for example, the reiteration of the distribution of surfaces and slopes, already described under Geomorphology, in the later analysis of distribution of settlement or communications. Each chapter is capable of indefinite extension by the method aptly described by Professor Wooldridge as 'scissors and paste synthesis'. In attempting advanced studies the method fails signally, particularly in consideration of 'underdeveloped' territories for which material available under the different headings may show wide diversity in both quantity and quality. A writer is frequently faced with the alternative of chapters of equal length, but of widely differing degrees of detail, or of chapters which are of uniform style of treatment, but of very contrasted lengths. The adoption of either alternative inevitably results in the justifiable criticism of lack of balance. In addition the standardized treatment and repetition involved in the method tends to the production of books which may be valuable works of reference for factual information, but hinder geographers in the creation of great magistral regional studies equivalent to the historians' studies of periods. The net result tends to be the extension of the 'gazetteer' concept of regional geography from the school to the university level, and the suspicion, even among geographers, that specialization in regional studies is a refuge for the less enquiring mind. At the same time there is the realization that great regional studies must require at least a considerable familiarity with all the systematic branches of the subject, a task so formidable that the majority of geographers tend to confine their research to the systematic field, sometimes losing sight of the links that bind their own specialized work to the rest of the subject.

In presenting a regional study of West Africa the authors make no claim to the full knowledge of the subject which has just been declared so important. On the contrary, they have learned from their experience in the region that even in the systematic fields to which they have given particular attention the commonly accepted principles do not always satisfy observed conditions. This book may perhaps be said to have originated from realization of a lack of knowledge which has stimulated the search for a way of presenting the West African milieu in a manner more satisfactory than the orthodox method described, and of attempting a balanced presentation despite the inequalities in the available material. Moreover, they make no claim to present a synthesis, accepting the view of Stevens that synthesis and true integration can never be performed by the geographer, but only by chemists and mathematicians – 'those who believe so have been carried away with a word and imagined it a thought'. Rather their task is to undertake analysis and to present the results of that analysis in a way in which something of the relationships of the features shown may be appreciated. One cannot satisfactorily relate all place features within the frame of a common purpose or link them all to a common theme. A choice must be made and a theme taken in order to determine that choice. Here the theme is man's occupation and development of the region, so that this study is concerned essentially with human geography. Yet physical geography is not neglected, for the attempt has been made to ascertain and describe those physical features which are relevant to man's activities. In part the work is a study of physical features as they are appreciated by West Africans themselves.

Clark maintained that one ought to begin one's studies in human geography by seeking to understand something of the 'furniture of men's minds'.[3] In West Africa this is particularly true. A feature of fundamental importance in understanding geographical relationships in the region is the emphasis which the people place on kinship, rather than on land, in the definition of the community. Before the 'Scramble for Africa' in the late 19th century, with its attendant introduction of European concepts of land tenure and of states with fixed frontiers, the major part of the continent was divided among tribal communities who in many cases had no clearly demarcated boundaries to the areas which they occupied, and possessed a high degree of mobility. This mobility had its counterpart in shifting agriculture, limited architectural achievement and, with certain exceptions, most of which occurred in West Africa, a lack of large towns or cities. The importance of understanding the nature of tribal communities in any study demonstrating the relationship of man to his physical environment suggests a method of geographical enquiry which might use the areas occupied by such communities as a major element of study, and take as its basis the examination of man's use and organization of space. Here the approach has been adopted of studying firstly the distribution and activities of the African population and of their physical limitations, then of examining a number of regions developed by selected African communities, and finally of studying the changes introduced by Europeans and some of the new forms of regional organization. The method, it is hoped, will achieve a closer linkage between the various elements of the subject matter, and eliminate the hiatus between physical and human treatments. The landscapes studied and portrayed in the community region sketches will be seen as the product of the communities concerned, each within its physical environment. These landscapes and the regions themselves may be seen as changing features according to the expansion, contraction and migration of the communities concerned and the newer influences of contact with the non-African world. An historical outlook is therefore also essential to appreciate the processes involved, and to assess the geographical implications of culture contact.

Kinship is one feature of special interest in West Africa. Another is the existence of broad, comparatively level erosion surfaces, divided from one another in most cases by steep escarpments. The understanding of the nature of these surfaces is fundamental to the understanding of the distribution of the West African peoples and of their agricultural techniques. Here one must face the problems of their origin, and in doing so the authors submit a viewpoint with which many geographers disagree, but which appears to provide the only satisfactory explanation in West African conditions. The existence of an African school of geomorphology with its theory of pediplanation is in itself a sufficient commentary on the special circumstances involved. The wide erosion surfaces, in conjunction with climatic conditions peculiar to West Africa, have also led to the formation of lateritic crusts on a scale not seen elsewhere, and human distribution and activity cannot be considered without reference to their existence. Linking, as it were, men and the land are a number of different agricultural practices whose common denominator is the employment of long fallows, an annual burning of vegetation refuse, and the constant shifting of cultivation. There can also be demonstrated a relationship with the seasonal rhythm of West African climatic conditions and with the soils, cultivated plants and wild flora peculiar to the high temperatures and varied moisture supplies of the inter-tropics.

In pointing to these special features forming the keystones of West African geography one must, however, beware of the dangers of correlating them with inter-tropical conditions generally. For example, some observers have claimed a correlation between the existence of the great escarpments, erosion surfaces and inselberg topography of Africa and the distribution of the inter-tropical climatic régimes. An examination of the surface forms of Europe, however, reveals in many places features of striking similarity. Walther Penck has already demonstrated the existence of inselbergs in Central Europe, and pediplanation may yet be of suitable application to the study of erosion surfaces in western Britain. It must be remembered that present climatic conditions in the temperate regions of Europe are abnormal in relation to the conditions under which the major landforms were developed, and present precipitation patterns are not those which assisted the production of these major forms. Climatic conditions have varied in West Africa also, but to a lesser extent, and the region has not been greatly disturbed by the younger orogenies, factors which have permitted the wider development of erosion surfaces and inselberg landscapes. Such forms are regarded in terms of precipitation rather than in terms of temperature, and essentially similar physical processes may have operated in Europe and in West Africa. The difference between the landscapes of the two regions may be only in degree, producing larger and more obvious escarpments and pediplanes in Africa than in Europe. To take a second example, shifting cultivation in Africa has been described as 'less a device of barbarism than a concession to the character of a soil which needs long periods for recovery and regeneration'.[4] It may well be true that given certain tools and techniques shifting cultivation is an excellent adaptation to inter-tropical physical conditions, but it is conceivable that given other tools and techniques different methods of cultivation are possible. Shifting cultivation has not been unknown in temperate lands. It was the basis of Celtic agricultural practice for a long period in the eastern highlands of Britain. In seeking features of agricultural practice peculiar to the inter-tropics in general, and to West Africa in particular, one must look less to the fundamental technique and more to the forms which that technique takes, such as choice of cultivated plants, length of fallow period and nature of fallow cover. In comparing the agricultural practices of Europe and Africa one must view them not as contemporary static features, but as contrasting systems of changing techniques, whose actual changes and rates of change have to be compared. Without historical perspective all comparison is virtually useless.

West Africa, therefore, can hardly be described as being unique in any one particular feature, although those features which have already been described are outstanding, and condition the thinking of the West African geographer. What is peculiar to West Africa is its particular combination of geographical elements and prominence of certain of those elements within that combination. The authors do not suggest that they have entirely succeeded in their task. The book is in the nature of an experiment, and is subject to all the imperfections of such an experiment. It is nevertheless hoped that a greater measure of correlation has been achieved than would have been the case with a regional study along more orthodox lines, and that some of the inferences drawn and conclusions reached will be of interest to the student of West African geography.

BIBLIOGRAPHICAL NOTES

[1] A. Stevens, The Natural Geographical Region, Presidential address to Section E, British Association, 1939, reprinted in *Scottish Geographical Magazine*, 55, 1939, pp. 305–17.
S. W. Wooldridge, Reflections on Regional Geography in Teaching and Research, *Transactions and Papers of the Institute of British Geographers*, 16, 1950, pp. 1–11.
[2] R. Hartshorne, *Perspective on the Nature of Geography*, Chicago, 1959, p. 122.
[3] K. G. T. Clark, Certain Underpinnings of our Arguments in Human Geography, *Transactions and Papers of the Institute of British Geographers*, 16, 1950, pp. 15–22.
[4] Lord Hailey, *An African Survey*, 2nd ed., London, 1945, p. 1 (revised 1956).

Acknowledgments

The authors wish to pay their tribute to the outstanding studies of West Africa's geography made by Professor R. J. Harrison Church and Professor J. Richard-Molard. Harrison Church's 'West Africa' is treated from a different viewpoint, to which the present work is intended in some sense to provide a complement. In a text in which there are many references, not all the points on which guidance has been obtained from the above authors have been acknowledged. Accordingly we wish to offer our especial thanks for the invaluable instruction which their works have offered, and our thanks also to those specialists in related fields of West African research whose published contributions have provided essential material to our study, especially to Dr H. Vine (soil science), Dr J. M. Dalziel, Mr R. W. J. Keay, and Professors A. Chevalier, R. Portères and A. Aubréville (botany and agriculture).

The Authors and Publisher wish to express their thanks to the following for permission to reprint or modify material from copyright works:

Basil Blackwell Ltd for Figure 13.6 (from K. Baldwin, *The Niger Agricultural Project*); Directors of Survey of Ghana & Nigeria, and the Etat-Major de la Defense Nationale for the aerial photographs; Edward Arnold for Figure 1.5 (from J. D. Fage, *Atlas of African History*); Geographical Journal for Figures 1.11, 1.5, 7.3, 7.5 and 7.8 (Papers by W. B. Morgan); Institute of British Geographers for Figures 1.11, 1.17 and 9.1 (Papers by W. B. Morgan); Journal of Tropical Geography for Figure 2.10 (Paper by W. B. Morgan); Northwestern University Studies in Geography for Figure 11.7 (from P. Gould, *Transportation in Ghana*).

The authors also thank those members of the technical staff of King's College without whose assistance the maps and diagrams could not have been completed, namely, Mr C. R. Polglaze, Mr G. Adika, Mr J. Davie, Mr R. Cunnington, Mr G. Zalavary and Mrs C. Lawrence.

Introduction

West Africa is generally described as that area lying west of the plateaux and peaks of the Cameroons and Adamawa, and south of the Sahara, or as the combined area of the former British and French West Africa together with Portuguese Guinea, Liberia, the Cape Verde Islands, and the islands of Fernando Po, São Tomé and Príncipe and Annobon. These two very nearly coincident areas are accepted as 'West Africa' in the authoritative text by R. J. Harrison Church who describes this usage as 'based upon a real physical separateness'.[1] The authors accept the definition partly for convenience and partly because of certain distinctions which lend some unity to the region defined. Yet they must demonstrate that the division from the rest of Africa is by no means sharp, and whilst hitherto it has had a certain utility in terms of a colonial human geography, changing political conditions may eventually lead to the necessity of dividing western Africa in other ways for the purpose of regional study.

As a term 'West Africa' is a European invention intended to include all those areas linked with Western Europe by trade operating from ports south of the Sahara and west of the Cameroons. To the British this was 'The Coast' or the 'Guinea Coast' originally extending as far south as Angola. It was that portion of the tropical world nearest to Western Europe from which the great overseas empires and the exchange of manufactures for tropical raw materials were developed. The interior lands not linked by coastal traffic, but if anything trading across the Sahara, were part of 'Central Africa' and were so described by one of their 19th-century visitors from Europe, Heinrich Barth.[2] For the French there was also the notion of a 'coast', but more importantly of a Sudan forming, as it did for the Arabs and Berbers, the southern fringe of the Sahara and part of a greater North Africa. The British, German, Portuguese, Spanish and independent territories were enclaves in a French whole, although this concept has had some criticism.[3] The idea of a West African whole is comparatively recent and dates mainly from the federation of the French West African territories, and the British recognition of a regional affinity between the Gambia, Sierra Leone, Ghana and Nigeria. Spanish Guinea still includes territories both within and outside the unit, whilst the Southern Cameroons have become part of the Cameroon Republic of Central Africa. For the West Africans themselves there was no notion of such a regional unit, although it would be a mistake to suppose that until the colonial era their horizons were entirely tribal. Trading contacts and the creation of large states such as Mali or Yorubaland enabled people to visualize greater units even if these were sometimes seen in social rather than areal terms.

A large part of the Sahara is included in several of the political units which comprise West Africa. Although for statistical convenience such portions of the Sahara may be contained in some of the assessments in this work, the authors' concern is with the area to the south. Some Negro peoples have long been resident in Saharan oases, yet generally there is an excellent correspondence between the area dominantly occupied by Negroes and the lands of more continuous occupation where some rainfall occurs every year. Saharan conditions are controlled mainly by the high irregularity of precipitation with a complete lack in some years. Except where groundwater is available, migration is a necessity and migration patterns are subject to some variation from year to year. To the south, movements are much more regular, for even with high rainfall variability there is at least some rainfall in each year and a pasture may yield a little nourishment even in bad years. From the viewpoint of human migrants the dividing line between North Africa and Africa south of the Sahara, or between Afrique Blanche and Afrique Noire, lies somewhere between these extremes. The line is indefinite and may in fact be subject to change of location as rainfall conditions change. The use of a more definite line, for example the isohyet of 15 inches (381 mm.)[4] may suggest a precision which is unsupported by other evidence. Moreover, isopleths of annual normals are perhaps the least useful lines to adopt in seeking a relation between human and physical phenomena. Botanically there is no sharp line. The widely dispersed low bushes and tufted grasses of the Sahara, where they do occur, occasionally include trees of the Sahel savanna or 'wooded steppe' to the south. As Keay remarks of the vegetation zones shown in the map of Africa prepared by the Association pour l'Etude Taxonomique de la Flore d'Afrique Tropicale: 'The areas mapped as Subdesert Steppe normally merge imperceptibly into Wooded Steppe on one side and into Desert on the other; on both sides there is interdigitation with the adjoining types.'[5] Indeed, in several instances the boundary between 'derived savanna' or 'forest savanna mosaic' on the one hand and rain forest or 'moist forest at low and medium altitudes' on the other is much sharper, but in the latter instance human interference has been more marked.

The relief of West Africa is dominated by plains or surfaces from 500 to 1500 feet (150 to 460 metres) above sea-level. There are higher plains and peaks higher still, but these are isolated and total only a relatively small area. If one examines a map (Fig. 0.1) showing the land of Africa above and below 1500 feet (460 metres) above sea-level there appears a general division of Africa south of the Sahara into a higher portion in the east, south and centre, although including the Congo basin, and a lower portion with higher plateaux and ridges west of the Cameroons. The high plateaux of Adamawa and the Cameroons oriented from north-east to south-west appear to offer an obvious divide, reinforced when one examines the botanical distributions by the discovery that with their distinctive montane species and forms they provide a break in the east to west zonal pattern. Again, as Rosevear suggests, the Cameroons massif has usually been regarded as one of the western boundaries of Central African fauna although

Distribution of Relief in Africa

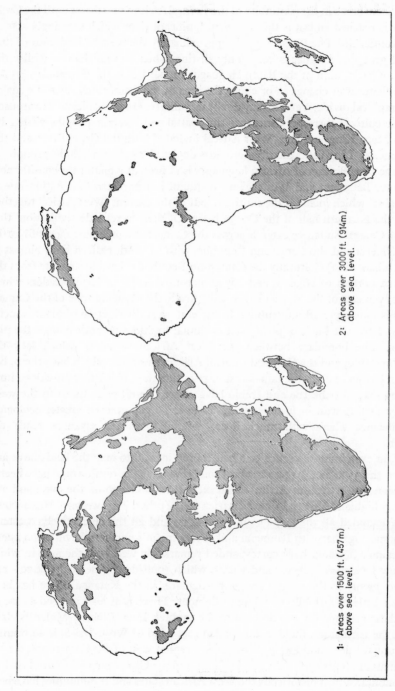

1: Areas over 1500 ft. (457 m.)
above sea level.

2: Areas over 3000 ft. (914 m.)
above sea level.

Figure 0.1

there is no break in the continuity of the Central African rain forest until the Cross River is reached and 'it is this rather insignificant river which seemingly acts as the frontier'.[6] The Cross River is approximately the western limit also of that small group of languages commonly distinguished as semi-Bantu, whilst the north-western limit of the Bantu languages proper lies in the Cameroons.[7] All these features of change in or about the area of the Cameroons suggest a major geographical divide. Yet one may doubt its validity. One's suspicions are aroused by the cultural correspondences of the coastal and riverain peoples visited by Miss Mary Kingsley. Her 'West Africa' included both the Cross River and the Ogooué.[8] Linguistic distributions are doubtful guides to ethnic groupings, and the classification of African languages is at present a matter for considerable dispute. Baumann and Westermann distinguish a northern 'civilisation ouest-africaine' which includes the southern half of the current 'West Africa' together with the northern half of the Congo basin. Of their 'cercles de civilisation' that of the Central Sudanese extends across the Cameroons, including most of Northern Nigeria and the Cameroun Republic, with its south-eastern limit almost at the Oubangui.[9] Culturally the Cameroun Republic is hard to separate from the eastern portion of Nigeria, and has numerous colonies of Hausa traders which exist even east of the Sanaga River. Botanically the montane zone of the Cameroons is only a partial interruption in the east–west distribution of plant associations. The same kinds of plant exist in similar locations on both sides of the plateaux. The boundary between the West African savannas, which lack the *Brachystegias*, and the East and Central African savannas, which have them, lies much farther east. In the rain-forest distribution the Cross River provides a limit set by man, for the Ibo and Ibibio have cleared an oil palm forest to the west, whilst farther west in Dahomey and Togo lies a gap of even greater ecological significance where with much lower rainfall totals the savannas reach the coast.

If, in examining the relief, one had chosen instead to map the land above and below the 3000 feet (915 metres) contour (Fig. 0.1) the result would have been a division into a western Africa which included the Congo on the one hand and a truly highland East and Central Africa on the other. This western Africa would have included all the major rain-forest areas and all the distinctively 'western' savannas together with Baumann and Westermann's northern 'civilisation ouest-africaine'. It would have corresponded remarkably well with the area in which yellow fever was endemic and within which (outside the Belgian Congo – and there mainly in the upland fringe, particularly in the Katanga) there has been only a little or virtually no white settlement. There is at least as good a case on all these grounds for one division as for another. Even Richard-Molard's claim that the harmattan, the dry, dust-laden east wind of West Africa, is an original feature[10] does nothing to distinguish a region west of the Cameroons, for the harmattan occurs also to the east in Chad, and the Cameroun and Central African Republics. Whilst historically the West African states and communities have been profoundly influenced by trans-Saharan contacts, so have the peoples to the east of Lake Chad, and contacts similar in character, although derived mainly from Arabia and north-east Africa, have influenced the peoples of the east coast. On a cultural basis, and perhaps on a botanic and crop distribution basis too, a western Africa, including much of the Congo and Chad basins, would perhaps be more satisfactory for study.[11] However, the political element is also of vital importance, not just for statistical convenience. Distinctive economic, political and social policies in the West African colonies led to separate patterns of development. One might on purely political grounds prefer to treat together all former French colonies, but this ignores the important locational element. French West Africa formed a federation distinct from the colony of French Equatorial Africa. Patterns of administration and economic development were similar, but contacts on the whole were few. The former British and Portuguese colonies and Liberia were in effect enclaves within the larger areal unit, having of locational necessity social and economic contacts. Much of the labour supply of the former Gold Coast came from French territory, whilst French Niger looked to export outlets via Nigeria. Again despite administrative differences many of the economic and social problems of the various territories have been similar or related. At present the colonial era is barely ended and thus the West Africa of current convention is the most convenient unit to adopt for study. As the newly independent states adopt new policies and alignments, however, the question of a satisfactory regional unit will have to be reconsidered. Almost certainly other boundaries will have to be chosen.

The West Africa of current convention has an area of over $2\frac{1}{2}$ million square miles ($6\frac{1}{2}$ million square kilometres) and a population probably in excess of 90 millions.* This gives an over-all density of at least 36 persons per square mile (14 per square kilometre) or an effective density, excluding the Sahara, of about 60 per square mile (23 per square kilometre). The peoples concerned existed in a vast number of groups or tribes until the colonial period, some politically well organized and others more social units with little or no administrative authority. The tribes and nations of former states still exist, but the peoples were regrouped towards the end of the last century and at the beginning of this into colonies and one nominally independent state. These colonies existed for approximately half a century and have led in turn to the existence of independent states with forms of government and economic organization not dissimilar from those of Europe. Social advance has been less rapid and many of the pre-colonial features survive. Indeed, in certain instances modern political organization conflicts with traditional social duties and ties. The colonies and one independent state which existed until the recent era of independence were:

FEDERATION OF FRENCH WEST AFRICA

Mauritania, Senegal, Soudan, Niger, Guinea, Ivory Coast, Dahomey, Upper Volta.

* 1964 estimate 96·1 millions, of which 59 per cent were in Nigeria.

TOGO (under separate French administration).

BRITISH WEST AFRICA

Gambia, Sierra Leone, Gold Coast (including British Togoland), Nigeria (including British Northern and Southern Cameroons).[12]

PORTUGUESE WEST AFRICA

Cape Verde Islands, Portuguese Guinea, São Tomé, Príncipe, The Fort of St John The Baptist at Ouidah.

SPANISH WEST AFRICA

Fernando Po, Annobon.

LIBERIA

Most peoples in West Africa depend on agriculture either directly or indirectly for their livelihood, the staples being grains (chiefly guinea corn, pennisetum, millets and rice), and roots (chiefly yams and cassava). The chief commodities exported which must help to pay the cost of economic development are also mainly agricultural, oil palm produce, cocoa, coffee, groundnuts and cotton. Manufactures are of very little importance for export trade, although there is a considerable production of hand-woven cloths and hand-made agricultural implements. Minerals are of some growing importance in overseas trade, but even in the major producing territories of Ghana, Liberia, Sierra Leone and Guinea they still provide a smaller share of national income than does agriculture. Internally fishing and pastoralism are more important than mining and make a vital contribution to diets which tend in several instances to depend over-much on starch foods. Yet agriculture, fishing and pastoralism all depend greatly on physical distributions. The West African may be said to be much closer to his physical environment than is, for example, the European or North American. He has undoubtedly learnt a long process of adaptation of tools and methods and has carefully selected seed. The very houses, built mainly of mud and, except in the case of the flat-roofed dwellings of the north, thatch roofed, seem to be part of the soil on which they stand. Frequently, as in the great African city of Kano, the borrow pits from which the building clay was abstracted are near to the houses themselves, and provide with their pools a local source of water for domestic washing in the dry season and a breeding ground for disease carrying insects. Yet this close affinity with the physical environment which is so apparent in West Africa should not lead one to suppose that adaptation to physical conditions is closer in West Africa than in those countries where the landscape appears more ordered. The greater importance of the subsistence element in the economy of West Africa, and the restriction of trade, with the high cost of transport over vast distances, have encouraged the local cultivation of as great a variety of crops as possible. Cotton may, for example, be grown where yields are low in marginal conditions solely because the lint produced is more cheaply acquired than that bought from importers. In countries with more highly developed marketing and transport systems the trend is towards fewer crops locally, towards those best suited to local conditions, costing least to produce in consequence. Thus except where subsidies or tariffs conflict, sometimes for the purpose of achieving a more balanced productivity, cropping in the economically more developed countries may appear more closely 'adapted' to the physical environment than in West Africa. Again, although cultivators have adapted their techniques with great care, the distribution of the tribes and other social groups in West Africa does not appear to correspond with physical distributions. The area occupied by a given West African community may contain a great variety of physical conditions and the community itself may be composed of cultivators employing many different techniques and growing different combinations of crops. In the Yoruba lands of south-western Nigeria the contrast between the cultivation of the northern and western savannas, consisting mainly of open grassland interspersed by shea trees, *Lophira*, *Daniellia* and oil palms, and that of the southern forests with grass restricted mainly to roadside verges, is immense. The fallows differ both in character and length. Lengths of growing season differ, and the savanna crop combination of yams, guinea corn and egusi melon may be contrasted with a forest combination of maize, yams and cassava. Several of the crops are grown in both the forest and grassland areas, but their relative importance in these respective zones may differ. The relations between man and physical environment in West Africa are apt to be much more complex than casual observation or reading make apparent. The 'tribe' is frequently not a tightly knit social and economic unit, and the method used by some authorities of plotting crops, agricultural techniques, house types and village farms by 'tribes' may produce very misleading results.

West Africa forms a compact mass 2200 miles (3500 kilometres) in length by 1200 miles (1900 kilometres) in width. Dakar and Victoria in the Cameroons are as far apart as London and Stalingrad or New York and Salt Lake City. Despite its European appellation of 'The Coast' this mass appears to be mainly continental in character for the coast is on the whole smooth and has few satisfactory harbours. Many ports are merely open roadsteads where even now the passenger must be landed by mammy-chair and surf canoe or the goods off-loaded by lighters. For long the approximate northern half of West Africa had contacts with the non-African world only across the Sahara. Not until the new ports built by Europeans extended their hinterlands by means of railways did the northern portions of West Africa look to the south rather than to the commercial and religious units of northern Africa.

Except in the south-east of this landmass in Southern Nigeria, in the north-east in Hausaland, and in the west in the Fouta Djallon, population densities are low as elsewhere in Africa. Locally here and there they may be quite high within each community nucleus. Even today, despite the great commercial and social changes, the tribal units surrounded by their 'no-man's lands' or zones of relatively low density are evident in the population pattern. Thus virtual islands of population are spread across this great mass, with between them huge gaps of low density and therefore low productivity. It has been suggested that these 'gaps' were the product of poor soils since it was assumed that with a close adaptation to physical environment population distribution in West Africa reflected the relation between man, mainly an agriculturalist, and the physical conditions. Study of West Africa's history and of changing agricultural techniques invalidates this notion. The 'gaps' have meant great distances between producing centres, and low tonnages and low passenger frequency per mile of railway or road route. Thus Richard-Molard concluded that the coastlands were the best endowed economically.[13] In the 19th century trade was especially limited since it could penetrate inland on a large scale only by the rivers, and the great concentrations of population with the chief markets lay away from river valleys. Only in the east and in the central coastlands have there been sufficient continuities of high population density to enable overland transport routes to be created in a dense network.

The sub-continental mass of West Africa consists for the most part of vast plains at low and medium altitudes. In a few cases at the medium altitudes of 1500 to 2000 feet (460 to 610 metres) above sea-level and in the plains across the upland remnants or larger inselbergs at 3000 to 4000 feet (915 to 1220 metres) remarkably level surfaces are apparent with broad, shallow valleys whose rivers flood considerable areas each year. Other surfaces or plains, particularly at the lower altitudes below 1500 feet (460 metres) have been greatly incised by their streams which have cut deep steep-sided, generally convex-sided valleys. The forms of youthful erosion thus appear at the lower rather than the higher altitudes. Streams may descend from older to more youthful valleys in appearance making their passage between these stages by 'gates' where escarpments or their equivalent in the form of heavily dissected hill zones divide one stage from another. The 'gates' with their rapids, water-falls and gorge-like cross profiles present the most youthful erosion forms of all. For man the isolation of distances is thus emphasized by the physical isolation of one plain or plateau level from another, by the difficulties of surmounting escarpment steps and of navigation where river courses are so frequently interrupted. Upon the plains the island mountains appear not only as considerable isolated plateaux of which the largest are in the Fouta Djallon in the west and in the Jos Plateau of Nigeria in the east, but in the countless rounded summits of bare rock usually of granite, exfoliated, showing the cracks of the joint planes, and supporting sometimes a small clump of apparently inaccessible trees. These, the 'bornhardts' of Africa, provided natural fortresses for peoples engaged in local wars and feuds in a land where the greatest trade until about 1870 was in slaves. At their base the springs of the pediments provided water which had to be carried to summit stores, but which today normally supply a pediment village which has replaced the decayed or even disappeared summit fortress.

The great central mass of West Africa and much of northern and south-western Nigeria consist essentially of crystalline metamorphic and igneous rocks, chiefly schists and gneiss together with granite intrusives, and exhibit residual features such as bornhardts together with boulder-capped knolls and quartzite ridges in great abundance. Yet some of the highest peaks occur on the softer metamorphics, particularly where these are capped by relatively resistant 'laterites' or ironstone crusts. The highest point in the west is Bintimani (6376 feet or 1943 metres) in the Loma Mountains of Sierra Leone. The highest peak in West Africa is the great volcano of Mount Cameroon in the extreme south-east with a summit at 13,350 feet (4069 metres), the only point in the region on which occasional falls of snow occur. Between and around the crystalline or basement complex zone are sediments, chiefly primary sandstones and Cretaceous sands and limestones. The erosion of these sediments has produced cuestas particularly within the Fouta Djallon, and in south-eastern Nigeria, whilst where the primary sandstones are level, huge steep-sided plateaux have been formed. The porous rocks frequently present rather arid surfaces, particularly during the dry season. The population of the great plateau of Bandiagara is thus confined mainly to the flanks where compact villages hug steep cliffs on their perches immediately above the pediment. Tectonic movements have produced huge basins particularly in the north in the central portions of the Senegal and Niger valleys and in the great Chad depression. Thus the Sahara is separated generally by a zone of depression from the better watered highlands to the south. In the south-east a huge tectonically depressed zone includes the basins of the Benue and Lower Niger and the Lama-Hollis depression of Togo and Dahomey. It is thus possible to discern major anticlinal and synclinal axes which have been of the greatest importance in the formation of the present pattern of rock exposures and relief.

Almost all of West Africa lies between 5° and 20° N. The winter of temperate latitudes is in consequence unknown and low temperatures are no longer a significant factor in plant growth. Wherever water is available growth may continue all the year round and some plants show bud, flower and fruit at the same time. Climate has been described as the most important factor in West African life.[14] Perhaps the most striking features to the visitor from temperate Europe or North America are apt by contrast to be those associated with climate. Certainly one may admit that both agriculture and pastoralism, the present bases of the West African economy, depend in their distributions on climatic limits and particularly on those limits associated with humidity and moisture supply. Extremely high temperatures in the sun may affect growth, particularly of very young plants, and a common practice amongst cultivators is to provide shade for seedlings. High air temperatures, especially when associated with high relative humidity, may bring physiological discomfort, and it is customary to avoid working during the hottest part of the day. Yet it is the distribution of rainfall in both quantity and incidence which above all else has been used as a criterion for distinguishing climatic regions or zones arranged in east to west belts. Perhaps because the botanists have been able to advance their work in West Africa more rapidly than have the climatologists, there has been a tendency amongst the latter and amongst geographers to adopt the botanic terms to describe their climatic regions, and even to take vegetation regions as climatic and thus easily deduce a relationship between the two. Broadly locational terms such as Sahel, Sudan and Guinea have been adopted by botanists, climatologists and geographers, and used in a variety of senses. The authors propose with some modification to follow the system of Richard-Molard.[15] They wish to recognize five main climatic divisions, adopting moisture supply and particularly the length of growing season for crop plants as the main criterion:

1) Saharan with rainfall only in some years;
2) Sahelian with rainfall in every year, but with a rainy season of less than $2\frac{1}{2}$ months on average so that in most years crop plants cannot be grown without irrigation;
3) Sudanic with one rainy season of $2\frac{1}{2}$ to 7 months;
4) Guinean with two rainy seasons totalling approximately 7 to 12 months.[16]

The locational terms may thus be used to define a system of rainfall regions, but a system which has been considered in relation to agriculture. One may develop this system further by adding:

5) West Guinean with one rainy season generally of 7 to 9 months. By considering other elements of importance one may subdivide regions 3) and 4) into:
3a) Sudanic proper with one rainy season of approximately $2\frac{1}{2}$ to 5 months and generally free from tsetse fly;
3b) Sub-Sudanic with one rainy season of approximately 5 to 7 months and with a high incidence of tsetse fly making cattle raising very difficult especially in the rainy season;
4a) Sub-Guinean with two rainy seasons totalling approximately 7 to 9 months and with a high incidence of grass fallows;
4b) Guinean proper with two rainy seasons totalling approximately 9 to 12 months, air of high relative humidity throughout most of the dry season, and woody fallows.

This system is highly generalized and may suffer some local criticism, but it provides a useful means or ordering some of the features, especially the climatic, which are directly important to man in West Africa. The terms defined above are used from time to time in the book and provide a locational frame of reference. The proposals for such a scheme are similar in principle to those of Phillips for a more detailed bio-climatic system.[17]

A remarkable feature of the dry season in West Africa is its extreme dryness in the regions outside the Guinean zone proper. The harmattan air which occurs

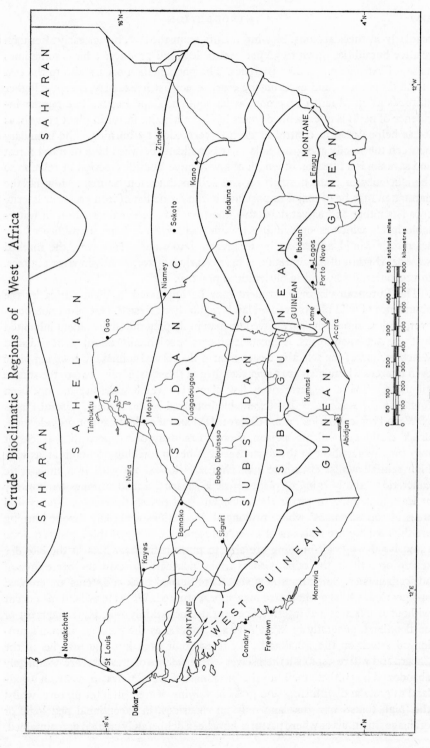

Crude Bioclimatic Regions of West Africa

Figure 0.2

regularly in these regions, blowing mainly from the east, brings early afternoon relative humidities down to 30 per cent or less, and produces a haze, sometimes a fog, of extremely fine dust particles. The phenomenon occurs also to the east of the Cameroons, and even on the coast somewhat irregularly, except at higher altitudes as on Mount Cameroon, as far south as Cape Lopez. The regular incidence of periods of extreme dryness has been a major factor in plant growth, as it has helped man to control or destroy vegetation by burning. The boundary between the woody and grass fallows or botanically between high or moist forest and savanna is a function of length of low relative humidity period in relation to the efficiency of plant destruction and soil modification by man. How far the harmattan may be of major importance in the formation of iron crusts or laterite caps is another and as yet debatable question. The seasonal variation in water-table levels which is only indirectly affected by the relative humidity of dry season air would appear to be of greater importance. However, the marked seasonal rhythm of precipitation is here clearly a factor, as it is in river régimes, in vegetation forms and in agricultural practice.

The European visitor or student may be impressed in West Africa by the abundance of wild plants even on lands regularly cultivated. One must not, however, underestimate the part played by man in shaping the environment inhabited by these self-sown forms. A constant process of soil modification, plant and seed selection, and of the selective destruction of the related animal life is taking place even in areas where men are fewer than five to the square mile (two to the square kilometre). There are, moreover, few plants for which some use has not been found, as the student of that invaluable botanical guide, Dalziel, 'Useful Plants of West Tropical Africa', must discover,[18] and if a plant cannot provide food, drink, clothing, medicine, poison, timber, ornament or weapons then at least it may provide fertilizer in the form of ash. If heavy leaching occurs in areas with high rainfall whilst elsewhere phosphorus is locked up with iron in lateritic concretions, the burning of plant refuse in clearing a field supplies temporarily at least something to repair the phosphate and potash deficiency. The typical trees of the 'savannas' where prolonged dry periods especially favour burning are thus mainly fire resistant or even 'pyrophilous'. Some of these plants despite extensive damage by burning are able to put out fresh suckers in the late dry season or early in the rains. Others have thick bark to resist the fierce fires of adjacent grasses. Sometimes new shoots are burned back and stems are crooked and gnarled, whilst a whole tree may appear stunted. Whilst grassland may occur without man's seasonal interference on extremely thinly soiled lateritic crust or on floodland, generally in West Africa it appears as the product of man's prolonged attack on the woodlands, for trees occur even into the margins of the Sahara and will re-establish themselves where patches of grassland are completely abandoned by cultivators. Thus the 'savannas' of West Africa are as much woodland as grassland with trees and grass in varying degrees in intermixture, whilst the 'high forest' has grassland only on roadsides, in exceptional pedologic or drainage situations or where pastures have been deliberately created or maintained.

As with the vegetation, so with the soils. The east to west zoning is still marked, with strong climatic and botanic influences. Leaching becomes more intense as rainfall increases, and high acidity is a feature of most soils in the Guinean zone, even in better drained sandy horizons. The accumulation of mineral salts, particularly of iron and to some extent of aluminium, appears to have occurred throughout the region, although the mineralized crusts of the Sahel and Sahara may be fossils. In the extreme cases, normally on comparatively level sites, an impervious crust is formed, commonly with only a thin soil horizon or no soil at all. Here agricultural conditions are at about their worst in West Africa. Two major phenomena are the occurrence throughout much of the Sahelian and Sudanic zones of extensive superficial deposits of wind-blown sand, usually in the form of dead dunes, and the occurrence in the wetter areas, on comparatively level surfaces on crystalline rocks, of clays. Relief brings its catenary variations with hill-top clays alongside slope gravels as does drainage with the 'firki' clays of ill-drained depressions and the 'tannes' or saline alluvial soils of estuaries.

The people of West Africa seen in relation to the physical environment of their region may provide one theme in this study of a place, but this relation has been changing rapidly in some localities during the last half century due to the economic, social and political revolution generated by contacts with the outside world and the temporary establishment of colonialism. Colonial contact with all that has implied in the changing use of land and the changing character of places must provide another. The contrast between the older African environments and the newer 'Europeanized' or 'Neo-African' environments is immediately apparent. These newer environments may be seen as distinct regions increasing in size at the expense of the older regions, incorporating some of the older elements and rejecting others, so that in many places our clues to the nature of the traditional African environment as it existed perhaps as late as 1880 are few and even distorted; whilst in others conditions have even now hardly changed, at least in certain major features such as agricultural techniques and housing. The handful of Europeans, at most never more than 100,000, and of Syrians or Lebanese totalling some 20,000, have introduced the means to a revolution which seems out of all proportion to their numbers, and which has extended in the form of new plants, new buildings, roads and transport, new forms of exchange, foodstuffs, clothing, domestic goods of all kinds, new social relations and forms of government throughout most of West Africa. Its effect has been to produce new social groupings and new states whose governments are eager to proceed as rapidly as possible with economic development. New powers have been created which may become of major political force within the next decade and which already, through such agencies as the United Nations, have some influence in world affairs. For the peoples of West Africa the disappearance of colonialism has meant emancipation. Yet it is that era of colonialism which marks the ending of many traditional African forms of economic, social and political development, and which therefore must also be appreciated for the understanding of the present-day geography of West Africa.

BIBLIOGRAPHICAL NOTES

[1] R. J. Harrison Church, *West Africa*, London, 5th ed., 1966, p. xxv.

[2] Heinrich Barth, *Travels and Discoveries in North and Central Africa*, 5 vols, London, 1857–58.

[3] J. Richard-Molard, *Afrique Occidentale Française*, Paris, 3rd ed., 1956, p. xiii.

[4] L. D. Stamp, *Africa, a Study in Tropical Development*, New York, 2nd ed., 1964, p. 270.

[5] R. W. J. Keay, *Explanatory Notes*, Vegetation Map of Africa South of the Tropic of Cancer, published on behalf of L'Association pour l'Etude Taxonomique de la Flore d'Afrique Tropicale with the assistance of UNESCO by the Oxford University Press, London, 1959, p. 10.

[6] D. R. Rosevear, *Checklist and Atlas of Nigerian Mammals*, Lagos, 1953, p. 36.

[7] H. Baumann and D. Westermann, *Les Peuples et les Civilisations de l'Afrique*, French translation by L. Homburger, Paris, 1957, map following p. 439 and pp. 449–71.
J. Greenberg, Studies in African Linguistic Classification, *Southwestern Journal of Anthropology*, **5**, 1949, and **6**, 1950.

[8] Mary Kingsley, *West African Studies*, London, 1899, and *Travels in West Africa*, London, 1900.

[9] H. Baumann and D. Westermann, op. cit., pp. 55–57, map opp. p. 88, and pp. 307–330.

[10] J. Richard-Molard, op. cit., p. 15.
'Il y a lieu de s'étonner de ce que ce souffle de l'est n'ait qu'exceptionnellement été reconnu comme l'un des traits les plus originaux de l'Afrique occidentale, l'un des plus décisifs. On ne comprendrait guère par exemple la répartition des croûtes ferrugineuses, la distribution des paysages végétaux et par conséquent la plupart des faits humains et même économiques sans l'*harmattan*.'

[11] A recent study of food and crops in Africa uses this 'Western Africa' region. See B. F. Johnston, *Staple Food Crops in West Africa and the Congo*, Stanford, 1956.

[12] References to West Africa before the secession of the Southern Cameroons from Nigeria in 1961 include the Southern Cameroons. References to the period after secession exclude them.

[13] J. Richard-Molard, op. cit., p. xiii.

[14] ibid., p. 26.
'Nul trait physique, en Afrique occidentale n'a une influence plus décisive que le climat sur la vie. Pasteurs ou agriculteurs, la presque totalité des hommes y sont paysans. Leur existence, leur civilisation sont directement liées au régime des pluies et à la terre.'

[15] ibid., pp. 14–26.

[16] The botanical use of the term 'Guinean' or 'Guinea' to describe the southern portions of the savannas is avoided except in quotation.

[17] J. Phillips, *Agriculture and Ecology in Africa*, London, 1959.

[18] J. M. Dalziel, *The Useful Plants of West Tropical Africa*, London, 1937, being an appendix to the *Flora of West Tropical Africa* by J. Hutchinson and J. M. Dalziel, 2 vols, London, 1927–48 (revised 1954–63).

PART ONE

PART ONE

CHAPTER I

The Peoples of West Africa

In dealing with man's role in developing the character of West Africa, it has been found desirable to study both the social and the demographic aspects together. Hence a study of peoples in which population is discussed as one aspect of the whole. No demographic account of West Africa can, in any case, be satisfactory if it fails to discuss the societies to which its statistical units belong, and which therefore directly affect the distributions studied. In West Africa the distribution of communities is as important a concept in geographic study as the distribution of people, for it is only within the framework of the community, of which they are a part, that the distribution and actions of the people can be studied. The distributions in West Africa of people and communities, and of people within the communities, are exceedingly varied and complex when studied in detail. Admittedly the broad outline appears simple and some valid generalizations can be made. The dangers of generalizing without the examination of detail, and of easy acceptance of certain apparent correlations between human and physical distributions are, however, great. The problems of population density and distribution in the Fouta Djallon expounded by the eminent French authority Richard-Molard should serve as a sufficient warning, for there it is the poor lands which are occupied by astonishingly high population densities even though the population must depend for its living on the soil.[1]

This study will begin with a discussion of the sources of information followed by general accounts first of population distribution and then of the communities. These will be followed by detailed discussion of distributions within the communities and finally by accounts of population movements, age structure, sex ratios and discussion of demographic problems and the various social and physical factors.

The sources of information available to demographers in West Africa

Before discussing West African population some account must be given of the sources of information, in order to show how little can be described and how much must be guessed. The first West African population census was taken in the Colony of Sierra Leone in 1802. Seven more censuses were made up to 1831, and from 1832 to 1851 a census was taken in nearly every year. These early attempts were prompted by the fear that the liberated Africans, who formed a large part of the colony's population, might be kidnapped and re-enslaved.[2] In most British West African territories decennial 'censuses' took place from 1871, but in most cases counts were restricted to only a few areas and the remainder of each 'census' consisted of estimates, based usually on tax returns. Thus counts were attempted in the Gambia Colony in 1851 and every ten years from 1871 to 1931, but the Protectorate was not included until 1901. In the Protectorate of Sierra Leone 'censuses' were made in 1901 and 1911, by estimating in the former case and counting in the latter case the number of houses, and multiplying by an 'average' number of occupants per house.[3] In Ghana the 1931 census was claimed to be the first in which the entire population was individually counted; 'either by enumerators who counted and recorded village populations on a form or by means of forms delivered to house-holders in which the head of the household or occupier inserted particulars of each individual'.[4] Earlier methods had included counting by heads of families who placed in a bowl a cowrie for each female or a grain of corn for each male member of the family.[5] The 1921 census included Togoland and the 1911 census was the first to include the Northern Territories. In the Colony the first count was that of 1891. In Nigeria the earliest count took place in Lagos in 1866. The first census of the whole country took place in 1921. In former French West Africa no census proper was ever taken of the majority of the African population. Europeans, 'assimilés' and urban populations were counted, but the African figures outside urban areas were mainly estimated. There was a quinquennial census ('recensement') of the non-native ('non-autochtone') population, but with regard to the native population there was only a 'dénombrement administratif' by cantons every four years, and a 'recapitulation générale' by subdivisions every five years.[6]

The population figures used as the basis for study are those issued by the Governments of the various territories concerned as referring to the following years:

Nigeria:
Northern Region	.	.	1952
Western Region	.	.	1952–3
Eastern Region	.	.	1953

Portuguese Guinea	.	.	1956
Former French West Africa	.	1956
(including Guinea)		
Togo	.	.	.	1956
Sierra Leone	.	.	1960
Ghana	.	.	.	1960
Gambia	.	.	.	1961

There have been some more recent estimates or censuses in some of the territories concerned, for example in Senegal in 1961, and in Nigeria in 1962 and 1963. At the time of completing the manuscript, however, the detailed break-down of these censuses was not available.

In the comparisons made between territories therefore up to nine years difference may be involved. The Ghana and Nigeria censuses make greater claims to accuracy than do the others, which admit to being mainly evaluations or estimates. In the Nigeria census, the greater part of the African population figures were returned on forms which included the name of the head of the household only, together with the number, sex, age, marital condition, tribe and religion of those who 'sleep' there, including 'hunters and farmers in the "bush"', but not 'sons and daughters and other relatives who are away (temporarily or permanently) with friends or relatives elsewhere in the town or village, or in a distant village'. Clearly the enumerator could not count all the persons in one household but had to rely on information given to him. In the Ghana census, too, the enumerators depended on the cooperation of heads of households. Such information could be falsified by misunderstanding or by the desire to evade taxation or by the desire of some heads of households or chiefs of districts to appear more important than was in fact the case. In the Northern Region of Nigeria the census was taken in May, July and August, before the movement of population from about the end of September. District counts lasted generally from 4 to 14 days. It was commented that '. . . most believed that the count must be more than 95% accurate' except in Ilorin Province where the 'undercount' may have amounted to more than 10,000 with half a million people recorded. Probably many of the Cattle Fulani were missed also. In the Western Region several 'unknown' villages were discovered, 'several houses in Ibadan and Ijebu-Ode were reported to be locked up throughout the census week although they were visited several times', there was opposition in one division and in others rivalry between villages which may have led to overcounting. The Western Region census took place in December and January at the height of the cocoa season, thus including seasonal immigrants already counted in the Northern Region census. The Eastern Region census took place in April and June, the period when most people are on their 'farms' – and probably the most suitable time for a count in the non-cocoa growing areas of the Western Region. In the Degema Division of the Eastern Region, the total was more than three times the previous estimate, and the figures were 'adjusted' after a recount of about half the Division. Nevertheless the claim was made for the Region that 'in total the figures are correct within 3%'.[7]

Further study of censuses elsewhere in West Africa reveals similar situations and possibilities for error. It seems from the evidence that the 1952–3 census of Nigeria may have been under the actual totals by a considerable margin. On the whole under- rather than over-counting appears to be the likeliest result, and with improvement in the efficiency with which the censuses are taken the errors should be smaller in the more recent censuses than in those of the past. In consequence figures for increase in population produced by comparison of two censuses are probably over-estimates and the true increase is likely to be less. Comparison of this sort rests on such an unsatisfactory basis that its value must be very doubtful. Trewartha and Zelinsky point out that 'large probable margins of error' exist in all African population counts which are generally on the side of under-enumeration and which are sufficient to 'mask' any discontinuity introduced into population maps by using material varying in publication date by as much as a decade.[8]

Information acquired in the censuses on age, occupation and tribe appear to be of very doubtful value. With regard to age, for example, it was apparently assumed by census officers that infants in Ghana in 1948 were physically more advanced than those of Nigeria in 1952–3. The Ghana instructions to enumerators in 1948 classified 'babies who cannot walk as less than one year old, and those who can, as one year but less than 16'. The Nigeria instructions stated: '*Under 2 years of age*. Where the age of the infant is not known it may be assumed that most unweaned babies and toddlers not yet walking firmly are in this age-group.' Another instruction concerning methods of discovering ages was as follows: 'In order to arrive at the ages of these last two groups (15–49 and 50 years of age and over) you must, in cases where the age is not known, try and relate their age to prominent events in your area.' The occupational problem is enormous since many people in West Africa combine two quite different sorts of occupation, e.g. cultivation and trading, and it becomes extremely difficult to decide which is the more important. Moreover, many, for the purpose of tax-evasion, prefer to be known in the humbler of any two capacities. With regard to 'tribe' the concept can, unfortunately, mean many different things. It can be confused with language, as is undoubtedly the case with the vast number of 'Hausas' recorded in Northern Nigeria. It might mean to the people enumerated 'family group', 'clan', 'people of a particular district', or 'people recognizing a common authority'. Many have undoubtedly tended to claim affinity with the local majority 'tribal group' in order to 'belong' to the district.

The most remarkable attempt to achieve accuracy has so far been the 1960 census of Ghana in which the country was divided into 6882 enumeration areas, all very much smaller than the divisions previously used, and 6,726,815 people were counted. Immediately following the main census a 5 per cent post-enumeration survey was conducted to assess the accuracy of the main census and collect additional information. The enumeration areas were also used as the basis of an industrial census in 1962 and an agricultural census in 1963.[9]

In former French West Africa many useful studies were made by intensive sample censuses. In Guinea these have been purely demographic, but in the Ivory Coast and Senegal social and economic information has also been sought. Such sample censuses, well conducted, offer the possibility of more accurate results for a few areas, which would serve as useful indicators of demographic, social and economic conditions and trends.

The picture to be drawn of population in West Africa clearly rests on uncertain statistical foundations. All comments made from figures are subject to the possibility of error in the enumeration. In consequence, the figures are not used as fully as would be those supplied by more reliable censuses. Except in certain cases, chiefly in urban areas, detailed analysis cannot be attempted. In many

Cercles and Administrative Divisions

Figure I.I

Population Distribution by Cercles and Divisions

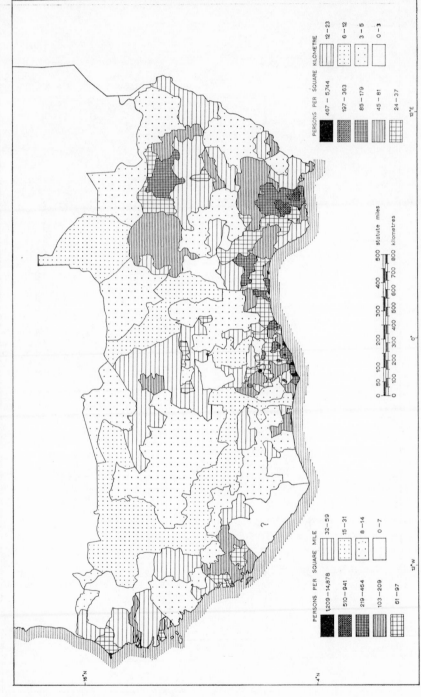

Figure I.2

cases approximate or 'round' numbers will be used in order to avoid giving the reader a false impression of accuracy.

The method of plotting West Africa's population distribution

Even a cursory examination of the distribution of West Africa's population indicates the existence of great concentrations of population, in islands of high population density, separated by extensive areas of very much lower density. In order to distinguish some of these in a population map (Fig. 1.2) showing densities by the smallest administrative divisions, the figures have been analysed by ranking and an attempt has been made to discover the appropriate points of division between high and low densities by seeking breaks in the rank order. The results of analysis are as follows:

Group	Density range per square mile	per square kilometre	Number of items
1	1209–14878	467–5744	10
2	510– 941	197– 363	12
3	219– 464	85– 179	35
4	103– 209	40– 81	49
5	61– 97	24– 37	42
6	32– 59	12– 23	59
7	15– 31	6– 12	40
8	8– 14	3– 5	41
9	0– 7	0– 3	22

An interesting feature is that the breaks in the ranking and between the density ranges given are approximately at 1000, 500, 210, 100, 60, 30, 15 and 7 (or 386, 193, 81, 39, 23, 12, 6, 3 in metric units), and very nearly in geometrical ratio.

The distribution of West Africa's population

More than half the area included politically in West Africa is desert and belongs geographically to the Sahara. The remaining area stretching southwards from the northern limits of the Sahel has, with few exceptions, a minimum density of 3 persons per square mile (1 per sq km) (group 9, with only a few items each large in area, overlaps) and averages approximately 60 per square mile (23 per sq km). This average is much higher than that of most other parts of inter-tropical Africa and reflects the greater agricultural productivity of West Africa. Some portions of West Africa are crowded by inter-tropical African standards and may be compared with densely populated areas in south-east Asia. In several of the Ibo and Ibibio districts in the south-east, for example, district densities, i.e. densities of areas smaller than the divisions and cercles used in Figure 1.2, are well over 1000 per square mile (386 per sq km) amongst communities who have no other local resource than their crops.

Figure 1.2 shows that the greater part of West Africa south of the Sahara has cercle or division densities of between 15 and 59 per square mile (6–23 per sq km) (groups 6 and 7). The area thus defined corresponds remarkably with the areas of cereal cultivation (Fig. 2.1, p. 74) and is interrupted by a number of 'islands' of higher or lower density groups. In the north is a vast area with 7 or less per square mile (3 per sq km) corresponding well with the area of nomadic pastoralism, where rainfall is too irregular for cultivation. In the south and south-east are various density groups mostly of 61 or more per square mile (24 per sq km) corresponding to the areas of root crop cultivation. The broad outline is clearly related to the agricultural basis and through agriculture to the environ-mental pattern, but there are several exceptions, and moreover there is clearly a distinction between groups 2, 3, 4 and 5 within the root crop economy. There are numerous factors affecting the densities which can be supported by cereals and roots. The most important is undoubtedly returns per acre, for roots produce approximately 10 times the weight of food per unit area produced by cereals. The agricultural factor in population densities will be discussed further during this chapter, but for a detailed survey of carrying capacity of the land, the reader is referred to the end of Chapter 2, Agriculture (pp. 125–8).

The marked east–west alignment characteristic of West African population distribution is apparent in Figure 1.2 and even more marked in Figure 1.3 where the method of presentation makes possible a more detailed picture. Two major factors produce this trend – the physical environment, through the marked dependence of the population on agriculture, and the space relationships of external trade. With certain remarkable exceptions the alignments of comparable conditions of moisture supply and of the secondary vegetation types characteristic of the greater part of West Africa are also east–west. With regard to external trade, the traditional markets for exchange with North Africa lay along the Saharan fringe in the Sahel and Sudan whilst the present markets for overseas traffic are along the coast. Whilst many northern centres have declined due to the disap-pearance of the trans-Saharan trade, some have flourished and others developed due to the construction of roads and railways to the coast and the growth of a traffic in groundnuts and cotton. In the south the Guinean environments provide favourable conditions for a traffic in the products of perennial plants, particularly oil palms and cocoa, in heavy demand overseas. The trade in these products has provided a means of increasing agricultural productivity in the areas affected. Before this development, there were few markets in West Africa to encourage the production of more than a very small surplus above the amount needed for sub-sistence. Thus the Sudanic and Guinean areas have become attractive to settle-ment. A further attraction lies in their possibilities for a higher production for subsistence than that of other areas, or for an equivalent production with less effort due to more favourable physical conditions. In the Sudanic areas, cattle keeping is possible and a symbiosis between pastoralists and cultivators makes manure available for the soil. In the Guinean areas a rainy season of nine months or more makes possible the cultivation of heavy yielding root crops or the double cropping of quick-growing plants. Here it must be admitted that the high forest was difficult to clear, particularly at its most luxuriant on the heavier soils.

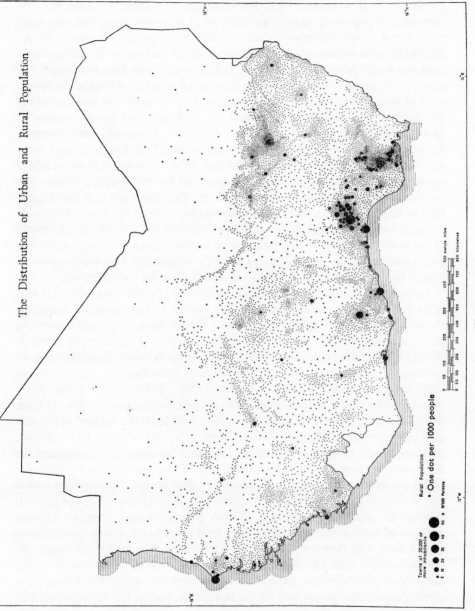

The Distribution of Urban and Rural Population

Towns of 20,000 or
more inhabitants

● ● ● ● ● ●
2 10 20 40 60 90

Rural Population
● One dot per 1000 people

'000 Persons

0   50 100   200   300   400   500 statute miles
0 50 100   200   300   400   500   600   700   800 kilometres

Figure 1.3

In some cases the more important 19th-century settlement concentrations appeared rather in the sub-Guinean fringe, and from there, people migrated into the forests as they became more attractive due to trading developments, the cultivation of perennials and the introduction of superior cutting tools. An additional factor in the migration to the Guinean areas has been warfare and the destruction of many sub-Guinean and sub-Sudanic settlements by attack, chiefly from the north. Many of the refugees looked to the more heavily forested districts for the greater protection which they could afford by impeding the movement of attacking forces, particularly cavalry. Lower population densities in the sub-Sudanic and sub-Guinean areas have been ascribed to the process of 'bowalization', that is to the formation of ironstone crusts and other forms of 'lateritic concretion' which have been judged infertile.[10] Whilst there are areas of ironstone crust difficult or even almost impossible to cultivate, there are others supporting dense populations, e.g. the canton of Labé in Fouta Djallon. The problems of the areas between the Sudanic and Guinean zones (e.g. the 'Middle Belt' of Nigeria) are complex and need discussion in detail for they differ greatly between one part and another. A common factor is the widespread occurrence of tsetse-fly hindering or preventing stock rearing in many areas, without the compensation, in the sub-Sudanic zone, of a sufficiently long rainy season to permit double cropping or the cultivation of the heavier yielding roots.

An important feature of the general distribution of population in West Africa is the contrast between east and west. The eastern half of the region, including the present territories of Nigeria, Ghana, Upper Volta, Togo and Dahomey, includes most of the great population concentrations and supports two-thirds of West Africa's total population. The dividing zone between these two areas of contrasting population distribution is aligned approximately from north to south in the longitude of Abidjan in the Ivory Coast. In the south this zone corresponds to one of the broadest areas of heavily forested country in West Africa, that of the eastern Ivory Coast. In the centre it includes the 'trough' of remarkably low rainfall extending northwards from central Ivory Coast. In the north a dividing zone is only apparent further eastwards between the Songhay and the Hausa-speaking peoples at the northern end of the Atacora Range where the Niger ceases to be navigable and is incised in deep gorges. The dividing zone is not, therefore, continuous, nor is it suggested that it contains any major physical barriers to population movement. Rather it is a meeting point of different cultures of eastern and western origins. In the north, the Hausa culturally are linked more with Bornu and the Nile basin peoples than with the Songhay and Malinké of the west. The western peoples have looked to the floodlands for the support of their densest population concentrations, whilst the Hausa have developed cultivation not only in the floodlands, but on the rainlands of their great plateau east of the Niger and Sokoto valleys. In the south the divide separates the peoples of the West Atlantic culture dependent mainly on the cultivation of rice, from those of the East Atlantic culture dependent mainly on the cultivation of yams.[11] In the centre, the Mossi- and Akan-speaking peoples have cultural contacts both with the north-west and the east. Possibly they represent a western limit of the cultures which tend to support higher densities of population – a limit which it may be possible to move further westwards. The lower population densities of the western 'Middle Belt' seem to be the result of social and political rather than physical conditions.[12] Similar factors appear to have affected the south-western portion of the Ivory Coast where some of the most primitive methods of cultivation in West Africa still exist and where many peoples are still largely dependent on the products of hunting and gathering. West Africa's population pattern is still in a state of change. Even in many cases where agricultural techniques have remained unaltered for long periods, the maximum population densities have not apparently been reached. Urvoy claims that without improving agricultural methods almost the whole of the Sudan could support 130 per square mile (50 per sq km). Harrison Church remarks: 'Population distribution is not, as in Europe, the result of long trial and error over many centuries by advanced peoples, in each type of environment. Tradition is stronger in West Africa than in most temperate regions. Attachment to the soil, even in poor areas, and dislike of nearby fertile but non-traditional areas, are important factors.'[13] West Africa's traditions and techniques vary from people to people. Population density problems can only be studied therefore by studying the communities of people in West Africa and understanding something of the differences which exist between them.

The concept of 'population density groups' expressed in Figure 1.2 tends to obscure the considerable local variation in density and the existence of a number of relatively dense nuclei which exist in the most favoured portion of each of the areas occupied by a distinct community. There is some suggestion of local variation and the existence of nuclei in the few 'island groups' in Figure 1.3. These are from west to east:

1) In the north:
   the Serer and Wolof, the Mossi, the Hausa.
2) In the centre:
   the Kabrai of Togoland, the peoples of the Jos Plateau.
3) In the south:
   the Yoruba and Ibo of south-western and south-eastern Nigeria respectively ('islands' within denser concentrations than the above).

'Islands' of local variation within the group densities or of high density over an area too small to be apparent in the divisions and cercles used in Figure 1.2 are apparent in Figure 1.3. The West African population map is clearly a patchwork of small nuclei. In this pattern, a varying combination of physical and social factors is at work. Firstly it has until recently been a common practice for a no-man's land or zone of less densely occupied forest or 'bush' to be left between any two communities, e.g. between the Yoruba and the Bini, or the Nupe and the Gwari, or the waste areas surrounding the Balante of Portuguese Guinea and the Bousansi of the Upper Volta.[14] Secondly, many communities have tended to expand as a shortage of land due to overcrowding has occurred in their original centre, e.g. the Tiv (see pp. 323–8). Thirdly some communities have been able to support high densities in their nuclei by drawing on the labour resources and even the crops of their neighbours. Thus the Hausa, particularly those of the southernmost state of Zaria, enslaved their neighbours and reduced the populations of surrounding districts. Several communities have been forced to reduce their area of occupation, due to attack, and thus have high local densities, e.g. the Serer and Mossi under pressure from the Wolof and Manding respectively.[15] Local variations in relief, soils and water resources are important in the location of high density nuclei. A dense population needs high local agricultural productivity. Level or almost level land is preferred together with light easily tilled but productive soils and a supply of drinking water satisfactory throughout the whole year. A marked feature of much of West Africa is the occurrence of level land on plateaux or hill-tops. There are few broad open valleys except towards the sources of major streams, and chiefly in the north. Floodland concentrations of population are few in West Africa and only two are apparent in Figure 1.3, both northern – the Senegal and middle Niger valleys. In consequence many of the major concentrations of population in West Africa occur on plateaux or hill-tops, that is, on erosion surfaces and their dissected remnants, as opposed to the valleyward concentrations common in, for example, Europe. This feature is of great importance in the present development of West Africa's productivity. Local high relief has often provided good defensive sites, e.g. the cliffs of Bandiagara, the rocky outcrops of Yorubaland, or the Atacora range of Dahomey, and West African valleys are frequently narrow, of convex profile and subject to malaria. The settlements of the Ewe provide a notable exception, occurring mainly in comparatively broad valleys in south-eastern Ghana and southern Togo.[16] Whilst heavy soils may be densely occupied today, as for example the clays of portions of the Ghana and Nigeria cocoa belts, they were not so occupied in the recent past. Only the introduction of commercial perennials like cocoa, giving best results on such soils, has made them attractive to settlement. The soils of south-eastern Nigeria have been described as 'of low fertility',[17] and yet these light soils derived from sedimentary rocks are capable of producing 5 tons of root crops per acre (12 tons per hectare) of land cropped and were early attractive to settlement. Today they are occupied by, though they do not entirely support, the densest population concentrations in West Africa. The drinking water factor has been of great importance in limiting agricultural distributions. Shortage of water in the dry season has prevented the permanent occupation of portions of the Ferlo of Senegal where cultivation is possible during the rains. Dry season water-deficiency and low-population densities also occur in the Volta basin and the Oti sandstone plateau of Togo. In these areas occur density groups of 14 or less per square mile (5 per sq km) (Fig. 1.2) comparable with pastoral districts. Even here, water shortage for part of the year is not the sole explanation, for the areas are in the 'Middle Belt' of warfare and slave-raiding and lie between powerful states.

A final feature of the population maps is that they show distributions resulting from and affected not only by traditional practice, but modern developments. The first portion of this book is concerned with traditional practice. In consequence, the remainder of this chapter will be concerned mainly with the older features of African societies and techniques, although not entirely, for in many cases separation of the old and new becomes impossible so closely are they linked. Recent changes in population distribution, contributing to the features shown in Figures 1.2 and 1.3, will be discussed in the second portion of the book in Chapter 9.

The communities of West Africa

West Africa's population is divided into a vast number of groups whose members recognize some common social bond or link. The distribution of these social groups or communities is indicated in Figure 1.4. The boundaries shown are necessarily generalized, and not all the divisions are as clear cut as the maps would suggest. Information for the map comes from a large number of sources and varies greatly in classification and content. Grounds for the definition of the communities vary, and in some cases, but not in others, the communities shown are subdivisions of larger groups. Figure 1.4 provides therefore no more than an indication of the distributions and a useful guide for the location of many of the communities named in the text.

The communities may be sub-divided into 'states' and 'tribes'. The states consist of groups of people, in many cases of diverse ethnic origins, over whom a common government has been established and which rules normally through local chiefs or which draws tribute from a number of subject peoples. The systems of government have some small resemblance to those of the mediaeval feudal states of West Europe. The distribution of communities with common government authority in each is shown in Figure 1.5, where it may be seen that there are two groups: the Sudanic in the north and the East Atlantic in the south corresponding broadly with the densest population concentrations and the most favourable physical conditions. The 'tribes' consist of any groups of people who feel that they have a common link whether it be cultural, political, economic or linguistic or a combination of any or all of these. Some of the tribes so defined have a common head, e.g. the Jukun of the Benue valley, usually with little practical authority. Others have no traditional head, e.g. the Ibo of south-eastern Nigeria, and are formed by a loose collection of groups usually with a common language and similar social organization. A tribe, however, is capable of absorbing within it other groups who are permitted to settle within the tribal area, or groups added by intermarriage or conquest. Some tribes are so small as to be collections merely of kinsfolk, others consist of peoples of extremely varied origins. 'Les termes d'état, peuple, nation aussi bien que ceux de tribu et clan, ont des significations précises qui ne correspondent pas, sauf exceptions, aux réalités ouest-africaines actuelles. En fait le groupe ethnique se définit par un faisceau très hétérogène de facteurs tenant des races, des langues, des religions, de

Distribution of Communities

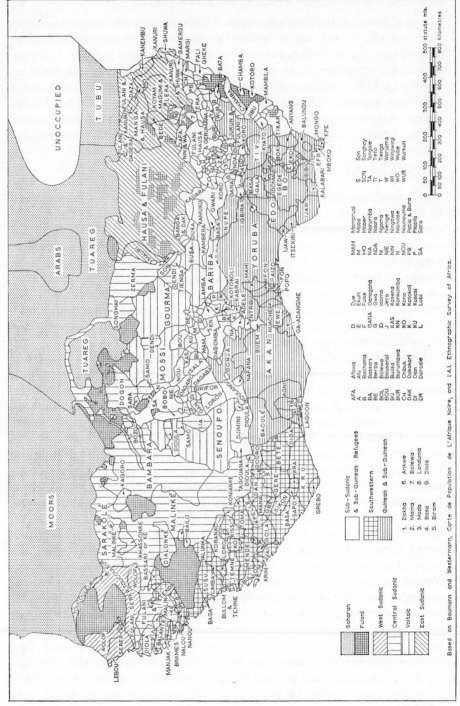

Based on Baumann and Westermann, Carte de Population de L'Afrique Noire, and I.A.I. Ethnographic Survey of Africa.

Figure I.4

l'histoire, des coutumes, des modes architecturales, vestimentaires, artistiques, du genre de vie, du régime alimentaire; ou de quelques-uns seulement de ces éléments et point des mêmes d'un groupe à l'autre.'[18]

There have been several attempts to classify West Africa's communities, of which the most notable have been the ethnic and linguistic classifications of Baumann and Westermann[19] and the linguistic classification of Greenberg.[20] None of these is satisfactory for geographic purposes and the method used in Figure 1.4 is based on the 'geographic' classification of J. Richard-Molard[21] in which recognition is made not only of social but also of economic and physical factors.

1. SAHARAN

The Saharan peoples, although living for the most part outside West Africa, are important to consider owing to their influence on neighbouring West African peoples by intermarriage, warfare and trade. There are three major groups: Moors in the west, Tuareg in the centre and Toubou in the east. Each of these is sub-divided into tribal communities not delimited on the map. All three groups are for the most part nomadic herdsmen formerly of great importance in their role as trans-Saharan traders, carriers, or 'protectors' of caravans. Both the Moors and the Tuareg have established 'empires' for a time in the lands of the middle Niger basin.[22]

The Moors consist mainly of a mixture of Arab and Berber peoples and call themselves Beidan, that is 'whites'. Their society is divided into castes. Below the noble warrior caste are the 'harratin' or freedmen and the 'abid' or slaves, all of whom are Negroes. Many of these live in fixed oasis settlements where they are occupied as cultivators and the remainder act as herdsmen. An important group of Moors who are neither cultivators nor nomads are the 'marabout' religious teachers and traders who travel as far south as the Ivory Coast and form small colonies in the south-western ports and in the larger inland trading and administrative centres such as Bamako in Mali. The 'marabout' or 'Almoravid' movement began in the 11th century and led to the formation of a fanatical religious group who established an empire in north-west Africa and Spain by 1102. The northern or Saharan Moors such as the Tormoz are true nomads, but the southerners live in a more humid environment, keep few camels, and, like the Fulani to the south, migrate only over small areas.[23] Moorish herds are bred and raised for meat, sale or as pack animals, and not as formerly in the case of the Fulani as an end in themselves. Dwellings consist of straw huts for slaves and tents, double (one inside the other) in the rains, and single (a cotton sheet spread over arched branches) in the dry season. A few mud and stone dwellings exist in the older settlements.

The Tuareg are pastoral Berber peoples who still speak a Berber language, Tamashek, and who probably established themselves in the uplands of Adrar des Iforas and Aïr and on the fringes of the Niger valley by the 7th century A.D.

Some Ancient West African States and Empires and their Nuclei

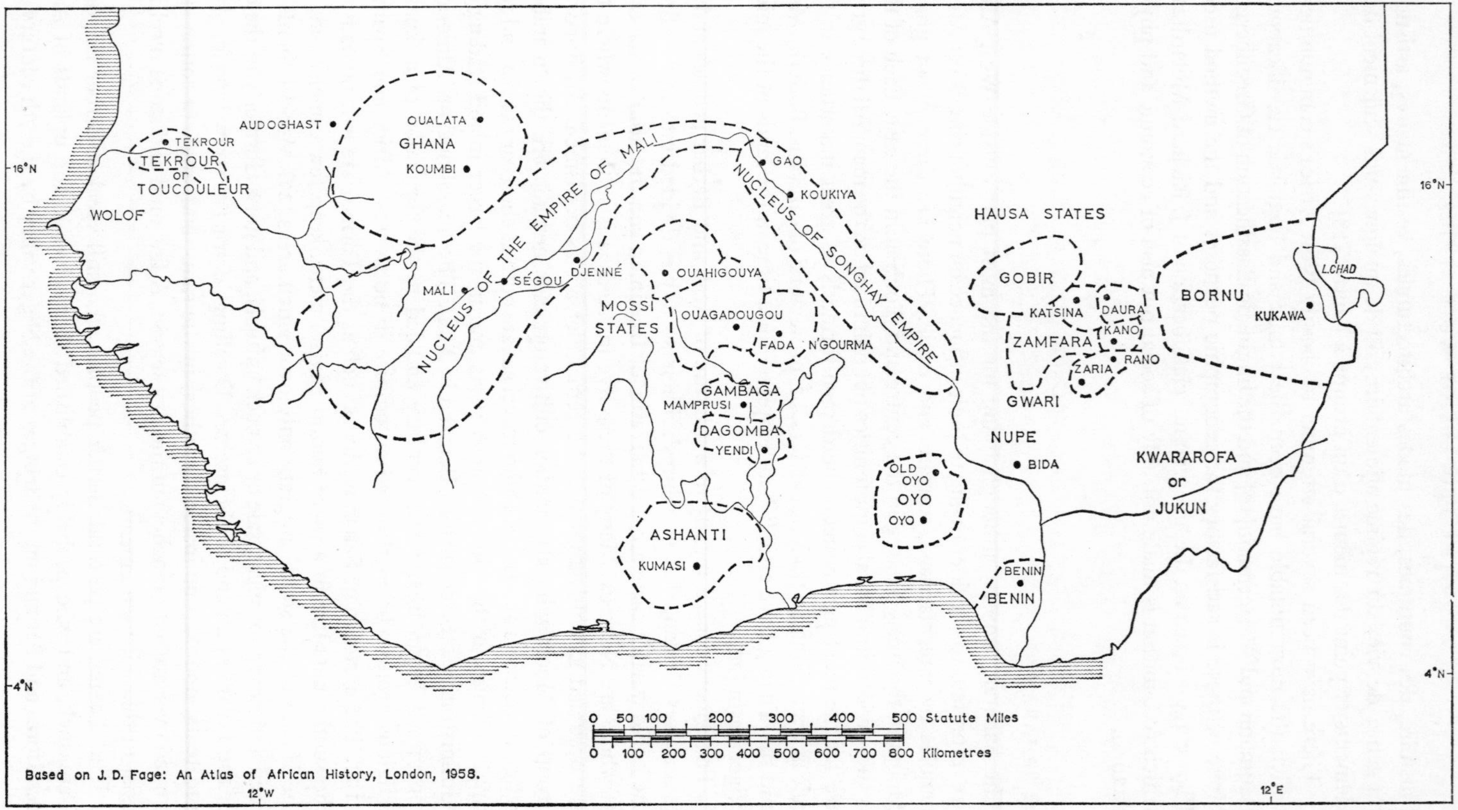

Figure 1.5

Based on J. D. Fage: An Atlas of African History, London, 1958.

Tuareg groups founded the 'Hausa' state of Gobir, and others intermixed with Negroes established the first Songhay empire in the Niger valley by the 11th century. A group of mixed Tuareg and Negro or mixed Kushite and Negro origin appears to have been the 'Zaghawa' pastoralists who influenced the development of the Bornu and Hausa states and whose name according to Palmer may remain in 'Sokoto', that is Sagwa-tu or Zaghawa-tu.[24] The Tuareg are also divided into castes:

the 'imajeghan' or nobles, that is, Tuareg proper;
the 'imrad' or vassals,
the 'irawellen' ('bella') or slaves and artisans.

The last two groups are of mixed or pure Negro origin. Outside the mud dwellings of the towns, the Tuareg live in skin tents or in hemispheric shelters made of mats.

The Toubou live on the eastern fringes of the Aïr massif and in the plains stretching northwards from Lake Chad to the Fezzan. Their northern groups, the Teda, occupy Tibesti and the Bilma oasis, a noted salt-producing centre. Their southern groups, the Daza, occupy portions of Kanem and Bornu. The Toubou are of mixed Negro and possibly Berber origin. In their few fixed settlements they occupy stone houses or caves. Temporary settlements consist of hemispheric shelters of branches and leaves, or rectangular box-shaped structures of mats.

2. FULANI (PEUL OR FULBE)

The Fulani are a Negro people speaking a language classified by Greenberg as of the 'West Atlantic' division of the Sudanic group (including Serer and Wolof) and occupied traditionally chiefly in nomadic and semi-nomadic pastoralism in the Sahel and Sudan. Some Fulani no longer speak the Fulani language, e.g. the Ouassoulounké of Guinea, the Khassonké of Mali and the Silmissé of Upper Volta, and probably three-quarters are of serf or slave origin, that is, absorbed from other communities. Labouret suggests that the Fulani may be of Ethiopian origin.[25] A common view is that they are of white origin and became negroid by intermixture. It seems, however, possible that even if such intermixing had taken place the main ethnic elements can still be of Negro origin as Greenberg suggests for the language. Fulani society may be divided into the nomads or cattle keepers (the 'bororoji' or 'mbororo') of the Sahel; the part nomad and part sedentary groups some of whom are independent, notably in the Fouta Djallon and northern Nigeria, whilst others live near Negro villages in the Sudan where they act as herdsmen; and the sedentary Fulani of the former Fulani states and of non-Fulani states, such as those of the Hausa, where they form aristocracies. Settled Fulani recognize a division into castes of which the lower groups are of Negro slave origin. Nomad Fulani are divided into tribes and dwell in hemispheric or box-shaped huts made of straw or branches with a thorn fence to

Areas formerly under Fulani Rule or Fulani Influence

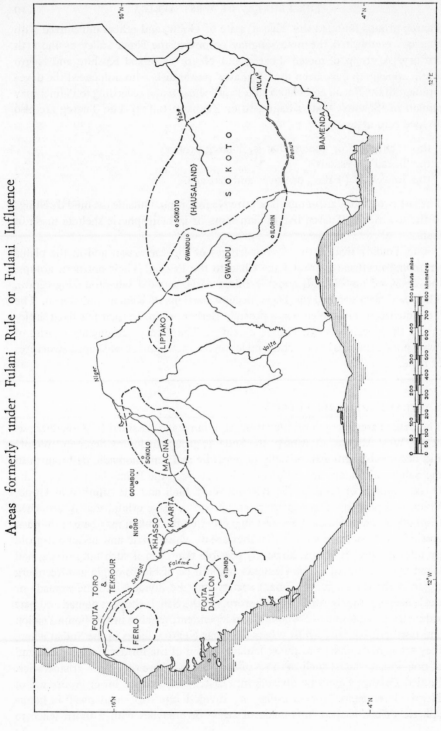

Figure 1.6

protect their cattle. The pastoral Fulani live for their cattle and seek to obtain as large herds as possible. They form nomadic groups of 10–20 households, usually possessing a permanent wet season settlement and occupied by those too old or otherwise unfit for migration. During migration only temporary conical shelters of straw are erected. About the 5th or 6th centuries A.D., the Fulani appear to have been settled in the present territory of Senegal where they founded the state of Fouta Toro, whilst a group, probably of mixed Fulani and Negro origin, founded the riverain state of Tekrour (Toucouleur). Possibly Berber attacks or a struggle between Fouta Toro and Tekrour resulted in emigration to the districts of the Ferlo, the lower Falémé, Khasso, Diomboko, Kaniaga, Kaarta and the Fouta Djallon. In the 13th century a few small groups moved as far east as Bornu. In the 15th century further migration took place, and settlements were made in Sokolo and Macina, between Goumbou and Nioro, and in Hausaland. By the 17th century Macina had become an important state, and a new Fulani state, Liptako, had been founded further east. During the period from the 11th to the 17th century the Fulani spread over the whole of the Sahel and Sudan. The Fulani tradition was anti-Islamic until the conversion of many of the leaders in the 18th century, resulting in the development of Islamic states in the Fouta Djallon and Fouta Toro and the 'holy war' proclaimed in 1804, which led to the establishment of Muslim Fulani aristocracies in Macina, Hausaland and most of the area enclosed by the great northward bend of the Niger, and from Hausaland as far south as the Ilorin Yoruba and as far east as Adamawa.

3. SAHELO-SUDANIC

The Negro peoples and peoples of mixed Negro, Berber and Arab origin of the Sahel and Sudan are mainly agriculturalists, some of whom keep animals or own them and leave them to the care of Fulani herders. Most of these peoples at the time of the establishment of the French and British colonial empires lived in states rather than in tribal groups. Of these states, the most notable have been:

1) Ghana or Auker, in the interfluve between the Senegal and Niger, 8th–13th centuries. The state had several capitals built mainly of stone (large pieces of schist cemented together with mud) but apparently unwalled, one of which was on the site of Koumbi Saleh and another on the site of Settah.[26] The founders of Ghana were probably the Sarakolé, Negroes of the central Sahelo-Sudanic group who include Berbers in their ancestry ('Sara-kolé' = 'white man'). The state was at the Sahelian end of the westernmost trade route across the Sahara and flourished on the export of gold from the Falémé basin, and ivory and slaves from surrounding districts, to Morocco or Barbary. The capital was the earliest recorded 'twin' town in West Africa, that is it consisted of two neighbouring towns, one Muslim and the trading centre, the other pagan and the residence of the ruler. To the northwest on the site of Tegdaoust lay Audoghast, an Arabo-Berber colonial foundation on the route to Ghana.

2) Mali, in the middle Niger basin, 13th–17th centuries. Mali was founded by Manding peoples who completed the final destruction of Ghana in 1240 and constructed an alternative market at Birou, or Oualata. The first capital was Jeriba on the Niger above the inland delta. Later the capital was moved downstream to Mali on the present site of Niani. The empire of Mali at its greatest extent included Ghana, the gold-producing area of the Falémé basin, the inland Niger delta plus the districts round the great emporia of Djenné and Timbuktu, and the Songhay section of the Niger valley as far south as Borgu.

3) Songhay, in the Niger basin below the inland delta, 9th–11th centuries and 15th–16th centuries. The first Songhay state developed by the conquest of the Niger basin below Timbuktu and the control of the central caravan route across the Sahara. The state was conquered by Mali, but later reasserted its independence, and subjugated the inland delta region and Timbuktu. An important feature in the establishment of power in the Songhay and other empires was the control of the salt traffic from Teghaza and Taotek and the copper production of Takedda, besides the import of cloths, metal and glass ware from the Maghreb. The traditional capital of Songhay was Gao or Koukou, consisting of two towns on the banks of the Niger. That on the west bank was occupied by the rulers, whilst the town on the east bank was Muslim and the chief market. In the 16th century Gao was recorded as having 7626 houses, and, like the capitals of Ghana, appears to have been without walls.[27]

4) The Hausa states, on the watershed between the Chad and Niger basins, 12th–19th centuries. Hausaland consists not of one state, but of seven. Of these Gobir lay to the west and included the basin of the Sokoto river and the adjoining pastoral lands, whilst Daura (the oldest), Kano, Zegzeg or Zaria, Katsina, Biram and Rano, lay to the east on the high plateau forming the watershed. Gobir was more pastoral and under Berber influence – the 'warrior' state – the others depended on agriculture and looked more to Negro influence. Kano and Katsina vied with one another as the chief market centres for the trans-Saharan trade, and the latter, in the 18th century, was renowned throughout the Sudan as a centre of learning. Zaria became the chief slave raiding state. Portions of Hausaland were conquered by the Songhay in the 16th century, by the Kwararofa or Jukun and by Bornu in the 17th. In the 19th century the traditional rulers were replaced by the Fulani dynasties. Each state had a capital city traditionally walled. Possibly, since several of the older towns of the western empires were unwalled, this tradition derives from influences from the Nile valley.

5) Bornu, in the Chad basin. The first state established in the Chad basin was that of Kanem founded east of Lake Chad on lands occupied by the Sao negro peoples by a group called the Magumi, of Zaghawa origin, in the 9th century. Islam was introduced from Egypt in the 11th century. By the 13th century an empire had been established stretching from the Niger to the Nile, and from

Fezzan to Adamawa. In the 14th century the Magumi and their followers were driven out of Kanem by a related group, the Bulala. A new Magumi state was founded in Bornu west of Lake Chad, and the capital of N'gazargamu (possibly Ksar Magumi, Ksar being a common word in the Sahara for a town or fortress) built in the valley of the Komadugu Yobe river. The Fulani sacked N'gazargamu in 1808 and the capital was moved to Birni Kafela, Ngornu and finally (1815), under a new dynasty from Kanem, to Kuka or Kukawa. The adventurer Rabeh, from the Nile Sudan, conquered Bornu in 1893 and established yet another capital at Dikwa. Kukawa was visited by Barth in 1853 and he described it as consisting of two towns, Kuka Futebe and Kuka Gedibe. The great market place lay outside the former, and the chief authority lay in the latter.[28] Much of Bornu's importance was in its position at the southern end of a caravan route leading across the Sahara to Tripoli, and in its control of the salt traffic (chiefly in the form of natron) from the Bilma oasis.

6) States of Moroccan origin. In the 14th century, the Dawi Hassan, a group of Moroccan Arabs, established themselves in Adrar and by the 16th century extended their conquests as far south as the Senegal river. They formed a warrior aristocracy and introduced Islam and Arabic customs and language to many peoples in Mauritania and the Hodh.

In the 16th century an army of Moroccan and Spanish origin invaded the Sahel and took Timbuktu in 1591, extending Moroccan power throughout the middle Niger valley in the course of the following century. The state which was created survived until 1770, when it was destroyed by Tuareg invaders.

The Sahelo-Sudanic communities of the present day may be divided into the Western (Serer, Tekrour or Toucouleur and Wolof), Central (Manding, Sara-kolé and Songhay), Voltaic (Mossi) and Eastern (Hausa and Kanuri). The Serer, Tekrour and Wolof have caste systems and were once grouped in petty states of which the chief were Cayor and Baol. The chief occupation is agriculture, but some cattle are kept, notably amongst the Serer. Settlement occurs by family groups occupying compounds consisting chiefly of rectangular huts. These appear to be a comparatively recent introduction for it is claimed amongst the Wolof that the original type of hut was round.[29] The Tekrour have structures of arched branches, straw and mats, similar to those of the Fulani.

The Manding form a large ethnic and linguistic group occupying the inland Niger delta and Upper Niger basin. They are divided into the Malinké to the west and in the Upper basin, the Bambara to the east and in the inland delta, and the Dioula who live in communities scattered widely throughout the western half of West Africa. The Malinké and Bambara are the inheritors of one of the oldest systems of cultivation in West Africa, and from their original Niger valley centres have tended to spread chiefly to the west and south-west. Thus other peoples have been forced towards the coast or absorbed, but in the process have, in many cases, adopted Malinké customs and Malinké rice cultivation. The Dioula are the traders of western West Africa occupying a position comparable to that of the Hausa in the east. Traditionally the Malinké settlement unit consisted of the large compound containing a number of round huts with conical roofs, whilst amongst the Bambara and Dioula the flat-roofed terrace house prevailed. At present a mixture of the two types is more common. Related groups include the Dogon or Habé, who live in terrace houses at the foot of the great escarpments of Bandiagara and Hombori, on sites chosen partly for their defensive value and partly for the abundance of local water supply, the Bozo who are fishermen on the Niger and Bani, and the Somono who are, in effect, a fisherman caste of the Bambara. Culturally linked are the Sarakolé, Soninké or Marka, who live in widely dispersed groups, the largest of which is to the north of the Malinké. The Sarakolé have depended in the past on slaves to perform their agriculture and keep their stock, whilst they themselves formed the ruling castes of the states which they founded. Many Sarakolé groups have adopted the language of other peoples amongst whom they form a minority, e.g. the Yarsé group amongst the Mossi. The Songhay to the north-east depend chiefly on the cultivation of the floodlands below the inland delta, and have a ruling caste which in the past intermarried chiefly with the Sarakolé. Songhay dwellings include a large version of the dome-shaped hut of arched branches covered with mats, rondavels with conical roofs, particularly in Ansongo and Niamey, and terrace houses, notably in Goundam. The Sorko fishermen of the Niger are related to the Songhay.

The Mossi form the largest community of the Voltaic group and had the highest densities of population in French West Africa. The plateau of the Mossi was divided originally between three 'states': Ouagadougou, Ouahigouya or Yatenga and Fada N'Gourma. The states were ruled by chiefs or kings advised by ministers, with societies divided into castes. Included within the Mossi are large numbers of people of highly diverse origins who have been absorbed into the community by conquest. Slaves were important to cultivate and keep cattle – for the latter occupation they were chiefly the Silmimossi of Fulani origin. Despite crowding, the Mossi population is highly dispersed in family compounds (soukala) made of clay and straw. Although constantly at war with the powerful states to the north and raiding the southern tribes for slaves, the Mossi have never been overrun by other peoples, and in consequence have enjoyed a security which has probably been the main factor in their high population densities. Related groups are the Gourma, the Bariba who have also been under Hausa influence, the Dagomba, Mamprusi, Nanumba, Dagari, Talensi, Nankana, Kusasi and Wala. The Senoufo are a Voltaic community who have adopted many Manding and Akan customs. They live well to the south, in sub-Sudanic and sub-Guinean environments.

The Hausa have been described as not an ethnic unit, but a nation in the making.[30] They are noted not only as cultivators and traders, but as smiths, textile workers and dyers, tanners and leather workers. Their compounds include both the rectangular terrace and rondavel house types made of mud. The Kanuri, similarly, occupy a mixture of rondavels and terrace houses, but the rondavel with a very tall slightly domed thatch roof close to the ground is traditional and not too dissimilar from the beehive thatch huts of the Mobber or of pastoral peoples living close by. Like the Hausa, the Kanuri have traditions of skill in textiles and leather work. The Shuwa arrived in Bornu as early as the 17th century, and the first groups intermarried and mixed with the Kanuri. Later arrivals, who came as allies against the Fulani in 1809, were given lands known as Ngomati lying to the south-east of Lake Chad where the majority still reside. The Shuwa are an Arabic-speaking part-nomadic pastoral people of markedly negroid appearance who live for part of the year in temporary grass shelters and for part in round huts over 30 feet (9 metres) in diameter and 10 to 15 feet (3 to 5 metres) high. These contain a large central raised floor where the family sleeps whilst the surrounding space is used as a stable, barn and slaves' quarters. The huts are usually grouped in a circle and with thorn fencing enclose a yard for livestock.

4. THE SOUTH-WESTERN PEOPLES

The south-western peoples of West Africa, situated between the Casamance River and the forest peoples of Liberia and the Ivory Coast, include a great ethnic variety. Many of these people have been crowded together as refugees on the coastal lowlands of the 'Rivières du Sud' where they have been able to introduce the cultivation of swamp rice. Inland there are large areas still depopulated by the slave raids or 'razzias' of the Sudanic conqueror Samory in the 19th century. Villages are small and highly dispersed and there are few groups with a chief having authority. The social structures have been described as 'archaic'[31] and were presumably introduced from the Sudanic centres of origin which many of these groups claim.

The communities concerned may be sub-divided between those of the 'Rivières du Sud', northern Sierra Leone and the associated interior lands, and the forest peoples of southern Sierra Leone, Liberia and western Ivory Coast. The former include the swamp rice cultivating Diola, comprising several sub-groups, of which the largest are the Bainouk, Balante, Manjak, Nalou, Baga and Mendenyi; the Landouman who dwell in escarpment refuges in north-western Guinea, and the Timne and Limba of Sierra Leone. All of these communities preserve the older social structures. Others, however, have been influenced by Manding peoples and have adopted Islam and in some cases a division between castes. These include the Susu, Dialonké (Yalunka) and Kouranko, together with groups only slightly influenced by Manding culture, living on the forest fringe, like the Kissi, Kpelle and Manon.

The forest peoples, with the exception of the Gagou and possibly also some of the ancestors of the Gouro, are also refugees from northern centres of origin. Their agricultural techniques are less well developed than those of surrounding peoples, and they depend much more on the produce of gathering and hunting. Some of the peoples have remarkably low densities of population – cercles of

Tabou and Sassandra in the Ivory Coast have respectively 4 and 7 to the square mile (1·6 and 2·7 per sq km), most are highly dispersed and have only a rudimentary administrative organization in the community as a whole. The peoples include the Kru with their numerous sub-divisions, some of which specialize in fishing, the Gouro and Gagou, and the Guéré and Dan who live in hill refuges.

Housing includes a great variety of types as must be expected amongst peoples subject to a variety of external influences and who are themselves of many different origins. Many of the Diola have rectangular terrace houses of the Sudanic type or courtyard houses. Amongst the other communities, rectangular, oval and round houses occur. A linear arrangement of houses or compounds is common, particularly in Liberia where street villages are widespread.

An important feature in the development of resources by the south-western peoples is the long period of contact of many of the communities concerned with Europe, and the development of an overseas trade as early as the 15th century.

5. THE SUB-SUDANIC PEOPLES

These, the 'middle peoples' of West Africa, the 'South Sudanese' of Richard-Molard, like the south-western peoples, consist of a large number of small communities of great ethnic variety, many of which preserve pre-Islamic cultures. Sub-Sudanic communities are frequently found in 'difficult' environments, e.g. thin-soiled bowal areas, or crowded on rocky plateaux and bornhardts easy to defend against attack. Many of them have fled from the Sudanic areas seeking sites too poor to attract invasion by other peoples or suitable for resistance against slave raiders. They include the 'palaeonigritic' societies of Baumann and Westermann, with less developed political organization than is usually found amongst Sudanic societies, and pagan religious beliefs. In a few areas of close contact with more advanced communities, small states have been formed, e.g. Dagomba and Wala in present-day Ghana. Housing consists mainly of small rondavels of mud, frequently on a base of stones, although terrace houses, even of a large fortress type, e.g. amongst the Somba of Dahomey, are not unknown. In the past, and still amongst a few communities today, little clothing was worn, the most common garments being of leaves or woven raffia or straw. In many cases, however, particularly in the hill refuges, agriculture is well developed, and includes manuring, terracing and irrigation techniques. Some communities keep small, hardy horses. Mining and the smelting of ores, particularly iron ore, was formerly widespread.

The Dogon, already classified amongst the Sudanic peoples, have many sub-Sudanic features, including the preservation of remnants of an early culture and the construction of stone dwellings on elevated sites at the foot of the Bandiagara escarpment. The Guéré and Dan, amongst the south-western peoples, also have some similarities. The Dagomba, Mamprusi, Nanumba, Dagari, Talensi, Nankana and Wala, to whom reference has been made above under Voltaic groups, are strictly classified from the geographical viewpoint amongst the sub-Sudanic peoples. Some of them, like the Talensi, occupy overcrowded hilly sites. The Nankana have a reputation as horsemen and keep cattle in addition to growing crops. Other adjacent communities include the Bobo, claimed to have the most archaic society of all,[32] Lobi, Birifor, Gourounsi, Ko and Kasena. In north-western Guinea are the Coniagui who have evolved a system of manuring part of their agricultural land by the regular movement of their huts. Near them are the Bassari who live in stone houses. Both these communities, however, belong more strictly to the south-western group. The Senoufo likewise are mainly sub-Sudanic in location although closely linked by origins with Sudanic peoples. Over 800,000 in number, the Senoufo may be divided into three groups, the most central of which, focusing on the town of Korhogo, formed in effect a small state. The Senoufo have been markedly influenced by Dioula immigrants who founded the great trading centre of Kong, probably in the 10th century. Malinké raids and immigration have also affected the Senoufo. Descendants of Malinké immigrants founded the important centre of Sikasso in the 19th century after the destruction of Kong.[33] In Togo and Dahomey there is a vast number of small yet distinct communities scattered throughout the hilly country of the Atacora Range, and frequently living in high density clusters of population separated by virtually unoccupied lands. The Kabrai and Naoudemba have local densities of 200 per square mile (77 per sq km), and employ the most intensive methods of cultivation to extract a living from the few fertile patches of soil available in their mountain retreats. Others, like the Konkomba, have been continually moving, until the advent of colonial authority, in search of fresh lands to cultivate, or away from enemies. In the 'Middle Belt' of Nigeria there is again a vast number of small communities, stretching from the Bariba confines in the west, eastwards throughout the adjacent portions of the Niger and Benue basins, the Jos Plateau and the plateaux of Adamawa and Bamenda together with their outliers. Examples are the Dakakari in the west, who resisted Fulani authority and the introduction of Islam, the Ari, Ningi, Burra and Warji who live on fortress-like hill-tops on the northern fringes of the Jos Plateau, the Birom and hill Angas or Kereng of the Jos Plateau proper, who build houses with stone foundations and formerly cultivated narrow terraces fringed by lines of stones, the Chibbuk or Margi, who formerly lived in tunnels in the hills of south-eastern Bornu, and the peoples of Adamawa, with their stone terraces and manure cultivation. Amongst the peoples of the Jos Plateau and amongst the Kamuku to the east, several of the older hill sites are separated from the crop lands by streams which, in the wet season when the cultivators must move between the village and the fields, become swollen torrents. In such cases stone causeways have been constructed, often V-shaped with the apex pointing downstream, with culverts, inclined stones to mark each edge when under water, and sometimes upright pillars at each end.[34] In the extreme south-east are the various peoples of Bamenda who have been classified by Baumann and Westermann as 'Semi-Bantu', but who occupy geographically a situation similar to those already described as characteristically sub-Sudanic. The 'grassfield' people of Bamenda cultivate steep hill-sides which they ridge and occasionally terrace, live in square-plan houses with pyramid roofs and possess a number of social features which link them as much with the Sudan as with the adjacent forest country to the south. The Tikar tribes who are politically dominant extend across West and East Cameroun where the Bamoun built the walled city of Foumban and their ruler Njoya invented a script of 300 signs at the beginning of the present century.

6. THE GUINEAN AND SUB-GUINEAN PEOPLES

There is much that is surprising about the Guinean and sub-Guinean peoples, as for example their development of comparatively advanced civilizations of the 'East Atlantic' type, although apparently separated from the more advanced Sudanic societies by a 'palaeonigritic' zone, and the occupation by several of the larger communities of two markedly contrasted environments – grassland and forest. A number of the communities like the Ewe and Ijaw are close to the palaeo-nigritic basis which appears common to most West African societies. Others show a combination of a number of different elements suggesting introduction from external sources possibly by invasion and conquest. Generally in West Africa it appears that a single distinctive tribe has an agricultural technique which limits its numbers to a certain range of environmental conditions suited to that technique and the associated crops. Yet the Yoruba, for example, occupy an area which includes a great range of environmental conditions, from the six to seven months dry season and grasslands of the north and west of their region, to the rain forest lands without a dry season and the swamps of the south and south-east. Possibly the answer is that the Yoruba, as such, consist rather of a collection of a number of peoples loosely knit into a state under the secular authority of the Alafin of Oyo and the religious authority of the Oni of Ife. Common language, common religious belief and even common political authority, do not imply common origins. Similarly peoples of several different origins are united, as Ashanti in the west, or loosely grouped, as Ibo in the east. Meyerowitz states of the Akan, of which the Ashanti were a part, that they were never a tribe, but a cultural group which split and reformed and absorbed parts of other groups.[35] An interesting feature is that the more advanced communities speak languages belonging to one linguistic group, the Kwa. These include the Kru (in the 'south-western peoples'), Agni-Twi, Fon, Ga, Gwang, Yoruba, Nupe, Edo and Ibo. The less-advanced groups can be divided into the peoples of the lagoons and the peoples east of the Ibo, nearly all of whom speak 'semi-Bantu' or 'Central Branch Nigero-Congolese'.[36] Greenberg indicates that the 'semi-Bantu' speaking area of the Cameroons may be a centre of origin of Bantu languages by suggesting that if 'proto-Bantu' were ever spoken, it would resemble one of the so-called 'semi-Bantu' languages. The more advanced communities have a tradition for building large settlements, virtually towns, since in most cases they include functions associated with towns outside West Africa, although the greater part of their population is agricultural.

In the west the most important group is the Akan, which includes the Ashanti, Agni and Gwang communities, each of which is sub-divided into several tribes. These peoples have founded a number of states including, to the north of the rain forests, Kumbu west of the Bandama, destroyed in about 1470, Bona between the Bandama and the Volta, conquered in 1595, and Gonja between the Black and White Volta. On the forest fringe between the Tano and the Volta, they founded Bono, which, according to Meyerowitz, flourished between about 1295 and 1740, and in the forest itself, Ashanti, created in 1701.[37] The Akan peoples developed a large export trade of gold and kola nuts, both northwards to the Sudan and southwards to European factors on the coast. They established the earliest recorded plantations (of kola) in West Africa, and were famed as metal workers. Houses are generally rectangular in plan and are often grouped on three or four sides of a courtyard. Cities were established at an early date, like Bono-Mansu, Famase-Akyerekyere and Twifo-Heman which were capitals of small but powerful states and centres of the gold trade. These each consisted of two settlement units, one occupied by the ruler and the other by traders, but without any defending wall. Each was divided into quarters, apparently on the basis of kinship, and had a more or less regular street plan.

To the east of the Akan are the Fon, who founded the state of Abomey or Dahomey, whose chief wealth in the 19th century came from the local control of the slave traffic, and people of mixed Ewe and Yoruba origin who founded the small states of Savi or Ouidah and Allada later conquered by Dahomey. Between Dahomey, the Niger and the great escarpments above Benin, are the Yoruba, occupying a plateau lying between 400 feet (122 metres) and over 2000 feet (610 metres) above sea-level, with a few related groups on the coastal lowlands to the south. Yoruba civilization appears to have been well developed before the arrival of the Portuguese on the neighbouring coast at the end of the 15th century. The Yoruba consist of a number of peoples speaking variants of a common language, most of whom once recognized an over-all authority. Most of them claim a common origin from Ife, the religious capital. The Yoruba groups built walled cities surrounded by farming hamlets and villages. The cities were and still are the centres of authority, trade and manufactures, chiefly cloth and metal work, notably in gold and bronze. Traditional Yoruba houses consist of long, narrow rectangular structures continuously surrounding a courtyard with a drain to remove storm waters. The Yoruba are noted for an early development of sculpture, not only in wood, but also in stone and bronze. Remarkable discoveries of stone and bronze heads of extremely fine workmanship have been made, chiefly at Ife and Esie. The Edo or Bini to the south-east were early influenced by Yoruba culture and founded the city of Benin well within the rain forest area. Benin, with its surrounding earth embankment over 20 feet (6 metres) in height with a deep ditch, became the centre of a powerful state whose influence extended from the Volta to the Niger. Like the Yoruba, the Bini built courtyard houses, established farm hamlets and villages round their city, and produced remarkable bronze castings. To the north of the Yoruba are the Nupe with traditions of craftsmanship in weaving, glass manufactures and metal work. The Nupe are also town builders, but live in rondavels of the Sudanic type, linked in groups by walls to form compounds. The Nupe established a state, absorbed other groups and in turn have suffered conquest and the loss of groups who moved away from the traditional centre. Tribal or political unity, as in the case of so many other communities, is again difficult to recognize. As Nadel remarks, 'What is the social reality to which the term Nupe people or Nupe tribe refers ? The three meanings of Nupe, people, language, and country, do not coincide. Disregarding the split-off sections we may say that the Nupe tribe inhabits, roughly, the same territory. But it is not, and never was, "one country" in the sense of a group united politically, or by facts of close contact and "common life", thus marked off from other, similar areas or groups.'[38] Nupe culture has close links with the cultures of the Yoruba and Bini. At the beginning of the 19th century, the Nupe, like the northern or Ilorin Yoruba, were conquered by the Fulani who established a new ruling house, and introduced Sudanic features into the social life, including Islam. It is doubtless this factor which has led Baumann and Westermann to classify the Nupe as 'Central Sudanic' when their earlier traditions are of contacts with the south rather than the north.

To the east of the Bini are the Ibo with their traditional centres east of the Niger on the savanna-ward fringe of the rain forest. The Ibo have never established a state. They consist of a vast number of small groups in the savanna and the rain forest, speaking several dialects of a common language. There is a traditional common recognition of the religious centres of Umundri and Arochu-ku, but no common authority. Even amongst small village groups over-all authority is only slight, except in the extreme south, notably amongst the Ikwerri Ibo. The rain forest Ibo live chiefly in dispersed hamlets and compounds, or, in a few cases, in small closely nucleated villages. The savanna Ibo, however, have built large settlement units several of which have over 30,000 inhabitants. These contain within them a dispersal of dwellings, but are sufficiently well-defined and include enough trading and small manufacturing functions to be dignified with the name of towns.[39] Ibo dwellings consist of rectangular mud-walled and thatch-roofed huts grouped in compounds and often surrounded by a wall. In the west, the Ika and Onitsha Ibo have been influenced by the Bini and build courtyard houses. Until the arrival of colonial authority at the beginning of the present century, the Ibo were in process of expansion from their densely popu-lated traditional centres chiefly to the east where colonies were established at the expense of the Ibibio and the peoples of the Cross river basin. To the north are the Igala, Idoma, Igbirra, Tiv and Jukun, sub-Guinean communities having cultural links with the Yoruba and under varying degrees of Sudanic influence. The Igbirra and Igala both built towns. The Igbirra capital of Panda, before its destruction by the Fulani, was in the shape of a half-moon, with walls 12 feet (4 metres) high and 6 feet (2 metres) thick, and defended on three sides by a ditch 10 feet (3 metres) in depth and on the fourth by a ravine. The king's palace consisted of a collection of rondavels occupying about 10 acres (4 hectares).

The total population of the town was probably 30,000.[40] The Jukun also built a capital town at Wukari and established a state – Kororofa or Kwararofa. Jukun conquests at one time extended the power of this state over the whole Benue valley and northwards into Hausaland and Bornu. H. R. Palmer claims a Bornu origin for the ruling castes of both the Igala and the Jukun, and for the introduction of iron-working not only to the Jukun, but also to the Hausa, Nupe and Songhay.[41] The Tiv must be described here geographically although culturally and linguistically their links are chiefly with the south-eastern 'semi-Bantu' speaking peoples. The Tiv have been moving northwards for more than a century from overcrowded centres of origin on the fringe of the rain forest into comparatively empty lands between the Idoma and the Jukun. The settlement units are small dispersed hamlets. Until colonial authority halted further movement, not only northwards, but also to the south-west, the Tiv were chiefly shifting cultivators continually in search of new lands, lacking any central authority and with no fixed boundaries. The system of land division, the settlement patterns and the direction of population movements depended on the recognition of different degrees of kinship.[42]

The lagoons peoples of southern Ivory Coast probably belong to a very ancient West African high forest stock. Many are short in stature and appear to be related to primitive cultivators and gatherers like the Gagou. Others are more closely linked with the Kru. The old 'palaeonigritic' cultures appear, however, to have been influenced by a variety of others, notably by the Akan through the group known as the Anyi. The largest communities are the Ebrié and Attié. Others include the Mekyibo or Veteré, formerly dominant in the lagoons of Assinie and Grand Bassam, the Arikam, Aladia, Abé and Ari. Many of these are engaged chiefly in fishing in the lagoons and rivers, and occasionally out to sea. They occupy nucleated villages, frequently containing several thousand people, and traditionally build houses on stilts along the water-line. Related lagoons peoples, the Dassa, Kpéda and Kotofon, are found in the coastlands of Dahomey.[43] Other important fishing peoples are found eastwards from the Ivory Coast. These appear mainly to be of mixed Akan, Ewe, Yoruba and Bini origins. In the Niger delta are the Ijaw and Kalabari who occupy permanent very closely nucleated villages, chiefly of rectangular palm rib huts, and establish temporary camps according to season along the coast, in the lagoons and the delta and along the banks of the lower Niger. On the delta fringe are the Itsekiri or Jekri, primarily fisherman and traders, and profoundly influenced by the cultures of the Bini and Yoruba.

The south-eastern peoples of Calabar, the Cross river basin and the southern Cameroons, excluding Bamenda, occupy dispersed settlements, and have low population densities, with the exception of the Ibibio. Until recently they mostly practised a form of shifting agriculture involving settlement movement, and preserved archaic cultural traits. In the Cross river basin and the southern Cameroons rectangular houses arranged in small street villages are widespread. The Boki, Yache, Ukele and Yala on the savanna fringe to the north are exceptional and have rondavels. The Ibibio occupy dense dispersals of compounds and have population concentrations of almost as high a density as those of the more overcrowded sections of the Ibo. The Efik early took advantage of the development of the slave trade to establish themselves as middlemen, and built the town of Calabar with its great slave barracoons and its two- and three-storey corrugated iron houses imported from Europe. Other similar slave ports were established on the Ibo, Ibibio, Ijaw and Kalabari portions of the coast and delta, notably Brass, Bonny and Opobo. The traditional garments of many of these south-eastern peoples were made of raphia fibre, and iron-working was only poorly developed as most of the iron used had to be imported from the north. On the coast of the Cameroons are a number of small fishing communities, with, inland, the scattered hamlet and village units of the Kpe and Mboko plantain and cocoyam cultivators. The fishing communities include the Duala, Limba, Mongo and Wovea who, working from temporary camps, catch chiefly crayfish, prawns and shrimps.

Settlement patterns and distributions

In this section it is proposed to give a more detailed account of the ways in which population is distributed by the description of settlement patterns. As Steel has commented in his study of population distribution in Ashanti, in a region where there is a lack of the basic population data, or where those data are unreliable, the study of settlement patterns provides a most useful approach to the problems of population distribution.[44]

I. SETTLEMENT PATTERN ELEMENTS

The basic population unit in settlement pattern distribution is the family which in most cases in West Africa is a large unit. The small family unit of a man, wife or wives and children may be distinguished in the social structure, but is rarely significant geographically. In the detailed study of population distribution, that is in the study of settlement patterns, the geographer is concerned rather with an 'extended family' or large family group occupying a body of houses or huts generally termed a compound. The family group usually consists of people related by blood and marriage, but may also include others not so related who are either servants or slaves or have been accepted into the group for social convenience. Compounds are of varying sizes and may be amorphous or may consist of structures arranged in regular patterns. Rooms may be in separate structures or joined together, and in many cases the compound is surrounded by a wall or walls. Some notion of the possible variations is given by Figure 1.7. Commonly a compound is occupied by about 20 people, but over 100 occupants is not unknown. The larger and more elaborate compounds are difficult in some cases to distinguish from hamlets or small villages, for the population of an apparent hamlet or village may consist of kinsfolk as closely related as those of a compound, whilst the settlement units concerned will serve similar functions. The only difference appears to be in the pattern of housing. Such for example is the case with the Owerri Ibo 'nchi', a settlement unit with the appearance of a closely

Generalised plans of compounds illustrating some variations in form
(no scales)

DOGON TYPE,
Bandiagara
(after Calame-Griaule, Bull. I.F.A.N.,1955, pp. 477-99)

A KONKOMBA COMPOUND
(after Froelich, Mem. I.F.A.N.,1954)

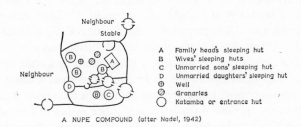

A Family head's sleeping hut
B Wives' sleeping huts
C Unmarried sons' sleeping hut
D Unmarried daughters' sleeping hut
⊕ Well
⊘ Granaries
◯ Katamba or entrance hut

A NUPE COMPOUND (after Nadel, 1942)

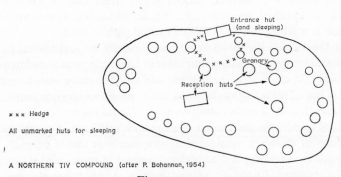

× × × Hedge

All unmarked huts for sleeping

A NORTHERN TIV COMPOUND (after P. Bohannan, 1954)

Figure I.7

nucleated circular village of small compound units, within which the inhabitants are for the most part close kinsfolk.

The hamlet is a collection of compounds in which a small number of large family units is grouped together usually for the purpose of mutual assistance in part of the labour of cultivation. Hamlets often occur as subsidiary purely agricultural settlements attached to large village or urban settlements. In such cases, as amongst the Yoruba, they may be occupied for part of the year only, or for the whole of the year by only part of the family, the remainder occupying a town house. Many hamlets, as for example those of the Konkomba, consist of widely separated compounds, for each is situated amidst its attached croplands. Nevertheless a hamlet unit exists, distinguishable physically by its relative degree of nucleation and by the pattern of paths joining the compounds of any one hamlet with another.

The village consists normally of a large collection of compounds whose occupants are entirely or mostly engaged in agriculture, but whose purpose in gathering together is non-agricultural or only indirectly concerned with agriculture. The purpose may be purely social, i.e. the preference for living in large groups. Usually the main purpose is for trading convenience, for defence or for administrative convenience. In the last case it is easier to establish control from a given centre over a small number of villages each with its own administrative head or council than over a large number of widely scattered compounds. This factor has not, however, applied in all cases. Amongst the Mossi, for example, there is a strong central authority and dispersed settlement. Defence, although no longer important, was a vital consideration in many parts of West Africa until the end of the 19th century. Most cases of the round village occur because of defence needs since a circular unit is the easiest to surround by a wall, embankment, or trench. In many areas the village is, in effect, the basic trading unit, the first collecting point of agricultural produce for sale in the regional markets. Many villages, therefore, possess a small market, either within or immediately outside the village itself or within the nearest town. The street village aligned along an important route is a development due to the importance of trading agricultural produce. There are, however, many cases of street villages where the trading factor is unimportant, and where the parallel alignment arises simply from convenience in marking out plots from a central path or road.

Like the village, the town is inhabited chiefly by agriculturalists for non-agricultural purposes. Boateng states that in Ghana, 'a town is a settlement which is the seat of a chief; it is the political and administrative and, therefore, social centre of life'. This is to give the word 'town' purely social significance, and Boateng admits that because the definition is 'static', and because of changing political and social trends, the distinction of a town on this basis is unrealistic.[45] The distinction of the town considered geographically is that it normally combines the functions of trading and administration and in most cases is a regional and not a local centre. In the recent past in West Africa it has also had a defence function, which in some cases, although not all, has been of prime importance. In Yorubaland and in Benin, for example, there is a settlement hierarchy with towns as the regional centres of administration and trade, serving surrounding villages and hamlets (Fig. 1.8). Agriculture still remains the chief occupation of the majority of the town's inhabitants, but the size of the town depends not so much on surrounding agricultural production as on the importance of its market and of its authority. Daily markets serve the townsfolk whilst 4, 5, 7, 8 or 10 day markets serve the surrounding district. Large seasonal markets provide for exchange between regions or nowadays serve the collection and despatch of export produce. Most towns are divided into quarters which are, in effect, large villages within which many of the inhabitants are kinsfolk. Quarters are often attached

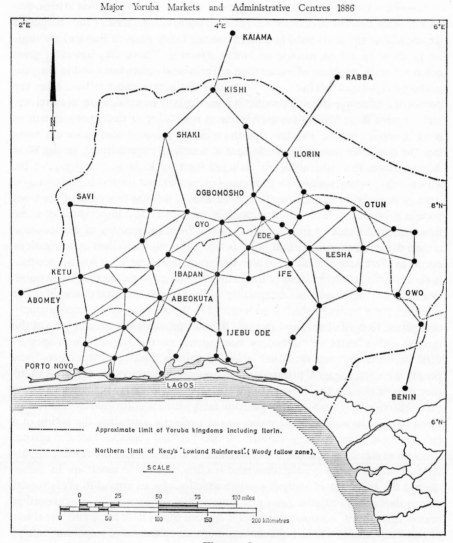

Major Yoruba Markets and Administrative Centres 1886

Figure 1.8

through kinship to nearby villages and hamlets, and each quarter normally possesses the use-right in a distinct area of land. Within the quarters, except where modern planning has brought changes, street patterns rarely exist. The quarters are usually mere collections of compounds. Between the quarters, however, there are often regular, sometimes straight streets, focusing on the centre of administration and the chief markets. The attraction of the greater variety of social amenities provided by the towns has become an important factor in the movement of population at the present day.

In seeking to define the different types of settlement unit in West Africa, one finds that the functional distinctions between town, village, hamlet and compound (equivalent to the traditional large farm unit of many parts of Europe) are similar to those found in Europe or North America. There are, however, great contrasts in the problem of recognition of functional distinctions and in the proportional difference between one functional distinction and another. Thus the proportion of people in basic production, particularly in agriculture, is extremely high in most West African towns, whereas it is small or virtually non-existent in most European towns. The fact that the majority are cultivators does not mean that the main function of the settlement is necessarily agricultural. In the West African town, the cultivators are gathered together in large numbers, not for agricultural purposes, as in the compound or hamlet, but for trading advantages, defence or social or administrative convenience. Thus the functions of the town remain primarily non-agricultural, and in most cases the importance of these functions is difficult or impossible to obtain from an analysis of occupational census data. Another important point is that although specialism in occupations occurs in West Africa, and indeed is an important feature in West African production, nevertheless agriculture is frequently combined with another occupation, or a man may undertake one occupation whilst his wife undertakes another. For example, petty trading, which is widespread in West Africa, is a normal auxiliary occupation to agriculture, and in some families provides the greater part of the income. Other 'extra' or 'secondary' occupations are the preparation of agricultural produce, seasonal or casual labour of various kinds, and transport. Even people who are engaged primarily in manufacture, services or the professions may own or possess the use-right in a small parcel of land, which they cultivate themselves, or may draw an income from land which is cultivated by relatives or hired labour. In addition, therefore, to the problems attending the taking of a census already discussed, West African occupational censuses face the further problem of classifying people with more than one occupation, the relative importance of which to the people concerned is often difficult to ascertain. In consequence the problems of analysing urban functions by an appeal to occupational census data are enormous. Finally, it may be that the extremely low proportion of non-agricultural occupations in West African towns is in large part the result of colonial contact. There is increasing evidence of the more important role of manufacture, and the great importance of internal trade in the past.[46]

2. DISPERSAL OF COMPOUNDS OR HAMLETS

This is the tendency towards an even distribution of population within a region which appears to be characteristic of communities with little development of either central administration or trade. It is associated essentially with the communities described by Baumann and Westermann as 'palaeonigritic' and may well be the oldest form of settlement distribution development in West Africa. Not all such communities occupy dispersed compounds and hamlets. Some have been forced to adopt nucleations by defensive needs, by being drawn into the trading orbits of other communities or by their occupation of areas with only a few highly localized sources of water.

The Guinean areas with their dense rain forest, difficult to clear, partly because of the high density of trees and shrubs and the lack of a dry season for burning, contain several examples of dispersal with, in many cases, low densities of population. In south-eastern Ivory Coast, the Bété and Gagou occupy dispersed hamlets and compounds in districts with densities of less than 7 per square mile (3 per sq km), excepting in those areas occupied by the Gagou where coffee plantations have been developed in recent years. In the neighbouring portions of Liberia dispersal also occurs, notably in Sapa where hamlets of about 20 huts are common. Defensive needs have brought the fortified circular village, chiefly to the north where attacks were more frequent, and many of the smaller hamlets and compounds are today being abandoned as people leave for the more developed centres.[47] In southern Iboland, chiefly in Aba and southern Owerri divisions, and in Ibibioland, dispersal occurs amongst extremely high densities of population. The density in Aba Division is 413 per square mile (159 per sq km), but several of the village group areas have densities very much higher (600–800 per square mile (230–310 per sq km)), and the support of many of the population is derived from farming distant areas by temporary migration, or by daily bicycle journeys to distant fields, or by remittances from relatives working in the towns. In southern Owerri village group area densities are lower (183 per square mile (71 per sq km) in Ohoba and 374 per square mile (144 per sq km) in Ngor-Okpala), although still much higher than in comparable areas in West Africa outside Nigeria. An interesting feature is that dispersal occurs despite the relative infrequency of surface water supplies. Many householders must walk distances of up to 10 miles (16 km) in order to obtain water for domestic uses.[48] Further north extremely high densities of population are concentrated into areas with an almost continuous dispersal of compounds. Okigwi and Orlu divisions have 755 and 873 persons per square mile (291 and 337 per sq km) respectively. In northern Owerri the village group areas of Mba-Itoli-Ikeduru and Mbaise have densities of 955 and 1108 per square mile (369 and 428 per sq km). Similarly in Ibibioland, there are the divisions of Ikot Ekpene (622), Uyo (670) and Abak (667) (respectively 240, 259 and 258 persons per sq km). Such densities are extraordinary in West Africa and are associated not with advanced communities, but with communities having little trade except for the export of palm produce, and a recently developed traffic in foodstuffs and textiles, little manufacture, and little or no central government. No satisfactory explanation has yet been put forward and is difficult to obtain because of the lack of adequate historical data. At least the soils are highly productive in root crops and oil palm produce, but their production

c

alone is insufficient to support these large numbers despite the export of the higher value yams in exchange for lower value cassava, thus increasing the quantity of food available. Clearly many Ibo and Ibibio depend on farming adjacent areas or on incomes from external sources, a situation which has developed only under colonial government. It would appear, therefore, that before such government was introduced, densities were probably lower, although undoubtedly still high by West African standards. Enough is known of Ibo history to show that the Ibo, until the advent of colonial government, have been in a state of almost continual expansion into the lands of their neighbours from their densely populated centre. A considerable natural increase in population at the centre seems likely, relieved by emigration to the perimeter. That expansion has now been stopped with, in consequence, increase in density in the centre and the creation of a problem in obtaining sufficient resources for the population's support. Possibly a similar situation prevails in Ibibioland, although the Ibibio have been pressed back on to their densely populated nucleus by the Ibo advance from the west across the Imo into Aba. Here the colonial government have relieved the situation.

Dispersal of compounds and hamlets is widespread in the savannas. As Labouret remarks, in a great part of the 'geographical Sudan' almost all the houses are separated by fields or gardens.[49] Dispersal is common amongst sub-Sudanic peoples such as the Lobi, Dagari and Gourounsi. Chiefs have little authority or are non-existent. The extended family is more or less independent and its members co-operate in the tasks of cultivation. Densities are of the order of 15–56 per square mile (6–22 per sq km) except in the Northern Territories of Ghana where in some districts much higher figures are reached. Lawra for example has 105 per square mile (41 per sq km), Kassena-Nankani 147 (57), Kusasi 147 (57) and Frafra 204 (79). These districts are separated by Tumu with only 16 (6) and limited on the south by eastern Dagomba 20 (8), western Dagomba 41 (16), eastern Gonja 11 (4) and western Gonja 7 (3). Here one has an example of a typical feature of West African demography – population density extremes side by side. The low density areas of Dagomba and Gonja are poor in soil resources. In the rains, the lower ground is mostly flooded, and in the dry season the higher ground is mostly destitute of domestic water supplies.[50] Hilton lists as important factors affecting population density in northern Ghana:

1. Slave raids
2. Wild animals
3. Trypanosomiasis
4. Onchocerciasis
5. Other epidemic and endemic diseases
6. Soil erosion and soil exhaustion.

He suggests that the last is possibly the most important.[51] The high densities of the northern districts arise partly from the fertility of the soils and partly from the tendency, as Hilton has shown, for the population of surrounding districts to move towards the watersheds. In northern Togo and Dahomey the

Somba groups have solved the problem of defence whilst preserving a dispersed distribution by the construction of their peculiar terrace houses equipped with small turrets.[52]

Amongst sub-Guinean communities, the Idoma and Tiv are remarkably dispersed, and show within their community area great contrasts in population density and, uncommonly in West Africa, the lack of a single high density nucleus, although densities are generally higher in the south, the source of Tiv migration, than in the north. On the southern boundary, the Bohannans have recorded a density as high as 550 per square mile (212 per sq km) contrasted with densities as low as 25 (10) north of the Benue.[53] Amongst the Tiv dispersal had obvious advantages in view of the tradition for continual movement of compound sites and migration to new agricultural lands. Movement of compounds is a feature of the settlement pattern amongst several low density dispersed communities, a feature which has become less common since the introduction of colonial government, and the modern development of trade and nucleated villages near markets. Even small villages were once frequently moved, causing confusion amongst colonial surveyors and administrators. At Bayare, south-west of Yola, for example, it was recorded in 1907–9: 'As the smaller villages are always changing their names, and often their sites, it is sometimes difficult to get reliable information concerning them, and new guides have to be obtained at frequent intervals.'[54]

In the Sudan, dispersal occurs amongst a number of communities with advanced agricultural technique such as the Serer, and amongst communities which have established states, e.g. Wolof and Mossi. Wolof hamlets generally average less than 100 people, and as they grow larger they tend to break up and form several distinct settlements.[55] Today there are a few small towns in the territory of the Mossi, and Ouagadougou, the centre of authority, has long formed a small nucleation, but traditionally the Mossi have lived, as most of them still live today, in scattered compounds grouped for social convenience in 'villages', although it is almost impossible in many cases to perceive where one 'village' ends and another begins. The 'villages' are in turn grouped in cantons and the cantons in provinces of which there are eight. Five of these were directly ruled from the centre and three were vassal units. Altogether over one million people were thus ruled over by a single authority in Ouagadougou. Population densities are 42 per square mile (16 per sq km) in Ouagadougou, 81 (31) in Koudougou, 43 (17) in Ouahigouya, 54 (21) in Tenkodogo, 48 (19) in Tougan and 97 (37) in Yako. Many of the cantons, however, have densities of over 120 (46).

In Bornu many of the Kanuri today occupy villages, although formerly the majority were in hamlets which tended to shift. At the beginning of the present century there was no town in the Bornu plains. There were only temporary straw huts grouped in scattered small villages and hamlets. The Shuwa Arab, Manga, Kanembu, Mobber and Koyam are still mainly semi-nomadic and undertake a little cultivation for only short periods in the year. The over-all density for Bornu Province is 35 (14) with only 23 (9) and 30 (12) in Bedde and Bornu

Divisions respectively. Potiskum and Dikwa with higher proportions of settled cultivators have 69 (27) and 52 (20) respectively.

3. NUCLEATION – VILLAGE SETTLEMENTS

Settlement within small villages with compounds grouped closely together is of frequent occurrence in the hillier districts occupied by the sub-Sudanic peoples,

Gourounga fortified village

Figure 1.9   *After Binger*

amongst fishing peoples, particularly on the coast, and on the margins of the northern floodlands.

Amongst the sub-Sudanic peoples the villages are rarely established on high summits, but usually occur on lower hill-tops, hill-sides or the pediments at the bases of escarpments. Peoples of the Guinea Highlands, the Atacora Ranges, the Jos Plateau and the Adamawa Highlands all provide examples. Local densities are extremely high. The Dogon of Mt. Sarnière east of Douenza, for example, have a density of 260 per square mile (100 per sq km) and the Naoudemba of northern Togo have over 500 (193). Even over comparatively large areas, densities can be high. The subdivision of Lama-Kara (1060 square miles (2745 sq km)), for example, has 171 (66) with its great concentration of Kabrai hill cultivators. Jos Division (1434 square miles (3714 sq km)) has 160 per square mile (62 per sq km). To the south, the Kukuruku or Afema, and the Igbirra peoples (sub-Guinean) of the low hills of Igbirra Division show extremely high densities in some divisions and occupy sites similar to those of the sub-Sudanic peoples. Three of the small districts have densities of 882, 834 and 747 per square mile (342, 322 and 288 per sq km).[56] The sub-Sudanic hill peoples are almost all either refugees or the descendants of refugees forced to crowd together in these dense concentrations perched on rocky slopes, often hidden amidst boulders, occupying sites offering some defence against the superior military techniques of their enemies. On such sites, they must make the maximum use of the little land available, and in many cases the few 'pockets' of soil are highly fertile and can continue to give good yields under careful methods of cultivation. Several of the Jos Plateau villages are quite large, larger even than many 'townships' although largely lacking urban functions. Gindiri village, for example, has 8000 inhabitants, and the 10 villages of Karam District all have between 4000 and 7000. The village units consist of compounds separated by small gardens, each surrounded by a euphorbia hedge with the main croplands outside the village. There are a number of other sub-Sudanic village communities not on hill sites, amongst whom living in a village is preferred to living in scattered compounds. The Bariba of Borgu, for example, live in small widely distributed villages and have an over-all population density for Borgu Division of only 7 per square mile (3 per sq km). The Batta and Bashama, with only about 15 per square mile (6 per sq km) in their district, live in villages in flat and marshy country in the Benue valley near Numan. Such areas of low population density are a frequent sub-Sudanic and also sub-Guinean feature, due in some cases to local water shortage, in others to disease, particularly sleeping sickness, and, above all else, to past depopulation by slave raiders. Thus in 1902 the following description was written of Kabba and Nassarawa Provinces:

'With regard to the depopulation of Northern Nigeria by the Fulani, which is so apparently manifest to the merest novice in the service, a traveller (in the country, for instance, between Kabba and Egga) would not, I am certain, come across 200 people en route, in what, even in my time, was a densely populated country. Again, in the Nassarawa country, a once fertile and populous province, one can now only view the remains and ruins of large and totally deserted towns, bearing witness to the desolation wrought by 100 years of internecine strife and slave-raiding by the Fulani.'[57]

The divisions of Kontagora(19 persons per square mile (8 per sq km)), Bauchi, 35 (14), and Muri, 24 (9), were alike devastated by the Hausa Fulani whilst in the west the Fouta Djallon Fulani took slaves from amongst the Susu, Baga, Nalou, Landouman, Tyapi, Badyaranké, Coniagui, Bassari and Dialonké. The cercles of Gawal and Dabola fringing the Fouta Djallon have densities of only 17 and 12 per square mile (7 and 5 per sq km) respectively.

Fishing communities generally occupy closely nucleated villages whose form depends greatly on the nature of the local terrain, and whose density depends partly on the local fishing resources and partly, in the several cases where agriculture is an additional occupation, on local soil resources. Thus the lagoon coasts of south-eastern Ivory Coast, south-eastern Ghana, Togo, Dahomey and Nigeria with their immense fish resources have the greatest concentrations of fishing peoples. Of the 25 administrative units concerned 16 have over 90 per square mile (35 per sq km). The Niger delta divisions with their vast areas of mangrove swamps and few sites suitable for settlement have densities of 35, 38, and 39 (14, 15 and 15). The lagoon cercles of south-eastern Ivory Coast have 14, 21, 35 and 64 (5, 8, 14 and 25). The two lower densities are in cercles with their main population concentrations on the coast. Lagoon fishing villages tend to be linear in shape following the shore line. Houses are often on stilts at right angles to the shore and in water at high tide. In the delta, the fishing villages are established on small islands of firm ground and make the maximum use of the area available above high-water mark. Delta villages thus tend to assume round or amorphous shapes. Houses are less commonly on stilts and are often grouped in rectangular compounds.

OKO JOKO

An Okrika fishing village near Port Harcourt

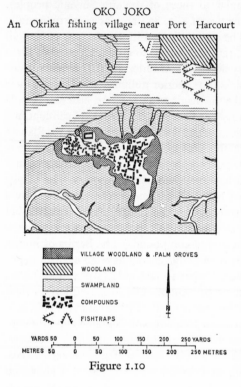

VILLAGE WOODLAND & .PALM GROVES

WOODLAND

SWAMPLAND

COMPOUNDS

FISHTRAPS

YARDS 50   0   50   100   150   200   250 YARDS
METRES 50   0   50   100   150   200   250 METRES

Figure 1.10

Sudanic floodland cultivators normally live in compact villages in the villages of the Senegal and Niger and overlooking the fadama of tributary streams like the Bosso and Sokoto. Along the banks of the upper Niger, for example, are strung the compact villages of the Malinké built on terraces at the edge of the flooded zone, of great agricultural importance. Each village is subdivided into quarters, each occupied by large compounds often fringed by gardens. In the middle Niger basin, villages tend to be small, occupy islands and levées and are frequently moved. Most villages have less than 500 inhabitants and very few have more than 1000. Densities in floodland cantons are comparatively high (50–130 per square mile, 19–50 per sq km) although no higher than in the more productive portions of the Sudanic rainlands. Away from the floodlands much of the area has too short a wet season for much crop production and thus over-all cercle densities are low:

Senegal valley: Bas-Senegal 33 per square mile (13 per sq km), Podor 17 (7), Matam 11 (4), Bakel 5 (2), Kédougou 6 (2), Trarza 4 (2), Brakna 5 (2), Assaba 5 (2), and Guidimaka 10 (4).

Upper and Middle Niger valley: Dalaba 41 (16), Dabola 12 (5), Siguiri 16 (6), Bamako 23 (9), Macina 13 (5), San 38 (15), Ségou 42 (16), Mopti 38, (15), Issa-Ber 23 (9).

Such low densities are extraordinary in regions where the most powerful states in West Africa were created. Richard-Molard even suggests that where a powerful state has existed settlement tends to be widely dispersed in regular low density, giving as examples the Manding, Songhay and Hausa empires.[58] In none of these cases is this statement wholly true, for in the cases of the Manding and Songhay empires population distribution was uneven, being concentrated by water-courses, whilst in the Hausa states, which with their much higher densities on rainlands are hardly comparable, a high degree of concentration appears always to have existed around the most powerful administrative centres. Higher local densities occur amongst the rice cultivators of the floodlands of the south-western estuaries. Here peoples like the Baga live in linear villages generally sited on levées or old beach ridges. The location of settlement is markedly related to soil distribution. 'Poto-poto' soils drained by fresh water are preferred whilst the more saline 'tann' soils are generally avoided.

Villages occur amongst rain forest communities normally in association with medium to high population densities. The 'small towns' of the Mende are in effect villages and rarely contain more than 2000 inhabitants. The Mende number nearly 600,000, approximately one-third of the population of Sierra Leone. Their three provinces of Moyamba, Kailahun and Bo have densities of 85, 91 and 199 per square mile (33, 35 and 77 per sq km) respectively with a remarkably even distribution of population. Little's study shows that in 1951, for example, the smaller districts had very similar densities to those of the larger units.[59] Village settlement appears also amongst the Urhobo with houses commonly ranged along streets, as amongst the neighbouring Bini, and amongst the Itsekiri, whose older settlements have irregular patterns whilst the newer settlements have adopted the street form.[60] Urhobo densities are high with 176 per square mile (68 per sq km) for the division. Street villages appear to be the most common form in the high forest regions, particularly in Southern Nigeria and the southern Cameroons. Amongst the Owerri and Ikwerre Ibo and in Arochuku, round villages occur in a few small districts. Those of Owerri consist of very closely built compounds and houses, and probably reflect the need for defence in a community once holding an important position in the trade in slaves and oil palm produce. Oratta district which includes the Owerri villages has a density of 395 (153) – one of the highest in village settlement areas. Other districts nearby also have round or circular villages as in the examples shown in Figure 1.11. Compact agricultural villages are of frequent occurrence in the Sub-Guinean savannas; for social reasons as in Figure 1.12, and in other cases for defence.

Atako's Village, Diobu District, North of Port Harcourt

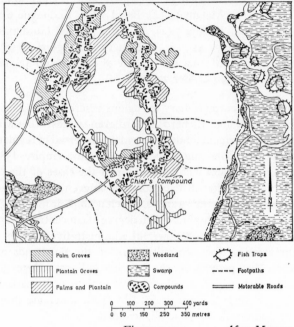

Chief's Compound

▨ Palm Groves		▨ Woodland		✿ Fish Traps	
▤ Plantain Groves		▨ Swamp		--- Footpaths	
▨ Palms and Plantain		⬭ Compounds		═ Motorable Roads	

```
0    100   200   300   400 yards
0   50   150   250   350 metres
```

Figure 1.11*a*   *After Morgan*

A village in Owerri township

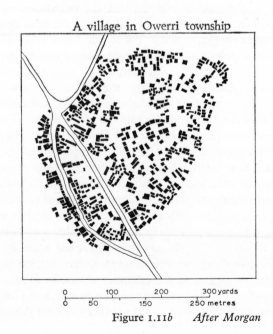

```
0        100       200       300 yards
0    50        150       250 metres
```

Figure 1.11*b*   *After Morgan*

An interesting feature of the development of village settlement patterns, is the founding of daughter settlements by families from the older centres. Where land is abundant this is achieved by founding the hamlet nucleus of the new

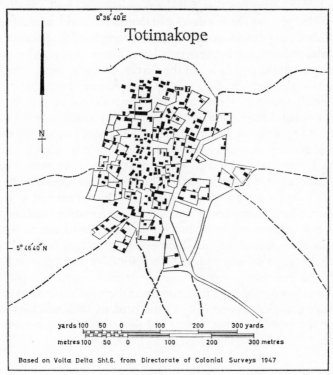

Figure 1.12

village in virgin or long fallow woodland. Elsewhere the new settlement is often located amidst the more distant croplands. Thus Bradbury describes the Urhobo settlements as being divided into:

1) The supposed parent settlement divided into wards which are subdivided into extended family units.
2) Other villages and hamlets derived from parent wards or immigrants from outside the district.
3) Villages and hamlets derived in turn from the above.[61]

The Ibo of Abakaliki Division distinguish the 'unuku' or original village, the 'ndiabo' or village founded by the first emigrants, usually several miles away, and the 'ndiagu' or village founded furthest away by later emigrants. In Nsukka Division, in overcrowded conditions, Bridges found settlement expansion from the original unit into adjacent croplands and was informed that when the settlement of such lands had reached its maximum, then movement to the more distant cropland would begin.[62]

In a few areas such as the Fouta Djallon and the Bamenda Highlands, a mixture of village and dispersal occurs where the village form appears to have been introduced by invaders and provides a local administrative centre. Here the village has an urban function, but the population is small, usually less than 5000, and trade appears to be less developed than in areas with true urban centres. Richard-Molard has given an account of the demography of the Fouta Djallon.[63] There appears little relation between population density and physical conditions. The greater part of the population of the Cercle of Labé occupies comparatively level surfaces with only thin, poor soils on concretionary ironstone – the 'bowé' (sing. – 'bowal'). Many of these bowé are almost devoid of population whilst others are crowded. Labé canton has 151 persons per square mile (58 per sq km) and Bantignel 174 (67). The eastern fringes of the Fouta Djallon and the Guinea Highlands providing comparable physical conditions are virtually empty. The bowé of the Fouta Djallon are used mainly for pasture. The greater part of the cultivation occurs in the valley bottoms. The chief factor appears to be political. The Fouta Djallon is not an upland refuge. The Fulani entered as conquerors and introduced large numbers of slaves from surrounding districts to act as cultivators and herders and serve them in their chief settlements. Similarly in Bamenda, invaders, chiefly of the Tikar-speaking groups, imposed their rule and created the larger villages such as Bafut, Njinikom and Banso or Kumbo on the interfluves. Population crowded round the more important political foci. Again high and low densities are juxtaposed and there are many areas of virtually empty pasture occupied seasonally by Fulani herders. Bamenda Division has 92 persons per square mile (36 per sq km) and the neighbouring division of Wum has 34 (13).

4. NUCLEATION – URBAN SETTLEMENTS

Whereas in most of inter-tropical Africa before the arrival of European influences towns were of rare occurrence, in West Africa towns were built by many peoples, notably by the Manding, Songhay and Hausa in the Sudan and Sahel, and by the Akan, Fon, Yoruba, Nupe and Bini in the sub-Guinean and Guinean environments. These towns did not exist alone, but were surrounded by an associated dispersal of compounds, hamlets and small villages. Many of the settlement patterns produced have been little modified under colonial government and can be studied in present-day examples. In Figure 1.13 are illustrations and plans of towns in the lands west of the Volta as they were recorded by L. G. Binger in his book, *Voyage du Niger au Golfe de Guinée*, Paris, 1888.

The West African towns appear to have arisen amongst communities with authoritative government, needing nucleated easily defended settlement units, and normally possessing well-developed trade and manufactures. Whereas dispersal is often associated with migratory communities, towns only occur amongst peoples needing some degree of stability in order to establish settled government and trade. Towns are also restricted mainly to areas of high

A sketch map of Bondoukou

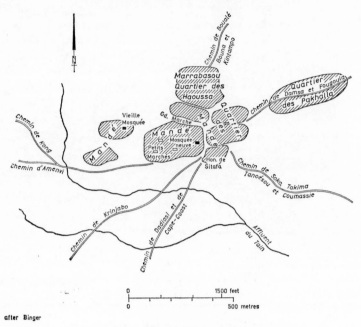

Figure 1.13a

Plan of Ngélé or Niélé

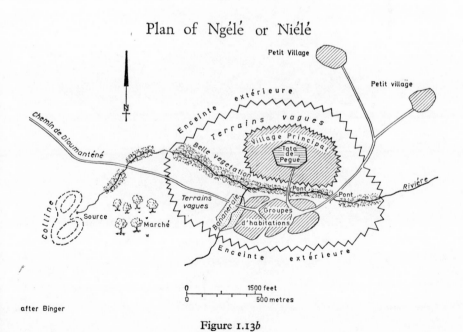

Figure 1.13b

A sketch map of Kintampo

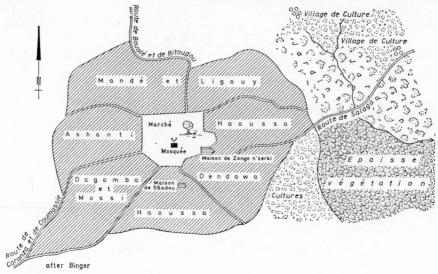

after Binger

Figure 1.13c

No scale on original map

A sketch map of Salaga

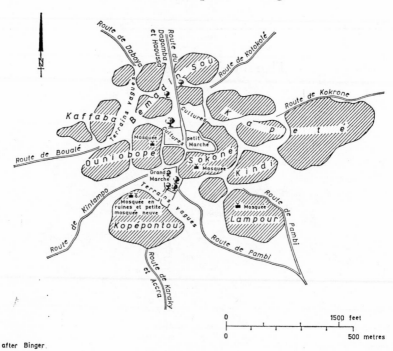

after Binger

Figure 1.13d

Figure 1.13*e*   *After Binger*

A sketch map of the town of Kong

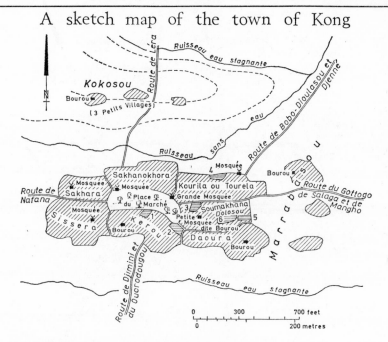

No.1. Habitation de Diarawary Ouattara, chef de Kong
No.2. Habitation de Mokhosia Ouattara, chef des captifs de Karamokho-Oulé Ouattara
No.3. Habitation de Karamokho-Oulé, souverain du pays
No.4. Habitation de l'almamy Sitafa, chef religieux de Kong
No.5. Habitation de Fotigué Dou
No.6 Seul groupe de cases où l'on fabrique du dolo

after Binger

Figure 1.13*f*

The tata of Sikasso

Figure 1.13*g*   *After Binger*

A sketch map of Ouagadougou

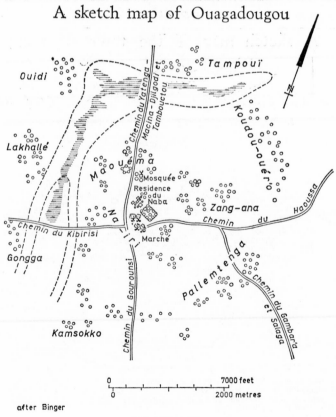

after Binger

Figure 1.13*h*

A sketch map of Sia or Bobo-Dioulasso

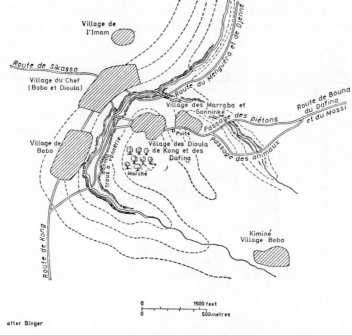

Figure 1.13*i*

agricultural productivity and to peoples able to realize that productivity by good
husbandry. The population needed to provide administrative and social services,
and to engage in trade and manufacture, must be provided with a surplus of
agricultural produce above the needs of the cultivators themselves. Nevertheless, in most cases cultivators form the majority of most urban populations, and
are commonly grouped in villages or quarters consisting mainly of kinsfolk or
of people accepted by the kin. Other quarters are occupied by distinct groups of
craftsmen, or by peoples from other communities settled as distinct groups
within the town for protection or in order to act as trading middlemen. Thus in
Barth's description of Katsina, the list of quarters includes those occupied by the
Hausa kinsfolk of Katsina itself, those occupied by craftsmen, e.g. saddlers'
and shoemakers' quarters, and those occupied by 'strangers', e.g. peoples from
Gobir, Bornu and Kontagora, and Arabs.[64] Many of the quarters have their
own markets, but there is always the great central market, in some cases, as in
many Yoruba towns, established close by the palace of the ruler. The relationship
between quarters and kinsfolk is often complex, and in many cases there is no
apparent relationship at all. Thus Lloyd, in discussing Yoruba lineages, shows
that whilst in some of the smaller towns of Ado Ekiti district the compounds
of each lineage form a quarter, in other cases quarters are occupied by members
of several lineages. 'The lineage is a feature of social structure; the town is one

of territorial structure. The lineage may be divided into segments; it is itself
part of a larger unit, held together by clanship ties. The town may be divided into
quarters and compounds, it may be part of a kingdom (now usually called district
for administrative purposes). The living male members of a lineage or its
segments live together in a compound or series of compounds which are usually
adjacent but may be scattered. The members of related lineages are scattered
through many towns and kingdoms. Conversely, the inhabitants of a town
come from many lineages of diverse origin.'[65] In Ibadan, until the recent

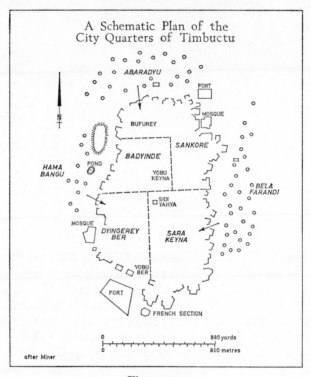

Figure 1.14

growth of Lagos, the largest Yoruba town and the largest town in inter-tropical
Africa, with a population of perhaps two-thirds of a million, there are few quarters
in the normal Yoruba sense. The town was founded by small armies of refugees
from the Fulani conquest of northern Yorubaland, and it developed as a stronghold offering protection from attack, adding other refugees. These peoples looked
not to kinship but to army groups as their social units.[66] Ibadan today is
divided not into quarters but into wards, whilst its surrounding villages are
grouped not by districts but by roads.

Conquest of surrounding districts, the exaction of tribute and the import
of slaves have led to the growth of some towns and the decline of others, with

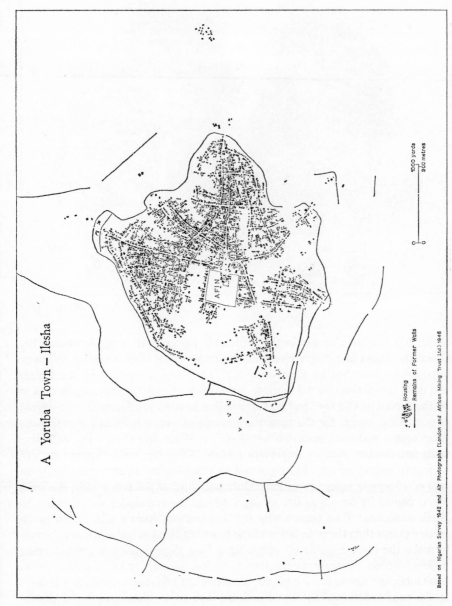

A Yoruba Town — Ilesha

AFIN

Housing
Remains of Former Walls

Based on Nigerian Survey 1942 and Air Photographs (London and African Mining Trust Ltd) 1946

1000 yards
900 metres

Figure 1.15a

Gateway of Ipara, in the Ijebu country

Figure 1.15b   After C. M. S. Gleaner, 1855

frequently marked changes in the settlement pattern. Thus the interfluve between the Ogun and Niger rivers in Yorubaland was once occupied by many
large towns described by Clapperton.[67] They were destroyed by the Fulani
and their populations forced to move southwards. Today the area once occupied
by the capital of Old Oyo and its surrounding hamlets is a forest reserve devoid
of settlement except for the temporary camps of hunters. Except amongst the
Akan towns, and some northern towns such as Timbuktu (Fig. 1.14), defensive
walls and ditches were an important feature. Kano has walls between 30 and
50 feet (9 and 15 metres) in height and 12 miles (19 km) in circuit enclosing an
area of 16 square miles (41 sq km). Only one-third of the area within the walls
was occupied by houses as late as 1933[68] and the remainder was farmed. As
Barth remarked: 'The reason why the fortifications were carried to so much
greater extent than the population of the town rendered necessary, was evidently
to make the place capable of sustaining a long siege (sufficient ground being
inclosed within the walls to produce the necessary supply of corn for the inhabitants), and also to receive the population of the open and unprotected villages
in the neighbourhood.'[69] Fortifications were often elaborate. Aerial photographs of the Yoruba town of Ilesha show the remains of several walls or
embankments with salients at the four main gateways. Another feature of Yoruba
towns, probably associated with defence, is an outer ring of woodland, the
'igbo ile' or home woodland. This impeded the movements of attacking forces,

provided timber and occasionally included burial places and religious groves (Fig. 1.15a).

Street patterns vary. The old Hausa cities usually had several main streets

Plan of Kano city and section of city wall, 1903

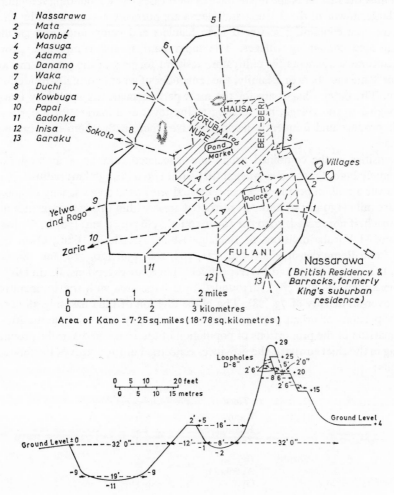

1	Nassarawa
2	Mata
3	Wombé
4	Masuga
5	Adama
6	Danamo
7	Waka
8	Duchi
9	Kowbuga
10	Papai
11	Gadonka
12	Inisa
13	Garaku

0   1   2 miles
0   1   2   3 kilometres
Area of Kano = 7·25 sq.miles (18·78 sq.kilometres)

Nassarawa
(British Residency & Barracks, formerly King's suburban residence)

Loopholes D-8"

0 5 10 20 feet
0 5 10 15 metres

Based on the diagram in *Annual Reports*, Northern Nigeria, 1902, p.165

Figure 1.16

converging on a centre. Kano in Barth's day appears to have had 6 such streets converging on the Dala, or oldest quarter, with other important streets leading to 14 gateways. The former Akan towns of Ghana had one long street oriented from north to south with side streets at right angles subdividing the towns into quarters, usually from 4 to 8 in number. The Yoruba streets were established commonly in the form of a cross with the great market at the centre. The main streets were oriented in most cases from north to south, along the trade routes leading to the Niger crossings and Hausaland, and from east to west, connecting one town with another.

Whilst the smaller Nupe towns have in most cases few surrounding settlements, the larger towns of the Yoruba and Hausa are normally encompassed by an extensive area containing scattered farm hamlets and compounds and an outer fringe area containing villages. The inner hamlets and compounds provide agricultural settlements for cultivators resident for part of the year in the town or for some members of a family, the remainder of whom normally reside in the town. The outer villages are for the most part permanently settled by families belonging to the village, but looking to the town as a market for a portion of their produce and frequently having relatives there with whom they can make contact.

Densities in the combined urban and associated rural areas are commonly extremely high. Prothero estimated that within 20 miles (32 km) radius of Kano city over a million people were concentrated with an average density of 360 per square mile (139 per sq km). 'In restricted areas within this zone densities must approach, if not exceed, 1000 per square mile' (386 per sq km).[70] In the highly urbanized Yoruba divisions of Ibadan, Oshun, Ife, Ilesha, Ekiti, Owo, Ijebu and Ijebu-Remo densities are 359, 371, 265, 198, 156, 120, 129, and 188 (139, 143, 102, 76, 60, 46, 50 and 73) respectively. There are exceptions. Benin Division for example has one 'city' surrounded by a large area with the comparatively low over-all density of 73 (28). The Nupe division of Bida has only 38 (15).

Proportions of urban population vary considerably between communities. A comparison of the proportions of population of the Hausa and Yoruba provinces living in the chief towns of the provinces concerned in 1952–3 gives the following results:

	Town	Percentage of provincial population
Hausa	Kano	3·9
	Katsina	3·5
	Zaria	5·8
Yoruba	Ibadan	27·7
	Abeokuta	13·0
	Oyo	9·2

32 per cent of the people of the Western Region of Nigeria and of Lagos Colony live in towns with 20,000 or more inhabitants, compared with only 3·6 per cent in the Northern Region. The Western Region has 3,045,000 or 47 per cent of its population in urban settlements with more than 5000 inhabitants and 23 per cent in only 10 towns each with over 50,000.[71] Yoruba urbanization is outstanding in West Africa and includes several towns of remarkable size within a community depending almost entirely on agricultural production. In 1952 Ibadan, for

example, had a population of 459,000, and Ogbomosho had 123,000. The largest indigenous town outside Yorubaland was Kano with 130,000. Kumasi, the largest town of Ashanti, had only 80,000. It has been found impossible to make an effective correlation between settlement function and size. There are a number of administrative and trading settlements in West Africa which are smaller than villages populated almost entirely by cultivators. Censuses generally adopt the

Awka

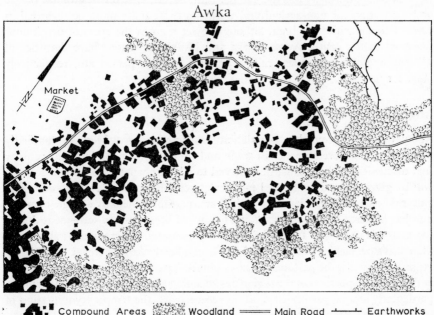

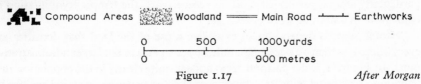

Compound Areas   Woodland   Main Road   Earthworks

```
0          500          1000 yards
0                       900 metres
```

Figure 1.17   *After Morgan*

figure of 5000 as the minimum size of a town. A preliminary examination of function and size in Yorubaland suggests that this figure is too low, and that 10,000 would probably be a nearer approximation. In the Yoruba towns proportions of urban male population engaged in non-agricultural occupations are low compared with Europe. Ife had only 36 per cent in 1952, Ogbomosho 33 per cent, Oyo 26 per cent, but there were some higher proportions in important administrative centres, notably Ibadan with 65 per cent and Abeokuta with 85 per cent. Outside Yorubaland towns generally have higher proportions of non-agricultural male population. In Iboland, for example, Onitsha had 97 per cent in 1953, and in Hausaland, Kano City had 92 per cent.

A peculiar case of urbanization occurs in Onitsha Province in northern Iboland. Almost the entire population is grouped in settlement units normally with over 10,000 population. These may be 3 miles (5 km) or more in diameter, nearly circular in shape with the perimeter defined by narrow belts of woodland, and occasionally by embankments and trenches. Within the unit population is dispersed and, except where recent changes have occurred, there are no streets. Yet each of the units is in effect a nucleation of settlement clearly separated from other units. In each case population is grouped together for social convenience, defence, administrative purposes and trade. The proportions of non-agricultural population are normally less than 20 per cent, nevertheless on the grounds of size and nucleation for non-agricultural purposes these units must be regarded as towns.[72] Densities are high, although lower than in the areas of continuous dispersal to the south. Awgu, Awka and Nsukka Divisions have densities of 356,440 and 392 per square mile (137, 170 and 151 per sq km) respectively (Fig. 1.17).

Migration

Many of the present-day population movements have been so markedly affected by the developments in trade and production of the last half century that discussion of them must be deferred to a later chapter. Here some account will be given only of traditional movements chiefly amongst pastoral and agricultural nomads. Migration over limited areas normally held by a single community has hitherto been a characteristic feature of West African settlement due to the methods employed for exploiting local resources. Where land is abundant, the cultivator, lacking manures and fertilizers, has looked wherever possible for virgin soils, whilst the pastoralist has sought fresh pasture. The marked dry season in the northern portions of the region has encouraged a regular seasonal movement, particularly among pastoralists and, in recent years, the temporary migration of cultivators in search of work elsewhere.

Pastoral nomads depend on so extensive a use of the land that densities are everywhere less than 10 per square mile (4 per sq km) in the larger administrative units. In Figure 1.2, the pastoral areas appear quite clearly in the population distribution. The Sahel with its extensive wet season pastures, occupied mainly by the Fulani, shows higher densities than the Saharan areas to the north. Linguère and Tambacounda, for example, which include large portions of the Ferlo, have densities of 5 and 7 per square mile (2 and 3 per sq km) respectively. In the Mauritanian Sahara, Tagant, Inchiri and Baie du Lévrier have densities of only 1 (0·4). Adrar has only 3 people for every 10 square miles (26 sq km). Occasional trading and agriculture settlements bring locally higher densities. Nioro in Mali has 12 persons per square mile (5 per sq km) and Zinder in Niger has 19 (7). Comparison of the figures is, however, of doubtful value due to the seasonal movement of population and the problem of timing the census. Moreover, the pastures vary in quality between one wet season and another, and population movement is modified accordingly. An account of the movements involved is given in Chapter 3.

The shifting of agricultural settlement is tending to disappear in West Africa due to changes in agricultural practice and the influence of modern administration. Shifting still occurs amongst the Bété and Gagou in the south-western Ivory Coast and in the neighbouring portions of Liberia where it is associated with densities of less than 7 (3) and dispersed settlement. It occurs also amongst some of the Boki and Anyang peoples in the east – Mamfe Division in the Cameroons has a density of 23 (9). The shift of settlement is not seasonal, but occurs after a period of years when the soils adjacent to the settlement cease to give adequate returns for the labour expended. Movement may, therefore, occur at irregular intervals, varying according to soil quality. Bohannan has described traditional migration amongst the Tiv.[73] The Tiv seek new land even from areas where there is no land shortage or move away from the rule of a man or group considered to be tyrannical. Bohannan distinguishes between 'steam-roller' migration in which land is taken from neighbours furthest away in kinship, 'leapfrog' migration in which a new settlement is founded near kinsfolk, and 'lonewolf' migration consisting of the movement of a family or small group to the land of 'strangers' on which they become 'guests'. In the case of the Tiv, the pace of migration has increased due to population pressure on local land resources in some areas and the security of colonial administration enabling greater ease of movement. Here changing conditions have been met by more migration instead of by a change in agricultural practice. It would seem likely that the movement of settlement was formerly a more common feature than it is now and was practised extensively throughout West Africa. Today even in areas of 'fixed' settlement, some local movement may occur if only over distances of a few yards. Clay houses with thatch roofs soon become worn by weathering and a new dwelling may be preferred. A new house may be built away from old cess-pits or from local gardens overgrown with tall shade trees. Erosion of the foundations, particularly in towns on pediment slopes, may encourage a move. Religious and social factors, e.g. the death of the head of a household, may also be important. Movement of individual families frequently occurs between one village and another. Gamble found frequent change of place of residence among the Wolof, for example, due to pressure on the land or social factors.[74]

Local agricultural population movements which are small, but which affect consideration of settlement patterns and the question of census-taking, occur between towns and neighbouring rural areas and between croplands dependent on rain and floodlands. Such movements frequently involve the building of temporary settlements or even structures intended to last for several seasons and only partially inhabited during the 'off-period'. There is in addition some traditional movement of labour, paid commonly in kind, for work on the croplands of neighbouring communities. Thus young Ibo men of Umueke in Okigwi Division undertake farm work in less crowded and more prosperous areas, whilst Tiv 'age sets' assist in hoeing mounds in return for food and beer.[75] Specialist labour groups occur such as the Urhobo who cut palm fruit in many Yoruba districts and establish temporary camps.

Large-scale migration by conquest has ceased today, but has produced some important population movements in the past. The Wolof of Senegal have encroached on neighbouring communities, the Malinké on the tribes of the southwest, and the Ibo on the Ibibio and Cross River peoples in the east.

Population increase

The problem of determining the rate of increase of West Africa's population has been made extremely difficult by the inadequacy of census material. However, some detailed local studies provide understanding of the nature of the problem and indications of the probable growth.

Detailed sample censuses recording birth and fertility rates, death and infant mortality rates, have been made in Guinea (1954–5), Bongouanou in the Ivory Coast (1954), the lower Senegal valley (1957) and the middle Senegal valley (1960), and sample censuses, recording social data including age groups, were made in a few French West African towns. The urban data give little indication of the general trend, but the age pyramids for Dakar and Abidjan (1955) are of interest in their reflection of the large number of immigrants aged approximately 20–40 years. The age pyramid derived from the sample censuses of Guinea indicates a youthful population likely to increase rapidly. The annual natural increase in Guinea is estimated to be 2·2 per cent in the rural areas and 2·4 per cent in the larger population centres, making possible a doubling of the population in about 30 years. So large a rate of natural increase seems to have been possible only in the last 10 to 15 years, with the great expansion in medical services lowering the death rate and increasing the number of live births.[76] Although the annual increase in Ghana between 1931 and 1948 can be estimated by comparison of census totals to be 1·8 per cent, a similar figure to the above, it appears to be too high when taking account of the possibilities of greater underestimation of population in the earlier censuses. It is possible too that the French sample censuses are not as precise as similar censuses in Europe. Even the most careful methods cannot elucidate all the details required from a largely illiterate population which views census-taking as inimical to its interests. However, it would seem probable that the populations of former French Guinea and of Ghana are increasing and probably at a rate greater than 1·5 per cent per annum.

In the middle valley of the Senegal the net reproduction rate was 1·78. Net reproduction rates for Guinea were estimated at the high figures of 1·5 in the rural areas and 1·4 in the major centres. In Bongouanou the rate was 1·7. Gross reproduction rates for the last three areas were 3·3, 2·6 and 2·8 respectively. These results occurred despite the high infant mortality rates of 226, 142 and 157 per thousand, again for the same areas. Similar high infant mortality rates occurred elsewhere, e.g. Bathurst (1954) – 115, Ghana (1951) – 118, Lagos (1953) – 82, Freetown and the Colony of Sierra Leone (1954) – 123.[77] Estimated crude birth and death rates per thousand in sample census areas in French West Africa were as follows:[78]

	Guinea 1954-5		Bongouanou 1954	Lower Senegal Valley 1957
	Rural	Major centres		
Birth rate	59	50	55	50
Death rate	37	26	23	27
Natural increase	22	24	32	23

Other death rate figures are Ghana (1951 – 10 per cent sample of compulsory Registration Areas only) – 19, Lagos (1951) – 16, Portuguese Guinea (1952) – 13. Expectation of life is low. In Guinea, the expectation at birth in rural areas is only 31 years and in major centres 36 years. The population is therefore likely to consist mainly of young people for a long time to come, and to incur few problems with regard to the support of the aged. Prothero has calculated fertility ratios for Northern Nigeria from existing census data showing the number of children aged 0–6 years and the number of women aged 15–49 years. These appear to be high and according to Prothero are consistent with 'the increases in population that have taken place since 1931' – presumably referring to the difference between the 1931 and 1952 census totals.[79] In the middle Senegal valley the death rate is high, but a high birth rate suggests an estimated doubling of the population in approximately 30 years.[80] Similarly the Agni population of the Ivory Coast is estimated likely to double every 25–30 years.[81]

Previous estimates of population increases, particularly where these have been derived by comparison of censuses taken at different dates, appear to be of doubtful value, as Kuczynski has demonstrated.[82] West African families have rarely been large partly owing to the tradition amongst many peoples of a long weaning period, during which the mother abstains from sexual intercourse, and partly owing to high infantile mortality rates and high death rates amongst mothers giving birth. Disease has taken a heavy toll, particularly the epidemic diseases of smallpox, meningitis and plague. Malaria is almost universal, and poor diets sometimes result in deficiency diseases such as kwashiorkor. Some areas are so badly infested with fly-borne diseases, such as sleeping sickness, onchocerciasis and filaria, that they are, as far as possible, avoided. Medical research and services have increased enormously since 1945, particularly in preventive work – for example, vaccination – and in the provision of better maternity facilities. An expectation of an annual increase of 1·5 per cent in future does not therefore seem unduly high, not when compared with apparent annual increases from population censuses and estimates of 6 per cent in Senegal (1955–60), 5·8 per cent in Nigeria (1955–63), and 5 per cent in Togo (1955–62).

BIBLIOGRAPHICAL NOTES

[1] J. Richard-Molard, Les Densités de Population au Fouta-Djallon, in Hommage à Jacques Richard-Molard, Présence Africaine, 15, 1952, pp. 95–106.
J. Richard-Molard, Démographie de l'Afrique Occidentale Française, L'Encyclopédie de la France d'Outre-Mer, Afrique Occidentale Française, Tome I, 1949, pp. 125–32.

For recent discussion of population censuses, mapping and densities, see K .M. Barbour and R. M. Prothero (ed.), *Essays on African Population*, London, 1961.

[2] R. R. Kuczynski, *A Demographic Survey of the British Colonial Empire*, vol. I, West Africa, 1948, Sierra Leone, Census-Taking, pp. 19–40.

[3] ibid., pp. 32–34.

[4] *Report on the Census of Population*, Gold Coast, 1948, p. 7.

[5] ibid.

[6] *Annuaire Statistique de l'Afrique Occidentale Française*, vol. 5, Tome I, 1950-4, 1956, pp. 40–43.

[7] Quotations and comments are made from the reports of the population censuses for the three regions of Nigeria, Northern and Western Regions 1952, Eastern Region 1953.
    Nigeria has had two more recent censuses. The first, in 1962, showed that the Northern Region had lost its demographic hegemony, and was suppressed. The second, in 1963, gave the surprising total of nearly 56 millions, and restored the North's demographic lead, but the district details are still unpublished. The problem of Nigerian censuses is that hitherto the number of seats allotted to each region in the Federal Parliament has depended on the census results.

[8] G. T. Trewartha and W. Zelinsky, Population Patterns in Tropical Africa, *Annals, Association of American Geographers*, **44**, 1954, pp. 135–62.

[9] E. A. Boateng, Some Geographical Aspects of the 1960 Population Census of Ghana, *Bulletin, Ghana Geographical Association*, **5**, 1960, 2–8.
    J. M. Hunter, A Note on the Post-Enumeration Uses of the 1960 Population Census Enumeration Area Maps of Ghana, *Bulletin, Ghana Geographical Association*, **8**, 1963, 27–32.

[10] J. Richard-Molard, *Afrique Occidentale Française*, 1949, pp. 27–30 and p. 45.

[11] H. Baumann and D. Westermann, *Les Peuples et les Civilisations de l'Afrique*, trans. from the German by L. Homburger, Paris, 1948, pp. 340–88.

[12] For discussion of population in the 'Middle Belt' of Ghana, see T. E. Hilton, *Ghana Population Atlas*, Edinburgh, 1960.

[13] Y. Urvoy, Petit Atlas Ethno-Démographique du Soudan, *Mémoires, L'Institut Français d'Afrique Noire*, **5**, 1942, p. 14.
    R. J. Harrison Church, *West Africa*, London, 5th ed., 1966, pp. 163–4.

[14] Démographie de l'Afrique Occidentale Française, op. cit., p. 130.

[15] ibid., p. 131.

[16] E. A. Boateng, Recent Changes in Settlement in South-East Gold Coast, *Transactions, Institute of British Geographers*, **21**, 1955, pp. 157–69.

[17] K. M. Buchanan and J. C. Pugh, *Land and People in Nigeria*, London, 1955, p. 38.

[18] J. Richard-Molard, Les Groupes Ethniques de l'Afrique Occidentale Française, *L'Encyclopédie de la France d'Outre-Mer*, Afrique Occidentale Française, Tome I, 1949, pp. 107–24, see p. 110.

[19] Les Peuples et les Civilisations de l'Afrique, op. cit.

[20] J. Greenberg, Studies in African Linguistic Classification, *South-western Journal of Anthropology*, **5**, 1949, and **6**, 1950 (7 articles).
    A general anthropological account using Greenberg's divisions with modification as a basis appears in G. P. Murdock, *Africa – its Peoples and Their Culture History*, New York, 1959.

[21] Les Groupes Ethniques de l'Afrique Occidentale Française, op. cit.

[22] For a general account of West African history see:
J. D. Fage, *An Introduction to the History of West Africa*, 3rd ed., Cambridge, 1962.
E. W. Bovill, *Caravans of the Old Sahara*, London, 1933.
Lady Lugard (Flora Shaw), *A Tropical Dependency*, London, 1905.

[23] See G. Doutressoule, *L'Elevage en Afrique Occidentale Française*, Paris, 1947, p. 22.

[24] H. R. Palmer, *The Bornu Sahara and Sudan*, London, 1936, pp. 5, 8 and 39.

[25] H. Labouret, La Langue des Peuls ou Foulbe, *Mémoires, Institut Français de l'Afrique Noire*, **14**, 1955, pp. 17–20 and 37–41.

[26] P. Thomassey and R. Mauny, Campagne de Fouilles à Koumbi Saleh, *Bulletin, Institut Français d'Afrique Noire*, **10**, 1951, pp. 438–62.

[27] R. Mauny, Etat Actual de la Question de Ghana, *Bulletin, Institut Français d'Afrique Noire*, **10**, 1951, pp. 463–75.

[28] H. Barth, *Travels and Discoveries in North and Central Africa*, vol. II, London, 1857, p. 304.

[29] Les Groupes Ethniques de l'Afrique Occidentale Française, op. cit., p. 116.

[30] Les Peuples et les Civilisations de l'Afrique, op. cit., p. 312.

[31] Les Groupes Ethniques de l'Afrique Occidentale Française, op. cit., p. 120.

[32] Les Peuples et les Civilisations de l'Afrique, op. cit., p. 405.

[33] An outstanding study is B. Holas, *Les Senoufo (y compris les Minianka)*, Paris, 1957.

[34] There is a reference to causeways among the Kamuku in O. Temple, *Notes on the Tribes, Provinces, Emirates and States of the Northern Provinces of Nigeria*, 2nd edition, Lagos, 1922, p. 207.

[35] E. L. R. Meyerowitz, *Akan Traditions of Origin*, London, 1952, pp. 124–9, especially p. 129.

[36] Studies in African Linguistic Classification, op. cit.

[37] Akan Traditions of Origin, op. cit.

[38] S. F. Nadel, *A Black Byzantium*, London, 1942, pp. 12–13.

[39] W. B. Morgan, The 'Grassland Towns' of the Eastern Region of Nigeria, *Institute of British Geographers, Transactions and Papers*, **23**, 1957, pp. 213–94.

[40] P. Brown, The Igbira, in D. Forde et al., *Peoples of the Niger-Benue Confluence*, London, 1955, p. 61.

[41] The Bornu Sahara and Sudan, op. cit., see especially pp. 27, 38–39, 83, 100–101, 148.

[42] P. Bohannan, *Tiv Farm and Settlement*, Colonial Research Series, London, **15**, 1954.

[43] Les Groupes Ethniques de l'Afrique Occidentale Française, p. 122.

[44] R. W. Steel, The Population of Ashanti: A Geographical Analysis, *Geographical Journal*, **112**, 1948, pp. 64–77.

[45] E. A. Boateng, op. cit.

[46] See especially E. P. Skinner, West African Economic Systems, in M. J. Herskovits and M. Harwitz, *Economic Transition in Africa*, London, 1964, pp. 77–95.

[47] G. Schwab, *Tribes of the Liberian Hinterland*, Cambridge, Mass., 1947, see especially pp. 29–41.

[48] W. B. Morgan, Farming Practice, Settlement Pattern and Population Density in South-Eastern Nigeria, *Geographical Journal*, **121**, 1955, pp. 320–33.
    Water-carrying has become a minor occupation. See R. K. Udo, Land and Population in Otoro District, *Nigerian Geographical Journal*, **4**, 1961, pp. 3–19, where he records the practice of water-carrying among the Ibibio people and the opposition of the carriers to the introduction of pipe-borne supplies.

[49] H. Labouret, *Paysans d'Afrique Occidentale*, 6th edition, Paris, 1941, p. 108.

[50] *The Gold Coast*, 1931, vol. i, p. 157.

[51] T. E. Hilton, The Population of the Gold Coast, *International Geographical Union*, Natural resources, food and population in inter-tropical Africa, Makerere Symposium 1955, 1956, pp. 43–49.

[52] P. Mercier, L'Habitation à Etage dans l'Atakora, *Etudes Dahoméennes*, **11**, 1954, pp. 29–79. See Fig. 13.

[53] L. and P. Bohannan, *The Tiv of Central Nigeria*, London, 1953, p. 10.

[54] Lt.-Col. G. F. A. Whitlock, *Delimitation of Boundary between Yola and the Cross River*, 1907-09, Cd. 5368, 1910, p. 5.

[55] D. P. Gamble, *The Wolof of Senegambia*, London, 1957, p. 14.

[56] R. M. Prothero, The Population Census of Northern Nigeria 1952: Problems and Results, *Population Studies*, **10**, 1956, pp. 166–83.

[57] *Colonial Annual Report*, Northern Nigeria, **409**, 1902, p. 79.

[58] Démographie de l'Afrique Occidentale Française, op. cit., p. 131.

[59] K. L. Little, *The Mende of Sierra Leone*, London, 1951.

[60] R. E. Bradbury, *The Benin Kingdom,* and P. C. Lloyd, The Itsekiri (in the same vol.), 1957, pp. 129 and 182, London.

[61] ibid., p. 143.

[62] A. F. Bridges, *Report on Oil Palm Survey*, Ibo, Ibibio and Cross River Areas (Kumba), 11th June 1938, unpub.

[63] Les Densités de Population au Fouta-Djallon, op. cit.

[64] Travels and Discoveries in North and Central Africa, vol. II, op. cit., pp. 77–82, and Appendix I, pp. 107-27.

[65] P. C. Lloyd, The Yoruba Lineage, *Africa*, **25**, 1955, pp. 235–51; see also P. C. Lloyd, *Yoruba Land Law*, London, 1962.

[66] See N. C. Mitchel, Some Comments on the Growth and Character of Ibadan's Population, *Research Notes*, Department of Geography, University College of Ibadan, **4**, 1953.

[67] H. Clapperton, *Journal of a Second Expedition into the Interior of Africa*, London, 1829, see especially pp. 12–35.

[68] C. R. Niven, Kano in 1933, *Geographical Journal*, **82**, 1933, pp. 336–43.

[69] Travels and Discoveries in North and Central Africa, vol. II, op. cit., pp. 118–19.

[70] R. M. Prothero, The Population Census of Northern Nigeria, 1952, op. cit.
For a more recent study see M. J. Mortimore and J. Wilson, *Land and People in the Kano Close-settled Zone: a Report to the Greater Kano Planning Authority*, Ahmadu Bello University, Zaria, 1965.

[71] For detailed study of the Yoruba towns see N. C. Mitchel, Yoruba Towns, in K. M. Barbour and R. M. Prothero, *Essays on African Population*, London, 1961, pp. 279–301.

[72] See The 'Grassland Towns' of the Eastern Region of Nigeria, op. cit. One might compare these towns with the 'village-towns' of Hungary, large settlement units containing widely separated dwellings and where the chief occupation is agriculture.

[73] The Tiv of Central Nigeria, op. cit., pp. 54–57. See below, p. 326.

[74] D. P. Gamble, *The Wolof of Senegambia*, London, 1957, p. 52.

[75] C. D. Forde and R. Scott, *The Native Economies of Nigeria*, London, 1946, vol. I, pp. 73–74.
The Tiv of Central Nigeria, op. cit., p. 51.

[76] A.O.F. – 1957, Tableaux Economiques, Haut commissariat de la république en Afrique occidentale française, pp. 109–10.

[77] United Nations, *Statistical Year Book*, 1955.

[78] A.O.F. – 1957, op. cit., p. 112.

[79] R. M. Prothero, The Population Census of Northern Nigeria, op. cit.

[80] J. L. Boutillier, P. Cantrelle, J. Causse, C. Laurent and Th. N'Doye, *La Moyenne Vallée du Sénégal*, I.N.S.E.E., 1962. There are, however, numerous exceptions to the general rate of increase within the valley. Le Blanc, for example, found in Amadi-Ounaré village evidence of the doubling of population only in 56 years (C. Le Blanc, Un Village de la Vallée du Sénégal: Amadi-Ounaré, *Cahiers d'outre-mer* ·17, 1964, 117–48).

[81] J. L. Boutillier, *Bongouanou, Côte d'Ivoire*, Paris, 1960.

[82] A Demographic Survey of the British Colonial Empire, vol. I, West Africa, op. cit.

Figure 1.14 is based on a diagram in H. Miner, *The Primitive City of Timbuchtoo*, Princeton, 1953.

Agriculture

The West African cultivator like his counterpart elsewhere in inter-tropical Africa is not a farmer in the European or North American sense but a gardener. His holding of scattered plots is rarely more than five acres in extent, often considerably less, and must produce fairly high total returns per acre to feed himself and his dependents and provide a small surplus for exchange or sale. (Individual crop returns in West Africa are frequently rather low, but here one is concerned with the total return of mixed and, in some cases, succession cropping.) Production is mainly, although in only rare cases entirely, for subsistence or highly localized exchange or sale. There are, moreover, some exceptional communities whose cultivators sell most of their produce. The cultivator does not normally own land, but has a 'use-right' in it which is sometimes shared.[1] His approach to agriculture is therefore quite unlike that of the farmer in, for example, Great Britain.

'The social system in Great Britain and the social system in West Africa are very different. The main differences between these two social systems are not only that the agricultural and craft industries in West Africa embrace the whole people, but that the basis of these industries is farming for subsistence on land held on a communal basis and not farming for sale and profit on land held on individual tenure.'[2] The total return per acre is remarkably high when one considers the poor quality of the seed, the shortage of manures, the lack of fertilizers, and the limitations of technique. High total return is the result of hand tillage and attention to individual plants in a system of mixed cultivation. This tillage makes use of only a few implements and is rarely assisted by the labour of animals. There is therefore a severe limitation on the acreage which can be worked and in only a few cases is that area sufficient to supply more than the bare necessities of existence. Many peoples experience an annual shortage of food for a few weeks at the end of the dry season and the beginning of the rains. Others must store food against the lean years when rains are poor or late. In West Africa there is little surplus available for expenditure on the improvement of agriculture. Improvement must in any case be regarded with suspicion by peoples whose hold on the physical environment is at best precarious. The failure of some recent attempts to deviate from established methods reinforces the claims of traditional practice.[3]

Implements

The chief implements are the hoe, the digging stick, the 'matchet' or cutlass and the sickle. Of these there is a great variety to suit local tillage methods, soils or the planting and harvesting of different crops. In forested areas or where the fallow consists of woody plants heavy cutting tools are needed. Very large trees may be removed by girdling and burning and their stumps left in the fields. Where the fallow consists of grasses, pulling and burning may suffice. Burning may loosen the ground before tillage by the expansion of moist soil during firing and may provide ash to fertilize the soil.[4] A dry period is essential for a system of cultivation so dependent on fire to clear the ground. In Ghana clearance without burning – 'the proka system' – takes place in the wetter areas, but consists mainly of the removal of the undergrowth in order to plant cocoyam and plantains.[5]

Steel matchets and axes were introduced by European traders. Their greater cutting efficiency when compared with tools of local 'soft' iron has undoubtedly eased the task of clearance, and has modified the development of fallow cover by keeping sprouts and bush 'whacked out', instead of letting the land rest under regrowth.[6] Other cutting tools include the sickle for harvesting grain and cutting thatching grass, and the long-handled pruning and harvesting knife of the cocoa farmer.

The hoe is the chief digging implement. The chief types include:

1) A long-handled hoe with a crescent-shaped blade (the 'iler' of French authors[7], 'hauya' in Hausa, 'kworemi' in Kanuri) used by the Sudanic peoples merely to break the surface of very sandy soils. The cultivator pushes the implement in front of him.

2) A long-handled adze hoe used, notably in Hausaland and Bornu, for breaking up clay soils.

3) A short-handled tanged adze hoe ('fantainya' in Hausa) for planting and weeding in clay soils.

4) A short-handled hoe with a broad slotted blade set at angles between 15 and 45 degrees ('galma' in Hausa) and used by Sudanic peoples for making small ridges in sandy loams.

5) A short-handled, tanged hoe with a broad blade set at 15 to 20 degrees used chiefly by sub-Sudanic peoples for making small ridges in light soils. As in (4) tillage is shallow and the action of turning the soil over bears some similarity to ploughing. Similar untanged hoes are used by the Wolof ('warango') and Serer ('vrenglie').

6) A short-handled hoe with a blade of various widths according to local soil conditions and set at 45 to 90 degrees (the 'daba' of French authors). This is the general purpose hoe used mainly for medium to deep tillage throughout West Africa, but chiefly by the sub-Guinean and Guinean peoples.

7) A long-handled hoe with a narrow blade ('ube' in Ibo), held vertically and used by Guinean peoples, notably the Ibo, to dig holes for yam planting in well-drained soils.

8) Various short-handled, small-bladed hoes used for weeding.

Other digging tools include long-handled dibbles and digging sticks used to make holes for planting, and the 'kofi' or long-handled 'spade' of the Baga rice growers of Guinea, and of the Diola of Lower Casamance. In northern Liberia a digging stick rather similar to the Baga 'spade', made entirely of wood, is also used for planting in wet ground.[8] The plough is little used, is of recent introduction, and will be discussed in Chapter 10.

Tillage

Tillage methods are related directly to crops, soils and moisture supplies. On the northern fringes of cultivation where rainfall totals are only between 20 and 30 inches, and particularly where soils are sandy, the surface is merely broken for planting. The upland rice cultivators of the south-west with a heavy rainfall in one short season also plant on the 'flat'. In Bornu and in parts of Mali planting may even be in hollows in order to collect moisture. Further south the Sudanic and sub-Sudanic peoples depend on cereals planted in ridges, which on the heavier soils and in the wetter areas may be as much as 2 feet (60 cm) high. The ridge provides free drainage during heavy showers, preventing waterlogging, and conserves moisture between showers. The Guinean peoples of the extreme south and south-east depend mainly on root crops planted in mounds. The mounds provide the maximum concentration of top soil for each individual large seed, conserve moisture and drain off the surplus of downpours. In the wetter areas with heavy soils mounds of 3 to 4 feet (90–120 cm) in height are common. Six feet (180 cm) is not unknown, particularly in floodlands. On light soils mounds are generally lower, usually between 1 and 2 feet (30–60 cm) in height. On very sandy soils low mounds are raised over holes filled with a mixture of top soil and ash. Whilst the general rule in West Africa appears to be ridges for cereals and mounds for roots, there are numerous exceptions. Many sub-Sudanic peoples plant their cereals in mounds, whilst others, notably in the Jos Plateau of Nigeria, have only recently adopted ridges for the purpose, due to external influence.

Raised beds a foot or more (30 cm) in height and 2 or 3 feet (60–90 cm) in width are used for the cultivation of groundnuts, and even in some cases for cassava. Generally, however, hardy crops like cassava or legumes are planted with little preliminary tillage, or, if interplanted, occupy the sides of the ridges or mounds, or even the troughs between. On steep slopes narrower beds are often constructed parallel to the contour and forming small terraces supporting a great variety of crops. Notable examples occur in the Bamenda Plateau in the Cameroons. In other hill regions, particularly in the Atacora of Dahomey, in the Jos and Adamawa Plateaux, and on the steeper hill-slopes of Houndé in

Upper Volta low stone wall terraces have been constructed against which soil has accumulated to form narrow field strips. Often in association are stone mounds about 2 or 3 feet (60–90 cm) in height which are probably the result of collection in order to clear the ground for cultivation.[9]

A notable feature in West African tillage is the contrast between the drier sandier areas of the north and the wetter and often heavier soiled areas of the south. In the former tillage is mostly associated with cereal cultivation and is shallow (3 in (75 mm) or less in depth). In the latter tillage is mostly associated with roots cultivation and is deep (6 in (15 cm) or more). Deep tillage also occurs in the wetter cereal growing districts where high ridges are made.

Manures

For the most part there is a shortage of animal manures in West Africa, clearly evident in the necessity for long periods of fallow in order to rest the land after cropping. In the wetter south, notably in the zone of woody fallows, grass pasture is difficult to develop and maintain. In most areas where woodland is still abundant, tsetse flies occur and carry trypanosomiasis to stock. This is a major problem of the sub-Sudanic and sub-Guinean zones where population densities are too low to maintain effective clearance of woodland, and thus limit the distribution of tsetse fly. Only in the drier areas of the north and on high plateaux where grass pasture is easier to develop and the fly less abundant or non-existent, are animals kept in large numbers. The divorce between stock rearing and cultivation which commonly obtains in West Africa, and the seasonal movement of stock, mean that even in the north manure supplies are available for only a small part of the year.

However, many peoples realize the value of animal manures and use them wherever possible. Cultivators like the Wolof, Songhay and Hausa encourage the pasturing of cattle on their cropland during the dry season. The Serer of Senegal keep cattle and have a regular rotation of pasture and cropping. The Kabrai and Somba of the Atacora also keep cattle, and allow them to roam over their fields in the dry season.[10] In south-eastern Nigeria the Ezza Ibo make compost in open circular pits using even human excrement.[11]

Green manures are applied in some instances. In Bamenda grass is frequently dug into the mounds used for planting. The Bobo of the Upper Volta use millet and rice stalks.[12] The Mbula of Northern Nigeria sow their seed amongst grass which is later cut down for manure.[13] Other forms of manuring include the use of ashes, household refuse, night soil, the digging of cess-pits on land to be cultivated, and even the use of river bed soil, e.g. in the case of the Jakara river in the Kano Province of Northern Nigeria.[14] A peculiar example has been described from northern Guinea. There the Coniagui fertilize their fields by the annual removal of their bamboo houses from field to field, and by movements of 10 metres or so within a field every two to three weeks during the dry season.[15] Where only small supplies of manure are available use is usually restricted to plots of land near the settlement producing 'kitchen-garden' crops.

D

On such 'compound land' virtually permanent cultivation is possible. An unusual source of manure is the termite mound. Several peoples, chiefly in the sub-Sudanic zone, pulverize the mounds and scatter the fine soil and organic matter over their land.

Fields

The field units of West Africa belong to ordered systems which give the appearance of careful planning. There are two main groups:

1) Fields on compound land.
2) Fields on the main cropland.

The latter may be subdivided into large units held by groups and smaller individual or family units. In almost all cases cropland fields are arranged in strips providing a convenient method of land division amongst members of the land-holding group and easy means of access. Compound land fields are of varied shape, since they are the product of holding by the individual or the family and not of subdivision within a group. Strip fields on compound land usually indicate new, possibly European influences.

Field shape and size vary according to the needs of the community, availability of land, type of crop and system of cultivation employed. Social traditions and organization, and systems of land tenure are also important factors. Detailed examples will be given in Chapter 7. Where land is abundant and holdings scattered they may be amorphous. Where, however, plots or larger field units are contiguous rectangular shapes are preferred for convenient demarcation and division. Rectangular shapes also suit better the common method of planting in rows. They are preferred amongst communities lacking instruments for land measurement and needing suitable reference points. The cropland paths provide easy lines of reference, and are often subdivided by pacing into a series of narrow frontages each giving access to a strip plot.[16] In some cases, notably in Ghana, the technique of land division leads to the creation of narrow strips of enormous length.[17] Except in the few cases of overcrowding the field systems are not static, but constantly changing as new fields are cleared and the old returned to fallow. It is this constant movement of fields which makes land use studies difficult, and which has given rise to the terms 'shifting cultivation' and 'rotational bush fallow' (see below).

Holdings and land tenure

Whereas the size of holdings is related to the area available and the limitations of technique, the pattern, that is the distribution and type of plots held, is related to the systems of land tenure and to the allocation of land to different forms of cropping (land classification below).

Size of holdings varies enormously, but to give a notion of the order of size one may say that a common holding of a basic family unit of about seven persons is approximately 3 acres (1·2 hectares) with an additional 10 to 20 acres (4 to 8 hectares) of fallow. Holdings can be as small as half an acre (0·2 hectare) and are rarely larger than 20 acres (8 hectares). Where additional labour is available small plantations or even large estates exist. Large estates maintained by slave labour occurred in the last century amongst the more powerful communities, particularly in the Sudanic 'empires'. In some cases chiefs or elders maintain small plantations with labour provided by the local community. The use of hired labour on larger holdings has tended to increase with the spread of commercial cropping.

It seems likely that holding sizes are smaller in the wetter than in the drier areas, since the possibility of planting roots in the wetter areas provides higher yields per acre, the task of clearance is heavier, and there is evidence of shorter fallow periods, especially in areas of higher population densities. The average area under crops per farmer in the Western Region of Nigeria in 1958–9 was 2·7 acres (1·1 hectares). The comparable average in the Northern Region in 1957–8 was 3·9 acres (1·6 hectares).[18]

There are several different systems of land tenure in West Africa. At one extreme, e.g. in the cocoa growing areas of Ashanti, almost all land is owned or rented by individuals or small family units. At the other extreme, e.g. the Tiv of the Benue valley, all cropland is held by large family units in community groups. In the latter case land is subdivided mainly on the basis of need. In the former much of the land is held by a few families who lease or rent it to others. Bridges distinguishes:[19]

1) Freehold.
2) Leasehold (including rented land).
3) Pledged: Land may be 'pledged' in return for a loan. The lender has the right of cultivation, but not development, until the loan is redeemed. Failure to redeem over a long period results virtually in transfer of 'ownership'.
4) Trusthold: The holder is free to pledge or sell with or without the permission of the community to anyone within the community.
5) Usehold: The holding of land on trust from the community with exclusive rights only during the term of occupancy.

It is commonly found in West Africa that different systems of land holding exist side by side. Thus a family may have a share of usehold land on which they produce their main crop, and also possess freehold 'compound land' for their kitchen-garden crops. One should note the tendency to put the little manure available on freehold rather than usehold land.

Amongst communities recognizing usehold the act of clearance establishes the right to plant a crop. Labouret[20] shows that the Toucouleur connect the word 'fire' with ideas of holding, possession and ownership. Amongst the Wolof and the Fulani of Senegal ownership is sometimes called the privilege of the axe. On usehold land fragmentation is common, since plots are commonly allotted one at a time to each cultivator in turn before a fresh allotment is made and repeated, until all plots are allocated. Thus a simple method of sharing out land is achieved, and is claimed by some West African peoples to divide fairly the different types of soil. It also gives each cultivator a share of the distances to be walked between the plots and the settlement. Distances of 5 miles (8 km) or even more may separate the plots of any one holding. Where land is abundant and fallows are long or where woodland is allowed to regenerate land holdings are often more compact, particularly where settlements are dispersed in small compound units. Excessive fragmentation is usually the product of the large settlement unit in which there is barely sufficient land to be divided amongst the members of the community.

In the Fulani states land is often held in trust for the community by the ruling authority. Taxes on harvests, rents and capitation taxes may be levied or service demanded in lieu of tax.[21]

Crops, trees and houses are not considered as inseparable from the soil on which they stand and may be owned by individuals. The pledging or leasing of land does not always give rights to the trees upon it which may be retained by the owner. The harvesting rights of trees on usehold land usually belong to the cultivator on cropland and to the community on fallows.

Land classification

Different types of land, suitable for the production of different crops or of varying degrees of fertility, are distinguished and classified by most agricultural communities. Thus the Wolof distinguish five different kinds of floodland according to their productive capacity, and recognize a number of soil types each carrying its own distinct and most suitable crop. Where land is abundant classification is usually on the basis of vegetation. Where land is barely sufficient for needs, or where little woodland remains, classification is on the basis of fallow or soils. For an example of the latter, the northern and western Yoruba have a detailed classification by means of different fallow grasses. Different stages of fallow are usually named, and where large clearances by a whole community are made such names become virtually field names. The Oratta Ibo have five field names according to the fallow stage.[22]

Land is also classified according to the use to which it is put. The basic distribution here is between cropland producing the main crops, and compound land producing secondary or reserve crops. These may be divided into a more elaborate classification system depending on distance away from the settlement and variations in use. As already discussed above the types of land thus classified are associated with different systems of land tenure.

Customary labour

Traditionally amongst many West African communities cultivation depends on the use of the family as a labour unit – in some cases consisting of two or more wives and their children. Additional labour may be obtained from outside the family. A number of cultivators may assist one another in some particularly heavy task, for example, clearance of woodland. Amongst some communities labour societies exist, often comprising the members of a particular, usually adolescent, age group, who may assist the older cultivators or work in turn on the holdings of other members. Until its use was prohibited slave labour was also of great importance amongst the more powerful communities and made possible the cultivation of large estates or plantations.

Field crops[23]

In this chapter attention will be focused on the 'traditional' crops important for subsistence or internal exchange. Consideration of export and recently introduced crops will be left until Chapter 10.

Generalized field crop regions are shown in Figure 2.1. These are based on dominant staples, but there is in fact a considerable overlap between one region and another. Dominance has been decided from statistical and descriptive, mainly anthropological, sources, where available, on the basis of acreage and not weight of food produced. The six regions shown are:

1) A northern cereals region in which the dominants are bulrush millets, guinea corn and *Digitaria* millets. This region occupies by far the greatest area and may be subdivided into a northern bulrush millet dominant sub-region and a southern guinea corn dominant sub-region.
2) A south-western rice region.
3) A mixed cereals and roots region in which the dominants are bulrush millets, guinea corn, maize, cassava and yams.
4) A roots region in which the dominants are cassava, yams, cocoyams, and in parts of which plantains are important.
5) Two small maize dominant regions in which root crops are also important.
6) A plantain and cocoyam dominant region.[24]

Physical limitations will be discussed in the next chapter. Here one should note that length of rainy season is the chief factor in cropping, for in West Africa it is moisture supply and not temperature which governs the length of the growing season. North of approximately the fourteenth parallel there are only three months in the year with more than 1 in (25 mm) of rain and rainfall totals are everywhere less than 20 in (508 mm). Cultivation can only be by irrigation save in years of exceptionally heavy and protracted rains. Southwards cereal cultivation is possible up to the limit of woody fallows which marks the northern limit of short (less than three months) and humid dry season conditions. Only maize, of all the cereals in West Africa, appears to produce abundantly in the

CROP DOMINANCE REGIONS

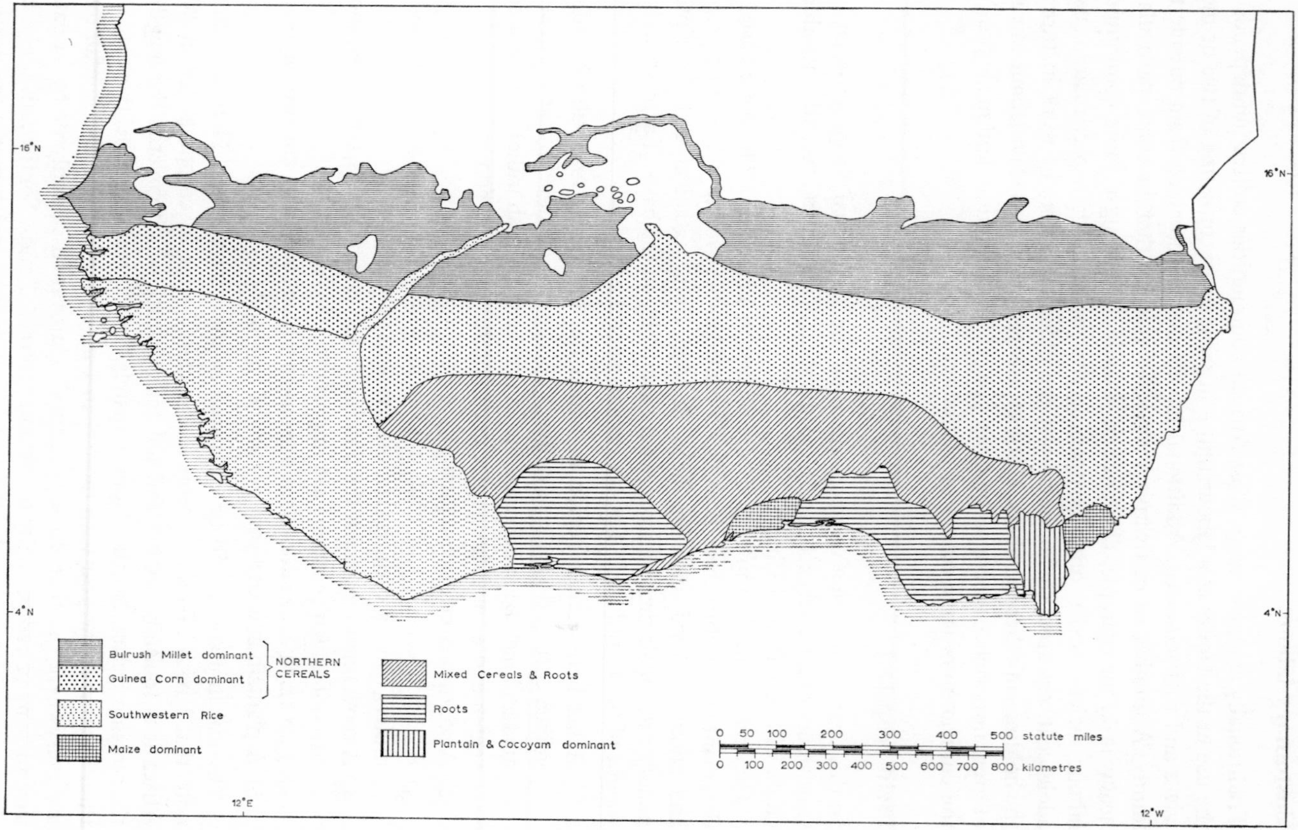

Figure 2.1

moister regions. Long wet seasons of at least seven months are suitable for the production of root crops which need a minimum of seven months in the ground to mature. The general northern limit of root cropping is marked by the isopleth of occurrence of double maxima of rainfall in 75 per cent of years recorded. This is the northern limit of high expectation of double maxima and of long rainy seasons. Root crops are grown north of this isopleth, but with only poor returns outside the floodlands. In the case of yams northern cultivators are unable to produce seed from the cut root after harvest, and must draw on the main crop for next year's planting. The south-western upland rice region corresponds largely to the south-western monsoonal climatic region of heavy rainfall (over 60 in (1524 mm)) with dry seasons of well over three months. Swamp rice is also grown and is widespread in West Africa. Upland rice occurs in a number of widely separated districts outside the region.

A number of West African crops appear to be of local origin.[25] Portères claims that West African rice (*Oryza glaberrima*) was developed from a wild species (*O. breviligulata*) in the inland Niger delta. For *Digitaria* millets he claims a centre of origin on the edge of the Fouta Djallon in the upper basins of the Senegal, Niger and Gambia. Guinea corn and bulrush millets may have originated in the Sudanic environment, although Chevalier claims a Saharan centre of origin. Several of the different varieties of yam also have a West African origin. The sub-Guinean environment provided the only conditions suitable for wild yams, with a long enough wet season and a short dry season in which the seed is less likely to suffer damage from disease than in the more humid areas to the south. The eastern portion of that environment between the Volta river and the Cameroons would seem to be the most likely area of origin, since yam culti-vation is concentrated mainly to the east, and corresponds in the distribution of its major area of concentration with an East Atlantic cultural grouping of people. The boundary between the rice and roots (traditional yams) regions at the Bandama river in the Ivory Coast is thought by Miège to be due to cultural and historical factors associated with the distribution of 'East Atlantic' and 'West Atlantic' peoples.[26] West African crop plants may be classified by origin as follows, although in many cases it must be recognized that doubt exists regarding the origins of many of the plants listed. Allocation has been made to the likeliest groups on available evidence.

I. CEREALS

Local origin

Guinea corn (*Sorghum* spp.)
Bulrush millet (*Pennisetum* spp.)
West African rice (*Oryza glaber-rima*)
Fonio, fundi, acha, hungry rice (*Digitaria exilis, D. iburua*)
Founi kouli (*Brachiaria deflexa*)

Introduced

Maize (*Zea mays*), 'Americas'
Asian rice (*Oryza sativa*), chiefly Indo-China
Finger millet, Tamba (*Eleusine cora-cana*), Central and Eastern Africa
Wheat (*Triticum durum, T. vulgare*), North Africa

2. ROOTS AND BULBS

Local origin

West African yams (*Dioscorea* spp.)
Tumuku, Hausa potato (*Solenostemon rotundifolius* (= *Coleus dysentericus, C. rotundifolius*))
Rizga (*Plectranthus esculentus* (= *Coleus dazo*))
Earth pea, Bambara groundnut (*Voandzeia geocarpa*)
Earth lentil, geocarpa groundnut (*Kerstingiella geocarpa*)
Yam bean (*Sphenostylis stenocarpa*)

Introduced

Asian yams (*Dioscorea alata, D. esculenta*)
Cassava, manioc (*Manihot esculenta*), Brazil
Cocoyam, koko, eddo, taro (*Colocasia esculentum*), South-east Asia
Cocoyam, tania, yautia, malanga (*Xanthosoma sagittifolium*), West Indies
Sweet potato (*Ipomoea batatas*), South America
Groundnut (*Arachis hypogaea*), Central America
Onion (*Allium cepa*), North Africa

3. FRUITS, NUTS, SEEDS AND LEGUMES (tree fruits under 'trees')

Local origin

Sesame, benniseed (*Sesamum indicum* – possibly Asian)
Black benniseed (*Polygala butyracea*)
'Benniseeds' (*Sesamum radiatum, Ceratotheca sesamoides*)
Black sesame (*Hyptis spicigera*)
Pumpkin (*Cucurbita pepo, C. maxima*)
Fluted pumpkin (*Telfairia occidentalis*)
Watermelon (*Citrullus citrullus*)
Egusi melon, yergan (*Cucumeropsis edulis*)
Sweet melon (*Cucumis melo*)
Calabash, gourd (*Lagenaria siceraria*)
Cowpea, niébé (*Vigna unguiculata* or *V. catjang*)
Bengal bean (*Mucuna aterrima* – possibly Asian)
Velvet bean (*Mucuna nivea*)
Horse-eye bean (*Mucuna urens*)
Winged bean (*Psophocarpus tetragonolobus*)

Introduced

Castor oil, ricin (*Ricinus communis*), South-east Asia
Lima bean, kissi (*Phaseolus lunatus*), South-east Asia
Haricot bean (*Phaseolus vulgaris*)
Black gram (*Phaseolus mungo*), South-east Asia
Indian butter bean (*Dolichos lab lab*), South-east Asia
Sword bean (*Canavalia ensiformis*), India
Soya bean (*Glycine soja*)
Pigeon pea (*Cajanus cajan*), North Africa
Tiger nut (*Cyperus esculentus*) South-west Asia
Tomato (*Lycopersicon esculentum*), South America
Pineapple (*Ananas comosus*), South America
Banana (*Musa sapientum*), South-east Asia
Plantain (*Musa paradisiaca*), South-east Asia

Local origin

Okra, gumbo, ladies' fingers (*Hibiscus esculentus*)

Garden egg, brinjal, aubergine (*Solanum melongena*)

West African black pepper (*Piper guineense*)

Grains of Paradise, Guinea pepper (*Aframomum melegueta*)

Introduced

Ginger (*Zingiber officinale*), South-east Asia

Turmeric (*Curcuma longa*), South-east Asia

Peppers (*Capsicum annum, C. frutescens*), South America

4. LEAF, STEM, FIBRE AND DYE PLANTS

Local origin

Rama, ambary, da (*Hibiscus cannabinus, H. lunarifolius*)

Roselle, Guinea sorrel (*Hibiscus sabdariffa* – possibly Asian) (also used as intoxicant)

Indigo (*Indigofera tinctoria* – possibly Asian)

West African indigo (*Lonchocarpus cyanescens*)

Henna (*Lawsonia inermis* – North African?)

Spinach (*Spinacia oleracea*)

Wild Amaranth (*Amaranthus viridis*)

Leaf benniseed (*Sesamum alatum, S. radiatum*)

Tea bush (*Ocimum viride*)

Bologi (*Talinum triangulare*)

Introduced

Cotton (*Gossypium* spp. – claims have been made for West African origin)

Java indigo (*Indigofera arrecta*), South-east Asia?

Sugar cane (*Saccharum officinarum*), South-east Asia

Tobacco (*Nicotiana rustica, N. tabacum*), South America

American basil (*Ocimum americanum*), Americas

Bush greens (*Amaranthus hybridus*), South-east Asia

Indian spinach (*Basella alba*)

Distribution and cultivation of major field crops

I. BULRUSH MILLET

At least eight species are cultivated in West Africa. Three of these are concentrated in the north-east, in Hausaland and Bornu. One is widespread throughout the Sudanic region. Four occur chiefly in the west, in the basins of the Senegal and Gambia, in Sierra Leone, Guinea, northern Ghana and northern Togo and Dahomey (Fig. 2.2).[27]

Bulrush millet has a remarkable capacity for drought resistance and can remain dormant during long dry spells. It is the dominant crop in the northern portion of the Sudanic region where the rainfall is less than 30 in (762 mm) and the rainy season is less than five months. Some varieties mature in less than 90 days (the 'fastest' in little more than 60 days). At its southern limit the crop is normally

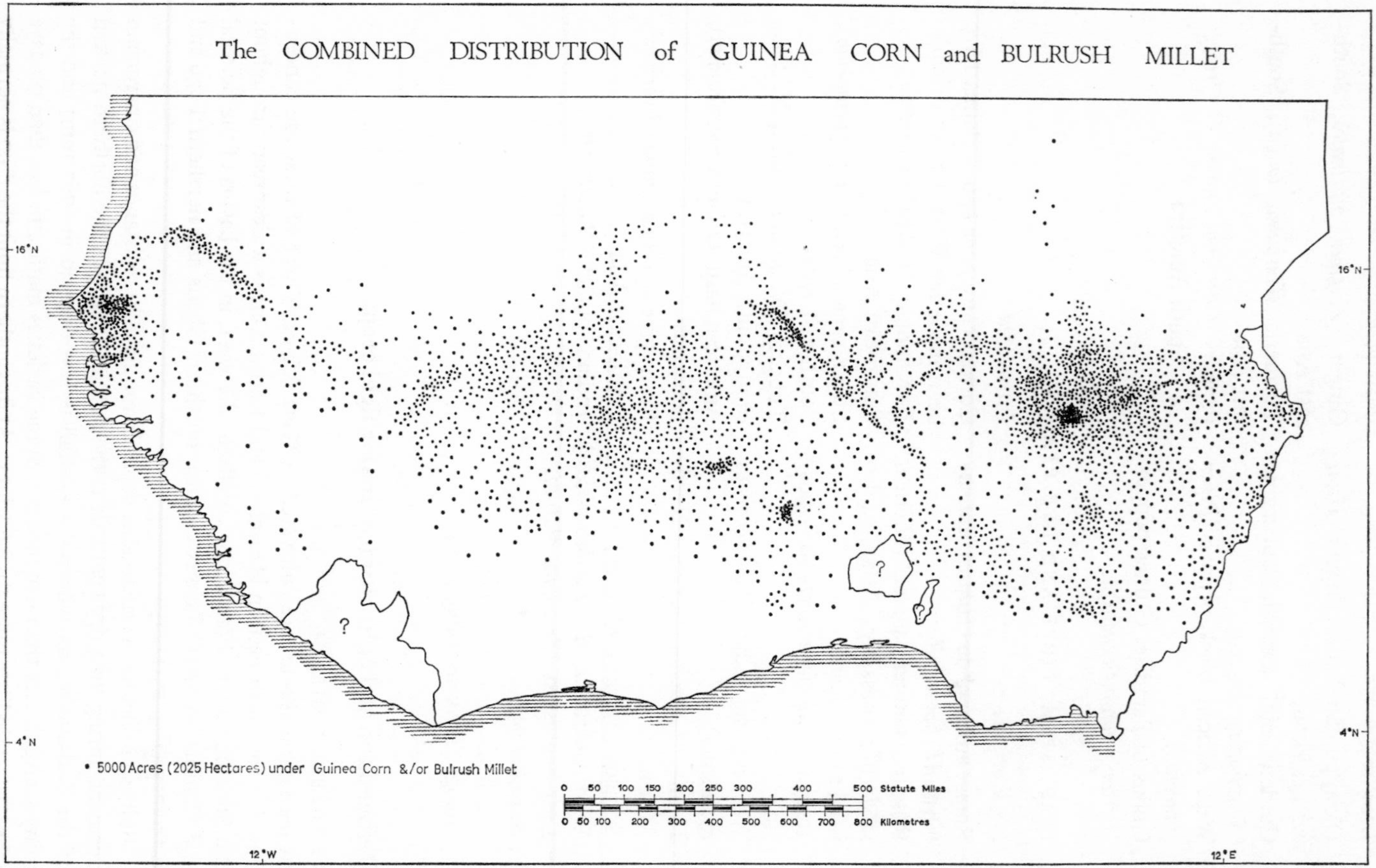
The COMBINED DISTRIBUTION of GUINEA CORN and BULRUSH MILLET
16°N
16°N
?
?
4°N
4°N
• 5000 Acres (2025 Hectares) under Guinea Corn &/or Bulrush Millet
0 50 100 150 200 250 300 400 500 Statute Miles
0 50 100 200 300 400 500 600 700 800 Kilometres
12°W
12°E

Figure 2.2

mixed with guinea corn to provide a catch crop if rains are poor and grain harvests at different periods of the year. Early and late varieties are commonly planted together. Vernacular names are often confusing, but there is a distinction in Hausa between 'gero' varieties harvested in 90 days, and 'maiwa' or 'dauro' varieties needing more than 130 days. One low-yielding variety matures in as little as 60 days, but is liable to damage by birds.[28] In the wetter areas 'gero' often precedes guinea corn in the same season, whereas 'maiwa' is either grown mixed with guinea corn or competes with it for land. Generally bulrush millets are reckoned to need less moisture in the soil for germination than any other crop. Yields average between 500 and 800 lb of grain per acre (560–900 kilos per hectare) (Bauchi Province, Northern Nigeria, an especially favoured area, 1961–1962, sample census average of over 1100 lb per acre). Part of the crop is used for local beer production.

2. GUINEA CORN

Dalziel lists at least twelve 'races' of *Sorghum* or guinea corn cultivated in West Africa.[29] The crop is widespread throughout the region with at least three months dry season. Like bulrush millet it is drought resistant, but is less tolerant of poor soils. It is a staple in most regions with between 30 and 50 in (760–1270 mm) of rainfall and with 6 to 9 months rainy season. There are many varieties maturing in 80 to 190 days. Generally sandy clays are preferred. In most cases the plant is grown for one season only, but sometimes the roots are allowed to remain in the ground for up to three years. Irvine claims that although this prevents fuller tillage of the land, the crops appear better able to withstand drought than those sown every year.[30] The crop is frequently first in rotations and is sometimes manured. Yields average between 700 and 1000 lb per acre (785–1125 kilos per hectare) (Bauchi Province, Northern Nigeria, 1961–2, sample census average, sole, i.e. not mixed, of 1282 lb per acre (1436 kilos per hectare)). The crop is favoured in many areas for the production of local beer. 'Masakwa' or Egyptian corn (*Sorghum durra* var. *niloticum*) is grown as a flood-land crop on clay soils, chiefly in Bornu. *S. caudatum* var. *colorans* is planted mainly to produce a red dye. The sweet sorghums, *S. mellitum* and *S. nigricans*, are grown in order to chew the stems.

3. FONIO, ACHA OR HUNGRY RICE

There are two cultivated species *Digitaria exilis* and *D. iburua*. *Digitaria exilis* is widespread at a great variety of altitudes in the sub-Sudanic and sub-Guinean regions with over 20 in (508 mm) of rainfall and 7 to 9 months rainy season. In the lowlands of Guinea it grows in areas receiving over 100 in (2540 mm). *D. iburua* is localized amongst the peoples of the Jos Plateau and of the Atacora Range. The more frequent occurrence of fonio at altitudes over 2000 feet (610 metres) is due to its association with peoples who have settled in mountain refuges

DISTRIBUTION of FONIO

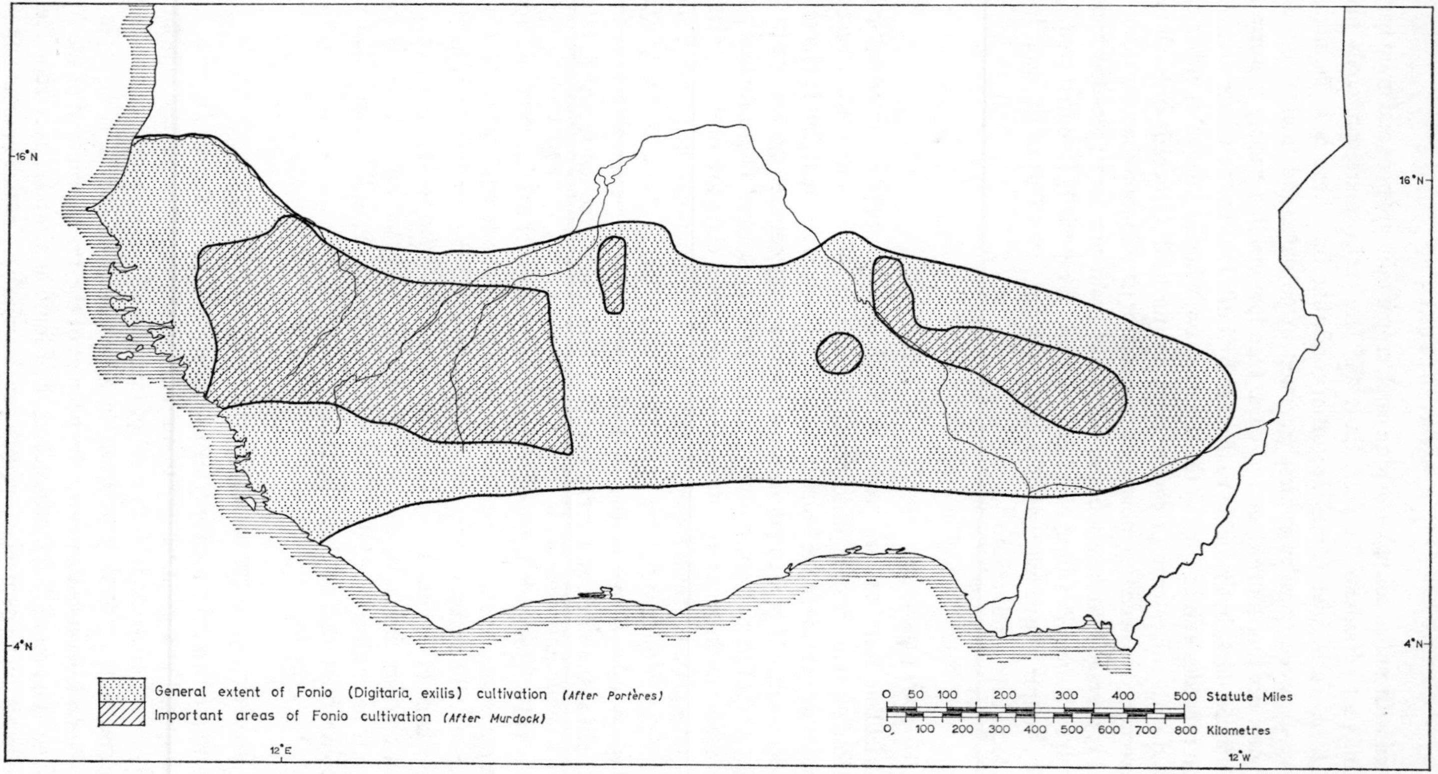
16°N
16°N
4°N
4°N
General extent of Fonio (Digitaria, exilis) cultivation (After Portères)
Important areas of Fonio cultivation (After Murdock)
0 50 100 200 300 400 500 Statute Miles
0 100 200 300 400 500 600 700 800 Kilometres
12°E
12°W

Figure 2.3

easy to defend from the attacks of slave raiders. The eastern limit of fonio coincides with the western limit of another hardy cereal which takes its place in Central Africa – tamba or finger millet.[31] This suggests incidentally a divide between West and Central African cultures established by two distinctly distributed crops.

Fonio ripens in 90 to 130 days. Unlike guinea corn and bulrush millet which, in areas of comparable rainfall are generally grown on ridges, fonio seed is scattered and lightly hoed into the soil. The planting procedure is very similar in the case of upland rice and the two crops are frequently grown by the same peoples. Fonio is often sown after rice in the rotation and is sometimes grown as a reserve against the failure of the main crop or as an early 'hunger breaker'. It is tolerant of a wide range of soil and rainfall conditions and frequently occurs on high plateaux at over 2000 feet (610 metres) above sea level. On the Jos Plateau fonio is frequently a staple with bulrush or finger millet as a reserve. In a few cases the crop is transplanted from seed beds into large manured mounds. Yields average 200 to 450 lb per acre (225–500 kilos per hectare). On the Jos Plateau bulrush millet has taken the place of fonio in some cases owing to its superiority for the brewing of local beer.

Fonio is often sown on the worn soils available at the end of a rotation, sometimes even after cassava. Because of its association in consequence with worn or poor soils it has been described as an exhausting crop.

4. RICE

West African rice (*Oryza glaberrima*) is still important throughout the south-western region, the Sudanic areas as far east as Lake Chad and in the floodlands of the Sahel. Its probable parent *O. stapfi* is cultivated in the south-west.[32] Asian rice (*Oryza sativa*) was introduced to the south-west and the Upper Niger by the Portuguese in the 15th to 18th centuries, and more recently throughout West Africa by Government agricultural departments. It has gradually increased its area chiefly at the expense of the indigenous rice.

Upland varieties produce a crop in 90 to 170 days. Generally they thrive in areas with a minimum rainy season of 5 months and a minimum rainfall total for the year of 30 in (760 mm). Below 30 inches they give way to acha.[33] The seed is sown after the rains have begun and once it becomes established, millets, maize, guinea corn, beniseed, cassava or cotton are often interplanted. Yields average between 400 and 800 lb of rice in husk per acre (450–900 kilos per hectare), but can be as high as 1500 lb per acre (1680 kilos per hectare).

Swamp rice is grown without the interplanting of other crops. It produces a crop in 140 to 220 days. There are two main types of floodland – riverain and coastal. In the riverain lands the seed is sown in damp ground, preferably clays, as the water recedes. In the coastal swamplands of the south-west a system of transplanting from nursery beds to fields lying under water has been developed, partly in order to avoid high salinity at the beginning of the rains. During the

DISTRIBUTION of RICE

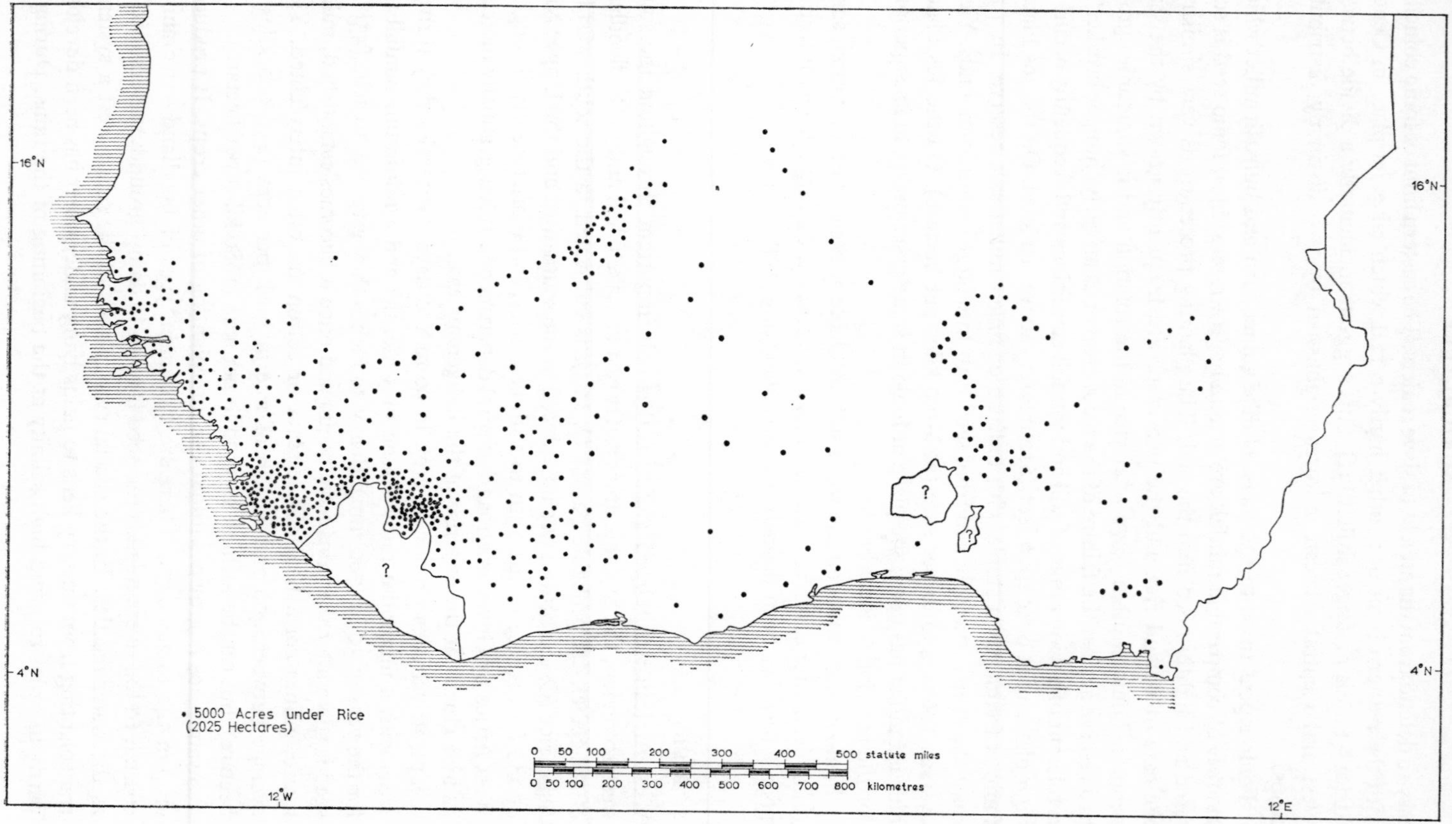

• 5000 Acres under Rice
  (2025 Hectares)

0   50 100   200   300   400   500 statute miles

0   50 100   200   300   400   500   600   700   800 kilometres

Figure 2.4

last century this system spread south-eastwards from the Casamance valley and the 'Rivières du Sud' to the Scarcies district of Sierra Leone, and has since been introduced into Ghana and Nigeria. Coastal swamp cultivation involves the clearance of mangroves, and the drainage and desalting of soils for at least three years before planting. It also involves a careful choice of site to avoid too great a concentration of salt water. Salt water flooding before the rainy season limits the growth of weeds with the exception of the salt resistant grass *Paspalum vaginatum*, which is especially troublesome in Sierra Leone. Rice is planted to nursery beds in May or June, and then transplanted, often by boat, in July and August when there is abundant fresh water after heavy rains. After September the water becomes brackish. The main harvest follows in December. In some entirely freshwater districts two crops are grown – the first sown directly in damp ground in May or June for harvest in October, and the second transplanted from nurseries in November for harvest in the following February or March. Generally swamp rice yields average 900 to 1700 lb per acre (1000–1900 kilos per hectare), but may rise to 4000 lb per acre (4500 kilos per hectare) where conditions are ideal.[34]

There are numerous swamp varieties of West African and Asian rice, suited to different soil and drainage conditions. Systems of 'fringe' planting of different varieties exist, utilizing lower and later exposures of floodland as water levels recede after flood peak.[35] Floating varieties are frequently planted in the bottom lands, and may grow in depths of water as great as 10 feet (3 metres). They ripen in 180–250 days, and can utilize basins subject to deep flooding where no other crop can be raised.

5. MAIZE

Maize was introduced from the Americas by two routes. The hard maize varieties of Central America came via the Mediterranean countries, the Nile valley and Bornu; the soft maize varieties were probably brought directly from Peru and Brazil by the Portuguese. The latter appear to have been introduced first to the inland of São Tomé and later to lower Dahomey via the slave trading settlements.[36]

Maize is widespread, mainly as a secondary crop, throughout the sub-Sudanic, sub-Guinean and Guinean areas although it is most abundantly grown in areas having between 40 and 60 in (1016–1524 mm) of rainfall and over 7 months' rainy season. The area of greatest concentration is in southern Dahomey and Togo. Best results are obtained on loams and in clearings with ample sunlight. Dry heat is injurious and humid air is preferred, although in extremely humid conditions the plant is susceptible to rust disease. Weeding is extremely important and wide spacing preferred. The careful interplanting of crops, offering the minimum of competition for soil nutrients, may be beneficial. Double cropping of maize is often practical where the rainy seasons last 9 months or more, particularly in south-western Nigeria and lower Dahomey.

There are numerous varieties maturing in 75 to 150 days. Quick-growing

DISTRIBUTION of MAIZE

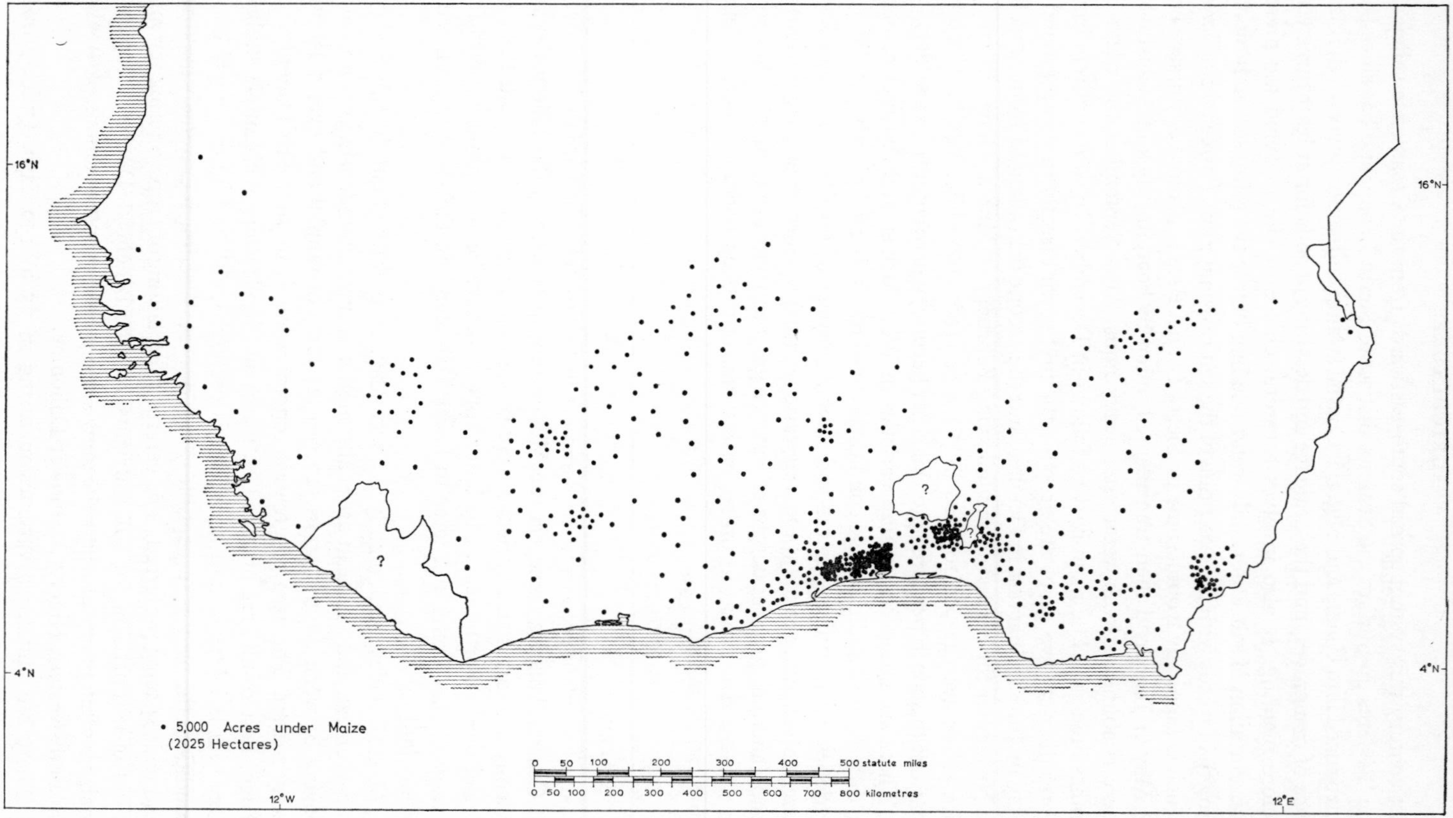

• 5,000 Acres under Maize
(2025 Hectares)

Figure 2.5

early varieties have tended to increase in popularity in recent years as a 'hunger breaker' or as a crop to harvest before millets, particularly where millets have suffered heavy losses to insect pests. Normally maize is planted on ridges in the first or second shifts of a rotation. In the Sudanic and sub-Sudanic zones it is frequently planted in floodland. Elsewhere it is often grown on fertilized compound land.

Yields average 450 to 1100 lb per acre (500–1230 kilos per hectare). In the Western Region of Nigeria in 1958–9 average yields for maize as a sole crop were 924 lb per acre (1033 kilos per hectare) for the first crop and 586 lb per acre (656 kilos per hectare) for the second. As a mixed crop the comparable yields were 547 and 493 lb per acre (613 and 552 kilos per hectare).

6. YAMS

Yams are the traditional staple crop of the Guinean and the greater part of the sub-Guinean areas east of the Bandama river. They are not a rain forest crop as some observers have suggested, but a rain forest tolerant crop with important centres of production in the savannas.

Dalziel lists 13 races of which only 2 are from south-east Asia: *Dioscorea alata* or water yam and *D. esculenta* or Chinese yam.[37] There is an enormous number of varieties and most of these mature in 200–300 days. At least 40 inches (1016 mm) of rainfall in 7 months or more are preferred, although continuously high humidities encourage disease. Soils should not be too heavy, preferably loams. Two of the commonest races cultivated are the White Guinea (*D. rotundata*), and the Yellow Guinea (*D. cayenensis*). These are planted in mounds between 2 and 6 feet (60–180 cm) in height. *D. rotundata* includes the fastest-growing varieties which generally have more northerly locations. In the Guinean areas with little or no dry season, yams may be planted in February to April at the beginning of the rains. Until then the seed yams are stored in racks to keep them dry. Seeds may be produced by cutting away the main tuber, and leaving the top to produce a new smaller tuber in 2 to 3 months. In the sub-Guinean areas yams are planted in October to December and left in the ground during the dry season. They do not rot in the ground as they sometimes do in the Guinean zone, and may thus be planted early before the soil is baked hard. Planting after the rains have softened the ground means a shorter growing season. The yam produces a vine which in well-wooded areas is normally supported by trees growing on the cropland, or by the stumps of dead trees. Elsewhere poles are used, or the stalks of harvested guinea corn or cassava stems. Great care is taken in yam cultivation. Mounds are frequently manured with household refuse and capped with grass to prevent erosion and retain moisture. The young shoot is shaded with leaves or grass. A practice in some areas is to open the yam mound about half-way through the growing period, and to remove all the smaller tubers in order to allow more development for the larger. Most of the Yellow Guinea Yam varieties usually need at least 270 days to mature. The White Guinea Yam varieties can mature in shorter

DISTRIBUTION of YAMS

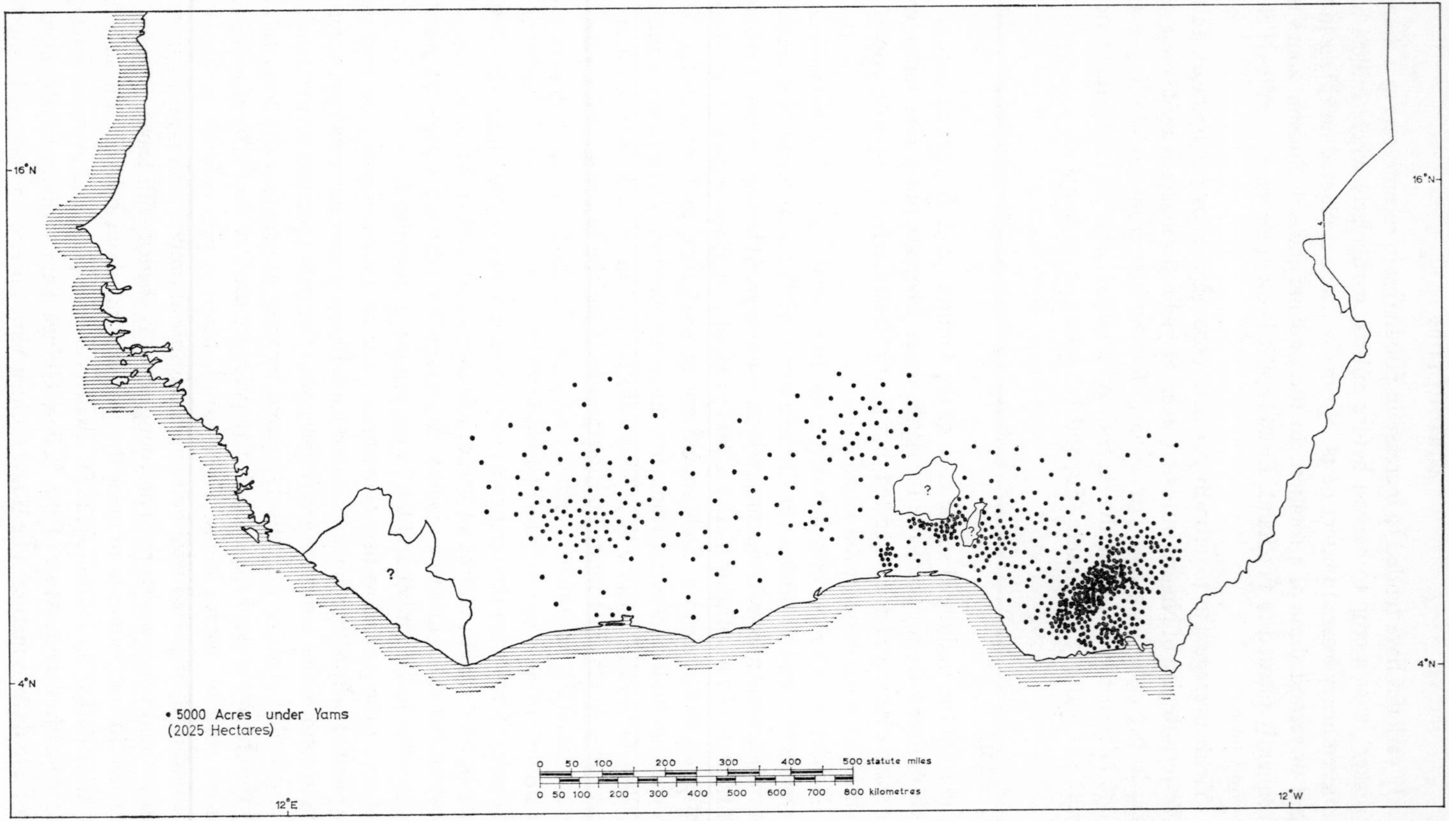

• 5000 Acres under Yams
  (2025 Hectares)

Figure 2.6

periods and are better suited to cultivation in the drier areas. The greater or water yam (*D. alata*) requires a large mound and will grow in lighter soil and under drier conditions. It is regarded as of poorer quality. The Chinese yam (*D. esculenta*) is of late introduction, has small tubers and is grown only in small quantities. It can be grown with a rainfall as low as 30 inches (760 mm) and thrives in the drier, more open districts. It is grown chiefly by the Ewe and Fanti. Yams make a heavy demand on soil, need long fallow or virgin land to produce abundantly, and are normally first in the rotation. Yam production averages between 5000 and 12,000 lb per acre (5600–13,440 kilos per hectare), but the seed rate is heavy (1500 to 4000 lb per acre (1680–4480 kilos per hectare)). In Nigeria in 1961–2 the highest yam yields were in Ilorin Province with averages for mixed cultivation of 15,438 lb per acre (17,391 kilos per hectare).

7. CASSAVA

Cassava is extremely tolerant of soil and moisture conditions and is grown throughout West Africa. Its cultivation is most developed wherever the traditional staple is the yam, which in many cases it has replaced as the dominant crop. It has spread in recent years, however, into the sub-Sudanic and Sudanic zones where, although yields are very low, it fulfils a useful function as a reserve against famine and resists locust attack. Although of early introduction cassava did not become popular in West Africa until its reintroduction by former slaves from Brazil who also imported the culinary technique necessary for its preparation as a foodstuff. Thus cassava has spread as the art of removing its prussic acid content and making cassava meal has spread.[38]

The attraction of cassava lies in its high productivity per acre even on light soils or at the end of a rotation (its normal place), combined with ease of propagation from stem cuttings and need for little tillage. Like fonio, cassava has been described as exhausting because it has often been planted in soils already worn by other crops. The crop takes 240 to 450 days to mature and can stay in the ground for periods up to three years. It thus supplies fresh food all the year round and has helped to solve crop storage problems. It is also a useful reserve against failure of other crops due to late or poor rains, and since propagation is from stem cuttings all the crops may be consumed. There are numerous varieties, which may be subdivided into the 'bitter', with hydrocyanic acid in all parts of the root, and the 'sweet', with hydrocyanic acid only in the rind. The leaves provide a useful fodder for animals in the Sudanic zone, and the crop suffers in unfenced fields from grazing livestock. Cassava may be made into 'fufu' or 'gari', a form of flour which will keep for long periods and can be transported cheaply over great distances. It is a popular cheap food in the towns, and recent urbanization encouraged its growth on a commercial basis. Production averages between 6000 and 11,000 lb per acre (6720–12,320 kilos per hectare) (Western Region of Nigeria, 1958–9, cassava, sole crop, 9025 lb per acre (10,108 kilos per hectare) average), although yields as high as 60 tons per acre (148 tons per hectare) have

DISTRIBUTION of CASSAVA

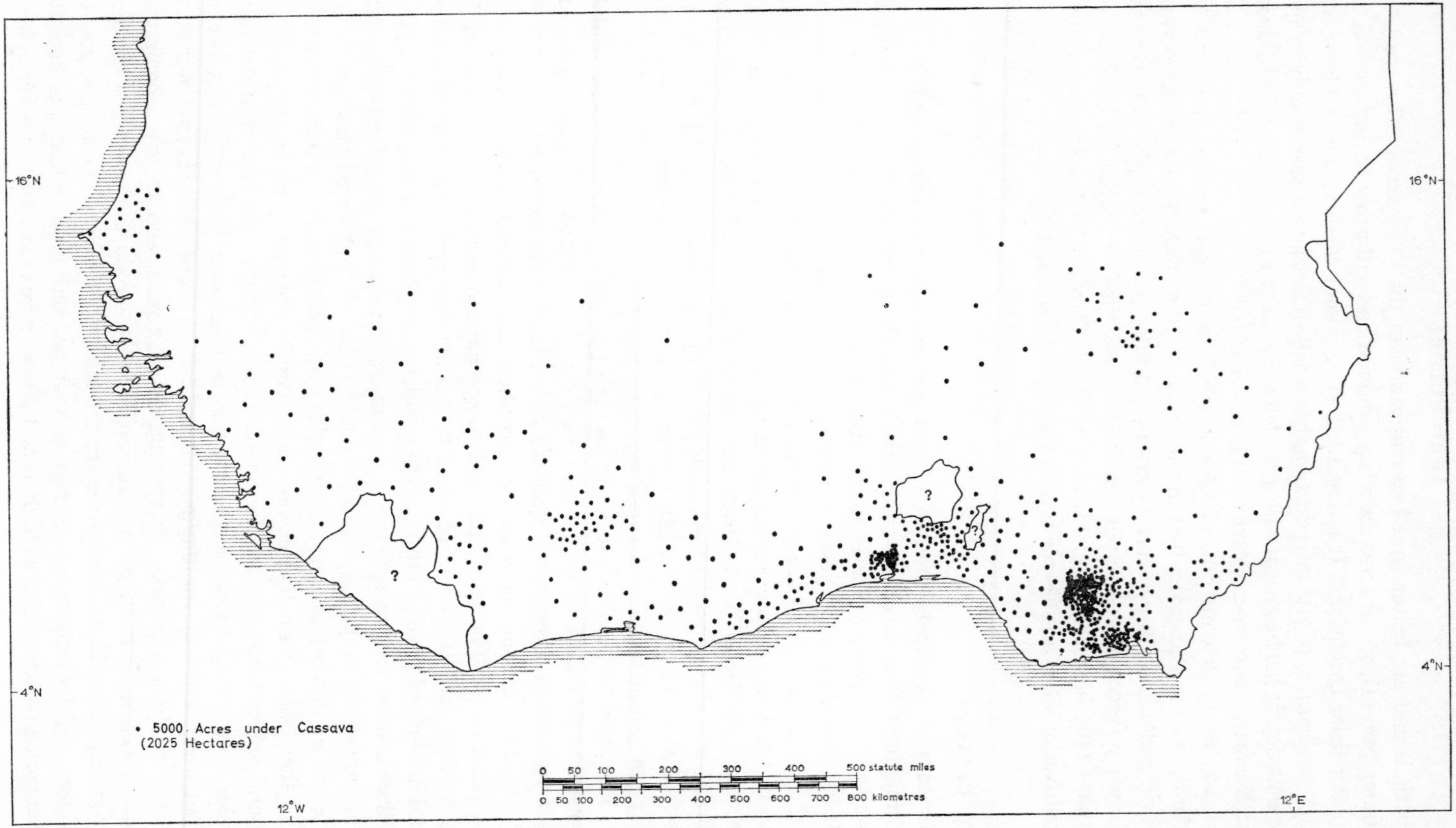

• 5000 Acres under Cassava
  (2025 Hectares)

16°N   4°N   12°E

16°N   4°N   12°W

0 50 100 200 300 400 500 statute miles
0 50 100 200 300 400 500 600 700 800 kilometres

Figure 2.7

been reported from Government farms. Yields are normally higher than those of yams in the Guinean zone, and the plant can survive shorter rainy seasons, yet in the sub-Guinean zone cassava yields are frequently lower than those of yams, and there the plant has made least advance.

8. COCOYAMS

Cocoyams occur mainly in the Guinean environment at altitudes up to 3500 feet (1070 metres) above sea-level. They need abundant moisture (normally over 50 in (1270 mm) of rainfall), and shade, making them a true 'rain forest' and 'gallery forest' plant. The crop thrives on clays or alluvium providing there is enough slope to permit drainage. It matures in 90–270 days and before the introduction of cassava was an important 'hunger season' (March–May) food in south-eastern Nigeria. Outside the southern Cameroons and southern Ghana, it is rarely grown on a large scale, and is usually a catch crop associated with tree cultivation especially with cocoa. Occasionally, e.g. in southern Iboland, the crop is manured. Of the two genera, *Colocasia esculenta* is older established. Its tuber contains an acrid substance and gives greater yields (2000 to 4000 lb per acre (2240–4480 kilos per hectare)). Cocoyams have tended to become widespread of recent years in the Guinean zone, partly because of their use as a cover plant for young perennials, and partly because their preference for shade makes them also a suitable inter-crop with mature perennials.

9. SWEET POTATO

The sweet potato is grown on floodland in many areas and is of greatest importance in Guinea, although it is also grown in Senegal, Mali, Upper Volta, the Ivory Coast and Northern Nigeria. The plant is a minor root crop in regions where cereals are dominant, and is valued partly for its speed of growth – maturing in 3 to 6 months – and partly for its keeping qualities when dried or made into meal. The tubers, however, are difficult to store. In the Guinean zone some sweet potato is grown on rainlands, notably in Ashanti and Southern Nigeria.

Yields range from 3000–8000 lb per acre (3360–8960 kilos per hectare).

10. GROUNDNUTS

Although a major export crop to be discussed in Chapter 10, groundnuts are also an important foodstuff in West Africa, and therefore need some reference here.

Groundnuts are grown in almost every part of West Africa, but their highest production occurs in the Sudanic and Sahelian zones. Of American origin, they were almost certainly introduced into Senegambia early in the 16th century, where they gradually replaced the earth pea, *Voandzeia*.[39] Planting is normally on special flat-topped ridges about one foot (30 cm) high, especially on sandy soils suited to the plant's habit of pushing the fruiting carpel into the earth. The

DISTRIBUTION of GROUNDNUTS

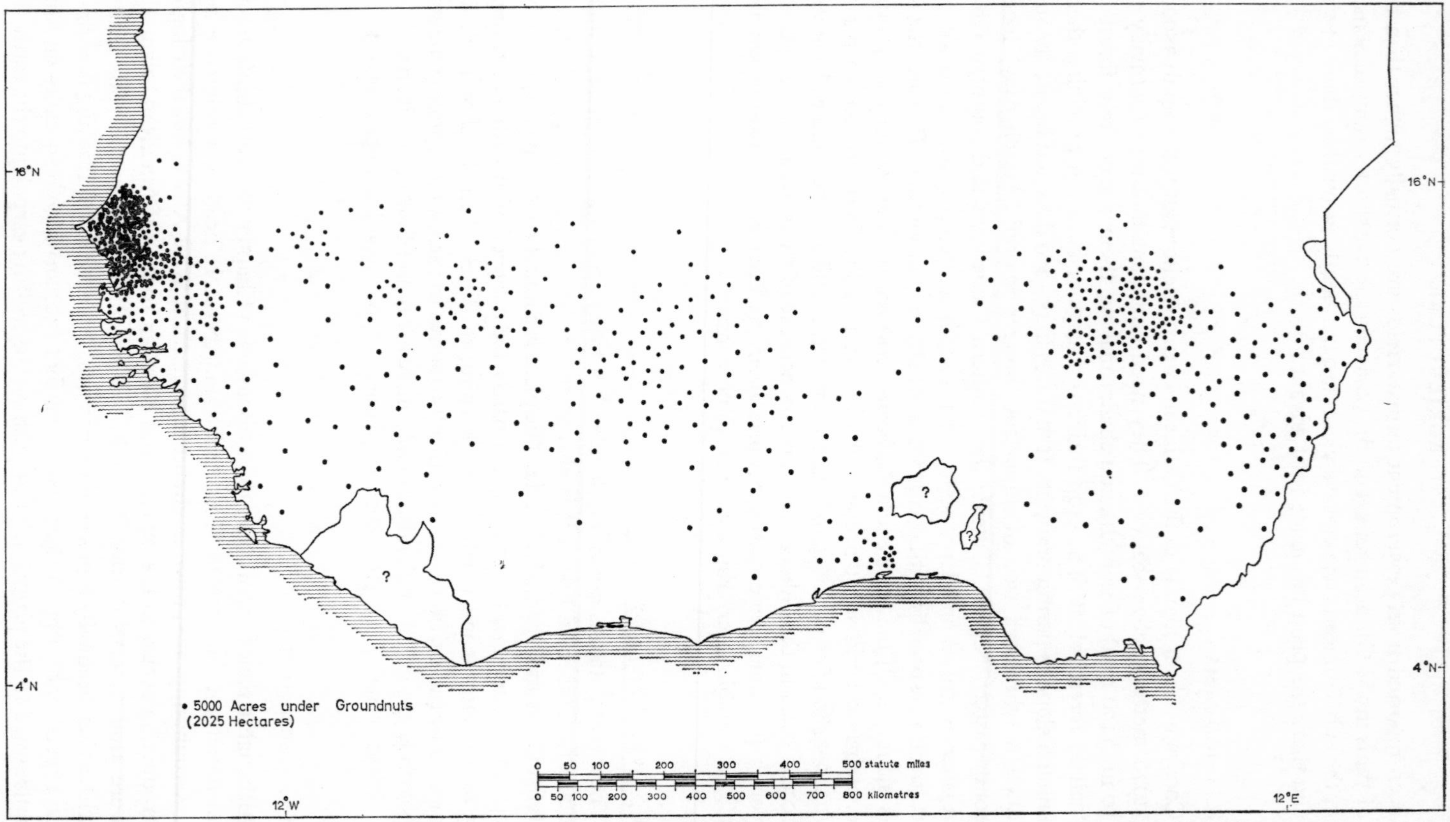

• 5000 Acres under Groundnuts
(2025 Hectares)

16°N
4°N
12°E
12°W

0   50 100 200 300 400 500 statute miles
0 50 100 200 300 400 500 600 700 800 kilometres

Figure 3.8

soils of former Saharan dunes in Senegal, Mali and Northern Nigeria are excellent, where the clay fraction is less than 10 per cent. There are two main types:

1) 'Running', more common, with good yield, and widespread on coarse sandy soils.
2) 'Bunched', lower yield, grown on less coarse soils, suitable for rotation with cotton.

Groundnuts mature in 90 to 120 days and produce 300 to 800 lb of decorticated nuts per acre (340–900 kilos per hectare). Since groundnuts are leguminous and a cleaning crop, they play a useful part in rotations, and are normally a mixed crop in the second or later shifts. Although groundnuts are planted in the first shift in some areas, it is normally reckoned that the richer soils after fallow result in too much leaf production. Often groundnuts will yield a crop on poor soil where most other crops fail, and are thus sometimes last in a rotation.

II. COTTON

Before the introduction of cottons by Agricultural Departments there were species long established in West Africa and still used to make local cloth. These include *Gossypium punctatum* ('Koroniba'), *G. obtusifolium*, *G. africanum*, *G. arboreum* ('Koroni ule'), *G. peruvianum* ('Meko') and *G. vitifolium* ('Ishan'). The last two are characteristic of the moister Guinea zone. A khaki fibre cotton is still widely grown in southern Dahomey, and is possibly related to the Nanking cotton of eastern Asia. Most of these cottons appear to be descended from long established Asian and American plants. *G. africanum* and *G. obtusifolium* may be related to an African plant *G. anomalum* or *Cienfuegosia anomalum* with a useless lint, occurring in the Sudan and Ethiopia.[40]

The numerous varieties have a wide tolerance of soils and moisture supply and the demand for cotton cloth has led to a widespread distribution of the earlier cottons in West Africa. The 'drier' varieties are more important and produce best on loams or clayey-loams with 35 to 50 in (889–1270 mm) of rainfall and a marked dry season for ripening. Yields are lower in pure stand than those of exotic cottons, but are generally higher under mixed cultivation. Cottons are ready for picking in 150–200 days, and in the wetter areas are best planted late in the rainy season in order to ensure ripening at a dry period. They may thus frequently follow an early crop (e.g. maize or millets) and be interplanted with a late crop (e.g. guinea corn or groundnuts). Times of harvesting and planting are distinct from those of any other crop, so that cotton has a useful place in the farming calendar. Yields are 200 to 400 lb per acre (225–900 kilos per hectare) of seed cotton.

12. PLANTAINS

Distributed throughout the Guinean zone are plantains, the fruits of *Musa paradisiaca*, which are eaten cooked, the staple food of many peoples of the Cross river basin and of West Cameroon. They are also important as a secondary foodstuff throughout southern Nigeria, south-western Ghana and Ashanti, in the southern Ivory Coast and in Liberia, and are commercially grown in association with cocoyams. 50 inches (1270 mm) or more rainfall with a rainy season of nine months or more are preferred, with deep loam soils. Planting is by suckers producing fruit in 360 to 540 days. After cutting fresh stems appear, and the clump may produce for more than five years with manuring. In most cases cutting down occurs after two or three years, and the land reverts to fallow. Yields are the highest of any cultivated plant, averaging 7000 to 16,000 lb per acre (7840 to 17,920 kilos per hectare).

Protected and planted trees

Trees and tree crops have long played an important role in West African agriculture, even before the development in the 18th century of a demand for intertropical timbers, rubber, cocoa and oil and coconut palm produce. The cultivator needs trees for fuel, building materials, tools, fruit, drink, edible fats and as a means of maintaining soil fertility by tree fallows. Trees have provided a defensive screen and a windbreak for his home. In many parts of the Guinean zone tree produce is greater both by value and quantity than field crops. Traditionally some oil palms and kola only were planted. Other oil palms, kola and useful trees were 'protected' on the croplands or around the settlement and even tended by pruning and manuring. The present tree distributions in West Africa are therefore mainly the result of careful selection in the development of fallows, cropland and settlement sites.

1. OIL PALM (*ELAEIS GUINEENSIS*) (WEST AFRICAN ORIGIN)

Portères suggests that the oil palm originated in the forest outliers of the sub-Sudanic zone and that its numerous varieties developed in the sub-Guinean and Guinean zones where today it is most densely protected or planted.[41] Productivity is highest in those areas with little or no dry season and a rainfall of over 60 in (1520 mm). In Bamenda the oil palm occurs at altitudes up to 3500 feet (1070 metres). Although planting occurs throughout Southern Nigeria, the only true plantations were made by the Krobo of Ghana, and they were later abandoned for cocoa planting.[42]

There are two main groups of oil palms:

1) those with thick-shell nuts, little pulp, and a high proportion of kernel (predominant in West Africa);

2) those with thin-shell nuts, abundant pulp, rich in oil, and a low proportion of kernel.

The trees begin to bear after five years. At about thirty years the yield gradually declines. The average weight of fruit produced annually per tree is 50 to 80 lb (23–36 kilos). Village palm groves average about 2000 lb per acre (2240 kilos per hectare). Local extraction methods by pounding and fermentation produce a 'hard oil' used mainly in cooking. Less commonly, a softer oil is produced by boiling and skimming. The extraction rate averages only 45 to 55 per cent of the oil content of the fruit. A little kernel oil is produced by roasting and boiling and is used mainly for medicine, soap manufacture and lighting. The fermentable sap is consumed as 'palm wine'. Its extraction often results in damaging or even killing the tree.

2. KOLA (COLA SPP.) (WEST AFRICAN ORIGIN)[43]

Of the large number of kola species there are two of outstanding importance. Cola acuminata or 'Abata', and C. nitida or 'Gbanja' or 'Goro'. C. acuminata with more than two cotyledons occurs chiefly in the eastern Guinean zone between Dahomey and Gabon. C. nitida with only two cotyledons is mainly western Guinean and is found in Ashanti, Ivory Coast, Liberia and Guinea. Kola nuts provide a sustainer and a stimulant obtained by chewing or by use in medicine. Long in demand in the northern 'empires', they gave rise to an early traffic, encouraged by their high value per unit weight, chiefly from Ashanti and the neighbouring portions of what is now Ivory Coast. The nitida varieties are generally preferred both for flavour and storage qualities, and their cultivation has been spread in recent years into areas formerly producing acuminata. Kola, particularly C. acuminata, needs shade plants in the early stages. It comes into bearing after five years and yields about 1000 nuts annually per tree. Planting was developed at an early stage of history by the Ashanti and Agni and by neighbouring peoples to the west for trade with the Sudan. It was probably the earliest planted and not merely 'protected' tree in West Africa.[44] Today the nitida kolas are commonly interplanted in coffee and cocoa holdings. C. anomala is a species planted in the highest parts of the southern Cameroons at altitudes of 3000–7000 feet (915–2135 metres) and traded locally.

3. SHEA (BUTYROSPERMUM PARKII) (WEST AFRICAN ORIGIN)

The tree is one of the chief sources of vegetable fats (obtained from the kernel) of the Sudanic and sub-Sudanic peoples. The fat is used for cooking and for soap and candle manufacture. The tree occurs in areas having between 20 and 60 inches of rainfall (510 and 1520 mm) and at least four months dry season. It bears fruit at twelve to fifteen years, growing slowly in secondary woodland and grassland where it is stunted and twisted by the annual burning. Larger trees

DISTRIBUTION of KOLA and KOLA TRADE ROUTES ABOUT 1910

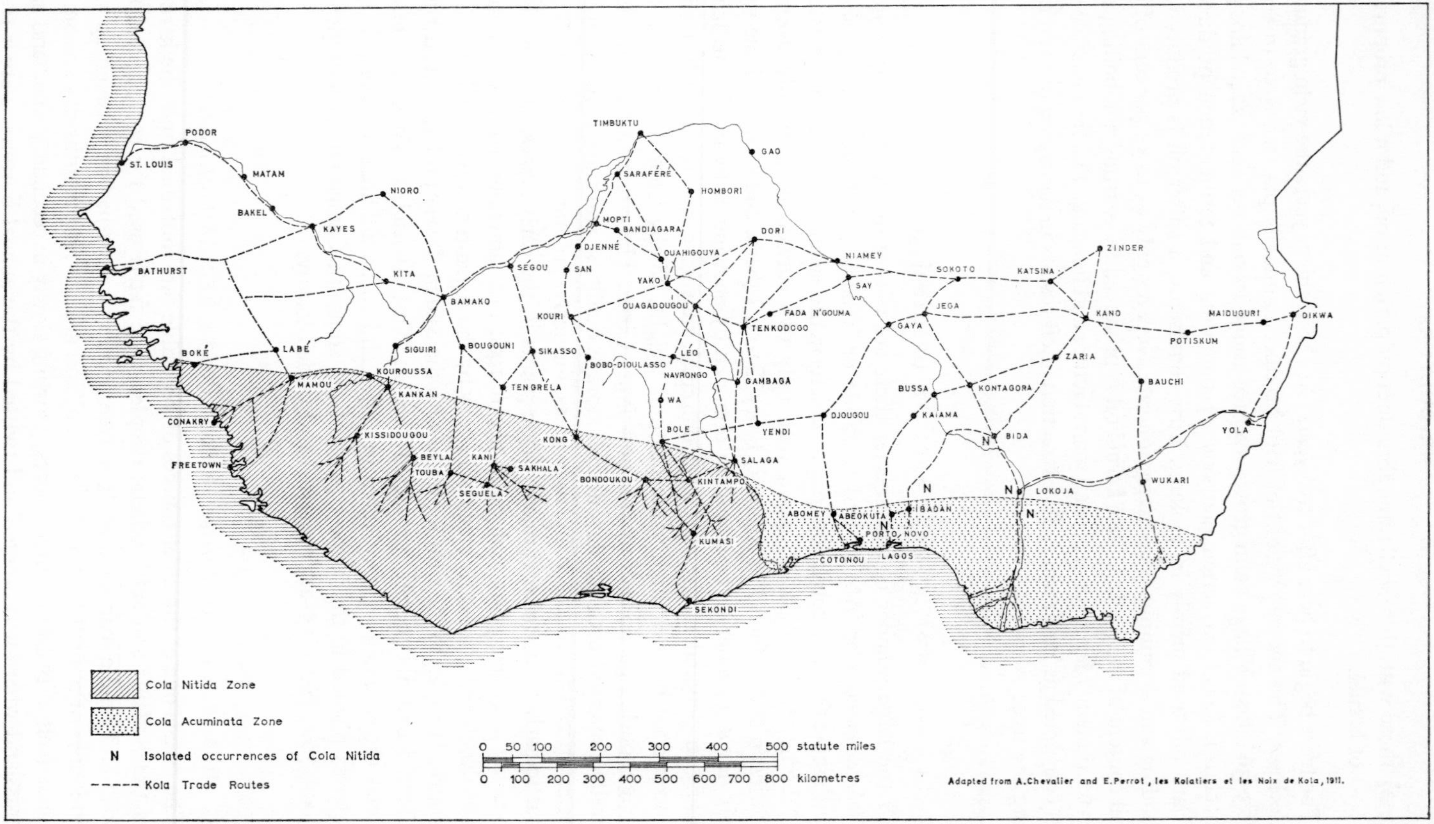

Adapted from A.Chevalier and E.Perrot, les Kolatiers et les Noix de Kola, 1911.

Figure 2.9

Cola Nitida Zone

Cola Acuminata Zone

N Isolated occurrences of Cola Nitida

----- Kola Trade Routes

with better yields occur in protected situations near settlements. Foliage remains on the tree for one or two months of the dry season, and can provide both fodder and shade for animals pastured on cropland after harvest.[45]

4. 'GAO', 'GAWO', 'KAD' (*ACACIA ALBIDA*) (WEST AFRICAN ORIGIN)

The 'gao', 'gawo' or 'kad' (*Faidherbia albida* of French authorities) is extensively protected on croplands and fallows throughout the Sahelian and Sudanic zones where it provides pods and leaves for forage. Only the Wolof appear to cut the tree down in their extensive clearances for groundnut cultivation.[46] It is found chiefly on cultivated land, fallows and village sites. The tree has the advantage of putting out fresh leaf at the beginning of the dry season and shedding leaves during the rains so that its growth is not detrimental to crops. Moreover, grain-eating birds are offered no shelter during the harvest season when the tree is still leafless or has only a little young leaf. Cropland benefits by the accumulation of leaf mould and manure from stock seeking shade, and from the 'fixing' of atmospheric nitrogen at the roots. One square kilometre (243 acres) of pastoral land in Niger will feed ten head of cattle. With a supplementary planting of 'gao' it will feed between sixteen and eighteen head.[47]

Other planted or protected trees include:

Local origin
Akee, akee apple (*Blighia sapida*) fruit, Guinean
African pear (*Pachylobus edulis*) fruit and shade, Guinean
Tamarind (*Tamarindus indica*) fruit, Sudanic
Yellow mango (*Irvingia gabonensis*) kernels for seasoning, Guinean
Yellow plum (*Spondias mombin*) fruit, Guinean
Cashew (*Anacardium occidentale*) fruit, Guinean
Oil bean (*Pentaclethra macrophylla*) kernel oil and shade, Guinean and sub-Guinean
Locust bean (*Parkia biglobosa*) pulp and seeds, chiefly south-western
Locust bean, dorowa (*Parkia filicoidae*) pulp and seeds, seeds make daudawa cake of Hausaland, Sudanic and sub-Sudanic
Awusa nut (*Tetracarpidium conophorum*) seeds and leaves, Guinean
Bitter kola (*Garcinia kola*) seeds, Guinean
African pepper (*Xylopia aethiopica*) fruit, seeds and timber, widespread
Baobab, kuka (*Adansonia digitata*) fruit and leaves, chiefly Sudanic
Iroko (*Chlorophora excelsa*) timber, Guinean and sub-Guinean
Mahogany (*Khaya senegalensis*) timber, sub-Sudanic and sub-Guinean (a more comprehensive list of West African timbers is given on pp. 539–40)
Horse-radish tree (*Moringa pterygosperma*), common hedge and fodder plant, Sudanic and sub-Sudanic

Introduced

Coconut (*Cocos nucifera*) fruit, coastal and Guinean settlements, south-east Asia

Papaya, paw-paw (*Carica papaya*) fruit, widespread, South America

Avocado pear (*Persea americana*) fruit, South America

Orange, lime, lemon, grapefruit (*Citrus* spp.) introduced via North Africa

Mango (*Mangifera indica*) fruit, Sudanic and sub-Sudanic, south-east Asia

Date palm (*Phoenix dactylifera*) fruit, Saharan, Sahelian, Sudanic and sub-Sudanic, south-west Asia

Desert date (*Balanites aegyptiaca*) fruit and kernel oil, Sahelian and Sudanic, North Africa

Breadfruit (*Artocarpus communis*) fruit, coastal, south-east Asia

Custard apple (*Anona squamosa*) fruit, coastal, West Indies

Soursop (*Anona muricata*) fruit, coastal, West Indies

Cassia (*Cassia* spp.) timber, village plantations, Sudanic, sub-Sudanic and sub-Guinean, south-east Asia

Teak (*Tectona grandis*) timber, village plantations, Guinean and sub-Guinean, south-east Asia.

Crop competition

Numerous factors affecting the choice of a particular crop or combination of crops have already been discussed. These have been mostly physical or agricultural. To a certain extent such factors must be of major importance in a region where amongst most communities the greater part of the crop is used for subsistence. Yet even before the era of colonialism food crops were sold or exchanged on local markets and thus acquired a commercial value. Today, with the growth of markets in towns and in the developing export crop regions, the commercial production of foodstuffs is increasing. Again consideration of crops as foodstuffs, that is consideration of taste, diet, nutrient and calorific values, is also important. Thus whilst yams, cassava and plantains each give approximately 10 times the yield per acre of bulrush millet, guinea corn or upland rice, the calorific yield per acre is only $2\frac{1}{2}$ to 4 times. In other words root crop or plantain yields need to be at least $2\frac{1}{2}$ times as great as those of cereals per acre for the same level of food production. Despite a lower over-all weight of production, bulrush millet and guinea corn combined yield in total in West Africa only slightly less food on a calorific basis than yams or cassava combined.[48] Moreover, the high productivity of roots is offset as competitive advantage by the longer growth period and by the general need for longer fallows. Rotations are generally longer under cereals than under roots, the proportion of fallow land is smaller, and although the cropped area may be greater, the amount of land which must be cleared every year is less. The return in money or exchange value and the labour cost involved are both important, however, in many areas. Thus in the Nigerian cocoa belt yams are often a favourite crop, despite the considerable labour involved in cultivation, because they give the highest cash return per acre of any crop other than cocoa.[49] In Abeokuta Province, however, upland rice is tending to replace yams in many areas because of high prices with increased popularity, and because the labour cost per acre is much less.[50] Cassava may require even less labour than rice and thus can frequently give a satisfactory cash return despite low prices (Table 1). The popularity of guinea corn in the Gambia may be judged from the fact that the crop yields the greatest return per unit of labour expended. Fonio or hungry rice and maize give the next highest returns and rice is a poor fourth.[51] Outside consideration of market prices, where sufficient land is available returns per unit of labour expended tend to be more important. Where lands are overcrowded returns per acre become of more importance. Both these factors are, however, subject to physical considerations and to problems of agricultural technique such as the most satisfactory crop combinations and rotations. An additional factor is the popularity of crops which, although low yielding, are quick growing, and thus give the first fresh foodstuffs of the cropping season. Cassava, with its property of remaining in the ground for periods of up to three years, is especially valued as a foodstuff for the 'hunger season', which normally occurs in the last two months before the first harvest. The hunger season lasts longest and is most acute in the Sudanic regions where, despite an additional floodland harvest, the period during which food storage is necessary is longer than elsewhere in West Africa.

Dietetic considerations other than those dictated by taste or culinary considerations enter very little into the question of crop competition. The roots may be lower in protein than the cereals which in turn have less protein than beans, but the protein content is either unknown or not considered. Beans give only low yields per acre, take a great deal of labour in cooking (many West Africans beans need several soakings in water to remove their high acid content) and are generally considered indigestible. A number of bean dishes are well known in West Africa, but are eaten chiefly as relishes to a main starch food.

Pests and diseases

Weeding is one of the great problems of West African agriculture and makes a heavy demand on labour. Mixed cropping helps to reduce the area available to weeds, and at the same time holds the soil under heavy downpours despite weed removal. Some of the major weeds like spear grass (*Imperata cylindrica*) are of European introduction, and several have appeared only in the last or in the present century (see pp.496–7). Most are, however, of local origin and form in effect the first stage of fallow regrowth. In the savannas local grasses quickly establish themselves, particularly the *Andropogons*. Weeds such as *Setaria verticillata* with spike-like inflorescences and *Heteropogon contortus* with twisted and bent arms are particularly troublesome. Wild relatives of cultivated plants such as wild rice, *Oryza barthii*, are big competitors on cropland and are difficult to eradicate. Examples of other troublesome plants are the *Commelina* spp., particularly *C. forskalaei* and *C. vogeli*, the Yoruba 'creeper that kills the farm crop',[52] and *C. benghalensis*, a pest of groundnut cultivation. In the Guinean zone soft stemmed forbs such as *Solanum torvum*, *Ageratum conyzoides*, *Physalis angulata* and *Cardiospermum halicacabum* are characteristic although there are some grass invaders such as *Paspalum conjugatum* and *Setaria chevalieri*. Animal and insect pests include birds (particularly the Sudan dioch), see p. 517, rodents which do extensive damage to oil palms, beetles which attack yams, aphis which infest guinea corn, and even fish which cause considerable damage in paddy fields. Locusts are a major pest in Sudanic and Sahelian areas. In the middle Senegal valley, for example, they have been estimated to cause 74 per cent of the crop damage attributed to pests.[53] Fungus diseases are a serious problem with oil palms and with several other plants, causing considerable losses both in the fields and in storage. Cassava is particularly susceptible to mosaic and the grains suffer from rust, blight and smut. Virus diseases cause marked reductions in the yields of yams, cassava, maize, groundnuts and cotton.

Crop storage

An important feature amongst almost all agricultural communities in West Africa is crop storage. Even in areas with nine months or more of rainy season, the harvests, except of cassava, may not occur all the year round and a crop must be stored for satisfactory use. At the other extreme on the northern margins of cultivation with only three months of rainy season or even slightly less, crop storage may be a vital necessity to ensure any food supplies. There are thus three main types of storage:

1) Storage of food crops for only a few weeks to offset temporary shortage or to keep until a favourable time for marketing, usually in woven grass bins.
2) Short-term storage for some months or even a year in order to keep a supply of the main crop and retain some food against the 'hunger season', usually in clay bins for grain or on racks for yams.
3) Long-term storage for several years, to offset the danger of famine due to loss of crop with failure of the rains or devastation by locusts or birds, usually in pits.[54]

Storage bins of grass or clay occur throughout West Africa and are one of the more prominent features of the villages. Without them harvests would have to be spread throughout the year and permanent settlement in areas with less than six months of rain would be impossible. In the drier areas rainfall variability is high and moisture supplies only just sufficient. At the same time locust and bird plagues are heavier and more frequent. Long-term storage is an essential method of balancing the supplies of good and bad years. In the moister areas with constantly high air humidities disease, particularly fungoid growth, is a greater danger and roots storage must be open to air circulation: hence the yam rack. The importance of cassava as a foodstuff which may be kept in the ground after maturity and harvested at any time can hardly be overestimated wherever storage is difficult to achieve. Again particularly in areas with long dry seasons,

...orage basket in Bornu

Nupe dwelling hut and short term storage bin

Figure 2.10a   *After Morgan*

Figure 2.10c   *After Morgan*

Short term storage bin near Randa
to south-west of Jos Plateau

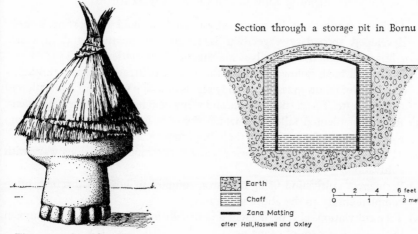

Section through a storage pit in Bornu

Earth

Chaff

Zana Matting

after Hall, Haswell and Oxley

0   2   4   6 feet
0   1   2 metres

Figure 2.10b   *After Morgan*

Figure 2.10d

gathered produce provides an invaluable supplement to eke out the supply of stored food. Some crops may be stored in a prepared or semi-prepared form. Thus cassava flour may be kept for periods of rather more than five months and the dried sliced roots may even be kept for a year.

For very short-term storage calabashes are still important in many, chiefly more remote, areas. Dumont suggests that calabash cultivation has declined, especially near road and railways, due to the competition of imported hollow-ware.[55].

The hunger season

Frequent references have already been made to the occurrence of a period of food shortage, usually at the beginning of the rains, when stores from previous harvests are low. Despite storage, or in some cases because of insufficient supplies in store due to a poor harvest, there is often a period each year when many peoples have little food or must depend almost entirely on the remains of a staple grain or on gathering. In the more humid areas with the longer rainy season this phenomenon is less obvious, for a greater variety of foodstuffs with a greater spread of harvests may be grown, together with cassava which may be left in the ground until required. Frequently the 'hunger season' appears to be rather a period of monotony in foodstuffs when only one grain or root remains, and when undernourishment rather than food shortage may occur. Quick-growing early crops, despite generally lower yields, are universally grown in order to obtain the first harvest as soon as possible.[56]

Systems of cultivation

There are seven major systems of cultivation in West Africa:

1) Shifting cultivation: in which virgin land or land supporting a well-developed secondary vegetation is sought for planting and in which cultivation sometimes involves movement of the settlement.
2) Rotational bush fallow: in which the area of cultivation rotates through a fixed area of fallow grasses or woody plants in which woodland is not allowed to regenerate. The settlement site and many field boundaries are permanent.
3) Rotational planted fallow: in which the only important distinction from rotational bush fallow is that the fallow cover is selected and planted.
4) Mixed farming: in which stock rearing is combined in various ways with cultivation.
5) Permanent cultivation using manures, compost or household refuse, often complementary to the above systems.
6) Tree cultivation, also permanent and usually associated with the rotational bush fallow system of cropping.
7) Floodland and irrigated cultivation, also often permanent and in many cases complementary to the above systems. Figure 2.11 shows generalized agricultural regions illustrating the distribution of the above systems. It should be noted that these regions are gradually changing both in character and distribution.

The first four of these systems are the chief means of cultivation in West Africa. The last three are either complementary to the first four or are practised

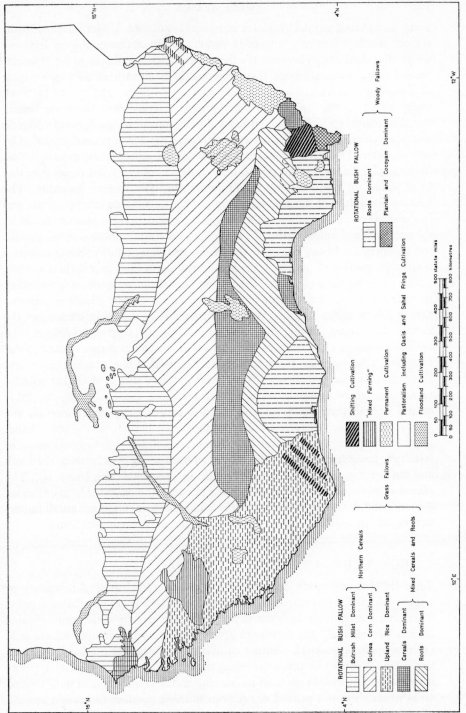

ROTATIONAL BUSH FALLOW

Northern Cereals
Bulrush Millet Dominant
Guinea Corn Dominant
Upland Rice Dominant

Mixed Cereals and Roots
Cereals Dominant
Roots Dominant

Grass Fallows

Shifting Cultivation
"Mixed Farming"
Permanent Cultivation
Pastoralism including Oasis and Sahel Fringe Cultivation
Floodland Cultivation

ROTATIONAL BUSH FALLOW

Roots Dominant
Plantain and Cocoyam Dominant

Woody Fallows

0   50 100 200 300 400 500 statute miles
0 50 100 200 300 400 500 600 700 800 kilometres

Figure 2.II

under exceptional physical, social or economic conditions. Under certain circumstances the first four may appear in various combinations producing land use
zones. The distinctions between the four chief means of cultivation are of fundamental importance, although they are sometimes difficult to distinguish from
one another and have frequently been confused. Their relations to physical,
social and economic conditions differ greatly. Nevertheless there are certain
common features which may be discussed here. Except in south-eastern Nigeria
and West Cameroun all West African cultivation has a 'rest period' produced by
lack of water. This varies from nine months in the north to two months or less
in the south. Part of this rest period is not only without rain, but desiccating due
to an influx of north-easterly air of remarkably low relative humidity. The
relative humidities of the dry season are of vital importance in crop raising and
in the character of the fallows. The longer the rest period the shorter should be
the proportion of fallow during the cropping season, since there is more time for
soil recuperation in any one year. Generally, therefore, fallows should occupy a
smaller proportion of the cultivable area in the north than they do in the south,
where cropping takes place throughout the year. In many areas, however, they
do not. There is evidence that a fallow under shrubs is more effectively restored
than a fallow under grasses. Moreover, methods of cropping complicate the
factors. The longer growing season in the south permits crop successions or even
double cropping. The variety of crops grown in most areas permits mixtures and
rotations. Thus land may frequently produce more than one crop in a season and
be kept in use for several seasons before it is rested due to declining returns.
Generally, where cropping takes place throughout the year rotations rarely
extend beyond three years, since the land is continuously under crop for the
whole time. Where there is a marked annual rest period, on the other hand,
rotations frequently extend over four or more years, since some recuperation of
fertility is possible each year. The contrast in manure supplies between the south
and the north is also of obvious importance in this connection (see p. 69). The
period a crop needs to mature, the returns per acre, the extent of local or market
demand, and the range of tolerance of soil and moisture conditions are all important factors in the development of mixtures, successions and rotations.

I. SHIFTING CULTIVATION

Since shifting cultivation depends on the use of well-developed secondary or
virgin woodland, it can only exist in areas of comparatively low population density.
There is a considerable variation in the population density which can be maintained, but generally the maximum appears to be 25 persons per square mile
(10 per square kilometre). Shifting cultivation is a vegetation selection system,
that is land is chosen for tillage according to the type, height and density of plants
it supports. The system depends on burning and flourishes best in well-wooded
areas where there is a marked dry season. Burning provides the easiest method
of clearance and returns mineral matter quickly to the soil. The result is the

development of a fire-conditioned or 'pyrophilous' vegetation, normally of two storeys (savanna woodland) consisting of old-established, fire-resistant trees and quick-growing plants, often including grasses, which are periodically destroyed. The wetter areas of the Guinean zone with little or no dry season and constantly high humidities are less suitable for this system of 'fire agriculture', except in their northern fringes where the forest is more deciduous in character, than areas further north. It seems likely that the earliest forms of cultivation were developed in the areas with savannas and a dry season of low relative humidities, and that Guinean agriculture is historically recent.

Shifting cultivation is located chiefly in the sub-Sudanic and sub-Guinean zones and in the deciduous fringes of the Guinean chiefly in the extreme east, in the Cross river basin and on the lower slopes of the plateaux of the Cameroons, in the west notably in south-west Ivory Coast and Liberia, and round the great sub-Sudanic plateaux and hills which once served as refuges from slave raids. In the last case it is a development of the last sixty years. In the former cases it is old established. In the east the Boki, Ekoi, and Anyang peoples depend on the shifting cultivation of plantains, cocoyams and maize. The heavy yield of plantains is a great advantage in this thickly forested region of the Cross river basin, since the task of clearance is heavy, and the area planted tends to be small (rarely more than two acres). Cocoyams combine well with plantains since they thrive in the shade provided by plantain leaves. After cropping for two to three years the land is abandoned for at least fifteen years. The creation of vast forest reserves in the region, however, has removed a considerable area from cultivation, and thus limited the extent to which shifting is possible. In some cases a cropping rotation within a small fixed area is now practised instead of former shifting. The settlement pattern is changing from the traditional dispersal to nucleation in small linear villages.[57] In the south-west the chief shifting cultivators are the Gagou, Gouro, Dan and Kru. Excepting the northern and central Gouro and some of the Kru peoples who are chiefly upland rice cultivators, the chief crops are plantains and yams. Again long fallows, the clearance of well-developed woodland and dispersed settlement, are traditional although changes have taken place due to external influences. Rice cultivators seem to have adapted themselves more easily to a system of short fallows than have plantain cultivators. Peoples in northern Liberia have tended to move to settlement sites nearer markets and routeways, and in the resultant crowding to have developed a system of fallows rarely more than six years in length. Gathering and hunting are still of great importance in the economy, and amongst the Gagou are of almost equal importance with cultivation. Tauxier describes the Gagou as a people who have depended entirely on hunting and gathering until the development (recently in their history) of the shifting cultivation of plantains and cocoyams.[58]

Elsewhere shifting cultivation has developed within the last sixty years on the pediments and plains surrounding the plateaux and inselbergs of the sub-Sudanic and sub-Guinean zones. Here, many peoples who were confined to hilltop sites for defence against the attacks of slave raiders, chiefly from the Sudan, have now abandoned their crowded fortress sites for the formerly unoccupied plains below. They have, at the same time, abandoned the careful system of cultivation necessary where little cultivable land was available, for a non-manuring shifting system. There are numerous cases on the fringes of Hombori, Bandiagara, the Atacora, the Kukuruku hills, the Jos Plateau, the Shebshi hills, the Mandara mountains and the plateaux of Adamawa. In most of these cases the cultivators plant a field for one or two years only, and then abandon it until it is covered with well-developed woodland. The chief crops planted are bulrush and *Digitaria* millets, guinea corn and, in the Jos Plateau and the regions further east, finger millet.

In general shifting cultivation is undertaken with only the minimum of tillage, since so large a proportion of the time available before planting must be spent in clearance. Only a few crops are planted making rotations impossible or at best very limited, and fields are soon abandoned. Little attempt is made to dis-tinguish soil types, and although planting is often in rows for the sake of conven-ience, fields are generally formless. The system is highly individual and suited best to a dispersed settlement pattern of scattered family units with little or no central authority.

2. ROTATIONAL BUSH FALLOW

Rotational bush fallowing is the chief system of cultivation used in West Africa though often closely associated with the permanent cultivation of either flood-land or of a small area of 'compound' or 'kitchen garden' land. It depends on the development of fallows which are never allowed to revert to woodland. Fields are rectangular, quite often with permanent boundaries, and the main settlement is fixed or moves only within the compass of a fixed site. The system supports population densities of between approximately 50 to 600 per square mile (19 to 232 per sq km). The area of fallows must normally be greater than the area planted, and consists of self-sown plants, grasses or shrubs, on land formerly under crops. The fallows change in character, i.e., in density, height and compo-sition, according to the number of years for which they are allowed to remain undisturbed. Fallows are judged strictly by their character rather than by the length of time which they have taken to develop, which varies greatly according to local physical conditions. A heavy demand for cultivable land may mean clearing fallow vegetation at a much earlier stage in its development than in areas where the demand is less. There is, in West Africa, a major distinction between the areas with grassy fallows and those with woody fallows. The woody fallows are restricted to areas with humid conditions after harvesting, where the seeds of shrubs and trees can establish themselves, or where root stock left in the ground can easily regenerate. Clearance by cutting and in some cases uprooting, followed by burning, is normally a heavy task taking several weeks. The larger trees are commonly left uncut and are sometimes used as tie poles for the yam vines. In the grass fallow areas, with dry conditions after harvesting, the pulling or cutting and burning of grass is easier and much more quickly accomplished.

In order to make the maximum use of the fallow area available rotational bush fallow cultivators employ crop mixtures, rotations and successions. Crop mixtures make possible a high density of plants per unit area cropped by combining plants making different demands on the soil. In other cases they spread the labour of planting and harvesting on one plot, or by close planting reduce the area which needs to be weeded. High densities may give low returns for each individual plant, but high total production per unit area. They provide some protection for the soils against erosion by heavy rains. Shifting cultivators frequently use crop mixtures although only to a very limited extent since they are usually restricted to a smaller variety of crops. Within a mixture the crops will occupy different positions on ridges or mounds. Thus in the south-east a common mixture consists of yams at the top of a mound, maize on the sides and cassava in the trough. Successions normally consist of planting individual crops one after the other over a period of a number of weeks in order to spread the labour of planting and in order to establish the most favoured or demanding crop before other plants can compete with it for moisture or soil resources. True successions, that is planting after harvest in the same plot during a single season, are uncommon in West Africa and are restricted chiefly to the zone with between seven and nine months rainy season. In the south and south-east the zone with a rainy season of nine months or more is dominated by root crops which normally remain in the ground for periods of over eight months. In the north the shorter rainy season normally permits only one crop in a year. Even in the intermediate zone a true succession is only possible with quick-growing varieties of cereals, chiefly maize, guinea corn and bulrush millet, and these varieties frequently give low yields. Crop rotations make possible the extension of the period of cultivation before abandoning a plot to fallow. The rotation may be of single crops or of crop mixtures. In some cases they are quite regular. In others they are what de Schlippe calls 'pseudorotations', that is an improvised order of crop mixtures which follow one another irregularly until the soil is exhausted.[59]

Crop mixtures, rotations and successions are most highly developed in the grass-fallow areas with long rainy seasons where the greatest variety of crops is available. To the north and south they are less well developed, although returns per acre are frequently higher due to the greater availability of manures in the north and the annual renewal of soils by the harmattan, and to the concentration on high-yielding root crops in the south. The different rotations and successions and mixtures of crops will be described within the framework of the crop regions discussed below.

A. Grass fallows

I. The northern cereals region

I.1. *Bulrush millet dominant sub-region.* On the rainlands between latitudes approximately 12° and 16° north bulrush millet is the dominant crop, usually grown in combination with other cereals, chiefly acha and guinea corn, and with ground-nuts and various legumes. The commercial developments of recent years have resulted in many parts of the sub-region in the extension of groundnut cultivation at the expense of cereals. Bulrush millet is generally preferred to guinea corn as a food, although the latter is normally reckoned superior for the brewing of beer. In the wetter areas guinea corn gives higher yields. In consequence the southern limit of the sub-region represents a balance between food preference, rainfall and drainage conditions. An additional factor is that bulrush millet is renowned for its keeping quality. This is of major importance in a region where food may have to be stored for twelve months or more.

In the west the Wolof depend on a combination of groundnuts, quick-growing and low-yielding bulrush millet ('souna'), slow-growing and high-yielding bulrush millet ('sanio') and a little guinea corn, normally of a quick-growing variety. Commercialism has made groundnuts dominant, frequently occupying between half and two-thirds of the cultivated area. Bulrush millets are, however, the traditional crop and are grown in combination with cowpeas or other legumes following groundnuts in the rotation. Groundnuts and millet normally alternate for periods of up to eight years before the return to fallow of four years or less. Some Wolof keep cattle which are pastured on the cropland in the dry season. Generally the Wolof have very little compound land. An interesting feature is the frequent cultivation of 'souna' in preference to 'sanio', even in moister areas where the latter would give higher yields, except in the extreme south in Saloum. The chief factors appear to be:

1) 'Souna' gives a quicker return, normally at a time of year when other foodstuffs are scarce.
2) 'Sanio' ripens late in the year when birds, especially the Sudan dioch or *Quelea quelea aethiopica*, make heavy depredations on the harvest.[60]

To the east in southern Mali on the rainlands fringing the lower portions of the basins of the Upper Senegal and Upper Niger, bulrush millet is grown in combination with groundnuts, fonio, upland rice and cotton, with maize, earthpeas and even cassava as minor crops. Upland rice and bulrush millet are frequently mixed, although often planted or harvested in succession, and are followed in the rotation by groundnuts and finally by fonio or cassava. Many cultivators in this sub-region own some livestock, but leave them to the care of specialist herdsmen. Occasionally bulrush millet has become a dominant crop amongst people traditionally mainly concerned with guinea corn, due to 'honey-dew' blight in the latter which does not affect pennisetums. This has occurred chiefly amongst some of the peoples of the Upper Volta.[61]

In Northern Nigeria bulrush millet occupies the greatest area for any one crop in Sokoto, Bornu, and Hausaland with the exception of Kano Province where there is a special case of permanent cultivation. In the northern sandy soiled areas of Hausaland and Bornu groundnuts, cowpeas and some guinea corn are combined with millets in a rotation. Cereals alternate with groundnuts for periods of up to four to six years and are followed by five to ten years fallow. 'Gero', early bulrush millet, is often sown first and harvested three months later. Guinea corn is commonly interplanted amongst a standing crop of 'gero'. 'Maiwa', late bulrush millet, is mixed with cowpeas. In Kano a little upland rice is planted on poor soils subject to waterlogging. In southern Hausaland cotton is a popular crop and replaces groundnuts on the heavier soils. It is normally grown alone after a crop of 'gero'. Many Hausa and Kanuri cultivators keep livestock, particularly goats, sheep and fowl, and may even own cattle. Many benefit from the use of their fields for dry season pasture by Fulani pastoralists. As in the west birds are a great pest especially with regard to late-ripening cereals. The Hausa cultivate in addition both compound land and floodland, the latter being especially important for sugar cane and onion production. The Mobber of Bornu migrate regularly between wet and dry season croplands.

Throughout the sub-regions trees play an important part in cultivation, particularly the 'dorowa' and the 'kad'. The latter is widespread throughout the region, and its presence on cropland is useful to attract cattle during the dry season. The former appears to be concentrated chiefly in the centre and east, particularly in Hausaland, where the leaves are recognized to be a valuable manure, and where exacting crops like cocoyam or cotton are often grown under its shade.

I.2. *Guinea corn dominant sub-region.* Guinea corn becomes the dominant crop in the wetter areas approximately 9° and 12° N., particularly in the centre and east. In the west it is less widespread being confined as the chief food crop chiefly to the Manding of the Casamance basin and to the Saloum Wolof. Elsewhere its place is taken by rice.

The Manding are in effect invaders of a region devoted chiefly to rice cultivation and have introduced their traditional crops of guinea corn and bulrush millet. Manding cultivators divide their main cropland into near and distant portions. On the distant portion groundnuts are mixed with guinea corn until the soils are almost exhausted, when bulrush millet and fonio are planted in successive years. On the near cropland 'sanio' bulrush millet, groundnuts, guinea corn and fonio frequently rotate, or if large numbers of cattle are pastured on the land during the dry season, then guinea corn becomes the chief crop followed by or mixed with groundnuts, and ending the rotation with fonio. Compound and floodland are important elements in the cultivation, and where an abundance of floodland occurs rice often replaces guinea corn as the staple food. The Saloum Wolof use rotations based chiefly on the alternation of guinea corn and groundnuts, sometimes replacing guinea corn by 'sanio' millet.

In the Upper Volta guinea corn is the traditional staple although replaced in several areas, particularly in the west, by bulrush millet due to 'honeydew' blight (see above). The position is unstable as a check in the disease after planting bulrush millet can lead to an increase in the planting of guinea corn. Amongst the Mossi cultivation on the main cropland lasts for four to ten years before returning to fallow. Guinea corn frequently begins the rotation, and may be grown mixed with beans for three years before planting groundnuts and finally bulrush millet or fonio. On well-drained soils bulrush millet often replaces guinea corn in the rotation. Where a well-developed fallow vegetation of ten years or more is cleared, beniseed is often planted first in order to put the soil in 'good heart' for the planting of cereals. Compound land is a very important resource in overcrowded Mossi with short fallows, and is used to produce a great variety of crops, of which the chief is maize. A little rice is cultivated in the floodland which in the extreme south is also used in a few areas to produce yams. In the western districts Savonnet makes a distinction between 'archaic', 'semi-evolved' and 'evolved' systems of cultivation.[62] Lobi and Koulango cultivators have 'archaic' methods rotating 1) yam and bulrush millet, 2) guinea corn, beans and earthpeas, followed by ten to fifteen years fallow and with little or no compound land. The Lobi and Koulango occupy areas marginal to the mixed cereals and roots region, and can just produce a yam crop on rainland. Yam returns are poor as the growing season is short and moreover does not permit the production of seed yams. However, the returns per acre are high compared with cereals, and help to compensate for the heavy work of bush clearance. The Dagari provide an example of the 'semi-evolved' system, using compound land, near and distant cropland. The distant cropland has a rotation of guinea corn and groundnuts for three to five years, followed by four to five years fallow in crowded areas and eight to fifteen years fallow in less densely populated areas. The 'evolved' system is used by the Bobo, again with three classes of land: 1) 'Ka' or manured village land, 2) 'Wa', also manured, nearly permanently cultivated and forming an *Acacia albida* park around each village and 3) 'Ma', the outfield, manured, with long fallow periods. 'Ka' and 'Wa' fields are often fenced or hedged to protect them from local sheep, goats and cattle, usually tended by Fulani shepherds or herdsmen.[63] On the unmanured main cropland guinea corn, maize and groundnuts are cultivated together for one year and followed by six years fallow, but on the whole the manured lands with their permanent culture are more important. Amongst the cultivators of the Upper Volta and surrounding districts are peoples like the Nankana who keep large numbers of animals. Their cultivation and their stock rearing do not appear, however, as closely integrated as in the examples cited below, and accordingly the areas they occupy are included within the guinea corn dominant sub-region. In the neighbouring district of Northern Mamprusi in Ghana over 90 per cent of the cultivated land is planted to early and late bulrush millet and guinea corn.[64] Lobi and Dagari are amongst the most mobile of West African cultivators, and in the last thirty years have moved across Upper Volta and the Ivory Coast into the western Gonja district of Ghana. Lobi have tended to use nearly permanent methods, and Dagari have used rotational methods, except in the emptier areas of Ghana's 'middle belt', where both have returned to extensive shifting with very long fallows. Yams have become the chief crop, but for commercial reasons.[65]

In Nigeria guinea corn is the chief crop of the southern extremity of Hausaland, in Zaria Province, of the peoples of Borgu, of the non-riverain lands of

Niger Province, and of the plains between the Jos Plateau and the plateaux of Adamawa, particularly in southern Bornu. Prothero has described an example from Zaria Province, the village of Soba, where guinea corn is the traditional staple, although commercial influences even before 1900 have made cotton of equal or greater importance.[66] Soba has three classes of cropland: 1) land within village walls, heavily manured and continuously cultivated, 2) permanent cultivation land, outside village walls and also manured, and 3) main cropland. In the last, ridges are made for planting and are shifted annually, with a rotation of i) cotton; ii) guinea corn; iii) cotton or groundnuts; iv) guinea corn, followed by fallows of at least five years. Some Bambara groundnut or earthpea is also planted. In southern Bornu guinea corn is the chief crop on loamy sands, where it takes approximately 40 per cent of the cropped area.[67] It is usually rotated with bulrush millet mixed with cowpeas and groundnuts. Elsewhere the Dakakari rotate guinea corn and hungry rice, the Kugama rotate mixed guinea corn and beans with groundnuts, and the Mumuye rotate 1) yams; 2) guinea corn or bulrush millet; 3) groundnuts, followed by three years fallow.[68] With the exception of the Mumuye who occupy an isolated 'roots dominated' island, yams are grown in a marginal area as a minor crop, and are expected to produce little at the end of a long period of cropping.

II. *The south-western upland rice region*
The region appears to have been the location of the development of an indigenous system of agriculture based on the cultivation of West African rice, both in upland and swamp conditions, and fonio. At one time it appears to have extended much farther eastwards. Meyerowitz claims that rice was formerly the chief crop of the Akan kingdom of Bono, in what is now Ghana, and that yams were introduced there in the early 17th century and later into Ashanti.[69] The introduction of Asian varieties of rice was confined until the 19th century to the area of traditional rice cultivation, west of the Bandama river in the Ivory Coast, probably because it was only in this region that people had the necessary technique of cultivation.

In Portuguese Guinea the Brames are upland rice cultivators who have invaded the area between the Rio Grande de Buba and the Rio Tombali, introducing rotational bush fallow cultivation of upland rice and groundnuts in place of the former shifting methods of the older occupants, the Beafadas. With increasing density of population at certain trading points, chiefly near the rivers, 'garden' cultivation in small units has become of increasing importance.[70]

Portères has drawn attention to a method of growing upland rice practised in the middle and upper Casamance and in Upper Gambia.[71] Slopes generally of 2°–8° are chosen and the rice fields are aligned parallel with the line of steepest gradient, about 300 feet (90 metres) long by 150 to 180 feet (45–55 metres) wide, usually facing south. Bands of 'bush' surround each field and interrupt the flow of surface water, whilst other bands 12–15 feet (3·7–4·6 metres) in width across the field subdivide it into plots 15–45 feet (5–14 metres) wide. Ridges and furrows are made parallel with the contour holding back moisture. At the top of the field there is a ditch taking off excessive water. At the bottom there is a large ridge. Rice is normally planted in the furrows, but in some cases it is planted on the ridges in the lower part of the field. Quick-growing varieties are preferred, and occasionally the varieties planted at the top of the field are quicker growing than those at the bottom. Cultivation is normally for two to three years, followed by one to two years of fallow. The same fields with the same separating bands of 'bush' are used each time. Within the area unfurrowed fields, otherwise similar in type, have been observed. To the north, where the rainfall is less, rice planting occurs in small basins. To the south in Guinea there are no dividing bands of vegetation, and there is less use of ridges and furrows parallel with the contour to retain moisture.

The Mende combine upland rice cultivation with oil palms, cocoa, ginger, groundnuts and some yam, guinea corn and beniseed growing. A little rice is grown, producing about an eighth of the total Mende rice production in Sierra Leone. Rice planting takes place in February and March, but the crop is not normally harvested until September. Early yams provide a useful stand-by food in July and August, supplemented by cassava planted the previous year. Except for yams and cassava, which are planted in small mounds, crops are generally planted on the flat. Rice usually begins a short rotation, often of only two years, which ends with cassava. Swamp rice cultivation has increased in recent years and provides a useful supplement.

In the Upper Niger basin the Malinké are also rice cultivators, chiefly on flood-lands. Many Malinké, however, have little or no floodland and depend on the cultivation of upland rice, either alone, or mixed with bulrush millet and followed in the rotation by cassava and fonio. Cultivation lasts from four to seven years and is followed by seven to fifteen years fallow. In Upper Guinea the Kissi, Guerzé and Toma plant rice with the first rains in May or even in June, normally first in the rotation and interplanted with or followed by groundnuts, guinea corn, maize or cotton.

In Liberia the Lomo, Mano, Sopa and Gio plant upland rice for one or two years, then fallow for three to seven years. The crop is often broadcast and afterwards hoed in. The Northern Gouro also plant rice, usually second in the rotation to yams. The Wobé, Guéré and Yacouba of the Ivory Coast follow rice with cassava and finally with plantains. Within the rice dominant zone there are however some exceptions, such as the Kru and Grebo, who depend mainly on cassava supplemented by fish, possibly due to local difficulties in harvesting grain due to high humidity.

III. *The mixed cereals and roots region (grass fallows)*
III.1. *Cereals dominant.* This sub-region extends across northern Ivory Coast, Gonja, Tamale and the eastern districts of Ghana, Togoland and Dahomey extending southwards to the coast, southern Bariba and Nupe. The rainy season is sufficient for satisfactory roots cultivation in most years, but the cereals, guinea

The Agricultural Lands of Mokwa (Nupe)

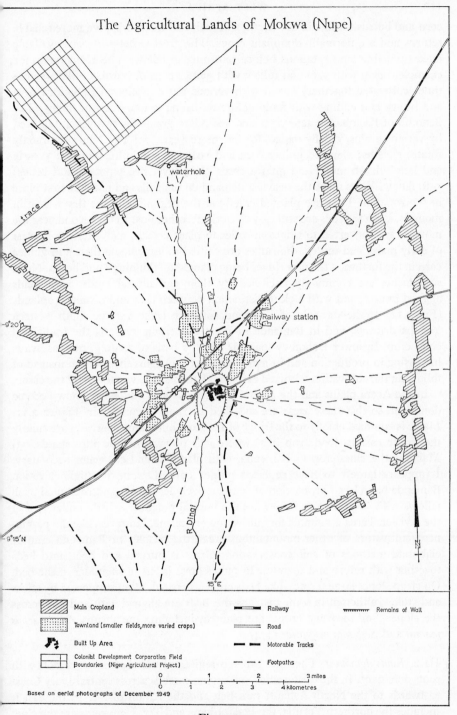

waterhole

trace

Railway station

9°20'N

9°15'N

R. Dingi

15°E

N

▨ Main Cropland	▭ Railway	▬▬▬ Remains of Wall
⋮ Townland (smaller fields, more varied crops)	═══ Road	
Built Up Area	▬ ▬ Motorable Tracks	
Colonial Development Corporation Field Boundaries (Niger Agricultural Project)	– – – Footpaths	

0   1   2   3 miles
0   1   2   3   4 kilometres

Based on aerial photographs of December 1949

Figure 2.12

corn and bulrush millet in the north, and maize in the south, give more reliable returns and are normally dominant crops. The great variety of crops available makes possible long rotations before returning to fallow. The Konkomba, for example, begin with yam and follow with guinea corn or bulrush millet (sometimes cultivated together) mixed with various pulses, followed by guinea corn and beans, and ending with fonio before returning to four years of fallow. The Senoufo of Kiembara rotate yams and secondary grains for two years, followed by various grains, chiefly maize, for five more years.[72] The Nupe commonly rotate: 1) yams; 2) maize, guinea corn and early and late bulrush millet; 3) early and late bulrush millet and guinea corn; 4) cassava, sweet potato and beans; 5–8) fallow. Yams make the heaviest demand on the soils and take the first place in the rotation. They are planted chiefly at the beginning of the dry season in mounds, when the soils are still easy to work after the rains. In the second year the mounds are converted to ridges in order to plant cereals, and after the harvest of early maize and millets the ridges are shifted to leave late millets and guinea corn in the furrows – the new ridges being planted to 'thinnings' and beans. Nupe settlements are commonly encircled by their agricultural lands, with fields aligned in arcs, and with a clear distinction between near and distant croplands (Fig. 2.12). In the 'dry belt' of Togoland, southern Dahomey, the south-western Yoruba districts, and in Bamenda in West Cameroun maize is the traditional chief crop. In lower Dahomey maize is still the basis of feeding, but cassava is increasing in production and in many places often begins the rotation instead of following the cultivation of mixed early and late maize as was formerly the case.

In the Accra plains and the coastal belt cassava and pulses have now become dominant, so that these areas are classified as 'roots dominant' in Figure 2.11. Maize is confined chiefly to the fringe of the more humid forest areas, particularly the 'south-eastern food crop belt' where it is often grown in pure stands.[73] Maize is the chief crop in Bamenda, with plantains and cocoyams secondary. It appears largely to have replaced guinea corn. Despite its high elevation Bamenda has a large proportion of comparatively level land, and rotational bush fallows with several years fallow are the normal practice. A little under half of the divisional area is suitable for cultivation or grazing. However, like the permanent cultivators of other mountainous areas, the peoples of Bamenda employ elaborate methods of soil conservation. Grass is burned and hoed into beds together with refuse and manure. In places grass is left to smoulder in the bed. On steep slopes large terrace-like beds are constructed, often supported by sticks and stones, although in some districts the beds are aligned with and not across the slope. 'Soil recovery crops' are planted, including the shrubs *Adenocarpus mannii* and *Sesbania aegyptiaca*.[74]

III.2. *Roots dominant*. There are two sub-regions of mixed cereals and roots with roots dominant. In the west a small sub-region extends across central Ivory Coast eastwards to the North Ashanti yam belt and the Afram plains. In the east it includes the northern Yoruba, the Igala, Idoma and Tiv. Here yams are the chief crop, although guinea corn occupies a greater area, partly due to a longer rainy season, partly in some cases to tradition, and partly to modern commercial influences, which have made several parts of the sub-regions food producers for the cultivators of cocoa and palm oil produce to the south. Within the sub-regions a normal rotation consists of three years: 1) yams; 2) maize, guinea corn and bulrush millets; 3) cassava and beans. The yams are grown in mounds which are re-hoed in the second year to form ridges. These are shifted or even allowed to break down for the third year of cultivation.

High population densities in many parts of the sub-regions are presumed to have resulted in a severe reduction of the original forest cover, and the emergence of broad open areas of fallow grassland so distinctive that botanists have delimited a zone of 'derived savanna' (see Chapter 5). In northern Yorubaland the shortage of standing trees or poles to support yam vines has led to the use of guinea corn stalks in their place. The rotation developed in consequence is: 1) early maize and guinea corn; 2) yams and maize; 3) cassava. After harvest the guinea corn stalks are bent and tied to form a trellis, the ridges are 'mounded', and the yams are then planted during the dry season. An additional possible factor is the local suggestion that the yams produce better yields by taking second place in the rotation. The Tiv often plant a piece of cassava stalk in the mound several weeks before yam planting in order to serve like guinea corn as a vine pole. The importance of benniseed cultivation (encouraged by the Agricultural Department) amongst the Tiv has led to a rotation of 1) yams; 2) guinea corn and bulrush millet; 3) benniseed, cassava and groundnuts, in the south, and 1) yams; 2) bulrush millet or guinea corn and benniseed in the north.

In overcrowded northern Iboland cereals are of little importance, and the mixed cropping of yams and cassava makes this area an extension of the roots region north of the zone of woody fallows. Amongst the north-eastern Ibo there is a specialist production of large yams in mounds between 3 and 6 feet (1–2 metres) in height. The largest of these tend to be located chiefly in well-watered bottomlands.

Upland rice has become increasingly important in recent years in south-western Yorubaland (Abeokuta), and swamp rice amongst the north-eastern Ibo (Ogoja), partly because of the low labour requirement compared with yams, and partly because of changes in diet (see below, pp. 494–5).

B. Woody fallows

IV. The roots region

The roots region extends throughout the two zones of woody fallow to the east of the Bandama river in the Ivory Coast. Yams could be grown as a major crop further westwards, but are at present only of secondary importance to rice. As suggested above, the western limit of the roots region has been claimed as a major ethnic divide between 'West Atlantic' rice growers and 'East Atlantic' yam growers[75], although distinctive climatic conditions may be of some significance, that is the tendency to a single rainfall maximum to the west and to a double maximum to the east.

Yams are the traditional crop, but cocoyams and cassava are important, especially the latter, which in the last half century has become one of the chief food crops of West Africa. Maize is the only cereal of any importance. Plantains take up a greater area than roots in a few parts of the region, notably in south-western Ghana.

Within the region one may distinguish between the cassava–maize system of the fringes of the woody fallow in southern Ghana and in south-western Yorubaland, the yams–maize–cocoyam–cassava system of eastern Yorubaland and Benin, and the yam–cassava system of the regions east of the Niger. In the first, maize is the traditional crop, but has been largely replaced by cassava, grown in many areas mainly for sale to urban markets. In the second, rotations have developed, such as 1) early and late maize; 2) yams and small crops; 3) cocoyams or cassava. In some cases cocoyam and cassava are planted in the second year and the land allowed to revert to fallow in the third. Yams are planted at the beginning of the rains, since earlier planting often leads to disease. In the last system yams and cassava are interplanted. Yams are planted in February or March and harvested in October to December. Cassava is planted after the yams have become established, in some cases not until the second or later rains, and harvested throughout the following year. In West Ashanti and Mampong, yams, cocoyams, plantains and maize are combined. Cocoyam is favoured because it keeps down weeds. In the Ghana portion of the region generally, and in south-west Ivory Coast, yams are less important than cocoyams and plantains. The importance of cocoyams and plantains is based on tradition reinforced by their use as shade plants for young cocoa.[76]

Throughout the region oil palms are a major crop and abundant on croplands where they are in effect 'interplanted' with the field crops. Commercialism has greatly changed the character of the region within recent years due to its suitability for the cultivation of perennials producing crops like cocoa, kola, coffee and palm oil and kernels. Proximity to the coast has been a factor of obvious importance.

V. *The south-eastern plantain–cocoyam region*

The area of rotational bush fallow, with plantain and cocoyam as the dominant crops, is small, being confined to the West Cameroun. Cocoyam is normally regarded as a woman's and plantain as a man's crop. *Xanthosoma* is planted first in most cases, and sometimes followed by *Colocosia*, formerly the sole cocoyam and chief root crop of the district. Plantain suckers are usually planted between the cocoyams, and cut down after each harvest, allowing fresh suckers to grow from the old root. Cocoyam is allowed to stay in the ground for five to six years, the cormels being harvested from the plant as required. Yams and maize are subsidiary crops, either following the main crops, or being planted separately. Fallows average four to six years, extending up to a maximum of just over ten years.[77] Elsewhere plantains and cocoyams are widespread in the roots region, and are particularly important in central and east Yorubaland and south-west Ghana.

3. ROTATIONAL PLANTED FALLOW

The only example of rotational planted fallow known to the authors occurs in south-eastern Nigeria amongst the Ibo and Ibibio speaking peoples. The cultivation system is based on the interplanting of yams and cassava, leaving the latter in the fields during the second and even third years, whilst the planted fallow is established. The Ibo of Umuahia and Aba districts plant 'echeku' (*Acioa barterii*), whilst the Ibibio of neighbouring districts plant 'nya' (*Macrolobium macrophyllum*). These small shrubs have deep tap roots and soon form a thick fallow cover. In clearance the stems are often allowed to remain in order to serve as yam stakes. The act of planting confers the right of clearance and of cropping the land so planted.

4. MIXED FARMING

'Mixed farming' is used for lack of a better term to connote systems of cultivation combined with the large-scale keeping of stock, chiefly cattle, sheep and goats. Only amongst some of the Serer people of Senegal does mixed farming consist of an integrated use of pasture and cropland. Elsewhere, except for dry season pasturing, stock rearing and cultivation are distinct occupations even when performed by the same people. Most cultivators in West Africa keep some livestock, usually sheep, goats and fowl, and in some non-Moslem areas, pigs. Occasionally a few cattle are kept, usually either for prestige or for sacrificial purposes. Some peoples like the Toucouleur and the Diawara of the Sudan own large herds, but do not keep them, giving them instead to the care of Fulani or Moorish herdsmen.

The groups of people amongst whom stock rearing and cultivation are of approximately equal importance are the Serer in the north-west, some of the sedentary Fulani communities of the Fouta Djallon, and the Shuwa of the north-east. Amongst the Serer the stock-rearing tradition had tended to decline in importance with the increase of commercial groundnut cultivation. Amongst the sedentary Fulani the tendency to mixed methods has been reinforced by the introduction of the plough and encouragement by French government authorities. Amongst the Shuwa there appears to have been little change in their economy over the past half century except for the development of new, stable villages in areas provided with well water by Government drillers. Marti notes the development of mixed farming amongst the Fulani of Bandiagara due to the freeing of Rimaïbé serfs.[78]

The Serer have compound land, enclosed farmland and open farmland. On the enclosed farmland, according to Pelissier[79], they rotate: 1) sanio bulrush millet; 2) groundnuts, and in some cases 3) pasture. There is no fallow. On this land the fields are divided by hedges, and the cattle graze on the pasture section or on fallow land proper during the wet season. During the dry season they graze throughout the enclosed and open farmland areas, and their feeding on crop remains is supplemented by the leaves of the 'kad'. In some villages flocks of sheep are kept and follow a similar grazing system. Portères gives a rotation of 1) groundnuts; 2) souna and cowpea (interplanted late); 3) groundnuts; 4) sanio. This is repeated twice and followed by two years of pasture fallow.[80] Thus there exists on part of the area cultivated an indigenous system of mixed farming, able to support population densities of between 100 and 190 to the square mile (39–73 per sq km) in a region of sandy soils and thorn bush. However, it is not a system which can be compared with mixed farming in Europe. For example, no fodder crops are grown.

In the Fouta Djallon, particularly in the Cercle of Labé, there are large numbers of Fulani families no longer able to depend on slaves to do the work of cultivation and commanding little or no paid labour. In consequence many of these families have combined cultivation with stock rearing, and encouraged by loans and education in new methods have acquired a plough and sometimes a harrow. Labouret provides an example.[81] A family of seven adults and four children has one large rice field and one large fonio field on the cropland, and also cultivates sweet potatoes, cassava and groundnuts. Another field near the compound contains cotton, sweet potatoes and bananas. In addition they keep twenty-one cattle, of which eight have been trained to plough, and eight sheep. A little seasonal labour is hired for not more than two months in the year, and provided with food and accommodation.

The Shuwa occupy the lands south of Lake Chad with dry season pastures near the lake and wet season pastures farther south on higher ground. The permanent settlement is usually located in between the wet and dry season pastures, near the 'firki' clay soils which are used for dry season cultivation, and are divided into owned holdings. Cattle and sheep are frequently penned during the heat of the day in the 'tum-tum' to protect them from flies. The 'tum-tum' has a central sleeping place for the family surrounded by the cattle stall. On the sandy soiled rainlands bulrush millets, cowpeas and groundnuts are grown, and are manured from the cattle stalls and from cattle penned on the cropland at the beginning and end of the dry season. On the moisture retaining 'firki' claylands dry season guinea corn or masakwa is cultivated. Formerly agriculture was undertaken only by slaves, whose place has now been taken by family dependants or hired labour. Much of the firki area is unused because of either inadequate or excessive flooding.

5. PERMANENT CULTIVATION

Permanent cultivation, that is cultivation without fallow, appears in two forms, outside floodlands, in West Africa. In the first it is a form of kitchen-garden cultivation with manures on 'near farmland' or compound land. In the second it concerns the cultivation of all or at least of the greater part of the cropland available, and is associated with a shortage of arable land, that is normally with high densities of population. This second form appears in the crowded mountain refuges of the sub-Sudanic peoples, in the densely populated portions of Iboland and Ibibioland in south-eastern Nigeria, and in the district around Kano in Northern Nigeria.

Compound land has already received some discussion above and several examples have been given in association with systems of rotational bush fallowing. The manures applied include household refuse, ashes, crop remains and animal manure. In addition the land is frequently the site of cess-pits. A high level of fertility is often maintained, and former compound land sites which have been abandoned are noted for their highly productive dark, even black soils. Both field and tree crops are frequently associated on compound land. The field crops normally consist of plants used in only small quantities for relishes or sauces, e.g. okra, peppers; a few plants needing special attention or even hand watering (particularly if being cultivated in marginal conditions), e.g. some varieties of yam, tobacco; plants grown in reserve in case of food shortage, e.g. cocoyams, sanio bulrush millets, fonio. Tobacco, chiefly *Nicotiana rustica* or Turkish tobacco, needs abundant manure and is a common compound land crop. In drier sandy soiled areas the improved moisture retaining properties of the well-manured soils of compound land have a special value for crops like cocoyam needing plenty of water. Useful fruit and timber trees are preserved on compound land, and a few, particularly the oil palm, are even planted there. Being close to the settlement they are normally protected from the 'bush fires' of the cropland. Manures are frequently heaped round the bases of the trees which eventually form dense, shady groves.

The sub-Sudanic hill refuge systems of permanent cultivation are best developed in the Guinea Massif, the Atacora Range, the Jos Plateau, and the plateaux of Adamawa. Tillage normally includes the careful construction of ridges and mounds, and occasionally box ridging, together with the heaping of stones in mounds or in lines along the contour to form terraces. True terracing rarely exists. The lines of stones are fragmentary, and in some cases in northern Dahomey and the Jos Plateau are not walls. In the Mandara Mountains, however, Stanhope White has observed terrace walls up to 10 feet (3 metres) in height, and extending vertically for some 2500 feet (760 metres). There is a careful selection of soils, the highest yielding crops normally being planted in the most fertile, and an elaborate development of crop rotations and of manuring. The traditional staple crop in most areas appears to be fonio, probably because this is an indigenous crop cultivated at a very early date, and the hill refuge peoples were amongst the first cultivators established in West Africa. In some parts of the Jos Plateau and in Adamawa the staple is the Central African or East African crop, finger millet. These crops do not reflect low fertility. The hill refuges frequently offer numerous small pockets of highly fertile soils derived from basic lavas. Guinea corn and bulrush millet have become widespread in the last half century, and are popular mainly because of their use in brewing beer. Yams, cassava, beans, grams and pulses have also been introduced. Groundnuts have become a useful commercial crop particularly in the Jos Plateau. Cereal plants are often sown, first in nursery beds, and the cereals afterwards transplanted. Manured land frequently occupies more than half if not all the area cultivated. In the deep soils of rapidly decomposing granites, cultivation is often permanent and yet without manures. Valley bottom lands provide annually flooded alluvium useful for crops with great moisture needs, e.g. cocoyam, okra, plantains, bananas and ginger. In some areas these floodlands are protected against stream erosion by stone walls. Amongst the peoples of the Mandara Mountains advanced agricultural techniques are remarkably well developed. Stanhope White lists:

1) The planting of soil-holding shrubs across lines of erosion.
2) Selective breeding of cattle.
3) Collection of manure and night soil and distribution on cropland together with ashes and refuse.
4) Rotation of crops.
5) Two years fallow after soil exhaustion followed by the planting of tiger nut or earth almond (*Cyperus esculentus* – introduced from Egypt), when fertility is regained.
6) Irrigated cultivation of onions.
7) Planting or protection of several trees and pruning of leaves for fodder.

With the more settled political conditions of the last half century there has been a tendency either to abandon the hills for the surrounding plains or to cultivate plains land in addition. At the lower levels the careful methods used on the better hill soils are abandoned for shifting cultivation over large areas (see under 'shifting cultivation'), or on the level lands of the Jos Plateau, for example, for a rotational bush fallow system with fallows normally of 2 to 6 years following rotations of 5 to 10 years.[83] Thus the Jos Plateau now has a mixture of permanent and rotational bush fallow methods as indicated on the map. Not all cultivators in hill refuges are in any case permanent cultivators. The Mumuye of northern Muri, for example, follow 3 years of cultivation with 3 years of fallow.

In the Ibo divisions of Orlu and Okigwi with 873 and 755 persons per square mile (337 and 291 per sq km) respectively and in the Ibibio divisions of Abak, Ikot Ekpene and Uyo with 677, 622 and 670 persons per square mile (261, 240 and 259 per sq km) the main cropland area is either less or no more than the area of compound land. An apparent increase in the population total over the last century has resulted in the sacrifice of cropland, in which use-right is commonly shared, in favour of compound land, in which use-right belongs to the family or individual. Thus permanent cultivation on manured soils, in close association with the development of oil palm groves, has become the chief feature of the agriculture economy.

The Kano close-farmed zone occupies approximately 2700–7500 square miles

(7000–19,500 sq km) around Kano City, with a radius of 30–50 miles (50–80 km). Up to 10 miles (16 km) radius, very approximately, the population density averages some 500 per square mile (190 per sq km). Holdings in this inner zone average between 2 and 5 acres (0·8–2·0 hectares). The basis of cropping is bulrush millet and guinea corn together with groundnuts. Cassava, sugar cane, cocoyams and sweet potatoes are also grown, particularly in the moister soils of the valley bottoms or of marshy depressions. A few animals are kept, and their manure and ashes and household waste are used to maintain continuous cultivation. Sometimes dwellings are removed and the old sites enriched by refuse are then cultivated.[84] Other additions to the soil are the leaves of various acacias and the 'dorowa', night soil from Kano City, and the fertile alluvium of the Jakara river which is enriched by its use as a sewer for part of the urban area. Holdings near surface water are frequently irrigated to produce crops, including onions, various vegetables and small quantities of wheat during the dry season. Many of the plots are subdivided by hedges which protect the crops from animals. Cultivation of this type is common to a lesser extent around many Sudanic cities. A related form of market gardening, usually with short fallows, occurs around other large urban areas in West Africa.

6. TREE CULTIVATION

Reference has already been made to tree cultivation in the case of oil palms growing on compound land. On the fallows and croplands, where they are self-sown, they form an 'oil palm bush', widely distributed throughout the region of woody fallows and amidst the modified remnants of 'forest' outliers in the savannas to the north. Densities of oil palms vary, in Dahomey, for example, between a mean of approximately 18 to the acre (45 per hectare) at the northern limits of the oil palm 'belt', and 100 to the acre (250 per hectare) in the south.[85]

In the fringes of the former forests of the Ivory Coast, eastern Liberia and western Ashanti kola became an important crop for exchange at a remote date in West Africa's history. *Cola nitida*, the species of this region, provided nuts finding the readiest market in the Sudanic towns. Many of the nuts were simply gathered in the forest, particularly in the southern areas in what is now Liberia. In the areas occupied or controlled by the Akan-speaking peoples, however, plantations were established, which in Bono and Ashanti were state-owned and worked by slave labour.[86] Similarly in Nigeria the Nupe early established small plantations of the less-favoured eastern species, *Cola acuminata*.

Today tree cultivation, particularly of cocoa, kola, oil palms and coffee has become well developed amongst the Guinean peoples due to the development of overseas trade. This, however, is clearly a modification of traditional agricultural practice by European influences and will be discussed in Chapter 10.

7. FLOODLAND CULTIVATION

Cultivation in annually flooded alluvium is a widespread feature in West Africa, usually in association with other systems of cultivation. The most common case is the planting of rice, sugar cane or maize in riverain alluvium as water levels decline, in most cases at the end of the rainy season. In Hausaland, for example, the riverain floodlands or fadama are generally divided into holdings of less than half an acre (0·2 hectare) each in size, producing rice, sugar cane, onions, wheat, peppers and cocoyams. They provide small supplies of fresh food after the main harvest on the cropland, and extend agricultural work into the long dry season. The shaduf is a common feature in irrigation in Northern Nigeria, and is frequently portable so that it may be transferred from one field to another.

There are, however, three regions in West Africa where floodland cultivation is more important than the cultivation of rainlands. They are the Sahelian floodplains of the Senegal, Niger and Chad basins, the floodplains and oases of the Sahel and Sahara fringe outside the great basins, and the alluvial floodlands of the estuaries particularly on the western coast between Cape Verde and Cape Mount, the 'Rivières du Sud' region.

In the 'walo' or floodplain of the Senegal between Bakel and Dagana the Toucouleur or Tekrour cultivators plant their chief crops of guinea corn, cowpeas and maize from October onwards as the water level retreats.[87] The flooded area normally covers 1,240,000 acres (501,820 hectares) (not including the 'djedjogol', a zone flooded only in occasional years) of which not more than 320,000 acres (129,500 hectares) are cultivated. With variations in flood level the cultivated area fluctuates between 200,000 and 600,000 acres (80,930 and 242,860 hectares). Flood cultivation lasts throughout the dry season from October to June when the final harvest takes place. In the latter month planting begins on the rainlands of the 'fondé' or levée, in most years above the floods, and of the 'diéri' or sandy soiled croplands above the floodplains.

Here the chief crop is bulrush millet harvested in November in widely dispersed fields with long fallows. There are also some Wolof and Sarakolé cultivators in the valley who plant chiefly rice and maize in the flooded areas, particularly in the lower portions of the 'fondé'. The Toucouleur own cattle and use the manure together with ash on some parts of both the rainlands and the floodland. Generally the cattle are kept by Fulani herdsmen who bring their own beasts to the fondé and the waterside in the dry season, where they are welcomed by the cultivators for the additional supply of meat, milk and manure. An interesting point is that although floodland yields are generally higher than those from rainland, more labour is required per unit area and there is a better financial return to the family as a whole from rainland.

The Songhay of Gao plant rice in the floodlands at the beginning of the rains in May to June. The rains are needed to soften the clays of the rice lands in order to make them easier to till. A little after planting the flood arrives, and rises in the two and a half months from July to September $8\frac{1}{2}$ feet (2·6 metres) out of its total normal rise of 12 feet (3·7 metres). Before the floods attain greater heights, dikes are built or repaired to control the flood level in the fields. By December all the rice has been harvested, the flood levels have declined, and in January the fields are used as nurseries to establish seedlings of guinea corn and bulrush millets.[88] These crops are planted out on the rainlands by the first rains and are harvested in September. The Songhay also own and keep stock, chiefly cattle, sheep and goats. The cattle are regarded as a form of wealth, and are neither sold nor killed, except when very old or on special occasions.

Similar practices are followed for rice cultivation in the inland Niger delta of Mali. At Mopti the flood lasts from the end of August to the beginning of January and covers the rice fields with between 5 and 6 feet (1·5–1·8 metres) depth of water. Planting takes place after the rains in July, chiefly of late varieties to be harvested at the end of December. In the north of the delta the flood is later and there is a danger of a delay in its arrival after the rains have finished in October. Moreover, the crop must be harvested by canoe in fields still under water. In the lakes zone the flood is so late that rice is not planted with the rains, but with the decline in flood levels and is sown from April–May onwards. With the great depth of flooding in places, wild floating varieties (*O. barthii*) are more important as sources of food than cultivated varieties.[89] However, in both the inland Niger delta and in the Gao area guinea corn and bulrush millet are the chief crops, and the importance of rice has probably been overstressed by observers. Barth observed little rice cultivation in the Sudan, and in Chevalier's experience of the last half century rice cultivation has spread *inland* from the Rivières du Sud, regarded by him as the cradle of cultivation of African rice varieties.[90]

In the Mauritanian Sahel valley floodplains, the 'hofrats' or flooded basins, and lands irrigated from wells, provide areas of cultivation which form in effect oases distinct from the great river basins to the south. Toupet has described an example in the Tamourt valley.[91] Here in the wadis barrages have been constructed to hold back sufficient water for flood cultivation. Wheat occupies the lower area, needing the moisture of one month's flooding, and bulrush millet is planted on higher ground needing a flood of only eight days. The staple crops are bulrush millets and beans planted together on the floodland as the water level recedes, and also in the 'hofrats', where the brief rains sometimes make a harvest possible. On the lands irrigated from wells with the aid of shadufs and channels, date palms, wheat, vegetables and tobacco are grown. However, production only equals consumption one year in five, and millets frequently have to be imported from Senegal. Pastoralism provides an important commercial resource, and many of the lower castes (serfs and former slaves) emigrate temporarily in search of work.

In the broad valley of the Dallol Bosso in the Niger Republic the distribution of cultivation depends on the depth of water-table. The optimum average depth is between 33 and 49 feet (10 and 15 metres). Above that level marshes often develop and the soil accumulates heavy concentrations of salt.[92]

Elsewhere crops of guinea corn and rice are raised in the fadama of Sokoto and Hausaland, wheat is cultivated in the valley of the Komadugu Yobe in the

Chad basin. The Bataci sub-group of the Nupe combine fishing on the Niger with marshland crops of maize, sweet potatoes, cassava and rice; whilst the islanders of Yauri grow onions for sale in manured beds watered by irrigation channels and handscoops.[93] Although rice is of only minor importance in Nigeria, the total production of over 250,000 tons (mainly swamp rice cultivated in Sokoto, Hausaland and south-eastern Nigeria) is comparable with that of Guinea.

Amongst the swamp rice cultivators of the south-west, the Balante, who are mainly in Portuguese Guinea, are noted for the clearance of mangroves and the development of annually flooded rice fields. They depend for their cultivation on the annual floods of fresh water to reduce the amount of salt in the soils. Rice is sown in nurseries in July, and planted out in the estuarine swamps as far north as those of the Casamance River in September to October. Harvesting takes place in December to January. Swamp rice cultivation has increased since the Portuguese and French established peaceful conditions on the coast. Traditionally many Balante regard guinea corn or bulrush millets as their staple foodstuffs, and endeavour to cultivate groundnuts and upland rice in addition.[94] Although it appears that swamp rice cultivation was established on this coast before the arrival of the Europeans, notably in the valley of the Rio Mansoa[95], nevertheless the system received its first great impetus to develop with the introduction of Asian rice by the Portuguese in the 16th, 17th and 18th centuries, and its second impetus with the stable political conditions of the 20th. Some Balante cultivate compound land, and have four types of cropland dependent on rains, sowing chiefly bulrush millets and groundnuts. Many keep livestock and these are pastured on the cropland in the dry season thus providing manure.

Floodland is also used in some cases for cultivation, especially of maize, outside the main areas described. In the lower Ouémé valley of Dahomey, for example, cultivators distinguish between the 'tikpla' or floodplain edge, with its crops of maize and beans planted as water levels decline, and the tigboji', or floodplain proper, formerly important for maize production on heavy soils, but now largely neglected except for fish ponds.[96]

Sahel fringe cultivation

Temporary fields have been established beyond the northern margins of permanent cultivation in the Sahel in years of favourable heavy initial rainfall. Shortage of dry season water supplies inhibits permanent settlement. The French 'peace' has encouraged this northward movement of cultivators in regions formerly dominated by pastoralists.

Land use

The study of land use in West Africa has not yet been sufficiently developed to allow the presentation of a survey of land-use patterns. The only statistical survey of a whole territory is that contained in the Nigerian Sample Census of Agriculture of 1950–1,[97] although descriptive accounts of territorial land use exist in such works as 'Soil conservation and land use in Sierra Leone',[98] and attempts to make statistical surveys by provinces or regions have been made in Northern and Western Nigeria each year since 1956. The 1950–1 Census was based on detailed surveys of a few small sample areas, chosen on the basis of a division of Nigeria into probable agricultural regions. The classes of land use distinguished were farm crops, tree crops, fallow, forest reserves, non-agricultural, grazing and uncultivated bush and waste. Grazing land was recorded only in Bamenda Province. The possible errors in estimates based on so few detailed surveys, which in themselves are probably of doubtful accuracy, are enormous. The survey merely indicates that the highest proportions of total area in field cropland by provinces are amongst the Ibo oil palm and root crop cultivators (23–36 per cent), amongst Yoruba cocoa farmers (28 per cent) and the Hausa groundnut and millets cultivators (20–25 per cent).

Elsewhere, except in Calabar, which includes a great contrast in land-use patterns between its eastern and western portions, field cropland varies between 2 and 11 per cent. The proportion of tree cropland is highest in the south-west where in the Lagos Colony it reaches 53 per cent, but unfortunately no attempt was made in the survey to assess the area under oil palms or under shea trees. The area under fallow varies between approximately one-third and nine times the area under field crops, having the highest ratios in the south central provinces of Benin and Warri, in the Cameroons and Bamenda and in Niger Province – all areas badly served with communications and with little development of commercial cropping. All the northern and north-eastern provinces were recorded as having less fallow than field cropland, which is possibly true in the north with its high proportion of permanent and flood cropland, but is more doubtful in the north-east. Areas with over 60 per cent uncultivated bush and waste include the whole of Northern Nigeria and the Cameroons. Ijebu Province in the south-west recorded 57 per cent since a large part of its area consists of swamp. However, in most cases the area of uncultivated land appears too high and must include both some pastures and some fallow. Forest reserves form the greatest proportions of total area in the south, where the best timber trees remain, and where forested lands were often left as a border no-man's land between rival communities. Non-agricultural lands include roads and building sites, and are only 3 per cent or less of the total area of any one province.

Land-use maps based mainly on small sample surveys have been made within Nigeria and elsewhere in West Africa, and one complete survey on 1:25,000 scale in the Gambia.[99] These have been useful in distinguishing types of land use, but except in the Gambia, and to some extent in Sierra Leone, have added little information on the areas of each type, partly because these have all been isolated examples, and partly because in only a few cases were the authors able to calculate the areas involved. An example is provided by Prothero's careful study of land use in Soba Village in the Zaria Province of Northern Nigeria.[100] Prothero distinguished five categories of land use: 1) Land under cultivation;

2) Land that had recently reverted to fallow after cultivation; 3) Fallow land of greater age; 4) Heavy bush; 5) Fadama or river floodplain. From air photographs the total area of Soba Village lands could only be estimated and nowhere were areas of the categories given. The boundary of the village lands could only be mapped approximately, and lengths of fallow could only be stated as 'probable'.

The student of land use in West Africa is at present hindered by a lack of base maps, by difficulties in obtaining the boundaries of village lands, by the difficulty of estimating lengths of fallow, by the temporary, unstable nature of much of West African cultivation and by the problem of interpreting aerial photographs. Notable exceptions are the land-use maps of Gambia and Sierra Leone, and some attempt has been made to indicate land use on the old coloured Gold Coast maps and the French West African sheets. The land-use maps of Sierra Leone are on a 1:16,000 (approx.) scale, and distinguish the following categories: 1) Woodland; 2) Farm bush; 3) Cultivation; 4) Dense stands of wild oil palm (*c.* 100 trees per acre (250 per hectare)); 5) Mangrove swamp (predominantly *Rhizophora racemosa*); 6) Mangrove swamp (predominantly *Avicennia*); 7) Mangrove swamp (predominantly *Rhizophora harrisoni*); 8) Swamp forest; 9) Swamp forest (predominantly *Raphia gracilis*); 10) Swamp forest (predominantly *Raphia hookeri*); 11) Riverine and aquatic grassland; 12) Swamp areas under water; 13) Swamp rice.

The land-use maps of Gambia are on a 1:25,000 (approx.) scale and distinguish: 1) Woodland; 2) Fallow bush; 3) Grass (including findo); 4) Groundnuts; 5) Groundnuts, sorghum and millet; 6) Sorghum, millet and other food crops; 7) High mangrove; 8) Low mangrove; 9) Grass marsh; 10) Barren marsh; 11) Reeds; 12) Standing water in marshes; 13) Rice (cultivated in 1956) and showing three categories: i) at least 90 per cent, ii) 30 to 90 per cent, iii) less than 30 per cent; 14) Rice (cultivated in 1946).

Whilst aerial photographs have been of great assistance where base maps are lacking, their value for land-use study is diminished by the fact that in most cases they are taken during the dry season in order to ensure clear skies for photographic work. Moreover, a photograph may well be taken whilst bush clearance, planting or harvesting are in progress, and interpretation becomes difficult, particularly after the long delay before prints become available for use in the field.

Nevertheless some useful pictures of the landscape can be presented through the study of land use by field work with the aid of aerial photographs. Buchanan and Pugh provide comparative land-use maps in their 'Land and people in Nigeria'. In this work detailed land-use material is provided for comparison in some of the community studies of Chapter 7. A recent and remarkable study has been published by the Institut Géographique National in Paris: J. Hurault, *Les Principaux Types du Peuplement au Sud-Est du Dahomey*, 1965, in which sample photographs are analysed in detail.

Population-carrying capacity of the land

A number of authors have displayed interest in the notion that there are limits to the productivity of West African soils under any given agricultural technique, and that these set limits to the number of people who can be supported by West African agriculture. Since agriculture is the mainstay of over 90 per cent of West Africa's population, either directly or indirectly, it is theoretically possible to calculate the maximum number of people West Africa or any part of West Africa can support by present techniques, assuming that no change takes place in them as population densities change. Unfortunately some authors have pushed this notion too far in that they have tended to label densities below or above their calculated maxima as 'under' or 'over' populated. In any one region there are a number of factors involved other than the cultivation of the lands available within that region. Moreover, the term 'overpopulation' is meaningless by implication unless the existence of an optimum population density is first established. Without this, 'overpopulation' is merely a value judgement, which is the case with most examples of its use, since the data are insufficient to establish optimum densities. Again, it can be established that agricultural techniques change in response to changes in demand for land and in intensity of use. The notion of a theoretical maximum is therefore based on ideal static situations which rarely obtain, and its use is solely as a simple aid to thinking with regard to the relationships of density and productivity.

Y. Urvoy suggested that peoples with the same technique in the same environment should have the same 'coefficient' of density.[101] He found a variety of densities within a given environment and suggested that these densities were associated with distinct communities having different social and political structures and different histories. He also suggested that without improving agricultural techniques, but simply by occupying all the cultivable land available, the whole of the Sudan between Senegal and Chad could support the 130 persons per square mile (50 per sq km) found south of Ouahigouya in Upper Volta.

It would seem useful as a guide to regional differentiation of population density problems to apply this idea of 'coefficient' of density to the agricultural regions already described, using the densities of cercles and divisions which are large enough to include wasteland. Only the densities of divisions with at least two-thirds of their area in the appropriate region have been used, and divisions markedly affected by commercial cultivation have been excluded. The results may be summarized as follows:

Shifting cultivation
Range 4–23 per square mile (1·5–9 per sq km) including divisions partly affected by rotational bush fallow methods and excluding Ikom, 50 (19), in the Cross river basin, because of commercial developments and recent changes in agricultural practice.

Rotational bush fallow

I. The northern cereals region

I.1. Bulrush millets dominant sub-region

Range 6–19 per square mile (2·3–7 per sq km) in the west and 23–31 (9–12) in Bornu. Maradi, Dosso and Tillabéry range 19–27 (7–10), but include some flood-land. The West Senegal cercles are all affected by commercial groundnut culti-vation. Many areas are unoccupied because of lack of dry season domestic water, e.g. the Ferlo of the Senegal, or because they have been left as strips of no-man's land.

Excluding such areas the over-all range of representative divisions and cercles is 12–30 (5–12).

I.2. Guinea corn dominant sub-region

Range 6–83 per square mile (2–32 per sq km), but most of the divisions' and cer-cles' densities are between 20 and 50 (8 and 19). In this sub-region large areas still remain unoccupied due to historical factors. A few small districts in Upper Volta and the Northern Territories of Ghana have extremely high densities, e.g. Zuarungu (Frafra) with over 200 (77). 'Effective' densities may be even higher, for Raeburn calculated that much of North Mamprusi was wasteland and never cropped, whilst only 14 per cent of the total area was tilled for crops in any one year.[102]

II. The south-western upland rice region

Range 13–93 per square mile (5–36 per sq km), but most cercles are between 30–50 (12–19). Sierra Leone has extremely high densities with administrative divisions recording more than 80 (31).

III. The mixed cereals and roots region

Range 8–184 per square mile (3–71 per sq km). Areas with lower densities are in all cases not fully occupied. High densities are usually associated with the commercial cultivation of food crops. A more representative range is estimated at 30–90 (12–35). Great local contrasts occur between small areas. Bohannan has calculated village group area densities amongst the Tiv as high as 550 per square mile (212 per sq km) and as low as 25 per square mile (10 per sq km).[103] Again several districts remain unoccupied due to historical factors.

IV. The roots region

Areas with little land to spare range 115–440 per square mile (45–170 per sq km). Where plenty of land is available the range is 11–19 (4–7). Grove estimated a maximum density depending on local resources in northern Iboland between 300 and 400 (116–154). Morgan estimated between 382 and 490 (147–190) in southern Iboland.[104] In both these areas densities are frequently over these maxima, and are maintained by incomes from external sources, chiefly emigrant labour, or by cultivating distant cropland. Many of the higher densities have been affected by commercial cultivation. An over-all range of 70–200 (27–77) would be more representative.

V. The south-eastern plantain–cocoyam region
Only two divisions are represented: Kumba, 33, and Victoria, 34 per square
mile (13 per sq km). The latter includes the commercial cultivation of bananas.

Rotational planted fallow
The densities here are included within those of the roots region above.

Mixed Farming
The mixed farming areas include Kaolack (Serer) 52 per square mile (20 per
sq km), Labé (Sedentary Fulani) 49 (19) and Dikwa (Shuwa) 52 (20).

Permanent cultivation
Kano Division has 240 per square mile (93 per sq km) (Prothero estimates 360
(139) within 30 miles' (48 kms) radius of Kano and over 1000 (386) in restricted
areas).[105] The Ibo and Ibibio permanently cultivated divisions range from
622–873 (240–337), but the latter derive some support from external sources. It
is impossible to use cercle or divisional densities for the people of the hill refuges,
since the areas involved in each case are too small, except in Jos (170 (66) but
including a considerable mining and immigrant trading population), Jema'a
56 (22), Southern 75 (29) and Bamenda 92 (36). The Kabrai of northern Togo
appear to support a local density of 237 (91).

Tree cultivation
In all cases, except those of recent commercial development for export overseas,
tree cultivation is too closely associated with other forms of cultivation for densities of population supported to be calculated.

Floodland cultivation
The areas of cercles and divisions are too large to produce figures restricted to
floodland areas. Urvoy calculates for the Niger valley between Tosaye and Say
between 50 and 130 per square mile (19 and 50 per sq km), and similar figures in
the cultivated portions of the delta. In the floodlands of the Gao district densities
are greater than 130 (50).

The present systems of agriculture appear to be supporting (in round figures)
about 20–50 per square mile (8–20 per sq km) in the cereals regions, about
30–90 per square mile (12–35 per sq km) in the mixed roots and cereals region,
and about 70–200 per square mile (27–77 per sq km) in the roots region. The
development of permanent or commercial cultivation within any of these regions
appears to have led to the support of even higher densities. The systems of cultivation are changing and despite the pessimistic forecasts of many students of
West African conditions, particularly in their views on soil fertility, it seems
that there is room for a considerable increase in population. Higher densities are
necessary in many areas for the development of essential modern services or, for
example, for the reduction of tsetse fly. Nash estimates that the minimum density

necessary in the Anchau area (guinea corn dominant region) of Zaria Province in Nigeria, in order to keep a level of clearing to control tsetse, is 70 per square mile (27 per sq km).[106] Stamp's estimates of maximum carrying capacity in the savannas of 88 (34) and in the 'forest' areas of 144 (56) seem unrealistic.[107]

Densities for productive land only would be higher than those already demonstrated, particularly in areas where the waste percentage tends to be high. Unfortunately the land-use survey work done so far is inadequate for the calculations to make such a comparison worth while. Not only is a more detailed and careful survey needed based on field work in conjunction with aerial photography, but the classification system used needs also to be more detailed and more precise. A calculation based on estimated areas under cultivation or cultivation and fallow is inadequate, because it neglects pastoral and timber resources and normally fails to distinguish true fallow from true wasteland.

The existence of a variety of systems of cultivation has been demonstrated, a variety even within similar physical environments. Other systems have been added and modifications have been made to existing practices by recent European influences. There is clearly no case for supposing that either shifting cultivation or rotational bush fallow represent in themselves rigid adaptations to existing environmental conditions or to 'poor' soils. Adaptations exist rather in points of detail within the broad systems of cultivation, and these points – concerning tillage, cropping and rotations – have been discussed. With the rapid changes which are now taking place within West Africa the possibilities for agricultural production cannot yet be estimated.

BIBLIOGRAPHICAL NOTES

[1] For a full discussion of the problems of land tenure see: T. O. Elias, *Nigerian Land Law and Custom*, 2nd ed., London, 1953.

[2] H. C. Sampson, E. M. Crowther and A. G. Doherty, *The West African Commission, 1938–39*, The Leverhulme Trust, 1943, p. 7.

[3] For a general discussion of agricultural practice and of European attempts to introduce new methods see: A. Pitot, L'Homme et les Sols dans les Steppes et Savanes de l'A.O.F., *Cahiers d'Outre-mer*, 5, 1952, pp. 215–40.
For invaluable physical and technical background information see: M. Gaudy, *Manuel d'Agriculture Tropicale* (Afrique Tropicale et Equatoriale), Paris, 1959.

[4] G. Schwab, *Tribes of the Liberian Hinterland*, Cambridge, Mass., 1947, p. 57.

[5] W. Manshard, Agrarische Organisationsformen für den binnenmarkt bestimmter Kulturen in Waldgürtel Ghanas, *Erdkunde*, **XI**, 1957, pp. 215–24.

[6] C. O. Sauer, The Agency of Man on Earth, in W. L. Thomas Jr., *Man's Role in Changing the Face of the Earth*, Chicago, 1956, pp. 49–69, p. 57.

[7] According to D. P. Gamble (*The Wolof of Senegambia*, London, 1957, p. 31 n.) the 'iler' has long been established in Senegal. The Saloum Wolof call the long-handled hoe 'jahai' and reserve the name 'iler' for a short-handled hoe with a heart-shaped blade.

[8] G. Schwab, op. cit., p. 55.

[9] For discussion of similar mounds in Israel see: Yehuda Kedar, Water and Soil from the Desert: Some Ancient Agricultural Achievements in the Central Negev, *Geographical Journal*, **123**, 1957, pp. 179–87, p. 184.

For discussion of terracing see: B. N. Floyd, Terrace Agriculture in Eastern Nigeria, *Nigerian Geographical Journal*, 7, 1964, pp. 91–108.

[10] J. Dresch, Paysans Montagnards du Dahomey et du Cameroun, *Bulletin de l'Association de Géographes Français*, 1952, pp. 2–9.

[11] J. W. Wallace, Agriculture in Abakaliki and Afikpo, *Farm and Forest*, 2, 1941, pp. 89–95.

[12] M. G. Savonnet, Système d'Occupation du Sol dans l'Ouest de la Haute Volta, *Symposium de Géographie*, Institut Français d'Afrique Noire, 1956, pp. 27–31.

[13] C. K. Meek, *The Northern Tribes of Nigeria*, London, vol. I, 1925, pp. 119–33, account of agriculture.

[14] ibid.

[15] M. de Lestrange, *Les Coniagui et les Bassari*, Paris, 1955, pp. 18, 20 and 38.

[16] W. B. Morgan, The Strip Fields of Southern Nigeria, *International Geographical Union*, Natural resources, food and population in inter-tropical Africa, Makerere Symposium, (1955), 1956, pp. 33–37.

[17] M. J. Field, The Agricultural System of the Manya Krobo of the Gold Coast, *Africa*, 14, 1943, pp. 54–65.
S. la Anyane, A Strip System of Farming in Ghana, *The Economic Bulletin*, 1960, pp. 6–12.
W. Manshard, Afrikanische Waldhufer– und Waldstreifenfluren, *Die Erde*, 92, 1961, pp. 246–58.

[18] *Agricultural Sample Surveys* of the Northern and Western Regions of Nigeria, 1955 onwards (mimeographed). These vary very much in content from year to year, hence the comparison between different years.

[19] A. F. B. Bridges, *Report on the Oil Palm Survey* in the Ibo, Ibibio and Cross River areas, 1938 (unpublished MS).

[20] H. Labouret, *Paysans d'Afrique Occidentale*, Paris, 1946, pp. 69–70.

[21] See Lord Hailey, *An African Survey*, London, revised 1956, Chap. XI, and *Native Administration in the British African Territories*, 1951.

[22] Bridges, op. cit.

[23] For invaluable studies of West African food crops see: B. F. Johnston, *The Staple Food Economies of Western Tropical Africa*, Stanford, 1958, and R. Schnell, *Plantes alimentaires et vie agricole de l'Afrique noire*, Paris, 1957.

[24] Another system of crop regions is shown in B. F. Johnston, Staple Food Crops in West Africa and the Congo, *Tropical Agriculture*, 33, 1956, pp. 214–20.

[25] On the origin of cultivated plants in West Africa see: R. Portères, Vieilles Agricultures de l'Afrique Intertropicale, *Agronomie Tropicale*, 5, 1950, pp. 489–507, Les Appellations des Céréales en Afrique, *Journal d'Agriculture Tropicale et de Botanique Appliquée*, 6, 1959, pp. 68–105, 189–233 and 290–339.
A. Chevalier, La Sahara, Centre d'Origine de Plantes Cultivées, in *La Vie dans la Région Désertique Nord-Tropicale de l'Ancien Monde*, 1938, p. 307.
H. C. Sampson, E. M. Crowther and A. G. Doherty, op. cit., pp. 16–19.
H. Labouret, op. cit., pp. 182–4.
For some controversial views see: G. P. Murdock, *Africa, its Peoples and their Culture History*, New York, 1959.

[26] J. Miège, Les Cultures Vivrières en Afrique Occidentale, *Cahiers d'Outre-Mer*, 7, 1954, pp. 25–50.
There can be little doubt that yams were cultivated in West Africa before the arrival of the Portuguese. There are references to widespread cultivation in São Tomé by 1506 and to a species originally from Benin in Th. Monod, A. Teixeira da Mota and R. Mauny, *Description de la Côte Occidentale d'Afrique par Valentim Fernandes* (1506–10), Centro de Estudos da Guine Portuguesa, 11, Bissau, 1951, pp. 138–9 and 191 n. 299.

[27] J. M. Dalziel, *The Useful Plants of West Tropical Africa*, London, 1937, pp. 538–40. Figure 2.2 shows the combined distribution in West Africa of bulrush millet and guinea corn for 1952–6 except in Liberia and Oyo Province, Nigeria, for which figures were not available. It should be borne in mind that the statistical bases of all the crop maps are extremely unreliable, being based at best on very small samples and at worst on mere guesswork.

[28] J. Miège, op. cit.

[29] J. M. Dalziel, op. cit., pp. 544–8.

[30] F. R. Irvine, *A Textbook of West African Agriculture*, London, 1934, pp. 99–106 (2nd ed., 1953). For additional useful information on this and other crops, see: T. A. Phillips, *An Agricultural Notebook*, 2nd ed., Ikeja, 1964.

[31] R. Portères, Les Céréales Mineures du Genre Digitaria en Afrique et en Europe, *Journal d'Agriculture Tropicale et de Botanique Appliquée*, **2**, 1955, pp. 349–86 and 477–510.

[32] J. M. Dalziel, op. cit., p. 534.

[33] J. Miège, op. cit.
An excellent general account of rice cultivation in West Africa is J. Dresch, La Riziculture en Afrique Occidentale, *Annales de Géographie*, **58**, 1949, pp. 295–312.

[34] B. F. Johnston, *The Staple Food Economies of Western Tropical Africa*, op. cit., p. 62, quotes yields of 1500–2000 lb per acre (1680–2240 kilos per hectare).

[35] R. Portères, Le Système de Riziculture par Franges Univariétales et l'Occupation des Fonds par les Riz Flottants dans l'Ouest Africain, *Revue Internationale de Botanique Appliquée et d'Agriculture Tropicale*, **29**, 1949, pp. 553–63.

[36] R. Portères, L'Introduction du Maïs en Afrique, *Journal d'Agriculture Tropicale et de Botanique Appliquée*, **2**, 1955, pp. 221–31.
A. Adandé, Le Maïs et ses Usages dans le Bas-Dahomey, *Bulletin, Institut Français d'Afrique Noire*, **15**, 1953, pp. 220–82.
M. D. W. Jeffreys – The Origin of the Portuguese word Zaburro as their name for Maize, *Bulletin, Institut Français d'Afrique Noire*, **19B**, 1957, pp. 111–35 – claims that maize was cultivated in West Africa before the Portuguese arrived.

[37] J. M. Dalziel, op. cit., pp. 488–93.

[38] B. F. Johnston, *The Staple Food Economies of Western Tropical Africa*, op. cit., pp. 178–9.
W. O. Jones, *Manioc in Africa*, Stanford, 1959.

[39] J. Fouquet, La Traite des Arachides dans le Pays de Kaolack, *Etudes Sénégalaises*, Institut Français d'Afrique Noire, **8**, 1958, p. 19.

[40] J. M. Dalziel, op. cit., p. 124.

[41] R. Portères, Vieilles Agricultures, op. cit.

[42] J. M. Dalziel, op. cit., p. 503.

[43] A. Chevalier and E. Perrot, *Les Kolatiers et les Noix de Kola*, Paris, 1911.
T. A. Russell, The Kola of Nigeria and the Cameroons, *Tropical Agriculture*, **32** 1955, pp. 210–40.

[44] M.-H. Lelong, La Route du Kola, *La Revue de Géographie Humaine et d'Ethnologie*, **4**, 1948–9, pp. 35–44.

[45] B. Ryssen, Le Karité au Soudan, *Agronomie Tropicale*, **12**, 1957, pp. 143–72 and 279–306.

[46] J. Fouquet, op. cit., p. 58.

[47] C. Lemaitre, Les Problèmes de la Conservation des Sols au Niger et le 'Gao', *Proc. 2nd inter-African soils conference*, Leopoldville, 1954, vol. I, pp. 569–80.
G. R. G. Kerr, Gawo: The Ideal Farm Tree, *Farm and Forest*, 1942, pp. 72–75.

[48] B. F. Johnston, *The Staple Food Economies of Western Tropical Africa*, op. cit., pp. 126–8.

[49] R. Galletti, K. D. S. Baldwin and I. O. Dina, *Nigerian Cocoa Farmers*, London, 1956, p. 324.

[50] A. Mabogunje, Rice in Southern Nigeria, *Nigerian Geographical Journal*, **2**, 1958–9, 59–69.

[51] M. R. Haswell, *Economics of Agriculture in a Savannah Village*, London, 1953.

[52] J. M. Dalziel, op. cit., p. 465.

[53] J. L. Boutillier, P. Cantrelle, J. Causse, C. Laurent and Th. N'Doye, *La Moyenne Vallée du Sénégal*, Institut National de la Statistique et des Etudes Economiques, Paris, 1962.

[54] W. B. Morgan, The Distribution of Food Crop Storage Methods in Nigeria, *Journal of Tropical Geography*, **13**, 1959, pp. 58–64.

[55] R. Dumont, *Types of Rural Economy*, Studies in World Agriculture, London, 1957, p. 89.

[56] For an account and bibliography see: B. F. Johnston, *The Staple Food Economies of Western Tropical Africa*, op. cit., pp. 203–12.

[57] J. H. Mackay, A Regional Survey of the Ikom-Oban Area, unpublished MS (1944).

[58] L. Tauxier, *Nègres Gouro et Gagou*, Paris, 1924.

[59] P. de Schlippe, *Shifting Cultivation in Africa: The Zande System of Agriculture*, London, 1956, pp. 207–10.

[60] R. Dumont, Etude de Quelques Economies Agraires au Sénégal et en Casamance, *Agronomie Tropicale*, **6**, 1951, pp. 229–38.

[61] L. Tauxier, *Le Noir du Soudan, Pays Mossi et Gourounsi*, Paris, 1912, pp. 30–31, 87–88 and 108–9.

[62] M. G. Savonnet, Systèmes d'Occupation du Sol dans l'Ouest de la Haute Volta, op. cit., pp. 27–31.

[63] M. G. Savonnet, Un Système de Culture Perfectionnée, Pratiqué par les Bwaba-Bobo Oulé de la Région de Houndé (Haute Volta), *Bulletin, Institut Français d'Afrique Noire*, **21B**, 1959, pp. 425–58.

[64] C. W. Lynn, *Agriculture in North Mamprusi*, Gold Coast Department of Agriculture, Bull., **34**, 1937.

[65] W. Manshard, Land Use Patterns and Agricultural Migration in Central Ghana (Western Gonja), *Tijdschrift voor Economische en Sociale Geografie*, **52**, 1961, pp. 225–230.

[66] R. M. Prothero, Land Use at Soba, Zaria Province, Northern Nigeria, *Economic Geography*, **33**, 1957, pp. 72–86.

[67] J. H. Mackay, *Bornu Survey*, unpublished MS (1945).

68] C. K. Meek, The Northern Tribes of Nigeria, op. cit. The Mumuye rotation given is based on Nigerian Agricultural Department reports, but E. R. Russell, Primitive Farming in Nigeria: The Mumuye Tribe, *Empire Journal of Experimental Agriculture*, **8**, (**29**), 1940, pp. 51–55, claims that the Mumuye repeat mixed guinea corn and bulrush millet for 2–3 years and end the rotation with a mixture of yams, maize and beans.

[69] E. L. R. Meyerowitz, *The Sacred State of the Akan*, London, 1951, pp. 46–48.

[70] A. Teixeira da Mota, A Agricultura de Brames e Balantes Vista Atraves da Fotografia Aerea, *Boletin Cultural do Centro de Estudos da Guiné Portuguesa* (Bissau), **5**, 1950, pp. 131–72.

[71] R. Portères, Les rizières de ruissellement en Casamance, *Revue Internationale de Botanique Appliquée et d'Agriculture Tropicale*, **32**, 1952, pp. 34–37.

[72] A most useful detailed study of Senoufo agriculture is in S. Coulibaly, Les Paysans Senoufo de Korhogo (Côte d'Ivoire), *Cahiers d'Outre-Mer*, **14**, 1961, pp. 26–59.

[73] H. P. White, Some aspects of food crop production in the Gold Coast, *Internationa*

Geographical Union, Natural resources, food and population in inter-tropical Africa, *Makerere Symposium 1955*, 1956, pp. 37–42.

[74] P. M. Kaberry, *Women of the Grassfields*, London, 1952, pp. 53–62.

[75] J. Miège, op. cit.

[76] W. Manshard, Agrarische Organisationsformen für den binnenmarkt bestimmter Kulturen in Waldgürtel Ghanas, op. cit., pp. 215–24.

[77] E. Ardener, *Coastal Bantu of the Cameroons*, London, 1956, pp. 39–48.

[78] M. P. Marti, *Les Dogon*, Paris, 1957, p. 95.

[79] P. Pelissier, Les Paysans Sérères, Essai sur la Formation d'un Terroir du Sénégal, *Les Cahiers d'Outre-Mer*, 6, 1953, pp. 105–27.

[80] R. Portères, L'Assolement dans les Terres à Arachides au Sénégal, *Revue Internationale de Botanique Appliquée et d'Agriculture Tropicale*, 30, 1950, pp. 44–50.

[81] H. Labouret, La Langue des Peuls ou Foulbé, *Mémoires, Institut Français d'Afrique Noire*, No. 41, 1955, pp. 25–27.

[82] For this and other observations on agriculture in the Mandara Mountains see: Stanhope White, The Agricultural Economy of the Hill Pagans of Dikwa Emirate, Cameroons, in either:
Empire Journal of Experimental Agriculture, 9, (33), 1941, pp. 65–72,
or: *Farm and Forest*, 5, (3), 1944, pp. 130–4.

[83] A. T. Grove, Land Use and Soil Conservation in the Jos Plateau, *Geological Survey of Nigeria, Bulletin 22*, 1952, pp. 23–28.

[84] M. J. Mortimore and J. Wilson, *Land and People in the Kano Close-Settled Zone: a Report to the Greater Kano Planning Authority*, Ahmadu Bello University, Zaria, 1965.
K. M. Buchanan and J. C. Pugh, *Land and People in Nigeria*, London, 1955, p. 112.

[85] R. Guérard, La Régénération de la Palmeraie Dahoméenne et l'Accroissement de la Production de l'Huile et des Amandes de Palme, *L'Agronomie Tropicale*, 6, 1951, pp. 66–71.

[86] E. L. R. Meyerowitz, *The Sacred State of the Akan*, London, 1957, p. 207.

[87] L. Papy, La Vallée du Sénégal, in Problèmes Agricoles au Sénégal, *Etudes Sénégalaises*, 2, 1952, Institut Français d'Afrique Noire, pp. 24–25. Papy uses the term 'walo' for the floodplain proper. Labouret (*Paysans d'Afrique Occidentale*, 6th edition, 1941, pp. 80–101) uses it for the delta only.
J. L. Boutillier, P. Cantrelle, J. Causse, C. Laurent and Th. N'Doye, *La Moyenne Vallée du Sénégal*, I.N.S.E.E., 1962 – a most detailed study, particularly of demography and agriculture.

[88] Notes et documents (on the Songhay), *Bulletin, Institut Français d'Afrique Noire*, 16, 1954, pp. 178–84.

[89] J. Dresch, La Riziculture en Afrique Occidentale, op. cit.

[90] A. Chevalier, Review of J. Dresch above, in *Revue Internationale Botanique Appliquée et d'Agriculture Tropicale*, 30, 1950, pp. 343–5.

[91] C. Toupet, La Vallée de la Tamourt, *Symposium de Géographie 1956*, Institut Français d'Afrique Noire, Dakar, pp. 37–43.

[92] Y. Urvoy, Petit Atlas Ethno-Démographique du Soudan, entre Sénégal et Chad, *Mémoires, Institut Français d'Afrique Noire*, 1942, p. 11.

[93] P. G. Harris, Notes on Yauri, Nigeria, *Journal of the Royal Anthropological Institute*, 60, 1930, pp. 283–334.

[94] R. Dumont, Étude de Quelques Economies Agraires, op. cit., pp. 235–8.
Rice cultivation in neighbouring Senegal has been described in P. Pelissier, *Les Paysans du Sénégal: les Civilisations Agraires du Cayor à la Casamance*, St.-Yrieix, 1966.

[95] A. Teixeira da Mota, A Agricultura de Brames e Balantes, op. cit.

[96] P. Pelissier, Les Pays du Bas-Ouémé, *Cahiers d'Outre-Mer*, **15**, 1962, pp. 204–54 and 313–59.

[97] *Report of the Sample Census of Agriculture*, Nigeria, 1950–1.

[98] E. A. Waldock, E. S. Capstick, A. S. Browning, *Sierra Leone, Sessional Paper No. 1*, Freetown, 1951.

[99] 1:25,000 Land Use Map of the Gambia, Directorate of Overseas Surveys, London. For discussion of the problems of producing the Gambia land-use map and other land-use maps elsewhere in West Africa see R. P. Moss, Land Use Mapping in Tropical Africa, *Nigerian Geographical Journal*, **3**, 1960, pp. 8–17.

[100] R. M. Prothero, Land Use at Soba, Zaria Province, Northern Nigeria, *Economic Geography*, **33**, 1957, pp. 72–86.
R. M. Prothero, Land use, land holdings and land tenure at Soba, Zaria Province, Northern Nigeria, *Bulletin, Institut Français d'Afrique Noire*, **19**, 1957, pp. 558–63.

[101] Y. Urvoy, op. cit., pp. 13–14.

[102] J. R. Raeburn, Report on a Preliminary Economic Survey of the Northern Territories of the Gold Coast (quoted in R. J. Harrison Church, *West Africa*, London, 1957, pp. 387–8).

[103] L. and P. Bohannan, *The Tiv of Central Nigeria*, London, 1953, pp. 9–10.

[104] A. T. Grove, Soil Erosion and Population Problems in South-East Nigeria, *Geographical Journal*, **117**, 1951, pp. 291–306.
W. B. Morgan, Farming Practice, Settlement Pattern and Population Density in South Eastern Nigeria, *Geographical Journal*, **121**, 1955, pp. 320–33.

[105] R. M. Prothero, Unpublished MS on Northern Region of Nigeria.

[106] T. A. M. Nash, The Anchau Settlement Scheme, *Farm and Forest*, Vol. II, No. 2 (1941), p. 77.
See also: K. M. Buchanan and J. C. Pugh, op. cit., pp. 78–79.

[107] L. D. Stamp, Land Utilisation and Soil Erosion in Nigeria, *Geographical Review*, **28**, 1938, pp. 32–45 (see p. 35).

Figure 2.10d is based on a diagram in D. W. Hall, G. A. Haswell & T. A. Oxley, *Underground storage of grain*, Colonial Research Series, No. 21, 1956.

F

CHAPTER 3

Stock Rearing

Although the keeping of animals plays an important part in the agricultural economy of several West African peoples, the rearing of cattle, sheep and goats by nomadic pastoralists is still considerable, and their herds are an important source of meat for the larger commercial markets. The seasonal migration of stock extends from the southern margins of the Sahara southwards into the sub-Sudanic zone. The area thus delimited contains the most abundant supplies of the best fodder grasses and trees, and a large part of it is north of the zone occupied by trypanosomiasis-carrying tsetse flies. As Doutressoule has demonstrated, nomadism is a necessity in order to make the fullest use of the pastures available.[1] In the better watered lands much of the area suitable for pasture is occupied by crops during the rainy season. In the northern portion, the most suitable for stock rearing, the proportion of fallow on agricultural land is low, and some weeks must elapse after harvest before a satisfactory cover of grasses is developed. Moreover, fallow pastures necessitate fencing to protect the croplands. The Somba of Dahomey are forced to the extreme of keeping their animals indoors during the rains.[2] Many pastoralists move northwards during the rainy season to avoid the greater incidence of disease associated with their southern pastures. The northern grasslands of the Sahel and southern Sahara provide sufficient fodder only for a short period, but they enable the removal of stock from the croplands during the growing season and their subsequent return during the rest period, providing manure for the Sudanic cultivator.

The Stock

I. CATTLE

There is some confusion with regard to the classification of cattle in West Africa as colour names are frequently used in preference to breed names. Indiscriminate cross breeding exists side by side with deliberate cross breeding for improvement in size or in milk production. Nevertheless a number of distinct breeds have been distinguished.

1) Humped (*Bos indicus*). Estimates of admittedly doubtful reliability suggest that of possibly 21 million cattle in West Africa, 14 million are humped. These are descendants of Zebu cattle presumed to have been introduced after the other

ESTIMATED DRY SEASON DISTRIBUTION of CATTLE in 1961

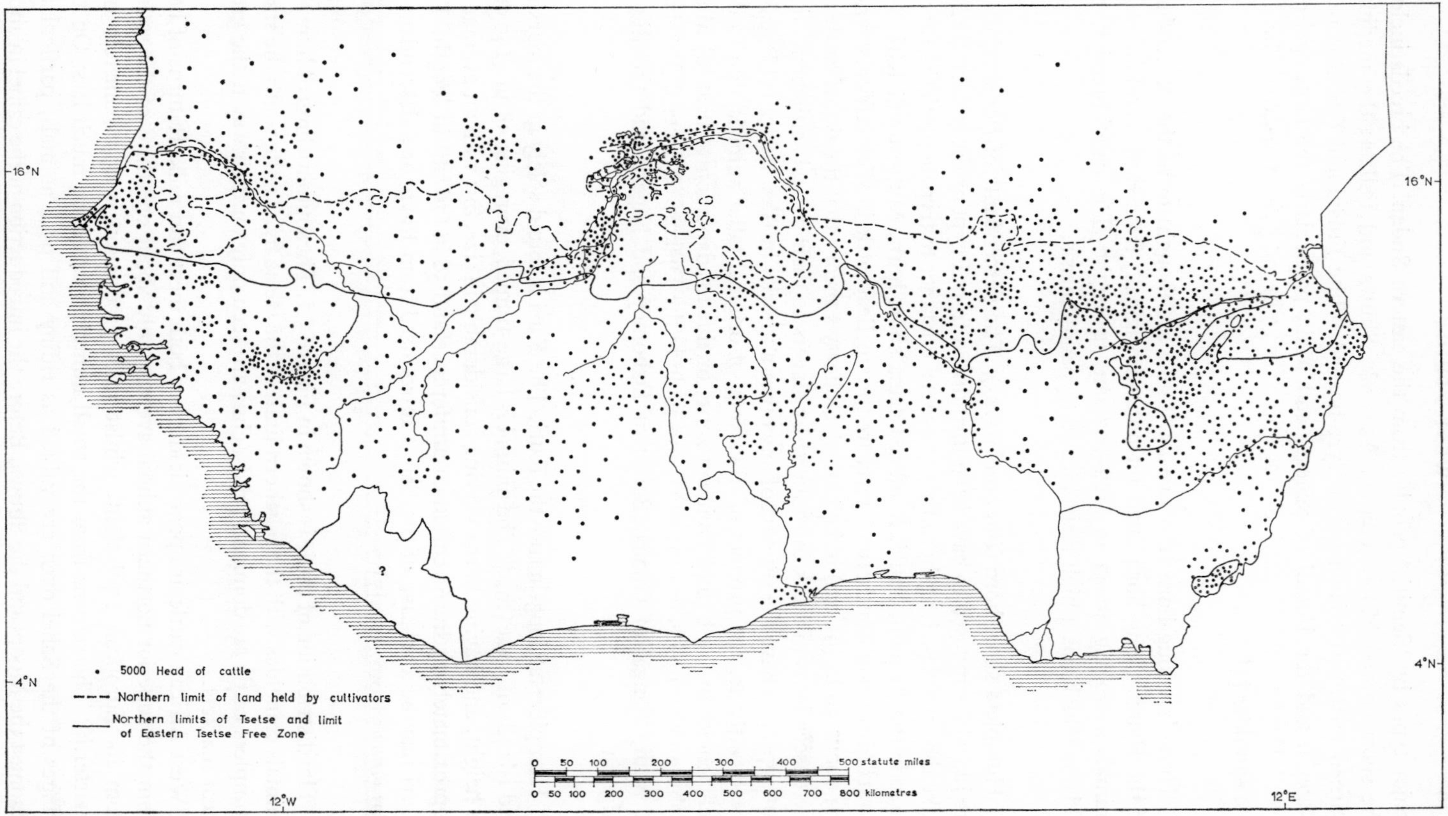

- 5000 Head of cattle
- - - - Northern limit of land held by cultivators
——— Northern limits of Tsetse and limit
of Eastern Tsetse Free Zone

16°N
4°N
12°E
12°W
16°N
4°N

0   50 100   200   300   400   500 statute miles
0   50 100   200   300   400   500   600   700   800 kilometres

Figure 3.1

major types by 'Semitic' peoples from the eastern Sudan. The breeds include the short-horned Moor, Tuareg, Azaouak, Shuwa and Fellata; the medium-horned Diali and Adamawa; the lyre-horned White Fulani and Red Bororo of Nigeria, and the Fulani of Senegal and Mali, particularly the large 'gobbra' breed. Heights of Zebu cattle average between 47 in and 55 in (120–40 cm) behind the shoulder.[3]

2) Humpless long-horn (*Bos taurus*). These are thought to be the descendants of the Hamitic long-horn cattle introduced originally from Egypt, and are small animals averaging 40–42 in (102–107 cm) in height. The chief breed is the Ndama which has a high resistance to trypanosomiasis.

3) Humpless short-horn (*Bos brachyceros*). The descendants of *Bos brachyceros* are likewise supposed to have been introduced from Egypt or the eastern Sudan. Like the humpless long-horn they possess a tolerance to trypanosomiasis. Breeds include the Lagoon, Baulé, Somba, Ghana short-horn, Muturu and Kiri. The dwarf Muturu of Southern Nigeria are the smallest cattle in West Africa, averaging about 36 in (91 cm) in height.[4] Doherty's theory that the dwarf cattle are the descendants of stock introduced by slavers to their coastal settlements does not appear to have the support of any other authority in West Africa.[5] Possibly these cattle are the product of 'dwarfing' of original taller animals, due to diet deficiencies in the humid Guinean zone, or due to adaptation to heat.[6] Many Zebu and humpless crosses exist, and include the Djakoré of Senegal, Bambara of Mali, 'Sanga' of Ghana, Borgu of Dahomey and Nigeria and the Biu of Nigeria.

4) Humpless tall long-horn – the Kuri. The Kuri is found solely in the marshes and islands of Lake Chad. The animal is large-framed, averaging 58 in (147 cm) in height, and having horns varying considerably in size, but with an average of approximately 25 in (63 cm) in circumference and 30 in (76 cm) in length. The Kuri may be a relative of the Sanga introduced from Egypt or a descendant of *Bos gaurus* from Asia.[7]

The distribution of cattle is shown in Figure 3.1. The southern limit of humped animals coincides with the northern limit of the tsetse fly. To the south the small humpless cattle are dominant, and Zebus are seen only on their way to the great meat markets.

West African cattle are poor yielders of both meat and milk. Returns of beef from the superior northern animal average only about one-third of the return from its European equivalent, whilst milk production is approximately one quarter.[8] The returns from the small humpless cattle are much less. On the fringes of the Sahel oxen are valued as riding and pack animals, particularly amongst the Moors and the Shuwa. Before the introduction of the camel in about the 3rd century A.D., oxen appear to have provided the chief means of transport across the desert and within the desert fringe.

2. SHEEP

The 14 million large sheep of West Africa belong mainly to the Sudan and the Sahel where they are reared by nomadic pastoralists, chiefly Fulani. To the south there are approximately 6 million sheep kept in small numbers by agriculturalists. The following breeds have been distinguished:

1) Hairy sheep. Once common in North Africa and subdivided into the large and long-legged animal of the north, and the small and short-legged animal of the south. The latter provides meat on ceremonial or festive occasions, but is otherwise valued only for its hair. The former may be further subdivided into the Moor of the west with its extremely long hair and useful skin, the Tuareg of the east raised mainly for meat and milk, and the Fulani of the south which provides chiefly meat.
2) Wool sheep. The wool sheep or Macina total about $1\frac{1}{2}$ millions and are localized chiefly on the pastures of the inland Niger delta. These sheep are possibly of Syrian origin and are valued for their fleece, used in the manufacture of cloth and blankets, and also exported. A related breed to the Macina is the Goundoum which was introduced into the Niger valley between Timbuktu and Niamey from the Lake Débo district of the inland delta in the 18th century.

Like the cattle West African sheep are poor yielders. Meat production per animal is about three-quarters by weight of European varieties, and the wool yield about one-tenth.

3. GOATS

Except in the valley of the Niger where different pastures are preferred, sheep and goats are generally kept together in West Africa. (There appear to be about 26 million goats – nearly twice the number of sheep.) In the more humid Guinean physical environment where there is a lack of suitable fodder there are a few sheep, but goats, which can be fed on a variety of household waste, are common. Quite often their movements have to be restricted by tethering, or by wooden frames attached round the neck and wider than a gate or doorway, in order to prevent damage to crops or stores. Goats have the widest distribution of any livestock in West Africa, and are an important source of milk and the chief source of meat for most of the population.

Again, as in the case of sheep, there is a distinction between the large breeds of the Sudan and Sahel and the smaller animals to the south. The smaller animal has a higher resistance to trypanosomiasis, but gives poorer returns in meat and milk. The Maradi or Sokoto Red and the Kano Brown goats provide the best skins for glacé kid leather, once an important item in trans-Saharan traffic. Many of these skins were exported from North Africa to Europe as Moroccan leather. Even today goat skins form a small, but valuable, export from West Africa and are in heavy demand locally for a variety of uses including water containers, bellows, saddlery, knife sheaths and footwear.

4. PIGS

There are probably about one million pigs in West Africa mainly of the black long-snout variety introduced from Iberia by the Portuguese, together with some recent crosses. These are confined to the non-Moslem areas, and are thus found mainly south of the Sudan, chiefly in the Guinean region and notably in the towns. Most pigs live on household scraps, and are too small in number to make much contribution to West African diet.

5. HORSES

Doutressoule classifies the approximately half-million horses of West Africa into the Pony, the Arab, the Barb and the Dongolaw. All of these are severely limited by the incidence of tsetse fly, and are restricted mainly to the Sudan, Sahel and high plateaux.[9] (With care and adequate feeding horses can survive in the Guinean zone where they are kept for racing or riding purposes.)

The Pony appears to have been introduced first, and survives in a variety of breeds amongst the widely separated peoples of the mountain refuges. It is curious that many of these peoples, regarded as amongst the most primitive in West Africa, should not only be noted for elaborate agricultural techniques, but also as horsemen. The pony breeds include the Baol of Senegal, the Bandiagara type of southern Mali, the Cotocoli of the Atacora, the Jos Plateau pony, the Kirdi of Chad and Adamawa, the M'Bayer and M'Par of Senegal, the Torodi of Niger, and the Bobo of the northern Ivory Coast.

Horses of a dominantly Arab strain belong mainly to the Sahara and are strictly outside the limits of a West African region. However, they have given several crosses with the Barb or Mongolian horse, confined chiefly to the regions west of the inland Niger delta. To the east is the Dongolaw, introduced in the 13th century by Arabs from the Upper Nile, the horse of the Songhay, Hausa and Kanuri.

West African horses have hardly ever been used as draught or pack animals, oxen, donkeys and camels being preferred. Horses are too costly to purchase and maintain for such purposes, but have been valued for warfare and ceremony or as riding animals for the nobility. The sacrifice of horses in Iboland at the costly ceremonies involved in 'taking title' stresses the notion of high value which is normally attached to them.

6. DONKEYS

Donkeys are the chief pack animals of the Sudan, too humid in the rainy season for camels. During the dry season they are used to convey goods even as far south as the Guinean regions. Altogether there are about 2 million donkeys in West Africa, and these are normally classified into six main breeds of which the tallest is the Sahel of the north, and the hardiest are the Gourma and Yatenga raised by the Mossi and Gourma peoples south of the great Niger bend. The Moba of Togoland also breed donkeys, but sell them at two years old to the Hausa, as they themselves have little use for transport animals.[10]

Except in the Sokoto district of Hausaland and in Government breeding farms, mules are not reared in West Africa. Many West African peoples refuse to keep an animal which cannot reproduce itself, despite its hardiness and strength.

7. CAMELS

There appear to be over 200,000 camels in the Saharan fringe of West Africa. In the dry season they come southwards as far as the Sudanic zone, sometimes in search of fodder, but normally in camel trains. Their chief use is to convey groundnuts from the Niger Republic to the railhead in Nigeria, and until recently from the former French Sudan to Senegal. Formerly they played a vital part in the economy of the Sudan, providing almost the sole means of transport across the desert to the markets of North Africa. At present their importance, and probably their numbers, are declining.

Doutressoule writes that the camel cannot live where millet grows. It prefers the poor fodder of the Sahara and needs water only every three to six days. The Tuareg, Toubou, Moors and Arabs all raise camels, and a few are owned by the Shuwa, but not by the Fulani. Many nomads undertake a regular transhumance to the salt-producing oases such as Bilma, chiefly in the period September to November. Of their eight major breeds the Manga and Gandiol are noted as the carriers, and the 'River' type has the greatest resistance to humidity, living near the banks of the northernmost portion of the Niger.

8. POULTRY

The chickens of West Africa are widespread and of unknown number. Few compounds are without them. Since they have to subsist on household refuse they produce only one-third to one-half the number of eggs produced by their equivalent in Europe. The eggs are small, averaging about half the larger European size. Eggs and chickens were, and in many cases still are, used for ceremonial purposes. In recent years they have begun to take a more prominent part in the diet. Although chickens are poorly fed, they are quite often elaborately housed, particularly for protection against wild animals.

Other poultry include the Muscovy or Barbary duck of Brazilian origin, Guinea fowl and turkeys.

9. DOGS

Most villages in West Africa have their dogs which depend chiefly on scavenging for food. In the north dogs are bred as guards and for hunting, or for sale chiefly to southern communities for sacrificial offerings. The market is large enough for there to be traders in dogs to the exclusion of all other animals or goods.[11] The Bedduwai of Bornu use dogs as guards for their flocks of sheep.[12]

10. OSTRICHES

A few ostriches are still reared in the Sudanic regions, but their importance has declined since 1904 when the colonial annual report for Northern Nigeria referred to 'ostrich farming, much mismanaged' in the north of Sokoto Province.[13] The birds appear to have been confined inside huts, and their feathers were frequently valueless due to rubbing.

The pastoralists

Whilst some selection of the better animals exists, the chief aim is undoubtedly to increase the size of the herd, particularly amongst the Fulani. Many pastoralists live off the milk of their cattle, sheep or goats, exchanging it for grain and other commodities, and selling only a small percentage of the annual increase of their herds.

Fulani pastoralists live mainly in the Sahelian zone, practising transhumance into the Sudan in the dry season. A number of small groups have sought mountain pastures elsewhere, notably in the Fouta Djallon, the Atacora, Jos, the Mandara and Alantika mountains of Adamawa, and the Bamenda Plateau of West Cameroun. The symbiosis between pastoralists and cultivators has led throughout the Sudanic zone to the occurrence of settled Fulani villages whose occupants effect liaison between the two communities. The sedentary Fulani make possible the exchange of animals for plant products, and eventually they adopt the life of the agriculturalist, in some cases becoming mixed farmers. Probably less than 8 per cent of the Fulani of Northern Nigeria, for example, are nomadic, although many more Fulani practise some form of pastoralism.[14] The nomadic pastoralists wander over areas of several hundred square miles (500–1000 sq km) each year in small groups of between 10 and 20 households. Frequently they have a 'home' or 'semi-permanent' settlement, normally located near the wet season pastures in the Sahel. The average size of cattle herd possessed by the individual is about 30 head, although some pastoral Fulani are entirely without their own stock and work as herdsmen for others.

The Moors of the west may be divided into the Saharan group of true nomads and the southern group who, like the Fulani, wander slowly over small restricted areas. The Saharan Moors frequently wander over areas of several thousand square miles (5000–10,000 sq km), and concentrate chiefly on the keeping of camels. The southern Moors concentrate mainly on cattle and sheep, and often employ herdsmen to keep and tend their animals. Whereas cattle are an end in themselves to the Fulani, to the Moors they are a means to an end, and may be butchered or sold wherever there is a commercial advantage in so doing.

The Tuareg and Toubou may be divided into the nomads of the desert–Sahel border zone and the Saharan groups who are mainly sedentary. The latter are to be found chiefly in oases, particularly in the great mountain massifs of Aïr, Adrar des Iforas and Tibesti, where they have been able to establish towns and villages supported mainly by cultivation. The former wander over vast areas with their herds of camels, cattle and sheep, each 'caste' in the community having distinct occupations.

Forms of transhumance

Transhumance in West Africa does not consist of a movement of animals from one place to another, but of a series of changes in the direction of movement in search of water and pasture.[15] In general this movement consists of an oscillation between the Sahel on the Saharan fringe and the Sudan, but there are numerous exceptions due to variation in local water supplies, distribution of pasture and needs for salt and exchange. Dry season pastures include former cropland in the Sudan, the poor grasslands of the dry or burnt 'bush' of the Sahel and Sudan, floodlands of the valley bottom lands, the shores of Lake Chad, the swamps of the inland Niger delta, and grasslands on moisture-retaining clay soils. Wet season pastures include the valleys and even the interfluves of the Sahel and Saharan fringe and numerous high plateau grasslands.

In Mauritania the Moors migrate between the Trarza and Brakna plains in the wet season and the north bank of the Senegal River. The plains consist of clays and stable dunes. The clays support thorn shrubs, acacias and grassland affording pasture for cattle and sheep. *Acacia senegal* and *A. arabica* are noted for the production of gum obtained by stripping the bark from the trees. Gum collection is thus associated with stock rearing and the annual migration to the dry season pastures and markets of the Senegal valley. There the north bank, or Chemama, is cultivated by the Wolof, Toucouleur and Sarakolé who exchange millets for animal products or deal in gum. The area most densely populated with cattle lies immediately north of the river, where pastures are abundant and the distances migrated usually small. The Guidimaka region in the south-east has intermittent streams, and these, together with a few small permanent lakes such as R'Kiz in Trarza and Aleg and Mal in Brakna, provide local dry season grazing centres of limited pasture. To the north the proportion of sands increases, and north of the Trarza the pasture is fit only for sheep, goats and camels. In the Mauritanian Adrar the northern nomadic Moors migrate with herds of cattle, sheep, goats and camels over huge areas and are based on small centres of cultivation in the oases. To the east are the sandstone plateaux of Tagant, Assaba and Affollé, with irrigated cultivation at escarpment-foot springs, some permanent pools providing dry season grazing and wet season pastures in the valleys and the plain of Regueiba. Amidst these dominantly Moorish lands there are several settlements of sedentary Fulani, particularly near Lakes Aleg and Mal, east of Brakna and in Guidimaka.

South of the Senegal the surface is divided between the croplands of the west and the Ferlo in the east. The low plateaux and valleys of the Ferlo with their park savanna dominated by acacias, particularly *A. stenocarpa* and *A. seyal*, form a region distinguished mainly by shortage of dry season water supply and by the activities of man. During the wet season it is cultivable, but permanent settlement is impossible over most of the area without deep wells, owing to the great depth of the water table, and the lack of surface water in the dry season. Only here and there in valley bottoms have shallower wells been established, water pits ('bouli') dug or small ponds used. Here, therefore, are lands used as wet season pasture and cropland by some 90,000 semi-nomadic Fulani. This mainly pastoral region forms a centre, a meeting place each year for the Fulani herdsmen, each group of whom occupies a distinct zone. Settlements concentrate chiefly on the 'seno' soils of former dunes where bulrush millet, groundnuts and cowpeas are planted. Crops needing more moisture are planted in the 'bardial' or clays of neighbouring depressions. The 'niargo' or skeletal soils of lateritic plateaux with their *Combretum* spp. are avoided. In the late dry season the pastoral groups move out to the fallows and harvested croplands of the perimeter and the salt licks of the Lower Ferlo, the Lake of Guiers and Sine-Saloum, and to the unflooded, and mostly uncultivated, portion of the 'fondé' or levée close to the Senegal river. Some groups stay throughout the year usually pasturing close to wells.[16] In the extreme south of Senegal, in Casamance, Fulani herdsmen follow the diminishing supplies of surface water upstream during the dry season.

In Mali there is an important distinction between camel transhumance within the Sahel and desert, and cattle, sheep and goat transhumance between the Sahel and the Niger valley. The Sahel consists essentially of the plains of the Hodh, Kouch and Aklé, limited to the north by sand dunes. The Kouch and Aklé regions are dependent on deep wells for water supplies. Here camels wander between open pastures and wells in the dry season, and migrate to pools during the rainy period. Cattle, sheep and goats find sufficient wet season pasture, but in the dry season they move mainly southwards to Macina in the inland Niger delta. A few migrate to the shores of Lake Maghi. To the north the plateau of Adrar des Iforas, with its locally higher and more regular rainfall, provides an island of Sahel in the Sahara, rising to over 3000 feet (915 metres) above sea level. Nomadic migration as far as this plateau is possible by the wadis, pools and shallow wells of the valley of the Tilemsi. In the south of Mali is the central Niger plateau with some permanent pools and a number of intermittent water-courses. Here rainy season pasture is provided, but in the dry season the herds of this region, like those of the opposite bank of the Niger, converge on the inland delta. Like the Ferlo the central Niger plateau has many pastures on cultivable land in areas lacking dry season water supplies. Here by contrast with the Ferlo the meeting ground for Fulani and Tuareg is in the dry season inland delta pastures. The 'bourgou' grass of the delta provides excellent pasture from March to June when the river starts to rise and movement outwards must begin again. As the floods subside stock re-enter the zone, entering the pastures as they become free of water. The cattle enter first, and the sheep, more susceptible to parasitic diseases, come later when the soil is drier.[17] The season of declining flood levels is also the season for agriculture, and much of the pasture land is suitable for cultivation. There is in consequence a conflict of interest revealed strikingly in the problems arising from the drainage schemes of the Office du Niger (Chapter 13). The Macina wool sheep occupy a special position in the delta. They are concentrated chiefly in the south and leave for the Sahel before the floods and the parasites and coarse grasses of the rainy season. Above all else the sheep are pastured on the bourgou. This is one of the few areas in West Africa where goats are not mixed with sheep for they are pastured in separate herds on shrubs and thorns.

To the east is the zone of 'dallols', wide valleys with intermittent streams and pools on the left bank of the Niger. In the dry season water is never far below the surface and huge areas of pasture are provided for the livestock of the neighbouring portions of the Sahel. To the south, the Niger valley and the banks of the small creeks of the Tera region also provide dry season pasture serving a transhumance which in most cases is entirely local. To the north-east is the vast Sahel of the Niger Republic, mostly fit only for dry season pasture. The great depression of the Azaouak, once occupied by a wadi, has water below the surface, but provides rainy season pasture only. The shores of a few lakes, such as Keita and Adouma, provide pasture all the year, and the valley of the Gulbi-n-Kaba is likewise frequented at all seasons. Most pastoralists, however, move south to the more humid lands of Damergou, to the valleys and cultivated lands of the Hausa and to the banks of the Komadugu Yobe in Bornu and the shores of Lake Chad. To the north the plateau of Aïr has some poor grasslands amidst the Saharan desert and some rich valley pastures providing the basis for a local transhumance. To the east are the sands of the Ténéré, nearly 200 miles (320 km) wide without water supplies. To the south-east are sands, hills and plateaux where the Toubou maintain good valley pastures near permanent ponds and lakes, and dig deep wells to supply their needs in the sandy grassland. In the latter there is an abundant supply of 'had' for the feeding of camels, one of the chief elements of Toubou livestock.

South of the Sudanic environments transhumance is on a small scale and mainly involves movement between the great plateaux and the valleys. In the Fouta Djallon for example the Fulani move their herds of Ndama cattle from the wet season pastures of the treeless bowé, that is the concretionary ironstone areas of the high plateaux, to the dry season pastures of the valley bottoms. In the latter are the agricultural settlements of former Negro slaves where an exchange of crops for animal produce may be effected. From January to April the cattle are kept in the valley. With the first rains they move up-hill reaching the plateaux levels by July and moving on to the bowé proper by October.[18] On the Jos Plateau there is a similar movement of cattle between valley bottom and uplands, although in many areas the movement is slight because of the abundance of good pasture and water supplies and the comparative freedom from disease. In the central portion of the plateau there is, however, no close symbiosis between pastoralist and cultivator. Many of the agricultural peoples look for their support to the land required also by the stock raiser. Unlike the cultivators of other mountain areas or of the regions to the north and south, they employ extensive methods of cultivation and use manure only for fuel. To the north the cultivators use cattle manure and also to the south in the north-western Pankshin area. Much manure is lost, however, because for the most part cattle are grazed on lands which are never cultivated.[19]

Stock rearing by cultivators

References have already been made in Chapter 2 to the rearing of livestock by cultivators and 'mixed farmers'. Mixed farmers like the Shuwa practise transhumance, and many cultivators in the Upper Volta and inland Niger delta districts confine their animals to the care of Fulani pastoralists who migrate seasonally with them. Other peoples like the Songhay keep many of their animals close to their settlements throughout the year, confining only milkless cattle to the care of the Fulani.[20] Amongst the Fulani themselves the practice of cultivation around the wet season settlements is increasing, and in many cases the wet season settlements are permanently occupied and the inhabitants are as much concerned with crops as with livestock. In Borgu cattle migration is only over short distances in order to obtain fresh pasture and is not a true transhumance. In the sub-Guinean environments there are some almost permanent pastures, and amongst people like the Somba every family keeps a few animals. In the Ivory Coast the Dioula have introduced the raising of cattle for meat and milk into the forest areas of the south. On the whole the southern environments, with the common occurrence of trypanosomiasis and other diseases, and lacking suitable pastures, are restricted for stock rearing chiefly to the smaller animals. Sheep, goats and chickens are valued for sacrifice and an occasional feast. A herd of cattle, even if these are only dwarf animals, adds to a man's prestige. Cattle rearing and fattening for market are, however, occupations of increasing importance with the growth of markets for meat in the export crop producing areas of the Ivory Coast, Ghana, Togoland, Dahomey and Southern Nigeria. The market for pork is increasing, and poultry and eggs, in many cases, now provide a significant part of the incomes of many cultivating families.

The pastures

The pastoral lands of West Africa are self-sown, but, apart from the regions liable to periodic flooding, are the product of burning and of their use as pasture. Most grasses provide their best fodder when young, and burning is frequently employed to remove coarse material and encourage the growth of young shoots. At the same time plants lacking protection against fires are either suppressed or eliminated. The grazing stock are selective and, where dense numbers exist, may reduce the most desirable elements in a pasture. Pasture deterioration is particularly marked if the dry season is abnormally long. Stock, however, may also spread seed in their droppings, and thus widen the distribution of certain species. Shrubs and the leaves of trees provide important pasture resources. Often the use of trees for feeding has encouraged their protection, propagation and consequent wider distribution, but extremely high densities of stock can result in sufficient pressure on food resources to reduce their number. Frequently shade trees improve the quality of the grass fodder beneath them by the dropping of leaves and protection from the direct heating of the sun.

The majority of West African fodder plants are grasses, and of these the most common are *Andropogons* and *Panicums*. In few areas are they suitable for hay or of much value for feeding except when young. There are few leguminous herbs, but a number of trees and non-leguminous plants are important, particularly in the dry season.[21] Generally tropical grass species are low in crude protein and high in fibre when compared with temperate grasses cut at similar stages of growth.[22].

The Saharan pastures are strictly outside the West African 'region', but reference should be made to the 'had' (*Cornulaca monocantha*) and *Traganum nudatum*, both important camel fodders. Desert grasses are chiefly annuals and include *Panicum turgidum* (like the 'had' a camel fodder), *Pennisetum dichotomum*, *Eragrostis bipinnata*, *Cynodon dactylon* (perennial, found in wadis), *Aristida pungens* and *Danthomia forskalii*.

The chief fodder plants of the Sahel and Sudanic zones include:

1. Rainy season pastures

1) Perennials

Andropogon gayanus and *A. tectorum*, Gamba grass, tufted with cane-like shoots growing up to 15 feet (4·5 metres) in height.
Aristida mutabilis, *A. longiflora*, *A. stipoides*, camel fodder on sandy soils.
Cenchrus catharticus, Kramkram, Bur grass.
Ctenium elegans, soon becomes coarse.
Cymbopogon giganteus, *C. rufus*, *C. proximus*, very coarse when mature.
Dactyloctenium aegyptium, Comb-fringe grass, good fodder for horses.
Digitaria horizontalis, *D. velutina*, weeds on cultivated land, excellent fodder for horses and cattle.
Hyparrhenia spp., suitable for fodder only when young.

Imperata cylindrica, Spear grass, generally giving a poor pasture, only edible when young.

Panicum albidum, often dried and fed to sheep.

P. maximum, Guinea grass, highly nutritive, palatable and heavy yielding, resistant to drought, introduced elsewhere in the tropics as a planted pasture grass.

Pennisetum setosum.

Perotis indica.

Urochloa lata, sometimes stored as hay.

2) Annuals

Brachiaria deflexa, tufted wild grass resistant to drought.

Eragrostis ciliaris, E. gangetica, E. pilosa, E. tremula, palatable and nutritive, but low yielding.

Hackelochloa granularis.

Pennisetum pedicellatum, Kyaswa grass.

Rottboellia exaltata, sometimes cultivated by the Mossi as a fodder for horses.

Sorghum arundinaceum, wild Guinea corn.

2. Dry season pastures

1) Perennials

Acroceras amplectans, A. zizanoides, found chiefly in marshes.

Cynodon dactylon, Bermuda grass, found at the edges of streams or pools, or sometimes as a weed on cultivated land.

Cyperus spp., not a grass, but of grass-like appearance. A good fodder when young, but frequently full of disease-bearing insects after flood peak, and normally left for 3–4 weeks before grazing.

Echinochloa stagnina, Bourgou, swamp grass giving best pasture on land flooded annually between 6 and 10 feet (2–3 metres) in depth. Rooting is improved by the trampling of animals.

Paspalum scrobiculatum, Bastard millet.

Pennisetum purpureum, Elephant grass, grows up to 12 feet (3·5 metres) in height in clumps, deep rooted and a useful means of binding soils against erosion, highly palatable.

Oryza barthii, Wild rice, forms large meadows in the Niger valley floodlands, edible when young.

2) Annuals

Coix Lacryma-Jobi, Job's Tears, heavy yielding grass growing up to 6 feet (2 metres) in height in swampy areas.

Echinochloa colona, 'Jungle rice', grows only up to 2 feet (60 cm) in height, excellent fodder.

Oryza breviligulata, Wild rice.

3. *Leguminous herbaceous plants*

Cassia mimosoides, grows up to 2 feet (60 cm) in height.

Mimosa pudica, a weed.

Zornia diphylla, deep tap root, often stored as hay, chiefly for feeding horses.

4. *Trees*

With their different periods of coming into new leaf, trees provide fodder throughout the year in the Sahel and Sudan. They also form a useful reserve when other fodder is scarce.

Acacia seyal, leaves and pods used as fodder in the dry season, particularly important in the Ferlo and Bornu when it forms pure stands.

A. albida, Kad or Gawo, particularly important in the latter portion of the dry season from February to April when most other acacias have little leaf (see p. 95).

A. senegal, young leaf used for fodder, chiefly in Mauritania.

A. arabica, leaves and pods used for fodder, especially in the Saloum valley of Senegal.

A. sieberiana, remains in leaf late in the dry season.

Adansonia digitata, Baobab, fruit and leaves used for fodder, to an extent limited by their use as human food.

Bauhinia rufescens, *B. thonningii*, pods and leaves used for fodder in many parts of the Sudan.

Moringa pterygosperma, Horse-radish tree, improved by pollarding.

Parkinsonia aculeata, Jerusalem Thorn, foliage fed to goats, chiefly in Hausaland and Bornu.

Other fodders include crops used otherwise as food for human beings, and the refuse left after harvest.

South of the Sudan pastures are more limited in area and distribution. Portères has listed fodder plants in the pastures of the plateaux of southern Ivory Coast[23] notably:

Anadelphia arrecta, perennial eaten chiefly in the dry season.

Brachiaria brachylopha, *B. fulva*, annuals eaten chiefly in the wet season.

Cassia mimosoides.

Cymbopogon citratus, Lemon grass (exotic).

Imperata cylindrica.

Sporobolus pyramidalis, Rat's Tail grass, perennial, good fodder only when young.

Other useful pasture plants include[24]:

Panicum repens, perennial, weed, common on sandy soils.

Paspalum conjugatum, Green grass, perennial, withstands drought.

P. vaginatum, in coastal swamps.

Setaria barbata, Bristly foxtail grass.

S. chevalieri, Buffel grass.

Stenotaphrum secundatum, Buffalo grass, perennial, common in sandy coastal areas.
Stylosanthes erecta, herbaceous legume.

Pastures have been developed by burning and by selection by feeding livestock. Where numbers of livestock are great and resources limited there is a danger that the better feeding plants will disappear. Portères claims that in the southern Ivory Coast 'overstocking' leads to the reduction or elimination of the preferred grasses and shrubs and their replacement by the coarse leaved plants normally avoided. The cattle transform the pasture into a shaved lawn from which emerge the plants not eaten.[25] He points to differences in the selection of plants between various breeds of cattle. For example Zebu cattle on their way to market from the north prefer *Cymbopogon citratus,* whilst the local Lagoon breed refuse it, but on the other hand will eat young *Imperata cylindrica.* The value of burning pasture grasses is still a disputed question. Jeffreys claims that at least in the more humid environments fires keep down the coarser grasses which mark the early stages in a return to forest cover, and also destroy ticks.[26] Pitot disagrees and claims that fires destroy all surface vegetation including seeds, leaving only the roots and rhizomes. Thus annuals are at a disadvantage compared with perennials and in consequence grasslands are progressively colonized by the coarser, more resistant plants. Pastures in consequence become poorer and eventually contain only a few grasses.[27] The issue has not yet been resolved. In defence of the herdsmen it should be pointed out that burning is a practical necessity in order to obtain young shoots which alone give satisfactory fodder amongst the grasses. It also reduces the number of ticks. Until controlled pastures with superior types of grass are introduced burning remains a necessity. Moreover, the bulk of the grasses suitable for feeding livestock are in fact perennial. Burning does not destroy humus. The rise in soil temperatures during the fire is in fact very slight, although exposure to the sun may bring a later increase of 5°–7° F. (3°–4° C.).[28] It seems probable that the deterioration of pastures noted by some observers is the result not of burning but of too heavy stocking. Heavy cultivation seems to have the effect of reducing perennials to the advantage of annuals. The appearance of perennials in cultivated areas in the savannas usually denotes a long fallow.

Environmental influences

Some reference to environmental influences has already been made, chiefly with regard to pasture. A good all year round supply of feeding stuffs is necessary to keep stock healthy. The floodland pastures of the inland Niger delta, for example, provide progressively poorer feeding from November to June, and by May the death rate among stock becomes high. By a more economic use of the superior 'bourgou' pastures, and by the provision of better water supplies in the Sahel enabling a longer period away from the floodlands, it is hoped to maintain a more even use of the pastures available.[29] However, under present conditions hardy animals are preferred and Doutressoule suggests that where food is plentiful stock can degenerate. For example, the horses of the sandy plains of Niger, or on the poor soils of Liptako or the Mossi region are less well fed and are hardier, more vigorous and more resistant to disease.[30] The shortage of lime or phosphorus frequent in very sandy soils or in fine clays has an adverse effect, and the general deficiency of salt needs to be rectified by importing it or by taking the stock regularly to salt-producing districts. Water supplies are often of critical importance in determining the choice of or length of stay in pastures. Large areas of the Sahel are rapidly 'grazed over' by animals moving from one water hole to the next. Camels can survive eight to ten days without water and need very little if the pasture is abundant. Even the hardiest cattle, however, need water every two to three days in the dry season, particularly in the dry harmattan air when evaporation rates from the body are high.

Trypanosomiasis or sleeping sickness is a major problem south of the Sahel. In Nigeria *Trypanosoma vivax* is involved in about 70 per cent of the infections of cattle, *T. congolense* is involved in about 30 per cent, and *T. brucei* in only a very small proportion. The chief vector is the tsetse fly. Of these *Glossina morsitans* is found only where there is game, that is where the human population density is low, whilst *G. palpalis* and *G. tachinoides* are found chiefly near streams and rivers and carry trypanosomiasis to both men and animals.[31] In the savannas tsetse seek shady woodlands and avoid open spaces, but in the more humid Guinean zone open conditions are generally preferred. Fulani herdsmen try to avoid the *morsitans* areas, but are often forced in the dry season to move their herds to waterside and thus expose them to the attack of *palpalis* and *tachinoides*. Open pastures are generally free of tsetse and good feeding can reduce the number of deaths from the disease. 'Animals well housed and fed may show transient febrile symptoms only, probably breaking down again at a later stage.' [32] Overwork, malnutrition and a prolonged rainy season will increase the death rate. The introduction of oxen to ploughing frequently results in their early death. Sheep and goats generally have more resistance to trypanosomiasis than cattle, and in consequence are more widespread in their distribution. Only a very high density of tsetse flies can prevent the raising of these animals. The goat, in consequence of its resistance to this disease and its ability to survive on a great variety of feeding stuffs, appears to be the ideal animal for stock rearing in wooded environments, and particularly in the Guinean areas. An important aspect of the problem of resistance to the disease is that immunity to one strain of trypanosome does not convey immunity to others. Thus even resistant breeds can suffer from the disease when exposed to other strains on a long transhumance journey or on a march to market. Increased density of population in infested areas would make possible the maintenance of bush clearings and keep the areas relatively free of tsetse. Clearance of river banks is a more difficult problem, partly because of the danger of accelerating erosion, and partly because riverine forest often includes many useful fruit and timber trees.

Contagious bovine pleuropneumonia is carried by a micro-organism spread by the movement of cattle for transhumance and trading. Outbreaks occur in areas of cattle concentration, particularly along trade routes and in great market centres. Bovine tuberculosis occurs, although the White Fulani cattle appear to have some resistance to it. Rinderpest is a virus disease of cattle which spread into West Africa from the Nile Valley and Ethiopia at the end of the 19th century. The dwarf short-horn cattle resistant to trypanosomiasis are more susceptible to this disease than the Zebu. Although East African coast fever is not present, other tick-borne diseases, notably heartwater, occur, and badly affect sheep and goats.

A number of diseases affect poultry in West Africa, including typhoid, cholera, fowl pox, and helminthiasis, but the most serious in recent years has been Newcastle disease or fowl pest, of which outbreaks were first reported in 1950 in Dakar, and elsewhere in West Africa in 1951. West African poultry are highly susceptible to the disease and many of the outbreaks have been devastating.[33]

BIBLIOGRAPHICAL NOTES

[1] G. Doutressoule, *L'Elevage en Afrique Occidentale Française*, Paris, 1947, p. 26.
Much of this chapter is based on Doutressoule's work which provides the most comprehensive account of stock rearing in West Africa. See also the most useful studies published by the Food and Agriculture Organization of the United Nations, Rome; H. J. Mittendorf and S. G. Wilson, *Livestock and Meat Marketing in Africa*, 1961; H. J. Mittendorf and H. J. Louwes, *Hides and Skins Marketing in Africa and the Near East*, 1963.

[2] G. Doutressoule, op. cit., p. 56.

[3] For a list of breeds, see I. L. Mason, *The Classification of West African Livestock*, Technical Communication No. 7, Commonwealth Bureau of Animal Breeding and Genetics, 1951.

[4] G. M. Gates, Breeds of Cattle Found in Nigeria, *Farm and Forest*, vol. XI, 1952, pp. 19–43. This paper is extremely useful for its descriptive material and its numerous illustrations.

[5] A. G. Doherty, Livestock Problems, *West Africa Commission, 1938–39*, Leverhulme Trust, 1943, p. 63.

[6] D. E. Faulkner and J. D. Brown, *The Improvement of Cattle in British Colonial Territories in Africa*, Colonial Advisory Council of Agriculture, Animal Health and Forestry, Pub. No. 3, H.M.S.O., London, 1953, pp. 13–15.

[7] G. M. Gates, Breeds of Cattle Found in Nigeria, op. cit. For a description of Kuri cattle, see K. Kone, Le Bœuf du Lac Tchad de la Région de N'Guigmi, *Bulletin des Services de l'Elevage et des Industries Animales de l'A.O.F.*, Tome I, 1948, pp. 47–65.

[8] G. Doutressoule, op. cit., p. 287.

[9] ibid., p. 238. See also I. L. Mason, op. cit., pp. 25–27.

[10] Doutressoule, op. cit., p. 268.

[11] A. G. Doherty, Livestock Problems, p. 65.

[12] C. K. Meek, *The Northern Tribes of Nigeria*, vol. I, London, 1925, pp. 115–19.

[13] *Colonial Annual Report* for Northern Nigeria, 476, 1904.

[14] C. E. Hopen, *The Pastoral Fulbe Family in Gwandu*, London, 1958, pp. 4–5.

[15] G. Doutressoule, op. cit., p. 27.

[16] P. Grenier, Les Peul du Ferlo, *Cahiers d'Outre-Mer*, **13**, 1960, pp. 28–58.

[17] G. Doutressoule, *L'Elevage au Soudan Français*, 2nd ed., Mortain, 1953, p. 75.

[18] G. Doutressoule, *L'Elevage en Afrique Occidentale Française*, op. cit., p. 54.

[19] A. T. Grove, Land Use and Soil Conservation of the Jos Plateau, *Geological Survey of Nigeria, Bulletin 22*, 1952, pp. 34–37.

[20] Notes et Documents, *Bulletin, Institut Français d'Afrique Noire*, **16**, 1954, pp. 169–84.

[21] Listed in A. Chevalier, Principales Plantes Fourragères du Sahara, *Revue Internationale de Botanique Appliquée et d'Agriculture Tropicale*, 1953, pp. 373–4, 596–7; E. Guernier, *L'Afrique Occidentale Française*, vol. I, 1949, pp. 135–42; G. Doutressoule, *L'Elevage en Afrique Occidentale Française*; J. M. Dalziel, *The Useful Plants of West Tropical Africa*, 1948; *Pasture and Fodder Plants in Sierra Leone*, Agricultural Notes No. 6, Sierra Leone Agricultural Department, 1954; and J. G. Adam, Contribution à l'Etude Floristique des Pâturages de Sénégal, *Agronomie Tropicale*, **12**, 1957, pp. 67–113.

[22] V. A. Oyenuga, The Composition and Agricultural Value of Some Grass Species in Nigeria, *Empire Journal of Experimental Agriculture*, vol. 25, 1957, pp. 237–55.

[23] R. Portères, Le Bétail et les Prairies des Plateaux du Néogène de la Basse Côte d'Ivoire, *Journal d'Agriculture Tropicale et de Botanique Appliquée*, e, 1956, pp. 891–902.

[24] *Pasture and Fodder Plants in Sierre Leone*, op. cit., and V. A. Oyenuga, Composition and Agricultural Value of some Grass Species in Nigeria.

[25] R. Portères, op. cit.

[26] M. D. W. Jeffreys, Feux de Brousse, *Bulletin, Institut Français d'Afrique Noire*, **13**, 1951, pp. 682–710, and This Burning Question, *Farm and Forest*, **6**, No. 3, 1945.

[27] A. Pitot, Feux Sauvages, Végétation et Sols en A.O.F., *Bulletin, Institut Français d'Afrique Noire*, **15**, 1953, pp. 1369–83. On the relationship of burning to laterization see also A. Pitot, Bowalisation et Feux de Brousse, in L'homme et les Sols dans les Steppes et Savannes d'A.O.F., *Cahiers d'Outre-Mer*, **5**, 1952, pp. 215–40.

[28] A. Pitot and H. Masson, Quelques Données sur la Température au Cours des Feux de Brousse aux Environs de Dakar, *Bulletin, Institut Français d'Afrique Noire*, **13**, 1951, pp. 711–32. For an excellent summary study see J. M. Ramsay and R. R. Innes, Some quantitative observations on the effects of fire on the Guinea savanna vegetation of northern Ghana over a period of eleven years, *African Soils*, **8**, 1963, pp. 41–85.

[29] G. Doutressoule, *L'Elevage au Soudan Français*, op. cit., p. 33.

[30] G. Doutressoule, *L'Elevage en Afrique Occidentale Française*, op. cit., p. 10.

[31] For this and other references to Animal Health, see D. H. Hill, Diseases in Nigeria Which Could Threaten North American Livestock, *Proceedings Book*, American Veterinary Medical Association, 90th Annual Meeting, Toronto, 1953, pp. 465–71 (see pp. 206).

[32] ibid.

[33] D. H. Hill, O. S. Davis and J. K. H. Wilde, Newcastle Disease in Nigeria, *The British Veterinary Journal*, vol. 109, 1953, pp. 381–5.

CHAPTER 4

The Non-Agricultural and Non-Pastoral Economy

The importance that must attach to agriculture and pastoralism in West African studies often obscures the fact that in most communities a considerable proportion of the income is derived from other activities. Gathering, to provide a vegetable supplement to the diet, is almost universal, and is especially important during periods of crop shortage. Hunting is more specialized, and for many communities is still the chief source of meat. Fishing is a widespread activity, but certain communities specialize in fishing to the exclusion of almost every other occupation, and export a large part of their produce to neighbouring peoples. Mining of local ores has tended to decline, but was once of vital importance in the supply of raw materials for tools and in the production of a valuable export, gold, for the trade with North Africa. Within each community there are specialists in a great variety of trades – metal working, textile manufactures, building, wood carving, pottery and basket manufacture, rope making, canoe building and the preparation of certain foodstuffs. Some of these specialisms are broad, that is they are restricted only to large groups such as all the men or all the women of a given community. In many cases the specialists are also agriculturalists or may even have a third occupation. In other cases there are true specialist groups within communities, skilled solely in the one occupation, and often of alien origin or forming a caste or co-operative society with its own customs and even its own deities. Much depends on the seasonal pattern of work. A long dry season in effect encourages most people to find some work other than agriculture for part of the year. A short dry season or no dry season at all may mean that agriculturalists have little time to spare away from their fields and must depend on the labour of others for their clothing, houses and tools. Trading has long been a leading occupation in West Africa, for, despite the traditional emphasis on subsistence production, few cultivators or herders fail to produce a small surplus to exchange for their additional needs. Local trading is universal, although more developed amongst certain communities by particular groups, for example women amongst the Yoruba. Lacking modern wholesale and retail organization, lacking an adequate transportation network, and serving a people on the whole poor, the greater part of traditional exchange is undertaken by petty traders, who frequently sell only minute quantities of any one commodity. Petty traders may move from one village to another trading in a ring of markets so that they always return to each village at regular intervals. The intervals are determined by the local calendars which, according to the community, may be based on 4, 5, 7 or 8 day weeks. Outside the local market cycle of petty trading, there is the more specialized trading between communities over long distances. This is normally concerned with produce possessing a high value per unit of weight, such as kola nuts or salt. Small communities of Sarakolé and Hausa traders have established themselves in most of the large commercial centres to act as agents for this trade.

Gathering

Although gathering plays some part in the economy of every West African community, it is of greatest importance in the north amongst Sudanic and Sahelian peoples, whose agriculture is affected by the shortness of the growing season and by a precipitation both marginal and highly variable. April, May and June are the months when the problem of food shortage is greatest. The Songhay begin gathering the seed, roots and leaves of aquatic plants in February and continue until August. In February and March they gather the seed of 'babata' (*Saccolepis interrupta*), an aquatic grass. In April they begin picking the roots of 'konkarou' (*Nymphaea lotus*) and the following month gather 'koundou' or 'bourgou' (*Echinochloa stagnina*). Over the next two months an enormous variety of foodstuffs is provided by gathering:

'houbey' (*Gyrandropsis pentaphylla*).
'daun' (*Ipomoea reptans*), the aquatic potato.
'karou' (*Aechynomene aspera*), an aquatic vegetable picked for its leaves.
'dani' (*Cenchrus biflorus*), a wild cereal.
'gansi' (*Echinochloa colona*), another wild cereal gathered abundantly and the cheapest grain in Gao market by the end of August.[1]

Wild rice (*Oryza barthii*) is regarded more as a weed to be eradicated than as a source of food, not only by the Songhay, but throughout the Sudan and Sahel wherever rice is cultivated. Even in Bornu where rice cultivation is a comparatively recent introduction wild rice is little valued.[2] Wild rice is the grain of scarcity gathered without cutting, in baskets or calabashes. Other important wild grains important throughout the sub-Sudanic and Sudanic areas are 'founi kouli' or *Brachiaria deflexa*, cultivated only in the Fouta Djallon, and elsewhere gathered, and *Digitaria debilis*, *D. velutina* and other *Digitaria* spp., the seeds of which are valued in scarcity, and which are sometimes cut to provide fodder for horses and cattle. *Digitaria* and *Brachiaria* are more important in sub-Sudanic areas, where they provide a small supplement to the diet or are gathered only in emergency. To the south the longer rainy season, with the greater abundance and variety of fresh food supply throughout the year, has made gathering important only as a source of supplementary foodstuffs or to produce small emergency supplies during the traditional hunger period, particularly in years of below average crop returns. It is only in the more heavily forested portions of the Guinean environment that gathering has played a vital part in southern economies, for in the heavier soiled portions agricultural occupation did not come in great density until the introduction of perennial cropping for overseas markets. Even there gathering has been severely limited, confined mainly to wild yams, frequently the survivors of former crops. Wild, mainly sub-Sudanic, yams include *Dioscorea praehensilis*, *D. dumetorum* [3] and *D. sagittifolia*.[4] The first two are also occasionally found in cultivation. All contain a bitter poisonous alkaloid and need to be sliced, washed and boiled before eating. Another tuber occurring in Sudanic areas and also needing treatment to remove poison is *Tacca pinnatifolia* or *T. involucrata*.

Amongst perennials the most important trees affected by gathering are the oil palm, kola and shea, also frequently protected or even planted and described under 'Agriculture'.

Other important gathered perennials are:

Pentaclethra macrophylla, oil-bean tree, Guinean, beans, fat, poison and timber.

Parkia biglobosa and *P. filicoidea*, African locust bean, Sudanic and sub-Sudanic, pulp, kernel, paste and tannin.

Lophira alata, Meni oil tree, Sudanic, sub-Sudanic and sub-Guinean, kernel oil used chiefly in south-west for cooking and timber.

Adansonia digitata, Baobab, Sudanic and sub-Sudanic, seeds, pulp, leaves (in soup), medicinal bark, fibre and cloth from inner bark.

Ziziphys jujuba, Jujube tree, Sudanic, pulp cakes and timber.

Raphia vinifera, etc., wine palm, Guinean and Sudanic gallery forest, palm wine, piassava (for brushes, ropes, etc.), poles, piassava oil for lighting and cooking.

Oxytenanthera abyssinica, African bamboo, Guinean and Sudanic gallery forest, poles, fencing.

Tamarindus indica, Indian tamarind, Sudanic, pulp cake, flowers and leaves eaten, medicinal bark and root, kernel oil, tannin, silk worm host.

Ximenia americana, wild olive, chiefly Sudanic and sub-Sudanic, fruit, kernel oil, tannin.

Balanites aegyptiaca, desert date, Sahelian fruit, kernel oil, edible kernels, roots and bark form a soapy lather with water and also provide a fish poison.

Borassus aethiopum, African fan palm, Sudanic and sub-Sudanic, palm wine, fronds for thatch and baskets, fibre, fruit pulp, germinating radicle eaten in famine.

Hyphaene thebaica, dum palm, Sahelian and Sudanic, fronds, fibre, edible rind of fruit, edible kernel, vegetable 'ivory', source of black dye.

Herminiera elaphroxylon, Ambatch or pith tree, mainly Lake Chad, floats, rafts and shields.

Boscia senegalenis, Sahelian, edible berries and leaves, useful in time of scarcity.

Bombax buonopozense, West African kapok, silk cotton, Sudanic and sub-Sudanic.

Ceiba pentandra, kapok, silk cotton, sub-Guinean and Guinean, introduced from the Americas, floss for stuffing cushions and quilts, seed oil, medicinal leaves and fruits, timber.

Khaya senegalensis, Mahogany, Sudanic and sub-Sudanic, timber, tannin, medicinal bark, seed oil.

Daniellia oliveri, Copaiba Balsam, Sudanic and sub-Sudanic, copal, timber, medicinal leaves, bark and roots.

D. thurifera, Niger Copal, Guinean and sub-Guinean, copal, timber.

Ricinus communis, Castor plant, widespread, occurs as a plant but can become a tree up to 30 feet (9 metres) high and frequently wild, castor oil.

Guiera senegalensis, Sabara, Sudanic – common on abandoned croplands, medicinal leaves, fruit and roots, commonly cut to provide fencing.

Numerous other plants are gathered and treated to provide food, medicines, poisons, dyes, fibre and even cloth. Moreover, one must not forget that in West Africa firewood, the chief fuel for cooking and heating, is in most cases gathered, and not grown and cut on a commercial basis. The existence of towns as large as Ibadan, with three quarters of a million people demanding firewood for cooking, has created enormous problems in gathering wood. It has to be collected from roadside pick-up points, distributed over a radius of at least 20 miles (32 km). Many fodders for livestock are also gathered, including the foliage and shoots of several acacia species, sold in northern markets such as Timbuktu as a fodder for sheep, and grasses such as *Rottboellia exaltata* (planted by the Mossi) [5], *Panicum albidum, Cenchrus catharticus* and *C. ciliaris* whose seeds are also used as human food. Other essentially gathered products, used locally or sold on the West African internal market, are insects such as locusts used for food, gum arabic, the product of the Senegal and Mauritanian acacias, bees' wax and honey and silk cocoons. The silk worms, *Epanaphe vuilletii, E. moloneyi, Anaphe infracta, A. venata* and *A. reticulata* inhabit such trees as *Tamarindus indica, Isoberlinia doka, Bridelia ferruginea, B. micrantha, Cordia millenii* and *Ficus platyphylla*. The silk found on *Tamarindus indica* is regarded as superior. The silk thread obtained is occasionally woven, but is normally embroidered on gowns.[6]

Hunting

Although hunting is practised more in the savanna regions than elsewhere, yet its importance in local economies is greatest in the heavily wooded areas where grass fallows are rare and few livestock can be kept. Before the planting of cocoa and other perennials in the Guinean areas of the Ivory Coast, Ghana and south-western Nigeria, the forests, which formerly occupied these areas, were the seasonal home of hunters and gatherers from neighbouring populous districts. In south-western Nigeria many of the local names recall hunters' camps or record the names of the animals hunted. The high forests of the Guinean areas are favoured by many animals as a refuge. For example the bush buck and duiker shelter and breed in the high forest, and spend the rest of their lives wandering in the savanna country. Moreover the high forest, with its thick canopy and poor undergrowth, offers less resistance than savanna to penetration by low built four-footed animals.[7] Even elephants penetrate the high forest, although chiefly in areas which have been recently cleared for cultivation. Hogs also occur and tree-haunting animals such as monkeys and lemurs. Animals which are virtually restricted to the Guinean environment include a large number of the bats, the common potto, six of the squirrels, two of the flying squirrels, a number of the mice and rats including the common rat, the brush-tailed porcupine, the two-spotted palm civet, the 'kusimanse', golden cat and tree hyrax. Several of the forest animals inhabit only a portion of the forest. For example, the royal antelope and Brooke's duiker occur only in the west, in Ghana and the Ivory Coast, whilst several shrews, eight species of bat, the Calabar potto, two galagos, the mangabey, eight squirrels, two flying squirrels, seven species of mice and rats, the black-footed and long-nosed mongoose and three of the duikers are restricted to West Cameroun. The Niger also acts as a barrier for some animals. For example Bate's dwarf antelope only occurs to the east of it. Some animals like the bongo and the forest hog occur in the west and also to the east in Cameroun, but are unknown in Southern Nigeria. Possibly more intensive hunting in Southern Nigeria has eliminated them. In the savanna a number of animals, particularly the porcupine, the otter, the cutting grass, a giant rat, various buck such as bush-buck and reed-buck, the roan antelope, wild cats such as the civet, the leopard, serval and lion, are widespread from the southern margins of the Sahara southwards to the northern edge of the high forest. In the southern savanna areas elephant are more common than elsewhere, and there are marked concentrations of waterbuck, kob and western hartebeest. The Sudan savanna is preferred by the jackal, fox, hunting dog, polecat, weasel, badger, the African wild cat, caracal, cheetah, black rhino, giraffe, Senegal hartebeest and the red-fronted gazelle. The Sahel is favoured by the jerboa, small crested porcupine, common jackal, striped hyena, scimitar oryx and dorcas and dama gazelles.

The preferred time for hunting is the dry season, mainly from November to March, after harvesting the main crops and when the number of drinking water sources is at a minimum. The movement of larger game particularly is very restricted during the dry season. In consequence the northern portions of West Africa are in this respect more favoured than the southern, and hunting in groups, using burning techniques to drive animals in a desired direction, is common during the dry season. Dogs are also frequently employed, and many northerners breed them for the purpose, particularly the Hausa. Guns are the chief weapons used, chiefly muzzle-loaders known in former British West Africa as 'dane-guns'. Other weapons include spears and bows and arrows. Traps are used extensively, especially locally made traps of the 'gin' type, running nooses, torsion spring traps using tree branches or twisted cloth and camouflaged game pits containing spikes. Several poisons are employed produced from local plants some of which are cultivated. Examples are:

GATHERED

Strophanthus gratus, arrow poison plant of the Cameroons, *S. sarmentosus* and
   S. hispidus, widespread arrow poison plants.
Sapium grahamii, hunting poison made from the root.
Adenium honghel, arrow poison made from the root.
Erythrophleum guineense, poison made from the bark.
Physistigma venenosum, Calabar ordeal bean.

CULTIVATED

Strophanthus hispidus, cultivated throughout West Africa for arrow poison.
Euphorbia poisonii, *E. unispina* and *E. kamerunica*, often planted as a hedge and
   commonly mixed with *Strophanthus* in preparing arrow poison.
Jatropha curcas, another ingredient with *Strophanthus* in the manufacture of
   arrow poison.

Amongst several communities, especially in the south, where the interval
between the last main harvest and the first clearance for the following season is
small, hunters form specialist groups who engage in little cultivation or in no
cultivation at all. They sometimes form guilds possessing monopoly rights in
certain methods or in the hunting of certain animals.

Today hunting is of declining importance due to the development of cattle
raising in order to supply the meat markets of the towns, particularly in the
former high forest areas, now largely cleared for the cultivation of perennial
export crops. High densities of population have resulted in the removal of most
large game, and thus the chief hunting districts are in the low density areas where
the size of the meat market is small. An example occurs in the Oban Hills of
south-east Nigeria where districts with less than 20 persons per square mile (8 per
sq km) produce smoked 'bush meat' for Ibo and Ibibio markets.

Fishing

Fish provide one of the chief sources of animal protein in West Africa, and
amongst many communities play a more important part in the diet than meat.
Fishing is a widespread occupation not only on the coast and in the large rivers
and lakes, but in every small stream. Many districts, having only limited local
fish resources, import fish from overseas or from West African sources 500 miles
(800 km) or more away.

Fresh-water and sea fishing may be considered separately. The latter is confined chiefly to coastal waters and lagoons. Deep-sea fishing is rare, partly because
of problems of navigation away from land, and partly because of the small size
of the craft used. The Wovea of West Cameroun were an important exception
formerly, for they hunted whales with harpoons in July and August.[8] Generally
the African inter-tropical fisheries are poorer than are temperate waters in

suitable edible varieties which can command a good sale. The West African fisheries, however, are the richest and may be divided into three regions:[9]

1) *The Mauritano-Senegalese*. The region extends from Cape Blanc to the Saloum, has low surface water temperatures (68°–77°F., 20°–25°C.), average salinity and small tidal range. Air movement is chiefly from the north and north-west. The coast is low and sandy with bars, excepting for the Dakar peninsula. The fishing is subdivided by a trough descending over 2500 feet (760 metres) in depth off Kayar which marks the true divide between the North Atlantic fish of the 'Grande côte', and the Central and South Atlantic fish of the 'Petite côte'. The trough appears to form a barrier to migration further south of the golden headed sea bream (*Pagrus ehrenbergi*) and the sea bream (*Dentex vulgaris*).[10]

2) *The 'Rivières du Sud'*. From Saloum to Sherbro Island surface water tempera-tures are higher (77°–81°F., 25°–27°C.), salinity is slightly lower and the tidal range is high (6–15 feet, 2–4·5 metres). The predominant wind direction is south-westerly. The coast has been drowned and rias with 'open' mangrove swamps are the chief feature.

3) *The Gulf of Guinea*. From Sherbro Island to the Cameroons surface water temperatures are generally high, salinity is a little higher than in the Rivières du Sud, and the tidal range is generally less than 5 feet (1·5 metres). The coast consists essentially of sand bars and lagoons with 'closed' mangrove swamps, interrupted by the Niger delta.

These three fishing regions together comprise a continental shelf of 100,000 square miles (260,000 sq. km) containing over 600 species of fish, of which about one third are edible. In 1955 about 100,000 tons of fish were caught, of which about 40,000 tons were landed in Senegal and about 30,000 tons were landed in Ghana. Much of this catch, especially that of Senegal, was provided by powered vessels using modern fishing gear. Their contribution will be discussed in Chapter 11.

The fishing off the 'Grande côte' belongs geographically to the north, rather than to West Africa. The 'Ngot' (*Temnodon saltator*), sea-breams and mullets make the greater part of the catch, and some of this is dried on the beaches and taken to interior and southern markets by camel. Coastal fishing is performed by a distinct Berber caste. Deep-sea fishing takes place from Port Etienne, M'Boro and Kayar chiefly from January to April. Fishing vessels from Europe and the Canary Islands also operate in these waters. The fishing grounds of the 'Petite côte' are amongst the richest in West Africa, and give abundant catches of 'sar-dines' (*Sardinella eba*) and shad or 'cobo' (*Ethmalosa fimbriata*). The season is from April to November, and fishing vessels from the large harbours can thus operate on both 'côtes'. The greatest concentrations of *Sardinella* are in May and July, and of *Ethmalosa* in August and September. Concentrations of the latter are

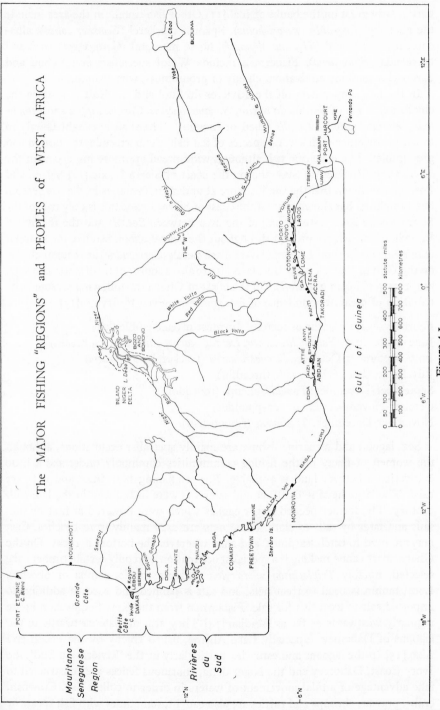

The MAJOR FISHING "REGIONS" and PEOPLES of WEST AFRICA

Figure 4.1

particularly great on the banks of Joal.[11] Other fish caught in the area include the anchovy (*Engraulis enerasicholus*), Spanish mackerel (*Scomber colias*), albacore, tuna or 'thon' (*Thynnus thynnus*), horse mackerel (*Caranx carangus*) and barracuda (*Sphyraena*). Fishermen include Wolof specialists and Lebou and Serer who combine cultivation, chiefly of groundnuts, with fishing.

In the less salty waters off the 'Rivières du Sud' and the Gulf of Guinea the chief catches are of *Sardinella aurita*, *S. cameronensis*, *Caranx hippos* and *Ethmalosa fimbriata* and *E. dorsalis* (shad or 'bongo'). The shad is caught chiefly in estuaries, together with several species of flat fish, the barracuda, the tarpon and grey mullet. The estuarine fish although widespread are more important in the west in the 'Rivières du Sud' and on the coast of Sierra Leone.[12] Salzen and Postel have shown that the shad is more abundant in estuaries in the dry season, but Longhurst has shown that off the coast of Sierra Leone this is only true of the Sierra Leone River estuary and of the area between Bonthe and the mainland. Elsewhere the fish are present throughout the year. Lagoon fish like the snapper (*Lutjanus eutactus* and *L. guiniensis*) and sea perch (*Serranidae*) are caught chiefly on the Gulf of Guinea coast. The lagoons are also a source of fresh water fish such as the carp (*Tilapia heudeloti*). Off the coast of Ghana the following seasonal distribution of greatest abundance of fish species is given by Irvine:[13]

February-May: months of scarcity for most marine edible fish
June-September: *Sardinella aurita*, *Dentex macrophthalmus* (sea bream)
June-September-October: *Scomberomorus* (mackerel), *Sphyraena*
July-September: *Pentanemus* (threadfin)
September-December: *Pomadasys* spp. (roncador)
October-November: *Elops* (ten-pounder)
November-December: *Trichiurus* (ribbon-fish).

Sea, lagoon and estuarine fishing are mainly specialist occupations, although the women of many of the fishing communities commonly undertake a little cultivation wherever land is available. For sea fishing both lines and nets are used. The large herring drift net and seine net were introduced in the late 19th century. The former needed larger canoes which were powered at first by mat sails and later by sails of cloth. Seine nets are used mainly from beaches. Cast nets are used to catch 'sardines' and shad wherever the bottom is rocky. On the Ghana coast canoe making is a specialist occupation, and only certain timbers are selected, notably *Triplochiton scleroxylon* (African maple, samba or obeche). Local tannin is used to treat nets, and salt is panned and used in addition to imported salt to treat fish for sale. Fishermen from the Keta Peninsula migrate regularly westwards as far as Abidjan.[14] They also migrate eastwards to the lagoons of Dahomey, especially Lake Ahémé, fished chiefly by the Pedah and Aizo.[15] In the lagoons and estuaries particularly in the 'Rivières du Sud', the Ivory Coast, Dahomey and the Niger delta, enormous fences are constructed to take advantage of a tidal movement of waters in order to collect fish. Crawfish, crabs, prawns, shrimps and turtles are also caught, sometimes with fish spears or harpoons. Crayfish are important in the estuary of the Cameroons river and in the Niger delta where basket traps are frequently used. The smoking and salting of fish at the chief fishing villages along the coast is an important industry in order to preserve the flesh for sale at distant markets. Frequently fish needs to be stored for several weeks before transport is available, particularly when heavy catches are landed towards the end of the rainy season, and local roads are impassable.

Whereas much of the deep-sea and coastal fishing takes place during the rainy season (April to November), fresh-water fishing occurs mainly during the dry season, and therefore provides a means of maintaining fish supplies throughout the year. The chief species caught are catfish (*Clarias* spp.), Nile perch (*Lates niloticus*), moonfish (*Distichodus* spp.), African carp (*Labeo* spp.), mormyrs (*Mormyrus* spp.), lungfish (*Protopterus annectens*), carp (*Tilapia* spp.), barbels (*Barlus* spp.), 'tinéni' (*Alestes nigrilineatus*), *Hydrocyon* spp. and *Citharinus* spp. Shellfish are also caught. The methods of catching include barrage fences, communal fish drives with handnets, spears and harpoons, dragging from the bank or canoes with nets, fixed nets, traps of which the cone type is the most popular, lines and poisons. At least sixteen species of plants from which fish poisons are prepared are listed in Irvine and Dalziel. Of these the most common are *Tephrosia vogelii*, a cultivated plant, *Balanites aegyptiaca*, *Mimusops ajave*, *Pentaclethra macrophylla* or oil bean tree, *Cassia sieberiana*, *Parkia filicoidia* or African locust bean, *Strophanthus hispidus*, *Adenium honghel*, *Schwenkia americana* and *Erythrophleum guineense*. Since fresh-water fishing is mainly a dry season occupation, it is widespread throughout West Africa, particularly in northern districts, where the dry season is of several months duration. On the larger rivers and on Lake Chad, however, there are peoples who specialize almost completely in fishing. These include the Bozo and Somono of the inland Niger delta, the Sorkawa of the Songhay section of the Niger, the Kede and the Kakanda on the Niger between the Sorkawa and the Benue confluence, the Wurbo and a group of Jukun on the Benue, and the Buduma and Bede of Bornu. The most valuable fishing grounds are normally not in the main streams, but in the lakes and creeks of the floodplains, which contain the floodwater of the main streams in the rainy season. Here chiefs, tribal groups and families have rights to fishing, which they either use themselves or let out to migrant fishing parties. Since fishing is so seasonal an occupation and depends on the different flooding periods throughout the courses of the larger rivers, it frequently involves extensive migration, and the construction of temporary camps on levées or sandbanks.

In the Lake Débo portion of the inland Niger delta, the Bozo and Somono move into fishing camps in December and January as the flood level declines. By April water levels have dropped considerably, the Fulani pastoralists enter the region, the Rimaïbe and Bambara cultivators arrive to fish with handnets, and the Bozo and Somono move away from the lake shore to levées and islands situated nearer the water. Shallow confined waters where the fish are confined behind levées, unable to reach the lowered levels of the main stream, provide the richest fishing grounds. The chief species sought is the 'tinéni', highly valued as a source of edible oil. For a short period fishermen and pastoralists dwell in a form of symbiosis, using neighbouring environments, and effecting an exchange of fish and meat products.[16]

On the Niger, below the gorge of the 'W', the Sorkawa, a fisherman caste of the Songhay, have their permanent bases along 75 miles (120 km) of the river's length from Ayuna to Bagarua, and along the Gulbi-n-Kebbi. Their migrations in search of fish, however, extend from Timbuktu to the coastal delta of the Niger over a distance of 1500 miles (2500 km). The Sorkawa distinguish between the western flood of January to May, which comes from the Upper Niger, and the eastern flood of June to October, which is of local origin in the Niger valley south of the Gulbi-n-Kebbi. In March the Sorkawa leave their bases in the Kebbi region, and move north into Zerma and Songhay as the levels of the western flood decrease. Many of the Sorkawa remain in Songhay until September. The eastern flood reaches its maximum from Kebbi southwards by August, and from September onwards the Sorkawa move southwards to take advantage again of declining flood levels. Navigation of the rapids between Samanadye and Leaba is difficult, and for the Auru rapids a pilot is needed. Canoes move as far south as Onitsha and the delta, and sometimes fishermen stay on the Lower Niger for four years or more. On the lower Volta the Ga and other fishing peoples also migrate seasonally in search of a catch. In southern Dahomey, in the delta of the Ouémé, ditches and canals have been cut, partly for fishing and partly for communication. In some cases they help to separate pasture from arable land.[17]

On Lake Chad the Buduma are the chief fishermen and fish in the rivers of the Shari-Logone delta, together with the Makari, when the waters are low, and in the lake throughout the year. The Buduma use papyrus (*Catagyna papyrus*) tied in bundles to make canoes, make floats of two calabashes joined with a stick, and make rafts, net floats, poles, shields and sandals of ambatch (*Herminiera elaphroxylon*), an extremely light wood. Buduma is a Kanuri name meaning 'people of the grass' for they mainly occupy the islands and peninsulas of the highly indented eastern and northern shores with their abundant papyrus and ambatch. The west shore affords fewer sites suitable for hiding a lakeside settlement, and there the ambatch cannot survive the 'harmattan' wind.

The extraction of minerals

Mining, the working of salt deposits and the panning of gold, were formerly occupations of vital importance in the West African economies. Today these occupations have declined, either due to the activities of modern European-controlled mining companies or to the competition of cheaper or superior imported metals and metal goods. The 'Guinea gold' of Bambouk, the territory of the Falémé basin in Senegal, of Bouré, on the head streams of the Bakhoy, and of Ashanti, was a major export to North Africa and Europe for several centuries. The Falémé workings have declined, and mining in Ashanti is now undertaken by European companies. Workings in Bouré stopped in 1940 when the rice import necessary to feed the miners ceased. As many as 70,000 people had obtained a regular living from the placer gold of the Bakhoy headstreams, of whom about one quarter were solely dependent on mining. As many as 30,000 of those employed were strangers coming from January to July to assist in the workings. The ore was obtained chiefly from pits and shallow galleries, but some panning of the streams took place from July to November.[18] Gold working, chiefly for the internal market, still survives in the numerous small valleys north-west of Ilesha in Yorubaland, and Yoruba goldsmiths have a high reputation for craftsmanship throughout Nigeria. Other alluvial gold workings occur in northern Dahomey and in the south-eastern Ivory Coast. In the Akan states of present-day Ghana gold was mined by pits and shafts and by panning in streams. The gold was exported northwards to Mali and Hausaland, and later southwards to the European trading posts on the coast.

Salt production occupied a place in the economy nearly as important as that of gold, and north-eastern districts, particularly in Northern Nigeria and Niger, still depend largely on locally produced salt rather than on the imported commodity. On the coast the heavy demands of the fish trade for salt for curing purposes are still met largely from local salt. Salt is panned on the coast of Mauritania, and obtained from the inland deposits of Taoudenni, Ijil and N'teret, whilst sea-water is still evaporated for salt in the Ada and Keta districts of Ghana. Rock salt has been cut for at least 1000 years at Taoudenni and Terhaza, valued sources of salt bars for Morocco and for the former states of Ghana and Mali. In Mauritania, Mali and Niger local salt or mixtures of earth and salt have an additional value in providing 'salt licks' for livestock. In Bornu there are salt-making centres in Manga, north-west of Nguru, Yusufari and north-west of Geidam, but the most important source for Bornu and the north-eastern districts generally is the oasis of Bilma. Over an area of 37 acres (15 hectares) more than a thousand small basins have been dug. Salt is extracted between March and October, after the dust storms of the dry season, and before the arrival of the October to December camel caravans bringing millets in exchange.[19] In the Ogoja Province of south-eastern Nigeria there are 'salt lakes' from which the salt is obtained by filtration and evaporation, and wells have been dug to tap brine.[20] Salt is also obtained from numerous vegetable sources in West Africa by burning, filtering water through the ashes and finally boiling. They are used wherever mineral salts are difficult to obtain, as normally the latter are preferred. Particularly important as sources are the aquatic and sub-aquatic plants. The Itsekiri, for example, formerly made salt from the leaves and shoots of the white mangrove, and from the shoots and roots of the red. In the 19th century slaves were employed to cut the mangroves needed for the industry.[21]

Iron mining in shallow pits and small quarries was once widespread in the concretionary ironstones of West Africa, which frequently form superficial deposits of great thickness. Iron smelters and forgers frequently formed and still form separate castes or tribal groups, normally despised by the Sudanic communities and respected by the Guinean.[22] Furnaces are made of clay and may be up to 15 feet (4·5 metres) in height as at Ouahigouya in Mossi territory. The blast is supplied by bellows, normally made of goatskin and operated manually. Fuel is provided by charcoal, produced by the slow burning of local wood under heaps of earth. A few districts managed to achieve more than a local reputation as sources of iron and iron goods. Banjeli, for example, in northern Togo supplied iron ware to the peoples of northern Dahomey and Togo, and to the Ashanti and Mossi. The ore was smelted by the Catalan method of alternate layers of ore and charcoal in furnaces between 6 and 9 feet (2 and 3 metres) in height. So great was the production that neighbouring peoples like the Konkomba produced charcoal for sale in Banjeli to maintain fuel supplies.[23]

Copper, tin, lead, silver, zinc and antimony ores have also been worked in a few districts in West Africa. Copper was worked in the Sahara at Tekada and at Kutu or Kwoto south of the Jos Plateau, where silver was also worked. Antimony was worked by the Jukun, and is still worked today for use as a cosmetic. The remains of old workings in silver, lead and zinc ores have been found at Abakaliki in south-eastern Nigeria and at Tozali near Muri in Northern Nigeria.[24] Tin smelting occurred at Liruei-n-Kano and Liruei-n-Delma in the Jos Plateau until about 1860 and 1910 respectively. The ore was washed from alluvial deposits and poured from the furnaces into clay tubes, made by using local straw as cores. 'Straw tin' was exported to Hausaland in the north and the peoples of the Niger and Benue valley in the south.

It was the sale of this tin that first attracted the attention of the Niger Company's representatives to the possibility of tin mining in the Jos Plateau, and led eventually to the suppression of local tin smelting by the Nigerian Government in the interests of the European mining community.[25]

Gravel and clay are quarried today throughout West Africa for building purposes. Gravels are normally obtained from river terraces, but clays for the manufacture of bricks or for use in making walls commonly occur on level land on hilltops. Since such land is often chosen for settlement sites, many towns and villages contain within the built-up areas the borrow pits from which the building clays were obtained. Kano with its numerous small ponds in borrow pits provides an outstanding example – and a health problem, for small ponds provide breeding grounds for the anopheles mosquito.

Manufactures

Whilst manufactures of all kinds were formerly widespread in West Africa, specialized production on a large scale was mainly confined to the larger states of West Africa, amongst whom the craftsmen were normally organized in guilds, and often located in special quarters within the larger towns.[26] Their products were sold not only in the markets of their own communities, but were exported, often over considerable distances. Formerly such manufacture played a very much more important part in the economic life of West African communities than perhaps it does today. The import of the cheap textiles, cutlery, tools and hollow-ware of Europe, America and later Japan not only destroyed much local industry, forcing the population back on to agriculture, but for a long time prevented any attempt to foster new industrial growth.

The most important traditional manufactures are iron goods and textiles which still flourish amongst many West African communities today, despite the competition of imported goods. Forges for the production of hoe blades, knives, pruning hooks, adzes, axes and spring traps flourish in almost every community. In a very few cases local iron is still used, but in most 'hoop iron' and scrap metal from imported wares is the chief raw material. The making of hoe blades seems likely to remain a local industry for a long time to come, for each community has its own preferred types, and more than 200 different patterns exist in Nigeria alone. Locally made cutting tools are often preferred, because, although usually made of softer iron than imported implements, they are easier for the peasant cultivator to sharpen. The spinning and weaving of locally grown cottons have been long established in West Africa. Cotton is woven on both horizontal and vertical looms. The latter, however, is more widespread and is almost the sole means of weaving cloth amongst Sudanic communities like the Hausa. It produces extremely narrow strips of cloth, often 9 in (23 cm) in width, which must be sewn together to make a robe or a sheet, or cut and sewn to make a hat or cap. Horizontal looms are used to make a variety of widths. The yarn is usually attached to a weight, which drags along the ground as the loom is worked, thus providing tension. Many original weaving designs exist, of which those of the Ashanti, Yoruba, Edo, Akwete Ibo and Hausa are of sufficient merit to find a market outside the regions in which they are produced. For traditional dress, the wearing of which is now increasing amongst the professional and managerial classes, local cloth is preferred and commands high prices. In many cases the local cloth has better wearing qualities than the equivalent imported commodity. In consequence cotton frequently commands a higher price on the internal than on the external market, a factor which has constantly hindered the development of a satisfactory cotton export trade. Cloth is also made from wool, normally imported, and from the hair of West African sheep. Local silk is used for embroidery (see p. 155).

An important industry connected with textiles is the manufacture of vegetable dyes. Blue dyes are made from cultivated *Indigofera* species and from the wild *Lonchocarpus cyanescens*; red dyes from the cultivated grain *Sorghum caudatum var. colorans*; and fawn and black dyes from the pods of *Acacia arabica* and *A. farnesiana*.[27] Imported aniline dyes compete in West African markets, but dye pits, using the local product, are still in widespread use.

Traditional metal manufactures include brass ware, notably amongst the Edo and Nupe, and bronze castings, of which the Ife heads of the Yoruba and the Benin bronzes of the Edo have achieved considerable artistic merit. Other highly skilled manufactures include glass-ware, particularly the beads made by the Nupe (although today the chief raw material consists of imported bottles);

G

jewellery, particularly the gold ornaments made by the Ashanti and Yoruba craftsmen; pottery, an almost universal manufacture; the preparation of calabashes for use as domestic utensils; wood and ivory carving; leather working noted particularly amongst the Hausa, and the weaving of raffia straw and other fibres into bags, hats, baskets and screens.

Additional important non-agricultural occupations which may be classed as manufactures are the building of houses, the construction of canoes by hollowing logs, and the production of rope, twine, fishing lines and nets. Soap making from local vegetable fats and lye is another widespread activity, which has tended to suffer from the competition of imported goods, but the brewing of beer from millet grain in the Sudanic and sub-Sudanic areas and the preparation of palm wine in the Guinean areas are still flourishing industries.

Trading[28]

Trading is probably the least specialized of all non-agricultural occupations. Many cultivators spend a large part of their time in selling goods, not only their own surplus of produce, but commodities of all kinds bought and sold whenever the markets are favourable. 'Africans frequently do not regard trade as an occupation (especially when it is carried on by dependents) and would not refer to it as such. They regard it as part of existence and not as a distinct occupation'.[29] Thus the great majority of the West African population, including even the children, is engaged in a trade, most of which is either local or concerned with making up the bulk for exports or breaking down the bulk of imports. West African producing units are small and income low. In consequence the millions of West African traders play a vital role in distribution. Local and even interregional exchange has always been small scale in a region where the cultivator himself produces the greater part of his own requirements. Thus the small or petty trader system is based on traditional needs and practices, and is described by Bauer as essential in an early stage of distributive economy with low income and low productivity per capita.[30] The tendency in some areas to buy one's requirements for the day only is an important factor. The system is costly in its use of labour, as are most West African forms of production, but is necessary in a region of widely dispersed and low per capita productivity. In some communities the market plays only a small part in the economy – 'peripheral markets' of Bohannan and Dalton – but in many others it plays a dominant role.[30]

Every town and small village has its market or markets, held daily or at regular intervals, often as part of a market system. In Akinyeli village north of Ibadan the market is held every eight days, and on each of six of the remaining seven days the women traders of Akinyeli go to one of the six neighbouring village markets, distributed approximately in a ring round Akinyeli. The remaining day is a day of rest.[32] Other market rings have been observed in Dahomey and in Northern Nigeria.[33] Local produce and the more common manufactures and imported articles are sold in these rural markets. Meat is often sold in specialized markets on the main livestock routes. Towns and large villages frequently possess daily markets in which there is an enormous variety of locally manufactured and imported wares, with permanent stalls, grain mills and booths occupied by tailors, bicycle repairers and blacksmiths. Seasonal variations in the types of goods sold and in the numbers of people frequenting markets are important. Markets are busiest when cultivators have a surplus to sell and cash to buy. In the Egba Division of south-western Nigeria markets are held every four days, and are traditionally situated between 4 and 6 miles (6–10 km) apart, although larger gaps occur today as the number of markets has been reduced by the introduction of motor transport.[34] In the past inter-regional trade was served by caravans operating chiefly from villages situated a few miles outside Abeokuta, the Egba capital. Each caravan was assembled in the village situated on the road leading from Abeokuta to the destination chosen. Caravans travelled as far away as Ilorin in northern Yorubaland, a journey of eleven days, alternating six days of travel with five days of rest.[35] Some of the urban markets are extremely large. For example, in the early 1950's Kumasi central market in Ghana had 15,800 sellers, whilst Aba central market and Onitsha's great market in south-eastern Nigeria had 7–8000 and 6000 sellers respectively.[36]

Amongst some West African communities there are large numbers of people who earn a living solely by trade and exchange of goods between major producing regions. The tendency to latitudinal zoning of crop regions is an important factor. The main markets tend to lie on approximately the same parallel, and the main trade routes are orientated from north to south. Thus Maiduguri, Kano, Jega (once one of the most important of Hausa markets, but by-passed by modern railway and road routes), Fada-n-Gourma and Ouagadougou are all near latitude 12°N., the approximate meeting line of Saharan camel and Sudanic donkey transport, lying only a little south of the northern limit of grain production on lands dependent on rain. From these markets Hausa traders operated caravans to markets on the northern edge of the Guinean zone where kola nuts, oil palm produce, yams and imported goods, particularly textiles, hardware, cutlasses, knives and spirits could be bought. In exchange they brought cloths, livestock, leather goods, salt and antimony. To the north Hausa traders moved across the Sahara to Tripoli in caravans 'protected' by the Tuareg, conveying feathers, skins, ivory, gold and slaves, and bringing back metal goods, glass ware and textiles. Today the trade has changed. The trans-Saharan traffic has declined, but kola nuts and Guinean foodstuffs are moved north by road and railway in exchange for northern goods, particularly livestock. In the west the counterpart of the Hausa is provided by the Dioula who form trading communities in most of the important marketing centres west of Ghana, and organize the kola traffic from Liberia and the Ivory Coast to Senegal and Mali. The 'azalai' or Saharan caravans still function, but mainly as exchangers of commodities between the Sudan and the Saharan oases. Caravans set out from markets like Timbuktu, Sokoto and Kano twice a year, normally in November–December and April–May for the salt-producing oases of Taoudenni and Bilma, carrying grain in exchange for salt and dates. In the 1890's 20,000 camels set out from Timbuktu in November alone, but by 1923 the number had been reduced to 2400.[37] Saharan salt can still compete with the European product in northern markets, partly because of local preferences in flavour.

The chief problems of traders were insecurity, the state of the roads and the medium of exchange. Until the creation of colonial governments insecurity provided a marked hindrance to the operation of caravans which frequently needed armed escorts. Wars were fought to control producing centres like the salt oases of the Sahara, to control markets and to obtain slaves. Thus trade to the coast, to Ashanti and to northern Yorubaland was constantly hindered and reduced by local warfare between the intermediate communities, who endeavoured to act as middlemen and fought one another for the possession of routes and markets. Roads had to be used mainly during the dry season, partly because of their muddy condition in the rains, especially where clays occurred, and partly because many rivers were unfordable when in flood. Only in more developed areas, such as southern Yorubaland, did plank bridges exist. River traffic by canoe was easier and cheaper, but outside the few major rivers – the Senegal, Niger, Benue, Volta and lower Ogun – appears to have been of only minor importance. Most of the great markets and the densely populated areas avoid the valleys, and in consequence cannot be served by water transport. Canoe traffic played an important role, mainly in the early stages of the development of the overseas export trade, particularly in the Senegal, lower Niger, lower Ogun and Cross Rivers, where the canoe fleets of West African middlemen conveyed gum, palm oil and palm kernels. The problem of a medium of exchange appears to have been solved in the 15th and 16th centuries, when European direct trade by sea began, by means of barter. However, there were many situations, due mainly to differences in seasonal productivity, where barter was unsatisfactory or impossible. Arab merchants trading across the Sahara used letters of credit, but amongst communities lacking writing some kind of money was essential, and a vast variety of different kinds has been used. In order to satisfy the demands of small-scale local trading the 'money' had to consist of extremely small units. Cowrie shells, imported from India, for example, were a common currency in the 19th century, but so low did their value become towards the end of the century that the weight of cowrie shells was frequently nearly as great as the weight of the purchases made.[38] Large numbers of people were employed in the markets to count the cowrie shells needed for major purchases. Other forms of currency have included slaves, iron bars, copper wire, manillas, trade spirits, pieces of cloth, gold dust, silver, Louis-Napoleons and Maria-Theresa dollars.

The traditional forms of transport

The traditional forms of transport in West Africa have differed from those common in other continents in two important respects. Firstly, over wide areas pack animals of any kind are unknown; secondly, there has been no traditional use of the wheel. The absence of pack animals in the southern part of the region follows from problems of fodder and disease (although horses were used for riding, and horse-drawn carts have been used between the European settlements in southern Ghana), but in the north camels, donkeys and oxen are still used. The importance of the camel in the trans-Saharan trade needs no emphasis, and the organization of the caravans has been described by Bovill.[39] Barth[40] refers to a steady speed of $2\frac{1}{2}$ miles (4 km) per hour by camel caravans in the Sahara, which is no mean rate of progress for pack animals under desert conditions, and it is still possible to see caravans moving at this speed to or from the northern markets such as Kano. Indeed, for the carriage of goods between Kano and centres such as Bilma, the camel caravan is possibly still easier to organize and to maintain than is motorized transport. The ox as a pack animal is used for the transport of tents and personal baggage by Fulani herdsmen moving cattle to new pastures. The donkey is the more common beast of burden, both for loads and for passengers riding bareback, and seated over the hind legs. Horses have usually been too valuable to be used as pack or draft animals. In the past they have been the basis of the state's cavalry power, and today are still symbols of class and prestige.

The wheel has usually been regarded as absent from West Africa before the advent of the Europeans. The Naval Intelligence Division handbook on French West Africa, Volume 1 (1943) says, 'Neither the Negroes nor the invaders from the north used wheeled transport.' More recently, however, Lhote has mapped the sites of paintings and engravings of wheeled chariots from Tripoli to Gao by way of Ghadames, the Hoggar and the Tanezrouft, and suggests that this was an established routeway five centuries before Christ, if not earlier.[41]. He also identifies place-names along the route with those cited by Pliny in describing the triumph of Cornelius Balbus. Whether or not these hypotheses are true, there is no doubt that knowledge of wheeled vehicles extended to the Niger bend. The subsequent disappearance of the wheel is therefore of particular interest. It can be argued that wheeled vehicles would not have been suitable for wet-season movement along muddy tracks, but the wet season is short along the northern margins, and mud would impede carts less than in Western Europe. The absence of paved roads is no explanation, as this applied also in other continents. It might have been expected that the wheelbarrow, at least, might have developed in West Africa, where it would have been suitable even in the forested southern districts where it could have been used on narrow paths. Pedler refers to one-wheeled chariots, constructed on the wheelbarrow principle, in which chiefs in Sierra Leone were pushed along bush paths, but no details of the origin of these vehicles are given, and they may have evolved only after the reintroduction of the wheel through Freetown. Pedler also mentions that middlemen trading in palm oil prefer the wooden cask to the more durable metal drum because the former has convex sides which permit it to be rolled easily along paths as if it were a one-wheeled container.[42] The widespread use of the bicycle in recent years, particularly for the transport of freight along forest paths, is a further indication of the suitability of simple wheeled transport for West African conditions. It is possible that West Africans failed to develop the wheel because it arrived too soon for it to be of practical value to them, and had been forgotten before their social structure had progressed to a point at which the interchange of bulky produce made vehicles desirable. The subjects in feudal savanna states, living by 'subsistence agriculture', did not need to move quantities greater than those which

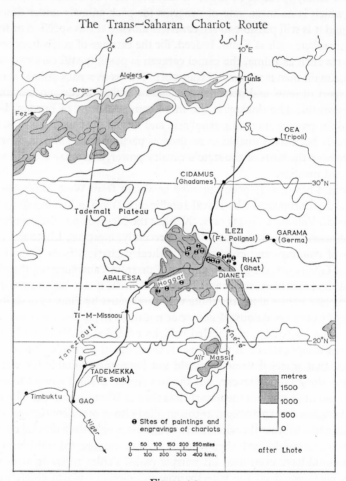

Figure 4.2

could be carried by donkey or by their own head-porterage; rulers could, if necessary, move larger quantities by using more animals or by impressed or slave carriers. The heavy loads of early Europe – stone and timber – were not required in a region where architecture did not have to contend with the problem of severe winter cold, and where more malleable building material than stone was readily available. Whatever the reason may have been, the wheel did not reappear, notwithstanding the trading contacts with the Mediterranean lands and with the eastern Sudan.

Over most of West Africa the common form of freight movement was by head-load porterage, and this remains the standard method of carriage of personal belongings even in the larger cities. In places the load may be carried on the shoulder, as in parts of Kontagora emirate in Northern Nigeria, where it is balanced on a type of staging made from an inverted calabash, but the usual practice is head carriage on a small pad of cloth or grass. A light-weight object such as a bottle or a bowl may require neither pad nor supporting hand, and is maintained in position by the superb sense of balance which most West Africans appear to possess. Normal individuals have no difficulty in carrying a head-load of 56 lb (25 kilos) for a daily distance of 15–20 miles (24–32 km), and this was the average basis on which carrier transport was employed in British territories and on which daily wage rates were calculated. Individuals with moderate loads will sometimes cover much greater daily distances: professional carriers could succeed in walking 40–50 miles (65–80 km) in a day if the spacing of villages or of water supplies necessitated this. Porterage has been described as a social evil, a political danger and an economic waste.[43] The first two of these comments should not be overstressed: under normal conditions the number of employed carriers was probably small before commercial crops were grown, and porterage was possibly no more damaging to the moral or political structure than the existence of travelling traders in medieval Europe. Only when carriers were required in great numbers, in the 20th century, did the problem begin to present itself, and it has already been cured by the economic necessity of developing other forms of transport. That porterage is economically wasteful is beyond doubt. It has always been an exceedingly costly form of transport. On the basis of a daily wage of 1s. 6d. (U.S. $0.21), the rate per ton/mile is approximately 2s. to 2s. 6d. ($0.17–$0.22 per ton/km); a wage increase to 5s. ($0.70) per day raised the transport costs to approximately 10s. to 12s. 6d. per ton/mile ($0.88–$1.10 per ton/km), which is a wholly uneconomic rate in relation to road haulage costs. Lugard has referred to head-porterage as an archaic and wasteful form of transport;[44] Hailey mentions that in the First World War the French employed 125,000 carriers to move 4200 tons of foodstuffs, and quotes an East African example where carriers moving loads over a distance of 500 miles (800 km) ate nearly all that they carried.[45] Unless the load carried has a high value/weight ratio, the distance over which it is economic to move freight is very low.

On the great rivers and in the coastal creeks and the lagoons movement has always been by water-craft. The most common form of vessel has been the canoe made from a hollowed tree-trunk, usually propelled by paddles in deep water and by use of a long pole in shallow reaches. These canoes can be of very considerable size, capable of carrying several tons of cargo and requiring a dozen or more paddlers when used in surf water. On the Niger and Bani boats made of planks stitched or nailed together appear to have been used for some considerable time. They can carry up to two tons of freight with a draught of only 4 in. (10 cm).[46]

Sails are not extensively used: on the sheltered lagoon waters small sails may be used, but strong stepped masts are rarely seen with indigenous craft. The sea-going boats, used mainly for fishing, similarly did not use sails as a regular feature. There may be several reasons for this lack of sail development. One is that the sheltered waterways of the lagoon and creek systems provided easy passage for craft of simple construction, and there was perhaps no incentive to venture into the rough ocean waters, nor to develop more advanced and complicated designs. A second reason is that when canoes did venture into the open ocean the heavy surf necessitated considerable man power (as well as skill in boat-handling) to get the craft to or from the beach. This involved maximum effort with paddles, which could not have been achieved with decked vessels, and so the advanced skills of handling sails, which inevitably follow from the decking of ships, were never forced upon the coastal peoples.

On inland waters there may still be found alternatives to the canoe, such as rectangular rafts, or the circular coracles used in the Ivory Coast. In some areas no boats of any type were built until very recently, and rivers were crossed precariously by lying on inverted calabashes or air-filled bladders, and paddling with arms and legs.

Slavery

Whilst the greater part of the labour force used in production and distribution consisted of free-men, slaves have long played an important part in the West African economy as labourers, as a medium of exchange, and as a trading commodity. The effect of slavery is still felt in the economy and in social organization today. Despite ordinances prohibiting slavery (passed in Southern Nigeria as late as 1916), many thousands of West Africans today may still be regarded socially as slaves or as inferiors because they are the descendants of slaves.

The chief use of slaves was as an export commodity to the Americas and North Africa (see p. 387), and as carriers on the major inter-regional trade routes. The value of a slave in West Africa was in fact proportional to his or her carrying powers.[47] Slaves were, however, used in large numbers in the kola nut plantations of Ashanti, in the food 'farms' of Ondo in south-western Nigeria and in northern Iboland, as diggers of wells in the Sahel and Sudan, as builders and maintainers of city walls, as cultivators in the large estates created by the rulers of the Sudanic states, particularly in Hausaland, and as cultivators and herdsmen of the Fulani of Fouta Djallon, Macina and elsewhere. Emancipation resulted in a severe disruption of the economy of Northern Nigeria in the period 1900–10, when vast numbers of slaves abandoned the cultivated lands of Sokoto, Kano and Zaria to return to their old homes. Many Sahelian villages, dependent on wells dug by slaves to depths as great as 100 feet (30 metres) or more, had to be abandoned when the labour force necessary for well maintenance was no longer available. Town walls were eroded away even without the edicts of authority against their maintenance. In the south emancipation frequently meant that the villages of the slaves became richer than those of their former masters, amongst whom agriculture was despised. Religious slaves, for example the 'osu' of Iboland, still play a part wherever traditional ritual is practised, and have been regarded as a distinct social group by the rest of the community.

BIBLIOGRAPHICAL NOTES

[1] Notes et Documents, *Bulletin, Institut Français d'Afrique Noire*, **16**, 1954, pp. 178–84.

[2] A. Schultze, *The Sultanate of Bornu*, trans. by P. A. Benton, London, 1913.

[3] J. M. Dalziel, *The Useful Plants of West Tropical Africa*, London, 1937, pp. 491–2. Much of the following material is based on this work. A comprehensive list of useful wild plants is in R. Schnell, *Plantes Alimentaires et Vie Agricole de l'Afrique Noire*, Paris, 1957, pp. 84–99 and 123–32.

[4] A. Chevalier, Sur un Igname Sauvage de l'Ouest Africain, *Revue de Botanique Appliquée et d'Agriculture Tropicale*, **29**, 1949, pp. 609–12.

[5] E. Guernier (ed.), *Encyclopédie de la France d'Outre-Mer*, Afrique Occidentale Française, Tome I, Paris, 1949, p. 136.

[6] J. M. Dalziel, op. cit., pp. 137, 138, 195, 201 and 281.
O. Temple, *Notes on the Tribes, Provinces, Emirates and States of the Northern Provinces of Nigeria*, 1922, pp. 413–14.
F. D. Golding, The Wild Silkworms of Nigeria, *Farm and Forest*, **3**, 1942, pp. 35–40.

[7] D. R. Rosevear, *Checklist and Atlas of Nigerian Mammals*, Lagos, 1953, p. 15. This book has been used extensively as a source of material for the hunting section.

[8] E. Ardener, *Coastal Bantu of the Cameroons*, London, 1956, p. 44.

[9] *Encyclopédie de la France d'Outre-Mer*, op. cit., Afrique Occidentale Française, Tome II, p. 178.

[10] J. Arnoux, Note sur la Pêche de Kayar, *Bulletin des Services de l'Elevage et des Industries Animales de l'A.O.F.*, **5**, 1952, pp. 41–53.

[11] A. Blanc, Les Clupéidés de la Petite Côte (Sénégal), *Bulletin des Services de l'Elevage et des Industries Animales de l'A.O.F.*, **2**, 1949, pp. 47–51.

[12] E. A. Salzen, Observation on the Biology of the West African Shad, *Ethmalosa fimbriata*, *Bulletin, Institut Français d'Afrique Noire*, **20A**, 1958, pp. 1388–426.
E. Postel, Note sur *Ethmalosa fimbriata*, *Bulletin des Services de l'Elevage et des Industries Animales de l'A.O.F.*, **3**, 1950, pp. 45–49.
A. R. Longhurst, Local Movements of *Ethmalosa fimbriata* off Sierra Leone from Tagging Data, *Bulletin, Institut Français d'Afrique Noire*, **22A**, 1960, pp. 1337–40.

[13] F. R. Irvine, *The Fish and Fisheries of the Gold Coast*, London, 1947, p. 19. For the Ghana fisheries see also W. Manshard, Die Küsten und Flussfischerei Ghanas, *Die Erde*, **89**, 1958, pp. 21–33.

[14] A. P. Brown, The Fishing Industry of the Labadi District, in F. R. Irvine, *The Fish and Fisheries of the Gold Coast*, 1947, pp. 24–44.

[15] A. Guilcher, La Région Côtière du Bas-Dahomey Occidental, *Bulletin, Institut Français d'Afrique Noire*, **21B**, 1959, pp. 357–424.

[16] See J. Gallais, La Vie Saisonnière au Sud du Lac Débo, *Les Cahiers d'Outre-Mer*, **11**, 1958, pp. 117–41.

[17] Comments on the Sorkawa are based on J. Rouch, Les Sorkawa Pêcheurs Itinérants du Moyen Niger, *Africa*, **20**, 1950, pp. 5–25.
The fishing ditches of southern Dahomey are described in J. Hurault, *Les Principaux Types de Peuplement au sud-est de Dahomey*, Institut Géographique National, Paris, 1965, especially pp. 50–52.

[18] See *French West Africa*, Naval Intelligence Handbook, B.R. 512, Vol. I, 1944, pp. 288–9.
J. Richard-Molard, *Afrique Occidentale Française*, Paris, 1949, p. 195.
H. Labouret, *Paysans d'Afrique Occidentale*, Paris, 1941, p. 220.

[19] Capt. Grandin, Notes sur l'Industrie et le Commerce du Sel au Kawar et en Agram, *Bulletin, Institut Français d'Afrique Noire*, **13**, 1951, pp. 488–533.

[20] J. W. Wallace, Note on the Salt Industry of Ogoja Province, in Agriculture in Abakaliki and Afikpo, *Farm and Forest*, **2**, 1941, pp. 89–93.

[21] R. Portères, *Cendres d'Origine Végétale*, Gouvernement Générale de l'A.O.F., Direction Générale de la Santé Publique, Organisme d'Enquête pour l'Etude Anthropologique des Populations Indigènes de l'A.O.F., Dakar, 1950.
P. C. Lloyd, The Itsekiri, in R. E. Bradbury, *The Benin Kingdom*, London, 1957, p. 175.

[22] P. Clement, Le Forgeron en Afrique Noire, *La Revue de Géographie Humaine et d'Ethnologie*, No. 2, 1948, pp. 35–58.

[23] J. C. Froelich, La Tribu Konkomba du Nord Togo, *Mémoires, Institut Français d'Afrique Noire*, **37**, 1954, pp. 39–48.

[24] Colonial Annual Reports, 704, *Northern Nigeria*, 1910–11, p. 74.

[25] J. D. Falconer and C. Raeburn, The Northern Tinfields of Bauchi Province, *Geological Survey of Nigeria, Bulletin 4*, 1923, pp. 43–45.

[26] P. C. Lloyd, Craft Organisation in Yoruba Towns, *Africa*, 1953, pp. 30–44.
R. E. Bradbury, *The Benin Kingdom*, London, 1957, pp. 26 and 34–35.
E. P. Skinner, West African Economic Systems, in M. J. Herskovits and M. Harwitz, *Economic Transition in Africa*, London, 1964, pp. 77–97.

[27] J. M. Dalziel, op. cit.

[28] An excellent account of trading and trade routes at the beginnings of European occupation is given in E. Baillaud, *Sur les Routes du Soudan*, Paris, 1902.

[29] P. T. Bauer, *West African Trade*, London, 1954, p. 11.

[30] ibid., pp. 27–29.

[31] For an important study with some valuable essays on West Africa, see P. Bohannan and G. Dalton, *Markets in Africa*, Evanston, 1962.

[32] B. W. Hodder, The Yoruba Rural Market Ring, University College, Ibadan, Department of Geography, *Research Notes*, **12**, 1959, pp. 29–36.
B. W. Hodder, Rural Periodic Day Markets in Part of Yorubaland, Western Nigeria, *Transactions & Papers, Institute of British Geographers*, **29**, 1961, pp. 149–59.

[33] P. Verger and R. Bastide, *Le Réseau des Marchés Nago (Dahomey)*, Nigerian Institute of Social and Economic Research, Conference, 1958.
M. G. Smith, *The Economy of Hausa Communities of Zaria*, Report, Colonial Scientific Research Council, 1955.

[34] A. L. Mabogunje, *The Changing Pattern of Rural Settlement and Rural Economy in Egba Division, South-Western Nigeria*, unpub. M.A. Thesis, University of London, 1958, pp. 113–20.

[35] ibid., pp. 109–11. 12 days are given for the journey to Ilorin in the original script, but a journey of alternating days of rest and travel must comprise an odd number of days.

[36] F. J. Pedler, *Economic Geography of West Africa*, London, 1955, pp. 139–40.

[37] Naval Intelligence Handbook, op. cit., Vol. II, pp. 209–10 and 378.

[38] One factor in devaluation was the considerable import of cowrie shells from India for use in the purchase of stores for British Naval Vessels.

[39] E. W. Bovill, *The Golden Trade of the Moors*, London, 1958 (a revised form of *Caravans of the Old Sahara*, 1933).

[40] H. Barth, *Travels and Discoveries in North and Central Africa*, London, 1857.

[41] H. Lhote, *The Search for the Tassili Frescoes*, London, 1959, pp. 122–33 and map p. 22.

[42] F. J. Pedler, op. cit., p. 112.

[43] R. J. Harrison Church, *West Africa*, London, 5th ed., 1966, p. 153.

[44] Sir F. D. Lugard, *The Dual Mandate in British Tropical Africa*, London, 1926, p. 474.

[45] Lord Hailey, *An African Survey*, revised 1956, London, 1957, p. 1536.

[46] E. Baillaud, op. cit., pp. 73–74.

[47] A. McPhee, *The Economic Revolution in British West Africa*, London, 1926, pp. 234–235.

CHAPTER 5

The Major Environmental Factors

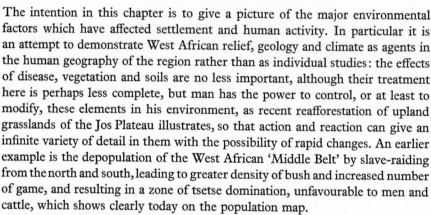

The intention in this chapter is to give a picture of the major environmental factors which have affected settlement and human activity. In particular it is an attempt to demonstrate West African relief, geology and climate as agents in the human geography of the region rather than as individual studies: the effects of disease, vegetation and soils are no less important, although their treatment here is perhaps less complete, but man has the power to control, or at least to modify, these elements in his environment, as recent reafforestation of upland grasslands of the Jos Plateau illustrates, so that action and reaction can give an infinite variety of detail in them with the possibility of rapid changes. An earlier example is the depopulation of the West African 'Middle Belt' by slave-raiding from the north and south, leading to greater density of bush and increased number of game, and resulting in a zone of tsetse domination, unfavourable to men and cattle, which shows clearly today on the population map.

The limitations on existence in West Africa in the second half of the 20th century are few. Given sufficient of the benefits of technological development, man can exist even in the Sahara in considerable comfort. Air-conditioned housing, fresh food supplies brought by aircraft, fresh water carried in special tankers, all contribute to a life which is comfortable even if unattractive to many, and extend and eliminate the boundaries of civilized existence. Primitive man was interested only in simple existence in the first instance, and recognized very clear boundaries beyond which this was not possible. The modern peasant is perhaps less conscious of the limitations, because of settled social conditions and of plants which can give him yields capable of keeping himself and his family, with the added security of modern communications to bring aid in case of disaster.

The original southern limit of settlement was the coast, to those who penetrated so far or who were driven to it. The northern limit was less clearly defined than it is today in terms of general or scattered settlement. Careful reproductions of Saharan rock paintings[1] confirm the greater humidity of the desert in prehistoric time, and show that existence was possible in many areas which today are almost completely arid. Not only was it possible, but in terms of life at the time it was probably comfortable and 'civilized', in that men would not have created these artistic works if resources had been so strained that every working hour was to be thought of as essential hunting time. The people living in what were then watered grasslands had sufficient leisure and cultural standards for

176

art to be an appreciated form of expression. According to Büdel,[2] the desert and desert steppe, which today stretches from about 12° N. to 32° N., would have been narrowed to a belt between 15° N. and 28° N. during the Würm glaciation. Today human activity continues well north of the 12° parallel, and in a more humid period may have extended well to the north of the 15° parallel. A latitude

Tassili Rock Paintings

after Lhote

Figure 5.1

value of 12° (or 15°) is, of course, arbitrary, as the climatic and vegetational boundaries in West Africa tend to be aligned not along the parallels but along a line progressively further south as one moves from west to east. The frescoes mentioned are in the highland areas of the central Sahara, where rainfall can be expected to have been heavier than on the lower ground, so that it is not implied that even a pastoral life existed across the whole of what is now desert. Nevertheless, with paintings of large herds of cattle, pictures of giraffe, antelope and hippopotami, it is clear that the present arid conditions were more restricted in prehistoric time than is now the case. This desiccation is clearly demonstrated within historical time. Such extensive medieval empires as Ghana, Mali and Songhay flourished in areas which would not be thought capable of supporting them today, and there is little doubt that the northern limit of settlement has retreated in the last few thousand years, although too much stress should not be laid upon this evidence of shifting empires. Farmer[3] has reminded us that Asian history shows capital cities 'in a sea of aridity in which there was nothing but nomadic population'. In the case of ancient Ghana, the Arab chronicler Bekri in the 11th century speaks of vast and prosperous fields,[4] implying a genuine desiccation since that date. This does not involve acceptance of Stebbing's hypothesis of the southward extension of the Sahara.[5] The northern limit of habitable West Africa has oscillated repeatedly, and a series of humid and dry periods have been identified.[6] The evidence of former humidity in the desert can be matched by evidence of past aridity in the savanna lands, as in the dead erg of Northern Nigeria described by Grove.[7]

Within historic time, most of the Sahara has been of no interest to West Africans, apart from the recognized caravan routes. The most significant of these was probably that in the west, coming southward from Morocco to Mauritania. By this route the Fulani may have reached West Africa. This and the routes further to the east remained important until the 20th century, when the diversion of trade southwards to the coast reduced the strength of the Saharan caravans and the quantities of produce carried by them. It became impossible to maintain all the watering points along these desert routes, as fewer travellers were prepared to contribute to the cost and slave labour was no longer available. Only the major routes, on which seasonal motor services operated, were to retain any importance.

Because the desert formed a northern limit to settlement, and the coast formed the southern limit, penetration by successive waves of migrants was necessarily from east to west in most cases. It is possible that the southern limit preferred by primitive man was not the coast, but the high forest margin. Difficulties of clearing would possibly make the dense forest less attractive than the more open woodland of the savanna areas. The density of undergrowth varies with the age of the forest as well as with the rainfall. Mature high forest may have relatively little undergrowth, and movement in the drier areas is not unduly difficult, as is shown by the existence of animals such as the African Forest Elephant (*Loxodonta cyclotis*), the West African Bushbuck (*Tragelaphus scriptus*) and the Bushcow (*Syncerus nanus*). Secondary growth, especially in the wetter areas, may be almost impenetrable for a time, when the access of sunlight, following the falling of a single large tree, leads to fierce competition between plants. The ground layer of vegetation may be more dense in the savanna than in mature high forest, but it may be argued that the latter is more difficult to clear for farmland. The tendency would therefore appear to be movement in a direction from north-east towards the south-west, the southerly component being assumed to appear if any wave, moving from east to west, was stronger than its predecessor and displaced it, not only westward but also southward into the forest zone, along the natural corridors of more open vegetation. Many West African peoples, even strong groups now on the coast such as the Yoruba, have a tradition of movement towards the south-west, even though this may be coupled with legends of local origin, such as that of Ife in the example mentioned. Among the more southerly peoples, an exception to this type of myth is the Tiv of the Middle Benue valley, whose history is discussed later (pp. 323–8).

Optimum living conditions would therefore appear to have lain between the desert and the high forest. Both these limits are reflections of climate, and in particular of moisture. Temperatures in West Africa can be said never to fall below the minimum for plant growth, although rarely they may do so for a few nights in October or November in the more northerly latitudes. Snow never falls, the freezing level over the region being at about 16,000 feet (4880 metres), and the highest point being 13,350 feet (4069 metres) on Mount Cameroon, where a few very short-lived falls have been recorded in exceptional storms. The vegetation is therefore not restricted by temperature to a growing season and a rest period, but may be forced into a seasonal rhythm by the presence or absence of water.

The rainfall of West Africa depends upon the interaction of three major air masses. Of these two are normally in contact with the ground, the Tropical Maritime and the Tropical Continental, the two meeting along the Inter-Tropical Convergence Zone (I.T.C.Z.). The former is warm, moist air which over West Africa blows inland in a general south-west to north-east direction from the ocean, and which has a very high relative humidity: Warri, in the Niger delta, and lying under this air mass throughout the year, shows mean monthly values of relative humidity between 95 and 99 per cent at 06.00 hours, and between 65 and 82 per cent at 12.00 hours. The latter air mass is warm and dry, blowing in the opposite direction, from the desert, with a very low relative humidity: Sokoto for the five months December to April inclusive shows mean monthly values between 23 and 38 per cent at 06.00 hours, and between 10 and 17 per cent at 12.00 hours. The Tropical Continental air overrides the Tropical Maritime to give the latter a wedged shape increasing in thickness southward. The sloping upper surface of the wedge has an average gradient of about 1:300, although steeper near the ground. Rain does not usually occur unless the wedge is about 5000 feet (1525 metres) thick, several hundred miles to the south of the location of the I.T.C.Z. on the ground surface. Rain occasionally falls in the areas covered by the shallow section of the wedge, but more often any cumulus clouds forming here are seen to dry out, and to disappear as their upper parts feel the effects of mixing with the dry upper air. Figure 5.2, after Garnier,[8] shows the pattern of rain belts across Nigeria at two seasons. South of the rain belt is a zone in which cloud amount remains high, but there is a considerable reduction in precipitation. This results from a marked inversion, which is at about 3000 feet (915 metres) in the south-east trades, and which is carried into West Africa (where it occurs at 6–7000 feet (1830–2130 metres)) from the south-west, following deflection north of the equator. Crowe[9] remarks that in July, when this 'dry belt' appears in West Africa, the south-east trades are at their strongest and the waters beneath them are at their coolest, so that the inversion is not dispersed on crossing the equator 'but roofs over the whole strong southerly air stream. Such a "roof" may be penetrated in three chief ways – (i) where a gigantic relief feature like Mount Cameroun (13,350 feet) bodily protrudes through the inversion and stimulates convectional overturnings around its flanks . . .; (ii) where more

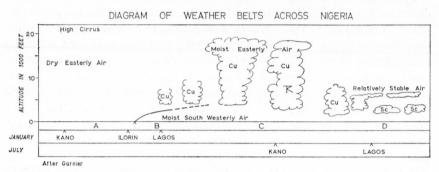

Figure 5.2

moderate elevations like the Fouta Jallon Plateau are encountered by strong persistent winds . . .; and (iii) by surface heating over a continental interior. . . .'

The dry belt in the Tropical Maritime air mass has important consequences. It leads to a 'little dry season' between two rainfall maxima in wet seasons, and this, if unduly prolonged, may have disastrous results agriculturally. Also the amount of rain dropped in the southern districts, by the double passage north and south of the wet zone, may be less than the amount dropped where the wet zone arrives, slows, halts and departs. It follows that the maximum mean rainfall totals will therefore tend to be not in the coastal districts experiencing Tropical Maritime air throughout the year, but in those parts of West Africa which lie a little to the north of the inversion zone at its greatest extent, that is, a little to the north of the transition from 2-peak to 1-peak rainfall régimes. In this zone the average intensity of rainfall may be at a maximum, as not only is the annual total greater than in the coastal regions, but the length of the wet season is less than it is further to the south.

The rainfall experienced at any place thus clearly depends upon its position at the time in relation to the I.T.C.Z., and the seasonal migration of the latter is therefore of the greatest significance. Over the main north–south mass of Africa the zone moves from about 20° N. in July to about 20° S. in January, but over West Africa the zone lies north of the coast everywhere east of Cape Palmas. These coastal lands therefore retain their high relative humidity throughout the whole year, even though in December and January rainfall may be very slight.

At Lagos the harmattan, the dry north-east wind representing Tropical Continental air at the surface, breaks through to the coast on only one or two days in a year, although 20 miles (32 km) inland it is much more common. Crowe quotes Solot[10] as implying that in these months no I.T.C.Z. exists in West Africa, and

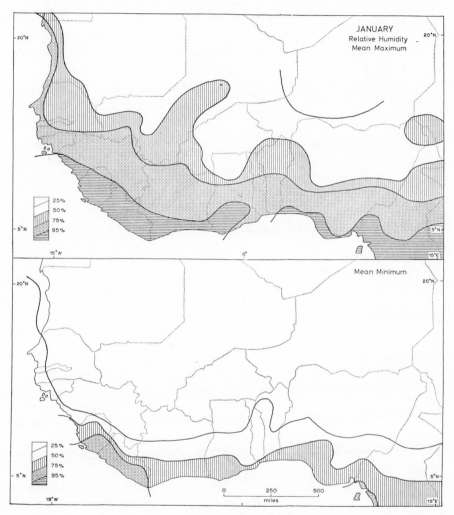

Figure 5.3

Garbell[11] as implying the zone to be present but inert. Crowe suggests that the wedge of humid air at this time is possibly no more than a rather widespread sea breeze, which has become recognizable owing to the general weakness of the circulation. This is not unreasonable, as sea-breeze effects can be felt up to 50 miles (80 km) from the coast when well-established. The wedge is too thin at this season to allow much cloud development, so that the inhabitants of the coastal districts have in the early months of the year a combination of high temperatures (mean daily maxima above 90°F. (32°C.)) with high relative humidity, which is much more exhausting than the combination of high temperature and low relative humidity experienced to the north of the I.T.C.Z. As the wedge is

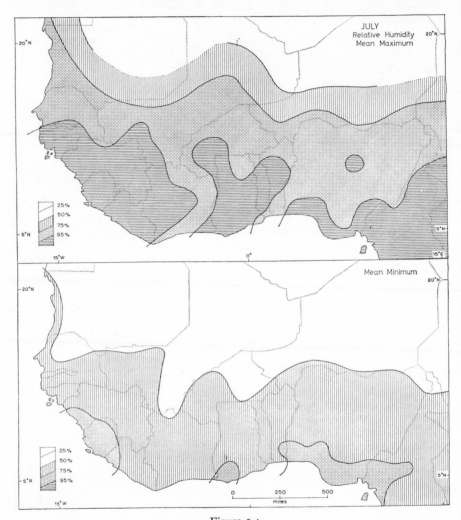

Figure 5.4

too thin to permit cumulus clouds to form, rainfall is slight, mean values for January being only 1·5 in (38 mm) in Tabou (Ivory Coast) which has a mean annual total of over 92 in (2340 mm), and 1·5 in (38 mm) in Warri (Niger delta) which has over 108 in (2750 mm) in an average year. Even at Debundscha, on the western side of Mount Cameroon, the January rainfall is less than 10 in (250 mm) although the mean annual total is of the order of 400 in (10,150 mm).

North-west of Cape Palmas it is clear that the land in January is north of the I.T.C.Z., and lies under the influence of the Tropical Continental air mass. Relative humidities along the coast may still be high west of the Fouta Djallon and the Guinea Highlands, of the order 80–85 per cent at dawn, but this is principally the result of breezes off the sea, and the protection of the highlands against the dry north-east winds. In the short distance between Conakry and Boké, along the coastal lowlands of Guinea, there is a difference in mean monthly relative humidity (6.00 p.m. values) for the first three months of the year, between 68 and 69 per cent at Conakry, and 41 and 46 per cent at Boké. The lower values continue north-westward to the southern coast of Senegal, but from Dakar northward the mean values are slightly higher, due to the effects of sea breezes blowing in from the Atlantic in the afternoons, raising the humidity and lowering the temperature.* The cool Canary current, flowing north to south, is a contributory factor to the early morning mists and fogs along this stretch of coast, most noticeable when the I.T.C.Z. is in the area and winds are indeterminate in character.

In the areas immediately south of the I.T.C.Z. contact with the ground, convection rain rarely occurs for the reason stated above, namely lack of depth in the wedge of humid air. The rain that comes is in the form of line squalls, which are localized disturbances rarely exceeding 150 miles (240 km) in diameter. Squalls tend to approach from the east or north-east at a speed of 30–40 miles (48–64 km) per hour, and the tracks of individual squalls can sometimes be plotted over long distances. A squall is frequently preceded by several days of uncomfortable heat and humidity, and clouds may build up on successive afternoons only to evaporate in the evenings. Once established, the squall moves steadily with intense lightning and thunder, presaged by a few minutes of high winds with velocities up to 60 miles (100 km) per hour. The rain front can be seen approaching as a curtain of water, and for the first ten minutes the rainfall is intense, occasionally reaching values of 6 or 8 in (150–200 mm) per hour for very short spells. After about ten minutes, the intensity diminishes, and steady rain may fall to give an inch (25 mm) or more of precipitation in the succeeding hour. The rain is accompanied by a fall in temperature.[12] The lateral margins of a squall are also sharply defined, so that while one place receives an inch (25 mm) or more of rain, another place, only a mile away, may receive nothing. The cause of the line squalls is not known for certain, but it has been suggested[13] that they are due to the action of a third air mass, the cool Equatorial Easterlies of higher altitudes. If, for any reason, these upper winds are deflected downwards, they will cause disturbances in the lower layers of the atmosphere. If a wedge of humid air is present, the Easterlies may 'undercut' the south-west winds, causing the upward motion of warm moist air, with attendant thundercloud formation. The east to west

---

* Strictly speaking, the sea breeze is too weak to overcome the Trade Winds. The sea breeze merely deflects the Trades to blow from a northerly direction, which makes air movement on the coast slightly on-shore in the afternoons. The morning land breeze effect causes an east to west movement.

passage of squalls, the intense rain front, and the lowering of temperature all accord with such an origin. This intervention in severe form is restricted to the period when the humid wedge is thin and the Easterlies are within range, that is to the beginning and end of the rainy season. In the dry season similar disturbances may be the cause of 'dust devils', although these are of much less intensity and on a small scale; the harmattan and the upper winds both having an easterly component have less interaction, and the extreme dryness of the Tropical Continental air means that clouds and rain cannot develop unless a very intense disturbance carries the lower air to very great heights. When rain falls from these very high clouds it rarely reaches the ground, but can be seen to disappear on its downward passage into warmer and drier air. However, the disturbance in the Easterlies is not necessarily as simple as this. The upper air need not penetrate to ground level, but may develop wave forms, moving from east to west, within itself; following intensive heating of the ground the surface layer, itself potentially unstable, may be overlain by unstable air within the wave form, leading to thundercloud development.[14]

The movement of the I.T.C.Z. therefore determines not only the length of the wet season, but also the type of rain experienced. It is clear that line squall rain is far less reliable than the steadier rainfall coming from convectional heating of a thick layer of humid air. The former is unreliable not only in time but also in space, on account of the routing of individual squalls along narrow tracks. The early rains are of great importance to a peasant farming community. At the end of the dry season the surface may be brick-hard, and the first squall of the year may drop 2 in (50 mm) of rain without dampening the soil a few inches below the surface. The ground is too hard for percolation to take place. Several squalls are necessary before the soil can be regarded as moist, even if the ground has been prepared in advance. In an area where the I.T.C.Z. is in movement, line squall rain will moisten the soil, assist the germination of seed, and will nourish the seedlings before giving place to the steadier and less violent rain of the main Tropical Maritime air mass. In regions where the I.T.C.Z. is stationary or indeterminate for a considerable period, or in any district where the northward movement of the I.T.C.Z. is for any reason temporarily checked, the line squall rain may be the only form of precipitation for the first few months of the wet season. In such a case agriculture is precarious. The early squalls may have dampened the soil sufficiently to encourage a farmer in the belief that the rains have become established. A 2 in (50 mm) squall on the first day of April may lead him to plant out his seed, which may germinate, sprout and shoot, only to wither and die for subsequent lack of rain. Rain in the latter days of the month may lead to the planting of reserve seed, the shoots of which may be beaten into the ground by a series of severe squalls. April may have had rainfall well above average, and yet the first sowing has been lost through drought, and the second may be destroyed by rain or even similarly by drought. The seasonal oscillation of the I.T.C.Z. is therefore an important factor in determining the suitability or otherwise of an area for assured agricultural occupation. It is sometimes stated

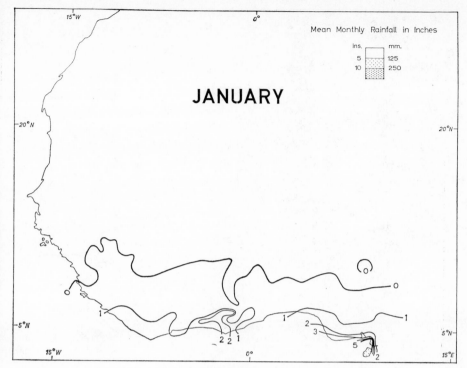

Figure 5.5*a*

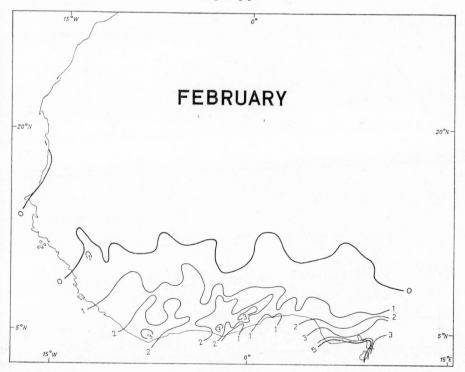

Figure 5.5*b*

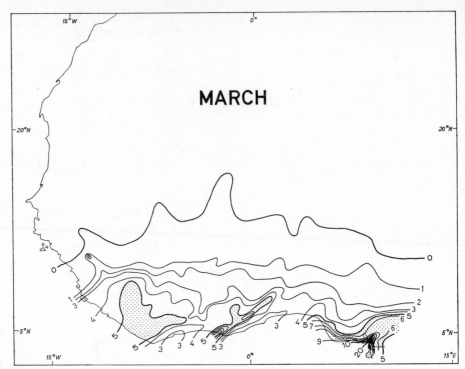

Figure 5.5c

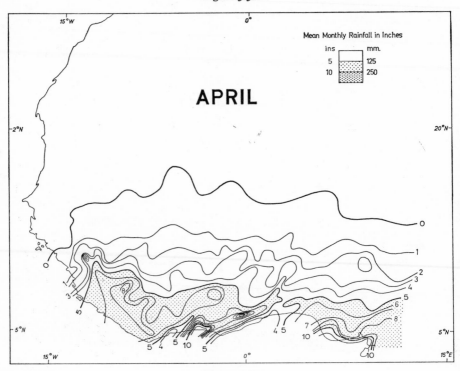

Figure 5.6a

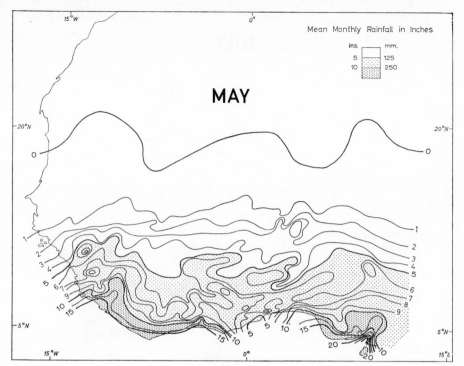

Figure 5.6*b*

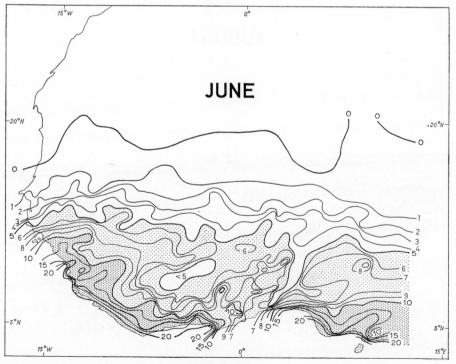

Figure 5.6*c*

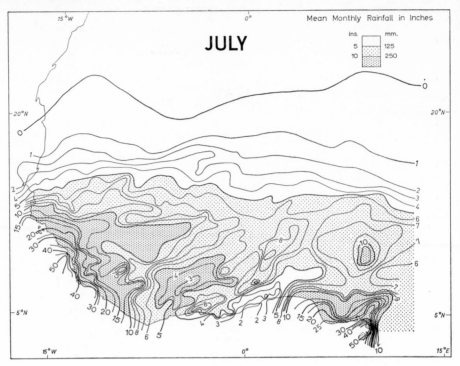

Figure 5.7a

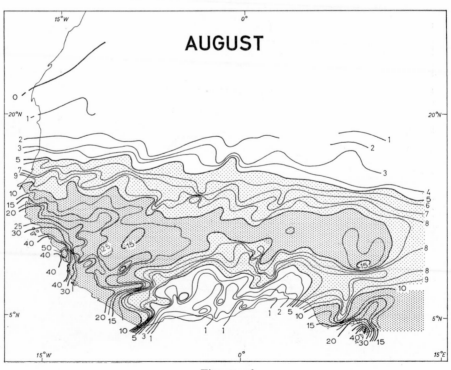

Figure 5.7b

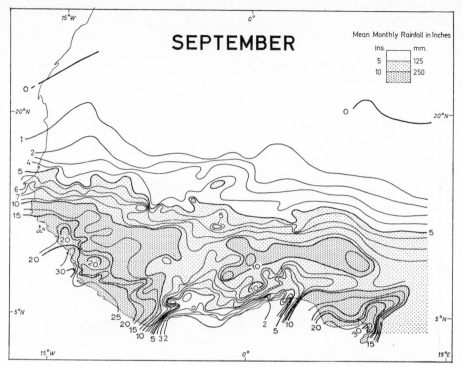

Figure 5.7c

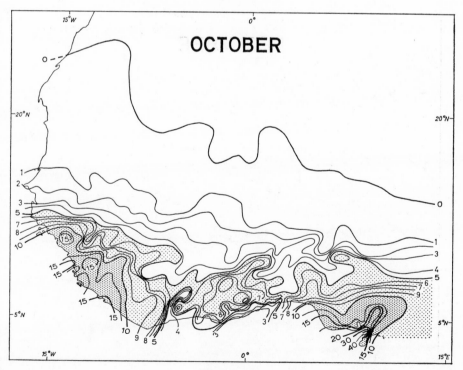

Figure 5.8a

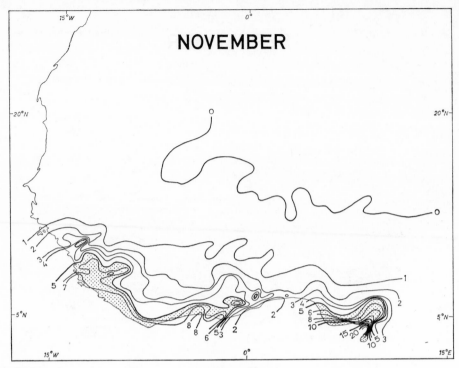

Figure 5.8*b*

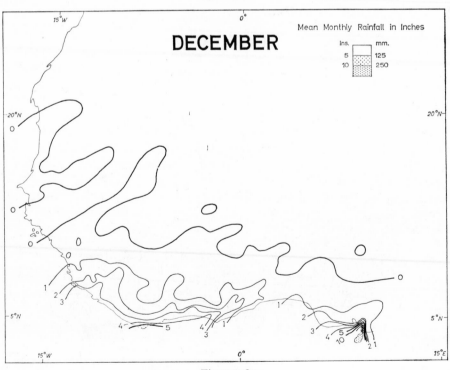

Figure 5.8*c*

that West Africa does not have weather, but only climate, 'weather' in the sense of day-to-day variation being largely precluded by the character of the N.E. Trades and the Tropical Continental air mass. Either this warm dry air is at the surface or it forms a stable layer above a wedge of moist air and renders inter-action impossible, or almost impossible. Use of mean monthly rainfall figures permits the construction of moisture balance graphs, but these vary in value for the critical sowing months, not because of weather uncertainty, but because of the change or persistence of type of rain. Rainfall almost everywhere in West Africa shows much greater unreliability than in the British Isles, for example, but the greatest variation from mean values is in the months at the beginning and end of the wet season.

The rainfall maps for the months January to December (Figs. 5.5 to 5.8), although drawn to show mean monthly isohyets, illustrate differences within West Africa in rate of movement of the I.T.C.Z. These can be seen by comparing the positions of the isohyets for 0 in and for 5 in (127 mm). The area between these two isohyets on any map may be roughly equated with the major squall zone. The zero isohyet remains virtually in the same position, a little north of Conakry, for practically the whole period from December to April inclusive.* Further east, however, the zero isohyet shows considerable variation of position from month to month. The 5-in (127-mm) isohyet, barely present in West Africa in December, reappears in March, in three different localities, and develops rapidly in April and May. The differences between the western and eastern areas of West Africa are readily understood. The eastern areas are affected by the southward passage of the I.T.C.Z. into the southern hemisphere. The I.T.C.Z. acts as though hinged in the Republic of Guinea for 6 months of the year, with the seasonal migration increasing eastward from there. Only in May does the front, which has become latitudinal with the northward progress of its eastern sector, move northward at a more or less constant speed over the whole of its length. The less regular return movement is in some ways less critical in that it is more rapid, so that variation of rainfall type and total operates for a shorter period of time.

The length of the wet season bears directly upon man's activities, as it deter-mines in large measure whether he can find water to keep himself alive, and whether there is moisture for sufficient length of time to allow the growth of crops to feed himself or of pasture to feed his animals. A comparison of Figure 1.2 (Popu-lation Density) and Figure 5.9 (Length of Dry Season) suggests that for pastoral peoples the limiting isopleth is that of 7 months of complete drought, and for agricultural peoples the normal limit is $5\frac{1}{2}$–6 months of drought. The uncertainty of squall rain in the marginal months of the wet season means that agriculture is precarious with this length of dry season, unless irrigation is practised in some form to ensure adequate watering of crops before the harvest. The Sahelian type of climate was described in the Introduction as having a regular wet season of less than $2\frac{1}{2}$ months, and requiring irrigation. This is the area suggested above

* In December there is still an area of very slight rainfall over the western districts of Senegal and Mauritania.

as capable of supporting pasture (which may be irregular poor scrub). The seven months of drought each have less than one-tenth of an inch (2·5 mm) on average; the 2½ months of rains may give the greater part of an annual total of up to 20 in (510 mm); the remaining period represents months with an average of less than 1 inch (25 mm) of rain each. The northern margin of the Sahelian zone is thus one of the limits of West Africa in terms of general human occupation as opposed to isolated settlements in the Saharan zone. Necessarily this northern limit has

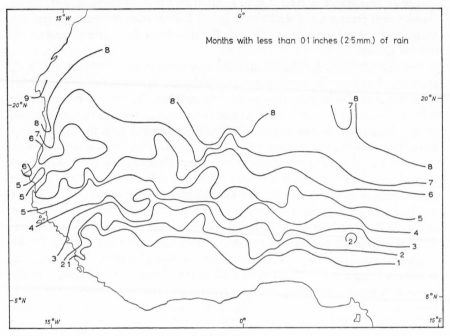

Figure 5.9

a pulsating character, varying with the season and with local reserves of drinking water. Slave labour in the areas of sedimentary rock was used to dig unlined wells as deep as 300 feet (90 metres), but in exceptionally dry years the water-table may fall below the level of a well of any depth and cause a temporary withdrawal of the population. The termination of slavery in Northern Nigeria in the 20th century, as a result of British occupation, led to the end of maintenance work on the deep wells, and to the collapse of some of these. This resulted in the migration of whole village settlements, and further encouraged the belief in 'the encroaching Sahara'. By the middle of the 20th century mechanical digging of boreholes to tap water supplies guaranteed the continued survival of settlements which had previously depended upon the continued yield of one of these deep wells, but this security was absent in the early years of colonial occupation when the sociological ideas of the imperial power outran its technological ability.

The seasonal shift of the I.T.C.Z. has had one other important result. The exact processes of laterization are still a matter for discussion, but there is no doubt that high temperatures and intense rainfall, even if the latter operates for only a few months in each year, contribute to deep weathering and the development of laterite. It is generally recognized that the formation of the great plains and of the landscape features that rise above them is intimately connected with the effects of deep weathering, and rotting of rock can be found to hundreds of feet in some areas. Deep weathering of this type may be found throughout the inter-tropical zone, downward leaching including silica. The end product varies in character, depending on the constitution of the parent rock, on the intensity of the processes at work, and on the nature of the latter, that is, whether the laterite has been formed in situ or is deposited material transported from elsewhere. Richard-Molard[15] stresses the importance of distinction between the latter two alternatives: the first is laterization, the second is the deposition of a layer of partly lateritic material. If cementation of the particles has occurred in the second case, this has been after deposition. There is also variation in the proportions of the more important constituent materials, so that hydroxides of iron, aluminium or manganese may be locally sufficiently concentrated as to constitute a workable ore. In West Africa, however, laterization can take the form of deep weathering, accompanied by the development of a hardpan layer at or just below the surface, or of the formation of a hardpan layer across transported material. Such duricrusts, usually of a ferruginous character, can be encountered in other parts of the world, but nowhere so well developed as in West Africa. The exact processes of formation are again uncertain, but the seasonal fluctuation of the water-table is unquestionably involved, and possibly the upward movement of moisture in the dry season to leave deposits of mineral salts following the evaporation of the water.[16] Nowhere else in the world is there so well seen the formation of these layers of sterile crusts inimical to life. Other regions have high temperatures, a marked dry season, and mean annual rainfall totals exceeding 35 in (900 mm), without having the marked development of this crust, carapace, cuirasse, or bowal: West Africa appears to suffer from its formation to an exceptional degree because, in addition, it is the only continental area which also has wide plains of great perfection, and the unusually strong and persistent dry harmattan wind, encouraging excessive dry season evaporation. Hence arises the characteristic presence of bowal south of a line from 14° N. in the west to 12° N. in the east, and north of a line from 8° N. in the west to 7° N. in the east. North of this zone the rainfall totals are too low: south of it the harmattan blows for too short a period of the year. This has been another limiting factor for human activity, arising from the nature of the climate and the landforms. Economic prosperity is not excluded from the whole of this zone, which locally includes some of the areas of greatest agricultural production, but these areas will be seen in many cases to have exceptional characteristics, such as drift soils or rainfall below the totals required for true bowalization. The bowal zone has been none the less the location of many of the major states of West Africa, notwithstanding the difficulties of agriculture and the danger of increasing crust formation, as a result of clearing vegetation and opening the soil, by tillage, to greater sun and wind action. Principally this may have been for negative rather than for positive reasons – to the north the climate was too dry for agriculture, to the south the forest was too thick for easy clearing, and too infested with pests for the health of man or beast. The open savanna grasslands offered the logical site for settlement, in spite of indifferent soils.

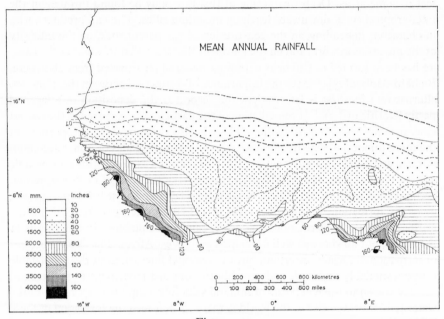

Figure 5.10

The duricrusts vary considerably in their mode of occurrence. Scaëtta[17] refers to their presence between 8° N. and 16° N. In the regions with a 2-peak rainfall régime, the crust is found at depths of $\frac{1}{2}$–3 metres ($1\frac{1}{2}$–10 feet) below the surface, and is covered by a zone of movable material on which the shallow-rooted forest stands. He states that the cuirasse is always formed at depth, except in Guinea, where a locally distinct type may be formed at the surface. He envisages both formation and destruction of the cuirasse as phases in a natural cycle, of which the half-way point is the maximum sub-surface development: during the latter half of the cycle the overlying horizons are stripped off, with consequent exposure of, and hardening of, the crust. Thick hardpan is found at the surface between 10° N. and 14° N., varying in thickness from $\frac{1}{4}$ metre (10 in) to several metres. In the southern areas the forest cover preserves the overlying layer and the crust never hardens. In the savanna a thin, mobile layer supporting degraded forest sometimes covers the crust: where the pan is exposed, soil may be restricted to pockets within hollows in the crustal surface, with a grass cover.

Between 14° N. and 16° N. crusts tend to be found only in locations where they

West Africa: Extent of Ferruginous Crusts

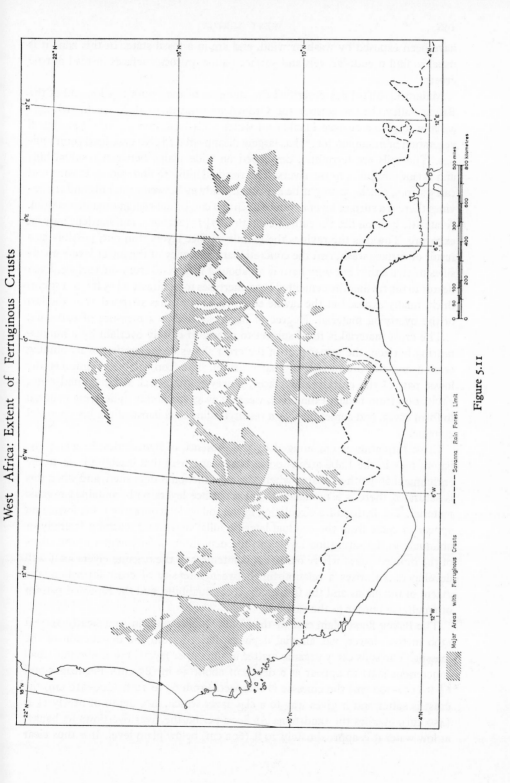

Major Areas with Ferruginous Crusts

——— Savanna Rain Forest Limit

Figure 5.11

have been exposed by wash or wind, and are in a fossil state. In this zone it is usual to find pseudo-gravels and surface patina on rock surfaces instead of true crusts.

Maignien[18][19] has described the cuirasses of the Fouta Djallon and of the Bafing valley. In the former the Ordovician sandstones have weathered sub-aerially to give a surface blanket on which soils have developed. The original vegetation of mountain forest has largely disappeared to give grassland communities. The soils are ferrallitic, developed on wide plains between residual hills and ravines draining to the rivers. The residual hills are undergoing erosion and carry strong crusts, as might be expected. Midway between the hills and the ravines there is a surface layer of about 28 in (70 cm) of soil rich in organic material. A lateritic horizon lies beneath at a depth of $7\frac{1}{4}$ ft (220 cm), and hardens only on exposure. Towards the ravines the mobile surface layers thin out, possibly as a result of surface wash, and the concretionary tendency of the lower layers intensifies to give a thin but very hard layer about 2 ft (65 cm) from the surface. Even nearer to the ravines the cemented layer increases to a cuirasse $1\frac{1}{2}$–5 ft (50–150 cm) thick, finally exposed at the ravine edge where wash has stripped away the last of the overlying material. Degree of hardness is thus a measure of exposure.

The crust material is itself subject to attack. If closely overlain by a humus-bearing horizon, the upper part of the crust shows disintegration of its binding cement and the production of coarse gravel. The iron released reinforces the lower part of the cuirasse. In places, however, the attack is by ground-water circulation from beneath the crust, wearing away the softer underlying material to form caves, and sometimes, as a result, leading to collapse of the unsupported cuirasse.

Crust formation is encouraged by the presence of hydroxides, in which the parent rock in the Labé area is poor. It appears there that leaching leads to the enrichment at depth of a layer where the clay fraction is deposited, and when this is saturated there is a tendency to thick surface layers with contained organic material. The hydroxides circulating in the soil and encouraging crust formation appear to come from the residual lateritic hills, suggesting leaching laterally or obliquely to the saturation level, and the deposition of hydroxides at the edges of the drained zones where oxidation is intense and the organic layers least well developed. So arises a relationship between intensity of crust formation, the extent of the plains and the frequency of residual hills, and the repeated pattern of a cuirasse border to the ravines.

The Bafing flood-plain east of the Fouta Djallon plateau, and nearly 1000 ft (300 metres) lower, has alluvial deposits derived from the destruction of the massifs. The soils carry organic matter in the upper layers, but numerous small concretions start to appear at a depth of about 33 in (85 cm). Between 5 and $6\frac{1}{2}$ ft (150–200 cm) the cuirasse is compact. From $6\frac{1}{2}$ to 10 ft (200–310 cm) the crust is softer and it gives way to a clay layer which, at a depth of nearly 15 ft (450 cm), overlies the sandstone. At flood period the river overflows its banks; at low water it is approximately 20 ft (600 cm) below plain level. It is thus clear

Soil Map of West Africa

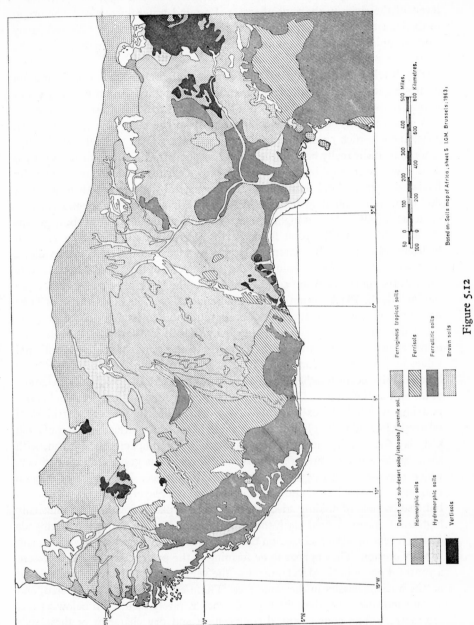

Desert and sub-desert soils/lithosols/juvenile soil.

Halomorphic soils

Hydromorphic soils

Vertisols

Ferruginous tropical soils

Ferrisols

Ferrallitic soils

Brown soils

Based on Soils map of Africa, sheet 5 I.G.M, Brussels, 1963;

Figure 5.12

H

that in the Bafing valley the cuirasse is formed between high- and low-water levels of the river, in the zone of seasonal ground-water fluctuation. The origin of the lateritic material is partly the wash from the surrounding hills and partly from soluble salts in the ground water, with deposition of hydroxide in the pre-existing alluvium.

The development of a cuirasse thus appears to be related to seasonal variation of ground water, to climatic factors, and to topography. Parent material is not necessarily significant, and crusts can be found on rocks of a variety of type.

A broad zoning of soil types is apparent from the map. The drier northern zones include rock pavements and sands, sometimes with skeletal soil development, but this is really beyond the limit of settlement. The most northerly settled zone is one of tropical brown or reddish-brown earths, followed successively by fersiallitic, ferrisol and ferrallitic zones. In general these are reddish in colour due to a high content of ferric oxide. Fersiallitic soils have a greater silicious content: ferrallitic have a higher percentage of sesquioxides. With these groups are also shown the Tropical Black Earths (Vertisols) and the major areas of hydromorphic soils. The latter are largely restricted to the main river valleys, the Niger delta, the Chad basin, and the inland delta of the Niger, and constitute some of the more important agricultural soils. The Vertisols are of several types but include the Black Cotton Soils of the Benue valley. The Black Earths of Togo have been described by Leneuf[20] and are notable as having pH values (5·9–7·2 at the surface) higher than the majority of soils in West Africa; most parts of the region, at least as far north as 14° N., have strongly acid soils with pH values in some cases as low as 4·3. The Togo Black Earths have been developed by relatively recent weathering on basic parent materials – volcanics, metamorphics and sedimentaries. The larger occurrences follow the Lama–Hollis depression, which includes limestones, and which lies in the 'dry corridor' of relatively low rainfall. The resulting profile has a black surface horizon of sand and clay 6–16 in (15–40 cm) deep, followed by a compact clay horizon, with some calcareous concretions and varnished ferruginous gravels, above bedrock, which may be 12–39 in (30–100 cm) below the surface. The wealth of mineral elements added to the structural stability of the upper layer, which is well drained but also capable of holding adequate moisture for plant growth, gives unusually high soil fertility. Azonal black soils are also found in the Cameroon Highlands on the recent basaltic rocks, or on the older volcanics where they have been laid bare by erosion. They appear to be forming at the present day, and to represent a youthful phase in the development of the very regular red lateritic soils found on the ancient basalts in the same area. These are very deeply weathered, and are not moisture-retentive: fresh parent rock is rarely seen, even below 33 feet (10 metres). The poor chemical composition and dry character of these soils makes them infertile.[21]

The broad zoning of West African soils should not disguise the fact that soil varies very considerably in character and fertility depending on its position on the slopes of the land surface. The Bafing valley example given above illustrates the variation in soil characteristics across a fairly uniform slope. From top to bottom of a valley side the changes may be much more marked, and the sequence of soil types in a catena is often reflected in the land use. Vine[22] demonstrated the agricultural importance of catena changes in the cocoa-growing areas of Nigeria: the hill-tops and upper slopes show deep clay and clay-loam soils on which cocoa flourishes, while the valley floor and lower slopes have sandy soils, sometimes with concretions, which tend to give lower yields. The effects of slopes on soils, and of soils on agricultural use, have been taken further by Moss[23] in a detailed study of part of south-western Nigeria. He also considers the location and mode of formation of the lateritic soils, in particular the mottled clays and the vesicular laterite, and comments on the hardening of the aerated sections on the margins of erosion surfaces, the break-up and attrition of the hardened material with the advent of a retreating scarp, and the deposition, on the lower surface, of this material. He refers to the correlation of laterites with erosion surfaces, but stresses that there is no certainty that the hard layers were produced under conditions similar to, or dissimilar from, those of the present day.

The methods of soil description used in temperate lands are not always suitable for West African soils. Nye[24] has shown that A B C horizons are not always identifiable. For his upper surface layers he used CrW, CrT and CrG, representing layers of soil creep in which worms are the significant movers, or termites similarly, or in which gravel is most apparent. For a soil at Ibadan he located an oxidation-reduction zone just below the CrG layer at 30–48 in (76–122 cm) above the sedentary S layers. The CrW layer was $\frac{1}{2}$–1 in (1·3–2·5 cm) thick at all points on the hill-slopes. The CrT layer varied in thickness from 6 in (15·2 cm) on the upper slope to 24 in (61 cm) on mid-slope, as a result of the rate of creep, but did not increase in thickness to the lower slope. The maximum particle size in the termite layer was 4 mm diameter. The gravel layer thickened all the way down the slope to 6 ft (2 metres) at the foot.

Nye carried out water absorption tests on this soil in the wet season, and showed that on the upper slopes water could be absorbed vertically at a rate of 11·2 in (28·5 cm) per hour for 30 minutes: the second half hour showed an absorption rate of 7·8 in (19·8 cm) per hour, followed by a rate of 3·25 in (8·25 cm) per hour for the second hour. The experiment was made well after the start of the wet season, and the ground was initially thoroughly moist: for the first storms of the year the rate of absorption would probably have been very much less.

It was noted in the experiment that lateral seepage between the CrG and S layers, at the level of maximum clay content, 27 in (69 cm) below the surface, started after 28 minutes when the soil had received 5·2 in (13·2 cm), and stopped when the absorption rate dropped to 3·25 in (8·25 cm) per hour. This very porous soil had no run-off in the rains and no lateral sub-surface flow under natural conditions, so clay eluviation is vertical. This is in contrast with the lateral movement noted in the Bafing valley.

An attempt has been made by Fournier[25] to calculate the danger of soil erosion for Africa south of the Sahara. This does not take active cognizance of

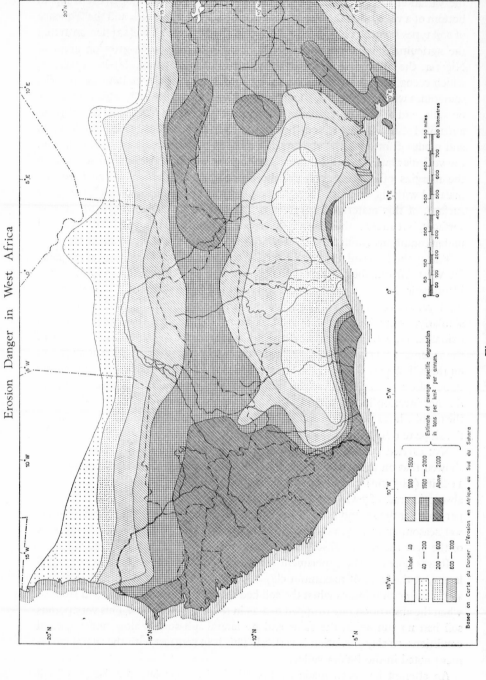

Erosion Danger in West Africa

Estimate of average specific degradation
in tons per km² per annum.

Under 40
40 — 200
200 — 600
600 — 1000
1000 — 1500
1500 — 2000
Above 2000

Based on Carta du Danger D'Erosion en Afrique au Sud du Sahara

Figure 5.13

the soil type or of the vegetation cover, but is based on considerations of topography and climate. The notable features of the resulting map, in West Africa, are the area of relatively little danger (less than 1000 tons per square kilometre removed per annum), from the Niger–Benue confluence to the western frontier of the Ivory Coast, and the belt of greater risk at approximately 12°–13° N. The former agrees closely with the two dry corridors noted earlier in the consideration of rainfall, and the latter marks, approximately, the belt of greatest rainfall intensity along the line of transition from 2-peak to 1-peak distribution. This is another demonstration of the significance of the I.T.C.Z. movement.

The climate has one other very important influence over man. Brown[26] has written: 'The Nigerian inherits almost all the disorders of temperate climates and only escapes the others by dying relatively young. On top of these he may suffer from a multitude of other diseases to which his ignorance of their causes, his poor standards of hygiene and his geographical situation on the globe make him liable.' Many of the diseases to which man is prone in West Africa are transmitted by insects or parasites whose life cycle is defined by limits of humidity and temperature. Malaria is transmitted by the anopheles mosquito, of which at least eight species act as vectors. The two most important are *Anopheles gambiae* and *Anopheles funestus*, the former being widespread, the latter restricted to inland areas. These mosquitoes will breed almost anywhere with a free water surface, provided that climatic conditions are suitable. Marshes, swamps, dry season pools, the water trapped between leaf and stem of many plants, all are suitable breeding grounds, and at least one variety of *Anopheles gambiae* can breed in highly brackish water in coastal swamps. Temperatures between 60° F. (16° C.) and 100° F. (38° C.) are optimum for the transmission of malaria, with relative humidities of 60 per cent or above. It is clear that most of West Africa is suitable for mosquito breeding in terms of temperature: in general terms of humidity only the Tropical Maritime air mass is favourable. In theory, therefore, the degree of exposure of man to malarial infection depends upon the length of the dry season, or rather upon the length of the period of exposure to the dry Tropical Continental air. In practice, mosquitoes are more widespread in the dry season than this simple statement suggests, because the breeding grounds may experience a microclimate very different from that of the surrounding air mass. Relative humidity may remain high in the curve of a folded leaf in which water is trapped, if the leaf itself is shaded by fringing forest along a water-course, and the effective period of freedom from breeding is therefore reduced. In the coastal regions breeding of mosquitoes may continue unchecked throughout the year, and the disease can be transmitted at all seasons, whereas in the forest the period of transmission may be only 8 to 9 months, and in the Sudan and Sahel zones only 5 months on average. Local conditions obviously cause wide variation. About 5 per cent of mosquitoes normally carry parasites, but the incidence rate varies from 0 to 20 per cent with season and locality. The most important of the malarial parasites is *Plasmodium falciparum*, the cause of malignant tertian fever. This is responsible for over 80 per cent of hospital cases of malaria, and in Nigeria of 96 per cent of malarial infections. The virulence of malaria was well shown by the experience of European sailors on the West Coast of Africa. The first English ships in the Benin River in 1553 lost 100 men out of 140[27]; in 1843 only nine Europeans survived from a complement of 48[28]. The effect of malaria on West Africans appears to be less violent, but this

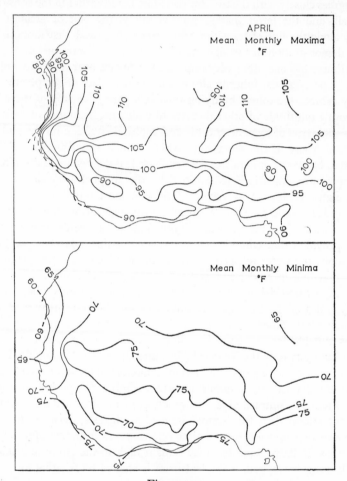

Figure 5.14

is largely because a certain degree of immunity is developed with age as the result of constant re-infection, and the adults seen are the survivors from the children infected. At least one-tenth of recorded deaths in childhood are from malaria: probably a much higher percentage is nearer the truth. The chances of survival even today are such that children under the age of five are frequently ignored in counting the number of individuals in a compound, as Census officials have found in making sample checks on the figures returned: only after the age of five is the likelihood of survival considered sufficient to justify the consideration of children as potential adults. Malaria, when not lethal, causes debility, lack of energy and loss of initiative. It may result in individuals never attaining more than 50 to 75 per cent of their potential ability in terms of physical and mental work,

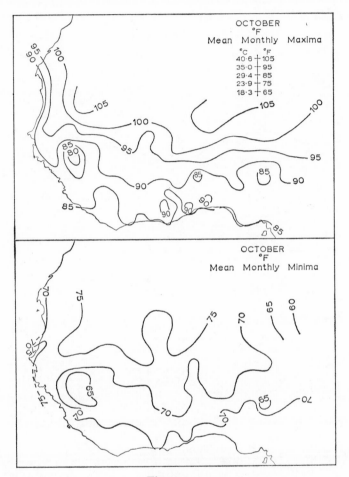

Figure 5.15

without necessarily ever causing prolonged or severe illness. In terms of the present day this means that there is an enormous economic loss experienced every year by the community; in terms of prehistoric man it meant that an individual had less chance of survival in the malarial areas because he expended less energy on the farm. The northern savanna areas with a longer dry season of low relative humidity were thus preferable to the southern forest country in the first instance.

Malaria is only one of the many diseases endemic in West Africa. Yellow fever

VAPOUR PRESSURE (MONTHLY MEANS)

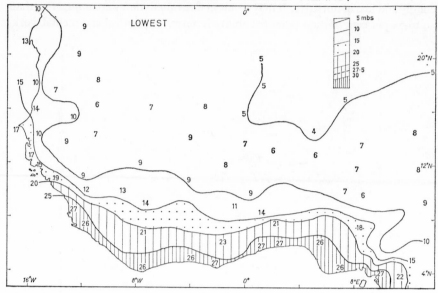

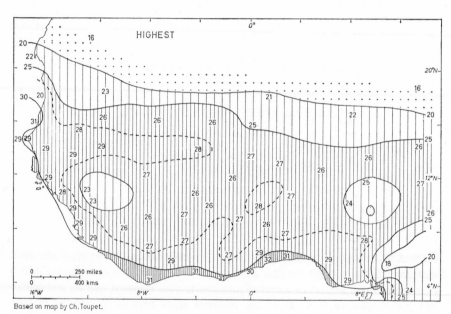

Based on map by Ch. Toupet.

Figure 5.16

is also mosquito-borne, the virus being transmitted by the mosquito *Aedes aegypti*. This would appear to be far less of a hazard to the West African peoples than to immigrants from other parts of the world. Europeans attacked by the disease rarely survive unless previously inoculated, and Syrians in West Africa have revealed the same vulnerability. The indigenous peoples appear to experience

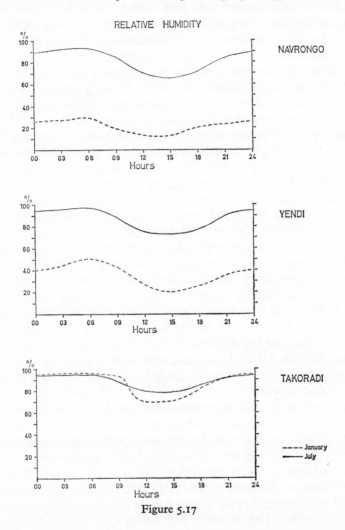

Figure 5.17

no more than a few days of mild discomfort with normal epidemics, and a mortality rate of less than 1 per cent. One attack gives lifelong immunity and in some districts from which yellow fever has never been reported up to 92 per cent of the population have been found to have experienced the disease.[29] Severe outbreaks of more virulent form can occur, such as one in Eastern Nigeria in 1952 in which some 600 Africans died. This disease is probably, therefore, of only minor importance as a physical factor affecting population distribution. It is probable that it occurs throughout West Africa south of the Sahara, although for the most part recorded only where immigrants have been infected.

Trypanosomiasis is widespread in West Africa. The disease is caused by the minute parasites called trypanosomes, particularly *Trypanosoma gambiense*, transmitted by biting insects from host to host. The latter include other large animals besides man. The parasites are conveyed by the tsetse fly, *Glossina* spp. Four species are of importance, their distribution depending in large measure on climatic conditions. *G. morsitans* is absent from the humid southern forests, and frequents the savanna areas. It can withstand hot and dry conditions, partly by taking refuge in riverine vegetation. *G. longipalpis*, by contrast, avoids areas with more than four months dry season and less than 45 in (1150 mm) of rain; it is therefore approximately confined to the areas of Tropical Maritime air, although apparently capable of surviving a short period of generally dry air by using local areas of higher humidity around streams. *G. palpalis* is the most widespread of the species, and thrives from the coast to the savanna, although of riverine rather than general distribution in the north. *G. tachinoides* avoids the forest and can tolerate a dry season of up to 7 months. *G. tachinoides* and *G. palpalis* transmit the disease in humans, *G. morsitans* in humans and in animals, and *G. longipalpis* only in animals. All therefore have an effect on man's distribution and well-being, both directly and indirectly, in that even where the disease in humans is not endemic cattle may be liable to infection with nagana. This widespread restriction on cattle-rearing has had major effects on the human diet, and is responsible for the general lack of protein and consequent malnutrition. In West Africa, as in other parts of the world, inability to rear animals for meat has led to the use for food of any creature capable of providing nutriment. Apart from the larger game animals, rodents, snakes, birds and the larger lizards are all utilized if need arises, and some of these are remarkably appetizing even to a western palate. The restriction on the keeping of cattle is itself a reflection of the movements of the I.T.C.Z., as the fly generally prefer high humidity and vegetation sufficiently thick to provide shade. Simple clearing of riverine vegetation is no general solution to the problem, even if it were possible, as in the southern areas of dense forest partial clearing produces conditions more favourable to *G. palpalis* than the original environment. In the northern areas clearing of riverine bush can be highly effective, as shown by the success of the Anchau Corridor scheme in Northern Nigeria,[30] but this requires constant attention to a planned programme, the value of which is not always readily apparent to village peoples even today. The success of the Anchau Corridor, where the incidence rate was reduced to a twentieth of its previous figure, was matched by the speed of fly advance into the treated zone when responsibility for clearing passed from the medical to the local administrative authorities. Prior to the arrival of modern medical knowledge no prophylactic measures would appear to have been taken against the tsetse fly. Because the infection of the southern areas was lethal to cattle, the early pastoralists, like those of today, were restricted to the northern

The Distribution of Tsetse Species in West Africa

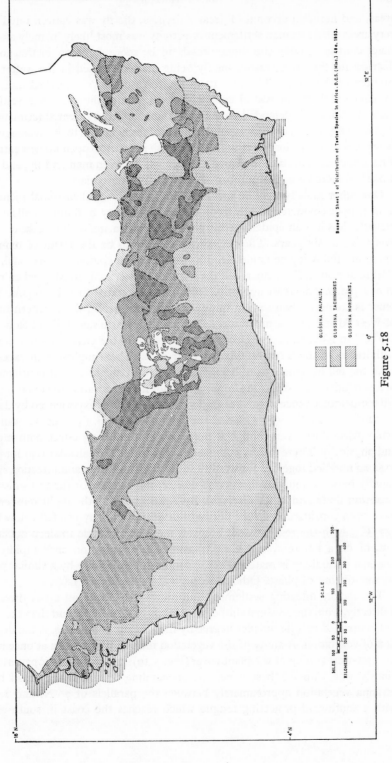

SCALE

MILES 100   50   0   100   200   300

KILOMETRES 100 50 0   100   200   300   400

GLOSSINA PALPALIS.

GLOSSINA TACHINOIDES.

GLOSSINA MORSITANS.

Based on Sheet 1 of Distribution of Tsetse Species in Africa - D.C.S. (Misc.) 4Ba. 1953.

Figure 5.18

areas, and here, on account of greater dryness, the fly was concentrated in the very areas where human settlement or activity was most likely, namely along the water-courses. Today the disease tends to be more common in the northern districts for the same reason, the fly being more dispersed in the wetter forest country of the south. The history of the disease shows a marked increase in incidence with the arrival of colonial powers, due to the change in settlement pattern from large, defended communities surrounded by cleared farmland (and therefore free of fly) to the scattered hamlets of farmers who took advantage of the new peaceful conditions to move into the bush in order to open up new farmland. This outward migration increased the contacts between man and fly, and led to a marked increase in the number of cases of trypanosomiasis.

One other malady may be included here, namely cerebro-spinal meningitis. This is not a characteristically tropical disease, but may be found in all latitudes. Nevertheless it is an epidemic scourge in West Africa, major outbreaks occurring every five to six years. The periodicity appears to be the result of temporary immunity following an epidemic. The rhythm of an epidemic is seasonal. Cases start to appear in December, and the number rises steadily to May, when reports of new patients decrease abruptly. It has been suggested that this regular occurrence is connected with mean minimum temperature. In the northern districts of West Africa night temperatures show minima which may fall to below 50° F. (10° C.) in November and December, as a result of the clear skies following the withdrawal of the Tropical Maritime air mass. These nights seem excessively cold, the fall in temperature being accentuated by the arrival of continental air of low relative humidity. One important factor in the sensation of cold is the diurnal temperature range at this season, as *sun* temperatures experienced by day may be 120°–130° F. (50°–55° C.), and the fall of 70°–80° F. (39°–44° C.) can cause acute discomfort, even though it may have a stimulating effect both mentally and physically. There is thus a tendency at the end of the calendar year for people to sleep huddled together for warmth in unventilated huts, and infection spreads rapidly between individuals (as also do lice, the vectors for the transmission of relapsing fever and other diseases). By April and May the night temperatures have risen considerably in the northern districts, and may not fall below 80° F. (27° C.), with the result that it becomes more comfortable to sleep outside the hut, or on a flat roof, and close transmission of infection ends rapidly. The seasonal periodicity is matched in the southern hemisphere by a similar pattern six months out of phase. Other diseases will be mentioned later.

The factors affecting settlement and mentioned above all arise, directly or indirectly, from the seasonal shift of the I.T.C.Z. No less important than the above, but controlled to a far smaller degree by the climatic conditions, is the distribution of vegetation. A study of the vegetation map of West Africa at once reveals the east-west zoning of the plant cover (Fig. 5.19) similar to climatic patterns previously seen. Among these zones the outstanding feature is the broad belt of savanna vegetation approximately between the parallels of 7° N. and 14° N., with a southward-projecting tongue which reaches the coast in south-eastern

West Africa: Vegetation Zones

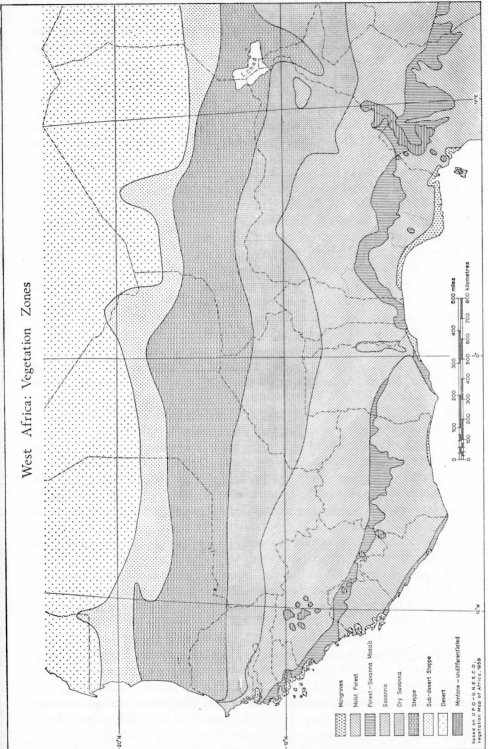

Mangroves

Moist Forest

Forest – Savanna Mosaic

Savanna

Dry Savanna

Steppe

Sub-desert Steppe

Desert

Montane – undifferentiated

based on U.P.O – U.N.E.S.C.O.,
Vegetation Map of Africa, 1959

Figure 5.19

Ghana. The savanna zone is not uniform in plant type, and Keay[31] shows three main divisions, the relatively moist savanna of the south, the northern savannas and the relatively dry savanna. Rosevear[32] refers to Guinea savanna, Sudan savanna and Sahel savanna. The Sahel savanna is classified as 'wooded steppe' by Keay, whose 'dry savanna' corresponds to the 'Sudan savanna' and who refers elsewhere[33] to the Southern and Northern Guinea Savanna. The savanna zones all display mixed grass and woodland, but there are considerable differences between the appearance of the northern and southern areas. The savannas here probably do not represent a natural climax vegetation. Originally it seems likely that forest, at least in 'islands', extended much further to the north than at the present day, and the present character is largely the result of man's activities. This does not contradict the earlier statement that climate partly determines the vegetation type. Every year man burns the grassland for one reason or another – to clear land for preparation for farming, to promote the growth of new shoots for cattle fodder, to drive wild game into the open, even from sheer habit or wantonness. There is no reason to suppose that early man was any less addicted to firing the grassland in the dry season, and he may well have shown an even greater tendency to do so, being more dependent on hunting than his modern counterpart, and possessed of less effective tools. The effectiveness of grass firing depends on the extreme dryness of the air and on the desiccated nature of the plant material after a short period of exposure to Tropical Continental air. All the savanna areas have a number of months each with less than 1 in (25 mm) of rainfall, and an increasing number of months, as one goes northward, of dry continental air. Under these conditions fire will spread through grass at high speed, although individual fires are usually not very extensive in area. The grass is burned down to ground level, but is not destroyed on account of the underground root-stocks. Trees lose their remaining leaves, and unless protected by thick bark may be killed. This is one reason why man himself has been a potent factor in moulding the appearance of the landscape, as the annual firing kills off the fire-tender tree species of the humid forest. The extension of the grassland in this way may have given rise to the 'derived savannas' which may be found locally as far south as 6° N. They are matched by the 'fringing forests' and 'gallery forests' found in the Guinea savanna. It is notable in the savanna lands that the vegetation alters in character with the minor features of the landscape, changing from grassland on the open plains to a more woody cover over rocky sites: Eyre[34] suggests that these rocky sites check the grass fires and allow the survival of heavier plant growth more closely representing the climax vegetation of the region.

The most southerly savanna area ('Forest-Savanna mosaic' in Keay's later map)[31] is the derived savanna zone. Its origin may be inferred from the uneven character of its southern margin and the sometimes abrupt transition from the high forest to the grassland, which clearly negates a purely climatic differentiation, but may represent local variation in soil. The grasses are tall, tussocky species such as elephant grass (*Pennisetum*) which can burn with intense heat in the dry season; many grasses will by then have the thickness of a normal pencil and the texture of dry bamboo.

However, it is not certain that cultivation and burning are today affecting the savanna-forest margin. Morgan and Moss[35] have shown that the boundary between the two is abrupt, but by no means simple: 'outliers' of forest, of considerable size in some cases, appear to be in a thriving condition notwithstanding an apparent preference by local farmers for settlement and cultivation within these forest areas. Over an 8-year period, the forest margin in those parts of Western Nigeria which have been studied in detail appears to show no encroachment by the savanna, in spite of increased population and greater pressure on the land. Agricultural practice appears to differ between the neighbouring savanna and forest areas, and the forest may well mark the local distribution of richer soils, thus explaining the farmers' preference for cultivation within it. Burning seems to be particularly effective on the poor soils across lateritic crusts, but the fires tend to die away on reaching the forest edge. This would be a reasonable consequence of soil differences, in that the grasses of the shallow soils would be dry enough for burning while the vegetation on the deeper patches of soil might still be too moist to burn easily. Fires may therefore die out over deeper soils, or over rocks, as Eyre suggests. Different factors may be expected to have different emphasis in time and place, and it is not yet clear whether there are critical levels of population density which affect forest degradation under specific conditions of soil or climate.

The southern Guinea savanna has the same high grasses, but with established woodland of trees up to 50 feet (15 metres) in height. These may be either fire-tender or fire-resistant. The former are encountered in the fringing and gallery forests along the moist valley bottoms and on the rocky hills respectively, and represent the remnants of the original high forest vegetation. The trees for the most part are deciduous in the southern Guinea savanna, but in the northern Guinea savanna an increasing proportion of evergreens occur. In these northern districts the grass is shorter, in the range 2–5 feet (0·5–1·5 metres) high, and the grass may be suppressed altogether in areas where the tree cover becomes continuous. The gallery forests of the northern savanna show affinities with the savanna rather than with the high forests of the humid south. The typical trees of the Guinea savanna include *Isoberlinia*, *Daniellia*, and the Locust-bean and Shea-butter trees, respectively *Parkia oliveri* and *Butyrospermum parkii*. The southern Guinea savanna is often called 'orchard bush', and the northern Guinea savanna, with its more frequent and larger trees, 'savanna woodland'.

The Guinea savanna often has greater rainfall than the forest zones to the south, although concentrated in a shorter wet season. The Sudan savanna, to the north, has less rainfall than the Guinea type, and a dry season possibly extending to 7 months. It is, none the less, more heavily populated, and corresponds approximately with the northern zones of denser population. The vegetation varies widely in composition; the grass is shorter and sparser than in the Guinea savanna, so that bush fires are of lesser intensity; *Isoberlinia* notably disappears away from the Guinea savanna margin; the kapok or silk-cotton tree (*Bombax*), the Baobab (*Adansonia*) and the branching dum palm (*Hyphaene*) occur in this zone; pure stands of the flat-topped *Acacia seyal* are found in ill-drained areas; and the genus *Combretum* produces low scrub. *C. micranthum* gives wide areas of almost monotypic scrub 5–10 feet (1·5–3·0 metres) high; *C. elliotti* is a small tree some 15–20 feet (4·5–6·0 metres) high, sometimes found in extensive and almost pure stands. The contrast between wet and dry season appearance is striking. In the middle of the dry season the trees and bushes in most cases are leafless, and the grass absent as a result of firing; unlike the grasses of the Guinea savanna, the grasses in this zone do not put out new shoots after burning. The arrival of the moist maritime air mass causes a transformation. The ground and the bushes burst into green growth, and by the end of the wet season the vegetative cover is relatively heavy, at least in general appearance, where it still approaches anything like its natural state. Pressure of population has largely cleared the natural cover in many areas, such as the densely-peopled district round Kano, which today seasonally alternates in appearance between an extensive and fertile garden and an arid waste. The shedding of leaves during the dry season is not universal: in some cases, such as *Acacia albida*, leaves are shed during the rains and new leaf is put out during the dry season. Many trees and smaller plants start to leaf or to flower a short time before the first rains arrive. Within the Sudan savanna belt the flat river flood-plains, liable to seasonal inundations, carry stands of tall Fan Palms (*Borassus*) among other trees: these flood-plains are known in Hausa as 'fadama'. The tree types within this zone vary from broad-leaved to thorny, and wide local variations occur. This is also probably due to man's interference, albeit indirect, in that the type of tree which survives may be dependent upon the intensity of the grazing. If cattle are not too numerous, they appear to encourage woody growth by eating down the grass in the rains and so reducing fire damage in the dry season. Over-grazing, however, leads to cattle consuming not only the grass but also the foliage of young seedlings: under these conditions only the thorny species tend to survive, and locally it causes southward extensions of almost pure acacia woodland into relatively well-watered districts.

The Sahel savanna may have short grass in the moister areas, and this is never burned, being too valuable as pasture for the cattle herds. The typical tree is the thorny flat-topped *Acacia raddiana*, with smaller bushes such as the Salt Bush (*Salvadora persica*). From a distance there may be an impression of extensive woodland, but the trees or bushes are rarely within touching distance of each other, and the soil may be almost completely bare over wide areas.

It has been suggested earlier in this chapter that the savanna areas would have been the most attractive parts of West Africa, for early man. It must be remembered in this connection that early man would probably have found heavier woodland where the Guinea and Sudan savannas now extend, firstly because of moister conditions in the past, and secondly because the effects of widespread burning would not have been apparent. The most open areas would then probably have been in what is now the Sahel savanna belt, and it is indeed in this zone that the sites of the medieval Sudanic kingdoms lie. The southward movement of vegetation zones under man's influence has probably been continuous for thousands of years: Eyre[36] stresses that Hanno's account of his voyage in the 5th century B.C. referred to extensive fires, even though their exact location has not been determined.

Northward the vegetation thins out to nothing, except for widely scattered solitary plants, and for patches of vegetation in places with locally higher rainfall. In the areas of subdesert steppe annuals will germinate, grow, seed and die within a few weeks after rain, the seeds if necessary waiting some years for the next rain-storm.

Southward the savannas give place to high forest, except in the coastal zone from eastern Ghana to southern Dahomey, where they reach the sea. The high forest varies in character, and has been variously subdivided, as, for example, into Rain and Dry Forest, into Evergreen and Mixed Evergreen-Deciduous Forest or into Tropical Rain Forest and Tropical Seasonal Forests.[37] Keay's later work[21] refers to Moist Forest at low and medium altitudes without detailed subdivision, and in terms of general human geography this is sufficient for present purposes. The character of the forest is well known. Normally there are three tiers of canopy, at about 120, 60 and 40 feet (37, 18 and 12 metres), trees having straight trunks and few branches below the crown; the latter is more spacious in the taller A layer than in the more crowded zones of the B and C layers. Below the lowest layer little direct light reaches the ground except when a large tree dies and falls, giving temporary light and space over a small area. The absence of light tends to an absence of low plants at ground level, and tree seedlings grow very slowly indeed, sometimes staying almost dormant for decades while waiting for the fall of one of the surrounding trees, after which there is a burst of sudden growth activity until the space is filled (usually not by one of the slow-growing dominants but by faster-growing secondaries which will be superseded and shaded out of existence within 20 years). The absence of grass and bush at ground level prevents fire damage. Lianas, epiphytes, stranglers and other plants have their individual adaptations for the acquisition of water as well as light, and the absence of a ground layer is not necessarily accompanied by space between the tree trunks at ground level – sometimes the tangle of plant material is sufficiently thick to require a 'matchet' for the cutting of a route through the forest. Sometimes movement is comparatively easy, depending on rainfall and forest age, as stated earlier. The shedding of leaves throughout the year preserves a surface layer of plant remains, which decomposes rapidly, and maintains the base-status of the soil in spite of leaching by heavy rains. The soils beneath the forest are leached and laterized to tropical red earths, but in a natural state the decomposition of the surface material may prevent too great an imbalance and soil acidity. The nature of the underlying parent rock appears important in this respect; granites may give brown forest soils and grits highly acid soils.

Initial penetration of the wetter forest by man must have been difficult. When necessary, men lived in the forest, practising shifting cultivation in a very primitive manner, so that regeneration of the forest after a year's farming presented no difficulty. The forest in its natural state contained a number of separate micro-climates at different levels above and on the ground, and shifting agriculture on a small scale would lead to only slight and temporary disturbance of these. Not until man had arrived in the forest in large numbers did the deterioration become serious, with the frequent clearing of farm patches and the practice of burning the material cleared; these changes have let in heat and light, have allowed the direct impact on the soil of heavy rain and, in the drier areas, the drying effect of the harmattan, while at the same time checking the leaf-fall on which the natural cycle was dependent. As in the northern zones of West Africa, man's influence on the forest in recent centuries has in many areas changed totally the nature and character of the vegetation and of the soil. In the extreme case, when trees have been extensively felled for the preparation of farmland, only the oil palm (*Elaeis guineensis*) survives, to give a vegetation type frequently referred to as 'oil palm bush'. This palm, although indigenous, is not a true inhabitant of the high forest, as it rarely grows above 50 feet (15 metres) and would normally be killed by forest shade. However, over wide areas, particularly in south-eastern Nigeria, there is a fairly thick woodland cover of oil palms, not in plantations, but in almost pure stands. This is particularly noticeable where high population pressure is felt on the leached and acid soils of the sandstone areas, where the oil palm can flourish under conditions inimical to most high forest species.

The continued existence of original high forest anywhere in West Africa is doubted. Probably the whole of the present forest area has been cultivated at some stage, with secondary growth over farm clearings. The most likely area for virgin forest is in Liberia, where population densities are still relatively low and pressure on the forest for cultivation or exploitation has not been widely experienced away from the vicinity of the larger settlements. Where large clearings have been made in primary forest, the combination of heat and wind may lead to hardpan development, giving increased run-off, with gullying and soil erosion, and making regeneration difficult even for secondary forest growth. Invasion by grass may lead to fires. Resultant alteration of soil structure and processes may lead to permanent changes in the vegetation, and perhaps to continued or accelerated leaching without the rehabilitating effects of leaf-fall. For this reason the establishment of tree crops is preferable to complete clearing of the forest for annual plants, in order to preserve at least some shade cover and some leaf addition. The oil palm, the raphia palm, cocoa, kola, coconut, coffee, rubber and citrus trees are therefore all to be expected and encouraged as major crops in the southern parts of modern West Africa, possibly combined with interplanted crops; plantation agriculture of this type is less likely to cause gross disturbance of the natural conditions than any other type of agriculture.

Between the moist areas of high forest and the savannas, the forest changes in character. Increasing numbers of deciduous trees are mixed with the evergreens, and in the drier areas with a dry season exceeding four months and with at least part of this time under the dry air of the Tropical Continental air mass, some of the deciduous trees shed their leaves in this season, giving a leaf carpet always liable to burning. This simultaneous shedding of leaves by many of the trees results in much stronger illumination of the ground and the growth of grass and ground plants, although these tend to die back in the drought. The drier margin rarely has trees exceeding 60 feet (18 metres) in height; the wetter areas may preserve the three-tier structure of the high forest, but with decreasing numbers of epiphytes in particular. Along the banks of water-courses, long tongues of fringing forest extend into the Dry Forest zone. These tongues, which have affinities with the moist high forest rather than with the surrounding vegetation, are thicker and less open than the Dry Forest. In part this is due to the greater amount of moisture available for growth, and in part it results from the greater amount of light reaching the ground laterally as well as vertically and so encouraging vegetative growth. The greater density of riverside vegetation is apparent even in the moist high forest.

On the coastal side of the high forest are other variants. 'Swamp Forest' is the name given to the vegetation cover of the fresh-water swamp areas. The forest cover in these areas, which may be seasonally or occasionally flooded, is similar in character to the moist high forest, although with more epiphytes and possibly impenetrable lower levels where the tree canopy is more broken. As elsewhere, the cover is thickest along the river banks. The plants present will vary with local site, being most typical of the high forest on any drier 'islands' in the swamp lands, and containing more palms such as the *Raphia* palm, in the wetter locations. The drier 'islands' may be important as settlement sites. In the brackish water of the estuaries and lagoons Mangrove Forest may occur, forming a dense tangled mass of tree stems, roots and aerial branches over a surface of soft mud. The Mangrove Forest is not found unless the mean annual rainfall exceeds 70 in (1780 mm), and it develops best where the mean total exceeds 100 in (2550 mm). Individual trees may exceed 100 feet (30 metres) in height, but the average height is about 40 feet (12 metres). The Mangrove Forest is almost completely impenetrable, and it forms a barrier between the drier land and the sheltered waterways of the rivers and lagoons, a barrier which impeded contact between the European sailors and the coastal peoples just as it had probably discouraged the latter, arriving overland at the coast, from nautical enterprise. On the sandbars separating the lagoons from the sea, and on the drier parts of the coast where mangrove is absent, there is frequently a low discontinuous cover of succulents, herbs and stunted bushes, with scattered coconut palms. This thin cover may thicken to a tangle of bushes, creepers and trees, the latter including exotics such as *Casuarina* and the cashew (*Anacardium occidentale*), with a variety of savanna grasses and annuals. Variation of soil type, resulting from the mode of formation of the sandbars, in some areas cause the alignment of parallel bands of vegetation, long narrow grassy glades alternating with largely impenetrable strips of thick vegetation, giving an unmistakable striped aspect from the air. In the 20th century these coastal strips have sometimes been developed for coconut plantations, or as pasture for small herds of the dwarf cattle immune to trypanosomiasis infection.

Montane vegetation of various types occurs on the highlands of West Africa. In the extreme S.E. of the region is Mount Cameroon, which has a zoned vegetation unique on the West African mainland. The zones vary in height round the mountain, rising higher on the wetter south-west side, where mean annual rainfall totals about 400 in (10,160 mm) per annum. High forest extends up to 5000–7000 feet (1515–2135 metres), with 'mist-forest' above about 4000 feet (1220 metres). Mosses, epiphytes and tree ferns give way to lichens and grasslands at higher levels, whilst some stunted trees, together with moss cushions and short grass become dominant above 10,000 feet (3050 metres). Other highland areas of West Africa do not show this perfection of zoning on account of lower altitude. The highlands of the eastern frontier of Nigeria and of the Cameroons show a sharp break from forest to grassland, generally at about 4000 feet (1220 metres), but tongues of gallery forest may be found in valleys up to 7000 feet (2135 metres). The abrupt change from high forest to grassland occurs mainly at the top of the great scarp surrounding the higher plateaux, and is comparable to the sharp change from high forest to savanna seen elsewhere at lower levels, but human interference has reduced the tree density of the savanna and has rendered difficult the distinction between savanna and montane grassland, which is probably represented in true form only above 7000 feet (2135 metres). The same sequence is seen on the Jos Plateau of Northern Nigeria, where destruction of the savanna trees has been recognizable since the opening of the tinfields to modern methods. The higher parts of the Fouta Djallon and of the Guinea Highlands also show the same abrupt change from forests on the flanks and in the marginal valleys to grassland over the summit areas. Each of these upland areas has its own vegetative characteristics, which will be considered later; each has also played an important part in the historical geography of West Africa.

One striking feature of the vegetation map of West Africa is the separation of the eastern and western forest areas by the belt of savanna country reaching the coast between Accra and Porto Novo. This has made the southern areas of Dahomey, Togo and south-east Ghana open to easier penetration by peoples from the north. It is perhaps not surprising that whereas most of the southern districts of West Africa failed to develop large organized states comparable with those of the northern savanna areas, this central area of savanna country was exceptional. The kingdom of southern Dahomey was large and powerful, and its neighbours on the east were the Egba kingdom of Abeokuta and the Yoruba kingdom of Oyo, both on the fringe of this southward extension of the grasslands; on the west the kingdom of Ashanti was in an approximately similar situation. The reasons for this savanna corridor to the coast are not clear. It has been variously suggested that it arises from the southward deflection of the harmattan winds by the Togo-Atacora mountains; from the drying effect of winds blowing onshore after crossing the cool waters welling up off this stretch of coast, as a result of the slight off-shore movement of the Guinea Current, deflected by Cape Three Points; and from the configuration of the coast, roughly parallel to the dominant wind for much of the year and therefore receiving less rain. The 'dry' corridor can be clearly distinguished from the maps of Mean Annual Rainfall and of Mean Monthly Rainfall, and it appears that here, at least, there is a stronger assumption of climatic control over the vegetation type than is thought to be the case with the main belt of savanna woodland. This association of climate and vegetation would seem to be confirmed by the presence of a second 'dry corridor' in the Ivory Coast, as shown by the rainfall maps. This is less well established than the belt previously mentioned, and the map of Mean Annual Totals (Fig. 5.10) shows only the northern part as markedly drier than the areas to east and west. This northern section of the western corridor is, however, reflected in the vegetation, the savanna extending in a broad tongue southward into the Ivory Coast.

The origin of the two dry corridors remains uncertain. The three factors involved for the eastern corridor sound plausible in relation to the area concerned, but none of them applies to the western corridor, and it is improbable that there are no causative factors common to both. It is tempting to suggest that the whole of the central part of the West African coastal lowlands should constitute a dry zone, stretching from near Cape Palmas to the Nigerian frontier, with an alignment of isohyets (and vegetation boundaries) related to the prevalent wind directions. To the east of this broad zone climate is associated with the seasonal shift of the I.T.C.Z., modified by the highland regions of Nigeria and the Cameroons; to the west is a separate climatic province in which the alignment of the coast in relation to wind direction, together with the alignment of highland areas inland, maintains an air mass boundary inland and a semi-monsoon system: the monsoonal rainfall of Freetown starts only when the Tropical Maritime air mass passes over the highlands and starts to move northwards across the interior plains. The extreme eastern and western areas of West Africa may therefore be climatically distinct in origin. Between them the dry zone is incomplete, being broken into two corridors, separated by a south-west to north-east belt of higher rainfall. The latter significantly starts over that part of the coastline, in the eastern Ivory Coast and western Ghana, where the coast is more nearly at right angles to the south-west winds; it extends inland across the higher areas of Ashanti where orographic rain could be expected, to the Togo-Atacora ranges and the main watershed of Dahomey. It is not possible to say whether this belt of higher rainfall would be located here without this alignment of coast, scarpland and highland ranges. The increased westerly component in the winds of July and August, noticeable over the whole length of the southern coastlands, would further contribute to the dryness of the central area occasioned by the extension over it of the inversion zone of the Tropical Maritime air, as the westerly winds blow parallel to the coast and give rain only on those coasts aligned from north-west to south-east in west and east. The generally high degree of unreliability of rainfall in this region suggests that, whatever the cause of the dry corridors, the dominant air masses are delicately poised.

The environmental factors set out thus far tend to the implication that climate, more than any other factor, has affected man's settlement and activity in the West

African region. Vegetation, it has been suggested, is less clearly controlled by climate, although obviously individual plants will require climatic conditions suitable to themselves, the present location of broad zonal boundaries being in large measure the result of man's own interference. The factor of disease depends on a combination of climate and man, in that the insect vectors are not entirely dependent upon natural climatic conditions, but may survive and, indeed, flourish in microclimates resulting from man's interference with the natural vegetation. The influence of soil type has been seen to be greatest in areas seriously affected by hardpan formation, this resulting from broad climatic conditions or locally as a result of forest clearing, and being dependent upon the presence of level ground. Where the ground is not level, conditions of soil and vegetation may vary considerably in a short distance, and a catena may be identifiable which is reflected in the land use.[38][39] The influence of parent material on soils can be seen in the tropics as in temperate regions, and marked changes over different materials are sometimes reflected in a complicated pattern. The extent to which this is found depends in part on the degree of weathering of the parent material. It is therefore appropriate at this stage to consider the land forms of West Africa and their broad effects upon human activity.

The greater part of West Africa approximately south of the fourteenth parallel consists of pre-Cambrian rocks. The major rock groups as distinguished by Haughton[40] are as follows (oldest at the bottom):

> Younger Granites
> Buem Formation
> Falemian
> Togo Series
> Nigritian
> Tarkwaian
> Birrimian Granites
> Pre-Birrimian Granites
> Pharusian
> Birrimian
> Dahomeyan

These, broadly grouped, are shown in Figure 5.20. The Dahomeyan includes the Basement Complex of Nigeria. The rocks of the pre-Cambrian are mainly metamorphic or igneous, but they include a few old volcanic rocks. The pre-Cambrian rocks are important today for their included minerals, such as the iron ore from the Marampa haematite schist of Sierra Leone, the magnetite quartzite of the Nimba Mountains, on the Guinea–Liberia frontier, of Dahomeyan age, and the auriferous conglomerates of the Tarkwaian in Ghana. The mineral industries are, however, of modern working only (with a few exceptions) and the early human significance of the formations lies elsewhere, as will be shown.

Palaeozoic sediments outcrop extensively in West Africa. Not all the sediments can be dated, as widespread continental deposits without fossils, occurring

West Africa : Geology

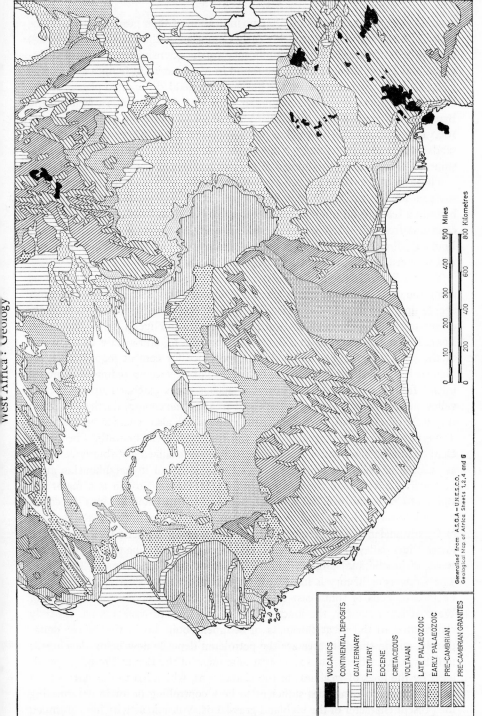

VOLCANICS
CONTINENTAL DEPOSITS
QUATERNARY
TERTIARY
EOCENE
CRETACEOUS
VOLTAIAN
LATE PALAEOZOIC
EARLY PALAEOZOIC
PRE-CAMBRIAN
PRE-CAMBRIAN GRANITES

0   100   200   300   400   500 Miles
0   200   400   600   800 Kilometres

Generalised from A.S.G.A.—U.N.E.S.C.O.
Geological Map of Africa Sheets 1,2,4 and 5

Figure 5.20

sometimes in isolated localities, offer no indication of their position in the time-scale. The oldest rocks are probably early Cambrian (a tillite in the Kayes area), but the beds of greatest human significance are the extensive sandstones of Ordovician and Devonian age. These are found in Mauritania; in Guinea and Portuguese Guinea, where they form the horizontally-bedded dissected plateau of the Fouta Djallon, traversed by rectangular fault systems; in western Mali, in the Bamako area, where the (Cambrian) Sotuba and overlying sandstones total 1000 feet (300 metres) in thickness; in southern Mali, where the Bandiagara sandstones exceed 1800 feet (550 metres) in thickness; and in the Voltaian sandstones of Ghana, also containing a tillite, and possibly of Cambrian age and later.

These sediments form a great, discontinuous ring of sandstone plateaux whose surfaces for the most part offer little prospect of agricultural prosperity. The bounding scarps have offered shelter in some cases, as at Bandiagara, and springs emerging from the scarp foot have nourished settled communities such as in the Fouta Djallon or, in the past, round the margins of the Hodh. These plateaux will be considered in greater detail in the next chapter.

The earliest Mesozoic sediments in West Africa are scattered occurrences along the coast of Ghana which may be of Upper Jurassic or Lower Cretaceous age, faulted into the pre-Cambrian. Lower Cretaceous sediments are repeatedly encountered along the coast eastward from Senegal to Nigeria. In Dahomey the Lama limestones, exposed in a depression parallel to, and a little to the north of, the coast, may have some modern importance for cement manufacture. In Nigeria is found the only extensive occurrence of Cretaceous sediments running inland from the coast. The Lower Cretaceous rocks extended up the Benue valley and the Gongola valley to the Chad area and the country north of Nigeria; they were overlaid by Upper Cretaceous strata which also extended up the Niger Trough, resting unconformably upon the basement rocks beneath. The coarse character of the basal beds of the Cretaceous, their localized distribution, and the association of volcanics with the Lower Cretaceous and its neighbouring areas in Nigeria, have led to the suggestion that the Benue Trough is a major rift valley of Cretaceous age,[41] representing the furthest extension into the continental interior of the major Lower Cretaceous disjunction initiating the division of Gondwanaland in this region: the alignment of the Upper Cretaceous of the lower Niger valley is seen as a non-faulted warping extending the Upper Cretaceous disjunction[42] aligned southwards from the Cameroons to the Cape. The Cretaceous history is important for several reasons. Firstly, in the Upper Cretaceous beds of south-east Nigeria are the only economic coal deposits of West Africa: secondly, the junction of the two lines of weakness has possibly contributed to the great thickness of sediment built up in the Niger delta: thirdly, within the delta area are the petroleum deposits now being developed: fourthly, the north-east to south-west alignment of the Benue Trough is paralleled by the lines of weakness in the Cameroons, which led to the extrusion of volcanic rocks in quantities sufficient to be a controlling factor in determining the present character of the highland grasslands. Volcanic activity has continued until the present day (Mount Cameroon erupted in 1959), but most of the volcanic sources ceased activity in Tertiary or Quaternary time. It has been estimated[43] that some of the younger cones of the Jos Plateau were active not later than 50,000 years ago.

Marine transgression intermittently covered much of the northern areas of West Africa from the Cretaceous onward. However, the *Continental Intercalaire*, of Late Jurassic to Cretaceous age, is a continental deposit which corresponds to the Nubian sandstones further east, and gives sandstone plateaux in a number of West African localities. A narrow belt of marine Tertiary deposits is found along much of the West African coast, widening slightly in Nigeria, where continued subsidence in the delta area led to a thickness of some thousands of feet. These beds included occasional deposits of phosphate and extensive deposits of lignite in Southern Nigeria, which may be of commercial value at a later stage.

Along the northern margin there are other important continental deposits dating from the Eocene onwards. In French literature these clays and sandstones are normally referred to as the *Continental Terminal*. The two great areas are in Mali and in the Chad Basin. Detailed reference to the former will be made later, in connection with the Inland Delta of the middle Niger valley. In the Chad Basin the depth of sediments is very considerable, locally exceeding 2000 feet (610 metres), and the fluctuating extent of the lake has left exceedingly flat plains over the inner parts of the basin. The lake varies considerably in area, and a very wet year can cause wide extension, as the average depth is very little: if restricted to 4600 square miles (12,000 sq km), in area, the average depth is about 4 feet (1·25 metres) and the maximum depth no more than 12 feet (3·75 metres) – extended to 8000 square miles (21,000 sq km), the average depth increases to 13 feet (4 metres). Intercalations of lateritic crusts with the sediments indicate repeated fluctuation in the past. These hardpan layers, and also clay lenticles, lead to perched water-tables in some districts, which have influenced settlement sites in a region where the depth to the water-table may exceed 300 feet (90 metres). Included with these continental sediments must be the windblown deposits of the northern districts. Major areas of dead dunes have been described by Grove[44] and others,[45] and these have had effects on settlement and farming practice.[46] Variations in the texture of aeolian drift have also caused major variations in soil type, as shown by the modern distinction between the Zaria and Northern Drift soils in Nigeria: the former, representing up to 14 feet (4·25 metres) of very fine material, are exceedingly difficult to work, being heavy and waterlogged in the rains, drying hard and cracking in the dry season, and being used for cotton, whereas the Northern Drift soils are of coarser texture and of lesser fertility, but admirably suited to groundnut cultivation. Sediments elsewhere may have a different significance, such as the riverine alluvium of the Jos Plateau, sometimes buried beneath basalt flows of Tertiary or later age, which is washed for the separation of cassiterite eroded from the Younger Granites. Vast quantities of sand have moved by longshore drift in very recent time to

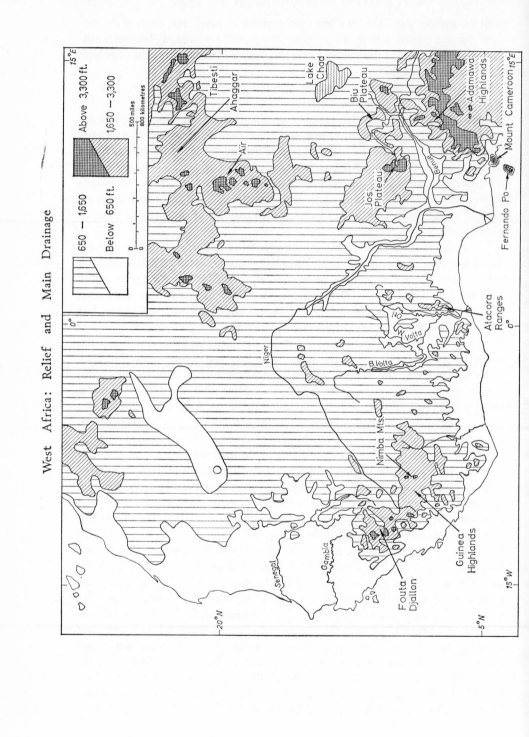

West Africa: Relief and Main Drainage

650 — 1,650   Above 3,300 ft.

Below 650 ft.   1,650 — 3,300

500 miles
800 kilometres

Tibesti
Ahaggar
Aïr
Lake Chad
Biu Plateau
Jos Plateau
Benue
Adamawa Highlands
Mount Cameroon
Fernando Po
Niger
B. Volta
Ho
W. Volta
Atacora Ranges
Nimba Mts.
Guinea Highlands
Fouta Djallon
Gambia
Senegal

15°E
0°
15°W
20°N
5°N
0°
15°E

Cyclic Surfaces of West Africa

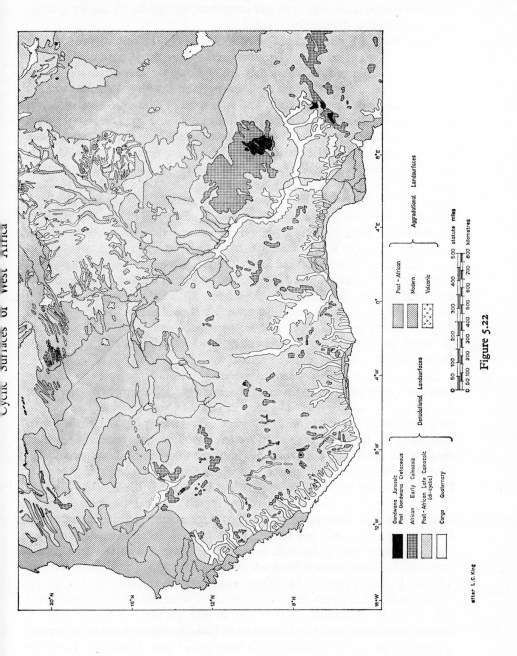

Denudational Landsurfaces

		Gondwana Jurassic		Post Gondwana Cretaceous

African Early Cainozoic

Post-African Late Cainozoic (di-cyclic)

Congo Quaternary

Aggradational Landsurfaces

Post - African

Modern

Volcanic

0   50   100   200   300   400   500 statute miles
0 50 100   200   300   400   500   600   700   800 kilometres

after L.C.King

Figure 5.22

build the coastal sand-ridge spits and complexes, so creating the lagoon systems between them and the mainland.[47]

An outstanding feature of the West African landscape is the existence of extensive plains of great perfection. In some areas these are depositional surfaces across young sediments, in others they are erosional surfaces across older sediments; over wide areas they are erosional surfaces cut almost indiscriminately across a variety of basement rocks and structures. These plains can be found at considerable altitudes, notably on the Jos Plateau of Nigeria, where they rise to some 4600 feet (1400 metres) and at varying altitudes in the highlands of the Cameroons.[48] Even older residuals rise above this uppermost surface, which is identified as the Gondwana by a number of writers, Jurassic in age according to King.[49] This is the oldest surface of recognizably wide extension in West Africa, although away from the two localities mentioned it appears only as a summit plane across higher residual masses, such as the Idanre Mountains of south-western Nigeria, Mount Agou in Togo and the Nimba Mountains of south-east Guinea. It is significant in the human geography of the region for two reasons. Firstly, its even form and high altitude (in its upper tracts) have resulted in mountain grasslands which have become important herding areas in the last century. Secondly, the highlands of the Cameroons, forming the physical eastern boundary of West Africa, have not formed a clear mountain barrier between different ethnic groups as might have been expected. Instead the mountain grasslands have provided, to some extent, a route for southward extension of Sudanic influences into equatorial Africa.[50]

The surfaces are usually separated one from another by scarps, or by narrow zones of broken country. In general the Gondwana surface owes its survival to the resistance to erosion offered by the rocks across which it is planed, so that the drop from the Gondwana to the next lower surface is abrupt. Round the southern margins of the Jos Plateau the scarp is some 2000 feet (600 metres) in height, a massive and forbidding wall which has been put to use in modern times for the generation of hydro-electric power, and which formed a natural refuge area for fugitive communities in early days. Below the scarp is the head of the next wide surface, rising to about 2400 feet (730 metres), and below a second, smaller scarp is the most widespread of the West African surfaces, ranging in height between 1400 and 2000 feet (425 and 610 metres), in altitude. All the West African surfaces vary in altitude, as would be expected with sub-aerial plains stretching in some cases for hundreds of miles; many have been gently warped. The full sequence from the Gondwana surface to the present cycle has not yet been identified, and correlation over the whole of West Africa has been attempted only in the broadest outline.[51] Studies in different parts of Nigeria suggests that six major cycles may be identifiable. In individual areas the number appears greater, on account of well-developed local phases due to warping. The great surfaces of the northern parts of West Africa have been the location of the major indigenous states, lying in the savanna zone of open woodland or grassland, with regular rainfall and at least seasonal relief from insect pests.

West Africa : Major Physical Regions

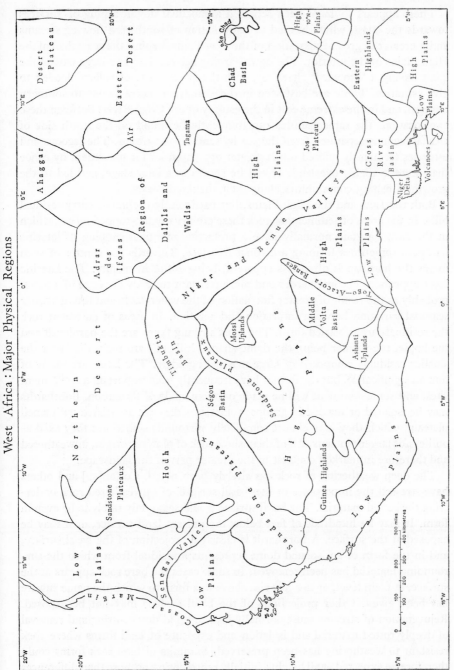

Figure 5.23

There appears to have been repeated monoclinal downwarping of surfaces towards the coast, which has led to rejuvenation of southward-flowing streams and a greater degree of dissection of the Low Plains behind the coast than of the High Plains of the interior. The downwarping has resulted in a large part of the coast having a 'drowned' character, with the lower parts of valleys flooded to give estuaries. These are best seen in the west from Sierra Leone to southern Senegal, and in the extreme east in the estuary of the Cross River. Between these two locations the same features can frequently be found on the north side of coastal lagoons separated from the sea by sand-ridge systems. The lagoons and estuaries frequently offered much greater opportunities for movement by canoe than were available overland, as will be shown at a later stage, and led to the growth of fishing communities along their sheltered coasts.

Both the Low and the High Plains, but particularly the latter, carry residual hills. In the areas of sedimentary rock these are usually flat-topped mesas, which in the savanna zone normally have a protective marginal capping of lateritic hardpan, sometimes forming a distinct free face. Towards the centres of such mesas the hardpan is often less apparent, being softer in quality. The lateritic layer appears to become harder and more resistant towards the edge of a mesa, probably as the result of greater fluctuation of the water-table and thus a greater seasonal variation between saturation and aeration. In areas of basement rock the residuals are of varied form. The most striking types are the bornhardt and the kopje, the former being the dome-shaped hills of bare rock, the latter the smaller residuals composed of large massive boulders. The latter are rarely of human significance, but the former have frequently been important as settlement sites, and some comment will be made on their mode of formation. Bornhardts may be isolated or massed in groups; sometimes they are associated with small plateaux which they may almost completely surround; sometimes they exist as outliers of larger plateaux. All of them show rock of plutonic origin, unweathered and therefore in marked contrast to the greater part of the landscape.

The deep weathering of rock has already been noted. Cotton[52] and others have stressed the importance of the 'basal surface' of unweathered rock under-lying the rotted material. The basal surface would seem only rarely to be even in form. It may be hundreds of feet below the present land surface, or it may be exposed at the surface. A bornhardt is clearly a projection of the basal surface, and in the form of an isolated dome represents a residual from which the sur-rounding material has been removed. In some cases the bare rock appears at the surface, at plain level, or as a low rise above it, a form to which the name ruware has been given. Other projections of the basal surface may not be exposed. Rejuvenation of streams must normally lead to rapid downcutting and removal of deeply rotted material and isolation and exposure of land forms where rock resistant to weathering has been preserved. Summits of bare rock forms could therefore be expected at all heights, initially representing no more than differences in the depth of weathering before exposure. In the field it is found that correla-tion appears possible between many of the summits, the bevels on the complex bornhardts and the surfaces on the larger residual masses, and summit planes continuing these surfaces can be postulated. This implies that erosion of the bare rock hills can occur as an extension of the general plain level.

It is possible to suggest the sequence of events following the rejuvenation of successive cycles of erosion. The exposures of bare unweathered rock are reduced to plain level in two ways, firstly by the recession of hill-sides, and secondly by general lowering of small residuals. The first method can be seen where some residuals show petrological boundaries some little distance in advance of the bornhardt sides, and the great residual mass of the Jos Plateau shows that the scarp in some places has retreated by as much as half a mile from the edge of the resistant Younger Granites to which the Plateau owes its existence. Retreat of this order does not imply the existence of bare rock exposures at the foot of the hill or of the scarp: the rate of retreat has been estimated[53] to average 1 foot in 150–300 years, and in the lapse of time following exposure to sub-aerial influences the rock newly exposed at plain level may develop at least a thin mantle of soil. The possible causes of retreat are several. The bornhardt normally displays two contrasting joint systems, one being a sub-rectangular system and the other a tendency to curved exfoliation joints. The latter may be due to relief of load following the removal of overlying material, and this may well be a major factor when exfoliating sheets are exposed at plain level; it may be due to partial failure of the rock on the dome sides following the removal of the material formerly there, that is, the response to outward pressure; it may be due to expansion of crystals in the rock following the advent of moisture and air; in a few very thin cases (a few inches only, whereas some shells may be 30 feet (10 metres) or more in thickness) it may be due to thermal effects, rock surfaces in the savanna regions heating to about 160°F. (71°C.) on occasion, with a nightly drop in temperature which can be as much as 130°F. (72°C.). The curved exfoliation joints can sometimes be found continuing a short distance below ground level. The formation of exfoliation joints seems to take place only shortly before exposure. The sub-rectangular jointing has several effects. If well developed before exposure, it may lead to sub-surface weathering along the joints and the division of the rock into a mass of corestones which, on later exposure, may have the form of a castle kopje; if accentuated after exposure as a result of outward pressure towards the hill-sides, it may lead to etching out of joints by sub-aerial weathering (including root pressure and greater water acidity if vegetation takes hold) so causing division of a bornhardt into two or more fractions – if these joints are sufficiently numerous, a bornhardt may be completely subdivided into a mass of large blocks while initially still retaining its curved outer profile. This is a second form of castle kopje. The greatest effect of the sub-rectangular joint system is probably the determination of the pattern of major stream flow by alignment along major joints, so subdividing an upland mass into a number of compartments[54] of different sizes, some of which develop as bornhardts and others, more quickly, into castle kopjes.

A large residual mass may tend to develop jointing only near its margin, where accentuation of the dormant joint system may be assisted by active stream incision, and a tendency towards slope failure. In the vicinity of a scarp, therefore, it is possible (although not inevitable) that division into compartments may be well illustrated on the residual side of the scarp, and bornhardts and other remnants may show a high frequency on the lower side of the scarp. Not all the latter will rise to the summit plane of the main residual mass; some will have experienced sub-surface rotting to below the plane level before exposure, and others, which may formerly have risen to the plane level, will decline rapidly in summit altitude as their sides retreat inwards or as sub-aerial weathering reduces them.

The pediplanation theory stresses the difference in type of water flow between the scarps or hill-sides and the plains. On the hill-sides the water flow is turbulent and highly erosive, water moving down every crack and gully, in turbulent fashion. On the plains the water ideally moves as laminar sheetflow, non-erosive, across the pediment slope, the pediment being the long slope, slightly concave upwards, at the plain head immediately below the hill-side. A pediment may be of very considerable width, sloping all the way to the flat flood-plain of the nearest stream or river. Because the water flow across the pediment is non-erosive, while the flow on the hill-sides is highly erosive, downward cutting is restricted to the hill-sides. It follows that a scarp area, particularly if represented not as a single scarp between upper and lower surfaces, but as a zone of residuals and compartments with active streams and youthful, steep-sided valleys, acts as a belt of localized downwearing. Inevitably this belt moves across country, cutting into the edge of a higher surface and extending the inner margin of the lower surface, and the effect is one of backwearing of scarps and of parallel retreat of hill-slopes although the processes are those of localized downwearing. The downward movement of material in this belt is not due entirely to the action of turbulent water flow. Water will cut down actively only if possessed of tools, in the form of load particles, with which to work; very often water running over the rock will be clear, with very little erosive effect, but this is only to be expected if the rate of slope retreat is of the order estimated. Periodically load will be supplied as a result of soil creep, of debris due to gravity spalling or failure of the rock surface due to unequal mechanical expansion or chemical reaction to atmospheric agents, and wherever load is supplied erosion will be resumed: each fractional increase of incision enhances the possibility of new development. Repeated study of any bare rock face may fail to exemplify active erosion by turbulent running water, but this may nevertheless be a potent factor. There are frequently numerous small rills or gullies on the scarp or hill-side, of which only a minority are continued by stream channels across the pediment – a very large number end at the scarp-foot knick, where the water apparently changes from its confined and turbulent flow to the laminar sheetflow of the pediment. The net result of this zoned concentration of downward action of all forms is the creation of a landscape of broad, old-age surfaces stepped one above the other, separated by the belts of youthful country or by scarps.

The pediment has been stated by King[55] to be the most important element in the African landscape. The tropical pediments of Africa are not in all respects identified with their desert counterparts of higher latitudes. West African pediments are rarely cut in bare rock, but normally carry a cover of soil or weathered material which may be thin close to the scarp foot but of considerable thickness lower down the gentle slope, where weathering has had longer to act. Indeed, the pediment has often never existed on bare rock. Rejuvenation may lead to the steady progression inland of the incised valleys of a new cycle, with the erosive downward action in localized zones as stated above. The new cycle will advance rapidly up major streams and their tributaries, and more slowly into the minor tributary valley systems: division into compartments may result in areas of unweathered rock, but over much of the land surface the new cycle will be operating on rotted material above the basal surface. In this case the hill-sides will retreat more rapidly, and the pediments will be developed on lateritic material in the first instance, apart from higher projections of the basal surface which will tend slowly to wear to the plain level. In more humid areas the pediment becomes straighter in profile and steeper in gradient, before disappearing as a clear land form in the most humid parts of the region.

The pediment is thus primarily an area of transport. Water passes across it as a smooth laminar sheetflow provided that the depth of flow does not exceed a few inches, a depth rarely attained even with the intense rain of line squalls. In its natural form the pediment appears to be designed for rainfall of fair intensity, allowing the rapid passage across country of large quantities of water in minimal time. The laminar flow means that the water in contact with the ground, checked in movement by plants, is (if moving at all) soaking vertically downwards, but the rate of seepage can be very slow, particularly at the beginning of the rains when the surface is baked brick-hard. Twenty-four hours of continuous sheetflow has been known to give no more than 9 in (23 cm) of percolation.[56] Some erosion inevitably takes place, but in the form of a gradual lowering of the pediment surface as the hill-sides above it retreat. The final landscape form will tend to be a mass of coalescing pediments all subject to slow reduction: on the interfluves the concave form gives place to convexity as a result largely of soil creep, and the old-age landscape may show little preponderance of either concave or convex forms.

The pediment is of great importance in the human geography of all but the most humid parts of West Africa. The long pediment slopes, not exceeding 6°-7° in gradient even at their steepest, provide the obvious site for agricultural activity, being well-watered and well-drained, with a soil cover, often not present on the hill-sides, and lacking the heavy vegetation of the flood-plains, which required much greater effort in clearing. Also the water-table is frequently close to the surface of a pediment still in active development, being most accessible at the scarp-foot knick or pediment head, where water can sometimes be found at depths of only two or three feet. After prolonged heavy rain, the water-table may intersect the surface so that the scarp-foot knick becomes a spring line.[57] Settlements nevertheless tended to avoid the pediment in favour of the hill

I

summit in areas lacking political stability, but the pediment remained the most rewarding land form from the agricultural point of view. In peaceful areas the pediment is the obvious place for house construction, and many of the older quarters of the larger towns are centred on pediment sites. The preservation of the pediment is thus clearly a matter of the greatest importance, the more so because it is the element of the landscape which is most vulnerable. Any disruption of the laminar flow of water may be disastrous. The building of two houses may cause the canalization of storm water flow between them, as well as the development of a footpath: water running over the latter assumes a turbulent flow, highly erosive; within a few years the pediment is traversed by a gully six feet or more in depth, concentrating more and more of the water flow as its side branches proliferate; in addition, if the gully is deep enough to transect the water-table, it rapidly lowers the level of ground water; if this falls below root level the vegetation cover will wither and die; and the A horizon of the soil, no longer bound by the vegetation, may blow or wash away to leave infertile badland even before extension of gullying has destroyed the original pediment form. When this occurs it is possible to find local changes in land use. On the original pediment surface, farms are increasingly confined to the higher parts of the pediment head, not yet jeopardized by the gully action. The lower parts of the original surface are at this stage only narrow infertile ridges between the gullies, but as the latter widen their flat floors are used by farmers for new plots. A two-tier agricultural pattern thus develops, the lower tier progressively increasing in size at the expense of the upper, and in due course the coalescing of the widening gullies may lead to a new surface, graded to the same drainage system, but at a more gentle slope than the original pediment. Regrading of the landscape can thus occur without the advent of a new cycle or a change in base level. A similar two-tier pattern of land use can be seen where marginal depressions lie between the hill-side and the pediment head.[58]

So-called primitive peoples in many parts of West Africa have appreciated the importance of pediment preservation, as is shown by the stone wall terracing in many districts. This terracing, most impressive on steep hill-sides, extends to pediments with slopes of no more than $2\frac{1}{2}°$. The magnificence of the terracing could be described as being in inverse ratio to the power and importance of the tribe responsible. Usually the terracing is seen on steep hill-sides or scarps, and it may run from top to bottom of a scarp, as it does near Kwong, on the south-east side of the Jos Plateau of Nigeria.[59] Individual terrace walls may be up to 6 feet (2 metres) in height, and terraces may be no more than a foot or two in width. The districts concerned are usually refuge areas to which have fled small, weak communities, individual tribes today often numbering only a few thousand. A weak group of this type had no choice of farming sites. Farms on the savanna woodland of the plateau surface were liable to be overrun by stronger peoples in search of slaves; farms on the savanna woodland of the plains below the scarp were equally liable to this fate. Consequently farming was restricted to the steep scarp slopes on which raiding cavalry could not operate, the settlements themselves being in narrow and easily defended valleys, often hidden by rocks and gallery forest. The scarp farms were terraced of necessity, and the extension of farming to the lower plains was safe only for a minimal distance: wherefore the need to preserve the soil over this safe distance was great and conservation was important. Today the pediments are in greater danger than at any previous time, not only because more people are living and farming upon them, but also because contacts with other parts of the world have led to the introduction of agricultural techniques not always suitable for the country. The plough can be disastrous if furrows are run up and down the pediment; clean weeding can lead to accelerated soil erosion which may be avoided by indigenous methods. Much research is still required on the most suitable methods of increasing agricultural production without damaging the natural environment.

The bornhardts rising above the plains are not always of simple form. In some cases they form a ring of domes around a small tableland; in other cases large residuals are bevelled to give a dome-on-dome form. The origin of these complex forms would appear in many cases to be cyclic planation by scarp retreat, as the bevels and upper plains can be correlated with summit planes across neighbouring residuals. The successive stages of this type of feature are seen in Figure 5.24. A cyclic scarp retreating rapidly across rotted material may be checked on an un-weathered mass, and may have made only slight inroads upon this before the advent of a later cyclic scarp. The first new cycle is then left represented by a bevel on the sides of the mass. Not all major residuals show such bevels – some, on very resistant rock, will withstand the arrival of successive cyclic scarps with-out modification. Where the lower dome shows marked exfoliation, this would seem to confirm that jointing due to relief of load takes place at a very late stage. Where a kopje stands on a dome, it may be that the former has evolved from sub-aerial disintegration of the upper dome during the greater period of exposure to atmospheric agents. It is, of course, conceivable that in some such cases the kopje and the dome have evolved in a single cycle by the exposure of sub-surface forms evolved at different depths and therefore under different degrees of decomposition; it is equally possible that some bevels may represent sub-surface or sub-aerial accentuation of disintegration along the plane of a major horizontal joint in the sub-rectangular system. It is unlikely that this is always so, however, as a number of the major bornhardts carry summit lakes in rock basins which must be free of joints through which water could soak away. The Addo Rock in Western Nigeria[60] carries two rock basin lakes and three bevels, and as the lakes are close to the dome sides it is clear that the rock is not traversed by major joints. The significance of these lakes as a settlement factor, and of the use of the tablelands as settlement sites, will be mentioned later (pp. 243–4).

The great plains have had their own effects on human history, and their per-fect form is well demonstrated by a statement[61] that in the Chad Basin a fisherman once caused the permanent diversion of river water from 1000 square miles (2600 sq km) of country by the placing of a fish trap: the latter, being of the customary pattern of a row of vertical sticks, created an obstruction which

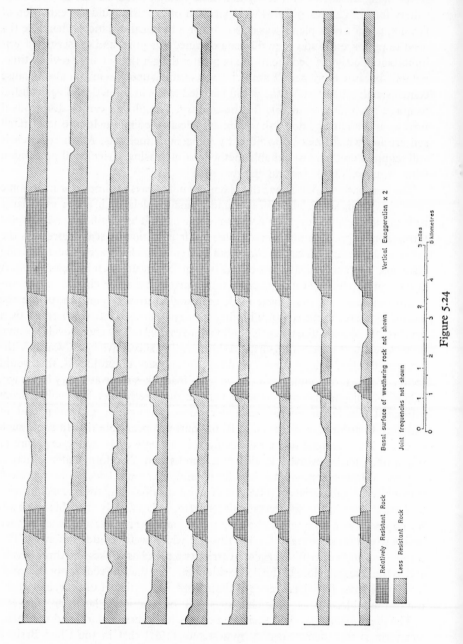

Retreating Scarps and Bevelled Bornhardts
Successive Stages of Surface Development

Relatively Resistant Rock

Less Resistant Rock

Basal surface of weathering rock not shown

Joint frequencies not shown

Vertical Exaggeration x 2

Figure 5.24

was too great for a river which was scarcely flowing over an almost level course. The flood-plain of a river with a very low grade tends to be wide, with an uncertain and indeterminate channel, and may be covered with a broad belt of fringing forest. The clearing of the vegetation may be laborious, complicated by the locally increased intensity of insect infestation as a result of higher atmospheric humidity and the presence of pools and swampy ground, so that the flood-plains, notwithstanding their alluvial soil, are not always sought by the indigenous peoples. A number of diseases, additional to those already described, are largely localized in river areas, and may incapacitate the inhabitants of riverine settlements. A variety of parasites may be introduced into the human body, as a result of fly bites to give *filariasis* of different forms. One of these is *onchocerciasis*, commonly called 'river blindness', caused by the worm *Onchocerca volvulus*, the embryos being transmitted by the black *Simulium* fly which frequents the river banks. This is common in the Lower Volta basin of Ghana and affects up to 85 per cent of the people in some districts of Nigeria – not all the infected individuals lose their sight, but 15 per cent of the inhabitants may be blind in some settlements. The filarial worm *Wuchereria bancrofti*, mosquito-borne, is very common and widely scattered, and can lead to elephantiasis, although fortunately few patients progress to this stage of disability. The Guinea Worm *Dranunculus medinensis* infests many West African districts. The embryos infect a minute fresh-water crustacean, and if this is swallowed the adult worm may develop in the human host, usually being about a yard in length and entwined in the tendons of the leg when ready for parturition, embryos being discharged through a sore at the ankle when the human host steps into water. The worm can cause great swellings of the leg and may incapacitate whole villages in badly affected districts. Infection seems less likely with running water than with stagnant pools. Modern wells are designed with concrete aprons sloping outwards to avoid contamination of well water by embryos ejected following the spilling of water over an infected leg. Bilharzia is also widespread, and probably millions of West Africans carry the worm *Schistosoma haematobium* or the less common *S. mansoni*. The former resides in the bladder, the latter in the rectum, and eggs are passed out of the human body with waste products, the resulting embryos seeking the snail *Physopsis globosa* which can exist in foul and muddy water. Minute worms, invisible to the eye, emerge from the snail and enter the human host through any skin area exposed in infested water. In some cases the resulting debility can be extremely serious, and the cure long and difficult; in others the patient suffers only minor discomfort. Not only are most West African rivers infested, but also the lagoons of the coastal districts, where more than three-quarters of the inhabitants may suffer from the disease. It is not surprising that watershed settlement is usually preferred to a riverine site.

   The wide almost flat plains have already been mentioned as being the areas best suited to the formation of lateritic concretions. It has also been stated that rotting of parent material may extend to hundreds of feet below the surface. This has contributed to the great depth to the water-table in some areas, which made

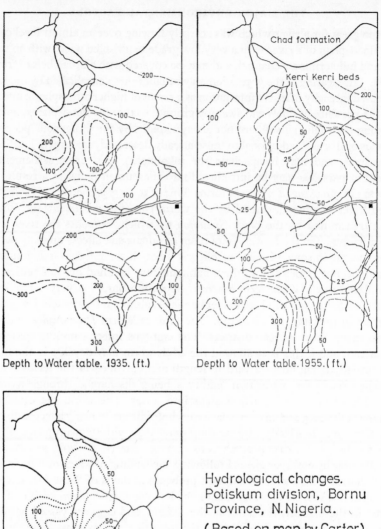

Depth to Water table. 1935. (ft.)

Depth to Water table. 1955. (ft.)

Chad formation

Kerri Kerri beds

Hydrological changes.
Potiskum division, Bornu
Province, N. Nigeria.

(Based on map by Carter).

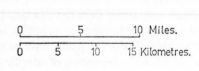

■ Damagum

Potiskum–Maiduguri rd.

0		5		10 Miles.
0	5	10		15 Kilometres.

Rise in Water table. 1935-55. (ft.)

Figure 5.25

necessary the digging of the very deep wells, and at the same time made this task physically possible. Modern deep boreholes have been preferred to surface reservoirs in such areas, firstly because of the difficulty of storing water where the underlying rock has rotted, and secondly because the wide valleys of the plains would create reservoirs of very great extent in relation to depth. Under such circumstances the loss by evaporation would be prohibitive. The northern savanna districts have mean annual evaporation losses of the order of over 60 in (1500 mm), which exceeds the mean annual rainfall, and large reservoirs would hold water for only a short period of the dry season. The only surface reservoirs likely to be wholly successful are those on unweathered rock in the youthful scarp zones, where loss through percolation would be at a minimum and the reservoirs would have greater depth in relation to surface area.

The depth to the water-table has shown some marked variations in the course of this century. It has been shown[62] that the water-table in parts of Bornu has risen by over 200 feet (60 metres) in 50 years, which is a phenomenal rate of change. This follows the establishment of colonial rule in Northern Nigeria, and the movement of peoples from Kano and from Bornu into the empty no-man's-land which had lain along the common boundary of these two hostile kingdoms. The clearing of the light forest cover by these immigrant farmers has resulted in a greater percentage of surface run-off and reduced percolation. As a result stream flow has been increased, and seepage through the stream bed has caused a ridging of the water-table beneath the main valleys and a lowering of the table beneath the watersheds. In one place the ground water has been raised to surface level, leading to inundation of the valley floor. Similar changes must have occurred in the past as population density increased and the forest cover was reduced; the southward withdrawal of the forest belts after the last glacial episode must likewise have affected the ground-water profiles.

A further effect of the wide plains is to be seen on the river régimes. It has been stated that the rate of run-off is high, even on rotted rock, at the beginning of the wet season, and the percentage of rainfall reaching the streams remains high throughout the year over the greater part of West Africa as a result of the intensity of much of the precipitation. Heavy falls of rain lead to sheetflow across the pediments and to sudden increases in stream volume. Flash floods are therefore common, as the sudden influx of water gives a peak flow which moves steadily downstream, and water levels may rise at the rate of several feet per hour, falling again with equal rapidity after the passage of the flood. With small rivers flash floods of this type rarely last more than one day. A river draining a larger catchment area may receive a succession of floodwaters from different parts of the basin, representing merely fluctuations in the normal seasonal rhythm of flow. Over much of West Africa even large rivers cease to flow in the dry season, at least in the northern districts, although water may be available a few feet below the stream bed. The length of the period of flow appears to be decreasing in many areas, coupled with an increase in the amount of sediment transported by the river. Very few measurements of stream flow have been made, but it would seem that the pattern of Bornu is being experienced elsewhere, namely that as increasing areas of natural vegetation are being cleared so the percentage run-off is increased and the percolation and ground-water storage reduced. This results in quicker response of river level to storms, and an increasing tendency for soil particles to be washed away, a matter which could rapidly assume serious proportions and has, indeed, already done so in crowded areas such as Iboland, where the sandstone cuestas have a barren aspect, while the rivers below the Udi scarp follow shallow braided courses over wide deposits of alluvial material.

On the great plains the low grade results in low speed of flow. In the north it is possible to find the abnormal conditions of stream flow decreasing with distance from source, in such cases as the inland drainage from the Jos Plateau towards the Chad Basin. On the sediments there is a steady percolation loss through the stream bed, as well as steady reduction of volume by evaporation, which may be very great in view of the river's width/depth ratio. These streams supply only $1\frac{1}{2}$ per cent of the waters of Lake Chad, and in some years fail to contribute to its volume. The low speed of flow is well illustrated by the floods of the Niger and the Benue. The Niger headwaters receive vast quantities of water between May and August, and the peak of the flood, 25 feet (8 metres) above low-water level, reaches Koulikoro, near Bamako, in October. By the end of December the peak flood reaches Kabara, on the river near Timbuktu, by the following June it has travelled to Gaya, in the Niger Republic, and by the second December it is in the lower course of the river in Nigeria. Even allowing for the great length of the river, this is a slow passage, with the best speed achieved between Koulikoro and Kabara, an average of nearly 200 miles (320 km) per month, or 7 miles (11 km) per day. This is the section of lakes and swamps, which are frequently stated to delay the flood passage. On the contrary, the rate of flow apparently decreases from Kabara to Gaya, in spite of increased gradient, and the average speed is only a little over 100 miles (160 km) per month at Gaya. Subsequently it accelerates again, but this is not unconnected with the additional floodwaters provided by the tributaries in the lower half of its course. There are, in effect, two flood peaks in the lower course, one from the current year's rainfall, reaching the river between June and November, and one from the previous year, still on passage to the sea. The river level is further complicated by the great volume coming down the Benue, but peak period here is between August and November (varying with position on the river). In the lowest part of the Niger course, below the Benue confluence, the level is least between February and June, when no floodwater is available. The seasonal rhythm of the river is utilized in the cultivation of flood-plain lands for rice and other crops; farms cover the alluvial levels, enriched by annual sedimentation and exposed at low water, when the river level falls by as much as 35 feet (11 metres) below flood level.

On arrival at the coast the Niger divides into a distributary system in the delta. The vegetation changes from high forest to swamp forest to mangrove swamp, with particularly thick undergrowth along the river banks. Life in the swamp area must of necessity be based on fishing rather than on farming, although some agriculture may be attempted on the drier 'islands' within the swamps. The villages are often on stilts above swamp level, or are house-boat settlements. Elsewhere on the coasts the swamp soils are sometimes used for agriculture, but this depends on a variety of local circumstances. A certain amount of sand gives

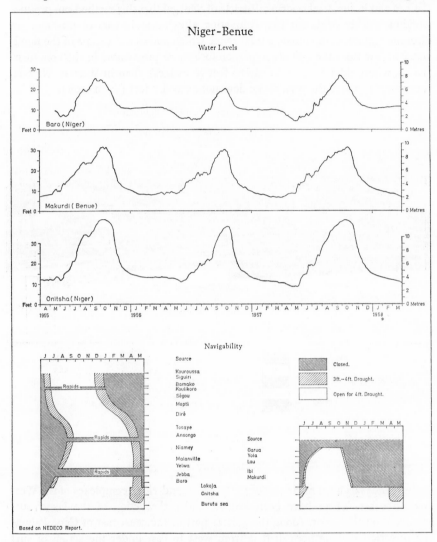

Figure 5.26

the black swamp mud (sometimes called the poto-poto) a greater degree of stability, but the greatest objections to agricultural development are the acidity and the salinity of the coastal swamps. The pH values in some coastal sites are as low as 4 after clearing of mangrove. Acid or saline soils can nevertheless be prepared for cultivation by repeated flushing with fresh water. This is best achieved by surrounding the area with embankments allowing rainwater to accumulate (not difficult when the mean annual total is 100 in (2500 mm) or above) and releasing the floodwater through the embankments at low tide, the process being repeated regularly over a number of years. It has been found in Portuguese Guinea and in the neighbouring districts of Senegal that this method can produce workable paddy fields for rice cultivation after several years of flushing. An essential feature is, of course, a tidal range which allows the escape of the floodwater at low tide; the technique is therefore more practicable in the area mentioned, where tidal range is nearly 20 feet (6 metres), than in Western Nigeria, for example, where the tidal range does not exceed 5 feet (1·5 metres).

Badagri   Sand   Ridges   and   Vegetation

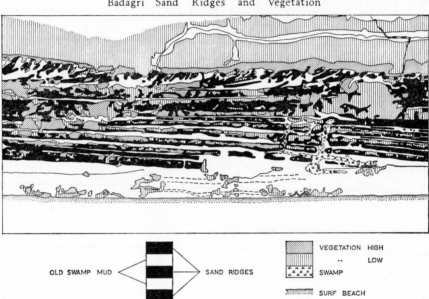

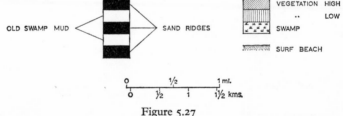

Figure 5.27

Reference has been made earlier to the great sand-ridge complexes of the West African coast. These have been formed under the action of the heavy surf prevalent on this coast. Along the greater part of the coast east of Cape Palmas the direction of longshore drift is from west to east under the action of surf motivated by the south-west winds blowing throughout the year. The sand barriers between the ocean and the lagoons of the Ivory Coast, south-east Ghana, Dahomey and Nigeria are, in reality, huge sandspits which have joined the mainland at their further ends. Their origin can be recognized from detailed study of any section[47] of the barrier, and Figure 5.27 shows the recurved ends of the first spit to grow, and the later sub-parallel developments, in part of Western

Nigeria. These sand barriers are breached in a number of places to allow passage to the sea of fresh water from the lagoons or major rivers, and the normal feature of such a breach is a submerged sand bar 11–12 feet (3·5 metres) below water level. Sand crosses the bar below water level, as is shown by the Opobo Bar, for example, where sand is restricted to the bar and thick black mud is found both to the north and south. On reaching the far end of the bar, which is curved in form, with the receiving end set back relative to the other, the sand resumes normal longshore drift along the beach. The direction of drift can be determined from the map by inspection of the regular setting back of beach alignment where breaks occur. The 12-foot channel itself appears to moves slowly along the bar in the same direction as the sand, reappearing at the leading end after each passage to the receiving end. The quantities of sand in the movement are enormous: the first attempt at cutting a canal at Abidjan failed immediately through silting, and the present Vridi Canal is kept open by the deflection of drift sand into the head of a submarine canyon offshore; the moles at the entrance to Lagos Harbour have checked the drift, causing seaward progradation of the western beach by a quarter of a mile (400 metres) in 50 years, with corresponding recession of the eastern beach; the Forcados channel to the Niger delta ports has silted from 25 feet (8 metres) to 11 feet (3·5 metres) in 40 years, and is to have a protective mole built to trap the drifting sand. The last example is of particular interest because part of the Forcados Bar was surveyed by the Marine authorities at regular monthly intervals, and the changes in sand volume calculated. It was found that the greatest monthly increment of new sand was $2\frac{1}{4}$ million tons, although admittedly the following month showed a decline of $1\frac{3}{4}$ million tons. The significant feature is that these are not absolute figures

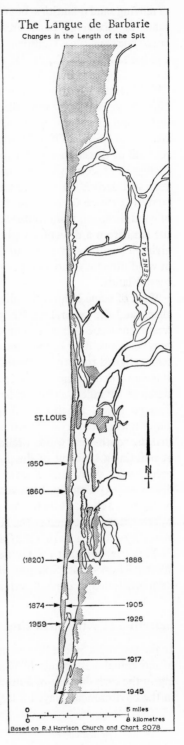

The Langue de Barbarie
Changes in the Length of the Spit

R. SENEGAL

ST. LOUIS

1850

1860

(1820)   1888

1874   1905
1959   1926

1917

1945

0   5 miles
0   8 kilometres

Based on R.J. Harrison Church and Chart 2078

Figure 5.28

of moving sand quantities, but represent only the excess of incoming over outgoing sand (or vice versa) in the area surveyed. As with many features of the African landscape the scale is continental, and must be remembered in the planning of port and harbour works. As the existing sand-ridge systems are related to present sea level, their size is in itself sufficient commentary on the quantities moved annually. The sand barrier of the Ivory Coast, or that of Dahomey and Western Nigeria, is well over 100 miles (160 km) in length and often of considerable width, and must have been built following the stabilization of sea level after the last glacial episode. Of additional interest in the Forcados Bar survey was a slight reversal of direction of sand movement in the middle of the wet season, even though the excess figure was less than 100,000 tons per month. For most of the year surf arrives on this stretch of coast from the south-west, giving a north-westerly drift on the west side of the delta. In mid-year there is a noticeable shift of wind direction from south-west to west, sufficient to bring the surf in towards the land from a direction slightly north of the perpendicular to the coast, thus giving a slight south-eastward drift of material. This is the same westerly shift of wind direction noted on p. 217 as contributing to the 'little dry season' of the coastal lands.

West of Cape Palmas the alignment of the coast in relation to wave direction alters, and the general tendency is for longshore drift to be towards the north-west from Cape Palmas to Portuguese Guinea. Local conditions may, of course, cause effective drift in the contrary direction. The coasts of Senegal and Mauritania, aligned roughly north–south, show a tendency to southward movement of longshore drift. This is particularly noticeable in the case of the Langue de Barbarie, 27 miles (43 km) in length, which deflects southward the mouth of the Senegal River. Small-scale maps indicate wind directions here as seasonally either south-west or north-east, and as the latter are offshore it might be supposed that the south-west winds would be the dominant force in raising waves capable of building a sandspit of this size. Some surf from the south-west does indeed occur every year, and if severe can trim back the spit end for considerable distances.[63] Usually, however, this south-west surf is less effective than the northerly swell aided by the on-shore breezes, from a little west of north, caused by sea-breeze deflection of the North-East Trades, and mentioned on page 183. It is worthy of comment that the Canary Current flows north to south, off the Langue de Barbarie, and that the Guinea Current flows west to east along much of the West African coast. Spit growth in the same directions has thus inaccurately been attributed to current action by several writers.

Selection of settlement sites

In the centuries before the arrival of Europeans, the factors affecting the location of individual settlements in West Africa were broadly similar to those operating in the early history of Europe. Alternatively expressed, the physical factors in the environment played a larger part than the cultural or the technological, and whereas the latter were already of major importance in Europe in Roman times, they remained relatively insignificant in West Africa until the last hundred years. Although the requirements of man from his environment are basically the same the world over, West Africa, like any major region, has its own physical character and its own characteristics in man's reaction to his surroundings.

In the selection of a settlement site the prime necessity was, initially, security against marauders, and it must be borne in mind that locally this remained a major factor even in the early years of the 20th century. The accidents of landscape and of climate have denied to West African peoples many of the typical types of site common in Europe, but have instead produced some types peculiarly characteristic of the region. In both Europe and Africa the early permanent settlements tended to be on hill-top sites (once man had passed beyond the cave-dwelling stage)* which had the advantages of standing above the level of river floods and thick riverine vegetation, and of being readily defensible. However, the characteristics of much of the West African landscape, described above, inhibit the development of a relatively close distribution of hill-top settlements, available hill sites being few in many districts. The dissected marginal lands of the European continent frequently show an ancient settlement on a spur easily defended from fortifications across its neck. This type of site can be found also in West Africa, but is less general because spurs do not exist over wide areas. The most striking features of summit occupance have been the establishment of fortress towns, large or small, and of scarp-face dwellings.

In Europe the defensive factor in site location is also admirably demonstrated on the lowlands. Repeatedly towns are seen which originated as settlements on the projecting tongue of a river terrace, standing above flood level, protected by the river on three sides and by fortifications on the fourth side. This type of settlement is more rare in the northern areas of West Africa because the climate reduces the value of a river loop as a protection. For much of the year the river bed may be dry, so that earthworks or stockades would be required to supplement the defensive value of the river bank: the river bed, of course, provides an open field of fire in the event of hostilities, readily available without the labour of clearing riverine forest, but this may be offset by risks of flood or of trypanosomiasis or onchocersiasis in which the vector is an insect preferring the shady conditions of riverside vegetation. Only in the case of the larger rivers which flow throughout the year may the river form an effective shield on one side of the settlement, or occasionally, as with the Nupe town of Jebba, on an island in the Niger, on all sides.

It is worthy of note that aspect has probably never had the same importance in West Africa as in Europe. This is, of course, a simple function of latitude, in that sun altitude is always considerable and the noon sun is sometimes north and sometimes south of the observer. Shelter from sun is therefore a more or

* Cave-dwellings containing artefacts have been identified at a number of sites, such as north of the Nimba Mountains, and at Ropp on the Jos Plateau; caves are still partially used where settlements adjoin the sandstone scarps.

less uniform problem throughout West Africa. There is no question of seeking sites which will experience maximum insolation: if anything, the tendency is in the opposite direction, or would be if there were any appreciable annual difference between different locations. Shelter from cold is also of relatively less importance over much of West Africa, as mean sea level temperatures are always high and only over restricted areas are altitudes sufficiently great to reduce them to figures requiring serious adaptation of settlement. In consequence it has been possible for settlements to become established on the exposed summits of bornhardts possibly some thousands of feet above sea level, with no fear of over-exposure to cold polar air nor risk of ice on bare rock surfaces, which would be impossibly dangerous in the conditions of a European winter. The need for shelter from low temperatures is replaced by the need for shelter from the physiological cold of the Tropical Continental air in the early part of the dry season. Avoidance of disease may be more important than shelter from the physical elements, and of the latter the one most to be considered for the individual dwelling is the high wind accompanying the line squalls at the beginning and end of the wet season. In view of the general movement of these squalls from east to west, huts are often built with doors facing south-west. The orientation of individual huts is a different matter from the location of village sites, and on the open plains of the savanna regions little can be done to avoid site exposure to winds from any direction. Nevertheless, many examples can be found in West Africa of settlements apparently deliberately sited in positions offering shelter from winds, such as the villages at the foot of the Bandiagara scarp in Mali, screened from the eastern line squalls and to some extent from the harmattan.

Water-supply appears to have played a part much less important than might have been expected, in that hill-top sites sometimes appear to have no permanent source of water. This need cause no surprise, in that it is typical of many prehistoric settlements in Britain and in Europe: Celtic settlements frequently show the same feature. The explanation can be seen in life today in those villages which are still occupied on their original sites. In the village of Gere, on the north side of the Jos Plateau, the women fetch water daily from streams nearly 2000 feet (600 metres) below the settlement, to replenish water stocks held in gourds and large earthen jars; even now, after half a century of settled social conditions in Northern Nigeria, the villagers are reluctant to abandon completely the hill-top stronghold of their ancestors. A hostile force moving over the plains would be seen at an early stage by a watcher on the summit, and would be unlikely to take such a settlement by surprise. Indeed, it is possible that the village would pass unnoticed to strangers moving over the plains, and, if seen, it is doubtful whether the average raiding party would attempt to force its way up narrow defiles blocked by defended stone walls, with no alternative route to the top. The chances are that any such attempts would be abandoned after a few days, unless the investing force were particularly strong, and the water storage of the settlement would probably last that length of time. A protracted siege would imply a force of such strength that resistance by a small village would be useless in any case. For small settlements, therefore, sources of water did not need to be within the boundaries, although manifestly this would be an asset, or even a necessity for communities of any size. Thus larger summit settlements show a predilection for sites with perennial sources of water, unusual though some of these might be.

The Oke Iho Tableland

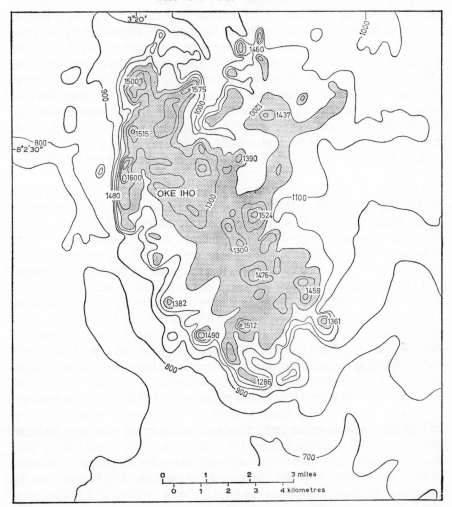

Figure 5.29

The settlement now at the foot of the Addo bornhardt in Yorubaland would appear to have abandoned the summit site only at the end of the 19th century, and the sacred shrine of the ancestors is still preserved at the hill-top. This bornhardt has two lakes on its long whale-back of bare rock, and one of these never fails, although water level varies seasonally. Similar examples are described by

Onawoye.[64] Permanent water supplies must have been essential for any community numbering some hundreds, as such a total would make a prolonged siege worthwhile to a raiding force. Slave-raiding was a characteristic of West Africa – as of other regions – from earliest times, long before the advent of the white peoples, and it persisted into the 20th century in areas remote from European influence. Well-water can be an important source of supply even in areas of crystalline rock, and can be obtained close to the foot of rocky hills, at the top of the pediment, thus adding to the defensive value of rocky outcrops. The larger residuals above the plains, in the form of small tablelands ringed by higher hills, offered excellent sites (Fig. 5.29). Many of the modern towns of medium size, such as Shaki in Western Nigeria, occupy this type of site. Idanre, also in Western Nigeria, is an example of the occupation of a double-tiered tableland with surrounding peaks of over 3000 feet (915 metres) in altitude. In this case the original town was on the upper level, and only relatively recently has it moved to the lower tableland, principally for greater ease of access: the upper tableland, with its approach defiles dammed, is to be converted to a high-level reservoir.

The need for building materials would seem to have been a localizing factor of little importance. The lateritic products of the deep weathering characteristic of so much of West Africa have provided the customary building material, reinforced in some districts with forest products. Roofing materials are at hand in leaves, in the grasses of the savanna belts, or in the ribs of palm fronds in the southern areas. It must be remembered that the grasses of the tropical savannas, often 10 feet (3 metres) or more in length and with basal diameters of a quarter or a third of an inch (6 to 8 mm), can have the consistency of cane if allowed to dry out completely, and furnish admirable raw material for thatching. This type of roofing, effective in colder and wetter climates, is quite adequate for West African conditions; among some peoples such as the Tiv of the Benue valley, thatching has attained standards of excellence in no way inferior to those developed in other continents. Stone in its unweathered condition being absent from large areas of West Africa figures but little as a building material, although in a few districts where it is readily available it is used extensively for house walls and for terrace walls on the farm. Very occasionally it has been used for what may be regarded as major engineering projects, as in the stone bridges near Bokkos. These bridges were built by a people unknown – the present inhabitants of this southern part of the Jos Plateau have no tradition of such works, and do not have in their tribal traditions any record of such building. The bridges were there when the present pagan tribes arrived in the area, and have therefore survived for an unknown number of centuries, a tribute to design and construction.

In the coastal areas the most important consideration was, in most cases, a dry site for housing with easy access to fishing canoes. Where the coast is rocky, raised beaches[65] are sometimes well shown, giving good sites for fishing settlements. In large part, the long, low, straight stretches of sandy beach separated the ocean from the lagoons, and threw the emphasis on to the sheltered smooth waters of the latter rather than on to the surf and swell of the Atlantic, both for fishing and for transport. Behind the lagoons were areas of swamp forest, and of high forest where the land stood above water level, with big timber trees furnishing admirable raw material for dug-out canoes. The latter probably developed at an early date, first with the hollowing-out of trunks by fire, later with wood-working tools made from iron derived from the local smelting, a little distance inland, of the lateritic ironstones. These craft, easily constructed and admirably suited to the lagoon conditions, appear to have remained virtually unaltered in design to the present day. Propulsion is by poles or paddles, assisted in the wider lagoons by small triangular sails.

The reasons for the selection of a site were no doubt often subconscious, and even today the articulate appreciation of the landscape features is not always to be found. The Tiv are discussed later in this book (p. 325), with reference to their tribal history and past movements. The tradition that the tribe originated in the foothills behind Obudu, where their north-westerly movement was temporarily checked by the power of the Jukun on the Benue valley plains, is sufficiently strong for these hills to be used as a reference point for geographical direction and situation. 'Towards Obudu' is therefore 'up', 'away from Obudu' is 'down', whether this be north-east towards Wukari, north towards Lafia, west towards Abakaliki, whether it be down the gentle slope towards the Benue or up the steeper rise from the river northward. The social background to geography appears to be more firmly established than the physical basis – although, in contrast, the only permanent names in the landscape are the hills and rivers, together with a few modern towns of 'foreign' creation, the scattered Tiv hamlets being known by the name of the resident elder member of the family.

Conclusion

The major factors of the physical environment have been set out in broad form, with some discussion of their importance. It has been suggested that for a combination of reasons, the savanna grasslands were probably the areas most favourable for early human activity, and that stronger groups would establish themselves there, with a retreat of weaker communities to the residual hills or to the southern forests. Nothing in this pattern is permanent, however: the seasonal burning of the savanna grass has tended to shift the vegetation zones towards the south; clearing of woodland has affected the water-table; the establishment of settled conditions has increased the incidence of some diseases. The interaction of man and his environment has caused the former to change his habits and preferences, and the latter to change its character. The movement of peoples and customs has caused geographical regions to expand or contract, to survive or disappear, and this was normal even before the advent of the Europeans on the coast, as shown by the rise and fall of the medieval empires.

The advent of the European was to introduce a new and formidable factor. Some of the West African diseases have already been described in relation to particular aspects of the environment. Many others are widespread, such as leprosy and venereal diseases. The latter, in some parts of Africa, affect over 90 per cent of the population, and were prevalent when outside contacts were first made. The most common form is gonorrhoea, which while not lethal produces ill-health and sterility. The majority of sufferers never seek medical advice, possibly because it is not appreciated that the disease exists – with such high incidence rates the symptoms and effects tend to be accepted as a normal concomitant of adult life. The disease has acted as a major control in restricting the population growth, through its sterilizing effects. The population has likewise been restricted in the past by the high death rate from all the major diseases. The colonial powers started the introduction of modern medical knowledge and techniques, and the reduction of the death rate, by the use of surgery, drugs and prophylactic measures. The reduction of the death rate by two-fifths in eight years in Ceylon, as a result of malarial control alone, is an indication of the power of the medical factor, and if this modern knowledge is applied rapidly and extensively in West Africa the increase in population that will result may further change the geographical scene. As malnutrition is already widespread, the food problems of the region are likely to increase enormously within the next decade, and consideration of agricultural practice and potential is therefore of the greatest importance.

BIBLIOGRAPHICAL NOTES

[1] H. Lhote, *The Search for the Tassili Frescoes*, London, 1959.
  J.-D. Lajoux, *The Rock Paintings of Tassili*, London, 1963.

[2] J. Büdel, Climatic Zones of the Pleistocene, *International Geological Revue*, **1**, 1959, pp. 72–79.

[3] B. Farmer, in discussion to R. J. Harrison Church, Problems and Development of the Dry Zone in West Africa, *Geographical Journal*, **127**, 1961, p. 201.

[4] El Bekri, *Description de l'Afrique septentrionale*, trans. M. de Slane, Algiers, 1913, cited in Naval Intelligence Division Handbook, *French West Africa, I The Federation*, 1943, p. 168.

[5] E. P. Stebbing, The encroaching Sahara: the threat to the West African colonies, *Geographical Journal*, **85**, 1935, pp. 506–24.

[6] See, for example, Y. Urvoy, Les Bassins du Niger, *Mémoires, Institut Français de L'Afrique Noire*, **4**, Paris, 1942.

[7] A. T. Grove, The ancient erg of Hausaland, and similar formations on the south side of the Sahara, *Geographical Journal*, **124**, 1958, pp. 528–33.

[8] B. J. Garnier, The moisture resources of Nigeria and their utilisation, *Report of a Symposium of the International Geographical Union, Makerere, Uganda, 1955*, London, 1956, pp. 28–32.

[9] P. R. Crowe, Wind and weather in the equatorial zone, *Transactions & Papers, Institute of British Geographers*, **17**, 1951, p. 33.

[10] S. Solot, The general circulation over the Anglo-Egyptian Sudan and adjacent regions, *Bulletin, American Meteorological Society*, **31**, 1950, pp. 85–94.

[11] M. Garbell, *Tropical and Equatorial Meteorology*, London, 1947.

[12] See S. Gregory, Rainfall over Sierra Leone, *Department of Geography, University of Liverpool, Research Paper No. 2*, 1965, p. 13.

[13] R. Hamilton and J. Archbould, Meteorology of Nigeria and adjacent territory, *Quarterly Journal, Royal Meteorological Society*, **71**, 1945, pp. 231–64.

[14] S. Gregory, op. cit., p. 10.

[15] J. Richard-Molard, *Afrique Occidentale Française*, Paris, 1949, pp. 26–32.

[16] J. A. Prescott and R. L. Pendleton, Laterite and Lateritic Soils, *Commonwealth Bureau of Soil Science, Technical Communication 47*, 1952, p. 35.

[17] H. Scaëtta, Limites boréales de la latérisation actuelle en Afrique occidentale, *C. R., Académie des Sciences*, **212**, 1941, pp. 129–30.
H. Scaëtta, Les types climatiques de l'Afrique Occidentale Française: leur rapport avec l'évolution du sol tropical, *La Météorologie*, 1939, pp. 39–48.

[18] R. Maignien, Formation de cuirasses de plateaux, région de Labé (Guinée française), *Transactions, 5th International Congress of Soil Science*, IV, 1954, pp. 13–18.

[19] R. Maignien, Cuirassement de sols de plaine-Ballay (Guinée française), *Transactions, 5th International Congress of Soil Science*, IV, 1954, pp. 19–22.

[20] N. Leneuf, Les Terres Noires du Togo, *Transactions, 5th International Congress of Soil Science*, IV, 1954, pp. 131–6.

[21] A. Laplante, Les sols foncés tropicaux d'origine basaltique au Cameroun, *Transactions, 5th International Congress of Soil Science*, IV, 1954, pp. 144–8.

[22] H. Vine, Nigerian soils in relation to parent materials, *Commonwealth Bureau of Soil Science, Technical Communication 46*, 1949, p. 4.

[23] R. P. Moss, Soils, slopes and land use in south-western Nigeria, *Transactions & Papers, Institute of British Geographers*, **32**, 1963, pp. 143–68.

[24] P. H. Nye, Some soil-forming processes in the humid tropics, *Journal of Soil Science*, **5**, 1954, pp. 7–21.

[25] F. Fournier, *Explanatory note to map of erosion danger in Africa south of the Sahara* C.E.E., C.C.T.A., 1962.

[26] A. Brown, in K. M. Buchanan and J. C. Pugh, *Land and People in Nigeria*, London, 1955, p. 41.

[27] A. C. Burns, *History of Nigeria*, London, 1929, p. 75.

[28] ibid., p. 102.

[29] Naval Intelligence Division Handbook, *French West Africa, I The Federation*, 1943, p. 133.

[30] T. A. M. Nash, *Tsetse flies in British West Africa*, London, 1948.

[31] R. W. J. Keay, Explanatory notes, *Vegetation map of Africa south of the Tropic of Cancer*, Oxford, 1959.

[32] D. R. Rosevear, *Checklist and Atlas of Nigerian Mammals*, Lagos, 1953, Foreword on vegetation.

[33] R. W. J. Keay, Ecological Status of Savannah Vegetation in Nigeria, in Management and Conservation of Vegetation in Africa, *Commonwealth Bureau of Pastures and Field Crops, Bulletin 41*, Aberystwyth, 1951.

[34] S. R. Eyre, *Vegetation and Soils*, London, 1963, p. 243.

[35] W. B. Morgan and R. P. Moss, Savanna and Forest in Western Nigeria, *Africa* **35**(3), 1965, pp. 286–94.

[36] S. R. Eyre, op. cit., p. 242.

[37] K. M. Buchanan and J. C. Pugh, op. cit., p. 34; Naval Intelligence Division, op. cit., p. 93; S. R. Eyre, op. cit., Chapters XV–XVI.

[38] K. M. Buchanan and J. C. Pugh, op. cit., p. 39.

[39] R. P. Moss, op. cit., pp. 152–3.

[40] S. H. Haughton, *Stratigraphic History of Africa south of the Sahara*, Edinburgh, 1962.

[41] J. C. Pugh and L. C. King, Outline of the Geomorphology of Nigeria, *South African Geographical Journal*, **34**, 1952, pp. 30–37.

[42] A. L. du Toit, *Our Wandering Continents*, Edinburgh, 1937, p. 101.

[43] J. C. Pugh, The Volcanoes of Nigeria, *Nigerian Geographical Journal*, **2**, 1958, pp. 26–36.

[44] A. T. Grove, op. cit. See especially Figs 1 and 2.

[45] J. R. V. Prescott and H. P. White, Sand formations in the Niger valley between Niamey and Bourem, *Geographical Journal*, **126**, 1960, pp. 200–3.

[46] W. D. Clayton, The swamps and sand dunes of Hadejia, *Nigerian Geographical Journal*, **1**, 1957, pp. 31–37.

[47] J. C. Pugh, A classification of the Nigerian coastline, *Journal of the West African Science Association*, **1**, 1954, pp. 1–12.
J. C. Pugh, Sand movement in relation to wind direction as exemplified on the Nigerian coastline, *Department of Geography, University College, Ibadan, Research Notes*, **5**, 1954.
J. C. Pugh, The Porto Novo–Badagri Sand Ridge Complex, *Department of Geography, University College, Ibadan, Research Notes*, **3**, 1953.

[48] J. C. Pugh, High-level surfaces in the Eastern Highlands of Nigeria, *South African Geographical Journal*, **36**, 1954, pp. 31–42.

[49] L. C. King, *Morphology of the Earth*, Edinburgh, 1962, p. 223.

[50] H. Baumann and D. Westermann, *Les Peuples et les Civilisations de l'Afrique*, Paris, 1948.

[51] L. C. King, op. cit., Fig. 119, p. 300.

[52] C. A. Cotton, The Theory of Savanna Planation, *Geography*, **46**, 1961, pp. 89–101.

[53] L. C. King, Canons of Landscape Evolution, *Bulletin, Geological Society of America*, **64**, 1953, pp. 721–52.
J. C. Pugh, Isostatic Readjustment in the Theory of Pediplanation, *Quarterly Journal of the Geological Society*, **111**, 1955, pp. 361–74.

[54] Lester King, A Theory of Bornhardts, *Geographical Journal*, **112**, 1948, pp. 83–87.

[55] Lester King, The Pediment landform: some current problems, *Geological Magazine*, **86**, 1949, pp. 245–50.

[56] For similar conditions in N.E. Africa, see J. A. Hunt, A general survey of the Somaliland Protectorate 1944–1950, *C. D. & W. Scheme D.484*, London, 1951, p. 55, cited in J. E. G. W. Greenwood, The development of vegetation patterns in Somaliland Protectorate, *Geographical Journal*, **123**, 1957, pp. 465–73.

[57] R. W. Clayton, Linear depressions (Bergfussniederungen) in savannah landscapes, *Geographical Studies*, **3**, 1956, pp. 102–26.

[58] C. A. Cotton, *Climatic Accidents in Landscape Making*, Wellington, N.Z., 1947, p. 95.
F. Thorbecke, Der Formenschatz im periodisch trockenen Tropenklima mit überwiegender Regenzeit, *Düsseldorfer Geographische Vorträge*, **3**, 1927, pp. 11–17.
J. C. Pugh, Fringing pediments and marginal depressions in the inselberg landscape of Nigeria, *Transactions & Papers, Institute of British Geographers*, **22**, 1957, pp. 15–32.

[59] J. C. Pugh and A. E. Perry, *A Short Geography of West Africa*, London, 1960, p. 198.

[60] A. Bernard, Afrique Septentrionale et Occidentale, *Géographie Universelle, Tome XI*, Paris, 1939, p. 413, plate.

[61] C. Raeburn and Brynmor Jones, The Chad Basin: Geology and Water Supply, *Geological Survey of Nigeria, Bulletin 15*, 1934.

[62] J. D. Carter, The rise in the water-table in parts of Potiskum Division, Bornu Province, *Geological Survey of Nigeria, Records*, 1956, pp. 5–13.

[63] A. Guilcher and J. P. Nicolas, Observations sur la Langue de Barbarie et les bras du Sénégal aux environs de Saint Louis, *Bulletin d'Information du Comité Central d'Océanographie et d'Etude des Côtes*, **VI**, 6, 1954, pp. 227–42.
A. Guilcher, Dynamique et morphologie des côtes sableuses de l'Afrique atlantique, *Cahiers de l'Information Géographique*, 1954, pp. 57–68.

[64] M. O. Onawoye, A note on some inselbergs around Bauchi, Northern Nigeria, *Nigerian Geographical Journal*, **3(2)**, 1960, pp. 33–37.

[65] S. Gregory, The raised beaches of the Peninsula area of Sierra Leone, *Transactions & Papers, Institute of British Geographers*, **31**, 1962, pp. 15–22.

Figure 5.16 is based on a map by Ch. Toupet in the West African Atlas to be published by the Institut Français d'Afrique Noire.

CHAPTER 6

Local Factors in the Environment

The major factors were set out for West Africa as a whole in Chapter 5, at the end of which it was stressed that even some of the natural boundaries within the major region are in a state of movement, and that geographical regions, in terms of man's activities, transcend and even modify the physical pattern of the environment. Nevertheless some detailed consideration of the landscape and climate is inevitable, because the scale of Africa involves generalized association of very different features which may have profound local effects. Also it is true that the main features of the relief are immovable in the landscape, and although physical boundaries may not be geographical boundaries in the true sense, they may nevertheless have their own effects upon the latter. In this chapter, therefore, an attempt is made to describe, set by set, the stage on which the human play has been, and is being, enacted, while remembering that the scenes are not complete in themselves but may be grouped in acts or may have relevance to more than one act. Necessarily, also, this chapter is in danger of being closely allied to the piecemeal regional treatment which the authors have already deplored.

The northern sector

THE MIDDLE NIGER BASINS

The medieval kingdoms of West Africa were situated mainly in the areas north of the river Niger. The Ghana empire, traditionally founded about the 4th century, and finally destroyed in the 13th century, had its capital between Goumbou and Oualata, in what is now the south-eastern corner of Mauritania. The capital city was said to have been a double or twin-town, one half housing Moslems and the other half housing the unbelievers (an interesting forerunner of the twin-towns of modern years) and to have been situated in prosperous farming country.[1] Ghana was succeeded by the Mali, or Manding empire, whose rulers moved to a capital on the Niger, below Koulikoro, where they cleared the forest[2] and encouraged agriculture. The Songhay empire, centred on Gao, was also concerned chiefly with districts north of the great river.

These areas today are desert or semi-desert, and, away from the river, among the least attractive parts of West Africa. The plains containing the upper basin of the Niger will be mentioned later. From them three rivers flow northward, the

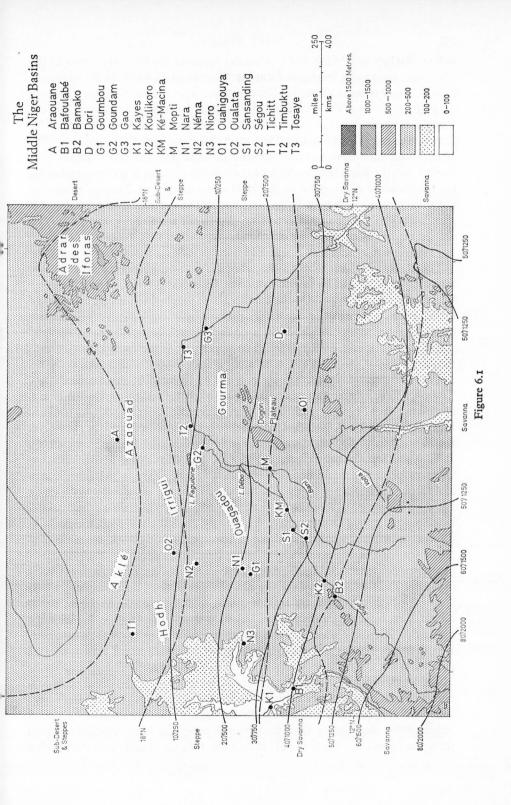

The Middle Niger Basins

A	Araouane
B1	Bafoulabé
B2	Bamako
D	Dori
G1	Goumbou
G2	Goundam
G3	Gao
K1	Kayes
K2	Koulikoro
KM	Ké-Macina
M	Mopti
N1	Nara
N2	Néma
N3	Nioro
O1	Ouahigouya
O2	Oualata
S1	Sansanding
S2	Ségou
T1	Tichitt
T2	Timbuktu
T3	Tosaye

miles   0   250
kms   0   400

Above 1500 Metres,
1000–1500
500–1000
200–500
100–200
0–100

Figure 6.1

Bafing, Bakhoy and Niger, the two former entering the sandstone mass of the
Manding Plateau and uniting to form the Senegal river, while the Niger takes a
north-easterly course to Bamako. Here it passes from the pre-Cambrian rocks of
the High Plains on to the belt of sandstones aligned roughly east to west. Modern
Bamako is situated in the gap where the Niger passes between the high cliffs,
forming the edge of the Manding Plateau on the left bank, and the sandstone hills,
which on the right bank are scattered some distance from the river. The site is an
ancient one, the Keita family which was to provide the Manding emperors having
been established at Kangaba, on the river above the site of Bamako, as early as
the 7th century. Not only does the site command the narrow river routeway, but
also it marks the end of navigation on the upper river, being the site of the
Sotuba rapids. The forty miles of channel across the sandstones to Koulikoro
are interrupted by rapids.

The character of the Niger valley shows a marked change on entering the
Ségou basin. This can be said to extend as far as Lake Débo, and to include a
variety of landscape types. On the southern side the Bani valley can be included
in the basin, although the two rivers do not unite until Mopti. The surface
materials are alluvial, brought down from the upper valleys of the two rivers and
spread as a great area of deposition. The upper part of the basin has older sedimentary deposits, laterized with time and partially capped with a hard carapace,
but downstream this is increasingly overlaid or replaced by more recent clays.
The river in the upper part of the basin is slightly incised below the flat plains,
but by the time Ségou is reached the river is capable of overflowing its banks at
flood periods. Below Ké-Macina the incision has disappeared, and the river gives
the impression of flowing above the general level of the surrounding country,
spilling over from its main channel to give a complex braided system of distributaries, of which the most important is the Marigot de Diaka, which flows north-
east through fen country towards Lake Débo. Urvoy shows a contoured sketch,
based on instrumental levelling of the Office du Niger, which shows the contours
making downstream convex curves where they cross the two main channels.[3]
This is not surprising in view of the general gradient, which is no more than
about 1:17,000 or approximately $3\frac{1}{2}$ in per mile (6 cm per km). Older distributary channels, abandoned by the river, leave its present course on the north bank
as far upstream as Ségou, where the old channel of the Fala de Molodo starts
a course which initially is almost due north. A little lower downstream, below
Sansanding, the Fala de Boky-Wéré follows a course more in keeping with the
present distributary system, keeping roughly parallel to the river for a considerable distance, passing a little to the north of Ké-Macina and thence aligned
parallel to the Marigot de Diaka in the direction of Lake Débo. The Fala de
Molodo also becomes a crest channel, and 100 miles (160 km) north of Ségou,
east of Sokolo, is well above depressions to both sides. These two channels have
dried out very recently, and have been the basis of modern irrigation schemes
based on the Sansanding Barrage, whereby water has been returned to them
from the Niger, the Sahel Canal serving the Fala de Molodo and the Macina

Canal serving the Fala de Boky-Wéré. This is the major project of reviving the 'dead' channels of the Inland Delta area, and is discussed in detail elsewhere.

Below Lake Débo the Niger valley is marked by a large number of lakes, chiefly on the right bank of the river. That these are lower than the river is shown

The Inland Niger Delta

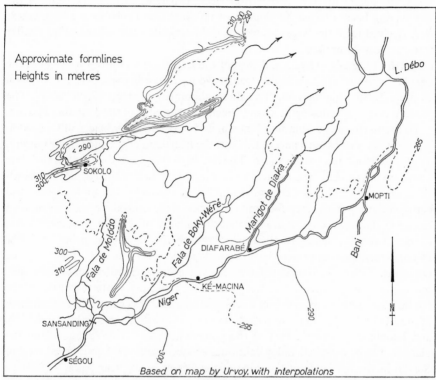

Figure 6.2

by the fact that Niger floodwaters pass to the lakes, but flow is never in the opposite direction. The lakes are relatively shallow. Between them are sand dunes, and it appears that the Niger re-established itself in this area after a dry period had led to erg formation, the lakes now representing the overflow of river waters into the hollows between the dunes. The gradient through the lacustrine sector is very slight indeed, and the variations in size of Lake Débo appear to be entirely dependent upon the annual flood and its subsequent decline. The lakes north-west of Goundam, where the Niger turns eastward, are of a different character, the largest being Lake Faguibine, which may be up to 50 miles (80 km) in length and 100 feet (30 metres) deep. These lakes are not inequalities in fen swamps, but lie at the leeward base of sandstone hills round which dunes have moved from the eastern side. From the western end of Lake Faguibine an old natural water channel extends north-westward, in which water flowed intermittently in the 19th century. This had been partly deepened by a Songhay emperor in the 15th century as a military supply canal, but the channel is clearly the remains of a natural waterway draining towards Oualata and the ergs of Irrigui and Aklé. The former is an area of old dead dunes aligned WSW–ENE, but Aklé has a live erg of active barkhans. Part of Aklé, however, shows clay deposits between and around dune bases, the height of clay on the latter being constant, with all the signs of the clay having been a lacustrine deposit of no great age. Probably the lake waters were derived from the Niger by way of the Faguibine channel and other similar features near Timbuktu.

North of the Ségou Basin and west of the lacustrine sector of the Niger is the erg of Ouagadou. This is a double feature, young dunes being superimposed upon an older fossil dune system. The dune alignment is again WSW–ENE. The western extremity runs up as a sand sheet over the edge of the Manding Plateau.

To the north of the Manding Plateau, and north-west of the erg of Ouagadou is the Hodh. The eastern part of this was the heartland of the old Ghana empire. Today the Hodh is a barren waste. The northern margin of the Hodh is the clear scarp, up to 600 feet (180 metres) in height, which marks the edge of the sandstone plateaux ringing the central Hodh. These scarps are known as *dahars*, and between the northern scarp foot and the dunes of the central erg is a narrow strip known as the *baten*. On this are situated the remains of abandoned villages, some of them fishing settlements, all clearly established on a former spring line. The fishing settlements appear to have been dependent on lakes now buried in the erg sands. Tichitt, in Mauritania, remains as a spring line settlement of some size, but many smaller oases with spring water lie along the western margin of the Hodh. The southern margin is of a different character, because the northern flank of the Manding Plateau is not a clear scarp but is partly delimited by the Bakhoy and Baoulé river valleys. East of the point where the latter emerges from the plateau, a large marginal valley continues eastward and turns southward west of Sokolo in the flat lands of the edge of the Ségou basin, near Nara. This large valley, dry at its upper end, meets the present Senegal valley at Bafoulabé but continues north from there to join the Kolimbine; the present Senegal valley between Bafoulabé and Kayes, much disturbed by falls and rapids, is clearly a very youthful feature due to river capture. The large valley, obviously an old course of the Senegal, skirts the western end of the Sarakolé massif (schists capped with dolomites in the west) which separates the south Hodh valley from the northern erg.

The northern Hodh is itself remarkable for the traces of an old drainage system. The Kolimbine valley, in the south-west, is of such a size that it is doubtful whether even a humid period over the whole of the Hodh could produce a river of adequate volume to erode it. This great valley, buried under dunes in the central Hodh, reappears in the vicinity of Nara, where the dunes of the erg of Ouagadou have partially encroached upon it. Urvoy suggests that the Niger at one stage flowed by this route before being diverted eastward.

It is clear, even from this brief summary, that conditions of wet and dry

periods have alternated in these areas north of the Niger, witness the alternation
of dunes, inundation and lake formation, and present aridity in Aklé. The diversion of Niger waters from the Hodh was too far back in time to affect the human
activity of this area; likewise the later flow of the Niger north-east to the vicinity

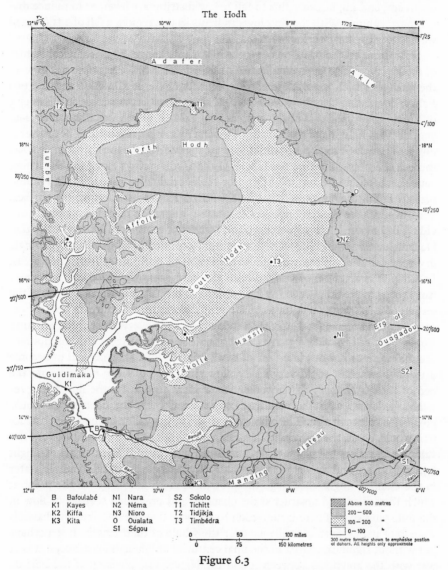

The Hodh

B	Bafoulabé	N1	Nara	S2	Sokolo
K1	Kayes	N2	Néma	T1	Tichitt
K2	Kiffa	N3	Nioro	T2	Tidjikja
K3	Kita	O	Oualata	T3	Timbédra
		S1	Ségou		

Above 500 metres
200 – 500   "
100 – 200   "
0 – 100   "

300 metre formline shown to emphasise position
of dahars. All heights only approximate

0   50   100 miles
0   75   150 kilometres

Figure 6.3

of Goundam and Timbuktu, and thence northward or north-westward into
Araouane and Aklé. It would seem that later still the ergs of northern Gourma
and the Timbuktu basin slowly became submerged to form a major lake. This
ultimately overflowed into the basin to the east, and cut the narrow valley at

Tosaye, to drain away much of the surplus water, and to lower the level of the river sufficiently to cause the abandonment of old distributary channels. A steady wearing down of the Tosaye sill under the action of the huge volume of water coming down the Niger would tend to slow but definite reduction of water level upstream, and might cause this to fall below distributary level, or to reduce distributary volume. With the very low gradients in this region, a fall of 1 ft (30 cm) would possibly have serious results.

There remains the problem of recent historical change. The geological history of the river explains the major features of the land surface, but does not explain the changes which have led to the settlements of the Hodh, Aklé and the two Fala valleys being abandoned in historical time. Mention was made in Chapter 5 of Stebbing's hypothesis of the encroaching Sahara, which was discounted, and yet the overwhelming of the old site of Ghana by erg is irrefutable. The answer is not yet known. Several possibilities suggest themselves. In the northern districts there is the possibility that the failure of the Hodh springs along the dahar foot could have followed as a result of a water-table, originally raised in the last humid period, falling below the critical level and no longer intersecting the surface. This would have the double effect of causing migration of peoples and of providing dry material for wind movement instead of moist soil. Mauny states that Oualata has two wells today where 15 existed a century ago.[4] Secondly, a single dry year could cause the permanent deflection of river water from wide areas. In Chapter 5 a reference was made to the permanent diversion of river water from 1000 square miles (2600 sq km) of land in the Chad basin as a result of the setting of a fish trap, on account of the very low grade of the stream bed. Reference has been made above to the very low gradients everywhere from Ségou to Tosaye, including wide expanses on both sides of the Niger. If a distributary channel were to dry out in a year of weak rainfall, thus allowing soil to become dry, the harmattan could very easily blow six inches of loose material into the bed of the distributary. This would be sufficient to prevent the flow being re-established, and with the resulting continued dryness the obstruction would possibly increase in size. The whole of the soil in the valley beyond the obstruction would be on the move within a few years, giving the beginnings of erg development, unless the channel were re-opened by man. The same result might follow from an unduly wet year: an unusually prolonged period of ample water in the channel might encourage the growth of reeds and sedge to the point at which they filled and obstructed the channel, and prevented seepage or flow in the following year. There is no reason to suppose that the distributary channels were kept under close surveillance over the whole of their length. It is perhaps not without significance that in the final centuries of Ghana's existence, it was at war with the kingdoms between it and the Niger. The blocking of the Fala de Molodo, intentionally or unintentionally, would well have encouraged the westward extension of the erg of Ouagadou: Aklé could similarly have been precipitated into barren aridity. Chapter 5 also commented upon man's contribution to the southward shift of the vegetation zones in West Africa, and this may have accentuated changes taking place for such reasons as the above. The very low gradients of the rivers also imply that any small earth movement would have widespread results. No accounts of movements of importance have been recorded in historical time, but a broad gentle warping giving a maximum uplift of 5 feet (1·5 metres) spread over 600 years and therefore not identifiable could reverse the drainage over a distance of nearly 20 miles (32 km) from the centre of any such movement, which would be sufficient to alter conditions permanently over a wide area.

There remains an additional detail which would not only appear to be inimical to Stebbing's hypothesis, but which has important implications for the future. Urvoy[5] gives details of the analysis of material from different parts of the zone under review, as follows:

LOCALITY	PHYSICAL ANALYSIS OF GRAIN SIZE		ANALYSIS OF FINE GRAINS				
	>1 mm	<1 mm	1·0–0·5 mm	0·5–0·2 mm	'limon'	'argile'	pH
Kolimbine Valley W. of Sarakolé massif	0·48%	98·52	10·20	46·00	17·02	26·78	7·3
20 km N. of Bafoulabé	0·13	99·87	1·30	57·06	5·04	36·60	7·3
30 km E. of Nioro	0·80	99·20	30·80	45·48	3·74	19·98	7·3
S. margin of Dogon Plateau	1·85	98·42	15·72	62·54	3·08	18·66	6·8
6 km S.W. of Ouahigouya	9·35	90·67	11·34	59·80	4·88	23·98	7·2
15 km S. of Dori	1·25	98·75	35·32	60·40	1·18	3·10	6·9

These figures suggest that the sands found here are unlike the sands of Saharan ergs. They have not been winnowed to give some degree of uniformity of grain size, but have a much more balanced composition, and offer possibilities for agriculture. Indeed, they are better suited to dry farming methods than are the clay deposits of the valley floors. It would appear that extension of irrigation into the ergs is therefore a much more reasonable proposition in the Sudanic and Sahelian zones of West Africa than would be the case in many other parts of the world. Urvoy adds that the erg sands of the Hodh, and of Irrigui, also show a much higher clay content than would be expected for their latitude. He thinks that the sands of the Hodh, of Ouagadou, and of Gourma are wind-borne from Azaouad or the Adrar des Iforas, while those of Azaouad and Aklé are fluviatile in origin. Whatever their origin, it is reasonable to suppose that while moisture was available in the soil, even a steady influx of this windblown material would not have been detrimental to agriculture, and would on the contrary have been beneficial. Only with the cessation of water flow would typical erg formation become active.

In references to ergs in this section it has been shown that the sand is not the pure sand of classical desert type. It must likewise be remembered that the true Saharan climate is found only in the extreme north of Mauritania, Mali and Niger, and the climate of what was old Ghana is still Sahelian in the north and Sudanic in the south. The whole of the Hodh receives a regular wet season, although in the north-east the mean annual total may not be more than 5 in (125 mm). The north-western Hodh may receive some rain in each of six or seven months, but in no month is the average likely to exceed 2 in (50 mm), and the mean total may be no more than 10 in (250 mm). In consequence of this moisture and the sand composition, the erg of the northern Hodh carries a scattered vegetation on its dunes, and is not a 'sand sea'. Nevertheless it remains an unattractive area today, as the lack of water means that there is now no compensation for high temperatures. Néma, below the dahar of that name, has a mean maximum daily temperature of 100°F. (38°C.) for the year, with seven months showing figures above this with a maximum of 109°F. (43°C.). These are screen temperatures, and sun temperatures may be 20°–30°F. (11°–17°C.) higher. This raises physiological problems in the maintenance of the moisture content of the body. Reasonably heavy work is possible in higher temperatures than these, but must be accompanied by adequate fluid intake. Once the latter became unavailable the northern Hodh became almost uninhabitable for an agricultural community. Seasonal herding in the southern part of the area is still possible, however.

The older valley of the Senegal in the southern Hodh is much less difficult country, with mean annual rainfall totals exceeding 15 in (380 mm) in the south. This is true Sudanic climate, the major rivers flowing for much of the year, and the vegetation is a mixture of wooded steppe and dry savanna which from a distance can give the impression of a comprehensive tree cover. This is workable land today.

THE EASTERN BASINS

East of Tosaye the landscape shows some points of similarity with the central basins, but the complicated series of changes in the Niger drainage is lacking. The Tilemsi valley flows approximately due south to join the Niger at Gao. In dimensions it is comparable with the old valley of the Niger in western Hodh, being 30 miles (50 km) wide over much of its length. In more humid times it collected the western drainage from the highland mass of the Adrar des Iforas, and the volume flowing southward must have been considerable. The Adrar des Iforas rise to over 3000 feet (915 metres), and are in effect a spur from the great mass of Ahaggar in southern Algeria, a mass of faulted pre-Cambrian rocks, principally schists, with the effects of repeated volcanic activity in the form of cones or lava flows. The highest summit of Ahaggar is probably about 10,000 feet (3050 metres) in altitude. The Ahaggar mass is largely surrounded by sand-

The North Eastern Basins

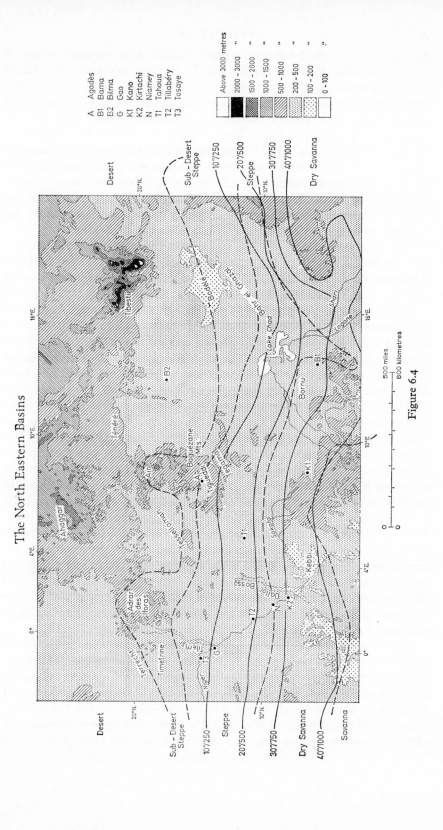

Figure 6.4

stone plateaux ('tassilis'), but these are absent on the south-west and the abrupt
edges of the Adrar des Iforas are of schists or granites, facing the lower scarps
of Terrecht and Timetrine overlooking the Tilemsi from the west. The valley
formed the upper part of the great trough followed by the Niger today, fed by
tributaries also of considerable size entering from the left bank. It was into this
already existing trough that the Niger overflowed at Tosaye to establish the
present course to the sea. A little below Gao the river flows on to pre-Cambrian
rocks on which it stays until Tillabéry, and it again crosses basement rocks between Kirtachi and the confluence with the Dallol Bosso. Both these stretches
are impeded by rapids. In the lower case the river follows an irregular W-shaped
course as it crosses the north-eastern extremity of the Atacora structure, and
alternates on sandstones and schists.

Centred on the meridian of 8° E., and aligned approximately north–south, is
the pre-Cambrian massif of Aïr, with younger volcanic rocks. The highest part
of this massif is the block of the Baguézane Mountains, bounded by abrupt scarps
on three sides. The surface of this plateau is at some 5000 feet (1525 metres),
studded with volcanic cones rising to over 6000 feet (1830 metres). Lower surfaces exist in the range 1650–3000 feet (500–915 metres). The valleys trenching
the sides of the Aïr massif show in marked contrast to the summits, the latter
being bare and the former wooded. The water-table is often only a few feet below
the valley floors. The streams which now flow in these valleys appear only for a
short period after each storm, in the form of flash floods. The eastern valleys
quickly lose themselves in the desert of Ténéré, where the sands from Tibesti
and the Chad basin extend up the eastern flank of Aïr. The western valleys lose
themselves equally, but in a wide clay plain, slowly adding to it the quantities of fine
material which they bring down. They direct flow towards the great Tessellaman
depression – sometimes a swamp – which provides rich pasture in the wet season
in contrast to the barren plains around it. The depression drains southward to
the Niger by a great wadi, steep-sided and wide-floored, which is known in its
southern part as the Dallol Bosso. Similar dallols drain the southern part of the
Adrar des Iforas, and the north-western part of Northern Nigeria, where the
Sokoto river runs as a dallol over 100 feet (30 metres) deep. Much of the country
between the Niger and the Dallol Bosso is impeded by sand, and east of the
Dallol sand increases northward to form static dunes south of Tessellaman. The
dallol country consists of sandstones with a hard duricrust capping, which preserves the steep edges of the dallols and gives a flat, barren aspect to the upper
surface.

South of Aïr is the Tegama, an area of sedimentary rocks culminating northward in the Tigueddi scarp which faces Aïr across the narrow plain of Agadès.
This is barren country across *continental intercalaire*, with little to relieve the
monotony of the plains. On these is the major watershed between the Niger and
the sea on the one hand, and the inland basin of Chad on the other, but it is very
uncertain and ill-defined, and thus typical of many of the major watersheds of
Africa, situated on plains of little relief. South again are high plains, trenched by

the major rivers but spread with sand which forms dunes in some districts. This was the country of some of the old Hausa kingdoms, on the edge of the High Plains of Hausaland, cut across the pre-Cambrian rocks of Northern Nigeria. The older rocks appear from beneath the younger sedimentary core at Zinder, but disappear to north and east beneath the blown sands of the western edge of the Chad basin. These sands stretch away northward for hundreds of miles into the Ténéré erg, with only a few isolated rocky hills breaking through the sand cover. Bilma has seven months with mean daily maximum temperatures exceeding 100°F. (38°C.) (the June figure is 111°F. (44°C.)) and a mean annual rainfall of less than 1 in (25 mm), although this occurs in the months July to September. However, monthly mean figures for relative humidity do not rise above 58 per cent even at 8.00 a.m., and the Tropical Equatorial air mass cannot be said truly to cover this area. Bilma is really a Saharan oasis. Farther north the erg gives way to hammada and reg, and the land becomes more rugged as it rises towards Tibesti. Agadès has a mean annual rainfall of only 7 in (180 mm), but this is partly the result of its site, and the mean figures for the western side of Aïr, if they were known, would probably be twice that figure. The southern areas have 15 in (380 mm) or more per annum, which is sufficient for arable farming as well as for pastoral activity.

The medieval kingdoms of the eastern basins were of a different character from those of the middle Niger. The earliest state of note would appear to have been a loosely-bound Tuareg kingdom with its capital at Agadès. The emphasis appears to have been pastoral rather than arable except on the oases, and there was no closely-settled farming community. The Songhay empire, based on Gao, was more typical of the middle Niger, and although its yoke was extended eastward to Agadès the connection remained short-lived and rather tenuous. The Hausa states in the 15th century came under the temporary domination of Kebbi, but their history is really tied to the High Plains rather than to the northern margins. Tuaregs, Bornu, the Fulani, the Moors, all held nominal authority at one time or another, and the lack of continuity over long periods may well be a reflection of the different character of this eastern sector.

Bornu deserves special attention, because it has survived to the present day from at least the 15th century. This may be not unconnected with the physical conditions. Lake Chad, albeit of varying size, is a permanent feature of the landscape, and some agriculture is always possible round its margins and in the floodplains of the rivers flowing to it. The lake has also provided assured dry-season pasture for cattle. The surrounding lands are of exceedingly low gradient, in part being the floor of the lake when this increases to maximum area, in part the further extension of this in the last humid period. Whereas the area of what is now the Republic of Niger shows relatively little evidence of recent change of climatic or other conditions affecting water supplies, the Chad basin is distinguished by the cessation of water flow from Lake Chad toward the northeast, by way of the long depression of the Bahr-el-Ghazal. This extends for nearly 400 miles (650 km) to the Bodélé depression, with a gradient of approximately 1 in 7500, which is more than twice as steep as the Niger in the vicinity of the Inland Delta. Archaeological finds indicate that there was a flow of water, presumably fairly regular, until the Middle Ages, and there are references[6] which suggest that canoe passage was possible as late as the 18th century. In 1830 water appears to have travelled 160 miles (258 km) towards the north-east, and in 1874 to have flowed 100 miles (160 km). The cessation of flow could be due to choking of the channel by sand, as suggested for some of the middle Niger distributaries, but it is more likely to be the result of the steady but continuing drying-out of this area. It has been suggested[7] that the Kabi tributary of the Benue is in process of capturing the Logone, which contributes a major part of the Chad water. Certainly some of the Logone floodwater flows via the Kabi to the Benue, but far from this being evidence of increasing diversion, it is now thought[8] that the flow by this route is much less than was formerly the case, and that the Logone is instead trenching into its earlier sedimentary deposits. The drying-out mentioned above would represent the continued slow fall of a water-table which was at its height in Upper Pleistocene time, when Lake Chad occupied some 120,000 square miles (310,000 sq km), comparable in size with the Caspian Sea today. The beach ridges marking the boundaries of the lake have been described[8][9], the most notable being the Bama ridge, 40 feet (12 metres) above the plain level, with a crest altitude given at various heights between 1144 feet (348 metres) and 1017 feet (310 metres), and which can be traced for over 300 miles (480 km). Another ridge east and north-east of the Shari river, and correlated with the Bama ridge, extends for 400 miles (645 km). Smaller ridges mark later marginal positions between the great ridge and the present lake. The evaporation from the lake at fullest extent must have been enormous, and must have given rise to local climate conditions very much wetter than those of today.

The western sector

In this sector the most striking feature of the landscape is the uneven line of scarps marking the edge of the sandstone plateaux. This scarp line was seen above in the great curve of dahars round the north side of the Hodh, approaching the Senegal river at its confluence with the Kolimbine. The scarp swings round abruptly to lie south to north, overlooking the plains to the west, and continues, with interruptions and stepped duplication, to north of Atar, near the south-east corner of the Spanish Sahara. The surface of the plateaux is everywhere dry and barren, and settlements – where any exist – are on the spring line at the scarp foot or in the deep valleys trenched into the scarp edge.

The decline of Tichitt, in the Hodh, has been mentioned above. It is an interesting commentary upon the decline of the Hodh that there is no mention in literature of Tichitt until a catalan map of 1444[10], nearly 700 years after the first reference to Ghana, and 200 years after the destruction of the latter. Today it is three-quarters in ruins. The other towns on the plateau margins are of moderate age – Chinguetti was founded in the 15th century or before; Ouadane, in the same

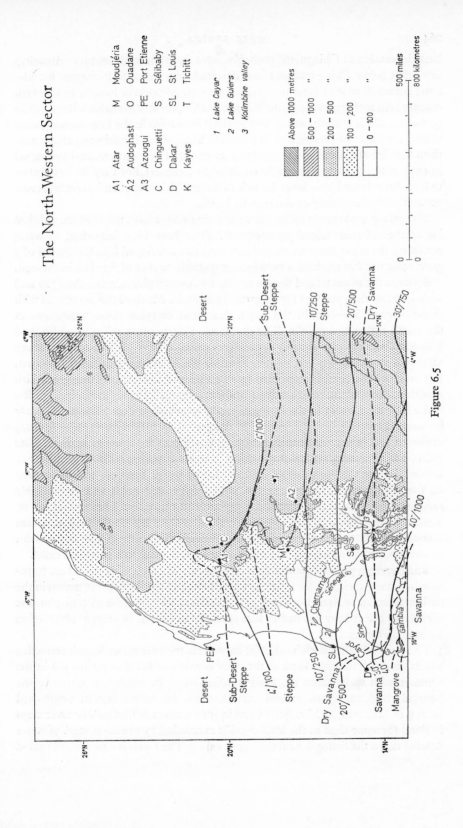

The North-Western Sector

A1 Atar   M Moudjéria
A2 Audoghast   O Ouadane
A3 Azougui   PE Port Etienne
C Chinguetti   S Sélibaby
D Dakar   SL St Louis
K Kayes   T Tichitt

1   *Lake Cayar*
2   *Lake Guiers*
3   *Kalimbine valley*

Above 1000 metres
500 – 1000   "
200 – 500   "
100 – 200   "
0 – 100   "

500 miles

800 kilometres

Figure 6.5

long depression as Chinguetti, probably dates from the 12th century; Abweir, a few miles below Chinguetti and now deserted, was also a 12th-century foundation; Azougui, now of little importance, was an Almoravid bastion in the 11th century; Audoghast, in the western Hodh, with water still available within 30 feet (9 metres) of the surface, was sacked by the Almoravids in the 11th century, after several centuries of prosperity – it probably had 5–6000 inhabitants, about one-third the size of Ghana, at the height of its power. These settlements have varied in their history: some have declined through conquest, but they do not appear to have been forced into decay by lack of water. This makes an interesting comparison with the history of the eastern Hodh.

The spring settlements along the west-facing scarps have not held the political importance of their inland counterparts. They have been important as water points on the trans-Saharan routes, but none has developed into the capital of a great state nor has attained a position comparable to that of Agadès, in the east.

Between the plateaux and the sea are the low coastal plains, 200 miles (320 km) wide and less than 500 feet (150 metres) in altitude. Much of this is covered with dunes aligned SW–NE, in the south dead and carrying some vegetation, in the north active and mobile. The dunes are ridges, often miles in width, and between them are clay-floored depressions called *aftouts* which become marshy after rain storms in the wet season. In some places these dunes reach the coast, but much of the coast is paralleled by depressions (*sebkras*) containing brackish mudflats, also capable of becoming marshy after rain. The only major indentation is the Baie du Lévrier in the extreme north, on which is Port Etienne. The bay has several good anchorages (as well as dangerous shoals) in its 27 miles (43 km) of length and is now developed as a deep water port for iron ore carriers. Port Etienne is a Saharan settlement, lacking in water supplies, with no genuine wet season. Before the construction of the railway to Ijil the port was dependent on the fishing trade, modern vessels with refrigerated holds and considerable range making good use of the fishing grounds off this coast. These could not be worked before the advent of powered craft, and were not established on a firm economic basis prior to the use of diesel-engined vessels in the 1930s, with longer range than steamers, and manifestly better suited to a waterless coast.

The northern part of Mauritania is true desert. The iron mines at Ijil are fortunate in having spring water from the scarp foot, and similar sources maintain the oasis settlement of Atar, but much of the lowland west of the sandstone plateaux is erg, and the railway has had to take special precautions to prevent obstruction by moving dunes.

The Senegal valley with its alluvial deposits is the only major feature attractive to settlement. The right bank of the river consists of flat clay plains, fed in the summer with water from the wadis leading from the sandstone scarps to the Senegal river, the mean annual rainfall totals increasing rapidly southward from 9 in (228 mm) at Moudjéria to 26 in (660 mm) at Sélibaby. The river stays in flood for some time as the local flood is succeeded by the main mass of water coming down the Senegal from the upper valley. The result is a prolonged period of available water, far in excess of expectations assessed in terms of local climatic conditions. In the Chemama, the north bank district of the bend of the river westward, the plain is flooded for a considerable period and Lake Cayar is a permanent feature, albeit varying widely in size. These features are matched on the south side of the river, where Lake Guiers is a permanent feature, and the prolonged annual floods cover a broad marshland area on the flanks of the river, which flows in multiple channels for the last 300 miles (480 km) to the sea. The lower part of its course is through country with sand dunes aligned SW–NE across the clay plains, giving marsh between the sand hills in the flood season. The gradient of the river in its lower course is exceedingly gentle. This would appear to have the advantage of slow withdrawal of the floodwaters, but it also has the disadvantage that salt water flows far up the river when the latter is not in flood, leading to brackish conditions. The salt content of many of the lower marshes is, as a result, too high for rice cultivation, and, prior to the construction of a permanent barrage, annual earth dams were built by the local people to keep the salt flow from entering Lake Guiers.

The country between the Senegal valley and the Gambia has no significant landscape features. The plains of Cayor in the west and of Ferlo in the east are unrelieved by any major interruptions. Much of the plain in the west has been spread with sand, which has accentuated the plain form by partially filling valleys and depressions. Towards the coast the sand increases in quantity and forms lines of dunes, for the most part inactive and covered with unusually thick scrub vegetation, which is itself a reflection of the high humidity along this coast and of the increasing rainfall southward. Small seasonal streams draining western Cayor discharge into depressions between and behind the dunes. East of Cayor the blown sand is less common, and most of the Ferlo is dry sandstone or sandy clay. The two valleys of the Ferlo and Sine Rivers drain the area, but much of the rain soaks into the surface and passes directly to the water-table, which over wide areas is between 100 and 200 feet (30–60 metres) down. The rainfall averages over 20 in (510 mm) per annum, but is concentrated in the June to October period, most of the total being accounted for in the months July, August and September. In this short wet season the valleys and depressions become marshy, in contrast to the dry, friable surface of much of the year, and the resulting pasture can be of good quality for a short time. Otherwise it is a zone of stunted gums and thorn-bush. It is, nevertheless, not without attraction to herdsmen for occupation during the wet season, having the advantage of lacking the tsetse fly which make more hazardous the areas farther to the south.

The southern and western districts are much more desirable, and traditional agriculture has been extended to cash crop production, especially of groundnuts. This is a relatively modern development, and the northern half of Senegal saw little prehistoric settlement away from the Senegal river and coast estuaries.

The uplands and the high plains

Passing reference has already been made to the Manding Plateau. This great sandstone mass stands between the Hodh to the north and the Upper Niger basin to the south; and between the latter basin, over 1000 feet (305 metres) in altitude, and the low plains of the Senegal valley below Kayes, only 150 feet (46 metres) in altitude when 600 miles (970 km) from the sea. The Plateau is, nevertheless, not a major watershed between the Niger and Senegal drainage systems, and is almost entirely within the catchment area of the Senegal. The watershed, difficult to determine precisely, characteristically lies on the feature-less plains of the Upper Niger basin, analogous to the indeterminate divide between Niger and Chad drainage mentioned earlier (p. 260) in the Niger Republic.

The western edge of the Plateau is the Tambaoura scarp, overlooking the Falémé valley, and the southern edge is a broken scarp overlooking the Niger, and continued as a series of flat-topped hills towards the Bafing valley. The upper surface of the sandstone is capped by a lateritic carapace, best seen in the southern districts. This results in a thin vegetation cover existing somewhat precariously on the meagre soils of the summits, and contrasting markedly with the forest of the valleys, even though in many places this has been degraded to indifferent woodland by man's activities. The major valleys, often with steep sides compar-able with the limiting scarps of the Plateau, are trenched below the upper surface by as much as 600 feet (180 metres). The upper Plateau is physically unattractive, and for this reason it should be remembered that the ancient kingdom of Mali, sometimes called the Manding empire, was centred on the Niger valley and not on the sandstone plateau.

To the south-west the sandstones are continued by the Fouta Djallon. This great mass rises to over 4000 feet (1220 metres). As elsewhere, the sandstones show marked development of lateritic duricrust and it is from here that the name bowal originates. The crests are broad, flat summits, trenched by deep valleys with steep sides, and as the mountains are subjected to the Tropical Continental air mass for a considerable period of the year, it will be appreciated from the account given in Chapter 5 that optimum conditions exist for bowal develop-ment. The hard crust, the lack of humus in the thin soils, the great depth to the water-table away from the valleys, with consequent lack of moisture except immediately after rain, all combine to produce a summit vegetation of grass and scattered dwarfed trees. In complete contrast is the gallery forest or fringing forest of many of the valleys, fringes of dense vegetation penetrating between blocks of almost arid aspect. The forest benefits not only from the high rainfall (over 100 in (2540 mm) per annum in many localities) but also from the springs emerging from the valley sides.

The history of the Fouta Djallon drainage is complex, and is not yet clear, but it has no direct bearing upon the human geography. Its indirect effects arise from the resulting division of the mountain area into blocks, and the use to which man

The Upper Niger Basin and the Surrounding Highlands

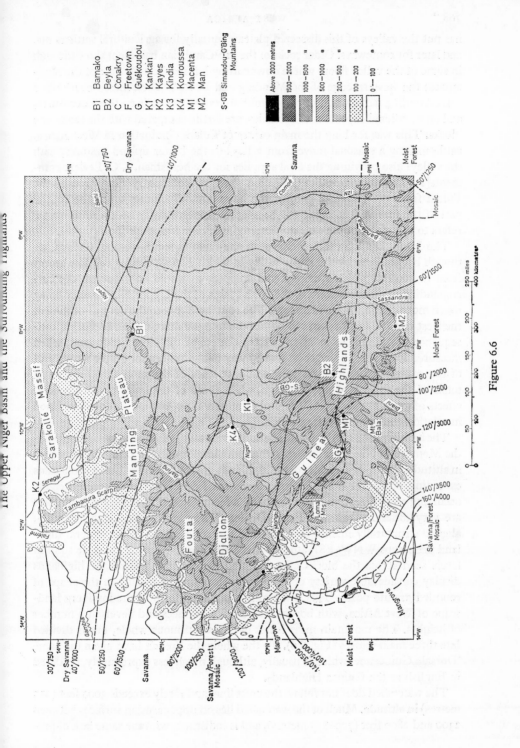

Figure 6.6

has put the valleys of this dissected plateau, initially for agricultural settlements, and later for routeways. Older rocks of the pre-Cambrian basement show through in some of the valley floors where downcutting has reached the base of the sandstones: the western edge of the Manding and Fouta Djallon massif overlooks a corresponding narrow belt of pre-Cambrian rocks. The soils on these exposures, and on occasional exposures of volcanics, are fertile compared with the sandstone blocks. This was for long the main centre of Fulani domination in West Africa, cattle making a seasonal move from valleys to the better upland pastures, with the valleys also providing the food supplies for the herdsmen. J. C. Leclerc comments[11] that the name Fouta Djallon signifies the country conquered by the Fulani from the Dialonké people: the latter are still numerous in the central part of the massif. The name has been applied increasingly widely until it now refers to the whole of the sandstone massif, which was not the local custom.

The Fouta Djallon reaches almost to the coast in south-western Guinea, although backed here by the major valley in which Kindia is situated. The ascent from the coastal plains is abrupt and stepped, as would be expected, the corresponding descent eastward to the High Plains of the Upper Niger valley being much more gentle, with wider steps. The contrast between the deep dissection of the west and the less broken country of the interior margin is an inevitable consequence of differences in distance from the sea to the river headwaters, when measured from the Guinea coast and by way of the Senegal or Niger rivers, and of the contrast in rainfall on west and east sides of the mountains, the mean totals of the former being very high, while those of the latter reflect the joint effects of greater exposure to Tropical Continental air, and the shadowed position in relation to the rain-bearing winds.

The highland mass of the Fouta Djallon terminates in the lower ground between the Mongo and Niger headwaters, where the level is only 1600 feet (490 metres) in altitude. South-east of this col the highlands are resumed, the Loma Mountains exceeding 6000 feet (1830 metres) in Sierra Leone, and comparable heights occurring elsewhere, notably in the Nimba Mountains. These eastern mountains are very different from the Fouta Djallon. They are of pre-Cambrian rocks, aligned structurally mainly in a NE–SW direction, although the general highland mass runs WNW–ESE athwart this structure. No longer are clear summit levels seen across the blocks of a dissected plateau, but instead the highlands display considerable variety of form, with the summits usually in the shape of rounded granite peaks. This is a highly accidented form of the inselberg landscape of West Africa, with bornhardts, erosion surfaces and bevels at a number of heights. The mountain mass is not even a continuous whole, but is divided into three main masses (Fig. 6.6). To the whole the French have given the name 'Dorsale Guinéenne' which is usually, although much less expressively, rendered in English as the Guinea Highlands.

The watershed does not follow the crest line, and rarely exceeds 3000 feet (915 metres) in altitude. Much of the watershed lies on upper erosion surfaces between 2300 and 2800 feet (700–855 metres), and is indistinct, with the same lack of precision already referred to as typical of many major watersheds in Africa. The higher peaks are usually on the coastal side of the watershed, detached from it by the extension of lower plains and valleys, which have encircled the residuals and have left them isolated in abrupt contrast with their surroundings. Peaks may be in the range 4000–6500 feet (1220–1980 metres). On the northern side of the watershed there are fewer isolated peaks and a greater number of small dissected plateaux, the remnants of older surfaces at heights between 3250 and 4000 feet (990–1220 metres) standing above the inland plains. Between these residuals, of both types, the lower plains are extended by deep valleys following the structural alignment at right angles to the watershed. Notwithstanding the high degree of dissection of the mass as a whole, it appears that a summit plane can be drawn across the highlands, sloping gently from the high southern peaks to the residual northern plateaux.

The largest of the three mountain areas is the massif north-east of Macenta. Through this runs the major watershed between the Atlantic and the Upper Niger drainage. The massif is distinguished by the 'Chaîne du Simandou' and the 'Chaîne du G'Bing' which prolongs it northward, a line of mountains approximately 100 miles (160 km) in length from north to south, but only a few miles wide. The peaks rise to over 5400 feet (1645 metres), with the highest, exceptionally, on the northern side of the watershed, but the general crest level of the chain is 2600–3900 feet (790–1190 metres) and the plains at the foot of the chain 2150–2300 feet (655–700 metres). The chain is too narrow to form a major barrier, and the cols at about 2600 feet (790 metres), used today by roads, cannot have proved any great impediment to early man. The major watershed ignores this mountain chain, and runs roughly west to east. It is not easy to decipher the water parting within the massif. In the north-west this is the result of the accidented topography, but of non-typical type: the southern peaks are not isolated residuals, but are on spurs from the northern mass, as though the southern ridges and the northern plateaux had been placed in direct contact. In the south the watershed is more typical, the streams originating on a marshy surface of indeterminate drainage between scattered hills and ridges of no particular plan. Leclerc refers to this as the 'Plateau des Sources'. At its margins the major rivers cut large valleys to the lower level of the adjacent plains. Between the two areas there is in effect a longitudinal depression aligned west to east, in the form of successive valleys separated by low cols. Eastward this runs on to the north to south line of the Milo valley, draining northward, and the Diani, draining southward, which almost divide the massif into two on the west side of the Simandou chain. These main routeways through the massif have prevented it from acting as a major social barrier. The 'Chaîne du Ziana' on the west side of the Diani valley extends southwards with peaks reaching successively higher altitudes and culminating in Mount Bala at 4560 feet (847 metres).

East of the Simandou chain the massif changes in character. Wide erosion surfaces at 2150–2450 feet (655–745 metres) surround Beyla, with only very slight undulations. This is in effect a large-scale example of the residual plateau described in Chapter 5. The planed surface is bordered from east to south by higher residuals, extending up to about 3750 feet (1140 metres) in altitude, and by the Chaîne du Simandou on the west. Between the surrounding higher mountain groups, the rivers from the plateau drop to the lower plains by way of broad valleys, with steep scarps on both sides but presenting relatively open and easy passage both to the plateau and the plains. A branch from the main watershed runs south-east from Beyla, dividing the drainage systems leading to the coast.

The third part of the Guinea Highlands lies on this south-eastern watershed, and consists of two sections. The greater of these is the Man Massif, between the upper valleys of the Cavally and the Sassandra, but the more striking part is the Nimba Mountains, on the border between Liberia and Guinea. These form a narrow ridge of characteristic shape for the southern flank of the Guinea Highlands, but of unusual height. The summit of the Nimba Mountains is the peak formerly marked as Mount Nouon, and now designated Mount Richard-Molard, which at 5748 feet (1752 metres) is the highest point in the Guinea Highlands outside the Loma Mountains. The Nimba Mountains do not lie directly on the watershed last described, but are to the south of it: the drainage, to the coast from its eastern and southern flanks, follows a circuitous route from north-west and north to flow eastward into the Cavally. The mountains are of geomorphological interest in that they show evidence of erosion surfaces at approximately 5250, 4250, 2625–2950 and 1800–1970 feet (1600, 1300, 800–900 and 550–600 metres).[12] They are also of economic interest because the chain owes its survival largely to the resistance to weathering and erosion offered by the quartzite forming its main ridge. This is a valuable magnetite ore which until recently remained unworked on account of its distance from the sea, but it is now being mined for export through Liberia.

The Man Massif is less imposing, its highest point being a little below 4500 feet (1370 metres). The 4250-foot (1300-metre) surface can be extended across the plateau summit, although this lacks the uniform planation of Beyla or of the Fouta Djallon. The massif is a compact entity, although subdivided by valleys into several major compartments which largely correspond with tribal distribution.

The mountain area has a relatively dense population. The Fouta Djallon has been a traditional Fulani stronghold for centuries: the Guinea Highlands, on the other hand, have sheltered a number of different tribes in the different massifs. The difficulties of the terrain have made some contribution to this, the mountains offering a relatively safe refuge, but this is not the only reason. As suggested in Chapter 5, the highland zone in this part of West Africa possibly acts as a barrier to the coastward movement of the Tropical Continental air, and this is restricted to the northern side of the mountains, while the south-western flanks of the highlands are under the Tropical Maritime air throughout the year. As a result there is no true dry season south-west of the highlands, and in the gaps between the massifs of the Guinea Highlands agricultural prospects have always appeared to be good: relatively fertile soils from the basement rocks, little lateritic hardpan, good water supply and some rain at all seasons. Guékédou, on plains at 1500 feet (460 metres) on the southern flank of the Highlands, receives nearly 100 in (2540 mm) of rain a year, with only one month of less than 1 in (25 mm), and Beyla, on the 2200 feet (670 metres) plateau of the Guinea Highlands, receives 70 in (1780 mm) a year with only two months below 1 in (25 mm). High forest extends into the valleys on the Atlantic side, thinning out upwards into mountain vegetation: the Highlands are not high enough to reach the true tree-line, but the summits are largely under grass, with only stunted trees, in the Fouta Djallon because of the rapid percolation of rain in the sandstones, in the Guinea Highlands as a result of the thinning of soil towards many of the summits. This highland zone is a boundary between two contrasting areas, the wet West Guinean and the sub-Guinean, the former coinciding approximately with high forest and the latter with a savanna woodland mixture. The discontinuous nature of the highland masses, combined with the structural alignment of mountain chains at right angles to the highland axis and parallel to the winds, has made the boundary a very ragged and uneven one, in which it is possible to some extent to experience the advantages of both sides. The northern watershed east of Beyla exercises a greater effect on the rainfall than the Man Massif and the Nimba Mountains, as seen in Figure 6.6; the rainfall distribution from July to October closely reflects the relief. Local variation within the broken hill country is, of course, inevitable.

To the north of the Highlands is the Upper Niger basin, a great plain ringed by upland areas. The plain itself is of extremely low gradient. Urvoy gives the altitude above Kouroussa and Kankan as 400 metres (1310 feet), and that at Bamako as 340 metres (1115 feet). River distance in each case is approximately 225 miles (360 km) giving a slope of 10 in to the mile (158 mm per km). Few residuals break the surface of much of the plains, the most notable exception being a line of hills, rarely exceeding 600 feet (180 metres) in height, which mark the Kouroussa dyke, and which continue in a SSE–NNW direction for 100 miles (160 km). This continues the line of the Simandou–G'Bing Mountains, and where it crosses the Niger it is responsible for the rapids which define the head of navigation. Some tabular sandstone residuals fringe the sandstone masses bordering the plains to west and north. The general surface of the plain is, however, far from even, the drainage system being incised by as much as 60 feet (18 metres) into a former surface. The latter carries a well-developed lateritic cara-pace, so that the incised valleys have steep sides below the protecting hard surface. Many of the valleys and ridges, on which the crust is less well developed, carry savanna woodland, separated by wide expanses of poor grassland, but richer grasslands are found along the major valleys in the flood-plains subject to annual inundation. The area commonly called the Upper Niger basin is not restricted to Niger drainage, part of it being drained by the Senegal system. The divide between the two catchment areas is imprecise. The rocks of the basement are pre-Cambrian, and from them alluvial gold has been widely dispersed within the basin. As with the placer deposits of the Falémé valley, north-west of the sand-stone uplands, the local people have worked the ores since early times, and the

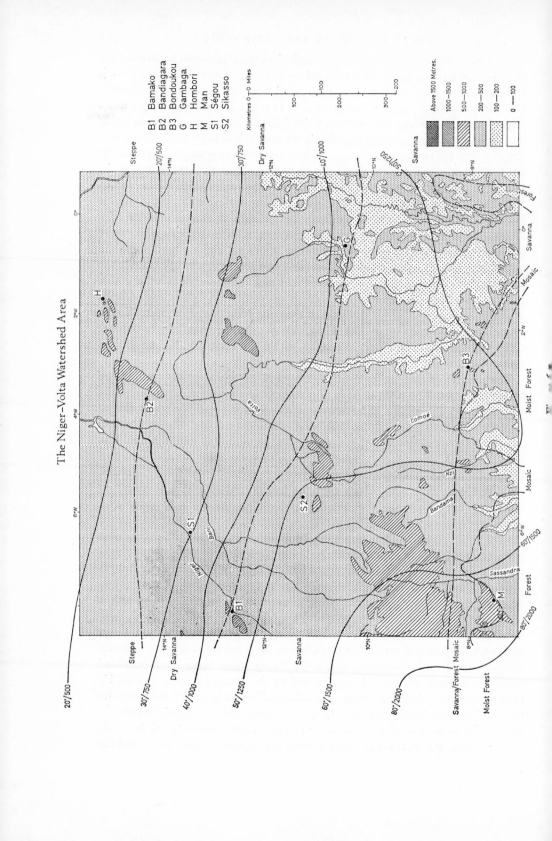

The Niger–Volta Watershed Area

B1 Bamako
B2 Bandiagara
B3 Bondoukou
G Gambaga
H Hombori
M Man
S1 Ségou
S2 Sikasso

Kilometres 0   0 Miles
100
200
300

Above 1500 Metres.
1000 —1500
500 — 1000
200 — 500
100 — 200
0 — 100

gold output contributed to the wealth of the medieval empires. The gold-bearing alluvium is not aligned along the present river channels, but along an older and higher drainage pattern referable to the upper surface.[13]

To the east of the Upper Niger basin, and south-east of the Inland Delta area, sandstone plateaux reappear. The Sikasso Plateau has a southern edge marked by the Banfora scarp some 500 feet (150 metres) in height, and this curves round to the north-east, where it is trenched and broken by the headwaters of the Black Volta. North of the river the scarp is resumed, passing north-eastward and increasing in height and magnificence. It is best known in the Bandiagara scarp, facing eastward near the northern end of the Dogon Plateau which lies between the Bani river and the Gondo plains. This long narrow plateau is not cut through by rivers, nor does it carry a lateritic carapace, in contrast to the sandstone plateaux of Manding and the Fouta Djallon. Its north-western side is inconspicuous, the sandstones emerging from beneath the younger rocks of the Ségou basin and rising eastward to give a cuesta form. At the northern end, where this is about 600 feet (180 metres) high, spring-line settlements cluster along the scarp foot. Beyond the end of the plateau the sandstones continue as a line of isolated residuals of increasing height, known as the Hombori Mountains, where the highest summit reaches 3117 feet (950 metres), nearly 2000 feet (610 metres) above the surrounding plains.

East of the plateau are the Gondo plains, a sand-covered strip thought to represent a former north-easterly valley of the Black Volta abandoned after a river capture and subsequently filled with blown sand. The latter increases in thickness towards the scarp, as is only to be expected in view of the harmattan direction, but does not lie directly against the scarp, being separated from it by a narrow trench which remains moist with spring water and is well vegetated with Sudanic forest species. The plains rise gently eastward to the Mossi country, which reaches over 1500 feet (460 metres). This is an area of high population density with a long history, and is considered elsewhere (pp. 348–51). That the surface is for the most part infertile is therefore somewhat surprising. Essentially this is a domed plain with an exceedingly well-developed lateritic carapace. On the margins this has a superficial cover of clay or sand. The central part of the plain is broken by the valleys of the present drainage system, to leave tabular residual hills, with thin scrub vegetation over the ironstone capping, standing above rough wastes of basement rocks, sometimes weathered, sometimes relatively fresh. The country between this formidable heart and the barren sterile margins consists of similar lateritic hills standing 500–600 feet (150–180 metres) above valleys floored with thick deposits of fertile clay, and separated from them by bad-land country of ridges and gullies. The contrast between the green valleys, with fringing forest or closely worked farms, and the infertile areas between them is very marked. Towards the north and north-east the even crested hills capped with ironstone give way to granitic domes of bornhardt type, and rocky hills surrounded by sand, the depth of which increases with distance northward.

The Guinea Highlands, the sandstone plateaux of Sikasso and Dogon, and the

Mossi uplands form a broken line of higher country following a SW–NE direction from the Nimba Mountains to the heart of the Niger bend. To the east of this line lie broad plains of monotonous aspect, relieved only by occasional bornhardts, kopjes and small plateaux. Bornhardts are more common in the west, and tabular hills in the east. This is High Plain country of the type described in Chapter 5 as characteristic of the area of basement rocks. The southern part has been warped gently towards the coast, and the Sassandra, the Bandama and the Comoé Rivers follow roughly parallel courses from north to south. Lateritic carapace is widespread, and would seem to be forming today. The southern margin of these plains is not easy to define, there being no clear bounding escarpments separating them from coastal lowlands, although there is a steepening of the river profiles, sometimes marked by rapids. The most suitable margin would appear to be the edge of the high forest, although this does not coincide exactly with the topographical boundary. The extension of the savanna woodlands southward from Bouaké is very striking, and it can be correlated with the western 'dry corridor' seen in Figure 5.10 and discussed on page 217.

The High Plains of the Ivory Coast and Upper Volta extend into Ghana. In the northern part of Ghana they show little difference of character from those described in neighbouring districts. The basement rocks pass eastward beneath the sediments of the Middle Volta basin, and the sandstones of the latter form an outward-facing scarp which looks northward and westward across the crystalline rocks: the Gambaga scarp in the north-east of Ghana is well-known, overlooking the plains of Bawku, and the Konkori scarp, 100 miles (160 km) west-south-west, is also distinctive, but between these two scarps, and to the south of the latter, the plains pass almost imperceptibly from the crystalline rocks to the Voltaian sandstones. The change in bedrock can be identified in part by the variation in soil character and population density, fertility over the sandstones being much reduced compared with that over the basement.

The extension of the plains south-eastward from Bondoukou into southern Ghana is more complex. In Western Ashanti the crystalline structure is aligned NE–SW, and erosion of the softer rocks has led to parallel, steep-sided ridges in some districts. Elsewhere erosion has made less progress, as on the Kumasi Plateau, where the surface is relatively undisturbed at between 700 and 1100 feet (210–335 metres) in altitude. The southern margin of the uplands is not distinct: the degree of dissection increases and the valleys open out southward between spurs of higher ground. The eastern part of the Ashanti uplands is of quite different character, consisting of Voltaian sandstones which rise to over 2500 feet (760 metres). The Mampong or Kwahu scarp faces south-west and overlooks not only the coastal lowlands but also the western uplands of Ashanti. The abrupt edge of the sandstones runs approximately north-west from Koforidua for nearly 150 miles (240 km) before turning northward as the Wenchi scarp continuing as far as the Black Volta. Incision of the rivers in the Volta basin has left the margin of the sandstones not only standing high above the crystalline areas to the south-west, but also overlooking the sandstones of the basin itself. The north-

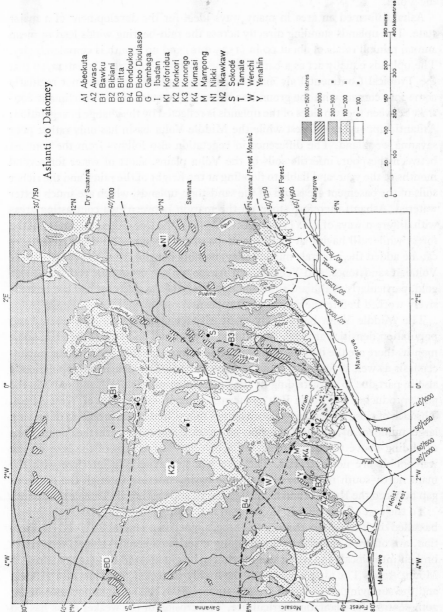

Figure 6.8

eastern edge of the Ashanti uplands is marked by the Afram scarp facing towards the Volta.

Ashanti formed an area in many ways ideal for the development of a major state. The uplands standing directly across the rain-bearing winds lead to mean annual rainfall totals of about 60 in (1525 mm) and no month is completely dry. The uplands equally act as a barrier to the dry north-easterly harmattan, so that the Tropical Continental air mass reaches the uplands, but does not regularly come into contact with the ground on the south-western side. The climatic contrast between the two sides of the uplands is reflected by the change in vegetation: Ashanti supports rain forest while the Middle Volta basin has only rather poor savanna woodland. The difference in vegetation also follows from the contrast between the poor, infertile soils of the Volta plains, short of water for several months of the year, and liable to flooding at the height of the rains, and the richer soils of the basement areas and of the sandstone uplands, which are much better watered. Ashanti therefore stood on the margin between two contrasting areas with different ways of life. Today it benefits from the tree crops and timber of the forest while still having at hand the crops of the savanna. To these advantages can be added the minerals mined today, notably bauxite from Nkawkaw, on the Voltaian sandstones, and Yenahin and Awaso, on the crystalline rocks, and also gold, particularly at Bibiani and Konongo. Some of the gold ores had been extensively worked before the arrival of Europeans.

The Middle Volta basin is by comparison unattractive to settlement, and population densities are low. In addition to poor soil and lack of water in some months there are the hazards of disease, this being a notably bad area for onchocersiasis as well as for malaria and trypanosomiasis. Low density of population is also in part due to slave-raiding by the powerful groups to north and south in the past, producing a 'Middle Belt' pattern here as in other parts of West Africa. The lack of close settlement is an advantage today, in that the problems of moving large numbers of people have not arisen in connection with the Volta Lake extending above the dam of the Volta Project. The effects of the lake on the water-table are not yet clear. The lake will not materially interfere with the main north–south routeway through the basin, entering through the northern gap between the Konkori and Gambaga scarps and passing via Tamale to Kumasi.

To the east of the Middle Volta basin is the long belt of highland which may be called the Togo-Atacora ranges. These, aligned in a general SSW–NNE direction, are of pre-Cambrian rocks, forming a series of parallel ridges, sometimes broken into blocks, and rising to a maximum height of 3366 feet (1025 metres) in Mount Agou. The ranges represent the highly-dissected remnants of a plateau, and the surviving areas of the plateau surface have had some importance in the 20th century for plantation agriculture. The erosion of the weaker rocks has led to the development of several major ridges aligned in the SSW–NNE direction, separated by steep-sided, deep, narrow valleys, and presenting scarps over 1000 feet (305 metres) high, facing across the plains on either side. These ranges, starting in south-eastern Ghana, cross Togo and northern Dahomey before dying away towards the Niger. Their structural continuation is responsible for the zig-zag course of the Niger river above the confluence with the Dallol Bosso.

The nature of the ranges has made them a barrier to movement between the populous districts of the Mossi kingdoms and those of the south-east. In the main part of the chain summits remain above 1500 feet (460 metres) in altitude, with the exception of the lower crest now used by the road between Sokodé and Blitta, and even this remains difficult as a major routeway. The accidents of land-scape are strengthened by the heavier vegetation encountered along the ranges, resulting partly from lack of incentive for clearing in the past, and partly from the heavier rainfall along the ranges, where mean annual totals can exceed 60 in (1525 mm). The forested character is all the more evident because of the poor savanna woodland which surrounds the ranges, and the rainfall totals, although much less than they would be if the ranges were aligned at right angles to the wind direc-tion, contrast sharply with the totals experienced in the 'dry corridor' to the south-east. In past centuries the ranges offered at least temporary refuge during hostilities between major tribal groups, notably the Ashanti and Dahomey king-doms. In this century they have offered Europeans economic opportunities in the form of plantation cultivation of coffee and cocoa at altitudes giving some slight relief of temperature, and in the form of potential timber extraction, mahogany afforestation having been started under German rule: the ultimate benefit will, of course, now be to the indigenous peoples.

Between the Atacora Mountains and the Lower Niger valley is an area of stepped and warped plains across basement rocks. In places these plains are magnificent examples of an old-age landscape, in others the land surface may be a confused combination of three or more cycles following successive rejuvenations. Above the plains rise residual masses of varying size and type: bornhardts are numerous in many districts, and reference has already been made (p. 244) to the small residual plateaux which have frequently served as sites for settlements of con-siderable size. The scarps surrounding residual masses and separating surfaces are sometimes hundreds of feet in height. In northern Dahomey the broken country around Nikki rises to about 2000 feet (610 metres) in altitude, on the major watershed between the drainage to the sea and the drainage to the Niger, and this figure is exceeded in a number of districts as the higher land continues south-eastward and then eastward into Nigeria. In general the southern margin of the plains is much more broken than is the northern margin, with an irregular and often abrupt transition from one surface to the next: where a number of surfaces are found in close proximity, in an area of resistant rocks, such as the Ilesha district of Western Nigeria, the landscape becomes rugged and difficult. In the present century road and railway construction has required careful align-ment through this marginal country.

There has been progressive southward tilting towards the coast, as shown by the regional dip of sedimentary rocks south of the basement areas. The same tilting would appear to have been responsible for the generally north–south align-ment of the major rivers, which is here, as in the Ivory Coast further west, possibly a pattern of very long standing, which has survived through a number of cycles[13], modified only by captures between adjacent river basins and by local uplift. It is possible that the watershed has progressively migrated northward, as each new cycle has reached the headstreams of the rivers flowing to the sea, before it has reached the headstreams of rivers flowing to the Niger. Examples of diversion to the coastal drainage of rivers flowing towards the Niger are not infrequent in West Africa, that of the Black Volta being well known (p. 273); on the high plains under discussion a striking example is the Pendjari river, which in northern Dahomey flows north-eastward for 100 miles (160 km) from the Atacora range before turning abruptly west and south-west to join the Volta system. It is also of interest to note that the highest summits are for the most part to the south of the major watershed in the western part of Nigeria. The watershed between Ilorin and Ogbomosho is at about 1300 feet (400 metres) in altitude, but the Olla Hills, south of Ogbomosho, reach 1844 feet (562 metres) and the Awba Hills, south-east of Oyo, over 2000 feet (610 metres). Further to the east the watershed is again relatively low, compared with summit heights of 2000 feet (610 metres) east of Ilesha rising southward to 2400 feet (730 metres), with the Idanre summits of over 3000 feet (915 metres) even further to the south, little more than 70 miles (115 km) from the coast. Falconer[14] describes it as follows: 'The primary watershed . . . is not defined by any range of hills or mountains, but by the crest line of a lofty plain which, like a low extended arch, slopes gently northward towards the Niger and southward towards the sea.' This even watershed reaches its greatest height between Shaki and Kaiama where it exceeds 2000 feet (610 metres) on the line of a prolonged SW–NE axis of uplift.

The plains show much greater diversity of climate and vegetation than of land form. The eastern 'dry corridor' crosses the plains from NE to SW, with mean annual totals of less than 45 in (1140 mm) extending from the north to the sea, and also occurring in the Niger valley in the lee of the major watershed. Immediately to the east of the Atacora ranges the rainfall averages over 50 in (1270 mm) per annum along the watershed to Nikki, but totals diminish rapidly northward. To the south-east of the 'corridor' the totals increase to over 60 in (1525 mm) along the southern margin.

These rainfall totals are reflected in the vegetation pattern. High forest is found only in the districts east of Ibadan and south of the watershed, and the greater part of the plains is under savanna woodland, much of it of an open character. This savanna zone no doubt contributed to the growth of the relatively large states which evolved here, particularly the Yoruba kingdoms in the east and the Dahomey kingdoms in the south.

If easier communications assisted these developments, they were also a disadvantage, in that strife between the Ashanti, Dahomey and Yoruba kingdoms was almost continuous; also the attacks of the Fulani on the Yoruba kingdom in the 19th century led to the sacking of Old Oyo and the southward move of the Yoruba rulers. The Fulani, indeed, penetrated to the southern margin of the plains as far as Abeokuta.[15]

The High Plains of Nigeria

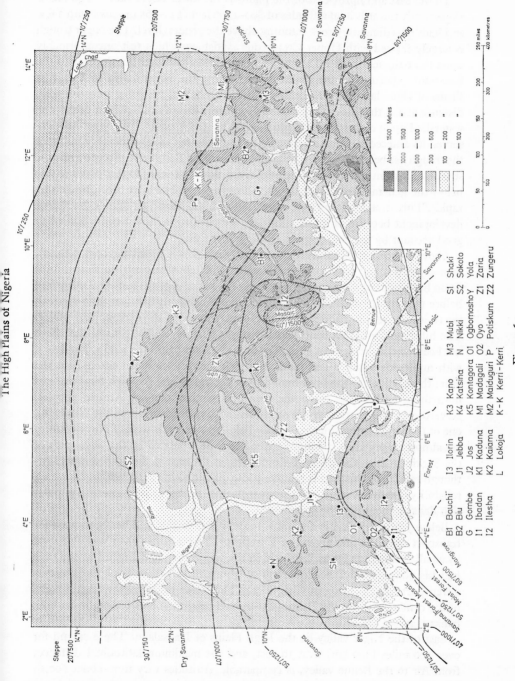

Figure 6.9

To the east and north-east of the plains is the lower Niger valley. The plains slope gently towards it, at altitudes of 800–1200 feet (245–365 metres), with a few residuals of sedimentary rock standing above the general level. The Niger trough is largely floored with Upper Cretaceous sandstones which rest unconformably upon the basement rocks. The sediments are not continuous, however, and the basement exposures of the plains extend across the Niger valley to the High Plains of Hausaland. The river flows on the crystalline rocks for a considerable distance across the line of the Kaiama–Kontagora axis of uplift, which carries the watershed up to over 1600 feet (490 metres) west of Kaiama. The Niger has preserved its antecedent course across this axis, although the sedimentary filling of the trough has been removed. The plains of northern Borgu give place to a narrow stretch of broken country in which the river, flowing some 500 feet (150 metres) below the general surrounding level, follows a gorge-like tract much broken by rapids. This stretch of the river, which hitherto has been a hindrance to modern development because of its unsuitability for navigation, is now to be turned to good account by the construction of the Niger dam.

Above and below this antecedent course, the valley is broad and open on sedimentary rocks, and with little gradient. East of Jebba scattered sandstone hills lie on both sides of the river, representing the remains of the last erosion surface before the current cycle, which is here at approximately 400 feet (120 metres), the residuals standing about 250 feet (75 metres) above the surrounding plains. The hills usually have a concretionary upper surface, and in general they have not been used as settlement sites. Towards the river banks the land is low-lying, with numerous swamps and pools in which mosquitoes breed throughout the year: these, added to the high humidity of the valley and the high temperatures normal to the latitude, make the area unattractive to many African peoples. Nevertheless the districts north of the river are now occupied by the Nupe[16], one of the larger groups of the Middle Belt. To the north-west of Nupe country are almost empty areas of savanna woodland, depopulated by the slave raids of the Sarkin Sudan (the Emir of Kontagora) at the end of the 19th century. Although rainfall in this area is relatively low (about 40 in (1015 mm) per annum), reliability is above average, and there seems to be no reason why a normal population density should not be supported.

Below Jebba the river is navigable for powered vessels, and has been used for transport since the first arrival of Europeans. The Kaduna river was also used by small steamers as far as Wushishi in the wet season, and Lugard at one time had his administrative headquarters at Zungeru. Discussion of the river as a transport route is given in Chapter 12. The Niger valley narrows again north of the confluence with the Benue, flat-topped sandstone hills closing in on both banks.

East of the Niger valley lie the High Plains of Hausaland. These extend for over 300 miles (500 km) west to east, and the maximum latitudinal distance, from Aïr to the Benue valley, is comparable. Altitudes vary from about 600 to 2800 feet (180–850 metres). Nearly all the area included under the general title of the High Plains consists of basement rocks, and the variety of the latter makes the perfection of planation all the more noteworthy. In places the more resistant rocks survive as residuals above the plains; sometimes they are responsible for scarps or steps which have preserved considerable areas of former cyclic surfaces; frequently they can be identified by outcrops of fresh rock at the level of the plains, in marked contrast to the deeply-weathered material of adjacent areas. At the margins of the High Plains the transition from crystalline to sedimentary rocks is not readily distinguishable, the plain surface passing unbroken from the one to the other. In the west, along the margin with the Niger trough, this transition occurs at under 1000 feet (305 metres); in the north-east the boundary of the Chad basin sedimentaries is at about 1400 feet (425 metres); and in the east the basement rocks pass beneath the sandstones of Gombe and Kerri Kerri at 1600 feet (490 metres). The northern districts have some superficial deposits overlying the crystalline rocks, in the form of sand carried southwards under drier conditions in the past, possibly simultaneously with the formation of the great erg of which the immobile vestiges can be seen between Kano and Lake Chad. These deposits are of considerable economic importance today, providing the sandy soils of the groundnut-growing districts of Northern Nigeria and the cotton soils of Zaria emirate farther to the south, where the proportion of fine material is very much greater. The latter soils, inevitably, tend to become waterlogged in the wet season and to crack and dry out in the rainless months, making them heavier and more difficult to work than the coarser soils to the north. Even further to the north the soils become less fertile, and there is a marked contrast between the closely-worked farms of the Kano emirate, with its high density of population, and the more barren localities of Katsina. The northward change in land-use is not unconnected with the relatively rapid decline in mean annual rainfall totals and a corresponding increase in the length of the dry season, combined with increases in temperature resulting from the reduced cloud cover. Most of the High Plains within the Nigerian frontier can be said to carry a savanna vegetation, although considerable local variations are readily apparent, depending not only on natural physical conditions but also on history and population pressure. To the north of the Nigerian frontier the trees become fewer and the vegetation is more truly sahel.

Major axes of uplift in the High Plains were first mentioned by Falconer[17], and these movements have affected the drainage patterns. The major watershed on the High Plains is between the areas draining to Lake Chad and those draining to the sea, but the divide is rarely on a notable feature. Usually it lies on the plains, and minor adjustments due to river capture by both systems can be identified. More notable are alterations of rivers leading to the Niger, some of which appear to have been diverted from original courses towards the north-west and to have been deflected towards the west and south-west. The Kaduna river is an example. The gradients on some of the rivers of plains are remarkably low: the Tubo river has an average slope of 1 : 3800 along a course of 150 miles (240 km), and quite small vertical movements are liable to cause major alterations of direction with slopes of such low angle. This can also have economic effects: firstly, by causing rejuvenation and stream incision, which may affect local water-table conditions and agricultural potential, secondly, in the case of minerals, by breaking the connection between lodes and alluvial deposits, it may make prospecting and development more difficult. The Hausas have long been familiar with the working of gold, although usually from localized alluvial deposits which have not lasted for many years, and, in this century, have added the mining of base metals such as tin, columbite, wolfram and tantalite. In many cases the source lodes of alluvial deposits have probably long since been eroded, but in others the sources may still be awaiting discovery, possibly in quite different and relatively distant catchment areas.

The High Plains were the location of the ancient Hausa states and the later Fulani emirates. Their advantages, in terms of the development of organized societies, have been discussed earlier. With regard to modern development, the High Plains, by virtue of their geomorphological form, have other advantages in respect of the expansion of the transport network: except in the junction zones between successive surfaces, roads and railways are not faced with steep gradients; watershed routes, when possible, are remarkably flat and require very little engineering; when bridging is required it is not usually necessary to erect high arches, and low bridges of considerable strength can easily be built; construction of airport runways presents little difficulty. It follows from this that railway development should be relatively inexpensive, and that the road transport can be in the form of heavy diesel-engined lorries, which represent the most economical form of motor vehicle. On the debit side of the account is the high percentage of run-off in areas where deep weathering has not occurred, with a consequent liability to flash floods, and when the latter are of unusually large volume following an exceptional storm, wash-outs of both road and railway may occur. Hausaland has been one of the most important areas of West Africa since medieval time, and with its present large population and its modern economic importance it continues to be one of the key areas of the region.

Totally surrounded by the High Plains is the Jos Plateau. This owes its survival to the resistance to erosion offered by the Younger Granites. The Plateau is in effect no more than the upper part of the staircase of surfaces seen on the surrounding plains, but there are valid reasons for regarding it as a separate and distinct entity. Firstly, the Younger Granites to which it owes its survival are mineralized, and are responsible for the modern economic importance of the Plateau as a producing area for tin and other base metals. Secondly, the scarp which surrounds the Plateau is of unusual height (over 2000 feet (610 metres) in some districts) which has led to interesting human and economic results. Thirdly, the Plateau has experienced repeated volcanic activity, although there are no active manifestations of crustal weakness today. Fourthly, the unusually high altitude of the Plateau has led to climatological and vegetational differences between it and the surrounding plains.

Although the resistance of the Younger Granites is responsible for the survival of the Plateau, the bounding scarps are not necessarily situated on the geological boundary. In the Monguna and Kaleri districts in the south-west of the Plateau the scarps have retreated about half a mile from the boundary. The scarp has a maximum height of about 2000 feet (610 metres) in the south-west, where it overlooks the Benue trough, the High Plains in this area being restricted to a narrow stepped belt. The scarp is well-defined on the western side of the Plateau as far north as the Kagoro Hills, north of the railway, and in the southern part of the eastern side, although the basal steps are higher in altitude and the scarp height correspondingly reduced. Round the northern half of the Plateau the scarp is less distinct, the lower surface running up the main valleys and breaking into the highland mass. In the north-west the streams are the headwaters of the Kaduna and Karami rivers, draining to the Niger, in the north those of the Kano and Delimi rivers, draining to the Chad basin; in the east those of the Bagel and Lere rivers, draining to the Gongola, and thence to the Benue. These valleys divide the northern part to give the appearance of separate hill groups, rather than of a continuous plateau surface. In places the Plateau shows a stepped character, this being particularly notable in the Toro district north-east of Jos on the road to Bauchi.

The general level of the Plateau surface rises gently southwards, from 4000 feet (1220 metres) at Jos to 4600 feet (1400 metres) between Ropp and Bokkos. This surface shows interruption round the margins where the headwater streams are working back into it, and elsewhere large areas have been disturbed in this century by open-cast mining, which has destroyed the continuity of stream profiles, and has led to severe gully development in some districts and to occasional marked alluvial deposition in the lower river courses. Above the surface rise hill groups or isolated residuals. A number of summits exceed 5000 feet (1524 metres) and the highest point on the Plateau is 5841 feet (1780 metres) in the Shere Hills. In addition to the granite residuals there are hills resulting from two phases of volcanic activity. The earlier flows were basalts which have been highly decomposed to leave clays, ranging in colour from white to purple. The basalt flows filled the existing valleys, and beneath them lie tin-bearing gravels. Originally more resistant than the granites, the basalts led to inversion of relief, and their remnants now stand as flat-topped hills above the general level, or as a thin veneer across low watersheds. The later volcanic activity was mainly but not entirely in the south-eastern districts of the Plateau, distinguished by ash cones and flows of unweathered lava.[18] Both periods of activity post-dated the formation of the Plateau scarp, over which the flows pass. The earlier phase was possibly early Tertiary, but the later phase may have been no more than 50,000 years ago.[19]

The major watershed of Nigeria lies on the Plateau surface, a few miles south of the Jos. As Falconer has remarked, 'There is no group of rocky mountains, no rugged peak at the hydrographical centre of the Protectorate, no lofty ranges forming the watersheds between the radiating rivers, only an undulating, swampy, alluvial plain diversified by a few short, broken ridges and low kopjes of granite boulders.'[20] This is comparable with the insignificant water partings noted on the High Plains.

Climatically the Plateau breaks the even alignment of isotherms across Northern Nigeria. The reduction in temperature consequent upon altitude is noticeable to African and European alike, and has contributed to economic development in the 20th century by making employment in the tinfields agreeable to the latter. It may well have assisted in earlier times in keeping the Plateau as a refuge area for small fugitive groups, the lower temperatures being uncomfortable for peoples accustomed to tropical conditions, and to whom small changes in temperature are more apparent than to peoples accustomed to the variations of temperate latitudes. Increased altitude also results in heavier rainfall, the south-western districts being considerably wetter than places some little distance out on the plains. This also has contributed to the modern economy with the construction of hydro-electric installations on the rivers of the south-western scarp.

The vegetation of the Plateau today is short grass used as pasture by large herds of Fulani cattle. The modern dairying industry has evolved as a result. It appears that the original climax vegetation was not true mountain grassland such as that of the higher parts of the Cameroons highlands farther to the east. Although originally there was probably fairly open savanna woodland on the thin soils, the trees have largely been removed by mining operations, or by the pagan peoples as fuel, and the modern grazing of the Plateau has contributed to the suppression of tree growth. In the rock valleys of the Plateau edge, trees are often abundant, hiding the village settlements from casual observation.

To the east of the crystalline area of the High Plains lies a continuous, but varied, zone of sedimentary rocks. In the north the plains merge into the even surface of the Chad basin. Reference to this has already been made (p. 281). The margins rise to about 1600 feet (490 metres) north of the Gongola bend, and to about 1300 feet (400 metres) near Kano, and altitudes decline gently towards the lake, at 830 feet (253 metres), and the lower land towards the north-east. The greater part of the southern half of the basin consists of the plains unrelieved by any eminence apart from fixed dunes. The dead erg of Hausaland has been described by Grove[21] together with the Bama ridge to the west and south-west of the lake, which marks an earlier shoreline (see p. 262 above).

The basin structure here would seem to be an ancient form. The basal sedimentary beds are of Cretaceous age, resting on the basement floor which reaches the surface on the margin of the basin but which is below −2500 feet (−762 metres) at Maiduguri, west of Lake Chad. An unconformity separates the Cretaceous rocks from the overlying sediments in the south-west, and in some districts Tertiaries lie in direct contact with the basement floor: it may be inferred that movement in the basin has been periodic.

The low gradients of the surface have been mentioned on page 231, and these lead to temporary flooding in many districts in the wet season. The short duration of the latter is, however, apparent from Figure 5.9, and local agricultural practice has been adapted to the conditions, as illustrated by Rosevear.[22] In

Bornu are found the deep hand-dug wells described on page 192, and in the Potiskum district of the south-west there has occurred the spectacular rise of the water-table discussed in Chapter 5 (p. 235).

The sedimentary rocks continue southward along the eastern margin of the High Plains, in the lower Gongola valley and its bordering districts. In eastern Bauchi the transition from basement to sedimentaries is barely noticeable, although there is a decline eastward. Between Bauchi and Potiskum the general level falls by some 300 feet (90 metres) in a distance of 14 miles (22 km), an average slope too small to be appreciated by the normal eye, but the drop becomes more distinct towards the Gongola and is abrupt towards the Benue valley, where there is a stepped scarp some 700 feet (210 metres) in height. The corresponding scarps in the lower Gongola valley are nearly 1000 feet (300 metres) high, but are between the plains carried eastward across the sandstones and the plains of the main valley floor. The drop is again stepped. In many ways this eastern part of the High Plains with the lower Gongola valley is not unlike the western margin with the lower Kaduna valley. Both have flat-topped sedimentary residuals above wide plains, with a series of stepped surfaces leading to higher altitudes; both have relatively low density of population, and are, socially, on the fringes of the Northern Nigerian central zone.

East of the Gongola bend lies the Biu Plateau, an extensive area of basalt with numerous volcanic cones. This plateau rises to about 2750 feet (840 metres), with a few cone summits exceeding 3000 feet (915 metres). Activity probably continued well into Tertiary time, but the existence of volcanics interbedded with Cretaceous beds in the lower Gongola valley[23] suggests that activity started in the Mesozoic, and this is one point of evidence used[24] in the hypothesis that the Benue trough (which also contains scattered cones and hot springs) has its origin as a rift valley of Lower Cretaceous age.

To the south-east of the Biu Plateau is a smaller area of plains cut across basement rocks on the west side of the Mandara Mountains. In the south, towards the Benue valley, these plains carry residual bornhardts and hill masses, such as the Kilba Hills,[25] with summit levels as high as 3700 feet (1130 metres) in the east, although lower towards the Gongola valley. The Mandara Mountains represent the northern part of the Eastern Highlands of Nigeria isolated from the rest of the upland mass by the Benue valley above Yola. Summit heights north of the river are nearly 5000 feet (1525 metres) above a fairly even upper level of about 4000 feet (1220 metres), which is readily perceptible from the west side. To the north of Mubi the summit level is lower, at about 2400 feet (730 metres), but is broken by a number of peaks not far below 5000 feet (1525 metres) near Madagali. The steep hill-sides in this district are renowned for the terrace farming of the pagan peoples, and for the independent spirit of these peoples, which evoked comment from Miss Perham in 1937[26] and which had not changed when one of the present writers visited Gwoza in 1956. The mountains are too far to the north and to the east for their alignment, almost parallel to the rain-bearing winds, to result in appreciably increased rainfall or correspondingly heavier

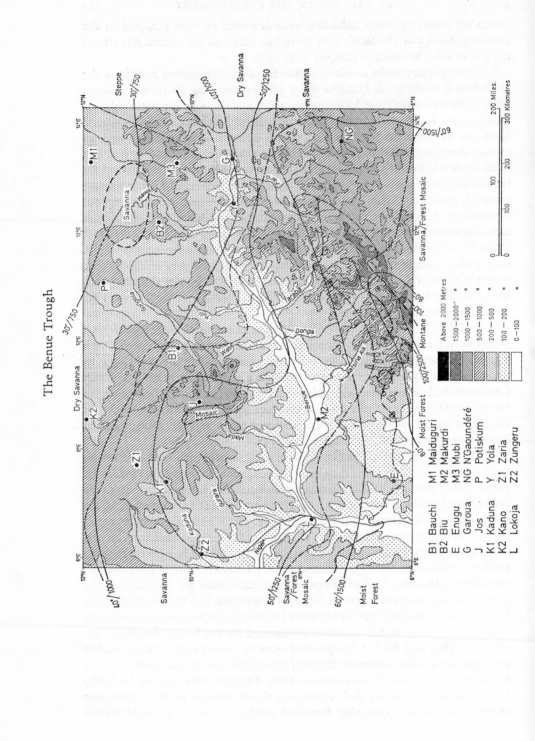

The Benue Trough

B1 Bauchi   M1 Maiduguri
B2 Biu   M2 Makurdi
E Enugu   M3 Mubi
G Garoua   NG N'Gaoundéré
J Jos   P Potiskum
K1 Kaduna   Y Yola
K2 Kano   Z1 Zaria
L Lokoja   Z2 Zungeru

Above 2000 Metres
1500 – 2000 "
1000 – 1500 "
500 – 1000 "
200 – 500 "
100 – 200 "
0 – 100 "

0   100   200   300 Kilometres
0   100   200 Miles.

vegetation, although the Biu Plateau to the west experiences relatively similar conditions; east of the Mandara Mountains, however, a slight rain-shadow effect leads to the southward extension of grassland vegetation.

The Benue trough contains rocks of Lower Cretaceous age which rest directly on the pre-Cambrian basement. Nowhere else in West Africa do rocks of this age form a link between the Atlantic coast and the interior, and this has been used with other facts to postulate a Lower Cretaceous rift valley here.[24] The Upper Cretaceous rocks subsequently deposited have been largely stripped by erosion. Few faults have been identified along the margins of the trough, but few un-weathered exposures have been seen either, and the location of the crystalline sedimentary boundary is inferred rather than surveyed. The Benue plains are extended on to the basement areas along the margins in some districts, but in others the eastern highlands come within a score of miles (32 km) of the great river. Sandstone scarps overlook the valley from the north, near the Gongola confluence, and from the south above the Niger confluence. The trough does not appear to have suffered transverse uplift such as that seen in the antecedent stretch of the Niger. In consequence the Benue has largely reached a graded profile for the greater part of its length, and provided that sufficient depth of water is available navigation is impeded only by shifting sandbanks and not by rapids. At the height of flood conditions river steamers can reach Garoua, approximately 1000 miles (1600 km) from the sea along the river course, a distance from river mouth without parallel in West Africa. The only permanent sandbank is at Lokoja, at the confluence with the Niger, and the importance of this is mentioned on page 585.

Much of the trough is notable for its high humidity during the rains, evaporation loss from the mile-wide river being considerable. The long dry season inhibits vegetation thicker than the savanna woodland, except as fringing forest along the water-courses, and man's activity in the more densely-populated areas has further contributed to the removal of large trees. The most striking example of this is in the Tiv country, where the even spread of hamlets over the whole countryside in lieu of scattered villages, has had noticeable effects on the landscape. The Tiv country is remarkably open, particularly in the southern districts which the tribe has occupied for the longest period of time, and few major trees remain in a landscape of gently rolling country, broken only by minor steps between three or four erosion surfaces and by the isolated residuals, often of mesa form, which stand above them. In places the provincial boundary can be recognized by the change in tree density, which reflects different pressure on the land and different custom on the two sides of an arbitrary line, itself significant only as evidence of an isolated moment in time. Once part of the moving boundary of an expanding geographical region, as the Tiv flood flowed vigorously into the Benue plains after the collapse of Jukun power, it has been fossilized by the authority of a temporary ruling power, which was accustomed to the established population groups of a distant continent, and whose social conscience had advanced so far beyond the purely acquisitive stage of colonialism that it rejected the idea of permissive expansion of energetic tribal communities at the expense of less mobile neighbours. In the Tiv Division of Benue Province the large trees under which Akwarra market is held are well-known for their size, having been deliberately left to provide shade. The Benue valley has been described in some detail by Grove.[27]

The coastal zone

The inland areas of Senegal have already been described. Cayor is separated from the sea by a marshy depression and the sandy beach unbroken by any stream outlet between the Senegal mouth and Dakar. The long southward-growing spit of the Langue de Barbarie has been built by longshore drift from north to south, and the river mouth itself impeded by a submerged bar across which sand moves from the spit to the mainland coast for its continued southward journey. The depth of water across the bar varies with the quantity of sand on the move, and when the bar has been at its largest, use of the port of St Louis has been severely hampered. This has been one reason for the decline of St Louis after the advantage of its early start and its river route to the interior. To the south of the river outlet the coast has been smoothed and the small valleys sealed by the great beach, which in many ways appears to be not unlike the beaches found farther to the east in West Africa except that here it has been driven hard against the mainland whereas in the Ivory Coast or Western Nigeria the beach system is separated from the mainland by creeks and lagoons. The complex of beach ridges, brackish lakes and sand dunes is widest at its southern end, where the Cape Verde peninsula acts as a gigantic groyne. This stretch of the coast has little human importance, even fishing villages being few in number.

The rocky Cape Verde peninsula, in character so different from the coast to north and south, provides the shelter for the excellent port of Dakar, which is discussed in Chapter 12. The cool Canaries Current moving southward offshore is constant to Cape Verde, and while causing mist and fog over the northern coast of Senegal its moderating effect on the tropical heat has contributed to the rise in importance of Dakar. To the south of Dakar the direction and nature of current flow is variable with the seasons. The change in air temperature on a voyage from West Africa to Europe as a ship enters the cool current is sufficient to waken a sleeping traveller. The cooler air in past centuries was said to contribute to the demise of many Europeans debilitated by too long a stay in West Africa. The change not only in air temperature but also in water temperature makes the 'turning of the corner' important even to the master of a freight vessel, to whom the ventilation of cargo holds in this section of the journey is a matter of concern. The metal hull of a ship quickly assumes the sea temperature, and if warm air is circulated in a hold of which the sides are cold, condensation takes place on the sides of the hold. If the cargo was loaded in the European winter

The South West Coastlands

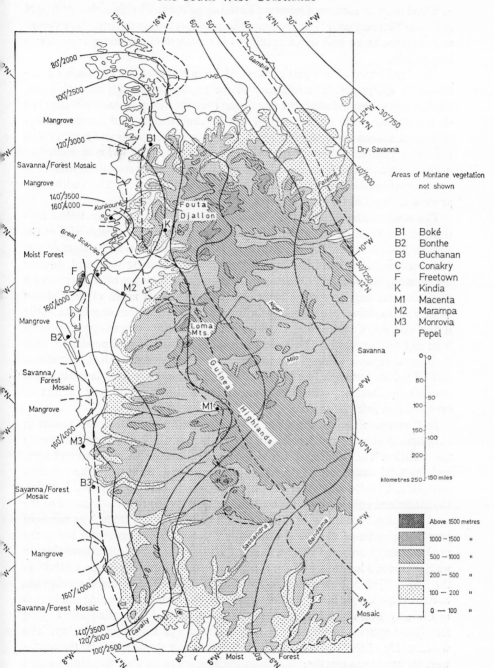

Mangrove

Savanna/Forest Mosaic

Mangrove

Konkouré

Great Scarcies

Moist Forest

Mangrove

B2

Savanna/ Forest Mosaic

Mangrove

M3

Savanna/Forest Mosaic

Mangrove

Savanna/Forest Mosaic

Cavally

Gambia

Falémé

Fouta Djallon

Niger

Loma Mts.

Milo

Guinea Highlands

Sassandra

Bandana

Dry Savanna

Areas of Montane vegetation
not shown

B1   Boké
B2   Bonthe
B3   Buchanan
C   Conakry
F   Freetown
K   Kindia
M1   Macenta
M2   Marampa
M3   Monrovia
P   Pepel

Savanna

Moist   Forest

Mosaic

| kilometres 250 | 150 miles |

Above 1500 metres
1000 — 1500   "
500 — 1000   "
200 — 500   "
100 — 200   "
0 — 100   "

Figure 6.11

for an outward voyage, on the other hand, warm air circulated over a cold cargo may lead to condensation of moisture on the cargo itself. The 'sweating' of freight in this fashion may easily lead to damage by moisture before the end of the voyage and attention to air and water conditions is therefore of considerable economic importance.

The significance of this part of West Africa in terms of climate has been discussed in Chapter 5. The tendency of the I.T.C.Z. to pivot round the Fouta Djallon means that although the dry season over the Senegal coastlands may last six months the mean annual rainfall may be considerable in the southern districts; it also means that there are rapid changes in rainfall totals and in vegetation type over relatively short distances. Thus Ziguinchor has twice as many wet days as Dakar, and a mean annual total of 64 in (1625 mm) compared with 23 in (585 mm); likewise grassland is found within a short distance of Thiès with mangrove and forest in the coastal districts of southern Senegal.

The coast south of Dakar has a short stretch of cliffed sediments unlike anything else in West Africa, and this is succeeded by the considerable area of the Gambia, southern Senegal and Portuguese Guinea, also distinct in West Africa, and consisting of the muddy estuaries of the rivers flowing westward, notably the Saloum, Gambia and Casamance. The outer beaches are often sandy, with sandspits and bars across the river channels: the sands north of the Saloum estuary are exploited commercially for ilmenite. The estuarine swamps are fertile if washed free of salt, and rice cultivation is becoming increasingly important here and farther south. The main valleys are reasonably well populated, with their broad expanse of alluvium and adequate water for crops such as groundnuts and oil palms, but their low interfluves suffer increasingly from lateritic crusts towards the interior, occasionally presenting a landscape of very indifferent grass over an infertile surface.

In Portuguese Guinea the slight change in orientation of the coast results in longshore drift being much reduced, the winds normally being at right angles to the coastline. The submerged bar at the river entrance is therefore absent here, and the tidal range, over 15 feet (4·5 metres), assists in making the estuaries navigable. Unfortunately there is little incentive to develop shipping facilities, the hinterland offering little for overseas trade, and the greater advantage of the tidal range has been its use in flushing salt from bunded rice fields. The northern part of the coast of Guinea is essentially the same, with mangrove lining the muddy sides of drowned valleys. Inland the valleys become progressively higher with southward location, and the coastlands become narrower as the foothills of the Fouta Djallon draw nearer to the sea. An arm of the highland reaches the coast at Cape Verga, but more important is the long ridge, extending south-west to Conakry and, in broken form, to the Los Islands. Mount Kakoulima, 3304 feet (1007 metres) in altitude, is only 20 miles (32 km) from Conakry. The western side of the Fouta Djallon shows a series of steps, which in the south-west are partly run together to give an initial scarp some 2000 feet (600 metres) in height.

The plains south-west of the Fouta Djallon are cut across sedimentary rocks, and extend up to 50 miles (80 km) from the coast, in the north. The plains are prolonged into the highland mass by narrow valleys trenching the stepped lower parts of the uplands. Reference was made on page 268 to the most important of these valley plains, namely the long north–south trough that almost bisects the Fouta Djallon and which extends for over 100 miles (160 km), although it is not the valley of a single river. The drainage follows the rectangular pattern previously described, which carves the highlands into a series of blocks. The northern part of the trough is occupied by the Kakrima river before it joins the Konkouré on its westward course; the southern part is occupied by a tributary of the Great Scarcies river. This trough is well-watered, both by the heavy rainfall and by the springs from the mountains; it is well-drained, rising to over 1000 feet (300 metres) in altitude, in contrast to many of the districts of the coastal plains which tend to become waterlogged in the rains; it is well vegetated, partly because compared with the mountain summits it tends to remain longer within the Tropical Maritime air mass, so that bowalization is less marked; also it tends to receive soil washed into it from above rather than to experience soil erosion. As a result it is today important economically for the cultivation of commercial crops, just as it was important in the past for the production of subsistence crops.

The coastal districts in Guinea carry a belt of forest-savanna vegetation between the sea, or the mangrove swamps where these occur, and the true savanna woodland inland. Southward this gives way to rain forest, the latter becoming established in the relatively short distance between Conakry and Freetown and occupying a zone up to 250 miles (400 km) in depth from the coast, stretching eastward as far as Ashanti in southern Ghana. In the western part of the zone the forest-savanna boundary approximately coincides with the watershed of the Guinea Highlands, of which the higher summits have montane grassland rather similar to that of the Fouta Djallon. Only along the coast does the forest give way to other plant communities, mangrove swamps commonly occupying the coastal fringe as far south as Bonthe, and a thin strip of mixed woodland and grass fringing the coast as far as Cape Palmas, albeit with occasional mangrove areas intervening.

The dissected plains between the Guinea Highlands and the coastal districts represent a landscape of inclined surfaces sloping in a NNE–SSW direction seaward from the watershed. Steps between these surfaces are not usually in the form of clear scarps: the rivers, flowing for the most part in the direction of maximum slope, have trenched their valleys into the plains, particularly where a lower surface is extending into a higher plain, to give an irregular junction zone of dissected country. The major surface on this Atlantic slope rises inland to about 1000 feet (300 metres) in altitude, and there is then a fairly abrupt change to higher levels, whether of the mountains or of their surrounding High Plains, the interval being not less than 500 feet (150 metres). This forms a contrast with the plains of the western Ivory Coast, where there is again a general rise inland of stepped surfaces, but with an intermediate cyclic surface at about 1250 feet

(380 metres) at its head, between the lower plains and the upper. The general slope is also different being NNW–SSE in the Ivory Coast.

The whole of Liberia, and almost the whole of Sierra Leone and the Ivory Coast, is part of the pre-Cambrian platform. Within this broad generalization lie a variety of distinct formations, which in Sierra Leone were identified and mapped between the wars. Prospecting in Liberia is but little advanced, but the iron deposits of the Bomi Hills, within easy reach of the coast, have been exploited since the war, the ore being railed to Monrovia, and more recently the ores of the Nimba Mountains have started to move by a new railway to the port of Buchanan. In Sierra Leone the iron ores from Marampa have been railed to Pepel for shipment, and the less accessible reserves at Tonkolili have yet to be developed. The pre-Cambrian of Sierra Leone also provides the gold, diamonds, chromite and platinum of that country. These minerals represent a modern accession to local wealth: previous interest had, for centuries, been restricted to the alluvial gold of both Sierra Leone and Liberia.

The coastal features deserve special mention on account of their unusual nature compared with the remainder of West Africa. The greater part of the coast of Sierra Leone is not unlike that of Guinea, Portuguese Guinea and southern Senegal, distinguished by open drowned estuaries free from impeding sandspits, although a sand bar beneath the surface usually hinders easy access, with the exception of the Freetown entrance. The harbour of Freetown is by far the best natural anchorage in West Africa, although not typical because of the protective barrier of the Freetown peninsula sheltering the harbour from the south-west winds and swell. The peninsula, which rises abruptly to peaks of over 2000 feet (610 metres), is a norite mass contrasting with the narrow coastal belt of Pleistocene sediments which fringe the pre-Cambrian rocks of the interior. The alignment of the high peninsula at right angles to the direction of the rain-bearing winds results in the very high totals for mean monthly rainfall at Freetown during the wet season. The resulting graph, similar in appearance to the monsoonal distributions of Asia, can nevertheless be matched by similar graphs from other West African stations such as Conakry. It represents the single-peak régime of this latitude accentuated by the distribution of highland close to the coast. Mean rainfall totals exceeding 50 in (1270 mm) a month bring their own problems in the form of severe gullying and soil erosion if the protective forest cover is removed, physical damage to crops and roads, and the difficulty of dry handling of merchandise of all forms. On the credit side is the greater ease of fresh-water flushing of bunded swamp land undergoing reclamation as potential rice paddy.

From Sherbro Island southwards the coast is mainly one of low, sandy beaches, with river outlets frequently deflected by longshore drift from south-east to north-west. Only in a few places is the monotony relieved by the cliffs of headlands reaching the sea, as at Monrovia, where part of the town is built on Cape Mesurado. The sand beaches and spits have not formed a continuous barrier between sea and lagoons as in the Ivory Coast or in Western Nigeria. Instead the Liberian coastline has a series of individual lagoons isolated from each other, and so not providing the advantage of a continuous sheltered waterway as in the two countries mentioned. Navigation is restricted to shallow-draft vessels on the lower reaches of the rivers, which are themselves obstructed by rapids where they pass from step to step of the dissected plains. A narrow strip of grass

Weather Statistics, Freetown

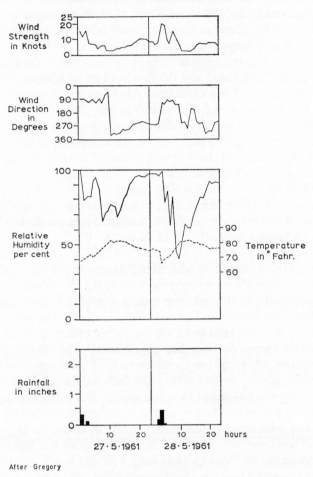

After Gregory

Figure 6.12

woodland fringes the Liberian coast, separating the forest and the ocean. This would appear to be due as much to man's interference as to purely environmental factors.

East of Cape Palmas the landscape changes. The coastline is initially rocky, cliffs being particularly notable for some 25 miles (40 km) west of the Sassandra mouth, but eastward a sand-ridge complex forms a smooth outer beach between the ocean and the lagoons. Longshore drift is west to east, and the river outlets

L

have been diverted.[28] As in Nigeria[29], the outer sand bar may vary in width up to three or four miles, and provides an effective shelter for the lagoon water-way. Evidence of a formerly higher sea-level can be seen on the outer beach, com-parable with raised beaches identified on the rocky coast of Sierra Leone[30] and Ghana[31]: equally the drowned lower valleys of rivers entering the lagoons indi-cate past lowering of sea-level. The shore of the mainland, north of the lagoons, is in many places rocky and cliffed, modern settlements tending to use the higher sites whereas the older villages are more frequently at lagoon level. The importance of the lagoons as routeways is discussed in Chapter 12, with an account of the development of modern transport facilities along this stretch of coast. Only since the cutting of the Vridi Canal and the development of Abidjan as a sheltered deep-water port has the Ivory Coast been able to engage in overseas trade with the prospect of large-scale activity, as surf is heavy and continuous over the whole length of the outer beach, and this made the coast one of the most danger-ous in West Africa. This unattractive nature to overseas traders was enhanced by the inhospitable character of the western peoples, when encountered, and by the poor visibility sometimes experienced in the drier months, making navigation hazardous. The western of the two 'dry corridors' of West Africa reaches the sea in the central part of the Ivory Coast, mean annual rainfall totals falling below 60 in (1525 mm), and in the dry season the harmattan occasionally breaks through to the coast and causes markedly low visibility.

The southward extension of the savanna zone in the Ivory Coast has been mentioned (p. 217) in connection with rainfall figures, but this is not due to rain-fall alone. The factors affecting vegetation include the type of soil, and notwith-standing the great depth of weathering usually found the bedrock also has pro-nounced effect. The granitic and gneissic rocks of the interior give soils with a high proportion of coarse sand and a low percentage of fine materials. The Ter-tiary rocks of the lagoon districts show approximately the same characteristics. By way of contrast, where the pre-Cambrian rocks of the basement are schists or ancient volcanics the clay content of the soil is high and the coarse element slight. The coarser soils will be leached the more quickly and will obviously have less moisture-retentive capacity. As a result the high forest flourishes on the clayey soils of the east with mean annual rainfall totals of under 50 in (1275 mm), and also on the clayey soils north of the confluence of the Bandama Rouge and the Bandama Blanc, although mean annual rainfall is only 45 in (1150 mm) and the dry season lasts four months. To the west of this latter area the forest is much broken by grassland, although the dry season may be only three months and the mean annual rainfall 55 in (1400 mm), the difference being the coarser sandy soil of the granite-gneiss areas. Figure 6.13 illustrates the relationship be-tween geology, rainfall and vegetation, and it can be seen that the dry corridor and the southward projection of the savanna are not wholly coincident although some relationship is obvious. The forest cover appears intact if the mean annual rainfall exceeds 55 in (1400 mm), but below this figure soil quality is important: how important cannot be stated with certainty, as human action also plays a part.

Ivory Coast: Relationship between Geology, Rainfall, and Vegetation

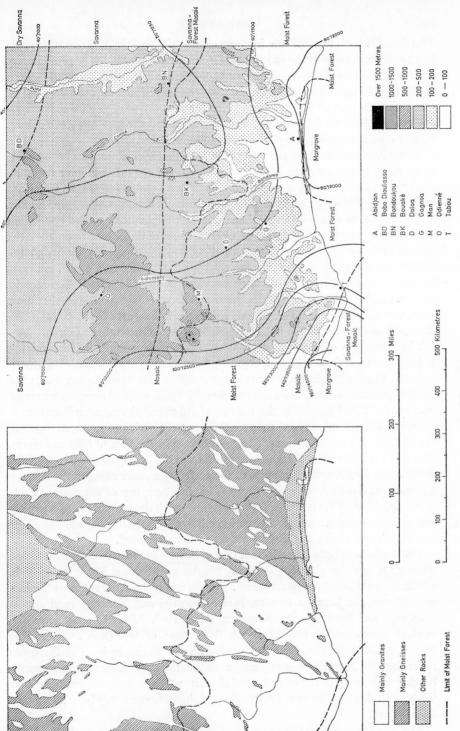

Figure 6.13

A   Abidjan
BD   Bobo Dioulasso
BN   Bondoukou
BK   Bouaké
D   Daloa
G   Gagnoa
M   Man
O   Odienné
T   Tabou

Over 1500 Metres.
1000 – 1500
500 – 1000
200 – 500
100 – 200
0 — 100

Mainly Granites
Mainly Gneisses
Other Rocks
Limit of Moist Forest.

300 Miles

500 Kilometres

The forest is itself not uniform in composition, although in the areas of crystalline rocks with above 75 in (1900 mm) of mean annual rainfall the general character is independent of soil conditions or topographical situation. In districts with less than 75 in (1900 mm), the trees vary with soil type and local water conditions. On the sandy soils of the lagoon margins the proportion of grass woodland increases irrespective of rainfall as the map shows, and the area has some affinity with the grass-woodland strip along the Liberian coast.

These relationships between vegetation and the physical features in the landscape apply elsewhere than in the Ivory Coast, but they do not have the same clarity. The forested zone of south-western Ghana extends across soils which are of the same general type as those of the eastern Ivory Coast, but the reappearance of the schists in south-eastern Ghana and in the countries to the east is not marked by a corresponding forest cover on account of the reduced rainfall of the eastern corridor. The forested regions of Ghana and the Ivory Coast, on the schists, are the most suitable for the cultivation of coffee and cocoa, and it is in these districts that the greatest production has been localized. Commercial timber, on the other hand, may be produced from anywhere within the forest zone, and although in the Ivory Coast this tends to be west of the tree crop districts, cocoa and timber are much more intermingled in southern Ghana.

The landscape of south-western Ghana is further complicated by mining activity resulting from a high degree of mineralization of the rocks of southern Ashanti. Physiographically the coast is not unlike that seen further west; the lagoon systems continue to Axim, and a rocky coast, with settlements on raised beaches and small lagoons at the mouths of individual rivers, extends eastwards to Accra. Behind this coastal strip lie the dissected plains of southern Ashanti, the NE–SW structural alignment being reflected in the plan of hills and rivers, although the latter show some modification from the ideally simple pattern. The plains are the confused lower steps of the surface sequence rising to the Ashanti Uplands previously described (p. 274). This has been one of the most densely populated parts of West Africa for a long time, with the advantages of adequate water, fertile soil and a marginal situation relative to the northern savannas. More recently the proximity to shipping services has been added.

The Tarkwaian beds of south-west Ghana include the auriferous Banket series, different in age and character from the nearby gold-bearing Birrimian rocks in which the gold occurs in quartz reefs. The former include the mines at Tarkwa and Abosso, the latter at Prestea, Bibiani, Obuasi and Konongo (and also at Navrongo and Bawku in the Northern Territories). Alluvial deposits are also worked commercially, particularly in the valleys of the Tano and Ankobra Rivers. Alluvial diamonds are also worked in the Birrim basin. The Birrimian rocks include manganese ores, mined at Nsuta: occurrences of manganese-bearing rocks are also known in several districts of the Ivory Coast but none have yet been exploited. The bauxite deposits of Ashanti have already been mentioned on page 276.

The forest is restricted to the west of the sandstone escarpment of the Volta basin and the southern end of the Togo Mountains. Along the coast eastward from Takoradi the forest-savanna mosaic reappears, passing into true savanna on the Accra plains and extending to the north-east along the dry corridor east of the mountains. The latter are forested, and have been described above (p. 276). Mangrove and swamp vegetation replace the grass woodland on the outer edge of the Volta delta. The delta appears small in relation to the size of the river, but the rock floor of the buried valley extends down to over 60 feet (18 metres) below present sea-level, and the infilling of this drowned valley is a partial explanation of the small deltaic extent. The outer coastline from Ada, through Keta to Lomé, appears, indeed, to have less relationship to the river delta than to the lagoon and sand-bar type of coast already described in the Ivory Coast and seen eastward as far as the west side of the Niger delta.

The open vegetation of the plains is due principally to the lack of rainfall. Marked differences of soil exist as between the Accra plains and the delta, and within the plains themselves, variations in soil texture, composition and water storage being readily apparent. In this area one is faced with the anomalous situation of irrigation being necessary only a few miles from a coast subjected to on-shore winds for the greater part of the year.

The coast of Togo and Dahomey has a smooth outer, sandy beach broken only by a few outlets. Behind this beach bar, which in places is only a few yards in width, lie the coastal lagoons forming part of the sheltered waterway to Nigeria. At this western end of the lagoon system depths are small, and dry-season conditions may show no more than 5 feet (1½ metres) of water in some of the lagoons and channels, compared with 30 to 40 feet (9–12 metres) in the lagoons of Western Nigeria. This means that although the water route has been of some importance in the past, it has diminished in value with the development of modern forms of transport. This contrasts markedly with the introduction of powered craft on, for example, the deep-water creeks between Lagos and Porto Novo, but the shallow depth and the construction of a good motor road along the coastal beach strip has led to diversion of business to the lorry.

Behind the lagoons rise low plateaux of Tertiary sediments, largely clays, which rise gently northwards. This gives a low plateau, known as the Terre de Barre, some 300 feet (90 metres) in altitude, broken into a number of segments by the rivers which have trenched through it on their way southward. The lower parts of these valleys have been drowned and, where not filled in with alluvium, provide extensions to the main lagoon system. The Terre de Barre has some economic importance, population density on the clay soils being relatively high. Water supply is the chief difficulty, rainfall totals being low and the clays providing rapid run-off when rain falls: many settlements rely on deep wells through the sediments. Only in western Togo does the Terre de Barre pass smoothly into the plains of the interior. Already apparent in eastern Togo, best displayed in Dahomey, and continuing eastward into Nigeria is a depression between the clay plateau and the inland plains, known as the Lama–Hollis depression. This rarely exceeds 100 feet (30 metres) in altitude, generally has a marshy floor, and

The Lagoon Coasts from the Volta to the Niger

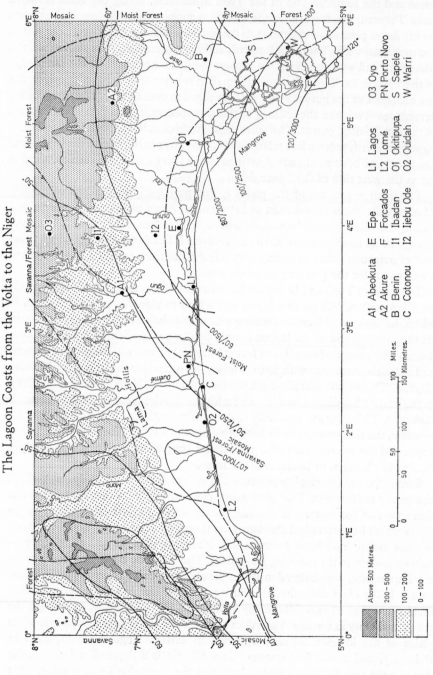

A1	Abeokuta	E	Epe	L1	Lagos	O3 Oyo
A2	Akure	F	Forcados	L2	Lomé	PN Porto Novo
B	Benin	I1	Ibadan	O1	Okitipupa	S Sapele
C	Cotonou	I2	Ijebu Ode	O2	Ouidah	W Warri

Above 500 Metres.

200 – 500

100 – 200

0 – 100

Figure 6.14

is liable to flooding in the wet season. Communication across it is always difficult and in a very wet year contact may be broken, except by canoe, between the plains and the plateau. The depression is important agriculturally and, potentially, industrially. It has a black fertile soil capable of yielding high returns, although not much used as yet on account of flood difficulties. The rocks of the depression include limestones and lignites, and both can be traced eastward into Nigeria, where the commercial use of the limestones is being investigated for cement manufacture. Northward from the depression the crystalline rocks emerge to form the lower plains of the sequence northward to the Niger.

In Nigeria there is some similarity between the southern margin of the crystalline area of the west and the sedimentary area to the south of it. The geological boundary can nevertheless be taken as dividing the High Plains from the dissected margin, because of the difference in form of residual hills and of the stream channels. The sediments decrease in age towards the coast, the oldest being Cretaceous, and there is a general dip towards the sea which accords with the idea of monoclinal downwarping of the continental margin.

The Lama–Hollis depression of Dahomey has a sequence including limestones, overlain by phosphates, and with lignite at higher levels, the whole exposed by the stripping of younger overlying beds. The depression can be identified as passing eastward in Nigeria[32], albeit less distinct than in Dahomey, but with the same general geological sequence. To the south of the depression is a ridge with crests exceeding 400 feet (120 metres), aligned approximately west-to-east near the frontier, but later turning to the south-east towards the lagoons. Phosphatic beds were recognized in the Ifo district many years ago[33], and lignites were reported south of Abeokuta[34], although not found subsequently. Although both the depression and the ridge become indistinct in places, the pattern reappears at its most distinct in Benin Province. The limestones are exposed in the Osse valley, and the scarp to the south rises to 950 feet (290 metres), although, as the whole of this area is clothed in high forest, this considerable surface feature is not readily apparent without instrumental readings. Benin City is only a little over 200 feet (60 metres) in altitude, and the river beds east of the town are as little as 60 feet (18 metres) above sea-level, but to the north-east of the Benin–Asaba road the land rises steadily to the crest of the Ishan Plateau at over 1300 feet (400 metres), with a northward-facing escarpment, all the more imposing because in the Uromi–Irrua district the differences in relief are accentuated by a vegetation contrast between thick forest over the clays which form the upper plateau beds and poor savanna bush on undulating sandy plains to the north. The margins of the plateau are markedly dissected, and the Lignite Series is frequently well exemplified in the steep-sided valleys which are sometimes several hundred feet deep.

To the north of the depression, the older sediments rise northward, with a maximum height of about 600 feet (180 metres) east of Abeokuta, where they form flat-topped hills with a pronounced northward-facing scarp. Dissection of the cuesta form is well advanced here, giving a marked contrast between the tabular sedimentary residuals south of the town and the rounded crystalline summits on the basement rocks to the north. Moss[35] has made an interesting study of the relationships between land forms, soils and land-use in this part of Nigeria.

The dissected nature of the sedimentary belt is partly a consequence of the repeated cuesta structure, and partly a result of successive cycles of erosion, possibly combined with some crustal movement. In places, as at Okitipupa, the land immediately to the north of the lagoons stands well above water level, giving a steep shore similar to that seen far to the west in the vicinity of Abidjan.

The western end of the dissected margin shows variation from the vegetational cover of the remainder of the zone. Elsewhere the usual cover is one of high forest which deteriorates on the sandier and more acid soils, and which varies to swamp forest in the wetter parts of the valley floors. In the west the effects of the dry corridor, better seen on the High Plains to the north, are apparent in the more open character of the woodland and a greater tendency to grass. Grass also becomes important on the margin of the Niger delta, where the forest has given way to derived savanna as a result of man's activities, notwithstanding the high rainfall totals.

Between this marginal zone and the ocean lies a coastal strip of a type already described. The outer beach is broken only once in a distance of some 120 miles (193 km), at the entrance to Lagos harbour. The sand-ridge system behind the beach varies in width from a few yards to about five miles (8 km). The mainland districts bordering the lagoons must also be included within this coastal belt, because in character and origin the lower parts appear to be associated with it. The valleys are drowned or swampy and the effect of northward extensions of the lagoon has impeded road construction along the mainland shore. In Togo and Dahomey the main west–east road runs along the beach bar; in Nigeria it runs well to the north of the lagoons, with southward branches to the more important lagoon settlements, such as Badagry. A striking feature of the mainland fringe is the zoning of the area into broad parallel bands, readily distinguished by alternation of thick forest and woodland, a pattern which in places extends inland for nearly 10 miles (16 km). The outer edge of this zone shows the modern lagoons as part of the banding, and it appears that the zone as a whole is one of repeated outward growth.

The sand-ridge system between the lagoons and the sea is also banded, but the individual bands are very much narrower and appear to indicate successive stages of spit growth. On the lagoon side there is evidence of repeated turning of the original spit end to give a series of recurves. The vegetation contrast between the narrow bands is exceptionally marked, open grassy glades miles in length being separated from one another by strips of almost impenetrable vegetation. Movement parallel to the beach is very easy, but movement at right angles can be extremely difficult. This has its advantages where small herds of dwarf cattle, resistant to trypanosomiasis, are pastured on the sand ridge. The geomorphological significance of the sand bar has been discussed above (p. 239), and some of its economic effects are dealt with later (p. 594).

Approximately at the change of direction of the coastline from east to south-east, the sand gives way to mud, and this continues almost to the Niger delta. The delta as a whole is an enormous mass of mixed sediments. Whereas the Volta has a disproportionately small delta in relation to river length, the Niger delta is large by any standard. The reasons for this are several. Firstly, the great

The Niger Delta and the Cross River Basin

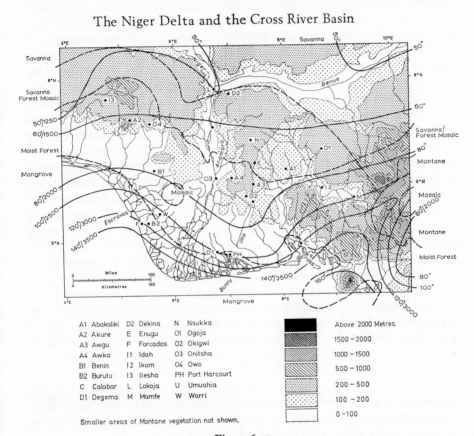

A1	Abakaliki	D2	Dekina	N	Nsukka
A2	Akure	E	Enugu	O1	Ogoja
A3	Awgu	F	Forcados	O2	Okigwi
A4	Awka	I1	Idah	O3	Onitsha
B1	Benin	I2	Ikom	O4	Owo
B2	Burutu	I3	Ilesha	PH	Port Harcourt
C	Calabar	L	Lokoja	U	Umuahia
D1	Degema	M	Mamfe	W	Warri

■	Above 2000 Metres.
	1500 – 2000
	1000 – 1500
	500 – 1000
	200 – 500
	100 – 200
	0 – 100

Smaller areas of Montane vegetation not shown.

Figure 6.15

area drained by the river and all its tributaries must involve the transport of vast quantities of material. Secondly, both the Niger and the Benue flow for consider-able distances over sediments which are physically softer than the basement rocks. Thirdly, if the hypothesis advanced on page 220 is correct, both the Niger and the Benue have been contributing to the delta for a very long time. The thickness of accumulated material has been put at as much as 40,000 feet (12,200 metres), and there are references to the 'Nigerian geosyncline' in geological literature.[36] The economic significance of these great masses of sediment lies in the possibility of mineral deposits. Seepages of bitumen were known in Western Nigeria many years ago, but only after the war did long-continued prospecting result in the tapping in quantity of petroleum and natural gas, and the first major field in operation is at the south-eastern corner of the delta. Development is now also making progress on the south-western side of the delta.

In the past the surface features of the area led to the localized siting of settlements on drier 'islands' within the delta, or as houseboat villages (p. 237), with agriculture more or less restricted to the drier patches of soil. Early contacts with overseas sailors led to the establishment of a number of ports on the delta coast but many of these have declined in importance. Quantities of water passing down the various distributary channels vary slowly, and this is a contributory factor in determining the type of entrance from the sea. The increasing obstruction of the western approaches to the delta ports has been described on page 239.

Between the delta and the Niger–Benue confluence at Lokoja the river follows a narrow and confined course unlike the wide open valleys of the river troughs above Lokoja. The restriction of the river between steep banks results in a very considerable rise in water level at times of flood, but with little or no accompanying increase in width. The variation between high- and low-water conditions is of the order of 30 feet (10 metres), leading to the exposure of sandbanks as the floodwaters fall. Local farmers make regular use of the exposed banks, planting crops as the river falls. The great variation in depth and the shifting sediment of the river bed have hitherto presented difficulties of bridging the lower valley which have made the cost of such a project uneconomic. However, the changing economic position of the country justified the expenditure on a major bridge to replace the ferry link between the road systems on opposite sides of the river.

A difference in character of the valley can be recognized above and below Onitsha. From the town to the delta is a plain of moderate width, with the Niger separated by a flood-plain from the Orashi River which flows along the eastern side of the former Niger flats. Above Onitsha higher land closes in immediately on the eastern bank, where altitudes of 300 feet (90 metres) can be found within a mile of the main channel, and although the hills temporarily recede where the Anambra joins the Niger, by the time Idah is reached sandstone cliffs rise on either bank, and summit altitudes of 700 feet (210 metres) lie close to the river. Between Idah and Lokoja the river flows on basement rocks in a gorge-like tract before the valley widens once more to a broken plain with sandstone residuals on the eastern bank.

East of the Niger lies the unusual feature of a broad belt of sedimentary rocks stretching from the interior to the coast. The sediments are of Upper Cretaceous age, with younger beds in the south. The geology of the central sector of this belt, including the main coalfield area, has been widely studied.[37]

The northern part of this sedimentary area is occupied by the Anambra basin. The main stream in its lower valley is below 200 feet (60 metres) in altitude, and most of the lowlands are at about 400 feet (120 metres), but the outer rim of the basin forms a scarp of appreciable height. The Dekina hills overlook the Lokoja confluence, and the Bassange escarpment faces north across the lower Benue valley before turning south-east and south, gaining in height as it does so, with the result that the Anambra headwaters exceed 1200 feet (370 metres). The southern edge of the Anambra basin is not more than 400 feet (120 metres) in altitude on the watershed between the Mamu and Imo valleys.

The scarp is the most easterly of a series. In the central sector dip-slopes face west and scarps face east. Here the Enugu–Nsukka scarp reaches 1900 feet (580 metres) before it diminishes and is overlapped by the Awgu scarp to the south, which in turn swings eastward from Okigwi to the Cross River.

The natural vegetation of this northern part, savanna woodland, is still visible in parts of the Anambra valley, but southwards it has largely given way to grassland as a result of population pressure. The southern part, for similar reasons, shows replacement of the original forest by oil palm bush, for reasons discussed later (p. 319).

The Mamu–Imo plains are overlooked by the Awka–Orlu scarp, rising to over 1200 feet (370 metres), but southwards this becomes firstly a plain area at about 500 feet (150 metres) and then a cuesta edge facing north-east. In the northern part of this scarp occur erosion gullies of great depth and area, some individual gully systems exceeding a square mile (2·6 sq km) in size and being hundreds of feet in depth.[38] The whole of this sedimentary belt west of the great scarp is poor, overcrowded land, saved only by the ability of the oil palm to withstand acid, infertile soil conditions. The rocks are largely sandy in character, apart from the coals of the Enugu scarp and the younger lignites which occur widely in the south but which are not rich enough to warrant economic exploitation. The sands may be put to industrial use in the manufacture of glassware and commercial bricks.

To the east of the scarp lies the Cross River basin. In the north this lies on Upper Cretaceous sediments, but it includes the whole of the Lower Cretaceous exposures in Eastern Nigeria as well as basement rocks along the eastern margin and Tertiary beds towards the coast. The watershed between the Cross and Benue basins reaches to within 25 miles (40 km) of the latter river in the north, which appears a surprisingly small distance in view of the size of the Benue. It has been suggested[39] that the Benue at an earlier stage of its history followed a course parallel to the edge of the eastern highlands and entered the sea by way of the present Cross Estuary, but it is doubtful whether this suggestion could be sustained. The existence of the Lower Cretaceous sediments here clearly has a bearing on the hypothesis mentioned on page 220, and it is of interest that volcanics have been found interbedded with the sediments and that faults aligned SW–NE have been inferred. The unusual lower course of the Imo River between Umuahia and Port Harcourt, remarkably straight for 50 miles (80 km), with no tributaries, suggests rapid headward erosion along a line of weakness by a stream which captured an earlier Imo flowing into the Cross. Erosion cycles appear to have advanced rapidly upstream on the soft sediments; the 100-foot (30·5-metre) contour extends as far as Ikom which allows navigation by river steamers well up-river from Calabar. Throughout the basin the vegetation is thicker than on the uplands west of the scarp, and is undeniably forest in the lower parts of the

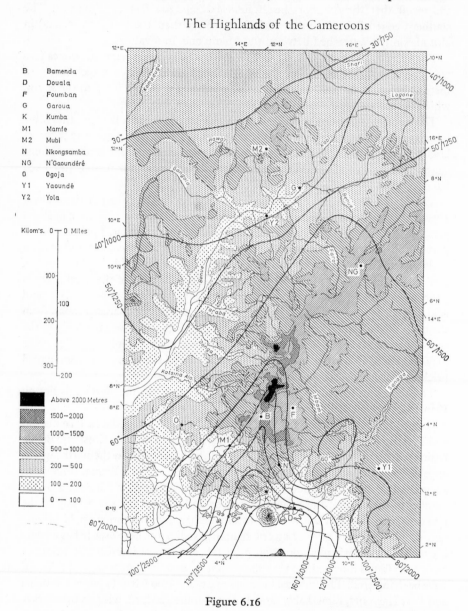

The Highlands of the Cameroons

B   Bamenda
D   Douala
F   Foumban
G   Garoua
K   Kumba
M1   Mamfe
M2   Mubi
N   Nkongsamba
NG   N'Gaoundéré
O   Ogoja
Y1   Yaoundé
Y2   Yola

Kilom's. 0 — 0 Miles

Above 2000 Metres
1500 — 2000
1000 — 1500
500 — 1000
200 — 500
100 — 200
0 — 100

Figure 6.16

valley, but the thinning effect of constant clearing is apparent in the northern and western districts.

The sediments include limestones which are now of importance for cement manufacture, and silver-lead ores near Abakaliki where workings existed long before the arrival of colonial administration and are thought to have been contemporary with the early Portuguese contacts with Benin.

Between the estuaries of the Cross and Bonny Rivers the coastline is one of muddy creeks and mangrove swamps with a smooth sandy beach and sand bars across the river mouths. There are no longitudinal lagoons as in Western Nigeria.

The outer edge of the Niger delta is at present undergoing active erosion, and large quantities of sand move eastwards along the coast. The difficulties of sand obstruction of the Forcados and Escravos estuaries, leading to the delta ports, are described on page 239 and similar problems may arise east of the Delta. The Fouché channel to Degema, west of the Bonny channel leading to Port Harcourt, has already become unusable, and it is probable that continued eastward encroachment by moving sand will ultimately imperil the Bonny channel also.[40]

The eastern margin of West Africa, in the physical sense, is the line of highland stretching from Cameroon Mountain north-eastward to the Mandara Mountains of the Chad basin, and will be described briefly here, although the southern and eastern parts of the highlands are politically now included with Central rather than with West Africa.

Mount Cameroon is the only active volcano in West Africa, and following six eruptions in the 19th century has been active five times in the 20th. Although reaching a greater altitude than any other of the great volcanoes along the line of weakness from the Gulf of Guinea north-eastward into the African continent, it is not the largest in size from base to summit. Nevertheless it is an impressive mountain, and with a summit at 13,350 feet (4070 metres) is the highest point in West Africa. It has multiple craters, and is built of basalts and ash, the basalts forming cliffed headlands along the coast, separated by beaches of black sand. The great mountain fails to reach the level of permanent snow. Vegetation is zoned with altitude, with forest up to 6000 feet (1830 metres), including tree ferns; above 6000 feet (1830 metres) trees become more scattered and stunted with the forest epiphytes being replaced by lichens; this zone is succeeded first by coarse, tussocky grassland with occasional dwarf trees, and above 10,000 feet (3050 metres) by turf and moss cushions.

The mountain, by virtue of its size and position, experiences rain throughout the year on its western side, where Debundscha averages nearly 400 in (10,160 mm) of rain per annum. The decline in mean totals is very sharp towards the leeward side, as seen on the rainfall maps of the previous chapter. Mount Cameroon is isolated from the remainder of the eastern highlands by a narrow belt of lowland.

The eastern highlands, from south to north, fall into six main groups namely

1) the Oban–Rumpi Hills
2) the Koupé–Manengouba Mountains
3) the Bamenda Highlands
4) the Mountains of Ogoja and Benue

5) the Adamawa Highlands
6) the Mandara Mountains described on page 285–7, and lying to the north of the Benue valley.

1) The Oban Hills[41] form a watershed at about 1500 feet (460 metres) between the southern headwaters of the Cross River and the headstreams of rivers flowing direct to the sea. Summits rise as high as 3800 feet (1160 metres). The hills lie on basement rocks, and are much like residual masses on the crystalline rocks elsewhere, except that they appear to lack the steep, exfoliating faces of typical bornhardt domes. Some mineralization is proved, but attempts at tin-mining[42] were abandoned, largely because of the difficulties of the high forest cover. Rainfall totals are well over 100 in (2540 mm) a year on the south-western slopes.

The Rumpi Hills lie to the south-east of the Oban Hills, with summits rising to 4800 feet (1460 metres). The major watershed is again at about 1500 feet (460 metres). Several erosion levels can be recognized in the hill mass. Volcanic rocks are widespread above the crystallines, and Kumba Crater is a notable feature with a steep rim of bedded ash.

2) The Koupé–Manengouba complex lies to the west of Nkongsamba, and has been described in detail by Gèze.[43] Koupé rises to 6791 feet (2070 metres), and the summit above the calderas of the Manengouba group is at 7382 feet (2250 metres). Between the two, and eastward, is a ridge of basement rock at about 4000 feet (1220 metres), and a lower ridge with a summit level of about 3400 feet (1040 metres) joins the mass to the higher areas to the north.

3), 4) These two groups together form a great triangular mass, roughly equilateral in shape, with sides of length 100 miles (160 km). Apart from valleys working back into the margins, all this mass lies above 3000 feet (915 metres), much of it above 6000 feet (1830 metres), and with summits over 8000 feet (2440 metres). For the most part the boundary of the highlands is a steep scarp up to 3000 feet (915 metres) in height. In the north-east this mass connects to the mountains of Adamawa by a narrow belt of land above 4000 feet (1220 metres) in altitude.

Volcanic activity has been widespread in the Bamenda Highlands and has been a major factor in determining the form of the landscape. It appears that the basement rocks lie at about 4000 feet (1220 metres) in altitude, with volcanics above, the latter including trachytes and rhyolites as well as basalts. There would seem to have been two phases of activity roughly comparable with those of the Jos Plateau on the opposite side of the Benue Trough. The younger flows extended well beyond the limits of the older flows, which are now largely decomposed to soft clays.

The exposures of basement rocks show a clear erosion surface at about 4000 feet (1220 metres) and this has been identified with the 'Gondwana' surface elsewhere in Africa.[25b] Locally this rises to close on 6000 feet (1830 metres) on the margin of the Benue Trough, where the Sonkwala hills overlook the plains of Tiv and Ogoja. Other surfaces can be identified at lower levels.

5) North-east of the Bamenda Highlands volcanic activity appears to have been much reduced in scale, and hill groups are composed almost entirely of crystalline basement rocks. The different hill groups are more distinct and isolated than farther south, and although summit levels can be recognized in some districts there is lack of continuity. Summit heights vary up to 8000 feet (2440 metres). Individual masses are still of considerable size, the Mambila Plateau having a maximum length of 60 miles (97 km), for example. There is everywhere a steep drop from a little below 4000 feet (1220 metres) to about 2400 feet (730 metres), although these limits vary. The Adamawa Mountains are notable as being the basement exposures at the greatest elevations in West Africa, and they probably lie on an axis of uplift represented by the major watershed running eastward for some 250 miles (400 km) past Ngaoundéré to the Massif de Yadé, largely above 3000 feet (915 metres) and with summits of over 5000 feet (1530 metres). Northward the highlands continue to the Benue, which is overlooked by the residual masses of the Verre Hills and the Alantika Mountains.

The highlands are not markedly mineralized. Their human significance lies firstly in the barrier which they have presented to migrations in a SE–NW direction, and which seems to have inhibited movement in this sense, with the possible exception of the Tiv. Secondly, the great extent of the high altitude areas has led to true montane grassland along the length of the mountains, which has resulted in their use as upland pasture by herdsmen, who have here been able to bring the cattle much farther to the south than elsewhere in West Africa. In recent years the competing claims of herdsmen and agriculturalists have been a matter of some concern. Thirdly, climatic zoning with altitude has led to modern commercial cropping, notably of coffee in the highlands, and the potential of the highlands for development by European settlers was appreciated by the Germans. It might be remarked that they also appreciated the commercial potential of the Tiko plains, east of Mount Cameroon, where they developed the extensive plantations of oil palms and bananas, in particular, which distinguished this area from the rest of the country when the Southern Cameroons (West Cameroon) was joined with Nigeria under British administration. Geographically there would seem to be little doubt that the union of the Southern Cameroons with the Cameroun Republic was a logical step.

BIBLIOGRAPHICAL NOTES

[1] Naval Intelligence Division Handbook, *French West Africa, I The Federation*, London, 1943, p. 168.

[2] ibid., p. 171.

[3] Y. Urvoy, Les Bassins du Niger, *Mémoires de L'Institut Français d'Afrique Noire*, **4**, Paris, 1942.

[4] R. Mauny, *Tableau Géographique de l'Ouest Africain au Moyen Age*, Thesis, Dakar, 1961, p. 210.

[5] Y. Urvoy, op. cit., p. 51.

[6] R. Mauny, op. cit., p. 207.

[7] J. C. Pugh and A. E. Perry, *A Short Geography of West Africa*, London, 1960, p. 23.

[8] A. T. Grove and R. A. Pullan, Some aspects of the Pleistocene paleogeography of the Chad Basin, in *African Ecology and Human Evolution*, ed. H. C. Howell and F. Bourlière, Viking Fund Publications in Anthropology, No. 36, 1936, pp. 230–45.

[9] R. A. Pullan, The recent geomorphological evolution of the south central part of the Chad Basin, *Journal of the West African Science Association*, **9**, 1964, pp. 115–39.

[10] R. Mauny, op. cit., p. 70.

[11] J. C. Leclerc, J. Richard-Molard, M. Lamotte, G. Rougerie and R. Portères, La Chaîne du Nimba, Essai Géographique, *Mémoires de L'Institut Français d'Afrique Noire*, **43**, Dakar, 1955, p. 248.

[12] ibid., pp. 225 ff.

[13] J. C. Pugh, The geomorphology of the northern plateau of Nigeria, *University of London*, Ph.D. thesis (unpublished), 1955, pp. 36–41 and 123–8.

[14] J. D. Falconer, *The Geology and Geography of Northern Nigeria*, London, 1911, p. 16.

[15] A. C. Burns, *History of Nigeria*, London, 1929, p. 35.

[16] See S. F. Nadel, *A Black Byzantium*, Oxford, 1942.

[17] J. D. Falconer, op. cit., Chapter VII.

[18] J. D. Falconer, The Southern Plateau Tinfields and the Sura Volcanic Line, *Geological Survey of Nigeria, Bulletin 9*, 1926.
R. A. Mackay, R. Greenwood and J. E. Rockingham: The Geology of the Plateau Tinfields – Resurvey 1945–8, *Geological Survey of Nigeria, Bulletin 19*, 1949.

[19] J. C. Pugh, The Volcanoes of Nigeria, *Nigerian Geographical Journal*, **2**, 1958, pp. 26–36.

[20] J. D. Falconer, The Geology and Geography of Northern Nigeria, op. cit., p. 41.

[21] A. T. Grove, The ancient erg of Hausaland, and similar formations on the south side of the Sahara, *Geographical Journal*, **124**, 1958, pp. 528–33. See also [8] and [9] above.

[22] D. R. Rosevear, *Checklist and Atlas of Nigerian Mammals*, Lagos, 1953, Foreword, pp. 28–30 and Plates 24–27.

[23] Geological Survey of Nigeria, *Annual Report 1950–51*.

[24] J. C. Pugh and L. C. King, Outline of the geomorphology of Nigeria, *South African Geographical Journal*, **34**, 1952, pp. 30–36.

[25] (a) J. C. Pugh, Fringing pediments and marginal depressions in the inselberg landscape of Nigeria, *Transactions & Papers, Institute of British Geographers*, **22**, 1956, pp. 15–31.
(b) J. C. Pugh, High-level surfaces in the Eastern Highlands of Nigeria, *South African Geographical Journal*, **36**, 1954, pp. 31–42.

[26] M. Perham, *Native Administration in Nigeria*, Oxford, 1937, p. 137.

[27] A. T. Grove, *The Benue Valley*, Kaduna, 1957.

[28] For this stretch of coast, see the following:
E. F. Gautier, Les côtes de L'Afrique Occidentale au sud de Dakar, *Annales de Géographie*, **40**, 1931, pp. 163–74.
M. Malavoy, Sur quelques particularités du littoral et des lagunes de la Côte d'Ivoire, *Comptes Rendus, International Geographical Congress, Warsaw*, **2**, 1934.
G. Rougerie, Etude morphologique du bassin français de la Bia et des régions littorales de la lagune Aby, *Etudes Eburnéennes*, **II**, 1951.

There is a very full bibliography in
P. Le Bourdiec, Contribution à l'étude géomorphologique du bassin sédimentaire et des régions littorales de Côte d'Ivoire, *Etudes Eburnéennes*, **VII**, 1958, pp. 7–96.

[29] J. C. Pugh, A classification of the Nigerian coastline, *Journal of the West African Science Association*, **1**, 1954, pp. 3–12.
J. C. Pugh, The Porto Novo–Badagri Sand Ridge Complex, *Department of Geography, University College, Ibadan, Research Notes*, **3**, 1953.
J. C. Pugh, Sand movement in relation to wind direction as exemplified on the Nigerian coastline, *Department of Geography, University College, Ibadan, Research Notes*, **5**, 1954.

[30] S. Gregory, The raised beaches of the Peninsula area of Sierra Leone, *Transactions & Papers, Institute of British Geographers*, **31**, 1962, pp. 15–22.

[31] N. R. Junner, Geology of the Gold Coast and Western Togoland, *Gold Coast Geological Survey*, Bulletin II, 1940.

[32] J. C. Pugh, Eastward projection of Lama–Hollis forms into Western Nigeria, *Journal of the West African Science Association*, **2**, 1956, pp. 77–80.

[33] R. C. Wilson and A. D. N. Bain, The Geology of the Western Railway, Section I, *Geological Survey of Nigeria, Bulletin 2*, 1922.

[34] R. C. Wilson, Brown Coal in Nigeria, *Geological Survey of Nigeria, Occasional Paper No. 1*, 1925.

[35] R. P. Moss, Soils, slopes and land use in south-western Nigeria, *Transactions & Papers, Institute of British Geographers*, **32**, 1963, pp. 143–68.

[36] For example, Dr F. Dixey, in discussion after
L. C. King, Pediplanation and isostasy: an example from South Africa, and
J. C. Pugh, Isostatic readjustment in the theory of pediplanation, *Quarterly Journal of the Geological Society*, **111**, 1956. See p. 370.

[37] A. D. N. Bain, The Nigerian Coalfield, Section I, Enugu Area, *Geological Survey of Nigeria, Bulletin 6*, 1924.
R. C. Wilson and A. D. N. Bain, The Nigerian Coalfield, Section II, Parts of Onitsha and Owerri Provinces, *Geological Survey of Nigeria, Bulletin 12*, 1928.
C. M. Tattam, A review of Nigerian stratigraphy, *Geological Survey of Nigeria, Annual Report 1943*, Appendix B.

[38] A. T. Grove, Land Use and soil conservation in parts of Onitsha and Owerri provinces, *Geological Survey of Nigeria, Bulletin 21*, 1951.
A. T. Grove, Soil erosion and population problems in south-eastern Nigeria, *Geographical Journal*, **117**, 1951, pp. 291–304.

[39] R. C. Wilson and A. D. N. Bain, The Geology of the Eastern Railway, Section I, Port Harcourt to Enugu, *Geological Survey of Nigeria, Bulletin 8*, 1925.
R. A. Reyment, *Aspects of the geology of Nigeria*, Ibadan, 1965, Chapter XIII.

[40] J. C. Pugh, Sand movement in relation to wind direction as exemplified on the Nigerian coastline, op. cit.

[41] J. Parkinson, The geology of the Oban Hills, Southern Nigeria, *Quarterly Journal of the Geological Society*, **64**, 1907.

[42] C. Raeburn, Tinstone in Calabar District, *Geological Survey of Nigeria, Bulletin 11*, 1927.

[43] B. Gèze, Géographie physique et géologie du Cameroun Occidentale, *Mémoires du Musée National d'Histoire Naturelle*, Nouvelle Série XVII, Paris, 1943.

Figure 6.12 is taken from S. Gregory, *Weather Statistics in Sierra Leone*, Occasional Publication No. 2 of the Department of Geography, University of Liverpool, 1967.

CHAPTER 7

Examples of Community Regions

In presenting a general portrayal of man and his environment in West Africa, the vast scope prevents in many cases a full appreciation of the integral part of each of the features presented. Smaller regions are useful for a clearer appreciation, and also for the presentation of variation within West Africa as a whole. A complete system of geographical regions is at present impossible to devise for West Africa, nor is the information available sufficient for a balanced description of all areas. Harrison Church's regions, for example, are defined mainly on political and relief grounds.[1] However, highly detailed work has been done in many areas, and, using communities as the basis for regional definition, a number of community regions has been selected, and these are presented as samples of smaller scale inter-relationship. Community regions have been chosen, because they enable the identification of a system of relationships between men, plants, animals and environment within areas. Moreover, they make possible the closer study of the distinctive contributions which different human groupings have made to the West African landscape. At a cursory glance this landscape appears chaotic and little modified by man. Yet research has revealed numerous attempts to order and change the environment, of which some detail will be given in the following studies.

Yorubaland

The Yoruba region may be divided into two major parts: the grassland and the high forest or rain forest, that is the grass fallows and woody fallows, for the distribution of vegetation owes much to man. A broad ridge of higher ground between 1000 and 2000 feet (300–600 metres) above sea-level lies in the north of the region and forms the chief watershed. To the south an erosion surface descends gradually, interrupted by the great basin of the Ogun River and the smaller basins of the neighbouring streams, by quartzitic ridges, by bornhardts and by several escarpments. The escarpments are most marked in the central and eastern districts where they divide the Ijesha from the Ekiti, and the Yoruba of Ondo from the Edo or Bini. The hills of Ekiti rising to over 2000 feet (600 metres) above sea-level form a south-eastward continuation of the main watershed and provide the highest densely settled ground in the region. However, relief has generally a local rather than a regional significance. Areas of broad level land

LOCATION of SAMPLE COMMUNITIES

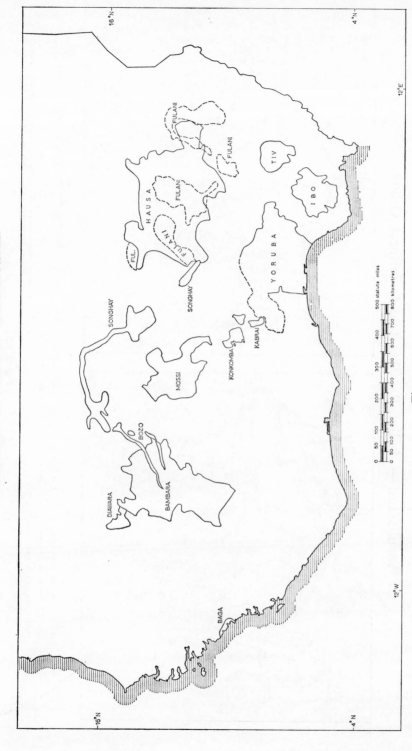

Figure 7.1

Yorubaland—Relief, Rainforest and Cultural Groups

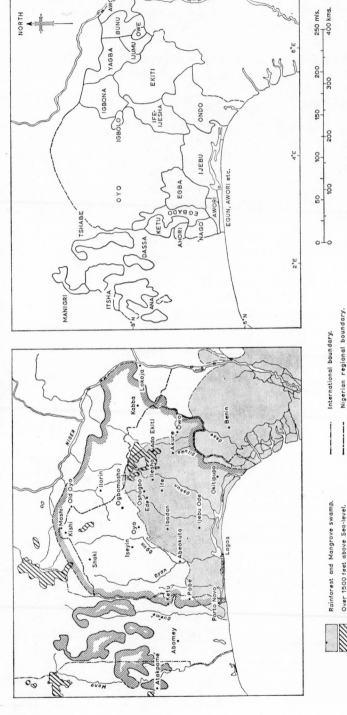

Figure 7.2

suitable for cultivation are of widespread distribution. The major distinctions are between the grass fallows and the woody fallows, where different patterns of occupance and different modes of obtaining a living have been developed. The varied products of the two fallow zones have long been exchanged. The peoples of the two zones have thus been economically linked, and yet their differences have appeared in an antithesis of political interests in recent Yoruba history.

The name 'Yoruba' is possibly of Hausa origin and appears to have been adopted as a collective term recently. The peoples concerned spoke a common language, and formed a loose federation at the beginning of the 19th century, under the nominal authority of the Alafin of Oyo, whose capital lay to the north of the Ogun basin on the main watershed. Here in 1826 was one of the most populous parts of Yorubaland, forming a great crescent of towns and villages around the northern perimeter of the Ogun basin.[2] In the west a north to south line of settlements lay on the road to the port of Badagry – the nearest port to the grassland. The woody fallow and rain-forest lands to the south-east were divided between a number of distinct groups, forming small states, of which the Egba, Owu, Ijesha, Ijebu and Ife appear to have been the most important. To the north-east were the Yagba; to the west the various Dahomeyan groups, such as the Ana, Sha and Ketu, together with the Adja and the old state of Allada.[3] The Oyo were the most powerful military group and used cavalry. They could regard the forest people as 'epo' or weeds.[4] But it must not be forgotten that, whilst secular authority lay in the grasslands, religious authority lay in the forest at Ife, the residence of the Oni, and the legendary centre of origin of the whole people. Moreover, some of the wealthiest trading towns, such as Owu, lay in the forest, although near to the grassland border. In the first decades of the 19th century, Fulani armies invaded northern Yorubaland, established a capital at Ilorin and destroyed Oyo and most of the neighbouring towns. The refugees fled southwards to the Egba domain in the southern grasslands and the neighbouring forest. Egba towns were destroyed and their population in turn forced southwestwards. In the north the abandoned lands of the watershed reverted to a woodland with species adapted to a marked dry season ('Guinea Savanna'). This woodland was maintained by the creation in the 20th century of a forest reserve in the Upper Ogun basin. In the southern grasslands increased density of population resulted in the removal of almost all woodland, leaving only a few scattered trees ('Derived Savanna'). In the forest land old settled areas, depopulated by warfare, reverted to forest, but new clearances were created, especially around the growing military camp of Ibadan founded c. 1820. The increasing refugee population in the forest lands resulted in the creation of an almost permanent woody fallow and croplands landscape. To this in the 20th century were added the plantations of cocoa trees and a rapid increase in removal of the forest, which, outside the forest reserves, remains confined mainly to settlement and roadside fringes, or to the steeper valley slopes.

The urban tradition of the Yoruba is old-established, although it would appear likely that the proportion of urban population increased during the 19th century with the need for defence. Yoruba groups had to fight not only against invaders, but against one another. Warfare was further encouraged by the demand for slaves, either for agricultural labour or for export. The traditional Yoruba town is divided into quarters occupied by lineages. Iwo, for example, with a population of 100,000 dwelling in an area of 2 square miles (5 sq km), is divided into four quarters and has 200 lineages in 500 compounds.[5] Main roads tend to separate quarters, and to focus on the compound of the ruler – the 'afin' – and the central market. The town is surrounded by one or more walls with gateways, and by a belt of woodland – the 'igbo ile' or 'home forest'.

The lineage ('idile' or 'ebi') is the traditional land holder, and its head apportioned plots according to need, except in Owo and Ondo districts where the land appears to have been held by the whole community. Formerly the 'ebi' land was in one piece, but today it has for the most part been subdivided into fields, worked by individuals or by the smallest family groups. Large joint clearances known elsewhere are rare in Yorubaland. The agricultural lands form a patchwork of fallows and tilled fields with oil palms and other useful trees. Each family works its holding by its own rotation of crops and fallows. In the immediate vicinity of many towns fields are smaller than on the main croplands farther away, probably because these nearer lands have been longer occupied and are in greater demand. Cropland occurs within the town walls, and thus once provided food during a siege and open land for occupation by refugees from the surrounding lands. Other classes of land include:

1) Town lands, occupied by the compounds.
2) 'Ile ilu' or public lands occupied by markets, cemeteries and public buildings.
3) 'Orubo' or land held by chiefs in office.
4) 'Ile adugbo' or quarter land, that is unallocated cultivable land and the groves of the ancestral spirits.

More distant croplands are normally worked, not from the town, but from the hamlet or 'aba', whose occupants are part of a town family. Some townspeople move to the 'abas' during the planting and harvesting seasons, but most movements between hamlets and towns are for festival occasions. Cocoa planting has brought an enormous increase in the number of 'abas', giving almost continuous settlement throughout the cocoa belt. The villages, which contain only a small proportion of the population, provide market facilities between the more distant croplands and the towns.[6]

Yams are the traditional staple, planted in February and March, in mounds one to two feet in height, with the vines trailed normally on stakes. Field units are often reckoned by the number of yam mounds. In Ekiti or Owo, for example, fields average 1500–2000 mounds or just over one acre (0·4 hectare).[7] In the grassland the chief secondary crops rotated or interplanted with yams are guinea corn, maize, egusi melon, cassava and okra. In the south-western woody fallows maize and cassava are the chief secondaries; in the eastern, maize and cocoyam.

Plantains are widespread, but are particularly common in the eastern woody fallows. Cassava is of rapidly increasing importance, and, with the spread of cocoa, is becoming a common crop on the poorer hill-slope soils useless for cocoa planting. Cassava has also invaded former fallows, for with ease of planting and the property of being available as required after a year's growth, more cassava is planted than need demands. The Yoruba cultivator can classify vegetation and soils, and use his knowledge to seek the best areas for planting a given crop. Even before the dissemination of advice by Government agricultural officers, the value of leguminous crops for 'nourishing' the soil was appreciated. Cotton is still grown to supply the local textile industry, and is localized mainly in the western grasslands with their longer dry season. Rice is of growing importance as a commercial crop, supplying a new demand, and requiring less labour in cultivation than yams. The chief centres of rice planting are in Abeokuta and Kabba provinces. Few livestock are kept. Surveys in 4 woody fallow districts in 1952 indicated averages of 12–19 fowls, 2–4 goats and 1–3 sheep per family.

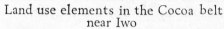

Land use elements in the Cocoa belt near Iwo

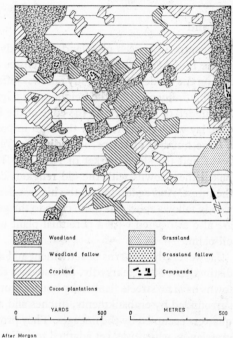

Woodland		Grassland
Woodland fallow		Grassland fallow
Cropland		Compounds
Cocoa plantations		

YARDS 0 ———— 500   METRES 0 ———— 500

After Morgan

Figure 7.3

However, it is cocoa which, above all other crops, has made the greatest impact on the economy and landscapes of the region, as will be shown in detail in a related area, the cocoa belt of south-eastern Ivory Coast and Ghana, in Chapter 13. With the wealth derived from cocoa, many Yoruba families have abandoned their traditional single-storied, narrow-roomed, courtyard houses for two- or three-storey buildings roofed with corrugated iron. The latter have been developed from a house type introduced in the last century by former slaves returned from Brazil, and later modified by the influence of British building. Cocoa has spread on the red clay 'ilepa' soils of the northern portions of the woody fallows. It thus occupies the area favoured by urban refugee settlement and adjacent to the grassland border along which so many of the great markets have been established. Here a traditional zone of population concentration has been enlarged and yet more intensively occupied, due to the commercial attractions associated with cocoa cultivation and the new urbanism and transport network. The broad tracks and the caravans of the past have been replaced by roads and lorries. There is some little evidence of retreat of the forest 'edge' in Egba Division, with the advance of agriculture[8], and, with more intensive occupation, the boundary zone between the woody fallows and the grassland has been more sharply defined. Thus the modern trends have re-emphasized the basic regional divisions, which are as outstanding geographical features of Yorubaland today as they have been in the past.

Iboland

The contrast between grassland and woody fallows appears equally in the lands of the Ibo. Again there are the old centres of culture and trade in the grassland and on the border of the woody fallows. Jeffreys points to a northern culture area, possibly influenced by the neighbouring Igala, and with an important centre at 'Umundri' or 'Umunri' on the edge of the former rain forest.[9] Near that same edge lay what were probably the most important trade routes in Iboland, linking a large number of towns, including the old-established iron-making centre of Awka and the slave market of Nike.[10] To the south-east a connecting route linked these towns with the old religious centre of Arochuku – built like Ife in the forest. And again, today, the highest densities of population occur within the woody fallows zone, but quite close to the grassland border. These high densities are also associated with a perennial plant whose product may be exported – the oil palm.

However, the patterns of settlement and agriculture, and the resultant regional distinctions, differ markedly. So also does the physical framework. The northern towns have no streets flanked by houses, but are groupings of dispersals, formerly surrounded by embankments, ditches and a woodland belt, and subdivided into quarters occupied by the lineages. They provided a system of defence in the open grasslands, which was yet adapted to a dispersal of dwellings.[11] In effect, they were the very simplest form of community, linked solely by defence needs. To the south the towns are replaced by dispersals, either of hamlets or of individual compounds, for the forest provided a protective screen. Divisional densities in the centre are over 600 to the square mile (230 per sq km), and some small village group areas have densities of over 1000 (385). The dispersal is virtually continuous, and it is for the most part impossible to discover from the distribution where one social unit ends and another begins. Only the small agglomerations of Owerri, Arochuku and the coastlands provide exceptions to the general pattern. The large holding, expressed in a common field, of the lineage or quarter, is still either a significant feature, or has left traces in field systems only recently changed (Fig. 7.5). Owerri still has its five fields and five quarters, with some tendency to rotate clearance and planting through holdings situated in some or all of the fields. In Umuahia scattered hamlets unite in the possession of large field units, although generally the field units in areas of dispersed settlement are smaller

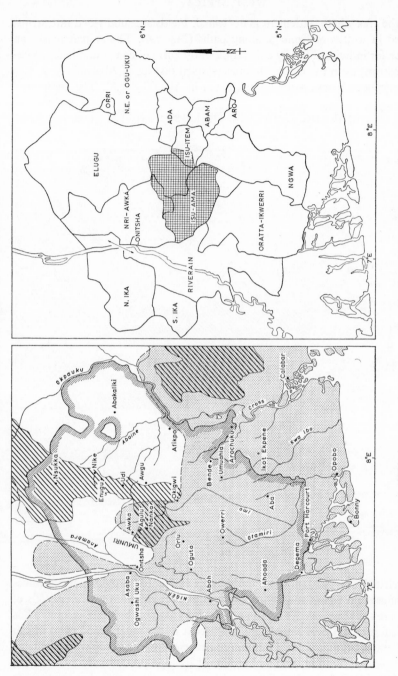

Rainforest and Mangrove swamp

Over 600 feet (180 metres)

Approximate boundary of Ibo area

Oriu and Okigwi divisions with >750 persons per square mile (>290 per sq. km.)

Based on D. Forde and G.I. Jones, Ibo and Ibibio speaking peoples, 1950. Keay, Outline of Nigerian Vegetation, 2nd. edition 1952; and G.S.G.S. 1:2M.

Figure 7.4

than in the area where settlement is nucleated. Fields are subdivided into strips, calculated in widths of frontage along paths (Fig. 7.6). The system makes an allowance for individual family cultivation in the form of compound land, sometimes in strips, as in the crowded Ameka–Isiagu district of Abakaliki (Fig. 7.7) or in amorphous blocks as in Umu Ocham in Aba (Fig. 7.8). The compound

Settlement and Land use in Eastern Diobu

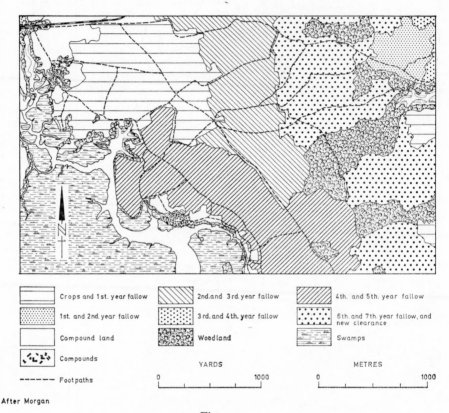

Crops and 1st. year fallow	2nd. and 3rd. year fallow	4th. and 5th. year fallow
1st. and 2nd. year fallow	3rd. and 4th. year fallow	6th. and 7th. year fallow, and new clearance
Compound land	Woodland	Swamps
Compounds		
Footpaths		

YARDS   METRES

0   1000   0   1000

After Morgan

Figure 7.5

land is virtually owned, supports the densest stands of oil palms, and receives all the household refuse and other forms of manure. The brown forest soils of Iboland are thus improved, and frequently acquire a much darker colour. Thus the most fertile and productive land is adjacent to the settlements, even within towns. Yams are the traditional staple crop, and cassava a new crop whose cultivation is rapidly increasing, mainly because of its high productivity even on the poor soils resulting from short fallows with overcrowding rather than for reasons of convenience, competition with another crop or commercial advantages. The two- or three-year rotations of Yorubaland involving a large number of crops are replaced by the mixed cultivation of yams and cassava, with a little maize or beans, which is allowed to become a fallow with cassava in the second year. Despite short fallows, yams are grown wherever possible, even for sale as a commercial crop, in order that the money earned may be used to buy larger quantities of the cheaper 'gari' or cassava flour. The oil palm is the most important of all plants in the economy, despite the importance of the yam as a staple food. It forms an almost continuous forest, thin on the cultivated lands, and dense in the groves which surround and intermingle with the settlements. As the last

Plot patterns in Eastern Diobu and Umu Ocham

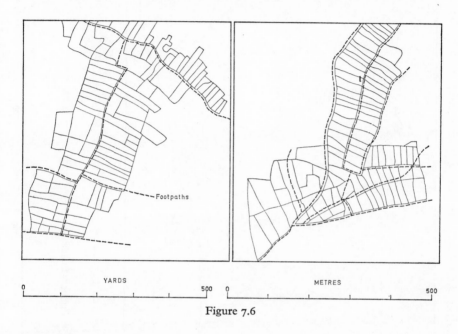

Footpaths

YARDS
0   500   0

METRES
                                                                                500

Figure 7.6

remnants of woodland are stripped away, so they are replaced by a forest of oil palms, whose over-all density is roughly proportionate to that of the Ibo population.

The keys to the high Ibo population densities, and to the distinctive crowded landscape of compounds and oil palms, lie in social organization and the character of the environment. The Yoruba organization into states with some measure of central authority is replaced in Iboland by a virtual anarchy of small groups. Thus family lands are replaced by group lands, and the town remains divided into quarters with a dispersal of families, united together only for defence, and by quarters only for land division. Moreover, this dispersal allows the existence of compound land between the compounds and its easy manuring. It is only by this means of achieving virtually permanent cultivation and dense stands of oil palms, on at least part of the land, that the high densities can be supported. R. K. Udo in

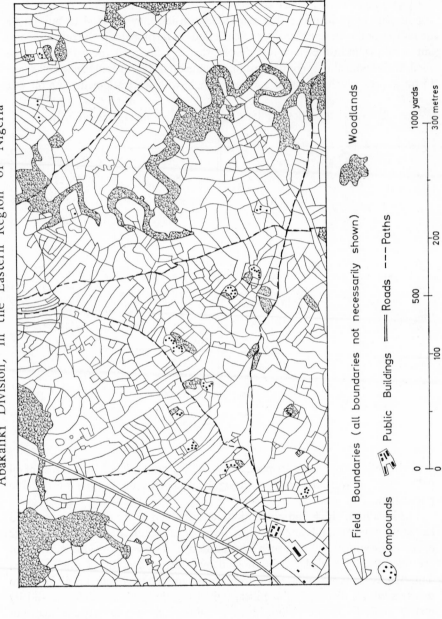

Field Boundaries in the Ameka – Isiagu District,
Abakaliki Division, in the Eastern Region of Nigeria

Field Boundaries (all boundaries not necessarily shown)

Woodlands

Compounds   Public Buildings   ══ Roads   ─ ─ ─ Paths

| 0 | | 500 | | 1000 yards |
| 0 | 100 | 200 | 300 metres |

Based on Aerial Photographs

an important paper[12] points to the close association of high population density, dispersal and individual land tenure, suggesting that dispersal represents the final stage in the disintegration of the nucleated settlement caused by high population density and the establishment of colonial rule. There is abundant evidence to support this thesis, although some dispersal was well established before colonial

Settlement and Land use in Umu Ocham, Aba in the Eastern Region of Nigeria

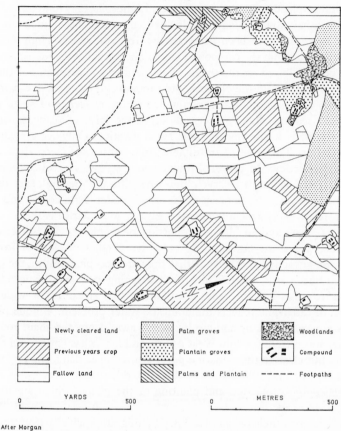

	Newly cleared land		Palm groves			Woodlands
	Previous years crop		Plantain groves			Compound
	Fallow land		Palms and Plantain			Footpaths

YARDS
0   500

METRES
0   500

After Morgan

Figure 7.8

rule, and there are difficulties in correlating the degree of dispersal with population density.

There is little ground over 1500 feet (460 metres) above sea-level in Iboland. In the north are two cuestas aligned from north to south with eastward facing escarpments. The high ground with its light soils, developed on soft Cretaceous sediments, is densely occupied. The Anambra lowlands in between, and the lowlands of the Niger valley to the west, and of the Cross river basin to the east, are less densely peopled. Here and there, particularly in the Anambra lowlands, are stretches of flood-plain wide enough to be worth cultivation, and yams are planted in tall mounds providing adequate drainage. To the south there is a plain of deep porous Tertiary sediments, deeply dissected by numerous streams draining southwards, and again densely populated. The acid sandy soils have been described as infertile, but soil fertility is a subjective concept. Thus the uplands of Elugu are called 'ana ocha', that is 'white' or 'barren' land, but the barrenness must owe much to an overcrowding which once encouraged the sale of some members of the upland communities as slaves. Light soils, easy to work with hoes, ideal for root crop cultivation, and supplied with an abundance of moisture for all or most of the year, have been preferred by Ibo cultivators. High yields are achieved, particularly on the compound lands. Shorter fallows and declining fertility have been followed by the threat of accelerated soil erosion, but the most severe cases of erosion, in the Nanka–Agulu region and on the Udi escarpment, appear rather to be the natural consequence of the existence of steep slopes, extremely soft sediments and a precipitation in the form of heavy downpours. Everywhere there is fertile land suitable for cultivation. Only overcrowding has reduced its value. The areas of unsuitable land, because of steep slopes, or of infertile sands, are few. In Owerri Province only 3·5 per cent of the total area has been classified as 'forest reserve', 'non-agricultural', 'grazing', and 'uncultivated bush and waste'. 35·5 per cent of the area is under 'farm crops', and 61 per cent under 'fallow'.[13] Probably nowhere else in West Africa is there so low a proportion of waste and so high a proportion of cropland. Here there are no interruptions by granitic outcrops, no extensive patches of clays or ironstone concretion. So attractive are the soils that they are occupied despite the general absence of surface water, the difficulty of constructing wells and the need to walk as much as 10 miles (16 km) from a settlement to a stream. The widespread distribution of catch-pits reflects the domestic water problem. Unique physical conditions are paralleled by unique location – away from the main routes by which maize was introduced into West Africa, and maize has never been of great importance, but close to the estuarine ports of the Niger delta, the region once termed the 'Oil Rivers'. The trade in palm oil and kernels is over 150 years old, and stimulated the protection and planting of the palms, which are today so distinctive a landscape feature.[14]

The Ibo occupied their present territory by migration, chiefly from the lands which today form their most densely populated nucleus. Whereas peoples like the Yoruba migrated, because of external pressure, or in response to the organized conquest of new lands, the Ibo appear to have migrated only due to internal pressure from overcrowding. The small communities were never organized to undertake conquest for its own sake. They sent some of their number outwards only as circumstances demanded, and in some cases sold them as slaves to their neighbours. Thus maximum densities were supported before migration began. The attractive environment of the homeland, and the lack of any but local contacts, produced an immense crowding of people. Thus began the migrations into

Owerri (Oratta-Ikwerri), and eventually across the Imo River into Aba (Ngwa), and from there across the Aba River to the Aza, where the movement was stopped by the British conquest. To the west migrants settled on the borders of Benin (N. and S. Ika). To the north-east they invaded the Cross River lowlands, and established a frontier on the Okpauku River. In the north-east the Ibo reproduced the grassland pattern of fortified settlements, in which compounds were loosely grouped together. To the south they reproduced the forest pattern of dispersal. Only the British peace brought dispersal also to the north-east, with the abandonment of the fortifications in order to settle on the croplands. The desire to live on or near one's own cropland, away from the authority of others, despite the necessity for combination with others for clearance and burning, appears to have overridden all other considerations, and to have been in different contexts a dominant factor in the evolution of the Ibo landscape.

The Tiv lands

To the pioneer work of Abraham, but above all to the more recent work of the Bohannans we owe much of our information on Tiv land and people.[15] The Tiv occupy approximately 10,000 square miles (25,900 sq km), consisting mainly of plains slightly dissected by streams flowing north and south to the Benue River, with the exception of the deep dissection of the great southern tributary of the Benue, the Katsina Ala, which almost bisects Tivland. The greater part of Tiv territory lies to the south of the Benue, and extends as far south as the western foothills of the Cameroons plateaux and the Sonkwala Hills. In the south the effectively occupied area reaches an altitude of over 1300 feet (400 metres) above sea-level, and includes several hills with peaks at over 4000 feet (1220 metres). To the north the Benue trough marks the lowest area at approximately 350 feet (107 metres). With light soils developed on the sedimentary rocks of the Benue trough and a rainfall of 40 to 50 in (1016–1270 mm) in a season between 7 and 9 months in length, physical conditions are suitable for growing a great variety of crops, including particularly roots like yams and cassava, and grains such as guinea corn, pennisetum and maize. Large-scale dry season burning and a tradition for migration into neighbouring emptier lands have resulted in the wholesale clearance of woodlands. The only survivors are fire-resistant species such as *Daniellia* and *Lophira*, and in much of the area grasses between 8 and 10 feet (2·4–3·0 metres) in height when mature are dominant. Dense woodland is developed only along stream banks, on steep slopes and hills, especially on the southern fringes, and in the 'marches' fringing the Tiv lands.

Although one writes of Tiv 'lands', in practice these are not easy to define for there are no strict limits. The concept of the frontier is unknown. There are no fixed boundaries between social groups except for those marked by aliens. There can in effect be no boundary, since traditionally the Tiv must always be moving. [16] The important feature to the Tiv is the location or relative position of the lineages, not their geographical position. Thus there is constant adjustment in

The Tiv Lands

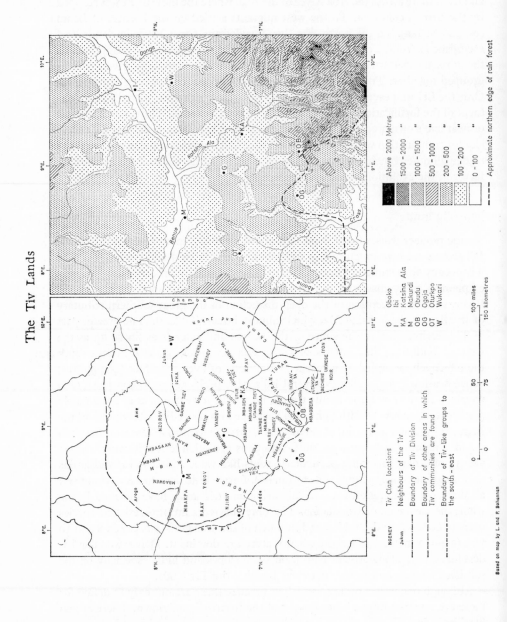

NGBENEV   Tiv Clan locations

Jukun   Neighbours of the Tiv

— — —   Boundary of Tiv Division

- - - -   Boundary of other areas in which
Tiv communities are found

—·—·—   Boundary of Tiv-like groups to
the south - east

G   Gboko
I   Ibi
KA   Katsina Ala
M   Makurdi
OB   Obudu
OG   Ogoja
OT   Oturkpo
W   Wukari

Above 2000 Metres
1500 – 2000   "
1000 – 1500   "
500 – 1000   "
200 – 500   "
100 – 200   "
0 – 100   "

— — —   Approximate northern edge of rain forest

0   50   100 miles
0   75   150 kilometres

Based on map by L. and P. Bohannan

position, but there should be no change in location. In northern Tivland or
Iharev very little adjustment of position is necessary since population densities
are low – about 25 per square mile (10 per sq km) – but in southern Tivland or
Kparev, with densities as high as 550 per square mile (213 per sq km), there is a
constant need to adjust position, or for the founders of new homesteads to emigrate. Although, as Buchanan and Pugh claim, the distribution of population in
Tivland is 'patchy',[17] there is an over-all general pattern of high density in the
southern homeland and low density on the more recently occupied perimeter.
One may agree with Buchanan and Pugh and with Briggs[18] that this pattern is,
at least in part, an example of 'arrested occupance' due to controls imposed by
the European administration and to a 'pile up' of population in southern districts, pushing later migrants to the north-west. This feature of a densely populated 'homeland' nucleus is well known elsewhere amongst the Yoruba, Ibo and
Hausa. Again one sees a reluctance to move far from the original home despite
a migratory tradition and despite increasing land-shortage. The placing of
administrative boundaries round the Tiv, and the building in the south of the
'Munshi' or Tiv wall, later a forest reserve, have done much to prevent further
Tiv encroachments on the lands of their neighbours. Similarly one may note the
attempts to found new settlements in the Nigerian 'Middle Belt' across the probable line of future Tiv advance. Within the division, however, the security provided by colonial administration has made for greater ease of movement and
there appears to have been some increase in the pace of migration. The over-all
density of Tiv Division was 73 per square mile (28 per sq km) in 1952, only a
fraction above the 70 per square mile (27 per sq km) minimum considered
desirable to maintain bush clearance in order to prevent tsetse fly infestation.[19]
Whilst the traditional solution of Tiv overcrowding has been a low density
advance on the perimeter, the future may be a period of density adjustment within the division.

The Tiv traditions claim that they came from the uplands to the south-east,
where they were either driven out by the Chamba, or large numbers left due to
internal strife. In the uplands there appears to have been a tradition for living in
nucleated settlements – hill forts surrounded by earthworks – some remains of
which still exist in southern and south-eastern Tivland. At some period during
the early 19th century they migrated northwards, adopting a dispersed pattern
of settlement. By 1852 they had reached the south bank of the Benue, and by
1879 they were reported on both banks. The British arrived in 1906 and administered Tivland as a part of Southern Nigeria until 1914 when it was transferred to the Northern Region.

The Tiv accept the notion that every man has the right to sufficient land for
his wives to cultivate. This right is held within the 'minimal tar' or smallest
land-holding unit whose members are descendants of a single ancestor. The whole
Tiv area is one 'tar', subdivided into the 'tars' of the larger family units, and
subdivided again into smaller 'tars' of the smaller family units.[20] Within each
'tar' the men must have sufficient land, and, if land is short, then more must be

M

obtained at the expense of the bounding land holders who are genealogically most distant. The loss of this latter group must be repaired in a similar manner with, as a result, a constant adjustment of land holdings outwards from a given overcrowded centre. This process described by Bohannan as 'steamroller migration' is the most common form of movement, although there are two other forms which have become more common since the establishment of colonial administration. These are the founding of new settlements well beyond the areas held by the bounding groups by 'leapfrog migration', and the movement of small family units or individuals to new areas as 'guests' in 'lonewolf migration'. These forms of movement may be of increasing importance in any attempt to solve problems of overcrowding in southern Tivland, without a readjustment of the entire land-holding pattern or settlement at the expense of neighbouring communities (p. 59).

Land is held by the group and shared amongst the members. There is even some shared labour. Yet essentially the greater part of the work of cultivation is performed by the individual. Each wife has her own strip within the field unit or units held by her husband. There are common features in the pattern of cultivation, and overcrowding within the group may affect the individual by a reduction in field size, reduction in the length of rotation period, reduction of fallow or even a change in cropping pattern. Yet each individual must judge the timing of operations and choose the crops. In Kparev each field is marked with a centre line or 'dechi'. Ideally 39 rows are marked off on each side of this with 58 yam mounds in each row, at one pace apart, between 18 and 30 in (46–76 cm) in height. The mounds are mostly made by the younger men. Grass and leaves are placed on the top of the mound to prevent erosion. Normally the whole family, making the compound unit, join together in November in pulling grass to clear their fields. In November the rains have finished in the north-west, but a few showers still occur in the south (Makurdi 0·5 in (13 mm), Ogoja 2·2 in (56 mm)). Damp ground is easier to clear and hoe, for many of the soils tend to harden very rapidly in dry weather. Despite this, grass pulling is generally later in the north and not earlier, as might have been expected. This is due mainly to the greater importance of grain crops in the north, especially guinea corn harvested normally in November and December when grass pulling would otherwise begin. Mounds are dug throughout the dry season and in some districts the work continues until May.

The Tiv staples are yams, main crop harvested in December and January, guinea corn, harvested mainly in November and December, and pennisetum, harvested in May and June. Yams are the most valued of these three, and normally occupy first place in the rotation. In many areas, however, shortage of wood has created problems in providing a trellis for the vines, and the practice has developed of planting a piece of cassava stalk in each mound several weeks before yam planting to serve the purpose. Seed yams are taken from stores in the compound, or from trenches or old mounds, and planted in the period February to May. Maize is also planted with the first rains (Makurdi 1·3 in (33 mm) in March, Ogoja 0·8 in (20 mm) in February), since quick-growing varieties are available to provide the earliest fresh food. After the harvest of the root crops, the mounds are levelled, and, with the first big rains in February or March, pennisetum is planted broadcast. The soil is turned over after sowing, and a month to six weeks later guinea corn is commonly interplanted. Some cassava may still be in the field from the previous season. The millet ripens quickly – some varieties are ready in 2 months, that is by early June – and is harvested by pushing down with a long pole and subsequent cutting. In some districts wood is so short that the stalks are used for fuel. In others the stalks are used as the base of ridges intended for the planting of guinea corn.[21] In some areas the yam heaps are not levelled for the interplanting of pennisetum and guinea corn, and there is an additional 'underplanting' of cowpeas.[22] Again, especially in the south, there is a considerable planting of benniseed in the second year, usually in a separate portion of a field or in a separate field. Fallowing normally follows the second year of cultivation in the overcrowded south, but in the north a third year of cropping frequently occurs, when benniseed is the crop most commonly planted. Benniseed is the commercial crop. Its planting has been encouraged by Government officers and it is generally recognized as the crop which pays the tax. More benniseed is grown in the south since population densities, i.e. the densities of tax payers, are higher. Other crops include cotton, indigo, tobacco, groundnuts, Bambara nuts, sweet potatoes, okra, peppers, gourds, roselle and black benniseed or 'ada' (*Polygala butyracea*, grown for fibre). Several of these minor crops are planted together with maize in compound land, often in association with useful trees. Tobacco is normally planted separately in small fenced plots. Some use is made of flood- or swamp-land, especially in the south, for the cultivation of maize and rice. In some cases ditches are dug for drainage or irrigation. Most flood-land and swamp cultivation in Tivland, however, is done by immigrant southerners. The main cropland is left to fallow normally after the second or third year of cultivation. Its readiness for re-cultivation is judged by the type of grass. At first 'ihila' (*Imperata cylindrica*) normally appears, but after two or three years this is gradually replaced by 'agom' or 'aper', grasses which are reckoned to indicate the restoration of soil fertility.[23]

The Tiv clearance of land has in many areas been remarkably effective, and even stumping has been undertaken in the more crowded areas in order to obtain the maximum possible use of land. In the overcrowded south almost the only trees remaining are those offering the greatest economic advantages, such as the oil palm. The result in such localities is the creation of a landscape mainly of grassland and crops, interspersed with apparently scattered groupings of rondavels, together with rectangular 'reception' huts, each grouping being oval or circular in shape and providing a compound. Many of these have hedges, fences or fruit trees, chiefly figs, mangoes and oil palms, arranged occasionally in a line or a ring close to compound land, containing a great mixture of crops, or standing singly within or close to the compound to provide shade. Each compound provides a social 'hub' so that paths link compound with compound and not village with village.[24] Yet there are the social groupings, and one compound may be closely linked with others socially if not physically. Large social groups possess markets which function once every traditional week of five days. Thus markets function despite the lack of Tiv nucleation and despite a migratory tradition, and in effect the few nucleated settlements are occupied mainly by strangers. From the sale of benniseed, cotton and, more recently, soya beans, the Tiv realize enough money to buy cloth, imported metal goods and enamelware. The markets are arranged in groups within which small markets adjacent to one another operate on different days, and there is at least one large market where Tiv, Hausa or Ibo exporters purchase not only the commercial crops listed, but also food crops. Despite the overcrowding of southern Tivland there is an export of food particularly of the more highly priced foodstuffs.

The lands of the Kabrai

In northern Togo are several granitic massifs rising over 2000 feet (610 metres) above sea-level and overlooking the plains of the Kara and Koumongou tributaries of the Oti. The two largest are Charé, 2555 feet (779 metres), and Farendé, 2227 feet (679 metres), separated by the Sossoa plain. These and the neighbouring smaller massifs are occupied by the Kabrai, who have removed the original vegetation, and developed a system of permanent cultivation, supplemented by crops from shifting fields in the plains. The Kabrai are mountain refugees, whose dispersed compounds are perched above steep slopes, offering a natural protection from attack. Pressure on local soil resources is great, and many devices are employed to obtain the maximum possible return from the area available. A rainfall of 50 to 60 in (1270–1520 mm), spread over 8 months, makes possible the cultivation of root crops, but the Kabrai are a northern people whose staples are guinea corn and groundnuts. Yams and cassava have been introduced only in recent years from the south, and are confined to the poorer soils of the plains with an irregular rainfall of between 40 and 50 in (1015–1270 mm). There, cultivation has developed due to the cessation of local warfare with the imposition of European rule, and, moreover, depends on the clearance of old fallows.

Permanent cultivation is not accompanied by nucleated settlement, but by the dispersal normally associated with moving peoples like the Konkomba. Here permanent cultivation is a response not to social and economic organization, but to the restrictions of an environment chosen because of its military value. Yet the environment is not unattractive to the cultivator, for between the granite outcrops the soils are deep and highly productive, even with only small applications of manure. The problem is the number of people. 110,000 Kabrai occupy 463 square miles (1200 sq km), much of which consists of outcrops of rock, and within which local densities are as high as 500 per square mile (192 per sq km). In the surrounding plains densities are less than 50 per square mile (19 per sq km). Despite the recent development of shifting cultivation in the plains and even of the emigration of 11,000 Kabrai to the eastern Mono plains, clearly the people are loath to leave the homeland in which they have expended so much labour to extract a living from the soil.

Even the steepest slopes are cultivated. Stone retaining walls have been constructed to hold up the soils or to protect them from stream erosion. Enjalbert remarks of these walls that they do not necessarily extend along the contour, and do not provide true terraces.[25] As in the Jos Plateau of Nigeria, they are fragmentary lines of stones, which effect partial terracing here and there, and modify slopes only slightly. Their construction has taken place as much in order to clear

Kabrai Lands

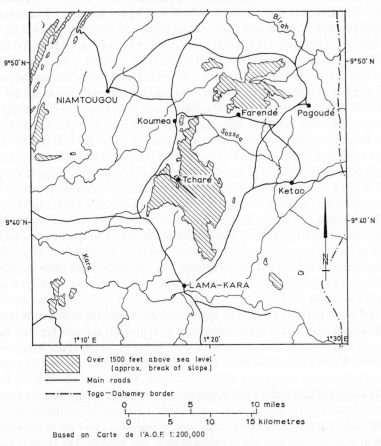

Figure 7.10

stones from the land, and demarcate fields, as to provide protective walling. Elsewhere the minute fields abut onto rock outcrops. Manures are applied to part of the land, and on the remaining fields weeds are dug in as a form of green manure. Goats, sheep and pigs are kept almost entirely for their manure supplies. Elaborate ridges and mounds, even box ridges, are constructed for planting. Little land is left to fallow and rarely for more than two years.

The compounds stand amidst the fields, although not all fields surrounding a compound belong to the family occupying that compound. Generally, however, the land surrounding the dwellings is divided into smaller fields, and fertilized with animal manures and household refuse. This compound land, with its rich moisture-retaining soils, can be planted to two crops a year – mostly bulrush millet and maize, interplanted in April and harvested in June and July, followed by late bulrush millet, sown in August and harvested in November and December. Other crops include cocoyam, tobacco, beans, earth lentils, earth peas and okra. Farther away from the compounds are the main croplands, planted to guinea corn and groundnuts, and fertilized with 'green manure'. The two crops are interplanted in April and May. Groundnuts are harvested from August to October, providing the chief commercial crop, and guinea corn from December to February. Guinea corn is less liable to lodge on main crop than on manured land. The lighter soils are also more suitable for groundnuts. Within the plateau are a number of alluvial basins, where the soils are generally too moist for good returns and need drainage. Here the Kabrai dig ditches and ridges, alternating their locations each year, and burying groundnut refuse as a manure and millet stalks in order to improve drainage. Groundnuts are the chief crop, with a little guinea corn and bulrush millet. The soils of the peripheral depressions of the massifs offer possibilities if drained, and here also ditching and ridging are practised. The French administration sought to effect improvements in productivity by introducing fish ponds and swamp rice fields into these lands. In the plains are the pastures for cattle and the long fallow lands, where the 'new' crops – yams, cassava and upland rice – are planted together with earth peas, and followed by guinea corn and groundnuts. Early yams are planted from December to February in mounds, and harvested from July onwards. Late yams are planted from February to May and harvested by December. Cassava is planted in the sides of the mounds in April and May, and harvested as desired after maturing. Rice and earth peas are planted in March and April, and harvested in November and December. In some fields cultivation is continued for another one or two years, by planting guinea corn and groundnuts, before allowing the land to revert to fallow. A few cattle are owned by the Kabrai, but these are mostly pastured in the plains under the care of Fulani herdsmen. Cattle are valued more for the prestige they confer, and for use in sacrifices and special feasts, than for their use as food. Again the French administration hoped to improve conditions by introducing stables and organizing the collection of manure. Trees are of some economic importance, especially the oil palm, kapok and baobab, but there is no tree cultivation – only protection.

The Kabrai lands provide an example of an environment in which conservation methods have been carried to great lengths in order to support a great density of population in a region of small resources. Possibly such methods may have a more general application in West Africa. Yet, as Dresch remarks, as soon as the Kabrai descend to the plains, where land is abundant, they abandon the methods of the hills and revert to the long fallows or shifting systems already employed there.[26] Possibly this represents a return to earlier practices, before the Kabrai were forced to take to the hills. However, one must beware of facile assumptions. The plains are, in part, only temporarily occupied, or where occupation is permanent, they carry lower densities of population. The use of manures and household refuse in the hills is as much a product of abundant supplies due to high densities, as it is of pressure on resources due to the same cause. Without the hill-top densities and permanent settlement, fallows become a practical necessity on the poorer, thin soils overlying the ironstone concretions of the plains. Moreover the more extensive methods of the plains mean lower costs of production in terms of labour. With abundant land more importance is inevitably attached to production per 'man-day' than to productivity per acre.

The lands of the Konkomba

To the masterly studies of the Konkomba by Froelich and Tait[27], the authors owe the basis of this account. Like the Tiv, the Konkomba are a migratory people, about 80,000 in number, in a sub-Guinean environment, whose movements in search of new land have been hindered but as yet little changed in character by the establishment of colonial rule. Unlike the Tiv, however, there appears no evidence of over-crowding on Konkomba lands. Admittedly soils may be poorer, and comparison of apparently similar environments may be deceptive. Yet, with highest densities of only 50 per square mile (19 per sq km) (within the lowest density group for agricultural peoples), and with the greater part of the occupied area with densities of less than 25 (10), population pressure would seem unlikely. Indeed the yam is still the staple crop, and a surplus is produced for sale to the Chokossi, a neighbouring community in the north. Cassava, a frequent indicator of poor soils, is little cultivated. Hungry millet, another 'poor soil' crop, is cultivated, but is not a staple and does not appear in all rotations.

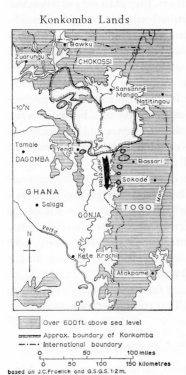

Konkomba Lands

Over 600 ft. above sea level
Approx. boundary of Konkomba
International boundary

0   50   100 miles
0   50   100   150 kilometres
based on J.C.Froelich and G.S.G.S. 1·2 m.

Figure 7.11

The Konkomba occupy the gently rolling hills eroded from shales and mudstones in the Oti basin of Ghana and Togo. Gradients are mostly slight, but in a few places there are small cliffs of concretionary ironstone. The alluvial sands and muds of the valley bottom are generally avoided, partly because of the danger of flooding, and partly to avoid waterside concentrations of tsetse fly. Flooding is so extensive that for above three months some hamlets are accessible only by boat. During the last century many Konkomba crossed the Oti, and moved east-wards onto the ferruginous shale uplands of the Buem formation, whose soils are claimed by Froelich to be less fertile.[28] Recent migration has been directed southwards towards the lands of the Bassari, to Gonja and to Kete Krachi where the Konkomba are now very numerous. The Konkomba have migrated partly in search of new land, and partly because of political pressure. They were driven out of their homeland, Dagomba, in the north-west, in the 16th century. From the 16th to the 19th century, they were attacked by the Ashanti and many were enslaved. Constant warfare resulted in a readiness amongst the Konkomba to take up arms against any invaders, or even against one another. The Germans only reduced them by punitive expeditions in which large numbers were killed. Many were sent to plantations in the Cameroons, or recruited as forced labour for work on the road between Atakpamé and Sokodé.

The Konkomba lands have known if vague limits, yet, as Froelich remarks, the lands 'have neither historic reality nor fixed frontiers, they exist only as a function of the Konkomba who dwell in them, and are limited only by the rights of neigh-bouring peoples'. The Konkomba have no common government, although they may join together in some political issue. Each head of family is a local authority, and a 'chief of the land' exercises authority in land apportionment between families. The population is dispersed in loose groupings ('litingbal') of com-pounds ('ledetchal'), situated on hill-tops close by the croplands and away from roads. Here there is no desire to participate in new developments, but a deliberate turning away to preserve tradition and keep the old subsistence and local exchange economy. The only nucleated villages in the Konkomba lands are inhabited by Hausa and Mossi 'strangers'. Within a 'litingbal' the 'ledetchal' are 100–200 yards (90–180 metres) apart. Each 'ledetchal' consists of rondavels, providing separate rooms for the family, and linked by a wall. When a son marries and acquires a family, he may erect his own 'ledetchal' some distance away. The site of the 'litingbal' is not fixed, and may be moved for a few miles at a time, or even greater distances, when emigration to new lands is attempted. Several markets, with more or less fixed sites, exist, each of which functions every 6 days, and attracts people from an area of about 12 miles (20 km) radius.

The fields are normally cropped for 4 years, and then abandoned to a fallow of at least 4 years, before cropping begins again. Two common rotations are:

   i) 1. yams, 2. guinea corn, 3. guinea corn, 4. hungry rice.
  ii) 1. yams, 2. bulrush millet and cotton, 3. guinea corn, 4. groundnuts.

Interplanted crops include maize, okra, cowpeas, earth peas, yam beans, hari-cot beans, tobacco, castor and calabashes. Yams and guinea corn occupy by far the greater part of the cropped area. Clearance and burning normally take place in November and December. Mounds are made with short-handled hoes, and the yam buts planted in January for harvest, according to variety, from August to March of the following year, although some early yams may be dug in July.

Guinea corn is planted in the remains of previous yam mounds in April for harvest in November and December, whilst bulrush millet, groundnuts, fonio, pigeon peas and beans are planted from May until July. A little rice is planted in the flood-plain of the Oti. The rains last from the middle of May until November, and by the use of numerous varieties of each crop, and by varying dates of planting, the labour of cultivation and harvest is well spread throughout the year. There is no period of serious food shortage, and gathering is chiefly for fruits, particularly of the shea tree to provide vegetable fat, for the poisonous *Strophanthus*, and for dye plants, chiefly *Indigofera tinctoria*. There is little meat in the diet, for few livestock are kept, and hunting is undertaken only in the dry season. There is an average of less than one cow per head of population, although a few men own small herds. In addition, there are sheep, goats, pigs and fowls. Cattle are tethered in the rains, but herded on a common pasture near water during the dry season. Fulani herdsmen are sometimes hired to tend the few larger herds. The small number of livestock mean, however, that killing is restricted to ceremonial occasions. Dogs are bred as hunting animals. Fishing is of great importance in the provision of protein foods. In the dry season, when the Oti and its tributaries are reduced to a few pools, the fish are concentrated and comparatively easy to catch. Groups of fishermen begin to work on agreed dates, and the river banks are divided up into virtual 'properties', the fishing rights of which belong to individual families. The task of fishing from any one bank may, however, be shared by several families, who will share their own rights in turn. Mobile net barrages are formed above and below a given site, and the two lines of nets are advanced towards one another enclosing the fish. Fence and cone traps and poison are also used. Fishing not only provides a local foodstuff, but a useful medium of exchange, for the surplus is smoked and sold in markets elsewhere. Another commercial product formerly was charcoal made by the Konkomba women. The charcoal used to find a market in Banjeli to the east, on the Buem ironstones, where it was exchanged for iron worked into hoes, axes, knives, hammers, arrowheads and other metal goods by Konkomba smiths. Tait suggests the possibility that smiths were formerly more common amongst the Konkomba, as there are the remains of old foundries and smelting sites in their former homeland.[29]

The Konkomba are one of the few communities still closely linked with the past. As frontiers become more controlled, as the road network is developed, and as land acquires a commercial value, so the pace of their migration must be slowed and finally halted, and their economy linked to the outside markets. Eventually the search by the communities for new land must be replaced by the movement of young men to the towns, and Konkomba loyalties give way to a broader national allegiance.

The lands of the Baga

The lands of the Baga are estuarine, part tidal mangrove swamp and part ridges of sand on the south-western coastlands, stretching from the left bank of the Rio

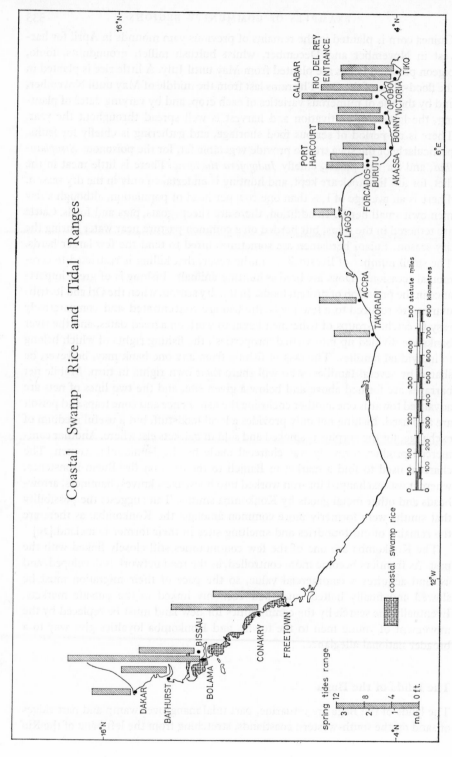

Figure 7.12

Nunez to Conakry. Here are the drowned estuaries of the 'Rivières du Sud', the 'Basse Côte' of the Republic of Guinea, with its distinction of high tides – at Conakry ranges of $12\frac{1}{2}$ feet (3·8 metres) at spring and $10\frac{1}{4}$ feet (3·1 metres) at neap tides. Northwards from Conakry the tidal range is even greater, reaching 19 feet (5·8 metres) at the spring tides of Bolama Island in Portuguese Guinea. This physical distinction has been used by man to produce a unique landscape of polders, enclosed by dikes, and subdivided into swamp rice fields. Amongst the rice growers of the region, the Baga are themselves unique, for in addition to swamp rice they are also cultivators of floating rice of West African origin, brought by them from the Mopti district of the inland Niger delta.

It is the tidal range which has hitherto defined the area available for estuarine swamp rice cultivation. There are two important effects. The first is that a high tidal range reduces the amount of free sulphuric acid occurring in mangrove swamp soils, whereas with a low range the accumulation can become sufficient to be toxic. Secondly, the invasion of the rice fields by salt water, during high tides in the 'rest' season, reduces the weeds.[30] Simple dikes are normally sufficient to keep out salt water during the growing period, whilst the first rains normally supply sufficient fresh water to reduce, at least temporarily, the salt content of the soils. Spring tide ranges of 10 feet (3 metres) or more appear to be desirable, and limit coastal swamp cultivation to the area. The southern limit appears to be Freetown ($10\frac{1}{4}$ feet (3·1 metres)) and the northern limit Bissau (8 feet (2·4 metres)). Nowhere else on the coast are comparable tidal ranges found, except in the extreme south-east (Calabar, 10 feet (3 metres)) where, other conditions being satisfactory, coastal swamp rice cultivation might profitably be introduced.

The Baga live in houses mostly made of dried mud and rectangular in shape, arranged in two rows, each facing the other, in their several villages. In part the distributions of local relief and soils are important, for sand bars or ridges or the line of firm ground between the rice fields of the swamps and the palm groves provide important locations. There are about 40,000 Baga altogether, a community produced by the joining together of a number of different groups, a community, moreover, which has lost many of its members to other tribes. As Denise Paulme remarks, Baga unity is geographic and not ethnic.[31] People of diverse origins, seeking refuge in these coastal swamps from the slave raiders of the north-east, have joined together in a common system of cultivation, and today, for the most part, speak a common language. The Baga were mentioned by the Portuguese as early as the 16th century, yet they have a tradition of immigration from the Fouta Djallon at a later period. Portères suggests that one group of Baga came from Mopti, and moved up the Niger and Tinkisso to the northern flank of the Fouta Djallon in the 16th and 17th centuries.[32] From there, due to Fulani attacks, they moved to the western flank, and thence down to the coast between 1720 and 1775. It seems likely that the migrants brought with them the floating variety of *Oryza glaberrima*, known as 'Baga-Malé', which is grown above all by the group known as Baga Foré or 'Old' Baga. It seems likely also that the existing groups, mentioned by the Portuguese, already practised swamp

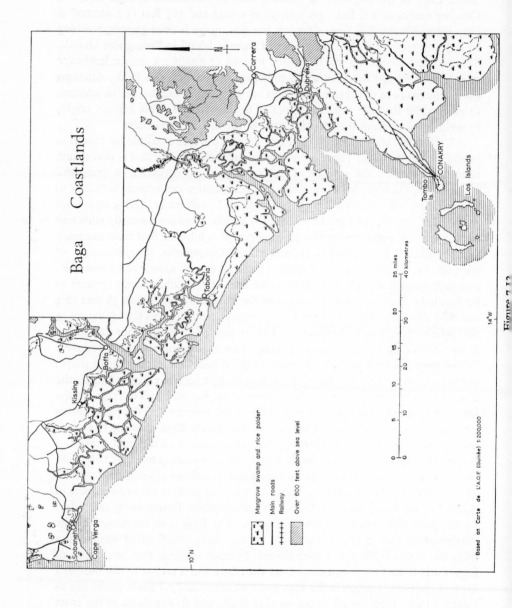

Baga Coastlands

Kissing
Boffa
Taboria
Correra
Dubréka
CONAKRY
Tombo Is.
Los Islands
Sobaneh
Cape Verga

10°N

Mangrove swamp and rice polder
Main roads
Railway
Over 600 feet above sea level

0   5   10   15   20   25 miles
0   10   20   30   40 kilometres

Based on Carte de L'A.O.F. (Guinée) 1:200,000

14°W

Figure 7.12

rice cultivation, and that the immigrants introduced floating rice as an additional crop. During the immigration period (15th to 18th centuries) the Portuguese introduced several analogous Asian varieties of swamp rice. Asian varieties were often preferred, because they shed their grain less readily, and are less brittle for milling. The Portuguese also introduced trade. For a time the Baga and several other peoples of the south-west coast gained a little importance and some wealth from the presence of numerous small trading posts on the estuaries. Here were the chief contacts between Europe and the Mali hinterland.

Swamp rice is normally transplanted from calabashes or basket 'pots' to nurseries near the compounds on the sand ridges in May and June. These nurseries are fertilized with ashes and household refuse. Quick-growing varieties are normally planted first, in order to obtain as early a harvest as possible. May and June are also the times for digging ridges in the rice fields, after the mangrove clearance and dike construction and repair of the previous two months. Ridge making does not, however, follow clearing on the same land, as in the case of upland rice and other crops dependent on rainfall rather than flooding. March and April are the last two months of the dry season, when the rivers and local water levels are at their lowest. At this time of the year the mangroves are easiest to cut, and the roots may be pulled up. Dike repairs, similarly, may be more easily effected. But the land cannot be put under cultivation immediately. It must wait for 2 or 3 years during which the salt water is kept out and fresh water supplied. Drainage canals are cut behind the dikes, to assist both water supply and removal. In May the rains arrive and river levels rise. The sluice gates, made of tree trunks and old canoes, built into the dikes and sealed with grass and mud, are closed as the tides rise, and opened as they fall. The rice fields extend at right angles to the linear village, so that each compound normally has easy individual access to the land, which is held on a family basis. The ridges are dug with the large iron-tipped spade, $7\frac{1}{2}$ feet (2·25 metres) in length, and normally manipulated by two men. With it they aerate, wash and turn the soil for over $1\frac{1}{2}$ feet (0·5 metre) in depth, and bury the weeds. Each year ridges and furrows alternate. The dikes enable a fixed depth of fresh water to be maintained on the land after planting, which continues with various varieties until October. In October the first harvest – of quick-growing varieties – takes place. The soil is then turned over, and a second planting made from nurseries for harvest in January and February. October marks the end of the rains and water levels drop. The sea water threatens to invade the rice fields at each high tide or by seepage. As the rice ripens in each field, so the sluice gates are opened and the grain cut. Harvesting continues until February, followed in some areas by the 'after crop' in March and April, and by rice still ripening in extremely low-lying and damp portions of the fields. Clearly locations at approximate tidal limits are preferred. Near the coast the sea-water invasion is earlier, and soils tend to be more heavily impregnated with salt. Beyond the tidal limits the mangrove swamps, which provide the soil accumulation for polder construction, do not occur. There is no rotation and no fallow. The soils are rested for 4 to 6 months each year, and to some extent renewed by flooding, the 'digging in' of weeds and the manure from transhumant Fulani cattle, pastured between January and May on the rice stubble, which is also rich in salt. The only dangers are destruction by crabs, salting by seepage or by penetration of the dikes, and silting of the estuaries. The last danger has, in many cases, resulted in the permanent submergence of many rice fields. Baga Malé floating rice produces only a small proportion of the total crop, but is extremely useful for planting in deeper water, and thus making a fuller use of available resources. Baga Malé cannot tolerate too rapid a rise or drop in water levels, possible even with the local dikes. Variations in the incidence of flooding and salt impregnation are all damaging. In consequence Baga Malé is a secondary crop, providing a supplementary food resource and is grown with less care, partly because only a limited time is available, and most of that must be given to swamp rice, and partly because only extensive methods pay where the risk of loss is great.[33] The seed is planted directly in the lowest portions of the fields at the beginning of the flood season, and given no further attention. In some cases the plant is harvested by canoe.

Additional resources are oil palm produce from the neighbouring groves, onions, various fruits, maize, cassava, sweet potatoes, yams, cocoyams and groundnuts grown on the highest floodlands, and planted as the water levels retreat. The upper floodlands receive less silt and debris from flooding, and in consequence are more easily exhausted. Hence their use for recently introduced secondary crops. An advantage is that these crops offer work at different times of the year – sowing in December and January and harvest April to September. Groundnuts are often planted on compound land, that is above flood levels, in June and July. Another important resource is fish. Fish are caught by the women, using traps and lines in the streams, channels and small creeks, which occur amidst the rice fields. Fish may damage floating rice growing in deeper water, but they provide an important element in the diet, and when dried are sold inland.

The Baga lands offer only limited commercial possibilities – rice, some dried onions, dried fish and a little vegetables and fruit are almost the sole saleable products. Yet they were once in a commercially favourable area, trading between Europe and the Upper Niger valley. Population densities are less than 20 per square mile (8 per sq km), in so far as they may be calculated, in a region where the land area fluctuates seasonally and annually. Yet much of the area is useless, because it is too salty or because it is occupied by less fertile sands. Large areas of only partially developed mangrove swamp exist, especially near the coast. Each family has an average of 5–8 acres (13–20 hectares) of cultivated land. Yet, despite the low density of population, there appears to be insufficient cultivation, for food reserves are frequently low, and many Baga have left due to loss of agricultural land following silting. Clearly at least 90 per cent of the area must be wasteland or uncultivated, yet many Baga seem anxious to leave and will sell their use-rights to land for small sums to Susu traders. Many of these seek land as a commercial venture in which to grow crops with hired labour. One Baga group has already been completely absorbed by the Susu, and only three remain. These are described by Denise Paulme as 'breaking up.'[34] The Public Works Department of the former French administration of Guinea sought to prevent the permanent loss of land, due to silting, by cutting drainage canals, and in 1954 the administration recommended the introduction of the Asian water buffalo. The buffalo, however, means a change of method, and it is more likely that the young Baga, who include most of those likely to be interested in new methods, will seek a new life altogether in Conakry. The lands of the Baga, giving 1100–1320 lb of swamp rice per acre (1250–1500 kilos per hectare), are not sufficiently productive for the tedious labour involved to remain attractive. Moreover, they have become a commercial back-water, and perhaps for that reason alone must suffer a constant drain of emigrants.

The lands of the Bambara[35]

The Bambara succeeded in creating an empire, which reached its greatest territorial extent in the 18th century, when it included most of the Upper Niger basin and the inland delta, and extended north to the margins of the Sahara, and south into sub-Sudanic regions to include Sikasso and Kong. Yet it has been impossible to delimit precisely the boundaries of the Bambara empire, 'for the frontier as we understand it has no meaning for the Negro. In effect empires have not sought to control this or that region; they have above all aimed at the exploitation of the greatest possible number of individuals, considered apart from their countries and race.'[36] The empire has been split between the states, which are the heirs of the French West African federation of colonies, but most of it is included in Mali where the Niger from Bamako to Ké-Macina forms as it were a central axis of the Bambara domain. To the west and the north are the Malinké and Soninké respectively, speaking related Manding dialects; to the east the Fulani of the former state of Macina, the Bozo fishermen and the Bobo; to the south-east the Senoufo.

Altogether there are about a million Bambara, approximately two-thirds of whom live in the central cercles of Bamako, Ségou and Bougouni where the densities of population are 23, 42, and 16 per square mile (9, 16 and 6 per sq km) respectively. Densities are highest in the Niger valley, especially on the fringes of the inland Niger delta, where floodland attracts both cultivator and pastoralist and where some of the greatest markets in West Africa have flourished. Despite their creation of a powerful empire, and despite the importance of trade and manufacture in their lands, the Bambara live mainly in villages averaging in size about 250 people and ranging in local (canton) averages from 120 to about 500. Traditionally the villages were sited to the north or east of a protecting tree, and consisted of compounds, mainly of rondavels with the occasional rectangular structure, and fortified, sometimes with as many as 3 earth walls, reaching a maximum height of about 15 feet (4·5 metres) and averaging about 6 feet (2 metres) in thickness at the base. There is only one town within the region with over 30,000 population, and that is Bamako, the capital of Mali, with 110,000 in 1961. Other towns lie within or fringe the Bambara lands but all with lower

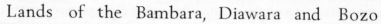

Lands of the Bambara, Diawara and Bozo

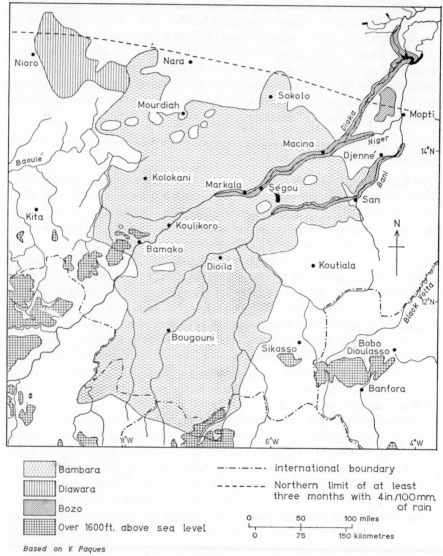

Figure 7.14

totals: Ségou 20,000, Mopti and Sikasso 14,000, and San 8,000. Formerly all settlements of any political importance had large periodic markets, or fairs of regional significance, plus small daily markets to serve local needs. French administration regulated the number of trading 'points', and controlled the types of goods sold. The control regulations were removed in 1946, when two co-operative organizations to guide production and trade were created, which have tended to take trade off private merchants. Except in the Sahel and in the desert fringe, the formerly extensive caravan traffic has been largely replaced by a trade which looks mainly to road and railway.

The Bambara are almost entirely an agricultural people, of very mixed origins, who live close to the lands of the pastoral Fulani. As elsewhere in the Sudanic zone there has developed an important relationship between pastoralist and culti-vator, which in turn has led from time to time to political union between the two groups. Fulani kingdoms were created in the 17th and 18th centuries by Baramongolo on the right bank at Sougou, and by Niangolo on the left bank at Sounsana near Mourdiah. The eventual union by conquest of the two Fulani kingdoms led to the formation of the Bambara empire which possessed a powerful army, a river fleet and even a corps of engineers. Slavery was the basis of Bam-bara military strength and of the central power, but the slave army was finally defeated by Toucouleur forces under El Hadj Omar in the middle of the 19th century.

The Bambara are in effect a union of past conquests, but a union of a number of peoples of various origins and occupying a variety of habitats. Three broad distinctions of habitat may be made: the Upper Niger valley, the inland delta and the Soninké Massif.

To the south are the valleys of the Upper Niger and Bani. Geologically the area consists mainly of schists with intrusions of quartzite, dolerite and granite. Occurrences of gold are widespread, and the panning of gold was formerly a major industry, together with pit mining. Ironstone crusts cap many of the inter-fluves, and generally support only thin soils and a savanna dominated through selection by shea trees, *Parkia*, *Erythrophleum*, *Afzelia* and *Andropogon* grasses. Cultivation exists, but is mostly confined to the slopes and the valley bottoms. There are vast virtually 'empty' spaces, occupied mainly by game and the tsetse fly. The rainy season lasts for 5 to 7 months, and cultivation does not depend entirely on floodland, although the latter provides an important supplement during the dry season. In the upper valley flooding is earlier than in the inland delta – generally August (at Bamako the peak is reached about September 22nd and levels begin to fall about October 15th). The flood period is also shorter and the fall in levels faster. In consequence floodland cultivation competes much more with rainland cultivation for labour time, and quicker-growing varieties of rice and other floodland crops are normally dominant. The lengthening of the growing period by flood control has been an important French contribution to the agricultural economy of the area. This is the chief area for the cultivation of guinea corn and *Pennisetum*. The chief rice varieties grown are of Asian origin. Maize and bananas are also grown especially on the floodland fringe or even on the floodland itself. Some cassava and yams are planted with *Digitaria* on the poorer soils, and groundnuts, beans, tomatoes, sweet potatoes, calabashes, gumbo, da and garden-egg as important secondary crops. The rainlands frequently supply less than half the crop return, although normally comprising well over half the acreage. Cropping lasts for 2 to 6 years or more before fallowing, and *Pennisetum*, groundnuts and other secondaries are the chief crops. Important plant indicators are 'ségué' (*Striga senegalensis*) showing soil exhaustion, and 'tiékala' (*Cymbopogon giganteus*) and 'wagha' (*Andropogon gayanus*) on richer soils.[37] On the floodlands rice, cotton and onions are grown whilst guinea corn, maize and tobacco are grown on manured compound land, tilled chiefly by the women.

In the inland Niger delta cultivation was governed traditionally by the flood, rising in the lowest portions in July to a November peak, and descending from mid-December to a minimum in June. The inland delta is the great rice producer of Mali, for over half the total rice crop comes from this small area, and still partly from the indigenous species *Oryza glaberrima*, and particularly from the floating varieties.[38] The delta is the location of an important symbiosis not only between pastoralist and cultivator, but between the Bambara and Songhay cultivators and Bozo and Somono fishermen.[39]

The Bambara occupy not only the riverain lands described, but the southeastern portions of the Soninké or Sarakolé Massif. This massif, mainly of schists, is for the most part covered by sand in its eastern half, where only low densities of population are supported, whilst in the north-east economies depend on pastoralism. Here the Bambara are living close to the limits of rainland cultivation, for the rainy season is effectively only 3 to $3\frac{1}{2}$ months, and they depend on quick-growing varieties of *Pennisetum* with some *Digitaria*. An important cultivation exists in valley bottoms, and in suitable soils in the valleys of former streams draining to the Niger. Wheat is an important crop, here planted in November for harvest in February. It is above all in this region that the Bambara own livestock obtained by exchanging grain with the Fulani, Tuareg or Moors. Even here, however, it is customary for the animals, especially cattle, to be in the charge of herders from the pastoral communities, especially the Fulani. The practice is, however, widespread throughout the Bambara lands. Another economic feature, of widespread importance, although of particular significance in the north, with its very short rainy season, is gathering. The fruits and leaves of the baobab, of *Parkia* trees and of numerous other plants are all gathered. The *Acacia albida*, with its dry season leaf, 'plays a major role in Bambara mythology'.[40]

By selecting from a variety of plants, especially from the grains, and by developing hand techniques suitable to the various habitats, the Bambara have succeeded in wresting a living from a hard environment, particularly in the Soninké Massif and on the fringes of the ironstone crusts of the Upper Niger valley. The French peace, by removing their enemies and the heavy exactions previously needed to maintain a powerful military organization, should have improved the Bambara cultivators' lot. In a sense it has done so, and yet has weakened the position of the Bambara, for at the time of the French invasion much of the economy depended on the labour of slaves, who were also recruited for the armies deployed by each village group. Gold mining, once an important resource, has declined, as have local industries, particularly those of the smelter and the blacksmith. The invasion of neighbouring lands, in search of loot and slaves, has been replaced by migration to the towns, to Guinea, Senegal, the Ivory Coast and Ghana chiefly as agricultural labourers. The number of migrants in officially registered movements alone from Bamako, Ségou and Bougouni averaged about 8000 a year between 1947 and 1950. The Bambara have already made a major contribution to the development of the groundnut producing region of Senegal, and of the coffee and cocoa growing region of the Ivory Coast.

The Diawara lands[41]

On the northern fringe of the Soninké Massif, on the very edge of the pastoral Sahel, the Diawara live in small villages of only a few hundred population each, and raise crops in a rainy season of only $2\frac{1}{2}$ to 3 months. The sand-covered schist plateau is crossed by wadis, reduced to dry sandy furrows with pools and marsh in the dry season, and contains a number of creeks and channels marking the courses of former tributaries of the Niger. Ores of iron, copper and chrome occur, of which the first have been particularly important. Their working has led to the removal of much of the local woodland. The industry died, not only because of overseas competition after the introduction of French rule, but because of short-age of charcoal. The rains begin in July and end in September, totalling 21 in (533 mm). Most of the rain occurs in heavy downpours, and much of the small moisture supply is lost to run-off, in addition to evaporation loss. Almost half the total rainfall occurs in one month – August. The interfluves are dominated by *Acacia* and *Bauhinia* savanna, including species which produce leaf during the dry season. In and about the villages and on abandoned settlement sites are *Ficus* spp., *Khaya senegalensis* and *Hyphaene*, the dum palm.

At the 1951 census the Diawara population was returned at a total of 43,000, but later estimates suggest that their numbers may be over 80,000. No count of any reliability has been made. The population density is low, and has been estimated for Nioro Division at only 12 per square mile (5 per sq km). It reflects the existence of large areas which are used either as open range or only for gathering or hunting. In the map, 'Distribution of communities' (Fig. 1.4), they have been grouped by language, location and type of economy with the Sarakolé or Soninké. By origins they should probably be grouped with the Malinké.[42] As with the Bambara, the village is the basic political unit, and villages were formerly organized in groups under a local authority, and each group provided soldiers – mainly slaves – to form an army. Classes were virtually castes, with at the head the noble and warrior caste, including the ruling royal families. Under these came the 'marabouts' or priests, the professional caste of doctors, poets, musicians and historians, the smiths and leather-workers and finally the slaves. Slavery is no longer permitted as an institution, and the former slave markets have disappeared, but a form of serfdom or limited bondage still remains.

Although smelting has now disappeared, as elsewhere in West Africa, forging
still survives and produces a variety of agricultural implements, cutting tools
and weapons. Spinning, weaving and dyeing using local vegetable materials still
flourish, local pottery and leather industries still have some importance, together
with wood carving, the preparation of calabashes and of leather goods and the
manufacture of ropes. The Diawara are less well served by modern transport
than many other Sudanic and Sahelian peoples, and, in consequence, the competition of imported commodities is less effective. Local industries have correspondingly greater importance.

The Diawara village consists of a collection of walled compounds containing
mainly rondavels and date palms, and divided from one another by narrow and
tortuous alley-ways. Enclosures are created for animals, which have a greater importance for cultivators on the fringe of the Sahel and living in widely separated
villages than for cultivators in areas with longer rainy seasons. Some of the huts
are used as stables. Others, raised on stones, are used as granaries, differing in
type between those for current use and those for reserve. Crop storage with a
long dry season is of vital importance, and great care is taken to prevent weevil
infestation and to guard against the attacks of rodents. Each compound also has
its verandah, its chicken house and its space for cooking and the preparation of
flour. During the last half century, with the French peace, there has been a tendency to create a number of new villages, and this has been especially marked
during the last 15 years in the marginal lands to the north. Here new settlements
have encroached on Moorish pastoral lands. The process has been described by
Boyer.[43] After a famine a group of people leave home to found a new settlement.
A site is chosen on a hill, on the edge of a wadi or at a hill foot. Wells are dug, a
space enclosed for animals, and rough shelters made of branches. Eventually mud
buildings are erected, and a village formed, focusing on the wells and on a space
which serves as a market.

Agriculture is the chief occupation regardless of caste. Land is held by the
nobles, who lease or rent a portion of it to others. Many of the villagers are
labourers, who work on a share basis for the land holders. Of the area cultivated,
the labourer is allowed the produce of a little more than a quarter, and the rest goes
to the holder. In return the holder must supply not only land for the labourer's
share, but also seed and food. Other arrangements are possible including simple
hiring for a payment in cash, kind or both. The chief crop is *Pennisetum*, the
quicker-growing varieties of which flourish in the shorter periods of rains on the
mainly sandy soils in a rotational cultivation with groundnuts and beans. Some
guinea corn and even maize are grown, but only on moisture-retaining black or
red earths in a form of compound land cultivation, using hand irrigation, or on
floodland. Other crops, associated with the moister soils, are rice, onions and
cassava. On the sandy soils cotton and *Digitaria* are grown, and the latter is
especially important as a reserve against failure of the rains or lateness in the
onset of the first showers. Clearance of the main croplands takes place at the end
of May, and sowing in June. In July and August weeding takes place and thinning

of the grain crop. Wherever the plantings have failed, the thinnings are used as replacements. Harvest takes place in the dry season, mainly in October and November. If the storage bins have insufficient grain in reserve during the growing period, then some of the green millet is picked, and 'ripened' in clay furnaces. The heating helps to reduce the toxic qualities of the immature grain.

Large herds of cattle, sheep and goats are held by the Diawara, but the herders are normally Fulani or Moors. During the dry season some pasturing of stock is possible on the stubble of the harvested fields, but transhumance is unknown, for the local pastures are good for most of the year. Horses, donkeys and a few camels are kept, but generally draught oxen are preferred to camels for local transport. Hunting and gathering are of great importance in the economy. In famines and in the all too frequent occurrences of food shortage during the growing season, the leaves and fruit of trees such as the baobab, tamarind and *Ximenia americana* are gathered, together with the young shoots of the dum or *Hyphaene* palm, and the seed of grasses such as 'cram-cram' (*Cenchrus biflorus*) and the wild *Digitaria*. Game hunting with dogs, spears and muzzle-loading guns is abundant, particularly in May at the end of the dry season. Buck, hares, birds, wild cats and hyaena are all hunted. Rats and insects are also caught and eaten. Little fishing is possible, and most of the fish supplies must be obtained from the south by trade.

Despite the hard physical conditions there is very little Diawara emigration. In contrast with the Bambara, the Diawara young men will only seek a few months' work in the nearest towns after harvest. They do not wander on any great scale to distant regions as agricultural labourers. The Diawara alternative has been to develop an extensive trade based on a commercial tradition developed at a period when a location on the fringe of the Sahel conferred opportunities to develop traffic across the Sahara or with the oases and salt-producing centres. Itinerant Diawara traders, dealing mainly in the produce of other regions, visit the towns of Guinea, Senegal and the Ivory Coast, and are especially numerous in Nioro, Kayes, Bamako, Bafoulabé and Kita. Thus an ancient tradition has adapted itself to modern expanding commercial conditions, and has provided a supplementary income to support a population otherwise dependent on only the poorest of resources.

The Bozo fishing grounds

The inland Niger delta of Mali is one of the great fresh-water fishing grounds of West Africa. The southern or non-lacustrine portion of the 'live' sector, from Diafarabé to Lake Débo, is the traditional home of the Bozo who have lived almost solely by fishing for several centuries. Here there are 7,700 square miles (18,000 sq km) of flood-plain, the clays and sands of the Pondo supporting a rich cover of grass, especially 'bourgou' (*Echinochloa stagnina*), a swamp grass which forms a large part of the Niger sudd. As the flood level rises in the Pondo, so the seeds of the grasses and the insects present on the grass are carried away by the water, and provide foods in abundance for the vast shoals of fish. The Pondo is divided into two portions by the Niger. To the north and west is the Northern Pondo, drained partly by the Niger, and partly by the Diaka creek, connecting the Niger at Diafarabé with the western end of Lake Débo. To the south of the Niger, and limited by the Bani, is the Southern Pondo with the Kouakourou creek. Fish movements are divided in the flood period between the two Pondos, and, as flood levels drop, between the Diaka on the west and the Niger on the east.

The Bozo form a distinct community of about 16,000 people. Their origin is unknown, but they appear to have been the earliest fishing people to establish themselves in the inland delta. At one time they probably occupied the whole delta region, but were pushed back into the Pondo by other fishing groups from the north-east and south-west, some of whom have even settled either permanently or temporarily amongst the Bozo. One is born a Bozo[44], but one may become a member of the other fishing groups, for they are 'castes' of communities whose main occupations are either agriculture or pastoralism. Of these groups the most important are the Somono (Bambara) chiefly to the south-west, and the Sorko (Songhay) and Soubalbé (Fulani) to the north-east. The Rimaïbé 'vassals' of the Fulani, occupying agricultural settlements in the north-eastern lakes portion of the delta, also engage in fishing for a short period of the year. All groups, however, recognize the pre-eminence of the Bozo in fishing, and the superiority of their rights in many parts of the Pondo. The use of fences or barrages, one of the chief means of catching fish, is virtually a Bozo monopoly, and fishermen from the other groups must pay a rental or fee to the Bozo for the privilege of using such fences. The Bozo are also the chief canoe builders, making canoes by nailing pieces of wood together reinforced with cord and sealed at the joints. They are thus regarded in the Pondo as the masters of the waters and of the fishing rights.

The Bozo live in villages and camps established on the levées above the highest flood levels. Some of the villages are also inhabited by Rimaïbé, or seasonally by Fulani pastoralists. The fishermen must move to the fishing grounds according to season, and there live in temporary camps. The fishing grounds are divided into fixed 'territories', or zones, each controlled by an extended family or clan chief. The zones have fixed limits, and the dates when fishing may begin are also fixed.[45] The chief fish caught are the 'tinéni' (*Alestes leuciscus*, *A. nurse*, *A. dentix* and *A. baremoze*), but many other species are also caught, including *Micralestes* spp. and the predators – *Hydrocyon*, *Lates* and *Bagridea* spp.[46] The Niger waters begin to rise in June, and, after rising above the banks of the main channel, flow into the broader flood channel, and eventually up the tributary creeks into the flood-plain. The 'tinéni' follow the rising waters, and are dispersed in the flood-plain after July. In July they breed, and the young fish appear in September, when the floods have just reached their maximum. There is food in abundance in the flood-plain, where even the fields of young rice may provide additional nourishment. At the very peak of the floods in October, just as the drop in flood levels is beginning, the 'tinéni' begin to leave the flood-plain, moving at night with the first full moon. This movement is a lateral migration by the tributary creeks and the flood channel into the main channel, where the 'tinéni' move upstream. The migration to the main channel continues with other shoals at the full moon in November and December. The shoals move from four zones:

1) The higher ground near the river in the Diafarabé district in the south-west.
2) The lower portions of the Southern Pondo and the southern half of the Northern Pondo.
3) The northern portions of the Northern Pondo and the creeks of the Mopti district.
4) Lake Débo.

Shoals from each of these zones pass slowly upstream – one calculation indicates at a rate of $5\frac{1}{2}$ miles (9 km) a day.[47] When the 'tinéni' move by the lateral creeks into the main stream, they have completed their growth, and possess reserves of fat, which are used up during the coming low-water period with its food shortage. October, November, December and January are the months for catching fat fish in order to extract oil (approximately 27 per cent of weight). After January the 'tinéni' are smoked or dried. The surviving 'tinéni' move upstream to Markala, where they are halted by the modern barrage – few are able to pass upstream by the fish pass – and then return in small groups to the Pondo.

Construction of fish fences begins as flood levels are about to drop in October. The fences are erected in the creeks and other small channels by which lateral movement to the main channel takes place. Their construction in the Niger itself is forbidden. Grass and tree branches are used to construct the fences in a V shape or in a series of V shapes pointing downstream. The barrages are also used as floodwaters rise together with small dikes with 'sluices' to control water levels. Not all the lateral channels are natural. Some have been opened by the deliberate breaching of the levées by the Bozo themselves.[48] Other methods of fishing include:

1) Seine nets used from the bank or from canoes, often weighted and supported by floats. Meshes vary in size according to the type of fish sought.
2) Dip nets usually mounted on wooden frames and used to gather fish from behind barrages or from the river or creeks at low water.
3) Basket traps.
4) Harpoons.
5) Lines.
6) Cast nets, a comparatively recent introduction and used chiefly by the Somono between Diafarabé and Markala. The cast net is disliked by many Bozo, because it is operated only by one man and encourages individualism and a break with traditional shared methods of the past.

The chief fishing season lasts from October until June. After June there is a little fishing, but the period is mainly one of rest, repairs to equipment and trading. In the Lake Débo area Rimaïbé and some Bambara cultivators leave their agriculture for fishing in April, after the main 'tinéni' shoals have moved upstream. The Bozo move away and share the camps of the pastoralists on the southern shore of Lake Débo and on the neighbouring levées, where they exchange oil, dried and smoked fish for butter and milk.[49] Here the Fulani have only recently established themselves in order to provide pastures for their cattle, and there have been disputes over property rights between fishermen and pastoralists and between the different pastoral groups.

Few Bozo undertake any form of cultivation, except for the planting near the main villages of a little tobacco, which they chew, and some ramie or da (*Hibiscus cannabinus*), providing fibre for the manufacture of lines and nets. There is also some ritual cultivation of fonio or 'hungry rice'(*Digitaria exilis*).[50] For the rest the sale of fish must provide meat, shea butter, yams, beans, fruit, salt from Rosso or Taoudenni, peppers, groundnuts, okra and kola nuts. Local ironsmiths make hooks, harpoons, knives and other tools, and construct the canoes, which at their largest can carry up to 2 tons of cargo and passengers.

In the fishing groups of the Bozo, one has an example of an economy closely adapted to and limited by the physical conditions peculiar to the inland Niger delta. Fishing has been made a specialism, and through that specialism a trade has developed with the neighbouring agricultural and pastoral peoples. The fish provide the basis of life for the Bozo, and an essential protein element in local diet. Yet the inland delta contains valuable floodlands, which could be used for rice fields, if flood levels were controlled, and are occupied here and there by both pastoralists and cultivators. Here then are elements which may compete in their demand to use the delta's resources, and which have already conflicted. Yet these competing elements also need one another, and their very movements always bring them together in the delta for the purpose of exchange. In this need it should always be possible to resolve the problems of competition.

Ouagadougou and Yatenga

The two Mossi states of Ouagadougou and Yatenga occupy the watershed between the Volta headwaters and the Niger. Here more than one and a half million people depend chiefly on the cultivation of cereals, grown in the sandy soils of a remarkably level plateau rising between 800 and 1000 feet (245–305 metres) above sea-level. The plateau has formed an island of ordered government for at least 500 years. Only the French have defeated the Mossi. Thus a culture which owes much to pre-Islamic influences has been preserved, retaining a dispersed distribution of population, despite the existence of states, and despite Sudanic location. Possibly the ordered government helps to explain the comparatively high population densities attaining 97 persons per square mile (37 per sq km) in Yako and 81 (31) in Koudougou, with local densities rising well over 100 (38). Comparison with Hausaland, providing a similar if rather higher Sudanic plateau, however, shows that such densities are not extraordinary, and do not necessarily imply pressure of population on local resources.

The Mossi created their first state in Yatenga by the 12th century, when they

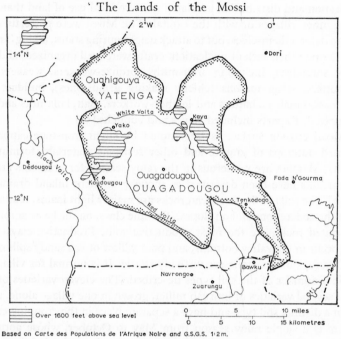

' The Lands of the Mossi

Based on Carte des Populations de l'Afrique Noire and G.S.G.S. 1:2m.

Figure 7.15

invaded their present lands from the east, subdued many of the local inhabitants and intermarried with them, and drove out the Dogon or Habé to Hombori. The conquerors created government by the Moro-Naba or chief, advised by a council each of whose members had a distinct office. Eventually six castes were created:

1) Nakomsé: descendants of the founder prince.
2) Naidamba: descendants of ministers of founder prince.
3) Yarsé: descendants of Muslim priests of founder prince.
4) Ninissi: descendants of the original inhabitants conquered by the Mossi.
5) Yem dado: slaves.
6) Saba: ironsmiths.[51]

The Mossi states were small enough each to assert effective authority from one small centre: Ouahigouya in Yatenga, and Ouagadougou. There was no devolution of authority, and therefore there were no intermediate administrative centres. Trading was insufficiently developed to promote any major nucleation outside the two small capitals. Indeed, as amongst some other West African communities, the traditional markets are not in the villages, but outside them, central to a group of villages. Here and there rectangular terraced houses exist, introduced from the north, but for the most part the dwellings consist of groups of 4 to 35 rondavels linked by walls. These groups or compounds are known as 'zaka', and a widely dispersed number of 'zaka' forms a 'village', a social unit whose location and distribution is related more to local use of land than to contacts with other villages or with the capital. The Mossi were powerful enough, not only to defend themselves, but to attack neighbouring states, taking Timbuktu in 1333. Despite their lack of nucleation, crafts were well organized, and undertaken by specialists, including ironsmiths, bronze-workers, weavers, dyers, tailors, potters, stone masons (chiefly making grindstones), builders, woodworkers, basket makers, hatters and leather-workers. Salt, kola nuts and copper were imported. Exports included slaves and eunuchs.[52]

The Mossi erosion surface is interrupted by slight ironstone-capped hills, and isolated outcrops of granite and other resistant materials, forming small bornhardts. Marshes are numerous in the rainy season, for gradients are slight, and the streams have been described as showing a 'latent inland drainage tendency'.[53] The soils of the Archaean rocks are mainly light loams, tending to be coarse on the concretions and on slopes. The fine clays, on the basic amphibolites and associated rocks, are the most productive soils. Productive clays needing drainage occur in the valley bottoms, and poor yellow or red sandy soils on sandstones. Outcrops of ironstone are virtually sterile. It is normal for village lands to include a number of the soil types described. The eleven varieties of guinea corn, and several varieties of bulrush millet, grown in one village alone, are each planted in a distinct soil type and have a separate place in the cropping calendar. [54] There is a single rainy season from May to October, whose approach is heralded by a few showers in February or March. Annual rainfall totals vary between averages of 20 in (508 mm) in the north and 32 in (813 mm) in the south. Totals, however, are less significant in agricultural practice than variation and incidence. Percentage deviations may be over 30, and even in years of sufficient rainfall total, the rains may fail at planting time. The last problem is serious enough for Mossi cultivators to retain a seed reserve against the possible need for a second sowing. A single growing season followed by a long rest period has meant a great dependence on food storage. Yet little attempt has been made to use floodland, despite the possibility of gaining an extra supply of fresh food after the main harvest. Only in recent years, and in response to changing market conditions, have there been attempts to develop market gardens in the floodplains, or to water vegetable plots from wells. A little swamp rice is planted – chiefly in the Volta valleys. There, fodder grasses are also grown, in order to feed the horses which were once a vital part of Mossi military power.

The staples are guinea corn and bulrush millets, with maize, beans, cotton, groundnuts, sesame and rice as important secondaries. Sample 'rotations' are:

    i) 1. Bulrush millet, 2. bulrush millet or guinea corn, 3. bulrush millet, 4. groundnuts, 5. fallow 4–10 years.

ii) 1. Guinea corn, 2. guinea corn, 3. guinea corn, 4. bulrush millet, 5. groundnuts, 6. fallow 4–10 years.

iii) 1. Guinea corn, 2. guinea corn, 3. guinea corn, 4. guinea corn, 5. cotton,
6. cotton, 7. guinea corn, 8. guinea corn, 9. guinea corn, 10. bulrush millet,
11. fallow 3 years or more.[55]

These can barely be described as 'rotations'. A greater effort to make a balanced
use of soils is effected by crop mixtures. Beans and sesame for example are
normally interplanted with guinea corn. Cassava and fonio are relatively unimportant, which suggests the possibility of a general maintenance of fertility
levels. Dubourg remarks of Taghalla, where famine occurs from time to time,
and where fallows are shorter, and cultivation has extended onto poorer soils,
that if soil degradation occurs, it is probably slow and is not catastrophic in
appearance.[56]

Factors influencing soil fertility include the annual deposit of harmattan dust,
the long rest period each year, and the supply of manure from cattle grazing in
the fields during the dry season. Many Mossi families own cattle in addition to
fowls, sheep and goats, but employ Fulani herdsmen, who receive the milk from
the cattle in payment. Much manure is deposited elsewhere since the cattle
migrate seasonally, and cattle ownership has more prestige than practical value.
As in Iboland the dispersal of homesteads enables the cultivator to develop 'compound land', fertilized with domestic refuse near his dwelling. In this land he
generally plants the slower-growing varieties of guinea corn together with maize,
tobacco and other 'kitchen-garden' crops. Other sources of foodstuffs are gathering, hunting and fishing, which, during the long rest period, are important
occupations among the Mossi. Gautier estimates that these three activities provide 17 per cent of the Mossi food supply, and are especially important in years
of poor rainfall incidence, when harvests are small.[57]

Perhaps the greatest problem of the Mossi is their distance from ports and
from the centres of most rapid economic development. They have no major
export crop and their long rest season has encouraged the temporary migration of
labour, which in some cases has become permanent emigration. Transport has
been a major factor. Although the railway from Abidjan reached Bobo Dioulasso
in 1934, it was not extended to Ouagadougou until 1951. In 1948 over 40,000
Mossi were absent in Ghana. By 1956 some thousands were in the Ivory Coast
(over 11,000 in Abidjan alone). Here social and economic disequilibrium are produced by a population movement which reduces pressure on the land and brings
in return the cash to pay for imported goods, but in which the migrant returns
home at a time of seasonal food shortage. Yet how much real pressure on the
land exists? The migration of the Mossi is paralleled elsewhere in Africa by
numerous migrations in search of seasonal labour by young people, chiefly young
men, who are in effect in search of new ways and who want social disequilibrium.

The lands of the Songhay

The Songhay are one of the few communities in West Africa dependent for the greater part of their food production on floodland. Their territory extends in a narrow strip along the middle course of the Niger, from the northern portions of the inland delta almost to the confluence with the Gulbi-n-Kebbi. The Songhay may be divided into two groups: the Songhay proper, a mixture of a number

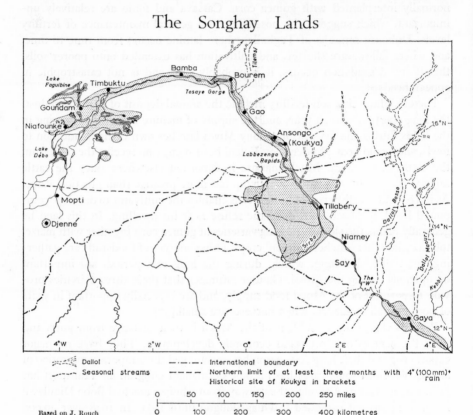

The Songhay Lands

Dallol
Seasonal streams

International boundary
Northern limit of at least three months with 4" (100mm)+ rain
Historical site of Koukya in brackets

| 0 | 50 | 100 | 150 | 200 | 250 miles |

| 0 | 100 | 200 | 300 | 400 kilometres |

Based on J. Rouch

Figure 7.16

of peoples, and the assimilated groups who live within Songhay territory and have accepted a measure of Songhay culture. All these peoples, with the exception of the Gow hunters, became dependent on the river for its supply of water for cultivation, for its fish, for its use as a trade route or as a path to conquest. The Songhay lands form a narrow strip of permanent occupation in the midst of the territory of the pastoral and nomadic Tuareg. Nomadism had been a constant factor in Songhay history, and, even today, Tuareg and Songhay live in a form of symbiosis. Songhay language and culture are permeated by Tuareg elements, yet the river remains the dominant economic and political factor, giving unity to the different Songhay groups.

From a little north of Tillabéry southwards, the annual rainfall averages more than 18 in (460 mm) in a season of $3\frac{1}{2}$ months or more. Cultivation, subject to considerable rainfall variation, is possible away from the river, and it is here that the Songhay lands reach their broadest extent. To the north the cultivator is entirely dependent on flooded or irrigated land. The tributary valleys, including the broad 'dallols' of the left bank, have flowing water for only a few weeks in the year. For the rest they are reduced to pools or to lines of wells, providing routeways for migratory herds of cattle. The landscape is monotonously level, yet there is a variety of surface materials including the sands and alluvium of the lakes portion of the inland delta, the clays of the narrow basins of Timbuktu, Gao and the valley south of the confluence with the Dallol Bosso, the sandstones of Tosaye and the basement complex from Kukya to the 'W' gorge. It is in the clay basins that cultivation has been most intensively developed. In the southernmost of these and on the adjoining strip of alluvium to the north, the Niger flood, which began in the Guinean uplands, has been delayed sufficiently by its long journey to occur in the dry season. Labour can thus be employed at separate times of the year on floodlands and rainland, and be kept in almost continuous employment.

The first 'Songhay' to settle in the region were Sorko hippopotamus hunters, who appear to have come from Lake Chad via the Benue valley, and settled on the islands of the Tillabéry archipelago. North of the Labbezenga rapids and at the southern end of the Gao basin they founded their most important settlement – Kukya. The Sorko traded with the Gow hunters of the interior lands and in the 7th century A.D. accepted the ruler of a Lemta (Berber) family whose leader founded the Za dynasty.[58] Some of the Sorko moved upstream and settled in the Mopti district. The kingdom of Kukya, 'Kuku' or 'Kawkaw' was described by Arab travellers of the 9th century as the greatest and most powerful state of the Sudan.[59] Islam was introduced in the 10th century and later the 16th Za was converted. A new capital was established at Gao in the fertile basin north of Kukya, and from there an empire of the middle Niger was created. Gao consisted of two towns, a market town frequented by Muslim traders on the left bank, and a royal town with Songhay traditions on the right bank. Wealth was acquired from trading with countries as far away as Egypt. Songhay merchants were established in numerous towns, including the great trading city of Djenné, and the valley provided a route from Mali, controlling the upper portions of the inland delta and the Upper Niger valley, to the Hausa of the plateau to the east. For a time Mali extended its rule over the Songhay, but in the 14th century there was a revolt, and the 20th Za took the title of Sonni or Si, by which the rulers of the new empire were henceforth known. Sonni Ali, 1464–92, conquered the middle valley from Bussa to Djenné and attempted to cut a canal from Ras el Ma on Lake Faguibine for 250 miles to Oualata, in order to make a passage for his fleet of war canoes. The succeeding Askya dynasty was defeated by the Moroccans or Arma, who today form a distinct group in the north-west. In the 16th century the Djerma or Zerma occupied the Zermaganda plateau in the south-east, possibly coming from Mali, and eventually occupied the adjacent 'dallols' and Niger valley. Other Songhay peoples moved further downsteam, and divided the two groups of Tienga or Tianaza settlement, confined to the rainlands and dallols, whilst a fishing branch of the Sorko, the Sorkawa, moved down the Niger and eventually settled on the confluence with the Gulbi-n-Kebbi, between the two major 'flood regions'. The Songhay empire was never re-established. Other peoples invaded the region, and founded settlements, including the Kurtey, a Fulani 'river' caste, Fulani and Tuareg nomads, and the Bella, Tuareg agricultural slaves. Some Songhay cultivators moved further upstream, founding new villages in the delta, whilst others settled on the rainland fringe of Gurma, or as traders in neighbouring towns.

The Songhay are not entirely dependent on cultivation. They also depend on the produce of stock rearing, fishing and gathering.[60] The Songhay lands may be divided into two major regions: Songhay proper above the Labbezenga rapids, and Dendi to the south. Dendi possesses cultivable lands above the flood limits. Songhay proper depends entirely on the river, and, in both the Gao valley and the inland delta, the chief crops are floodland guinea corn and rice. In the delta the flood period lasts from August until January. Floating rice is sown directly in the fields in July. Water levels are in many cases controlled by dikes. Swamp rice of the Kobé variety is planted in nurseries in May, replanted in June or July and harvested with floating rice in October. As the flood levels decline in February and March guinea corn is planted – sometimes replanted from a nursery watered by handscoops. Bulrush millets are sometimes interplanted, and in a few villages wheat and barley are grown on artificially watered land. Other crops include maize, beans, cotton and tobacco. With the exception of maize, grown in small basins near the normal upper limit of flooding between November and February, December and January are usually avoided by cultivators, as a young or standing crop may be eaten by locusts which swarm at that time of the year. Other pests are fish and birds, especially the Quelea. Late varieties of floating rice may be lost to these. Another problem is the considerable variation in the height of flooding, and the danger of too rapid a drop in the flood levels. Rice crops, especially floating rice, are especially liable to suffer damage, which even diking cannot altogether prevent. In consequence much of the rice cultivation is essentially extensive in character, for laborious preparation too often ends in failure.[61] Hence constant friction between the Songhay cultivator and the French administration, which sought to introduce more productive methods requiring more labour, even attempting in 1946 to force the building of dikes by legislation.[62] In the Gao region bulrush millet is the chief crop, although both guinea corn and rice are important. As flood levels decline in February and March bulrush millet and guinea corn are planted, and benefit during their period of growth from the short rainy season before harvest in September. Rice is planted in the high 'fisi dogey' floodlands in September, when the rise in flood levels is normally slower than in the preceding months, and the crop is less likely to be damaged. An early crop is available by November, harvested by boat, and the last of the late crops is normally harvested by the end of December. The preparation of rice fields begins during the previous flood, when the grass is cut below water level. With the drop in flood levels, the rains arrive to keep the clay soils moist, so that they may be dug with the large long-handled hoe or spade, the 'beri gourou', used like the spade of the coastal swamp dwellers of the south-west. In Dendi rice cultivation is replaced by a remarkable concentration on bulrush millets, grown on both floodlands and rainlands. Guinea corn, groundnuts, earth peas, cotton, okra and sesame are also important. Bulrush millet is planted, well after flood levels have declined and the soils have been drained, in June or July and harvested in October. The rainlands are also planted at about the same time, and, in some cases, the water supply is supplemented by scooping water up from the river into a series of channels arranged in steps. On the 'fari' croplands, situated round the villages, the dry season resting period is long, and the cattle provide manure. Cultivation may last 10 years followed by 10 to 20 years of fallow. In some villages cowpeas and a little cassava are also planted, but generally cassava is despised as a foodstuff, and the traditional bulrush millet preferred. The land immediately round the villages is often irrigated and fertilized with manure and household refuse. Here numerous vegetables are grown, and groundnuts, which provide a commercial crop. Only Dendi has a crop to export and sufficient land to satisfy all requirements. Songhay proper has no export crop, and barely sufficient land to support its population. Holdings average less than an acre (0·4 hectare) per family.

The small nucleated villages of the Songhay are located near the river, not only in order to control the valuable floodland and obtain domestic water supplies, but also to control fishing rights and the valuable 'bourgou' pastures. From March to June the Tuareg and Fulani nomads bring their herds of cattle to the river-side pastures, and occupy land which could otherwise be planted to bulrush millet or guinea corn. The cultivators have constantly sought to increase their acreage at the expense of the pastoralists, but the French administration, seeking to avoid conflict, prevented further clearance, and reserved certain pastures for the nomads. Cattle tracks through the cultivated lands are between 200 and 300 feet (60–90 metres) wide, and fixed by hedges in order to prevent the animals straying into the fields. The Songhay themselves own about one cow and two or three sheep or goats per head. A few families also own horses, donkeys and camels. Livestock are kept on open pastures and on the croplands after harvest by the children, or confined to the care of the nomadic pastoralists, with the exception of milch cows and calves, which remain in the village. As elsewhere in West Africa the possession of cattle conveys prestige, and few Songhay will sell or kill them, except at special festivals. In the Dori district stock rearing is the chief occupation.

Fishing is the occupation chiefly of the Sorkawa, a branch of the Sorko, the original hippopotamus-hunting 'caste'. The Sorkawa come north in March as the flood levels decline and fish from temporary camps. In September to December they move south for the declining flood levels of the Niger below Bussa. Some Sorko fish, especially in the valuable 'tinéni' grounds of the inland delta, but many Sorko despise all forms of 'fishing' other than hippopotamus hunting, forbidden by the French administration, and in consequence have become cultivators.[63]

Gathering, especially of grass seeds, makes a large contribution to the Songhay economy, particularly in the north, where holdings are small. The dependence of cultivation on the flooding régime results in the occurrence of the main bulrush millet and guinea corn harvest from September onwards, and the main rice harvest from October. Harvesting may continue for three or four months as crops planted at successively lower levels are cut, but a long period without fresh food still occurs. By July and August wild grains are sold in greater abundance than cultivated grains in Songhay markets, especially *Echinochloa colona*, *Cenchrus biflorus* and *Digitaria* spp. Wild roots are also valued, including the 'aquatic potato' (*Ipomoea reptans*).

The Songhay economy is distinct, for the pattern of flooding on which it depends is unique. The advantages of developing a fixed agriculture and fixed settlement in the organization of a powerful Sudanic state were great. Yet the agricultural wealth of the river attracted too many conquerors, and contrasted too markedly with the poverty of the surrounding pastoral and hunting lands. Hence the agricultural-pastoral symbiosis, and hence also constant attempts by herdsmen to impose their authority on the cultivators. Today the northern location of Songhay, which was of such advantage for the trans-Saharan trade, no longer assists the economy. The trade has almost disappeared, and the crowded floodlands can barely support a population virtually thrown back on agriculture. Moreover, the control of the Middle Niger, once so valuable a political asset, has become an economic disadvantage, because of distance from the modern commercial centres. Perhaps here the river may again provide the answer, for, canalized and dammed, it may yet provide a great highway, and a major source of power to assist a developing economy.

Hausaland

Almost all peoples who today speak Hausa as the sole or main language may claim to be Hausa. Yet by tradition the Hausa proper are the freemen of seven states or 'bakwai': Daura formed about A.D. 1000 or 1050, Biram, Kano, Rano, Katsina, Zaria (Zazau or Zegzeg) and Gobir. On the southern fringe are the bastard or counterfeit seven, the 'banza bakwai', communities who have adopted Hausa customs and dress and Hausa political organization and laws: Kebbi, Nupe, Gwari, Yelwa, Ilorin (Yoruba), Kwororofa and Zamfara. The Hausa kingdoms owe their origins to the movement and settlement of a number of agricultural and pastoral peoples, and their history is associated with the early development of walled cities and of metal-working and manufacturing techniques. Hausa myth suggests

that a pastoral people, the Zaghawa, invaded the Sudanic region in about the
10th century, introducing a new religion, possibly introducing the horse, and
bringing well-sinking techniques.[64] The Zaghawa imposed their rule on the
agricultural peoples they conquered, and founded the Habe dynasties, creating
a serf caste and a noble caste. Although Daura was the first of these new states,

Hausaland—Relief and Approximate Limits

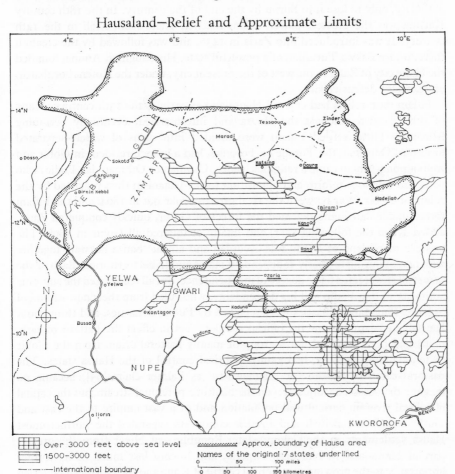

Figure 7.17

the claim has been made that Gobir, lying to the north and mainly Sahelian, was
the only true state of freemen, whilst the other six states of the great plateau
between the basins of Sokoto and Bornu were mainly agricultural and servile.
The capitals or 'birni' of the states were centres of trade, industry and military
force. Thus there is a tradition that Kano was founded by iron-workers, whilst
Zaria was the chief slave market and the chief slave catcher. Katsina and Kano
both became great markets, with important trans-Saharan connections, and for a

time the former city was renowned as a centre of learning. The seven states never appear to have been united, except for short periods, by the military ascendancy of one of their number, or by conquest from an outside power. In the 15th and 16th centuries Kano conquered most of Hausaland, and even imposed its authority on the Songhay. In the 17th century the Jukun or Kwororofa imposed their authority, only to lose it to Bornu by the end of the century. In the 18th century Katsina was the greatest power. Islam reached Kano from Mali in the 14th century. It was introduced into Zaria in 1456, and was followed by the creation there, under Bakwa Turunku, of a powerful state. His daughter, Amina, founded the Habe city of Zaria to the west of the present city, under the Kofena bornhardt, an excellent defensive site.

Fulani pastoralists had entered Hausaland as early as the 13th century. Many of them settled amongst the Hausa and intermarried, eventually becoming Muslims. These settled Fulani were divided into clans of widely-separated locations. One clan, the Torobe or Toronke, had a branch resident in Gobir and from amongst them came a religious leader, Usuman or Othman dan Fodio, who preached religious reform and opposition to the paganism then practised by the rulers of Gobir. War between the rival groups broke out in 1804, and the Fulani forces under dan Fodio defeated the forces of Gobir, quickly conquered Zaria, added Kano the following year, and finally conquered all Gobir in 1808. The western marchland of Bornu was occupied and all the 'banza bakwai', together with neighbouring formerly-independent states and tribal territories. Each of the new emirates created had a degree of independence, but all recognized the supreme authority of dan Fodio and his descendants, who ruled from their new capital of Sokoto. The Habe dynasties were replaced by Fulani dynasties, and throughout Hausaland Islam became the official religion. Yet in effect the pattern of early myth had been repeated, for a group of mainly pastoral origin from the Gobir Sahel, claiming nobility, had gained political control of the Hausa states. The pastoral camp of Sokoto (or 'Zaghawa-tu' as Palmer claims[65]) became no longer a dry season headquarters on the bank of a perennial stream, but the capital of a local riverain agricultural population and of a vast empire to the east and south. Finally the British and French conquests separated the northernmost Hausa settlements in the Colony – later Republic – of Niger from the greater part of Hausaland in Northern Nigeria, and Sokoto lost much of its former importance to the growing commercial centre of Kano and the Northern Nigerian capital of Kaduna.

The Hausa cultivator has widely differing soil and climatic conditions according to location. Hausaland consists essentially of the basin of the Sokoto river and its tributaries, to the west, and of the great plateau to the east. The Hausa Plateau consists of a comparatively level surface at 2000 to 2400 feet (600–730 metres) in the south, sloping down to below 1500 feet (460 metres) in the north. It is slightly dissected by broad valleys of mature streams, and is fringed to the west and south by another surface at 1600 to 2000 feet (490–600 metres), forming a 'step' between the plateau and the Niger trough. To the south-west rises a still higher plateau, that of Jos, with a general surface level at about 4000 feet (1220 metres) and granite hills rising above to nearly 6000 feet (1830 metres). The

Cultivation Aligned on Dead Sand Dunes, Hadejia

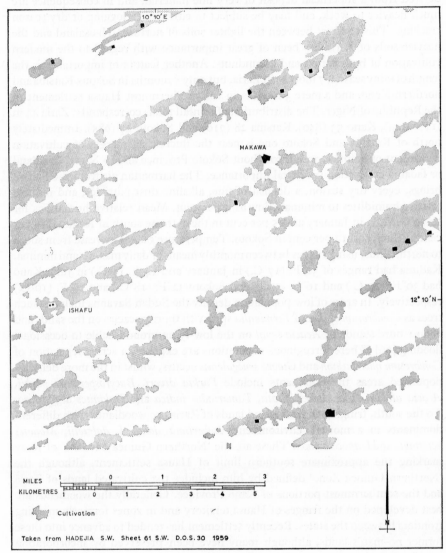

Figure 7.18

plateau consists mainly of schists, quartzites and granites, the 'Basement Complex', overlain in its northern part by the sands and deposits of a former southerly extension of the Sahara. The Sokoto basin consists mainly of Tertiary and Cretaceous sediments, commonly with ferruginous cappings and overlain by sandy deposits. Sands are of widespread occurrence in the northern portions, particularly in Kano and Sokoto, and settlement patterns have been much influenced by the dune formations (Fig. 7.18). To the south the Zaria soils are derived from a superficial deposit of very fine material, and in consequence are much heavier to work, and may be subject to either waterlogging or dry season cracking. This contrast between the lighter soils of northern Hausaland and the heavier soils of Zaria has been of great importance with regard to the modern cultivation of both cotton and groundnuts. Another feature of importance is the length of rainy season, 7 months in Zaria, but only 5 months in Sokoto, Katsina and northern Kano, and a mere 3 months in the northernmost Hausa settlement in the Republic of Niger. The distribution of rainfall totals corresponds: Zaria 44 in (1170 mm), Kano 33 (840), Katsina 28 (710) and Sokoto 27 (685). Immediately north of Katsina and Sokoto one is near the fluctuating margin of cultivation dependent on rainfall, and, throughout Sokoto Province and in Niger, floodland or fadama cultivation is of vital importance. The harmattan air from the Sahara brings, every dry season, a deposit of fine, alkaline dust particles, and reduces relative humidities to minima as low as 4 per cent. Mean relative humidities for 12.00 G.M.T. in January are 15 per cent in the extreme south in Kaduna, 13 per cent in Kano and 12 per cent in Sokoto. Temperature ranges increase from south to north. Thus, using ranges between monthly means of daily maxima and minima, Kaduna had ranges of 30°F. (17°C.) in January and 14°F. (8°C.) in July, Kano had 30°F. (17°C.) and 16°F. (9°C.) and Sokoto 32°F. (18°C.) and 18°F. (10°C.) respectively. In areas of low population density the Sudan Savanna includes such trees as *Combretum* spp. and *Terminalia* spp. with thorny acacias on the sands and almost pure stands of *Acacia seyal* on the low-lying ground liable to occasional flooding.[66] Where ferruginous concretions are exposed, a scrub vegetation of *Combretum micranthum* and *Guiera senegalensis* occurs, whilst in the more densely-populated areas the dominants include *Parkia diveri*, *Butyrospermum parkii*, *Acacia albida*, *Adansonia digitata*, *Tamarindus indica* and *Balanites aegyptiaca*. To the south, fringing the cultivated lands of Zaria are woodlands with different dominants in a moister environment: *Isoberlinia doka*, *I. dalzielii*, *Monotes kerstingii* and *Uapaca somon*. These are the 'Northern Guinea Savanna' of Keay marking the approximate southern limit of Hausa settlement, although the 'Northern Guinea Zone' defined by him includes the cultivated lands of Zaria and the southernmost portions of Kano Province. Generally the woodlands are best developed on the fringes of Hausa territory and in zones formerly marking frontiers between the states. Recently settlement has tended to advance into these former no-man's-lands, although many have been preserved by incorporation into forest reserves.

The Hausa settlements may be classified into the 'birni' (plural = birane) or city, normally the political centre of a former state and frequently today a provincial or divisional centre; the 'gari' (plural = garuruwa) or local market town; and the 'kauye', 'tunga', or 'unguwa', a village which is a political and economic satellite of a city or town. Of the Hausa cities the four largest in 1952 were

Settlement and Cultivation in North West Niger Province – Abandoned Towns

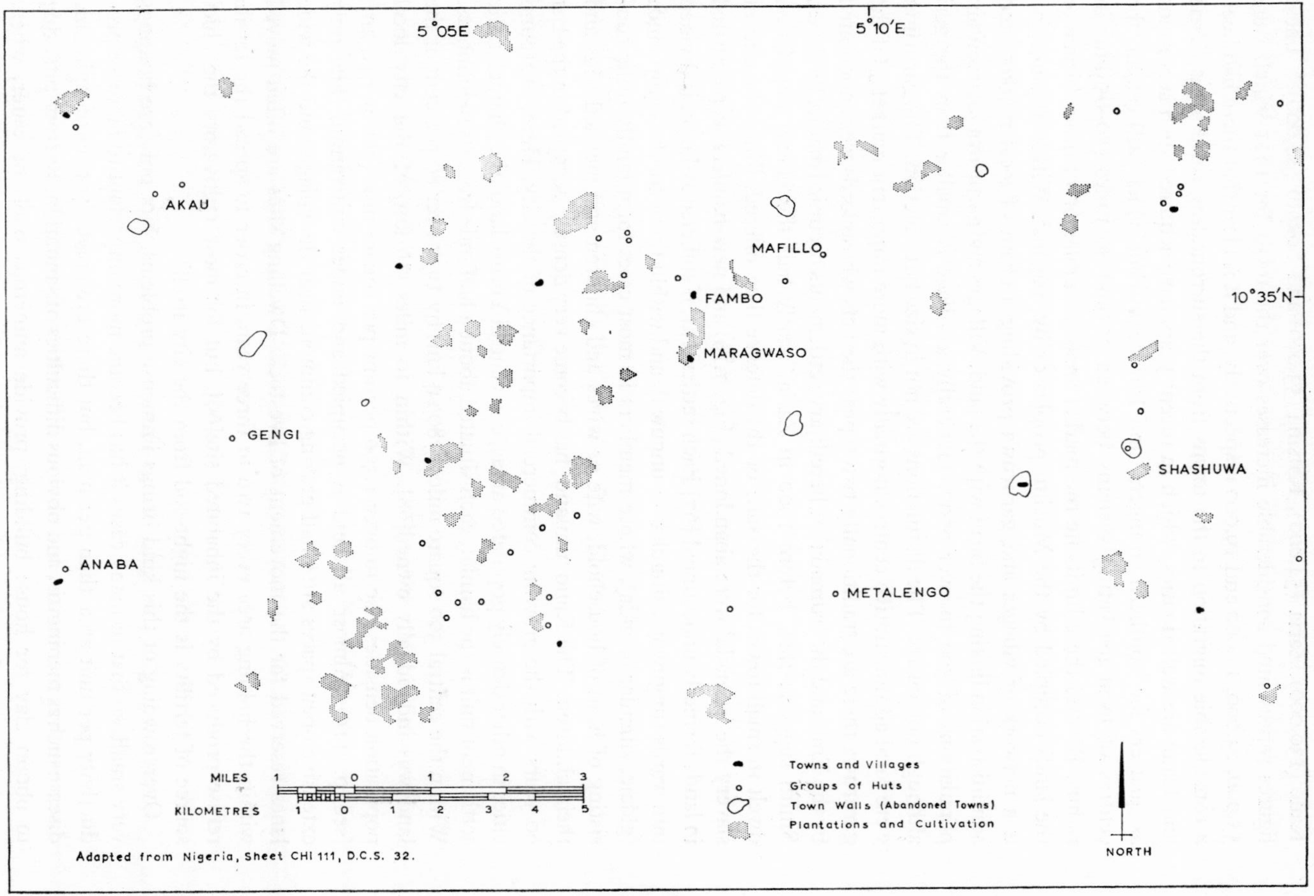
5°05E
5°10'E
10°35'N
AKAU
ANABA
GENGI
MAFILLO
FAMBO
MARAGWASO
METALENGO
SHASHUWA
MILES 1 0 1 2 3
KILOMETRES 1 0 1 2 3 4 5
Towns and Villages
Groups of Huts
Town Walls (Abandoned Towns)
Plantations and Cultivation
NORTH
Adapted from Nigeria, Sheet CHI 111, D.C.S. 32.

Figure 7.19

Kano (130,000), Zaria (54,000), Katsina (53,000) and Sokoto (48,000).* These figures represented considerable increases over the totals for 1921 which were 55,000, 23,000, 17,000 and 19,000 respectively, and it is clear that there had been a considerable migration to the towns from the surrounding rural areas. Zaria and Kano are walled cities, which in recent years have acquired such accretions as quarters for 'southern strangers' and Europeans, but which still remain the centres of local marketing systems between 30 and 40 miles (50–65 km) in radius. Beyond these limits lie the market areas or 'umlands' of other birane or the lands occupied by the Muslim peoples or by 'pagans'. Within the umland is a network of villages and garuruwa providing a chain of local markets and administration linking the birni with the land. Villages and garuruwa may contain populations of 500 to over 6000. Generally a village is smaller than the gari although not always. The distinctions are not in size but function. The garuruwa were local administrative centres normally with more important markets. Of the garuruwa there are traditionally two types: the fiefs whose lords were appointed by the Emir and the 'rumada' or hereditary settlements occupied mainly by slaves. Smith suggests that, before 1900 in Zaria, nearly half the Hausa population dwelt in small towns for the sake of the defence they offered. Since the end of slavery the 'rumada' were abandoned (Fig. 7.19) and new hamlets were created in lands formerly unoccupied.[67] Each settlement, if sufficiently large, is divided into wards (unguwoyi, singular = unguwa), and within these are the compounds (gidaje, singular = gida), whose members in most cases form family units con- sisting of head of household, wife or wives and children and married sons and their children. The Kano 'umland' has become very densely occupied in the last 60 years with the growing commercial importance of the city. Here, as around cities in other densely populated areas, e.g. central Yorubaland, the characteristic settlement unit is the hamlet, each situated about a half mile from its neighbours. Within the central 300 square miles (780 sq km) by 1937 over 80 per cent of the land was individually owned[68]. Within 10 miles (16 km) of the city local population densities rise to over 1,300 persons per square mile (500 per sq km) (see p. 119). Almost all land is occupied and under cultivation. The only extensive open spaces are small grazing commons near the villages and the wide lanes reserved for the movement of livestock. Dwelling sites are often moved within the holding area every two to three years in order to spread the fertile refuse produced by the inhabited site[69], but for most cultivators the chief source of fertility is the night-soil from the city itself.

Overcrowding of this kind brings immense problems. Not only are holdings very small, so that in many cases it has become more important to increase pro- ductivity per unit area than per man, but there are grave dangers of epidemic disease such as meningitis, and obvious difficulties of sanitation. Borrow pits, dug to obtain clay for house building, provide numerous pools of water, where mosquitoes may breed, and have become foci for the spread of malaria. At the

* According to the census of December 1963 Kano had 295,432 people, and Zaria had 166,170.

same time, resettlement of people in less crowded areas may mean exposing them
to the risk of sleeping sickness infection wherever there are woodlands infested by
tsetse fly.

The pattern of settlement is still mainly traditional in character. In Barth's
time Kano was powerful enough to offer protection to surrounding hamlets,

Nucleated Settlements as Foci of Cultivated Lands:
an example from Northern Nigeria

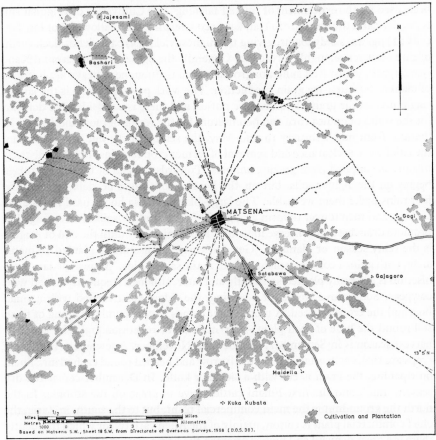

Figure 7.20

when other neighbouring areas were devastated by war. On the 9th March 1851,
Barth observed that beyond Kano were clusters of huts, tobacco and corn fields,
with 'detached farms', spread about over the cultivated country.[70] Dense woodlands were left in between the 'umlands', or tributary areas providing a 'no-man's-
land', or occupied the sites of towns, villages and cultivated land, depopulated by
warfare. Nucleation has been encouraged by the practice of forming a co-operative
work unit ('gandu' or 'gaya') for clearing, planting and harvesting fields, whilst
in the 'gandu' the families share not only the agricultural work, but domestic

duties. Commonly after harvest the families separate, only to reunite before the onset of the next rainy season. Many families move seasonally between the large compact settlement or gari, and an agricultural settlement or 'garin gona', in order to reduce walking distances. Formerly slave labour was used, not only to assist the 'gandu', but to work large estates owned by the Fulani aristocracy. Former slave owners have frequently been forced to reduce the areas they held for cultivation and to employ hired labour. In some cases the personal estates of the Emirs have been used for the experiment of 'mixed farming'.[71] Cultivators distinguish soil types. In Zaria the chief are: 1) jan kasa, red lateritic soils, shallow and of low fertility; 2) jigawa, sandy loams, giving the highest yields; 3) bakin kasa, black earth, of rare occurrence, highly fertile.[72] Generally the lighter red soils around Kano (jangargari), whilst well suited to groundnut cultivation, need heavy applications of manure for intensive grain production. The work pays, for Kano is the largest single market for grains and also for pulses, and there is a considerable demand for the stalks of guinea corn and pennisetum for the repair of roofs and fences. In 'bazara' from mid-February to mid-May, the season of the hot dry harmattan, the chief work is clearance and removal of former crop remains. In many districts manure is supplied from grazing animals. Towards the end of the season tillage begins on the lighter soils, but on the heavier soils must be delayed until the first rains make them workable. The large-bladed Hausa hoe is used to slice the surface, and turn it over to form a ridge. Only the sandiest soils are not ridged to promote drainage and conserve moisture. From mid-May until the end of August is the rainy season or 'damina'. 'Gero' or early pennisetum is planted immediately, with guinea corn interplanted later in the same fields. 'Maiwa' or late pennisetum is generally planted separately and later, although frequently mixed with cowpeas. Some three weeks after sowing, the ridges are trimmed with a small hoe, and the crops thinned. A month later comes weeding and the piling of fresh soil round the base of each plant – the 'maimai' or repetition.[73] The 'kaka' or harvest season is in September, October and November. A few weeks before the crops are ripe, earth is taken from the furrow and heaped round each plant. Then, on ripening, the grain is cut with a sickle or knife. In December comes the dry season, 'rani', and the first Fulani cattle arrive to graze on the stubble. In the north the groundnut is the main commercial plant, but to the south, in Zaria, the chief commercial plant is cotton, mainly of the Allen variety, for which frequently there is a great demand and higher prices in the home market. Of the minor crops the chief are maize, sweet potato, cassava, sugar cane, artichokes, peppers, tomatoes, indigo, pumpkins, rice, tobacco, henna, gourds and the hibiscus fibre plant. Indigo is normally grown in separate fields on the heavier soils, and a crop may produce for several years without replanting. Maize, sugar cane and sweet potatoes are grown mainly in the fadama. Fadama holdings are very small, averaging only $\frac{1}{2}$ acre (0·2 hectare), compared with 5 to 8 acres (2·0–3·2 hectares) under crops dependent on the rains. Yet they are highly productive, produce crops not otherwise available, and provide periods of planting, weeding and harvesting later than those of the main crops. Irrigation from streams and wells is used on only a small scale, assisted by shadufs or small containers attached to ropes. The chief irrigated crops are of high value such as onions, rice and tomatoes. A little wheat is also grown by irrigation in a few places. Wheat has been grown for a long time, and 19th-century visitors to Kano found bread on sale in the markets. The manuring of land round Kano, and in the fields of the compound land, helps the soil to hold moisture, and thus makes possible the growing of crops with heavier moisture demands, even without irrigation, such as maize and okra. In Niger the Hausa settlements depend greatly on their fadama or 'garka' cultivation of date palms, bananas, cotton, potatoes, rice, onions and vegetables, for the growing season on rainlands, usually on former sand dunes, is too short for crops other than pennisetum, groundnuts and beans. In Tassao Haoussa village three large fields are used for pennisetum cultivation, divided into small strips called 'gona', and tilled with the 'hauya' or hoe, pushed in front. Each field bears crops for 3 years, and has 6 years fallow.[74] Hausa cultivation has provided for several centuries a stable output of foodstuffs and fibres, and a considerable surplus of production to support its aristocracy, its armies and its artisans, and to exchange for the produce of other communities. It is above all in the quality of their manufactures and in the development of commerce that the Hausa have excelled. Hausa industry and skill produced high-quality metal goods, especially agricultural implements, knives, weapons, armour and ornaments. Mineral deposits in neighbouring lands, especially the tin ores of Jos, were developed and exploited. Distinctive patterns of weaving were produced and high-quality leather goods, especially from goatskins. Hausa traders developed commerce as far to the south as the lands of the Yoruba and Ashanti. To the north they established themselves in Mediterranean ports, above all in Tripoli, and exchanged the produce of the West African Sudan for that of Europe. In the Sahara their agents arranged for the movement of salt from central Saharan oases. By trade contacts the Hausa language became a *lingua franca* of that portion of West Africa which lies between the Bandama river and Timbuktu in the west, and the Cameroons in the east, whilst Kano and Katsina became, in their day, the greatest trading emporia of Africa south of the Sahara.

The pastoral Fulani regions of Hausaland

Within the region developed by the Hausa and by neighbouring communities, groups of pastoral Fulani have established certain rights in seasonal pastures and in arable lands, and migrate regularly between the areas they need to use. In the broadest sense, the regions occupied by the Fulani are in large part occupied also by other peoples, chiefly Hausa cultivators. Yet although there is this overlap of communities, which has been of economic advantage to both, each has its own regional pattern, defined in terms of its distinct way of using the physical environment. Within the territories of the Hausa and their neighbours are three sectors occupied by Fulani speakers: the western, or western Sokoto; the central, or Katsina, eastern Sokoto and northern Zaria; and the eastern, or western Bornu.

Pastoral Fulani Regions of Hausaland

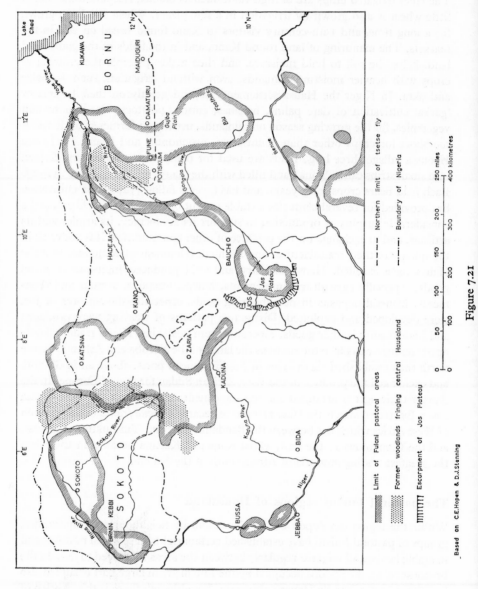

Based on C.E.Hopen & D.J.Stenning

Figure 7.21

Legend:

▓ Limit of Fulani pastoral areas

▒ Former woodlands fringing central Hausaland

IIIIIII Escarpment of Jos Plateau

--- Northern limit of tsetse fly

-·-·- Boundary of Nigeria

Map labels:

Lake Chad

BORNU

KUKAWA O

MAIDUGURI O

DAMATURU O

FUNE O

POTISKUM O

Gujba Plain

Biu Foothills

Yobe River

Gongola River

Komadugu River

HADEJIA O

BAUCHI O

JOS Plateau

Jos Plateau

Niger

KANO O

KATSINA O

ZARIA O

KADUNA

Kaduna River

SOKOTO

Sokoto River

SOKOTO O

BIRNIN KEBBI O

Rima River

BUSSA O

JEBBA O

BIDA O

Niger

Benue

12°N

10°N

12°E

10°E

8°E

6°E

0   50   100   150   200   250 miles

0   100   200   300   400 kilometres

There are in addition smaller sectors in south-eastern Sokoto, in the Jos Plateau and in Adamawa. The three major sectors are difficult to delimit, because within them the pastoral Fulani live side by side for at least part of the year with Hausa cultivators and settled Fulani, because the pastoral Fulani migrate seasonally, and lastly because, although the migration pattern has certain elements of regularity, it may change from year to year, according to variations in pastoral and water conditions, and according to changing relations with the settled peoples. Yet, despite the problems of delimitation, the groupings of Fulani exist, and in association exist the trackways, the pastures, the briefly occupied arable lands, the permanent Fulani villages, the temporary camps and, here and there, the hedges needed to protect crops from migrating herds. All these features lend a distinction to the landscape, which areas not occupied by pastoralists do not possess. Moreover, each of these regions possesses a combination of features attractive to pastoral Fulani settlement and migration in terms mainly of water supplies, pastures, markets for the exchange of dairy produce for grain, supplies of natron and salt, and protection from the ruling authorities. With regard to the last feature, the establishment of rule by the settled Fulani over most of Hausaland in the first quarter of the century has been of the greatest importance.

There are over 3 million Fulani speakers in Northern Nigeria, of whom more than 2 millions are in the Hausa provinces of Kano, Katsina, Sokoto and Zaria and in the adjoining western portion of Bornu. Of the 2 millions only 104,000 were recorded as 'cattle Fulani' in the printed version of the Northern Region census of 1952. Of these, 53,000 were in Sokoto Province, where Hopen[75], with access to more detailed records, calculated that there were 72,000 Fulbe n'ai or cattle Fulani in the same year. Allowing the same margin of error throughout this would give an estimate for the Region of some 150,000. Of these probably 60,000 are in the western sector, 70,000 in the central and 20,000 in the eastern. These totals include a small number of 'Busije' or sheep-herding Fulani recruited from cattle Fulani who have lost their stock. It is interesting to compare these figures with the estimate in *The Native Economies of Nigeria*[76] of 700,000 Fulani speakers of whom two-thirds depended mainly on pastoralism. In no case recorded by Hopen in Sokoto are the pastoral Fulani more than 6 per cent of the gross population, and they are dispersed in small groups over vast areas with no density higher than 4 per square mile (1·5 per sq km).

The pastoral Fulani do not depend on their livestock alone. The majority plant small plots of 'gero' or quick-growing pennisetum to provide additional support. Some plant extensive crops of gero, guinea corn, rice, groundnuts and beans and only a few have no arable holdings. Even these 'pure' nomadic pastoralists turn to agriculture from time to time. Pastoralism can only survive without agriculture where large herds are maintained. For most families (averaging 6 persons) in Sokoto the average herd of 30 head of cattle is insufficient to provide them with a living without some grain. If a large herd is re-established the family may return to pure pastoralism. Losses by disease must be 'made up' by cultivation. Most Fulani are now permanently settled either as Fulbe ladde, 'bush' Fulani or settled cultivators keeping some livestock, or as Fulbe siire or 'town' Fulani. Most of the last group belong to the Torobe clan from amongst whom came the leaders of the Fulani revolt at the beginning of the 19th century.

The three Fulani sectors are almost all Sudanic: only in their extreme northern fringes is the rainy season barely $2\frac{1}{2}$ months so that Sahelian conditions marginal for cultivation prevail. Moisture supplies throughout most of the area of the Fulani sectors are sufficient for agriculture. Pastures exist on lands as yet unclaimed by cultivators or uncultivable or lacking a dry season water supply to support a settled population. In the last case until the advent of deep wells or bores, nomadism alone makes possible the use of such lands. In the western sector are the great undulating plains of Sokoto with few perennial streams and interrupted by conical and flat-topped hills rising a few hundred feet above the general level. Regular bush burning helps to maintain wet season pastures, but the Fulani are anxious to preserve pastures, even of coarse grasses, rather than destroy them. Much of the burning is undertaken by Hausa cultivators who set fire to crop stubble to make cultivation easier, or create fire lines in the upland grasses to assist in their hunting. In the flood-plain of the Sokoto river, and to a lesser extent in the flood-plain of the Niger, are grasses of great value as dry season pasture. The numerous islands of the Sokoto river flood-plain provide isolated pastures where cattle may be kept away from crops, but in the rest of the flood-plain there is competition with the cultivator for land, and strips of arable land isolate long stretches of river and flood-plain from the pastoralist. The central sector is part Sokoto plains and part a dissected hill zone on the western 'edge' of the high plains of Hausaland at about 2000 feet (610 metres) above sea-level. Here the great forest reserve of the Sokoto–Katsina boundary is a remnant of the former extensive forests of the no-man's-land between Zamfara and Katsina, where herders could find pasture for their animals away from the croplands. To the east, within Katsina and northern Zaria Provinces, there are patches of uncultivated ground affording pastures between the extensive areas of arable. Some of these occur in troughs with wet season swamps between the dune remnants of a former southward extension of the Sahara, and are used mainly during the dry season. The eastern sector consists of similar pasture lands between former dunes in Hadejia and of the former 'Great Forest' in the west of the Chad basin marking a no-man's-land between the Hausa states and Bornu.[77] In the latter area a plain at about 1000 feet (300 metres) above sea-level slopes gently down to the north-east. It is only slightly incised by the broad troughs of the Yobe and Gana rivers, and its surface is interrupted only by dead dunes orientated WSW–ENE, in between which impermeable layers of clay in the troughs support either wet season swamps or 'tabkis', the small ponds invaluable for watering cattle, particularly where they contain water during the dry season. On uncultivated land trees with a canopy between 30 and 40 feet (9–12 metres) in height, thorns and medium height grasses are predominant. Acacias are especially common and many of these provide dry season fodder.

The Fulani entered the western and central sectors as early as the 13th century.

The Torobe clan of settled Fulani established themselves mainly in the north-west, in Gobir, and the pastoral Fulani gradually penetrated into the regions they now occupy. In the last quarter of the 18th century the ruler of Gobir raided the Fulani settlements and camps in his territory, and some of the pastoralists fled eastwards to Bornu. In 1804 the Fulani rebellion broke out and the result was the creation by 1809 of a Fulani empire in Hausaland consisting of two king-doms – a western with the Niger as its central axis and an eastern consisting of Hausaland, Adamawa and the former western districts of Bornu. Within the new possessions of the settled or Torobe Fulani, the pastoral Fulani received new privileges and changed their way of life. To the east, in the frontier zone between Hausaland and Bornu, districts taken by the Fulani were settled by a distinct group of Bororo'en pastoralists with larger herds and favouring migration over greater distances. These districts were in part retaken by Bornu and in part were in dispute during the 1830s. Some Bororo abandoned their pastures. By 1846, however, the Fulani rulers of Hausaland and the rulers of Bornu agreed on peace terms, and eventually the Shehu of Bornu gave grazing rights to the Bororo from the gates of Kukawa to the gates of Potiskum.[78] Before the Fulani jihad the pastoralists were subject people who lived in large and mobile camps, wore mainly hides and skins, and had only a little contact with the agriculturalists. After the jihad the pastoralists were protected by the ruling group, except in Bornu, where grazing rights had to be obtained from the Shehu. Slaves became available in large numbers to plant grains at a permanent location to which the pastoralists could always return. Except in the western region, where there was a need for defence against the independent state of Kebbi, and slave agricultural settlements were walled, the migrant groups could afford to split into smaller units, were able to develop better trading contacts with cultivators, and could afford to wear cotton cloth. In 1887 the pastoralists suffered enormous losses in cattle from an epidemic of rinderpest. Only a few groups in south-western Bornu, dwelling away from the main trade routes, were able to avoid the disease. By 1908 the British government of Northern Nigeria began to introduce schemes to gain administrative control of the migrants, the most important of which was the introduction of effective collection of taxes. In addition they sought to elimin-ate slavery, thus forcing Fulani families either to cease cultivation or to combine cultivation with cattle rearing. The tendency to do the latter has been encouraged by the tax policy introduced in 1915. Under the new system taxes were collected by chiefs who were paid a percentage of the collection and who established per-manent settlements in the areas occupied during the rainy season. By 1918 the number of such permanent villages where taxes were collected had increased, and attempts were made to define Fulani village areas and the limits of their rainy season pastures. In the 1920s non-Fulani immigrants began to settle in the Fulani villages and increased the area under cultivation. In such communities many Fulani have ceased to migrate, derive only a small proportion of their incomes from keeping livestock, and have come increasingly under either Hausa or Kanuri influence.[79] In some cases large permanent villages are surrounded by a ring of fixed hamlets which mark the former temporary camps of minor chiefs which were established around the large camp of powerful Fulani leaders.

The few pastoral Fulani groups who still migrate move by small family units which tend to come together in lineages or groups of 'friendly' families during the dry season, when pastures are short, and to disperse during the rains. In some cases rainy season pastures are established near the permanent agricultural village where the gero is planted so that the family stays together. In other cases the family is split in order that some members may cultivate longer-growing crops, and the others may take the cattle to pastures isolated from crops. The cattle are then brought on to the cropland immediately after harvest to eat the crop refuse and provide manure. Migration is most developed in the western and eastern sectors. In the centre there is less migration and a much more important contact with cultivators. In the densely populated portions of the Hausa agricultural areas cattle lanes, hedged to protect the crops, give access from wet season pasture on well-drained scrubland or, in the north, to dry season pastures on the clay of the lower ground, in portions of uncultivated fadama or floodland, and on the croplands. The Hausa cultivators in many cases offer gifts to pastoralists willing to graze their cattle on harvested cropland. Others, near the towns, specialize in fattening cattle for market by feeding them with groundnut tops, bean straw, guinea corn and bran. In turn the Fulani value the contact not only for feeding livestock during the dry season, but also for the opportunity to sell milk products for grain, salt and household material and to purchase bran and natron for their livestock. In recent years another valued service has been that of the Veterinary Department, particularly in its provision of inoculation against rinderpest. In the western and eastern sectors the migrant families still occupy the traditional westward facing homestead, with its semi-circular back fence giving protection against the east and north-east wind, the 'cold' and dusty harmattan. The womenfolk live in shelters at the rear, the calves are attached to a rope in the centre and the men sleep in the front. In the eastern sector Stenning distinguishes three types of movement:[80]

1) Transhumance, or movement southwards in the dry season and northwards in the rains.
2) Migratory drift, or change in the orbit of transhumance.
3) Migration proper or movement away from the normal orbit altogether to an area hitherto uncrossed and known only by repute.

Movement amongst the Bororo'en is nearly continuous and is little impeded by cropland, for there is little demand by agriculturalists as yet for land in western Bornu. In consequence there is less contact with cultivators than exists even in western Sokoto. Stenning distinguishes four physical regions of importance in the movements of livestock:[81]

1) The Gana river zone with wet season pastures and some dry season water supply available from holes dug in the dry river bed.

2) The central Fune–Damaturu zone of wet season grazings with dry camp sites on former sand dunes.
3) The Gyba Plain of dry season grazings, unusable during the rains because of tsetse fly infestation.
4) The Biu foothills zone with standing water and some grazing throughout the dry season.

The movement between northern and southern grazings is much more developed in Bornu than elsewhere. Animals must frequently be watered from wells between 6 and 60 feet (2–18 metres) in depth. During the rains the arduous work of hauling up water in calabashes is avoided, but by then cattle may be infested with ticks, and in some areas tsetse fly appear. In the western sector orbits are more between river and uplands than north and south.[82] In 'rumirde', the rainy season proper (July–September) there is abundant upland pasture, but cattle must move a little every 3 to 10 days in order to reduce the risks of foot infection and fly-borne disease. In 'yawirde', the hot humid season after the rains (October–November) the herds move on to croplands as the harvests take place, and then by the end of the season some move down to the flood-plain of the Sokoto river. In 'dabirde', the cool dry season (December–February) cattle graze on farmlands and in the Sokoto flood-plain. In 'chedirde' the hot dry season (March–April) pasture is short and there is little milk available. Some families move as far south as the Niger despite the danger there of liver-fluke. Finally in 'setinirde' the stormy period before the rains proper (May–June) the first rains arrive, some fresh grass appears and cattle begin to move on to higher ground. Some stay on islands in the Niger in order to avoid an early return and the possibility of damaging young crops.[83]

The average pastoral Fulani family has only a small income derived from the sale mainly of milk and milk products, and occasionally from the sale of livestock. Meat is eaten only on pastoral and ceremonial occasions. Cotton is bought in the local markets, and the womenfolk spin yarn and then pay Hausa weavers to manufacture cloth. Some are forced to sell livestock in order to pay their taxes. Others try to grow more grain in order to have a surplus for market. *The Native Economies of Nigeria* estimated that cattle sales appeared either to equal or to be greater than natural increase so that the herds of pastoral Fulani tended to be nearly stable.[84] Here and there some increase in stock has been effected by medical improvements, but as yet there has been little attempt to control breeding and thus improve the quality of the animals. Controlled ranching to make the fullest use of northern pastures would seem a possible solution, but would be very difficult to organize in view of the present patterns of migration. Moreover, the trend is towards increased grain production and the splitting of the family into herders, undertaking only a limited seasonal movement, and cultivators. Indeed if the estimates by Hopen and in the census are fair, then the numbers of pastoral Fulani today are so small that there is every reason, in view of the other evidence presented, to suspect that they are dwindling and may soon disappear. In their place is appearing a group of 'mixed' farmers holding both cattle and croplands and for at least a small part of the year using manure to maintain soil fertility, and for the rest of the year maintaining their cattle on more localized areas of pasture.

BIBLIOGRAPHICAL NOTES

[1] R. J. Harrison Church, *West Africa*, London, 5th ed., 1966.

[2] H. Clapperton, *Journal of a Second Expedition into the Interior of Africa*, London, 1829.

[3] J. Bertho, Note Accompagnant la Carte de la Répartition de la Population dans la Zone Côtière Comprise entre le Niger et le Volta, *Premier Conférence International des Africanistes de L'Ouest*, Compte Rendue, Tome II, 1951, pp. 115-17.

[4] S. Johnson, *The History of the Yorubas*, London, 1921, pp. 12-14.

[5] P. C. Lloyd, The Traditional Political System of the Yoruba, *Southwestern Journal of Anthropology*, **10**, 1954, pp. 366-84.

[6] For a study of social structure and land tenure, see:
R. Galletti, K. D. S. Baldwin and I. O. Dina, *Nigerian Cocoa Farmers*, 1956, Chap. 5, 'The Social Conditions', pp. 67-131.

[7] C. D. Forde, *The Yoruba-Speaking Peoples of South-Western Nigeria*. London, 1951, p. 56.

[8] A. L. Mabogunje, *The Changing Pattern of Rural Settlement and Rural Economy in Egba Division, South-Western Nigeria*, unpub. M.A. thesis presented to the University of London in 1958.
A. L. Mabogunje and M. B. Gleave, Changing Agricultural Landscape in Southern Nigeria – The Example of Egba Division, 1850-1950, *Nigerian Geographical Journal*, **7**, 1964, pp. 1-15.

[9] M. D. W. Jeffreys, *The Awka Report*, unpub. MS., 1931.
See also D. Forde and G. I. Jones, *The Ibo and Ibibio-Speaking Peoples of South-Eastern Nigeria*, London, 1950.

[10] W. R. G. Horton, The Ohu System of Slavery in a Northern Ibo Village Group, *Africa*, **24**, 1954, pp. 311-36.

[11] W. B. Morgan, The 'Grassland Towns' of the Eastern Region of Nigeria, *Transactions and Papers, The Institute of British Geographers*, **23**, 1957, pp. 213-24.

[12] R. K. Udo, Disintegration of Nucleated Settlement in Eastern Nigeria, *Geographical Review*, **55**, 1965, pp. 53-67.

[13] *Preliminary Census of Agriculture*, Lagos, 1951.

[14] For discussion of population distribution and soil quality see: R. K. Udo, Patterns of Population Distribution and Settlement in Eastern Nigeria, *Nigerian Geographical Journal*, **6**, 1963, pp. 73-88.

[15] R. C. Abraham, *The Tiv People*, Lagos, 1933 (2nd ed. 1940).
L. and P. Bohannan, *The Tiv of Central Nigeria*, London, 1953.
P. Bohannan, *Tiv Farm and Settlement*, Colonial Research Series, **15**, 1954.

[16] P. Bohannan, op. cit, pp. 43-46.

[17] K. M. Buchanan and J. C. Pugh, *Land and People in Nigeria*, London, 1955.

[18] G. W. G. Briggs, Soil Deterioration in the Southern Districts of Tiv Division, *Farm and Forest*, **2**, 1941, pp. 8-12.

[19] T. A. M. Nash, The Anchau Settlement Scheme, *Farm and Forest*, **2**, 1941, pp. 76-82.
See below pp. 660-1.

[20] P. Bohannan, op. cit., pp. 8–14.
L. and P. Bohannan, op. cit., pp. 50–51 and 54–57.
See pp. 31 and 39.

[21] See the invaluable study in P. Bohannan, op. cit., pp. 16–20.

[22] The Leverhulme Trust, *The West African Commission, 1938–39*, 1943, pp. 23–24.

[23] P. Bohannan, op. cit., p. 19, botanical names of 'agom' and 'aper' not given.

[24] P. Bohannan, op. cit., p. 3.

[25] H. Enjalbert, Paysans Noirs: Les Kabré du Nord-Togo, *Cahiers d'Outre-Mer*, **34**, 1956, pp. 137–80. This article has provided the greater part of the material used in the essay on the Kabrai.

[26] J. Dresch, Paysans Montagnards du Dahomey et du Cameroun, *Bulletin de l'Association de Géographes Français*, **222–3**, 1952, pp. 2–9.
Other useful works include:
J. C. Froelich, Densité de la Population et Méthodes de Culture Chez les Kabré du Nord-Togo. *Comptes Rendus du Congrès International de Géographie*, Lisbon, 1949, Tome IV, pp. 168-80.
J. C. Froelich, Généralités sur les Kabré du Nord-Togo, *Bulletin, Institut Français d'Afrique Noire*, 1949, pp. 77–106.
D. V. Sassoon, The Cabrais of Togoland, *Geographical Magazine*, 1950, pp. 339–41.
The change to less intensive systems of production in areas of lower population density is a common phenomenon in Africa. See R. M. Netting, Household Organisation and Intensive Agriculture: the Kofyar Case, *Africa*, **35**(4), 1965, pp. 422–9. For general discussion see E. Boserup, *The Conditions of Agricultural Growth*, London, 1965, pp. 66–69.

[27] J. C. Froelich, La Tribu Konkomba du Nord-Togo, *Mémoires, Institut Français d'Afrique Noire*, **37**, 1954.

[28] D. Tait, *The Konkomba of Northern Ghana*, London, 1961.

[29] J. C. Froelich, La Tribu Konkomba du Nord-Togo, op. cit., pp. 17–18.

[30] Report on Mangrove Swamp Clearance in Sierra Leone, *Proceedings of the 2nd Inter-African Soils Conference*, Leopoldville, 1954, vol. II, pp. 1095–7.

[31] D. Paulme, Des Riziculteurs Africains: les Baga, *Les Cahiers d'Outre-Mer*, **10**, 1957, pp. 257–78.
D. Paulme, Structures Sociales en Pays Baga, *Bulletin, Institut Français d'Afrique Noire*, **18**, ser. B, 1956, pp. 98–116.

[32] R. Portères, Un Problème d'Ethno-botanique: Relations entre Le Riz Flottant du Rio-Nunez et l'Origine Medinigérienne des Baga de la Guinée Française, *Journal d'Agriculture Tropicale et de Botanique Appliquée*, **2**, 1955, p. 538.
R. Portères, Historique sur les Premiers Echantillons d'Oryza glaberrima St. Recueillis en Afrique, ibid., 1955, pp. 535–7.
R. Portères, Linguistique et Migrations du Riz dans l'Ouest Africain, *Farm and Forest*, 1946.

[33] R. Portères, Les Riz Flottants de l'Espèce O. sativa L. et leurs possibilités d'Exploitation en Afrique, *Agronomie Tropicale*, **9–10**, 1946, pp. 467–503.

[34] D. Paulme, Des Riziculteurs Africains: les Baga, op. cit.

[35] Numerous studies have been made of the Bambara and their lands. An important early work was:
C. Monteil, *Les Bambara du Ségou et du Kaarta*, Paris, 1924.
A useful summary work with extensive bibliography is:
V. Paques, *Les Bambara*, Institut International Africain, Paris, 1954, on which this account is largely based.

[36] ... 'car la frontière telle que nous l'entendons n'a pas de sens pour le Noir. En effet les empires n'ont pas ambitionné de dominer sur telle ou telle région; ils se sont avant

tout donné pour but l'exploitation du plus grand nombre possible d'individus, abstraction faite des pays et des races', V. Paques, op. cit., p. 2.

[37] V. Paques, op. cit, p. 28.

[38] For discussion of rice cultivation see pp. 81–83, 109–10 and 121–2.

[39] See pp. 345–8.

[40] V. Paques, op. cit., p. 31.

[41] An excellent study of the Diawara is G. Boyer, Un Peuple de l'Ouest Soudanais, Les Diawara, *Mémoires, Institut Français d'Afrique Noire*, **29**, 1953.

[42] ibid., pp. 71–72.

[43] ibid., pp. 81–89.

[44] J. Daget, La Pêche dans le Delta Central du Niger, *Journal de la Société des Africanistes*, **19**, 1949, p. 1079.

[45] P. Malzy, Les Bozos du Niger et Leurs Modes de Pêche, *Bulletin, Institut Français d'Afrique Noire*, **8**, 1946, pp. 100–32.

[46] For a thorough account of the fish of the inland delta and the movements of the shoals, see J. Daget, Mémoires sur la Biologie des Poissons du Niger Moyen, I – Biologie et Croissance des Espèces du Genre Alestes, *Bulletin, Institut Français d'Afrique Noire*, **19**, 1952, pp. 191–225.

[47] ibid.

[48] J. Daget, La Pêche à Diafarabé, Étude Monographique, *Bulletin, Institut Français d'Afrique Noire*, **18**, ser. B, 1956, pp. 1–97.

[49] J. Gallais, La Vie Saisonnière au Sud du Lac Débo, *Cahiers d'Outre-Mer*, **11**, 1958, pp. 117–41.

[50] For ritual cultivation see M. Griaule and G. Dieterlen, L'Agriculture Rituelle des Bozo, *Journal de la Société des Africanistes*, **19**, 1949, pp. 209–22.

[51] Based on J. Dubourg, La Vie des Paysans Mossi: Le Village de Taghalla, *Cahiers d'Outre-Mer*, **10**, 1957, pp. 285–324.

[52] See E. F. Gautier, Les Mossi, Chap. V, *Afrique Noire Occidentale*, Paris, 1943, pp. 131–50.
For an excellent description of Mossi villages, life and trade see E. Baillaud, *Sur les Routes du Soudan*, Toulouse, 1902, pp. 233–58.

[53] N. Leneuf, Les Sols du Secteur Cotonnier de la Haute-Volta, *Proceedings, 2nd Inter-African Soils Conference*, Leopoldville, 1954, vol. II, pp. 971–91.

[54] J. Dubourg, op. cit.

[55] See A. J. Duhart, Rapport sur l'Etat Actuel de la Conservation des Sols en Territoire de la Haute-Volta, *Proceedings, 2nd Inter-African Soils Conference*, Leopoldville, 1954, vol. II, pp. 1291–1300.

[56] J. Dubourg, op. cit.

[57] E. F. Gautier, op. cit.

[58] J. Rouch, *Les Songhay*, Paris, 1954.

[59] R. Mauny, Notes d'Archéologie au Sujet de Gao, *Bulletin, Institut Français d'Afrique Noire*, **13**, 1951, pp. 837–52.

[60] Notes on the Songhay, Notes et Documents, *Bulletin, Institut Français d'Afrique Noire*, **16**, 1954, pp. 178–84.

[61] C. Grandet, Les Sédentaires du Cercle de Tombouctou (Territoire du Soudan), *Cahiers d'Outre-Mer*, **10**, 1957, pp. 234–56.
R. Portères, Les Riz Flottants de l'Espèce O. sativa L. et leurs possibilités d'Exploitation en Afrique, op. cit., pp. 467–503. For a study of cultivation in the inland Niger delta, see C. Grandet, La Vie Rurale dans le Cercle de Goundam (Niger Soudanais), *Cahiers d'Outre-Mer*, **11**, 1958, pp. 25–46.

[62] J. Rouch, op. cit., pp. 21–22.
J. Rouch, Contribution à l'Histoire des Songhay, *Mémoires, Institut Français d'Afrique Noire*, Part II, **29**, 1953, p. 166.

[63] J. Rouch, Les Sorkawa pêcheurs itinérants du moyen Niger, *Africa*, **20**, 1950, pp. 5–25.

[64] For a Hausa history see:
E. W. Bovill, *Caravans of the Old Sahara*, London, 1933.
E. W. Bovill, *The Golden Trade of the Moors*, London, 1958.
Flora L. Shaw (Lady Lugard), *A Tropical Dependency*, London, 1905.
H. R. Palmer, *Sudanese Memoirs*, Lagos, 1928.
H. R. Palmer, *The Bornu Sahara and the Sudan*, London, 1936.

[65] H. R. Palmer, 1936, op. cit., pp. 37–39.

[66] Excellent accounts of the vegetation are available in:
R. W. J. Keay, *An Outline of Nigerian vegetation*, 2nd edition, Lagos, 1953, pp. 26–34.
D. R. Rosevear, *Checklist and Atlas of Nigerian Mammals*, London, 1953, pp. 19–32.

[67] M. G. Smith, *The Economy of Hausa Communities of Zaria*, A Report to the Colonial Social Science Research Council, Colonial Office, 1955, pp. 102–7.

[68] C. D. Forde and R. Scott, *The Native Economies of Nigeria*, London, 1946, p. 145.
D. Whittlesey, Kano: a Sudanese Metropolis, *Geographical Review*, **27**, 1937, pp. 117–99.
See also above pp. 55–56.

[69] C. D. Forde and R. Scott, op. cit., p. 146.

[70] H. Barth, *Travels and Discoveries in North and Central Africa, 1849–1855*, 5 vols, London, 1857–58.

[71] See below pp. 511–14.

[72] M. G. Smith, op. cit., p. 2.

[73] In addition to Smith, op. cit., see also:
C. K. Meek, *The Northern Tribes of Nigeria*, vol. I, London, 1925, pp. 119–33.
The Leverhulme Trust, *The West African Commission, 1938–39*, 1943, pp. 21–22.

[74] G. Nicolas, Un Village Haoussa de la République du Niger: Tassao Haoussa, *Cahiers d'Outre-Mer*, **13**, 1960, pp. 421–50.

[75] C. E. Hopen, *The Pastoral Fulbe Family in Gwandu*, London, 1958, pp. 4–5.

[76] C. D. Forde and R. Scott, op. cit., p. 200.

[77] D. J. Stenning, *Savannah Nomads*, London, 1959, p. 26.

[78] D. J. Stenning, op. cit., pp. 64–70.

[79] ibid., pp. 81–97.

[80] ibid., p. 206.

[81] ibid., pp. 209–11.

[82] C. E. Hopen, op. cit., pp. 17–39.

[83] ibid., pp. 33–39.

[84] C. D. Forde and R. Scott, op. cit., p. 209.

PART TWO

CHAPTER 8

The Invasion of West Africa by Alien Peoples and the Introduction of Modern Commercialism

North African contacts

Even before the 15th century, when the Portuguese undertook the series of voyages which revealed the west coast of Africa to Europe, West Africa had been invaded by Berber, Moorish and Arab peoples who entered as pastoralists, traders or conquerors. The Sudanic lands had become a part of the Islamic world before the first European landed on the West African shore. Labouret suggests that the introduction of the camel into North Africa, as the power of Rome was declining, gave the Saharan Berbers the mobility required to attack the surrounding lands.[1] Berber or 'white' rulers appeared for a time in the ancient state of Ghana, and dynasties of mixed Berber and Negro origin have been suggested in Mali and Bornu. Travellers like El Bekri, El Idrisi, El Omari, Ibn Battuta and Ibn Khaldun wrote accounts of the lands of Ghana, Mali and Songhay, whilst a West African, Abderrahman es Sadi, born in Timbuktu in 1596, wrote a history of the Sudan.[2] Through Berber and Arab contacts a trade was established with North Africa. Gold, slaves, ivory, goatskins and gum were exported across the Sahara in exchange for salt, cloth, beads, copper and metal ware and books. By the year 1057 Ibn Yacin had united the Western Sahara, as far south as the Senegal river, into the Empire of Almoravid or of the 'marabouts', which by the 12th century had been extended to include Muslim Spain. An Arab architect from Granada built a mosque at Gao and another at Timbuktu at the beginning of the 14th century.[3] North African contacts brought trade and greater wealth to the Sudanic states. They influenced the organization of those states and the building of towns, and may indirectly also have influenced the development of the sub-Guinean and Guinean states. From North Africa writing and Islam were introduced into the northern half of West Africa, and a number of plants, including varieties of cotton, citrus fruits and even maize. The North African peoples resided in West Africa only in small groups, many of which intermingled with the Negro peoples. They established no conquests linked directly with states across the Sahara. Their influence was localized mainly in a few Sudanic states, and although it brought an important political revolution, its economic effect was small. Camel transport across the Sahara limited traffic to a few commodities of high value. Lady Lugard quotes Ibn Khaldun's claim that 12,000 laden camels passed through the oasis of Tekada to Mali every year in the middle of the 14th century[4], thus conveying approximately 16,000 tons of

379

merchandise. The figure appears high, for the supplies of water in desert oases and the availability of pasture imposed limitations unknown by sea-transport. Moreover, transport by camel was more costly than by ship. The export of agricultural produce, which has produced so profound an economic change in the present century, was only possible by sea.

The Portuguese discoveries

Despite Genoese and French claims to early discovery of West Africa, it was the Portuguese who first organized a series of voyages, by which the whole coastline was made known, and from which regular trade was developed, and settlements established. At the end of the 14th century Portugal had asserted its independence, and continued the war against Islam by the capture of Ceuta in Morocco in 1415. Prince Henry, a younger son of King John, was appointed governor of the town, and made Duke of the province of Algarve in Portugal. Prince Henry was well placed as governor of Ceuta to obtain knowledge of the Moorish lands and of the regions beyond. In Algarve he established a small town at Cape St Vincent near the port of Lagos. 'According to common belief, the Infant purposed to make of it an especial mart town for merchants. And this was to the end that all ships that passed from the East to the West, should be able to take their bearings and to get provisions and pilots there, as at Cadiz. . . .'[5] Henry sent out a number of expeditions to search for Guinea, in order firstly to add to knowledge, secondly to find new markets, thirdly to find the limits of Moorish power, fourthly to find if there were any Christian rulers who might become allies of Portugal, and finally to spread the Christian faith. Madeira was colonized in 1420, but had been discovered before 1367.[6] Cape Bojador, the southern limit of previous European navigation, was rounded in 1434, the Azores in 1439, and Cape Blanco and Arguin Island discovered in 1443. To a certain extent the voyages were stimulated by trade rivalry, for French and Castilian traders were active in the Canary Islands, and Castilian merchant ships took advantage of Portuguese discoveries on the west coast of Africa to proceed there for trade. By 1446 the Portuguese had passed the southern limits of the Sahara and reached Cape Verde and the Rio Grande or Geba river. By the time of Henry's death in 1460, Sierra Leone had been discovered and possibly Cape Palmas. The building of a fort on Arguin Island was begun in 1448, and textiles, corn, horses and metal goods were exchanged with the Moors for civet, malagueta pepper, gum, gold, salt and slaves. The trade of Guinea became sufficiently lucrative to attract Fernão Gomes, a Lisbon merchant, to obtain, in 1469, a five-year monopoly beyond the Cape Verde Islands, providing he explored nearly 400 miles of new coastline each year. This contract was later extended to 1475, by which year the Equator had been crossed, the islands of Formosa (Fernando Po), São Tomé, Ano Bomo (Annobon) and Príncipe discovered, and virtually the whole coastline of West Africa made known.

Portuguese trade

Between 1475 and 1479 Portugal and Castile were at war, but by the Treaty of Alcaçovas, signed at the conclusion, Portugal recognized Castile's claim to the Canaries, whilst Castile agreed not to dispute Portugal's possession of the West African coast, the Azores, Madeira and the Cape Verde Islands. Castilian inter-lopers continued to trade in West Africa until after the discovery of the Americas and the Treaty of Tordesillas in 1494. Portugal, however, had at least the *de jure* monopoly in the last two decades of the 15th century, and established a number of trading posts on islands and peninsulas, giving some security against attack. Santiago in the Cape Verde Islands, discovered a little before 1460, was colonized, and the port of Praia constructed. Special trading privileges were accorded to the colonists to encourage settlement, and trading posts were established on the mainland at Joal, Portudal, Rio Fresco, Beziguiche, Sierra Leone, Farim, and on the Rio Grande and River Gambia.[7] Attempts to found a fort at the mouth of the Senegal followed, but the river proved difficult to navigate. Advances inland by the Senegal route, in order to establish a post at the market of Oudane, and in order to mine the gold of Bambouk or 'Wangara', failed.[8] The Gambia, easier to navigate, provided the best line of penetration into the interior and the richest trade. Santiago's sphere of interest extended as far south as Cape Palmas. From there as far east as the Volta, trading was dominated by the settlement of El Mina. The discovery of the gold production of the present-day Ashanti during the monopoly of Fernão Gomes led to the termination of that monopoly and the construction of the castle of São Jorge de Mina in 1482.[9] El Mina castle became a fortified warehouse, the chief supplier of gold to Portugal, the residence of a royal governor and a garrison. At the beginning of the 16th century the Portu-guese also built forts at Axim and Shama, and created a system of alliances with local communities by 'gifts' – the 'dação' or 'dash' of modern parlance.[10] Slaves were imported from São Tomé to headload textiles, and cloth was brought in exchange for gold. To the east, Benin was first reached in 1483, and trading relations established two years later. Initially Benin was attractive because of its red peppers. Trading posts were established on the present Ologbo Creek and later at Gwato on the Benin River, and in 1486 Christian missionaries were allowed to enter and build a church.[11] The island of São Tomé was made a Portuguese captaincy in 1485, and was populated by Jews, convicts and exiles from Portugal. The island of Fernando Po was occupied about 1493. Settlements were established on the east coast, where they were deprived of the breeze from the open sea and subject to mosquito infestation. Disease gave the island a bad reputation, a reputation which Benin also acquired. With the developing prefer-ence for East Indian pepper in the Portuguese market, the Portuguese settle-ments in the Benin area were reduced after 1506. Instead, settlement concen-trated on the island of São Tomé which enjoyed a good reputation for health, became the leading slave market of the western coast of Africa and a plantation sugar producer. Above all São Tomé had the advantage of being in the belt of

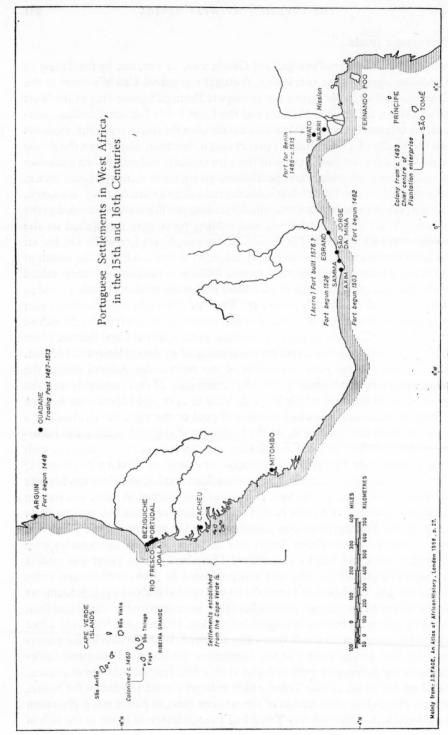

Portuguese Settlements in West Africa, in the 15th and 16th Centuries

SÃO ANTÃO ⌀
CAPE VERDE
ISLANDS

⌀ Bôa Vista

Colonised c.1460
RIBEIRA GRANDE ⌀ São Thiago

Fogo ⌀

ARGUIN ●
Fort begun 1448

● OUADANE
Trading Post 1487-1513

Settlements established
from the Cape Verde is.

BEZIGUICHE
PORTUDAL
JOALA
RIO FRESCO

CACHEU

MITOMBO ●

[Accra] Fort built 1576 ?

EGRAND ●
Fort begun 1526

SAMMA ●
SÃO JORGE ●
DA MINA
AXIM ●
Fort begun 1503
Fort begun 1482

Port for Benin
1486–c.1515

GWATO ●
WARRI ● Mission

FERNANDO POO ⌀

PRÍNCIPE ⌀
Colony from c.1493
Chief centre of
Plantation enterprise

SÃO TOMÉ ⌀

16°N
4°N
8°W
0°
6°E

MILES
0 50 100 200 300 400

KILOMETRES
0 100 200 300 400 500 600 700

Mainly from: J.D.FAGE, An Atlas of African History, London 1958. p. 27.

Figure 8.1

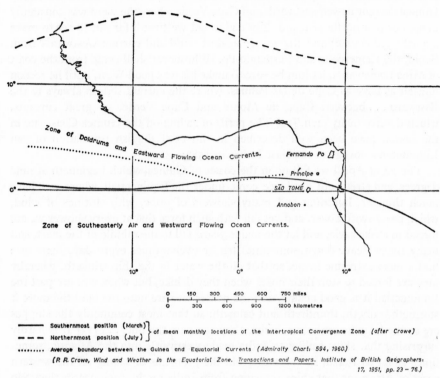

São Tomé – Location in relation to the Intertropical Convergence Zone
and the boundary between the Guinea and Equatorial Currents

Figure 8.2

prevailing south-east winds, offering a quick westward and homeward passage to shipping. Fernando Po was too far into the bight and to leeward of the south-westerly belt. Through São Tomé were imported the manillas and cowrie shells, which were to serve as currency until the present century.

Problems of navigation

The discovery of the route to India in 1497 brought a decline in interest in West African trade except in Mina gold, São Tomé sugar, and slaves, generally from the shores east of the Volta. Navigation was difficult. From March to September the rainy season with its storms was avoided, the gentler airs of the North-East trade or 'tread' winds, i.e. of constant direction, were preferred. Thus only one voyage could be made a year. Ships set out in September or October, taking three or four weeks to reach the Gambia, and sometimes longer, depending on the number of calls. With numerous stopping points en route, a vessel might take three months to reach the Gold Coast, and begin the voyage home in February or

March. The problem was in the return voyage, after two months or more trading, frequently with a number of the crew disabled by sickness, and against the north-east wind. Points of especial difficulty were: off Cape Palmas where the strong Guinea current flowed eastwards; off Cape Verde where the wind was constantly in the north or north-east, and ships had to sail westwards far out to sea to make a northward course; and the voyage against wind and current westwards from Benin, the Cameroons and Fernando Po. 'Whosoever shall come from the coast of Mina homewards, let him be sure to make his way good West, until he reckon himself as farre as Cape de las Palmas, where the currant setteth always to the Eastward . . . between Cape de Monte and Cape Verde, go great currants, which deceive many men.'[12] The perils of sailing off the Guinea Coast late in the season have been well described in the 1598 English translation of van Linschoten's voyage to the East Indies in 1583:

'The 24 of Aprill we fell upon the coaste of Guinea, which beginneth at nine degrees, and stretcheth until wee come under the Equinoctiall, where wee have much thunder, lightning and many showers of raine, with stormes of wind, which passe swiftly over, and yet fall with such force that at every shower we are forced to strike sayle, and let the maine yeard fall to the middle of the mast, and many times cleave down, sometimes ten or twelve times every day: there wee find a most extreame heate, so that all the water in the ship stinketh, whereby men are forced to stop their noses when they drinke, but when wee are past the Equinoctiall it is good againe, and the nearer wee are unto the land the more it stormeth, raineth, thundreth and calmeth: so that most commonly the shippes are at the least two monthes before they can pass the line. . . .'[13] It is hardly surprising that ships sailing to India made westwards into the Atlantic, some-times as far as Brazil, in order to avoid the problems of sailing off the western coast of Africa, or that ships returning from India rarely came nearer than São Tomé. The Guinea Coast was thus bypassed, and did not provide intermediate ports for victualling ships en route to the Cape of Good Hope.

The 'interlopers'

Despite the small number of products offered by West African trading, vessels of the other European sea powers sought to compete with the Portuguese. Guinea supplied approximately one-tenth of the world's gold supply[14], and large numbers of slaves. If the Portuguese preferred Asian pepper, West African peppers were still an attractive commodity to other European peoples, less well provided with spices. During the 16th century voyages by the English and French became increasingly frequent, and by the end of the century they were joined by the Dutch, Brandenburgers, Danes and Swedes. It was during the 16th century that the expansion of the West African slave trade began, due to the heavy demand for labour in the plantations and mines of the Spanish possessions in America. The slave trade became more lucrative than the gold traffic, and provided the chief cargoes of the coast for over two centuries. In 1580 Portugal was brought under Spanish rule, and did not become independent again until 1640. The Dutch revolted against Spanish rule in 1572, and extended their war to the Spanish and Portuguese colonies. By 1642 they had taken all the Gold Coast forts, together with Arguin, Gorée and São Tomé, and created colonies of sugar planters in Brazil, who were supplied with slave labour from Africa. In 1648 the Portuguese recaptured São Tomé, and six years later finally drove the Dutch from Brazil. However, the Dutch retained their hold on many of the most profitable sources of slaves in West Africa, and developed an export trade to the Spanish colonies in America. The French and English likewise acquired colonies in America, and an interest in the slave trade. Like the Spanish and Portuguese before them, they sought a monopoly in the trade of their colonies, and therefore tried to establish trading posts in West Africa. All the powers concerned created, chiefly in the 17th century, trading companies with exclusive privileges. Thus in 1618 James I gave a charter to the 'Company of Adventurers of London trading into Africa', which sent ships to the Gambia. With Jobson's voyage of 1620, however, 'the golden bubble of the untold wealth to be had for the asking was pricked for ever'.[15] In 1631 the English built a fort at Cormantine on the Gold Coast, but did not establish Fort James on the Gambia until 1664. In 1634 and 1635 monopoly trading rights were given by the French Government to three companies, who divided the west coast of Africa between them. The French concentrated on the coast of Upper Guinea north of Cape Palmas, particularly at the mouth of the Senegal, where St Louis was founded in 1659. In 1677 Arguin and Gorée were taken from the Dutch, and Gorée became the French naval headquarters. By 1713 the French became the strongest power in Upper Guinea, although rivalled by the English on the Gambia, and by numerous competitors on the 'Windward Coast' (Gorée to Sherbro Island – the coast of the 'Rivières du Sud').

Trade in the 17th century

On the Gold and Slave coasts of Lower Guinea, the Dutch West Indies Company and the English Royal African Company struggled to control the more profitable trade in gold and slaves. Towards the close of the 17th century the Dutch held eleven forts on the Gold Coast, including El Mina Castle taken from the Portuguese in 1637. The English held ten, including Cape Coast Castle taken from the Dutch in 1664. These forts were interspersed, so that Dutch and English forts were frequently close to one another, competing at the various trading points frequented by the middlemen – the coastal tribes. Of the remaining interests, the Swedes had been removed by 1657, the Danes concentrated their trading mainly east of Accra, whilst the Brandenburgers held two forts in the west between 1685 and 1709. The concentration of forts on the Gold Coast was produced by the greater profit in trade to be obtained there. However, it was also fortunate for the traders that the conditions were somewhat healthier and less

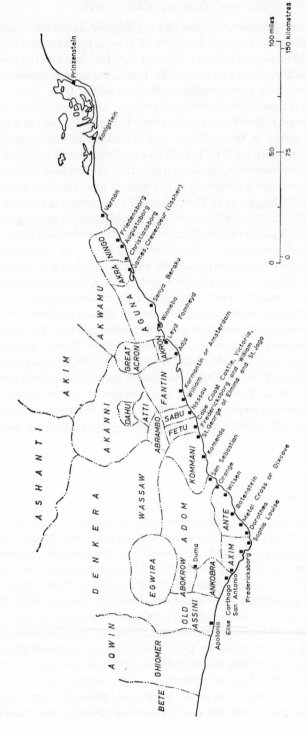

Forts of Ghana

Prinzenstein

Königstein

Vernon

Friedensborg
Augustaborg
Christiansborg
James, Crevecoeur (Ussher)

Senya Beraku

Wimneba

Leyd Fomheyd

Adja

Kormantin or Amsterdam

William

Nassau

Cape Coast Castle, Victoria,
Fredericksborg and William

St. George of Elmina and St. Jago

Komenda

San Sebastian

Orange

Witsen

Botenstein

Metal Cross or Dixcove

Dorothea

Sophia Louisa

Duma

Elise Carthago
San Antonio
Fredericksborg

Apollonia

PRINZENSTEIN KÖNIGSTEIN VERNON NINGO AKRA (AKRA) AKWAMU AKIM AGUNA AKRON FANTIN AKRON GREAT ACRON ATTI DAHU ABRAMBO SABU FETU KOMMANI AKANNI ASHANTI DENKERA WASSAW ADOM ABOKROW OLD ANTE AXIM ANKOBRA ASSINI EGWIRA AOWIN GHIOMER BETE

—————— Approximate boundaries of States and Tribal Areas at the beginning of the 18th century,
adapted from "A Map of the Gold Coast from Issini to Alampi" by D'Anville, 1729.

◼ Forts from "Forts of the Gold Coast Past and Present" in Atlas of the
Gold Coast, Gold Coast Survey Department, Accra, 1949

Figure 8.3

0   50   100 miles

0   75   150 kilometres

humid than on the coasts to the west and east, for here the rainfall is less than at any other point south of Senegal. Even so Bosman could remark:

'The great difference betwixt the European air and this, is so observable, that few come hither who are not at first seized by a sickness which carries off a great many, and that chiefly because we are so wretchedly unprovided with what should comfort and nourish these poor men . . . .'[16]

In Bosman's day Akim had become the chief source of gold, selling chiefly to the rival Dutch, English and Danish forts at Accra. 'At this place alone sometimes more gold is received, than on the whole coast besides; and its traffick would be yet enlarged, if the negroes of Aquamboe and Akim could agree, as they are generally at a difference.'[17] East of the Volta the ports of Great and Little Popo and 'Fida' (Widah or Ouidah) were amongst the chief sources of slaves, despite the great difficulty in landing due to surf. 'Fida' alone could supply one thousand slaves every month.[18] Forts were not constructed on the Slave coast, and much of the trading was done by individuals and not by large monopoly companies. The local rulers appear to have been more powerful than their counterparts on the Gold Coast, and 'insisted that the European establishments should be made of mud and thatch, and that they should be built close to their palaces in towns a few miles inland where they could be under their supervision.'[19] Thus the controllers of the trade were the local rulers and dealers, and not the European factors, as was the case on the Gold Coast. On both the Slave and Gold Coasts little attempt was made to penetrate into the interior, or to deal other than through middlemen. The Dutch imported miners to the Gold Coast in 1694, but the miners were attacked by neighbouring people, who were doubtless incensed by this attempt to avoid dealing with African traders, and who claimed that the ground was sacred. In Senegal, by contrast, the French succeeded in penetrating inland as far as Bambouk in search of the gold of the Moors and of inland markets, from which the trade of the Upper Niger valley might be diverted to the coast.

The 18th century – British and French domination

In 1713 the Treaty of Utrecht was signed, giving England the contract to supply up to 4800 slaves a year into Spanish America. By 1785 the slave trade had grown to enormous proportions, for 74,000 a year were being taken from the western coast of Africa, from Senegal to the Cape of Good Hope, of which 38,000 were in British ships. The nearest competitors were the French, with an annual export of about 20,000 slaves a year. The slave trade provided an essential commercial link between Africa, the American colonies and settlements, and Western Europe – the 'South Atlantic System' – for Europe exported manufactured goods to West Africa in exchange for slaves, sold in the Americas for cotton and sugar. Many argued in its favour on the grounds that it was the only remedy for African indolence in order to make the fertile tropical world fruitful.[20] The voyage to the West Indies suited shipping sailing from West Africa, for it was in any case essential to sail as far west as convenient before turning for Europe. From the West Indies the return passage to Europe on the Great Circle meant a voyage along the American seaboard, often with New England, with its ships' stores and timber, and its sugar and slave interests, as the last landfall before crossing the Atlantic. A great part of the slave traffic in the 17th and 18th centuries came, not from the Slave, but from the Gold Coast. In part this was due to the large numbers of prisoners taken in the warfare to gain the position of chief middleman in the trade. Of the numerous wars which took place the most significant for future commercial development were: 1) the defeat of Denkera by the Ashanti Union at the beginning of the 18th century, followed by the conquest of the southern subject states of Denkera, giving Ashanti control over the western half of the Gold Coast; 2) the Ashanti conquest of Akim, the chief source of gold in the 1730s; 3) the Ashanti invasion of the Fanti coastal states by the beginning of the 19th century, and direct interference with trading at the forts. Throughout the 18th century the slave trade increased enormously, and as it increased so the power of the Dutch declined, due to the attacks upon their trade and possessions by the British and French, and due to the competition between independent Dutch traders and the Dutch West Indies Company. The British Royal African Company was dissolved in 1750, and replaced by an association which all British merchants wishing to trade in West Africa could join. Parliament gave an annual grant towards the upkeep of British forts. Whilst Dutch influence was declining the British fought the French, capturing during the Seven Years War all the French posts in Upper Guinea, although Gorée was returned to France in 1763.

The problem of colonies

In 1764 the first West African colony was created, the British colony of Senegambia, which failed, partly because the greater part of the trade was allowed to fall into the hands of French merchants. The French eventually recaptured St Louis and the British took Gorée, but at the Peace of Versailles in 1783 France's possessions in Senegal were all returned to her except for a share in the gum trade of Portendik. Britain's only remaining major sphere of interest in Upper Guinea became the Gambia. Britain took the Senegal colonies again during the Napoleonic wars, and again returned them in 1815. Britain's reluctance to establish colonies in Senegal, at the end of the 18th century and the beginning of the 19th, arose only in part from the failure of Senegambia. More important was the realization that, despite the loss of the North American colonies, British overseas trade had increased more rapidly after 1783 than ever before. The value of a monopoly in colonial trade was offset, at least in part, by the costs of administration and defence. Colonies appeared to be necessary only where naval bases were required to protect merchant shipping and interests. Moreover many commercial interests in Britain were against the establishment of colonies in West Africa, on the grounds that control of the trade would pass from

British merchants to the settlers. Not only had Senegambia proved a failure, but also the colony of Bolama Island off the coast of what is now Portuguese Guinea. Bolama was occupied in 1792 by 275 British settlers, most of whom soon died from disease and famine. The colony was in consequence abandoned. The west coast had a bad reputation, and few Europeans could be induced to settle there, unless enormous gains were offered. Barring the trade in gold and slaves, there was little activity offering sufficient profit, and many companies engaged in the West Africa trade had failed financially, particularly French companies in Senegal. Besides, the Americas, India and South-east Asia all offered much more hope for the intending emigrant or overseas trader.

The abolition of the slave trade

The abolition of the overseas trade in slaves by the major interested powers came at a time when the few attempts at colonization had either failed completely, or at least had yielded no large profit to either settlers or merchants. It served to discourage enterprise in West Africa still further. In 1772 the Lord Chief Justice declared that the state of slavery was not allowed by the law of England. In 1804 the Danish Government forbade its subjects to engage in the slave trade, the British Government did likewise in 1807, the United States Government in 1808, the Swedish Government in 1813, and the Dutch Government in 1814. The abolition movement succeeded, but not because of a declining interest in the slave trade, for many of the merchants and plantation owners strongly opposed abolition, and the numbers of slaves transported to the Americas at the beginning of the 19th century were greater than ever. The chief factors were: the interest of a number of men of good standing in public life, the formation of abolition societies and the interest of other public bodies, and the wakening conscience of large numbers of people in Western Europe and North America. The British Government put a small patrol of naval vessels permanently in West African waters, and sought agreement with other powers whereby the patrol could detain and search all suspected shipping. Perhaps the patrol did lessen the increase in the slave trade, or at least prevent British merchants taking part. Nevertheless the number of slaves exported was greater than ever by the 1830s, and the number of interceptions was small. Even as late as 1849 it was estimated that over 67,000 slaves were exported from the western coast of Africa, of which less than 5000 were captured by British cruisers.[21] However, the patrol maintained the British interest in West Africa, and led, by its actions, to the development of the settlement at Sierra Leone, originally founded in 1787, and which eventually became a colony for slaves taken from the intercepted ships. It also led to the founding of temporary bases in Fernando Po at Clarence Cove (Santa Isabel), an excellent harbour in a breached volcanic crater, and at San Carlos. Moreover the desire to take more effective action against the slave traders led eventually to the annexation of Lagos. The Fernando Po bases were leased from the Spanish Government which had taken over Portugal's rights there and in Annobon in 1778. They were

o

used by the British navy only from 1827 to 1834, although British influence continued for several years, due mainly to the appointment of Beecroft as Governor in 1843, and later in 1849 as British Consul for the Bights of Benin and Biafra, and due also to the existence of a Baptist mission on the island from 1841 to 1858. Fernando Po was reckoned 'too hot' and too far to leeward to be of much use to the patrol. The journey to Whydah (Ouidah) on the Slave Coast took two or three days longer than from the more distant island of Príncipe. Thus, although the slave vessels constantly moved eastwards and southwards towards the Equator before turning westwards to America, interceptions were difficult, and, once a slave vessel was running before the south-easterlies, it was almost impossible to catch. Sierra Leone proved an unfortunate port of disembarkation, partly because of a high incidence of disease, and partly because of the difficulties of sailing there from the Bights. The average time taken to sail from the Bight of Benin to Sierra Leone was reckoned at one month, and many of the slaves taken by the naval patrol died on the journey. In 1842 it was suggested that it would be better to land the freed slaves in the West Indies, and to use Ascension Island as a patrol base.[22] The use of steam vessels for patrol work was difficult, because by 1842 coal was available only at the Cape Verde Islands, Sierra Leone and Fernando Po. Elsewhere only wood could be procured.

The reduction and final destruction of the slave trade came with the abolition of the legal status of slavery in those countries which had imported slaves from West Africa. The abolition of slavery occurred in all British dominions by 1840, French dominions by 1848, Dutch dominions and the United States by 1863, Portuguese Africa by 1878, Cuba and Puerto Rico by 1886 and Brazil by 1888. The volume of trade declined rapidly after 1850 as the Governments concerned took action. A big reduction was achieved when the Brazilian Government forbade the import of slaves in 1856. By 1864 the estimated export was only just over 7000, most of whom were sent to Cuba.

The end of the overseas slave trade did not end slavery in West Africa, which still continued, although on a smaller scale within the region, wherever communities existed powerful enough to obtain such labour. Despite the early general abolition of slavery within British dominions, ordinances either abolishing or modifying slavery were not issued in the Gold Coast until 1874, the Gambia until 1894 and 1906, Sierra Leone until 1896, Northern Nigeria until 1901 and 1904, and Southern Nigeria until 1916. Although the legal status of slavery has been abolished, the social recognition of slavery still exists. Moreover, forced labour has frequently been used by authority of the colonial governments, particularly for road and railway construction.[23]

Interior exploration[24]

The interest in Britain in abolishing the slave trade was linked also with a desire to know more of West Africa. It was impossible to plan the development of the region, and difficult to encourage trade or found colonies for former slaves, when so much of the interior remained unknown. In 1788 the 'Association for Promoting the Discovery of the Interior Parts of Africa' was founded, and until 1830, when it was absorbed into the Royal Geographical Society, did much to promote or assist the work of discovery. The first travellers sent out by the African Association all sought information about the great river of West Africa, the Niger. They were anxious to establish whether it flowed westwards into the Senegal or Gambia, or eastwards into the Nile, some inland lake or perhaps, after changes of course, into the sea. Between 1788 and 1793 four travellers were sent to Africa – Ledyard, Lucas, Hornemann and Houghton – but all failed to reach the Niger, and three died before completing their journeys. The fifth traveller, Mungo Park, started from the Gambia towards the end of 1795, and after a most arduous journey reached the Niger at Ségou the following July. Destitute, and unable to reach the sources of the Niger because of local warfare, Park was forced to turn back. Park established that the Niger flowed eastwards, and brought to England a valuable first-hand account of the country of the Malinké. To discover more of the course of the Niger he was sent, at Government expense, on a second expedition in 1805, accompanied by forty Europeans, most of whom were soldiers. On reaching the Niger at Bamako only Park, six soldiers and a carpenter remained. A canoe was purchased and 'improved' in order to sail down the Niger to the sea. Eventually Park and four survivors set sail only to perish in the Bussa Rapids. In 1816 Tuckey's expedition attempted to ascend the Congo in order to determine whether it was connected with the Niger, and again lost a large number of men due to fever. The Frenchman Mollien discovered the sources of the Senegal, Gambia and Rio Grande in 1818, and four years later Major Laing located the sources of the Niger. Laing succeeded in reaching Timbuktu in 1825 but was killed. Two years later the Frenchman Caillié also reached Timbuktu, but managed to return and to bring back an account of the city and of the country seen en route. However, the biggest contribution to the knowledge of West Africa of this period came from the 1822 expedition of Denham, Clapperton and Oudney, who crossed the Sahara from Tripoli to Lake Chad, and travelled extensively in Bornu and Hausaland, visiting both Kano and Sokoto. This expedition provided the first reliable account of the country between the Niger and Lake Chad, and demonstrated that east of Timbuktu the Niger must turn south. In 1825 Clapperton set out to reach the Niger and Sokoto from the south. He landed with four companions at Badagry and crossed Yorubaland. Three members of the expedition died and only Clapperton and a servant, Lander, reached Bussa and eventually Sokoto. It had been hoped to persuade the ruler of the Hausa, Sultan Bello, to assist in abolishing the slave trade, but discussion proved fruitless. On the return journey Clapperton died, but Lander brought back Clapperton's journal, together with his own account of the journey, and provided the first description of northern Yorubaland and of its ancient capital of Oyo, shortly before destruction by the Fulani of Ilorin. In 1830 Lander returned with his brother to Bussa, where they obtained a canoe and sailed down the Niger to the 'Oil Rivers', thus finally establishing the course of the river and the existence of its delta. Numerous expeditions were sent up the Niger after the exploit of the Landers, but these were as much trading ventures as journeys of exploration, and will therefore be discussed below in relation to the attempts to develop trade and agricultural production.

The last journey of the first phase of exploration, that is the phase of exploration partly for its own sake and partly to learn more of the internal slave trade or to persuade rulers against it, was that of Richardson, Barth and Overweg who set out from Tripoli across the Sahara in 1849. Richardson died near Kukawa, the capital of Bornu, whilst travelling alone, but Overweg explored Gobir and Maradi, whilst Barth visited Katsina and Kano, and both eventually reached Kukawa. From Kukawa Overweg went to Lake Chad whilst Barth travelled to Yola, Kanem, Musgu and Masena. In 1852 Overweg died, and Barth set out for Sokoto and Gwandu via Zinder and Katsina. From Gwandu he continued his journey to Say on the Niger and thence north-westwards to Timbuktu. Barth stayed in Timbuktu for nearly six months, and left in March 1854 to return to Sokoto and Kukawa. On his return journey he met another explorer, Vogel, who had intended to join Barth. It had been thought that both explorers would then journey southwards to the Benue, where they would meet Baikie's expedition in the steamer *Pleiad*. Unfortunately Barth had stayed over-long in Timbuktu having known nothing of that expedition. He spent only two hours with Vogel before continuing his journey to Kukawa, from where in 1855 he eventually returned across the Sahara to Tripoli. Barth had seen more than any man of the West African Sudan, and brought back with him a most detailed geographical account, in which locations and distances were recorded with astonishing accuracy, despite the fact that Barth made no astronomical observations. Barth obtained not only a large quantity of geographical information, but also linguistic, sociological and historical material, and discovered the 'Tarikh-es-Sudan' of Abderrahman es Sadi. Today the five volumes of Barth's *Travels and discoveries in North and Central Africa, 1849–55* provide one of the most valuable records for the historical geographer, giving an account of the Sudan without parallel for any other portion of West Africa.

The temporary decline of political and commercial interest in West Africa

Although geographers, travellers, missionaries and abolitionists could find much to interest them in West Africa at the beginning of the 19th century, the reduction of the slave trade brought a decline in commercial activity, and certain political interests and claims were either abandoned or sold. West Africa had little else to offer except men. Gum and ivory provided only a small traffic. Cotton was grown but not exported. No timber industry had yet been organized, and the trade in palm oil for the manufacture of soap, candles and lubricants was in its infancy, and largely in British hands. The trade of the Gold Coast was still of some value, but 'Guinea' was no longer the chief source of gold for Europe, and many of the old forts fell into disuse, and were abandoned during the first half of the 19th century. In 1850 the Danish forts and possessions on the Gold Coast were ceded to Britain for £10,000, and in 1871, after an interchange of possessions four years earlier, the Dutch West African properties were likewise sold to Britain.[25] Although exports from the whole western coast of Africa to Britain increased after the abolition of slave trading by British subjects in 1807, the value of such exports compared with the value of slaves sent to the Americas was small. Abolition by the various European powers in turn left the slave-trading field mainly to American vessels, until eventually the United States, and finally other American powers, also abolished the traffic. As European traders found themselves no longer able to profit from carrying slaves, so their interest in West Africa declined, despite the increase in exports to Europe, notably in palm oil. Moreover, high profits were needed to attract men to a region with so notorious a reputation for disease. Thus European export traffic to West Africa declined at first – in the Gold Coast, for example, from £1,500,000 worth of goods imported in 1806, to only £600,000 worth in 1810.[26] After 1830 the position began to improve, as the export trade in palm oil, groundnuts and ivory increased, although the gold export declined. Thus between 1831 and 1840 the exports from Cape Coast increased in value from £90,000 to £325,000, and imports rose correspondingly from £131,000 to £423,000.[27]

The temporary reduction of trade and the increased difficulties of operating the export of slaves had important effects within West Africa itself. According to Bourret[28] there was greater pressure on the communities, who had earlier benefited by the traffic, to gain a greater proportion of control over what trade remained. This, in part at least, may have been a major factor in the struggle between the Ashanti and Fanti, and the attempt by the Ashanti to maintain their own sea-port in Elmina. The African Company sent an expedition to Kumasi in 1817 to negotiate with the Asantehene, and sent Dupuis in 1820 as resident. Unfortunately, Dupuis' treaty was never ratified as the Company was disbanded in 1821. Similarly, to the east, Oyo maintained a route to a port controlled by allied interests in Badagry, whilst neighbouring powers fought one another to control the valuable import traffic of guns, ammunition, textiles, metal ware and liquor. The incentive to maintain an export traffic in any commodity, even slaves, was high when in return guns, which gave power over neighbouring communities to their possessors, could be obtained. To some extent the wars to gain greater control of trade succeeded in reducing it, and in the Gold Coast influenced both the Danes and the Dutch in their decision to sell their trading rights and properties. Although the African Company had been abolished, and the British Gold Coast settlements placed under the Governor of Sierra Leone, the Gold Coast was regarded as a liability by the British Government. Only seven years after assuming responsibility, the forts were handed over to a committee of merchants, who were given a grant for administrative expenses.

The slave settlements

The first true settlements of alien colonists on the coast of West Africa were created by philanthropic societies in order to provide homes for former slaves. The original ex-slave settlers, together with their European or American organizers, came from America and England. The first experiment in founding such a settlement was made in 1787 at Sierra Leone by an association of British philanthropists. This settlement failed due to numerous deaths from local disease, the difficulties of adapting the settlers to their new life in West Africa, and local hostility.[29] Despite this failure the philanthropists persisted, enlisting the aid of business men in their enterprise. In 1791 the Sierra Leone Company was founded to manage the colony. A new site was cleared, a fresh group of settlers was despatched from Nova Scotia, and a Governor and Council appointed to rule. Despite a French attack and a revolt, the colony survived, although commercially the venture was a failure. However, in 1800 the British Government gave the Company a royal charter and a subsidy, and in 1808 took over control of the small territory as a crown colony in order to establish a naval base to protect British shipping, and later to victual anti-slavery patrols.

Great interest was aroused in the United States by the British settlement of Sierra Leone, and in 1816 a number of philanthropists formed the American Colonization Society, which proposed to send Negro emigrants to Sierra Leone. A commission sent to Sierra Leone in 1818 reported favourably, but the first shipload in 1820 were refused permission to land, and moved southwards to Sherbro Island where in a few weeks many died, including all the leaders. The remainder managed to obtain asylum in Sierra Leone. In 1821 an extensive tract of land, including the site of Monrovia at Cape Mesurado, was acquired by another expedition. However, the first settlement attempted at Bushrod Island was successfully opposed by local Negroes, and the colonists fled to Perseverance or Providence Islands. From there in 1822 they moved onto the higher ground of the Cape Mesurado promontory, where they built houses and fortifications. The site lacked a good supply of spring water and the settlement depended on cisterns, but the position lent itself to defence. The colony was constantly under attack, and in consequence it was organized as a military settlement.[30] In 1823 a stone fort, with a wooden tower and six cannons, was erected to ward off future attacks of the De and Mamba. Various other settlements were founded from the United States on the coast, mostly south-east of Monrovia, and by 1837, with the exception of Maryland near Cape Palmas, all were controlled by a central authority in Monrovia. Each settlement claimed a width of coastline and sought to extend its territory inland at approximately right angles to the shore. Thus Liberia followed a pattern, not uncommon in America, of strips each with access to the coast, laid out geometrically in parallel lines (see Fig. 8.4). In 1847 the settlers and the American Colonization Society declared their possession a sovereign and independent republic. Britain recognized the new republic of Liberia the following year, but the United States did not do so until 1862.

Agreement with the British and French on frontiers was long delayed, and friction developed between the Liberians of American descent and those who belonged to the pre-colonization communities. Moreover, the Government of

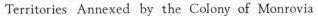

Territories Annexed by the Colony of Monrovia

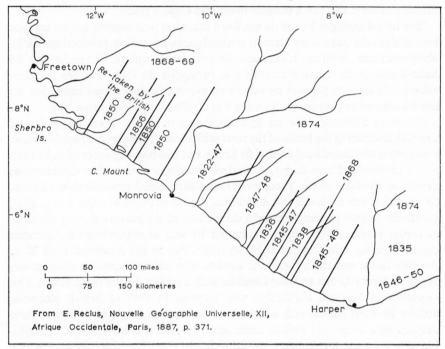

From E. Reclus, Nouvelle Géographie Universelle, XII,
Afrique Occidentale, Paris, 1887, p. 371.

Figure 8.4

Liberia lacked capital to develop the country and construct roads or railways into the interior. By the end of the 19th century there were nearly 12,000 Liberians of American origin of whom 2500 were in Monrovia. The total number of 'civilized' Liberians, however, that is of American and of mixed American and local origin, amounted to over 50,000.[31]

The first settler colony – Senegal

Experience in founding ex-slave colonies and the general decline in trade both tended to discourage enterprise in West Africa at the beginning of the 19th century. After 1815, however, French interest revived, partly because of the loss of possessions in America and Asia, and partly because of the desire of certain traders and politicians to create plantation colonies in Africa with its supposed abundant labour, whose movement overseas was now prevented. Besides it was feared that American sugar and cotton production would decline without further slave supplies. Senegal, France's chief possession in West Africa in 1816, consisted of a few trading posts, of which the chief was St Louis on its sandbank, standing only a little above the level of the river, extremely dry, supporting neither trees nor grass, and subject to dysentery and fever in the high water season.[32] Thus the attempt was made to change Senegal from a trading to a planting colony. In 1816 a memoir described Cape Verde:

'Sur un sol analogue à celui de nos îles à sucre, on peut espérer que les travaux bien dirigés du cultivateur africain obtiendraient les mêmes productions qu'ils obtiennent aux Antilles. L'excédent de population qui surcharge les îles de Saint-Louis et de Gorée fournirait à la presqu'île du Cap Verd ses premiers colons et la culture, gagnant de proche en proche, procurerait au commerce un nouvel aliment et préparerait les voies à la civilisation des indigènes.'[33]

Governor Schmalz drew an optimistic picture of the potential wealth of Senegal, comparing the banks of the river with those of the Ganges.[34] American seed cotton was introduced around St Louis, but was not very successful. In 1822 a new Governor, Baron Roger, authorized the development of an experimental garden on the bank of the Taouey river, and distributed concessions to settlers. Some export was achieved, but difficulties, mainly of physical origin (see p. 489), eventually ruined the enterprise. In the middle of the century further attempts at cotton planting were made, prompted by fear of depending on American cotton supplies, and stimulated by shortages due to the American Civil War. Another factor was rivalry with the British, who had attempted to plant cotton firstly in Sierra Leone and the Gambia, and, by 1859, in the Gold Coast. The Governor of Senegal, Faidherbe, was 'warned' in 1858 of British economic activity in West Africa, and asked for an increase in the local budget to help develop new crops.[35] Failure came again to cotton cultivation (see p. 498), but this time the factors were not entirely physical. The chief factor was undoubtedly the competition of groundnuts, the export of which had begun in the 1840s. Oilseeds were in ever-increasing demand in Europe, and Marseilles, with its olive oil interests and its trading connections with West Africa, was rapidly becoming the chief centre in the world for vegetable oil processing. Groundnuts were comparatively easy to grow in Senegal, found a ready market at the river ports and on the coast, and could be exchanged for cheap European textiles. The import of textiles meant that local cotton production tended to decline. At the same time cultivation of groundnuts on one's own account was more attractive than working on plantations, so plantation cotton-growing was limited too. Ill-health and political insecurity played their part in discouraging European settlers, whilst the shortage of cotton in France during the American Civil War was in fact met to a large extent by supplies from India. Once the Civil War was over, prices fell again, and French textile manufacturers were no longer interested in West Africa.

Faidherbe had opposed many of the grants of land to plantation owners, believing that the future of Senegal lay in African peasant production.[36] The groundnut export began from Senegal in 1842 with a first shipment of 840 tons.

The French Occupation of Senegal in the Nineteenth Century

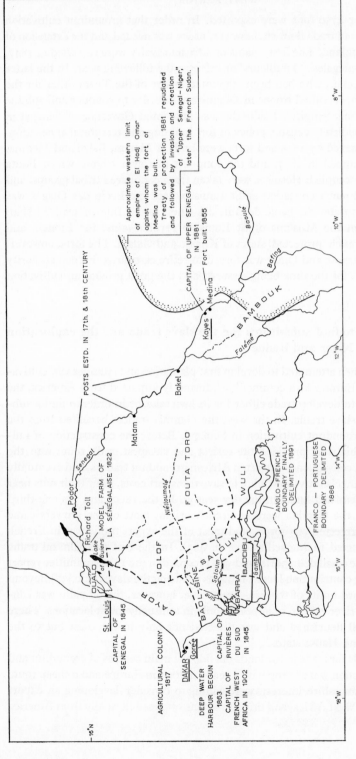

Figure 8.5

- - - - Approximate boundaries of the Ouolof States in 1820 according to Mollien
(adapted from map in D. P. Gamble, The Wolof of Senegambia, London, 1957.)

——— Southern colonial boundaries

The foundations of the colony of Senegal lay in the annexation of the Ouolof States: Ouala in 1866, Cayor in 1863, and Jolof in 1890.
The chief obstacle to expansion into the interior was the empire created by El Hadj Omar (1797–1864) (1857 and 1859 attacked
the French Forts of Medina and Matam respectively and repulsed). Ségou, the capital city of his son Ahmadu, was captured in 1890.

Ten years later 4750 tons were exported. In order that groundnut cultivation should spread and trade flourish, however, peace was needed and the extension of French power inland. The first Spahis or African cavalry were recruited in 1847, and the first Senegalese 'Tirailleurs' or infantry the following year. In the latter year El Hadj Omar, who had been appointed leader of the Tijani order for the Western Sudan, recruited troops in Dinguiraye in order to conquer and subdue the peoples of his 'empire'. Faidherbe was appointed Governor of Senegal in 1854, and immediately began a policy of fort building and territorial annexation. Trarza was annexed by 1858 and forts were built at Matam, Bakel and Medina. Dakar was occupied in 1857, and the conquest of Cayor begun, whilst Fouta Toro was also occupied. Hostages were taken from conquered tribal groups, and were given a French education at St Louis, where the Ecole des Otages was opened in 1855 (later the Ecole des Fils des Chefs et des Interprètes). El Hadj Omar called on the Muslims of St Louis to revolt against the French, and attacked the French 'protected' states of Khasso and Galam. The forts, however, served their purpose and Omar was forced to retire eastwards. French authority in Senegal was, for the time being, assured and the great groundnut cultivation could expand.

The attempt to find substitutes for the slave trade and the exploration of the Lower Niger and Benue

Whilst the French attempted to develop first plantation and later peasant cultivation to supply Europe with commodities, formerly imported from America, the British sought to develop trade either for its own sake, or in order to find a substitute for the slave traffic. In the west the Gambia traders benefited from the expansion of groundnut cultivation in Senegal. Before the construction of railways the Gambia river provided the easiest and cheapest trade route into the interior, and, in consequence, attracted African groundnut traders, and eventually temporary 'strange' cultivators, who, to save transport costs, grew their nuts near the river and returned home in the dry season. In the 1860s and 70s one-third of the nuts on the Gambia were of French origin, most of the growers came from French protected territories, and most of the export traffic was in French hands and directed to Marseilles (see p. 483). In the east the palm oil traffic flourished at the small delta ports, and was recorded in the 1842 committee report as making a big contribution locally towards reducing the slave trade.[37] Beyond the savanna-ward limits of the rain-forest zone, however, the oil palm was confined chiefly to river valleys, or appeared only in unusually moist locations. There slave traffic still flourished and was directed not only to the coast but to the Upper Niger and Hausa states.

The essentials for trade in the lands outside the main centres of groundnut and palm oil production were a crop with a ready market in Europe and a cheap route to the coast. Lancashire interests were willing to consider developing an export of cotton from West Africa, and other products obtained normally from America through Liverpool. The discoveries of the Lander brothers revealed the existence of a waterway navigable for shallow-draught steam vessels as far as the country of the Nupe, with further possibilities up the Benue. A Liverpool merchant and shipowner, MacGregor Laird, took out an expedition with Richard Lander as guide in 1832, which spent three years exploring the Lower Niger and Benue, and visited the delta ports, the Cross river and Calabar, and the mouth of the Cameroons river. Of the 48 Europeans in the expedition 38 died. Some exploration had been achieved, contacts made and knowledge gained, but the expedition could hardly have been described as successful, except in one respect – the smaller of the two ships used, the *Alburkah*, was the first ocean-going steamer constructed entirely of wrought iron (with the exception of her decks), and showed that the Niger could be navigated by such vessels.[38] In 1836 and 1837 Consul Beecroft explored the Lower Niger, travelling nearly as far upstream as Bussa, but the next large-scale expedition did not occur until 1841. James McQueen, a geographer, and Thomas Fowell Buxton, an abolitionist, had both pleaded for the development of civilization in Africa through the cultivation of habits of industry and the creation of extensive British contact with the Niger peoples.[39] Buxton proposed a Niger expedition, which would make treaties to open the way for trade and the development of agriculture. Despite opposition the Society for the Extinction of the Slave Trade and the Civilization of Africa, the Church Missionary Society and the British Government supported the scheme. The expedition was sent under the command of Allen and Thomson in 1841, taking two missionaries, one of whom, Samuel Crowther, was of Sierra Leone origin, and the equipment for a model farm. The vessels used were fitted with water-tight compartments, which, since the circulation of air was impeded, were supplied with air pumped by fans and conveyed by tubes. The air supplied was first filtered through an iron chest containing chemicals to remove the 'deleterious gases'. The first attempt at air-conditioning proved almost completely useless, and occupied valuable space in the crowded ships.[40] 'As auxiliary to the benevolent purposes proposed by the African Society', i.e. Society for the Extinction of the Slave Trade, 'an Agricultural Society was formed with the intention of establishing a model farm in such a locality as might be selected by the Commissioners.'[41] A West Indian superintendent was appointed and farm stores and implements, cotton ginning and pressing machinery taken on board. Fourteen liberated West Africans were added to the farm complement at Sierra Leone. Land was purchased from the Attah of Idah on the lower slopes of Mount Patti, near the present site of Lokoja, and overlooking the confluence of the Benue and Niger. Despite the doubts of the missionary Schön, the West Indian superintendent thought the soil 'as good as the soil in America . . .', and it was resolved to show the local community 'how to grow indigo and cotton properly'.[42] It was proposed to plant between 300 and 500 acres, but clearance was slow due to illness amongst the settlers. By July 1842 only 20 acres of land had been planted, chiefly to cotton and a few yams, using local seed, the previous cropping with imported maize and cotton having entirely failed. Trouble had broken out amongst the settlers, most of whom did not wish to undertake much manual labour, and preferred to leave when offered the opportunity to do so. The settlement was therefore abandoned. Not only the farm, but the entire expedition failed, and out of the 162 Europeans who originally entered the Niger, 54 died of 'fever'. Traders, missionaries and the British Government all concluded that the death rate was too heavy to make further penetration of the Niger worth while. Expeditions were, however, attempted elsewhere. For example, in 1850 some traders and manufacturers combined in the purchase of two vessels to be sent from Liverpool to West Africa (chiefly to Dahomey) in order to obtain cotton. In 1849 Laird founded the African Steamship Company, and in 1854 sponsored another expedition to the Niger Valley. This expedition was led by Dr Baikie, a naval Surgeon Commander. He believed that quinine used as a prophylactic would enable Europeans to avoid or resist attacks of fever, and proved it by bringing every member of the expedition back to the coast alive.[43]

Baikie's expedition hoped to assist Barth, but failed to find him. It carried out a successful exploration of the Benue, however, and, as a result of this expedition, MacGregor Laird entered into a contract with the Government to maintain a steamer on the Niger for five years in return for an annual subsidy.

In 1857 Baikie and Glover sailed in the *Dayspring*, to open up the trade of the Niger Valley, despite the opposition of Liverpool and other traders on the coast, who feared that their trading posts and contacts would be by-passed. The *Dayspring* was wrecked at Jebba, but another vessel was sent out, and trading posts were erected at Aboh, Onitsha and Lokoja. At Onitsha a mission site was established, and at Lokoja a consulate was established by 1866. Numerous troubles and setbacks were encountered, and the consulate was withdrawn in 1869 because it could not be adequately protected, but the foundations of future British supremacy on the Niger and of the development of inland trade had been laid.

Missionary influence on the invasion of West Africa[44]

The earliest Christian missions in West Africa were Roman Catholic, introduced by the Portuguese. A bishopric was founded at Santiago in the Cape Verde Islands as early as 1533, and the diocese included the coast from Cape Verde to Cape Palmas. An embassy obtained permission for missionaries to enter Benin in 1516, and Roman Catholic influence persisted in Benin and in the delta for several centuries, together with Portuguese trading interests. French Roman Catholic missions were most developed in Senegal by the beginning of the 19th century, and had declined or even disappeared elsewhere.

It appears that by the beginning of the 19th century the Protestant churches were the most active in the crusade against the traffic in slaves, and their missions the most active in West Africa. In more than one case annexation of territory by a European power followed missionary activity. In other cases the missionaries discouraged colonialism, and were frequently opposed to the policies of the traders. The missionaries had a profound influence on the evolution of the politi-

cal geography of West Africa, sought to modify local customs and social organization, and introduced in many areas new crops and implements, or even, as in
the case of Abeokuta, improved on local technique in warfare.

The part played by the missions in abolishing the slave trade, in founding ex-
slave settlements, and in encouraging expeditions to West Africa to promote an
alternative trade, has already received some comment. The first major British
mission in West Africa was that founded by the Church Missionary Society in
Sierra Leone in 1806. From this was founded Fourah Bay College in 1827, later
the first European University College in West Africa, and the diocese of Sierra
Leone in 1852. The Church Missionary Society, through its contact with Yoruba
slaves in Sierra Leone, who after liberation had eventually returned home,
founded a resident mission in Badagry in 1844, and in Abeokuta in 1846. The
Wesleyan Mission followed in the following year, and the Baptist Mission in
1850. Townsend of the C.M.S. mission assisted the Egba rulers in their request
to the British Government in 1848 for protection to enable them to navigate the
Ogun river and the Lagos lagoon. Townsend was also a member in 1849 of a
Church Missionary Society delegation to the Foreign Secretary, to advocate the
appointment of a British Resident at Abeokuta, the stationing of an armed boat in
Lagos lagoon, and the construction of a fort at Badagry.[45] In the Dahomeyan
attack on Abeokuta in 1851 much of the material used for defence had been
supplied by the British through missionary intercession, whilst the American
Baptist Bowen encouraged the Egba fighters.[46] The British bombarded Lagos
in 1851, and replaced the ruler Kosoko by an earlier ruler who had been deposed
– Akitoye. A C.M.S. mission was established at Ibadan in 1853, and the follow-
ing year at Onitsha on the Niger. In 1864 Crowther was consecrated the first
Bishop of the Niger territories. On the Gold Coast the Basel Missionary Society
began work in 1827 in the area of Danish influence, and twenty years later the
Bremen Society founded a station east of the Volta amongst the Ewe, thus
laying the foundation of the future German Togoland. The Wesleyans brought
British influence west of the Volta into the Fanti states and founded a mission at
Kumasi as early as 1839. To the east the earlier missionary endeavours were less
successful. The Baptists moved into Fernando Po, after it had become a base
for the anti-slavery patrol and a settlement for liberated slaves. In 1858 the
Spanish authorities drove them out, and they removed to the foot of Mount
Cameroon, where they founded the settlement of Victoria. Even this was eventually lost, however, for the Cameroons became German in 1885, and the mission
was eventually handed over to the Basel Missionary Society.

In assessing the part played by the missions in the modification of West
Africa, their contributions not only in the religious, social and political spheres
should be considered, but their introduction of education and medicine, and
their import of plants and seed from overseas. Thus Fourah Bay College helped
to train many West Africans in British territories, who later occupied important
Government and judicial posts, and who helped to lay the foundations for future
independence. The Basel Mission tried to introduce new crops, and in 1857 was

responsible for the first important introduction of cocoa into Ghana (see pp. 474 and 626). Many missions had developed experimental farms, which served not only to try new plants, but provided examples of new techniques, or even courses of instruction for West African cultivators. It might be added that one of the earliest vernacular newspapers, *Iwe Irohin*, was started by a mission in Abeokuta in 1859.

The palm oil trade and the Oil Rivers

A regular export of palm oil from West Africa began at the end of the 18th century. Liverpool, which had been pre-eminent amongst British ports in the slave trade, became the leading oil importer. The oil was used for the manufacture of soap and lubricants. By 1801 the largest shipment to Liverpool was only 96 casks (each cask or 'puncheon' weighed 12 cwt – 610 kilos), but by 1813 shipments of over 700 casks were made.[47] With the abolition of the slave trade, the slave dealers became oil importers. The ships of other nations, particularly of the United States, Spain and Portugal continued, however, to carry slaves to the Americas, and the slave trade remained more attractive to West African merchants. In the Niger delta ports, the chief source of both slaves and oil in the middle of the 19th century, the arrival of slave traders put an immediate stop to all dealing in palm oil. The loading of the oil vessels was constantly delayed by the procuring of slaves.[48] In consequence it became the oil traders' interest to destroy the slave traffic, and British naval forces in attacking slave vessels were promoting British trading interests. Fernando Po became of great importance not only as a naval base, but in its provision of the deep-water harbour of Port Clarence, at which the ocean-going ships were supplied with oil by smaller vessels capable of navigating the delta creeks.

In 1840 approximately 12,000 tons of palm oil were shipped from West Africa to Liverpool, of which three-quarters came from the Niger delta.[49] In 1854–5, 25,000 tons were shipped in twelve months from the delta and the Cameroons alone, of which over 16,000 tons came from Degema (New Calabar) and Bonny.[50] The Bonny river became the world's chief source of palm oil, and one of the chief foci of British commercial and political interests in West Africa. The oil was purchased chiefly by barter, and bargaining and the collection of cargo frequently took several months. Traders without a base in Fernando Po at first laid their ships up in the creeks, and roofed them over with grass mats. The crew were thus forced to stay in the Oil Rivers for several months, during which a heavy death rate was frequently experienced. A relay system was introduced in which the ships arrived in pairs, one remaining to load, manned only by a skeleton crew, and the other returning or trading elsewhere. By about 1850 the 'hulks' were established. Old ships were dismasted, roofed and moored permanently in lagoons or creeks, to act as collectors of oil, which was quickly transferred in large quantities to the trading vessels. Finally came the 'Beach' or shore warehouse, known at much earlier dates in the Gambia and on the Gold

Coast.[51] In exchange Britain exported a great variety of manufactures, of which the chief items by value were:

Exports to West Africa (£) [52]

	1827	1841
Cotton manufactures	41,840	183,632
Arms and ammunition	46,923	91,247
Hardware and cutlery	2,252	19,378
Iron and steel manufactures	11,152	17,864
Empty casks and staves	5,817	17,282
Brass and copper manufactures	3,391	16,452

Rum, spirit and wines were also exported, although the importance of the alcohol traffic was undoubtedly exaggerated at the time. Much more important was the export of arms and ammunition, for the communities who could obtain European weapons became very much more powerful than their neighbours. This last trade gave most power in consequence to the coastal communities, encouraged a struggle to control the ports, and effected a political revolution in the coastal hinterlands of West Africa. It was to control the sources of military power that the Ashanti sought to gain control over the coastal communities of the Gold Coast, and asserted their right to Elmina. Similarly the Ibadans emerged as a military power amongst the Yoruba under pressure of Fulani attack, and fought their neighbours in order to ensure a supply of weapons from Lagos and the lagoon ports.

The French empire in West Africa

At the beginning of the 19th century French activity was confined chiefly to the coastlands and lower valley of Senegal. The urge to enlarge the field of such activity came after the final defeat of Napoleon, with the return of peace to Western Europe, and the loss of empire in Asia and America. French textile mills were demanding more cotton. Oil was needed to lubricate the machines of the new industrial age. The decline of the slave trade suggested that these products were best obtained from the source of labour, that is, chiefly from West Africa. Attempts to extend French power and the area tapped by French traders inland up the Senegal failed, partly because of the difficulties of navigating the Senegal river, and partly because French forces based on St Louis were insufficient to defeat the forces of the interior Muslim states. Accordingly French merchants sought to develop trade elsewhere along the coast.

In 1838 the only French trading posts of any importance south of Senegal were in the valley of the Rio Nuñez, from which they exported groundnuts and coffee. Between 1838 and 1842, however, treaties were concluded with local rulers near Cape Palmas, on the Ivory Coast and at Bonny. In 1843 fortified trading posts were constructed at Assinie and Grand Bassam, and nine years later at Tabou. Ouidah in Dahomey had been re-occupied in 1841, and commercial relations established with the state of Dahomey. In 1849 Boké on the Guinea Coast was bombarded and captured. Seventeen years later a French protectorate was created over lands on the lower Mellacory river, and a fort was built at Benty. Thus French influence, and eventually political authority, was brought to a number of points on the west coast of Africa by traders. British and French trading posts virtually claimed monopoly rights in the traffic of alternating hinterlands. Thus was the foundation laid of the present distribution of states and territories, each with a relatively narrow coastal frontage and an extensive hinterland, a distribution which ignores all previous ethnic and political groupings.

The French were particularly active in Dahomey and the Lower Niger valley, with the valuable palm oil trade. A treaty was concluded with Dahomey in 1851, and protectorates established over Porto Novo in 1863 and Little Popo (Anécho) in 1864. In 1868 the ruler of Dahomey also ceded Cotonou to the French. Here the French merchants conflicted with the British merchants in Lagos, for both sought to gain the trade of Yorubaland. For a time the French abandoned their Dahomeyan possessions, partly due to a decline in trade due to the wars between Dahomey and the Yoruba states, partly due to the British blockade of Cotonou, and partly due to a temporary lack of interest in colonial affairs after France's defeat by Prussia in 1870. Similarly the French garrisons were withdrawn from the Ivory Coast in 1871, and the forts left to the merchants. On the Niger and Benue two French companies, the Compagnie Française de l'Afrique Equatoriale and the Compagnie du Sénégal, had established a number of trading posts. Political control had not, however, followed by 1870. The British traders on the Niger united together in 1879, and formed the National African Company in 1882, which was large enough to buy out both the French companies by 1885. This was not sufficient, however, to prevent the revival of French claims. Lieutenant Mizon made treaties in the Benue valley in 1892, and the treaty of 1898 gave the French the right of navigation on the Niger between Bussa and the sea, together with the right to establish certain landing places and store sheds in order to make navigation free of British interference.

Between 1870 and 1880 France was recovering from her defeat by Germany, but after 1880 she returned to West Africa to establish, not spheres of influence as in the past, but colonies ruled directly by French authorities. France was not alone in attempting to establish political rather than economic control. Britain, Germany and Portugal were concerned in the new colonial movement. No longer were African interests to be left in the hands of a few individuals or private companies or societies. Instead the authority of European governments was to be established, chiefly by the use of force, partly in order to obtain trade monopolies, or control of a major share of trade, and partly for the sake of national aggrandizement. In the late 19th century the acquisition of colonies was regarded as a gain of wealth in raw materials and manpower. For France, which had lost the demographic hegemony of Europe, and its position as the major military power to Germany, the creation of a large overseas empire seemed a practical necessity.

In Senegal the basis for conquest had been laid by Faidherbe, under whose rule the work of constructing a deep-water harbour at Dakar was begun in 1863. Dakar was on the mainland, not on an isolated peninsula and island like St Louis, or on an island like Gorée. In 1866 the Messageries Impériales began a regular service via Dakar between France and South America. In 1880 the territory of Upper Senegal was made partially independent of the administration in St Louis, and a capital was established at Medina. The following year the capital was moved to Kayes, and protection claimed over the entire left bank of the Niger as far downstream as Timbuktu. The chief line of French advance into the interior became the Senegal, as Faidherbe wished, and the attempt was made to create an empire, comprising the entire African Sudan stretching from the Atlantic to Ethiopia. To some extent the line of advance looked physically easier than the penetration of the evergreen rain forests and thick woody fallows of the Ivory Coast and Nigeria. Again, the French may have been misled by the optimism expressed by many explorers with regard to the economic future of the Sudan. Here were the most powerful states and the best conditions for producing cotton. Here also were floodlands on the edge of the Sahara desert, and across that desert the floodlands of Egypt offered rich possibilities. In the event, the Sudan has never realized the productivity of export crops, the returns per acre, or the high densities of population, which are today associated with the woody fallows. The Faidherbe policy limited the expansion of other powers into the interior, gave quick territorial gains, and linked all the conquests together into one continuous area. Nearly two-thirds of the labour force and over three-quarters of the wealth, in terms of resources available over the next half century, went to the other powers, chiefly to Britain. Bamako was taken in 1883, and ten years later Kaarta, Ségou and Macina had been occupied. In 1894 the French had occupied Timbuktu. By 1896 they were in Say. Samory, the ruler of the southern Manding peoples, was captured in 1898, and the Fouta Djallon was taken in a campaign lasting from 1887 to 1896.

The Berlin Agreement of 1885 stipulated that no new annexation or protectorates on the African coastline would be valid, unless there were effective occupation. The French accordingly were not slow to establish a number of points of effective occupation on the coast, whilst leaving the interior conquest mainly to forces operating from Senegal. Moreover, they were encouraged to act as rapidly as possible, by the intervention of German treaty makers and forces on the west coast. Conakry was occupied in 1887, the Ivory Coast forts were re-occupied in 1886, and a more effective occupation was made of possessions in Dahomey in 1885. French control of the coastal states led to a war with Dahomey, resulting in the latter's defeat in 1893, and the constitution of the colony in 1899. The conquest of Dahomey led to a race between the French and British to claim Borgu, but major quarrels over territory were finally settled by the Convention of 1898. Delimitation of the boundary from the Gulf of Guinea to the Niger did not take place until 1912, however, and France retained the right to lease two pieces of land on the Lower Niger for use of her traders. In 1895 the first civil government of French West Africa was established. Dahomey was attached in 1899 to the federation of five colonies: Senegal, 'Haut Senegal-Niger', Guinea, Ivory Coast and Dahomey. In 1910 the military territory of the Niger was detached from 'Haut Senegal-Niger', and in 1919 the Colony of the Upper Volta was created. Mauritania was formed, and added to the West African union in 1922. The Upper Volta was incorporated into the Ivory Coast in 1932, and then restored as a separate colony in 1947.

The French empire in West Africa was neither an ethnic nor an economic unit. Its curious shape reflects its coastal and alien origin. The territorial divisions of this empire were frequently modified to suit administrative convenience. Each territory was divided into 'cercles', which, like the 'départements' of France, bore no relation to geographical distributions. French policy, far from fitting the new administrative apparatus to old institutions, and thus preserving them, sought to destroy the old affiliations and loyalties in order to assimilate the colonies into a single French political and, where possible, social unit. At first, due to the speed of conquest, the French were forced to recognize and employ traditional authorities, but gradually, as more administrative officials were added to the colonial service, direct administration was introduced. The administration was highly centralized, and focused on the Governor-General in Dakar, whose office was created in 1902, and to whom all colonial governors were responsible. A hierarchy of government was created from Governor-General down to village headman, replacing all previous systems of government. West Africans were encouraged to abandon old loyalties, and to become French citizens. Those born in St Louis, Rufisque, Gorée and Dakar became so automatically, and yet by the outbreak of the Second World War less than 0·6 per cent of the total population of French West Africa were French citizens, and most of those by virtue of birth in the communes cited above. To further the process of assimilation, Senegal was brought into the French political system by being given the right to send a delegation to the National Assembly as early as 1848. Thus French West Africa was absorbed into a scheme for creating a greater France overseas, increasing France's total manpower and material resources. The scheme failed. Although West African troops assisted France in both World Wars, the territories were poorly developed, short of the materials needed for their own economic improvement, and short of sufficient labour to provide any increase in output. Population densities are low, productivity is scattered, and in areas of higher density more work must be expended per unit of production because of the need to cultivate marginal lands. Manufacture is left to the 'parias', the low castes, or the corporate societies.[53] Moreover, few West Africans understood or appreciated the ideal of becoming a French citizen. Of the French West African war effort after 1942 Richard-Molard remarked:

'Tout cela pour des résultats dérisoires. Ce n'est pas par la contrainte, sans le moindre matériel, selon des méthodes néolithiques que les pays tropicaux peuvent produire. Le slogan rageur en Guineé, chez les Blancs opposants, était "deux millions d'esclaves pour deux liberty-ships par an".'

The British empire in West Africa

In 1843, on the recommendation of the Select Committee on the West Coast of Africa, the British Government agreed to accept more responsibility for the actions of its subjects in West Africa, and resumed direct control of the British forts on the Gold Coast. Treaties were negotiated with the rulers of the coastal communities, which provided for the introduction of the general principles of British law. In return the coastal peoples received 'protection' from the British Government, and many of their rulers agreed in 1852 to accept taxation. Both the concept of a 'protectorate', and the area involved, were vague. Even by 1865 the limitations of British authority around the Gold Coast forts were undefined.[54]

Despite the creation of the 'West African Settlements' as early as 1821, the British Government was reluctant to assume authority in West Africa. After the Ashanti campaign of 1824–6, the Gold Coast settlements had been handed over to a committee of London merchants, and as late as 1865 it was thought expedient not to extend the boundaries of Lagos Colony.[55] Policy vacillated. In 1843 the Gambia was detached from Sierra Leone. In 1866 it was reunited with the other British settlements in order to economize in the cost of administration. Whereas the Parliamentary Select Committee of 1842 had recommended that the British Government should take over the administration of the British settlements, the Select Committee of 1865 recommended the abandonment of all the settlements except Sierra Leone. Lagos had been captured in 1851, and annexed in 1861, in order to destroy the slave trade of Yorubaland, but the 1865 committee recommended that there should be no further annexations, and that West African communities, already ruled or protected by the British, should be prepared for their own self-government. Despite the adoption of these recommendations by the British Government, the Dutch forts on the Gold Coast were acquired in 1871. Since Ashanti laid claim to one of the forts, Elmina, which was regarded as a vital port, and since this port was now held by the British, who were in effect allies of the Fanti, the result eventually was an Ashanti invasion of the coast states. In reply the British invaded Ashanti in 1873, forced the renunciation of Ashanti claims to the coast states, and obtained a promise that the road to Kumasi would be kept open for trade. In 1874 Disraeli's Government changed policy again and decided that all 'protectorates' in the Gold Coast should be annexed, and, together with Lagos, be made into a new crown colony. A second British military force was sent to Ashanti in 1895 and a British protectorate imposed. In 1900 the Ashanti revolt was suppressed, and the territory was annexed the following year.

Britain's paramount position on the Niger was first asserted by the uniting in 1879 of all the firms interested in the Niger trade into the United African, later the National African, Company. The subsequent buying out of French companies enabled the British to claim at the Berlin Conference in 1885 that the entire trade of the Niger was in their hands, and thus secure recognition for their claims. The

British company received a royal charter, empowering it to administer the territories of the Niger valley, but not of the delta. The latter eventually became the Niger Coast Protectorate, administered directly by the British Government. The race to claim as much territory in Africa as possible, which developed in 1885, stimulated the British into political activity. In that year the National African Company forestalled the Germans in Sokoto, by making commercial treaties with the rulers. In 1888 the fear of French intervention led to the extending of a protectorate over Yorubaland. By 1896 the whole of the protectorate was under the authority of the colonial government of Lagos, which had been created ten years earlier. In the delta the Royal Niger Company* obstructed the Germans and French in their attempts to develop trade, and fought against the more powerful trading communities, who saw their middleman position threatened by the opening of navigation up the Niger and Benue. In 1897 the Company brought the Emirates of Nupe and Ilorin under its rule, and prepared to come into conflict with the French who had come down the Niger valley as far as Bussa. The British Government intervened by providing the money necessary for the formation of the West African Frontier Force. In 1900, because the Government had already paid for the defence of Northern Nigeria and because it was felt that the Company sought to establish a virtual trade monopoly, the Government bought out the Company's administrative and military assets. A protectorate was declared over Northern Nigeria, whilst in the same year the Niger Coast Protectorate was renamed the Protectorate of Southern Nigeria. Effective government over what is now the Eastern Region of Nigeria was not established until late, that is not until after the Aro Expedition of 1902. Similarly Northern Nigeria was not brought under complete control until after the military campaigns of 1900-4.

In the west the Gambia was given its own administration in 1888, but no attempt was made to increase the area of the colony after the failure of the claims to territory in what is now Portuguese Guinea. France was allowed to occupy territory on each side of the Gambia, and eventually it was even suggested that the Gambia should be exchanged with France for a portion of the latter's territory elsewhere in West Africa. Merchants with interests in the territories affected naturally objected to the proposals for exchange, and finally in 1891 a delimitation agreement was made by which Britain's right to both banks of the river as far inland as the limit of seaward navigation was recognized. Sierra Leone became a distinct colony with its own administration in 1888. In the 1860s claims to a 'protectorate' along the coast had been maintained, partly at the expense of Liberia, and a treaty of delimitation with France in 1894 defined the landward limits. After the suppression of the 1898 rising the whole interior was declared a protectorate, and British government introduced.

The British empire in West Africa was created by a combination of commercial and philanthropic interests, and it was only in 1885 that political interests became a major consideration. British commerce had been the first to lose interest in the slave trade, and looked in the 19th century to areas of high productivity, particu-

---

* Chartered in 1866: formerly the National African Company.

larly of palm oil. In consequence Britain's empire comprised all the more productive areas and, with the exception of the Ivory Coast and Liberia, all the more important woody fallows or rain-forest areas, where perennial crops could be grown. It also included all the more heavily populated territories, with the exception of the Mossi region, the longest stretches of inland waterway navigable from the coast, and most of the more important ports. French, German and Portuguese competition prevented the unification of the empire, which remained split into four colonies, whose shape reflects the pattern of conquest by sea-borne invaders. As in the case of the French empire, the British territories were formed with little reference to the distribution of West African communities. The frontiers largely ignore the existence of tribal groups and even divide former states. Even had there been a desire to consider ethnic factors, the rate of advance was so rapid after 1885 that it would have been impossible in most areas to acquire the necessary information before agreement between the opposing powers had to be reached. Little was known of the conquered lands and peoples. Most of the early delimitations were based on false assumptions with regard to West African relief and drainage, and most of the early survey work was of a very doubtful character.[56] In the period of rapid expansion meridians were frequently used to define boundaries, whilst attempts to use tribal frontiers were frustrated by the frequent disagreements between tribes as to the location of their dividing zones or lines. There were disagreements between surveyors with regard to determination of location by astronomic methods. Some rivers referred to in treaties were non-existent, or occupied broad flood-plains, where a maze of meandering channels made delimitation impossible. Arcs were also frequently used where important towns lay near a frontier, and might thus have been separated from their agricultural land or from their local commercial hinterland.[57]

Although at first direct methods of government were applied in British territories, gradually each colony acquired its own form of administration, and use was made of existing systems of government. Legislative councils consisting at first mainly of British officials were created in the Gambia in 1843, in the Gold Coast in 1850, in Lagos in 1862 and in Sierra Leone in 1863.[58] Unofficial members of these councils were at first British residents, but during the 1880s some West Africans were nominated to membership. Between 1922 and 1925 the election of West African legislative councillors was introduced, and after the Second World War the elected unofficial members were made majorities. Rule through existing forms of government, or 'indirect rule', was developed in British territories mainly as a result of experience gained in Northern Nigeria. There a lack of sufficient finances and men made the use of the Fulani emirs and their officials essential to preserve order and administer justice. The existing system was therefore preserved, but under the supervision of British Residents. Indirect rule needed autocratic rulers and could be applied wherever the people possessed powerful leaders or chiefs. In the Eastern Region of Nigeria peoples like the Ibo had no chiefs, and the attempt to foist 'warrant chiefs' upon them in order to make indirect rule work was a failure. The introduction of indirect rule to Ashanti and the restoration of the chiefs may have prevented the disintegration of Ashanti society, but in the Northern Territories it was difficult to secure recognition for the authority of many of the chiefs of the small communities, particularly in cases where their rights were doubtful. Indirect rule undoubtedly helped to preserve West African society in British territories, but in doing so it also hindered social and economic changes necessary with the alteration of methods of production and distribution. Moreover, other systems of government were required if the West African territories were to take an independent place in the modern world and there was a growing class of West Africans who desired democratic government of a European type.

Other empires in West Africa

Although the Portuguese had been the first to chart the coast of West Africa and the first to found settlements there they had ceased to take an active interest in West African affairs until the political 'scramble' of the late 19th century. A few fortified trading posts had been maintained at Cacheu and Bissau on the Guinea coast, on the Bissagos Islands and at Ouidah on the Slave Coast. The Cape Verde Islands, São Tomé and Príncipe were also Portuguese possessions. In Guinea Britain attempted to found a settlement at Bolama at the beginning of the 19th century and later laid claim to the islands and shores. Portugal protested, and the matter was submitted to arbitration. The verdict was given to Portugal, whose government then proceeded to organize a colony of Guinea under its own governorship. The Cape Verde Islands derived a short-lived importance from the coaling station of St Vincent. Economic development – of salt, livestock, iron ore and cinchona plantations – has been prevented or hindered by the lack of sufficient drinking water. The islands have had to depend partly on rainwater cisterns, partly on the distilling of sea water, and partly on imported water. São Tomé and Príncipe retain some small importance as exporters of cocoa, coffee and sugar to Lisbon. Eleven acres (4·5 hectares) of Portuguese territory were held at Ouidah until 1961, the sole remainder of Portugal's claim to the whole of Dahomey.

Spain acquired her West African interests only in the late 18th century, when, in 1778, she obtained the cession of Fernando Po and Annobon from Portugal in order to develop entrepôts for the slave trade. During the same period a settlement was founded at Corisco Bay on the river Muni, which became the nucleus of Spanish Guinea. At first the Spanish did little in Fernando Po, and permitted the British to administer the island from 1829 to 1844. They then decided to resume their rights, refused to sell the island to Britain, and encouraged the development of cocoa and cinchona planting, employing mainly Nigerian immigrant labour.

The most recent and short-lived of the West African empires was that of Germany. German contact with the west coast dates back to the 17th century when the Brandenburgers and the Prussian Company of Emden held the trading posts of Grossfriedrichsburg and Takrana. Later the Elector of Brandenburg

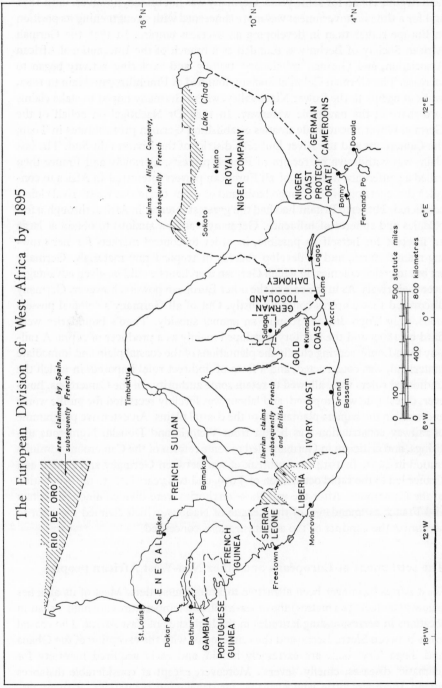

The European Division of West Africa by 1895

Figure 8.6

held Arguin Island for some years. Germany was not united, however, until 1871 and for a time its government was more concerned with strengthening its position in Europe rather than in developing an overseas empire. In 1878 the German African Society of Berlin was founded as a branch of the International African Association, and German missionary, trading and exploring activity began to increase. The German Colonial Society, founded at Frankfurt-am-Main in 1882, sent out agents to the Lower Niger valley, where Germany hoped to stake claims to a share in the navigable waterway. In 1884 Dr Nachtigal on behalf of the German Government made treaties establishing German protectorates in Togo, the Cameroons and the River Dubréka district of the Rivières du Sud. The last claim was withdrawn on receipt of French protests. Germany and France then called a conference in Berlin of all European powers interested in Africa to consider the question of the Congo basin and of other territories where rival claims conflicted. Hitherto Britain had had the greatest interest in Africa, through a few colonies and spheres of influence. Germany was now anxious to obtain as large an interest for herself as possible, in order to control markets for her growing manufactures, and to develop sources of tropical raw materials. Germany set out to create colonies, in which German merchants would be given advantages over their rivals. As in the case of the other European powers, however, Germany discovered that empires could be costly. Out of all Germany's colonial possessions, only Togo did not require an annual subsidy. Togo's boundaries were fixed by 1899, and the territory developed mainly as a producer of copra. A railway from Lomé, serving chiefly the plantations of the coastal plain and immediate hinterland, was constructed, and a form of 'indirect rule' imposed, in which the traditional rulers were allowed to retain some authority. In the Cameroons, however, direct rule was imposed, and labour was forcibly recruited for public works and work in the banana plantations of the coastal plains. An extensive programme of railway construction was begun from Victoria and Douala. Numerous uprisings, and criticism in Germany, led to some reform of the Cameroons administration in 1907. In 1914 the outbreak of war between Germany and Britain and France led to the rapid occupation of Togo, and two years later to the occupation of the Cameroons. After the war these territories were divided amongst Britain and France as 'mandates' of the League of Nations, which claimed the right to scrutinize the conduct of the administrations concerned.

The settlement of Europeans and other Non-West African peoples

West Africa has never been attractive to European settlers. Most of its area lies below 2500 feet (760 metres) above sea-level, and temperatures are higher than in locations in corresponding latitudes in the highlands of East Africa. The coastal areas between Sierra Leone and the Cameroons, with the exception of the Ghana and Togo 'dry' belt, are extremely humid, and early acquired notoriety for 'climatic' diseases, chiefly 'fevers'. Moreover, except at considerable distances inland, there was little land available for developing plantations, without displacing existing occupants, and West Africa offered less produce and poorer trading opportunities than elsewhere in the inter-tropics. Until the 19th century there were only a few small colonies of Europeans established along the coast wherever profit margins appeared high enough to over-ride other considerations.

Until the 20th century the number of Europeans in West Africa was extremely small, and consisted almost entirely of traders, officials, missionaries and soldiers. Even by 1960 the number of officials and soldiers was far greater than that of the total of other groups, except in Ghana and Nigeria, where West Africans had largely replaced them. Only in the Ivory Coast and the German Cameroons has there been any considerable number of settlers who attempted to live by agricultural production. Other non-officials have been chiefly Europeans engaged in mining in the Jos Plateau of Nigeria and the gold fields of Ghana.

Fear of disease and the climate appears to have been the main discouraging factor. Between 1812 and 1823, for example, there were 95 officers in the service of the British Company of Merchants on the Gold Coast. During this period 44 of the men died of some disease, 4 were killed in action and 28 returned to England. The annual death rates and invaliding rates on the Gold Coast towards the end of the 19th century have been estimated as follows:[59]

	Deaths per 1000	Invalided per 1000
1887	54	208
1888	55	555
1891	32·7	175·2
1897	76·6	155·1

It should be appreciated that most of the Europeans concerned were young men in the prime of their life. The number of old men had always been small, and retirement frequently took place at an early age. In the Gambia in 1825, of 199 soldiers who arrived in May, 160 had died before the end of December. The following year 200 more soldiers were landed at St Mary's Island at the beginning of the rains, and between 21st June and 21st December, 116 more had died. Of 399 soldiers, there were only 123 survivors in two years, of whom 33 were permanently unfit for any further service.[60] Senegal was notorious for yellow fever and cholera epidemics in the mid-19th century, in which as many as one-third of the European residents of the coastal settlements died. Between February 1825 and June 1828 Sierra Leone had 5 governors each of whom died in the service and only one of whom survived longer than 12 months. Freetown earned the title of 'White Man's Grave', and the anti-slavery cruisers which operated from there were known as the 'Coffin Squadron'. Quinine was in general use by 1840, but was taken too irregularly to be effective. The evolution of preventive treatment for malaria and yellow fever, based on Ross's discovery of 1898 and on the work of the American yellow fever commission in 1900, did much to lower death rates. So did the provision of better sanitation and the improved location of housing, for many Europeans were living in overcrowded towns and close to mosquito breeding grounds.[61] Some recognition of the relationship between disease and location had been made in the latter half of the 19th century, when the fevers were still thought to be climatic. Sanatoria at cooler altitudes had been erected on the Green Mountain in Ascension Island, at Basileh at an altitude of 1000 feet (300 metres) above sea-level in Fernando Po, at Aburi in the Gold Coast, where the Basel Mission maintained a station, at Hill Station above Freetown in Sierra Leone and at Buea in the Cameroons.

By 1951 there were almost 95,000 people of non-African origin living in West Africa, of whom about 82 per cent were of European or American (almost entirely United States) origin, and the remainder chiefly from the Lebanon and India. The proportion of non-Africans was thus less than 0·2 per cent of the whole, but their contribution to the development of West Africa, and to the present changes in its landscape, was out of all proportion to their numbers. Of the 95,000 non-Africans in 1951, 62,000 were in French West Africa, where a greater measure of 'settlement' has been encouraged than elsewhere, and fewer West Africans had been employed in managerial and administrative posts than in British territories. In all territories the non-African population was almost entirely urban, for example, there were 23,000 non-Africans in Dakar alone. Even in French West Africa, out of a total occupied population in 1951 of 34,026, only 868 were engaged in agriculture, fishing and forestry, 9328 were in the armed services, 8567 were in commerce, 6666 were in public services and administration, and 4981 were in industry. Similarly in Nigeria in 1952–3, of 8412 occupied non-Africans, 4431 were in professional, technical and related posts.

A comparison of the largest non-British territory, French West Africa, with the largest British territory, Nigeria, in 1951–3, shows the same proportion of females in both cases: 38 per cent. Admittedly the proportions of women and children were much higher than before the war due to the improvement in medical services and living conditions. Nevertheless, it remains true that, except for the Lebanese and Indians, West African expatriate communities were composed chiefly of young men engaged primarily as managers and administrators, many of whom served only for a few years. 31 per cent of the non-African population of French West Africa in 1951 was aged between 20 and 29 years. In Nigeria 33 per cent of the 1953 non-African population was aged between 25 and 34 years, and 35 per cent had resided in the country for only 1 year or less.

In each territory the nationals of the occupying power have predominated, but only in a few cases have they been willing to undertake socially 'inferior' work, even where this was remunerative. In consequence, opportunities have existed in commerce, particularly in the retail trades, for other non-Africans. In Sierra Leone in the 1890s the 'mercanti' of Southern Italy peddled their wares in Freetown and in the surrounding villages. They were followed by the Syrians, chiefly Lebanese, who went firstly to French West Africa, attracted through their trading contacts with the French in the Levant ports. Baillaud, for example, refers to a colony of Syrians in Conakry at the end of the last century buying rubber at higher prices than those offered by Europeans, because of lower overheads with a lower standard of living.[62] Many of them moved to the British territories about 1900, partly owing to heavy taxation, and large numbers of their friends and relatives joined them between 1921 and 1931. By 1951 there were over 15,000 Syrians in West Africa, nearly 10,000 of whom were in French West Africa. A few Indians were brought to West Africa, chiefly Nigeria, as clerks and skilled workers, but now all are engaged in trade. The Syrian and Indian traders compete with the West Africans in trading and money-lending. They are frequently petty middlemen, and, in the retail trades, are engaged chiefly in selling textiles and groceries. In 1950 they were said to have handled 40 per cent by value of the imports into the British West African territories.[63] There has been a tendency by West African colonial governments to protect African commercial interests, and to restrict the immigration or trading activities of Syrians. Their commercial importance may mean the imposition of further restrictions, now that West African territories have acquired independence.

For the non-African population as a whole independence has meant loss of many of the managerial positions held. Africanization departments of the Civil Service were created in Ghana and Nigeria, which lost almost their entire European government staffs. Yet, despite this tendency, the number of non-Africans in West Africa has been constantly increasing, and may well increase still further as more 'development' occurs. Thus in French West Africa the number of non-Africans increased from 32,000 in 1946 to 62,000 in 1951 and 88,000 in 1956. In Ghana the numbers increased from just under 7000 in 1948 to over 13,500 in 1960.

Trade in the late 19th and 20th centuries

The late 19th century witnessed the realization of higher productivity and the growth of overseas trade in West Africa. With the development of production and exchange, came the introduction of new methods of transport, new ways and standards of living, education, medical services and numerous other material improvements. Modern trading and transport will be discussed in detail below. Here a few features will be discussed which will set these developments into perspective with the European invasion of West Africa already treated.

The missionaries and traders of the mid-19th century had hoped that West Africa would become a major cotton producer. Instead the import of cheap textiles from Europe tended to reduce cotton production. Only from Northern Nigeria has any considerable export of cotton developed. Attempts as late as post-1945 to encourage cotton production in the Inland Niger Delta of the former French Sudan have not been very successful, and the agricultural scheme there has until recently concentrated mainly on rice. The first major exports were palm oil from Southern Nigeria and groundnuts from the Senegal and the Gambia. These supplied oils for lubrication, lighting and food. The market was threatened by the exploitation of mineral oils, but the discovery of the technique of manufacturing synthetic fats and their cheapness, compared with animal fats, increased the demand for vegetable oils enormously. Not only were groundnuts and palm oil in demand, but also palm kernels. The export of the last from Lagos alone rose from 2500 tons in 1865 to over 75,000 tons in 1902. Between 1894 and 1900 there was a slight drop in the export of palm produce due to a loss of labour to rubber gathering, but the rubber industry soon declined in the face of plantation competition from Malaya and only revived during the wartime periods of rubber shortage (p. 537).

Towards the end of the century the export of coffee and cocoa began from the Ivory and Gold Coasts and later from Southern Nigeria. With French protection and an excellent market in France itself coffee became a major export from the Ivory Coast. In the British territories better prices could be obtained for cocoa. By 1956 cocoa earned £51,000,000 for Ghana and accounted for well over half the total exports by value. Not the least important aspect of this trade was that 19 per cent of the earnings came from the United States. Groundnut products were the largest single export by value from French West Africa in 1956, but coffee came a close second, and cocoa production was increasing rapidly in the Ivory Coast. Palm produce was the chief export of Nigeria, followed closely by cocoa, and then by groundnuts. Mineral exports have also been developed, chiefly from the beginning of the present century. Ghana is an important exporter of gold, manganese and diamonds, and should become a major aluminium producer. Nigeria exports tin, Sierra Leone iron ore and former French West Africa iron ore and bauxite. Liberia and Nigeria have become large-scale rubber exporters. Although attempts have been made to produce other commodities in order to diversify the export economy, their production is at present completely dwarfed by that of the commodities cited above.

The growth of overseas exchange brought the rapid expansion of port facilities and the introduction of steam vessels, needed off a coast where sailing conditions were difficult. Railways, and later roads, were constructed to tap inland markets and open new regions suited to export crop production or containing exploitable minerals. Except for regions far inland, such as the groundnut producing area of Northern Nigeria, roads have become more important than railways in the last 30 years, and, in the two cocoa 'belts' of Ghana and south-western Nigeria, have provided a relatively dense network of modern transport facilities. River traffic has never become of great importance, for the few navigable waterways are distant from the major producing regions.

In the non-British territories, productivity and the direction of trade have in the past been strictly controlled. Whereas in 1956 only 35 per cent of Ghana's exports by value were directed to Britain, 75 per cent of French West Africa's exports went to France which also supplied 75 per cent of the imports. The Anglo-French Convention of 1898 gave equal treatment to British and French traders in Nigeria, the Gold Coast, the Ivory Coast and Dahomey for 30 years. In 1935 French import restrictions were extended to Dahomey and the Ivory Coast. Some easing of restrictions was undertaken in 1954 and 1956, and attempts were made to encourage French West African sales in other, mainly dollar, markets, but even today the former French West Africa territories, excepting Guinea, remain largely a closed commercial market.

Inland traffic and marketing in West Africa have been affected in more ways than by the introduction of overseas goods and production for overseas export. Firstly, in some cases, the growth of export crops has become an exclusive occupation, so that the cultivator must obtain food from elsewhere. Even where this is not so, the export crop cultivator frequently spends part of his income on foodstuffs. Secondly, the development of non-agricultural occupations, such as mining, and the increase in the urban proportion of the population, even though many urban dwellers still cultivate, has further increased the foodstuffs market. The needs of this market are met partly from overseas sources, which supply rice and 'luxuries' such as sugar, wheat flour, dried and tinned fish and tinned milk, and mainly from local commercial production of staples within the export crop regions, or on their immediate perimeter, or in the vicinity of the towns. The greater wealth derived from export crop production, or from food production for the internal market, has led in turn to an increase in demand for the local luxury, the kola nut, which is now transported by train or lorry instead of by porters, donkeys or camels. Similarly the meat markets have expanded, the movement of livestock from north to south has increased, and there is a greater demand for locally-made cloths used to make traditional styles of dress, in favour with the growth of national sentiment. The vast increase in circulation has brought a boom in the import of motor vehicles, of oil, and of oil products. More and more capital is accumulating in West African hands, although at present the chief avenues of investment are trade, transport and building, and not production.

Today West Africa is a basic producer, dependent on overseas sources for almost all her manufactured goods. The prospect of improvement of standards of living, low by European or North American standards, is affected by shortage of capital and by dependence on overseas markets. The economies of West Africa are susceptible to the slumps and booms of world exchange, although the existence of an agriculture capable of producing all of West Africa's food requirements should the necessity arise provides a useful safeguard against famine in the event of a general trade slump. West African politicians are naturally desirous of increasing the variety of West African productivity, and wherever possible of introducing manufacturing industries. Few such industries exist at present, and these few depend mainly on the use of local agricultural products. Not only are there problems of capital, but of power, transport and labour. Generally, coastal locations have great advantages over interior locations as future sites, yet, with the exception of Hausaland in Northern Nigeria, coastal regions or the immediate hinterlands are wealthier, and the interior regions are more in need of capital investment. Of all the West African territories Ghana was easily the richest, and until independence had demanded less capital from overseas sources than any other West African territory for her much greater measure of economic development. Already Ghana's economic strength has attracted more overseas investment than has the comparative weakness and greater need of several other territories.

BIBLIOGRAPHICAL NOTES

[1] H. Labouret, *Paysans d'Afrique Occidental*, 6th ed., Paris, 1941, pp. 28–32.

[2] See F. L. Shaw (Lady Lugard), *A Tropical Dependency*, London, 1905, and E. W. Bovill, *Caravans of the Old Sahara*, London, 1933.

[3] J. Richard-Molard, *Afrique Occidentale Française*, Paris, 1949, p. 101.

[4] F. L. Shaw, op. cit., p. 117.

[5] G. E. de Azurara, *The Chronicles of the Discovery and Conquest of Guinea*, translated by G. R. Beazley and E. Prestage, vol. I, 1896, p. 21, Hakluyt Society, no. 95. For a detailed account of the Portuguese discoveries see E. Prestage, *The Portuguese Pioneers*, London, 1933.

[6] See Duarte Pacheco Pereira, *Esmeraldo de Situ Orbis*, translated and edited by G. H. T. Kimble, 1937, p. 100, n. 4, Hakluyt Society, Series II, no. 79.

[7] See J. W. Blake, *Europeans in West Africa 1450–1560*, 2 vols, London, 1941, Hakluyt Society, Series II, nos 86 and 87; also J. W. Blake, *European Beginnings in West Africa, 1454–1578*, London, 1937.

[8] See E. Reclus, *Universal Geography*, edited by A. H. Keane, vol. III, West Africa, London, 1896, p. 153.

[9] Harrison Church notes that the castle must have been one of the world's first pre-fabricated buildings, the stone blocks being cut in Portugal and numbered to indicate their position in the eventual building, R. J. Harrison Church, *West Africa*, London, 5th ed., 1966, p. 361. Some of the stones were cut in Portugal, but part of the structure is in fact of local stone. See also W. E. F. Ward, *A History of the Gold Coast*, London, 1948, pp. 60–63.

[10] J. W. Blake, *Europeans in West Africa*, op. cit., vol. II, p. 383n.

[11] J. Bouchard, Les Portugais dans la Baie de Biafra au XVIème Siècle, *Africa*, **16**, 1946, pp. 217–27.

[12] R. Hakluyt, *Principal Voyages*, Maclehose edition, London, 1904, vol. VI, p. 151.

[13] *The Voyage of J. H. van Linschoten to the East Indies*, vol. I, London, 1885, Hakluyt Society, no. 70, p. 15.

[14] J. D. Fage, *An Introduction to the History of West Africa*, 3rd ed., Cambridge, 1962, p. 55.

[15] Richard Jobson, *The Golden Trade*, 1923, Penguin Press edition with an introduction by D. B. Thomas, 1933, p. xiii.

[16] W. Bosman, *A New and Accurate Description of the Coast of Guinea*, translated into English, London, 1705, p. 106.

[17] ibid., p. 69.

[18] ibid., p. 343.

[19] J. D. Fage, op. cit., p. 73.

[20] P. D. Curtin, *The Image of Africa: British Ideas and Action, 1780–1850*, London, 1965.
For details of the Slave Trade, see E. Donnan, *Documents Illustrative of the History of the Slave Trade to America*, 4 vols, 1931; vol. II, p. 598, n. 6 quoting from Report of the Lords of the Committee of the Privy Council, 1789, part I.

[21] *Report from the Select Committee on Africa (Western Coast)*, 1865, p. 466.

[22] *Report from the Select Committee on the West Coast of Africa*, 1842, part I, p. 127, q. 2477; p. 137, q. 2624–8; pp. 452–3, q. 7203–8; p. 543, q. 8407; pp. 695–7, q. 10550–63.

[23] For further comments on slavery see pp. 422–6.

[24] For the history of the exploration of West Africa in the first half of the 19th century see:

M. Perham and J. Simmons, *African Discovery*, London, 1942.

Mungo Park, *Travels in the Interior Districts of Africa, 1795–1797*, London, 2 vols, 1815–16.

Mungo Park, *Journal of a Mission to the Interior of Africa in the Year of 1805*, London, 1915.

Proceedings of the Association for Promoting the Discovery of the interior parts of Africa, 2 vols, 1810.

A. G. Laing, *Travels in the Timanee, Kooranko, and Soolima Countries in Western Africa*, London, 1825.

Dixon Denham, *Narrative to Travels and Discoveries in Northern and Central Africa in the years 1822, 1823 and 1824, by Major Denham, Captain Clapperton and the late Dr Oudney*, London, 1826.

Hugh Clapperton, *Journal of a Second Expedition into the Interior of Africa from the Bight of Benin to Soccatoo*, London, 1829.

R. Caillié, *Travels through Central Africa to Timbuctoo and Across the Great Desert, to Morocco, 1824–28*, 2 vols, London, 1830.

R. L. Lander, *Journal of an expedition to explore the course and termination of the Niger*, London, 1832.

H. Barth, *Travels and discoveries in North and Central Africa, 1849–55*, 5 vols, 1857–8.

R. M. Prothero, Heinrich Barth and the Western Sudan, *Geographical Journal*, **124**, 1958, pp. 326–39.

[25] Sir E. Hertslet, *Map of Africa by Treaty*, 3 vols, London, 1909; vol. I, p. 65.

[26] Quoted in F. M. Bourret, *The Gold Coast*, 2nd ed., Stanford, 1952, p. 18.

[27] *Report from the Select Committee on the West Coast of Africa*, 1842, part III, p. 15.

[28] F. M. Bourret, op. cit., pp. 18–19.

[29] For further details of the slave settlement see below, pp. 425–6.

[30] See rules of Ashmun's 1822 proclamation quoted in Sir Harry Johnston, *Liberia*, vol. I, London, 1906, pp. 136–7.

[31] Sir H. Johnston, op. cit., pp. 371–2.

[32] C. Schefer, *Instructions Générales Données de 1863 à 1870 aux Gouverneurs et Ordonnateurs des Etablissements Français en Afrique Occidentale*, Paris, 1921, Tome I, p. 81 (description of the Island of St Louis in 1782).

[33] ibid., p. 254.

[34] R. Pasquier, Les Essais de Culture du Coton au Sénégal, Institut des Hautes Etudes de Dakar du Department d'Histoire, no. I, extrait des *Annales Africaines* de 1955, p. 6.

[35] ibid., p. 7.

[36] ibid., p. 14.

[37] *Report from the Select Committee* . . . 1842, op. cit., part I, pp. 89–90, q. 1588-97; p. 92, q. 1649–52; pp. 93–94, q. 1697–1702; p. 101, q. 1877–8; p. 115, q. 2255.

[38] MacGregor Laird and R. K. Oldfield, *Narrative of an Expedition into the Interior of Africa by the River Niger in the Steam Vessels Quorra and Alburkah in 1832, 1833 and 1834*, 2 vols, London, 1837.

[39] James McQueen, *A Geographical and Commercial View of Northern Central Africa*, Edinburgh, 1821.
Thomas Fowell Buxton, *The African Slave Trade and its Remedy*, London, 1839.
K. O. Dike, *Trade and Politics in the Niger Delta, 1830–1855*, Oxford, 1956, pp. 61–62.

[40] W. Allen and T. R. H. Thomson, *A Narrative of the Expedition to the River Niger in 1841*, London, 1848, 2 vols; vol. I, pp. 28–29.

[41] ibid., p. 38.

[42] ibid., pp. 300–5.
Journals of the Rev. J. F. Schön and Mr. S. Crowther, London, 1842, pp. 114, 117–18, 124 and 353.

[43] W. B. Baikie, *Narrative of an Exploring Voyage up the rivers Kwora and Binue in 1854*, London, 1856.
See K. O. Dike, op. cit., p. 169.

[44] A useful commentary on the role of the Christian missions in the history of West Africa is in J. D. Fage, op. cit., pp. 119–22.

[45] S. O. Biobaku, *The Egba and their Neighbours 1842–72*, Oxford, 1957, pp. 35–37.

[46] ibid., pp. 44–45.
T. J. Bowen, *Adventures and Missionary Labors in Several Countries in the Interior of Africa from 1849 to 1856*, Charleston, 1857.

[47] N. H. Stilliard, *The Rise and Development of Legitimate Trade in Palm Oil with West Africa* (unpublished thesis, University of Birmingham, 1938), p. 14, quoted in K. O. Dike, op. cit., p. 49.

[48] K. O. Dike, op. cit., p. 54.

[49] *Report from the Select Committee* . . . 1849, op. cit., part I, p. 33.

[50] W. N. M. Geary, *Nigeria under British Rule*, London, 1927, p. 80.

[51] For a general account of the early trade see A. McPhee, *The Economic Revolution in British West Africa*, London, 1926, pp. 69–71.

[52] *Report from the Select Committee* . . . 1842, op. cit., part II.

[53] J. Richard-Molard, op. cit., p. 183.

[54] *Report from the Select Committee* . . . 1865, op. cit., p. 5, q. 71–75.

[55] ibid., pp. 78–80, q. 1803–05, q. 1818–25, q. 1867–71.

[56] The problems are amusingly expressed in a novel by Joyce Carey, a former member of the British colonial administration in Nigeria:
'Jarvis was a keen mapper. He had had, however, unusual difficulties with his latest map. He had found it impossible to use a plane table in the high jungle, and he had to rely on dead reckoning for distances; also it was hard to find out the local names of places. He was obliged to stop every traveller and to ask at every hut for names. But villagers did not always understand what a strange white man meant by pointing at the earth and uttering a sound like a dog's bark. They answered sometimes, 'I don't know', or simply 'Dirt, grass'. Thus one saw on Jarvis' map such places as Town Town, River River, Idontknow Village, Begyourpardon Rock, which was an important landmark, Dirtland, a fertile and prosperous tract on the River Water; and Forgodsakeplease Lake, which was surrounded by swamps and ought to be avoided by transport columns.' Joyce Carey, *Castle Corner*, London, 1938, p. 168.

[57] For a detailed account of boundary problems in the case of Nigeria see J. R. V. Prescott, The Evolution of Nigeria's Boundaries, *Nigerian Geographical Journal*, 2, 1959, pp. 80–104.

[58] For an account of methods of government see Lord Hailey, *An African Survey*, London, revised 1956. For an account of 'indirect rule' see Lord Lugard, *The Dual Mandate in British Tropical Africa*, London, 1922; M. Perham, *Lugard: the Years of Authority, 1898–1945*, London, 1960, and *Native Administration in Nigeria*, London, 1962.

[59] R. R. Kuczynski, *Demographic Survey of the British Colonial Empire*, vol. I, West Africa, London, 1948, pp. 533–7.

[60] ibid., p. 384.

[61] For health in relation to the location of settlement see pp. 451–3.

[62] E. Baillaud, *Sur les Routes du Soudan*, Toulouse, 1902, p. 319.

[63] Lord Hailey, op. cit., p. 412.

1. The Richard Toll rice-growing scheme in Senegal.

2. A modern Wolof groundnut growing village near Thiès in Senegal. Note inner dark zone of manured soil surrounding village.

3. The port of Dagana on the Senegal River. Note floodland and rain land cultivation.

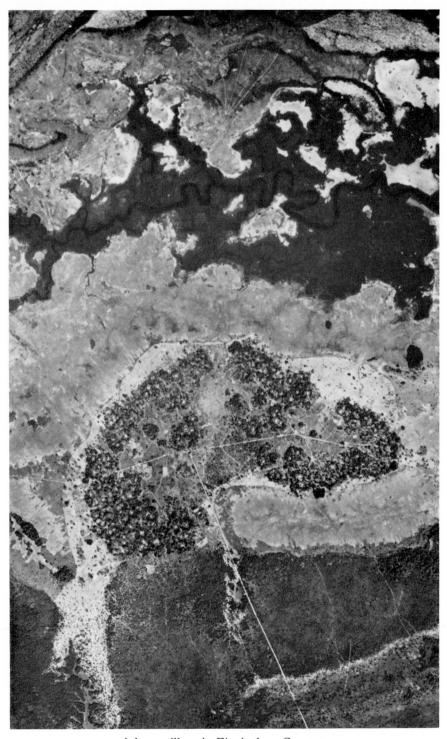

4. A large village in Ziguinchor, Casamance.

5. The barrier beaches of Ziguinchor in Casamance.

6. Abidjan.

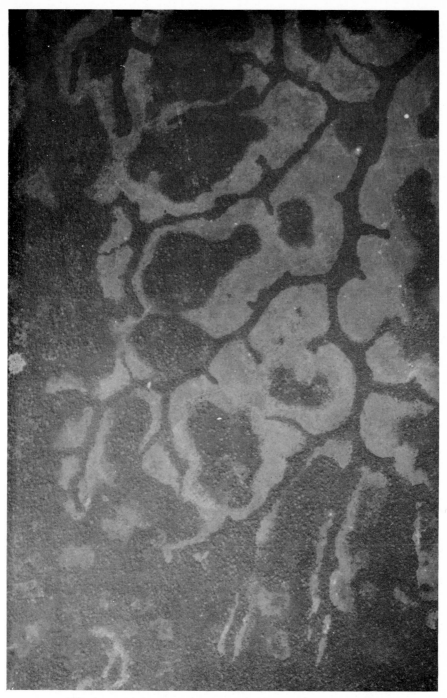

7. The forest-savanna boundary near Gagnoa in the Ivory Coast.

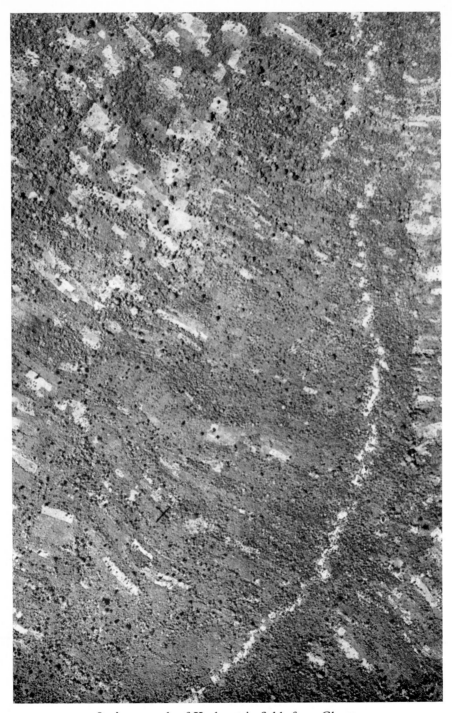

8. An example of Krobo strip fields from Ghana.

9. Djougou, Togo: the strip fields of high density agriculture, interrupted by quartzitic ridges with a superimposed drainage pattern.

10. Lanlate, Western Nigeria: a Yoruba village with geographically separated quarters in derived savanna. Note the close proximity of residual hill masses.

11. Timbuktu: a 'Tuareg' town with colonial grid-iron pattern quarters added. Note the fields near the lakes, and the more distant fields separated from the town by an open space.

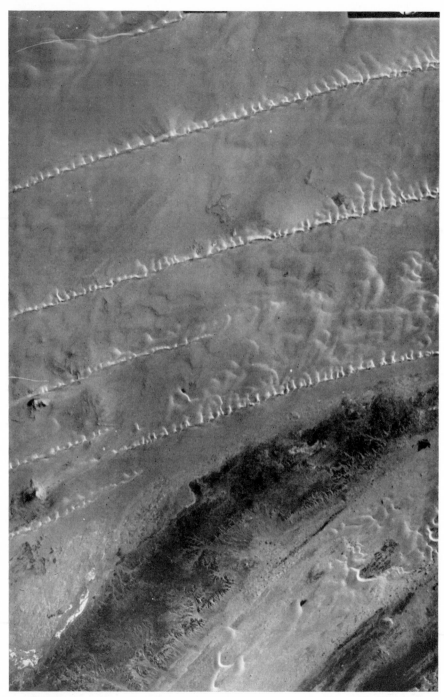

12. Niger Republic: Seif dunes (top) and bare rock (below) near Bilma oasis.

CHAPTER 9

Changes in Population Distribution, Settlement Patterns and Demography

Before the establishment of European political authority in West Africa, the most favoured areas for settlement appear to have been:

1) The Sudanic environments, with sufficient moisture for one cereal crop a year, supplemented by a small floodland crop, together with annual addition to soils of harmattan dust, a supply of manure from the cattle of nomadic pastoralists, and favourable situations for trans-Saharan traffic.
2) The sub-Guinean environments, with sufficient moisture for more than one cereal crop a year, or for the cultivation of roots, and yet with a climax vegetation not too difficult to clear.
3) The lighter-soiled portions of the Guinean zone, particularly in south-eastern Nigeria and Benin, where conditions were similar to those of the sub-Guinean environments.
4) The floodlands of the Sahel and Sudan.
5) The refuge hill areas of the sub-Sudanic and sub-Guinean zones.
6) The floodlands of the estuaries of the south-west, suitable for rice cultivation.

Within the first three of these favoured areas settlement tended to be concentrated more in the east than in the west.

Today the same pattern still prevails, as one may appreciate in Chapter 1 where Figures 1.2 and 1.3, showing the present distribution, provide the basis for discussing traditional features, but with certain exceptions. The exceptions include: the high densities of the Guinean environments, even on the heavier soils, particularly in Ashanti, southern Dahomey and south-western Nigeria; the large concentrations in the westernmost Sudanic areas in Senegal; the high coastal densities. The European occupation established the main trading centres on the coast, destroyed the former trans-Saharan traffic, revolutionized production and trade, and established a new pattern of transport and markets. Population moved towards the coast and the immediate hinterlands of the ports, to the western portions of the Sudanic environments, and into the formerly less densely-occupied Guinean areas, with the exception of south-western Ghana and south-western Ivory Coast. This movement was accelerated by the development of export crop production: groundnuts in western Senegal and the perennials – oil palms, cocoa and coffee – in the Guinean areas. The districts affected attracted population because of the higher incomes to be gained from cultivating export crops and the greater availability of imported commodities. They not only gained a large increase in their settled population, but also a seasonal influx of migrants in search of work during the 'slack' period on Sudanic and sub-Sudanic croplands. Elsewhere export crop production, with its accompanying local increase of population, developed in districts served by the new internal transport system, notably in the groundnut and cotton growing areas of Northern Nigeria, and to some extent in the areas served by the Dakar–Niger, Guinea and Ivory Coast–Upper Volta railway systems. The sub-Sudanic and sub-Guinean zones became less attractive, for they offered little export produce and have hitherto been largely neglected by modern transport developments.

The economic changes effected stimulated internal trade, and encouraged increasing production for market rather than for subsistence. The most attractive locations for settlement became those nearest railway stations, alongside roads or near urban centres. Political changes rendered hill-top refuges no longer necessary, and produced new administrative centres, besides encouraging the 'fixing' of settlements which formerely had tended to move. At the same time, in areas remote from the new markets, greater security encouraged greater mobility and dispersal of population away from fortified positions to the croplands. Social changes made agriculture less attractive to many, and encouraged an urbanward movement of population. Towns have been slowly changing in character from agglomerations of quarters, occupied mainly by agriculturalists, to commercial cities with distinct business, retail, residential and, in some cases, administrative and industrial zones. Thus under modern political, economic and social influences, trends already well developed in Europe and North America – centripetal population movement and the emergence of zones in cities – are beginning to appear in West Africa.

Early effects of European contacts

The first population movements arising from European influences resulted from the development of an overseas trade, chiefly in slaves, but also to a lesser extent in gold, ivory and wax. Trade brought the establishment of 'factories' or warehouses at small anchorages where merchant ships would call regularly. Many of these were situated on islands, often distant from the mainland, such as the Cape Verde Islands and São Tomé. Others, however, were established on the estuarine shores of the south-west, or on the beaches of the Cameroons. Beside the often fortified trading posts, large villages and even towns were established, mainly by local peoples seeking to benefit from the new traffic. Such settlements provided recruits for the defensive forces needed to guard the trading privileges obtained, and supplied labour for handling goods, supervising the slave barracoons, carrying loads to and from interior markets and watering and revictualling the ships. A commercial agriculture began near the anchorages, cultivating chiefly maize in order to supply food to both the slave barracoons and the ships. The town of

Dondou, established close to the Portuguese fort of El Mina in the 15th century, provides an example. Dondou was one of the earliest settlements of virtually detribalized people in Africa. Its inhabitants were allies of the Portuguese and had their own system of government. The town was divided into three wards each under a 'brasso' or African governor.[1] Slaves were imported into El Mina and Dondou from São Tomé and Arguin in order to carry pots and cloths to Ashanti to be exchanged for gold. The amount of trade depended much on the labour available in Dondou, and oppression by the Portuguese or, later, by the Dutch usually resulted in the desertion of the town's inhabitants and in consequence a decline in trade.

Besides settlements like Dondou, other purely African trading posts were founded, particularly during the 17th and 18th centuries, and many of these became important towns. Whereas European trading posts were established successfully in the less humid climatic conditions of the coast between Cape Three Points and Lagos lagoon, farther east conditions in the Guinean environment were much more trying, and the Portuguese attempt to found a post near Benin had proved abortive. Here on the Slave Coast between the Volta river and the Cameroons numerous small African ports profited from their access to the highest densities of population in West Africa. A coast which formerly had been occupied only by scattered villages was occupied at suitable points offering firm ground in the deltas of the Niger and Cross rivers by small detribalized groups, serving the needs of local slave dealers. Included amongst these ports were Ouidah (where European forts were built, but subject to the rulers of Dahomey), Porto Novo, Badagry and Lagos on the lagoons west of the Niger delta; Brass, Bonny and Degema or New Calabar in the delta; Opobo on the lagoons to the east; Calabar on the Cross river, and finally the Cameroons ports including Douala. Laird and Oldfield have left a description of the delta settlements in the 1830s, with their narrow strips of levée with a morass in the rear. So little room was available for cultivation that the bulk of food needed had to be imported from the interior. Only fish provided a local resource.[2] Calabar was founded in the 17th century by Efik tribesmen forced to leave the territory today occupied by the Ibibio. They settled eventually on the left bank of the Cross river estuary near the mouth of the tributary Qua river. The site consisted of a terrace, providing firm ground above flood-level, backed by swamps, and forming in effect a narrow easily-defended peninsula. Here the Efik settlers founded a number of small villages, known collectively as Calabar or Old Calabar, and from these they attempted to gain control of the overseas traffic of the Cross river basin. The hinterland provided large numbers of slaves, chiefly from Iboland (particularly from the interior trading settlement of Arochuku), and palm oil and kernels brought down the river by dug-out canoes.

The early trading brought not only new coastal settlements, but considerable displacements of population in the struggle to control ports and the routes leading to the coast, and in the warfare and destruction of settlement involved in providing slaves for export. Between 1680 and 1786, 2,130,000 Negro slaves were imported into the British American colonies alone, and by the latter part of the 18th century 70,000 slaves a year were exported from Africa to America, almost entirely from the western coast.[3] 1768 appears to have been a peak year with an export of 104,000 slaves from Africa, of which over half were taken in British ships.[4] Mortality on the voyage was frequently of the order of 15 per cent, and further heavy mortality occurred in the barracoons and en route from the point of capture to the coast. Add to this the large numbers killed during slave raids and it seems likely that the loss of population involved was of the order of ten times the number exported overseas. Most of the slaves taken came from the coastal and immediately inland districts, in the west from the Rivières du Sud, particularly from the Gambia and from Senegal, and in the south chiefly from the Niger and Cross river delta district, whose 'Eboes' (Ibos) and 'Quas' (Ibibios) were particularly prized as labourers on the plantations of the West Indies. It seems likely that high densities of population were nearer the coast between the Niger and Cross rivers than in any other part of West Africa in the 17th and 18th centuries, for the Ibos and Ibibios appear to have settled in the Guinean environment at an early date. West of the Niger the Guinean forests were little settled,* except in Benin and on the sub-Guinean fringes, until the export crop developments of the late 19th century. Depopulation by slave-raiding was also widespread farther inland, due to the demands of markets in Hausaland, the states of the Upper Niger basin and in Senegal. Warfare, with consequent population movement, occurred in the sub-Sudanic areas until the first decade of the 20th century. In Senegal the development of French trading posts led to a coastward movement of the Wolof and the growth of the states of Cayor and Baol.[5]

The development of trade led to the founding of settlements, not only on the coast, but at suitable inland trading points, and to a displacement of population consequent on the warfare to control trade routes and ports. Settlements like Bakel and Medina on the Senegal, Barracunda on the Gambia, and Kita and Nioro on the watershed between the Senegal and Niger basins became important trading posts, centres of authority directing trade and exacting tolls from caravans and canoes. The Sarakolé, who early developed a great interest in the coastal trade, founded numerous settlements on the major routes, or settled in small colonies in established market towns. The Moors and Wolof fought to control the Senegal river, whilst the Malinké gradually invaded the western coastlands and sought to obtain dominion over the coastal tribes, particularly where these were on important routes. In the Gold Coast the coastal tribes fought one another to control trade, and in turn fought Ashanti. The Ashanti peoples conquered many of the tribes to the south of them, and pressed the coastal tribes into a contracting area until the war of 1873. In Dahomey trade brought wealth to small states like Allada or Ardra and Ouidah, in which large market towns were established. Both states were conquered in 1724 and 1725 by the Fon of Abomey, who destroyed the towns and later extended his power as far eastwards as Abeokuta, where

* The Yoruba city states of Ilesha, Ife, Owu and Ijebu-Ode were important exceptions, although well inland.

he was stopped by the Egba. The Egba and the Ijebu to the east both controlled important routes and developed flourishing markets at their capitals of Abeokuta and Ijebu-Ode respectively. Farther inland the town of Ibadan became an important market and military power, especially after the destruction of the neighbouring trade centre of Ijaiye, and frequently fought the towns of Abeokuta and Ijebu-Ode in order to gain control of the routes to Badagry, Lagos, Ikorodu and Epe, by which guns and liquor were imported, and slaves and palm oil exported. Farther east numerous trading towns developed on or near the Niger, like Onitsha at the head of a route leading across northern Iboland to the Cross river. Owerri was founded on a route across southern Iboland, Arochuku became an important collecting point on the Cross river, and the Umon tribe established their chief town on an island in the Cross river in order to interfere with all traffic between the interior and the coast.[6] The abolition of the slave trade during the 19th century stopped the drain on West Africa's population resources, but it also resulted in the decline of some market towns like Salaga (in present-day Ghana). Between 1877 and 1885 the population of Salaga was claimed to have been reduced from 20,000 to 10,000.[7] Elsewhere new slave markets were founded. When Ouidah was closely watched by the naval squadrons in the 19th century, the king of Abomey established a new slave port at Cotonou. In West Cameroon, the cessation of the slave trade and the development of a market for palm produce brought a move of population away from the foothills to the oil palm districts of the plains. With the abolition of the slave trade came the return of many former slaves from the Americas. Some returned independently, like the 'Brazilians' who settled in small colonies in established ports and villages along the coast as in Lagos, or founded new settlements like Porto Seguro (in present-day Togo). Others were brought by philanthropic and other societies and settled on the coast of Liberia, notably at Monrovia, and, together with captives freed from slave ships, at Freetown in Sierra Leone. The first freed slave colony in Sierra Leone was founded in 1787 at Granville by 377 former slaves and Europeans on an area of 256,000 acres obtained from King Tom. The 'Province of Freedom', modelled on Granville Sharp's notions of ancient Israel and medieval England, was intended to settle the English black poor in Africa.[8] A heavy death rate and poverty of resources led to the virtual abandonment of the settlement by 1788. Further small immigration increased the numbers, but the settlement was destroyed by local tribes in the following year, and the inhabitants fled, chiefly to Par Boson's town 12 miles (19 km) up river. In 1791 the Sierra Leone Company formed a new settlement at Fourah Bay, and the following year brought over 1000 negroes from Nova Scotia together with 119 Europeans. By 1794 there was the settlement of Freetown with about 400 houses, a Nova Scotian settlement between one-third and $2\frac{1}{4}$ miles ($\frac{1}{2}$–$3\frac{1}{2}$ km) distant and the original settlement of Granville Town. Some Nova Scotians had settled up river where they planted rice. Krus came to the new colony to work as labourers, servants or seamen, and 'Mandingoes' and Timnes came for the purposes of trade. Many of the trading immigrants established new villages on the peninsula, but large numbers

of Krus came only temporarily, and an Act of 1816 sought to establish a town
especially for these seasonal residents. In 1847 the British Government persuaded
some of the Krus to emigrate as labourers to the West Indies. In 1800 550
Maroons, a group of rebellious Jamaican slaves, were landed and settled first at
Granville Town. Attacks by tribesmen forced their withdrawal to Freetown, but
later they were able to re-occupy their former lands. In 1808 a Vice-Admiralty
court was established in the Colony to deal with captured slaves brought in by
naval vessels and large numbers of Africans liberated in this way soon increased
the Colony's population, despite the heavy death roll due to disease and privation
amongst the immigrants. In 1817–19 West Indian troops were discharged in
Sierra Leone, and many of these founded the settlements of York, Kent and
Wellington, whilst others settled in Freetown itself, or moved to African villages,
the islands of Los and the Gambia. Some of the liberated Africans returned home,
particularly the Yoruba, and by 1844, 600–800 of these had returned, chiefly to
the districts around Badagry and Lagos. By 1822 the Colony had a population of
over 15,000, 5643 of whom were in Freetown itself, and the remainder in the
numerous small settlements and villages of the outlying districts of the peninsula.

Political factors

The development of effective government in West Africa by the colonial powers
brought important demographic and distributional changes. The new forms of
government brought the suppression of the internal slave trade and eventually,
in most areas, of slavery itself. They also brought peace to large areas, and
encouraged changes in production, trading, and social and political conditions.
Two of the limiting factors on population increase, warfare and slave-raiding,
were removed. Medicine was introduced. Hitherto, local migration of peoples
in large groups or in families had been an important feature of West African
demography, due mainly to the pastoral and agricultural methods employed, and
partly, in over three-quarters of the area, to the existence of marked seasonal
contrasts in moisture distribution. The resulting lack of stability in population
distribution was unsuited to the new political and economic developments. New
fixed patterns of settlement began to replace the old mobile patterns. At the
same time, in those areas where economic changes were greatest, a demand for
labour was created, and both seasonal and permanent migrations were encouraged. These were made possible both by the guarantee of peace and the introduction of new methods of transport.

Colonial governments early sought to 'immobilize' the population, partly by
endeavouring to find owners of the land, as in Senegal from about 1857 onwards[9], and partly by trying to establish fixed sites for many settlements,
especially where these were the residence of a local ruler or governing body. They
also tried to nucleate the population. The problem of administering a scattered
and mobile people is revealed in the report of one administrator in the Lagos
colony in 1900, who explained that the people of Erele or Ikale had scattered

among their farms and deserted Erele, formerly a large town. 'Major Ewart and I have endeavoured to persuade them to rebuild their town, they did so and straightway left it again. I can understand their liking to be near their work, but it makes it very difficult to discuss any question with them.'[10] In West Cameroun under the German administration, small communities, like the Ambele and

Izi Ibo Settlement Pattern

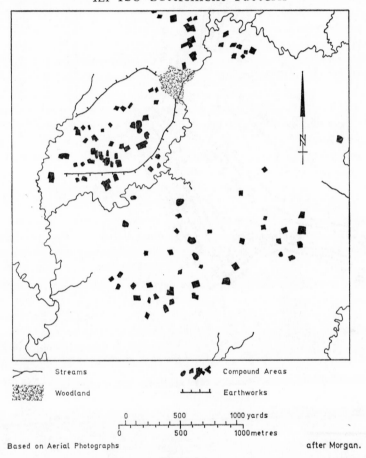

Streams		Compound Areas
Woodland		Earthworks

0   500   1000 yards
0   500   1000 metres

Based on Aerial Photographs   after Morgan.

Figure 9.1

Wechu clans of the Menka-Widekum area, were forced to concentrate so that their movements could be watched, and forced labour more easily recruited. Several villages were moved to important routes followed regularly by adminis-trators. After the siege of Agadès in 1916, the French forced the Tuareg nomads of Aïr to move southwards and take up a sedentary existence in the districts of Tanout and Zinder. Some 30,000 tribesmen were moved, and many of these crossed the frontier into Nigeria. Routeways and wells were neglected and the

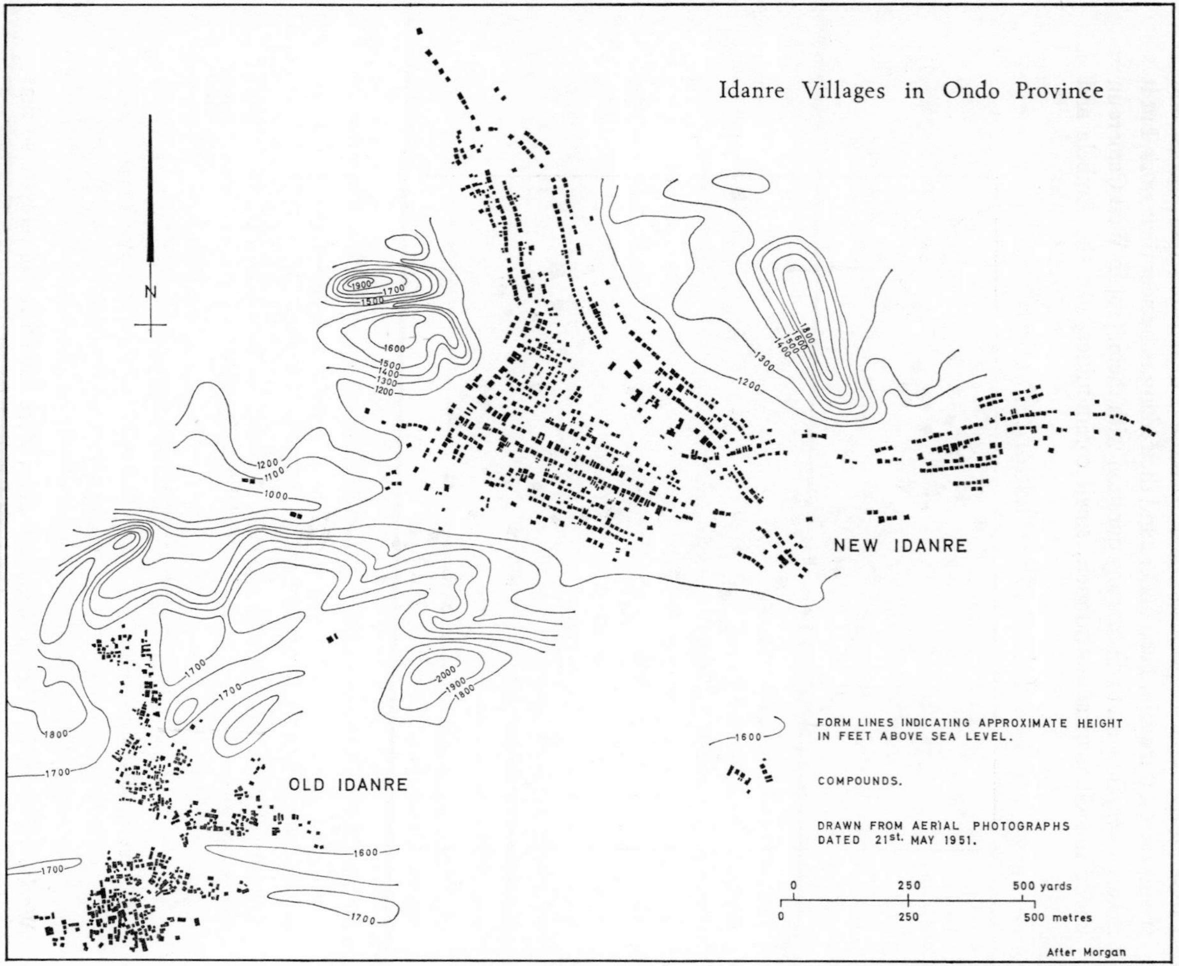

Idanre Villages in Ondo Province

NEW IDANRE

OLD IDANRE

FORM LINES INDICATING APPROXIMATE HEIGHT
IN FEET ABOVE SEA LEVEL.

COMPOUNDS.

DRAWN FROM AERIAL PHOTOGRAPHS
DATED 21st. MAY 1951.

0   250   500 yards

0   250   500 metres

After Morgan

Figure 9.2

number of camels dwindled. In 1922 the policy was reversed, and attempts were made to persuade the Tuareg to return to their former homes.[11] In areas remote from administrative control and unaffected by the new economic influences, the greater security provided by the colonial government encouraged increased mobility and dispersal. In north-eastern Iboland the Ibo left their small walled villages for compounds scattered throughout their croplands[12] (Fig. 9.1). On the northern fringe of the Benue valley peoples moved down from the hills, and settled in dispersed compounds and hamlets in the plains.[13] The Tiv have increased the pace of their migration away from the more crowded areas.[14] In other areas the development of well-nucleated market centres was frequently accompanied by a dispersal of the rural population. Thus the establishment of French authority in Senegal led to dispersal amongst the Serer and the occupation of small villages.

Political policy frequently encouraged a downhill movement of population away from old defensive sites, although the difficulties of obtaining a livelihood on such sites often led to voluntary movement to the broader and better watered surrounding lowlands. Figure 9.2 provides an example from Western Nigeria. Thus security brought the downhill movement amongst the Guéré and Dan from the 'pitons' of the Guinea Highlands of the Ivory Coast, and amongst many of the Jos Plateau 'pagans'. Peoples such as the Kadar were persuaded to settle in the plains by District Officers, partly because the new sites offered more cultivable land, and partly because the new distribution made the people more accessible to British administration. Hill-top sites afforded excellent lookouts, and even defences against the visits of District Officers. In the Kabba Province of Northern Nigeria all villages near the small government station of Iddo were moved down from the hills in 1911 by the persuasion of the Assistant Resident. Three years later the village of Ogamnana was destroyed when its inhabitants disobeyed the Resident's injunctions, and sought to rebuild it on a hill-top. In some cases downhill movement was slow or unattractive because of traditional attachment to the home district or even because of more fertile soils.[15]

The introduction of the new political authority encouraged mass resettlement in many cases, particularly in the Fulani Emirates where thousands of slaves were released and abandoned the estates of their northern masters in order to return to their former homes. Thus in 1905 there was a movement of population in Sokoto from the cities to the land, and the Sultan was recorded as having taken great pains to restore enslaved peoples to their deserted towns.[16] Frontier districts, formerly unhabitable, in northern Kano Province, Katagum, the 'Ningi bush' north of the Jos Plateau, and in the areas round Argungu and Silame were re-settled between 1902 and 1908, partly by immigration from French territory.[17] Slaves also left the Emirates of Kano, Zaria, Bida and Ilorin for their former homes. In the French Sudan (Mali) and Niger the power of the Moorish and Tuareg tribesmen was curbed. Fulani pastoralists and Negro cultivators moved northwards to wet season pastures and cultivable lands in the Sahel. In Senegal the creation of the French Protectorate enabled the Wolof, who had previously been resisted, to migrate into Serer country with its richer soils and heavier and more reliable rainfall.[18] The establishment of frontiers, which ignored ethnic and former political distributions, led to few demographic changes. Perhaps the most marked of these was the settlement of Tuareg refugees in Northern Nigeria after 1916. In some cases, however, frontier locations were an advantage. The Sarakolé, for example, established villages, whose inhabitants were engaged in smuggling, on the Senegal borders between Gambia and Portuguese Guinea.

Mass migration at the expense of neighbouring peoples, frequently involving warfare, was stopped by the colonial authorities. The north-eastward and south-eastward movements of the Ibo ceased with the British occupation, whilst the southern frontier of the Tiv was finally delimited by an earth ridge, known as the Tiv or Munshi wall – today a long strip of forest reserve. Although frontier zones which could be moved according to the strength of the forces opposed on each side were known in West Africa before the arrival of Europeans, fixed frontier lines were unknown. The establishment of such lines, combined with the policy of 'immobilization', created severe demographic problems for peoples such as the Tiv, who had hitherto been in a state of almost continuous expansion. And yet within the area occupied by the Tiv, so variable are the population densities that the pace of migration has in fact increased since the British occupation, due to the problems of population pressure created in the south by the fixing of the boundary, and due to the security and greater ease of movement provided by the new administration.[19]

Another effect of the changed political conditions was the decline of some centres, which had lost their administrative importance, and growth of others, often new creations of the colonial governments. Thus Dikwa and Kukawa, formerly major centres of administration, are now mere villages. Agadès is merely a local route centre and minor administrative town, whilst Timbuktu has little, except local trade and some tourist traffic, to support a population of only 7500. In their place are the new centres of political authority. The capital of the French Sudan, formerly Kayes on the Senegal river, was transferred to Bamako in 1908 after the construction of the railway to the latter by 1904. Bamako is at the lower limit of navigation on the Upper Niger and has the advantage of being backed by a high escarpment, the plateau summit of which, Koulouba, provided a suitable and comparatively healthy location for Government offices, some European residences and the Hospital. In 1833 Bamako was a mere village with a population of about 1000 located on an alluvial fan at the foot of the escarpment. There was nothing to distinguish it from other villages, until the French chose it as an important station on their railway from Kayes, and saw sufficient advantage in its nodality to make it the capital of the French Sudan. By 1910 the population of Bamako had increased to 6500. By 1931 it was 20,000, by 1955 68,000 and by 1960, when it became capital of Mali, 120,000. In Northern Nigeria the construction of capitals, firstly at Quendon near Lokoja, and then at Lokoja itself, secondly at Jebba near an important crossing of the Niger, thirdly at Zungeru, the most northerly point with river communication to the Niger, and finally at Kaduna, resulted in population shifts between the sites selected. An army of African troops, clerks, servants, carriers, labourers and traders moved from one capital to the next as British authority extended northwards. Zungeru was a failure. The site proved less healthy than expected, and the Kaduna river was navigable only for less than two months of the year. Kaduna, situated on the southern edge of the plateau of Hausaland, was in closer contact with the Hausa states and healthier, but it lacked people in the surrounding districts, initially to provide adequate supplies of fresh produce. In 1912 when the railway to Kano was completed, Kaduna was merely a watering point on the railway at the top of the steep gradient from Zungeru – the longest climb on the route. At this watering point the only settlement of any size was a small Gwari village. In 1913 Kaduna became the capital of the Northern Provinces, the Gwari village was removed, and a planned township erected for the local population, together with the Sabon Gari for immigrants, chiefly clerks and traders, from the south. In order to encourage the growth of the town, it was announced in 1926 that all Africans taking up land within 5 miles (8 km) radius of Kaduna would be excused the payment of tax for five years. Many came to escape Native Authority regulations, hoping that residence in Kaduna would imply the protection of the station magistrate. Although there has been a large influx of traders and artisans, in fact, Kaduna had nothing to foster its growth, other than its political and railway significance. The location of a suitable administrative site frequently involved shifts for at least a few years until a suitable place was discovered. When the British advanced into Bornu in 1902, they agreed to the rebuilding of the old capital of Kukawa, since the existing capital of Dikwa lay in the German Cameroons. Accordingly the Shehu of Bornu moved to Kukawa, but the Civil Resident resided first at Mongonu, secondly at Magumeri nearer the caravan routes, and only in 1904 moved to Kukawa itself. Two years later it became obvious that the population of Bornu was not attracted by the site of Kukawa, little trade had developed and the district was unhealthy. Accordingly both the Shehu and the Resident moved to Maiduguri, on a healthier site on a sandy ridge above the river Alo, affording a good supply of water, and located on the main route westwards to Potiskum and Kano, and near the German frontier.

Whereas the French have tended to establish new towns as centres of political authority, the British have in many areas preserved the old centres. This has been partly due to the existence of many more large urban centres in British than in French territory, and partly to a policy of preserving local political institutions and organization. Indirect rule has, however, expressed itself in the building of the 'Townships', small in population, but large in area beside the old towns. In the 'Townships' lived the Residents, the advisers of the African rulers in the towns.[20] The 'Townships' with their widely distributed houses with servants' quarters attached, often focusing on the administrative offices, sometimes possessing the railway station, a military camp and their own commercial quarter, were a distinctive feature of British West Africa, and were well developed in important regional centres such as Kumasi, Ibadan, Zaria and Kano. In Northern

Nigeria they frequently had a quarter for 'southerners', occupied as clerks and stewards, close by. In Southern Nigeria they were in some cases adjacent to a quarter for northerners, traders and followers of the small force of soldiers, normally consisting of Hausa recruits. Different situations brought different distributions. In Kano the 'Township' area formed a single entity on the eastern side of the city. In Ibadan problems of acquiring land have resulted in the spread of the various township units in separate locations around the old city limit.

Economic factors

The re-orientation of trading in West Africa from movement focusing chiefly on northern markets, for local sale or transport across the Sahara, to movement focusing on the coast ports, led to a shift in the growth of markets and of their associated settlements towards the coast. The vast increase in the volume of trade resulted in an extremely rapid urban development, and the new means of transport by river, railway and road produced a concentration of population at certain nodal points. The old Sudanic and Sahelian markets declined, with the exception of those with good coastal connections or serving as administrative centres. Thus Kano, Sokoto and Gao continued to expand, whilst Timbuktu, Djenné and Katsina declined. In the Sahel and on the fringes of the Sahara, the populations of many of the small oasis settlements were reduced, despite a brief influx of cultivators and pastoralists from the south, for the routes they served, as small markets or as watering places, became only little used. The competition of cheap European and later Asian wares brought the decline of many of the old metalworking and textile centres and the consequent emigration of artisans and traders.

THE ESTABLISHMENT OF THE PORTS

In the early stages of West African trade inland transport was poorly developed and costly, since it involved head loading. In consequence, port hinterlands were small in area and many small harbours were created, frequented by the shallowdraught vessels in use. Moreover, the political and commercial rivalry of the interested powers led to the development of harbours and trading posts in close proximity to one another. Hence the existence of Portuguese, British, Dutch and Danish forts, with their associated landing beaches and settlements all in close proximity to one another at several points on the Gold Coast. Hence also the rivalry on the Gambia river of the British port of St Mary or Bathurst and the French port of Albréda. The changed political situation of the 19th century, with the formation of colonies and spheres of interest, together with the introduction of steam vessels, led to the removal of rival harbours, and concentration at fewer points. The ports still tended to be small, and depended for their trade on river communication with the interior, as in the case of St Louis and the Senegal, Bathurst and the Gambia, Forcados, Burutu and the Niger, and Calabar and the Cross river. Or they were established near comparatively rich, easily tapped,

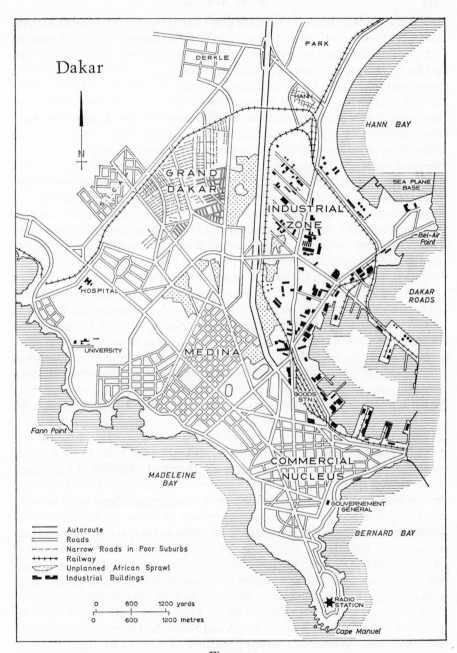

Figure 9.3

local hinterlands, as in the case of Cape Coast Castle and Accra trading to Ashanti, Porto Novo connected with Dahomey, or Badagry, Lagos and Epe, the outlets for Yorubaland. Many of the ports had only poor landing places on confined creeks or lagoons, with entrances difficult to negotiate, or on beaches exposed to heavy surf where ships had to be unloaded by canoes and lighters. As the volume of traffic and the size of vessels increased, so the choice of harbours became more restricted, and the leading ports became still fewer in number. Another factor was the problem of the regular imposition of customs duties. Thus, for example, the Nigerian overseas trading ports were reduced in the present century to eight, and the once important Badagry, Brass, Bonny and Opobo were reduced to coastal trading and fishing centres. Finally the costs of modern means of transportation, of harbour works for modern shipping and of handling facilities, together with the problem of choosing railway and main-road termini, led to the concentration of development at a very few favoured sites, to which large populations were soon attracted. These comprise the chief ports of West Africa which are, from west to east, Dakar, Kaolack, Bathurst, Bissau, Conakry, Freetown, Monrovia, Abidjan, Takoradi, Tema, Lomé, Cotonou, Lagos and Port Harcourt.

In this process of change even former major ports declined in importance, whilst new harbours were created elsewhere, with, in consequence, important changes in population distribution. For example, in 1880 St Louis was the largest town between Rabat in Morocco and Freetown. It was the capital of an expanding colony, sited on an island and sand bar at the head of an important river route leading into the interior. The dangerous bar at the river mouth made St Louis easy to defend from sea-attack, and the surrounding floodlands protected it from the mainland. But the bar made the harbour difficult to enter for merchant ships, the climate was unhealthy, and water shortage limited expansion. A boat was employed to bring water from the Senegal valley for storage in cisterns.[21] Moreover, the experiments in colonial settlement in the interior, which might have brought prosperity, had all failed. Despite the building of a mainland suburb at Sor and the construction of a reservoir fed by an aqueduct 15 miles (24 km) in length, St Louis was doomed once the decision had been taken to build the Senegal railway to the deep-water terminus at Dakar on the Cape Verde peninsula. The Central Government left for Dakar in 1902, and St Louis became the capital of Senegal and Mauritania. Its population declined from over 22,000 in 1910 to 18,000 in 1921. Since the latter date, however, there has been a considerable increase due to the expansion of Government offices in St Louis and its evolution into the chief fishing port of West Africa. By 1954 the total was 39,000. Further expansion has been limited by the removal of Government offices to Dakar, as capital of independent Senegal, and Nouakchott as capital of independent Mauritania. Even so, by 1961 the population of the town had reached nearly 49,000. Dakar (and Gorée) increased over the same period from 25,000 in 1910 to 32,400 in 1921, 54,000 in 1931 and 383,000 in 1962. Dakar was the product of the railway and the need for a deep-water anchorage.[22] At first Rufisque (nearly 50,000 in 1961), situated at the point where the railway turns away from the shore

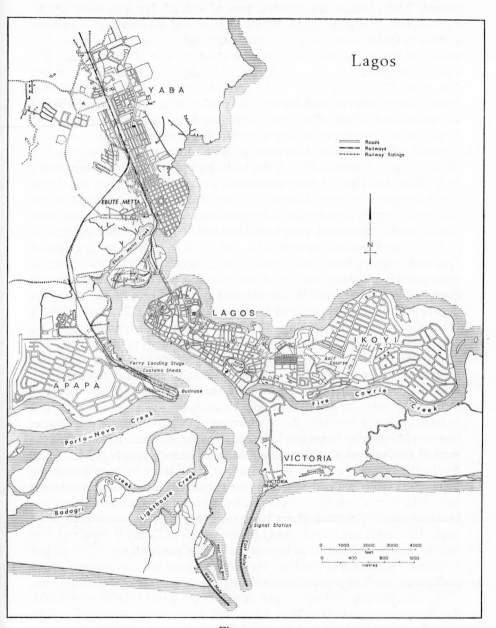

Figure 9.4

towards Thiès, became the principal port of Senegal, but here there was no harbour, only an exposed beach. Whilst Rufisque had the advantage of nodality in relation to the newly-developing groundnut trade, it could not accommodate modern shipping. At Dakar the Miocene volcanic rocks of Cape Manuel and Point Dakar provide shelter for a harbour with depths averaging nearly 30 feet (9 metres). The construction of the northern breakwater in 1898 made the harbour completely enclosed. Dakar is the product of the French penetration of the Sudanic zone. Political relations permitting, it has become the outlet of the Upper and Middle Niger basins by a combination of rail and river routes. It was the chief centre of French settlement in West Africa, and, as Whittlesey described it, the only town in West Africa in the European sense of the term with a clear distinction between functional zones. Today, Abidjan, Accra and Lagos would also merit the same description. The chief problem in its expansion has been water supply, for no adjacent surface sources are available, and local sub-surface supplies are limited. Geophysical research, however, has shown that bores at Tiaroye could provide 140,000 cubic feet (4000 cu m) a day, whilst wells at Pout could supply a further 50,000 cubic feet (1400 cu m) daily. Of the remaining ports Conakry, Abidjan, Takoradi, Cotonou, Lagos and Port Harcourt have all developed large hinterlands by rail and road systems. Lagos has the most productive hinterland both in quantity and variety of produce in West Africa. With a population of 665,246 according to the 1963 census (1962 estimate, 450,000), Lagos today is larger than Dakar and the second largest city in West Africa. The main problems of expansion of settlement in Lagos have been water supply and the confinement of the island site with the surrounding mangrove swamps of the mainland. These problems were met by the construction of the Iju river reservoir 17 miles (27 km) from Lagos by 1915, the drainage of swamps and reclamation of the foreshore, the construction of the Carter Bridge and Denton causeway, connecting Lagos and Iddo islands to the mainland, and the development of new suburbs at Apapa, Ebute Meta, Yaba and recently at Suru Lere. Today the Carter Bridge has become a bottleneck to traffic necessitating the building of another bridge to relieve the congestion. Abidjan, the capital and chief port of the Ivory Coast, has seen one of the most astonishing population increases in recent times. The trade of the Ivory Coast has increased enormously since 1945. This traffic was served chiefly by the wharfs of Grand Bassam and Port Bouet, until the completion in 1950 of the Vridi Canal with a depth of 30 feet (9 metres) for a width of 900 feet (275 metres), giving the new port of Abidjan access to the sea. The population of Abidjan, including its suburbs of Adjamé and Treichville, has increased from 46,000 in 1945 to 257,500 in 1964. Freetown, with the finest natural harbour in West Africa, with a deep-water channel of over 60 feet (18 metres) in depth, still had only 128,000 in 1963, although this represents an increase of 63,000 in 15 years, with the increasing tempo of development of the resources of Sierra Leone. Bathurst with only 29,000 (1964) is almost moribund within the narrow political confinement of its hinterland. Accra, the capital of one of the richest countries in West Africa, has 491,000 including the

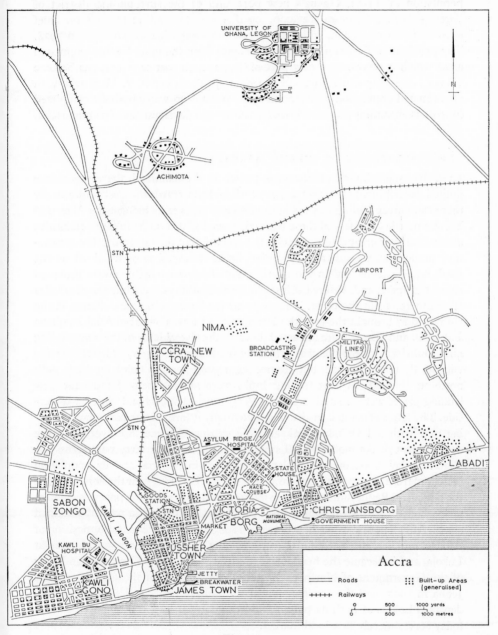

Figure 9.5

population of Tema, Ghana's new port, and of the surrounding district of 'Greater Accra'. Takoradi (123,000, together with Sekondi in 1960) is the chief exporting port of Ghana, with an artificial deep-water harbour opened in 1928. The problem of Takoradi is its great distance from the more heavily-populated areas which it serves. The new port of Tema, built east of Accra, has become Ghana's chief importing port and an important cocoa exporter. Monrovia, with an estimated population of 80,000 in 1961, and a deep-water harbour completed in 1948, is expanding only slowly due to the limited development of its hinterland.

THE DEVELOPMENT OF INLAND MARKETS

Until the establishment of European power on the mainland, there was only a limited development of market towns which looked towards the coast. Admittedly there were great trading centres in the Sudanic areas and amongst the Akan and Yoruba peoples, but few of these were concerned with a traffic in large quantities of material over great distances, with the exception of the salt trade. Transportation methods were crude and expensive, being restricted to pack animals in the north and head loading in the south. Only the few navigable rivers provided cheap transport, and, before the introduction of railways, were important arteries of commerce from the coast. The trade on the Lower Niger and Benue in the 19th century brought the growth of small market towns like Ibu, Aboh, Onitsha and Idah, and people were attracted down to the riverside from the surrounding hills. Onitsha, for example, was originally sited on a hill-top away from the river with its fly-borne disease, but controlling a good landing point for trade with northern Iboland. At first trading hulks were moored below, and later new landing places were created at Laird's Port, Abutshi Wharf and Onitsha Waterside. The latter expanded in size until eventually it formed one continuous housing unit with old Onitsha. Onitsha's big expansion came, however, with the development of the modern road system, and its role as a ferry port across the Niger. Today it has one of the largest markets in Nigeria, and its population increased from 18,100 in 1931 to 76,900 in 1952. At Lokoja, near the confluence of the Niger and Benue, hulks were also moored, and later a trading post was created, near which an African settlement was established, occupied in part by liberated slaves. After a period of decline between 1868 and 1879, due to the opposition of African middlemen in the Oil Rivers, trading companies built warehouses at Lokoja, and it became the headquarters of the Royal Niger Company, and later of the Government of Northern Nigeria. The removal of the Government to Jebba in 1900, and the construction of the railway between Lagos and Kano, deprived Lokoja of both its political and commercial importance, and the town today serves merely as a local market.

The introduction of railway and road transport brought a vast increase in traffic, the creation of new market centres, and the rapid expansion of some of the older towns, together with a remarkable shift in settlement. Moreover, railways and roads were better able to serve the existing population distribution with its tendency for the higher densities to be located on watersheds. The railway from Thiès in the Senegal to the frontier post of Kayes served to make Kayes, which had previously been a small military and trans-shipment post, into a thriving market town with a population today of over 20,000. Older centres away from the railway, like Bakel, declined or grew only slowly. Bakel in 1955 had a population of only 2300. Thiès, founded as a military post in 1863, owes most of its growth to the railway. The Dakar–St Louis railway could not follow the short coastal route, because of the difficulties in constructing it across the sand dunes. Inland from Rufisque the easiest route up to the plateau of Cayor was via the 'Ravin des Voleurs', cutting through the westward-facing Thiès Escarpment. Here, at the head of the gradient from Rufisque, Thiès provided the first important inland market for the rapidly-increasing groundnut traffic, and later became the junction point for the railway to the Niger. Thus in addition to its trading functions, the town acquired the railway workshops for the Niger railway (1923), and in 1934 the workshops for the Dakar–St Louis railway in addition. The town grew from 2400 inhabitants in 1914 to 13,000 in 1929, 24,000 in 1945 and 69,000 in 1961.[23] In south-eastern Nigeria the town of Aba, with a population of 57,800 in 1953 (131,000 in 1963), is another railway creation. In 1906 it was described as a small 'bush station' in the colony report. In 1916 the railway from the Enugu colliery to Port Harcourt was opened, and Aba became one of the many small halts on the line. The railway was built on the shortest route to the coalfield from one of the few suitable delta port sites, linked by firm ground with the mainland. It ignored other possible productive areas, and lay between the two areas of highest population density in south-eastern Nigeria, in a 'corridor' of lower density. The main roads from these higher density areas met the railway at Aba, which became a connecting point between road and railway of great importance in the movement of palm oil and kernels. Nearby, the Aba river supplied sufficient water for the railway, and for the growing needs of the township. The central position of the town in relation to the Ngwa Clan made it a suitable divisional headquarters. The Government Reservation was laid out in 1921, and two years later more land had to be acquired for the increasing numbers of Ibo traders and labourers. By 1936 Aba had become the largest traffic centre in the Eastern Region. Other important 'new' inland markets are Bobo Dioulasso (50,000 in 1961) which was the railway terminus for the Upper Volta from 1934 to 1954, and Kindia (25,000 in 1961), an important railway point for bananas in Guinea. Amongst older market centres which have been given a new importance by modern transport and trading developments, Ibadan, Kano and Kumasi are outstanding. Bowen put Ibadan's population in the 1850s at 70,000, equal to Ilorin, but less than Owo, 'the largest town in Africa'.[24] Ibadan's military power made it a centre of great political importance to the British, who placed a Resident there in 1893. From 1901 to 1905 Ibadan was at the head of the railway from Lagos, and became an important local nodal point by the construction of roads to surrounding towns and villages. The first 'trunk road' in Nigeria was that built from Ibadan to Oyo in 1905. Ibadan became the centre of a road and railway system, serving an area in which cocoa planting was becoming increasingly popular. It became the chief cocoa market of Nigeria at the junction of the railway and the road through Ife and Ilesha to Owo, the 'axis' of the cocoa belt. Its previous history, its political importance and size, and its nodality, made it the natural choice for capital of the Western Region, in effect taking the place of Oyo, 30 miles (50 km) to the north, the former headquarters of the secular head of the Yoruba. By 1921 Ibadan had a population of 238,100 which increased to 387,100 ten years later, 459,200 by 1953 and 627,379 in 1963. Kano's development came later, for the railway from Baro on the Niger was not completed until 1911, and the through connection to Lagos via the ferry at Jebba until the following year (the ferry was replaced by the Jebba Bridge in 1916). Like Ibadan, Kano became the chief railway station and nodal point for a rapidly-expanding export crop zone – the groundnut-producing zone of Northern Nigeria. By 1921 the population was 49,900, not greatly in excess of Barth's estimate in the 1850s of 30,000, although possibly the latter was exaggerated. By 1931 the population had reached 97,000, increased to 130,200 by 1952, and 295,000 by 1963. Kumasi occupies a similar position being an important railway and road focus in the cocoa belt of Ghana and an important regional capital. Bowdich had estimated Kumasi's population at 12,000–15,000 at the beginning of the 19th century.[25] By the 1870s it was estimated to be as high as 70,000, although the estimate may be exaggerated.[26] In 1874 Kumasi had been partly destroyed by the British, and the population was reduced by emigration. The 1901 census recorded only 3000. The railway from Sekondi reached Kumasi in 1903, and by 1911 the population was 18,900. In 1923 the line to Accra was completed, and by 1931 Kumasi had a total number of 35,800 inhabitants. By 1960 the total had increased to 190,000 including the suburbs.

TRANSPORT CHANGES AND THE RURAL POPULATION

The political and economic factors which have encouraged the growth of West African towns and cities have also brought some redistribution of villages and hamlets by the desire for easy access to market or to an urban centre. The construction of railways brought the development of small nucleations at the halts established as collecting centres for local products. Every line in West Africa supports these small local markets and loading points, meeting places between local roads or tracks and the railway, rarely containing more than a thousand inhabitants, except at the season when large quantities of produce have to be moved. Similar small collections of huts and market stalls appear also at many level crossings (road/rail bridging does not occur in West Africa), which again have some local nodality, and at which traffic may be halted and drivers and omnibus passengers seek refreshments. In some cases halts have had to be artificially established at regular intervals along a route lacking nucleated settlements. In only one case, however, has there been ribbon development alongside the railway – since the trains only serve a series of established points – and that is between Lagos and Abeokuta where 1800 plots of land between mile 33 and mile 60 on the old track were measured, and allotted as agricultural holdings, chiefly to reservists.[27] Today the railways are playing an increasingly important role in the movements of foodstuffs for internal trade, as may clearly be seen in Buchanan's map of yam traffic in southern Nigeria.[28] Here again, by supplying cheap foodstuffs to the export crop belts, they make possible increased settlement in less favourable areas such as Ilorin, Kabba and Ogoja.

Roads, however, have had an even more remarkable effect, for they act as feeders from producing centres, as well as through routes, and traffic can be made to halt to pick up passengers or goods at any point upon them. Settlement and cultivation have both tended to be attracted to roads, to move away from areas without them, and to follow them into previously unoccupied areas. The Lever-hulme Commission commented: 'In Northern Nigeria, as in England, a new arterial road brings about a "ribbon" development of clearings for cultivation.' Since the new roads tended to avoid valleys and seek watersheds, the Commission thought that such settlement constituted 'a serious threat to the country because the new land opened up will be more liable to denudation and erosion than that lower down the slopes'.[29] The threat seems unlikely to be serious, because the watershed areas of West Africa contain the more level land, whilst the land 'lower down the slopes' usually tends to be steep and is in fact more likely to be eroded. Settlement shift has been illustrated in a number of cases. Steel quotes a remark-able example in Ghana, where the straightening of a section of the Kumasi–Accra road and railway construction resulted in the building of the New Juaso township, leaving Old Juaso to the District Commissioner, the clerks and the police.[30] Figure 9.6 illustrates the development of the new village of Akuse at a road junction, also in Ghana. In the development of export crop cultivation, the pattern of the transport system has clearly been as potent a factor as soils and moisture supply in the distribution of planting and settlement. Figure 9.7 shows the influence of the transport factor in Senegal. Without adequate cheap transport, to an exporting port, equipped to handle the commodity produced, export crops cannot be grown, no matter how favourable the physical conditions. Southern Ondo Province in Nigeria, a potential cocoa-growing area, still awaits an adequate road system. Another feature of modern road development is the extension of the market areas of the town and the decline of nearby village markets, which are replaced by local picking-up points for lorries. Some of these nearby villages have in effect become outer suburbs of the towns. Thus in Ghana the village of Kwama no longer possesses a regular market, but sends its com-mercial crops in bulk to Kumasi. The village has become a 'dormitory' for Kumasi and its population has been increasing.[31] Another interesting feature at Kwama is the desire of the inhabitants to resettle on the new Accra–Kumasi road, 2 miles (3 km) to the north, where they wish to have their village replanned as a unit, with good housing and modern social amenities. The result of the trend towards main roads is a marked tendency to a ribbon development of housing and croplands, with long street villages which, in the more densely-populated areas, merge into one another. Nowhere is this more apparent than in south-eastern Nigeria where the main road from Onitsha to Port Harcourt and Oron via Aba has become one long line of Ibo and Ibibio villages. In many cases the houses are screened from the road by trees, but the problems of maintaining fast traffic and of creating adequate social conditions in these long sprawls will become pressing in the near

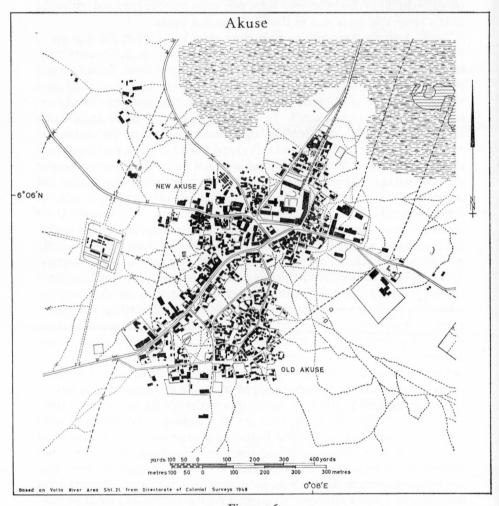

Figure 9.6

future. Similar problems arise in other newly-developing countries, where only a few adequate all-season roads exist, for example in Malaya where the main roads from Singapore are likewise attractive to new village settlement. Village settlement in some areas, notably in south-eastern Nigeria and the cocoa belts of Ghana and south-western Nigeria, is becoming a form of suburban development, radiating out from the large towns along the main roads. The only advantages in such a pattern are accessibility and the supply of main services. The growing tendency of modern settlement to seek the areas adequately served by modern transport

The Transport Factor in Senegal
The Influence of the Railway on the Spread of Groundnut Cultivation

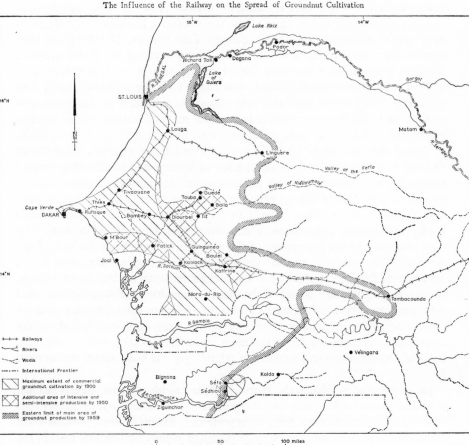

Figure 9.7

means the gradual abandonment of the more distant areas, the reduction of the occupied area, and, in consequence, the reduction of the area in cultivation, despite a need to increase productivity.

THE INFLUENCE OF COMMERCIAL CULTIVATION

The development of commercial cultivation, in particular the cultivation of export crops, has been the most potent factor in the redistribution of population in West Africa. In Senegal groundnut production has been responsible, once peaceful conditions were assured, for the occupation of an area stretching from the Gambia in the south to the borders of the Ferlo in the north-east and to the Lower Senegal river in the north. In 1956 population densities in the centre of the area reached 123 per square mile in the cercle of Thiès and 116 in Diourbel. Fringe densities were lower. Kaolack, for example, had 52. It is impossible to compare with much earlier figures, but there seems a likelihood that densities have more than doubled since the beginning of the century. The richer southern portion occupied by the Serer has been slowly invaded by Wolof growers. Between 1929 and 1937 the Serer district of Sine-Saloum received 175,000 permanent immigrants, mainly Wolof, who today form the majority group. The wasteland zones which separated the villages have tended to disappear, and villages have also become smaller. Indeed the units of settlement are hamlets rather than villages, and form a vast dispersal throughout the more level lands, separated here and there by shallow valleys and forest reserves. In northern Gambia a particularly dense concentration of hamlets and small village market centres has been established near the border, for here immigrants from Senegal provide a large part of the growing season labour force. The digging of wells and boreholes in the Ferlo, initially to serve the needs of transhumant cattle herds, has brought an invasion of cultivators even into the Ferlo itself. The only hindrance to the occupation of the area has hitherto been the lack of dry season drinking water. In this movement religion has been an important factor. Mouridism, founded in Baol by a Toucouleur religious teacher about 1886–9, teaches that agriculture is one of the essential conditions of sanctification, and demands total submission of the individual to a religious chief. Planned Mouride settlements occupied mainly by young people have been established on the eastern and southern fringes of the main groundnut-growing area. Touba, the Mouride headquarters and a centre of pilgrimage, was built within the western Ferlo.

Cocoa planting in Ghana, the Ivory Coast, and south-western Nigeria has had even more remarkable results, for evergreen rain-forest areas, mainly on clay soils in a Guinean environment, have been preferred. Except on their savanna-ward fringes some of these areas were once occupied mainly by hunters, and, in the Nigerian cocoa belt, for example, hunting rights persist almost unchanged at the present day.[32] 'During the past century a great part of the Western Region has changed from unappropriated forest land, in which tribal wars were fought and hunters wandered over large tracts, to settled and cultivated land over which families and individuals claim more or less exclusive rights.'[33] Around Ibadan the former high forest, the Igbo-Ipara or Ipara 'wilds', was gradually destroyed by settlers, and the process of destruction accelerated rapidly with the introduction of cocoa.[34] However, the first settlements of the Nigerian cocoa belt antedate the introduction of cocoa. The town of Ife, for example, was founded several centuries ago, and large towns, such as Owu, existed in areas which were converted to wilderness by warfare. Moreover, extensive settlement occurred of refugees from the Fulani invasion of the sub-Guinean savannas to the north, during the last century. Densities are high. The lowest divisional density is that of Owo with 129 persons per square mile. The highest is Oshun with 359. Comparable densities do not occur in the cocoa-growing districts of Ghana, where settlement of similar areas appears to have been more recent, and almost entirely due to cocoa planting. Nevertheless, an extensive movement of population has taken place, occupying firstly the Akwapim-Ewe Range, then areas to the north-west. As Boateng comments, the development of the cocoa industry and of the railway shifted the economic centre of gravity in south-eastern Ghana to the west, and introduced a new type of settlement, the commercial centre, which grew at the expense of surrounding areas.[35] Examples of population densities in cocoa-producing districts at the census of 1960 were: West Akim 119, South Akim 224, East Akim Abuakwa 135, West Akim Abuakwa 209, Amansie 128, Kumasi West 92, Kumasi South 279, Kumasi North 117, Brong Ahafo Central 82 and Ho 115. Akwapim with 219 is a district of former importance in cocoa cultivation, and nearby New Juaben is still a leading cocoa-marketing centre, but social factors appear to have been at least of equal importance in the local high population density.[36] By comparison of the 1931 and 1948 population censuses, Hilton claimed to have distinguished a belt of large population increases, stretching from Ahafo through Kumasi to Krachi and Nanumba, and pointed to local densities of over 100 in the cocoa areas of north-central Bekwai, Kumasi, Ashanti, Akim, south-western Mampong and near Berekum.[37] The Volta river district has suffered a decrease in population since 1931, due to the attraction of neighbouring cocoa-growing areas, but decreases do not appear to have occurred in districts badly affected by swollen shoot disease between 1931 and 1948 except perhaps locally. Between 1948 and 1960, however, Akwapim suffered considerable emigration. In the coffee- and cocoa-growing districts of the Ivory Coast also, dense settlement appears to have been very recent, and has affected only small areas. Cercle densities tend on the whole to be lower than in Ghana, reaching a maximum of 43 per square mile in Bouaké and a minimum of 11 in Abengourou. It is interesting to reflect that part of the planting has been undertaken by the Agni, a people closely related to the Ashanti of Ghana. In Ghana and the Ivory Coast the settlement pattern consists mainly of villages and hamlets in almost continuous distribution in the more heavily-populated areas, and aligned chiefly along main roads elsewhere. In south-western Nigeria this pattern is replaced by the large Yoruba towns, surrounded by hamlets and even individual compounds, dispersed throughout the local market area.

In Northern Nigeria the groundnut-cultivating districts, concentrated mainly in Kano and Katsina Provinces, are unique, being situated farther inland than any other export crop-producing area. At the beginning of the century, each village in Katsina Emirate was surrounded by a wilderness, and the western border of Katsina was marked by an extensive wasteland. With the completion of the railway to Kano and the development of a market for groundnuts, cultivators began to clear the formerly unoccupied lands and establish new villages. Settlements were founded near the railway line to Gusau, opened in 1929, and later

near the extension to Kaura Namoda. Here, a low but sufficient precipitation and
the sandy soils, marking a former southward extension of the Sahara, provided

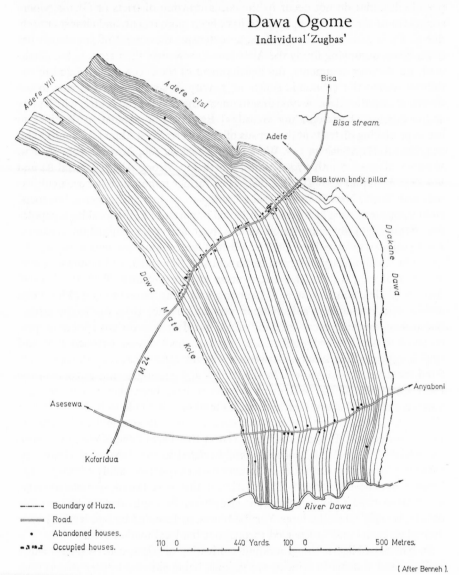

Dawa Ogome
Individual 'Zugbas'

Bisa

Adefe Yili

Adefe Sisi

Bisa stream.

Adefe

Bisa town bndy. pillar

Djakane Dawa

Dawa Mate Kole

M 24

Anyaboni

Asesewa

Koforidua

River Dawa

- - - - - -   Boundary of Huza.
========   Road.
•   Abandoned houses.
▪ ▪ ▪ ▪   Occupied houses.

110   0   440 Yards.   100   0   500 Metres.

(After Benneh).

Figure 9.8

ideal conditions. With the construction of the road feeder system to the railways,
'ribbons' of dense settlement were created amidst once sparsely settled pastures
and waste. Across the border in Niger, groundnut cultivation, with its accompanying new villages, developed in the southern areas, particularly in Zinder and

Maradi. In Northern Nigeria population densities rose to 230 in Kano Division, 157 in Katsina and 115 in Kano Northern. The two chief producing cercles of Niger have rather lower densities – 25 in Maradi and 19 in Zinder – for conditions are more marginal, and the proportion of uncultivable land is much higher.

Commercial cultivation for the inland market has also produced its new settlements. In Senegal and the Ivory Coast these occur as suburban hamlets whose occupants are engaged in market gardening. In Ghana and Nigeria, however, whole districts on the fringe of the more densely-populated areas have been affected by the growth of food production for market in recent years. This tendency has helped to slow down the emigration of people from Ilorin and Kabba provinces in Nigeria, and has encouraged extension of the 'huza' system of cultivation of the Manya-Krobo in Ghana. The huza system of purchasing a tract of land and subdividing it into long strips began about a century ago, due to strife with neighbouring Akan peoples. The Krobo area tends to be extremely dry for part of the year, and settlement occurs in long lines near the streams. Each stream forms a back line to the huza tracts of land, which are then cleared in strips towards the interfluve, until a common boundary is established. Some holdings have as many as four different types of land use: 1) uncleared woodland; 2) fallow; 3) food crops, interspersed with young cocoa and oil palms; 4) mature cocoa and oil palms. Food production for sale, in order to obtain money to purchase more land, is the chief aim of the Krobo cultivator, and the three principal markets of the Manya-Krobo country probably feed 'half the non-agricultural population of the whole Gold Coast'.[38] With overcrowding the Krobo are now settling elsewhere, and have founded colonies in Kwahu, Akwamu, Akim Abuakwa and Akim Kotoku (Fig. 9.8).

Migration of agricultural labour to commercial cropping areas will be discussed in detail later in this chapter, but some idea of the effects may be given at this point. The main labour-exporting centres are in a block in the centre and include Upper Volta, the Northern Territories of Ghana, the Sokoto Province of Nigeria and the neighbouring portions of Niger and Mali. The 1948 census of Ghana recorded that 2·9 per cent of the population (121,256) was foreign-born and 1·3 per cent (52,541) was born in other British countries – mainly Nigeria. Of the populations of the Colony and Ashanti, 3·8 per cent and 8·5 per cent were born in the Northern Territories respectively. Approximately a quarter of the people born in the Northern Territories were enumerated elsewhere. In 1960 it was found that 10 per cent of all males and 6 per cent of all females were immigrants from other countries, and that long-distance migration was more common than short-distance migration. Each year about 35,000 migrants have moved into the groundnut areas of Senegal, 20,000 into the Gambia, probably over 60,000 into the Ivory Coast with a total immigrant population of over 300,000, 150,000–200,000 into Ghana where more than half a million are foreign-born, and possibly over 60,000 into the cocoa-growing areas of Nigeria. The figures are very approximate for there are considerable fluctuations from year to year, the attempts at counting, either by census questions or at border control posts, can only be under-estimates and the figures for south-western Nigeria can only be a guess (see pp. 3–9 and 732–3).

THE INFLUENCE OF MINING AND INDUSTRY

European mining developments have had much less effect on population movement and the founding of new settlements than agriculture, partly because mining accounts for only a small proportion of West Africa's productivity, and partly because the work is on the whole unpopular. Migrants prefer either agriculture or urban occupations. In Ghana the gold workings of southern Ashanti and the Colony have involved the construction of villages near the mines and the introduction of labour from elsewhere, originally Krus from Liberia and the Ivory Coast, in addition to local labour for mining and carrying. 17,000 men were employed in the gold mines in 1948, of whom over 3000 were in Obuasi, whose population had more than doubled since 1931. The total number of miners in Ghana in 1948 was 19,000 – a reduction by 20,000 from the 1938 figure so that recent population increases in mining towns probably owe more to commercial and other urban attractions. An enquiry in 1939 discovered that 32·5 per cent of the labourers came from the Colony and Ashanti, 55 per cent from the Northern Territories and contiguous French territories, and 12·5 per cent from other West African territories.[39] One may note the building of mining settlements at Lunsar in Sierra Leone, the Bomi Hills in Liberia, Jos and Bukuru in Northern Nigeria, and Enugu in south-eastern Nigeria. Coal mining began at Enugu in 1913 and three years later the railway was completed to Port Harcourt. Enugu thus began as a mining town, and by 1931 had acquired a population of 13,000. The Eastern Region or Eastern Provinces, as they were then called, were first distinguished as a political unit in 1939. Enugu was chosen as the capital, and received its House of Assembly in 1946. The result was a remarkable increase in population to 138,457 in 1963.

Modern industry as yet has had little effect on population distribution. In 1954 there were only 28,152 salaried workers employed in manufacture in the whole of French West Africa. The greater part of these was in Dakar. In Lagos in 1950 there were 20,463 people engaged in manufacture. The effect of industry so far has been felt mainly at the major ports, where workers' quarters have been built and industrial zones created, and at inland towns like Thiès, where large railway workshops have been established. The planning of industrial sites and the preparation in advance of factory estates, with all main services to attract industry, are interesting recent features, a notable example being the Apapa Estate at Lagos.

Physical factors in the changing distribution

WATER SUPPLIES

There are few settlements in West Africa without a water supply problem, due to the tendency to watershed location, combined with the existence of a marked dry season in a greater part of the area. The distributional zones can be sub-divided into:

1) areas lacking sufficient moisture for cultivation without using surface or sub-surface resources;
2) areas having sufficient moisture for cultivation but:
   a) lacking drinking water supplies in the dry season;
   b) liable to sudden short periods of shortage in the dry season. A frequent problem here is the immense distance of many settlements from their regular source of surface water – up to 10 miles (16 km) – and in consequence a great expenditure of labour in fetching water. In such cases a large part of the domestic supply comes from the roof during rain storms, and is stored.

European efforts so far have been concentrated on developing irrigation schemes in zone 1, digging wells and bores in zone 2a, and constructing reservoirs, filled mainly by streams, for the supply of the larger urban areas in zone 2b.

In the field of creating new settlements dependent on irrigation schemes, the most remarkable achievements have been in the Office du Niger Scheme in the Inland Niger delta. Villages with an average population of 300 have been constructed of local brick, and by 1955, 25,000 colonists were settled in three centres, irrigated by canals from the barrages of Sotuba and Sansanding. About 45 per cent of the settlers are of local origin and 25 per cent are Mossi.[40] Other schemes described below have involved the migration to new villages of large numbers of people. Plans for future development involve considerable redistribution – for example the Office du Niger has planned to irrigate $2\frac{1}{4}$ million acres (900,000 hectares) over the next century. That would involve building villages for about half a million colonists.

The sedimentary basins, which occupy so large a part of the area of the Sahel, contain extensive underground water resources, which have been tapped on a limited scale by French and British engineers, in order to provide for the needs of pastoralists and cultivators. Even with modern equipment wells are difficult to dig – and also to operate – at depths greater than 250 feet (75 metres). Wells up to this depth were dug before the colonial period by slaves, and when slavery was abolished, the wells fell into disuse, collapsed, and the villages which depended on them were abandoned. At Pong Tamale, however, in northern Ghana, reservoirs excavated by local peoples between shales and an ironstone crust have been cleared out, and put back into use.[41] Modern wells depend on relatively high water table zones fringing the ancient shield lands, or on local seepages, e.g. from under sand dunes near Cape Verde. The greater part of Senegal, including the Ferlo, south-eastern Mauritania, western Mali, and a zone lying between the Adrar des Iforas and the river Niger, stretching eastwards across Niger, must be bored in order to use deep water supplies up to 1000 feet (300 metres) or more below the surface. Systematic water prospecting and well digging began in Senegal in 1904, and by 1913 almost 1000 had been dug, chiefly to improve water supplies to existing towns and villages and also to extend the area of cultivation. Between 1918 and 1939 one organization alone, the Société de Prévoyance de Kaolack, dug another 1000 wells. In Northern Nigeria well sinking by the Geological Department began in Sokoto Province in 1929, and by 1935, 800 wells had been sunk supplying about a half million people with drinking water.[42] The use of deep bores began in Senegal in 1938, and 14 had been sunk by 1951. These were intended, as were many of the wells, to supply drinking water for cattle, but villages soon developed at such vantage points for water and trade, and wherever possible cultivation was undertaken, particularly of groundnuts. Hence the phenomenal growth of M'Bar from a hamlet of 20 in 1939 to a village of 2750 in 1949, or of Sadio from 300 to 1200 over the same period.[43] A quadrilateral system of water points at approximately 12-kilometre intervals has been developed in Senegal. This has markedly affected the settlement pattern. Similar intensive development of water resources elsewhere in the Sahel will probably result in similar quadrilateral patterns, and will also result in a diminution of the pastoral area as agriculture gains.

Elsewhere in West Africa where supplies of water are more abundant and more reliable, although subject to marked seasonal changes in flow, the creation of modern towns created water supply problems. Only in Yorubaland had indigenous towns of 70,000–100,000 population been built before the colonial era, and in these an immense amount of labour must have been used in fetching and carrying water. Impluvia were a necessity to obtain every drop of water possible. Without modern reservoirs, pipe-lines and pumping stations, towns of 250,000 people and more would have been impossible. Water supplies have always been an important limiting factor. Gorée, for example, depended on rain-water storage in cisterns. Even these were insufficient for the entire dry season, and supplementary supplies had to be brought by boat from the springs at Hann on the mainland. Some settlement from Gorée was made on the Cape Verde peninsula, even before 1821, in order to obtain better water supplies and to grow vegetables. Dakar and Rufisque depended initially on local sand-dune seepages and well-water was used to irrigate local market gardens, producing essential food supplies. Even with modern bores, wells and pipe-lines tapping an extensive area, the water for fire hydrants and sewers at Dakar has to be pumped from the sea at Bernard Cove in order to conserve fresh water. Until the construction of the Iju river works in 1915 Lagos faced a constant water problem. Local wells were inadequate, and the population depended to a large extent on rain-water storage. During the dry season many of the inhabitants had to buy water.

HEALTH PROBLEMS

Colonialism introduced medical and sanitary services into West Africa, but it seems likely that the effect of these was restricted to a few small, mainly urban areas, until the expansion in health services after 1945. In the Gold Coast of 1900–10 even in the towns there was no sanitation or planning, rain was the chief source of water, mortality was high, and the medical services were provided by men amongst whom several were described as 'the dregs of the profession'.[44] Writing of the medical situation in Sierra Leone shortly after 1945 Kuczynski claimed:

'The position in the Protectorate is apparently about the same today as it was in the Colony a century ago, the only difference being perhaps that the better informed doctors today realize our complete ignorance of the state of health.'[45]

As late as 1950 Nigeria, with a population of approximately 30 millions, had only 344 medical practitioners, and the annual expenditure on health services was 2s. a head.[46] In French West Africa in the same year there were 599 practitioners to serve the needs of 17 millions. This, however, was an improvement on 1938, with 368 medical practitioners for an estimated 15 millions. It seems doubtful whether by 1950 medical services in West Africa could have been considered adequate even for as much as 3 per cent of the population (in England and Wales there was approximately one medical practitioner for every 1200 people). Before 1945 preventive health services were poor. Rates of vaccination, for example, were extremely low. In Sierra Leone the number of vaccinations per year decreased from 26,700 in 1920 to 8,400 in 1931, increased to 266,000 in the following year, and decreased again to between 50 and 60 thousand a year until the outbreak of war. Although by 1939 a great deal of sanitary and preventive medical work had been done in towns like Lagos, Accra and Dakar, in others conditions were still deplorable. Up to the outbreak of war little reclamation work had been done in Bathurst, for example, which remained an overcrowded and at times waterlogged island, where, in 1942, 10 per cent of the population slept in the streets. Its condition was little different from 1865 when '. . . in the rains, the Europeans die, and in the cold weather, the Africans . . . '.[47] Gourou's claim that the urban areas in the tropics are healthier than the rural because of their better medical services was true only in a few cases in West Africa.[48] Many of the towns were, and still are, poorly equipped for medical treatment, grossly overcrowded, with inadequate water supplies and only elementary forms of sanitation. By 1956 the capacity of Ibadan's piped water supply was only 4 gallons (18 litres) per head daily, compared with approximately 48 gallons (220 litres) in Lagos. Work under construction in Ibadan allowed for an increase to only 8 gallons (36 litres), assuming the population remained static.

It is hardly to be expected that the improvements in the social services introduced by Europeans can have had much effect on the demographic trend, at least up to 1950. Indeed the population movements produced during the colonial period, and the local increases in density, seem rather to have increased the incidence of disease and consequent mortality. Figures for death and birth rates or of disease incidence can be trusted only in rare instances, but there are other sorts of evidence suggestive of a worsening disease situation. Firstly there seems little doubt that European ships introduced the common European rat and, in consequence, plague.[49] As early as 1835 local population movement had its effect, for a colony of liberated Africans, brought to Bathurst from Sierra Leone, introduced small-pox.[50] In Nigeria's 'Middle Belt' the abandonment of nucleated villages for dispersed hamlets and compounds meant that settlements were no longer surrounded by open farmland, were more subject to infestation with tsetse fly, and the inhabitants therefore more likely to contract sleeping sickness.[51] In the densely populated areas meat resources are poorer, except for those with higher incomes, and there is ample evidence of the increasing importance of cassava in the diet (see p. 526). In such areas the problem of malnutrition must be even greater than elsewhere. Movement of seasonal labour on a large scale between different environments has led to the carrying of parasites and of infectious diseases elsewhere. Thus new strains of malaria parasites were introduced into Bathurst in 1942. In 1918 an influenza epidemic spread in two months from Lagos to the Cameroons. In Sierra Leone mining districts have proved centres of small-pox infection, from where the disease is carried to the rest of the country by labourers returning home.

Health considerations have affected the planning of settlements considerably, but few settlements have been in any way affected by planning, and these hitherto have been occupied mainly by the European community. The discoveries of Ross with regard to the transmission of malaria, and the founding of Government medical services, led Government and local authorities to consider questions of siting and drainage. Sanitary segregation had been advocated as early as 1830, but it was not until the end of the 19th century that separate European reservations were created, distant by a quarter mile or more ($\frac{1}{2}$ km) from African townships, and European traders were encouraged to move away from their premises. In Northern Nigeria Lugard himself examined the question of siting of British stations, insisting that they must be to windward, have an uncontaminated water supply, and that all millet crops must be cleared from the site. Provision was also made for the incineration and burial of refuse, for the disposal of the contents of latrine buckets, and for the erection of latrines for the use of the African population.[52] In many towns throughout Nigeria, regulations were made against the planting of tall crops on the peripheries, in order to reduce insect infestation, extensive drainage schemes were undertaken and old borrow pits filled in.[53] Dakar received its 'cordon sanitaire', dividing the administrative and commercial town from the African quarter of Medina. The brush was cut to eliminate mosquito breeding places, eucalyptus and casuarinas were planted in low places to lower the water-table, ravines were filled, and marshes within 12 miles (20 km) radius of the centre were drained. Lagos developed the European residential zone of Ikoyi, separated from the township by the MacGregor Canal, and until the introduction of pipe-borne water maintained a sewage tramway. After 1945 the improved prophylactic treatment of malaria made segregation less necessary on medical grounds, nor was it politically desirable. The former European residential areas, particularly in British territory, became the residential areas for those with higher incomes, regardless of race.

The post-1945 period has been marked by a great increase in medical activity, particularly in the field of preventive medicine. This increase has been most pronounced since 1950 with intensive campaigns against small-pox, yaws, onchocerciasis and sleeping sickness. In an area badly infected with sleeping sickness in northern Ghana, for example, the vectors *Glossina palpalis* and *Glossina tachinoides* were eradicated between 1940 and 1943, by clearing trees which provided a dry season habitat for the fly. Numerous surveys have been conducted in order to discover the incidence of certain diseases, and to recommend the most effective courses of treatment. In French West Africa in 1955 the number of vaccinations given against small-pox was $7\frac{1}{2}$ million, against yellow fever over 4 million, and against tuberculosis 95 thousand. In most territories in West Africa the numbers of hospital beds and maternity beds have doubled in the last ten years, and attendances at clinics and hospitals have increased enormously. Perhaps one of the most important developments has been the creation of medical teaching institutions like the University Hospital in Ibadan.

The growth of urbanism

The proportion of urban population is low in West Africa. If, for convenience, one counts the population of all settlements of 10,000 or more inhabitants as urban, then no large political unit has an urban population higher than 10 per cent with the exceptions of the Western Region of Nigeria, and of Senegal. In 1952 the Western Region recorded nearly 40 per cent, and in 1955 Senegal recorded 20 per cent. Provincial percentages in the Western Region were extraordinarily high: Ibadan 65, Colony 62, Oyo 56, Ondo 32, Ijebu 27. The northern provinces of the Eastern Region might also have recorded high percentages due to the concentration of population into the 'grassland towns'. The Census of the Eastern Region failed to recognize the existence of many of the towns as units and recorded the population in many cases by quarters, so that no true picture of the proportion of population in settlements of 10,000 or more inhabitants can be obtained, although these loose agglomerations, with certain exceptions, are hardly urban in the modern sense. Ghana (1948) had a percentage of 8, (in 1960, 23 per cent of the population was recorded as 'urban', i.e. in settlements of 5000 or more), Gambia (1951) 7, Sierra Leone (1948) 3, Ivory Coast (1956) 9, Dahomey (1955) 8, Guinea (1955) 4, Mali (1955) 4, Upper Volta (1955) 2, and Niger (1955) 2. Mauritania and Portuguese Guinea had no large urban settlements, and Liberia must remain a matter for speculation. The high southern Nigerian figures indicate the existence of indigenous towns, of which over a half of the inhabitants are dependent more on agriculture than any other activity. By the

Western Region Places of 5000+ People by
Proportion of Occupied Males in Agriculture

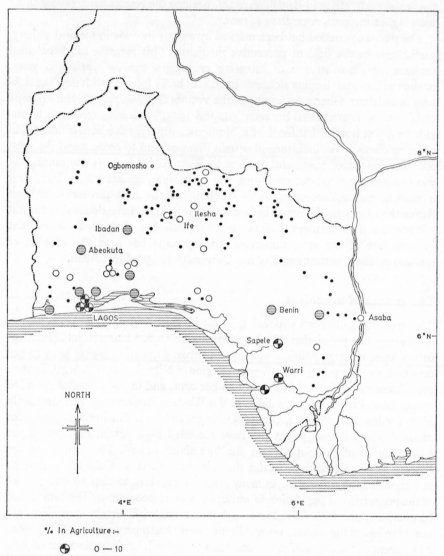

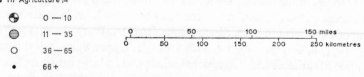

Figure 9.9

criteria of Chapter 1 the population is 'urban' and not 'rural', although in many cases mainly agricultural. In European terms these are not true towns, but the mainly agricultural population does enjoy certain urban advantages. In Figure 9.9 the proportions of occupied males in agriculture indicate the extent to which the Yoruba urban economies have changed, and contrast the modern ports and railway foci with more traditional centres.

An interesting related feature is that in Nigeria the modern towns, with the four exceptions of Port Harcourt, Enugu and Aba in the Eastern Region and Jos in the Northern Region, are developments of towns existing before the colonial period. Elsewhere in West Africa, with rare exceptions, the towns are new creations. Even an important commercial centre like Medina at the head of navigation on the Senegal was replaced by the railway centre of Kayes. The new routes by-passed the old river bank markets of Senegal and Mali. Dresch makes the generalization that west of Dahomey the large towns of today are all of recent foundation.[54] These new creations have new functions associated with modern administration and commerce, and many are important centres for education, medicine and professional activities. Such criteria may be used to define them and their relative importance as Manshard has attempted.[55]

It is unfortunately impossible to demonstrate changes in the urban proportion of population because of the probable census errors discussed in Chapter 1. Great increases can, however, be shown in the size of certain towns. For example, between 1931 and 1962 Abidjan has increased by 18 times, Cotonou by 11, Bouaké by 8, and Dakar and Thiès each by 7. Most towns have increased by at least half as much again since 1931. A few like Bida and Ilorin in the 'Middle Belt' have shown temporary decline due to emigration. With the exception of the Nigerian towns, all the towns with great increases are European creations. Of the Nigerian towns with a 4-fold increase or more between 1931 and 1952 only Benin, Ife, and Onitsha are traditional centres, and these, as in other cases of urban increase in Nigeria, have acquired new commercial sectors as a result of trade developments. The rapid growth of all towns is a response to the rapid development in commercial facilities, not necessarily to any great increase in productivity. The new towns, or the new sectors added to old towns, are required in the change-over from an economy looking almost entirely to internal markets, to an economy of which a large proportion looks to overseas markets.

The new towns are inhabited mainly by recent immigrants, many of whom do not regard them as home and return frequently to the rural areas. Instability of population and a high proportion of males are characteristic features. This instability is not, however, seasonal but confined to movement during holidays or on retirement from work. For example, in Dakar and Abidjan the proportions of population classified as 'resident' are 86 per cent and 88 per cent respectively. In both there is a great bulge in the 15–40 years age groups, and the proportions of population aged over 65 are below average. The numbers of males per 1000 females amongst the African population in 1955 were very high – 1120 and 1400 respectively. The Ghana census of 1948 also provided evidence of migration.

	Population	Males per 1000 females	Born in the town (%)	Neither born in town nor in the province (%)	Duration of residence (%)	
					1 yr	1–5 yrs
Accra	M. 72,000	1170	46	33	17	23
	F. 61,000		63	17	10	21
Sekondi-Takoradi	M. 25,000	1300	20	34	19	30
	F. 19,000		25	20	16	31
Kumasi	M. 31,000	1140	28	47	21	26
	F. 27,000		32	39	16	27
Cape Coast	M. 11,000	950	59	17	11	26
	F. 12,000		70	9	9	18
Koforidua	M. 8,900	1010	32	27	15	26
	F. 8,800		35	19	16	26
Obuasi	M. 9,000	1350	18	55	15	32
	F. 6,700		23	48	17	30

Recently-published figures for 1960 provide an interesting comparison and some additional data:

	Population	Males per 1000 females	Born in the town (%)	Born in another locality same region (%)	Born in another region in Ghana (%)	Born in another country in Africa (%)
Accra	M. 207,130	1141	45·5	2·5	32·9	19·1
	F. 181,266		55·2	3·4	30·1	11·3
Sekondi-Takoradi	M. 66,445	1169	30·6	32·1	19·3	18·0
	F. 56,868		34·6	39·2	16·3	9·9
Kumasi	M. 115,249	1121	37·0	18·3	29·7	15·0
	F. 102,923		33·0	19·8	29·3	7·9
Cape Coast	M. 28,346	992	61·4	15·3	17·0	6·3
	F. 28,568		69·0	16·7	11·0	3·3
Koforidua (New Juaben)	M. 27,455	1042	41·6	22·6	23·2	12·6
	F. 26,360		46·3	26·1	19·5	8·1
Obuasi	M. 14,582	1216	28·2	20·2	37·9	13·7
	F. 11,996		26·4	22·7	43·5	7·4

The least stable population is in the town of Obuasi with its mining interests; the most stable in the old-established settlement of Cape Coast, which between 1931 and 1948 increased by 31 per cent, or only 1 per cent more than the difference between the 1931 and 1948 census totals for all Ghana. The Lagos census of 1950 showed that only 40 per cent of the population were born in the town, but another 34 per cent were born in the Western Region, that is, had immigrated from nearby districts, and 71 per cent of the population were of the local Yoruba community. With certain exceptions, notably in Ghana, the greater part of urban migration comes from local districts. In Abidjan 50 per cent of the 1955 population consisted of the 'Eburnéo-Béninian' and 'West Atlantic' local communities, and in Dakar 43 per cent of the population was Wolof and 12 per cent Lébou. Kumasi acts as a major centre for immigrants – partly seeking work on the cocoa plantations, but in many cases moving no farther than Kumasi itself. As the links between the traditional communities and the individual weaken, the urban population may be expected to become more stable. Lombard suggests that a tendency to greater stability is already noticeable in Cotonou, where in 1952 more and more men were bringing their wives and children, and the number of males per 1000 females was as low as 1110.[56]

Cotonou (109,000 in 1964) has been increasing very rapidly. Part of the explanation for greater stability may lie in the fact that many of its inhabitants immigrate from other towns – Porto Novo, Ouidah, Allada and Abomey – and these people are already used to urban life.

The new towns have a number of distinct zones or sectors:

1) The trading and business sector extending from the port or railway station towards the periphery.
2) The administrative sector normally on the periphery.
3) The residential sector for the higher income or 'managerial' population (formerly the 'European' sector).[57]
4) The suburbs for the lower income or employed population.
5) The outer suburbs of recently-occupied shanty towns and villages.

The first three sectors are normally planned, in most cases with the colonial grid-iron street pattern, although there have been a few recent attempts to 'landscape' the distribution of houses and use curves. The fourth sector is also always planned in the new towns, and forms a monotonous grid-iron pattern of streets and lots of equal size, in which, in many cases, the houses are more sleeping quarters than houses in the fullest sense. Many of these suburbs are built on reclaimed or drained land, as for example Medina, the largest single suburb in former French West Africa, which was created on the periphery of Dakar in 1941 after an epidemic of plague. Treichville, the new suburb of Abidjan, is estimated to contain over 25,000 inhabitants in an area grossly overcrowded, and only poorly provided with water and sanitation.[58] Where, as in Nigeria, the commercial centres are established in the older towns, then the older towns themselves take the place of the suburbs. New housing, however, invariably occupies grid-iron locations, although normally less rigid in pattern. A distinctive feature here is 'quarter' separation of 'strangers'. Lagos, for example, has its Sabo for northerners, and the northern towns have their Sabon Garis occupied by southern clerks and traders. In Ghana, Kumasi has its Zongo, occupied by northern immigrants. Separation between some African communities, as formerly between European and African, is still a marked feature of West African towns despite the modern trend of grouping by economic or social position. The outer suburbs are unplanned sprawls, usually containing very low standards of housing and often forming virtual slums – Port Harcourt, for example, with its Diobu, and Abidjan with its Adjamé. At Aba a recent unplanned settlement has developed near the railway station taking advantage of the fact that the main planned town is limited in its expansion by the railway track. These unplanned suburbs often extend along main roads on the outer periphery, and limit planned expansion unless ruthless slum clearance is undertaken. As the towns have grown so have nearby villages, which act as transition points of settlement between the rural and urban areas, and house cultivators producing food for the urban market. Between 1936 and 1950 the combined population of the Dakar villages of Ouakam, Yoff, N'Gor, Tiaroye, Camberène, M'Bao and Youmbel had increased from 12,600 to 24,500. The village of Ouakam in 1923 consisted of five small scattered quarters. By 1951 three of these were joined together as a continuous housing unit, and the old track between them had become an important commercial street. Dagoudane Pikine, 6 miles (10 km) from Dakar, is an artificial village created to take people removed from the town by clearance projects. It has become, with its population of about 20,000, a small satellite town.[59] Savonnet has shown that the villages near Thiès have immigrants who lodge with relatives and cultivate on their land, until they are allowed by the local authority to build their own house. These immigrants then seek temporary work in Thiès itself, and also continue cultivation, but on their own plots. Eventually they obtain a permanent occupation, and finally move into the town itself.(60)

The rectangular patterned streets and the formal rows of houses in the new urban areas are evidence of the planning which is so marked a feature of 'Europeanized' settlement patterns. It is particularly marked in the former French West African territories where even very small towns, such as Tambacounda in Senegal (7100 in 1961), are markedly rectilinear.[61] Such planning occurred as early as the beginning of the century when Lugard devised a 'type plan' for towns in Northern Nigeria. In 1911 the Governor of Northern Nigeria wrote:

'In consultation with the Senior Sanitary Officer and other officials I have devised a plan for native towns . . . The main principles of the design are straight lines, broad avenues, large open spaces, a uniform size of building plot. Such towns could be extended almost indefinitely, and, if the design be carefully followed large open spaces, suitable for parks, gardens, or recreation grounds, would automatically be provided. Each building plot faces on a broad thoroughfare and the back of each lot is divided from the next by a lane 15 feet wide, which is intended principally for the removal of rubbish and night soil.

'Three townships, on those lines, have already been laid out at various points on the Baro–Kano Railway. They are proving very attractive to the natives, and some difficulty in fact, is being experienced in laying out with sufficient rapidity the building plots that are applied for. It is proposed to pursue this project not only in regard to new townships but also with a view to the improvement of old centres of population, and there seems to be no reason why, without undue interference with the traditions and customs of the natives, the people of Northern Nigeria should not be induced to live under conditions which will conduce to their good health and material improvement.'[62]

In 1939 the Government of Nigeria published a report[63] in which a schematic layout for new towns was recommended, having the following zones:

1) Administrative and business.
2) Industrial.

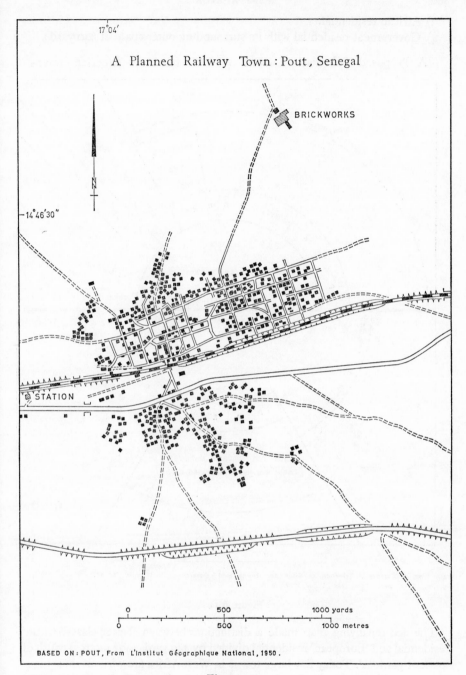

A Planned Railway Town : Pout, Senegal

17°04'

BRICKWORKS

N

14°46'30"

STATION

| 0 | 500 | 1000 yards |
| 0 | 500 | 1000 metres |

BASED ON : POUT, From L'Institut Géographique National, 1950.

Figure 9.10

3) African residential.

4) Government residential with its surrounding outer space of 440 yards.

A Proposed Schematic Layout of 1939 for New Nigerian Towns

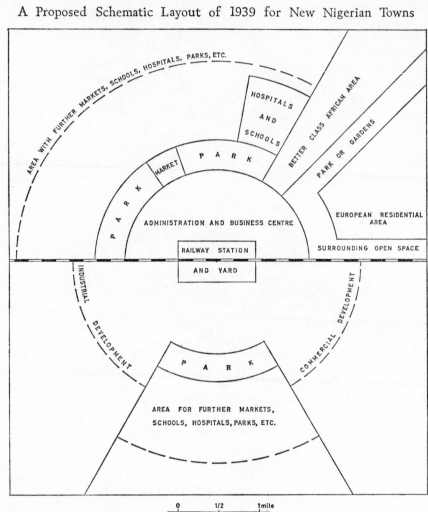

Drawn from a Diagram in Selection of Sites for Towns and Government Residential Areas,
Nigerian Government Publication, Lagos, 1939

Figure 9.11

The accompanying map made a distinction between 'better-class African' residential and 'European' residential divided by 440 yards (402 metres) width of 'park or gardens'. Today few large towns in West Africa are without their planning committees or even planning authorities. In former French territory the planning of future development has been enforced in several of the larger townships. Dakar, for example, has its Service Temporaire d'Aménagement du Grand

Dakar, which has produced development plans for the entire Cape Verde peninsula. Lagos has its Central Planning Scheme for slum clearance involving the movement of 20,000 people over 5–7 years to the Suru Lere Rehousing Estate. Planning may create its grid-iron monotonies in Medina, Treichville, the new railway towns and even in the new villages of recently-settled land, but there can be little doubt of the necessity for forethought in the problems of future expansion. Uncontrolled building has produced slums, insanitary conditions, and has led to encroachment onto main roads, once the value of land is realized. Thus in Epe in south-western Nigeria in 1902 it was discovered that in some cases street widths were reduced from 20 feet to 6 feet.[64] Development can be blocked by an unfortunate layout or by certain landowners. The railway, for example, presents an almost insuperable obstacle in a territory where there are no bridges, only level crossings. The suburb of Medina blocks the expansion of the city of Dakar proper, whilst in Thiès and Ibadan lands owned by church missionary societies have prevented building development in certain directions.[65]

An interesting feature is the trend in housing throughout the new towns of West Africa to rectangular forms, chiefly one storey, although peoples like the Yoruba tend to favour large two-storey structures, often subdivided into 'flats'. It is claimed locally that the modern Yoruba type of housing was introduced by returned slaves from Brazil, and the oldest forms are to be found in the Brazilian quarters of Lagos. The old type of European house of two storeys, with living quarters entirely in the upper portion, or of one storey on stilts, is also disappearing, to be replaced for the most part by smaller bungalows or two-storey houses in which both levels are occupied.

The rapidly-growing modern towns are the centres of political power, the foci of new loyalties which may eventually cut across the former 'tribal' pattern, and the areas most subject to external influence and to change. They provide the 'high life' so attractive to many of the rural population, and concentrate within them the most rapid developments in architecture, social services, education and medicine, which so impress the visitor. The rural areas are not entirely neglected. In a few, remarkable changes have taken place, particularly in the export crop regions. But even in these areas the amount of change has not been nearly as spectacular as in the towns, despite the fact that West Africa's economic strength is almost entirely rural. In consequence two very distinct worlds are developing in West Africa, the urban and the rural, with a social and economic change between them far greater than that which exists in the industrial nations. In some territories, notably in Senegal, Mali, Guinea and the Ivory Coast, there are fewer major centres, and only one large town or primate city which plays a dominant role in the economy. The lack of units in between the very large and the very small results in part from a functional hiatus and the alien character of many primate cities. It represents a transition stage in development.

Migration

Traditionally West African peoples migrated in search of land. Today, with a few exceptions, they migrate in search of wage-labour.[66] The exceptions concern forms of share-cropping and tenancy or short-term leasing of land. Large-scale migrations are recent phenomena, which have increased in size as export crop production has increased, and towns have grown in commercial importance. They are the product of local labour shortage whenever a demand is made for increase in productivity, and of seasonal labour surpluses, chiefly in northern areas, especially after the ending of local warfare and slave-raiding. On the whole West Africa lacks surplus labour, even for agricultural enterprises. Lack of labour has been a constant hindrance to West African economic development, and is a common feature elsewhere in Africa, where population densities are low, and sufficient land is still available for traditional systems of cultivation. Except in extremely overcrowded areas, labour is rarely forced out by local pressure on resources. As long as there is sufficient land, there is no labour available, unless the new enterprises can offer higher real incomes than those obtained from traditional agriculture. With the exception of portions of Mossi territory, Sokoto and Iboland, where labour is forced out either by overcrowding or by seasonal problems, migration is produced more by the factor of attraction.[67]

The earliest large-scale migration, concerned with a new form of production, began in the early 19th century in the Senegal and Gambia. The migrants were in effect share-croppers, endeavouring to produce groundnuts for export in order to purchase imported goods in or near their ports of entry. Every March–June the 'navétanes' of Senegal and the 'strange farmers' of the Gambia came to acquire land, and eventually share the crop with the landlord after about six months' work. Governor Macdonnell recorded their presence in the Gambia as early as 1852:

'It is a fact, that at least one-third of the produce exported is raised by natives, who travel from distances of 500 and even 700 miles in the interior to visit the Gambia along the banks of which they hire, from the various chiefs in whose countries they settle, small tracts of ground, which they cultivate. Most of these visitors from the interior remain from two to three years near the Gambia, till, by their labour and the produce of their farms, they have earned sufficient to enable them to purchase those goods, the desire for which had induced them to leave their homes.'[68]

In 1852 migrants had to walk – hence residence for 'two to three years'. Today many can take advantage of modern transport methods and migrate every year. Moreover, payment of a share of the crop for the right to use the land has changed to work of 2 to 4 days a week on the landlord's groundnut plot. Although wage-labour is not involved, the effect of the arrival of the strange farmer in the Gambia was to change the groundnut trade from barter to a cash transaction, in which, in 1843, sioce French merchants were chiefly concerned, the 5-franc piece became recognized as legal tender.[69] Less than 600 strange farmers were recorded in 1903, but numbers rose to a peak of over 32,000 in 1915, due to high war-time prices. They decreased to just over 3000 in 1943, when prices were higher in Senegal. Numbers rose to nearly 20,000 in 1945, and have since fluctuated between 10 and 20 thousand each year. Before returning home the strange farmers use about half their income to purchase cotton piece goods, which they trade over the border in order to increase their earnings. About half the strange farmers are normally from Senegal, and the rest are Gambians from the Upper River Province, and men from Portuguese Guinea and Guinea. In October there is, in both Gambia and Senegal, a second seasonal immigration, chiefly of younger men, who enter as extra wage-labour solely for the harvest. These are the 'baragnini' of Senegal.[70] A small number of strange farmers stay in the groundnut districts for ten years or more, and remit part of their earnings home. A few come from as far away as Upper Volta, and a few Gambians migrate as 'navétanes' to Senegal, but movement in any direction depends much on relative prices. In Senegal 30,000–60,000 navétanes are employed in any one year, coming from northern Senegal, Mali and Guinea. Many of these navétanes do not receive a temporary right to cultivate land for themselves, but are employed as wage-labourers. The Tekrour or Toucouleur of the middle Senegal valley are an important source of labour for the groundnut planters. Many of them, however, migrate to the towns or even as far afield as Bouaké in the Ivory Coast where they are employed mainly in the textile industry.[71]

Labour shortage, except during the dry season in certain areas, has long been a problem of development. The supply of labour for porterage and later for railway and road construction has always been short. Forced labour was used on the Thiès–Niger, Dahomey, Baro–Kano and Eastern Railways. It was also used in the Nigerian tin mines as late as 1942, in plantations in the Ivory Coast, and in Togoland and the Cameroons under German rule. The forced labour regulations in the Ivory Coast were not repealed until 1946, when the Syndicat Interprofessionel pour l'Acheminement de la Main d'Œuvre was formed to recruit and arrange transport for labour to the coffee and cocoa plantations. Forced labour has been recruited in Liberia for work on the Lower Congo Railway (under the former Congo Free State), and in the cocoa plantations of Fernando Po. 'Free' labour from Nigeria has been recruited for Fernando Po since 1957 at the rate of up to 800 labourers a month. In 1956 it was estimated that 25,000 immigrant labourers were at work on the island.[72] Nearly 1000 Nigerians were recruited also in 1953 for work in the Gabon timber industry.

By 1951 the Ivory Coast was receiving 50,000 seasonal labourers from Upper Volta, 25,000 from French Niger, and probably 50,000 from Nigeria (chiefly from Sokoto Province). In 1952–3 a census in Sokoto Province recorded 250,000 migrants, mostly moving in November–January, of whom 72 per cent originated in the Province (chiefly northern Sokoto), 17 per cent from French territory and 10 per cent from the rest of Nigeria.[73] 52 per cent of these were seeking money, 16 per cent seeking food, and 24 per cent going to trade. Of the total, less than a fifth were migrating for the first time. The migrants were divided into those travelling to the Zamfara valley, either from French territory or from within Sokoto Province itself (14 per cent), and those, usually without their families, migrating to the cocoa belts of Ghana (17 per cent) and south-western Nigeria (25 per cent), to south-eastern Nigeria (18 per cent), to the tin mines of the Jos Plateau (10 per cent), and to various other occupations elsewhere in Northern Nigeria. At destination 45 per cent of the migrants became labourers and 24 per cent petty traders. Maximum distances were 600 miles (950 km), and much was accomplished on foot. The existing trading system in kola nuts was thought to provide contacts in the reception areas. The earlier migrants to plantations in the then Gold Coast and in the Ivory Coast included former slave traders deprived of their occupation.[74] In Ghana some immigrants have bought cocoa land, but many work under the 'abusa' system, whereby they receive a third share of the crop for the work performed. Other immigrant labourers are paid a fixed sum for work done, contract in advance to do a particular job for an agreed sum of money, are daily paid, or are paid an annual fixed sum as wages. Some abusa labourers have established cocoa plots, sold their rights in the crop and then bought fresh land outright with the money.[75] In the Nigerian cocoa belt, immigrant labourers from Northern Nigeria, from fringing Yoruba districts, from Benin and from the Eastern Region, work as paid labour, or have established their own cocoa plots. The chief influx of labour comes after the groundnut and millet harvests, chiefly from October onwards, and the immigrants return north in February–March. These migrants do the work of harvesting the cocoa crop. Weeding of cocoa plots is done chiefly by southern Nigerians, who immigrate after planting their own food crops for the March–September period.[76] In the Victoria Division of the former Southern Cameroons in 1953, more than one-fifth of the total population of nearly 86,000 were strangers, of whom most were employed on the plantations. The immigrants came chiefly from the French Cameroons, the Bamenda and Mamfe Divisions and the Eastern Region. It should be added that local migration for paid work on food-growing land is now becoming an increasingly important phenomenon, in place of the former work for presents of food and beer. Specialist labour for fruit cutting or planting yams is frequently hired. Hired labour has become particularly important in districts formerly depending on slaves.

Long-term or permanent emigration, chiefly from rural areas to the towns, as already described above, is becoming an increasingly important feature, not just from the areas around the towns, but even from areas situated at some distance where economic opportunities and social conditions are more limited. Thus the northern areas with their long dry season, their swarms of insect and bird pests and their problems of food storage are becoming centres not only of seasonal, but of long-distance nearly permanent emigration. For example, the Toucouleur or Tekrour of the middle Senegal valley, despite their extensive areas of floodland cultivation, emigrate in large numbers. 20 per cent of the population has been estimated absent at one time, and of these emigrants 80 per cent are estimated to have sought work in Dakar where they form the second largest group to the local Wolof and Lébou.[77]

Recent resettlement and demographic change

There are many resettlement schemes in West Africa in which the movement of population, and not the agricultural development, is the primary objective. Such schemes have been particularly well developed in Northern Nigeria (see pp. 659–62). At Shendam on the southern margin of the Jos Plateau, for example, the attempt is being made to organize the settlement of a few of the people moving from the overcrowded foothill refuges to the plains. It is hoped to avoid the practice of poor farming methods in the new lands by encouraging rotations and manuring, a combination of food and commercial crops, the development of communal grazing and forest lands, and the cultivation of swamp rice in fadama. In the Anchau 'corridor', south of Kano, 610 square miles (1580 sq km) have been cleared of tsetse fly, and sixteen new villages and a town have been built. Protection against tsetse has been given, not only to the settlers, but also to the people of the more densely-settled areas of Zaria Province, to the west, by the creation of this fly-free zone. In Kontagora the Native Authority Land Settlement Scheme was begun in 1948 to organize the occupation of lands thought to be 'under-populated'. The Bamenda–Cross river–Calabar scheme included in part a resettlement project for the eastern portion of the Kwa Falls area, with over 100 families, cultivating chiefly oil palms, under the guidance of a planning authority. Other smaller resettlement schemes occur in the Gwoza area of Bornu Province, the Koza area of Katsina Province, and the Ruruma area of Zaria Province, for mixed farming, and also at Agangari in Sokoto Province where two dams have been constructed, providing water for a settlement scheme involving 300 Fulani and 5000 cattle.

The trend towards planning and control of population movement is evident in the resettlement schemes and in the establishment of town planning authorities. The days when men could claim virgin or long fallow land from the 'bush' have gone from most of West Africa, and the new states are seeking to develop planned economies, in which a great deal of control is exercised over future trends in population distribution. As suggested in Chapter 1, population increase seems likely in the future, due to the increasing tempo of medical activity, although it is impossible as yet to produce reliable and widespread census evidence of increased fertility rates or declining death rates. It is not yet evident that the increase will be rapid, despite the claim of one observer that the kind of population growth which occurred in Europe and elsewhere in the latter part of the 18th and in the 19th centuries will also occur in West Africa.[78] It is doubtful whether either the capital or the resources are available for an increase in production comparable to that which took place in 19th-century Europe. However, the urbanward trend and the movement to wage-labour occupations are clearly evident, and the general redistribution of the population into settlement patterns more like those existing in countries with a greater degree of commercial and industrial development may be expected.

BIBLIOGRAPHICAL NOTES

[1] J. W. Blake, *Europeans in West Africa 1450–1560*, 2 vols, Hakluyt Society, Series II, vols 86 and 87, London, 1942.

[2] Macgregor Laird and R. K. Oldfield, *Narrative of an Expedition into the Interior of Africa by the River Niger, in the Steam Vessels Quorra and Alburkah in 1832, 1833 and 1834*, London, 1837.

[3] Sir H. H. Johnston, *A History of the Colonization of Africa by Alien Races*, London, 1930 (first edition 1899), pp. 153–4.

[4] C. M. Macinnes, *England and Slavery*, Bristol, 1934, pp. 89–90. In 1789 the annual export of slaves was estimated to be 52,200 from West Africa including the Cameroons and 22,000 from the western coast of the Cameroons, see above, p. 387.

[5] D. P. Gamble, *The Wolof of Senegambia*, London, 1957, p. 14.

[6] Hugh Goldie, *Calabar and its Mission*, Edinburgh, 1890, p. 100.

[7] E. Reclus, *The Universal Geography*, vol. III, West Africa, translated by A. E. Keane London, 1896, p. 252.

[8] P. D. Curtin, *The Image of Africa, British Ideas and Action, 1780–1850*, London, 1965, pp. 99–101.

[9] See H. Labouret, *Paysans d'Afrique Occidentale*, 6th ed., Paris, 1941, pp. 57 et seq.

[10] *Colonial Annual Reports, Lagos*, 1900–1901, p. 6.

[11] Naval Intelligence Handbooks, B.R. 512, *French West Africa, II The Colonies*, London, 1944, p. 377.

[12] W. B. Morgan, The Grassland Towns of South-eastern Nigeria, *Transactions and Papers, Institute of British Geographers*, 23, 1957, pp. 213 and 224.

[13] A. T. Grove, *The Benue Valley*, Ministry of Natural Resources, Kaduna, 1958, p. 10.

[14] L. and P. Bohannan, *The Tiv of Central Nigeria*, London, 1953, p. 57.

[15] For discussion of the factors influencing downhill movement see M. B. Gleave, Hill Settlements and their Abandonment in Western Yorubaland, *Africa*, 32, 1963, pp. 343–52, and M. B. Gleave, The Changing Frontiers of Settlement in the Uplands of Northern Nigeria, *Nigerian Geographical Journal*, 8(2), 1965, pp. 127–41.

[16] *Colonial Annual Reports, Northern Nigeria*, 516, 1905–6, pp. 361 et seq.

[17] *Colonial Annual Reports, Northern Nigeria*, 409 (1902), 476 (1904), 516 (1905–6), 594 (1907–8).

[18] D. P. Gamble, op. cit.

[19] See L. and P. Bohannan, op. cit., pp. 54–57.

[20] For Derwent Whittlesey's comments see Kano, A Sudanese Metropolis, *Geographical Review*, 27, 1937, pp. 177–99, and British and French Colonial Technique in West Africa, *Foreign Affairs*, 15, 1937, pp. 362–73.

[21] J. P. Nicolas, Deux Ports d'Estuaire: St. Louis du Sénégal et Douala, *Bulletin, Institut Français d'Afrique Noire*, 19, ser. B, 1957, pp. 259–74.

[22] On the development of Dakar see:
C. Moraze, Dakar, *Annales de Géographie*, 1936, pp. 607–31.
D. Whittlesey, Dakar and Other Cape Verde Settlements, *Geographical Review*, 31, 1941, pp. 609–38.
D. Whittlesey, Dakar Revisited, *Geographical Review*, 38, 1948, pp. 626–32.
J. Dresch, Villes d'Afrique Occidentale, *Cahiers d'Outre-Mer*, 3, 1950, pp. 200–30.

P. Mercier, L. Massé and A. Hauser, L'Agglomération Dakaroise, *Etudes Sénégalaises*, no. 5, 1954 (Social and Demographic Aspects).

[23] For a detailed account of the growth of Thiès see G. Savonnet, Une Ville Neuve de Sénégal, Thiès, *Cahiers d'Outre-Mer*, 1956, pp. 70–93.

[24] T. J. Bowen, *Adventures and Missionary Labors in Several Countries in the Interior of Africa from 1849 to 1856*, Charleston, 1857, pp. 197 and 218.

[25] T. E. Bowdich, *Mission from Cape Coast Castle to Ashantee*, London, 1817.

[26] E. Reclus, op. cit.

[27] *Colonial Annual Reports, Southern Nigeria*, 1906, p. 59.

[28] K. M. Buchanan and J. C. Pugh, *Land and People in Nigeria*, London, 1955, p. 116.

[29] The Leverhulme Trust, *The West Africa Commission, 1938–9*, 1943, p. 50.

[30] R. W. Steel, The Population of Ashanti: a Geographical Analysis, *Geographica Journal*, **112**, 1948, pp. 64–77.

[31] R. M. Lawson, The Changing Pattern of Life in an Ashanti Village, *Annual Conference Proceedings, West African Institute of Social and Economic Research*, 1954, pp. 33–36.

[32] R. Galletti, K. D. S. Baldwin and I. O. Dina, *Nigerian Cocoa Farmers*, London, 1956, p. 125.

[33] ibid., p. 107.

[34] See H. Ward Price, *Report of Land Tenure in the Yoruba Provinces*, 1932, part II, Ibadan Division, par. 139, par. 149 et seq.

[35] E. A. Boateng, Settlement in South-East Gold Coast, *Transactions and Papers, Institute of British Geographers*, **21**, 1955, pp. 157–69.

[36] With regard to New Juaben, the Gold Coast Census of Population, 1948, p. 27, claims that the growth of population was due to the development of cocoa growing, but R. J. Harrison Church, *West Africa*, London, 5th ed., 1966, p. 379, whilst admitting the importance of cocoa states: 'The high density in New Juaben results from the desire of Ashanti people to live within its borders despite its small size.'

[37] T. E. Hilton, The Population of the Gold Coast, *International Geographical Union, Natural Resources, Food and Population in Inter-Tropical Africa, Makerere Symposium, 1955*, 1956, pp. 43–49.
T. E. Hilton, *Ghana Population Atlas*, Edinburgh, 1960.
For later survey see D. Grove, *Population Patterns, Their Impact on Regional Planning*, Kumasi, 1963.

[38] M. J. Field, The Agricultural System of the Manya-Krobo of the Gold Coast, *Africa*, **14**, 1943, pp. 54–65.

[39] R. R. Kuczynski, op. cit., p. 425, n. 2, quoting the Report of the Labour Department, 1939–40.

[40] A. Hauser, Colons Africains au Soudan, *Annual Conference Proceedings, West African Institute of Social and Economic Research*, 1956, pp. 45–51.

[41] The Leverhulme Trust, op. cit., p. 50.

[42] H. A. Cochran, The Technique of Well Sinking in Nigeria, *Geological Survey of Nigeria, Bulletin 16*, 1937, p. 8.

[43] P. Merlin, L'Hydraulique Pastorale en A.O.F., *Bulletin des Services de L'Elevage et des Industries Animales de l'A.O.F.*, 4, 1951, pp. 169–201.

[44] R. R. Kuczynski, op. cit., pp. 478–9.

[45] ibid., p. 239.

[46] A. Brown, Disease as an Element in the Nigerian Environment, in K. M. Buchanan and J. C. Pugh, op. cit., pp. 41–57.

[47] R. R. Kuczynski, op. cit., pp. 363–76.

[48] P. Gourou, *The Tropical World*, London, 4th ed., 1966.

[49] R. Rosevear, *Checklist and Atlas of Nigerian Mammals*, Lagos, 1953.

[50] R. R. Kuczynski, op. cit., p. 368.

[51] A. Brown, op. cit. For an excellent general discussion of the problems of migration and disease see R. M. Prothero, *Migrants and Malaria*, London, 1965.

[52] *Colonial Annual Reports, Northern Nigeria*, **476** (1904), pp. 231–2 and 348, **704** (1910–11), p. 728.
For early references to sanitary segregation see P. D. Curtin, op. cit., p. 190.

[53] *Annual Medical and Sanitary Reports*, Northern and Southern Provinces, 1914.

[54] J. Dresch, Villes d'Afrique Occidentale, *Les Cahiers d'Outre-Mer*, **11**, 1950, pp. 200–30.

[55] W. Manshard, Verstädterungserscheinungen in Westafrika, *Sonderdruck aus Raumforschung und Raumerdnung*, 1961, pp. 27–41.
See also A. Mabogunje, The Evolution and Analysis of the Retail Structure of Lagos, Nigeria, *Economic Geography*, **40**, 1964, pp. 304–23.
For attempts to define urban fields by studying the areas affected by urban services see W. Manshard, Die Stadt Kumasi (Ghana), *Erdkunde*, **15**, 1961, pp. 161–80, and D. Grove and L. Huszar, *The Towns of Ghana*, Accra, 1964.

[56] J. Lombard, Cotonou, Ville Africaine, *Bulletin, Institut Français d'Afrique Noire*, **17**, 1954, pp. 341–77.

[57] In 1950 Dresch distinguished the 'white town' from the 'black town' but admitted that segregation was not total, and that there existed a 'bourgeoisie' of Africans and coloured or peoples of mixed origin living in the 'white town'.

[58] J. Dresch, op. cit.

[59] J. Gallais, Les Villages Lebous de la Presqu'île de Cap-Vert, *Les Cahiers d'Outre-Mer*, **7**, 1954, pp. 137–54.

[60] G. Savonnet, Les Villages de la Banlieue Thièssoise, *Bulletin, Institut Français d'Afrique Noire*, **17**, 1955, pp. 371–87.

[61] For an excellent study of a small European created town see J.-F. Dupon, Tambacounda, Capitale du Sénégal Oriental, *Cahiers d'Outre-Mer*, **17**, 1964, pp. 175–214.

[62] H. Hesketh Bell in *Colonial Annual Report, Northern Nigeria*, **704**, 1910–11, pp. 709–10.

[63] Government of Nigeria, *Selection of Sites for Towns and Government Residential Areas*, 1939.

[64] *Colonial Annual Reports, Lagos*, 1902, p. 43.

[65] In Thiès mission land to the north of the railway has resulted in the existence of an undeveloped wedge penetrating nearly to the town centre. In Ibadan a row of mission properties aligned within the old wall has hindered expansion on the south side of the town.

[66] See 'Movements of Manpower' in International Labour Office, *African Labour Survey*, Geneva, 1958, pp. 127–38.

[67] J. Rouch, Problèmes Relatifs à l'Etude des Migrations Traditionelles et des Migrations Actuelles en Afrique Occidentale, *Bulletin, Institut Français d'Afrique Noire*, **22B**, 1960, pp. 369–78.

[68] Quoted in R. R. Kuczynski, op. cit., pp. 333–9.
See also Lord Hailey, *Native Administration in the British African Territories*, 1951, part III, p. 347.

[69] H. R. Jarrett, The Strange Farmers of the Gambia, *Geographical Review*, **39**, 1949, pp. 649–57.
Sir J. M. Gray, *History of the Gambia*, Cambridge, 1940, p. 384.

[70] H. Labouret, op. cit., p. 225.

[71] C. Le Blanc, Un Village de la Vallée du Sénégal: Amadi-Ounaré, *Cahiers d'Outre-Mer*, **17**, 1964, pp. 117–48.
A. Diop, Enquête sur la Migration Toucouleur à Dakar, *Bulletin, Institut Français d'Afrique Noire*, **22B**, 1960, pp. 393–418.
Prothero gives a figure of 30,000 labourers on Fernando Po *c.* 1960 out of 42,000 population. See R. M. Prothero, Population Movements and Problems of Malaria Eradication in Africa, *Bulletin, World Health Organisation*, **24**, 1961, pp. 405–25.

[72] For forced labour see:
Lord Hailey, *African Survey*, revised 1956, pp. 1362–4, 1368–76, 1384–5, 1401 and 1412.
H. Fréchou, Les Plantations Européennes en Côte d'Ivoire, *Les Cahiers d'Outre-Mer*, **8**, 1955, pp. 56–83.
J. Tricart, Les Echanges entre la Zone Forestière de Côte d'Ivoire et les Savanes Soudaniennes, *Les Cahiers d'Outre-Mer*, **9**, 1956, pp. 209–38 (chiefly pp. 230–4).

[73] A. A. Igun, The Demographic Consequence of Social Change in West Africa, *Annual Conference Proceedings, West African Institute of Social and Economic Research*, 1955, pp. 52–67.
Details taken from R. M. Prothero, Population Patterns and Migrations in Sokoto Province, Northern Nigeria, *International Geographical Union, Natural Resources, Food and Population in Inter-Tropical Africa, Makerere Symposium, 1955*, 1956, pp. 46–54.
For further information see:
J. Rouch, Migrations au Ghana, *Journal de la Société des Africanistes*, **26**, 1956, pp. 33–196.
R. M. Prothero, Migrant Labour in West Africa, *Journa .of Local Administration Overseas*, **1**, 1962, pp. 149–55.
R. M. Prothero, Population Movements and Problems of Malaria Eradication in Africa, op. cit.

[74] J. Rouch, Problèmes Relatifs à l'Etude des Migrations Traditionelles et des Migrations Actuelles en Afrique Occidentale, *Bulletin, Institut Français d'Afrique Noire*, **22B**, 1960, pp. 369–78.

[75] Polly Hill, Systems of Labour Employment on Gold Coast Cocoa Farms, *Annual Conference Proceedings, West African Institute of Social and Economic Research*, 1956, pp. 54–67.
Polly Hill, *The Gold Coast Cocoa Farmer, a Preliminary Survey*, 1956, Chapters I–III.
For estimates of numbers of immigrants into Ghana, see above p. 447.

[76] R. Galletti, K. D. S. Baldwin and I. O. Dina, op. cit., pp. 206–11.

[77] A. Diop, op. cit.

[78] A. A. Igun, op. cit.

Figure 9.8 is taken from G. Benneh, The Agricultural Geography of the Main Forest Zone of Ghana. Unpublished thesis for the Ph.D. degree of the University of London, 1964.

CHAPTER 10

The Impact of European Influences
on Agriculture and Pastoralism

European contacts with West Africa have led to an invasion of the region by plants and man and to a small extent by animals. The development of an overseas trade has introduced commercialism into agriculture, encouraging production for distant markets, either overseas or within West Africa itself. Changes in methods of transportation and the relocation of population, particularly the movement to the towns, have reinforced the commercial trend. The acquisition of political control has in turn led to the assumption by colonial governments of responsibility for the improvement of agricultural productivity. Attempts have been made to change the methods of cultivation, the crops and even distributions. The tempo of these changes in agriculture is increasing rapidly. West Africa is in the midst of an agricultural revolution of which the future results are difficult as yet to forecast.

The early indirect influence

Even before the creation of colonies in the 19th century, Europeans began to influence the pattern and progress of West African agriculture. American crop plants began to arrive in the 16th century, mainly by the agency of Portuguese traders. Hard maize varieties were introduced indirectly via the Nile valley, but the soft maizes, cassava, groundnuts, the sweet potato and American cottons appear to have been brought directly to the early coastal settlements. Many of the Asian plants listed in Chapter 2 were introduced, probably from Ethiopia or East Africa, before the 15th century. Ethiopia is itself a possible centre of some of the crops listed as 'indigenous', particularly the sorghums and pennisetum millets, but the problems of distinguishing centres of origin for the vast number of varieties have not yet been resolved. However, the Portuguese and the traders of other European nations at later dates made further introductions from Asia, notably of rice. The introductions of the 16th and 17th centuries were intended mainly to provide a variety of foodstuffs at the small coastal stations, and later to provide food for the frequently large slave populations awaiting transportation to the Americas. Most of the early European trading posts in West Africa were situated on the Gold Coast in order to develop the important gold trade with Ashanti. Here the marked dry season favoured the cultivation of cereals, and maize spread rapidly in the region between the forests of the Gold

Coast and Yorubaland, becoming a staple food of the population of southern Dahomey by the 17th century.[1] Cassava, although a useful crop for feeding slaves, did not prove so popular with West African cultivators until the crowding of population in the coastal areas began in the late 19th century, and brought the problem of shorter fallows. Probably, as Jones suggests, satisfactory methods of preparing cassava meal were not introduced until the arrival of Negroes from Brazil from about the last quarter of the 18th century (see p. 87). The sweet potato, although widespread, is still rarely a staple food, whilst groundnut production did not develop on a large scale until the commercial expansion of the 19th century. American cottons were planted chiefly by cultivators already growing Asian varieties, whilst the Asian rice was adopted most rapidly in the southwest by peoples who already depended on *Oryza glaberrima*. There was little early overseas trade in cultivated plants. Gathered produce was much more important. For a short time there was a small demand in Europe for West African peppers, the 'grains of paradise', obtained from the Grain Coast or from Benin. However, the trade was short-lived, due to Indian competition, and failed to give rise to extensive pepper planting. Plantations producing export crops were confined entirely to the island of São Tomé, where sugar cultivation was established as early as 1540.

The beginnings of direct modification

In the 18th century little further attempt was made to modify West African agriculture, except for the encouragement of food production near the slave ports. It was only in the 19th century that a large-scale introduction of new crops began, and that cultivation for export was encouraged. Trade was the mainspring of European modification of the traditional systems of cropping. The abolition of the slave trade led to a demand for commodities which could replace the traffic in human beings. The expansion of industry in Europe created a demand for overseas markets, which could in turn supply raw materials. The inter-tropical countries became a major source of fibres, particularly cotton, and of vegetable oils for lubrication and lighting. West Africa provides the nearest inter-tropical environments to Europe with a large surplus of oil seeds, chiefly from the oil palm, self-sown in the fallows, and secondary forests near the coast from the Casamance river to the Cameroons. The resultant increase in value of oil palm produce in West Africa encouraged the better protection and even planting of the palm. A small trade developed in copra or dried coconut kernels, chiefly in Dahomey, and attempts were made to encourage the planting of cotton and to introduce American seed, whilst the foundations of an export traffic in groundnuts were laid, beginning in the Gambia about 1830.

In many cases West African communities welcomed the new developments, and requested the introduction of new crops. In Senegal French Government agencies introduced a variety of plants as early as the 1820s. In the areas of British influence, plants were introduced by missionaries, and by traders like

MacGregor Laird and Robert Jamieson of Liverpool, with interests in cotton and oilseeds. Commercial and philanthropic societies were organized to import seed and give instruction in planting. The expedition to the river Niger of 1841 took with it cotton seed and apparatus to establish a model farm for a society interested in the promotion of cultivation in West Africa.[2] Numerous individual attempts were made to encourage cultivation. Campbell, Governor of Sierra Leone from 1834 to 1837, established 'Government farms', subdivided them into 4-acre (1½-hectare) holdings, and induced men to clear and cultivate them.[3] The Royal Niger Company established a plantation at Asaba on the river Niger in 1888 for experiments in commercial botany.[4] The British Cotton Growing Association was formed in 1902 to erect ginneries, introduce seed and create experimental or model farms for the purpose of instructing cotton cultivators.[5] Government botanic gardens were also founded, where exotic plants were established and in some cases acclimatized. From the latter developed the colonial agricultural departments, whose influence on West African agriculture during the present century has been of vital importance in developing the new trends. The policies adopted by these departments may be divided into two types.[6] The first of these derives from the West Indies, and lays emphasis on the development of plantation agriculture, even at the cost of importing food to support the labour force required. The second derives from south-east Asia, and lays emphasis on the encouragement of peasant cultivation, with attempts to improve production mainly by adaptations of methods proved successful in Europe, e.g. the introduction of mixed farming and, more recently, mechanization. The first is associated with territories having only low densities of population, where large areas can be occupied by colonial settlers. The second is associated with crowded areas, where the greater part of the land is already in the hands of peasant cultivators. In the more densely-populated Sudanic and eastern Guinean zones there has been little or no attempt to establish plantations. Only in the less populous western Guinean areas of Guinea and the Ivory Coast, and in West Cameroun, has any measure of plantation production been achieved. Nevertheless the two traditions have influenced departmental policies in the West African territories. Early British and French attempts to modify agriculture in West Africa owed much to West Indian experience, and it was only in the later stages of development that notions derived from experience in India or Indo-China became of major importance.

The introduction of crops and development of local crops for export[7]

The major crop plants introduced by European agency for subsistence or internal exchange production have been listed above in Chapter 2. Crops introduced for export production must now be discussed and further comment made on local crops developed for the same purpose.

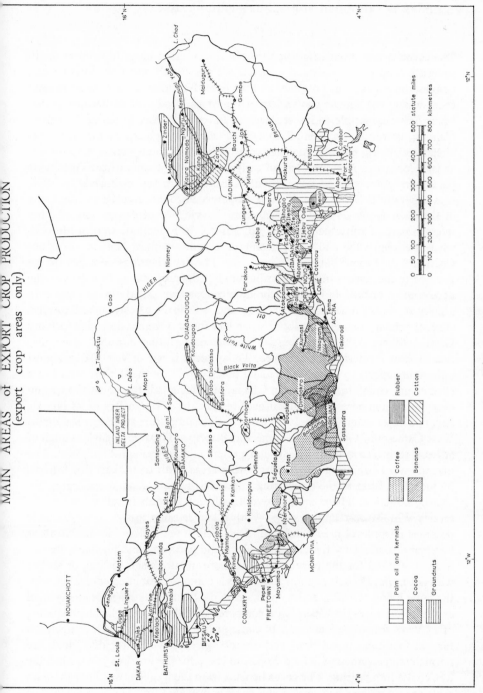

MAIN AREAS of EXPORT CROP PRODUCTION
(export crop areas only)

Palm oil and kernels

Cocoa

Groundnuts

Coffee

Bananas

Rubber

Cotton

0   50 100   200   300   400   500 statute miles
0 100 200 300 400 500 600 700 800 kilometres

Figure 10.1

A. CROPS INTRODUCED FOR EXPORT PRODUCTION

1. *Cocoa* (*Theobroma cacao*)

The cocoa tree is a native of the forest of the Amazon basin in tropical South America. The chief cultivated varieties are the South and Central American Criollo, the Amazonian Forastero and the hybrid Trinitario. Most West African cocoa was of the Amelonado variety of Forastero, producing rather low quality beans, less susceptible to insect attack or fungoid disease. Much of the earlier planting, however, has been affected by disease and replaced by newer, better-yielding varieties, notably 'Amazon' cocoa, which has some resistance to swollen shoot. Cocoa was introduced at an early date to São Tomé, where Portuguese plantations were worked with labour recruited from the mainland. In 1879, it is generally believed, one of these labourers introduced cocoa to Mampong in the then Gold Coast. However, there is evidence of earlier and of other more important introductions (see pp. 401–2). Introductions were made elsewhere between 1890 and 1910, notably into south-western Nigeria, the Ivory Coast and the former Southern Cameroons. The first plantings were close to the ports or to the centres of seed distribution, but the crop spread rapidly with the development of road and railway communications, particularly in the areas with a rainy season of nine months or more and with loam or clay soils. Extensive areas of primary or well-developed secondary forest were cut down in the Ivory Coast, southern Ashanti and central Yorubaland resulting in a shift of population to areas formerly little occupied. Today cocoa is one of West Africa's most important exports by value, and a major dollar earner for the sterling area. It has effected an economic revolution in Ghana, producing half the world's supply on nearly 4 million acres (1·6 million hectares), in the Western Region of Nigeria and, to a lesser extent, in the Ivory Coast. Minor producers are Togo, Dahomey, West Cameroun, Guinea, São Tomé and Príncipe. The tree needs a rainfall of at least 50 in (1270 mm) a year, and prefers constantly high humidities. The savanna-ward fringes of the cocoa-growing areas, with their short dry seasons, frequently subject to the desiccating effects of the harmattan, are marginal for cocoa production. There cocoa trees normally survive only in valley bottoms, or on heavy moisture-retaining clays. With a longer rainy season cocoa normally occupies fairly level interfluves with deep well-drained clayey loams. Shade is necessary, particularly for the young plant, and cocoyams and plantains are frequently planted for the purpose. In the more mature stage shading or shelter with *Gliricidia*, *Parkia* or *Pentaclethra* trees is common, but inter-cultivation with the taller kola trees often assists in reducing the light. Tree spacings are as small as 5 feet (1½ metres) in West Africa, compared with the normal plantation spacing of 15 to 18 feet (4½–5½ metres). In consequence there is too much competition for soil food, and insect pests and disease can spread very rapidly. Fields are normally interplanted with food crops and cocoa for the first five years, when the tree comes into bearing. The cocoa benefits from the frequent weeding, although roots are sometimes damaged, and a cover is provided for the soil, reducing the rate of erosion. New cocoa plots begin to produce abundantly by about the tenth year, and reach a peak in most areas between 18 and 22 years. After 35 years the decline is frequently very rapid. After 40 or 50 years the cocoa plot is abandoned. In some cases decline is hastened by the planting of food crops between cocoa trees, as the yields of the latter become smaller. In such cases roots are often lopped off close to the trunk. The rate of cocoa planting is subject to variations with fluctuations in price. The long period necessary for plots to come into economic bearing has resulted in maximum production being achieved during a boom in world prices, although, when, as in the 1930s, the plantings of several 'cycles' are still productive, the decline on older farms is not sufficiently rapid to affect a dwindling market, and so cocoa prices are then depressed.[8]

Yields average between 350 and 500 lb of dried cocoa per acre (400–560 kilos per hectare) in the better areas, but have tended to decline in recent years, partly owing to the age of many of the trees with declining rates of planting, as most of the suitable land has been taken, and partly owing to disease. At present 20 years' fallow is needed before plots may be replanted with cocoa. In consequence many of the older areas of the cocoa 'belts' of Ghana and Nigeria are declining in production, whilst few new areas remain to develop. The main production thus moves gradually across the zone of planting, northwards in Ghana from Akwapim to Ashanti, and eastwards in Nigeria from Ilaro and Ibadan to Ilesha and Ondo. The most serious of the diseases are the swollen shoot viruses, transmitted by mealybugs, which first appeared between 1910 and 1915 in the Eastern Province of Ghana. The disease spread from Ghana westwards to the Ivory Coast and eastwards to Nigeria. The only defence appears to be the cutting out of diseased trees and the creation of 'cordons sanitaires' round diseased areas. Cutting out involves considerable opposition from growers, despite compensation for the loss of crop and grants to assist in the replanting of cocoa. By 1961 over 100 million trees had been cut out in Ghana. Production in the Eastern Region, the most affected area, had declined from 128,000 tons in 1936–7 to 43,000 tons in 1958, but had recovered to 82,000 tons by 1962, due to replanting. The early establishment of control in Ashanti and fresh plantings in unaffected districts helped, however, to maintain total production at 220,000 tons (plus 15,000 tons marketed in French West Africa) in 1953–4 compared with 300,000 tons in 1936–7. Despite further cutting out, heavy rates of planting in the early 1950s gave a record export of 428,000 tons by 1962 declining to 382,000 tons by 1964. Nigeria's export in 1964 was 196,000 tons and that of the Ivory Coast was just under 100,000 tons. In Nigeria swollen shoot disease was first discovered in 1944, and by 1950 1½ million infected trees had been destroyed in an unsuccessful attempt to control the spread of the disease. Nigerian cocoa suffers badly from 'black pod', a fungus disease estimated to account for an annual average loss of 15 per cent of crop, and from attack by capsids, chiefly *Sahlbergella singularis* and *Distantiella theobroma*. Capsid attack is heaviest on the savanna-ward fringes of the Nigerian cocoa belt, where the damage done results in the opening of the tree canopy, allowing more light to penetrate into the cocoa plot, and favouring the growth of chupons, the favourite food of the capsids. As the canopy opens, grasses invade the cocoa plot, and finally a thicket develops, which completely suppresses the cocoa.[9] Work has begun on the suppression of black pod and capsids by spraying with chemicals. At present it is estimated that more land is going out of cocoa production than is being planted. However, cocoa 'farms' have now been

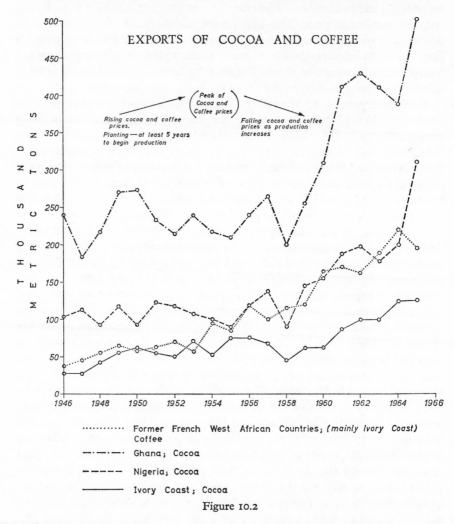

EXPORTS OF COCOA AND COFFEE

Peak of Cocoa and Coffee prices

Rising cocoa and coffee prices.
Planting—at least 5 years to begin production

Falling cocoa and coffee prices as production increases

THOUSAND METRIC TONS

············ Former French West African Countries; (mainly Ivory Coast)
　　　　　　　Coffee

—·—·—· Ghana; Cocoa

— — — — Nigeria; Cocoa

——————— Ivory Coast; Cocoa

Figure 10.2

established in Eastern Nigeria, particularly in Umuahia, and, on a very small scale, in the more humid portions of the Northern Region.

Cocoa plots are generally small, averaging only 2 to 6 acres (1–2½ hectares), although holdings as large as 200 acres (80 hectares) are not unknown. Many cocoa growers are in effect tenants, leasing or renting their holdings. On most holdings hired labour is necessary, chiefly for the task of harvesting and preparing the beans by fermentation. The chief harvest period is at the end of the rains from September to December, but one or two other pickings may be made during the remainder of the year. Cocoa growers are normally food growers in addition, planting chiefly cassava, since this crop will grow on poor hill-slope soils unsuited to cocoa, and needs little labour for planting or attention during growth. On the whole, however, cocoa makes heavy demands on land and a heavy seasonal demand on labour, and food must be imported into the producing areas, particularly when the large immigrant labour force arrives for the harvest. In consequence neighbouring districts unsuited to cocoa production are growing yams, cassava, maize and guinea corn for sale in cocoa district markets, instead of solely for local consumption. Since cocoa is a perennial it docs not allow a ready transference from commercial cropping to subsistence food production. Production is inelastic and, in consequence, the cocoa cultivator is more depen- dent on overseas markets with their fluctuations in demand than his Sudanic groundnut- or cotton-growing counterpart. The post-war development of mar- keting boards with a price stabilization policy has, however, done a little to offset the economic problems of sudden price fluctuations.

2. Coffee (Coffea spp.)

In part at least the lesser importance of cocoa in the former French West African countries is due to the great encouragement given to the cultivation of coffee, which has similar physical requirements. The chief cultivated variety known to commerce is *Coffea arabica* or Arabian Coffee, a native of Ethiopia, which thrives best at altitudes between 1500 and 5000 feet (450–750 metres) above sea-level, on deep loams with at least 50 in (1270 mm) of rainfall well distributed throughout the year. Shade is essential, usually with *Gliricidia*, *Erythrina* or *Ficus* species. Arabian coffee is the least resistant to disease of all cultivated species, and in consequence is normally only successful when grown on plantations, using care- ful methods of cultivation combined with frequent spraying against coffee-leaf disease. Little Arabian coffee is grown in West Africa. The chief centre of pro- duction is in Guinea. A little is grown in West Cameroun at Santa in the Bamenda Highlands, where plants have been introduced from the neighbouring formerly French territory. The chief variety of coffee grown in West Africa is *Coffea robusta*, developed from a wild species *C. canephora* or Congo Coffee, discovered in French Equatorial Africa in 1880 and in the Congo in 1895. Robusta is a hardy lowland coffee, resistant to coffee-leaf disease, but inferior in quality to arabica. However, recently it has been in great demand for the manufacture of 'instant' coffees, for which its stronger flavour is suited. The higher proportion of robusta in the Ivory Coast compared with Guinea is reflected in the classifica- tion of beans for export. In 1954 only 2 per cent of Ivory Coast coffee was in the first class ('Prima' and 'Supérieur') compared with 96 per cent for Guinea. Even by 1963 only 0·7 per cent of Ivory Coast coffee was of 'Prima' class, although 84 per cent was classified as 'Supérieur'. Robusta needs at least 60 in (1525 mm) of rain and prefers deep loams, but can tolerate a short harmattan. The plant is remarkable for its early fruiting tendency, producing its first fruit in two years and by the fifth year normally yielding over 600 lb of beans per acre (675 kilos per hectare). Most of the coffee production of the Ivory Coast, producing 3 per cent of the world supply and 90 per cent of West Africa's crop, is robusta. The first coffee planted in the Ivory Coast, however, was Liberian or *C. liberica*, derived from a local wild plant found only at low altitudes, widely planted in West Africa in the latter half of the 19th century. It was perhaps Liberian coffee which was planted by the Danes together with cotton in small plantations near their ports or on the southern edge of the Akwapim Hills in Ghana in the 1780s (see p. 498). Some growers preferred Liberian coffee, partly because the berries were larger and partly because it was more tolerant of direct sunlight. The first Liberian coffee plantation in the Ivory Coast was established in 1881, and became the nucleus of a small plantation industry owned by Europeans. Liberica and robusta coffees are also grown in Liberia which has a small export overseas. Other species of coffee of lesser importance include:

1) *C. excelsa*, first cultivated in 1904 in French Equatorial Africa, needing shelter and shade, of similar quality to robusta.
2) Abeokuta coffee, probably a variety of *C. liberica*, formerly of some little importance in south-western Nigeria.[10]
3) *C. stenophylla* or Sierra Leone Upland, of limited production in Sierra Leone at altitudes up to 2000 feet (600 metres) above sea-level, and producing a good quality bean.

A major pest of most varieties in West Africa is the berry borer, but, with the exception of virus disease in the Ivory Coast, diseases and pests of coffee have not presented so serious a problem in West Africa as in the case of cocoa.

In British territories there was some coffee planting in the late 19th century, but low prices brought failure, and most of the plantations were abandoned before 1905. Cocoa rapidly took the place of coffee in the humid areas in British possession. Higher prices since 1953, however, have encouraged some increase in coffee planting, particularly in Sierra Leone, Western Nigeria and Ghana. In Western Nigeria some 6700 acres were planted to coffee in smallholdings by 1958, chiefly of robusta. Production was very low, barely 250 lb per acre (280 kilos per hectare). By 1962 Ghana was exporting nearly 4000 tons and Sierra Leone 2400 tons (decreased from a peak of over 5000 tons in 1960). In the corresponding areas in former French territory coffee growing was greatly encouraged by French protectionism. In the Ivory Coast African cultivators showed little interest at first in export crop production, and the Government sought mainly to encourage African planting of cocoa rather than coffee. After 1930 the price of cocoa dropped, whilst that of coffee was maintained by protective measures. In consequence there was some increase in coffee planting encouraged by Provident Societies. Although cocoa production rose until the outbreak of war, after the war coffee production increased much more rapidly and eventually surpassed it.[11] By

1962 coffee exports from the Ivory Coast were approximately twice the value of cocoa exports, and by 1963 the export of coffee had risen to nearly 180,000 tons.

In Guinea coffee production by Africans was early encouraged by Government, and developed in the 1930s as part of a 5-year economic plan. At present an increase in coffee production in Guinea is affected by the problems of clearing fresh land. Cultivators clear sufficient land only for rice planting, and then plant coffee on the resultant fallows after the rice harvest. It is believed that rice only exhausts the top soil and that coffee draws its nutriment from sub-soil.[12] No manures are used in cultivation, and long fallows are needed before coffee may be replanted. Togo and Dahomey also have small coffee exports of approximately 10,000 and 2000 tons respectively.

3. Bananas (Musa spp.)

The bananas of international trade have all been introduced to West Africa. The Ivory Coast is the largest producer with an export in 1964 of 137,000 tons. Until 1961 Nigeria was the second largest exporter of bananas in West Africa, but production was concentrated almost entirely in the Southern Cameroons (West Cameroun). In Guinea, the leading producer in the early 1950s, there has been a

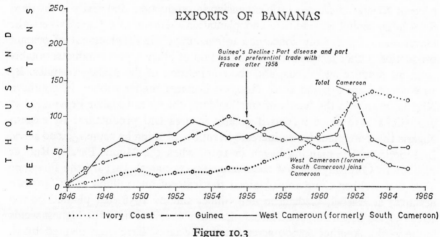

Figure 10.3

dramatic fall in banana exports from 96,000 tons in 1955 to 58,000 tons in 1961. Most Guinea bananas were grown on European plantations. Decline came chiefly from management and labour problems, and since independence from the loss of French preference.

The chief variety of banana grown is the Gros Michel of the West Indies, which flourishes best on formerly forested land at altitudes up to about 3000 feet (900 metres) above sea-level, with a minimum rainfall of 40 in (1020 mm), and preferably on deep loams. Shelter is needed from strong winds and, especially in West Cameroun, from the low temperatures associated with the sinking of cold air down mountain slopes. Diseases include Panama disease (*Fusarium oxysporum*), cigar-end (*Stechybidium theobromum*) and leaf spot (*Cercospora musae*). In the Ivory Coast the Canary or Chinese banana (*Musa Cavendishii*), introduced from the Canary Islands, is important. A few are also grown in Guinea where the 'camayenne' variety was evolved from an introduction made in 1898. The Canary banana has some immunity to Panama disease, but needs to be grown at higher altitudes than the Gros Michel to get the best results. The fruit is smaller and sweeter, but needs more careful handling when transported.

4. *Rubber*

Although in the past the greater part of the rubber exported from West Africa was gathered from wild forest vines, cultivated rubber has become of increasing importance in recent years, particularly in Liberia and southern Nigeria. Attempts were made to cultivate rubber plants in West Africa as early as the beginning of the present century, notably in Ghana and southern Nigeria, where local vines were tried and later Ceara rubber (*Manihot glaziovii*). Para rubber (*Hevea brasiliensis*), a native of the Amazon basin of Brazil, quickly proved its superiority, but after initial plantings, notably in the Sapele and Calabar districts of Nigeria, there was little expansion in production, due partly to the need for a large capital expenditure and plantation methods in a region where the Government was mainly concerned to encourage the development of peasant production. Other factors were the attraction of other export products, notably palm oil produce and cocoa, and the competition of the Malayan estates. By 1956 there were 250,000 acres (100,000 hectares) under rubber in southern Nigeria, mostly in the hands of smallholders, chiefly in Calabar Province, but plantations have since increased greatly in area and production. In eastern Nigeria there are plans for an increase in rubber planting by some 150,000 acres. In Liberia rubber planting began in 1910, when the Mount Barclay Rubber Plantations Company planted 2000 acres (800 hectares). In 1926 the Firestone Tyre and Rubber Company obtained the lease of one million acres (405,000 hectares) at Harbel, Gedetarbo and Sinoe, and by 1958 had planted 90,000 acres (36,500 hectares). The Harbel plantation claims to have the highest yields in the world. Another 60,000 acres (24,300 hectares) have been planted by B. F. Goodrich, north of Monrovia. Independent producers in Liberia had some 51,000 acres (20,600 hectares) in production by 1961. New leases are being granted to overseas companies, and rubber production is rapidly increasing.

Para rubber is a lowland tree thriving on deep soils, under a rainfall of more than 80 in (2030 mm), distributed throughout the year, with a minimum temperature of about 70°F. (21°C.) Modern growers employ elaborate grafting techniques to develop a high-yielding tree with a marked resistance to most diseases. On a well-spaced plantation trees should average about 60 to the acre (150 per hectare). On Nigerian smallholdings trees are grown from seed, give lower yields and are frequently overcrowded, resulting in poor renewal of bark over the area tapped. Tapping begins after five years, and the tree is cut every second or third day throughout the wet season, and allowed to rest for one or two months during the drier period of the year. Since 1945 the tapping of wild rubber has virtually ceased in Nigeria, and production from Para rubber has steadily increased, with a small drop in 1952 due to a decrease in prices. In addition to smallholdings there are some European-owned estates, chiefly in the Delta area and Calabar Province, and several 'partnership' estates, promoted by the regional development corporations. By 1957 Nigerian export production had overtaken that of Liberia, and in 1964 over 70,000 tons were exported. Rubber planting is being developed not only in Benin and Calabar Provinces of Nigeria, but also in West Cameroun where a hard rubber is produced suitable for tyre manufacture. A good market is being developed in Nigeria by tyre retreading and shoe factories, and the 1953 mission of the London Rubber Trade Association recommended a substantial expansion in rubber production.[13] In 1964 Liberia exported 43,000 tons, almost all of high-quality grades.[14] Rubber has been of vital importance in the Liberian economy, since it has provided until recently three-quarters by value of Liberia's exports. Some rubber planting has also taken place in the southern Ivory Coast, chiefly in plantations, in the 'forest' portions of Guinea, and in Ghana, where two major plantations, the Prestea and Dixcove Estates, are being developed. It is apparent that the political problems of southeast Asia, and the nearness of West Africa to Europe, have at last promoted the development of a rubber industry in West Africa, which in a few years should be a major world producer.

5. Sugar cane (Saccharum officinarum)

Although grown entirely for internal consumption today, sugar cane is of interest as the first West African export crop grown on plantations worked by slave labour in the islands of Fernando Po, São Tomé and Príncipe. Canes were introduced from the East Indies via Madeira, and planted, together with ginger, in Príncipe in 1520. São Tomé became the chief producer of the islands, and for a short time experienced enormous prosperity, based on the export of sugar and slaves. The loss of the slave trade to other powers, the decline of influence over the mainland sources of labour, and the competition of West Indian production, all resulted in a decrease in sugar cultivation in the islands, and it was not until the planting of quinine and cocoa in the 19th century that their economies revived. Today the production of sugar cane on large estates, normally employing irrigation, is being revived, notably in Sierra Leone, Ghana and Nigeria, in order to reduce sugar imports. In Nigeria 6500 acres (2600 hectares) have been developed for cane at Bacita in Ilorin Province, where a mill is producing white sugar for Nigerian consumption.

6. Other crops introduced for export production

i) Sisal (Agave sisalana)

Sisal, a native of Central America, has leaves which may be cut for fibre production after 3 years' growth. Cutting may subsequently take place over a period of about 5 years. Sisal is suited to climates with a long dry season, and was introduced firstly into Mali in 1908, and later into central Ivory Coast, Guinea, Upper Volta and Senegal. The crop has never proved popular with peasant producers, owing to the difficulties of handling and the generally low prices. It is grown on plantations, which suffer a constant problem in the recruitment of labour attracted to work elsewhere. The success of other crops has been largely responsible for the failure of sisal in West Africa to achieve more than a very small production.

ii) Quinine (Cinchona spp.)

Quinine, a native of Peru, thrives best on uplands 2000 feet (600 metres) or more in height, with a well distributed rainfall of at least 70 in (1780 mm). Plantations were established in São Tomé in the 19th century. Quinine was first planted in French West Africa in the Man region of the Ivory Coast in 1942, after 2 years' exploratory work by a mission under Professor Portères, at a time when the import of prophylactic and other drugs was extremely difficult. Further plantations were made in the Sérédou area of Guinea. Despite the development of new drugs for the prophylactic treatment of malaria, quinine still has important medical uses, but the future development of the plantations must be extremely limited.

iii) Soya beans (Glycine soja)

were introduced into both French and British territories after 1945, chiefly into the Benue Valley, central Ivory Coast and Upper Volta. Nigeria had a small export of 27,000 tons in 1963.

iv) Tea (Camellia sinensis)

A plantation has been established at Buea in West Cameroun, but the area in West Africa suited to tea cultivation (altitudes of 2000 feet (600 metres) or more with a rainfall of over 85 in (2160 mm) well distributed throughout the year) is extremely small.

v) Cashew nut (Anacardium occidentale)

Nearly 2000 acres (800 hectares) of plantations have been established in Eastern Nigeria at Oji, Mbala and Ajali, where the acid sandy soils are particularly suitable. The crop has also been found useful in checking gully erosion. Planting has taken place on a similar acreage in the Upper Ogun Estate in Western Nigeria.

B. LOCAL CROPS AND INTRODUCED VARIETIES DEVELOPED FOR EXPORT PRODUCTION

1. *Groundnuts* (*Arachis hypogaea*)[15]

The chief commercial groundnut-growing areas are in Northern Nigeria, with an over-all production of unshelled nuts in excess of 1,100,000 tons, and in Senegal, with rather less than a million. The export of groundnuts from West Africa began in the 1830's, chiefly from the districts served by the river Gambia trading posts. Production was encouraged by the heavy demands for cheap fats made by the soap industry in Europe. The French Government imposed import duties on most other varieties of oil seed, and, in consequence, the oil mills of Marseilles provided the chief market. Senegal, the nearest of French possessions to Marseilles, with extensive areas of land suitable for groundnut production, rapidly became the largest producer. The construction of a deep-water harbour at Dakar, and the opening of the railway between Dakar and St Louis by 1885, led to the extension of cultivation on to the sandy soils of Cayor. From 1900 groundnut cultivation advanced southwards and extended into lands served by the Dakar–Kayes railway (1907–23). This area, like the districts of southern Senegal and the Gambia, is more humid, and too long a rainy season can result in poor crops of the quick-growing 'running' varieties of groundnut characteristic of Senegal. In the Gambia, for example, the disastrous rainy season of 1893 was followed by poor crops in 1894, 1895 and 1896, since the seed nuts had also been adversely affected.[16] In Nigeria commercial groundnut cultivation began in the Northern Provinces with the opening of the Kano to Baro railway in 1911, and production was extended as branch lines were laid. By 1908 Marseilles was the world's chief market for groundnuts, and Senegal the most outstanding producer. In 1913 Senegal exported 238,000 tons of nuts in shell, against 19,300 from Nigeria. After 1945 Britain became the world's largest importer of groundnuts and by the middle 1950s Nigerian total export production approximately equalled that of Senegal (some 400,000 tons per annum, shelled basis). By 1963 Nigerian export totals surpassed those of Senegal, although the latter was still above in treated produce. Figures were:

	1963 Exports (tons)		
	Shelled groundnuts	*Groundnut oil*	*Groundnut cake*
Nigeria	613,000	70,000	88,000
Senegal	260,000	102,000	161,300
Niger	80,000	2,000	6,000 (estimated)
Gambia	40,300	—	700

Nigeria and Senegal together produce over three-quarters of the world's exports and their total production is probably nearly half as large again as the amount exported – the remainder being consumed within West Africa. An important difference between the two main producing areas is in the degree of concentration on the crop. For Northern Nigerian growers groundnuts are a cash earning

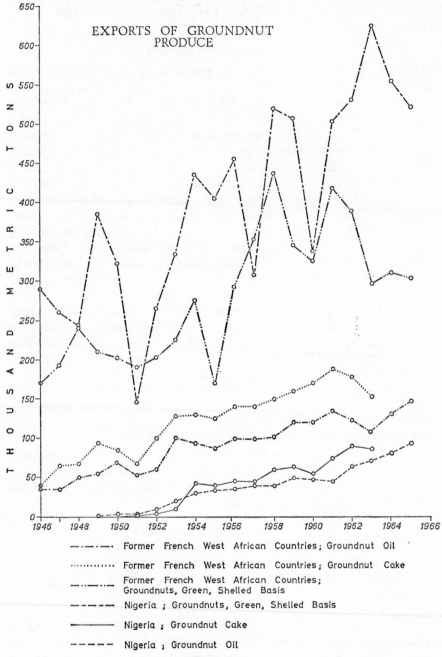

EXPORTS OF GROUNDNUT
PRODUCE

—·—·— Former French West African Countries; Groundnut Oil

············· Former French West African Countries; Groundnut Cake

—··—··— Former French West African Countries;
Groundnuts, Green, Shelled Basis

————— Nigeria ; Groundnuts, Green, Shelled Basis

——— Nigeria ; Groundnut Cake

— — — — Nigeria ; Groundnut Oil

Figure 10.4

extra, rarely occupying even one-third of the cropland. For the Senegalese grower they are more important than food crops and may take as much as two-thirds of the cropped area.

French authorities on groundnut production have always maintained that returns per acre are decreasing in the older cultivated areas and that production is only maintained by extensions of the area under the crop.[17] However, in 1963–4, the Thiès region, one of the earliest producers, had the record highest yield per acre of the seven groundnut regions distinguished. Moreover, whilst the area under groundnuts, with small fluctuations, has tended to increase, it is difficult to point to declining returns when production is so variable. A complicating factor is that as production spreads so heavier soils come into use, and on these growers tend to pick early, with in consequence lower yields, in order to avoid the labour of harvesting on soils baked hard.[18] Other important factors have been not only great variations in rainfall totals and the incidence of disease, but also fluctuations in export and home prices, and the disturbance of trade during wartime. In 1964 the chief producing districts in Senegal were the same as those of 1935, namely the regions of Sine-Saloum (44 per cent of commercial production), Thiès, Diourbel, Casamance.

However, the fear in 1945 of declining returns with a rapidly-increasing demand for vegetable oils led the French and British Governments to encourage every means of increasing production. Mechanized cultivation schemes were introduced (see pp. 521–2). Research has been undertaken into the crop rotations and mixed farming methods, in order to preserve soil fertility, and into breeding new varieties with higher yields. Generally running varieties are preferred on sandy soils, e.g. the 'dior' of northern Senegal, whilst erect and semi-erect varieties are bred for heavier soils under higher rainfall conditions, such as the 'dek' clays of central Senegal. The erect varieties permit mechanical weeding. Mechanization has therefore been introduced mainly into the wetter districts. Most cultivators sell all their nuts, and purchase fresh seed from Government agencies. In consequence, the introduction of new varieties is easy to effect.

The cultivation of groundnuts, more than of any other crop, has involved the movement of vast numbers of people. The seasonal migration of 'strange farmers' or 'navétanes', from Senegal into the Gambia, is vital for the maintenance of the latter's production. In Nigeria population movements have taken place, from overcrowded districts in Kano and parts of Sokoto Province, to the new groundnut settlements along the railway tracks. Similar migrations have occurred in Senegal, where location near the railway was perhaps reinforced by the 'arrêté' of 4 September, 1935, which forbade the conveyance of groundnuts by lorries, confining feeder transport for the railway to donkeys and camels. Notable in recent years has been the pioneer colonial settlement of the Mouride Brotherhood in the Touba district north-east of Diourbel.[19] Further advances into the Ferlo district in the east of Senegal are possible, providing water can be made available for domestic use during the dry season. The Government of Senegal has an extensive boring programme in the region, which will serve the needs of both

R

cultivators and pastoralists (see p. 509). Other important groundnut-producing areas are in Mali, Upper Volta and Niger, but all of these have export problems due to transport costs and dependence on the ports of other territories.

2. Oil palm (Elaeis guineensis)

The export trade in oil palm produce (oil and kernels) began in the late 18th century (a small import into Liverpool was recorded in 1772)[20], depending mainly on gathering from self-sown palms rather than cultivation. Amongst some peoples, particularly the Ibo, it is customary to plant an oil palm on the birth of a child, but the remaining palms, providing the greater part of the produce, are left untended in the croplands, or at most are manured and protected from fire in the compound land. The Krobo of Ghana made plantations, but the introduction of cocoa led to their neglect.[21] Nevertheless the area under oil palms has undoubtedly been increased since the development of trade with Europe, by the occupation of the Guinean lands with all their commercial advantages, and the subsequent extension of the fallows – the environment best suited to the oil palm. Production increased with the rising demand in Europe for soap and truck grease, declining after 1860, with the development of mineral oils. It revived by the end of the century with the production of margarine initially depending mainly on palm kernel oil, and the use of palm oil as a flux in the tinplate industry. Finally the invention of the hydrogenation process made possible the use of palm oil in the manufacture of a variety of edible fats.

In many parts of West Africa, particularly in southern Nigeria, the area under wild and planted palms has reached the limits set by physical conditions and trading convenience. Further increases in production must mainly be met by more efficient methods of preparation and the establishment of plantations of superior varieties. The need to improve the quality of the product is also generally recognized, and this may be met by the application of the same methods used to increase quantity. At present the tendency is to plant or encourage the thick-shelled dura varieties of oil palm, which give more oil by crude methods of extraction (although less by pressing) than do the thin-shelled and more saleable kernels, usually the perquisite of the women. Oil production is frequently low on compound land, despite the large numbers of trees, due to the close stands and interplanting of food crops. Palm wine extraction from the upper portion of the stem frequently involves excessive or 'cabbage' tapping, resulting in death. The chief oil palm disease of Nigeria is 'Orange Spot', due to nutritional deficiency. Other diseases include fungus parasites, chiefly Ganoderma and Fusarium spp.[22] Generally, however, it must be admitted that plantation oil palms suffer much more severely from disease than farmland or compound grove palms. African methods of preparing oil, by boiling or fermenting the fruit, extract only 45–55 per cent of oil content, and normally give an impure product high in free fatty acid (F.F.A.) content suitable chiefly for soap making and fetching only low prices. The average production of oil per acre under African methods is estimated to be about one hundredweight (125 kilos per hectare), compared with approximately a ton under plantation methods (2½ tons per hectare). In Nigeria plantations produce between 6 and 7 per cent of the total. Elsewhere in West Africa plantations provide only a negligible proportion of production. With the competition of plantation palm oil from elsewhere, notably from the Belgian Congo, and the incentive of higher prices for top grades, many attempts have been made to improve production. Colonial Agriculture Departments have introduced higher oil-yielding, thin-shelled varieties from the East Indies. Attempts have been made also to select and breed improved local strains. Seedlings have been issued to cultivators who have been encouraged, wherever possible, to develop plantations with a spacing of 50–60 trees per acre (125–50 per hectare), and intercropping only in the early stages. In the Southern Cameroons in 1903 the Germans tried to enforce a regulation that 25 oil palms should be planted for each standing hut and 50 for each new one. During the 1939–45 war the French authorities in Dahomey tried to force owners of 'empty' land to plant selected palms. Less than 18 per cent of these remained by 1950, owing to the difficulties of bare root planting of oil palm seedlings.[23] The 'ball of earth' method gave success in 90 per cent of cases, but cultivators were opposed to interference, and disliked the new varieties of palm with their poor kernel production. The greatest advances have been made in preparation techniques, firstly by the introduction of hand presses extracting 65 per cent of the oil contained in the fruit, with a lower F.F.A. content, and later by the introduction of the power-operated Pioneer Oil Mills extracting over 85 per cent. Despite local opposition there were some 125 Pioneer Oil Mills operating in Nigeria by 1957, each capable of producing about 250 tons of oil a year. By 1964, 86 per cent of the palm oil exported was of Special or Plantation Grade, compared with less than 1 per cent only fourteen years before. However, many of the mills were badly sited, and dependence on peasant production normally results in a mill working at less than capacity. Opposition has come from the women who lose their perquisites of kernels and a portion of the oil, and from farmers who find only good quality fruit is accepted. Financial losses have occurred and the Western Region Production Development Board even closed all its mills for a time (about 20 per cent of the Nigerian total) pending an investigation of the problems involved.[24] Plantation production by African cultivators has also been hindered, mainly by the land tenure problem involved (i.e. the introduction of ownership) and by local customs permitting the communal cutting of all palm fruit in a given district at certain periods of the year – chiefly at the time of tax collection.

Handling is mainly by barrels from the producers to bulk oil storage plants whence the oil is transferred to tankers specially constructed for the purpose. The Eastern Region of Nigeria (the former 'Oil Rivers Protectorate') is the chief exporter of palm oil in West Africa. The Western Region, however, is the biggest exporter of kernels, for a large part of its oil finds a ready market locally and in Northern Nigeria.[25] Similarly Sierra Leone is a palm kernel exporter (the chief agricultural product sent overseas) and consumes all its own small oil production from its thin pericarp fruit. Of the total West African export in the peak year 1956 of 205,000 tons of palm oil and 640,000 tons of palm kernels, Nigeria produced 90 and 70 per cent respectively. Nigeria has been able to maintain these proportions although export production has declined in recent

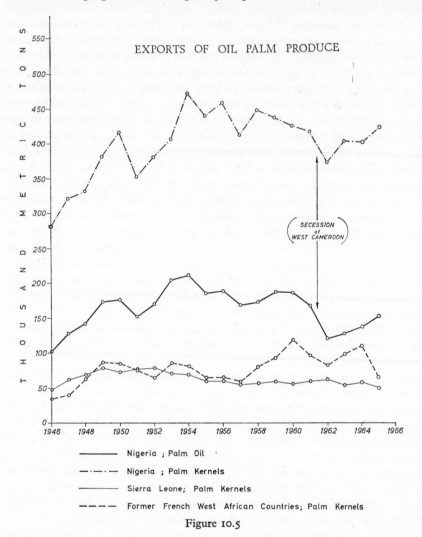

EXPORTS OF OIL PALM PRODUCE

Nigeria ; Palm Oil

Nigeria ; Palm Kernels

Sierra Leone; Palm Kernels

Former French West African Countries; Palm Kernels

Figure 10.5

years, particularly palm oil, which, in 1964, reached only two-thirds of the 1956 figure. Total production of palm oil to supply local needs in addition to the export market is estimated to be at least double the export total. Research organizations to develop oil palm produce have been set up in West Africa, notably the West African Institute for Oil Palm Research (W.A.I.F.O.R.) with its headquarters at Benin in Nigeria, and the Institut des Recherches pour les

Huiles et les Oléagineux (I.R.H.O.), operating chiefly in the Ivory Coast and Dahomey.

3. Cotton

The cultivation of cotton is old-established in West Africa. An internal cotton trade existed before the arrival of the Portuguese, and by the 16th century cotton cloth was exported to Europe through merchants in the Barbary Coast ports. A trade in West African cloths was also developed by European merchants on the Coast, particularly from Benin.[26] An export of indigenous raw cotton began in the 1850s from Abeokuta through the port of Lagos. The American Civil War stimulated the trade, but later exports decreased with American competition.[27]

The export from Abeokuta is the sole important case of an export of local cottons. All other exports have been of varieties introduced chiefly by Government agents. These include the American Upland (*Gossypium hirsutum*), the Egyptian varieties of *G. peruvianum*, Sea-Island (*G. barbadense*) and Indian cottons (*G. herbaceum*). Possibly the earliest cotton plantations in West Africa were those established in southern Ghana in the late 18th century, notably on the northern fringe of the Accra Plains and at Cape Coast (see p. 498). In 1817 American cotton plantings were made near St Louis. Plantings were also made in the experimental garden of Richard-Toll on the bank of the Taouey. The harmattan, salinity of the soils, floods and ignorance of the cultivators with regard to the techniques needed in the environments of the Senegal valley resulted in an early failure.[28] In the 1860s a small cotton export from Senegal began with the encouragement chiefly of mill-owners in Alsace, and money was given to the Roman Catholic mission at N'Gazobil to grow cotton by plantation methods, but again adverse physical conditions and insect pests brought failure.[29] The last major private attempt at plantation production was that of the Diré Cotton Company in the floodlands of the Inland Niger delta in 1919.

Modern cotton production by peasant cultivators, growing exotic strains, dates from the 1890s, when the boll weevil brought a decrease in American exports. The most important developments occurred in Nigeria, which today produces almost all of the West African export. The British Cotton Growing Association began the distribution of Egyptian and American seed to peasant growers in 1903, developed experimental farms, and introduced ginneries. The greatest effort was made in the south-west, owing to its proximity to the port of Lagos. However, it soon became apparent that production of American strains in the drier environment farther north was more reliable than the highly fluctuating yields from the more humid south, where, moreover, commercial cottons suffered badly from intercropping.[30] Optimism was expressed about the cotton potential of the north. The chairman of the British Cotton Growing Association stated in 1905:

'We have pursued our enquiries throughout the British Empire, and the one place which offers the greatest possibility of providing the millions of bales of cotton which are required is Northern Nigeria; we are absolutely convinced that in Northern Nigeria alone lies the possible salvation of Lancashire. . . . It is not improbable that at some future date Northern Nigeria will produce at least seven million bales, or sufficient to supply the whole requirements of Great Britain, and to leave an equal quantity over for other cotton consuming countries.'[31]

Elsewhere in West Africa other crops competed, e.g. groundnuts in Senegal and Gambia, cocoa in Ghana, whilst Guinea, Sierra Leone and the Ivory Coast were thought too humid. In French West Africa, cotton growing was promoted by the Office du Niger, the Institut de Recherches du Coton et des Textiles, and the Compagnie Française pour le Développement des Fibres Textiles, but on floodland, where rice proved a more attractive crop. Even in Nigeria, however, the costs of the B.C.G.A. establishments proved too high, whilst groundnuts competed for land. Despite low prices, cotton production gradually increased, mainly by the encouragement after 1916 by the Empire Cotton Growing Committee (later Corporation), which was subsidized by the British Government. The building of the railways was vital to Northern Region cotton growing. Development took place mainly in the Zaria district, where the soils are rather heavy for the types of groundnut most favoured for cultivation for export.

The varieties introduced into West Africa include:[32]

1) Allen, a medium staple cotton of the American Upland variety introduced into Nigeria from Uganda by the B.C.G.A. in 1912, and from Nigeria to French West Africa in 1925. Today it is the most widespread of the export cottons.
2) Triumph, an Upland variety introduced from the Belgian Congo to French West Africa about 1920 and grown chiefly under irrigation.
3) N'Kourala, an Upland variety introduced into the Sikasso district about 1900.
4) Long staple Egyptian varieties (Mitafifi introduced in 1917), mainly grown under irrigation, and producing little today, owing partly to a high liability to disease, and partly to the competition of other crops on floodland.
5) Karangani, a dwarf tree cotton, introduced about 1930 by the Office du Niger.
6) Sea-Island, introduced 1900–10 into German Togo and Southern Nigeria. Very little success was obtained.

Attempts have also been made to improve earlier introduced cottons like Ishan and Budi (from India) and establish them in various districts in West Africa, notably in the Ivory Coast.

Nigeria's export of 32,000 tons of cotton lint in 1964 probably represents about two-thirds of total production. The remainder is used for local cloth manufacture which creates a market often offering higher prices for raw cotton than the export market. About 4500 tons of raw cotton were exported from Mali in the same year.

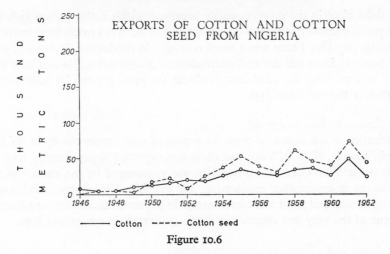

Figure 10.6

4. *Ginger* (*Zingiber officinale*)

Although of Asian origin, ginger has long been established in Africa. It is widely grown in West Africa, particularly where soils are not highly acid. The chief centres of export production are the Moyamba, Bo and Bombali districts of Sierra Leone, and an area immediately west of the Jos Plateau and north-west of Kafanchan in the middle belt of Nigeria. In Sierra Leone the crop is usually grown on separate plots, that is, not in rotation with other crops. In 1964 Nigeria exported over 2000 tons of ginger compared with about 600 tons from Sierra Leone.

5. *Other local crop developments*

i) *Coconut*

West Africa has only a small export of copra, the dried kernel of the nut and fresh nuts, chiefly from São Tomé and Príncipe, Ghana and Togo, where the Germans established a few plantations on the sandy soils of the coastlands. Dahomey and the Ivory Coast also produce a little. Copra has never been important as a source of vegetable oil in West Africa and the greater part of world export production comes from south-east Asia and Oceania. Wilt disease has been a serious problem of plantations, particularly in south-eastern Ghana.

ii) *Benniseed*

Almost the entire export of benniseed from West Africa comes from Nigeria – 24,000 tons in 1962. A high-quality oil is extracted, and is used to manufacture margarine and cooking fats, and to provide a substitute for olive oil. Benniseed grows wild in Nigeria's 'Middle Belt', and has been encouraged there as a peasant commercial crop by the Nigerian Agricultural Department. It normally takes the third place in the rotation, partly because it yields better on less rich soils, and partly because it is second in importance to food crops to the local cultivators – chiefly the Tiv. There was a small recession in production in 1950–1, which Buchanan claimed was due to the introduction of soya beans, planted later in the year, and enabling the cultivator to obtain the same income by spreading his work over the two crops.[33]

iii) Castor (Ricinus communis)

Cultivation of the castor oil plant for export of seed occurs chiefly in the Cape Verde Islands, Nigeria, Togo and Dahomey, exporting approximately 1000 tons each per annum. Castor oil production was encouraged by the French in 1915 for its use in aeronautical engineering, and has since filled a small market using the oil in soap and paint manufactures and in pharmaceuticals. Castor appears to be one of the very few commercial crops cultivated on compound land.

iv) Awusa Nut (Tetracarpidium conophorum)

The awusa plant is a wild vine indigenous to the Guinean Zone. The kernels yield a quick-drying oil useful in paint manufacture. Planting has been mainly successful on farm settlement schemes in Western Nigeria.

v) Fruit

There is in West Africa a small, but growing export of fruit and fruit juice, chiefly pineapples, grapefruit and oranges. The development of local canning and bottling industries has been the chief incentive. Nigeria exports orange juice and Guinea exports orange essence extracted from the rind. Both territories have developed plantations in order to ensure a regular supply of fruit to the factories, but as yet plantation production provides only a small share of the total. Ghana exports various citrus fruits and lime and grapefruit juice. The export trade from West Africa is very small, and has suffered from overseas competition and rapidly increasing home demands for both fresh and canned fruit.

vi) Kapok

Pre-war kapok exports came almost entirely from the gathered fibres of the indigenous *Bombax* tree. In Mali and Niger a few plantations of *Ceiba pentandra* were created, but failed due to fire damage and high labour and transport costs. The main centre of commercial production is the Dosso cercle of Niger.

vii) Urena lobata

Urena lobata, the source of Aramina fibre, has provided the most successful jute substitute yet discovered in West Africa. The plant is a quick-growing shrub flourishing chiefly in sub-Guinean areas. It has been tried chiefly in Ghana, notably on the Ejura State Farm, and may also be suitable for smallholding production, since it is already grown on smallholdings in the Congo (Leopoldville).[34] Other local fibre plants which have been tried include da (*Hibiscus cannabinus*) and bolobolo (*Clappertonia ficifolia*).

The introduction of crops and development of local crops for subsistence or internal exchange

I. RICE

Attempts have been made since the beginning of the present century to improve the production of rice in West Africa, and to increase the area under the crop. Agricultural officers, impressed by high per acre production in the floodlands of south-east Asia, have sought to introduce Asian varieties and to promote the cultivation of swamp rice wherever possible. Moreover, in swamp rice cultivation ploughs or even mechanical implements can be used. In Sierra Leone the policy was reinforced by the notion that the cultivation of upland rice led to excessive soil erosion and, therefore, that a move from the uplands to the swamps would bring an improvement in the use of soils. Moreover, the urge to plant rice was encouraged by the war of 1939–45, which brought to a temporary end the dependence of some areas on imported foodstuffs. The groundnut cultivators of Senegal, for example, were greatly dependent on the rice of Indo-China, with an average import of 55,000 tons a year from 1931–40. In consequence, it became of vital importance to increase local food production, and particularly the production of rice.

There has, however, been some resistance to abandoning upland for lowland rice cultivation, both in Sierra Leone and the Ivory Coast. A major problem is the danger of schistosomiasis or bilharzia infection, to which the cultivator working in fresh water is exposed. Peasant producers, in the valleys of the Niger and its tributaries in Northern Nigeria and in the coastal swamp lands, were offered the seed of exotic varieties, encouraged to use ploughs drawn by bullocks, given instruction in new methods of establishing nursery beds and planting, and, in some cases, provided with drainage control by the construction of barrages and dikes. Schemes for clearance or preliminary tillage by machines were introduced, particularly in the coastland of Sierra Leone and in the Upper Niger basin. These culminated in elaborate projects to develop flood control and cultivation by Government organizations, either in partnership with peasant cultivators or directly instructing them. The largest project of this kind is that of the Office du Niger in the Inland Niger delta. At Richard-Toll in the Senegal valley a rice plantation has been created in which mechanization has been introduced into every possible phase of production.[35]

Mechanization has in fact been regarded as the chief solution to the problem that increased rice production by peasant cultivators means a decline in groundnut exports. Asian rice was imported because it was cheap. In West Africa there is neither the abundance of swamp land nor the dense crowding of population to effect similar low-cost production. Moreover, there is the problem of introducing strains adapted to local conditions. In some cases it has been possible to replace varieties of *Oryza glaberrima* or old-established *O. sativa* by homologous recently-introduced *O. sativa* plants. This has been especially important in the floodland cultivation of rice, where distinct varieties are planted at varying heights above the water levels established by drainage control.[36] Chevalier, however, doubts whether, with a few exceptions, Asian varieties can be established in West African biological conditions, and wonders whether the qualities valued in the exotic plants can be maintained.[37] He points to worm infestation of rice straw before harvest in Senegal, the invasion of fields by weeds, especially wild rice, attack by birds, and the replacement of rice by millets in the floodlands of eastern Niger. In the mangrove swamps of the coast there are added problems. The clearance of mangrove swamps and their replacement with rice fields by African peasant cultivators has so far been attempted satisfactorily only in the area between the Casamance river and the Sierra Leone peninsula. This region has tides twice daily, with an average range of approximately 13 feet (4 metres), and even here the area affected by tides and available for cultivation is extremely limited. The remaining areas of the mangrove swamp in West Africa, particularly in southern Nigeria, where Government schemes are being attempted, have very little tidal range. Soils may become toxic with the formation of free sulphuric acid if mangroves are cleared in an area lacking free tidal conditions.[38]

Despite an increase in the purchasing power of groundnut cultivators since the last war, with regard to imported rice, and despite a great increase in rice imports with lower prices near ports than the West African product, rice production in former French West Africa increased from just under 400,000 tons in 1934 to 424,000 tons in 1948 and 615,000 tons in 1955. Imports increased from 1945 until by 1955 they amounted to 109,000 tons, a figure almost equal to the annual import in 1936 and 1937. Clearly, even taking into account an increase in population or an improvement in standard of living over the same period, rice has become an increasingly popular element in the West African diet. Probably the increased demand may be accounted for not only by an increase in the number of groundnut cultivators, but also by an increase in urbanization, since rice in Senegal has tended to become the food of townspeople. In Sierra Leone, rice production appears to have increased little since before the war despite Government mechanization schemes and encouragement. The 1955 production was estimated at 247,000 tons compared with 270,000 tons in 1933 and 200,000 tons in 1935. Rice imports have increased, reaching 36,741 tons in 1956 – partly due to the increasing demand for rice, and to a loss in production with the movement of agricultural labour to the diamond fields. Production in Portuguese Guinea was estimated at 29,000 tons in 1950 compared with 24,000 tons in 1933.

In Nigeria production reached 246,000 tons in 1950. There has been a big increase, especially in southern Nigeria, where the crop was hardly cultivated before 1939. Since 1950, however, there has been only a slight increase. In 1965 for example, the estimated production was 250,000 tons. Wartime encouragement of increased food production led to the expansion of upland rice in the Western Region and swamp rice in the Eastern Region, chiefly in Ogoja Province. The chief factors are the availablity of inland swamps in the Eastern Region, the provision of cheap rice mills, especially in the Eastern Region where more than

130 are in operation, and the growing popularity of rice as a foodstuff particularly in the towns. An additional factor in the case of upland rice is its low labour requirement compared with the traditional local crop, yams. Much of the crop is grown by 'strange farmers' or seasonal migrants.[39] In the 1950s approximately one-fifth of Nigerian rice was 'red' rice (*Oryza glaberrima*) grown in the northern fadama. Most of the swamp crop is produced from BG 79, a 5-month maturing variety introduced from British Guiana by the Agricultural Department. The chief upland variety is Agbede, a white or Asian rice, introduced 80 years ago into the Western Region.[40]

2. MAIZE

The greatest concentration of maize cultivation is in southern Togo and Dahomey and south-western Nigeria, from where an export began about 1900. In 1939 Dahomey exported 45,000 tons and French Togo 25,000, but the Nigerian export had ceased, and, after the war, French West African exports of maize to Europe were forbidden because of the danger of food shortage. The importance of maize as an export crop encouraged the early introduction of a vast number of varieties, chiefly from the United States, and later from Central America and the West Indies. Imported varieties are used for breeding experiments to produce high-yielding maizes adapted to local conditions, with a high resistance to disease, particularly to maize rust (*Puccinia polysora*).

3. TOBACCO

Tobacco has been known in West Africa since the second half of the 16th century, when *Nicotiana rustica* was introduced by the Portuguese from Brazil. *Nicotiana tabacum* was introduced from the Antilles early in the 18th century, but even today coarse rustica leaf is often preferred locally. A few European tobacco plantations have been established in French territory, but the chief stimulus to the cultivation of improved varieties came with the building of tobacco factories (in Nigeria as early as 1933), improved techniques and the issue of seed. The greater part of commercial production consists of air-cured leaf from the Sudanic and sub-Guinean areas. The chief producing districts are in Ghana, southern Ivory Coast and Western and Northern Nigeria, especially Shaki-Oyo (flue-cured and dark air-cured) and Zaria, Kano and Sokoto Provinces (mainly bright air-cured).

4. OTHER CROPS

A large number of minor crops has been introduced or modified by plant breeding and selection. Here one can only mention a few. In Mauritania the attempt has been made to improve date palms, and to develop new plantations. The work has been undertaken by the Institut Français des Recherches Fruitières. Mineral discoveries have, however, attracted labour away from the groves, and date production may decline. In Nigeria the Agricultural Department helped to promote the cultivation of 'nitida' kola, chiefly in the Abeokuta district, from where there has been developed a considerable export to the Northern Region. There is also a small overseas export of kola from both Ghana and Nigeria. Sierra Leone, similarly, has a small export of nuts, chiefly to the Gambia. The establishment of a small urban European population and changing tastes amongst the African community have encouraged the development of market gardening. Examples of market garden crops are the potato (*Solanum tuberosum* – limited by higher temperatures especially at night, and normally grown only at altitudes of 4000 feet (1220 metres) or more above sea-level), radish (*Raphanus sativus*), onions and leeks (*Allium* spp.), spinach (*Spinacia oleracea*), vegetable marrow (*Cucurbita pepo*), tomato (*Lycopersicon esculentum*), lettuce (*Latuca sativa*), cucumber (*Cucumis sativus*), cauliflower and cabbage (*Brassica* spp.), carrot (*Daucus carota*), beetroot (*Beta vulgaris*), artichoke (*Cynara scolymus*), aubergine or egg-plant (*Solanum melongena*) and the avocado pear (*Persea gratissima* – the fruit of a tree, but normally sold with vegetables as market garden produce). Only a relatively small effort has been put into breeding new varieties of yams and cassava, or encouraging their even wider growth, although these two crops have played vital roles in recent agricultural developments (see pp. 524–7).

The introduction of weeds

Whilst many of the weeds which affect West African cultivation are of African origin, other weeds have been introduced during the period of European contact with West Africa by Europeans and by Arabs, and many of these now have become major pests. The development of modern railways and roads, providing rapid transport over great distances, has undoubtedly encouraged the wider spread of the more persistent weed plants, and intensified the difficulties of cultivation. Chevalier lists four weeds of American origin as of especial importance:[41]

1) *Imperata cylindrica,* Spear grass
This plant was introduced either by Europeans, or by Arabs and Berbers, during the last few centuries, and has spread rapidly with the development of communications and increased movement of human beings since 1900. A quick-growing plant, with a deep root stock, spear grass is extremely difficult to eradicate once established.

2) *Andropogon leucostachyus*
A grass spread rapidly by burning. *A. leucostachyus* flowers before the end of the rainy season, and the seed heads normally survive grass or 'bush' fires. The seeds are scattered by the wind, and quickly become established in burned areas where there is little competition.

3) *Acanthospermum hispidum*, 'Tax grass' or 'Star bur'

'Tax grass' was introduced into Senegal after 1900, shortly after the introduction of the head tax, although its first appearance on the West Coast was about 1875. The most favourable environment for this weed is in the fallows following the cultivation of either cassava or cotton. The rapid increase in cassava cultivation in recent years is undoubtedly favouring the extension of the plant.

4) *Lantana camara*, Wild sage

Lantana was introduced by Europeans as an ornamental shrub, and may frequently be seen forming a thorn hedge. The plant spreads rapidly, may be dispersed by birds, and, once established on fallows, is an obstacle to the regeneration of trees.

Other important introduced weeds include:

1) *Solanum verbascifolium*

Of American origin, *S. verbascifolium* has become widespread in Southern Nigeria and Ghana in recent years, and during the last decade has spread as far west as Guinea. It is especially serious on lands used to grow food crops.

2) *Cynodon dactylon* or Bermuda grass

Although a good fodder plant, Bermuda grass tends to eliminate other plants, is deep rooting and difficult to eradicate.

3) *Tridax procumbens*, introduced from central America, appearing in Northern Nigeria in 1905.

4) *Eupatorium microstemon*, introduced from the West Indies, possibly since the war.

The development of plantations

Until about 1920 there was little European interest in the improvement of West African agriculture in order to satisfy the needs of the internal market. The chief interest lay in the increased production and improvement in quality of crops intended mainly for export to Europe. Even in the late 19th century such improvement seemed, to those interested in the development of West Africa, best effected by plantations owned and managed by European colonists. The earliest plantations for sugar cane were on São Tomé. By about 1550 São Tomé had 80 sugar mills and a population of 50,000 most of whom were slaves. After a decline between 1800 and 1850, when large numbers of settlers emigrated to the more prosperous territory of Brazil, commercial activity revived with the establishment of cocoa, quinine and coffee plantations. The sugar plantations are an isolated case where peculiar climate conditions and relative freedom from disease made European settlement easier.

Other early plantations include the attempts in the 1680s to grow indigo on Bance Island, Sierra Leone, the sugar plantation failure on Bolama Island in 1792, and the plantation on Tasso Island, Sierra Leone, at the end of the 18th century, which was worked by slave labour.[42] The Danes tried to develop plantations in southern Ghana. In the 1780s, plantings of cotton and coffee were made close to the Danish ports, and on the southern fringe of the Akwapim Hills. More attempts, chiefly to plant coffee, were made in the early 19th century, particularly at 'Daccubie' in the Akwapim Hills, some 16 miles (26 km) north of Christiansborg, where 80,000 bushes were planted. These attempts were promoted in part by the desire to find an alternative to the export of slaves, and partly to extend the area of Danish occupance. The Akwapim Hills were attractive because they had heavier soils than the Accra Plains and also because they were cooler and healthier. The chief problems were political. The plantations were beyond the limits of the friendly Ga state, and were raided, firstly by the Akwapims, and secondly by the armies of Ashanti. A final attempt to plant coffee – in 1835 – was badly affected by a locust plague in 1838. At Cape Coast a cotton plantation was created early in the 19th century at Napoleon. By 1840 coffee had replaced cotton. Over 3000 bushes had been planted, of which 800 were in bearing.[43]

From 1816 to 1831 attempts were made to encourage the 'surplus' population of St Louis and Gorée to settle in the Senegal valley and on the Cape Verde peninsula, in order to plant cotton, sugar and food crops for sale to the French settlements. In 1817 a colony of 200 immigrants of the Société Coloniale Philanthropique was established on Cape Verde. In 1822 the model farm of La Sénégalaise, later the botanical garden of Richard-Toll, was founded, concessions made, roots and seed distributed, and subsidies offered on the cotton produced. The scheme failed (see pp. 396 and 489). For a time indigo planting had some importance, but by 1827 it was suggested that the colony of Senegal would be best used for cattle raising, in order to export salt beef to the Antilles.[44] In 1858 cotton planting was again attempted in Senegal. Local cultivators preferred groundnuts as a commercial crop, or if they grew cotton at all, grew it for their own use. After 1860 grants of land to establish plantations were made to traders and former soldiers already in Senegal, and to religious bodies and industrialists from Alsace. The governor Faidherbe anticipated later trends, for he supposed the future of Senegal lay in production by African cultivators, and he opposed many of the attempted land grants. By 1860 disease, pests and lower prices brought the abandonment of almost all the plantations. Similarly, in Nigeria, the Lokoja model farm of 1841, although intended mainly as a demonstration farm to encourage local cotton cultivation, was in effect a plantation, which failed due to disease and organization problems, as did the 'experimental plantation' in Sierra Leone, a few years earlier.[45]

From 1880 onwards plantation agriculture was attempted by European companies, notably the Royal Niger Company. Cocoa and coffee estates were established at Abutshi, Onitsha, Appakka and the Creek in 1889 and 1890. European and African owned rubber plantations were begun in Benin Province from 1904. Later two European oil palm estates were developed in Calabar Province. Coffee planting was begun in the Lagos Colony. Falling prices, health problems amongst European personnel, and political difficulties, brought decline to most of these enterprises. Attempts to develop large-scale oil palm plantations were frustrated by the Government of Southern Nigeria which preferred to encourage peasant agriculture. Companies interested in such plantations had to look elsewhere, notably to the Belgian Congo. In 1900 the Director of Kew commented:

'These territories (of British West Africa) can never, properly speaking, be colonized. Nor will they, in all probability, afford much scope for British planting enterprise, at least not until the higher levels of the interior have been made accessible by railways.'[46]

However, despite the many difficulties, there are today in Calabar alone three large oil palm plantations, one of which is privately owned, and three rubber plantations, two of which are privately owned. Other plantations, locally owned or operated on a partnership basis between regional government and expatriate interests, exist elsewhere, chiefly producing rubber and sugar. In Sierra Leone a Government-owned oil palm estate was established at Masanlis in 1928, and, after a period of economic depression, was eventually leased to the United Africa Company. In the Gold Coast a few concessions were made for the planting of rubber, cocoa, oil palms and fruit. In French territories successful European owned and managed estates for the production chiefly of coffee, bananas and cocoa were established. Little expansion has taken place since before the war, however, and the total enterprise remains very small. In 1954, 61·6 per cent of the area under commercial banana production in French Guinea was in non-African hands, but the total non-African area concerned was in fact only 7000 acres (2800 hectares). In the Ivory Coast the non-African owned proportion of the area under coffee production in 1954 was 6·6 per cent, and of the area under cocoa production only 1·8 per cent.

Plantation production of export crops has declined. Banana production has been to some extent an exception, because the grower could not sell to a local dealer, but had to carry all the risks of shipment to the country of destination. The provision of special marketing organizations, usually in the form of co-operatives, to handle the special problems of small-scale growers has, however, brought an increase in the peasant grower's share in recent years, particularly in the Ivory Coast, now the leading exporter. In the Ivory Coast the plantation production of bananas, coffee and cocoa at the beginning of this century advanced westwards and to the north from the original areas of marked concentration in Gagnoa, Grand Lahou and Abidjan. Sisal, kapok and kola were also tried, and a large plantation company was formed, the Société des Plantations Réunies de l'Ouest Africain, which acquired 10,700 acres (4330 hectares). In 1930 came a slump in which cocoa prices dropped catastrophically. Planting ceased to expand and European growers concentrated mainly on coffee. The war brought the abandonment of many holdings, and the abolition of forced labour in 1946 brought wholesale desertion of labour from the plantations. Between 1949 and 1951 coffee virus disease destroyed large numbers of plants. By 1959 there were approximately 220 European planters in the Ivory Coast, occupying 75,000 acres (30,350 hectares) chiefly in the centre and west, on the leached sandy soils of the coast, and on the poor acid soils of the granites and crystallines. Holdings were not large, therefore, and averaged only 340 acres (137 hectares). Labour came chiefly from amongst the Mossi of the Upper Volta and was available for only a few months each year. African planters, who, in many cases, have modelled their holdings on those of Europeans, have tried to offer more attractive conditions to labour than those offered by the Europeans, or by planters in Ghana. African production of coffee and cocoa has increased since the war, whilst that of the Europeans has declined, despite a subsidy to holders of plantations of more than 62 acres (25 hectares).[47] Of the total available for cultivation and pastoralism in former French West Africa of 659,000 square miles (1,708,000 sq km), only 422 square miles (1093 sq km) or 0·06 per cent was the private property of non-Africans in 1956 (including properties for business, manufacture and residence).

The most determined attempt to establish plantations was that made by the Germans in Togoland and the Cameroons. In West Cameroun, on the fertile volcanic soils of the lower slopes of Cameroon Mountain, and on the Tiko plains, almost all the cultivable land available was divided into estates totalling 250,000 acres (100,000 hectares), planted to bananas, cocoa, oil palms and rubber. Other crops tried in the Cameroons were coffee, kola, tobacco, cotton and ramie (*Boehmeria bivea*), a fibre introduced from south-west Asia. Only bananas proved really successful. In 1946 the estates were bought by the Nigerian Government, and leased to the Cameroons Development Corporation, now responsible to the Government of West Cameroun. In addition, in West Cameroun there are private plantations controlled by the United African Company and by Elders and Fyffes.[48] Even in West Cameroun, however, the peasant share of the banana production for export has increased with the provision of a marketing organization suitable for small-scale growers and a producers' co-operative union.

The only territory in West Africa today almost entirely dependent on plantation production to maintain overseas trade is Liberia. Rubber planting by alien enterprises began in Liberia in 1910. In 1926 the Firestone Tyre and Rubber Company was granted a 99-year lease of one million acres (400,000 hectares) of which 90,000 acres (36,400 hectares) were planted by 1960. Some 2700 smallholdings existed by 1961, owned by Americo-Liberians, and totalling some 51,000 acres (20,600 hectares). A further large concession for 80 years was made to the B. F. Goodrich Company in 1954.

Undoubtedly, whilst problems of marketing, transport, disease and physical distribution have markedly affected plantation agriculture, the most important single question has been the availability of labour, which is related in its turn largely to the distribution of population. In the Ivory Coast and most of Guinea population densities are of the order of 10–50 per square mile (4–19 per sq km), insufficient to provide labour for anything but a small plantation development. In the Ivory Coast 'authorizations of recruitment' of labour were made in 1925–46, and a syndicate was formed in 1950 to arrange for the transport of workers. The peasant production of cocoa in Ghana drains the labour resources of a vast area stretching as far north as the Niger, and even attracts labour away from the Ivory Coast, where both European and African planters have to offer high wages and good working conditions in order to compete for Mossi labour with Ghana. In West Cameroun, under German rule, plantation development depended on a policy of enforced migration of labour from the neighbouring highlands.[49]

Botanic gardens

It was by the agency of botanic gardens, for the most part established by colonial governments, that many of the major crop introductions were effected, although one should not forget the many crop introductions and plantings of local crops and trees made by missionaries, merchants and early colonial administrators. In southern Ghana, for example, the tamarind tree is today an indicator of former Danish settlement, rows of tamarinds being planted across the Accra Plains and alongside the avenues leading to their plantations.[50]

The first really effective botanic garden in West Africa was established by the French at Richard-Toll in Senegal. After the agricultural failures of 1825–7, the garden was virtually abandoned until re-established on an adjacent site by Faidherbe in the middle of the century. From this refoundation dates a constant attempt to introduce, breed and select plants suitable for cultivation in West Africa. Other botanic gardens were founded, and from these original nuclei developed the agricultural departments of the present territories. At Victoria in the Southern Cameroons the Germans founded one of the largest botanic gardens in West Africa. A botanic garden for the introduction of a variety of plants, especially rubber, was founded at Ebute Metta near Lagos in 1887. The objects also included:

'The growth of specimens of indigenous trees and plants of marketable value (or likely to prove so) that may serve on development as visible means of instruction to the natives of the Colony and of the interior Kingdoms who visit the Government from time to time.'[51]

Further objects were the provision of a practical agricultural school, the distribution of seedlings, the introduction of exotic timber trees, notably Eucalyptus, the oil-yielding 'cajeput' tree or Melaleuca, and Casuarina, and finally the introduction of model kitchen-gardening. In 1888 the Royal Niger Company founded a public botanic garden at Asaba for the distribution of seeds and plants to both European and African cultivators. Five years later another garden was founded at Calabar, and by 1902 yet another at Olokemeji, between Abeokuta and Ibadan. In the Gold Coast a botanic station was founded at the Government sanatorium of Aburi in 1889, and a curator from Kew appointed to teach cultivation and crop preparation methods. Plants were distributed to both European and African growers, particularly cocoa seedlings. A second botanic garden was established shortly afterwards at Tarkwa.

Forestry departments

Despite the emphasis by early West African colonial governments on the development of export crop production, forestry departments were frequently created before agricultural departments, or the two were developed as one organization in which more importance was attached to the work in forestry. The chief factor was undoubtedly the importance in export traffic, at the turn of the century, of gathered produce, particularly palm oil kernels, rubber and timber. The rapid destruction of rubber vines led several colonial governments to consider the problem of conservancy. In Southern Nigeria the suggestion was made in 1897 that forest conservancy should be practised along 'somewhat similar lines to that in India'[52], and undoubtedly the success of the Indian Foresty Service was of great influence in deciding on a conservation policy. An Inspector of Forests was appointed to Southern Nigeria, and the first reserve constituted at Ibadan in 1899, to preserve timber and bring improved rubber yields. In the location of early reserves, great importance was attached to accessibility, and sites near railways were preferred. Land with good stands of timber, preferably unclaimed by cultivators, was desired. Hence the first reserves were established in the 'no-man's-land' zone between the rival powers of Ibadan and Abeokuta.[53] In 1901 the Botanical Departments of Lagos Colony and Southern Nigeria were amalgamated to form the new Forestry Department, staffed with officers trained in India. The chief aims were: to place 25 per cent of the area of Nigeria in reserve, to develop village wood lots, produce and enforce regulations governing the treatment and felling of trees, bush burning and the use of soils, and to encourage the planting of rubber. Today, departmental activities are largely restricted to the reserves, which total 29,000 square miles (75,000 sq km) or 7·7 per cent of the total area. Even in attaining this total, large areas of land under very long fallows, or regarded as reserve for future agricultural expansion, were incorporated, and the land thus lost to cultivation. This was particularly the case in the Oban Hills of Calabar Province and in central Benin Province. Opposition to Government agricultural and forestry schemes developed on the grounds that the Government was chiefly interested in taking away the cultivators' land. Fines for illegal felling of timber increased the department's unpopularity. The business of developing small wood lots outside the reserves, and of enforcing rules on the use or misuse of trees, is now the prerogative of the Native Authorities. The department has supplied seedlings and established exotics, has made numerous roadside plantings, and has established trees on mine dumps in the Jos Plateau, and in echelon strip formations in Katsina Emirate to form protective belts against the prevailing wind and blown sand. Dum palms have been planted to hold the soils along the northern frontier. Taungya methods of establishing forest plantations (persuading or paying local farmers to grow food crops intermixed with tree seedlings for the first two years) have also been tried.

In the remainder of West Africa, forestry services were established later. In the Gold Coast, the forest law of 1911 was opposed and withdrawn. The securing of reserves under a Forests Ordinance was not attained until 1927, following a Forestry Bill of the previous year, providing that reserves should be constituted, but should be the property of the stools or chiefdoms. Barely 6000 square miles (15,500 sq km) of present-day Ghana are in forest reserve. Sierra Leone has less than 1000 square miles (2600 sq km) of reserve and Gambia none. The French West African Forestry service was organized under a decree of 1923. 39,400 square miles (102,000 sq km), or 3·6 per cent of the total area of French West Africa, excluding true desert, was in reserve. Locally, however, higher proportions were achieved – 14·1 per cent in Dahomey, 8·8 per cent in Senegal, and 8·1 per cent in the Ivory Coast. Forests have been planted on the Saharan fringe in order to prevent sand encroachment, but the greater part of forestry work has been undertaken in the Ivory Coast, where there are estimated to be 27,000 square miles (70,000 sq km) of primary forest, besides extensive well-developed secondary areas. The original intention was to ensure the continuance of timber production, but today, in addition, a line of reserves has been established on the edge of the dense forest zone in order to prevent the encroachment of the savanna. Other modifications of agricultural practice and land use include planting woodland on abandoned groundnut areas, fixing the gradient limit to cultivation at slopes of 30° (decree of 1935), forbidding bush fires in the Fouta Djallon, and attempting to 'improve' lateritic crusts by fire control and the encouragement of woodland growth.[54]

The more successful exotics introduced by the forestry departments were:

Teak, *Tectona grandis*, quick-growing, yields a useful timber and thinnings used for firewood, common in West Africa especially in southern Nigeria, in village and town wood lots, intended primarily to supply fuel, thus solving the problem of the decreasing area of secondary forest, native of India.

Cassia spp., especially *C. siamea*, planted mainly for fuel or windbreaks, often round teak plantations, native of south-east Asia.

Neem, *Azadirachta indica* (*Melia azadirachta*), an evergreen able to withstand drought, quick-growing, useful for timber and fuel, much planted in avenues, chiefly in Sudanic townships, native of India.

Dalbergia sissoo, produces a useful wood for the manufacture of implements, handles and walking sticks, can withstand droughts and will grow on very stony soils, native of India.

Gmelina arborea, deciduous, useful for planking, grows best in moist forest, the chief exotic of Eastern Nigeria where used for pit props, native of India.

Eucalyptus spp., several species introduced into West Africa, including *E. alba* (White Gum) to the swampy areas near Lagos in 1899, *E. calophylla* (Red Gum), *E. citriodora* (Lemon-scented Gum), *E. globulus* (Blue Gum), and *E. grandis* (Rose Gum), the most important exotic in West Cameroun, native of Australia.

Pinus caribaea, Caribbean Pitch Pine, prefers moist environments with only a short dry season, grows on sandy soils in coastal situations, introduced into Sierra Leone in 1957, good timber, native of Central America.

Cupressus macrocarpa, heavy timber, useful fuel, planted in West Cameroun, native of California.

The development of agricultural departments

With improvement in communications the work of the botanic gardens brought results in the rapid creation of an export trade in crops grown by peasant cultivators. A government department was needed to advise and guide production in order to attain the standards required by overseas markets. For example, by 1918 the Gambia's prosperity lay in the export of groundnuts, and an agricultural department was created, the chief duties of which, in the early stages, were inspection of the crop and the organization of seed storage. In the Gold Coast the work of the agricultural department included cocoa marketing, produce inspection, and the organization of co-operative marketing societies. Until 1937 there was no agricultural station in the cocoa belt proper at which research could be carried out on the ecology of the crop.[55] Nigeria's agricultural department concentrated on export crops until the appointment of a director with India experience in 1921. An example of types of change in organization which have taken place may be taken from Ghana.[56] From 1889 to 1905 the policy was limited to the 'importation of exotic plants and observations of their behaviour under local conditions'. From 1905 to 1915 instruction and demonstrational work were added to the duties of the department, and agricultural demonstration or model farms were created. From 1915 to 1922 specialists in many different fields of agricultural research were added to the staff, and the Agricultural Department thereafter gradually became 'the recognized machine by which a progressive policy of development must be formulated and put into effect'. In 1927 voluntary inspection of cocoa was introduced, in 1934 compulsory inspection, and in 1937 a grading scheme. But crop inspection, grading and price differentials for different grades were not enough. Departments had to study and guide export crop production directly, and eventually were led to a policy of planned modification of the whole of West Africa's agriculture. The new policy was further encouraged by the realization of the intimate relationship in many areas between export crop and local crop production, and by increases in food imports. In the Northern Region of Nigeria in 1927, for example, the threat of famine resulted in the expansion of pennisetum and sorghum planting at the expense of cotton and groundnuts. Regulations were made in most territories to enforce the rejection of certain agricultural practices and the adoption of others. H. Martin Leake in his studies in tropical land tenure commented with regard to Nigeria:

'As has been seen in other territories, the pressure of the world's markets, with their insistence on a graded product, is driving Government more and more to supervise production in all its stages.'[57]

Examples of such regulations have been cited above in discussing export crops. One should note here the order of development, beginning with regulations prescribing the areas in which, and the dates within which, cotton may be grown (in order to control disease and pests), e.g. Nigerian Ordinance 55 of 1916, giving power to declare areas in which only American cotton might be grown, and to order the eradication and burning of all cotton and hibiscus plants by certain dates. Later one has the prohibition of the cabbage tapping of oil palms, and eventually the enforced planting of certain crops, the prohibition of others (particularly poisons and narcotics), the cutting out or uprooting of diseased trees or plants, and the enforcement in some areas of ridging, terracing or other forms of erosion control. The final result of this tendency to guide is the evolution of planning and control over selected areas, that is the development of planned agricultural schemes, in which the cultivators are either in some form of partnership with the authority, or are paid labourers working in effect on a plantation. Today agricultural department organizations are widespread and elaborate.

Marketing and producers' societies

Between the wars societies of all kinds developed amongst growers, particularly those concerned with export crops, in order to provide jointly the capital needed to supply water, or provide social services. Producer's societies were often concerned with improving the quality of the product and thus provided a medium for instruction or the dissemination of Government policy. Co-operative societies often organize their own marketing, and give the grower a greater share of the proceeds from crop sales. In many cases they receive seed or fertilizers from Government agents, and distribute these amongst their members. They also provide a means of loaning capital to private agricultural enterprises. In Nigeria the co-operative movement is growing rapidly and has spread from cultivators to artisans, to the retail trade and even to banking.

The development of such societies in former French West Africa provides a suitable example.[58] The cultivators of Senegal, Mali, Niger and Upper Volta, particularly in the marginal areas, have always needed to store a large part of their produce to ensure a dry season and early rainy season food supply, and to guard against poor harvests in any one year. Many local chiefs organized granaries on a village or communal basis. The development of such granaries was encouraged by French administrative officers and their use became more widespread with their prescription by a circular of 1902. In 1909 the stock-raisers and cultivators of Baol in Senegal formed a society to dig wells, whilst the cultivators of Sine-Saloum combined to buy seed and make a reserve for the future. In 1910 a decree recognized the granary committees as assurance societies, the Sociétés de Prévoyance. Their aims were defined by article 2 of the decree:

1) To take all measures contributing to the development of agriculture, of stock-rearing, of fishing and gathering, and to the improvement of the

conditions in which the harvest, preparation, circulation, conservation and
sale of products are effected.

2) To organize the sale of the produce of their members.

3) To assist or provide loans for those members in need.

4) To permit their members by loans in kind or cash to maintain and develop
their cultivation and improve their methods, tools and land.

The Sociétés de Prévoyance bought implements and either sold or loaned them
to their members. They distributed seed supplied by the research stations, introduced new crops, undertook constructional works, established food and seed
reserves, selected seed and organized sales. They also gave loans to develop cultivation, and provided accident and sickness insurance. To assist in the provision
of capital to these and other agricultural societies, a loan organization was
founded (regulated by a decree of 1931), the Crédit Agricole Mutuel. This public
body, through the giving or withholding of loans, could very much affect agricultural development in West Africa. Two later organizations to provide capital
loans for agricultural development were the Fonds d'Investissement et de Développement Économique et Social (F.I.D.E.S.) – afterwards replaced by F.A.C.
(Fonds pour l'Aide et Co-operation) – to provide economic and technical
assistance to states which have signed agreements of co-operation with France,
and the Fonds d'Équipment Rural et de Développement Économique et Social
(F.E.R.D.E.S.). The latter provided money for the smaller development schemes
of agricultural communities, e.g. irrigation, water supply, terracing schemes, the
building of granaries, stalls for livestock and markets, and the provision of
equipment to prepare agricultural, forest or livestock products.

In addition to the financial influence of the loan organizations, several West
African governments today have price stabilization policies, usually exercised
through Government marketing boards. By this means they hope to avoid effects
similar to those of the last great slump in agricultural prices between 1929 and
1933, and the consequent social and economic upheavals. Marketing boards
license buyers and control the purchase and movement of various grades of
export produce. When prices are high the grower receives less than market price
and the surplus is retained by the board. When prices are low the grower is
subsidized out of reserve funds. A portion of the marketing board funds is
commonly spent on research into methods for the improvement of quality and
quantity in the crop grown and of preparation and handling methods. Some
boards even construct roads and encourage the development of certain social
services. In the Western Region of Nigeria cocoa reached an average price in
May 1954 of £483 15s. 5d. per ton f.o.b., declining to about £240 in the latter
half of 1955 and less than £200 in January, 1956. 1954–6 Market Board prices
for Grade I cocoa were £200 per ton and the maintenance of that price (and
corresponding prices for lower grades) cost the Board in 1956 some £4 million.
Prices were reduced to £150 for Grade I for the 1956–7 season, but by August,
1957, the Board had to pay out at least another £1½ million. The Cocoa Marketing

Board has financed an economic survey of cocoa-producing areas, endowed a university agricultural department, and allocated funds to research and road construction. Despite payments to growers at times of low prices, the Boards have, however, functioned chiefly as instruments of taxation, providing considerable capital reserves for expenditure on new schemes for economic development.[59] Marketing boards were not set up in French West Africa but, since independence, some of the territories have tried to create bodies to control trading, grade produce and fix prices. Thus, the governments of Senegal and Mali, for example, monopolize groundnut marketing through the Office de Commercialisation Agricole (O.C.A.) and the Société de l'Importation et de l'Exportation (SOIMEX).

Stock-rearing and veterinary services

Excepting the attempt by a European firm, African Ranches Ltd, to rear cattle at Allaguerno and Rigachikun in the Bornu and Zaria Provinces respectively of Northern Nigeria in 1914[60], attempts to improve rearing in West Africa have come from government agricultural and veterinary departments. Stock-breeding has been undertaken by both departments, but generally the veterinary departments have been responsible for animal health, whilst the agricultural departments have been responsible for the practical application of livestock policy in relation to cultivation. Government agricultural and veterinary officers have tended to regard stock-rearing as complementary to cultivation and not as a separate activity. In consequence, they have sought, wherever possible, to bring the two activities together, and have even begun the experiment of mixed farming.[61]

The attempts to reduce outbreaks of disease amongst livestock by immunization have probably had the most profound effect on stock-rearing, by increasing numbers, and by making it possible to drive animals through disease-infected areas, thus enlarging the market area. Immunization camps have been constructed near large markets and on well-frequented animal trade or transhumant routes, particularly near political borders. Vaccination against rinderpest in cattle in Nigeria has been claimed to be so successful that losses from starvation due to overstocking are greater in some areas than losses caused by the disease.[62] As yet, however, little success has been obtained in the immunization of the Ndama and Muturu breeds of cattle against the disease. Vaccination methods have also been used against contagious bovine pleuropneumonia, but the disease spreads rapidly along drove routes, and a greater control of herd movements is needed. Inoculation with the drugs Ethidium, Dimidium and Antrycide, particularly the last, has been tried against *Trypanosoma congolense* and *T. vivax*. Attempts have been made to reduce sleeping sickness by eradicating or limiting the distribution of tsetse fly through clearance or resettlement schemes. Dipping has been applied to prevent tick-borne diseases.

Livestock breeding and selection is an important means both of controlling or reducing the incidence of disease, and of producing animals giving better returns of meat, milk, wool and hair. Attempts to introduce livestock from outside Africa have usually failed, because of lack of disease resistance, and because of climatic factors. For European breeds of cattle, milk yields decline with environmental temperatures of over 70°F. (21°C.), and weight is lost at over 75°F. (24°C.). Zebus on the other hand can tolerate up to 90°F. (32°C.) or 95°F. (35°C.).[63] The present policy is to concentrate on the selective breeding of suitable indigenous resistant strains, and to experiment with a few cross-bred animals. Some cattle, resulting from cross-breeding with French Montbéliards, have been introduced from Cameroun, whilst artificial insemination has made possible a crossing of British Holstein and local strains at the Vom Veterinary Department on the Jos Plateau. At El-Ouladji in Mali, crosses with Charollais, Normand and Tarentaise cattle have been produced. A great deal of success has been obtained in attempts to produce a beef animal suited to the southern tsetse-infested savannas by the selective breeding of Ndama cattle. Multiplication centres, like the stock-farms at Ilorin and Fashola in south-western Nigeria, have been established to breed bulls suitable for sale and crossing with local stock. The Pong Tamale Veterinary Department in the Northern Territories of Ghana has been attempting to improve and distribute Ndama cattle since 1922. At Shika near Zaria in Northern Nigeria attempts are being made to evolve dual purpose cattle for mixed farming areas from local zebu breeds. Even on Government stock-farms, however, there has been a high annual wastage due to trypanosomiasis. At Pokoase, Ghana, in the sub-Guinean zone, West African shorthorns have been kept in an area of severe tsetse infestation by the use of fly-proof pens.[64] The French West African Departments crossed merinos with local wool sheep, and produced an animal with a better fleece, still retaining a high disease resistance. Alpine goats have been crossed with local goats. Pure Large White Yorkshire pigs are raised around Dakar, and a cross has been produced with the local 'Iberian' animal, whilst the Berkshire pig has been introduced into southern districts of West Africa and crossed with the indigenous breeds. Middlewhite and Wessex saddlebacks are raised in the piggeries of Freetown. To improve poultry, Rhode Island Red, Indian Game and Light Sussex birds have been introduced. Of these, the Rhode Island Red has produced the most successful cross, suited to rearing in African compounds. Pure European birds soon succumb to disease when raised under these conditions.

Undoubtedly, the disease problem could be reduced if adequate improved pastures and fodders were available. Too heavy stocking in some areas, or the rapid decline in the quality and quantity of pasture available, due to failure of rains, have led to heavy losses. The problem is how to provide and maintain improved pastures when the greater part of West African livestock are transhumant. Moreover, without irrigation, which would prove costly, sufficient water for pasture is available for only part of the year in the zone of grass fallows, due to the existence of dry seasons of four to eight months. Admittedly, pastures last longer in the more humid south than in the drier north, and are capable of supporting more animals per unit area. Estimates suggest that 15 acres (6 hectares) per head of cattle are needed in the Sudan or Sahel, whilst 6 acres (2½ hectares) are sufficient in the sub-Guinean zone. Attempts to institute pasture improvement employing fencing are normally made in the latter, therefore, despite the high incidence of sleeping sickness. Exotic grasses have been introduced, and the possibility of developing and maintaining permanent or rotational pastures without the annual burning has been demonstrated. Model farms with large numbers of cattle, labourers and good technical services are, however, in a different position from that of the African pastoralist or cultivator. Whilst the annual burning may be deplored, there is no solution without the permanent settlement of the pastoralists, and the successful development of mixed farming. In the Jos Plateau it is possible to pasture cattle all the year round. So great, however, are the numbers, that local authorities have had to introduce licences for the poorer dry season grazing, and force many herds to migrate elsewhere.

Many Fulani cattle herders occupy permanent settlements, particularly in the Fouta Djallon and in the Sokoto Province of Nigeria. Herdsmen, however, are employed to migrate with the cattle, sheep and goats between local and more distant pastures. The provision of permanent pastures in the drier northern areas seems unlikely for some time to come outside the floodland zones, for there are problems of high incidence of disease in the rainy season, and competition for land by agriculturalists. A possible answer is the stall feeding of animals throughout the period when pastures are not available, but that will need a considerable increase in crop production and in the area under crops in order to produce fodder. Concentrates from crop waste (particularly from groundnuts, the waste from which feeds European cattle) should prove useful. The distribution of concentrates to livestock owners has been attempted, notably in the Eastern Region of Nigeria. Such an increase of fodder crops will mean the use of more elaborate farming equipment, and new methods of cultivation, including a capital investment which, for the West African household, will be very high. In the Sahelian areas of former French West Africa extensive grass pastures remain unused because of lack of water. In order to make a better use of Sahelian pastures, and reduce transhumance movements, the French authorities undertook an extensive programme of boring and of digging wells to provide increased water supplies. With funds provided by F.I.D.E.S. and F.E.R.D.E.S., several of the Sociétés de Prévoyance and the Service de l'Hydraulique have dug wells and put down deep bores. Wells are cheaper, can be dug in a greater density than bores, and have thus been preferred in order to make a maximum use of pasture for cattle. Bores cost several million francs, need a powered pump and the services of a mechanic, but have been useful in areas where the water-table is between 300 and 1000 feet (100–300 metres) in depth. In many cases motor pumps are too expensive and windmills are used, but unfortunately, these break down rather frequently. Conditions favouring bores exist over large areas of the Sahel. Estimates indicate that a cow can pasture up to 12½ miles (20 km) from a water point, drinking every two days. The area enclosed by a 12½-mile (20-km) radius is 300,000 acres (120,000 hectares) approximately, which should support, on French estimates, between 12,000 and 24,000 cattle. To supply this number of cattle with water, a continuous output of up to 700 cubic feet (20 cubic metres) an hour would be needed. Most of the bores put down in French West Africa give more than 1000 cubic feet (28 cubic metres) an hour, and the aim has been to provide such bores at least at 25-mile (40-km) intervals in rectangular distribution throughout the possible area.[65] Such a pattern with smaller intervals than 25 miles (40 km), has begun to develop in Senegal on the southern and western margins of the Ferlo. The new water points, both wells and bores, have attracted pastoralists and cultivators and resulted in the growth of new settlements. The well settlement at M'Bar, for example, grew from 20 people with no cattle in 1939, to 2750 people with more than 1000 cattle in 1949. By 1954, 30 deep bores, each supplying 8–12,000 head of cattle, had been completed in Senegal. Elsewhere in the Sahel a large number of wells has been dug and trial bores put down. In the Upper Volta and Dahomey, barrages have been constructed to provide reservoirs on well-established cattle routes. In Nigeria the Agangari Fulani Settlement Scheme depends on the use of two reservoirs created by building dams (see p. 465). Small reservoirs have also been created in southern Nigeria to provide better water supplies for livestock.

In the Yalunka area of northern Sierra Leone, attempts have been made since 1951 to settle Fulani and their herds in square mile (2½ sq km) blocks at a density of 1 cow to 7 acres (3 hectares). The cattle are chiefly improved stock from the Veterinary Department farm at Musaia. Local swamps are used for dry season grazing and their moisture-retaining capacity improved by means of earth bunds. Attempts have also been made to plant upland pastures with *Pueraria* and *Stylosanthes* grass. Cultivation has been encouraged, ploughs introduced and the lots have been separated from one another by barbed wire.[66]

The stable political conditions brought by colonial governments, combined with the growth of purchasing power in the areas of export crop production, which are mostly coastward, have resulted in a regular migration of cattle from the pastoral area to the markets of the new towns and of the export crop areas. Nowadays, most animals only walk part of the journey and travel the rest by rail, but many still walk the entire journey, which, in extreme cases, may be more than 1000 miles (1600 km). Losses amongst stock are heavy, and the loss in weight amongst the survivors is high. There has, therefore, been concern to improve the conditions of the traffic, to protect animals weakened by long journeys against disease, to immunize livestock against new disease vectors in the areas which they traverse, to provide fattening pastures and local stock-rearing as near the markets as possible. Hence again the interest in the pastures of the more humid areas.

The creation of a dairying industry, providing milk for most of West Africa's population, raises again the problem of permanence in order to supply the dairy centres and the markets regularly. There are, however, several small dairy enterprises in West Africa. That of Vom on the Jos Plateau provides an interesting example, with its central dairy manufacturing butter, and dependence on over 40 separator units, scattered over the southern districts of the plateau. There are in addition a number of associated cheese and clarified butter fat units. The milk is obtained from Fulani herds, many of which do not migrate over great distances and the grazing season on the plateau is relatively long. There still remains, however, the problem of a pronounced seasonal rhythm in production with the marked drop in milk supplies during the dry season.[67] Some dairy development has taken place in the large towns, due chiefly to the enterprise of Lebanese who keep zebu cattle in fly-proofed stalls, and supply them with fodder purchased locally.

Other developments mark a return to the early ranching idea. In the Obudu Hills of south-eastern Nigeria, the Eastern Region Production Development Board has established a cattle ranch, and a similar scheme has been tried on the Ogun River Estate in Western Nigeria. Piggeries have been developed, particularly by Lebanese, in the non-Muslim large towns, although even Kano and Dakar have well-developed piggeries in which concentrates are used for feeding.

The sole attempt at a large-scale livestock development scheme, comparable with the large-scale crop-raising schemes to be discussed below, was in the Gambia, where it was proposed in 1948 to establish an egg scheme in which 10,000 acres (4000 hectares) of forest and bush should be cleared to create a poultry farm capable of 'producing in 2 or 3 years' time 20 million eggs per annum, to be followed by subsequent expansion if justified by results'.[68] It would appear that the food requirements of the birds were underestimated, and the yield of grain per acre overestimated. The scheme was established in the Sandhills Region, south of Bathurst, with well-drained, but poor soils. There was a shortage of feeding stuffs, which in turn helped to make food short, in a country where the margins of food production are normally very small. In 1950 over 35 per cent of the birds died from fowl typhoid, and the following year the project was wound up with a loss of some £628,000.

Mixed farming

A system of mixed farming, combining the rearing of livestock with crop raising, and depending on keeping the land permanently in use, either as pasture or as arable, could have advantages over the present systems, assuming it could be established in West African conditions. The earliest notions of mixed farming in West Africa developed with the introduction of ploughs from the beginning of the present century. The plough, drawn usually by two oxen, could till four times the area a man could hoe in the same time. In this, it offered the possibility of an increase in productivity per cultivating family. The major problems in the introduction were seen to be the availability of capital, availability of land, the problem of combining the keeping of draught animals with cultivation, feeding problems, and the existence over large areas of extensive root systems and tree stumps. The second and last of these problems restricted successful introductions to the less heavily-populated portions of the Sudanic zone, and in fact most success has been achieved in the treeless floodlands of the Upper Niger basin. The third problem involved the evolution of some system of mixed farming, and the first Government agencies to provide loans.

Objections to ploughing in the tropics have been raised by some students of tropical problems on the grounds that ploughing involves too deep a tillage[69], which will in turn lead to soil erosion. These fail to take into account that (a) ploughing need involve no more than a mere scratching of the surface, (b) existing tillage by hoes is frequently deeper than the 3 to 6 in (75–150 mm) commonly ploughed in Western Europe. Moreover, outside the floodlands, the introduction of ploughs has been most successful on the comparatively light soils of the Sudanic zone, where, on the whole, deep tillage is traditionally avoided. However, this probably reflects problems of the distribution of draught power.

Ploughing was introduced into the Fouta Djallon in 1915, but was welcomed only by the less wealthy chiefs with medium to small holdings, who, unable any longer to command labour due to abolition of slavery, saw the advantage of replacing slaves by oxen. In 1918 there were 9 cultivators owning 18 ploughs and 5 harrows. By 1928 the numbers in Guinea had increased to 3563 cultivators with 4231 ploughs and 2131 harrows. Most of the increase had occurred, however, in the Upper Niger basin and after the economic crisis of 1929 to 1931 ploughing began to decrease in the Fouta Djallon, but continued to increase in the swamp rice lands of the Upper Niger. By 1934 there were 8000 ploughs in Guinea, 5000 of which were in the Upper Niger districts.[70] In the Fouta Djallon ploughs always had little advantage over hoes, except where large holdings were worked, and even there frequently more land was ploughed than could be kept free of weeds. Overcrowding of population with fragmentation and subdivision made for small fields, most easily worked by hand hoeing. Fodder for draught oxen became a problem during the growing season. Where rice was grown in floodlands, however, large areas were available for rapid expansion, and holdings and fields could be of a size worth ploughing. The flood-plain soils are generally heavier and make hoeing arduous, yet they are without stones, ironstone concretions, tree stumps and root systems which would impede ploughing. Moreover, excellent dry season pasture is available. The ox-drawn plough has spread since 1939 into the Inland Niger delta, where in the Mopti region there were 2530 by 1951. Here on heavy soils three men normally operate the plough – a guide in front, a man to steer, and a man to add weight to the plough, and regulate the depth. Three oxen are normally used to draw the plough in these heavy soil conditions.[71]

The French authorities have rarely claimed to be achieving anything more than the introduction of plough cultivation, except perhaps in small experiments like that of M'Pesoba (Mali) where although cattle pastures did not rotate with arable land, the cattle returned to the hamlet each night and manure was collected.[72] The British authorities in Northern Nigeria were less interested in introducing the plough for its own sake than in developing a system of mixed farming. In 1928, after four years' research work at the Government Farm at Samaru near Zaria, there were three mixed farmers, and after a very slow rate of increase the number rose rapidly from 1945 onwards reaching 10,943 by 1952, and 35,000 by 1964. Most success was achieved in Zaria Province, where at first mixed farms consisted of about 12 acres (5 hectares) of cropland, and had a pair of bullocks and a plough. In Kano Province much of the land was already under a system of permanent cultivation. In Sokoto the soil was thought too poor, except in the floodlands, where bullocks were used to puddle the rice fields of, for example, the Kworre scheme. In Ilorin mixed farming was delayed by the need to find suitable trypanosomiasis-resistant cattle.[73] It was claimed that more land could be cultivated than on the 'normal' holding (estimated to be 3 acres ($1\frac{1}{4}$ hectares) under crop), and that the manure supply would increase yields. A survey of the Bomo Village Area near Zaria indicated that mixed farmers cultivated approximately twice the area cultivated by hand tillage farmers (15·5 to 7·4 acres – 6·3 to 3·0 hectares), and obtained slightly higher yields. However, increase in productivity was limited in most of Northern Nigeria by problems of marketing. Moreover, two oxen could supply sufficient manure for only 4 acres ($1\frac{1}{2}$ hectares) a year, and had to obtain the greater part of their fodder from a considerable area of rough grazing land, no estimates of which were given in the works cited.[74] Indeed, feeding has been a major problem wherever abundant natural grazing has been lacking or seasonally deficient, for in such cases a farmer must raise crops to feed his livestock in addition to feeding himself and his family. Thus part of any increase in productivity achieved by mixed farming may have to go into draught power, and food shortages may occur at the same time for both men and oxen, frequently at the beginning of the rains when the work demands on both are at their heaviest. Since 1945 the mixed farming scheme has been modified. Holdings have become larger. For example, in the Kontagora Resettlement Scheme of 1947 each settler family received 33 acres (13·3 hectares), of which 20 acres (8 hectares) had to be cleared and stumped, and put under an eight-year rotation of:

1. Cotton. 2. Guinea corn. 3. Guinea corn. 4. Groundnuts. 5. Pennisetum. 5–8. Grass ley.

Two working bulls, two heifers and a plough were supplied to each farm unit. Four cattle multiplication centres were set up in 1953 to provide high-grade cattle for mixed farmers. For a time, the scheme proved attractive, despite the attempt to enforce the ploughing of large acreages, but the problem of weeding still remained. Four cattle could provide manure for 8 acres ($3\frac{1}{4}$ hectares) a year when sufficient for $12\frac{1}{2}$ acres (5 hectares) was needed. The oxen needed fodder during the dry season, and were in poor condition when they needed to do their heaviest work. In several districts, particularly round Kano, the introduction of mixed farming has involved the redistribution of holdings in order to obtain units of sufficient size.[75] Comparison with mixed farming elsewhere in the world is difficult, especially with that of Europe or North America, for in West

Africa, besides the enormous environmental differences, there are no imported cattle feeding stuffs. After over twenty years' effort the number of mixed farmers in Nigeria is as yet only a minute fraction of the total farming population. Possibly more rapid results may be achieved by encouraging the permanent settlement of Fulani – a development in which there has been some success in recent years.

Fallows, fertilizers and the problems of soil management

Mixed farming was attempted, partly in response to the idea that the soils needed manure to provide better results, and partly in order to put land in permanent use, and eliminate bush burning and the bush fallow harbouring tsetse fly. The better use of soils, and the development of pastures or green manures to replace traditional fallows, became important elements in the policies of agricultural departments between the wars. The idea that tropical soils were highly productive, current in the 19th century, had been succeeded by the view that they were on the whole poor, and were rapidly worsening, or even being removed by erosion, wherever 'wasteful' methods of 'shifting cultivation' were practised. Most observers in West Africa, particularly the French[76], regard bush burning as a means of impoverishing vegetation, 'laterizing' the soil and developing a 'carapace ferrugineuse', that is, ironstone concretionary capping or 'laterite shield'. Vine disagrees with these views, and D'Hoore claims that fire agriculture produces only a 'relative accumulation' of free sesquioxides in the surface layer of soils by the removal of non-sesquioxide elements, and not an 'absolute accumulation' of sesquioxides in more than one soil horizon leading to the formation of the carapace ferrugineuse.[77] Attempts to exclude burning may lead to an intensification of forest, and, outside the Guinean environments, would enable tsetse flies to increase their range. In the more humid Guinean environment, the tsetse prefer open conditions, and, in consequence, such attempts may help to reduce their spread.[78]

The elimination of fallowing and burning seemed possible in northern areas by the introduction of mixed farming. In the south, where the keeping of cattle faces many problems, the answer seemed to lie in green manuring – found unsuitable in the north because the green manure crop had to be sown at the busiest time of the year due to the short growing season. It was, however, difficult to persuade communities to grow a crop in order to bury it. The peasant cultivator prefers to see a return for his labour. Plants tried include *Tephrosia candida*, *Cassia siamea*, *Calopogonium*, *Mucuna aterrima*, *Canavalia ensiformis*, *Dolichos lablab*, *Crotalaria* and *Centrosema*. Some success was obtained in south-eastern Nigeria in increasing the area of *Acioa barteri* fallows (see p. 115), but elsewhere the development of a green manure crop was slow or failed altogether. In 1933 a Nigerian agricultural officer commented:

'If a green manure crop which has been allowed to grow through the dry weather and produce its seed is subsequently burnt, the effect on the succeeding maize crop is just as good as when the manure crop is buried green in November before it seeds or dries up.'

– and in 1936 the comment was made that it was doubtful whether the green manure, *Calopogonium*, could maintain a higher fertility level than weeds.[79] The Leverhulme Trust mission of 1938–9 recommended the development of the existing system of mixed cropping, rather than the introduction of revolutionary green manuring and mixed farming. Nevertheless, green manuring was still being attempted in the 1950s, particularly in large Government farming schemes, using mechanization, where leguminous crops have been ploughed in. Doubt about the value of green manures compared with bush fallows was still being expressed in 1955.[80] E. W. Russell commented that natural fallows were as good as planted fallows for benefiting crops and that grass fallows were as good as legumes.[81] Another possible solution to the problem of the fallows is the use of composts. Market gardens at Enugu in south-eastern Nigeria and croplands round Kano are supplied with composts manufactured from night-soil residues and market waste.[82]

Artificial fertilizers[83] have been applied to West African soils on Government experimental farms since the beginning of agricultural department work. Results, particularly with the application of superphosphates, have been encouraging, and most territories have schemes for the distribution of cheap 'mixed' fertilizers and for the demonstration of their application on special plots. Some territories have even distributed free artificial fertilizers in order to promote their use more rapidly. Artificial fertilizers have been used in large quantities in major Government farming schemes, notably in Senegal, where phosphates and potassium ammonia compounds have been applied. A major problem in using artificial fertilizers is that great care must be taken in application – a danger with free distribution amongst peasant cultivators. The effect of a fertilizer depends on how it is put in the soil in relation to the crop plants. Phosphates, and to a lesser extent potash, may become 'fixed' in the soils by the formation with the sesqui-oxides and clay minerals of highly insoluble compounds. In areas liable to the accumulation of free sesquioxides there are obvious dangers. There are, more-over, considerable regional differences in the fertilizer response of soils.

Attention was drawn to the problems of soil erosion in West Africa as early as the 1920s. In Nigeria, for example, the Forestry Department pointed to gullying on the Udi Plateau, but little was done until 1928, when headward retreat of the gullies threatened the Udi–Enugu road. Several hundred acres were declared pro-tected, and 85 acres (34 hectares) enclosing the gullies were 'ditched', at first with straight ditches 1 foot wide, 1 foot deep and 6 feet long (30 × 30 × 180 cm) along the contours, and later with crescent-shaped ditches. Small earth dams were constructed and soil-holding perennials planted, chiefly exotics.[84] E. P. Stebbing drew attention to the supposed encroachment of the Sahara in Northern Nigeria in the 1930s, and suggested that the water-table was being lowered. He cited as evidence the large number of dying trees, diminishing water supplies, and the exodus of population from the desert.[85] Tree planting was begun on the international boundary in Katsina Province in 1934, the intention being to provide a continuous belt of dum palms, backed by strips 1 mile (1·6 km) wide and a few miles long, containing a variety of tree species, chiefly *Dalbergia sissoo*. All dwellings were removed from the demarcated area, but it was found impossible to prevent all cultivation, and the strips had to be abandoned. Jones and Grasovsky disputed Stebbing's evidence, suggesting even the possibility of Saharan retreat (see p. 178), and doubting whether a forest belt would in any case serve the purpose intended.[86] The exodus of population is in any case known to be due to French policies, the decline of caravan traffic and the decay of wells with the ending of slavery (see p. 192). Prothero has discussed soil erosion problems in north-western Nigeria, noting that many wells tapped only unreliable perched aquifers, and that some districts report increased surface water in the dry season, probably due to increased run-off following widespread vegetation clearance.[87] In many areas soil erosion problems have been serious enough to require the organization of special services. The Government of Nigeria took the step of inviting a geographer, A. T. Grove, to make a survey of soil erosion and related problems in the Jos Plateau.[88] Anti-erosion measures included:

1) the re-establishment of woodland or adequate grass cover on all non-arable land;
2) attempts to re-settle cultivators from overcrowded areas and limit the number of stock permitted on grazing land;
3) the introduction of ridging, terracing and wave-bedding in areas either affected or likely to be affected;
4) control of drainage, particularly where a large run-off occurs from impermeable surfaces, e.g. roads;
5) the establishment of forest reserves on watersheds and steep slopes;
6) the limiting of cultivation to slopes of less than certain prescribed gradients;
7) the forbidding of cultivation near stream banks;
8) the control or forbidding of bush burning.

Such measures inevitably meant putting land out of cultivation, labour for which there was no direct return, the reduction in the area of crops planted or stock grazed, and interference with traditional practice. As the worst cases of erosion were commonly in areas of high population density where land was short and production per head was often low, such measures were often bitterly opposed by the communities affected.

Agriculture and dietetic problems

A minor but significant factor in Government agricultural policies has been the problem of West African diets. In the early stages of developing an agricultural policy, the view was taken that diets were not only deficient in certain elements, but were low in quantity, that is in calorific value, and, in many areas, were particularly low at the seasons of heaviest work. Attempts were made, therefore, to encourage a higher output of foodstuffs, particularly during the last war when imports were reduced, to devise better methods of crop storage, and to introduce supplementary crops, which could be harvested at times of traditional food shortage. The recognition of marked protein deficiency in many West African diets assisted in the encouragement of the improvement of stock-raising and pastures, and the attempts to develop mixed farming and dairying. The cultivation of beans and other legumes has been encouraged, not merely in order to improve crop rotations and add nitrogen to the soil, but also to help solve this deficiency problem. It has also been suggested that export crop production has tended to reduce food cropping. Whilst there is evidence of a greater dependence on food imports in export crop-producing regions, Johnston suggests that food production has probably increased at about the same rate as population growth, and that some export crop expansion was at the expense of such activities as hunting and fishing rather than food cropping.[89]

Work on crop diseases and pests

·Some account has been given above of the diseases affecting certain export crops. Work on the prevention of disease and the limiting or destruction of pests has been undertaken in connection with all crops. Such work includes not only the breeding of disease-resistant varieties, changes in dates of planting and harvesting, and the elimination of hosts, but also the use of chemicals. Enormous damage is done to grain crops by birds every year, particularly in the Sudanic zone, and the former French West African agricultural departments had special sections for bird destruction and control. Locusts also provide a special problem. Red and Migratory Locust swarms originate from the Middle Niger districts, and Desert Locust swarms from the Sahara. France, the United Kingdom and Belgium formed an international convention for locust control in 1947. In French West Africa a Service Fédéral Anticridien was created, with a section in each territory of the federation. A network of warning posts was devised, and mobile groups organized to destroy locusts in the Sahara, particularly in those areas favoured for re-grouping or breeding. Special mention should be made of work on diseases of cocoa, particularly swollen shoot, black pod and capsid attack, by cocoa research units in Ghana and Nigeria, on coffee diseases and pests in the Ivory Coast and Sierra Leone, particularly rust and berry borer, on oil palm diseases and pests by the West African Institute for Oil Palm Research, on cotton stainers, boll-worms and boll diseases in Northern Nigeria, on the Panama, sugatoba and cigar-end diseases of the banana in Guinea, the Ivory Coast and the Cameroons, and on maize diseases by the West Africa Maize Research Unit.

A minor, but not unimportant, point is that the pest problem has worsened due to increased educational opportunities. As the proportion of children going to school has increased, so the number of children available for scaring birds and animal pests has decreased. In some areas awned varieties of millet, generally avoided by birds, are now preferred in cultivation.

Market gardening[90]

Market gardening, or the production of vegetables and fruit for sale on small-holdings, has increased rapidly in recent years round most large towns. Agricultural departments are fostering their development and encouraging the application of fertilizers and irrigation. At Dakar market gardening produces not only vegetables but even flowers for the local market. There the fertile black earth fringing the swamps of the Niayes is ideal, although comparatively infertile sands have been made productive with the aid of manure, composts, green manure and chemical fertilizers. Irrigation from wells or local swamps is used, and windbreaks have been constructed to protect the crops. A useful windbreak here is 'ethel' (*Tamarix articulata*), introduced from California in 1943 by the American builders of the Yoff aerodrome, after having been introduced to America from Southern Algeria. In Northern Nigeria small vegetable gardens are frequently irrigated by shaduf from local streams, or by buckets and channels from wells.

Irrigation and floodland cultivation

The first attempt by Europeans to develop irrigation in West Africa was at Richard-Toll, where from 1822 onwards a 'noria' or Persian wheel was employed, but few other attempts were made to use surface or ground water for cultivation or to develop floodlands. The French, however, were early impressed by the possibilities of developing irrigation in their Sahelian and Sudanic valleys, particularly in the valleys of the Senegal and in the inland delta of the Niger. Having achieved little success in their campaign to increase upland cotton production between 1903 and 1913, under the guidance of the Association Cotonnière Coloniale, it was decided to attempt the cultivation of cotton by irrigation, and in 1919 a mission, directed by the engineer Bélime, was sent out to the valleys of the Senegal and Niger. Between 1925 and 1929 the first experimental hydraulic works were constructed at Sotuba on the Niger, and in 1929 a project to irrigate large portions of the Inland Niger delta was planned, intended eventually to comprise 1,250,000 acres (500,000 hectares) of cotton and 1,100,000 acres (450,000 hectares) of rice. The plan was approved in 1931, and the following year the Office du Niger was created to undertake the work. A barrage, dikes and canals have been constructed, and by 1956 there were 70,000 acres (28,000 hectares) under rice and 12,000 acres (4850 hectares) under cotton (see pp. 645–52). In the delta of the Senegal river the major problems were the invasion of sea water and the need to reduce the salinity of the soils. Cultivation was possible on the lands below the confluence of the Taouey and the Senegal, providing dikes were constructed, and the fresh water of the Lac de Guiers used for irrigation. From 1916 onwards an earth barrage was built across the Taouey each year to keep sea water out of the Lac de Guiers, and protect African cultivation and pastures round the lake shores. In 1938 the Mission d'Aménagement du Sénégal was created, and in 1945 it undertook the task of developing the delta, building a barrage across the Taouey three years later. Mechanized rice production was begun in 1952 on the first of four irrigated 3700-acre (1500-hectare) units. By 1962 a total of 13,500 acres (5500 hectares) was under rice entirely mechanically cultivated with a yield of just under 2500 lb per acre (2800 kilos per hectare) after heavy losses due to the quelea bird. Wild rice infestation, salinity of floodland soils in the tidal portion of the Senegal valley, and locusts, have all been major problems. Costs have been enormous, particularly due to the need to pump fresh water. After heavy financial losses the scheme was taken over by a public company in 1960, and all deficits were borne by the Senegal Government. Imported rice is now cheaper than that produced by the scheme, and there is, in consequence, a tendency to experiment with other crops, notably cotton, sugar and tomatoes.[91]

In addition to these two large schemes the French authorities have constructed a multitude of smaller schemes. In the Senegal valley the M.A.S. has diked several areas of fondé and walo, and constructed sluices to control water levels. Small pumping stations have been erected to provide water for the higher parts of the fondé.[92] There is also an M.A.S. plan for achieving hydrological control of 6000 square miles (15,550 sq km) of the valley by means of a large regulatory dam and three submersion dams. Improved navigation would also be achieved. In the Niger valley the Service de l'Agriculture has introduced schemes to make the maximum use of floodland available for the cultivation of rice, and to control the extremely irregular supplies of floodwater. Excluding the portions of the Inland Niger delta, which are not normally flooded, and which are controlled by the Office du Niger, the Service de l'Agriculture was faced with the development of two distinct floodland regions:

1) the flood-plains of the upper valley, long and narrow, and enclosed by uplands;
2) the vast flood-plains of the delta crossed by the Niger and Bani with numerous old channels, tributaries and distributaries.

In the former, there is a succession of flood-plains, each containing tributaries whose flow is regulated by the floods of the main stream. Here control has been exercised by barrages on the tributaries, and by canals supplying tributary water to the flood-plain, together with dikes and sluices controlling the floods of the main stream. In the latter, the numerous channels, with their natural levées, subdivide the floodland. To control the floodwaters small barrages and sluices have been constructed across the channels, and dikes to enclose breaches in the levées. In the upper valley, by 1949, 15,000 acres (6000 hectares) had been affected by flood control, and in the delta 110,000 acres (44,500 hectares). Work is under way on a further 150,000 acres (60,000 hectares). In the Sahelian zone seasonal wadis can be improved for irrigation by the construction of earth barrages. By 1949, 27,000 acres (11,000 hectares) had been affected and work has been proceeding on barrage irrigation for a further 75,000 acres (30,500 hectares). So far well or bore irrigation has not proved practical, as few wells or bores can provide more water than is needed by men and animals for drinking purposes.

In the remaining territories of West Africa, a few irrigation schemes and schemes of flood control have been developed, but the areas involved are at present extremely small. The major achievements in the control of water supplies for cultivation have been in the coastal and estuarine swamps of the south-west, particularly in Portuguese Guinea, Gambia and Sierra Leone. In Sierra Leone, between 1938 and 1955, 9000 acres (3500 hectares) of mangrove swamp were cleared by hand in the southern creeks under a rice-growing development scheme. The scheme was implemented, partly to produce more rice to satisfy local demand, and partly to counter excessive clearance of hill-slope land with the consequent danger of soil erosion. Four main areas of swamp rice production may be distinguished:

1) the Scarcies and Bonthe polders;
2) the Little Scarcies river banks;
3) river banks in the Bonthe and Pujehun districts;
4) the flooded inland depressions or 'boli lands' of the central Makeni area.

The swamp rice area is being extended in Sierra Leone by (a) improving the access of wet season tides to areas of poor drainage, not sufficiently reached by fresh water, and (b) empoldering swamps with little fresh water supply, where tidal water is always too saline for the growth of rice.[93] Reclamation of saline swamps has been undertaken in the Scarcies and the Colony and in 1952–3, 800 acres (325 hectares) were empoldered – 500 acres (200 hectares) by mechanical excavators.

In Liberia, as in Sierra Leone, Government officers and advisers have condemned the 'wasteful' use of forest lands by cultivators, and recommended a swamp rice programme. Work on inland swamps was begun in 1953, partly on a Government demonstration farm and partly on private holdings.[94]

In Nigeria, several rice irrigation schemes have been attempted, including the Edozighi Scheme on 2500 acres (1100 hectares) in the flood-plain of the Kaduna river, and the Sokoto Scheme in the flood-plains of the Sokoto and Rima. The latter scheme included mechanized tillage, and was a financial and agricultural failure, with returns of only some 750 lb per acre (840 kilos per hectare), in part due to damage from excessive flooding and from fish. Increased wheat imports and the growing demand for rice have stimulated interest in irrigation schemes. Other Nigerian schemes, totalling some 50,000 acres planned, are in Hadejia and on alluvium near Lake Chad.

Mechanization[95]

Except in the crowded areas of the south-east, in parts of Sierra Leone, in western Senegal, and in the Mossi and Hausa districts, there is no land shortage in West Africa. The limitation on productivity has lain in the limit to which the cultivator can extend the area under cultivation with his present techniques. The use of equipment making possible the cultivation of greater areas per cultivating family might, therefore, realize an increase in productivity, which would be desirable, providing the peasant family can either itself consume or find a market for the increased production. At present most of West Africa is too badly served by transport to be able to market increased surpluses. Peasant diets are slow to change. The main dietetic problem is not in the quantity, but in the type of food and the regularity of its supply. Even if the capital were available, training schools established and maintenance assured, the mechanization of peasant agriculture would at present for most areas of West Africa bring little useful return and at a high cost.

Mechanization of agriculture was introduced into West Africa after the 1939–1945 war. The use of machines for various purposes in warfare had undoubtedly impressed those concerned with West Africa's economic development. Elsewhere, in Europe, parts of Asia and the Americas, there was a great increase in the use of agricultural machines during the post-war period. In British territories alarm was felt over the future production of oil-seeds, and a quick increase in productivity was thought to be needed, an increase only obtainable by large schemes directed by Government agencies. In French territories similar alarm was felt, and schemes were planned to increase the output, not only of oil-seeds, but also of rice, in order to be less dependent on Asian food supplies and cotton, and to reduce the expenditure of American dollars. For such schemes the labour demand would be heavy, and labour shortage had always hindered or even prevented plantation development. Mechanization could, therefore, make up for the labour shortage, or, by undertaking the more arduous work of clearance and tillage, could make the schemes more attractive to intending settlers. Furthermore, it was hoped that mechanization might eventually mean lower production costs.

Baldwin has made a study of one of the larger schemes involving mechanization – the Niger Agricultural Project at Mokwa in Niger Province.[96] Here machinery was found too expensive for clearance, and was used for ploughing and ridging. Both steam ploughs using cables, and diesel or petrol engined tractor-drawn ploughs, had the same problems with roots, tree stumps, ant-hills, and the thick grass of October. The labour of planting, weeding and harvesting was performed by hand, and so were the clearance operations. In consequence, machinery was little used for most of the year, and whilst tillage operations took place, labour was little used. In effect double the labour power required was available, and half of it was idle at any one time. Without seasonal labour, mechanization and hand cultivation could not be geared together. Furthermore, the machines suffered heavy damage in this new environment, and the costs of maintenance and of supply of spare parts from Britain were high. Mechanization costs contributed to the heavy net loss incurred by the scheme of £11 5s. 10d. an acre (U.S. $78.06 per hectare) in 1952 and £10 15s. 10d. an acre (U.S. $74.60 per hectare) in 1953. Mechanization of rice production at Richard-Toll in Senegal seems to have had some success, but here conditions are different. It is possible to mechanize most stages of cultivation, and the area to be tilled is level and without tree roots and stumps. Even the moisture supply is controlled. Trials have been made with the use of aircraft. They were found rather costly for sowing seed, but useful for distributing fertilizers and weedkillers.[97] Mechanization seems most successful in its application to the cultivation of swamp rice, and tractors have been usefully employed by the Office du Niger and by the Agricultural Department and Co-operatives in Sierra Leone.[98] In the Casamance groundnuts scheme of the Compagnie Générale des Oléagineux Tropicaux in southern Senegal, mechanized cultivation has incurred some financial loss, although farther north the Mouride colonists have had some success (see p. 639). In Nigeria tractor cultivation in combination with peasant farming has been most successfully developed on northern floodlands, where in 1964 some 13,000 acres were tractor ploughed for wheat and rice. Tractor hire has, however, proved very costly, and has been subsidized since 1961. In Western Nigeria a small portion of the tobacco holdings is likewise ploughed by tractor.

The problems of servicing and maintenance, of employing skilled engineers and drivers at rates which are not exorbitant, and in some cases even of obtaining fuel and lubricants cheaply, are all of great importance in any mechanized scheme. The machines, too, must be adapted or modified for the environment in which they are to operate, and this quite often involves preliminary trials or even a pilot scheme. Mechanized cultivation seems possible in at least one instance, and may be adapted eventually for other applications. Charter has suggested mechanical bush clearing by pollarding instead of stumping.[99] Tricart has described a case of the use of a tractor by peasant cultivators in the Ivory Coast.[100] With the possibilities of future developments in view a school of mechanized agriculture was started in Lagos in 1954. In Ghana, where great importance has been attached to the development of mechanized large-scale agricultural schemes an assembly plant is already producing tractors to meet local demand.

Government farming schemes

Some of the post-war agricultural schemes developed by the Government agencies will be described in Chapter 14 on the economic and political development in the new states. Here it should be noted that they represent the most recent stage in the attempts to change West Africa's agriculture. There are several different types of scheme:

1) The co-operative or group farming scheme in which resources are pooled,

and advice, encouragement and financial assistance given by Government agencies.

2) The group farming scheme which is directed by Government agencies, but in which the cultivators are regarded as partners or shareholders. The 'partnership' is rather limited in practice since the plan of agricultural operations even down to small details is usually made solely by the Government agencies.

3) The Government agricultural scheme or state farm employing wage-labourers as cultivators, developed chiefly in Ghana, on former mechanized scheme lands.

All three types of scheme bear some resemblance to plantations, particularly the last. In effect they represent a return to plantation methods of cultivation in an attempt to achieve greater efficiency in production. Private enterprise failed to achieve more than a small measure of plantation agriculture in West Africa or was prevented from doing so. The greater part of the task of developing export crops was left to the peasantry. The West African governments have thus taken over the work which private enterprise was unable to undertake, and are trying to obtain success, either by a compromise with peasant cultivation, as in the first two types of scheme, or by the application of more modern techniques as in the last. That such schemes are concerned not only with export crops, but with food for consumption by peasant export crop producers, is an interesting paradox with parallels elsewhere in Africa.[101]

With independence West African governments have in some cases sought to promote a new type of scheme generally referred to as the 'farm settlement'. Many of these owe much to Israeli experience and guidance. Farm settlements have been tried in Ghana, where they have been associated with the activities of the Builders' Brigade, and generally represent an attempt to increase food production on former Agricultural Department experimental farms, using modern techniques, particularly tractors. Two kinds of co-operative organization have been tried:

1) collective ownership of all plots;
2) individual ownership of adjoining plots worked collectively wherever mechanical equipment is used.

In Western and Eastern Nigeria farm settlements have been tried mainly in order to train a new type of cultivator, and so make agriculture an attractive industry to school leavers.[102] Here they again involve the use of tractors, and also the scientific study of farming. Generally, however, holdings are too small to justify the use of a tractor on each, and in consequence a co-operative system has to be tried, with problems of competition for use at favourable times. Costs have been very high (see p. 708). In Togo a similar but smaller and lower-cost scheme has been organized by the Young Farmers' Clubs, in which the holdings are about 100 acres (40 hectares) each. On the whole such schemes have had only limited success so far, for they have failed as yet to make a significant contribution to West Africa's economic and agricultural problems.[103] In part they represent the attempt to enlarge the scale of African farming, that is to create large supposedly more efficient units, in part to introduce science into African farming, and in part to create agricultural cadres which will lead peasant farming in an era of rapid change.

Some aspects of local response to changes in agriculture and pastoralism

Whilst the promotion solely of commercial cropping for export or internal markets may be condemned as too one-sided an agricultural policy in countries most of whose productivity is devoted to crops for subsistence or local exchange, and in which there appears to be a need for better-balanced diets and improved farming techniques, nevertheless it is significant that such promotion has met with a far greater response than the attempts to improve farming methods or promote local food production. The attraction of immediate cash rewards seems to provide the greatest stimulus in West African agriculture today. Food cropping has, however, increased considerably, almost entirely as a commercial enterprise, which owes its development to the original policy of increasing export crop production. The development of commercial cropping has led to the movement of cultivators to a few especially favoured areas, whose distribution is determined by physical circumstances and questions of accessibility to market, and to a certain extent by the organization of seed supplies and Government propaganda. Hence the emergence of certain well-recognized export crop regions, of which the chief are the Senegal and Northern Nigeria groundnut regions, the Northern Nigeria cotton region and the southern cocoa, coffee, oil palm, and banana regions. On the fringes of these are commercial food-producing areas, a few of which, as in the case of rice production, are directly under Government control, but most of which have been developed by local peasantry to supply the needs of the export crop producers and of urban populations. Thus in Southern Nigeria yams and cassava are grown on the northern and southern fringes of the cocoa region and on the northern fringe of the main oil palm region, chiefly for sale. Ilorin, Kabba, Benue and Ogoja Provinces are the chief producers. Buchanan's map of tonnages of yams railed illustrates the point.[104] Mixed farming, green manuring and soil conservation methods have met with only a small response or even proved unpopular since they offer no immediate return for the cash and labour expended. Fertilizers have gained a little popularity in a few areas where higher returns have been demonstrated. Improved methods of preparation are slowly gaining ground due to cash inducement or legal enforcement.

In pastoralism circumstances are similar. The changes consequent on the introduction of new stock, of selective breeding, and of medical treatment, and on the attempts to improve or control the use of pastures, are not as startling as the development of the great meat markets of the growing towns, and the greatly increased migration of animals from the northern pastures to the slaughter-houses. Drove roads have been established over enormous distances throughout West Africa, and a stimulus to improvements in stock-rearing has been effected, which should eventually bring results. In the 1950s the higher prices fetched by fatter beasts encouraged increased movement of livestock by rail.

The changing pattern of West African agriculture due to the introduction of commercial cropping is, however, creating new problems which are meeting with a variety of responses from West African cultivators. The land-use patterns are changing. Instead of the mixture of woodland, fallow and cultivated land, with scattered villages, compounds and hamlets characteristic of several areas hitherto, a dense network of small plots with little fallow area and new forms of woodland or secondary grasses with dispersed, but closely-situated compounds or hamlets or larger nucleated villages is being created. In the Sudanic lands the savanna woodlands of the favoured areas are being removed as new roads are built, and in their place are great expanses of cultivated land interrupted by grass fallows. In the Guinean environments new types of forest have been created. In Ashanti and Yorubaland there is a hill-top forest of cocoa and kola interspersed with useful trees, cultivated land and fallows, subdivided by forest remnants in valley bottoms and reserves. In Benin, Iboland and Ibibioland there is a vast oil palm forest. Here and there villages and towns have their perimeters of useful trees, whilst forest remnants again appear in valleys and reserves. Cultivated land and fallows here provide not an interruption, but a lessening in the density of oil palms.

The export crop regions have tended not only to increase in area, but also to move as older worn-out areas, or areas in which perennials like cocoa have ceased to produce, are abandoned, and fresh lands are planted elsewhere. The oil palm region has tended to be the most constant, for there is very little evidence of expansion or movement since 1900, but cocoa has shown remarkable shifts in both Ghana and Nigeria. In Ghana production in the once important Densu and Birrim basins has declined, due partly to disease, and partly to age. The centre of maximum production has moved north-westwards to the districts around Kumasi. In Nigeria production has declined in the older centres on the westward fringe of the cocoa region, particularly in Ilaro, and planting has advanced east-wards into the Ilesha, Ondo, Akure and Owo districts. New roads in southern Ondo should advance plantings farther to the south-east. In Senegal the original centres of groundnut cultivation were in the north-west, chiefly in the Senegal valley. With the construction of railways, and later roads, the crop moved firstly towards the coast, and then advanced across Cayor and into Baol, Sine and Saloum, and eventually to Kaffrine and Koungueul. Since 1935 the main centres of production have on the whole remained stable.

The development of expanding or moving regions of export crop production, with some secondary food crops, is a response to European influences, reminiscent of the development of plantation crop production in, for example, Brazil. In effect modern commercial cropping has inherited something of the tradition of shifting cultivation. Not all commercial crop production shifts, however, or if it does, in most cases it shifts quite slowly. The smaller settlements and their associated cultivated areas tend to be permanent, or at least longer established than the equivalent agricultural settlements of the older subsistence or local exchange economy. The commercial cultivator must in fact look to stable features in the environment – roads, railways and markets. These have tended in West Africa to be insufficient to meet the rapid increases in demand, and in consequence suitable sites for commercial croppings have rapidly become overcrowded. Under such conditions fallows have become short, there is little if any land left for further settlement, and population and cropping distributions have become stabilized. The new situation demands certain responses and these are:

1) Interplanting foodstuffs amidst the commercial crop, often in the form of succession cropping.
2) Reduction of the main cropland area whilst retaining the same amount of compound land, thus increasing the proportion of land manured and virtually owned.
3) The cultivation of food crops which will produce a good return, even on the poorer soils remaining after the richer loams have been planted to commercial crops – the outstanding example of such a food crop is cassava.
4) Cultivation at greater distances from the settlement, often on rented or leased land.
5) The development of land ownership and of modern forms of leasing and renting land.

The interplanting of food and commercial crops, and the reduction of the main cropland area, are the results of land shortage with the competition for holdings and settlement sites in a favoured commercial crop region. Reduction in the main cropland area normally results in the shortening of fallows, and the cultivation of crops like cassava, adapted to poorer soil conditions. The great increase in cassava cultivation, which has taken place since about 1900, thus arises directly from European influences. An important factor is the growth of demand for cassava or gari flour in the towns, although outside Ghana, southern Nigeria and Senegal most urban markets as yet do not appear to draw on an area greater than that contained within 50 miles (80 km) radius. Gari keeps well and is easily transported. Moreover, amongst many communities the alternative root crop, yam, is by tradition planted by men, and it is the men who have tended to migrate in search of non-agricultural occupations. Cassava is easy to plant, and the entire root may be eaten, since propagation takes place from stem cuttings. It is a common practice to plant more than is required, and to pick the plant whenever needed, leaving any surplus in the fallow. Cassava is one of the few plants which will give fresh food all the year round and comparatively high yields on poor soils. Its disadvantage is its poor nutritive value. It has the lowest proportion of digestible protein of almost any West African crop. Cultivation at greater distances from the settlement involves the construction of temporary homes for the growing period, a tendency to concentrate on quick-growing crops, and frequently the use of bicycles. 'Bicycle cultivation' is now a phenomenon of the margins of overcrowded districts in the Eastern Region of Nigeria. Land ownership changes arise from the attachment of a commercial value to land with the production of commercial crops, or from the competition for land in over-crowded districts. In the first case, research in the Nigerian cocoa region has shown that 12 per cent of the cultivators concerned held almost half the cocoa-growing area, whilst only 4 per cent held one-third of the food-growing area. A few families have holdings as large as 200 acres (80 hectares). Speculation in cocoa land has developed, and many cultivators obtain a living by first establish-ing cocoa 'farms' and then selling them to the highest bidder. Shortage or even lack of fallows is not unknown. Of 480 farms surveyed, one-quarter had no fallow at all on food cropland, but employed a ten-year rotation of which two or more years were under cassava.[105] Renting or paying a share of crop is common in cocoa areas. In the 'abusa' system of Ghana, for example, the tenant cocoa farmer may pay two-thirds of the harvest. In Sierra Leone tribal authorities are clear-ing swamps for rice planting, and then letting out 'farms' for a cash rent. In the latter case ownership derives from the increasing proportion of compound land, or from a failure on the part of the original holders of the use-right to redeem a debt for which land has been pledged. Even outright purchase of land has developed. Many are forced to sell or pledge land, with increasing poverty as the cultivated area is reduced. In certain 'colony' districts, e.g. the Colony of Sierra Leone, Gold Coast Colony, Lagos Colony and Senegal, European land laws were introduced early, or Crown grants were made, sometimes in order to encourage permanent occupation and fixed settlement. Of a land bill about to be introduced in the Gold Coast Colony in 1910, the Northern Nigeria Lands Committee remarked:

'Civilized communities in Asia are accustomed to the continuous occupation and cultivation of their lands and to the practice of good husbandry. The Bill about to be introduced whilst preserving to the natives of the Colony their right to use public land for shifting cultivation in the manner in which they are accustomed, encourages them to settle permanently on cultivated land by assur-ing to them the right of proprietorship therein (a "settler's right") if occupation is continuous.'[106]

In the greater part of the Sudanic areas, Muslim land law prevails side by side with older customary usage. In the former French territories ownership of land is, on the whole, encouraged, because it is thought to favour increase in productivity. An owner using his land as security can borrow capital from the banks.[107]

In Iboland individual land tenure has become commonplace, and is frequently associated with dispersal of settlement and holdings in areas of high population density. Where Government officers have tried to encourage consolidation and ownership of holdings as a step towards improving local agricultural practice, the result is often dispersal, which, unfortunately, is at variance with the need for the closer grouping of settlement in order to cheapen the cost of introducing modern services.[108]

Clearly the changing state of agriculture has provoked new problems and new responses. The emergence of systems of agriculture adapted to meet the different conditions must await the fuller development of the changes at present taking place and the results of agricultural research. As yet only a marked drop in fertility under a fixed system with no possibility of moving elsewhere will make conservation measures, including extra labour or capital expenditure, acceptable to the West African cultivator. It may well be that eventually the present trend towards land ownership will in turn encourage the development of a system of commercial farming in the European sense.

BIBLIOGRAPHICAL NOTES

[1] A. Adandé, Le Maïs et ses Usages dans le Bas-Dahomey, *Bulletin, Institut Français d'Afrique Noire*, **15**, 1953, pp. 220–82.

[2] W. Allen and T. R. H. Thomson, *A Narrative of the Expedition to the River Niger in 1841*, London, 1848.

[3] *Report from the Select Committee on the West Coast of Africa*, part I, London, 1842, p. 563, q. 8898.

[4] J. H. Holland, The Useful Plants of Nigeria, Part I, *Bulletin of Miscellaneous Information*, Additional Series 9, Royal Botanic Gardens, Kew, 1908, p. 35.

[5] *Report of the Northern Nigeria Lands Committee*, Cd. 5102, 1910, pp. xviii–xix.

[6] The Leverhulme Trust, *The West African Commission, 1938–39*, 1943, pp. 31–33.

[7] For general information on West African crop plants the following works will be found useful:
J. M. Dalziel, *The Useful Plants of West Tropical Africa*, London, 1937.
F. R. Irvine, *A Textbook of West African Agriculture*, London, 1934, 2nd ed., 1953.
L. S. Cobley, *An Introduction to the Botany of Tropical Crops*, London, 1956.
H. F. MacMillan, *Tropical Planting and Gardening*, 5th ed., London, 1949.
On the development of export cropping there are numerous references. See for example:
F. J. Pedler, *Economic Geography of West Africa*, London, 1955.
A. McPhee, *The Economic Revolution in British West Africa*, London, 1926.
R. M. Prothero, Recent Developments in Nigerian Export Crop Production, *Geography*, **40**, 1955, pp. 18–27.
R. M. Prothero, Agricultural Problems in Nigeria, *Corona*, September 1953, pp. 328–33.
United Africa Company Ltd, *Statistical and Economic Review* (contains several articles).
S. La Anyane, *Ghana Agriculture*, Accra and London, 1963.

[8] R. Galletti, K. Baldwin and O. Dina, *Nigerian Cocoa Farmers*, London, 1956, pp. 5–6.

[9] D. Clayton, *Report of an ecological reconnaissance at Fada, near Ibadan*, 1956 (unpublished MS.).
On pests and diseases of cocoa see D. H. Urquhart, *Cocoa*, London, 1955, Chaps 11 and 12, and J. B. Wills (ed.), *Agriculture and Land Use in Ghana*, Accra and London, 1962, Chap. 19.

[10] For a discussion of the classification of Abeokuta coffee see A. E. Haarer, *Modern Coffee Production*, London, 1956, pp. 24–25.

[11] A. Köbben, Le Planteur Noire, Etudes Eburnéennes, Institut Français d'Afrique Noire, 5, 1956. For a discussion of the varieties of coffee planted in the Ivory Coast see E. Sibert, Les Caféiers de la Côte d'Ivoire, Paris, 1932.

[12] R. Portères, Les Arbres, Arbustes et Arbrisseaux Conservés comme Ombrage Naturel dans les Plantations de Caféiers Indigènes de la Région de Macenta (Guinée Française) et Leur Signification, Revue Internationale de Botanique Appliquée et d'Agriculture Tropicale, 29, 1949, pp. 336–55.

[13] London Rubber Trade Association, Mission Report, London, 1954. See also International Bank Mission Report, The Economic Development of Nigeria, Lagos, 1954.

[14] A useful source of information on the production of rubber and other commodities in Liberia is H. B. Cole, The Liberian Year Book, 1956, London, 1957.

[15] See detailed study by Y. Péhaut, L'Arachide au Sénégal, Cahiers d'Outre-Mer, 14, 1961, pp. 5–25.

[16] A. McPhee, op. cit., p. 37.

[17] See for example P. Pelissier, L'Arachide au Sénégal, Etudes Sénégalaises, Institut Français d'Afrique Noire, 2, 1952, pp. 49–80. This article provided invaluable information.

[18] J. Fouquet, La Traite des Arachides dans le Pays de Kaolack, Etudes Sénégalaises, Institut Français d'Afrique Noire, 8, 1958, p. 40.

[19] P. Pelissier, op. cit.

[20] A. McPhee, op. cit., pp. 31–34.

[21] J. M. Dalziel, op. cit., p. 503.

[22] J. M. Waterston, Observations on the Influence of Some Ecological Factors on the Incidence of Oil Palm Diseases in Nigeria, Journal of the West African Institute for Oil Palm Research, 1, 1953, pp. 24–59.
H. R. Rudin, Germans in the Cameroons, 1884–1914, London, 1938, pp. 258–61.

[23] R. Guérard, La Regénération de la Palmeraie Dahoméenne et l'Accroissement de la Production de l'Huile et des Amandes de Palme, Agronomie Tropicale, 6, 1951, pp. 66–71.

[24] Nigeria, Overseas Economic Surveys, H.M.S.O., 1957, pp. 109–12.

[25] For further discussion and a diagram showing oil palm produce hinterlands of the ports together with the proportions of oil and kernels exported see W. B. Morgan, The Nigerian Oil Palm Industry, Scottish Geographical Magazine, 71, 1955, pp. 174–7.

[26] See A. McPhee, op. cit., pp. 44 and 66.

[27] A. McPhee, op. cit., p. 45.

[28] R. Pasquier, Les Essais de Culture du Coton au Sénégal, Institut des Hautes Etudes de Dakar, Travaux du Département d'Histoire, 1, 1955, pp. 6–7.

[29] ibid., pp. 16–21.

[30] R. R. Irvine, op. cit., pp. 147–57.

[31] Colonial Annual Reports, Northern Nigeria, 516, 1905-6, pp. 416–18.

[32] For a discussion of cotton varieties see:
A. Chevalier, Le Cotonnier en Terrain Non Irrigué et Irrigué en A.O.F., Revue Internationale de Botanique Appliquée et d'Agriculture Tropicale, 31, 1951, pp. 319–20.
E. Guernier (ed.), L'Afrique Occidentale Française, Encyclopédie de la France d'Outre-Mer, vol. I, Paris, 1949, pp. 75–76.

[33] See K. M. Buchanan and J. C. Pugh, Land and People in Nigeria, London, 1955, pp. 141–2.

[34] P. Ahn, The Production of Urena Lobata Fibre in Ghana, World Crops, 15(3), 1963, pp. 92–97 and 103.

[35] See comments in J. Dresch, La Riziculture en Afrique Occidentale, *Annales de Géographie*, **58**, 1949, pp. 295–312.

[36] R. Portères, Le Système de Riziculture par Franges Univariétales et l'Occupation des Fonds par les Riz Flottants dans l'Ouest Africain, *Revue Internationale de Botanique Appliquée et d'Agriculture Tropicale*, **29**, 1949, pp. 553–63.

[37] A. Chevalier, Le Riz a-t-il un Grand Avenir en Afrique Occidentale? *Revue Internationale de Botanique Appliquée et d'Agriculture Tropicale*, **31**, 1951, pp. 321–2.

[38] Sierra Leone Report in *Proceedings, 2nd Inter-African Soils Conference*, Leopoldville, 1954, vol. II, pp. 1095–7.

[39] A. L. Mabogunje, Rice Cultivation in Southern Nigeria, *Nigerian Geographical Journal*, **2**, 1958–9, pp. 59–69.

[40] J. E. Y. Hardcastle, Development of Rice Production and Research in Nigeria, *Tropical Agriculture*, **36**, 1959, pp. 79–95.

[41] A. Chevalier, Mauvaises Herbes Envahissantes, Fléaux Redoubtables pour l'Agriculture en Afrique Tropicale, *Revue Internationale de Botanique Appliquée et d'Agriculture Tropicale*, **31**, 1951, pp. 390–9.
See also C. D. Adams and H. G. Baker, Weeds of Cultivation and Grazing Lands, in J. B. Wills (ed.), op. cit., pp. 402–5.

[42] P. D. Curtin, *The Image of Africa, British Ideas and Action, 1780–1850*, London, 1965, pp. 67, 110–12, 127–8.

[43] C. D. Adams, Activities of Danish Botanists in Guinea, 1783–1850, *Transactions of the Historical Society of Ghana*, **3**, 1957, pp. 30–46.
Report from the Select Committee on the West Coast of Africa, 1842, part II, p. 41, q. 10681.

[44] C. Schefer, *Instructions Générales Données de 1763 à 1870 aux Gouvernements et Ordonnateurs des Etablissements Français en Afrique Occidentale*, 1921.

[45] *Report from the Select Committee on the West Coast of Africa*, 1842, part I, p. 715, q. 10681.

[46] J. H. Holland, op. cit., p. 42.
See also The Leverhulme Trust, op. cit., pp. 25–29; R. K. Udo, Sixty years of plantation agriculture in Southern Nigeria: 1902–1962, *Economic Geography*, **41**, 1965, pp. 356–68.

[47] Details of plantation production in the Ivory Coast are from H. Fréchou, Les Plantations Européens en Côte d'Ivoire, *Cahiers d'Outre-Mer*, **8**, 1955, pp. 56–83.

[48] K. M. Buchanan and J. C. Pugh, op. cit., pp. 154–8. For a detailed study see E. Ardener, S. Ardener and W. A. Warmington, *Plantation and Village in the Cameroons*, London, 1960.

[49] See H. R. Rudin, op. cit., pp. 227–8 and 315–37. On labour problems in the Ivory Coast see H. Fréchou, op. cit.

[50] C. D. Adams, op. cit.
J. M. Hunter, A Specimen Observational Traverse, *Bulletin of the Ghana Geographical Association*, **7**, 1962, pp. 41–53.

[51] Quoted from the Moloney-Dyer Memorandum in J. H. Holland, op. cit., p. 24.

[52] J. H. Holland, op. cit., p. 39.

[53] W. B. Morgan, The Influence of European Contacts on the Landscape of Southern Nigeria, *Geographical Journal*, **125**, 1959, pp. 48–64.
See also J. D. Kennedy, The Development of Forest Legislation in Nigeria – an Outline, *Farm and Forest*, **3**, 1942, pp. 31–34.

[54] P. Bellouard, L'Action du Service Forestier en A.O.F. en Matière de Conservation des Sols, *Proceedings, 2nd Inter-African Soils Conference*, Leopoldville, 1954, vol. I, pp. 581–94.

[55] The Leverhulme Trust, op. cit., pp. 39–41.

[56] *Report of the Committee on Agricultural Policy and Organisation*, Accra, 1927.

[57] H. Martin Leake, Studies in Tropical Land Tenure, *Tropical Agriculture*, **9**, 1932, pp. 8–12; **10**, 1933, pp. 1–6.

[58] Based on E. Guernier, *Afrique Occidentale Française*, Encyclopédie de la France d'Outre-Mer, 1949, vol. II, pp. 315–23.
See also 'The Co-operative Movement' in International Labour Office, *African Labour Survey*, Geneva, 1958, p. 572.

[59] Overseas Economic Surveys, *Nigeria*, October 1957, pp. 112–14.
See criticism in P. T. Bauer, *West African Trade*, Cambridge, 1954, description and comments in D. E. Carney, *Government and Economy in West Africa*, New York, 1961, pp. 103–12, and below, p. 572.

[60] J. H. Mackay, *Bornu Survey*, undated MS. in University of Ibadan Library, pp. 434 and 570.

[61] See pp. 511–14, and T. Shaw and G. Colville, *Report of Nigerian Livestock Mission*, London, 1951.

[62] D. H. Hill, Diseases in Nigeria which could threaten North American Livestock, *Proceedings Book*, *American Veterinary Medical Association*, Ninetieth Annual Meeting, Toronto, July 20–23, 1953, pp. 465–71.

[63] See account in D. E. Faulkner and J. D. Brown, *The Improvement of Cattle in British Colonial Territories in Africa*, Colonial Advisory Council of Agriculture, Animal Health and Forestry, Publication No. 3, H.M.S.O., London, 1953, pp. 12–13.

[64] ibid., pp. 48–49.

[65] P. Merlin, L'Hydraulique Pastorale en Afrique Occidentale Française, *Bulletin des Services de l'Élevage et des Industries Animales de l'A.O.F.*, **4**, 1951, pp. 169–201.

[66] A. K. Murray, The Fula Cattle Owners of Northern Sierra Leone, *Tropical Agriculture*, **35**, 1958, pp. 102–13.

[67] K. M. Buchanan and J. C. Pugh, op. cit., pp. 125–7.

[68] Colonial Development Corporation, *Report on the Gambia Egg Scheme*, London, Cmd. 8560, 1952.

[69] P. Gourou, *The Tropical World*, trans. E. D. Laborde, 4th ed., 1966.

[70] M. Barthe, Le Labour Attelé en Guinée Française, *Agronomie Tropicale*, **6**, 1951, pp. 73–76.

[71] G. Jourdain and A. Fofana, Le Bœuf de Labour dans le Région de Mopti, *Bulletin des Services de l'Élevage et des Industries Animales de l'A.O.F.*, **5**, 1952, pp. 59–64.

[72] R. Dumont, *Types of Rural Economy, Studies in World Agriculture*, London, 1957, pp. 93–94. For draught oxen in Senegal see P. Nourissat, La Traction Bovine au Sénégal, *Agronomie Tropicale*, **20**(9), 1965, pp. 823–53.

[73] J. G. M. King, Mixed Farming in Northern Nigeria, *Empire Journal of Experimental Agriculture*, **7**, 1939, pp. 271–84 and 285–98.

[74] H. D. L. Corby, Changes Brought About by the Introduction of Mixed Farming, *Farm and Forest*, **2**, 1941, pp. 106–9.
An interesting criticism of the early period is made in W. R. Crocker, *Nigeria, A Critique of British Colonial Administration*, London, 1936, pp. 131–2.
Another account is in O. T. Faulkner and J. R. Mackie, *West African Agriculture*, Cambridge, 1935, pp. 64–75.
The Northern Nigeria Agricultural Department maintains that the object of the Mixed Farming Scheme is not only to maintain but to improve fertility, see P. C. Chambers, Progress with Mixed Farming in the Northern Region, Nigeria, *Conference of Directors and Senior Officers of Overseas Departments of Agriculture and Agricultural Institutions*, 1958, paper No. 4 (Wye College).
Haswell comments on shortages of fodder in the Gambia. See M. R. Haswell, *The Changing Pattern of Economic Activity in a Gambia Village*, London, 1963, p. 55.

[75] Agricultural Department, Nigeria, *Annual Reports*. K. M. Buchanan and J. C. Pugh, op. cit., pp. 122–5.
H. Vine and V. J. Weston, Progress of Work on the Management of Soil since 1948, *Proceedings, 2nd Inter-African Soils Conference*, Leopoldville, 1954, vol. II, pp. 1057 and 1070–2.

[76] See, for example, J. P. Harroy, *Afrique – Terre Qui Meurt*, Paris, 1944.
P. Gourou is a notable exponent of the view that tropical soils are poor – see *The Tropical World*, op. cit., p. 13 et seq.

[77] H. Vine, Is the Lack of Fertility of Tropical African Soils Exaggerated ? *Proceedings, 2nd Inter-African Soils Conference*, Leopoldville, 1954, vol. I, pp. 389–412.
J. D'Hoore, Le Facteur Humain et l'Accumulation de Sesquioxydes Libres dans les Sols Tropicaux, ibid., pp. 241–55.
For a criticism of the use of bush fallows and of shifting cultivation see F.A.O., Shifting Cultivation, *Unasylva*, **11**, 1957 and *Tropical Agriculture*, **34**, 1957, pp. 159–64.

[78] T. A. M. Nash, The Probable Effect of the Exclusion of Fire upon the Distribution of Tsetse in Northern Nigeria, *Farm and Forest*, **5**, 1944, pp. 8–12.

[79] Agricultural Department, Nigeria, *Annual Reports* for 1933 (p. 19) and 1936 (p. 24).

[80] C. F. Charter, The Mechanization of Peasant Agriculture and the Maintenance of Soil Fertility with Bush Fallows, *C.C.T.A. Conference on the Mechanisation of Agriculture*, Entebbe, June, 1955, paper published Kumasi 1955, pp. 2–3.

[81] E. W. Russell, The Fertility of Tropical Soils, *Conference of Directors and Senior Officers of Overseas Departments of Agriculture and Agricultural Institutions*, Wye College, 1958, paper No. 5.

[82] T. M. Greensill, The Application of Commercial Methods of Vegetable Growing in the Eastern Region of Nigeria, *Tropical Agriculture*, **33**, 1956, pp. 18–34.

[83] D. P. Hopkins, Fertilisers, *World Crops*, **17**(2), 1965, pp. 83–85.
H. L. Richardson, The Use of Fertilisers, *Symposium on Soil Resources of Tropical Africa*, African Studies Association of the United Kingdom, Sept. 1965 (to be published).
P. H. Nye and M. H. Bertheux, The Distribution of Phosphorus in Forest and Savannah Soils of the Gold Coast and its Agricultural Significance, *Journal of Agricultural Science*, **49**(2), 1957, pp. 141–59.

[84] W. D. McGregor, Anti-Erosion Operation at Udi, *Nigerian Forestry Department, Bulletin* 1, 1928, pp. 39–42.
J. R. Ainslie, Soil Erosion in Nigeria, *Empire Forestry Conference in South Africa*, paper printed in Kaduna, 1935.
R. A. Sykes, A History of the Anti-Erosion Work at Udi, *Farm and Forest*, **1**, 1940, pp. 3–6.

[85] E. P. Stebbing, The Encroaching Sahara: the Threat to the West African Colonies, *Geographical Journal*, **85**, 1935, pp. 506–24.
See also E. P. Stebbing, *The Forests of West Africa and the Sahara*, London, 1937.

[86] A. Grasovsky, A World Tour for the Study of Soil Erosion Control Methods, *Imperial Forestry Institute, Paper 14*, Oxford, 1938.
B. Jones, Desiccation and the West African Colonies, *Geographical Journal*, **91**, 1938, pp. 401–23.

[87] R. M. Prothero, Some Observations on Desiccation in North-Western Nigeria, *Erdkunde*, **16**, 1962, pp. 111–19.

[88] A. T. Grove, Land Use and Soil Conservation on the Jos Plateau, *Bulletin of the Geological Survey of Nigeria*, **22**, 1953.
Grove's work on problems of desiccation, water supplies, and on sand and agricultural distributions in Northern Nigeria is considerable. See also:
Land and Population in Katsina Province, Kaduna, 1957.
The Ancient Erg of Hausaland and Similar Formations on the Southern Side of the Sahara, *Geographical Journal*, **124**, 1961, pp. 528–33.

Population Densities and Agriculture in Northern Nigeria, in K. M. Barbour and R. M. Prothero (ed.), *Essays on African Population*, London, 1961, pp. 115–36.

[89] B. F. Johnston, Changes in Agricultural Productivity, in M. J. Herskovits and M. Harwitz (ed.), *Economic Transition in Africa*, London, 1964, pp. 151–78.

[90] T. M. Greensill, op. cit.
A. Chevalier, Sur une Entreprise Moderne des Environs de Dakar pour la Production des Fleurs d'Europe et des Légumes Difficiles à Réussir, *Revue Internationale de Botanique Appliquée et d'Agriculture Tropicale*, **30**, 1950, pp. 307–10.

[91] R. J. Harrison Church, Problems and Development of the Dry Zone of West Africa, *Geographical Journal*, **127**, 1961, pp. 187–204.
R. J. Harrison Church, Observations on Large-scale Irrigation Development in Africa, F.A.O., *Agricultural Economics Bulletin*, **4**, 1963.

[92] See L. Papy, La Vallée du Sénégal, in Problèmes Agricoles au Sénégal, *Etudes Sénégalaises*, Institut Français d'Afrique Noire, **2**, 1952.

[93] T. E. Tomlinson, Relationship between Mangrove Vegetation, Soil Texture and Reaction of Surface Soil after Empoldering Saline Swamps in Sierra Leone, *Tropical Agriculture*, **34**, 1957, pp. 41–50.
H. D. Jordan, The Development of Rice Research in Sierra Leone, *Tropical Agriculture*, **31**, 1954, pp. 27–32.

[94] U.S. Foreign Operations Administration, *Liberian Swamp Rice Production: a Success* Washington, 1955.

[95] For general discussion see: J. W. Y. Higgs, R. K. Kerkham and J. R. Raeburn, *Report of a Survey of Problems in the Mechanization of Native Agriculture in Tropical African Colonies*, Colonial Advisory Council of Agriculture, Animal Health and Forestry, Pub. No. 1, London, 1950.
J. E. Mayne, Progress in the Mechanization of Farming in the Colonial Territories – II, a Visit to the British Territories in West Africa, *Tropical Agriculture*, **32**, 1955, pp. 95–99.
H. P. White, Mechanised Cultivation of Peasant Holdings in West Africa, a Note, *Geography*, **43**, 1958, pp. 269–70.

[96] K. D. S. Baldwin, *The Niger Agricultural Project*, Oxford, 1957.

[97] R. Chateau, L'Utilisation de l'Avion en Riziculture à Richard-Toll, *Riz et Riziculture*, 1957, pp. 11–13.

[98] For a discussion of mechanized rice cultivation in Sierra Leone see J. W. D. Goodban, The Organisation and Economics of Rice Mechanisation in Sierra Leone, *Conference of Directors and Senior Officers of Overseas Departments of Agriculture and Agricultural Institutions*, Wye College, 1958, paper No. 15.

[99] C. F. Charter, op. cit. A successful use of mechanization in bush cultivation is discussed in V. Zelensky, Un Essai de Caféiculture Mécanisée en Moyenne Côte d'Ivoire, *Agronomie Tropicale*, **12**, 1957, pp. 7–66.

[100] J. Tricart, Deux Types de Production Agricole aux Environs d'Odienné (Haute Côte d'Ivoire), *Bulletin, Institut Français d'Afrique Noire*, **19**, ser. B, 1957, pp. 284–294.

[101] See, for example, W. B. Morgan, The Lower Shire Valley of Nyasaland: a Changing System of African Agriculture, *Geographical Journal*, **119**, 1953, pp. 459–569.

[102] A. Seager, Engineering Aspects of the Western Nigerian Farm Settlement Scheme, *World Crops*, **17**(3), 1965, pp. 20–27.
Ch. A. P. Takes, Problems of Rural Development in Southern Nigeria, *Tijdschrift van het Koninklijk Nederlandsch Aardrijkskundig Genootschap*, **81**(4), 1964, pp. 438–52.
G. J. O. Ojo, Trends Towards Mechanised Agriculture in Yorubaland, *Nigerian Geographical Journal*, **6**(2), 1963, pp. 116–29.
J. T. Coppock, Agricultural Developments in Nigeria, *Journal of Tropical Geography*, **23**, 1966, pp. 1–18.

For discussion of problems of school leavers and the development of agriculture see A. Callaway, Unemployment Among African School Leavers, *Journal of Modern African Studies*, **1**, 1963, pp. 351–71.

[103] F.A.O., Africa Survey, *Report on the Possibilities of African Rural Development in Relation to Economic and Social Growth*, Rome, 1962, p. 65.

[104] K. M. Buchanan and J. C. Pugh, op. cit., p. 116.
The role of yams in West Africa's economies is discussed in D. G. Coursey, The Role of Yams in West African Food Economies, *World Crops*, **17**(**2**), 1965, pp. 74–82.

[105] R. Galletti *et al.*, op. cit., p. 156.

[106] *Northern Nigeria Lands Committee*, 1910, Cd. 5102.
See also Lord Hailey, *An African Survey*, London, revised 1956, Chap. XI; Lord Hailey, *Native Administration in the British African Territories*, pt. III, London, 1951 (numerous references).

[107] Lord Hailey, 1956, op. cit., pp. 795–7.
The case for private enclosure and land resettlement in Nigeria is put in D. C. Igwe, The Need for Enclosure and Land Resettlement in Nigerian Agriculture, *Tropical Agriculture*, **31**, 1954, pp. 57–68. That for public or Government enclosure is put by H. A. Oluwasanmi, Land Tenure and Agricultural Improvement in Tropical Africa, *Journal of Farm Economy*, 1957.

[108] R. K. Udo, Disintegration of the Nucleated Settlement in Eastern Nigeria, *Geographical Review*, **55**, 1965, pp. 53–67.

The Development of Gathering, Fishing, Mining, Manufacturing and Commerce

The history of the European occupation of West Africa has been at least in part a history of the development and increasing importance of the non-agricultural and non-pastoral occupations. Something of the extent of those occupations and their contribution to the traditional economy before the European invasion has been shown. On the whole that contribution was small and concerned mainly with basic food-producing activities, such as gathering and fishing, or with the manufacture of textiles or the working of metals, chiefly for agricultural implements or weapons. Much traditional industry was only small-scale, expensive in labour and limited to local markets. Only the more valuable products, such as ivory, precious metals and drug-containing plants, could pay the cost of long-distance transport. The European revolution in transport, combined with the creation of larger political units with ordered government over great areas, promoted commerce, which in turn promoted the further development of many of the older occupations, and the introduction of several new means of production. In some areas the new frontiers, with their limited control of migration and their tariffs, hindered existing trade. In many areas the immediate result of conquest was the disappearance of some existing craft or industry in the face of competition from imported goods or the interference of alien promoters of new and larger enterprises. Yet on the whole the 'other occupations' have gained rather than lost over the past half century, and the general gain to the whole of West Africa, in the supply of cheaper goods reaching a wider market, and in the introduction of modern industrial and mining techniques, has been immense. One may regret the passing of many handicrafts and of much fine traditional workmanship, but one must appreciate the gains of a peasantry who in the past could purchase little more than the local market had to offer and their small surplus allowed. Traditional industries were, on the whole, closely related to the needs of agriculturalists, and, being small-scale, were widely distributed, and for the most part in rural locations. They were village crafts, and their character was no different even in the larger agglomerations of the Yoruba, Ashanti or Hausa. The new industries are associated mainly with the towns and especially with the sea ports. Their growth has thus helped to promote those urbanward and coastward trends of population movement which have already been discussed.

535

Hunting and gathering

The effect of the entry of Europeans on game was much less marked in West Africa than in East or South Africa. The higher population densities of West Africa must already have lowered animal densities, except in a few localities where population density was very low, or where slave-raiding reduced population sufficiently to allow game to increase. There was an extensive arms traffic as early as the 18th century, chiefly in flintlock guns, and this continued in the same weapons throughout the 19th century. This traffic increased hunting efficiency at an early date, yet few West Africans were able to afford or were permitted to own the more efficient sporting rifles developed in the 19th century. In consequence, excepting in some of the lower population density areas of the former French West Africa, there has not been the wholesale slaughter of wild life which has taken place in other parts of Africa, partly because there were few efficiently-armed hunters. There has long been a small export of 'elephants' teeth' or ivory, but taken almost entirely by African hunters, and only a little by Europeans. In the first half of the 19th century ivory was one of the more important exports amounting by 1841 to over 100 tons sent from the 'west coast' (including Gabon, the Congo basin and Angola) to Great Britain alone. In the 1830s, ivory collection was the main object of many trading voyages, and palm oil only a secondary consideration. The Ivory Coast with its low population densities and dense forest near the coastline, particularly in the south-west, was the chief source, although ivory was shipped from most West African ports.

Gathering has played a more important part in the development of overseas trade, and was for many territories in the 19th century the chief source of foreign currency. In Senegal and Mauritania, for example, the trade in gum arabic, gathered from acacias, led to the founding of French trading posts on the coast and on the banks of the Senegal river. The commercial foundations of St Louis, Portendik and Rufisque were in the gum trade, and it was their existence and the demand for oil-seeds in Europe, which, at a later stage, led to the traffic in ground-nuts.[1] Perhaps the most spectacular developments in the gathering of export produce were in the rubber industry, which enjoyed its first boom in the 1890s, followed by other booms in times of scarcity and high prices, notably in the two world wars. The chief sources of gathered rubber in West Africa were the vines, *Landolphia heudelotii* (chiefly in the savannas), *Landolphia owariensis* (a rain-forest vine), and *Clitandra cymulosa* (in the rain forests and savanna fringes – of good quality, but the latex was difficult to coagulate), and the trees, *Funtumia elastica* (the only true rubber tree of the rain forest) and *Ficus vogelii* (a source of poor-quality resinous rubber). Rubber was gathered and exported from numerous locations, particularly from areas of dense forest. Senegal, Guinea, Sierra Leone, Liberia, the Ivory Coast, Ghana, Togo, Dahomey and Nigeria were all producers. Latex from *Funtumia elastica* was of high quality and was known as 'Lagos Rubber', or if from Sierra Leone or the Ivory Coast as 'Manoh Twist' or 'Manoh Cube'. Some plantations of *Funtumia* were established, chiefly by Europeans, in Ghana, Nigeria and the Cameroons, but most rubber was obtained from wild trees. In southern Nigeria the rubber rush led to severe over-tapping and destruction of trees and vines, together with the abandonment of agricultural land and of the preparation of palm oil and kernels. There was insufficient labour to sustain both oil palm production and rubber tapping. As rubber boomed so oil palm produce declined (Fig. 11.1). 'Strangers' entered from surrounding districts and from as far away as Ghana, and sustained themselves in their camps by hunting, so that the numbers of wild animals were severely reduced.[2] Despite legislation and the work of forestry officers, the attempts to control rubber tapping were unsuccessful, and by 1899 it was estimated that 75 per cent of the rubber plants in the forests of the Lagos hinterland had been killed.[3] The small rubber boom of 1939 to 1944 affected chiefly the Ivory Coast, Guinea and Nigeria. So great was the need for rubber in Europe, that much low-grade material was accepted, including rubber from *Landolphia florida* and *Carpodinus hirsuta*, both of which yield an extremely resinous product, commonly used to adulterate higher-quality rubber.

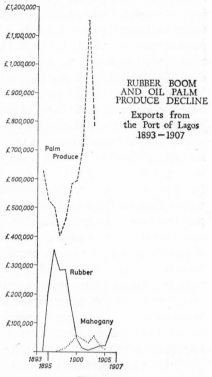

Figure 11.1

Probably the chief gathered product exported overseas today is piassava, the fibres obtained from the leaf-sheaths of the raphia or wine palm, and used chiefly for making brushes, brooms and mats. An important source is the coastal swamplands of Sierra Leone, the best quality being obtained from the Bonthe district where great care is taken over the preparation, especially the retting, of the fibres. Piassava is an important minor export of Sierra Leone – over 5000 tons in 1962, valued at some £245,000. Other gathered produce for export includes some palm oil and palm kernels; some kola nuts; shea butter and nuts, in which a small export trade developed before the last war, chiefly from Dahomey, Togo and Mali; gum copal from *Copaifera demeusei*; 'Guinea grains' or 'Grains of Paradise' (*Aframomum melegueta*), the gathered spice, exported chiefly from the Ivory Coast in the last century and earlier; beeswax; kapok from eight species of trees, but chiefly *Bombax buonopozense* in the savannas and *Ceiba pentandra* in Guinean secondary forest; and the red dyewoods, used chiefly to dye wool – Camwood (*Baphia nitida*) and barwood (*Pterocarpus soyauxii*).

Timber

The West African timber industry has hitherto had much in common with gathering, despite modern organization, and the construction of sawmills and plywood mills. The timbers for export are almost entirely obtained from self-sown species, and planted species such as teak and cassia are cut chiefly for the internal market. Undoubtedly the internal market for wood fuel and for building timber makes the heaviest demands on West African timber resources, and, as yet, planted trees in small timber or fuel lots make only a small contribution to the total. West African forestry departments have done much to promote the establishment of small wood fuel lots, chiefly of teak and cassia near the villages. Estimates of local cutting vary. One estimate from Nigeria was of a fuel wood consumption in the early 1950s of some 50 million tons a year for a population of about 30 millions.[4] With this heavy demand for wood fuel there is the problem of increasing urbanization, for as the towns increase in size and in their demand for fuel, so the distances from which wood must be fetched increase. Attempts have been made to control cutting by creating Forest Reserves or Forest Estates (see pp. 502–4), and it was estimated by 1953 that not less than 80 per cent of the trees felled in Nigeria on permit for commercial use came from outside the Forest Reserves. Regeneration has been promoted by the tropical shelterwood system of admitting light to the forest floor to encourage the growth of seedlings, and by taungya plantations in which tree seedlings are placed amongst crops.[5] Timber felling for the export trade concentrates chiefly on softwoods valued for the manufacture of plywoods and veneers and for making crates and boxes, and on harder woods suitable for cabinet making, for constructional purposes, or for special purposes such as the manufacture of handles for pick-axes or hammers. Costs are high, for in the rain forest, where most cutting takes place, normally only two or three valuable timber species are found per acre, and the trees required are difficult to find and identify. The species are, moreover, very unevenly distributed, and transport costs are considerable. The four most important timber exporters in West Africa are Ghana, the Western and Mid-West Regions of Nigeria and the Ivory Coast. Of these, Ghana, the largest producer, must move all its timber to port by railway or road. In the Ivory Coast and Nigeria some of the logs at least may be floated down streams or along coastal creeks or lagoons. It was fortunate for the Ghanaian industry that the port of Takoradi was so favourably located for timber exploitation. Again the commercial timbers of West Africa are generally slow-growing, and are difficult to replace. Estimates generally allow 80 to 100 years for growth to maturity of many of the trees. Plantings are few and in pure stands only for exotics. The mahoganies or *Khaya* spp., for example, are thought to be best planted with a mixture of *Erythrophleum* and teak.[6] Approximately half of the total African export of timber comes from West Africa and of that proportion more than half comes from Ghana and a little over a quarter from the Western Region of Nigeria. The main export is of softwoods. By value the cabinet woods for which West Africa is noted are of much less importance today than they have been in the past. Most of the timber is exported as logs, but there is an increasing export of sawn wood, especially from Ghana, and plywood and veneers, chiefly from Nigeria.[7] The greatest demand is in Western Europe where the market is still generally for logs in order partly to maintain existing mills. High-value logs have been preferred, and the development of an export of the cheaper softwoods has thus helped to promote the construction of West African sawmills.

The chief species of value in the timber trade are:

CABINET WOODS

Mahogany or Acajou	*Khaya anthotheca, K. grandifoliola, K. ivorensis, K. senegalensis* – chief species exploited is *K. ivorensis,* mainly in Ghana and Ivory Coast
Mahogany or Sapele wood	*Entandrophragma candollei, E. cylindricum, E. macrophyllum, E. rederi, E. utile* – the chief commercial species are *E. cylindricum* and *E. utile*
Makoré	*Mimusops heckelii*
Guarea	*Guarea cedrata*
Avodiré	*Turraeanthus africana*
Iroko or Invule	*Chlorophora excelsa, C. regia*
African Blackwood	*Dalbergia melanoxylon*
West African ebony	*Diospyros mespiliformis*

VERY HARD WOODS

Azobé or Ekki	*Lophira procera,* used chiefly for pit props and building
Kusia or Opepe	*Nauclea diderrichii*
Denya or Okan	*Cylicodiscus gabunensis*
Sasswood or Erun	*Erythrophleum guineense* ($= E.$ *suaveolens), E. ivorense*

MEDIUM WOODS

Red cedar, Niangon or Nyankom	*Tarrietia utilis*
African walnut or Dibétou	*Lovoa trichiloides*
Papao, Apa or Lingué	*Afzelia africana*
Satin wood, Black Afara, Idigbo or Framiré	*Terminalia ivorensis*
Bété	*Mansonia altissima*
Moringui or Ayan	*Distemonanthus benthamianus*
Dahoma	*Piptadeniastrum africanum*

SOFTWOODS

Limbo or White Afara	*Terminalia superba*
Obeche or Samba	*Triplochiton scleroxylon,* one of the chief timbers for crates, boxes and plywoods and the chief wood exported from Nigeria by value
Agba or White Tola	*Gossweilerodendron balsamiferum*
Bahia or Abura	*Mitragyna ciliata,* a marsh-loving tree
Ilomba or 'White Cedar'	*Pycnanthus kombo*
Silk Cotton	*Ceiba pentandra,* light, easily worked, used for paper pulp in the Ivory Coast
Umbrella Tree	*Musanga smithii*; used for paper pulp in the Ivory Coast, propagated in pure stands by layering
Copaiba balsam or Sandan	*Daniellia oliveri*; suitable for packing cases, widespread in the southern savannas

Fishing

The creation of improved trading conditions led not only to the expansion of commercial agriculture but to the expansion of commercial fishing. Particularly favoured locations have developed very large markets in fish and fish products, using mainly traditional methods, but supplying distant centres, chiefly by road. Thus large fishing industries have grown in the Inland Niger delta of Mali, on the shores of Lake Chad and on the coasts particularly of Senegal, Ghana, the Ivory Coast and Nigeria. Wherever there is a wealthier peasantry close at hand, the fishing industry has flourished, and this is particularly the case in Senegal and in Ghana. The growth of the fishing industry in favoured locations and the extension of their market areas have not, however, reduced local fishing output by competition. The industry is highly seasonal, and there is a considerable locational variation in season of maximum haul as already discussed (pp. 158–62). Again the market for fish is enormous, for it provides a source of animal protein which, in many places, is cheaper than meat. Hence the considerable fish import into West Africa, with which a more rationalized West African industry may hope to compete.

With the great increase in the size of fish market hinterlands, the need to preserve fish has increased, and in most areas preservation by drying, smoking or salting has become a considerable industry. Traders have tended to form syndicates, pooling their capital resources and purchasing or hiring lorries. Thus the Lake Chad fisheries of Bornu now sell mainly to syndicates of Ibo traders, who send smoked fish by road and railway as far south as the Eastern Region. A similar large-scale export of smoked and dried fish takes place from the Inland Niger delta of Mali to Upper Volta and Ghana. The fishermen themselves frequently form groups, or work for a company. In the coastal fisheries motor vessels are coming more into use, and for marketing purposes and the protection of their interests many of the 'smaller' fishermen have preferred to join co-operatives. Co-operatives have been particularly well developed in Ghana, where, in recent years, the incomes and profits from fishing have become smaller. The most extreme case, and perhaps the most successful, of co-operation in fishing is provided, however, by the community of Aiyetoro in Nigeria. Here belief in apostolic Christianity has led to the sharing amongst the 3000 members of the community of all profits from fishing. The result is a communally run township with free food and electricity in which no money is credited to individuals.

Deep-sea fishing on a large scale has been attempted so far only by European vessels off the coast of Mauritania and Senegal, and chiefly for North Atlantic fish off the 'Grande Côte' north of the Kayar trough. Port Etienne has been developed to serve the needs of some of these vessels. Off the 'Petite Côte', West African fisheries proper have been developed since 1955 for the 'thon' (albacore or tuna), chiefly by Bretons and Basques. The catch is frozen in Dakar and sent by refrigerator vessels to France.[8] Fish processing, including drying white fish and the treatment of sharks, takes place at Port Etienne, St Louis, Dakar, M'Bour, Joal and Sangomar, and with the canning and freezing industry of Dakar commercialization of fishing has proceeded further in Senegal and Mauritania than anywhere else in West Africa. Similar developments have begun to take place in Ghana, where the size of the market warrants a considerable expansion of the industry, and some commercialization has begun in Sierra Leone and in the Ivory Coast. In Ghana five new fishing harbours have been built at Tema, Elmina, Takoradi, Miamia and Ada, and refrigeration facilities have been provided.[9] Fishing vessels are being built at Sekondi and trawlers have been bought from Britain and the U.S.S.R. A more rationalized industry may, however, require less labour, and one observer forecast that the developments at Tema must spell economic disaster on the Fanti coast.[10] Government interest in promoting the fishing industry expressed itself as early as 1945, with the creation of a research station at Accra and in 1949 of a Fisheries Department. The most recent development is a survey of the possibilities for tuna fishing within 1000 miles (1600 km) of Tema by a Californian firm on behalf of the Government. Other surveys and studies have been undertaken by Russian and Japanese experts. In Sierra Leone a Fisheries Development Officer was appointed as early as 1943, when a Brixham smack was purchased to develop the marine fisheries. In 1949 a trawler was acquired and a cold storage plant erected in Freetown. In Nigeria a fishing harbour has been established at Lagos, and the catch is canned, frozen or used to manufacture fertilizer.

An equally important development has been the great improvement since 1945 in the fishing techniques of the great majority of small independent fishermen. These include the use of improved lines and hooks, nylon nets with better designed mesh, and outboard motors for canoes. The attachment of motors to small fishing vessels has greatly extended their range and speed, and reduced the numbers of men needed to operate them.

In many territories fresh-water fishing has been promoted by Government development schemes. Perhaps the most important of these has been the attempt to promote fish farming by creating large ponds behind earth dams. In Northern Nigeria, for example, such ponds are about 6 feet (2 metres) deep and have been established entirely by hand labour. The ponds have been stocked with *Tilapia*, which have a sufficiently rapid rate of growth, and care has been taken to avoid location on laterite with the possibility of iron contamination, and to have water as alkaline as possible.[11] It is hoped that the construction of the Volta dam will lead to the development of the largest fresh-water fisheries scheme in West Africa, for the new lake will have an area of over 2000 square miles (5200 sq km).

Mining

It was not until the late 19th century, when the colonies were created, that mining developed under European supervision. Previously Europeans obtained West African minerals solely by trade, and their influence was reduced to stimulating an existing industry, chiefly in the production of gold. The importance of the gold traffic may be measured by the density of trading posts on the Gold Coast, and the struggles there for trading supremacy compared with other locations. Some very early attempts to develop European gold mines were made in both the Gold Coast and at Bambouk on the upper Falémé, but all failed. The first successful European mining operation began at Tarkwa in the Gold Coast in 1878. At first European mining operations differed little from traditional mining, except in their scale and their dependence on an overseas market. Hand labour was used for all operations, and often the ores had to be head-loaded. Workings were frequently on the site of existing mines or quarries. In many cases traditional mining was either displaced by competition, usually of imported metals, or was removed by legislation, where this could be enforced. In some cases, where traditional mining already depended on the overseas market, competition from other mines overseas, able to produce more cheaply, removed the industry, and in other cases ores were either worked out, or worked to a point where the costs became too high.

IRON ORE

Iron ores are widespread in West Africa, but are particularly abundant wherever lateritic crusts have been formed on metamorphic rocks. Many of these occurrences have a high iron content when compared, for example, with the Liassic ores of Western Europe, but are too remote from markets to be worth working. Until recently all major workings depended on access to a port able to provide ore-loading facilities, but it seems likely that in the near future attempts will be made to develop modern iron and steel manufacture in West Africa, and this may alter the evaluation of existing ore bodies. The import during the last century of hoop iron from Western Europe almost entirely destroyed the existing iron industry, and until the demand for overseas ores increased in Europe and

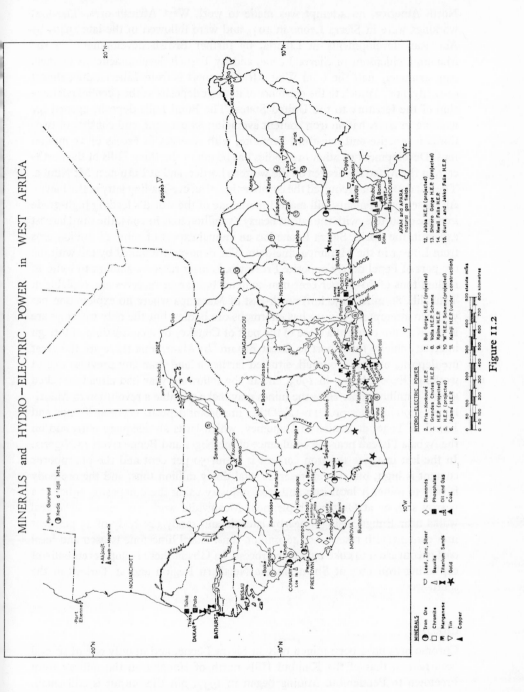

MINERALS and HYDRO—ELECTRIC POWER in WEST AFRICA

MINERALS

- ◉ Iron Ore
- ☐ Chromite
- ☒ Manganese
- ▽ Tin
- ▲ Copper
- ◁ Lead, Zinc, Silver
- ◮ Bauxite
- ◭ Titanium Sands
- ★ Gold
- ◇ Diamonds
- ◈ Phosphates
- ◭ Oil and Gas
- ▲ Coal

HYDRO—ELECTRIC POWER

2. Fria–Konkouré H.E.P.
3. Grandes Chutes H.E.P.
4. H.E.P. (projected)
5. H.E.P. Scheme (projected)
6. Ayamé H.E.P.
7. Bui Gorge H.E.P. (projected)
8. Volta H.E.P. Scheme
9. Kpime H.E.P.
10. 'W' H.E.P. Scheme (projected)
11. Kainji H.E.P. (under construction)
12. Jebba H.E.P. (projected)
13. Shiroro Gorge H.E.P. (projected)
14. Kwali Falls H.E.P.
15. Kurra and Jekko Falls H.E.P.

AFAM and APARA natural gas fields

0 50 100 200 300 400 500 statute miles

0 50 100 200 300 400 500 600 700 800 kilometres

Figure 11.2

North America, no attempt was made to work West African ores. The first workings were in Sierra Leone in 1933 and were followed in the late 1940s by American developments in Liberia, by further British developments in the Marampa chiefdom of Sierra Leone, and by French developments in Guinea. Approximately half the total West African export is from Liberia, due, almost certainly, not so much to the existence of its large deposits as the peculiar relationship of the territory to the United States. The Bomi Hills deposit, opened for working in 1951, has an iron content averaging 68 per cent, and consists of two-thirds magnetite and one-third hematite, with reserves in excess of 35 million tons. Development of other ore bodies has begun in the Bong Hills of the north-east, in the Mano River area on the western border, and at Putu near Mt Nimba. The last deposit has required the construction of an ore-loading jetty at Buchanan. All these developments will make Liberia one of the world's leading high-grade iron ore exporters, with the sale of nearly 15 million tons in 1965, the third largest export in the world. Sierra Leone has an annual export of some $1\frac{1}{2}$ million tons from Lunsar in the Marampa chiefdom. The deposits are linked by rail with the ore port of Pepel nearly opposite Freetown. Lunsar reserves amount to some 20 million tons of 60–65 per cent iron content, but larger reserves are available at Tonkolili, 80 miles (130 km) north-east of Marampa where no exploitation has yet been attempted. Guinea has enormous ore bodies, but the only workings are in the Kaloum peninsula close to the port of Conakry by a consortium of foreign interests, chiefly for export to Great Britain. In Mauritania there are the great ore deposits of Fort Gouraud, situated farther inland than any previous export working. Export began in 1963, and in the following year had already reached almost 5 million tons. Here the mines may make possible a revolution in Mauritania's economy (see pp. 711–12). Other important deposits occur at Kompa and Kandi in Togo, at Banjeli in Dahomey, which lacks an adequate port, and on the Agbaja Plateau near the confluence of the Niger and Benue rivers in Nigeria. In the last instance the iron content is about 50 per cent and the phosphorus content is high, but proven reserves total thirty million tons, and the ore body is easy to mine. A local iron and steel industry using these deposits, either at a nearby site, or at Onitsha, is planned. Meanwhile work has begun on a steel works near Enugu, using a nearby lateritic and sandy ore body of 43 per cent iron content with reserves of 46 million tons. Local limestone is used and local coal is converted to coke by a new process. In Ghana there is hope eventually of exploiting iron ores at Shiene in the Northern Region and at Tarkwa in the south-west.

CHROME

Chrome ores have been mined only in Sierra Leone, and in only one of several occurrences, that of the Kambui Hills north of Hangha on the railway from Freetown to Pendembu. Mining began in 1937, but the output is still small, amounting in 1962 to about 4000 tons of about 44 per cent chrome content, and shipped mostly to the United States. Other chrome ore occurrences are known in both Togo and Dahomey.

MANGANESE

Ghana is the chief West African exporter of manganese, with an output of some 250,000 tons a year, nearly all from the Nsuta mine near Tarkwa. Mining began in 1917, due to wartime demands in Great Britain for manganese steels. The workings had the advantage of being located close to a railway, and only 40 miles (65 km) from the new port of Takoradi. At Grand Lahou in the Ivory Coast, however, manganese workings which began an export in 1960 are already producing over 100,000 tons a year.

TIN

The only major tin workings in West Africa are in the Jos Plateau of Nigeria, although other smaller workings occur in the Northern Region at Liruei-n-Kano and Nassarawa, and in the Aïr Plateau of Niger. The occurrence of tin mining in Bauchi Emirate, for the production of 'straw tin', was discovered in 1884, and an expedition was sent to the Jos Plateau in 1902.[12] A tin 'rush' developed when prospecting licences were taken out for 3186 square miles (8251 sq km) of territory by 70 companies and subsidiary societies. At first the tin was head-loaded to Loko on the Benue, but a light railway was completed to Bukuru on the tin-fields from the main line at Zaria in 1914. The earliest workings were in valley alluvium, but that source was soon exhausted. Today most workings are in old alluvial deposits, lying under a thick overburden of clay or earth, or even under lava. Most excavation is by drag lines, hydraulic rams and gravel pumps. Water has to be strictly conserved in the long dry season, and there is only one dredge working. Hand-working still accounts for a large proportion of the production. Power is supplied by four hydro-electric installations constructed by a private company. Nigerian production of tin concentrates has been about 10,000 tons a year (1964: just under 9000 tons – second in Africa to the Belgian Congo), but output is at least partially governed by international agreement. The policy has been to prolong the life of the workings rather than take undue advantage of boom conditions. When tin prices were high in the early 1950s, many of the Nigerian mining concerns worked their least accessible ores, and reserved their more accessible for the anticipated period of lower prices. In 1961 the Makeri tin smelter on the Jos Plateau began to treat the greater part of Nigerian concentrates, so that today Nigeria exports chiefly tin metal.

COLUMBITE, PYROCHLORE, TUNGSTEN AND RADIO-ACTIVE MINERALS

The only major workings of these minerals have been on the Jos Plateau, where they occur either in association with tin, or nearby in isolated occurrences, or in association with other minerals. Nigeria supplies 80 per cent of the world's supply of columbite, with an export of some 2000 tons a year. Only very small quantities are needed to manufacture special heat-resisting steels. Practically all the columbite exported is separated from tin by washing and other methods of sorting at the tin workings, but columbite also occurs in the Jos Plateau in association with wolfram, and at Egbe in Kabba Province in association with tantalite. Tungsten has been worked from 1934, reaching a production peak of an estimated 155 tons of tungsten content in 1939. After the war production virtually ceased, but was resumed again from 1951 to 1953 with an average annual output of 13 tons. Pyrochlore occurs in a number of deposits, the chief of which is in the granites of Liruei-n-Kano. Niobium and uranium also occur in the granites of Jos and Liruei-n-Kano, but workings must depend at present on a considerable rise in world market prices.

COPPER

Until recently the only copper workings in West Africa were in two small deposits in Sierra Leone and the Ivory Coast. It was known as early as 1931 that there was a vast ore body at Akjoujt in Mauritania, but it was not until 1948 that a syndicate was formed to begin operations. In 1953 a mining company was formed, and the work of boring for water and of railway construction began. The Akjoujt copper ores are estimated to consist of some 8 million tons of cupricoxide and 17 million tons of copper pyrites. They are located near enough to the railway to Ford Gouraud from Port Etienne to make linkage by a branch line possible, although export by rail via Nouakchott has been suggested. Other copper and iron deposits are located near Akjoujt, and provide Mauritania with a great northern minerals zone whose development will depend mainly on port facilities, access to a railway and local water supplies.

LEAD, ZINC AND SILVER

The chief lead, zinc and silver deposits occur at Abakaliki and Zurak in Nigeria. The Abakaliki deposits extend for some 350 miles (560 km) in a broad belt through Benue, Ogoja and Adamawa Provinces. Recent production began in 1957 with an output of some 1000 tons of ore. The main problem is to develop cheap transport to the railway to Port Harcourt. High costs forced the cessation of earlier workings in 1932. The Zurak lode in Adamawa was discovered in 1928 and workings continued until 1937 when operations were hindered by faulting at depth.[13] Again transport costs, by lorry to the Kudu river and canoe to Lokoja, were high. Other lead–zinc ores in Nigeria include a lode at Tozali in Muri and another at Orofu, about 40 miles (65 km) south of Ibi on the Benue river where African workings were closed down by the Nigerian Government.[14]

BAUXITE

Guinea is at present the largest producer of bauxite in West Africa, and may well remain so if plans for the extension of production are completed. Ghana, however, is also a major producer, and with the completion of the Volta River Project may even lead in output. The bauxite deposits of the Iles de Los were discovered in 1912, but major excavation was not begun until 1949. The workings are easy to operate by the use of powered shovels, and Kassa provides a deep-water port. The ores are mostly shipped to Canada for processing. With an output of some 400,000 tons a year and reserves of only 9 million tons, the Los deposits are expected to last only until about 1975. Vast new deposits have, however, been discovered at Fria, in the Kindia–Dabola area, and at Sangaridi, near Boké. Work has begun on the development of new mines, railways, harbour works, hydro-electric and alumina plant by an international consortium at Fria (see p. 684). In 1962 Guinea exported 1,370,000 tons of bauxite and nearly 400,000 tons of alumina.

Ghana probably has some 234 million tons of workable bauxite altogether 200 million tons of which are in cappings some 20 to 50 feet (6–15 metres) in thickness on the hills near Yenahin, about 40 miles (65 km) west of Kumasi. At Awaso some 30 million tons of bauxite are being worked in deposits 70 feet (21 metres) thick and the ore sent by rail to Takoradi. Output is about 250,000 tons a year of ore, averaging 53 per cent aluminium content. The only other major deposit is of 4 million tons at Mount Ejuanema near Nkawkaw. However, the smelter at Tema will depend on imported alumina, probably until about 1975. The ultimate capacity of the Tema smelter, using entirely local ores, is intended to be 210,000 tons of aluminium ingots a year.

TITANIUM

Titanium sands containing ilmenite and zirconium occur on the western coasts from the Cape Verde peninsula at least as far south as the Casamance river. Workings were begun in Senegal in the Second World War, and production rose to over 13,000 tons a year, but has now markedly declined. A small deposit was being worked at Cape St Mary in the Gambia, but has been worked out. It was linked with Bathurst by 15 miles (24 km) of railway, the only line in the Gambia. In Sierra Leone ilmenite deposits occur in the Freetown peninsula and in the gravels of the Little Scarcies, but have not yet been worked.

GOLD

Ghana is the only considerable gold exporter in West Africa (fifth in the world in 1965 with an export worth nearly £11,000,000 or $31,000,000), but there have been numerous other workings in Mali, Dahomey, Sierra Leone, Nigeria and Liberia. Most of these used traditional methods, and much of the output was panned from stream gravels. Since the war, whilst the Ghanaian output has slightly increased, the output of the other territories has declined to only minute proportions, although, in addition to export, there is some small production of gold for the internal jewellery industry. In Ghana modern mining operations began mainly in the 1880s, and were chiefly in the 'banket' or conglomerate deposits of Tarkwa and the alluvial deposits of the Ankobra river. Despite the nearness of these deposits to port, production was greatly stimulated by the completion of the railway from Sekondi to Tarkwa in 1901. A major problem was the acquisition of labour. Mining was not popular, and higher wages could be earned from time to time in railway construction or in the cocoa-growing districts. At first Kru and Fanti labourers were chiefly employed, but after the conquest of Ashanti it was possible to import labour from the Northern Territories and Upper Volta, chiefly Mossi. The chief lode or quartz mines are at Obuasi, Prestea, Bibiani and Konongo. Obuasi has been the largest single producer in the past, although other centres are more important today. Generally the ores are of high grade, and the mines relatively shallow. As older workings decline, new ore bodies have been developed so that output has been maintained.

DIAMONDS

Ghana is second in the world in the quantity of diamonds produced, but low in total value, for 90 per cent of the stones produced are industrial. In 1963 Ghanaian production was 2·7 million carats, compared with production in Sierra Leone of 1·7 million. But, with a higher proportion of gemstones, the Sierra Leone export was worth rather more than that of Ghana. Liberia has an export of just under 1 million carats, mainly of industrial quality, and mostly from districts near the Sierra Leone border. With a large estimated loss of diamonds from the Sierra Leone workings, it seems likely that a proportion of the Liberian export is of Sierra Leone origin. Again some of the Sierra Leone diamonds may find their way to Guinea, which has a small export, about half of which are industrial, and obtained chiefly from Kissidougou and Beyla in the south-east. The Ivory Coast also has a small, fluctuating production (200,000 carats, almost entirely of industrial quality, in 1964). Most diamond workings are alluvial, and many are operated by hand. In Ghana the first discovery in the Birrim valley was in 1919, and three years later diamonds were also found in the Bonsa valley near Tarkwa. Whilst the Bonsa workings are operated by Africans using very simple methods, the Birrim valley gravels are excavated and sorted mechanically by four European companies, who produce a little less than half the total output. In Sierra Leone the diamonds also occur in river gravels, chiefly in the Sewa and Moa drainage basins in the east. There are some important workings where the railway crosses the Sewa and Moa valleys, but the most extensive diamond panning operations take place in the valleys of the head-streams of the Sewa, chiefly in the Sefadu district. Proximity to Guinea and Liberia has been a major problem so long as one company, the Sierra Leone Selection Trust, was able to claim a monopoly. Failure to apply effective control led to illicit digging on an enormous scale. Recent action by the Sierra Leone Government, removing the monopoly and licensing African diggers has, however, altered the position (see pp. 714–15). In Guinea the first diamond discoveries were in 1934, again alluvial, and the stones are recovered chiefly by hand-workings organized by European companies.

PLATINUM

Only a little platinum has so far been mined in West Africa, and that chiefly from the stream gravels of the Freetown peninsula at York and Hastings. Mining began in 1929, the first mineral working in Sierra Leone. After 1935 returns declined, and by 1949 mining had ceased.

PHOSPHATES

Three important phosphate deposits are being worked in West Africa: a tri-calcium deposit at Akoumapé, between Lomé and Anécho in Togo, a calcium deposit at Taika, 70 miles (113 km) from Dakar, in Senegal, and an aluminium phosphate deposit at Pallo near Thiès, also in Senegal. Shipments from Akoumapé began only in 1961, but in 1965 were the largest from any one source in West Africa at 982,000 tons. In 1964 Senegal exported 702,000 tons of calcium phosphate, 95,000 tons of aluminium phosphate and 17,500 tons of dehydrated aluminium phosphate. The production map has changed considerably since 1960 when the only major deposit was at Pallo.

With marked phosphate deficiencies in many West African soils, applications of a suitable phosphatic fertilizer should be of benefit to agriculture. In many cases the problem hitherto has been the high cost of artificial fertilizers, particularly when imported. In certain areas a local fertilizer industry may reduce costs, and the hope of improving productivity by promoting the use of fertilizers has led to the application by some governments of fertilizer subsidies.

OILS AND BITUMENS

Exploration for oil is taking place throughout West Africa, for there is a number of extensive basins of sedimentary rocks where oil occurrences are possible. The largest of these is in southern Nigeria between the old metamorphic blocs of Yorubaland in the west and the Cameroons in the east. Here the only major oil strikes so far have been made, and oil production began in the Niger delta in both the Eastern and Mid-Western Regions of Nigeria. Bitumen and oil traces were observed on Mahin beach in 1884, and attempts were made to explore for oil at Agabu near Okitipupa in 1907. At present the most important oilfields are at Oloibiri, Bomu and Ebubu connected by pipe-line with Port Harcourt, and an offshore field near Soku at the mouth of the Escravos river. Over £60 million

T

were spent on exploration before the first well began to produce in 1956. Production costs are high, but the oil has the advantage of being free from sulphur. Port facilities are poor, and large tankers cannot reach Port Harcourt. An ocean terminal has been built at Bonny, linked by pipe-line with Bomu, although even at Bonny dredging has been necessary to allow tankers as small as 18,000 tons to pass fully loaded over the bar. Production was nearly 6 million tons in 1964. Part of the oil is refined at Eleme near Port Harcourt for the Nigerian market. Oil consumption in Nigeria, as in most West African countries, has been increasing rapidly in recent years, not only to supply the enormous expansion in road transport, but also the dieselization of the railways and the use of diesel electricity generators, chiefly for stand-by purposes or for small local electricity 'markets'. Natural gas has been found at Afam and Apara in Eastern Nigeria and is being used to generate electricity and for industrial purposes on the Trans-Amadi estate. A small export of gas to Britain has been made, using a special tanker. In addition, the gas has an important potential for ammonia and nitrate manufacture. Exploration is progressing, particularly elsewhere in the Niger delta, and beyond it, even up to seven miles (11 km) offshore, in the southern sediments of the Western Region, and to a limited extent in the Northern Region, where the great geological basins of Sokoto and Bornu offer possibilities. In the Ivory Coast and Ghana there is a sedimentary basin extending from Eboinda to Bonyere, where drilling began as early as 1895. Only indications, however, have so far been found, and modern larger-scale exploration did not commence until 1956. At Eboinda bitumen-bearing sands in beds between three and ten feet (1–3 metres) in thickness were worked from 1942 to 1946, and since 1952. Oil traces have also been found in the great sedimentary basin of Senegal, where some exploration is now taking place, and not only in Senegal, but also in the Gambia. Bituminous schists were also found in Mali north of Gao, when a bore was made for water on the trans-Saharan route to Colomb-Béchar.

COAL

There is a general absence of Carboniferous strata in West Africa. Lower Carboniferous limestones occur in the north in the basins of Tindouf and Taoudenni, and some Carboniferous sediments occur between Cape Coast and Dixcove in Ghana. Coal of Upper Cretaceous age was first found in the valley of the Ofam river near Udi in the Eastern Region of Nigeria in 1909. The Udi coalfield was proved in 1912, and by 1915 operations had begun. In 1916 the Eastern Railway from Port Harcourt to Enugu was completed, and coal was supplied to the Nigerian and Gold Coast railways. Nigerian coals are non-coking (although a new process, it has been claimed, will be able to coke some of them) and sub-bituminous, and can be made to yield gas and tar-oils. Reserves are estimated at over 60 million tons. Six seams occur in structures gently inclined upwards to the east, and underlying a cuesta, whose eastward-facing escarpment permits adit mining. The two central seams are conjoint with a total thickness of five yards (4½ metres), and are the only seams worked. Until the introduction of modern coal-cutting machinery in the Hayes mine, mining was done entirely by hand labour, recruited from amongst the Ibo of the surrounding densely-populated districts. Difficulties include a superabundance of water, and the fact that the associated Cretaceous sandy limestones and sandstones are very soft and crumble easily, making mining conditions hazardous. Over half the coal produced is used by the railway, and the rest is divided chiefly between the Electricity Corporation of Nigeria and exports. Reduction in railway demands with dieselization were offset, until 1958, by increased demands for electricity generation. Since then there has been additional competition from natural gas, and output declined from 925,000 tons in 1958 to less than 700,000 tons in 1964. The lower coal measures have been traced northwards from Enugu to Ankpa in the Kabba Province of the Northern Region, and there are several known occurrences of workable seams, giving an estimated reserve in the Northern Region (Kabba and Benue Provinces) of some 180 million tons. Poorer quality upper coal measure seams occur in the plateau west of the Enugu escarpment, and younger Cretaceous coals occur in the Gombe Division of Bauchi Province, also in the Northern Region.

Extensive lignite deposits of Eocene age occur in the Mid-West and Eastern Regions between Ubiaja and Nnewi, and in Benin Province. The Benin reserves are estimated at some 72 million tons, and the seams are thickest (about 20 feet (6 metres)) near Asaba. They may be developed for chemical purposes, but with both coal and oil resources there is little need in the immediate future. Other lignites have been proved in the Tahoua and Tanout regions of Niger, near Ouagadougou in the Upper Volta, and in Sierra Leone, where with treatment they might be used for fuel on the railways, or be developed for electricity generation.

LIMESTONE

Outcrops of limestone, of a quality suitable for cement manufacture or for building purposes, are few in West Africa. Most limestone occurrences are of Cretaceous age or younger, and are frequently soft or liable to crumble. The demand for cement for building purposes is, however, already considerable, and growing rapidly, as more permanent housing than that offered by traditional methods is preferred. Moreover, building in concrete has a technique not so dissimilar in essence from building in clay, and is fairly easy to adapt to indigenous practice. The oldest cement works in West Africa is at Bargny near Rufisque in Senegal, with an output from marly limestones of some 80,000 tons a year. In the Eastern Region of Nigeria a cement works at Nkalagu near Enugu with a capacity of 100,000 tons a year began production in 1957, and already new works have been built, not only in the Eastern Region, but in both the Northern and Western Regions, at Takoradi in Ghana and at Bobo Dioulasso in Upper Volta.

CLAYS

West Africa has a great abundance of clays, worked for millennia as building materials and as the raw material for pottery and statuary. Until recently workings have been small-scale, but the demand for building bricks has increased, although not to the same extent as for cement, and brick-works have been established with both European and African capital in most territories. A few attempts have been made to develop local pottery industries, to produce a greater variety of products, or to produce more abundantly. European glazing and firing techniques have been introduced. More modern pottery has been produced at Abuja in the Northern Region and at Ado-Ekiti in the Western Region, whilst at Ikorodu near Lagos there is a mechanized ceramics plant established in 1953. China clay is worked on a small scale in the Jos Plateau, and a little is sent by rail to Ikorodu.

GLASS SANDS

Glass sands are being sought in several localities in Northern Nigeria. So far only the sands of Port Harcourt in Eastern Nigeria have been exploited, for the manufacture of beer bottles.

Development of water resources

Numerous references have already been made to the use and development of water resources for agriculture, fishing and transport, and to the digging of wells and boreholes (pp. 449–50). However, at this point a brief survey is required of the recent development of water resources for domestic and industrial purposes. Traditional methods of obtaining a domestic water supply normally require considerable carrying, and for the most part depend on streams or rivers with some additional supply from catch-pits. Such sources of water all too frequently proved sources of disease, particularly in densely-populated areas. In large towns, unless a considerable stream were near, great distances had to be walked to the various sources of supply, and in most cases settlements were established on hill-tops or plateau surfaces, well away from permanent streams. Wells were dug, particularly in the sedimentary basins of the Saharan fringe, but well maintenance and the digging of new wells depended on slave labour. Recent attempts to stabilize the moving population of many northern districts, and to use cultivable land in areas lacking dry season water supplies, have demanded the digging of wells and boreholes by modern methods. The growing urbanism has called for piped water supplies, even though in most cases the taps, stand pipes or 'water points' are public, and have to be shared between many houses. Reservoirs have been made for most of the larger towns, and in some cases there is an attempt at biological control of water purity, or at filtration, or both. The reservoirs have proved a notable addition to the landscape, particularly in the cases where their surrounds have been 'landscaped', and gardens made. However, with all these improvements the magnitude of the work to be undertaken may be appreciated from the fact that only the very few capital cities or large ports have a supply with a capacity over 30 gallons (140 litres) per head daily. Many large towns have less than 10 gallons (45 litres) per head and population is increasing far faster than new capacity is being created. Thus in Lagos, for example, in 1959 a capacity of 12 million gallons (55,000 cubic metres) daily could supply 44 gallons (200 litres) per head to 272,000 people. In 1963 a capacity of 18 million gallons (82,000 cubic metres) could supply only 27 gallons (122 litres) per head to 675,000 people. Even an earlier estimate of 450,000 population would have meant a slightly reduced supply, at a time of greatly increased industrial demand. An extra capacity of some 6 million gallons (27,000 cubic metres) is being constructed, but even this will only bring daily per head supplies to 36 gallons (164 litres). Industrial development in West Africa will call for large quantities of water, and their supply will be a costly undertaking for authorities which are far from wealthy, and which, in several cases, need to bring water from considerable distances, or have physical problems of storage, or problems of maintaining water purity.

Generally the water supply position is easier in the south with a longer rainy season. In the northern districts enormous reservoirs are needed for storage of water for periods of six months or more, and unless these reservoirs are covered there is a considerable loss by evaporation. In such cases underground water supplies, as at Dakar, will be preferred, but there are limits to such resources, and not every densely-populated district is situated on or near a sedimentary basin. With the general lack of piped water, there is also a lack of modern sanitation and methods of sewage disposal. Lagos, like the few other towns with modern amenities in West Africa, has somewhat better provision, and a firm of consultants has been employed to investigate the possibility of installing a public system. Generally modern sewage disposal has meant simply septic tanks for the housing of wealthier people. Lagos was once noted for its light railway, which was used, amongst other purposes, for the removal of night-soil and garbage to a jetty from which it was dumped in the sea, sometimes to be washed back on shore.[15]

There is a great need in the West African countries for more thorough study of water resources, and, where possible, to take an inventory to guide future planning of their use. Hydrological studies have so far been restricted to special needs in specific cases, such as the schemes of the Office du Niger, or the development of hydro-electric power in Guinea and Ghana. The most comprehensive study generally available is that of the Niger and Benue in Nigeria, made by the Netherlands Engineering Consultants, in which there are accounts of every aspect of hydrology.[16]

Electricity

As yet electricity supplies in West Africa are small, of limited distribution, and frequently expensive. Many West Africans, even where supplies are available, cannot afford them, and still depend on oil for lighting and wood for heating, even though the oil nowadays is mainly imported paraffin. The greater part of the electricity supply is from thermal electric plant, fuelled with imported coal, except in Nigeria, and in a few cases with local wood, or from diesel or gas turbine sets fuelled with imported oil – again Nigeria has its own natural gas resource. Wood fuel has been kept in store at some power stations to guard against interruption in coal supplies. Most power stations have been built to serve a single city or mining or industrial enterprise. Until very recently no attempt was made to link them by any form of 'grid', and in consequence, except where stand-by generators were available, failure at the power station meant failure of the supply for at least a portion, and sometimes for the whole, of the area served. Such failures, in a region where little capital, engineering equipment or skills are available, have been frequent, and stand-by generators are vital for at least essential services dependent on electrical power. Prolonged failure of electricity supplies has often meant failure of domestic water supplies or industrial stoppages. Thermal stations normally need large quantities of water, but with only very small producing units the problem of developing very large sources for the purpose has not yet been faced. The largest developments have been at ports where sea water is available for cooling, and, in some cases, a large river to provide fresh water. In most towns the generating plant is located next to the reservoir providing the piped water supply. West Africa has vast water power resources, and at first it may seem surprising that thermal electric or diesel generation has been preferred. The main difficulties hitherto have been capital and the size of the market. Thermal electric and diesel sets have been cheaper to acquire and install, and are suitable for serving small, but expanding urban markets. Hydro-electric installations need dams and reservoirs to ensure dry season flow, and are best developed on sites providing very large quantities of power. One of the earliest hydro-electric power stations was built to use the power of the Félou falls on the river Senegal in order to supply a small demand at Kayes. The first large hydro-electric scheme, however, was on the Jos Plateau of Nigeria, where today four installations, with altogether some 20,000 kW capacity, provide power for tin mining, and for other uses, by means of a local grid. Generally the demands of mining or of smelting have provided the chief incentives to develop large schemes, as in the example of bauxite mining and aluminium smelting in Guinea and Ghana. The first major scheme to provide power for general purposes was that at Ayamé on the Bia river in the Ivory Coast, chiefly serving Abidjan. The first thermal generators in West Africa were installed in the 1890s. The Lagos power station, for example, was built in 1896. Power was produced mainly for lighting in the European reservations and in the streets. Increase in capacity and consumption was very slow until after the Second

World War, when industrial demands for electricity began to be felt, and a great variety of domestic electrical equipment, including air conditioners, was introduced. By 1962 the total West African production for the year had reached some 1635 million kWh or about 19 kWh per head – very low compared with many other regions of the world.[17] Nigeria produced 48 per cent of the total, but with a population more than half that of West Africa as a whole, had a production per head rather less than average, as the following figures show:

Electricity production in 1962

	million kWh *(partially estimated)*	*kWh per head*
São Tomé and Príncipe	6	86
Ghana	431	62
Liberia	90	60 (if population 1·5 M.)
Senegal	172	57
Ivory Coast	120	35
Cape Verde Islands	7	35
Sierra Leone	52	24
Gambia	6	20
Nigeria	786	16
Dahomey	11	6
Niger	13	5
Togo	8	5
Mali	17	4
Guinea	12	4
Upper Volta	14	3
Portuguese Guinea	n.a.	n.a.

Nearly half of Nigeria's electricity production is consumed in Lagos, which, with its growing industrial estate, and its great port, is the largest single market for electricity in West Africa.

For the future in West Africa there is likely to be a big increase in hydro-electric power generation, linked with high voltage transmission lines. Apart from the schemes in Guinea and Ghana described elsewhere (pp. 682–4), the largest scheme attempted is that in Nigeria for the construction of dams and hydro-electric plant at an estimated cost of £121·5 million on the Niger and Kaduna rivers. The scheme is to build a dam at Kainji on the Niger 60 miles (100 km) above Jebba, creating a fish reservoir, and supplying electricity as far south as Lagos and as far north as Kano. A second, smaller work, at Shiroro on the Kaduna, would not only generate electricity but control the discharge of the Kaduna in order to improve on the navigational advantages in the Niger already resulting from the Kainji dam. By 1980 a third dam is planned for Jebba. Additional proposals include the development of an irrigation scheme from the reservoir to provide not only export crops but commercial food crops for the increasing population of southern Nigeria.

Manufacture[18]

The development of modern manufacturing industries in West Africa dates back to the period between the wars. As yet manufacture is of only minor importance in West Africa's economies. The country with the highest proportion of its labour in industry is Senegal, with production in 1962 valued at £109 million, a total of over 30,000 employees, and an ability to satisfy the home market in all or most of its demand for many manufactured foodstuffs, for shoes and for cement, and with a growing output of textiles. Ghana's industrial census of 1959 showed a total turnover of some £22 million and 24,000 employees (risen to over 50,000 by 1962). The Ivory Coast in 1961 had a production of some £17·5 million and 14,000 employees. Nigeria's industrial output was rather larger than that of Ghana, and in 1960 there were 48,000 employees, but these totalled only some 0·5 per cent of the male labour force. These figures all refer to modern industrial manufactures. Totals for all forms of manufacture including handicrafts are much higher. In Ghana in 1960, for example, there were some 235,000 persons employed in all forms of manufacture out of a total employed population of some 2½ millions. Of these only just over 30,000 were employed in modern industry. Generally many of the old crafts have disappeared, some of which, like iron smelting, were of vital importance. Few of the craftsmen concerned may, however, be said to have had the sort of skill required for modern manufacture. The greater part of the population is agricultural and has acquired biological, not mechanical, skills. Education has provided a means to introduce not industrial and mechanical thinking but academic thinking as an avenue either to teaching or to administration. Certainly education is of vital importance in developing West Africa, but hitherto 'schooling' has led to little improvement in either agriculture or manufacture. In this, education policy has been in no way to blame, for there has been and there still is little market for skilled engineers or scientific agriculturalists, whereas there is a very large market for administrators, lawyers, doctors and teachers. West Africa lacks anywhere an industrial environment in which to train workers, and must depend for the provision of its few skilled engineers on imported labour or on sending a few students overseas. For its semi-skilled operatives, West Africa must depend on local training for specific purposes, so that it must continue to produce operatives with the narrowest industrial experience who can hope to acquire no more than the barest knowledge of the methods of a particular operation. For the development of future industry there is in consequence normally an acute skilled and semi-skilled labour problem, and training of suitable personnel, with higher costs in consequence, is frequently involved.

Apart from the labour problem in terms of skills, manufacturing industry in West Africa has tended to suffer from general, even unskilled labour shortages, and in particular from seasonal movements of labour. Since the Second World War the demand for work in industry and for higher wages has increased, and there has grown a small movement of people away from the land. In the past and still in a few cases today, however, part of the labour available was tied to the land, particularly to its own land, and sought work only during periods when no cultivation could take place, or in order to earn money only for some specific purpose impossible to realize with the limited profits of agriculture.[19]

The markets for manufactured goods are small. Purchasing power is low, with an estimated income per head barely a twelfth the average for the countries of Western Europe. Products for the West African market need to be cheap and to have great popular appeal. The small market for luxury goods is too small to satisfy by local industry, except for handicrafts. Indeed much of West Africa's manufacturing industry has hitherto concentrated on serving overseas markets by refining or treating raw materials in such a way as to reduce the proportion of transport cost in the cost of the material delivered in Europe or North America. There are few places in West Africa with adequate power resources, and power costs are usually high. Moreover, capital costs tend to be very high, for plant must be shipped from Europe or North America, and in many cases erected by labour with little or no experience under the supervision of technicians receiving enhanced 'overseas' salaries, and for whom housing and other amenities must be provided. The initial capital cost per worker in West Africa is inevitably higher than in the industrial countries, and there are few or no related industries. Spare parts must be imported. As in the case of agricultural machinery, break-downs are extremely costly, and the costs of maintenance are generally high. The problem of West Africa is that with less capital, only small markets, and less to attract industry generally, the costs of industrial development are very much higher than in Europe or North America.

Yet it has been justly observed that 'in a sense, the obvious appeal of industrialization in West Africa is a fact more important than the grounds on which it is based'.[20] The development of some manufacturing industry may be regarded as necessary on political grounds alone. Economically there are several advantages despite high initial costs. There is a need for each of the new states to acquire as it were a pool of skilled and semi-skilled labour. The service and maintenance of public utilities is not enough. Some engineering development will help to reduce maintenance costs elsewhere, with less need to depend on imported 'spares' or costly overseas technicians. Some industrial progress will help to stimulate other developments, particularly in transport, the supply of fuels and electricity, and services. In a few cases, notably in south-eastern Nigeria, the rural areas are overcrowded, and alternative means of employment to agriculture are attractive to peoples who must otherwise emigrate from their home region. It has been suggested that industry could absorb workers who are 'under-employed' in petty trading, but until a considerable increase in earning capacity has taken place such petty trading is essential to break goods down into quantities small enough for the market. Finally industry will help to diversify economies and give a measure of stability. In general the range of agricultural raw materials and minerals produced is limited, particularly for the export trade. Greater diversification would help the economies, might reduce the imports of certain commodities, and assist development expenditure by enabling the overseas currency earned to be spent elsewhere. It should not be forgotten that the proportion of population engaged in handicrafts in the past was almost certainly rather higher than today, and has been reduced by the import of cheap manufactures. There is still a very small reservoir of craftsmen, and some of their crafts, notably weaving and wood-working, are capable of considerable development both for the internal market and for an export trade of a luxury 'handmade' character.

Incentives to industrial development take the form, in most countries, chiefly of 'tax holidays' for an initial period, usually of five years. These may be given mainly to new forms of industrial production which governments particularly wish to foster, classified in Ghana, for example, as 'pioneer' industries.

INDUSTRIES CONCERNED WITH AGRICULTURAL RAW MATERIALS

The largest of the raw material industries are those concerned with oil-seed processing, particularly groundnuts and oil palm fruit and kernels. The first decorticating mills for groundnuts were introduced into Senegal during the 1914–18 war and were followed shortly after the war by the first oil mills to satisfy local demand. Originally these were built in the chief markets of the producing districts in Kaolack, Diourbel, Ziguinchor and Louga, but from 1924 onwards mills were established at Dakar.[21] A small export of groundnut oil began in 1927, but was stopped in the general economic depression and did not begin again until 1936 when markets were found firstly in North Africa and latterly in France. In 1938 a restriction was imposed on the import of groundnut oil into France in order to protect the Marseilles industry. During the war, however, shortages and problems of cargo space brought the removal of the restriction, and a beginning was made on the development of a large-scale modern industry at Dakar. By 1948 the production of oil reached 60,000 tons and 4000 workers were employed. Tankers were used for oil conveyance – chiefly to North Africa – and were loaded by pipe-lines. In addition the oil mills had developed by-products, including the supply of materials otherwise wasted to soap factories, and the manufacture of cattle cake. However, the by-products, particularly the cattle cake, are difficult to sell locally, and deteriorate when shipped overseas, so that costs in this respect tend to be higher than those of the metropolitan industry. Elsewhere oil mills were built in Mali at Koulikoro in 1941, and later at Bamako, in Upper Volta at Bobo Dioulasso in 1942, and in Niger at Maradi in 1942. Total production for French West Africa reached 115,000 tons by 1956 of which 16,000 tons were consumed locally and the rest exported. Problems are a high cost of freightage, because tankers return to West Africa empty, and fluctuations in the supply of groundnuts and in market prices. There is very little wastage. Even the groundnut shells are used – as fuel in the mills. Today the oil mills treat not only groundnuts, but also oil palm fruit, shea nuts, castor oil seed and cocoa butter.

In the former British territories groundnut oil mills have been erected in Northern Nigeria and decorticating plant in the Gambia, but generally nuts in shell are preferred in the British market until a profitable outlet for the by-products is assured. Nigeria has lagged behind Senegal in the development of manufactures based on groundnuts. There has been rather a concentration on the improvement of processes for producing palm oil, for the fruit as such was never exported. The 'pioneer' oil mills, using centrifugal force for extracting oil, were introduced after the war to replace the former boiling methods or the Duchser hand process. Despite some local resistance in Nigeria, there were six mills working by 1949 each producing 350 tons of oil a year. By 1956 there were 125 such mills (100 in the Eastern Region), in addition to larger plant at Sapele and Calabar supplied by estates.[22] There were also 5000 handpresses still in operation. The oil is stored in bulk in seven plants located in the ports for loading on to tankers. These plants are all operated by a company partly controlled by the Central Marketing Board and known as Bulk Oil Plants of Nigeria Ltd. The tankers are small and have no return cargo. Other oil mills to deal with palm produce have been erected by the Institut de Recherche des Huiles et des Oléagineux (I.R.H.O.) in Dahomey and in the Ivory Coast at Abidjan.

Other industries which refine or concentrate local agricultural produce include cotton ginning, chiefly in Zaria Province, Northern Nigeria, but also in the Ivory Coast, Upper Volta, Mali and Senegal, meat processing, tanning, decorticating rice, the removal of fibres from sisal, and the extraction of sugar from cane – a fast-growing recently-introduced industry. At Bacita in Ilorin Province, Northern Nigeria, and at Asutsuare in Ghana, refined white sugar is being produced. Most of these industries are of minor importance as yet and are still small-scale. In Northern Nigeria there is, however, a considerable industry preparing goat skins for export, and in Liberia, southern Nigeria and the Ivory Coast the preparation of latex is a rapidly-growing industry as rubber production increases.

PROCESSING OF MINERALS

Some reference has already been made to these industries under 'Mining' on pp. 542–52. The reduction of waste material in the ores, ideally the extraction of the mineral itself, are important for the reduction of transport costs and should be done as near the mines as possible. Notable examples are the washing of tin ores, the separation of the several minerals contained in them at Bukuru in Northern Nigeria, the treatment of concentrates at Makeri and Embel, the concentration of iron ore in the Bomi Hills of Liberia and at Marampa in Sierra Leone, the preparation of phosphates in Senegal and Togo, of alumina at the Fria plant and on the Los Islands of Guinea, the extraction of gold in Ghana, and the washing of coal at Enugu.

The production of metals has virtually disappeared in the last half-century, but is being revived firstly by the schemes for aluminium manufacture in Guinea and Ghana, and secondly by the development of an iron and steel industry in Nigeria and Liberia and the building of a steel scrap plant at Tema in Ghana. Other products from industries processing minerals include cement, chiefly in Senegal and Nigeria, and the manufacture in several centres of concrete blocks. At Abeokuta in south-western Nigeria pre-stressed concrete posts, poles and beams are made. At Port Harcourt, Enugu, Wellington in Sierra Leone and Takoradi clinker grinding factories using imported raw material are also producing cement. Glass manufacture, mainly producing bottles, has begun at Port Harcourt and at Tema in Ghana.

SECONDARY INDUSTRIES USING LOCAL AGRICULTURAL RAW MATERIALS

Secondary industries are of rapidly-growing importance in West Africa. The oldest and the most widespread is the manufacture of textiles, which, in its 'cottage' form, producing hand-loom cloths, still survives, and serves a large West African market. The earliest cotton spinning mill appears to be that built in Bouaké in the Ivory Coast in 1923. This plant has since been completely modernized and together with four other mills supplies a local demand for cotton thread. After the Second World War another cotton mill was erected in Rufisque, and in 1953 two modern factories began production on the outskirts of Dakar. Today there are eleven textile mills in Dakar and Rufisque satisfying nearly half the Senegalese market and exporting a large part of their produce. In 1954 a hosiery mill was established at Abidjan in the Ivory Coast, and other mills producing silk goods and hosiery have also been built. More recently a calico printing factory has been constructed at Dadja. At present it uses cloth imported from Japan, but eventually it will manufacture cloth from local cotton. In Nigeria some attempt to develop a cottage industry was made when the Department of Commerce and Industries introduced the broad loom after the Second World War. Textile training centres were created to train operators in the use of the looms. In 1949 a factory was built at Kano to weave drills and Bedford cord, and other small spinning and weaving mills have since been established in Lagos. Two large spinning and weaving mills have been erected in Kaduna, another cloth mill in Kano and a fourth in Lagos. The Arewa textile factory at Kaduna is a notably successful result of partnership between Japanese and Nigerian Government interests. Clothing is manufactured in Lagos, Enugu and Port Harcourt, and new mills are being built in Onitsha and Aba. Altogether there are 19 textile mills in Nigeria, with a total of some 162,000 spindles and 4600 looms. Present capacity appears to be fully up to the requirements of the Nigerian market and may even be excessive. Although the textile industry has been considered by some economists as a form of manufacture suitable for introduction into countries beginning industrial development, there are several problems in West Africa, including the heavy demand of the industry for power, the competition of imported textiles and the lack of trained skilled personnel. Thus an attempt to develop a textile industry in Nigeria shortly after the Second World War failed because the costs of the enterprise then were too high, despite the supposed cheapness of labour. The Eastern Nigerian developments are particularly notable since power there is relatively cheap and there is a big demand for alternatives to agriculture. In Ghana, Tema is a growing textile centre. Another form of textile manufacture is the production of rope and bags from sisal. A factory to produce rope and bags was built in Dakar in 1938, and other mills exist at Bouaké in the Ivory Coast and Kankan in Guinea. A jute mill has been built at Jos, whilst jute bags are made at Kumasi and coir bags at Badagry, Western Nigeria.

Secondary industries, using fats produced from local oil-seeds, were not established in West Africa until after the Second World War with the exception of a few small soap-making factories. Soap works exist at the chief ports: Dakar, Lagos (Apapa), Abidjan, Porto Novo, Freetown and Takoradi, and use chiefly palm oil. In recent years the market within West Africa for margarine has increased considerably, particularly in the more prosperous cocoa-growing areas, and in response to the demand margarine factories have been erected at Abidjan and at Apapa.

Despite technical and marketing problems two factories for the manufacture of cocoa products have begun operation at Takoradi. Production, however, may remain small for some time, and cannot hope to take up Ghana's enormous cocoa surplus. Chocolates and sweets are now being made at Dakar, Niamey, Tema, Lagos and Kano.

Canning and bottling industries using local fruit and fruit juices, both for export and for the internal market, have been developed at many locations, but notably in Guinea, in the Ivory Coast (especially at Abidjan), in Ghana and in Nigeria. At Ibadan it was hoped that canning would provide a market for citrus fruits and pineapple grown as an alternative to cocoa destroyed by swollen shoot disease. It was thought that the canning factory would be able to depend entirely on local produce, but eventually it was found necessary to develop a pineapple estate in order to ensure adequate supplies. The home market for canned fruit is still rather small, and Nigeria has found it difficult to secure an overseas market. At Abidjan and Dakar locally-caught tuna fish are canned for export. Abidjan also has factories for the manufacture of instant coffee, for which the stronger-flavoured and generally cheaper West African coffees are preferred. As yet there are few industries based on dairy produce. The most striking development is at Vom on the Jos Plateau of Northern Nigeria, where milk is collected and processed at a central dairy, where a powdered form is produced, and also butter and cheese.

In southern Nigeria the remarkable growth of the rubber industry has encouraged the hope of using local latex to supply the big demand for tyres and remoulds. There are in West Africa a number of remould factories using imported latex, but it is only in Nigeria that West African latex is used. A factory to make tyres has been built at Ibadan, using mainly local raw material. Other tyre factories are at Lagos, Ikeja, and on the Trans-Amadi industrial estate where natural gas is used to raise steam for rubber processing.

The preparation of local tobacco and the manufacture of cigarettes, sometimes with an admixture of imported tobacco, is another widespread industry, but is developed on a large scale chiefly in Nigeria, where one of the first tobacco factories in West Africa was established at Oshogbo in the Western Region in 1933, and the largest factory is at Ibadan with an output of over 200 million cigarettes a month. Most of the tobacco used comes from Oyo Province and from the Northern Region. In Zaria there is a large leaf drying plant and a recently-built factory for cigarette manufacture.

Despite the existence of a traditional industry for the manufacture of footwear, the production of boots and shoes by modern methods is a comparatively recent introduction and exists chiefly at Rufisque, Abidjan, Apapa and Kano. The market is small as yet, but promises to grow rapidly as people cease to go barefoot and wear shoes. In part the growth in demand is connected with changes in taste and social distinctions, but shoes do enable the wearer to avoid a number of diseases associated with the feet, notably hookworm.

At Bimbresso to the west of Abidjan in the Ivory Coast a paper pulp mill using local timber was erected in 1949 – the only one of its kind in West Africa until 1965, when another was erected in Ghana. The chief source of timber for wood pulp in the Ivory Coast has been the local 'umbrella tree' (*Musanga smithii*), which occurs locally in almost pure stands. However, eventually it is planned to use mixed sources of timber. The main product is cement bags, chiefly sent to Rufisque, and paper and cardboard for a paper box factory at Tiaroye, Dakar. The manufacture of paper has also begun at Takoradi. Veneer and plywood production has already had reference (pp. 538–9).

At Labé in Guinea a perfume industry has been developed on the basis of the plantation production of oils and essences, using chiefly essences of oranges and of jasmine.

SECONDARY INDUSTRIES USING IMPORTED AGRICULTURAL RAW MATERIALS

The largest of the industries in this category is undoubtedly brewing. Alcoholic drinks provided one of the earliest items of trade between Europe and West Africa. As yet, spirits produced by modern distilleries are still imported, but considerable quantities of beer, chiefly of 'lager' type, are brewed from imported raw materials, particularly at Dakar, Abidjan, Accra and Lagos. As yet West African breweries supply only a small portion of local demand which is still met mainly by imported beers, chiefly from Holland, Denmark and Germany. Until recently there was no manufacture of bottles or beer cans in West Africa, and until such an industry was developed it was dearer to import empty bottles than to import bottles filled with beer. In consequence the West African breweries depended on the 'empties' of imported beers, and their collection still provides a minor, but widespread, local trade. However, glass manufacture has now begun at Port Harcourt, and cans are being made at Abidjan. Closely associated with beer brewing is the widespread and highly competitive industry of bottling imported soft drinks and mineral waters, and, in Dakar, the brewing of vinegar.

Wheat bread and biscuits command an increasing market, and bakeries have been established in many towns, particularly in southern Nigeria, Ghana and Senegal. Several flour mills are now in operation, chiefly at the ports.

SECONDARY INDUSTRIES USING OTHER IMPORTED RAW MATERIALS

Articles made from plastics, particularly polyethylene, polystyrene and polyvinyl chloride, can command a good market in the more prosperous portions of West Africa. For an industry in West Africa raw material is easy to import and labour costs are not high. Moreover, an initial installation can be quite small and units added as the markets expand. Small plastics factories have been established at Conakry, Abidjan, Takoradi, Ibadan, Apapa and Enugu. The unit at Ibadan was one of the first, being built in 1957 to produce tubes, pipes and conduits, with production extending later to a variety of articles including bowls, beakers, cups and combs. At Tema in Ghana and in a few other centres there are factories producing plastic footwear.

The largest chemicals industry is in Dakar, including the manufacture of explosives, paint, matches, liquid gas, storage batteries and dyes. Nearby at Rufisque there is a pharmaceuticals industry supplying part of local requirements. Chemical industries are being developed at several other locations, notably Port Harcourt, and include the manufacture of varnishes, matches and insecticides.

Oil refining is a comparatively recent introduction with the growth in importance of motor transport and diesel power for the railways and electricity generation. Refineries have been built so far at Port Harcourt (using Nigerian oil), Tema, Abidjan and Dakar.

ENGINEERING AND METAL INDUSTRIES

The chief engineering centre in West Africa is Dakar, and other centres of major importance are all ports, for here are not only the requirements of shipping, but the chief centres of manufacture, and the chief railway termini with their repair yards for locomotives and rolling stock. Dakar has the best facilities for ship repairs, but has been developed as a naval port. Other major facilities exist at the other large ports, particularly at Lagos. Abidjan has developed a number of metal industries in the last decade, notably the manufacture of aluminium ware and sheet, using laminated strip imported from Cameroun, of nails and of metal boxes. Nails are also made in Accra, and metal boxes at Lagos and Dakar, and aluminium sheet is rolled in Port Harcourt. Lagos also has a light engineering factory which can produce steel work and building frames. Other products include metal doors and window frames, pipes, storage tanks and wire. The manufacture of corrugated iron or aluminium sheet for roofing is at last beginning to satisfy a large part of West African demand.

ASSEMBLY PLANT

Some modern large-scale industries, particularly the manufacture of motor vehicles and of bicycles, have important although as yet small markets in West Africa. Costs of transport are high, particularly of the finished product. Such costs may be reduced by exporting the parts ready to assemble and paint, and, in consequence, attempts have been made to develop factories for the assembly of such goods at a few of the great West African ports. Labour must be trained, but the task is generally not as great as that of training labour to produce the original parts. Plant for the assembly of motor cars and of lorries has been erected at Apapa and Agege (Mushin) near Lagos, at Abidjan and at Tema. Bicycle factories have begun production in Abidjan, Tema, Agege, Port Harcourt and Zaria, to supply the considerable West African market. At Nsawam in Ghana a tractor assembly plant, made in Czechoslovakia, produces tractors for the new agricultural schemes. Other assembly industries include sewing machines and radios. Such industries will make possible the introduction of some manufacturing skills, and may in time be linked with further local developments in engineering.

INDUSTRIAL DISTRICTS AND ESTATES

Only Dakar has acquired a sufficient degree of industrial development for there to be industrial districts. The oldest of these lies immediately west of the harbour and east of Medina, and is the main groundnut crushing and chemicals centre, but has in addition a great variety of light industries, including the milling of flour from millets, maize and wheat, the manufacture of furniture, and the preparation of foodstuffs. To the east, immediately north of Tiaroye, is another industrial sector extending in a ribbon along the road from Dakar to Rufisque, between Tiaroye-sur-mer and the satellite town of Dagoudane Pikine. This is the most recently-developed industrial area, mainly of light industries, such as paper box manufacture, which have sought cheaper, but convenient, locations away from the crowded harbour area. Finally at Rufisque and between Rufisque and Bargny, there is another, but much smaller, industrial district whose origins, like those of the Dakar industrial quarter, are connected with port development and the groundnut traffic.

A large number of West African towns offer industrial estate facilities, but major developments of this kind are taking place chiefly at Abidjan, Tema, Lagos and Trans-Amadi (Port Harcourt), that is at large ports. At Abidjan the main industrial sector lies immediately behind the wharves of Petit Bassam Island and west of the residential suburb of Treichville. At Lagos 230 acres (93 hectares) of land in Apapa, immediately behind the wharves, in part reclaimed, has been laid out with roads and services and all lots have now been taken. 40 acres (16 hectares) have been reclaimed for industrial sites along the Ijora Causeway and 200 more acres (81 hectares) have been set aside at Iganmu. Other industrial estates have been opened at Mushin, Illupeju near Oshodi, and Yaba, the only 'fully packaged estate in Nigeria'.[23] Tema is a complete new port to the east of Accra offering the best deep-water harbour in Ghana and easy access to the capital city. Here again planned provision has been made for industrial development. Trans-Amadi has the unusual distinction of electricity supplies from a natural gas generator at Afam plus a supply of gas for special industrial purposes.

Commerce

The early features of the commercial development of West Africa by Europeans have already been described in the historical account (pp. 398–417) for the first contacts were essentially commercial in character. Moreover, the development of trade, with the struggle between coastal middlemen and interior producers, plus the question of the slave trade, led in large part to attempts to conquer or to extend protectorates over West African territory. The present commercial organization of both internal and external trade must, however, be described for an appreciation of many of the major factors which are modifying productivity and settlement in West Africa, and thus changing the character of the region.

The overseas trade of West Africa has increased enormously in volume since 1800, but in some respects has changed little in character. Under the colonial régime overseas trade was dominated by the metropolitan country, particularly in the case of the French West African territories, and as yet under independent governments there has been very little change, except in the case of Guinea. As in the 18th century the chief import items are still cloth, hardware, various metal goods and provisions, including ales and spirits, although capital goods including machinery are of rapidly-increasing importance. The chief items of export have changed, however, from slaves, gold and the products of gathering, to vegetable oils, cocoa, coffee, oil-seeds and ores – particularly of iron, tin and bauxite. West Africa's import trade has, therefore, changed less in character than her export trade, except for the increased demand for capital goods, a demand which should grow enormously with attempts to promote economic development. One may expect that greater trade deficits will be incurred as even greater capital expenditure takes place and large quantities of capital are borrowed from abroad.

The total overseas trade of West Africa in 1962 was worth some U.S. $1364 millions of exports and $1747 millions of imports.[24] Of this the only states or colonies with more than $50 millions worth of trade in either direction were:

	Exports ($ millions)	Imports ($ millions)
Nigeria	472	568
Ghana	291	333
Ivory Coast	193	146
Senegal	124	155
Liberia	68	132
Guinea	64	73
Sierra Leone	58	85

These seven territories were responsible for 93 per cent of the exports and 85 per cent of the imports. West Africa made a net loss on total traffic, and there was a number of notable trading deficits; Nigeria (—$96 millions), Liberia (—$64 millions), Ghana (—$42 millions), Mali (—$36 millions), Mauritania (—$33 millions), Senegal (—$31 millions), Upper Volta (—$28 millions) and Sierra Leone (—$27 millions). The only surpluses were the Ivory Coast (+$47 millions) and Portuguese Guinea (+$3 millions). All of the deficit territories, however, have considerable programmes for economic development, which may well alter their balance of trade position over the next several years. All the trading figures shown represent considerable increases over the pre-war totals. The traffic amounts to about 30 per cent of total African trade and 1 per cent of world trade. It must be remembered, however, that this low proportion of world trade is not a reflection of West African productivity, most of which finds its way into the internal market or is used for subsistence. There is a danger when describing the economy of West Africa of overstressing the importance of export products. If necessary West Africa can both feed and clothe her population entirely from her own resources. Overseas trade is needed to gain extra commodities, luxuries, and the equipment to increase productivity. Its amount reflects the kinds of produce which West Africa has been able to offer, and the world demand for them in relation to the amount of labour and land which West Africa has been able to put into their production.

West African export produce consists almost entirely of primary goods despatched either raw or partially prepared for manufacture overseas. With the one exception of Nigeria, each territory has only a small range of such goods, and usually either one or two items only are dominant. Thus comparing export dominants of the territories with the largest volume of trade:

(Figures give per cent of total export trade value for each territory in 1962)

Nigeria	cocoa 20, groundnuts, 19, oil palm produce 16, oil 10.
Ghana	cocoa 58, timber 11, gold 10.
Ivory Coast	coffee 42, cocoa 23, timber 20.
Senegal	groundnut produce 88.
Sierra Leone	diamonds 43, iron ore 31, palm kernels 15.

Vegetable produce is dominant and mostly for foodstuffs. Minerals are important only in Liberia and Sierra Leone, and to a lesser extent in Ghana and Nigeria, although they are of growing importance in Guinea and Mauritania. An important trend in mineral production is the decreasing proportion of production of precious metals, and the increasing proportion of iron and aluminium, in both of which West Africa should become a major producer during the present decade. Diamond production has on the whole been well maintained in Ghana, Sierra Leone and Liberia, and there are deposits of radio-active minerals in several territories, unworked in view of the abundance on the world market. The dependence on primary produce has been of the greatest importance for economic development in view of post-war world price movements. The prices of most primary goods increased from 1946 to 1954, due at first to general post-war shortages, and later to shortages at the time of the Korean war. From 1954 until 1964 prices have declined, especially of cocoa, and to a lesser extent of palm kernels and coffee. Groundnut prices in the franc zone have on the whole been maintained, but palm oil prices fell as early as 1953 with only a slight recovery in 1956. Generally incomes from export produce since 1954 have not increased as output has increased, and in several cases have declined. Ghana has had severe problems with the dramatic fall in cocoa prices, so that despite enormous increases in cocoa exports, earnings have increased very little. Not only has this

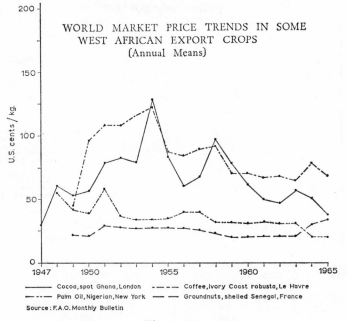

Figure 11.3

affected the earnings of overseas currency needed for the purchase of capital goods, but it has also affected Government revenues, a large portion of which is derived from the taxation of export produce. Moreover, as earnings per unit weight, especially of cocoa, have dropped, so an increasing proportion has been taken by freight and handling charges.

The great dependence on the export of agricultural raw materials has led to problems in handling freight and a markedly seasonal development of trade and of financial transactions. This is particularly so with the annuals, but rather less so with the perennials. Thus although groundnuts are moved from November to March, there is a very marked peak of movement in December. The cocoa peak is spread over November to January, with less heavy movements in October and February, totalling altogether about 90 per cent of the crop, and the remainder

moved from May to August. Oil palm produce is moved all the year round, although with a peak in April to June, and cotton moves mainly from November
to January, with some cotton from the areas with longer rainy season moving
between February and May. Goat skin and cattle hide supplies depend in part on
killings governed by Muslim festivals. These are fixed by the Muslim year of
354 or 355 days, so that the incidence of peak supplies becomes progressively
earlier in each Christian year by an average of some 10 days. The biggest produce
movements are concentrated in the dry season period, November to January,

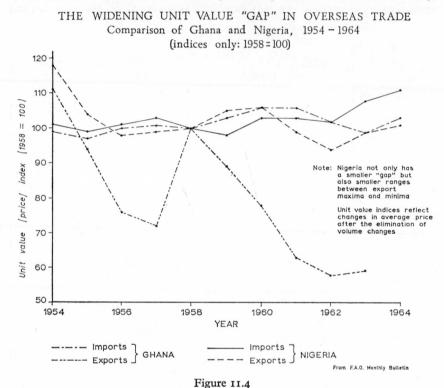

THE WIDENING UNIT VALUE "GAP" IN OVERSEAS TRADE
Comparison of Ghana and Nigeria, 1954 – 1964
(indices only: 1958 = 100)

Figure 11.4

when there is considerable traffic congestion, the most important exception being
the oil palm produce export peak in April to June.

There is some movement of produce which should strictly be classed as 'export',
but which is between West African countries and might also be classed as 'internal
exchange'. Again the main movements are of primary goods, including rice from
Mali to Senegal, kola nuts from the Ivory Coast to Upper Volta and Mali, and
livestock from Upper Volta and Mali to Ghana, and from Chad to Nigeria. A
small movement of manufactured products has developed, however, from Senegal
and from the Ivory Coast to other countries in the West African portion of the
franc zone, and includes soap, textiles, cordage and canned fruit.

Imported goods in West Africa consist of a much wider range of commodities

FOOD REQUIREMENTS and IMPORTS in WEST AFRICA in 1960

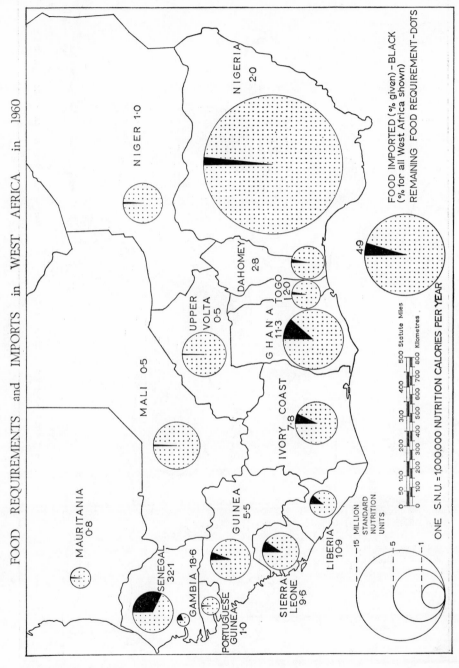

Figure 11.5

IMPORTS of SUGAR, RICE, WHEAT and WHEAT FLOUR in 1960

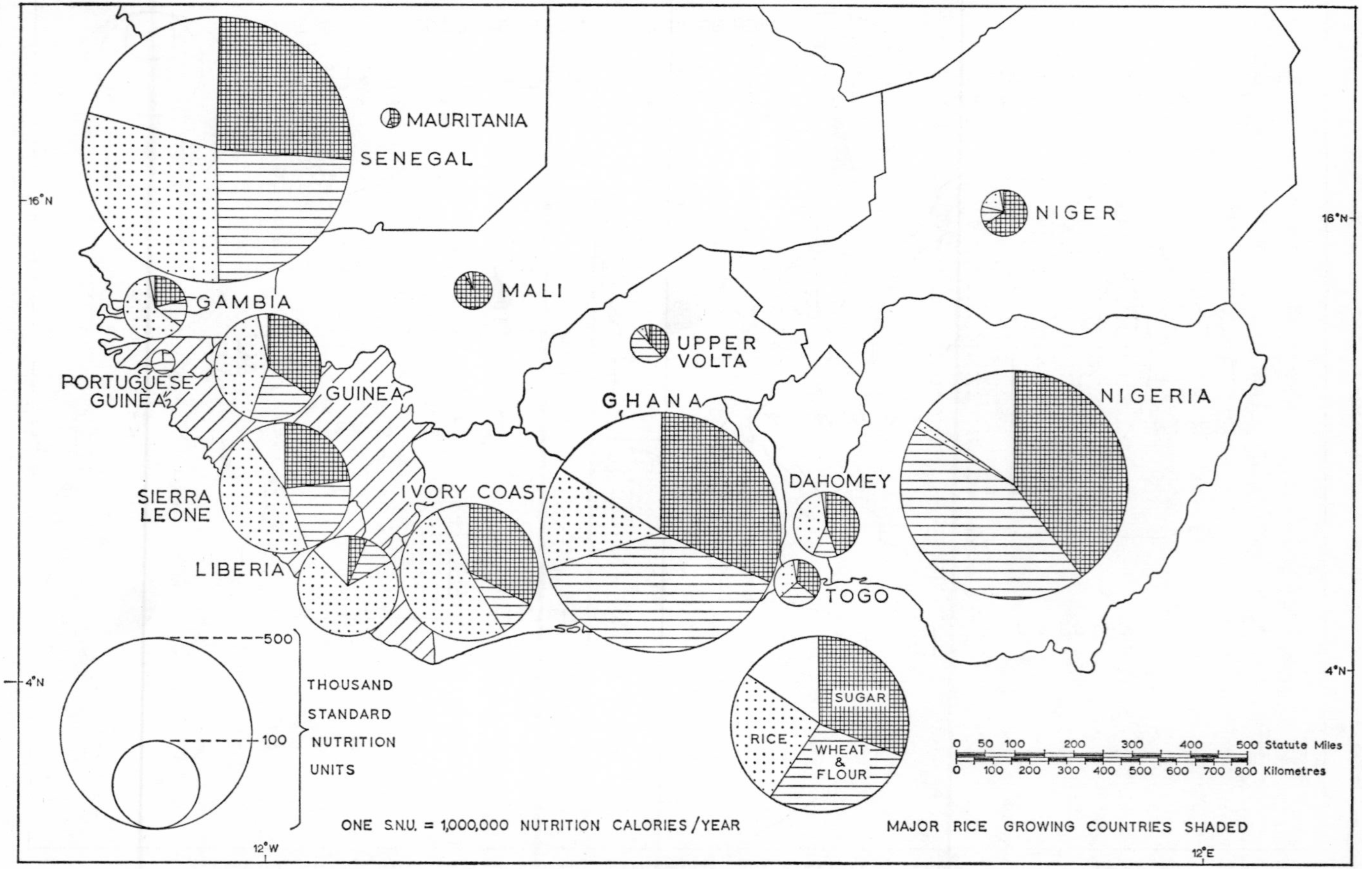

MAJOR RICE GROWING COUNTRIES SHADED

ONE S.N.U. = 1,000,000 NUTRITION CALORIES/YEAR

THOUSAND
STANDARD
NUTRITION
UNITS

Figure 11.6

than exports. The chief items are textiles, especially cotton piece goods; provisions, especially sugar, grain, flour, dried fish and canned goods, hardware, haberdashery; and capital goods, including agricultural implements and machinery, electrical gear, locomotives and rolling stock, metals and metal goods, motor vehicles, transport, building and maintenance equipment, and building materials (especially cement and corrugated iron). Other major imports include mineral fuels and lubricants, bicycles, motor vehicles especially lorries, oil lamps, chemicals and pharmaceuticals. Food was one of the most costly items in several countries. Amongst the countries spending high proportions of their import expenditure on food in 1961 were Senegal 30 per cent, Ghana 19, Mali 16, Ivory Coast 13, Liberia 12, Sierra Leone 11 and Nigeria 10. Thompson and Adloff noted an enormous increase in food imports into French West Africa between 1938 and 1953. Thus rice increased by 80 per cent, tinned milk by 300 per cent, flour by 400 per cent and preserved meat by 1900 per cent.[25] The proportions of import expenditure on food do not vary entirely with incomes, although there is a tendency for higher imported food consumption in higher income areas, especially in the towns. An important factor in Senegal is that the chief export crop, groundnuts, is an annual and requires considerable labour. Introduced into local crop rotations it has reduced the area under food crops considerably. Moreover, between the wars the French developed an import of cheap rice from Indo-China, which today has been replaced by imports from various sources, including the United States, Brazil, Egypt and Mali, and amounts to about one-fifth of the imported food bill. In Ghana and the Ivory Coast cocoa and coffee have reduced the need to grow one's own food, but cocoyams and plantains are the normal accompaniment of young plantations, and cassava, an easy crop to plant and tend, is frequently planted in ground locally unsuitable for cocoa. In Ghana and the Ivory Coast the foods imported are much more of the 'luxury' variety, or have a high protein content. Sugar, wheat flour, dried fish, canned meats and fish, and bottled beers are the chief items. The import of cotton cloth has been encouraged by the considerable manufacture of clothing to suit West African taste by local tailors, using imported sewing machines. Designs are specially printed for the West African market. Sources are Japan, United Kingdom, France, Holland and Germany. There is a growing demand for cloths of synthetic fibres, particularly nylon, for the manufacture of women's blouses.

Generally overseas trade has been dominated by the metropolitan powers, and, even with independence, this dominance may be slow to change, due to the problems and costs of changing the elaborate trading network developed. Proportions of dominance vary. In the 1950s France took 65–70 per cent of both the import and export trades of French West Africa, whilst Britain took 50–55 per cent of the export trades and 45–50 per cent of the import trades of her West African territories, and Portugal took only 25–30 per cent of the export trade and 40 per cent of the import trade of her dependencies. In 1961 the approximate percentages of the import trade by value of each West African country controlled by the former metropolitan or major interested power were as follows:

Ivory Coast 70, Mali 68, Senegal 67, Upper Volta 61, Dahomey 59, Liberia 54 (United States), Niger 50, Sierra Leone 45, Gambia 44, Togo 41, Nigeria 38, Ghana 37, Guinea 29. The continued dominance of France in the import trade of her former possessions, with the exception of Guinea, is quite remarkable. Political independence has very little affected the economic situation. Britain's share of the import trade of her former possessions has, however, declined, and is in all cases a smaller proportion than the United States' share of the import trade of Liberia.

To a considerable extent the trade of West Africa is controlled by Government agencies, and thus directed to some extent in its markets. Generally Government controls are more marked in the former British than in the former French territories. The British system has been to set up marketing boards to control the purchase, grading, marketing and export of the chief items of vegetable export produce (see p. 506). The boards have the legal power to fix the prices of a particular crop in advance of harvest and to license buying agents. The system has been criticized adversely by Bauer in his major study of West African trade, in part on the grounds that it discourages private savings and investment and deprives producers of incentives to adjust their acreages and methods in relation to world demands, even encouraging inefficiency.[26] Bauer claims that the price policy of the Cocoa Marketing Boards from 1947 to 1950 served to destabilize producer incomes, and that policies pursued up to 1952 suggested that some of the boards were unlikely to permit large-scale drafts on their reserves for the maintenance of producer prices on falling markets. Certainly some of the boards seem to have been more concerned with accumulating large reserves, some of which have depreciated in value. Moreover, as produce prices have dropped so have the maintenance payments of some boards. Taking cocoa production in Ghana and comparing the period 1926–39 with the period 1947–52, when the Marketing Board was operating, the producer received 73 per cent of f.o.b. value in the former period, but only 57 per cent in the latter. In French West Africa there were no marketing boards, and in the territories formerly in the federation until recently controls were few, with the exception of Guinea. However, Senegal and Mali now have boards monopolizing groundnut marketing and controlling other trade items. There are a number of preferential duties in the former French territories, and in effect the West African franc zone forms a closed trading system with 70 per cent of the traffic in the hands of one shipping group.[27] Moreover, a form of price equalization has been practised, which has markedly directed trade towards the metropolitan power. Thus after 1954 prices paid by France for certain French West African commodities were higher than the world prices. An important exception was coffee which, although it has found and still finds a market in France, is on the whole unsuited to French tastes. The 'robusta' coffee of the Ivory Coast, with its stronger flavour than that of 'arabica', has found a growing market in the United States where it is sold in the form of 'instant coffee'. On the whole there are few preferential duties on import goods, although general duties tend to be high, for a large part of budget

revenues is obtained from import duties. However, there are local buying preferences which tend to preserve metropolitan trading interests, and the influence
exerted by the large trading companies on the whole also favours the metropolitan
power.

The organization of overseas trading is largely in European hands, and one
company in each of the franc and sterling zones tends to dominate trade –
approximately 70 per cent in the franc zone and 40 per cent in the sterling zone.
Coste has described the traffic between north-west Europe and West Africa in
some detail in a study of the movement of goods by the Holland–West Africa
Line.[28] Thus dried stockfish is exported from Bergen and Oslo; beer and
salted pigs' trotters from Copenhagen; beer and cement from Hamburg; beer,
cloth, foodstuffs and alcohol from Amsterdam plus Ruhr motor vehicles,
machines, cloth and glass, Swiss milk, Eindhoven electrical goods and Czechoslo-
vakian beer and glass; machinery, metals, cement and building materials from
Antwerp; and finally wines, spirits and glass from Bordeaux plus Parisian motor
vehicles. In return timber, cocoa, coffee, rubber and cotton are shipped to
Europe. Groundnuts travel from Senegal, almost entirely by French ships, to
Bordeaux or Marseilles. In Nigeria one company, with its own shipping,
dominates the vegetable oil and oil-seeds trade, but Holland–West Africa ship
some palm oil. The company prefers to use mainly small tramp steamers, picking
up cargoes at a number of ports, with little depth of water at quayside or with
open roadsteads. A few large vessels are used for calls at the major ports. On the
journey out only the few specialist ports for handling import traffic are visited.
Return cargoes, however, may be found at a large number of small ports, many
of which only have an export trade. A major problem is the poverty of facilities
at many ports and long delays in loading and unloading cargoes, with, in consequence, queues of shipping waiting three weeks or more. An example of export
trade organization by a single firm is offered by the United Africa Company's
handling of the palm oil traffic of Nigeria.[29] The oil producers sell their product
in local village and hamlet markets where women traders or 'sub-middlemen'
buy small quantities, and bulk them in four-gallon (18-litre) kerosene tins. The
women traders then sell to middlemen (frequently also women) in the urban
markets, who blend the oils received to raise the grade of low-quality oils so that
they are just within a higher range. The middleman thus obtains not only a
trading profit, but a generally better price for the oil. A few of the middlemen are
Syrian traders, and in some cases sub-middlemen sell directly to factors who buy
in their own names, but are allowed to use company premises. Middlemen sell
directly to the company's agents in out-stations or in the local buying centres.
There are other competing buyers and generally the middleman goes to the
buyer or company with the best range of merchandise for sale. Thus part of the
price of the oil is taken in goods and part in cash. Traders return with the merchandise to take a further profit. Transport costs and the lesser bulk of return
journeys from local buying centres to the hamlets are important factors. Frequently reduced rates obtain, so that a trader may be able to offer merchandise

bought from a company's trading centre at a lower price than the company's local out-station. The oil bought is treated and bulked in drums or other large containers for conveyance to the bulk oil plants, where it is stored ready for shipment by tankers.

Some references have been made in the above accounts to the organization of import trading, for both export and import traffic are intimately connected. The availability of merchandise may determine the limits of export crop production, and conversely the forecast of a poor year for export crops may discourage traders from importing large quantities of goods, and lead to the imposition of higher freight charges. The market is extremely sensitive to small changes in the price or production of export crops, for savings are small and the average cash incomes of the West African territories have been estimated to range between £25 and £75 (U.S. $70–210) per head a year. The luxury goods market is very small, for the minority of wealthy Africans, Levantines and Europeans may be estimated at only 0·01 per cent of total population. However, there is an increasing sale of certain kinds of goods, which before the war were luxuries, and are now regarded more nearly as necessities or as adjuncts of a slightly better standard of living. These include bicycles, electric and oil lamps, sewing machines, cooking stoves fuelled either by wood or oil, radios, electric or charcoal irons, watches, fountain pens and imported beers and cigarettes, together with bread and canned foodstuffs including milk. Since the quantity, quality and prices of imported merchandise so affect export crop production, there are clearly advantages in a coastward location. However, the attraction of imported merchandise has helped to encourage seasonal migration from more distant areas – from Senegal and Mali to the Gambia, for instance, not just for the cash return from groundnut cultivation, but for access to the imported merchandise of the Gambia for conveyance home and resale. This factor is important also with the movement of Mossi migrants to Ghana and of Sokoto migrants to the Western Region of Nigeria. The purpose is both to earn during an otherwise slack season, and to obtain access to better markets and shops.

There are many other important features of trading practice of which the chief are loans by middlemen – who frequently depend on credit from company buyers – to sub-middlemen and producers, and the practice, where the market price of export produce is rising, of selling imported merchandise at a loss in order to obtain the cash to buy export goods. The financial risks involved in these transactions are tremendous, particularly in the latter case where merchandise has been obtained on credit. Security for loans can take the form of depositing deeds and property, but this is only satisfactory where titles are certain. In Nigeria, for example, titles may be doubtful outside Lagos or the Colony Province and in consequence these areas attract produce buyers intent on building in order to offer security when they need capital.[30] Interest rates on loans are requently exorbitant. For small borrowers, and especially for producers, the growth of the co-operative movement, of co-operative and Government banks and loan agencies and of small savings movements, such as that maintained by the post office, have all been important factors in weakening the economic hold of the middlemen.

The internal trade of West Africa must reach a large, but as yet uncalculated volume. The chief items in the traffic, other than imported goods, which are in a sense re-exchanged, are foodstuffs, locally brewed beers and palm wine, textiles, matting, thatching materials, firewood and timber, oils for lighting, locally-made pharmaceuticals, pottery and metal goods especially agricultural implements and knives. In some districts barter still occurs, or forms of coinage normally no longer regarded as legal tender are used. The exchange of foodstuff surpluses in village and hamlet markets functioning every 4, 5, 7, 8 or 10 days is universal throughout West Africa. The traditional market rings serve much the same purpose of exchange that they have always served. In the main export crop-producing areas, however, the local trading has been intensified to deal with the distribution of foodstuffs imported from neighbouring areas. The fringes of the cocoa- and coffee-growing districts have specialist commercial food crop areas producing yams, cassava, rice and plantains. Moreover, there is a considerable seasonal movement of foodstuffs, chiefly from areas with long growing seasons to areas with short growing seasons, where food, chiefly grains, must be kept in storage for long periods. Maps of the tonnages of yams railed and of rice distribution in Nigeria reveal the relations of food crop production to the main export crop zones.[31] Within Nigeria there is a considerable traffic by rail from the Western to the Northern Region, in palm oil for cooking and lighting, and in kola nuts. In the latter case Government agencies have helped to promote an internal exchange based on the former traditional trade so important elsewhere in West Africa (see pp. 166-8). In Ghana, White has analysed the movements of staple foods by road, and shown that about 80 per cent of total shipments originated within 75 miles (120 km) of Accra, whilst Gould has illustrated the movement of goods by road for internal exchange in great detail.[32] Yams, groundnuts, guinea corn, pennisetum, rice and fish move southwards, whilst salt, kola, plantains and citrus fruits move north. In addition a little copra and some palm wine move from the coastal areas as far north as Kumasi. Gould's analyses of commodities moving to local markets and their percentages of total movement gave:

1) *A northern market, Bawku:*
   rice 27·9, guinea corn and pennisetum 26·5, groundnuts 19·5, firewood 12·6, vegetables 4·0, cowpeas 2·9, clay pots 2·5, milk 1·7, cooked sweet potatoes 0·7, cloth 0·6, shea butter and dawa-dawa (locust bean preparation) 0·3, miscellaneous (kola, tobacco, sticks, hats, calabashes, chickens, etc.) 1·8.

2) *A central market, Dormaa-Ahenkro:*
   plantains 23·2, cocoyams 18·6, palm wine 10·9, firewood 8·3, vegetables 7·1, cassava 5·4, tomatoes 3·9, maize 3·5, coffee 2·9, maize flour 2·2, cocoa 2·2, oranges 1·9, cooked cassava 1·3, eggs 1·2, cloth 1·1, palm oil 1·1,

ANALYSES of COMMODITY FLOW into BAWKU MARKET, GHANA

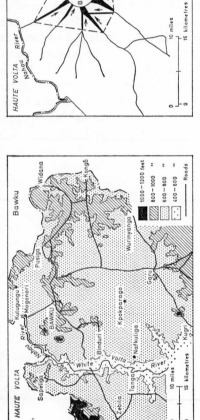

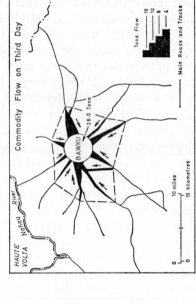

Commodity Flow on Second Day

Commodity Flow on Third Day

Commodity Flow on Market Day

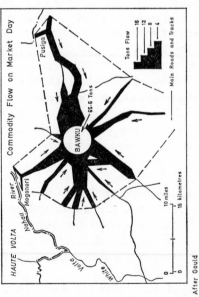

After Gould

Figure 11.7

poultry 1·0, miscellaneous (fruit, kola, leaves, palm kernels, clay pots, etc.) 4·3.

3) *A southern market, Dunkwa:*

cassava 24·9, firewood 17·5, plantains 11·1, rice 9·7, palm wine 7·6, vegetables 7·6, charcoal 3·9, yams and cocoyams 3·6, palm kernels 1·7, sugar cane 1·6, pineapples 1·5, maize 1·2, cooked cassava 1·2, coconuts 1·2, oranges 1·0, miscellaneous (sweet potatoes, poultry, meat, brooms, mats, stools, sponges, bread, kola, etc.) 2·1.

Tricart has drawn attention to the enormous extent of the kola nut traffic within the Ivory Coast, Liberia and Guinea, and has commented on the development of a commercial mixed cropping in the savannas of the Ivory Coast, with the modern sale of rice, yams and vegetables.[33] The movements northwards of kola nuts into Mali are much greater than the southward movements of dried fish in exchange. According to Tricart this explains the normal practice of lorries picking up foodstuffs in the Sikasso–Ferkessédougou area for transport southwards at very low prices. In consequence the estrangement between Mali and Senegal, and the tendency to divert some of Mali's export traffic from Dakar to Abidjan, met fewer problems than one would otherwise expect. The growth of urbanism has also encouraged a considerable internal traffic in foodstuffs, not only locally from 'market gardens', but from considerable distances. One estimate is that half the towns of Ghana receive food supplies from places more than 50 miles (80 km) away, and a quarter of the towns from places at distances of over 120 miles (190 km).[34] Meat, and dried, smoked or salted fish, all find considerable markets, especially in the export crop areas. In some cases of meat sales, the markets specialize in meat only. The meat traffic is highly organized. Cattle, sheep and goats travel partly on the hoof, grazing at pastures specially provided en route, or on roadside verges, and may travel, for example, from Fort Lamy to places as far distant as Lagos, over a thousand miles (1600 km). When prices in the meat markets for fatter stock rise, cattle move by rail. There is a general preference for tougher meat, and imported meat from Europe or New Zealand is often regarded as too soft to chew. Drove routes frequently follow main roads, diverging here and there for suitable pastures, or straighter if steeper routes. All animal movements over long distances are, however, generally focused on major river crossings by rail or ferry. Thus in Nigeria the Jebba and Makurdi bridges over the Niger and Benue are vital focal points in the animal traffic. Meat markets are usually located on the perimeter of a town, and usually on the side from which the animals approach. Frequently there are pastures nearby and a village where reside the Fulani agents of the livestock owners and dealers.

In discussion of both internal and external trades one should not forget the importance of the petty traders, mostly women, who in their millions make possible the initial bulking of small quantities of goods offered for sale, and break down commodities into small enough quantities to suit the pocket of most West African buyers. Nor should one forget that almost every West African engages at

MAIN LIVESTOCK TRADE ROUTES of WEST AFRICA

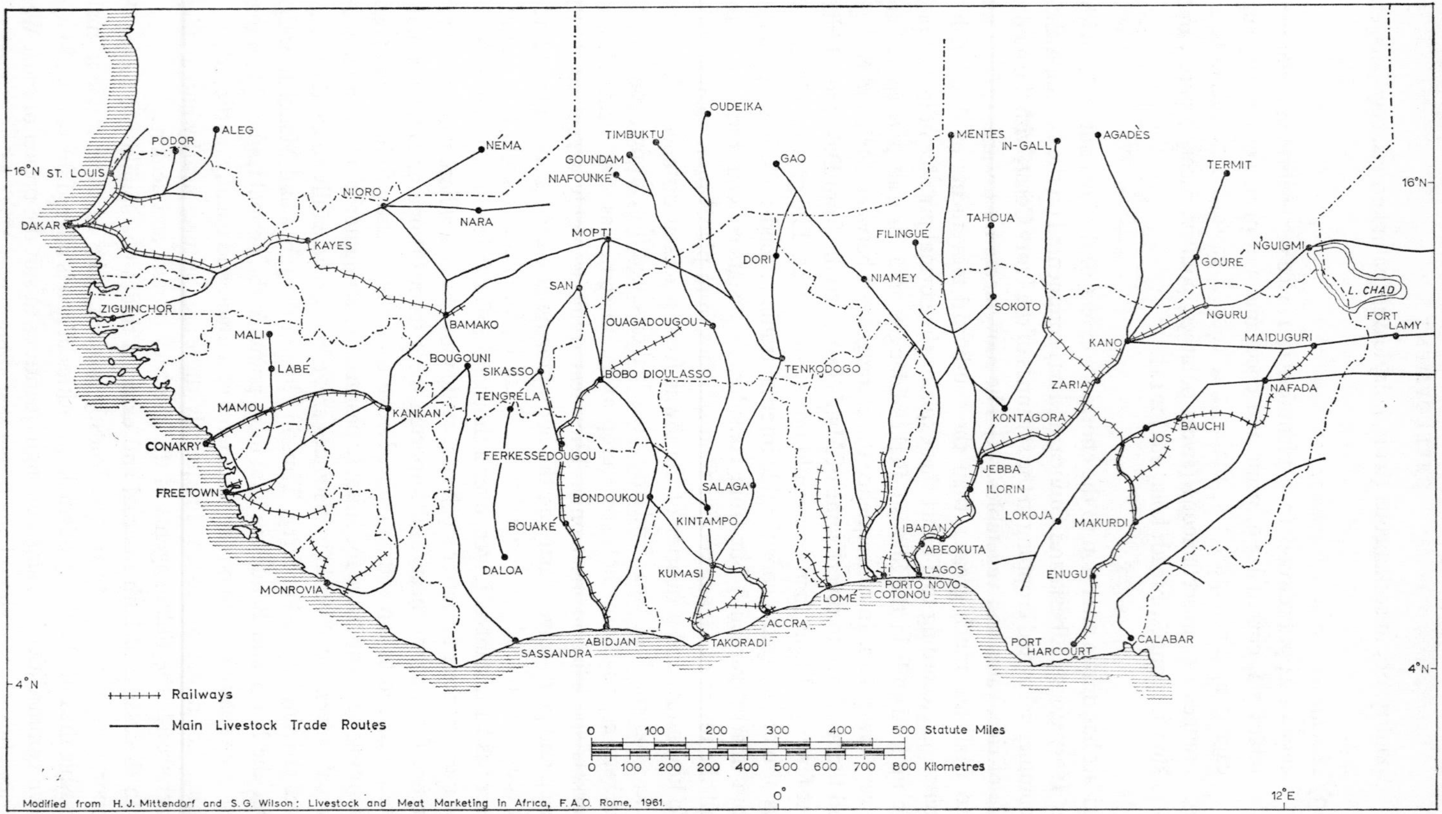

+++++ Railways

——— Main Livestock Trade Routes

Modified from H.J. Mittendorf and S.G. Wilson: Livestock and Meat Marketing in Africa, F.A.O. Rome, 1961.

Figure 11.8

some time or the other in petty trading, whenever the opportunity of making a small profit presents itself. Petty trading is essential as long as there are buyers who can afford at any one time no more than a few lumps of sugar, one or two cigarettes, or flour by the cigarette tin full. They undertake the greater part of market trading, and even retail goods on spaces rented in front of retail stores. One attempt has been made to map their distribution in a street in Ibadan.[35] Without them it would be impossible for the big trading companies to reach the small producers and consumers, who provide the greater part of the market. If and when the amount of work available and productivity and incomes increase, the need for petty traders will disappear, and they may be able to find employment elsewhere. At present, however, they provide a means of exchange, which could not otherwise be done so cheaply. They themselves find in the market a social amenity which many may be loath to surrender.

Today the West African countries are seeking to preserve and extend their trading links with Europe by association with the European Economic Community. Twelve countries (Dahomey, Ghana, Ivory Coast, Liberia, Mali, Mauritania, Niger, Nigeria, Senegal, Sierra Leone, Togo and Upper Volta) have also formed their own common market for goods and services to promote inter-West African trade.

BIBLIOGRAPHICAL NOTES

[1] The association of the gum trade with transhumance is discussed on p. 141. An excellent account of the trade is G. Désiré-Vuillemin, Un Commerce Qui Meurt: la Traite de la Gomme dans les Escales du Sénégal, *Les Cahiers d'Outre-Mer*, 5, 1952, pp. 90–92.

[2] Lagos Colony, *Annual Report for 1900–01*, p. 10.

[3] W. M. N. Geary, *Nigeria under British Rule*, London, 1927, p. 57.

[4] D. R. Rosevear, 'Forestry', in *The Nigeria Handbook*, London, 1953, pp. 174–205 (ref. p. 193).

[5] ibid., pp. 193 and 198–9.

[6] J. M. Dalziel, *The Useful Plants of West Tropical Africa*, London, 1937, p. 324 (quotation from Metzger, *Die Forstwirtschaft in Togo*, p. 66).

[7] On the African timber industry there is a useful chapter in G. H. T. Kimble, *Tropical Africa*, vol. I, New York, 1960, 'The Wealth of the Woods', pp. 195–224. See also G. von Wendorff and L. Okigbo, *Some Nigerian Woods*, Lagos, 1962 (with illustrations of prepared surfaces).

[8] C. Toupet, Dakar, *Tijdschrift voor Economische en Sociale Geografie*, 49, 1958, pp. 35–39.

[9] See T. E. Hilton, The Coastal Fisheries of Ghana, *Bulletin, Ghana Geographical Association*, 9(2), 1964, pp. 34–51.

[10] E. R. Rado, A Social and Economic Survey of Bentsir Quarters, Cape Coast, *Proceedings, West African Institute of Social and Economic Research*, 1954, pp. 37–45.

[11] K. K. Zwilling, Farming Fish, *Nigeria Magazine*, 44, 1954, pp. 315–28.

[12] A. F. Calvert, *Nigeria and its Tin Fields*, London, 1910. B. W. Hodder, Tin Mining on the Jos Plateau of Nigeria, *Economic Geography*, 35, 1959, pp. 109–22.

[13] P. A. Bower *et al.*, *Mining, Commerce and Finance in Nigeria*, London, 1948, p. 32.

[14] P. A. Bower *et al.*, op. cit., p. 128.

[15] N. Miller, *Lagos Steam Tramway 1902–1933*, London, 1958.

[16] Netherlands Engineering Consultants (NEDECO), The Hague, *River Studies and Recommendations on Improvement of Niger and Benue*, Amsterdam and The Hague, 1959.

[17] United Nations, *Statistical Yearbook*, 1960.

[18] A valuable article on industrialization in West Africa has appeared in United Africa Company, *Statistical and Economic Review*, **23**, 1959.
Two very useful accounts are:
W. A. Hance, *The Geography of Modern Africa*, New York, 1964, pp. 246–67.
A. Sokolski, *The Establishment of Manufacturing in Nigeria*, New York, 1965.
General problems are discussed in A. B. Mountjoy, *Industrialisation and underdeveloped Countries*, London, 1963.

[19] For thorough discussion of Africa's labour problems see International Labour Office, *African Labour Survey*, Geneva, 1958.

[20] United Africa Company, *Statistical and Economic Review*, **23**, 1959, p. 2.

[21] J. Suret-Canale, L'Industrie des Oléagineux en A.O.F., *Les Cahiers d'Outre-Mer*, **11**, 1950, pp. 280–8.
E. Guernier, *Afrique Occidentale*, Encyclopédie de la France d'Outre-Mer, vol. II, Paris, 1949, pp. 164–6.
A. Hauser, Les Industries de Transformation de la Région de Dakar, in P. Mercier *et al.*, L'Agglomération Dakaroise, *Etudes Sénégalaises*, **5**, 1954, pp. 69–83.
Y. Péhaut, L'Arachide au Sénégal, *Cahiers d'Outre-Mer*, **14**, 1961, pp. 5–25.

[22] United Africa Company, *Statistical and Economic Review*, **9**, 1952, and **13**, 1954.
W. B. Morgan, The Nigerian Oil Palm Industry, *Scottish Geographical Magazine*, **71**, 1955, pp. 174–7.
See p. 487.

[23] S. P. Schatz, Aiding Nigerian Business: The Yaba Industrial Estate, *Nigerian Journal of Economic and Social Studies*, **6**(2), 1964, pp. 199–217.

[24] United Nations, *Statistical Yearbook* (various dates).

[25] V. Thompson and R. Adloff, *French West Africa*, London, 1958, p. 461.

[26] P. T. Bauer, *West African Trade*, London, 1954.
See also F. J. Pedler, *Economic Geography of West Africa*, London, 1955, pp. 202–3.

[27] Thompson and Adloff, op. cit., p. 429 and Chap. VI.

[28] M. Coste, Le Fret Maritime Entre les Ports de la Mer du Nord et la Côte Occidentale d'Afrique, *Cahiers d'Outre-Mer*, **9**, 1956, pp. 350–62.

[29] United Africa Company, *Statistical and Economic Review*, **3**, 1949.

[30] R. Galletti, K. D. S. Baldwin and I. O. Dina, *Nigerian Cocoa Farmers*, London, 1956, pp. 123–4, 537–9.

[31] K. M. Buchanan and J. C. Pugh, *Land and People in Nigeria*, London, 1955, pp. 116–20.

[32] H. P. White, Internal Exchange of Staple Foodstuffs in the Gold Coast, *Economic Geography*, 1956.
P. R. Gould, *Transportation in Ghana*, North Western University, Studies in Geography, 5, Evanston, 1960, pp. 116–34. Figures quoted for Dunkwa do not add up to 100 per cent. Perhaps some very small items have been omitted.

[33] J. Tricart, Les Echanges Entre la Zone Forestière de Côte d'Ivoire et les Savanes Soudaniennes, *Cahiers d'Outre-Mer*, **17**, 1956, pp. 209–38.

[34] B. M. Niculescu, Food and Roads in the Gold Coast, *Proceedings, West African Institute of Social and Economic Research*, 1956, pp. 68–73.

[35] K. M. Buchanan and J. C. Pugh, op. cit., p. 69.

CHAPTER 12

The Development of Transport

The first effects of European contacts

The initial impact of Europeans would seem to have had little effect on the traditional forms of transport. The ships of the European nations for some time remained small enough to cross the bars of the larger rivers or to lie only a short distance offshore. The local canoes needed no adaptation in order to serve as links between ship and shore, and were the vehicles by which freight moved to the coast. When Europeans penetrated inland, other than by water, they did so on foot with porters to move their loads. While the chief items of trade were palm oil and slaves, no difficulties presented themselves. The palm oil moved principally by canoe, and the slaves walked.

The ports at this early stage needed nothing in the way of improvement to make them usable. In the west the great estuaries provided natural harbours, so that, even with considerable tidal ranges, small sailing ships could use them at all times. In the east, where tidal ranges were smaller, the absence of any break in the coastline for long distances necessitated anchorage offshore in any case. The sheltered anchorage of Lagos was available to ships drawing less than 12 feet (4 metres) of water, and the numerous entrances to the Niger delta, and the river mouths between the delta and the Cross river, also provided sheltered moorings. Until the late 19th century there were no heavy loads to put ashore, and so no necessity for quays or cranes.

The beginnings of modern port development were seen in 1863 with the completion of the first jetty at Dakar, and this developed into the best-equipped port in West Africa. Lighthouses were established soon after the first jetty, making it a relatively safe port of call, although the Almadi Reef has continued to claim victims under conditions of poor visibility. Shipping services using the South Atlantic began to make regular calls at the port, and the great naval base was started in 1898. By 1910 it was a well-equipped modern port capable of accommodating any ship then afloat. It remains the only West African port with a graving dock (although Lagos has a small floating dock), and its services are unequalled in the region. Elsewhere, apart from the construction of a number of jetties, nothing was done in the way of port improvement until well into the 20th century. Such changes as took place in the latter part of the 19th century were largely the result of the change from sail to steam propulsion, which led to an

U

Lagos Port
Original Entrance

Based on Chart 2812

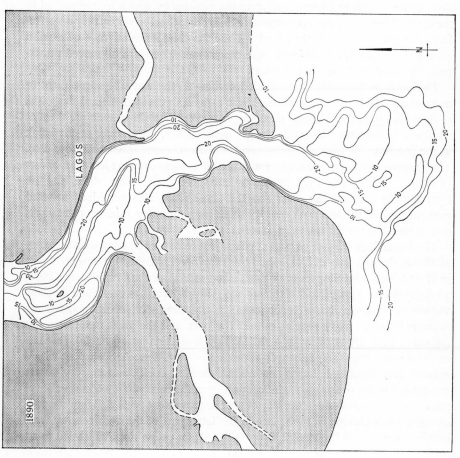

Figure 12.1a

Lagos Port
Improved Entrance

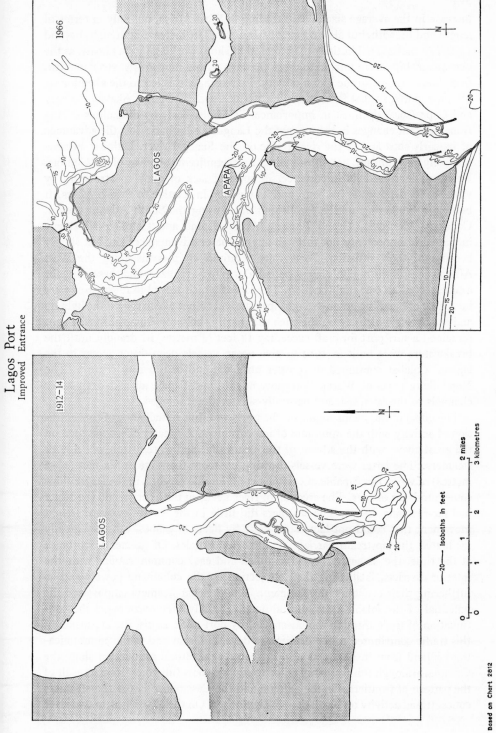

1912—14

1966

LAGOS

LAGOS

APAPA

—20— Isobaths in feet

0   1   2 miles
0   1   2   3 kilometres

Based on Chart 2812

Figure 12.1*b*

increase in the average size of ship trading to West Africa, not only in terms of length and breadth, but also in terms of draught. The increase in draught beyond 12 feet (4 metres) led initially to increased offshore working by surf boats, as the new steamships were unable to cross the bars across most of the river mouths, from Sierra Leone to the Cross estuary. Increasingly this led to the abandoning of minor ports, so that famous trading stations such as Opobo, Akassa, Badagry and Cape Coast declined in importance. St Louis, beset by difficulties arising from constant changes in the form of the Langue de Barbarie, lost the advantage of its early start and of the river traffic on the Senegal river. Bathurst became relatively insignificant, notwithstanding the magnificent routeway of the Gambia. Freetown increased its importance, in spite of lack of quay construction, by virtue of its deep-water harbour, and its position in relation to British Africa. It became a bunkering station for British ships using the South Atlantic routes. Conakry, Monrovia, Grand Bassam, Accra, Lomé and Cotonou all slowly increased in importance not through any virtue or advantage of site but simply because of their situation. Ports were required at intervals along the West African coast if the region's latent potential was to be realized, and these ports for a time served an essential function. The jetties which served in most cases were incapable of handling ocean-going ships, but had cranes which served the lighters and surf boats which lay on their lee side partly sheltered from the surf. Lagos remained a surf port for craft exceeding 12 feet (4 metres) in draught until the breakwaters were built in 1912 to give ocean vessels deep-water access to the lagoon. Calabar continued to prosper until the end of the 19th century. The Niger delta ports of Warri, Forcados, Burutu and Sapele all had deep-water channels to the open sea, and naturally-sheltered anchorages.

The effect of the steam engine on the ports was thus initially one of concentration of activity with the minimum of improvement. A greater effect was seen on the great rivers with the advent of the steam tugs and of the stern-wheel river steamers. The latter were vessels drawing no more than five or six feet ($1\frac{1}{2}$–2 metres) of water but capable of carrying considerable cargoes, in the larger ships some hundreds of tons. The creation of river fleets on the Senegal and the Niger had far-reaching effects. The steamers did little in the way of outward freight movement that could not have been done by fleets of canoes, but they greatly facilitated the upstream carriage of imported articles. Of greater importance at the time, the steamers produced quick and easy communications with the interior districts, facilitating their subjection by the colonizing powers and so furthering their economic development. The Senegal steamers emphasized the potential of the inland areas, and although initially they encouraged the continuation of trade through the unsatisfactory port of St Louis, the expansion of this traffic contributed to the decision to develop Dakar and to the communications inland from it. Steamers also increased agricultural production along the Gambia, although this routeway failed to expand to its full potential as a result of the pattern of frontiers. On the Saloum and the Casamance rivers the steamers concentrated activity on Kaolack and Ziguinchor. On the Niger system two river fleets came to serve a vast area of the interior. The Niger valley to Lokoja became the main artery to what is now Northern Nigeria, sustaining the seasonal pulsation of trade with the coast. At extreme low depth of the river, the steamers halted at Onitsha; as the floodwaters raised the level they could reach Lokoja, Baro and Jebba on the Niger, and increasing distances on the Benue. With the pacification of all West Africa the Benue fleet was able to travel as far as Garoua, in what is now the Republic of Cameroun, for two months of the year. The organization of the river fleet initially suggested an annual military operation (in some years this was indeed its precise function). The critical factor in the use of the Benue has been the depth over the bar which crosses it at its junction with the Niger. Once water-depth permitted, small steamers entered the river and laid fuel depots for the larger vessels which were to follow them as the flood rose, the return journey to the coast being with cargoes of local produce. Continuation of the operation upstream allowed use of the large vessels to be extended to the maximum, followed by withdrawal as water level subsided. It was essential that steamers should leave the Benue before the depth across the Lokoja bar was too slight. Lokoja thus became at an early stage of European penetration an important storage base and a fuel depot for the river fleets, but after 1912 it was to lose much of its importance (see p. 592). The Benue route still preserves its importance in the economy of the upper river areas, as inward transport of fuel oil, for example, would be prohibitively costly if arranged overland from Douala to Garoua. The importance of the river in the early administration of the region can be seen from a study of any early map of political boundaries. There was a tendency for provinces to be established on the axis of the river, and rectification to units of better social organization followed with stability of government at a later stage.

The beginnings of modern forms

RAILWAYS

The impetus to port improvement on a major scale came with the period of railway construction. The Berlin West African Conference of 1884–5 referred to effective occupation of territory, and it is frequently stated that this was widely interpreted as being unmistakably demonstrated by the presence of railway lines. The Dakar to St Louis line had already been completed in 1885, partly as a commercial link between Dakar Port and the Senegal river traffic, and later lines (with one exception) were not started until the last few years of the 19th century, or the early years of the 20th century. The time-lag between the Conference and the construction of lines suggests that the political implications of the former were perhaps less pressing than is sometimes supposed.

The Dakar–St Louis line provided a through route from Dakar to Kayes, the head of navigation from St Louis on the Senegal river. It had long been apparent that political control of the Upper Niger basin would require efficient communications via the Senegal valley, and the first suggestion for a railway had

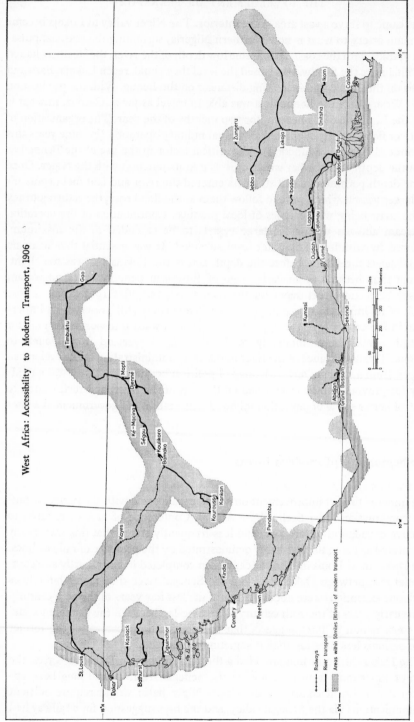

West Africa: Accessibility to Modern Transport, 1906

Figure 12.2

been in 1857. A line was equally necessary if economic development were to proceed, although this seems to have had little initial significance. The completion of the line to St Louis permitted the easier transport of heavy construction materials to Kayes, and a new railway line, for which works had started in 1881, was extended up the valley from near Kayes. The history of this construction is one of misfortune and mismanagement, and the first train did not run until 1893, but by 1904 the line was in operation to the Niger at Bamako and Koulikoro. These lines in final form were metre gauge. The significance of this route to the Upper Niger area is obvious, and its connection to Dakar by means of a line from Kayes to Thiès, completed in 1923, ensured an economic routeway to the ocean which was to last through the days of French colonialism only to be deliberately broken (albeit temporarily) in the early years of independent governments. The main delays in the completion of this line should not detract from the achievement. In 1904 the through route was in operation. At this time nothing comparable existed elsewhere in West Africa. The 2 ft 6 in gauge line from Freetown, started in 1895, did not reach Makeni until 1906; the line northward from Lagos, started in 1898, had progressed only as far as Ibadan; the line from Sekondi, started in 1898, had reached Kumasi in 1903. Elsewhere lines were only just beginning – 1900 from Conakry, reaching Kankan only in 1914, 1902 from Lomé, 1902 from Cotonou, and 1903 from Abidjan.

The arrival of the Kayes line at Bamako permitted further extension of river transport. Steamers were assembled on the Upper Niger and opened the river routes to Kouroussa and Kankan, and downstream to Gao. The course of the river was broken by rapids at several points, and later also by the Barrage des Aigrettes between Bamako and Koulikoro and by the Sansanding Barrage, but canals were constructed to circumvent the artificial barriers. All-season navigation of the whole river system is still not possible, but the importance of a through routeway is none the less considerable. Of particular value is the rail and water route from Dakar through to the Inland Delta area. The navigation of this part of the Niger system has never rivalled that on the Lower Niger and the Benue, partly because a through route to a port is not available, partly because of the alignment of the river, parallel to the coastline, so that passage along the river does not carry freight any nearer to the ports of the south. This was appreciated by the French, who planned to complete an interlocking transport system connecting the Middle and Upper Niger basins with the coast. The Dakar–Niger and Conakry–Niger lines reached the great river; the Abidjan–Niger did not, nor did the line from Cotonou, which has the unfortunate name of the Benin–Niger Railway, taking its name from the Bight and not from Benin town. It is unlikely that these lines will be extended in the near future to complete the planned network, particularly in view of current work on the Niger Dam in Nigeria, which will open a water route from the upper river to the Delta ports.

PORTS

The improvement of ports inevitably accompanied the construction of railway lines. The steam derrick allowed the overside unloading of steel railway lines and sleepers (wooden sleepers were abandoned relatively quickly in view of termite action) into lighters for carriage to jetties, but heavy items of equipment such as locomotives and rolling stock could not easily be handled except by heavy-lift cranes mounted on a quay, or by the use of coupled derricks in still water, that is, with the ship moored alongside a wharf or in smooth water behind a breakwater. Heavy-lift derricks for overside working were not fitted to normal ocean-going vessels until the 1930s. Early equipment therefore had to be assembled ashore from imported sections, and the importation of completed locomotives and rolling stock was a later feature. The greater influence of the railway was the concentration at the ports of export freight in quantities which made direct loading into ocean vessels highly desirable. Dakar and Conakry had quays available by the turn of the century, but the British West African ports had no comparable facilities.

The Gold Coast maintained two major ports, Sekondi and Accra. The railway from Sekondi had reached Kumasi in 1903. The line was first built to carry the heavy equipment required for the Ashanti gold mines, and by providing communications with the coast encouraged the mining companies in their investment in the area. It must be remembered that the Ashanti Wars were still of very recent memory (the extension of the line from Obuasi to the Ashanti capital of Kumasi was largely a political move), and roads did not exist, as the internal combustion engine had not yet reached West Africa and there was no wheeled transport in this region. The railway line inland was therefore the only effective link between the outer world and the Ashanti kingdom. The port of Accra was of long standing, and had been the capital of the Gold Coast since the British administration moved from Cape Coast in 1876. The more open vegetation of the Accra district led to some road construction and the use of wheeled transport, and the construction of the wharf allowed the use of lighters and surf boats for movement of freight between ship and shore. Accra, as the chief cocoa-exporting centre, remained important after the rise of Sekondi, which had no access to areas away from the railway. The railway from Accra was not started until 1909, and by serving the main cocoa-producing districts it increased Accra's economic status.

The ports of Nigeria have shown varying fortunes. The early ports have been mentioned above, and the decline of some of these with the arrival of the steamship. Initially the most important ports were Burutu and Forcados, on the Forcados river, one of the main western distributaries of the Niger delta, and Calabar, in the extreme east. The natural advantages of all three ports were considerable. Calabar had no obstructing bar across the estuary of the Cross river, and could therefore moor in sheltered anchorages vessels drawing 20 feet (6 metres) of water. Forcados and Burutu had even better moorings, with a depth of over 20 feet across the Forcados entrance, and serving the whole of Northern

Nigeria by means of trans-shipment into river steamers. Lagos was the only challenger to this trio, by virtue of its sheltered site and the relatively densely-populated areas of Yorubaland behind it, added to the natural routeways east and west through the coastal lagoons. It had one major disadvantage, namely the 12-foot (4-metre) depth across its entrance bar, which required overside trans-shipment by vessels lying offshore into surf boats or lighters. Much of the cargo destined for Lagos was at this stage trans-shipped at Forcados to coasting vessels of less than 12 feet draught. It was recognized that the advantages of Lagos

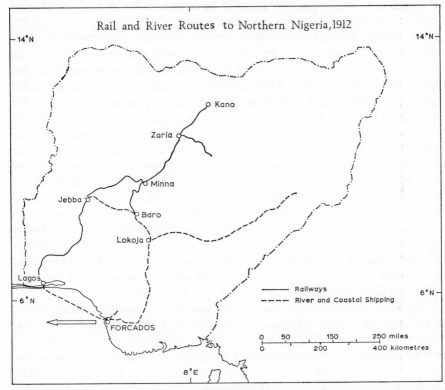

Figure 12.3

justified its development, this being particularly the case as the railway, started in 1898, was extended inland, and in 1907 construction of the entrance moles and training walls were started at Lagos, a task not completed until 1916, although ships were using the deep-water channel by the beginning of the First World War. Lugard had already developed the Niger river route to serve Northern Nigeria, opening a narrow-gauge railway line from Wushishi (the effective head of navigation on Kaduna river) to the then administrative headquarters of Zungeru as early as 1901. This early line was abandoned with the completion of the 3 ft 6 in gauge line from Baro, on the Niger, to Minna (1910), Zaria (1911) and Kano (1912). This rail-river route, based on the good Delta ports, could easily have continued to develop: railway extension on the High Plains of Hausaland was relatively simple and inexpensive, requiring a minimum of engineering works, as shown by the rapid construction between 1910 and 1912, when in addition to the main Baro–Kano line there was also built a 2 ft 6 in gauge line from Zaria south-east to Rahama, and a 3 ft 6 in gauge line from Jebba, on the Niger, to join the Baro–Kano line at Minna. This latter section provided a direct link between the Northern Railway and the Western Railway from Lagos to Jebba, the river crossing being made by ferry steamer. The sections from Ilorin to Jebba and from Jebba to Minna had been built in the face of considerable criticism, running as they did through the relatively lightly-populated country of the Middle Belt and offering little prospect of freight. Nevertheless the connection proved to be justified by later events, notably the onset of silting at the Forcados entrance, and the growth of wide bars bringing the minimum depths across the Forcados to only 9 feet (3 metres) by 1948 (tidal range is 4 to 5 feet (1·2–1·5 metres)) which destroyed the Delta ports as major gateways to the country. They have become only part-cargo ports, with ocean-going vessels completing loading at Lagos (a reversal of earlier practice!), but their early improvement is contemplated because of the importance of the river route to the Middle Belt in particular. A breakwater has been completed on the south side of the Escravos entrance to trap the sand moving up from the south by longshore drift. The influence of physical geography is reflected not only in the problems created by longshore drift, but also in the difficulty of supplying the materials to counter it. The Lagos moles required some 2 million tons of rock, which had to be brought from Aro Quarry, near Abeokuta, over 50 miles (80 km) to the north of Lagos, and the nearest point at which good unweathered rock could be found in quantity. The rock for the Escravos breakwater was brought over 100 miles (160 km) from Oluwagba Quarry, half a mile from Okitipupa.

The importance of Lagos steadily increased as the Delta ports declined, and was confirmed with the replacement in 1916 of the Jebba train ferry by the great bridge. The northern freight traffic had largely continued to move via Baro and the Delta ports until the completion of the quays on Lagos Island: while export cargo sent to Lagos had travelled by coaster to Forcados for loading, there was no advantage in using the through route by railway in preference to the river route direct to Forcados. The transformation of Lagos into a deep-water port served by the railway, coinciding as it did with the progressive transformation into shallow-water ports of Forcados, Burutu and Warri, led to a rapid reversal of role and importance. The original deep-water berths at Lagos were the Customs Wharf, and a number of small private wharves on Lagos Island; the coastal steamers brought coal to the power station at Ijora on Iddo Island, between Lagos and the mainland, and joined by road bridge to both. The railway terminus was also at Iddo.

No further extensions were made to the Western and Northern Railway systems apart from the completion, between 1912 and 1914, of the 2 ft 6 in line from Rahama to Bukuru, on the Jos Plateau. This involved climbing the edge of the Plateau, in a district where it was only some 1500 feet (460 metres) high, by a very steep and winding route. This little line, known as the Bauchi Light Railway,

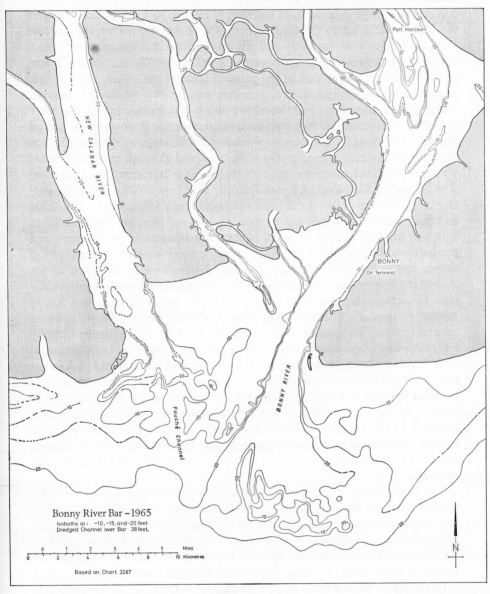

Figure 12.4

was the only economic link between the Plateau tin fields and the outer world until 1927. Up its tortuous track was carried much of the heavy machinery used in the mines, and the tin ore descended in the opposite direction. It was not closed until 1957. It derived its name from the former extent of Bauchi Province, which at one time included the Jos Plateau, but for much of its life it had no other connection with Bauchi town or Province.

A second change in importance was seen in Eastern Nigeria. The discovery of the Udi coalfield led to the construction of a railway from Port Harcourt to Enugu, carrying coal outwards and pit props (from the coastal mangroves), machinery and imported goods inwards. This line rapidly drew to itself and to Port Harcourt a large part of the palm oil trade of the region, and Calabar, notwithstanding its long history as a trading port, quickly found its hinterland reduced to its immediate neighbourhood and to the basin of the Cross river served by river steamers. Port Harcourt, situated on the Bonny river about 40 miles (65 km) from the sea, has deep-water quays for cargo working, with room for the relatively easy extension of port facilities, and although its original traffic was of a specialized nature its prosperity appeared to be assured from the start. The Udi coal could be sold without difficulty anywhere in West Africa for railway or power station use (until labour troubles made delivery dates unreliable and this market was largely lost outside Nigeria) and the port was established with the frequent sailings of small colliers. Its subsequent development and prosperity will be described later. The Bonny estuary has all the advantages of shelter and a deep-water channel. Its chief disadvantage is the threat of bar growth across its mouth: the bar is already present, although water depth is sufficient for ocean-going vessels to cross at high tide (the tidal range is 6 feet (2 metres) on the bar). The movement of sand eastward into the Bonny entrance appears to be on the increase, as shown by the blocking of the Fouché Channel and the closure of the direct route to the neighbouring minor port of Degema.[2] This danger has been appreciated only since the Second World War, and does not appear to have been appreciated when the port site was selected. In any case it is doubtful whether it would have affected the choice: all the Nigerian coast is affected by longshore drift, and the Bonny estuary is one of the places least impeded. In addition it is one of the few places where firm ground can be found in close proximity to a deep-water channel. Calabar shares these two advantages, but was too remote from the railway to hold its earlier pre-eminence in Eastern Nigeria.

The development of the coalfield had an additional impact on the country's transport system. With the arrival of the Eastern Railway at Makurdi, in 1924, the river port became the fuel depot for the Benue river, further diminishing the significance of Lokoja, which had already lost its function as the storage base for Northern Nigeria when the Western Railway from Lagos to Jebba was extended to Minna and so provided an all-season through connection with the coast.

Elsewhere in West Africa the construction of railways led to the same concentration of shipping activity into the larger ports. Conakry, situated on an island, sheltered to some extent by the Iles de Los and by an artificial breakwater, with deep water and good unweathered rock, is one of the better natural port sites of West Africa. It is an interesting reflection that its site would probably be con-

sidered indifferent were the mainland coast of West Africa of a different character. As it is, it has a reasonable routeway to the interior, on firm land through the
swamps and lowlands of the adjacent mainland, and the combination of all these
factors selected it as the coastal terminus of the Guinea railway. Started in 1900,
this was built with difficulty through the Fouta Djallon to the interior plains of
the Upper Niger basin, reaching Kouroussa in 1910 and Kankan in 1914. Choice
of routes was restricted by the frontier with Sierra Leone. The purpose of the
railway appears to have been mainly political, to facilitate control of the inland
areas and to channel their trade towards Conakry instead of through Sierra Leone
to Freetown, but it has also created its own traffic to some extent by encouraging
agricultural developments along its length, in particular the growth of citrus
fruits and bananas in the valleys of the Fouta Djallon foothills. The growth of
Conakry was matched by a decline in the relative importance of Benty, which has
moderate channel conditions (15 feet (4½ metres) of water), but which is almost
isolated in the southern extremity of the country's coastal lowlands.

The Ivory Coast had a number of small surf ports, notably Tabou, Sassandra,
Grand Lahou, Grand Bassam and Assinie. Of these Grand Bassam had the longest history as a port of call for ocean vessels, dating intermittently from the beginning of the 18th century. The Ivory Coast had had less contact with the outside
world than most other parts of West Africa, until the mid-19th century. Grand
Lahou, Grand Bassam and Assinie stood at the points where the sand-ridge
complex separating the sea from the coastal lagoons was broken respectively by
the Bandama, Comoe and Bia rivers. Grand Bassam was the port through which
moved the trade to and from the Ebrié Lagoon, which provides a sheltered east to
west routeway nearly 80 miles (130 km) in length. A lighter wharf was built at
Grand Bassam in 1901, and for thirty years this handled the greater part of the
Ivory Coast trade, even after the building of the railway, which was started at
Abidjan in 1903. Abidjan is situated on an island in the lagoon, and on the adjoining mainland, and following the decision to make it a railway terminus an attempt
was made to convert it into a deep-water port by breaching the sand complex
with a canal. A wharf was built at Port Bouet, on the coast south of Abidjan, and a
pilot canal cut between 1905 and 1907, but this silted up immediately after each
of several attempts, due to the large quantities of sand moved into its mouth by
longshore drift, and the canal project and the Port Bouet wharf were abandoned.
Thus Abidjan, alone of the West African railway termini, failed to develop as a
port after the construction of the line (opened as far as Bouaké, 196 miles (315
km) inland, by 1913), freight continuing to move along the lagoon waterway to
and from Grand Bassam. This lack of normal development was due principally
to the unrest in the territory, which was not completely pacified until 1915: heavy
fighting occurred in 1910 north of Abidjan as a direct result of the railway construction, local religious susceptibilities being affronted by its alignment. There
was thus no clear indication of immediate trade expansion justifying the cost of
port construction on a modern scale, and it is remarkable that the French should
even have attempted a deep-water canal at such an early stage.

Thus it can be seen that the timing of each phase of development varied from country to country, as is only to be expected. Senegal had, by 1910, passed into a later phase than the one here under discussion. By that year Dakar had been built as a modern port served by a transport system of combined rail and river services which extended 1000 miles (1600 km) into the interior and served the Upper and Middle Niger valleys. This was a system capable of improvement, but already of modern form. By way of contrast, the Ivory Coast in 1910 had only the Grand Bassam jetty and the lighter service to Abidjan, whence started a short and incomplete railway, the construction of which in that same year was delayed by fighting only 50 miles (80 km) from the lagoon. The Ivory Coast was still in this pioneering phase of development in the 1930s as far as the ports and railway were concerned, although motor roads were by then altering the national transport pattern to a more advanced phase. Liberia remained in the early stage of this phase until 1945, having until then no harbour works or railways, and very little in the way of roads.

The histories of Togo and Dahomey showed their own characteristics. In Dahomey, Ouidah was an ancient trading port at which European companies had maintained representatives since the latter part of the 17th century. It became the leading slave port on the Bight of Benin, and continued to export slaves until 1863. France did not take full responsibility for southern Dahomey until 1892, and consequently transport facilities were late on the scene. Railway construction inland from Cotonou was started only in 1900, on a metre gauge, reaching Savé, 169 miles (272 km) inland, in 1912. The first trains ran in 1902. A wharf was built at Cotonou to handle the overseas trade of the colony, and this effectively ended Ouidah's history as a port. Modern Ouidah is now on a lagoon 3 miles (5 km) from the sea and the old site. A second railway was brought into operation between 1907 and 1913, from Porto Novo to Pobé. This eastern line remained isolated from the central railway, and some freight crossed Lake Nokoué, from Porto Novo to Cotonou, by canoe or launch. The absence of a through line resulted in much of the trade for eastern districts following the traditional routeway from Porto Novo through the coastal lagoons to Lagos, and this continued after the construction of the Savé line, the lagoon route offering a good channel over its full distance. The Porto Novo railway and the lagoon route to Lagos were analogous to the Abidjan railway and the lagoon route to Grand Bassam. Unlike other West African lines, the Central Dahomey Railway had the disadvantage of starting away from a firm site on the mainland or on an adjacent island, and the initial construction through the sand ridges and the Terre de Barre presented some difficulties, although these were easily overcome. In Togo the German administration dated from 1884. Three railways were built from Lomé, where a wharf was built for handling cargo from lighters and surf boats. Rail construction started in 1902, and trains were running along the short coastal line to Anécho by 1905 and north-west to Palimé by 1907. Both were built to carry commercial products, and the Palimé line was successful not only in checking the movement of Togo crops to Ghana for export, but also in attracting cocoa grown in Ghana for sale and export to Lomé. A third line was built northward, and the 106 miles (171 km) to Atakpamé were in use by 1913. This line had less obvious direct economic motives, and was intended primarily to facilitate the administration of the northern part of the colony. All three lines are of metre gauge. The Germans thus established, in that part of the colony under their full control and administration, a higher density of railway than anywhere else in West Africa. The early establishment of plantation agriculture under white control may in part have contributed to this rapid creation of a railway system. The coastal strip produced palm oil, and to some extent coconuts also, and the lands served by the western line already had plantations of cotton, sisal and rubber. The unwillingness of the British Government to allow the introduction of alien plantation ownership inevitably acted against any equally rapid development of transport services in any of the British territories. Both the Togo and Dahomey railways in their coastal lines experienced difficulty with corrosion of rails and other metalwork as a result of salt spray blown inland from the breaking surf.

The Sierra Leone Government Railway has the very narrow gauge of 2 feet 6 inches. Construction was started in 1895 and the early sections were opened in 1899. Completion of the line to Pendembu (227 miles (365 km)) was achieved in 1906, and a branch line of 83 miles (134 km) was completed by 1911. This line was intended to serve the oil palm districts in the southern part of the coastal lowlands, but the railway could not compete economically with transport down the rivers to the coast, and it has lost money steadily since it was first built. The Freetown terminus remained unimproved, having only lighter wharves, principally as a result of the excellence of the natural sheltered harbour, which allowed overside working into lighters at all stages of the tide and without regard to the conditions of surf and swell. The railway has gained some of the freight trade from the rivers and minor ports since the silting of Bonthe became serious[3] and access by ocean-going vessels impossible.

It might be remembered that at the end of this phase of development, the railway was still the only form of transport, apart from porters and water transport, that reached into the interior. Lugard[4] stressed that 'the development of the African Continent is impossible without railways, and has awaited their advent'. He also notes that 'one railway train of average capacity and engine-power will do the work of thirteen thousand carriers at one-twentieth of the cost'. He urged that although standards of track materials should be maintained, quality of the fittings should be lower than in Britain: station platforms, turntables, even bridges, in his view, should wait (ferries could substitute for major bridges), not because of any social discrimination between Britain and Africa, but because of the need for the railways to start earning immediately. It is difficult to question his view that in the early stages it is a waste of money to spend large sums on anything more than the essential minima, particularly when lines were built across lightly-populated areas with little potential traffic, as in the Middle Belt of Nigeria or the desert margins in Senegal. Lugard stated 12 miles (19 km) per hour for the period of daylight as the necessary target for railway operation in a

new territory. These were sensible recommendations, and although this advice
was not always followed, as in the case of the early replacement by a bridge of the
Jebba Railway Ferry, in general they were adopted. Narrow-gauge lines permitted the use of steeper gradients and sharper curves than would have been the
case with standard gauge track; relatively light-weight locomotives allowed the
use of lighter rail than in Europe, and of less ballasting – an important consideration in areas where deep decomposition of the rock made ballast material difficult
to obtain; tunnels were everywhere avoided, if necessary by a deviation of a few
miles; everywhere the line was single-track, with passing places only at stations,
so that expensive signalling equipment was not required, trains being operated
on a staff system. Road crossings did not have to be bridged nor equipped with
level-crossing gates, because there were no roads, nor did lines have to be fenced.
All these factors contributed to cheapness of construction and operation, and
it needed modification only at a much later date. The greatest disadvantages of
the railways were those common to all single-track lines: the breakdown of one
train delayed almost every other train on the railway, while the breakdown of the
track cut communications completely. The latter is by no means uncommon
today, and reflects the lack of knowledge of basic facts of the physical environment. A railway engineer may be required to bridge a river of which the average rate of flow is not known, and of which the area of catchment is unmapped
and the average monthly rainfall totals unknown. Because the railway system
is single-track, and staff operated, a stop at every station is normal, so that even
today the limited accommodation 'express' trains may average little more than
20 miles (32 km) per hour.

The advent of the internal combustion engine

The internal combustion engine revolutionized the economic development of
West Africa, its effect there being totally different from its effect in Europe. In
the latter, there already existed a number of alternative methods of transport,
namely canal or river craft, railways, and road traffic, the latter being horse-
drawn wheeled vehicles which had lost the long-distance passenger traffic but
retained the local carriage of passengers and freight. Electric tramways were a
specialized form of road transport. The motor engine, whether in a private car, or
a lorry or any public service vehicle, merely improved a transport form which was
already in existence, and long-distance haulage, competing with the railways for
both passengers and freight, did not develop until after the First World War. The
motor engine in West Africa did not improve an existing form of transport, but
introduced an entirely new element into the transport network. The number of
transport vehicles increased much more slowly than in Europe, partly because
of difficulties of fuel and of repairs, but more particularly because there were
no roads on which the vehicles could run. Outside the towns, the first road in
Nigeria, for example, dates from 1905, when a road was constructed for some 30
miles (50 km) northward to Oyo from the then railhead at Ibadan. This road was

initially used by bullock-carts, the bullocks being trained on a partnership basis by the British Cotton Growing Association and the Nigerian Railway.[5] However, tsetse flies killed the animals within a year, and the service was replaced by a motor lorry, which, in spite of its limited capacity, halved the cost of transport compared with head-porterage.[6] In Northern Nigeria, ox-drawn carts from Zungeru to Zaria cost 1s. 9d. per ton/mile, against 2s. 9d. by head-porterage, but the early lorries were more expensive than the carts.[7] An attempt to use a steam traction engine was unsuccessful, the roads being too uneven in surface.[8] Pack animals, both oxen and donkeys, were also used in the early days of colonial administration, but proved unsuccessful in most areas. Hailey[9] summarizes the position in the non-British territories of West Africa as follows: 'the major routes in the Ivory Coast date from the period of the First World War; in Senegal and the Sudan the construction of roads of a modern type dates from about 1924. In Dahomey a beginning had been made before 1914, but the more important roads date in their present form from about the year 1925. In the Niger territory there was until 1934 only one road practicable throughout the year, namely that between Niamey and Zinder.'

Because the use of motor vehicles necessitated road construction, and this was difficult and expensive in the forested country of the coastal margins, expansion of the network was inevitably slow. It was also inevitable that in some territories the roads did not duplicate any of the routes served by the railways. In part this was the natural desire of Colonial Administrations to maintain the earning capacity of the railways without competition, but it was also common sense to ensure that all funds available for road construction were spent on projects of expansion. Thus it was natural for the roads to be built as feeder services to the railway lines, widening the area within reach of economic forms of transport, and augmenting rail receipts in the process.

Road materials offered no problem. Laterite was at hand almost everywhere, and the usual method of road construction made good use of it. Initially, however, road construction involved no more than the clearing of the vegetation, and the grading and compacting of the natural soil to make a surface. This was – and is – quite satisfactory in areas where there is a dry season of at least several months, in that it provides a dry-season road which will tolerate traffic flow of up to 100 tons per day. For a 10–12 feet (3·0–3·7 metre) carriageway costs in 1950[10] were £100–£200 per mile (U.S. $175–350 per km) in Nigeria, and annual maintenance about £60 per mile ($105 per km). The maintenance is essential, because the surface deteriorates rapidly in the rains, and anthills and vegetation re-establish themselves. A dry-season road of this nature may disappear if left without maintenance for one or two years. For traffic between 100 tons and 500 tons per day, a 3–6 in (75–150 mm) layer of compacted laterite is added and the carriageway widened to 12–14 feet (3·7–4·3 metres). Construction costs are twice as much (£200–£400 per mile, or $350–700 per km, in 1950) although maintenance remains much the same. The result is officially an all-season road, although passage in the rains may be difficult, or even impossible if attempted within twelve hours of heavy rain. With very little or no foundation material beneath the laterite, drainage is not good, and the weight of a heavily-loaded lorry after rain may cause such deep ruts in the road (which harden with dry weather) that smaller vehicles following in the same track may find themselves resting on the central road surface with their wheels out of contact with the ground. Even if a road of this type is closed for a day after heavy rain, the surface still gives trouble, although of a different kind. The prepared surface depends for its binding properties on the clay constituent of the laterite, and in the dry season this grade of material dries out and blows away. Once this binding effect is lost, the surface develops transverse corrugations with a wave length of 18–24 in (45–60 cm). On a badly-corrugated surface very low and very high speeds are both possible, but between 15 and 50 miles (25–80 km) per hour the vehicle is subjected to a vibration of such intensity that it may begin to disintegrate. The customary method of maintenance to prevent corrugation becoming too serious is daily brushing with a chevron-shaped broom hauled by two men, which re-distributes the loose surface material. Where traffic exceeds 250 tons per day the surface needs to be brushed twice a day. Above 500 tons per day the road surface must be dressed with tar or bitumen. This gives a road which is not a metalled or tarmacadamized road of the British type, but which is sealed against moisture changes, neither inward percolation by rain nor outward drying by evaporation being possible while the surface remains intact. Width is about 16 feet (5 metres). Such a road is much superior to the laterite-surface type, but is correspondingly more expensive. 1950 figures were £600–£1200 per mile ($1050–2100 per km) to construct and £100–£140 ($175–250) per annum to maintain. This type of surface has its disadvantages. In the rains the laterite margins tend to wash away, so that there is a shallow step down from the tar surface to the laterite margin: repeated traversing of this step by heavy lorries causes scalloping of the road edge as the surface breaks. This is followed (as in any other break in the tar seal) by the rapid development of pot-holes, which may be of considerable depth.

The figures for construction given above were the 1950 costs in Nigeria. In the early days of road construction costs were sometimes very much less. A good road engineer or administrative officer, if gifted with a persuasive manner, could so convince the local people of the advantages that would follow from road construction that voluntary labour (or, at least, labour ordered to the site by the local chief and not on the Government payroll) might provide the greater part of the working force. A famous road engineer of early days in Yorubaland is reputed to have spent nothing on labour or compensation of land, although both would be considerable items of present-day expenditure.

The expansion of the road network was at first largely restricted to feeder roads from the railways then existing to major towns within reasonable distance of the line but not scheduled for branch rail services. Rapid expansion was impossible, as there were insufficient local men of sufficient wealth and worldly experience to buy and operate vehicles, so that the early cars and lorries were Government owned or were operated by the large foreign trading firms. By 1913 Ghana, for example, had only 218 miles (351 km) of road and 100 motor vehicles, mainly acting as 'feed' vehicles to the railway. This planned allocation to the roads of a function complementary to the railway was general in the British West African territories, and marks the preliminary phase of the modern transport network. There was no question of competition – the roads were actively prevented from

The Road and Rail Network of Ghana, 1932

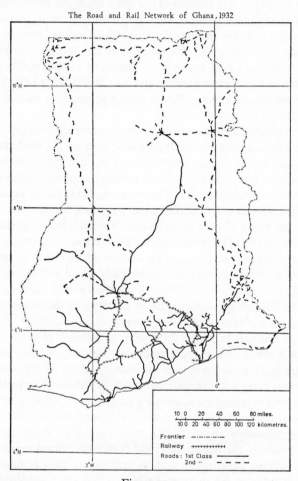

Figure 12.5

competing. In Ghana, as the number of roads increased, deliberate gaps were left between the various road systems so that through traffic was impossible, and this policy, which forced freight and passengers to travel by train, was largely maintained in southern Ghana until 1938. The railway from Accra to Kumasi was completed in 1923, and the Central Railway line in 1927. A trunk road from Accra to Takoradi was completed only in 1935, and legislation protecting the railway from road competition was enacted in 1936. If it is assumed that the function of an efficient transport system is to offer the cheapest possible rates for reliable carriage between different points, it cannot be said that southern Ghana had such a system even as late as the outbreak of the Second World War. The potential benefits of motor transport were better seen in the Northern Territories of Ghana. As the railway was not extended north of Kumasi, which it had reached from Sekondi in 1903, one of the first of the trunk roads was opened from Kumasi to Tamale in 1921, and was subsequently extended to serve the whole of the Northern Territory. Costs in 1921 for freighting produce over this road were 5s. per ton/mile (U.S. 70 cents per ton/km), but this figure fell to 3s. (40 cents) by 1924 and to 1s. (14 cents) by 1930 as a result of improvements in road and vehicle maintenance and management, and was to fall lower still. Thus Ghana between the wars had, in effect, different phases of transport development in the north and in the south.

Difference of phasing also existed within each part of the country. In the north there was the contrast between the head-load porter on the bush paths and the lorry on the new roads; in the south there was, in addition to the contrasts between the carrier, lorry and train, the difference between the ports of Takoradi and Accra, the two coastal termini of the railway. Accra remained an open port with a wharf for lighters and surf boats, but Takoradi, first used in 1928, represented a modern phase of port development. Takoradi is a completely artificial port, created by the use of local stone to build protective breakwaters which allow moorings in a sheltered anchorage. The subsequent additions of quays has not satisfied demand, and much overside working of cargo is still carried on, but the port provided for the first time in Ghana a certainty of safe handling.

All the West African territories were to display this dichotomy of transport phasing, although the phases varied in time, with the exception of the Gambia and Portuguese Guinea, in which there were no railways to affect Government policy, except a short line in the Gambia serving the ilmenite workings (see p. 547). With these exceptions, the preliminary phase in the evolution of a modern transport pattern was usually marked in British territory by the extension of the railway system and of accompanying feeder roads, but with no trunk roads capable of competition. In Nigeria railway extension between the First World War and the depression of 1930 led to the completion of the Eastern Railway from Enugu to Makurdi, on the Benue river, and thence northward to join the Lagos–Kano line at Kaduna Junction in 1927. A branch line from Kafanchan reached the Plateau tin fields at Jos in 1927. In 1929 a line was completed from Zaria north-west to Kaura Namoda, and an extension north-eastward from Kano to Nguru was finished in 1930. In the extreme south-west of the country a small branch line to Ilaro was also completed in 1930. The train ferry at Makurdi was replaced by the great bridge, half a mile in length, which was completed in 1932. These lines were built for clear economic reasons; to carry coal to the tin fields, to serve the groundnut-producing area of Kano Province, and to evacuate the expanding cotton crop in the districts north-west of Zaria. It is immaterial now that by the time the railway reached Jos the mining companies had already resorted to hydro-electric power, generated by the rivers plunging over the 2000-foot (600-metre) scarp surrounding the Plateau. If this had been foreseen, the line would probably not have been built, because for most of its length it crosses parts of the Middle Belt which offer little in the way of passenger or freight traffic. The particular value of this line was that it offered an alternative route for export production, and led to the expansion of Port Harcourt as an alternative to Lagos. It has been difficult to expand the facilities of Lagos with sufficient rapidity to keep up with demand, and this difficulty would have been greatly accentuated if Port Harcourt had not existed as an alternative national gateway.

To serve Nigerian railways, both those already existing and the extensions listed here, roads proliferated, but still in the feeder capacity. The two great north–south roads could not develop as main routeways until the railway bridges at Jebba and Makurdi were complete, and although the former had been finished in 1916 the road on both sides of the river received little attention. Indeed, the main road east of Jebba was still little more than a dry-season road as late as 1950, and although Nigeria never adopted the 'gap' policy of Ghana, the effect on this major road route was much the same. The main road through Makurdi was inevitably delayed until the bridge was completed there. If the absence of main roads prevented competitive road traffic, the extent of Nigeria encouraged widespread road development on a provincial or regional basis. In the north the railway itself operated a road service from Gusau, on the Kaura Namoda line, for over a hundred miles north-west to Sokoto, and private operators established services on the other roads as they were built. Road construction on the High Plains of Hausaland presented no great difficulties on account of the perfection of sub-aerial planation. Although the larger rivers required bridges, or drifts across the river bed, few culverts were necessary on the major roads (which usually followed the watersheds between the catchment basins). As a result heavy lorries were a reasonable proposition from the start, and 10- and 12-ton diesel-engined vehicles were in operation by the early years of the Second World War, giving freight rates to the railway at figures low enough to make production economically competitive. On the Jos Plateau the development was of different form, because the country was more rugged and broken, and laterite was not available. The majority of roads in the tin fields were built by companies or by the private miners for their own use, and were little more than roughly-cleared tracks with rock filling in patches of loose ground. These 'roads' in many cases were maintained only for the two wheel tracks in order to save expense, the life of alluvial mining leases being uncertain and high road expenditure being therefore unjustified. Culverts were of brushwood and mud, and bridges were non-existent – vehicles drove through rivers on a rough boulder causeway provided that water depth was not excessive. As the ratio of run-off to percolation is high on the Plateau, flash floods after rain are common but usually short lived, so that roads are not blocked for long. The mining tracks, in terms of standard of construction, should be dry season only, but as the washing of the tin-bearing gravels is possible only in the wet season the tracks may receive their heaviest use in the rains. Vehicles are therefore frequently of the 15-cwt truck type, usually of the American 'pick-up' design, light enough to get over wet ground, and with sufficient clearance and robustness of construction to ride undamaged over boulders and ant-hills. By way of contrast, heavier vehicles have been employed in the main mining areas of the Plateau by the big companies, where proved depth of stanniferous alluvium, worked by drag lines and by sluicing, offer an assured life for mines on the open and almost level surfaces at places such as Dorowa and Bukuru, contrasting with the manual panning of small streams in rocky valleys on the Plateau edge.

In south-eastern Nigeria and in south-western Nigeria road networks developed fairly early, especially in the former. This was facilitated by the heavy clearing of the forest which had already taken place over wide areas, as a result of population pressure, to leave only the oil palms on which the prosperity of the region depended. The movement of palm oil by road to the railway was added to the movement by water to the Niger, and lorries also carried the oil to the river. In Yorubaland, the more open network of roads followed the increasing cultivation for export of cocoa, cotton and palm oil, although much of the latter tended to be consumed locally instead of being exported, and the cotton production of this region was largely abandoned after 1925. At this stage produce still moved to Lagos by train: the Ijebu Ode to Lagos road was not completed until after the Second World War.

This phase of development as exemplified by Nigeria is typical of much of West Africa. One result of the colonial power establishing full control over wide areas was the systematic growth of products for export and of foodstuffs for internal exchange. Freedom of movement outside the immediate tribal area existed as never before, and offered economic possibilities on a scale undreamed of hitherto. The railways of the preceding phase had introduced the ideas of wider horizons and of cash crops (for internal or external consumption); the feeder roads and the vehicles operating thereon widened enormously the area capable of taking advantage of the economic possibilities which the railway represented.

In the Gambia and Sierra Leone the pattern was slightly different. The former has never had railways, and the roads were built as feeders to the river. Vessels with 19 feet (5·8 metres) draught can reach Kuntaur, and with 12 feet (3·7 metres) draught can reach Georgetown, 176 miles (283 km) up-river. Five-ton launches can pass out of the country and into Senegal. The evacuation of groundnuts by water is so obviously the cheapest form of transport that a road parallel to the river is only now being planned. Sierra Leone in this phase built no extensions to the Government railway, but developed a number of roads which acted principally as feeders to the canoes and launches on the north–south rivers instead of to the east–west railway. Water competition had always prevented the railway from making any profit, and now merely increased the losses incurred, to the point where tolls were put on some roads in an effort to divert traffic to the railway. The road system succeeded in expanding economic production, irrespective of the route employed to evacuate the produce. Sierra Leone also at this time added to her transport system a feature unique in British West Africa, namely a major railway not owned by the Government. This was the line of 3 ft 6 in gauge completed in 1933 from the iron deposits of Lunsar and Marampa to the port of Pepel, 57 miles (92 km) away. This line carries some $1\frac{1}{3}$ million tons of ore per annum to the special loading berths at Pepel. It is significant that this special wharfage was built for a product too difficult to load by use of lighters.

Dahomey in this phase saw the extension of the railway system by the link from Cotonou to Porto Novo which joined the central and eastern lines in 1930. The central lines were extended northwards to Parakou in 1934, and short-lived 60-cm gauge branch track lines were completed in 1927 to join Abomey and Zagnanado to the main line, and in 1931 to join Grand Popo inland to Athiémé and eastwards to the metre-gauge system. The reasons for this use of very narrow gauge are not clear: construction costs are much the same as for the metre gauge, and the disadvantages of the break in gauge are considerable. Before the advent of lorries these minor lines might have been justified, but they had little economic justification when they were paralleled by roads and lorries were available. The Bohicon–Abomey line was only 6 miles (10 km) in length, and the Zagnanado branch only 25 miles (40 km). It is not surprising that all the 60-cm lines were taken up during the Second World War when materials for the maintenance of the metre-gauge lines were in short supply. No further lines were built, and extension of the transport system was by road development, in particular by the construction of a main road northwards from Cotonou, branching to give roads to the north-west and north-east of the territory. Of these the latter was the more important, running to Malanville on the Niger, 557 miles (896 km) from Cotonou. At Malanville a ferry joins this road to Gaya and the road system of the former Niger Territory. This inter-colonial road showed little initial traffic, but was to become a main artery of trade, since for political reasons the trade of the Niger Territory was encouraged to remain within the boundaries of the Federation of French West Africa instead of crossing the international frontier with Nigeria. The other important road at this stage was the coastal highway running west to east, coming to Cotonou from Lomé and passing eastward from Porto Novo into Nigeria. This road was not of good quality, and little was done between the wars to improve its surface. The reasons for this appear to be clear. Firstly, the policy of transport development in French West Africa was one of creating a self-sufficient inter-territorial network of integrated services, whereby produce could be exported and necessary goods imported without crossing international boundaries. Secondly, the narrow longitudinal extent of both Togo and Dahomey made it possible for vehicles using the international road from Nigeria to Ghana to pass through both territories without even requiring to buy petrol, thus making no financial contribution whatsoever to the cost of road upkeep. This consideration still applies, and in the latest phase of transport expansion the coast road has been given a good metalled surface which makes through traffic fast enough to traverse both countries without even an overnight stop.

The history of Togo in this same phase is very similar. The French administration started the extension of the Central Railway northward from Atakpamé, but after reaching Blitta in 1933 the financial consequences of the economic depression prevented its further continuation. Beyond railhead the main road through the territory was improved to give a through routeway from Lomé to Ouagadougou, in Upper Volta, a further example of the inter-colonial planning of the French administration. Roads were not only built to serve the producing areas, but were built parallel to all the railway tracks, a pattern in direct contrast to that of the British West African territories, but apparently economically sound none the less. The coastal road was in the same indifferent state as in Dahomey. No improvements were made to port facilities at Lomé. At this stage the transport facilities of Togo did not attain a very high individual standard, but the road and rail network was sufficiently close on the ground to provide an efficient service not only for Togo itself but also for some of the Upper Volta trade and some of the Ghana trade. Cocoa from Ghana continued officially to move in considerable quantities until fiscal controls were introduced at the frontier, and have, subsequently, still moved in quantity, albeit unofficially.

In the Ivory Coast, construction work on the railway was resumed in 1923, and the line reached Ferkessédougou (347 miles (558 km) from Abidjan) in 1930 and Bobo Dioulasso (494 miles (795 km)) in 1934. This extension was intended to increase the overseas trade of the colony, and any such increase would clearly require a better arrangement than the loading of lighters at Abidjan and transshipment at Grand Bassam. The wharf at Port Bouet was therefore re-built in 1932, and an extension made to it from the railway at Abidjan, with the loading of lighters for working to ships lying offshore. Simultaneously with work on the wharf construction the excavation began in 1931 of the Vridi Canal some three miles west of the original canal attempt, intended to give ocean-going vessels access to the lagoon and to quays at Abidjan. The canal project was suspended during the Second World War, but its start marks the beginning in the Ivory Coast of the phase of port development, namely the construction of deep-water quays. Meanwhile development continued in the colony with the construction of a small jetty at Sassandra, and by the opening in 1923 of the Asagny Canal connecting the Ebrié Lagoon with the Bandama and Grand Lahou, thus allowing the establishment of regular launch and steamer services along the lagoon routeway. Hand-in-hand with the later stages of this development was the extension of the road network and the growing numbers of motor vehicles. The most important routes were the main road northward, in part close to the railway, to Bobo Dioulasso, joining the road east to west from Fada N'Gourma and Ouagadougou to Sikasso and Mali; and the road running in a general north-westerly direction from Abidjan to Man and on into Guinea. Among others, the north–south road just west of the frontiers with Ghana deserves mention. No good road connection was made with Ghana and none with Liberia, following the usual French policy, but a number of good or indifferent roads crossed the other boundaries. In the west roads were built down to Tabou and Sassandra, although these ports became of reduced importance with the rise of Abidjan and Port Bouet, and the expansion of economic crops such as coffee and cocoa was closely bound up with the extension of the road system. The timber resources of the country were less dependent on the roads, and their exploitation began in the pre-motor age, logs being floated out to the ships lying offshore. The motor tractor was used at a later stage to assist log haulage to the rivers. The internal road system was largely laid out during the First World War and immediately afterwards, and the relatively high frequency of roads is probably not unconnected with the late pacification of many districts.

The pattern of roads in Guinea offered a complete contrast to the feeder network of Ghana, for example. The most important road, from Conakry to Bamako in Mali, was never far away from the railway for the whole of the distance from Conakry to the Niger at Kouroussa, whence the road follows the left bank of the river. The second great road entered the territory in the north-west, from Senegal, and followed the Tomine valley up into the Fouta Djallon Highlands, to pass through Labé to join the other road and the railway at Mamou. It left them again 92 miles (148 km) up-country, at Dabola, and continued in a general south-easterly direction to join the Ivory Coast road system at Man. These two main roads were part of the inter-territorial route pattern of French West Africa, and the minor roads were largely tributary to them rather than to the railway, although between Conakry and Kouroussa it is obviously difficult to differentiate. The Guinea roads have without question greatly facilitated the growth of economic crops away from the railway, although this was not, it seems, their prime purpose. Because some of these roads traverse the mountain country of the Fouta Djallon they also contributed to the growth of the Highlands as a tourist or holiday area for officials and others working in the West African territories.

Senegal, already noted as having more advanced transport services than the other West African colonies, began the development of an extended network before the arrival of the motor lorry. A rail link from Thiès to Kayes was started in 1907, and the line had progressed over 250 miles (400 km) from Thiès before the First World War stopped construction work. A branch to Kaolack was added in 1911. The connection to Kayes was completed in 1923, and the short branch lines serving the groundnut-producing areas were built between 1929 and 1931. The main roads of Senegal run alongside all the railways; along the left bank of the Senegal river; north to south from Matam on the Senegal through Tambacounda, on the Thiès–Kayes railway, and on to Labé in Guinea, with a branch westward to serve the Casamance valley. The duplication of routes was not, however, as competitive as the map suggests, the roads being mainly of poor surface quality in order not to provide an attractive alternative to rail haulage. In effect the advent of lorry transport meant improved carriage of produce (especially groundnuts) to the railway, except in the extreme west, where the Thiès to Dakar road was given a tarmacadam surface at a relatively early stage.

The improvements in internal communications were accompanied by improvements in the ports of Dakar and Kaolack. The latter is the head of navigation for

ocean vessels on the Saloum river, and came into existence in the ten years
before the First World War as a result of the branch railway to the river. Its
activity has increased with the growth of road services to the groundnut-producing district to the north, and inevitably it has benefited from the completion of
the railway to Kayes and Bamako, although this has been at the expense of
smaller ports such as Rufisque rather than of Dakar. Kaolack suffers from the
presence of a bar at the Saloum mouth, so that effective draught is restricted to
11 feet (3·5 metres), and the port is in much the same position as the Delta ports
of Nigeria: part-cargoes are loaded at Kaolack and the remainder at Dakar. Dakar
remained the leading port of West Africa, with growing industrial development,
partly the processing of materials for export. Extension of quays and the provision of heavy cranes and other services continued throughout the period of road
and rail expansion, and the area of the sheltered harbour was increased by the
construction of moles and breakwaters. The construction of these was helped by
the presence of sound, unweathered volcanic rock on the Dakar Peninsula, so
that the raw material for harbour works travelled only a few miles, by rail, from
quarry to site, which is another point of marked contrast to most ports elsewhere
in West Africa. It is significant that the Senegal railway had already started
transition from steam to diesel and diesel-electric traction during the Second
World War. This change was due partly to lack of local fuel, partly to periodic
difficulties of water supply, and partly to greater mechanical efficiency of the
diesel units. The tendency to abandon steam for diesel is characteristic of all the
West African lines, particularly in the drier northern areas, but Senegal was the
first territory to make the change. At an earlier stage the Dakar–Niger Railway
had made use of articulated locomotives, giving greater power and adhesive
weight but capable of operating on relatively light tracks. Similar locomotives
were employed on heavy goods trains in Northern Nigeria prior to the renewal of
the section between Jebba and Kaduna with heavy rail.

The northern territories can be considered at this stage. Adjacent to the advanced colony of Senegal was Mauritania, lacking virtually all modern forms of
transport. Only one road of note was established, the so-called Imperial Route to
Morocco, running northwards from St Louis and keeping east of the frontier
away from the coast. Occasional vehicles used the southern part of this road, but
stretches of it were no more than a rough track having affinities with the trans-
Saharan routes of the territories farther to the east. The usual transport form in
Mauritania was the camel or the horse. The only modern forms were the river
craft on the Senegal river and the motor vehicles operating from St Louis. Port
Etienne was a sheltered bay serving as a fishing base.

Very similar conditions existed in the Niger Territory. Transport conditions
have remained in traditional form over most of the country to the present day,
with the camel being the chief agent of transport. Only along the southern
margin are recognizable 'roads' in existence, along the east to west route from
Lake Chad to Zinder and Birni n'Konni to Gaya and Niamey on the Niger. The
Niamey road continued on the left bank of the river into former French Soudan,

and became a trans-Saharan route. West of the Niger roads ran to Ouagadougou and southward to Dahomey, and over these roads much of the territory's trade was routed. Two roads ran south into Nigeria, to Kano and Sokoto, and caravans, of course, crossed the frontier where they pleased. The routes through Nigeria were economically the most desirable, but official policy diverted even bulky traffic such as groundnuts to the Dahomey route to and from Cotonou, with results which will be mentioned later. The trans-Saharan route northward through Agadès to Algeria carried little trade, and motor vehicles, including a regular bus service from Fort Lamy, preferred the route through Niamey and Gao.

Mali, the former French Soudan, in distinct contrast to the other northern colonies, was relatively advanced at an early date. Development of its transport pattern has been largely dealt with above in connection with neighbouring territories. The railway from Dakar to Bamako and Koulikoro opened the country for economic expansion, and the river steamers, averaging roughly 100 miles (160 km) a day, provided a link between this railway and that at Kouroussa and Kankan, as well as with the river in parts of the Niger valley as far as Niamey and beyond. The railway enters the country when it crosses the Falémé Bridge, 396 miles (637 km) from Dakar, and covers another 405 miles (652 km) to Koulikoro. From Koulikoro steamer services cover 1294 miles (2082 km) to Gaya, in Niger. The scale of operations, in terms of distance, is typically African. South of the river a system of roads connected with those of the neighbouring colonies, and as motor vehicles increased in number these southern and better-watered districts grew in economic prosperity. Produce moved in two directions, either southward to the French ports on the coast, or northward to the river services of the Niger or Bani and thence to the Dakar railway. North of the river, on the other hand, the motor vehicle made little impression. The trans-Saharan routes carried little traffic. The northern three-quarters of the country still rely largely on the camel for such movement of men and produce as is necessary. Until the Second World War the caravans to the salt workings at Taoudenni, setting out twice a year, were of considerable size, 5000–6000 camels, but the competition of manufactured salt has since reduced even further the importance of these deposits. Early in the century caravans were four times the size quoted.

The development of competitive transport forms

ROADS AND RAILWAYS

The final phase of development of transport in West Africa may be taken as that in which different services compete actively for traffic. In general, 'underdeveloped' countries face the problem of selective investment in one or other form of transport, whereas the more advanced nations have the need to share or apportion the traffic between the various forms existing. The initial impact of the motor vehicle was not to create alternatives to railways or river traffic, but rather to bring new business to these services. As has been shown, this was deliberate policy in some territories: in others it was a natural development in an expanding economy. Even where, as in most of French West Africa, roads were built alongside rail or river routes, duplication of services was not intended and was, indeed, frequently not possible, as road maintenance was sometimes too indifferent to make long-distance road haulage an economic proposition, and in addition the lack of skilled drivers and mechanics resulted in frequent breakdown of motor vehicles, making long hauls not only unreliable but also uneconomic. The low standard of driving will inevitably persist for some time because of the high rate of increase in the number of vehicles. The United Nations Statistical Yearbooks show, for example, that the numbers of vehicles of all types in West Africa roughly doubled between 1952 and 1958. The demand for motor drivers exceeds the supply. The difficulty in the past has not merely been one of inexperience, but also lack of 'feeling' for machines. The West African driver has not usually shown, in the past, the sense of awareness of slight changes in sound which indicate that mechanical trouble is impending but has not yet become serious. Equally he has not shown an appreciation of the power, lethal as well as mechanical, which he directs. For both reasons accidents tend to be more frequent than in Europe, and also more serious. These defects of vehicle management may be the result of youth passed in the non-mechanical world. The West African child does not have the mechanical toys of his European counterpart, nor the experience of mechanical appliances inside and outside the home. This background of mechanical inexperience is already changing rapidly, but the accident rate will probably not fall to European levels for a long time. Accidents are likely to remain frequent because the road conditions encourage the deterioration of vehicles unless these are operating only on the tar surface or tarmacadamized roads of the larger towns and main routes. Hawkins[11] put the average life of Nigerian commercial vehicles at four years, but Hogg and Roelandts[12] suggest three years, with the average life of a lorry as 2·2 years. Diesel vehicles last longer than petrol vehicles, and the diesel lorry probably averages 37,500 miles (60,500 km) per annum against 30,000 miles (48,000 km) by a petrol-driven lorry. Diesels in Uganda were stated[13] to be more expensive than petrol-engined lorries in terms of repairs, maintenance and depreciation, but fuel consumption in Northern Nigeria has been quoted as 25–30 per cent less. Most operators appear to make no allowance for depreciation, and it could be suggested that this is covered in part by the high insurance premiums, in view of the large number of vehicles that end their active life other than as a result of age. Strict cost accounting is, however, rare among private operators, and the economics of road transport in West Africa are now recognized as being very different from those in more developed areas.

In part this difference arises from the lack of distinction in West Africa between passenger and freight transport. Passengers and freight are not only interchangeable, but they are in large measure indivisible. This is because very large numbers of travellers are petty traders, often working over regular circuits, and carrying their wares with them. Local custom of buying and selling is one of dealing in small quantities – in the extreme case, in very small quantities, such as a few matches, a few lumps of sugar, single cigarettes. This is a logical feature of a society largely lacking in capital, and it is not without significance that in the colonial days the smallest coin in British West African currency was the anini, or tenth of a penny. Petty traders with minimal capital may therefore invest the whole of their resources in a very heterogeneous assortment of local or imported products, carried in a single large container, or may invest in bundles of yams, live goats or chickens, or bundles of dried fish. The trader is unwilling to let these articles out of his sight as they represent his assets and his independence. He is therefore reluctant to place them in the guard's van of a train, but the nature of his 'luggage' is such that he cannot place his articles in an overhead rack. The quantities in which he deals are too small for the individual hiring of a 10-ton rail wagon. Given a choice between rail and road travel, the trader will choose the latter because he travels with his belongings. The 'mammy wagon' of West Africa is a lorry chassis with a locally-constructed wooden body, which allows several tons of freight to be loaded on to the floor of the truck after which beams are placed from side to side to act as seats, passengers sitting above their packages. If local produce is available for profitable carriage, more bags of, for example, groundnuts or cocoa will be carried and fewer passengers and luggage. If freight is plentiful, passengers may be added merely as paying space fillers between produce and roof. The 'fare' paid by the passenger is a matter for individual bargaining, as is also the 'rate' for transport of freight. The figures finally agreed are not determined in relation to the actual cost of the road transport, but are largely arbitrary and may vary even from hour to hour. The rate asked depends partly on the quantities of freight seeking carriage and on the number of vehicles available at the time, but these are not the only considerations. For example, if alternative transport by rail is available, lorry rates are fixed to undercut the railway or to quote a lower door-to-door rate than is possible with use of railway and local transport to and from the stations. Rates vary with seasons, because less freight is offered in the rains than in the dry season and rates are therefore higher in the latter.

Another factor is the possibility of return loads, which is important where there is a marked one-way movement of bulky agricultural produce. The effects of this imbalance are considerable. Between Maiduguri in Nigeria and Fort Lamy, in the Chad Republic, the rate per ton/mile was 10d. to 1s. 3d. (U.S. 12–18 cents) northward and 1½d. to 2d. (1·75–2·25 cents) southward.[14] With imbalance of this magnitude, dealers in secondary (return) goods are in a much stronger bargaining position than shippers of primary produce. In some areas the latter will undertake regular dealing in other trades, such as cement marketing, if necessary selling the produce below economic price, because a small loss on the cement combined with a low carriage rate for the primary produce is financially more advantageous than one-way trade with a high carriage rate. Another common form of return cargo is the illicit carriage of cut-price passengers who will be off-loaded before reaching control posts. This also assists smuggling across frontiers, as personal head-loads of foot passengers are not examined for duty, whereas lorry loads should be. Passengers may therefore be dropped off a short distance from a frontier on one side and picked up again on the other. West African territories never had such tight distinctions of function as those used in vehicle control in Uganda and described by Hawkins[13], and this has avoided that element of high transport costs which is the result of an excessive percentage of empty journeys.

Social factors also affect the rates charged. The high percentage of petty traders among road passengers means that a crowded lorry may in effect be a travelling shop. Frequent and prolonged stops at small villages in the course of a single journey are no hardship to the passengers. On the contrary, they offer opportunities for business activity. Stops need not incommode the driver, who in some cases will have at least a part-ownership interest in the vehicle and who may also be carrying some goods for his own trading en route. These trading functions of some vehicles may explain the existence of 'tramp lorries' analogous in some ways to the 'tramp steamers' of earlier years at sea: lorries which will go wherever trade offers, and which will drive along a new road just because it is there and may offer business prospects.[15] Petty trading is important in the life of the people for two reasons. Firstly it meets the demand for small quantities and secondly it helps to create a 'middle class', in that enterprising operators starting with virtually no resources can, on the basis of small but repeated profits, build up their assets and accumulate capital to the point where they can enter business on a larger scale. Lorry owning is in itself a symbol of prestige, and there are a number of one-vehicle operators. Frequently, ownership is by a syndicate of related individuals; frequently, also, operators fail in business because of insufficient capital to cover maintenance costs, so that several successive breakdowns result in the permanent withdrawal of the vehicle from service.

The social aspects of travel also explain why the 'mammy wagon' survives after the introduction of long-distance buses. The latter operate at fixed fares, whereas a wait for a glutted transport market may enable lower lorry fares to be bargained; buses do not have luggage-carrying facilities for items such as live-stock; nor do buses make frequent stops of any duration. Bus passengers tend to represent a different non-trading class of custom, and to be successful need a high density of population or a society sufficiently advanced to have large numbers of junior officials, or of comparable grades in commerce or private business. The higher grades in government and in the large trading companies are usually assisted by loan schemes to purchase their own cars and for prestige reasons will travel in these rather than by bus.[16] The function of transport in meeting social needs has been demonstrated in Togo, where the railway administration trebled the number of passengers by introducing cheap rates on 'trains marchés', stopping at every station for periods long enough to allow a short organized market. Most of the travellers were market women whose average journey was less than 25 miles (40 km).

Another factor to be considered is that of time. In the past the expenditure of time has been of less importance than the expenditure of capital, the latter being in short supply. Increasingly, however, the monetary value of time has been appreciated, and the realization that capital locked up by time is unproductive.[17] Most West African trade is not yet at a stage where speed is vital, but nevertheless steady movement tends to be of importance. This does not necessarily apply to cash crops of an imperishable nature: the annual stock-piling of the groundnut crop in Northern Nigeria to give the 'pyramids' of Kano is a well-known example, the stocks of bagged nuts being steadily reduced throughout the year as the railway removes them. Some deterioration takes place during the delay, but the quantity is relatively unimportant, and as world supply is seasonal there is no economic gain to be obtained by rapid railing involving a great capital outlay on the railways. Stock-piling will still take place somewhere, and in the case of export crops of this nature it is the large company whose capital is 'frozen', and not the producer's. In the case of individual traders, however, capital is often too small to allow temporary stagnation, and resources must be kept in movement producing small but continuous returns on small investments. This is another factor favouring road transport at the expense of the railway, as not only can traders move immediately with their goods, but they can vary their programme and itinerary en route if promising opportunities appear to present themselves. The consideration of time applies also to the small shopkeeper, who may prefer slightly higher rates for road transport of individual packages of piece goods, for example, rather than the lower railway rates, because his turnover is accelerated by quicker delivery.

The tendency for traffic to turn from rail to road transport is understandable for short journeys, but would not be expected for long journeys. It was calculated[18] that the average cost of lorry transport, excluding maintenance, was 4·42 pence per ton/mile (U.S. 3·2 cents per ton/km) in Nigeria in 1959, whereas railway costs declined from 14·53 pence at 50 miles (10·2 cents at 80 km) to 7·77 pence at 100 miles (5·3 cents at 160 km) and to 4·39 pence at 200 miles (3·1 cents at 320 km). Above 200 miles (320 km) rail costs fell progressively to 2·70 pence at 400 miles (1·9 cents at 640 km) and to 1·75 pence at 800 miles (1·2 cents at 1290 km). Notwithstanding these figures, some bulk produce such as groundnuts moves 700 miles (1100 km) by road from Kano to Lagos, apparently in defiance of all economic laws. Some of the reasons have been given above. Others have included ill-judged railway rates. Many railways initially adopted *ad valorem* rates for railway freight, a system which worked well enough before the advent of road competition, but once the alternative was available the lucrative freight moved to the roads at more realistic transport charges, leaving the railways with low-value bulk produce, loss on which could no longer be met by profit on high-value goods. Subsequent adjustments to rates nearer actual costs have had varied effects. A rise in the tariff for kola nuts from Western to Northern Nigeria caused an instantaneous change to road haulage for the 700-mile (1100-km) journey: there had in any case been a 30-mile (50-km) road journey from the Shagamu district to the railway, so terminal costs of loading and unloading were unchanged, and groundnuts offered a return freight. Once established, traffic of this long-distance nature may persist; an early reduction of the rail tariff for kola nuts brought back only part of the freight, and the lorry operators substituted piece goods and manufactured articles for nuts on the northward journey, and introduced the greater security of locked vans in reply to further reductions in railway rates. Long-distance haulage appears now to be a permanent feature of the West African transport system – as the only means of transport over wide areas, road transport has the vehicles and facilities for servicing in the country, and will undercut rail costs to close a gap in an established route circuit or will compete directly over particular routes if rail rates make this economically possible. This has led to reductions of railway charges over sections with powerful road competition, as in the Ivory Coast, or to protective action, as in Ghana, where recent restrictive legislation prohibits the movement of timber by road if alternative rail transport is available. Frost and Stewart[19] found that in 1950 in Nigeria intraregional traffic was by road and inter-regional traffic by rail, but this pattern has largely changed. By 1959[20] the railways' share in the import/export trade had declined rapidly. In the previous ten years the percentage of exports handled by the railways fell from 94 to $67\frac{1}{2}$ per cent at Apapa, and of imports from 92 to $51\frac{1}{2}$ per cent. Corresponding figures for Port Harcourt were 98 to $69\frac{1}{2}$ per cent, and 91 to $40\frac{1}{2}$ per cent respectively. It is perhaps significant that in Senegal[21], where 200,000 tons of groundnuts were moved by road instead of by rail, the average load per lorry was only about 2 tons, suggesting that other part-cargoes or passengers were carried simultaneously.

In the latest phase of transport development, therefore, the roads move into full competition with other services, and on the whole appear to surpass them. This is, however, a generalization requiring much qualification, as shown by the extension of the Nigerian Railway from the Jos Plateau to Maiduguri. The cost of this line has been estimated at £19·4 million against a road cost of £9·6 million, but maintenance costs of a road would have been £0·5 million higher per annum. Whether or not the line will show a profit is not known. The disparity in road rates in opposite directions in this area has already been mentioned, and it is to be hoped that imports into the Chad basin will be balanced by bulk produce exports, particularly of groundnuts, cotton and cattle. Prior to the construction of the Maiduguri–Fort Lamy road, annual freight movement into Chad by this route was thought to be about 1000 tons per annum. The road (open on alternate days in each direction) increased this 50 times, and it has been estimated[22] that by 1970 it will have increased to 250 times. The economic results of the construction of the new line will be watched with interest elsewhere in West Africa, as the only other post-war line, the extension from Bobo Dioulasso to Ouagadougou, completed in 1953, did not result in a large increase in traffic as had been hoped. French policy decided against further new lines unless 150,000–200,000 tons of freight per annum could be clearly foreseen.

Mention has been made of the maintenance costs for railways being less than for roads. Millard[23] gave 1958 construction costs of roads in average undulating bush country as £8000–£10,000 per mile (U.S. $14,000–17,000 per km) for one-lane asphalt, £15,000–£23,000 per mile ($26,000–40,000 per km) for two-lane asphalt, £10,000–£20,000 per mile ($17,000–35,000 per km) for a single-line railway. Annual maintenance costs for 1957 in the Cameroons were cited by Devegue[24] as 180,000 francs C.F.A. for a single-line railway compared with 300,000 francs C.F.A. for a road carrying a lesser tonnage. The figures suggest that railways offer a better proposition than roads in terms of investment provided that enough freight offers to make the lines pay. It might be added that the railways also lose considerable money through non-payment of fares, as trains can be boarded without passing ticket inspectors, and a bargain struck later between the passenger and the train guard. In Nigeria in 1945 this loss was probably of the order of £80,000 per annum. In favour of road construction is the cheap cost of dry-season road construction and maintenance, as given earlier, and the enormous saving of cost that can result – or the enormous encouragement to growth of economic crops. Figures from the Ivory Coast[25] compare charges per ton/kilometre as follows:

Bush path. Carriers. 400 francs C.F.A. with no return loads.
Track. Land Rover. 80–100 francs C.F.A. with no return load.
Rough Road. 5-ton lorry. 20–30 francs C.F.A. with return load.

Annual cost was put at 42,000 francs C.F.A. as 6 per cent interest on construction cost of the road, plus 18,000 francs C.F.A. for maintenance, a total of 60,000 francs C.F.A. per annum. As the saving per ton/kilometre is 370–380 francs C.F.A., a total of 160 tons per annum will cover costs, and over 160 tons a profit to clear the capital outlay. Some of the Ivory Coast roads created in this way showed 500–1000 tons per annum developed within a few years. Agricultural production increased as new areas were brought within economic reach of modern transport, prices paid to farmers rose, agricultural officers and equipment had easier access, prices of imported articles fell in the area, better access to schools and dispensaries became available. These improvements have long been recognized by bodies such as the Cocoa Marketing Boards which have built speculative roads in the areas known to be suitable for the growth of cocoa with a view to encouraging production. Depreciation of vehicles on these minor roads, is, of course, heavier than on surfaced highways, and this is recognized by the Boards in the payments made for transport of cocoa.

One further factor needs to be mentioned. The extension of the 'spheres of influence' of roads has increased more rapidly than the roads themselves, by a large post-war increase in the number of bicycles used. A bicycle in some areas is an investment in transport, in that it is used for the carriage of freight along bush paths where formerly only carriers could operate. A bicycle fitted with wooden racks to hold petrol cans filled with palm oil can transport 14 gallons (64 litres) of oil over considerable daily distances at rates below that of head porterage.

x

PORTS

Improvement of ports has proceeded rapidly since the war, to cater for the great increases in tonnage of overseas trade. Among the ports of British West Africa, Freetown was at last given a deep-water quay in 1953; Takoradi was extended in 1953, with additional quays and special loading equipment for bauxite and manganese; Tema, another artificial port similar in nature to Takoradi, came into use in 1958 and diverted trade from Accra; Lagos Port was enlarged in 1955 by the extension of the wharves at Apapa and by the development of an industrial estate on the reclaimed land behind them; Port Harcourt has been further developed not only for freight travelling by railway but also to allow exports of petroleum from the nearby oil field; the Delta ports are scheduled to have a revised interest in direct overseas trade with the completion of the protective mole south of the Forcados Channel to prevent further silt accumulation on the bar.

Elsewhere changes have been at Conakry and Abidjan. At Conakry a mineral-loading pier was added to handle iron ore produced by open-cast methods only five miles from the port, and annual shipments are expected to reach 1,500,000 tons; a wharf for bauxite loading has been built on Kassa Island, and export, which started in 1952, reached nearly 500,000 tons within five years; the shipment of bananas increased nearly fourfold in the ten years 1946–56; and the port handled 1,600,000 tons in 1956 compared with 100,000 tons ten years earlier. Abidjan has been transformed by the completion of the Vridi Canal in 1950. The problem of longshore drift, which blocked earlier attempts at canal construction, has apparently been solved by the NW–SE mole at the canal entrance diverting sand out to sea towards the head of the Trou sans fond Canyon. It is yet to be seen whether there will arise the problem of erosion east of the canal, similar to that which faces Lagos east of the entrance moles. In 1949 Abidjan handled 418,000 tons of cargo by way of Port Bouet, and ten years later 1,400,000 tons. Deep-water quays within the sheltered lagoon have made Abidjan an excellent port. Dakar has diminished in relative importance in the former French colonies, following the development of these ports, but cargo handled increased from 1,300,000 tons in 1946 to 4,000,000 tons in 1956. An artificially-sheltered port is being constructed at Cotonou to serve Dahomey and the Niger Republic, replacing the old jetty and the lighter service to ships lying offshore. This major enterprise is intended to provide complete port services for Dahomey, thus freeing the country from the necessity of using Lagos and the lagoon route to Porto Novo for heavy imports. To the west a second port has been constructed at Kpémé, 22 miles (35 km) east of Lomé, in the form of a pier 1300 yards (1200 metres) long to deep water outside the surf. Intended principally for the export of phosphate from the open-cast workings at Hahotoe, 14 miles (23 km) inland, which are producing nearly a million tons per annum, it is also intended to be used for the importing of petroleum.[26]

Liberia has perhaps shown the greatest transformation since the Second World War. Breakwaters and deep-water quays built at Monrovia with United States aid were completed in 1948, and a railway constructed to the iron mines on the Bomi Hills. A second railway has been constructed to move iron ore from the Nimba Mountains to the new port of South Buchanan. Before the war there were about 27 miles of road in and around Monrovia. Since the war over 1000 miles of road have been constructed, including the important international road via Ganta to Nzérékoré in Guinea, which has diverted some agricultural produce, especially groundnuts, from Guinea to Monrovia for export. Liberia, however, not withstanding the transformation of the economic scene, cannot be said to have advanced very far towards the development of a modern transport system.

RIVER TRANSPORT

Major improvements of river transport in West Africa cannot be considered to be economic unless all-season operation is possible. In view of the seasonal flow of all the major rivers, this requires large control dams to maintain water depth, with circumventing canals and locks such as those previously constructed on the Upper Niger. Two great schemes deserve special mention. The first is the revised Volta Dam scheme, creating the Volta Lake which may encourage the development of water transport in the Northern Territories of Ghana, although the major export production of the country is to the south. The second is the Niger Dam under construction at Kainji, some 60 miles (100 km) north of Jebba. The by-pass locks will give Niamey river connection with the Delta ports for nine months of the year. The elimination of the large variations in depth due to seasonal flood will also allow the dredging of a deeper channel, and Mississippi experience shows that 20,000-ton tows are possible on a 9-foot (3-metre) draught. As a groundnut train carries only some 500 tons, an all-season 9-foot channel to Baro, coupled with the revival of the Delta ports as termini for full ocean-going cargoes, would put the rail-river route back into full competition with the Lagos–Kano railway. Scientific river administration could add 15 per cent to the present carrying capacity. Night sailing could add 60 per cent to the total, but would require navigational aids in quantity. Dredging could add an additional 30 per cent, but can be done only below the major dams, and no major project is as yet scheduled for the Benue, although the possibilities have been investigated.[27] As over 250,000 tons move annually by the river fleets of Nigeria, half of this being to the Republic of Cameroun in the short season on the Upper Benue, the full possibilities are seen to be considerable. The improvement of the Benue would give a water transport system complementary to the railway, and if fully developed such a system usually operates at one-quarter to one-half the cost per ton/mile of rail haulage.

On a much smaller scale, it may be remarked that some local watermen have, in the last fifteen years, enormously improved the carrying capacity of their canoes by fitting them with outboard motors, thus increasing the speed and the number of journeys made. This applies particularly to canoe ferries carrying passengers and loads across the great rivers, as fuel stocks do not then have to be carried in the canoe. Like the petty trader, or the 'bush' mechanic and the carpenter engaged in building local lorry coachwork, this is an example of an emerging middle class of intelligent self-employed men adapting themselves to new techniques to create a business in spite of minimal initial capital.

Hovercraft have been tried experimentally on the Niger. Obviously they are not affected by changes in sandbanks and channels, and require no dredging. It is probably too early as yet for their commercial use to be profitable.

AIR TRANSPORT

International passenger services came into infrequent but regular operation between the wars, although with many halts for refuelling, and with limited capacity. Modern long-distance services appeared after the Second World War, with aircraft capable of uninterrupted trans-Saharan flight. Kano had already added motor bus services to the surviving camel caravans, and it now became an important international airport en route from Europe to West, Central and South Africa. With increasing range, aircraft now fly direct from the main coastal centres to Europe.

Local services have proliferated in the same period. A deliberate policy of cheap rates (one company had the slogan 'You too can fly') and economy in fittings brought air fares within reach of middle-class Africans as well as of commercial or government employees. Where air services compete with railways, there is little difference in passenger fares, but considerable differences in time. The passengers on local services may even include the more successful market traders.

Air transport is less impeded than road or rail in the rains, provided that tarmacadam runways are available, and that alternative landing grounds are not too far away if a plane's arrival coincides with that of a line squall. Internal carriage of freight and passengers increased about five times between 1948 and 1958, freight being considerable. In the latter years of French West Africa, refrigerated planes flew some 3000 tons per annum of fresh meat from Bamako, Niamey and Fort Lamy to the coastal towns, and in respect of meat supplies to the ports this is an economic proposition, as the alternative of rail transport is not always present, and trekking of cattle 'on the hoof' results in very considerable loss of weight. Doubts have been expressed[28] about the effects of this airborne meat trade, in that it leads to the development of cross-bred animals produced for weight and quality of carcass. Previously the cattle were trained for six years in Mali, and only those capable of walking 20 miles (30 km) a day for one month, swimming rivers when required, and feeding as they walked, were sent southward. The essential feature of these animals was stamina and endurance. In the forest country individual animals could be diverted to remote villages, where they represented the only source of fresh meat, and supplied the essential protein in the local diet. The heavier cross-bred cattle are incapable of trekking; their meat arrives in the coastal towns, but cannot be carried by refrigerator van to all the remote villages without great expense and much road construction, and one

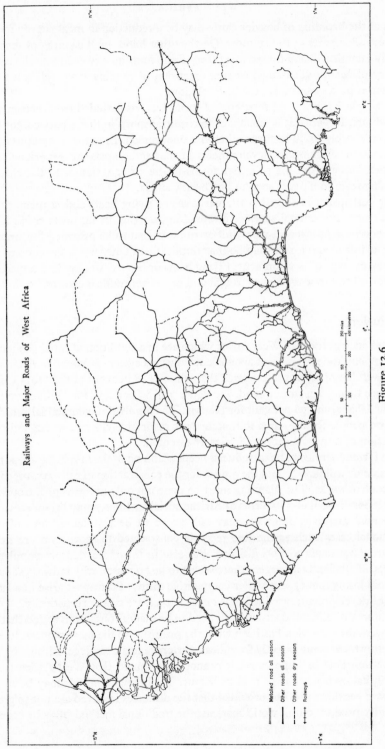

Railways and Major Roads of West Africa

Metalled road all season
Other roads all season
Other roads dry season
Railways

0   50   100   150   200   250 miles
0   100   200   300   400 kilometres

Figure 12.6

result of the breeding of heavier cattle may be a reduction in meat supply to the less accessible parts of the country. On the other hand, local canning of meat is already established, and tinned meat from Kano finds its way even into the cattle country of Mali, which suggests that extension of canning may well solve the problem if prices can be kept sufficiently low.

Air freight has not been restricted to meat, but has included fruit, cotton and groundnuts. In part this is analogous to road transport, in that a part-cargo may be taken cheaply to fill in space otherwise unoccupied. In part it is symptomatic of the speed of transport development, in that some areas are experiencing a direct transition from the primitive forms to the air age, similar to the change from dog team to aircraft seen in northern Canada.

It is perhaps surprising that the early use of flying boats and seaplanes was not pursued. For coastal services it would appear that flying boats could have made good use of lagoon waters, but as runways had to be provided for aircraft from the inland services it may be that duplication of airports is uneconomic at the present stage of development. Flying boats or hovercraft may find a place in the over-all transport system as freight and passenger traffic increases.

Conclusion

In states such as those of West Africa which are in a condition of rapid economic development, the provision of an efficient transport system is essential. A United Nations Bulletin[29] in 1962 showed that whereas 48 per cent of the Ivory Coast was more than 5 km from a road, the figure was 69 per cent for Guinea, 70 per cent for Ghana, and 76 per cent for Nigeria. The number of commercial vehicles per 1000 people for the same four states was respectively, 4·2, 1·8, 2·2 and 0·7. Expansion of transport services is clearly essential.

The form of service to be introduced needs planning in the first instance, as the governments will have to find the money for the construction of railways, roads or river control works. The planning must be done not only in terms of European-style economics, but also in terms of African social customs, capital resources and commercial methods. Railways may still prove to be justifiable, not only in exceptional cases such as the line recently constructed to move iron ore from northern Mauritania to Port Etienne, but also in the more densely-populated districts. If efficiently managed, there seems to be no reason why railways should not avoid losing money, even after competitive forms of transport arise in a later phase of development, provided that rates charged are costed realistically.

A number of difficult decisions will need to be made. It has been stated that in some areas the transition has been from the primitive to the most modern forms of transport, changing directly from head porterage to air carriage. Although this may be desirable in some cases, it cannot be disputed that West Africa lacks local capital even more than it lacks labour. Traditional methods may be more expensive per ton/mile, but provided that the distances involved are not so great as to price produce out of world markets, the traditional methods may be economically justifiable in lieu of vast capital outlay. This applies also to mechanical appliances for loading and unloading of vehicles, which can be more efficient than porters but will also usually be more expensive and raise costs to a dangerous level. The suggestion that mechanization is essential because manual labour is degrading must be resisted in West Africa as in Western Europe. There is also the danger that new states may establish air lines and shipping lines for prestige reasons, and that these may require large subventions either to cover the operational losses or to purchase expensive aircraft or ships. A modern aircraft or ship of the types used in West African services may cost £1½ million (U.S. $3½ millions), a sum which would pay for 3000 miles (5000 km) of laterite road at a construction cost of £500 per mile ($750 per km). There is no doubt at all that the latter would bring a vastly greater benefit to the state concerned, particularly as the present over-provision of ships and aircraft means that foreign operators would willingly supply such services at moderate cost. It is, of course, equally important that expenditure on road construction should not exceed the financial ability of the state to give the roads adequate maintenance, without which they will rapidly deteriorate.

In terms of road traffic, it is also important that specialization should not be introduced too soon. The use of buses as opposed to 'mammy wagons' is economically justifiable only when society has sufficient passengers of the type who prefer bus travel. The use of specialized freight vehicles may destroy the possibility of a return cargo and so increase prices of the commodity carried. A bulk cement carrier may be more efficient than the carriage of cement in paper sacks, but if the latter is a regular return cargo for vehicles taking groundnuts in the opposite direction, the cost of both groundnuts and cement may rise alarmingly. The time for specialization must not be forced too soon. In some trades specialized vehicles are required earlier than in others: heavy timber is an obvious example of an early need, and petroleum products are another. Petroleum tankers reduce costs, as the big 44-gallon (200-litre) steel drums are difficult to handle when full and are expensive to replace when damaged, and bulk transport also reduces possible contamination. Nevertheless, with newly-constructed roads the steel drum is still a necessary method of carriage, as filling stations equipped with storage tanks, for bulk unloading, do not appear until traffic density is known to be heavy enough to repay capital expenditure. Bulk transport will also follow on the expansion of processing industries. The shelling of groundnuts is a first stage in processing, reducing bulk and transport costs. The second stage is the provision of plant to extract the groundnut oil in the country of origin, which leads to transport of oil in lieu of nuts. Initially the oil will be carried in drums or containers, but bulk tankers for vegetable oils already operate in the West African shipping industry and may appear on a smaller scale in the road transport industry.

Finally, it must be remarked that in the interests of economic betterment it is desirable to alter some of the established trade routes. It is, for example, unrealistic to move groundnuts from the southern Niger Republic by the compli-

cated route through Dahomey to Cotonou, instead of by the obvious route to the
Nigerian Railway. The longer route is, of course, a survival from the colonial
period of French administration, as is also the routeing of trade from Chad to
Douala. Some attempt is made to preserve the old routes by the use of Customs
barriers or preferential tariffs, but these are not wholly effective. Smuggling
across unmarked frontiers is a simple matter, and considerable trade uses the
cheaper route by illegal means. Equally, local produce or imported goods will use
longer routes if smuggling across a frontier brings a higher purchase price or
avoids high taxation. The extent of illicit movement across frontiers can only be
estimated, because even legal inter-territorial trade is very poorly documented.
Mauritania started separate statistics only in 1961. In other cases the data are
often confused so that even figures which should be reliable may show wide
variation. Documented trade between the Gambia and Senegal for 1958 showed
a value of imports into the Gambia of 13 million francs c.f.a. (Gambia figures)
or $23\frac{1}{2}$ million francs c.f.a. (Senegal figures). Trade from Gambia to Senegal
was 38 million francs c.f.a. (Senegal figures) against $104\frac{1}{2}$ million francs c.f.a.
(Gambia figures). The wide divergence of the latter lies principally in textiles,
where Senegal cited 6 million francs, and Gambia 59 million francs, but the
Central Bank of West Africa in February 1962 estimated that contraband probably raised the total imports from 38 million francs (the Senegal figure) to 360
million francs.

Most contraband crosses the frontiers by porterage or bicycle, along the bush
paths, although larger individual amounts may be worked through a Customs post
by a private arrangement between a lorry driver and the Customs officials. Because tariffs on imported articles vary widely between states, contraband trade is
particularly active in these articles. French sugar imported directly into Lomé
has been more expensive than the same sugar imported into Ghana and then
transported illicitly to Lomé. Fromont[30] quotes cement costs per kilo in Chad
as 29,000 francs c.f.a. imported via Pointe Noire and 15,000 francs c.f.a. imported via Nigeria. Equalization of tariff rates by agreement between the states
of West Africa would remove the financial incentive which at present diverts
transport capacity which could be better employed. Agreement on prices paid for
primary produce would also remove the financial incentive to smuggle: some
4000 tons of cocoa are estimated to walk annually from Togo into Ghana, and
very large quantities of groundnuts from the Niger Republic into Nigeria. 70,000
tons of kola nuts are thought to move northward across the Nigerian frontiers,
and Sautter[31] estimated that in 1955 13,000 tons of dried fish passed annually
from Chad to Nigeria compared with the official figure of 1000 tons.

The quantities of contraband will increase as processing and manufacturing
industries become established to serve local demands, unless agreement is
reached which will remove incentives. It is wasteful of effort to have two trade
networks in operation, one diverting trade from the strictly economic route for
fiscal reasons. It also tends to bring the law into disrepute. Thirdly, as the U.N.
Economic Bulletin for Africa for 1961 stresses, a high proportion of State revenue

in West Africa is obtained from Customs levies, and the implementation of economic plans is very much dependent on the smooth running of the Customs. The Customs Union of West African States (U.D.O.A.) originally agreed to the Customs receipts at the ports being shared between the coastal and inland states of former French West Africa, and to the absence of Customs barriers along their common boundaries, but disagreement over the division of the Customs receipts led to State Customs posts being established everywhere within eighteen months. This involved the internal states in the establishment of warehouses at the ports and a complicated system for the refund of Customs dues collected by coastal states on transit material. The worst feature of disagreement was the breaking of the Dakar–Niger Railway at the frontier, disrupting the trade of Mali and leading not only to temporary air and road transport increases between Mali and the Ivory Coast but also to increased smuggling across the Senegal–Mali frontier. Agreement for the restitution of the railway link came two years later.

International agreement on the question of Customs charges and produce prices would seem to be essentially in the interest of all West African states. Equally important as transport systems develop will be international agreement on the control and use of the great rivers. It is also to be hoped that planners will consider the closer linkage with their neighbours of at least the roads of the countries formerly under British administration.

BIBLIOGRAPHICAL NOTES

[1] For information on West African ports, see:
G. Alexandersson and G. Norström, *World Shipping*, London, 1963, pp. 370–9.
H. P. White, The ports of West Africa, *Tijdschrift voor Economische en Sociale Geografie*, 50, 1959, pp. 1–8.
H. R. Jarrett, The port of Bathurst, *Proceedings, 17th International Geographical Congress*, Washington, D.C., 1952, pp. 157–61.
B. E. Thomas, Railways and ports in West Africa, *Economic Geography*, 1957, pp. 1–15.
H. R. Jarrett, The port and town of Freetown, *Geography*, 40, 1955, pp. 108–18.
K. M. Buchanan and J. C. Pugh, *Land and People in Nigeria*, London, 1955, pp. 215–22.
J. C. Pugh and A. E. Perry, *A Short Geography of West Africa*, London, 1960, pp. 150–1.
H. P. White, New ports in Dahomey and Togo, *Geography*, 46, 1961, pp. 160–3.
Naval Intelligence Division, *French West Africa, vol. I, The Federation*, 1943, pp. 357–70; *vol. II, The Colonies*, port details.

[2] J. C. Pugh, Sand movement in relation to wind direction as exemplified on the Nigerian coastline, *University College, Ibadan, Department of Geography, Research Notes*, 5, 1954.

[3] H. R. Jarrett, The port and town of Freetown, op. cit.

[4] Sir F. D. Lugard, *The dual mandate in British Tropical Africa*, London, 1926, p. 462.

[5] Colonial Annual Report, *Southern Nigeria*, 1906, p. 267.

[6] Colonial Annual Report, *Southern Nigeria*, 1907, p. 85.

[7] Colonial Annual Report, *Northern Nigeria*, 1906–7, p. 535.

[8] Colonial Annual Report, *Northern Nigeria*, 1907–8, pp. 600–1.

[9] Lord Hailey, *An African Survey, Revised 1956*, Oxford, 1957, p. 1586.

[10] H. W. W. Pollitt, *Colonial Road Problems*, Colonial Research Publication No. 8, London, 1950.

[11] E. K. Hawkins, *Road Transport in Nigeria*, Oxford, 1958.

[12] V. W. Hogg and G. M. Roelandts, *Nigerian Motor Vehicle Traffic*, Nigerian Social and Economic Studies No. 2, Oxford, 1962.

[13] E. K. Hawkins, *Roads and road transport in an under-developed country*, Colonial Research Study No. 32, London, 1962.

[14] United Nations: *Transport Problems in Relation to Economic Development in West Africa*, Economic and Social Council, Economic Commission for Africa, 3rd Session, E/CN 14/63, New York, 1960, Chapter III.

[15] See in Joyce Cary, *Mister Johnson*, London, 1939, the arrival of the first lorry on a new laterite road before the construction labourers have returned to their base village.

[16] Not always wisely. See in Chinua Achebe, *No longer at ease*, London, 1960, the increasing indebtedness of a young African Civil Servant, accentuated as a result of prestige ownership of a private car.

[17] E. K. Hawkins, *Roads and road transport in an under-developed country*, op. cit., p. 24.

[18] Nigerian Railways Corporation, *Report and Accounts* for the year ended 31.3.59.

[19] A. R. Frost and I. G. Stewart, *The National Income of Nigeria 1950–51*, London, 1953.

[20] International Bank, *Economic Survey of Nigeria in 1959*, Baltimore, 1960.

[21] United Nations, op. cit., p. 92.

[22] idem, Chapter IV, estimate by Chad Chamber of Commerce.

[23] R. S. Millard, Road development in overseas territories, *Roads and Road Construction*, 1959.

[24] R. Devegue, La modernisation de l'entretien de la voie au Chemin du Fer du Cameroun, *Industries et Travaux d'Outremer*, 1957, quoted in United Nations, op. cit., Chapter IV.

[25] United Nations, op. cit., p. 115.

[26] H. P. White, New ports in Dahomey and Togo, op. cit.

[27] Netherlands Engineering Consultants (NEDECO), The Hague, *River Studies and Recommendations on Improvement of the Niger and Benue*, Amsterdam and The Hague, 1959.
Federation of Nigeria, *Proposals for Dams on the Niger and Kaduna Rivers*, Lagos, 1959.

[28] G. Jourdain, M. Drahou and M. Revillon, Le Marché du Gros Betail dans le Moyen-Soudan, *Note d'Information, Banque Centrale des Etats de l'Afrique de l'Ouest*, No. 59, 1960.

[29] United Nations Economic Bulletin for Africa, *Economic Development in Africa: Aims and Possibilities*, New York, 1962.

[30] P. Fromont, *Les transports dans les économies sous-développées*, Paris, 1955, cited in [10] above.

[31] G. Sautter, *Le Chemin de Fer Bangui–Tschad*, Brazzaville, 1959, pp. 80–83.

CHAPTER 13

The New Regions of West Africa

In Chapter 7 a number of community regions was studied, and the communities living in them described, together with some of their more important environmental inter-relations. African traditional agricultural and pastoral techniques were shown to have effected a profound modification of West African geography. The invasion of Europeans with their new technology has effected further modification, and has produced changes already described in social and political organization, in population distribution and in economy which have also affected West African geography. These changes are not uniformly distributed. They differ in type and degree between one part of West Africa and another. In consequence European influences have created new regions which exist side by side or overlapping with the older community regions. These new regions are distinguished more by economic than by social features, although still influenced by traditional factors. Here, as in Chapter 7, sample regions will be described in order to present some of the inter-relations of the variety of features involved.

Broadly, European influences may be divided into two groups – the indirect and the direct. In the former group the new regions have been created by the West African peoples themselves through adopting new crops, new methods of cultivation or a new system of trade and transportation. In the latter group Europeans or West Africans, trained in the use of new techniques, have deliberately sought to create new patterns of land use by introducing revolutionary systems of cultivation divorced from traditional practices. In the latter planning has been applied. In the former the new developments were left to individuals or families, with little or no control by a central authority. In most cases a change in agriculture has been the chief feature. In view of the economic dependence of West Africa on agriculture this is hardly surprising. Even mining has failed to exact so profound an effect, mainly because it is highly localized. Only on the Jos Plateau of Nigeria may mining be demonstrated to have brought widespread land use changes.

In all these developments the policies of the colonial and of the metropolitan governments have been of great importance. In the case of direct influences, notions derived from experience of wartime planning and organization and from the example of the totalitarian powers have affected the nature of the schemes attempted. Capital, to provide the equipment needed for new forms of production, distribution and marketing, has come chiefly, although not entirely, from overseas. In the former British West Africa the chief Government source consisted of treasury grants and colonial loans, until the Colonial Development Act of 1929, followed by the Colonial Development and Welfare Acts of 1940 and 1945. The French created a colonial development fund, on the lines prescribed in the British 1929 Act, by 1935. After the war they created F.I.D.E.S. (see p. 506) to provide funds for large-scale schemes. The major post-war contribution by colonial governments to the problems of economic development in West Africa has been the introduction of large-scale planning.[1] As early as 1945 the Colonial Office asked for ten-year development plans from the colonial administrations, in order to apportion C.D. & W. funds. In some cases quick results were demanded, and large planned schemes were initiated, despite acute labour and transport problems, and despite a lack of important data on the application of the new methods in different physical and social environments. This lack of data, particularly in ecological fields, led to the failure of many schemes, the most spectacular of which were the large-scale mechanized projects. The pace of change by direct influence has in consequence been slowed, and a greater emphasis has been put on experimental work. The most profound and widespread changes have been effected over a longer period, chiefly since the beginning of the present century, by indirect influences, mainly through the medium of peasant cultivators.

Geographical changes produced indirectly

THE COCOA REGION OF GHANA, TOGO AND THE IVORY COAST

Despite important differences in Government policy between the countries concerned, which have affected the development of export cropping and of the associated land use in different ways, the areas in which cocoa is produced on a large scale in southern Ghana, Togo and the Ivory Coast, form in effect one region or one group of regions. The perennial crop, cocoa, together with some coffee in the Ivory Coast, provides their chief cash resource and their chief export commodity. Being a perennial, cocoa forms in itself a long-term agricultural feature, and is associated with distinctive methods of cultivation, patterns of fallow, and settlement type and distribution. Within the area physically suitable, cocoa and coffee have been established wherever transport facilities offer a remunerative return. As the road and railway networks have spread, so has the distinctive perennial crop landscape, thus creating and extending a region which may be defined by its appearance. Here and there soils have been abused or worked out, or disease has destroyed the trees. Areas so affected have been abandoned by perennial crop growers, but may still be said to possess landscapes profoundly modified by perennial cropping, and thus to belong to the region.

The region is discontinuous and changing in shape. Its boundaries are moving. Its distinctive land use may be divided into:

1) lots planted to cocoa or coffee – the 'farms';
2) associated lots under other, normally food, crops;

3) fallows;

4) woodland in reserves or on unused or unusable land;

5) land under housing, other buildings, public open spaces, and roads and railways.

The region may also be distinguished by its higher densities of population, its

The Cocoa Region of the Ivory Coast, Ghana and Togo

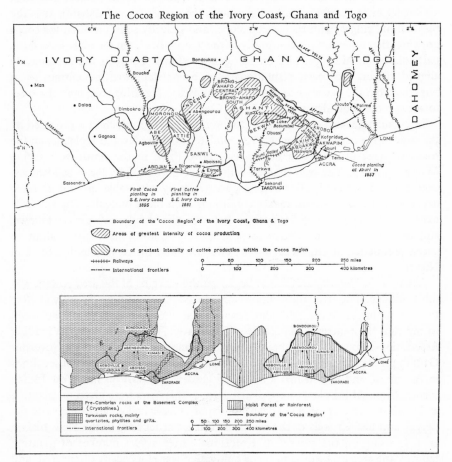

Figure 13.1

vast number of small villages located on or near main roads, the greater proportion of commercialism, and especially the importance of imported goods, its greater wealth than that of surrounding regions, the large numbers of motor vehicles and cycles, and the annual immigration of labour together with permanent labour of external origin.

The region is within the rain-forest zone. The savanna-forest boundary of woody fallows against grass fallows forms the normal northern limit of cocoa cultivation. North of that limit only poor crops of cocoa can be produced without a ground-water supplement to rainfall resources. Formerly many extensive areas of high forest were cleared by the cocoa planters themselves, who preferred, where available, virgin land for their 'farms'. The area lies almost entirely between the Bandama and the Volta rivers and consists mainly of crystalline rocks, forming low plateaux and basins, divided by residual, chiefly quartzitic, hill ridges aligned from NE to SW and from NW to SE. At one point the residual hills meet in the crater of Lake Bosumtwi, the sacred lake of Ashanti. It is the residual hill ridges, with their steep slopes and gravelly soils, unsuited for cocoa growing, that interrupt the continuity of the 'Cocoa Belt'. On the more level land, particularly on hill-tops, and on the gentler slopes, between the rectilineally aligned ridges, the cocoa plantations have been established, benefiting, as in Nigeria, from the occurrence of clays, for moisture-retaining soils help the trees to survive the short dry season.

In Ghana a general northern limit to intensive cocoa production is provided by the edge of the crystallines, where the sandstones of the Kwahu Uplands, on the southern edge of the Volta basin, rise above them in the south-west facing Mampong scarp. The well-drained soils of the porous Volta basin sandstones, except in well-watered valley bottoms, are generally unsuitable, and the extreme dryness of the 'dry' season makes conditions even more difficult. The approximate coincidence of the boundaries between the woody and grassy fallows, and between the Volta sandstones and the crystallines, has made a limit to cocoa production in Ghana even more effective than the corresponding limit in Nigeria.

Again, as in Nigeria, cultivation began on the margins of the area ecologically most suitable. The Basel missionaries introduced cocoa seedlings as early as 1857 to their station at Aburi. Although few of these survived, enough was achieved to indicate the potential importance of the crop. The Basel Mission Trading Association imported more beans from Fernando Po, and in 1887 Governor Griffith procured pods from São Tomé, arranged for the distribution of seedlings in Akwapim, and established a botanical garden at Aburi on the West Indian model. From Aburi plants were distributed, and lessons were given on planting and tending, and on curing the beans for export. Cocoa had greater success on the deeper and heavier soils to the north of Aburi, particularly in the New Juaben area, focusing on the market of Koforidua. After a vast number of planting failures, the area best suited to cocoa cultivation was empirically discovered, and cultivators learned to distinguish satisfactory soils, and discovered something of the plant's heavy moisture requirements.

Whereas in Nigeria cocoa planting tended to develop around or near small settlement units, in Ghana, except in certain special cases of planned land development, cocoa plantings were normally at some distance from the settlements. The difference in distribution followed from a difference in settlement pattern between the villages of the Akan-speaking peoples, and the towns, with their associated 'abas' or farm-hamlets, of the Yoruba-speaking peoples. The people of Ghana's cocoa-growing area either developed cocoa cultivation on the more heavily-wooded lands, fringing their existing fields, or developed new villages with cocoa plots, necessarily at varying distances because of the size of the settlement units. In one Akim village pre-war study showed that the distribution of cocoa 'farms' was comparatively uniform up to a distance of 3 miles (5 km) from the village, although most bearing farms were in the first $1\frac{1}{2}$ miles ($2\frac{1}{2}$ km). The distribution was explained as due to the exclusion of unsuitable land, the custom of retaining a 'belt of forest' round the 'farm' wherever possible, and the nature of local land tenure. The village contained just over 1000 people and was described as presenting 'an approach to the model cocoa village'.[2]

It has been suggested that the 'forest trees provided shade for cocoa'.[3] There may have been some cases of only slight clearance in between trees with broad canopies, which were allowed to stand in order to shade the seedlings. In most cases, however, only a few tall trees were allowed to remain, and shade for the young seedlings was provided by cocoyam (*Colocasia* or *Xanthosoma*, chiefly the latter in recent years) and plantains. In many cocoa-growing villages these were the staple foodstuffs, and were supplied mainly from plots of young cocoa. New plantings of cocoa have thus been in part encouraged by their association with food crops. Shade for the later stages of growth came from various trees either planted with the cocoa, or allowed to grow instead of being weeded out between the plants. Of these the chief are: 'Mother of Cocoa' (*Gliricidia maculata*), Coral Flower (*Erythrina senegalensis*), African Locust Bean (*Parkia filicoidea*), and the Oil bean (*Pentaclethra macrophylla*). The interplanting of kola has been less important than in Nigeria, despite the fact that kola trees are widely grown in southern Ghana, and that Ashanti was formerly the chief producer of the preferred nitida varieties, and still has a small export trade to the Upper Volta and Mali. But Ashanti led in production when the caravans could obtain free passage from there to the chief market – Hausaland. Today Western Nigeria, with its railway to Hausaland, has become the chief producer, and in consequence has had more encouragement to combine the crop with cocoa. In addition the 'Entente' territories surrounding Ghana look more to the Ivory Coast for their supplies. The spread of cocoa cultivation has thus encouraged the spread of cocoyams and plantains, and of the shade trees, plus the small cocoa plantations themselves, all of which have replaced the original forest. Together with the cocoa plots have spread the croplands, cropland fallows and cocoa fallows. All these plant combinations occur in patches, either in fields or plots or on the sites of former fields or plots, scattered about the village units. The villages themselves are usually located on or near a motor road, and in consequence often assume linear forms. Formerly the Ghanaian villages had tended to have few outside commercial contacts, and only a restricted intercourse for administrative and social purposes with other villages and centres of authority. Today, wherever cocoa can be grown, the village depends economically on its road link with the market, even in many cases for essential food supplies.

The fallows resulting from cocoa cultivation show distinctive successions of plants. Ahn has described the succession under different conditions of clearance in the western forest areas of Ghana.[4] Cocoa or food 'farms' are often succeeded by a thicket in which plants such as *Rauwolfia vomitoria*, *Bridelia micrantha* and thorny climbers are dominant. After long periods of cultivation, many of the species associated with this thicket stage are reduced in frequency, and others, notably *Combretum macrocarpum* and *Ricinodendron heudelotii*, become prominent.

Cocoa planting was not injected into the traditional system of shifting cultivation. Tree planting involved long-term occupance. Moreover, the new cultivation was strictly commercial and for an external market. New problems of land tenure were created, and a new class of cultivator came into being. As planting moved westwards from the original nucleus in Akwapim to the forests of Akim in the late 1880s, the planters were strangers who often bought land outright from local chiefs.[5] Land became a form of investment, and the profits of earlier plantings were used to purchase land farther to the west. Although individual tenure was universal, there was some variation in the form of holdings, expressed mainly in field patterns. Field patterns amongst matrilineal societies were thus often amorphous, the product of a high state of individualism. Among patrilineal societies the company system brought regularity and is expressed today in strip fields of enormous length.[6] In such cases the linear development of settlement reaches its extreme form, but with each dwelling on its occupant's land. The patterns of settlement and land division are similar to those developed for commercial food cropping by the Manya-Krobo (see p. 447). Companies of cocoa growers are usually combinations of strangers, formed temporarily for the purchase and subsequent division of land. There are today in Ghana 'several hundred'[7] such companies, migrating from one area to another as land is worked out. The companies purchase areas of several hundred acres, and divide them into strips of standard agreed widths. The cultivators do not mark out their entire strips, but work along them, measuring with a rope as they go. A single main path is established, often serving as a sort of base line, along which the dwellings are established. Further division may take place, longitudinally between heirs, or laterally on sale, so that a complex pattern may be produced within the framework of strip border lines. In order to distinguish boundaries 'ntome' trees (*Dracaena arborea*) are often planted along the lines. In some cases lateral subdivision takes place in order to divide the land between a cultivator and his sons or son. In such circumstances, when a cultivator has finished working his portion, he then begins fresh plantings on the other side of the portion granted to his son, and the latter, on completing his, begins cultivation again on the other side of his father's second portion. Alternating plots are thus created, until the whole strip is used, when it is either abandoned, or cultivation begins on the original plots again.

Cocoa planting in Togo is, in a sense, an extension eastwards of the Ivory Coast–Ghana cocoa belt, for at least in part it was encouraged by Ghana's success, and it is confined to the wetter mountain districts of the west, chiefly around Klouto and Palimé. Originally the crop was established in German-owned plantations, but today it is grown mainly on African smallholdings. As in Ghana, immigrant labour is employed, chiefly Kabrais.

The contrast provided by the south-eastern cocoa-growing districts of the Ivory Coast is instructive, for it illustrates the significance of political factors. Throughout the area physical conditions are broadly similar to those in Ghana. The woody fallows zone extends uninterruptedly across the border, climatic conditions and soils are broadly similar, and the majority of the inhabitants of the cocoa-growing areas are Akan speaking, and had created small kingdoms similar in many respects to the Akan kingdoms of southern Ghana. In the 19th century trade with Europe developed through coastal intermediaries, and the Agni peoples of Sanwi, Ndénié and Moronou, together with their neighbours the Attié and Abé, produced chiefly gold and kola nuts for export, as did the Ashanti. Again, as in southern Ghana, the end of the 19th century was marked by the development of rubber gathering for export, a development which resulted in a greater penetration of the forests than hitherto, and the establishment within them of camps and trading posts, some of which became the sites of permanent settlements in the succeeding timber cutting and cocoa and coffee planting era.[8] The Sanwi state, for example, was adversely affected by the imposition of direct administration in 1903, the collapse of the rubber market between 1913 and 1918, and the decline of caravan traffic with the north, due to the opening of the railway between Abidjan and Bouaké. Emigration to Ghana began, attracted by the demand for labour in the mines and in public works. This emigration was intensified with the French military recruitment campaign of 1916–17. At the end of the 19th century the French had regarded the south-eastern Ivory Coast as an area mainly suited to the commercial development of coffee growing by Europeans, for wild species occurred there, and a relative (*Coffea robusta*) of the local wild plants had been successfully introduced from the Congo. Coffee had a protected market, and French growers were not only protected from local competition, but various means were employed to ensure their labour supply (see p. 501). Whilst the Agni and their neighbours thus had greater difficulties in entering into coffee production than the French, they were provided with an alternative by the colonial government, which in 1908 made the cultivation of cocoa obligatory.[9] The result was the spread of cocoa growing despite some opposition to the crop, mainly on political grounds. The high prices of 1916 were attractive, and many planters achieved commercial success. In the late 1920s coffee seedlings were distributed to African farmers, especially of the more easily-cultivated 'gros indénié' variety. African growers began to gain a share of the coffee export, which enjoyed French protection, so that coffee prices in the Ivory Coast, after 1930, did not decline as markedly as did those of cocoa. Nevertheless, for many African growers, cocoa was the pioneer perennial export crop, and, moreover, extensive plantings had been made in periods of rising prices. In consequence, cocoa production continued to increase, especially from the Abengourou and Dimbokro districts, and the cocoa export was still maintained at a far greater level than that of coffee.

Since 1945 European coffee planting has declined whilst African coffee planting has boomed (see pp. 499–500). Production since 1949 has increased rapidly, so that today coffee exports exceed those of cocoa in tonnage, and comprise more than half the total export of the Ivory Coast by value.

The cultivators of the south-eastern Ivory Coast thus have two commercial crops. Whilst both are capable of growing on the same land, and, indeed, compete for land according to their market value, or replace one another after destruction by disease, there is a general tendency to plant each on distinctive soils. Thus the heavy Assié-Blé, or humid black earths, generally occupying the more level grounds of the flatter hill-tops or valley bottoms, are preferred for cocoa. The lighter Assié-Kokoré, or porous, gravelly, red earths of the slopes, are preferred for coffee. The oldest cocoa plantations are generally in valley bottoms. From 1935, after the full effects of the cocoa slump had been felt, most planting in the south-east was of coffee, and despite some return to cocoa, Sanwi and some of the adjacent lands are today more a coffee than cocoa producer, although both crops are grown on neighbouring plots. Perhaps partly because of early reaction against Government attempts to enforce cocoa cultivation, and partly because of high humidity spoiling beans or making necessary the use of drying ovens, Sanwi has a lower proportion of its commercial cropland in cocoa than northwards in the neighbouring district of Ndénié, or farther westwards still in Moronou, where cocoa is dominant. West of the Bandama river very little cocoa is planted and the area may be considered as lying outside the cocoa region proper. Here coffee is the dominant commercial crop, particularly in the Gagnoa, Daloa and Man districts, together with bananas in Gagnoa and Sassandra. To some extent, the division between the south-western and south-eastern portions of the Ivory Coast, noted by Miège in the case of food crops, also exists in commercial cropping (see p. 75).

Coffee and cocoa growing can be made complementary, for not only are there different soil preferences, but there are different times for undertaking the main agricultural tasks. Thus for cocoa the first weeding is in June and the main picking in November, December and January, whilst for coffee the first weeding is in October and the main picking in February and March. New plantations are continually being cleared, at an estimated rate of 80 square miles (200 sq km) a year, and this despite the stopping of the Government premium on new plantations after 1954. Immigrants have entered the south-eastern Ivory Coast in large numbers. In 1953 a third of Sanwi's fixed population was estimated to consist of strangers. Altogether people from 31 distinct communities may be found in Sanwi, Ndénié and Moronou, mostly living in long ribbon villages, many of which still have the older type courtyard houses of the Akan-speaking peoples. With the increase in cocoa and coffee cultivation has come an increase in the planting of the easiest grown of all food crops – cassava – and the increased development of compound land for kitchen-garden foodstuffs. At present large areas remain to be exploited, and migratory planting is the most common practice, giving high returns to the planters at comparatively little cost. It is on the post-war boom in cocoa and coffee that the agricultural prosperity of the Ivory Coast, and its present political prominence amongst the former member states of French West Africa, is based.

In Ghana there was no protected coffee market, but there was eventually a system of Empire preference, and a rapidly-expanding United Kingdom demand for cocoa. Cocoa growing was introduced into Ashanti shortly after annexation in 1900. A railway had been constructed between Sekondi and Tarkwa in 1900 to serve the gold mining industry. For military purposes it was extended to Kumasi in 1903, and was responsible for the concentration of cocoa production in Western Ashanti. Feeder roads were built and lorries introduced. In 1919 with the then high world cocoa price of £80 a ton, the Ten Year Development Plan was introduced, in which the main item was transport improvement, including the building of the Accra to Kumasi railway, completed by 1923, and the Huni Valley railway completed by 1927. By the early 1930s, however, lorry rates were below railway rates, and cultivation began to look less to location near the railway, and more to the expanding road system.

By the late 1930s there were estimated to be over 300,000 plots in Ghana, averaging about 3 to 5 acres (1 to 2 hectares) each, and each producing about one ton of cocoa. Many were poorly drained, had little or no pruning, were never sprayed, and suffered from a lack or an insufficiency of shade trees. Capital for improvement was lacking, and most growers were in debt to money-lenders, whilst the owners of larger areas under cocoa were for the most part merely absentee landlords. It is, however, difficult to generalize, not only because of the lack of reliable data, but because of the marked differences between one district and another shown by detailed sample studies.[10] Many 'farmers' appear to have held several cocoa plots, planted at different dates. In the early stages of the development of cocoa planting, the 'typical farmer' found himself the possessor of a new cocoa 'farm' every few years, and, in consequence, of an abundant food supply. By 1912 cocoa growing was expanding faster in Ashanti than elsewhere, partly due to physical suitability, partly to the railway and partly to the greater availability of immigrant labour, chiefly from the north. Estimates indicate that altogether there may be as many as 250,000 seasonal labourers from the Northern Territories and Upper Volta working in the cocoa belt. In the 1918 to 1939 period cocoa growing spread rapidly between Kumasi and Koforidua and in north-western Ashanti, but foodstuffs were becoming short, encouraging the development of commercial food growing in neighbouring areas (e.g. Manya-Krobo) unsuited to cocoa production, and encouraging also the rapid extension of new cocoa plots, with their interplanted foodstuffs – cocoyam and plantains. In many cases existing plantations were neglected in favour of new plantings, and production declined earlier than need have been the case.

With large numbers of neglected or little-tended holdings, a readiness to abandon poor-yielding properties for new plots, and the planting of trees as closely as possible, conditions were ideal for the spread of certain diseases, especially swollen shoot. Diseased plantations were noted in the older cocoa-growing areas as early as 1915. Severe losses were sustained in the older areas particularly in the more marginal areas climatically. Krobo, Ashanti, Akim and Bekwai all suffered heavily and cocoa has almost entirely disappeared from Akwapim.[11] The disease had made severe inroads before any attempt was made to prevent or cure it. Until 1937 there was no agricultural station in the cocoa belt proper at which the necessary research could be performed. Technical officers were unable to cope with the problem, and the suggestion that the diseased parts of the trees should be cut out opened the canopy with disastrous results. The disease discouraged many growers, but its chief effect, other than reducing production, was the acceleration of migration to areas such as Akim Abuakwa, where the disease was not serious, and above all to Central and South Brong-Ahafo, where planting has boomed. The only effective methods of control, the Government agricultural officers suggested, was the cutting out of diseased trees, and the destruction of complete holdings over wide areas. Opposition to this policy, since even a diseased plantation could give some yield whilst new areas were being cleared, led to increasing opposition to the colonial government, and support for the nationalist parties, strengthening the move towards Ghana's independence.

THE GROUNDNUT-PRODUCING REGION OF SENEGAL AND THE GAMBIA

Just as cocoa has brought an economic revolution to Ghana and the Ivory Coast, leading to profound geographic changes, so the groundnut has fulfilled a similar role in Senegal and the Gambia. Again the area affected is near the coast. Indeed only one major inland area has suffered a comparable transformation, and that consists of the cotton- and groundnut-producing districts of Hausaland – the product as much of favourable railway freight rates as of suitable physical, agricultural and social conditions (see p. 445 and p. 611). The history of groundnut exports has already been described (see pp. 483-6), but the effects on the agricultural economy, on social conditions and on political developments remain to be studied in some detail.

The first groundnut plantings for export were in the Gambia and in the valley of the Senegal, because of the availability of cheap river transport and French commercial interest. Later Cayor became the chief centre, with the development of trade from the port of Rufisque and, later (1885), the construction of the railway to St Louis. The traffic was stimulated by the development of an oil extracting industry at the ports. Attempts to extract oil for export had been made as early as 1834. The trade was for long largely in French hands, and looked mainly to the port of Marseilles, where thrived the largest oil-seed processing industry in Europe. Despite French dominance, the industry not only survived in the British enclave of the Gambia, but even attracted growers away from Senegal, because of the offer of special commercial and transport conditions. As the oilseed industry developed in Britain, with the growing need for margarine and synthetic cooking fats, so the Gambia's importance increased, but the Gambia despite its continuity of surface with Senegal is a special case. Like the Ivory

Coast in relation to Ghana, it occupies a distinctive position in relation to Senegal in the production of a commercial crop, due to its political distinction. Its cultivators have included a higher proportion of seasonal migrants, and its industry has been more susceptible to price fluctuations.

The groundnut needs little rainfall, but this does not mean that it is restricted to low rainfall areas. On the contrary, providing the soil is well drained, it can be grown almost everywhere in West Africa. Soil conditions are more critical than

The Groundnut Producing Region of Senegal and the Gambia

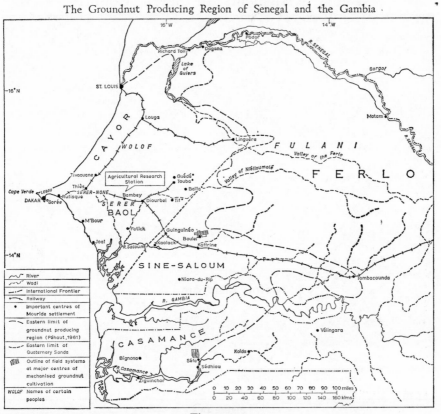

Figure 13.2

rainfall, especially for the heavier yielding 'running' varieties, favoured by African commercial growers, and, unlike cocoa, the plant was already well established, being grown for food throughout the Sudanic zone, especially on the light sandy soils of former dunes, preferred also as settlement sites. In the hinterland of Rufisque and Dakar, especially in the former Wolof kingdom of Cayor, and in the Serer districts of Baol, ideal soils occurred, and close to an exporting port. The Wolof concentrated on groundnuts at the expense of other crops and of soil fertility, seeking fresh soils in formerly wooded areas, and abandoning their clearances when the soils were exhausted. The Serer raised the groundnut from a minor to a major position in local crop rotations, expanded cultivation into neighbouring areas physically suitable, especially into the border forest lands between villages, and permitted the immigration of vast numbers of 'navétanes' or seasonal labourers, and of permanent settlers, including a majority of Wolof together with some Bambara. In some areas, however, notably in the Gambia, pennisetum millet cultivation is still very important, even to the extent of preferring to plant groundnuts late rather than early, despite lower yields, in order

Wolof Settlements in Serer Country

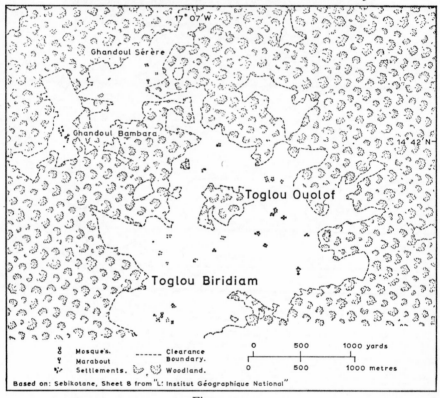

Figure 13.3

to avoid a peak labour demand in June and July when priority in planting and weeding is given to millet.[12]

Behind the dunes of the Senegal coastland, occupying a strip up to 15 miles (24 km) wide, containing marshy depressions or 'niayes', are the western plains, including Cayor in the north and Baol between the 'forest' of Thiès and the Saloum river. Here lacustrine deposits and recent sandstones are mostly covered by sand dunes, aligned regularly from north-east to south-west. The only relief is that of the dunes themselves, and of the 200-foot (60-metre) escarpment at Thiès, for the valleys are slight, being filled with sand, especially in their upper portions. The former acacia savanna of Cayor has been almost entirely removed for Wolof groundnut and food crop cultivation. On the light sandy soils ground-nuts can be planted in the first shift in the rotation, whereas on heavier soils they normally succeed better in the second or later shifts. Wolof growers planted groundnuts for the first two years, followed by souna pennisetum millet, and finally sanio, before three to four years of fallow. Cowpeas were sometimes inter-planted amongst the souna. At the northern extremes, particularly in Louga, the varieties need to be very quick growing, and cereal cultivation tends to predom-inate over the commercial crop. However, in the south, wherever heavier soils occur, quick-growing varieties are also frequently preferred, as the harvest must take place before the soil dries and becomes a hard mass. Frequently cultivation begins with souna millet, and groundnuts follow. The rapid spread of groundnut cultivation in Cayor is not to be explained simply by the development of the European market, of the St Louis railway, and of the ports of Rufisque and Dakar. The plant was already widespread as a local food crop although grown only on a small scale. Another plant, the 'earth pea', or *Voandzeia subterranea*, was already widely grown, and the methods of cultivation were similar. In consequence, as demand rose, the groundnut replaced the 'earth pea' in local crop rotations. There were already centres of commercial cultivation at Podor and Matam, at Cape Verde, and on the banks of the Gambia. Again the running varieties not only succeeded on the extremely light soils, but provided a soil cover against erosion, and were an excellent cleaning crop before planting cereals. Groundnut trash is often left on the ground after harvest to lengthen the period of protective cover for the soils. Constant improvement in quality has been made possible by the development of the Bambey seed station, and the compulsory sale of all nuts pro-duced, so that growers must purchase new seed each year. Moreover, since 1935 legislation has been invoked to protect trees, control bush fires, and reduce soil erosion.

In the 1880s the French advanced into the Soudan, and, by the end of the century, laid the railways which gave their forces mobility, enabled trade to flourish, and extended the hinterlands of their ports. Bamako was taken in 1883 and Macina ten years later. In 1907 work was begun on the railway to provide Dakar with a vast Sudanic hinterland. A junction was developed at Thiès. Thiès is in the Serer-None country, immediately to the south of Cayor. The area was once only sparsely populated, and the remnants of the 'forest' of Thiès remain in numerous forest reserves. Groundnut cultivation had already begun to spread amongst the Serer-None from Thiès, and their lands had been invaded as early as 1885 by Wolof immigrants, who settled near the fortified post of Thiès, and created their own distinct villages. The Serer-None villages consist of groups of hamlets of rectangular huts, with an abundance of *Borassus* palms in the fields, a concentration of millet fields round the settlements, and a scattering of trees. The Wolof villages are large nucleated units, generally also of rectangular huts, although rondavels are traditional. The groundnut fields are generally larger, and few trees remain, except round the villages themselves. Between 1890 and 1895 Bambara refugees from the attacks of Samory came into the Serer-None area, but

Changes in the Settlement Pattern of the Diourbel Area with the Expansion of Groundnut Cultivation

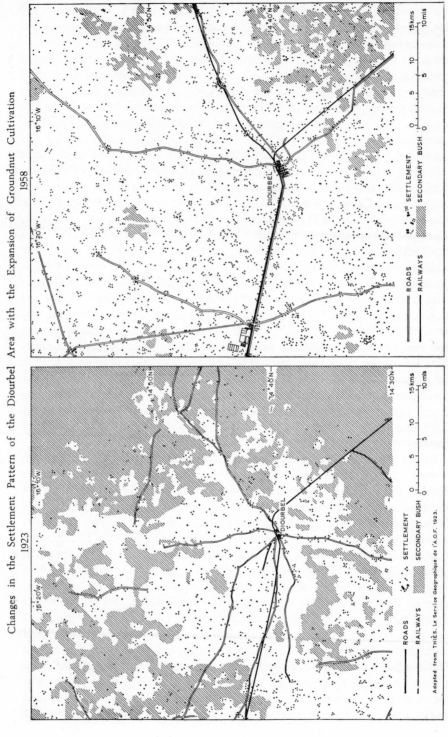

Figure I3.4

copied existing Serer-None and Wolof settlements in their village and field patterns. As the railway to Kayes was built across Baol to Bambey, Diourbel and Kaffrine, groundnut cultivation advanced southwards amongst the Serer, and south-eastwards outflanking the Ferlo. The branch to the port of Kaolack, created in 1883, was built in 1911, and gave an alternative outlet to this newly-developing southern area of production, today the largest groundnut-growing area of Senegal. Here soils derived from Quaternary sands, of maritime, alluvial and fluvial origin, provided favourable conditions for growth. Soils with more than 10 per cent clay content in depressions were avoided. Between 1929 and 1937 Sine–Saloum received 175,000 immigrants, chiefly Wolof, who became permenent settlers engaged in either commercial cultivation or trade.

Sine–Saloum produced 44 per cent of the total tonnage in the 1964 season, due less to any decline in the older areas from soil exhaustion than to an increase in the total area planted. The Serer territory of Baol is a parkland dominated by *Acacia albida*, in contrast with the nearly treeless areas occupied by the Wolof to the north. Pelissier[13] has portrayed the ideal Serer agricultural pattern, depending on a rotation of food crop, commercial crop and pasture on the main croplands, together with food crops and cotton on land immediately round the village, and pasture land and separate guinea corn fields on the heavier soils. Fields near the villages are called 'pombod', are fertilized with household refuse, and planted mainly with 'pod', or quick-growing pennisetum millet and interplanted beans. A few pombod plots support guinea corn, cotton or cassava, and all are frequently surrounded with a thorn hedge, especially alongside roads used to take cattle to water. The main croplands are divided into virtually a three-field system of: 1) 'matche' or slower growing, but heavier yielding, pennisetum; 2) groundnuts; 3) pasture fallow, but in some areas a four-course plus pasture system is used involving the rotation: 1) groundnuts; 2) souna; 3) groundnuts; 4) sanio; 5–8) pasture.[14] Again, hedges are used to prevent livestock straying on the cropland. Additional pasture is provided by surrounding uncultivated land, pasture land near surface water, and cropland after harvest, including the 'pombod'. Manure is thus spread over the croplands during the dry season. Three main varieties of guinea corn are grown: 'lock', harvested in December, 'rein', harvested in November, and 'm'boratel', harvested in September–October. Generally guinea corn is less important than pennisetum millet, and occupies separate fields. Of the three varieties listed, 'lock', which produces best on the heavier soils, appears to be the most important. Formerly groundnuts were only a pombod crop on a few plots near the dwellings, and the pennisetum millet crop was grown in fields, established in different locations each year, in the area otherwise available for pasture. Groundnut cultivation has caused the following changes, as Pelissier shows: 1) an increase in the area cropped; 2) the introduction of a more methodical and more systematic use of land, i.e. the 'three-field system'; 3) an economic change involving the development of specialized use of portions of the land; 4) population pressure on land resources involving the need for a more rational use of soils, i.e. soil selection; and 5) the occupation of former boundary or inter-

vening woodlands by other Serer or Wolof growers, raising population densities to
the present general levels of 75 to 130 per square mile (30 to 50 per sq km). New
villages are smaller, and many groundnut-producing settlements consist of dispersals of isolated compounds. In some of the newly-cleared areas, where abundant land is still available, the cattle pastures are separate from the cropland, and
in no way associated in rotation. In some of the older, now overcrowded areas,
permanent pastures, and even the pasture field in the rotation, have disappeared,

Land Use in a Groundnut growing
district near Sare Yewtu, Gambia

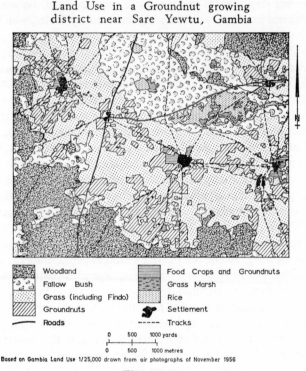

Figure 13.5

and groundnuts may be repeated more frequently in the rotation than any other
crop. Many cultivators now employ seasonal labour. The 'navétanes' from Mali,
or from overcrowded Cayor, may work as labourers on Serer or southern Wolof
holdings, or may acquire plots to work for themselves, by offering so much labour
to the land-holder. Dumont[15] gives a common rotation near Kaffrine of
groundnut and pennisetum millets alternating for eight years, followed by up to
four years fallow. For the Saloum Wolof, Gamble[16] cites two rotations:

    a) 1, groundnuts; 2, sanio; 3, guinea corn; 4, groundnuts; 5, guinea corn;
      6, fallow.

    b) 1, sanio; 2, groundnuts; 3, sanio; 4, groundnuts; 5, fallow.

In the Gambia rotations are very similar. Cropping frequently shows a markedly zonal pattern round the villages with an inner concentration of early millet (Fig. 13.5). Some villages have changed their locations in response to the development of new routes, but the distances moved have been small. Large areas of woodland still exist, and generally the impression is of a much slower advance of agriculture into the woodlands than in Senegal. Swamp rice is of increasing importance, especially in floodlands strongly affected by tides.

The most recent extensions of the groundnut zone have been into the western and southern fringes of the Ferlo, and south of the Gambia into Casamance. The Ferlo invasion has owed much to two developments: the introduction of bores for domestic water, and the organization of colonial agricultural settlements by the Mouride Brotherhood (pp. 444 and 485). Moreover these more recently-settled lands have in some cases been the site of developments in mechanized groundnut production, beginning with the Boulel experiment of 1948.[17] At Boulel the attempt was made to educate Mouride colonists in modern agricultural practice, and promote the co-operative organization of cultivation. The area was formerly used by Fulani pastoralists, was cleared originally for another scheme, and was abandoned because of poor soils and too short a rainy season. Large parallel rectangular fields were created at right angles to the roads. The first fields were $1\frac{1}{2}$ miles ($2\frac{1}{2}$ km) long by $\frac{1}{3}$ mile ($\frac{1}{2}$ km) wide, but later units were reduced to 1100 yards by 270 yards (1 km by $\frac{1}{4}$ km).[18] Narrow corridors of trees and bushes were left between the fields to act as windbreaks, and thickened by planting cashew, thus creating a rectilinear bocage. Groundnuts were planted in the first year, followed by pennisetum millet in the second and third, the last crop being ploughed in. Tractors were used for ploughing, but weeding had still to be done mostly by hand. The discipline of the Mouride social system has assisted the development of co-operation between the tractors and the cultivators, but the scheme must still be open to criticisms of mechanization combined with peasant cultivation expressed elsewhere (pp. 521–2). An attempt to copy the Boulel or Kaffrine system has been organized by the Mourides at Guédé near Touba, with pennisetum millet at the head of the rotation. Finally yet another mechanized scheme has been developed by the Compagnie Générale des Oléagineux Tropicaux (C.G.O.T.) in the moister and more thickly-wooded area of Sédhiou in Casamance, where the longer rainy season allowed tillage after the beginning of the rains, when the soils were easier to work. Elsewhere in Casamance, the Balante have developed the part played by groundnuts in rotations on main cropland dependent on rains, combining: 1) maize; 2) pennisetum; 3) groundnuts; 4) pennisetum; 5) groundnuts. When soils are exhausted the rotation becomes: 1) groundnuts; 2) fonio or 'hungry rice', or just one year of groundnuts and guinea corn intercropped. Where rice is cultivated the rotation becomes: 1) rice; 2) rice; 3) pennisetum and groundnuts; 4) groundnuts.[19] Still farther south groundnut cultivation, although on a smaller scale, has been invading Portuguese Guinea and Guinea, and the claims have been made that groundnut cultivation has been tending to replace upland rice on steep slopes, especially as swamp rice provides another food resource, that groundnuts and 'savanna' have been replacing the oil palm and secondary forest, and that the groundnut cultivation has impoverished poor soils still further.[20]

Intensive cultivation and pressure on land resources have led to a shortening of fallows, and to a demand for fertilizers. The French agricultural services experimented with sulphate of ammonia and potassium chlorate, and a hopeful development appears to lie in the use of local phosphate resources, for a rich deposit exists near Thiès at only shallow depths. As the commercialization of agriculture has been intensified, so local changes in settlement and road patterns have taken place. These have been mainly associated with the immigration of Wolof and of navétanes from many areas into Baol, and with the development of the organization of the Mouride Brotherhood. Settlements have become dispersed, scattered compounds at short intervals, or organized in streets. Access to road and railway station have become important, and market centres like Thiès and Louga have grown, together with the ports. An important factor has been the fixing of the number and location of trading posts by legislation, and legislative support for donkey rather than lorry traffic. The same price is paid for all groundnuts, irrespective of distance, encouraging growers far inland who are in effect subsidized. The principle of a guaranteed price to protect the industry has in any case been accepted since the early 1930s.

All groundnut sales are controlled by the Office de Commercialisation Agricole which, in the 1963–4 season, bought 63 per cent of the commercialized crop through co-operatives, 36 per cent through private traders and less than 1 per cent directly from the few large growers. Of the total crop, estimated at 936,000 tons, 53,000 are thought to have been consumed, 24,500 put by the growers into storage, and 80,500 taken into reserve by the Centres Régionaux d'Assistance au Développement (C.R.A.D.). 16,000 tons were lost in store and transit, and a net 7000 tons were taken out of further reserves, to make a total commercialized crop for decorticating or crushing of a little over 769,000 tons. Thus quite a large proportion of the crop is held back for seed, or in order to create a reserve to reduce some of the fluctuation in output.[21]

Rufisque was important for a while, and Kaolack, the port of Baol, is the biggest exporter of nuts, but despite the oil refineries at Kaolack, the greatest centre of the industry is still Dakar, which not only exports nuts, but crude and refined oil, and by-products from its mills. Dakar has slowly taken a large share of the oil mill industry from Marseilles, and is not only the political, but also the financial centre of the new state of Senegal. The groundnut growers depend considerably on imported foods, since the plant has taken the place of food crops in the rotations. Moreover, the development of the associated vast commercial and transport system has encouraged the development of commercial food cropping on a large scale, especially around towns and above all in the Lébou lands. Behind the line which was once defined by earthworks to mark their independence from Cayor, the Lébou have developed a market-garden zone, which has extended into the niayes, and whose produce supports an income derived otherwise mainly from fishing. Old villages have expanded and new villages built in modern rectilinear patterns, which in a sense are urbanized outliers of Dakar. Yet despite the efforts of the Lébou, heavy demand for cheap foodstuffs, especially rice, combined with groundnut prosperity, have led to a considerable importation, chiefly rice, wheat and sugar. For many, imported rice is now preferable to the old-established millets. For some the taste has been acquired from brief residence in the Gambia or from contact with rice-eating navétanes from Guinea. But, as in the cocoa areas, the effect is the same, the import of foodstuffs even at the expense of local foods, and this despite the rotation of pennisetum and guinea corn with the commercial crop.

Directly produced changes

THE MECHANIZED GROUNDNUT-PRODUCING REGIONS

The need felt in Europe after 1945 for a quick increase in vegetable oil production led to the despatch of research missions to West Africa to advise on future action and to the preparation of plans for large-scale agricultural production. The report of the Vegetable Oils and Oil Seed Mission of 1946[22] to the Colonial Office suggested that the key to increased export crop production in West Africa lay in the availability of consumer goods, particularly textiles. It was thought that, from a short-term point of view, this would have more influence on the volume of exports than any technical improvements in agricultural production. The West African Oilseeds Mission of 1947[23], however, proposed the immediate introduction of mechanized groundnut cultivation, and, in order to avoid disturbing existing areas of production, suggested six locations of very low population density due to lack of domestic water supplies, tsetse fly infestation, or depopulation by slave raids:

Location	Country	Area
Western Gonja	Ghana	2000 square miles (5200 sq km)
Northern Ashanti	Ghana	2000 ,, ,,
Damaturu, Bornu	Nigeria	2000 ,, ,,
Kontagora	Nigeria	2000 ,, ,,
Western Kiang	Gambia	30,000 acres (12,000 hectares)
Upper Niume	Gambia	5000 ,, (2000 hectares)

Reference was made to the benefits of mixed farming, to the raising of soil fertility to a higher level, and to 'placement planting' of artificial fertilizers in the form of a pill. The French Government produced the Plan de Modernisation et d'Equipment, which provided, amongst other matters, for the creation in 1948 of the Compagnie Générale des Oléagineux Tropicaux (C.G.O.T.). Schemes were proposed for the use of machines and fertilizers to produce groundnuts, and work was begun in three locations in Casamance totalling 200,000 hectares (770 square miles) in 1949.

In 1948 an advisory mission reported to the Nigerian Government on a visit to agricultural schemes in the Sudan.[24] It recommended that difficulties of water supply and transport and the narrow margin between price and cost of production ruled out Damaturu, and that Kontagora should receive priority. It preferred a partnership between tenant labourers and the Colonial Development Corporation to paid labour, and proposed

a) A rotation of: 1) grass; 2) grass; 3) groundnuts; 4) guinea corn; 5) groundnuts.
b) The combination of animal husbandry with cultivation.
c) The building of villages, each containing 100 families, and obtaining water from wells.

In 1949 a company, the Niger Agricultural Project Ltd, was formed to produce oil-seeds for export and food crops for sale within Nigeria. In the Gold Coast the Gonja Development Corporation was formed, to operate a smaller scheme on similar lines. Within five years the Niger Agricultural Project had to be taken over by the Northern Nigerian Government, and the whole programme of cultivation severely reduced and altered, whilst the Gonja Scheme was reduced to a small experimental project. The C.G.O.T. scheme in Casamance has also been reduced, but still continues at a huge cost disproportionate to the meagre results.[25]

These schemes of mechanized groundnut production in West Africa have failed, or survive only at a high cost. However, it is instructive to observe the patterns of agriculture and land-use created in them and the forms of settlement attempted, for here are new features in the geography of West Africa, which, if the schemes had been successful, would have been repeated over huge areas.

In Nigeria 32,000 acres (13,000 hectares) were selected near Mokwa, a small Nupe township, for the attempt by the Niger Agricultural Project Ltd. The Company was to clear the land, to plan and control agricultural operations, whilst the farmers were to be peasant settlers on holdings allotted to them by the Company.[26] The area chosen was virtually uninhabited, and yet near the railway, where workshops and stores could be established. The relief consisted of gentle slopes, supporting thick 'Guinea Savanna' woodland on thin sandy soils. The rainfall was greater than in the main groundnut-producing areas of Northern Nigeria (Mokwa 42 in (1070 mm), Gusau 37 in (940 mm)), and the rainy season longer. However, this was an advantage where machines were to be used for tillage, for cultivation could take place in May after the soils had been moistened, and the groundnuts were not planted until June. Moreover, the 'bunched' varieties, generally suited to the wetter conditions, were preferred for mechanical cultivation. The trees were removed, chiefly by hand, since mechanical methods proved too costly, and the logs were burned where they fell. Hand labour had also to be used to remove stumps, roots and ant-hills. The first clearing was imperfect and a subsequent clearing removed as many as 300,000 stumps from 4000 acres (1600 hectares). Straight-sided 24-acre (10-hectare) fields were created (Figs. 13.6 and 2.12) in parallel lines, and separated by tree belts, meant to serve as windbreaks. Each field was divided into two 12-acre (5-hectare) blocks, and ploughed in straight lines by tractors – originally, for a short period, by steam-tackle, but this could only operate on land completely free of roots. In some fields the furrows were oriented down the slope, and cross ridges were made at intervals varying with the slope angle. The crop rotation introduced was: 1) guinea corn; 2) groundnuts; 3) guinea corn; 4) 'cash crop'; 5-8) grass fallow. Each settler had 24 acres (10 hectares) under fallow and 24 acres under crop, subdivided into four field units. Machines were to be used only for ploughing and ridging. Weeding, sowing and harvesting were to be done by hand. Model villages, linear

Plan of Typical Farming Block

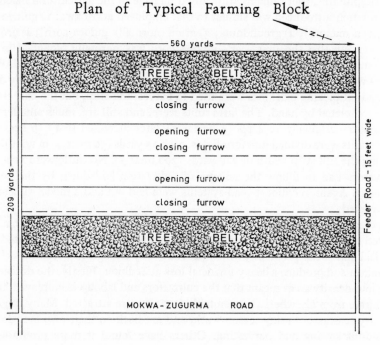

Based on diagram from "The Niger Agricultural Project" by K.D.S. Baldwin

Figure 13.6

in pattern, were built and supplied with wells. Roads were cut between the blocks, giving access to the farms from the villages.

The C.G.O.T. scheme in Senegal was intended originally to develop locations in Kaffrine, Nioro and Sédhiou. After a few months' effort the 25,000-acre (10,000-hectare) concession at Kaffrine was abandoned, because it was thought that the soils were too poor and the rainy season too short to make use of machines economic. A small portion of this scheme, at Boulel, was taken over by the Mouride sect, who farmed the area with some success. The Nioro concession was thought to be too densely populated, and in consequence it was decided in 1948 to concentrate on the Sédhiou location in Casamance, where Séfa provided a small river port and there was a road to Ziguinchor. Here woodland with a density of 140 trees of 8 to 12 in diameter per acre (350 trees of 20–30 cm diameter per hectare), mainly *Parinari excelsa* and *Daniella oliveri*, was cleared, chiefly by the use of teams of three tractors with a chain. Clearance time was only 6 hours an acre (15 hours per hectare), but the cost was high. Field strips 270 yards (250 metres) wide by 1100 yards (1000 metres) long (approximately 52 acres (21 hectares)) were created in parallel lines divided by tree belts. Later, widths were reduced to 220 yards (200 metres), in order to counter damage by wind.[27] Roots were cut out to depths varying between 12 and 16 in (30–40 cm), but, despite this, root remains still caused damage to the agricultural machines. The rotation introduced was similar to that employed at Mokwa: 1) guinea corn (as green manure); 2) groundnuts; 3) grain (normally guinea corn); 4) groundnuts – except that the first year's guinea corn was normally ploughed in as a green manure, and it was not proposed originally to allow a fallow period. Phosphates were applied in between two ploughings, and the seed was sown by drills. Groundnut picking machines were used to harvest the crop, but the harvest had to be completed by hand. The farm units were, and still are, much smaller than at Mokwa – originally 10 acres (4 hectares), later increased to 15 (6 hectares). These units were divided into four fields, each 55 yards (50 metres) in width, thus rotating the full strip width of 220 yards (200 metres). No cattle were kept, and cultivators had to follow the scheme of cultivation laid down by the central authority. Again, rectilinear road systems were laid out and a model village was constructed.

In creating a new form of production the groundnut scheme planners had also created new landscapes, yet, in modifying the previous forms, they created new physical and social problems, which proved costly enough to wreck the scheme at Mokwa and produce a heavy financial loss at Sédhiou. Firstly, the decision to clear low-density areas meant that the cultivators and labourers employed had to immigrate from elsewhere. Few suitable settlers were attracted. Many migrants seek dry season, not rainy season work, and are back on their own land for the groundnut sowing and harvesting. Others have found it more profitable, or perhaps more certain for the future, to work as navétanes on peasant holdings. Or again, work on the Nigerian or Ghanaian cocoa holdings, or in the rapidly-growing West African towns, has generally proved more attractive. Clearance of the original forest proved more difficult and expensive than expected. There were ant-hills and over 100 stumps or trees per acre (over 250 per hectare) to remove. Stumping or bulldozing of trees could take place only from April to July, when the ground was soft after the first rains. When dry, that is at harvest time, the soils became extremely hard. In consequence harvesting had to take place early enough to dig up the nuts before the soils hardened, but not so early that the nuts were too small to be worth picking. The problem lay in deciding when the last rains of the season had fallen. Weeds regenerated rapidly, and could only be controlled by ploughing twice. At Sédhiou one of the local grasses, *Pennisetum subangustum*, spread rapidly in the first year of cultivation, and caused the failure of a great part of the crop. The soils were light and easy to work when moist, but the high quartz content subjected ploughs to rapid wear, and the soils were easily eroded. The rectangular patterns of the fields, ploughing and ridging, which ignored the relief and drainage pattern, encouraged the acceleration of erosion by water and the formation of gullies. These rectangular patterns had been made necessary at Mokwa by the use of steam-tackle, and had proved easier at both Mokwa and Sédhiou for planning layout. At Mokwa water frequently collected on the roads forming divides between the fields, until it eventually broke through, forming gullies up to 6 feet (2 metres) wide and 3 feet (1 metre) deep, after only two seasons of cultivation. Occasional intense showers of up to 1 in (25 mm) in a quarter of an hour provided heavy run-off. In 1954 when the Niger Agricultural Project was handed over to the Northern Region Agricultural Department soil conservation work was begun and bunds were erected.[28] Again, in both areas, the prolific lateral root system caused heavy damage to equipment, a problem made worse by the lack of skilled operators, the high cost of spares, and the difficulty of obtaining them. Disease was an additional problem, for introduced plants, particularly guinea corn, were less resistant to diseases than local varieties. Guinea corn was damaged by stainer insects, and groundnuts by rosette disease and leaf hoppers. Finally, there was the huge extra cost of mechanization itself, caused not only by the factors cited above, but by the lack of work in the 'lay-off' period when hand labour was used. Whilst a report to the British Colonial Advisory Council recommended that tractors should be used to supplement hoe tillage at the beginning of the rains, and not for weeding, harvesting or threshing, since too costly, Baldwin showed that mechanization could not succeed unless all related operations were mechanized. Mechanized clearance and tillage could not be geared to hand weeding and harvesting, unless large quantities of seasonal labour were available.[29] For the settlers themselves the new villages proved artificial unsuitable units, and since the settlers were of several different origins and looked back to their old homes for their social ties, no coherent community could be formed.

THE IRRIGATION REGION OF THE INLAND NIGER DELTA AND UPPER NIGER VALLEY OF MALI

For Mungo Park, Heinrich Barth and many other explorers, the Niger lands of the Sudan gave promise of an agricultural future based on the use of flood-waters or irrigation equal to, if not greater than, that of the valley of the Nile. The apparent agricultural wealth of the West African Sudan attracted the imperialists of the 19th century, particularly those who foresaw the need for larger cotton supplies for the textile industry of Western Europe. They supposed Sudanic soils and climate to be ideal, and imagined a large reservoir of labour there, hitherto exported to the plantations of North America. For such, especially those who had had experience of India, all dark soils became 'black cotton soils', population totals were grossly overestimated, whilst the great northward bend of the Niger

Y

into the southernmost extension of the Sahara appeared to provide an oasis bridgehead, inviting the development of a railway route from there northward to France's possessions in North Africa.

The failure to establish colonial cotton cultivation in the valley of the Senegal, and the lowering of world cotton prices following the end of the American Civil War, deterred many from attempting the experiment. From 1903 until 1913 some

The Inland Niger Delta Scheme

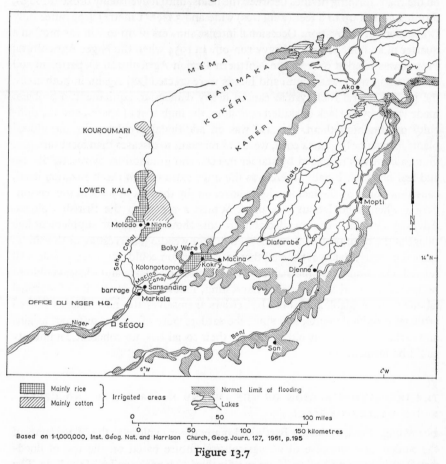

Figure 13.7

attempts were made, in collaboration with the Association Cotonnière Coloniale, to improve cotton production on lands dependent on rainwater, but these attempts failed, and in 1913 an irrigated cotton-growing scheme was begun at Ségou, but stopped on the outbreak of war. In 1917, under the auspices of the Government of the French Soudan, a trial planting of Egyptian cotton in the inland delta of the Niger was made, and in 1919 and 1920 a mission, under the engineer Bélime, undertook to make recommendations on the proposal to develop the area for cotton cultivation.[30] The area was surveyed, levelled, and mapped, and the existence of extensive areas below river level, well away from the river, demonstrated. By 1923 the deltaic nature of the area was appreciated, and its division into 'live' and 'dead' sections. The following year two former channels of the Niger were discovered: one parallel to the present course, the Boky-Wéré channel, and one orientated from north to south, the 'Fala de Molodo'. Both were blocked, but it was suggested that they could be opened for use as canals to supply floodwater to cotton lands, whilst other old channels or 'valley' tracks could drain off excess water.[31]

Already in 1922 an experimental cotton station had been created at Niénébalé, a village below Koulikoro on the right bank of the Niger. This was followed by a Government pilot scheme in 1925 of 15 families on 500 acres (200 hectares), one-third of which was irrigated, mainly from a small tributary stream. Despite poor results this scheme was expanded to 3750 acres (1500 hectares) by 1940, of which again one-third was under irrigation.

The Inland delta scheme, planned and developed in the 1920s, depended on an appreciation of the physical geography of the area, in the light of French demand for cotton and the need to create agricultural holdings and introduce settlers on to newly-irrigated lands.

The vast plains of the Inland Niger delta fall into three portions:

1) The live delta or Pondo extending below Sansanding between the Niger, Diaka and Bani, with a narrow belt on the left bank of the Niger and Diaka, and on the right bank of the Bani.

2) The dead delta, abandoned after the capture of the Upper Niger waters by the breaching of the Tosaye quartzite sill, and lying to the north-west of the live delta.

3) The lacustrine or Sahelian section of the delta, extending in a narrow arc on the north-eastern side of the live delta.

The Pondo is divided by the Niger into northern and southern portions, of which the northern is Macina, divided into eastern and western sections by the Diaka. Macina is regularly subject to flooding, difficult to control without the construction of bunds. Soils are normally rather heavy, and are generally heavier farther away from the river. They are also more moist than in the dead delta, due not only to the flooding, but to the maintenance of high water-table conditions beyond the floodwater period by the balancing effect of creeks and lakes. The dead delta consists of two portions; in the west, Kouroumari and Kala linked by the Molodo channel, and in the east, the much larger sector of Méma, Kokéri, Farimaka and Karéri, not linked by any one channel. The dead delta soils consist mainly of lacustrine deposits, more permeable than those of the live delta, drier, and with a much shorter season during which water is available. The lacustrine portion of the delta provides a much smaller area subject to annual flooding, and with variations between one lake shore or creek floodland and another. The existence here of a number of smaller areas of floodland, rather than a large

The Irrigation of the Inland Niger Delta

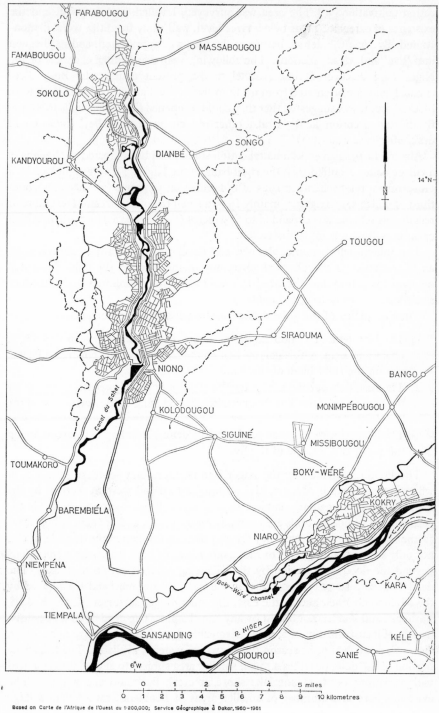

Based on Carte de l'Afrique de l'Ouest au 1:200,000; Service Géographique à Dakar, 1960–1961

Figure 13.8

continuity, plus the lack of a linking channel, suggested development preferably by a number of smaller schemes. Difficulties of flood control, except in certain areas, notably between San and Mopti, suggested more localized schemes in the Bani flood-plain and southern Pondo. The availability of channels, which had merely to be cleared rather than cut afresh, led to the suggestion that Kala and Kouroumari, with their drier conditions, should be suitable for cotton cultivation, and West Macina, especially in the Kokry and Macina proper districts, with their wetter and heavier soils, should be suitable for rice, provided a bund was constructed to control flooding. The mean 'turbidity' or silt content of the Niger is only one-tenth that of the Nile, so that there was no prospect of an annual renewal of soils, but for the sort of perennial irrigation scheme envisaged by Bélime this was an advantage, for there was no danger of silting. Large applications of fertilizer were needed, however, and, apart from phosphate deposits near Timbuktu and in Senegal, all these must be brought by an expensive rail, river and road haul from Dakar. Another advantage lay in the regulating effect of the numerous creeks and overflow channels, which continued to provide water even after flood levels on the Upper Niger had dropped. No large dams and reservoirs were needed, only barrages to prevent the effects of the flood being felt too soon, thus drowning the young rice, and to delay the drop in floodwaters towards the end of the growing season until the rice was mature. In so level a terrain, in any case, large dams and reservoirs were almost a physical impossibility. Such barrages would also help to reduce the range of the flooding, with variability of moisture supply from year to year.

Above the delta, at Sotuba near Bamako, and at Sansanding near the uppermost portion of the delta, sills of harder rock, associated with rapids, afforded suitable sites for barrage construction. Sotuba was too far away to affect the delta, but a small barrage was built there between 1925 and 1929 to provide a pilot scheme of irrigation on the Baguinéda plain. Thus two pilot schemes, one at Niénébalé and the other at Baguinéda, using different sources of water, provided invaluable data before the main scheme was begun. The Baguinéda area was irrigated in 1930, and by 1938 consisted of 7500 acres (3000 hectares) of rice, 7500 acres of various crops such as cotton, maize, cassava and groundnuts, and 3750 acres (1500 hectares) of pasture, supporting 5600 people in 15 villages. The plan for the main scheme was drawn up in 1929. It was to consist of 2,500,000 acres (1,000,000 hectares) of irrigated land, of which rather more than half was to be under cotton, on the left bank of the Niger, and mainly in the dead delta. It was estimated that at least 300,000 immigrants would be needed over a period of 25 years, to be installed at a cost, then, of 340 million metropolitan francs. An organization especially for the purpose, the Office du Niger, was created in 1932.[32]

The Office du Niger, made financially independent, was created in order to build a barrage at Sansanding, to develop a number of irrigation schemes dependent on the Sotuba and Sansanding barrages, and to supply them by means of several canals, to construct bunds to drain certain areas, for example Lake Horo, in order to use the alluvium of the former lake bed for cultivation and pasture, to install rice mills and cotton ginneries, to build settlers' villages, and to provide medical and education services. Work was begun on the barrage and the 'canals' (artificial channels plus the former river channels) in 1934. The Canal du Sahel and the Canal du Macina, both with artificial sections less than 15 miles (25 km) in length, were completed in 1935, but the barrage, with its navigable by-pass canal, was not completed until 1947. Water could be obtained and some small irrigation effected, however, even before the completion of the barrage, and, as early as 1935, work was begun on the first rice-growing centre of 16,500 acres (6600 hectares) at Kokry, and in 1937 on the first cotton-growing area of 20,000 acres (8000 hectares) at Niono in the Lower Kala district. The outbreak of war in 1939 interfered with the programme, but the Vichy government gave a further 600 million francs to the Office du Niger to bring irrigation to 500,000 acres (200,000 hectares), mainly for cotton production. The scheme was to be linked with a project to construct a trans-Saharan railway to provide a direct route to the Mediterranean.[33] Although the old and new delta surfaces were remarkably level, the cost of clearance, development and tillage was high. In the old delta area there were great problems to be faced in stumping and uprooting trees, and levelling ant-hills. Generally clearance was easier and costs lower in the areas already subject to flooding in the present delta, although here bunds had to be constructed. Thus the Kokry rice-growing area was early favoured by natural conditions. In 1942 the Bankani–Lake Horo centre was created, to grow mainly guinea corn on 10,000 acres (4000 hectares) of floodland, and to raise cattle on 20,000 acres (8000 hectares) in the former lake bed. This area of cultivation was, however, outside the main body of the scheme, and ceased to be under the Office du Niger in 1948.

In 1945 it was realized that very little had resulted from the efforts of the Office du Niger for the vast expenditure made. Despite the pilot schemes, insufficient knowledge of agronomic and pedological conditions had brought about a general failure of the initial stages of the irrigation project before the Sansanding barrage was completed. Moreover, it was almost impossible for the colonists to till the area given to them with the tools provided. Many of the settlers were Mossi, who came from a quite different environment, in which floodland cultivation was normally of only minor importance. Many of them solved their problems of tillage by bringing in relatives or employing hired labour, so that in some areas overcrowding occurred. Some settlers used their little profit to set up as shop-keepers, and employed others to work their holdings for them.[34] Cotton culti-vation had proved less remunerative than rice, for which there was a growing demand in both Senegal and Mali. Much of the original scheme to grow Allen and Kourala varieties of American upland cotton in the south, with an annual rainfall of about 10 in (250 mm), and Egyptian cottons in the drier north, had to be abandoned. Rice had suffered a number of initial failures of exotic varieties, but new varieties were developed from local and imported strains, which even-tually proved suitable. In 1945 it was decided to stop all further expansion, and to carry out essential research on the major problems for the following five years. It was also decided to give agronomic work priority over hydraulic engineering. The original plan was reduced to a scheme to develop 1,100,000 acres (440,000 hectares), using mechanical methods in combination with peasant cultivators. By 1948 there were 15,000 acres (6000 hectares) under cultivation in the Lower Kala area, of which one-third was annually under cotton, and the rest under fallow, green manure, rice, and guinea corn. An additional 1500 acres (600 hectares) was under cultivation on the left bank of the Fala de Molodo, and another 3700 acres (1500 hectares), outside the scheme, were under guinea corn and pennisetum. There were over 5000 people at the cotton ginning and market centre of Niono, whilst, serving the irrigated land, there were 19 villages, containing approximately 5700 people. The area also supported 3500 cattle, of which half were for draught purposes, 4200 sheep and goats, and a number of horses and donkeys. About 700 ploughs were in use. To the south-east there were nearly 25,000 acres (10,000 hectares) under cultivation in the Kokry district, of which approximately 23,000 acres (9200 hectares) were under rice. The Kokry district supported 11,300 people in 30 villages and 5900 cattle, of which 4000 were for draught, together with a small number of sheep, goats, donkeys and horses. Nearly 1600 ploughs were in use and 375 harrows. Holdings were of 15 acres (6 hectares), differing in emphasis on either rice or cotton, according to district, and were each intended to support a family of about six persons, giving a density for cultivable land of approximately 250 persons per square mile (96 per sq km). Higher densities did not allow enough land for the production of a commercial crop, in addition to land needed to satisfy local food requirements. Mechanization, with the aid of the Marshall Plan, was thought to be the answer to tillage problems, and especially to satisfy the need to dig deeply in order to bury weeds, such as wild rice, which proved a great pest. Moreover, only tractor-drawn ploughs could dig in the green manures, and, by their speed of working, could make possible the early sowings thought desirable by the organizers of the scheme. The answer to low fertility of soils was the raising of cattle, and the application of green manuring techniques and large quantities of artificial fertilizers, especially West African phosphates. The scheme, it was thought, should be supported, not so much as a cotton producer, but as a food producer, to make good the all too frequent shortages experienced in the surrounding territories.

The completion of the Sansanding Barrage in 1947 gave the water control needed to regulate the supply to the irrigated lands, especially to the rice-growing areas. However, the area under cultivation increased only slowly, even after the completion of the post-war period of five years' research. By 1955 only about 110,000 acres (44,000 hectares) were in the scheme, including fallows, after 23 years of effort, and even by 1962 the total acreage was barely 120,000 (50,000 hectares) including 18,000 acres (7000 hectares) mechanically cultivated and employing hired labour. The total expenditure by the Office du Niger was estimated at 1957 values by Hance at some £28,600,000[35], or approximately £250 per acre (U.S. $1750 per hectare). Harrison Church computed it by 1962 at

£36,500,000 or over £300 per acre ($2100 per hectare).[36] By 1957 rice occupied some 60 per cent of the total controlled area whilst cotton occupied only 15 per cent. Since 1962 there has been some decline in the importance of rice, due to political and trading difficulties between Mali and the chief market, Senegal, and also due to increasing difficulties of cultivation, with greater infestation by wild rice, and a worsening problem of losses to the quelea birds. Emphasis has once more swung to cotton, to be grown in rotation with wheat and kenaf or da. The rice acreage remains unchanged, although attempts have been made to raise yields by improved transplanting.[37] A sugar plantation is also planned, and cattle are to be pastured on fallows and on waste land. A major costly item is fertilizers, for irrigated land is too valuable to keep long either under fallow, or green manure crops. Yet, artificial fertilizers have had to be brought long distances, and, with the exception of phosphates, imported. Admittedly, more people have been attracted to the scheme than there have been land and homes available. There has been no shortage of labour, but the attraction has been achieved at enormous cost, in which clearly there was no longer any hope of repaying the capital expenditure. Yet, unless all of the initial expenditure was to be wasted, the scheme had to be maintained by further expenditure, and the attempt made to lower the capital outlay per acre by increasing the acreage under irrigation. Claims have been made for higher income than elsewhere locally as a result of the scheme – even up to £260 ($730) a year in a few households, but the economic effect is very difficult to judge in a system of closed marketing.

In 1961 the Office du Niger came under the control of the Government of Mali, and plans for expansion were made as part of Mali's over-all development planning. These involve increasing the irrigated area to 162,000 acres (65,000 hectares), the employment of manual labour in place of agricultural machinery, more cotton, less rice and the introduction of sugar cane. Thus even on irrigated land where the hazards of the roots or of a high incidence of abrasive materials in the soils are absent, and where the land is level, mechanized tillage has been proved too costly in present terms.

The schemes of the Office du Niger have tended to overshadow the large number of small enterprises created in the delta and in the valley of the Niger by the Service de l'Agriculture.[38] These small irrigation units have taken advantage of, and been adapted to, local conditions and needs. By comparison they have been cheap, and proved more productive for the capital expended. In the delta these smaller schemes are confined to the Pondo, including the plains between the Diaka and the Niger, the Pondory region between the Niger and Bani, the plains of San and Mopti, and the lacustrine section, including the neighbouring flood-plains of the Niger. They are either on land already subject to annual flooding or on its margins. In the valley above Sansanding the schemes have been developed on a number of small flood-plains, drained by tributaries of the Niger. The aim of the Service de l'Agriculture was to make more efficient use of flood-plains under some cultivation, in order to produce more foodstuffs, chiefly rice, and secondly guinea corn and pennisetum. The increased food production was intended partly to satisfy local needs, but more importantly for sale to cultivators in the major export crop areas of Senegal, Guinea and the Ivory Coast. Work began in 1943, and was stimulated by the development plans of 1949–50. The areas involved were:

	Acres	Hectares
Upper Valley	21,000	8,500
Central Delta		
Diaka–Niger plains	90,000	36,000
Pondory plains	100,000	40,000
San plains	50,000	20,000
Mopti plains	22,000	9,000
	262,000	105,000
Lacustrine or Sahelian sector		
Lacustrine region proper	52,000	21,000
Neighbouring flood-plains	40,000	16,000
	92,000	37,000
Total area under irrigation schemes of the Service de l'Agriculture	375,000	150,000

By 1955 the total area involved was well over three times the area effectively under the schemes of the Office du Niger.

The three basic divisions into Upper Valley, Central Delta and Lacustrine Sector indicate three broad physical divisions affecting the planning of the schemes. The plains of the Upper Valley are long and narrow, enclosed between the Niger and the neighbouring uplands, and crossed by tributary streams. Flooding is variable, rarely extends across the entire width of any one plain, and frequently arrives too late for satisfactory rice cultivation. Flow in the lower courses of the tributary streams is governed both by the moisture supply of their headwaters and by the régime of the Niger. In the delta the levées of the distributaries limit extensive flooded areas, where the rise in levels can be too quick for the completion of sowing, or may asphyxiate young plants, and where the end of the flood period may come too early. In the lacustrine sector there is a great contrast in flooding conditions, from those of the lakes nearest the river, which have small ranges between highest and lowest levels, to those farthest away which have considerable ranges, and which fluctuate markedly from year to year. Until the French hydraulic works were introduced, all rice and other floodland crops were subject to the caprices of the water levels, with, in consequence, extremely low yields in abnormal years. In the Upper Valley the system of control introduced was designed to isolate the plains from the Niger floods, by constructing dikes or improving existing levées. Barrages were built across the tributaries in order to regulate the rise and fall of their floodwaters. Water was thus better distributed, and the growing season prolonged. Higher yielding Asian varieties of rice have been introduced, chiefly from Indo-China. Cases have been described in detail by Bernus in the village of Kobané in the Siguiri basin of Guinea, situated on the left bank of the Niger below Kouroussa, and by Strasfogel in the village of Gouni on the right bank below Koulikoro.[39] At Kobané the flood-plain is protected by a dike. The Koba tributary of the Niger, which crosses the plain, is controlled by a small barrage, above which a small channel diverts water to the rice lands. Only Asian rice is planted in the fields, which are laid out with geometrical precision. Ploughing takes place when the soils are moist after the first rains. When the rice begins to grow, flooding begins, and, when the rice is ripe, the sluices are closed, and the dike opened. A rice crop, sown in June, will normally be harvested in November. On the edge of the flood-plain onion gardens take advantage of the improved water control, but need some supplementary irrigation by hand. Of the total area under cultivation, the flood-plain provides only 27 per cent, although its yields per acre are generally higher than those of the other lands dependent on rain, and the harvest is a little later in the year. Strasfogel follows Viguier in distinguishing three types of flood-plain in the Niger valley: the 'open' without a levée, the 'closed' with a levée above most flood levels, and the 'semi-open' with a levée regularly crossed by floodwaters. Of these Gouni has a flood-plain in the last class, together with cultivable lands on terraces at two levels above flood limits. Rice is an important crop, but on the mainly sandy soils, the more important are guinea corn and pennisetum. In the delta, dikes and sluice gates are used to prevent too rapid a rise in flood levels, and to hold back floodwaters at the end of the season, until the rice is mature. In some of the distributary channels grills have been placed to prevent the entry of fish, which will damage the young plants. An example is provided by the plains of Mopti, Soufouroulay and Djibitaga, watered by the Taikiri-Diabi distributary of the Bani.[40] When the Bani is in flood the sluice gates are closed to prevent a sudden rise in the Taikiri-Diabi. Despite the measure of control achieved, Asian varieties of rice have not proved as successful here as varieties selected from the West African *glaberrima* species, which are better adapted to the flooding and soil conditions peculiar to the inland delta. Local varieties of rice, particularly the 'Kobé' type, are also preferred in the lake flood-plains, where cultivation only takes place as flood levels decline. Hydraulic works are used to retain lake waters, and prevent a rapid decrease in levels, in order to prolong the growing season. In the lacustrine sector, near the Niger, where flood levels are fairly regular, and the range is small, simple earth dikes are built to prevent early 'drowning' of the crop, and to hold back floodwaters as the river level drops.

The Niger basin has been the subject of considerable study with a view to increasing greatly the pace of agricultural development. Proposals include a controlling dam nearer the source which would provide a better balanced, more regular water supply to the inland delta and improved navigation, and further developments in water control on the fringes of the inland delta, notably in the lacustrine sector.

THE DEVELOPED SWAMPLANDS OF SIERRA LEONE

Sierra Leone contains some 500,000 acres (200,000 hectares) of swampland, consisting of mangrove swamps along the coast, and inland fresh-water grassland and raphia swamps. Much of this area may be drained and cultivated, and, under both tidal and fresh-water conditions, rice has proved quite productive. Rice in Sierra Leone has so far proved remarkably free of pests and disease, although weeds have proved very troublesome in the fresh-water swamps. The Agricultural Department, with its early West Indian tradition of encouraging the development of plantation crops for export, failed to encourage rice production and swamp clearance until the 1920s, when a subordinate officer of the Madras Department of Agriculture was engaged to undertake research on rice cultivation in the Great Scarcies.[41] Other surveys followed, and work was begun to ensure a production sufficient to satisfy Sierra Leone's needs and to encourage swamp improvement, partly in order to offset the apparent loss of hill lands to soil erosion, thought to be due mainly to decreasing fallow periods with increasing population densities.

Swamp drainage work began even before support and encouragement were offered by the Department of Agriculture. In about 1880 Temne cultivators at the mouth of the Little Scarcies river began to employ the methods already used in Guinea in order to develop tidal swamps. By the 1920s these developments were extensive along the lower courses of both the Great and Little Scarcies. A commission of enquiry reported in 1927[42] that both tidal and inland swamps were capable of development, that production per acre was higher than elsewhere, that the land was available for planting each year, that 'bush and forest land' was valuable for other purposes, and that productivity was restricted mainly by the lack of sufficient labour for cleaning the grain. The commission recommended the introduction of rice-cleaning machinery, the establishment of a rice experiment station, and a survey of existing and prospective rice-growing areas. Surveys were undertaken in 1930 and 1938-9, the methods used by the Scarcies cultivators were introduced into the Provinces, and the agricultural research station of Rokupr was opened on the Great Scarcies in 1934. During and since the war the demand for rice has increased enormously in Sierra Leone, and prices have risen. In consequence, it has become economic to undertake more costly schemes, to apply artificial fertilizers, and even to mechanize. Clearance and drainage schemes have been initiated, not only by the Department of Agriculture, but by local authorities, anxious to profit by this new form of commercial agriculture.

Of the mangrove swamps there are 35-40,000 acres (14-16,000 hectares) under cultivation along the Great and Little Scarcies comprising almost all the land available.[43] The remainder is either too saline or subject to too heavy flooding. In the Southern Provinces, of 137,000 acres (55,000 hectares) of mangrove estimated suitable for cultivation, less than 10,000 acres (4000 hectares) had been taken by 1950, mostly north of the Bagru river estuary, although considerable clearances have been effected since, both by individual cultivators, supported by

Agricultural Department loans, and by local authorities. The mangrove swamps may be divided into two groups – the *Avicennia* and the *Rhizophora*. The soils of the latter tend to suffer from harmful concentrations of ferrous sulphate, whilst

Swamp Rice Production in Sierra Leone

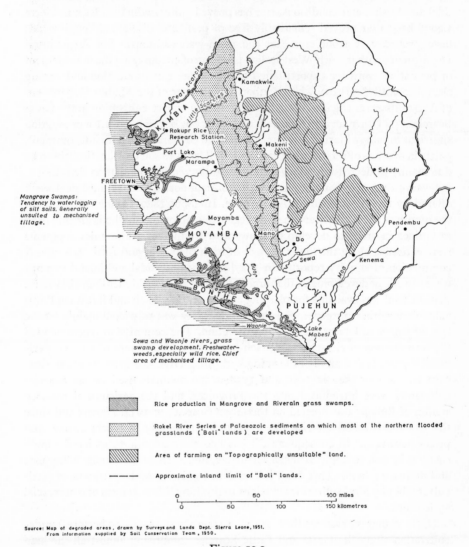

Mangrove Swamps:
Tendency to waterlogging
of silt soils. Generally
unsuited to mechanised
tillage.

Sewa and Waonje rivers, grass
swamp development. Freshwater-
weeds, especially wild rice. Chief
area of mechanised tillage.

Rice production in Mangrove and Riverain grass swamps.

Rokel River Series of Palaeozoic sediments on which most of the northern flooded grasslands ('Boli' lands) are developed

Area of farming on "Topographically unsuitable" land.

Approximate inland limit of "Boli" lands.

0   50   100 miles
0   50   100   150 kilometres

Source: Map of degraded areas, drawn by Surveys and Lands Dept. Sierra Leone, 1951.
From information supplied by Soil Conservation Team, 1950.

Figure 13.9

the rather heavier soils of the former are more affected by salinity. If free tidal conditions are no longer permitted high acidity may occur, and free sulphuric acid be formed.[44] Some soils are subject to marked seasonal fluctuations in acidity, which rises with high water levels and falls with low. This feature has proved of importance in choosing the period suitable for transplanting rice seedlings from the nursery.[45] In the Scarcies mangrove clearance involved the cutting of trees and the digging up of a layer of roots. Planting can take place after three to five years of drainage. Fertility is maintained by silt deposit from the rivers, whilst weeds are checked by the dry season invasion of salt water. Between the two extremes of too short a fresh-water period near the sea and too short a salt-water period inland occurs an area of optimum conditions lying between 6 and 15 miles (10–25 km) from the coast. In some places river bank erosion has resulted from clearance, and a problem of erosion control has been created for which 'mangrove hedges' may prove a solution. Crabs are an important pest, and losses can only be reduced by the local method of planting a large number of seedlings in each widely-spaced stand.[46] In the Moyamba and Bonthe districts many swamps do not require empoldering, since natural flooding from fresh water is adequate. By 1950 over 5000 acres (2000 hectares) of such land had been cleared. In the Kambia district extensive bunding has been undertaken. Mechanization of tillage has proved quite successful, particularly in the Scarcies. The clearance of roots necessary for rice cultivation permits satisfactory ploughing. Crawler tractors are preferred, since wheeled machines tend to break through the dry soil crust. As in mechanization elsewhere, there is a problem in co-ordinating hand labour tasks with those performed by the machine. The control of weeds by salt water, reducing the hand labour requirement, is significant here.

Inland there are fresh-water swamps adjoining the mangrove areas of the Sewa and Waonje rivers totalling 63,000 acres (25,000 hectares), less than 4000 acres (1600 hectares) of which have been developed. Here the fertile black alluvial soils support grasses, chiefly *Saccharum spontaneum*, which are much easier to clear than mangrove. However, clearance permits an invasion of wild rice – *Oryza barthii* – which is so difficult to control that cultivators move on to a new site after three years. Here, as in the Inland Niger delta, the answer to weed infestation has been claimed to be deep digging, for which mechanical cultivation has been claimed to provide the best method. Flood ranges are high – a rise of 20 feet (6 metres) is not exceptional – and in consequence bunding is mostly impractical. On the floodlands of Lake Mabesi the attempt has been made to improve drainage by increasing the effectiveness of the outflow with enlarged channels, and by constructing bunds and using pumps. Raphia palm swamps are not commonly cleared, since they provide the piassava of commerce, a source of palm wine, and thatch for houses. The northern flooded grasslands or 'bolis' occur mainly on the Rokel River Series of softer and less permeable rock materials. Local uplands are almost useless, due to thick lateritic crusts, whilst slopes have been degraded by too heavy cultivation. Only a small fraction of the 'boli' lands is under rice cultivation, and even this is subject to abandonment every three years in search of fresh sites, due to weed infestation. Some reduction of weeds has been achieved by the planting of dry season crops, such as sweet potatoes, quick-growing varieties of cassava, maize, tobacco and groundnuts after the rice harvest. The first inland swamp clearance scheme began at Kamakwie in 1946, and 1-acre (0·4-hectare) lots were created for renting to cultivators. The surrounding uplands were initially reserved for cultivation on principles laid down by the schemes's organizers to prevent soil erosion. In 1948 model holdings of 2 acres of upland and 2 acres of swamp were created. Generally, however, the Mende cultivators have 7 to 8 times as much land under upland rice as in swamps. Although it is a general practice to plant a small swamp area, the extension of that area at the expense of upland crops has been opposed by Mende farmers on the grounds of the heavier labour involved in trying conditions. Yet, since the work of clearing grass swamps was much less arduous than that of clearing mangroves, and since it was thought essential to increase rice production and decrease upland cultivation, the Agricultural Department pressed forward with its policy of inland swamp clearance. By 1957 100,000 acres (40,000 hectares) of inland swamp were in production, compared with 160,000 acres (65,000 hectares) of tidal and riverain swamp, and 390,000 acres (155,000 hectares) under upland rice.[47] The upland area was claimed to have been reduced by about one-fifth over 10 years, whilst there was also some reduction in the cultivated area of southern grass swamps.[48] The Government made possible the increase in the swamp rice area and the decline in the upland rice area, by buying all swamp rice offered to it at high fixed prices, leaving the upland rice to satisfy local markets. Rice imports were also controlled, to prevent competition, for the excess cost of home over imported rice was £30 (U.S. $84) a ton. The return of paddy from inland swamps was only 800 lb per acre (900 kilos per hectare), compared with 1500–1800 lb per acre (1700–2000 kilos per hectare) from the tidal and riverain swamps, and this even with artificial fertilizers sold to cultivators at one-third of cost. Of the total rice output rather less than 5 per cent came from land under mechanical cultivation. The area of swamps ploughed mechanically increased from a little over 2000 acres (800 hectares) in 1952 to 15,623 acres (6327 hectares) in 1957, beyond which little further immediate increase is planned. In the Southern Provinces the costs of mechanical cultivation in 1957 ranged from £6 2s. 9d. to £8 1s. 5d. per acre (U.S. $42.46–$55.81 per hectare), of which the cultivators paid £3 ($21) and the Government the rest. 3500 acres (1400 hectares) of inland swamp were cultivated by co-operatives, using lighter tractors at a cost of £5–£6 per acre ($35–$42 per hectare). The estimated costs of the Government's mechanization and rice subsidies according to Jack[49] were:

	£	$ U.S.
Government mechanical cultivation schemes	32,000	89,600
Co-operative „ „ „	12,250	34,300
Artificial fertilizers	2,500	7,000
Purchase of rice handled by Government mills	96,000	268,800
Difference in price of rice handled by private traders	187,000	523,600
Cost of official rice policy	329,750	23,300

A more recent estimate of the costs of mechanical cultivation in the Bonthe area is £5 per acre ($38 per hectare), of which the cultivator still pays only £3 per acre ($21 per hectare).[50]

SOME RESETTLEMENT SCHEME REGIONS IN NIGERIA

Most schemes concerned with agricultural improvement in Africa have tended to concentrate on the production of a particular crop or crops, or on the improvement of irrigation or drainage facilities. Their other aspects, the building of roads and settlements, the creation of new communities, and the provision of amenities, whilst by no means neglected, have been secondary to some main agricultural objective. In Nigeria, particularly in the Northern Region, mostly since 1945, a

Location of Major Resettlement Schemes in Nigeria

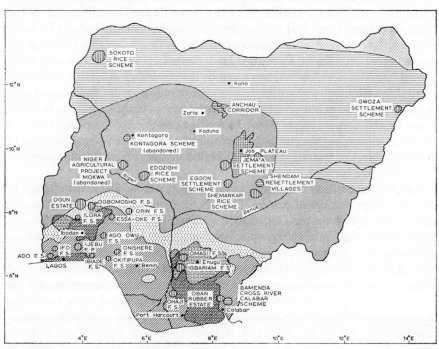

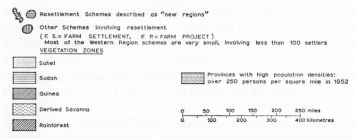

Figure 13.10

number of schemes have been undertaken whose main objective was resettlement, the creation of new communities, with agricultural development taking second place. Of these the most important in the Northern Region have been at Shendam, Kontagora and Anchau, but others have flourished, notably at Jema'a, west of the Jos Plateau, Eggon to the south, and at Gwoza in Adamawa Province. Some resettlement has been involved also in many agricultural schemes, notably in the Niger Agricultural Project, in the farm settlements of southern Nigeria, in irrigation schemes in Sokoto, Niger and Plateau Provinces, and in several small mixed farming settlement units. In southern Nigeria the only settlement scheme as such of any size, until the creation of the more recent 'farm settlements', was the Bamenda–Calabar–Cross River project in the Eastern Region which was abandoned in March, 1955. The purpose of all these schemes was, as Prothero has remarked, to strike 'a favourable balance between population and resources, particularly the fuller exploitation of the latter through modifications in the methods of production'.[51] Areas defined as 'underpopulated' were to be occupied by people drawn from 'overpopulated' areas, thus increasing productivity, and relieving pressure on a crowded land. Some impetus to the movement, of special importance at Anchau, was given by the researches of Nash, which indicated that a minimum population density of 70 per square mile (27 per sq km) was needed to keep down bush regrowth on stream banks cleared in order to be rid of tsetse fly and sleeping sickness.[52] In Anchau one-third of the population had sleeping sickness, but the population was too scattered for anti-tsetse measures to be practicable. Concentration was needed into a number of settlements connected by a tsetse-free corridor.

The Anchau Settlement Scheme, begun in 1937, was the first major attempt to resettle a large number of people. The scheme involved an area of 700 square miles (1800 sq km), the building of 16 new villages and the model town of Takalafiya, and the moving of 4300 people. Existing villages in the area were improved, wells dug, new markets built, new methods of refuse disposal introduced, and trees planted. The total population involved was 50,000, and the cost worked out at £1 per head. A complete survey was made of farmland and vegetation, and the distribution of potentially-good agricultural land was calculated, using vegetation distribution as an indicator. Composting was introduced, and a rinderpest immunization camp for cattle established. A great increase in the numbers of cattle brought into and through the district by Fulani herders was effected, with, in consequence, an increase in manure supplies. The Anchau fly-free corridor was established after 10 years' work, and took in an area approximately 70 miles long by 10 miles wide (110 by 16 km), from which tsetse fly had been removed, mainly by the clearance of 540 miles (870 km) of stream banks. The new higher density of population maintained clearance, and kept down secondary growth to a reasonable height. The scheme created a new region with its own peculiar landscape. It also suggested that in some parts of West Africa there are areas of insufficiently high density of population to maintain satisfactory health standards, and that the answer to this particular problem was the creation of an 'island' of population concentration. If Nash's estimate of 70 per square mile is a fair general indication of the density level required, then most of West Africa suffers from too low densities.

Whereas the Anchau Scheme had sought to improve health and increase population density by resettlement, the Shendam Scheme, begun in 1948, sought by the development of a comparable area (600 square miles (1550 sq km) – later extended to 1100 square miles (2850 sq km)) to provide a model of settlement organization and agricultural practice suitable for people migrating from heavily-populated to low-density areas. Within Shendam and neighbouring divisions some movement of peoples from the overcrowded plateau to the neighbouring lowlands had already taken place. Migrants did not repeat the intensive methods of cultivation used in the uplands, and adopted shifting methods, clearing considerable areas of woodland. Such clearance might have been thought to have assisted the removal of tsetse fly from the district, but was criticized by agricultural officers as wasteful and even disastrous.[53] Grove claims that the immigrant peoples had produced a retreat of the savanna woodland, clearing away all trees except the shea and the dorowa. They abandoned the terraces or contour ridges and ceased to manure their home lands. They occupied the new area either permanently or seasonally, and planted crops of groundnuts, beniseed and rizga, followed by guinea corn for three to five years until productivity ceased to be worth the planting.[54] The scheme began with the settlement of 50 ex-servicemen and their families in a new village, Sabon Gida, south of Inshar. Later settlers have been drawn from Hill and Plain Yergam and Montol peoples, and even from amongst the Tal Pai and Angas of neighbouring Pankshin Division. The settlers were intended to build their own villages, and do most of the work of clearance and cultivation themselves, although clearing of woodland was carried out by hired labour at first. The organizers provided the plan of cultivation and organization into communities, water supplies, roads and a little grain in the first year. The old road from Inshar to Ibi still existed, and provided comparatively easy access. A rectangular village plan was marked out round a well, and the area cleared was divided into 20-acre (8-hectare) holdings in 1-acre plots. It was hoped that half the area would be under commercial crops and that composting would be used to preserve soil fertility. The holdings were in contour ridged strips approximately 140 yards (128 metres) wide by 1 mile long (1·6 km), and separated by grass strips 30 feet (9 metres) wide. Eucalyptus and citrus trees were planted around the village and a cattle pen built. Cattle keeping and composting together with attempts to plough met several difficulties, however, of which the worst was trypanosomiasis infestation, which was considerable despite the clearance of woodland effected. Water supplies proved a major problem, as wells tended to dry up for part of the year. The difficulty was eased by the construction of a dam creating a reservoir. Without sufficient manure or compost to maintain fertility, the attempt to foster virtually permanent cultivation on 20 acres (8 hectares) could not succeed. Holdings were increased to 32 acres (13 hectares) in two equal blocks, one under cultivation using rotations for four years, and the other under planted fallow. In addition some 'fadama' floodland was ploughed for rice cultivation. By 1952 eight other settlements were established. At one of these, Mabudi, the holdings were cleared on a grid system measuring 300 yards (275 metres) square, and giving each settler 18½ acres (7½ hectares). At another, Dorowa, the water supply problem was solved by siting near perennial lakes. By 1956 the total population involved was 3561 and requests had been received from outside the scheme area for planned layouts of villages and holdings. Where required it was agreed to increase the size of holdings to 40 acres (16 hectares). The scheme has on the whole been successful, for it has continued to grow, accommodating nearly 10,000 settlers in over 40 villages by 1964. However, it has succeeded mainly because it provides water in areas otherwise only open to seasonal settlement, and is serviced by roads giving access to markets for agricultural produce.

The Kontagora Resettlement Scheme aimed at a more economic use of 'underpopulated' areas by the development of a form of mixed farming. Quick results were to be obtained by high capitalization. Land was cleared by hired labour, a model village constructed, and each settler presented with a cleared holding, a plough, a yoke of trained oxen, seed and some food. The scheme was initiated in 1947 with the selection of a site at Tungar Maidubu, west of Kontagora town, and holdings of 20 acres (8 hectares) each were cleared in 1948, with a further 10 acres (4 hectares) allowed for fallow to be cleared with the profits of the early working. In the first year the aim was to settle 20 families on 400 acres (160 hectares), and then to build other villages and establish fresh clearances. By 1950 three villages had been established and 1300 acres (520 hectares) cleared. Most of the work, even of clearance, was done by hand, although some small earth dams were built, mainly by scraper machinery, and water had to be pumped. Some tractor-drawn ploughing was done, but a tractor tried for advance work broke down. Two important features were the clearance of riverine vegetation and surrounding 'belts' in order to remove tsetse and allow the keeping of draught oxen, and the enforcement of a planned rotation of crops: 1) cotton; 2) guinea corn; 3) guinea corn; 4) groundnuts; 5) pennisetum; 6, 7, and 8) grass ley.

Home farms producing a variety of crops, including yams, beans, rice, earth peas (Bambarra groundnuts), sugar cane and sweet potatoes were also cultivated.

The first settlers were Hausa, but later settlers were chiefly Kambari, drawn from Kontagora division and claimed to be more satisfactory as cultivators in the scheme. Even the Kambari, however, could not reconcile their traditional methods to the methods laid down by the organizers and to the attempt to promote grass leys and mixed farming. Grain crops did well, but the commercial crops, groundnuts and cotton, gave only poor results. By the end of 1955 the number of settlers had been reduced to 220, and by April of the following year only 96 remained. The scheme in consequence was wound up.

The Bamenda–Calabar–Cross River Scheme in the Eastern Region was devised in 1946 to settle Ibo from overcrowded Owerri and Onitsha Provinces on holdings in a thinly-populated area in eastern Calabar Province. The main settlement of 5900 acres (2350 hectares) was intended to support 200 families, partly by the cultivation of food crops, and partly by the operation of a 1000-acre (400-hectare) oil palm plantation. Each settler family was expected to tend 5 acres (2 hectares) of oil palms, 2 acres of compound land (less the area occupied by the buildings) and 10 acres (4 hectares) of rotational crops. Each family was thus expected to work rather less than 17 acres (7 hectares), and with little or no fallows. The settlers were not recruited in the overcrowded areas, but came from amongst workers who had opened the area to commerce by road building. Such men had been used to family holdings of 4 acres ($1\frac{1}{2}$ hectares) or less, and had, in any case, already shown a preference for leaving the land. They were less likely to be attracted by the prospect of becoming pioneer cultivators than by the possibility of earning more than could be obtained at home. When this possibility was not realized, and when the amount of work required was appreciated, opposition to the organizers manifested itself. Settlers concentrated on their own holdings and failed to tend the 5 acre (2 hectare) palm lots. The organizing authority was obliged to bear the cost of maintaining the plantation, and, with increases in wages and salaries, it overspent and was forced to halve the size of the scheme. In 1950 there were 115 settlers and their families on some 2900 acres (1150 hectares) in the east, leaving 3000 acres (1200 hectares) in the west to be leased to the Eastern Region Development Board for the development of a palm oil plantation and of a rice-growing area on 650 acres (260 hectares) in the Massagha Swamp. In March 1955, after considerable difficulties with the settlers and heavy financial losses, the Resettlement Scheme was finally abandoned. In 1962 the Palm Grove Rehabilitation Scheme was begun to improve oil palm production and consolidate holdings. Some 16,000 acres have been planted in the first three years of operation.

The Volta River Project and its associated region

This review of regions modified by modern economic and political developments closes with an account of a number of areas in southern Ghana in which modification has barely begun. These areas are linked by the most ambitious and costly of all African large-scale development schemes – the combined power/mining/industrial/transport/port/agricultural project called the Volta River Project.

As early as 1915 the possibility had been considered of using the Volta river to generate power, and again in 1924 more serious consideration was given by the then Gold Coast Government to the possibility of power generation in order to smelt some of Ghana's vast bauxite reserves. The Volta basin narrows downstream until it enters the Ajena gorge where the river cuts through the NNE–SSW trending ridges of resistant rocks, chiefly quartzite, associated mainly with the Togo–Atacora ranges. The catchment area of the basin is 150,000 square miles (390,000 sq km), but most tributaries towards the north of the basin cease to flow for as much as seven months in the year. At Ajena the gorge flow varies in the peak months of September and October from 125,000 to 390,000 cusecs (354 to 1105 cu metres per sec), but falls as low as 1000 cusecs (3 cu metres per sec) in the driest month. A dam in the gorge at Ajena or at Akosombo was needed to level out the discharge. In 1941 bauxite working was begun at Kanayerebo near Awaso, exporting via Takoradi, and by 1945 and 1947 private interests acquired concessions to develop other deposits. In 1951 an investigation of the potential value of the Volta reported favourably to the Government on the possibility of

The Volta River Scheme

Figure 13.11

power development, in 1952 the White Paper entitled the Volta River Aluminium Scheme was issued, and, four years later, the report of the preparatory commission on the project.[55] The original project envisaged the building of a dam at Ajena. The final decision was to build a 370-foot (113-metre) high rock fill dam at Akosombo at a cost of £70 million (U.S. $200 millions). The advantage of the Akosombo site over that of Ajena was that dam construction could be completed in four years instead of seven. Behind it a reservoir has formed over 200 miles (320 km) in length and covering an area of 3500 square miles (9000 sq km). The flow will generate 883,000 kW by means of six sets, and allowing 710,000 acre feet (875 million cubic metres) of water per annum to be drawn off for an irrigation project. Approximately 40 per cent of the power generated will be required by the aluminium smelter located at the new port of Tema, and intended to have a capacity of 135,000 tons of aluminium a year. Alternative settlement has had to be provided for 80,000 people living in the area to be flooded, who must lose their homes and holdings, and will need to be resettled. For this purpose 52 new villages have been built of 'core' houses (roof for 4 rooms, walls for 1) and advice and help has been given to settlers by the Department of Social Welfare and Community Development.

The entire scheme, it is estimated, will cost £173 million – £70 million for power, £60 million for the smelter, £35 million for Tema port, and £8 million for resettlement. Until 1959, however, the support from overseas financial interests necessary to provide part of the capital was not forthcoming. Despite the enormous power potential available from the Volta Gorge, and the proximity of the power site to the coast, with bauxite resources already being worked not too far away (207 miles (333 km)), British and American interests and the World Bank were hesitant to offer their support. Nor were the vast easily-worked reserves at Yenahin or Ejuanema particularly attractive prospects to investors. Possibly the influence of past failures of large-scale schemes in Africa south of the Sahara had their influence, together with uncertainty before independence with regard to Ghana's political future. Certainly by 1956 world aluminium production had almost caught up demand, and the future estimated rate of increase in consumption of 5 per cent per annum would have been better supplied by the development of a number of small schemes rather than of this huge producing unit. Moreover, the scheme involved, for complete success, the building of new towns, road and railway extensions, bridge construction, additional dams and power-producing units in the Bui Gorge (93,000 kW), 120 miles (193 km) above Akosombo, and at the Kpong rapids, and even envisaged an irrigation and a flood-land agricultural project. Fortunately the climate of opinion altered and construction of the Volta dam began in 1962. The Kpong Rapids Project involves the building of a run-of-the-river plant with a head of only 40 feet (12 metres) and must depend on the stabilizing of flow by the dam at Akosombo. The Bui Gorge dam was to have been built by a construction team from the U.S.S.R. at a cost estimated (1960) at nearly £20 million.

Work on providing a new harbour at Tema 17 miles (27 km) east of Accra was thought essential, not only for the Volta River Project but to provide the increase in harbour facilities which it was anticipated Ghana would need with increasing overseas trade. Work was begun on an access railway from Accra in 1952 and completed in 1954. Stone was conveyed 20 miles (32 km) from quarries in the Shai Hills to construct the breakwater. Full facilities became available by the end of 1960, when the population of Tema was already over 27,000. Tema is a fast-growing industrial centre with a new steel works and a variety of manufactures including a clinker-grinding plant for concrete production, the manufacture of pre-fabricated concrete panels and of aluminium cutlery. The aluminium smelter began operations in 1967. The site was chosen in order to use imported ore, and postpone the capital expenditure needed to exploit Ghana's bauxite resources. In addition to the harbour for ocean-going shipping, there is also a harbour for fishing vessels, designed to encourage an expansion in the local fishing industry. Another important development was the completion of a bridge over the Volta river at Adomi in 1956, giving access by road to the opposite bank for future dam construction, and providing a through road to Togo, Dahomey and Nigeria.

The dam was completed in 1964 when the reservoir began to fill. The possibilities for agricultural development, for fishing, for transport and for the control of disease will be considerable. With regard to the latter, river blindness or onchocerciasis occurs in the Volta basin and is carried by the simulium fly which only breeds in river rapids or tumbling water. The development of the great reservoir should remove some of the fly breeding grounds. The fish resources of the new lake, it is estimated, will provide 20,000 tons per annum, and will help to reduce the considerable expenditure on imported smoked and tinned fish. Agriculture will be affected in two ways. Firstly, the reservoir level will rise and fall between the periods of maximum and minimum river flow, creating a strip of floodland on the lake periphery suitable for rice and sugar production – a survey for a rice- and sugar-growing scheme in the Lower Volta flood-plain was completed in 1962. Secondly, below the future dam site are the Accra Plains, where, it is calculated, there are 440,000 acres (180,000 hectares) which could be rendered productive by irrigation. Here the most important soils for agricultural use are:

1) The Akuse clay, poorly drained, low in available nitrogen and phosphates and very heavy when moist.
2) The much lighter red Tertiary sands.
3) The valley bottom clays.

Rainfall in the area is low and the rainy season short. Accra, for example, averages less than 29 in (740 mm) of rain in only six months, each with 2 in (50 mm) or more, and divided by a marked dry period in August and September. Moreover, the relative variability is high, and irrigation is essential to aid crops in dry spells and water crops with heavier needs than either pennisetum or sorghum. To some extent the pilot schemes at Kpong and Nungua have shown the way, and demonstrated the methods of irrigation and drainage needed for which the clay offered several problems. Cattle, including both Shorthorn and Zebu breeds, can thrive on the plains, and offer the possibility of mixed farming. Both ranching and market-gardening schemes are planned. Phillips claims:

'Contrasted with the Groundnut Scheme (in East Africa) there has been a thorough and comprehensive initial survey taking several years and costing £1·35 million – of considerable value should the project come into being. Compared with the initial and the continuing survey in the Gezira (Nile valley in the Sudan) the Volta survey has been much fuller because the subjects for investigation were much wider – from the mining of bauxite and the production of aluminium to the agricultural, social and health aspects.

Notwithstanding its special features, the Volta survey must remain a model for the preliminary examination of large-scale multi-purpose projects.'[56]

BIBLIOGRAPHICAL NOTES

[1] See Barbu Niculescu, *Colonial Planning: a Comparative Study*, London, 1958.

[2] W. H. Becket, *Akokoaso, a Survey of a Gold Coast Village*, London, 1944.

[3] K. Gyasi-Twum, Ghana, Gold Coast or 'Cocoa Coast', *Tijdschrift voor Economische en Sociale Geografie*, **50**, 1959, 130–6.

[4] P. Ahn, Regrowth and Swamp Vegetation in the Western Forest Areas of Ghana, *Journal of the West African Science Association*, **4**, 1958, pp. 163–73.
Similar successions have been described by Clayton in Nigeria, see W. D. Clayton, Secondary Vegetation and the Transition to Savanna near Ibadan, Nigeria, *The Journal of Ecology*, **46**, 1958, 217–38.

[5] Polly Hill, *Migrant Cocoa-Farmers of Southern Ghana*, Cambridge, 1963.
Polly Hill, The Migration of Southern Ghanaian Cocoa Farmers, *Bulletin, Institut Français d'Afrique Noire*, **22B**, 1960, pp. 419–25.

[6] Polly Hill, Obomofo-Densua: a Company of Cocoa Farmers, *Economic Research Division, University College of Ghana, Cocoa Research Series*, No. 9, 1957.
Adidiso: a Company of Cocoa Farmers, ibid., No. 10, 1957.
The Boah Family of Cocoa Farmers, ibid., No. 11, 1958.
The Nankese-Shai Company of Cocoa Farmers, ibid., No. 12, 1958.
Companies of Cocoa Farmers in the Nankese Area, ibid., No. 13, 1958.
John Hunter has mapped different patterns in close proximity and described them in a remarkably clear paper, Cocoa Migration and Patterns of Land Ownership in the Densu Valley near Suhum, Ghana, *Transactions and Papers, Institute of British Geographers*, **33**, 1963, pp. 61–87.

[7] Polly Hill, Obomofo-Densua, op. cit., p. 1.

[8] Part of the following study of the south-eastern Ivory Coast is based on G. Rougerie, Les Pays Agni du Sud-est de la Côte d'Ivoire Forestière, *Etudes Eburnéennes*, **6**, 1957.

[9] A. Köbben, Le Planteur Noir, *Etudes Eburnéennes*, **5**, 1956.

[10] Polly Hill, Systems of Labour Employment on Gold Coast Cocoa Farms, *Proceedings, West African Institute of Social and Economic Research*, 1956, pp. 54 and 67.

[11] For a detailed study of the effects of swollen shoot and other diseases on a cocoa-growing community, see J. M. Hunter, Akotuakrom: a Devastated Cocoa Village in Ghana, *Transactions of the Institute of British Geographers*, **29**, 1961, pp. 161–86.

[12] Several of the points made in the text are taken from J. Fouquet, La Traite des Arachides dans le Pays de Kaolack, *Etudes Sénégalaises*, **8**, 1958, and Y. Péhaut, L'Arachide au Sénégal, *Cahiers d'Outre-Mer*, **14**, 1961, pp. 5–25. See also the remarkable study by P. Pelissier, *Les Paysans du Sénégal: les Civilisations Agraires du Cayor à la Casamance*, St.-Yrieix, 1966.
For comparison with the Gambia see two studies by M. R. Haswell, *Economics of Agriculture in a Savannah Village*, London, 1953, and *The Changing Pattern of Economic Activity in a Gambia Village*, London, 1963.

[13] P. Pelissier, Les Paysans Sérères, *Les Cahiers d'Outre-Mer*, **6**, 1953, pp. 105–27.

[14] See J. Fouquet, op. cit., p. 37, and R. Portères, L'Assolement dans les Terres à Arachides au Sénégal, *Revue Internationale de Botanique Appliquée et d'Agriculture Tropicale*, **30**, 1950, pp. 44–50.

[15] R. Dumont, Etude de Quelques Economies Agraires au Sénégal et en Casamance, *Agronomie Tropicale*, **6**, 1951, pp. 229–38.

[16] D. P. Gamble, *The Wolof of Senegambia*, London, 1951, p. 32.

[17] Cultivation using a tractor was tried in 1921 and 1922 and abandoned in the latter year, see J. Fouquet, op. cit., p. 34.

[18] P. Pelissier, L'Arachide au Sénégal, *Etudes Sénégalaises*, **2**, 1952, pp. 49–80. For a more personal view of Mouride colonization, see R. Dumont, *False Start in Africa*, London, 1966 (*L'Afrique Noire est Mal Partie*, Paris, 1962).

[19] R. Dumont, op. cit.

[20] J. G. Adam, Lutte Contre le Déboisement en Région Forestière de la Guinée Française par les Cultures Arbustives, *Revue Internationale de Botanique Appliquée et d'Agriculture Tropicale*, **32**, 1952, pp. 37–44.

[21] J. Fouquet, op. cit., pp. 95–97 and 130–2. Banque Centrale des Etats de L'Afrique de l'Ouest, *La Commercialisation de l'Arachide au Sénégal en 1963–64*, Note d'infor-mation, no. 115, Paris, February 1965.

[22] B. A. Keen, C. E. Rooke and J. McFadyen, *Report of the Mission Appointed to Enquire into the Production and Transport of Vegetable Oils and Oil Seeds Produced in the West African Colonies*, Colonial No. 211, London, 1947.

[23] G. F. Clay, W. B. L. Monson, D. McKenna and F. Sykes, *Report of the West African Oilseeds Mission*, Colonial No. 224, London, 1948.

[24] A. T. Weatherhead and D. W. H. Baker, *Land-usage in the Sudan in its Relation to a Nigerian Mechanized Groundnut Scheme*, Government Printer, Kaduna, 1948.

[25] V. Thompson and R. Adloff, *French West Africa*, London, 1958, pp. 374–6.

[26] For the Niger Agricultural Project see specially K. D. S. Baldwin, *The Niger Agri-cultural Project*, Oxford, 1957, an invaluable, critical account; also, *Some Agricultural Development Schemes in Africa and Aden*, Colonial Office, London, 1953, Appendix I.

[27] J. G. Ossewaarde, The C.G.O.T. Groundnut Scheme in French West Africa, *Tropical Agriculture*, **33**, 1956, pp. 86–94.

[28] J. E. S. Palmer, Soil Conservation at Mokwa, Northern Nigeria, *Tropical Agriculture*, **35**, 1958, pp. 34–40.

[29] J. W. Y. Higgs, R. K. Kerkham and J. R. Raeburn, *Report of a Survey of Problems in the Mechanisation of Native Agriculture in Tropical African Colonies*, Colonial Advisory Council of Agriculture, Animal Health and Forestry, Publication No. 1, London, 1950.
K. D. S. Baldwin, op. cit., p. 180.

[30] M. Bélime was a public works engineer who had seen service in India and had some knowledge of British Indian irrigation works.

[31] See E. Bélime, *La Production du Coton en A.O.F.*, Paris, 1925.
G. Spitz, *Sansanding: Les Irrigations du Niger*, Paris, 1949, on whose work much of this section is based.

[32] The following account is drawn mainly from Georges Spitz, op. cit., but the authors have also drawn on:
E. Guernier, *Afrique Occidentale Française*, Encyclopédie de la France d'Outre-Mer, 2 vols, Paris, 1949.
A useful account in English is in R. Dumont, *Types of Rural Economy*, Studies in World Agriculture, London, 1957.

[33] R. J. Harrison Church, The History of Projects for a Trans-Saharan Railway, *London Essays in Geography*, ed. L. D. Stamp and S. W. Wooldridge, London, 1951, pp. 135–50.

[34] R. Dumont, Types of Rural Economy, op. cit., pp. 99–101.

[35] W. A. Hance, *African Economic Development*, New York, 1958, pp. 38–40.

[36] R. J. Harrison Church, Observations on Large Scale Irrigation Development in Africa, F.A.O., *Agricultural Economic Bulletin for Africa*, **4**, 1963, p. 33.

[37] Office du Niger, *Le Delta Resuscité*, Ségou, 1962.
R. J. Harrison Church, Observations on Large Scale Irrigation Development, op. cit., p. 34.

[38] See E. Guernier, op. cit., pp. 338–40, and R. Clerin, La Riziculture au Soudan Français, *Agronomie Tropicale*, **6**, 1951, pp. 400–6.

[39] E. Bernus, Kobané, un Village Malinké du Haut-Niger, *Les Cahiers d'Outre-Mer*, **35**, 1956, pp. 239–63.
S. Strasfogel, Gouni, *Centre National de la Recherche Scientifique, Centre de Documentation Cartographique et Géographique*, Tome 1, 1950, pp. 9–106.
P. Viguier, La Riziculture Indigène au Soudan Français, *Agronomie Tropicale*, **4**, 1939, pp. 339–78.

[40] E. Guernier, op. cit., p. 239.

[41] Leverhulme Trust, *The West African Commission, 1938–39*, London, 1943, pp. 41–42.

[42] R. B. Mackie, M. T. Dawe and C. F. Loxley, *Report of the Rice Commission on its Enquiry into the Position of the Rice Industry*, Sierra Leone, Sessional Paper No. 7 of 1927.

[43] Extensive use has been made in this section of E. A. Waldock, E. S. Capstick and A. J. Browning, *Soil Conservation and Land Use in Sierra Leone*, Sierra Leone Sessional Paper No. 1 of 1951.

[44] Report on Research in Sierra Leone, *Proceedings of the 2nd Inter-African Soils Conference*, Leopoldville, 1954, vol. 2, pp. 1095–7.
M. G. R. Hart, A. J. Carpenter and J. W. D. Jeffery, Problems in Reclaiming Soils in Sierra Leone, *Sols Africains*, **10(1)**, 1965, pp. 71–75.

[45] T. E. Tomlinson, Seasonal Variation of the Surface pH Value of some Rice Soils in Sierra Leone, *Tropical Agriculture*, **34**, 1957, pp. 287–94.

[46] H. D. Jordan, The Development of Rice Research in Sierra Leone, *Tropical Agriculture*, **31**, 1954, pp. 27–32.

[47] For inland swamps see J. Geldhaf, Practical Inland Swamp Improvement in the Eastern Province of Sierra Leone, *Sols Africains* **10(1)**, 1965, pp. 83–101.
For an account of the Sierra Leone Government's rice policy see D. T. Jack, *Economic Survey of Sierra Leone*, 1958, Government Printer, Sierra Leone.
See also H. D. Jordan, Rice in the Economy of Sierra Leone, *World Crops*, **17(4)**, 1965, pp. 24–31.

[48] H. P. White, Mechanised Cultivation of Peasant Holdings in West Africa, *Geography*, **43**, 1958, pp. 296–70.

[49] D. T. Jack, op. cit.

[50] H. E. G. Morgan, The Mechanical Cultivation of Rice in the Grasslands of Sierra Leone, *Sols Africains*, **10(1)**, 1965, pp. 117–21.

[51] R. M. Prothero, unpub. MS. on *Development Schemes in Northern Nigeria* 1954.
Some Agricultural Development Schemes in Africa and Aden, Colonial Office – reprinted in C. K. Meek, *Land Tenure and Land Administration in Nigeria and the Cameroons*, London, 1957, Appendix I.

[52] T. A. M. Nash, The Anchau Settlement Scheme, *Farm and Forest*, **2**, 1941, pp. 76–92.

[53] E. O. W. Hunt, *An Experiment in Resettlement*, Kaduna, 1951, pp. 3–4.

[54] A. T. Grove, Land Utilisation and Soil Conservation on the Jos Plateau, *Geological Survey of Nigeria, Bulletin 22*, 1952, pp. 51–58.
A. T. Grove, *The Benue Valley*, Kaduna, 1957, pp. 78–80.

[55] Sir William Halcrow and others, *Report on the Development of the River Volta Basin*, London, 1951.

The Volta River Aluminium Scheme, Cmd. 8702, London, 1952.
The Volta River Project, Report of the Preparatory Commission, London, 1956.
See also useful accounts in:
W. A. Hance, *African Economic Development*, New York, 1958.
J. Phillips, *Agriculture and Ecology in Africa*, London, 1959.
Commander Sir Robert Jackson, The Volta River Project, *Progress* (Unilever Quarterly), **50**, (282), 1964, pp. 146–61.

[56] J. Phillips, op. cit., p. 350.

CHAPTER 14

The West African States

Within eight years the whole of West Africa, with the exception of the Portuguese and Spanish territories, has gained its independence – or the right of government by authorities located in West Africa, and not supervised by any outside higher authority. New states have been created, which have continued the policy developed by the colonial powers of trying to substitute territorial for group loyalties, and of trying to make larger organized regions than those made by earlier states and tribal groups. The new states are thus on the whole opposed to earlier traditions which may threaten their disruption, yet they may seek to revive certain traditions in order to create an 'ethos' which will encourage pride in the nation and develop a large body of support for the new governments. Some of the new states are very small, having barely a million population, whilst Nigeria, with its 55·7 millions, dwarfs them all. Partly because of the feeling of insecurity which a small size gives, once some understanding of the world situation has been grasped, partly because of the common share in a general African independence movement, and partly because opposition to colonialism has engendered opposition to the colonial units themselves and their frontiers, there has been some tendency in West Africa to develop a pan-Africa movement, and to seek wider unions than those offered by the existing states system. Perhaps the most ambitious attempt to give expression to this movement is the creation for all Africa of the Organization for African Unity (O.A.U.) with its headquarters in Addis Ababa. As yet, however, such wider unions are only slightly developed. They have not involved the creation of a single authority over the states involved. Moreover, whilst there has been considerable sympathy for groups split at the end of the 19th century by colonial frontiers, the new governments, inheritors of the former colonial areas, seem as yet in no mood to make territorial concessions for the sake of tribal reunification. Indeed, despite the pan-Africa movement, the net immediate result of independence has been the creation of ultimate authority in smaller rather than in larger units. The federation of French West African territories has been broken into its separate former colonial pieces. Guinea left the proposed French Union immediately, and made an alliance with Ghana. The federation of Senegal and Mali (former French Soudan) was soon broken, and Mali has looked for support to the Guinea–Ghana alliance. However, better relations between Mali and Senegal have since been resumed, whilst the Guinea–Ghana alliance has also been broken. Future speculation is concerned

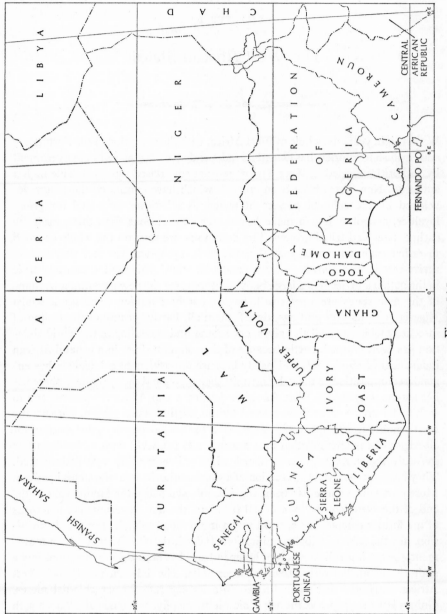

Figure 14.1

not only with the question of how closely such alliances may develop, and over-shadow or even destroy links with metropolitan powers in Western Europe, but with the question of whether a unit as large as Nigeria can survive or whether it must, like the French federation, break up into its regional parts if not into smaller units.

Common policies of colonial development for a French West Africa or a British West Africa have ceased. The weighing of the needs of Ghana against those of Nigeria within the orbit of a common fund for expenditure on all British territories in West Africa no longer obtains. The common pattern of economic development has been rejected in favour of a separate pattern. Separation has now gone so far that, whereas in 1945 the problem was to choose the site of one university college to serve the needs of British West Africa, in 1960 not only has each territory, except Gambia, its own college, but each region of Nigeria has built its own distinct institution with different policies for future development. For the geographer the significance of such separation of development policies lies in the possible future differences in regional organization and in form. New political movements may well create both new functional and new formal regions[1], just as the colonies themselves substituted new patterns for and superimposed new distributions on the old. Moreover, West Africa's geographic position in the world has changed with the changing relations of the great powers and the new political importance of the African states. The future economic development of these states depends no longer on the economic policies of directing metropolitan authorities, but on the competing generosities of rivals for world power, on the good offices of the World Bank and the United Nations, and on general world economic trends. When the Volta River Scheme was first mooted the decision of the British Government was of crucial importance. In 1960 the British Government was a participant in the discussion of the scheme's future – no longer the final arbiter – and only a minor contributor to the total estimated cost. Yet for some states the French Union, and for others the British Commonwealth, have remained valuable political associations despite opposition to action in Algeria or to the policy of Britain at one time in relation to South Africa or, at another, to Rhodesia. Common interests with other French Union or Commonwealth countries are too important for division to be desirable.[2]

A survey of the main features of the new states will provide therefore a conclusion to this study of geographic change. This survey must be brief and in a sense tentative, for political and economic changes follow one another with astonishing rapidity. Since the conclusion is concerned essentially with change, that is with the time element, each state will be taken in order of its date of attaining independence.[3]

Liberia

Liberia has been a 'free, sovereign and independent republic' since 1847, and yet has only been governed effectively from one centre since the end of the last war. In the main this delay in establishing effective government has been due to lack of resources, particularly capital, and to the inexperience of the governing groups or 'Americo-Liberians' who constitute probably less than 2 per cent of the total population of possibly 1,500,000. In part, however, the situation reflects Liberia's geographical circumstances and the essentially colonial character of the foundations of the present government already described. The Americo-Liberian settlements were coastal, frequently located on capes, although usually near to a large river providing a route for trade with the interior. Thus Monrovia looks to the St Paul river, Grand and Little Bassa to the St John, Greenville to the Sinoe, and Harper to the Cavally. The settlements were linked with one another only by the sea, and Harper with its territory of Maryland joined the new colony only in 1857. The coastal strip up to about 40 miles (65 km) in width is termed the County Jurisdiction, and within it the constitutional and statutory laws of the republic apply, together with the common law of the United States and of England. The Hinterland is governed in part by local rulers, in part by provincial and district commissioners appointed by the president, and in part by the president himself, who from time to time dispenses summary justice on tour. On the whole, however, the government in Monrovia still finds it difficult to exert its authority in the Hinterland, and local chiefs, courts and councils are mainly responsible for both administration and tax collection. Traditional forms of government are better preserved here than almost anywhere else in West Africa, just as the alien government of the Americo-Liberians preserves the early 19th century United States model, although with the modification of one-party government. As attempts are made to develop the country as a whole, the form of government must inevitably be amended, and possibly the American tradition will disappear or be severely modified as the great majority of Liberians take their share of authority.

At present this first independent territory has a government closer to the colonial model than that of any other West African territory, and is amongst the least developed economically. One should not, however, exaggerate Liberia's lack of development relative to that of other West African countries. Her exports are generally greater in value than those of Guinea, for example, with an equally large or even larger population, and her budget is greater. Liberia's problem is the concentration of her economic development into a few small areas, leaving most of the country untouched and virtually unknown. There is no adequate large-scale map coverage, although most of the country has been photographed from the air. There is little knowledge of resources beyond that supplied by a number of scientific expeditions, mostly alien, and there has been no population census. To develop the huge hinterland the Government in Monrovia must look to outside help, almost entirely to the United States, supplying aid under the

'Point Four' programme, and loans from such agencies as the United States Export-Import Bank. The port of Monrovia, the only 'free port' in West Africa, is itself mainly the creation of post-war construction by the United States, which provided a 2000-foot (600-metre) long deep-water wharf. The roads also are again mainly the product of United States investment, by the Firestone Company

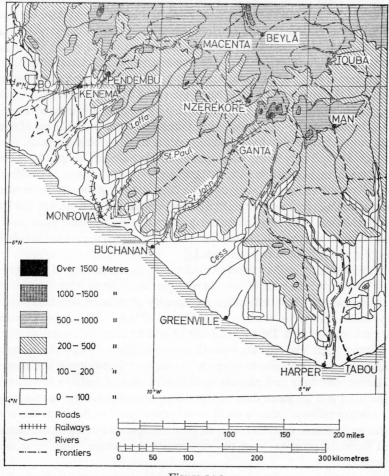

Figure 14.2

and by the military. By 1958 there were only 2000 miles (3200 km) of road in Liberia, the chief of which were: 1) from Monrovia to Ganta on the northern border linking with N'Zérékoré in Guinea, and giving Monrovia an international hinterland; 2) branches to the Firestone Plantation and to Robertsfield, the former United States military base; 3) from Monrovia to the Bomi iron ore workings – linked also by railway; 4) a northern branch to Zorzor, with its gold workings, and a link into Guinea.

Liberia's 43,000 square miles (111,000 sq km) consist essentially of a wide coastal plain rising to some 400 feet (120 metres), interrupted by low hills and backed on the north-north-east by the escarpments of plateaux averaging between 1500 and 2000 feet (450 and 600 metres) in height, and forming a southern 'foothills' fringe to the Guinea Highlands on the northern border. The unusually wide coastal plain (20 to 40 miles (30 to 60 km)) with its heavy rainfall (200 in (5000 mm) in the west and 100 in (2500 mm) in the east) might have been supposed to offer advantages for the development of export crops, but although it has been used for rubber, coffee and citrus plantations, and is a source of oil palm produce, the total area exploited is small compared with that available. Liberia has long been unattractive to commercial development, because of the limiting highlands of the interior with no valley route to the Sudanic zone, as in Guinea, or long navigable river. Only small shallow-draught vessels can sail far up Liberian rivers. There appear to be population densities comparable with those of Sierra Leone, but the population has produced only a small surplus of goods, traded chiefly locally, and only in the north and north-east is there an extensive inter-regional trade, mainly in kola nuts. Lack of a great trade, lack of a considerable demand for imported goods, have made the development of plantations or manufactures, needing large numbers of labourers, extremely difficult. On the Firestone plantations, after more than thirty years of development, most workers are still seasonal and provide their labour only long enough to earn the small sums needed for rather limited requirements.[4]

The main project under current development is the mining of iron ore on Mount Nimba and the completion of a new port together with an iron and steel mill at Buchanan. These will make the country even more dependent on the United States market, to which its major exports of Bomi Hills ore and plantation rubber are already sent. By 1968 Liberia should be exporting some 25 million tons of ore a year. The African Fruit Company of Germany has plantations on the Sinoe river, and may also be interested in harbour development at Greenville and Harper. But these new projects underline the lack of nodality at Monrovia, and the need still for more than one, possibly several ports. Without adequate trunk roads or railways focusing on Monrovia the country is still not a satisfactory political or economic unit, and with its small budget and small export earnings it still finds its earnings from the registration of foreign shipping a useful supplement.

Liberia is still feeling the effects of considerable government debt and a credit squeeze, due to inability to repay short-term loans incurred in order to improve communications, power supplies and social services. The problem has been worsened by delays in iron ore development, and the decline in world rubber prices. The United States has sent advisers to reorganize Liberian government finance.

Ghana

After a half century of colonial government Ghana became independent in 1957, the second territory in West Africa to acquire its own government, 110 years after Liberia. Whereas Liberia is still ruled by a minority group whose traditions were imported from overseas, the original ruling party in Ghana was elected by universal adult suffrage. Although the form of government was modelled on that of Great Britain, the rulers of Ghana derive their support and many of their traditions from the country itself, and already there have been a number of modifications of government away from the British pattern. Ghana was thus the first truly independent power of West Africa, the first major independent Negro power, and the first colony to attain independence. Ghana's achievement encouraged others and was followed, particularly in West Africa with its comparative lack of European settlement, by the attainment of independence by many other former colonies. To some extent Ghana was seen as a model, and as a leader in the general movement towards independence in Africa. Thus her first President, the Asagyefo, Dr Nkrumah, saw Ghana not only as a member state of the British Commonwealth, but, despite her small size with only 7·8 million people in 1965, as a leading African state to which eventually others might be linked in some association. Some linkage was achieved with Guinea and Mali, but 'pan-Africanism', the ideal of uniting all Negro peoples, depends on the uniting of newly-independent governments, naturally hesitant to surrender the freedom of action they recently acquired in order to create a larger organization. Moreover, differences in resources, economic development and political organization create difficulties in uniting the new states and tend to preserve them, and thus preserve, with some minor modifications, the old colonial frontiers. Thus the frontiers which divided African communities are still maintained by the modern independent African inheritors of colonial government. New loyalties are demanded, tribal loyalties rejected. Yet in a sense this is a continuation not just of colonial history, but of previous African history, for the 'tribes' and 'states' of pre-European West Africa were themselves formed by conquest and the division of former peoples. What is new for some portions of West Africa is the notion of the attachment of a land to the people, of a fixed frontier.

Three divisions of Ghana have commonly been distinguished. These may be recognized in the apparent climax vegetation or dominant fallows as coastal savannas, rain forest and northern savannas; in relief as coastal plains, Ashanti plateaux, and Volta basin and plateaux; and in the former administrative divisions of the Eastern and Western Regions in the south (now including Central), Ashanti in the centre (now with Brong-Ahafo) and the Northern Region (now divided into three units). These different kinds of division do not coincide, although the administrative divisions correspond more nearly to those of relief than to those of vegetation. The former colony of the Gold Coast was the product of a unity imposed on diverse peoples by conquest from the coast. Ghana became virtually an enclave within the French West African Empire. The coastal groups

z

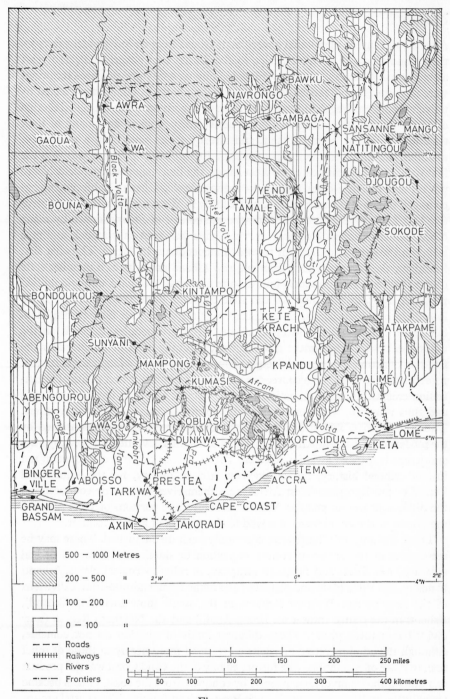

Figure 14.3

had a certain common economic interest, and looked to the invaders for assistance against the interior power of Ashanti. The Ashanti peoples, however, had links with peoples in the Ivory Coast, and had created an interior state, which now became subordinate to a coastal authority. To the north various peoples and territories without any major linkage, other than religious belief amongst some, were added in 1901 to form the new colony. To achieve a true unity in which all minority interests would have been satisfied would have been impossible. The majority interest, that of the coast, that is of the peoples of the former colony, prevails. Leaders of the many peoples and states of the northern regions expressed their doubts with regard to independence in 1955. Yet alone these small groups can hardly survive politically or economically, and a new government needs to be strong, needs to oppose the forces which immediately on independence seek to disintegrate the territory. It cannot achieve the impartiality of the alien power although it may obtain majority support. In the east the former British Togoland was incorporated into Ghana in 1956 after a plebiscite which gave 58 per cent support for the union. There is still a group there favouring union with the Togo Republic. This problem of the minorities, however, is not peculiar to Ghana. It is common to almost all the West African territories.

On a per capita basis Ghana is the wealthiest state in inter-tropical Africa, with an estimated income in 1961 of £71 (U.S. $200) per head and with a government revenue (1963–4) of £16·4 ($46) per head. Until 1961 there was steady economic growth, despite an estimated population increase of some 2·5 per cent per annum, and despite planning which was somewhat unrelated to economic structure, inherited, as Birmingham has remarked, from the former colonial rule.[5] The new planning, which was intended to be better related to economic structure and future needs, led, through over-ambition and extravagance, almost to economic disaster. A large part of Ghana's wealth is derived from its export trade, and to this cocoa alone contributed 58 per cent by value in 1962. Gold and timber each contributed only about 10 per cent. Other exports included bauxite, diamonds and manganese. Thus a country which is mainly agricultural has only one major agricultural export product. With the exception of timber, of which Ghana is one of the biggest producers in Africa, all other important exports are minerals. This one agricultural export, cocoa, has given Ghanaians a higher income than that enjoyed by other West Africans. However, falling cocoa prices since 1954 have been of great concern. The 1962 cocoa export was double that of 1958, and nearly 70 per cent more than that of 1959, yet it was worth less on the world market. However, new markets for cocoa are developing. For example, Ghana was able to sell 43,000 tons to the U.S.S.R. in 1965–6. High export earnings have encouraged the import of foodstuffs, especially of meat. Ghana is probably the biggest importer of meat in Africa, but hopes to reduce the import by developing ranching in the Accra Plains, and by promoting fishing – five new fishing harbours have already been constructed. Other than meat and fish the chief foodstuffs imported are wheat flour, rice and sugar. A sugar scheme has been started at Komenda with a 9000-acre (3600-hectare) plantation, and sugar and rice cultivation are planned for the Lower Volta flood-plain. Cocoa has also made possible an accumulation of capital to pay for welfare improvements, education and research, and even to a small extent to offset falling cocoa prices. The Cocoa Marketing Board contributed 14 per cent of the cost of the 1951–7 development plan, and gave another £5 million to health and education services. Cocoa also maintained to some extent the traditional relationship of Ashanti, the producing hinterland, and the coast with its middlemen and its European contacts. Ashanti and the coastal regions are closely knit by rail and road transport whose main lines form an approximate triangle from Takoradi to Kumasi, and thence to Accra. To the north of Kumasi there is no railway, and only few all-weather roads. Where cocoa found its northern limit so does the Ghanaian transport system, giving a remarkably sharp contrast between a densely populated, prosperous south, and an undeveloped, mostly empty and poor north. The leaders of the Convention People's Party, formerly the government party of Ghana, were drawn mainly from the south, that is from the area most under British influence, in which commercialism is most developed. Much of the opposition was drawn from Ashanti with its cocoa wealth, and yet with its old traditions of statehood and military power. The leading opposition newspaper was for a time the 'Ashanti Pioneer'. Ashanti, moreover, with its large seasonal immigration of cocoa labourers had become a major centre for the penetration of influences from outside Ghana, and had contacts with such peoples as the 'Agni' of the south-eastern Ivory Coast. Since the main strength of the opposition United Party was drawn from Ashanti, much of the political struggle has been regional rather than ideological, a normal feature of West African politics which finds its extreme expression in Nigeria.[6] If the northern regions can acquire greater wealth and a greater degree of literacy, one may see the development of opposition there also, an opposition which may be strengthened by the strong Muslim influences, with the possibility of widespread support from the more northerly states of West Africa.

The attempt to counter regional opposition has resulted not only in political centralization, but also in the attempt to link the country in one general plan of economic development. The co-operative organizations have been strengthened to assist in the promotion of a socialist type economy. Much of the cocoa crop, for example, has hitherto been handled by the Ghana Co-operative Marketing Association with funds loaned from the Co-operative Central Bank. The National Co-operative Council has supported the Government in its efforts to introduce more planning into the economy, and the former mechanized farming scheme at Damongo became the site for a model co-operative farming scheme with settlement units containing 100 families each and employing co-operative methods for cultivation, processing, marketing, the purchase of supplies and even for savings. Part of a recent Russian aid programme had been training in the organization of a model state farm, and state farms have played an increasingly important role, especially in food production, totalling 24,000 acres (9600 hectares) in 1964, 5600 (2240) of which were under rice. There is in addition in Ghana a

Farmers' Mutual Co-operative Insurance Scheme, and there are also marketing and even industrial co-operatives. To assist in the latest development plan a Builders or Workers Brigade of young volunteers was organized in 50 camps and field units. The immediate inspiration for this may perhaps be found in Israel, which in recent years has given Ghana some considerable technical assistance and helped to promote, for example, the Black Star shipping line, and a small 'kibbutz' farming unit. The Brigade was to be converted mainly into a land army, although it was also employed in other activities including manufacture. Its members were trained in the methods of co-operative farming for two years before moving to large-scale co-operative farm settlements.

Another feature is the encouragement of voluntary labour through town and village Development Committees. In Ghana there is little prospect of a rapid growth of indigenous capitalism, despite the relatively high incomes. To promote development the Government had itself had to invest in and control enterprises, and there was some pressure from Government supporters for nationalization. There have, however, been difficulties in operating the Government corporations. In January 1965 it was announced that losses of up to £15 million had been recorded up to the end of 1963 in the 32 state-owned enterprises, chiefly in the Ghana Airways, the state farms corporation and the mining corporation. Despite these losses the number of such enterprises increased to 52 by February 1966, and more were planned. However, the Government also sought to promote foreign investment or loans from all possible sources, including both the United States and Russia, although certain of its actions were not very encouraging. In 1960 five gold mines were prevented from closing, despite their claim that operations were unprofitable, and the Ghanaian Government offered to buy them. Since 1960 the mines have had constant difficulties, including inability to obtain import licences, delays in the shipment of stores and high rates of taxation. The military government of 1966 has, however, eased the situation. By contrast, the terms offered to the American VALCO consortium to develop the Volta River Project, the keystone of Ghana's economic development, have been generally regarded as generous. The Government's hand in economic affairs was strengthened enormously by the British-created marketing boards, through which it was possible to control the income of the producer, to bargain more effectively with consumers overseas, and to effect considerable public savings, providing funds to assist development. The boards have been criticized on the grounds that fixed prices limit producers' incentive either to improve or expand and reduce private saving.[7] Yet they have provided a concentration of capital not otherwise available and essential for development. The Cocoa Marketing Board operated at a loss in 1956 and 1957, and kept up the price paid to growers despite a fall in world market prices. Greater stability of prices is both an economic and a political advantage in Ghana. Not only is there control of resources and marketing, but also of labour. The Industrial Relations Act requires all workers to join unions, yet strikes are outlawed. Nevertheless, labour demonstrations took place in 1965 as a protest against aspects of Government policy. But as Kwame Nkrumah

stated on April 8th, 1961, the Trades Union Congress, together with the United
Ghana Farmers' Council, the National Co-operative Council and the National
Council of Ghana Women were integral parts of the Convention People's Party.
The proscription of the Convention People's Party, following the military coup
of February 24th, 1966, has led to the reorganization of the functions of many of
these bodies.

To attain the rapid improvement in productivity and the balance in economy
desired Ghana needs both a considerable national effort and foreign investment,
gifts or loans. Centralization, the over-riding of minorities, press censorship and
the formation of a presidential type of government by the declaration of the
republic in July 1960 must all be seen in relation to Ghana's economic and political problems. The economy is too dependent on cocoa. More could be done to
promote other agricultural products, but the Government has been concerned
to develop some measure of industrialization on the basis of the hitherto little-
developed resources of bauxite and water power. The Volta River Project has
been the chief element in the policy of economic development of Nkrumah's
government. It provides large quantities of electricity, supplies power to an
aluminium smelting plant, and has promoted the development of mines, a
harbour, railways and roads. It will also make possible the irrigation of portions
of the Accra Plains. The main burden of the cost of the new aluminium industry
has fallen on the United States, chiefly on a private consortium, VALCO. For this
American organization with its huge capital resources, the risks of capital investment in Ghana and of over-production of aluminium are apparently more than
offset by the possible returns from this enormous scheme. Certainly the concentration of aluminium production to be achieved in Ghana may well make for
lower costs than at many other sites already producing. Ghana hoped to achieve
great improvements in education, agriculture and industry through her Seven
Year Development Plan which, it was intended, would change her manpower
structure and free her from a hitherto colonial type of economy. However, the
balance of payments deficit of £79 million (U.S. $220 million) by 1965, the
failure of most state-owned corporations to make a profit, the declining rate of
growth, increased unemployment and rapidly-rising food prices showed the
failure of the plan, and the need for a fresh economic policy.

Guinea

The Republic of Guinea was the first of the former colonies of French West Africa
to attain full independence when a majority of its electorate voted against joining
the new Franco-African community in the referendum of September 1958. The
French administration abandoned Guinea very rapidly, and some of the new
members of the Franco-African community, established in October 1958, broke
off their former ties with Guinea and sought to isolate the new state. In part this
new situation with its important political and geographical implications was the
result of political struggles within the former federation of French West Africa.

Before the referendum the chief political party in Guinea was the Rassemblement Démocratique Africain (R.D.A.) which was also the chief party in the Ivory Coast and the former French Soudan, and was important in the Upper Volta, Dahomey and Niger. The president of the R.D.A. and later of the Ivory Coast, Houphouët-Boigny, supported the idea of the Franco-African community and of the break-up of the former federal structure with a capital at Dakar. Many of the other

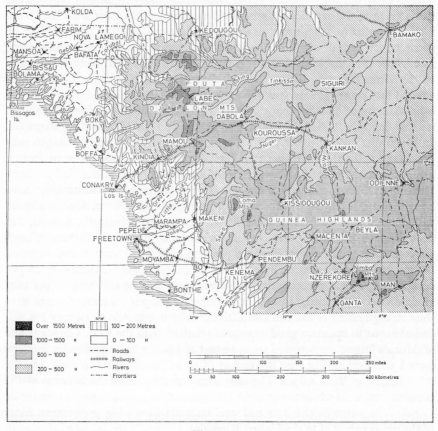

Figure 14.4

R.D.A. leaders disagreed with him. The leader in Guinea, Sekou Touré, was formerly president of the French West African general trade union or Union Générale des Travailleurs de l'Afrique Noire (U.G.T.A.N.) where he was influenced by left-wing organizations. Sekou Touré urged his supporters to vote against joining the Franco-African community, as did the Prime Minister of Niger, Djibo Bakary. However, the latter failed and was overthrown.

Guinea has some 3,357,000 people (1963 estimate) grouped into a large number of small tribal units. The Fulani of the former plateau state of Fouta Djallon are the largest group, but are composed of many diverse elements recruited from amongst the surrounding peoples. Few are Fulani proper. In consequence except for the problems set by distance – for Guinea with 95,000 square miles (246,000 sq km) is slightly larger than Ghana, yet with less than half Ghana's population – Guinea has not been difficult to unite under an authoritarian government. Presidential power is greater even than it was in Ghana. Sekou Touré has declared that the Government and the Assembly exist only to carry out the decisions of the Democratic Party of Guinea (P.D.G.), the name given to the expelled Guinea section of the R.D.A. Under the Three Year Plan, instituted in 1960, some £43 million ($120 million) was originally to be spent, 20 per cent of which had to come from 'human investment', that is, from free labour.[8] Unable to obtain assistance from France, the United Kingdom or the United States, Guinea turned elsewhere. In November 1958 Guinea entered into an association with Ghana by which Ghana offered a £10 million loan. A number of other loans and gifts has been obtained from elsewhere, notably from the U.S.S.R., China, the U.S.A. and the United Arab Republic. In November 1960 the cost of the Three Year Plan was estimated at £56 million ($157 million), of which £47 million ($131 million) were to come mainly from communist countries. Advisers from Eastern Europe and Russia have been assisting in Guinea's economic development, and Chinese agriculturalists have been maintaining a large demonstration rice-growing scheme. Guinea's trade with France and with other West African countries, principally Senegal, has been reduced, and has increased with communist countries. Whereas in 1958 the communist countries received 0·8 per cent of Guinea's exports and supplied 0·7 per cent of her imports, by 1959 the proportions were increased to 16 per cent and 9 per cent respectively. The franc zone in 1959 still took 51 per cent of exports and supplied 74 per cent of imports. Despite all these changes with their strengthening of Russian and Chinese influence in Africa, Guinea has still endeavoured to maintain good economic relations with the west. Guinea is one of Africa's largest exporters of iron ore and of bauxite both worked by foreign-owned companies. The iron ore export of some 720,000 tons in 1962 was the third largest in West Africa. The only major working is in the deposits of the Kaloum Peninsula where the quarries are operated by the Compagnie Minière de Conakry, in which British iron and steel interests have a big investment. Most of the ore is exported to the United Kingdom. Guinea is the leading exporter in Africa of bauxite with a 1962 production of some 1·4 million tons. The ore is mined chiefly on the Islands of Los. Some exploitation has taken place at Sangaridi in the Boké district and further workings may be established at Kindia and Dabola. At Kimba near Fria, a project has been under way since 1957 to produce alumina from local ore and export began in June 1960. Nearly half the capital invested is from the United States and over a quarter from France. The building of hydro-electric power stations at Souapiti and Amaria on the Konkouré river has begun, but already the Kimba alumina plant is operating with a capacity of 480,000 tons of alumina a year (equivalent to about 100,000 tons of aluminium). The long-range plan is for an output of 1,200,000 tons of alumina, the world's largest. Additional exports are 'Canary Island type' bananas, oranges and orange oil, pineapples, palm kernels and kola nuts (chiefly to other West African countries). There is therefore some variety in Guinea's export trade although the territory does depend rather heavily on minerals.

Most of Guinea drains inland and most of her major road and river routes lead to Mali or Senegal. The narrow coastal plain, with the capital and only major port of Conakry, is hemmed in by the Gangan Massif and by the enormous massif of the Fouta Djallon, which, with the Guinea Highlands, provides the main watershed of West Africa. Here the valleys provide the main areas for the production of export crops and the main routes between the high plateau surfaces with their 'bowé' and steep escarpments. The railway between the two major relief blocs of the Timbi Plateau and the Dalaba Massif links interior Guinea of the Upper Niger and Upper Senegal with coastal Guinea, yet the separation is emphasized by the great administrative importance of Kankan, the site now of major political conferences. The south-eastern portions of Guinea are even further separated from the capital. They drain by the great tributaries of the Niger towards Mali, and routes tend to focus on Kankan, but they consist essentially of numerous valleys and small basins on the northern fringe of the Guinea Highlands, and each has its own small market and administrative centre. Palm kernels are a major export of the N'Zérékoré district, but are sent via Monrovia, not Conakry. The Guinea Highlands have proved, with their steep slopes, dense forest, and lack of level upper surfaces, less accessible and less attractive to settlement than the Fouta Djallon. Development is thus even more valley-ward, and linked with the coast only by the very few favourable routes. The frontier with Sierra Leone and Liberia has served to increase the isolation of the area until the building of the road from Monrovia to N'Zérékoré. Thus Guinea also has a major problem in achieving real unity, not so much from the diversity of her population, as from her regional diversity and lack of a suitable focal point.

Mali

The Republic of Mali (formerly French Soudan and Soudanese Republic) became independent in association with Senegal in the Mali Federation in June 1960. The Mali Federation had existed within the Franco-African community since January 1959. The Federation had originally been proposed as a much wider organization by the leaders of Senegal, Mali, Dahomey, Upper Volta and Mauritania the previous December. The Mauritanian leaders were, however, lukewarm from the beginning, and the leaders of Upper Volta and Dahomey changed their minds, and decided to align themselves with the the Ivory Coast whose leader, Houphouët-Boigny, opposed federalism and favoured direct links with France. Such an arrangement had been favoured by the French Government when the new community had been created. Poor, land-locked Mali had, however, much to gain from federation, whilst the Ivory Coast with its new harbour at Abidjan, and its wealth from cocoa and coffee, gained least, and even faced the

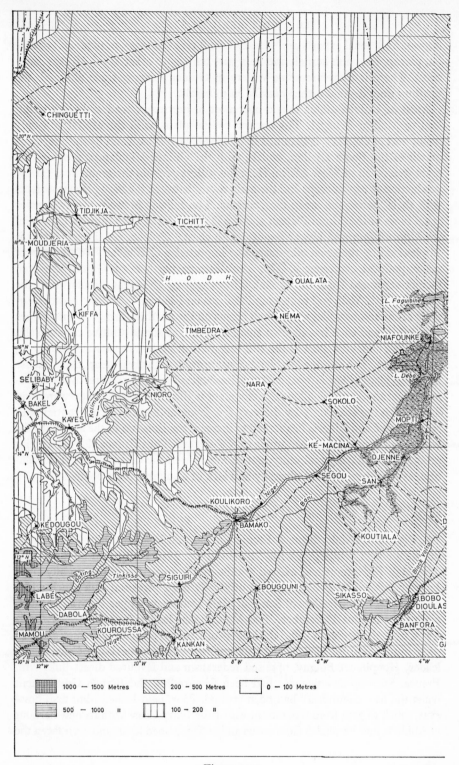

Figure 14.5

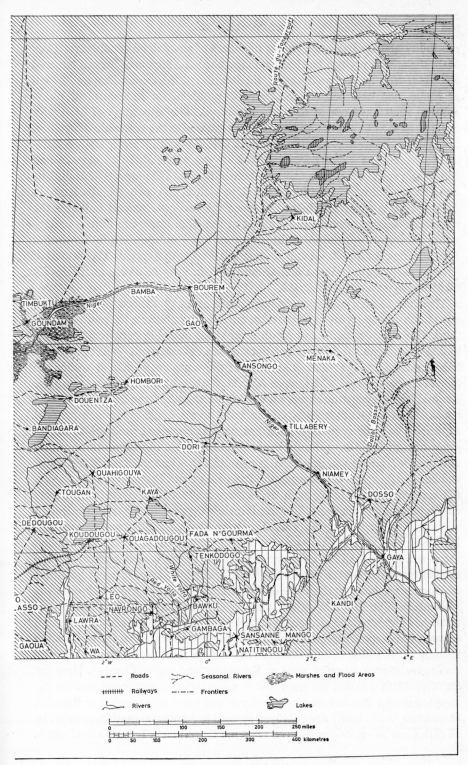

Figure 14.5 *continued*

possibility of subsidizing the poorer members of any federal community. Thus Mali, the territory which had been amongst the main targets of French imperial ambitions with its supposed wealth, the location of the former Empire of Mali or Melle, had now become an economic problem, for its control of trans-Saharan routes had ceased to be an advantage. The association of Mali with Senegal seemed to offer at least part of the answer to the economic difficulties. Senegal has the greatest measure of industrialization of the former French territories, possesses a major port connected by the only railway to Bamako and Koulikoro, and is a major importer of foodstuffs, one of the exports of Mali. The Federation succeeded in achieving independence, but two months later, in August 1960, a quarrel developed between the two governments in which the leaders of Senegal opposed the attempt of the Mali leaders to form a unitary state. The result was that Mali became completely independent in September 1960 severing both political and trading relations with Senegal. The new Mali joined the 'union' of Ghana and Guinea, but in 1963 resumed more friendly relations once more with Senegal.

Mali has an area of some 465,000 square miles (1,200,000 sq km) with a population of only 4·5 millions, but these are mostly confined to the south-western third. Her chief economic and political problems derive in part from her land-locked position and from the limitations of her environments – most of Mali is Sahel and desert. 850 miles (1400 km) of the northern frontier is within the Sahara and contiguous with that of Algeria, so that the French were for a time alarmed by the sympathy expressed in Mali for the F.L.N. movement. However, neither Mali nor its associates, Ghana and Guinea, could give much material expression to their sympathy. Mali has no major mineral production; only a small output of gold from alluvial workings in Bambouk. Her exports are ground-nuts, cotton, rice, kapok, dried fish, gum arabic, shea butter, livestock and skins, and her chief markets are Senegal, the Ivory Coast and France. Of these exports rice and livestock are of special interest, since they satisfy markets in the export crop regions nearer the coast. The rice is mainly the product of modern irrigation schemes. The livestock export is based on the traditional transhumant pastoralism. It is estimated that Mali possesses nearly 4 million cattle and over 8 million sheep and goats. Mali has huge tsetse-free areas of wet season pasture, and the northernmost dry season pastures in the inland Niger delta. It could become a major meat producer for the whole of West Africa. The major problem is distance. Mali needs high profitability per unit weight products. Much of her export traffic has hitherto depended on favourable railway freight rates, with a distance of 750 miles (1200 km) by rail from Dakar to the south-western crop-producing districts. This Dakar route was closed to Mali for three years but there was an alternative shorter route by river to Kouroussa and rail to Conakry. Here the major problem was that the track was in a poor state of repair and awaited the completion of a Russian scheme to relay it and build an extension to Bamako. Meanwhile Mali's traffic was conveyed by road to Abidjan at exorbitant rates. In an endeavour to operate at reduced rates the Government formed a road transport co-operative. However, in June 1963 the railway to Dakar was re-opened and trade with and via Senegal began once more. Despite the various moves against French interests and despite the new association with Guinea and Ghana, Mali is still subsidized by France, and without French aid Mali would be in even greater economic difficulties. In this respect the removal of French military bases has meant a considerable economic loss, but political pressures in the new African states constantly over-ride economic considerations. Military equipment and training have since been provided by France, the U.S.S.R. and the United States. In March 1961 the Mali Government signed an agreement with that of the U.S.S.R. by which the latter provided a long-term credit of £16 million ($45 million), and in June a loan of some £6 million ($17 million) was obtained from the United Arab Republic. Several other loans and gifts have been obtained, particularly from the E.E.C.

Senegal

Separated from Mali in August 1960, in 1963 Senegal was provided by its National Assembly with a new constitution, by which Léopold Senghor, the former President of the Legislative Assembly of the Mali Federation, became elected the President of the Republic of Senegal, holding all executive power. The constitution proclaimed that the Republic would spare no effort to achieve African unity, and asserted its own unity in the motto, 'One people, one aim, one faith'. Since the separation Senegal has moved towards a better understanding with France. Senegal, of all the West African states, has the oldest association with France, and has benefited most from French investment. The first great export crop boom – in groundnuts – took place in Senegal, and resulted in an early breaking down of tribal barriers in the mixing of Wolof and Serer cultivators in the groundnut-growing areas. In Senegal's capital and great port of entry, Dakar, France sought to create a port for much of the Sudan, and also the federal capital for the whole of French West Africa. Nearly a quarter of Senegal's population is urban, and the country, in proportion to its size, is the most highly industrialized in West Africa, possessing oil milling, soap and sisal manufactures, textiles, fish canning, sugar refining and confectionery, scrap-iron smelting, engineering including the assembly of agricultural machinery, oil refining, chemicals including explosives, paints, fertilizers, liquid gas and dyes, the re-moulding of tyres, cement manufacture and brewing. Quarries have exploited Senegal's phosphate, limestone, ilmenite, rutile and zirconium resources, and systematic exploration for oil has been taking place since the discovery in September 1959 of a natural gas field. Senegal also has the finest education system of the former French West Africa, including the only university. Senegal's population of some 3,360,000 maintained an import trade in 1963 of some £56 million and an export of some £40 million. Although the value of overseas trade is much smaller than that of Ghana and the value of exports less than that of the Ivory Coast, yet this trade is overwhelmingly superior to that of either of its immediate neighbours, Mali and Mauritania, which hitherto have depended mainly on Dakar for port facilities. Senegal's major problem is that nearly 90 per cent by value of her export trade is in one commodity, groundnuts, which also provides more than a fifth of the national income. The state is in consequence

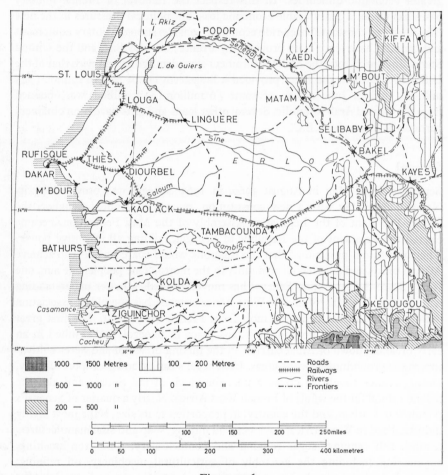

Figure 14.6

dependent on the great oil-seed markets, particularly Marseilles, and would prefer to diversify her trade. Moreover, she faces a considerable economic problem, as France has ceased to pay the special price for groundnuts, and Senegal must sell at the lower world market prices. Almost half the E.E.C. aid given to Senegal is to support the grower's price for groundnuts.

Physically Senegal is very limited, for much of the territory has only a very short growing season. There is a longer growing season in the south, in Casamance, but Casamance is separated from the railway and the main roads to

Dakar by the enclave of the Gambia. The Gambia has an excellent river route in one of the most productive of the groundnut-growing sectors, and annually attracts labour from Senegal despite the latter's prosperity. Political union between the Gambia and Senegal was heralded as a logical step by Léopold Senghor in November 1959, but as yet the Gambia remains a Commonwealth country. Communications still remain a major problem in Senegal, despite railway modernization and the replacement of steam locomotives by diesel. Not only is Casamance isolated, but so are the districts of Kédougou in the southeast, and the districts fringing the Ferlo in the north-east. The only good navigable river, the Gambia, is mainly controlled by another government, and the river Senegal, which provides only shallow-draught navigation for a short period, is shared with Mauritania. Again, Senegal depends on food imports, so great is the concentration of cultivators on groundnut planting. Approximately one-third of the import cost is in food, beverages and tobacco. Rice is the chief foodstuff imported, and its increasing use by the Senegalese population has made the country dependent on overseas rice-growing areas, and to some extent on other West African territories with a small surplus. The Richard-Toll Cultivation Project, completed at a cost of some £5·5 million ($15 million), contributes only some 15,000 tons of rice, and production is low for an irrigation scheme, averaging only just over one ton to the acre (2½ tons per hectare). Richard-Toll, however, is only the first of perhaps several schemes to be established in the Senegal valley, once adequate control of river flow is achieved. The attempt is to be made of converting the greater part of the project to sugar cane production. The Mission d'Aménagement du Sénégal (M.A.S.) has prepared a long-term plan of control, involving the building of four dams, the improvement of navigation, and more intensive use of floodland. Already at Guédé, 80 miles (130 km) above Richard-Toll, there is a 2500-acre (1000-hectare) rice and cotton scheme in operation.

Togo

The Republic of Togo was created out of the former French trusteeship or mandated territory of Togoland in April 1960. With only 1,642,000 people Togo is one of the smallest of the newly-independent states of West Africa, and it has been suggested that the territory will never be able to support itself, and will need to depend on the colonial powers. In consequence of its apparent lack of viability and its ethnic links with Ghana it should therefore, it has been claimed, form another region of the latter – as an independent state it is only an example of the 'balkanization' policy of the imperialists. In December 1965, however, Togo was admitted to the Conseil de l'Entente (see pp. 695 and 700). The first Prime Minister of Togo, Sylvanus Olympio, descendant of returned Brazilian Africans, had counted himself as an Ewe and helped to form a political party, which in 1939 pressed for the unity of all Ewe in the three territories of the then Gold Coast, British Togoland and French Togo. In 1952 this policy was changed

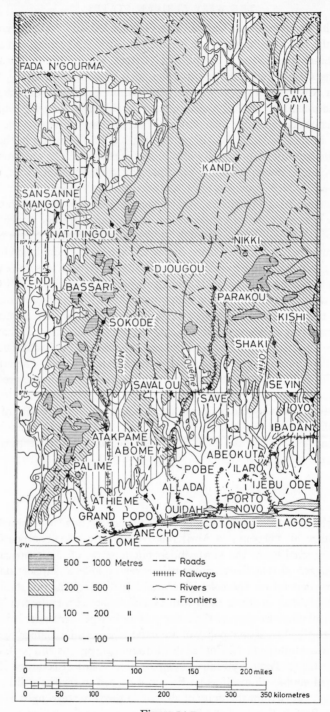

Figure 14.7

THE WEST AFRICAN STATES

to the unification of the two Togos and the party emerged as the Comité de l'Unité Togolaise. In 1956 hopes of unity were destroyed by the narrow vote in British Togoland in favour of remaining in Ghana. The Unité Togolaise party became an opposition group to the Government party under French auspices, the Parti Togolais du Progrès. Olympio and his supporters were able from time to time to use Ghanaian territory as a political base[9] and, no doubt, it was hoped in Ghana that if Olympio came to power there would be a closer accord between the two countries. In April 1958 an election in Togo was held under United Nations auspices to decide the Government for independence, and Olympio's party was returned, but with a changed policy favouring Togo independence and abandoning the idea of unity. Relations between Ghana and Togo were estranged until August 1960, when some measure of agreement was reached on the improvement of communications and increased economic co-operation. Eventually, however, political differences in Togo culminated in the assassination of Olympio.

Togo's budgetary expenditure per head of population is the lowest in West Africa. In 1962, for example, it reached less than £3 ($8.40). Overseas trade in 1965 amounted to only £10·5 million ($29·4 million) in exports and £16·2 million ($45·4 million) in imports, whilst the F.I.D.E.S. appropriation over the 1947–58 period amounted to £15 million or only about £1 5s. ($3.50) a head per year. Until 1959 French financial assistance had constantly been necessary in order to balance the budget. Togo's small size and relative poverty are not her only problems. There are major problems of ethnic and geographical diversity, and there is also the problem of shape. Togo is 375 miles (500 km) long but only 75 miles (120 km) wide at its greatest extent. In consequence much of this small territory is well inland. Fortunately for the future state the original Franco-British division of 1914 into two almost equal portions, with Lomé in the British portion, was abandoned in 1919 for a division which gave the major share including Lomé to France. The result for Togo is the possession of a small port and the original German railway and road systems with their subsequent modifications. Thus whilst Togo had been able to develop more or less independently of French West Africa, British Togoland had to be developed from the Gold Coast. The railhead is at Blitta, approximately half-way between Lomé and the northern border. An important branch line to the north-west taps the Togo–Atacora Mountain region in the Palimé district, the chief source of the two most important export crops: coffee and cocoa. North of Blitta the territory is extremely poor, and ethnically attains its greatest diversity in the numerous small tribes occupying the many plateaux and bornhardts. Here the peoples have little link with the coast, and more in common ethnically with neighbouring peoples in both Ghana and Dahomey. The Moba and Gourma granite plateaux of the extreme north are separated by the Oti river from the rest of Togo, and their peoples have close contacts with neighbours in Upper Volta. Cocoa and coffee have hitherto provided over 50 per cent of the exports by value, with palm kernels and copra adding to the variety of produce exported with about

10 per cent each. There is little possibility of industrial development and the wharf at Lomé provides a landing only for small vessels. However, in 1961 the mining of phosphate deposits began at Hahotoe Akoumapé, only 25 miles (40 km) in a direct line from Lomé. In 1965 the output was 982,000 tons, already greater than that of Senegal which has a longer history of phosphate working. Development schemes in Togo include agricultural planning in the Oti and Mono valleys, and a new deep-water port at Lomé.

Dahomey

Geographically and economically Dahomey's position is little different from that of Togo. The revenue and the value of the overseas trade are about the same and the problems of shape, distance and communications are all similar. In consequence, like Togo, Dahomey has a problem of economic viability and has tended to seek support from union or association with other West African territories. The Dahomeyan Government has also tried to preserve many of its economic ties with France.

Dahomey has a population of 2,250,000, most of whom live in the southernmost provinces. The largest group consists of some 800,000 Fon or 'Dahomans', and the next largest a related group of 300,000 Adja. There are, however, several other large tribal units, some of whom are part of larger groups in neighbouring Nigeria, including the Yoruba or 'Nagots' (200,000), the Bariba (210,000), the Aïzo (100,000) and the Somba (110,000). There are numerous smaller groups, notably some of the fishing communities of the lagoons, and some of the sub-Sudanic 'refugee' and riverain communities in the north. The export trade in 1965 was valued at £4·8 million ($13·4 million) and imports at £11·8 million ($33·0 million). Approximately one quarter of the imports by value are foodstuffs, for, as in Ghana and in neighbouring Nigeria, particularly in the two southern regions, the African cultivators are tending to concentrate more on export crops, and are neglecting local foodstuffs in favour of the preferred imports. Of the total value of the export trade 75 per cent is provided by oil palm produce, so that, as in Togo, the bulk of the overseas earnings comes from the produce of the south, but, unlike Togo, from less variety of goods. Dahomey is 415 miles (668 km) long by a maximum width of 77 miles (124 km), and its northern territories and peoples have more affinity with neighbouring areas and peoples in Togo, Upper Volta, Niger, or Nigeria than with the south. The Benin–Niger railway extends as far north as Parakou 272 miles (438 km) inland, but from there northwards traffic must depend on the road to Malanville. To the north-west there is a road from Tchaourou via Djougou and Natitingou to Fada N'Gourma in Upper Volta, and in the south two small railway extensions serve the Pobé and Segboroué districts and the coast. Cotonou, the capital, chief port and largest town, was merely an open roadstead until 1964 when a modern deep-water port was completed capable of handling four times the former traffic. Large F.A.C. grants have been necessary to develop Dahomey, which is still poorly provided with medical and educational services. The largest development project financed by F.A.C., other than the deep-water port at Cotonou, is that of the Ouémé valley agricultural scheme, begun in 1946 to improve the productivity of an area of some 400 square miles (1000 sq km) with a population of 85,000. A campaign to increase the area cultivated, mainly through the creation of collective farms, was begun in 1962. Despite development schemes the Dahomeyan economy has failed to advance. By March 1966 the Government had incurred enormous debts, food production had declined and the country was still highly dependent on a single group of commodities: oil palm produce.

The Dahomeyan leaders originally supported the idea of a general Mali federation, but when it became clear that such a federation did not have the support of states such as the Ivory Coast, the Dahomeyans changed their minds. For them the aid of France is regarded as essential, and they have in consequence joined the pro-French 'Conseil de l'Entente' or 'Benin-Sahel Entente' of the Ivory Coast, Upper Volta and Niger, formed in 1959. Each member state has adopted a similar constitution, providing for presidential government and a one-chamber legislative assembly, elected in Dahomey and the Ivory Coast on a majority list, i.e. the party with the most votes takes all seats in the Assembly. The Ivory Coast, the leading member of this group, has offered economic assistance to the others through a 'solidarity fund', to which each member contributes according to its means, and the four members have entered into a Customs union and political association – the only major association to arise from the remains of French West Africa, and paradoxically formed by the four anti-federalist states. The coup d'état of October 1963 brought a modification of the Dahomeyan régime to a semi-presidential type, in the creation of which the Army has played a major role. In December 1965 a second coup resulted in the completion of the Army's revolution with General Soglo's assumption of supreme power.

Niger

The Republic of the Niger became independent on August 3rd, 1960, two days after Dahomey. The new republic is even poorer than Dahomey, with a smaller budget per head of population, limited resources, and location at least 800 miles (1300 km) from the coast. Like Dahomey, therefore, Niger has sought the support of other neighbouring territories and of France, and in consequence has favoured membership of the 'Conseil de l'Entente'. For a short period the dominant political party led by Djibo Bakary favoured other policies, but this party was ousted just before the referendum, and replaced by a group favourable to France.

Niger has the comparatively large population of 3,117,000, but occupying an area of some 495,000 square miles (1,280,000 sq km), the second largest territory of the former French West Africa. Nomadism is still an important way of life for many, and livestock play a major role in the economy, with an estimated 7 million sheep and goats, and 3·5 million cattle. The greater part of the population

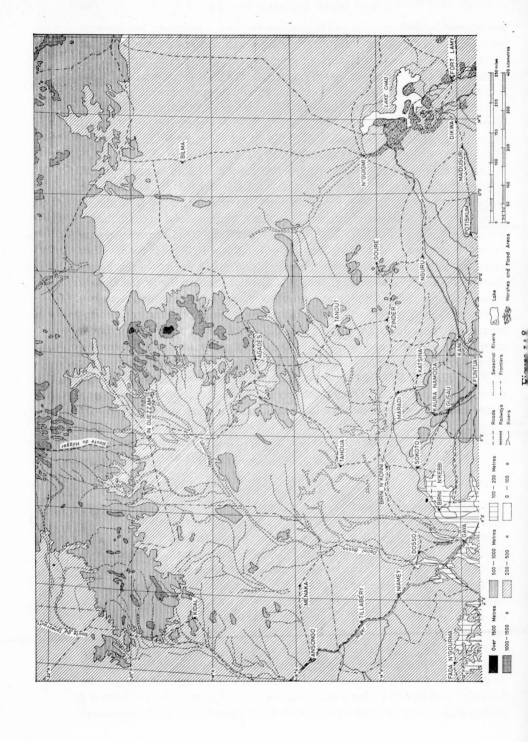

Figure 14.8

is confined to two broad regions: Djerma Ganda in the south-west, almost bisected by the river Niger, and containing the capital of Niamey, and the southern border districts of Gobir, Damagaram and Mounio. Other smaller more populated districts include the plateau of Aïr in the centre, and the pasture lands of Tessellaman and Northern Azaouak in the north-west. The populous centres are not only diverse both geographically and ethnically, but are widely separated from one another by areas of thorn bush as in Ader, sandy plains as in northern Gobir, or by sandy desert such as the Ténéré. The south-western region is occupied mainly by the related communities of Djerma and Songhay totalling some 400,000. Some of them are fishermen who migrate regularly to southern Nigeria, some are cultivators whose interests, both economically and ethnically, are similar to those of the Songhay of Mali, and others are traders in Ghana. The peoples of the southern border are mainly Hausa numbering about one million and forming the northernmost extension of the peoples of the former Hausa states, and Fulani numbering probably 400,000. The Hausa areas of Gobir, Damagaram and Mounio are the most productive lands of Niger. Their relation to the Hausa lands once made them subject to the claim of being within a British sphere of influence, but French rights were recognized over lands north of a line from Say to Baroua on Lake Chad, allowing the French a well enough watered route between their West and Equatorial African possessions. The importance of the Hausa areas may be gauged from the fact that their chief product, groundnuts, provides 75 per cent by value of the export trade (officially worth £7 million ($19·6 million) in 1963, but difficult to estimate, because goods exported to other French Union territories are not declared to Customs). Zinder, the great groundnut market, was the capital of Niger from 1900 to 1926, and is still more important than Niamey commercially, although it has less than two-thirds of the latter's population. Damagaram, the district of which Zinder is the chief centre, is the most important source of gum arabic, one of the chief minor export commodities. From Zinder the main trade route southwards leads to Kano, from Maradi in southern Gobir the route leads to Katsina, and from Mounio to Nguru. Thus some of the export traffic passes through Nigeria, despite attempts to develop a route through Dahomey. Aïr with its capital of Agadès is remote, a Saharan centre for Tuareg herdsmen and for traders, a stopping place on the trans-Saharan bus service, which has lost all its former importance. There is still a camel traffic in Niger which is particularly important for linking small oases and salt-producing centres like Bilma with markets in Gobir, Damagaram and Northern Nigeria. Modern Niger looks to its links with France and the Ivory Coast for economic support, and with Dahomey for contact with the coast. But the political and economic outlooks implied are from the vantage point of Niamey, which belongs to the Niger valley. The rest of Niger looks elsewhere and an effective unity economically and politically will be difficult to achieve. The relief of Niger's poverty at so great a distance inland by poor roads will likewise be difficult, although there is a possibility of oil exploitation and a little tin and wolfram are mined near Agadès. The main resource problem is water, both for domestic use and for agriculture. Economic development depends considerably on the prospects for irrigation, the building of small dams and the development of boreholes.

Upper Volta

The Republic of the Upper Volta is probably the poorest member of the Conseil de l'Entente. In 1962 the state exported only £2·5 million ($7 million) worth of commodities chiefly groundnuts, livestock, shea butter, cotton and dried fish, mostly to Ghana. Her imports were worth £12·5 million ($35 million) and this for a population of some 4·7 millions on 106,000 square miles (275,000 sq km) giving the highest population density of the former French West African territories. The budget revenue in 1960 was the lowest in West Africa on a per capita basis, being less even than that of Niger, and barely 8 per cent that of the Ivory Coast. Much of the Republic's income comes from the 150,000 seasonal or long-term emigrants to the cocoa and coffee plantations of the Ivory Coast and Dahomey.

In some measure Upper Volta's poverty is surprising, despite evidence of over-crowding on agricultural land, for most of the territory has a sufficiently long rainy season to grow the chief grains of West Africa, and there is a railway from Ouagadougou, the capital, via the market of Bobo Dioulasso to the port of Abidjan. Soils, however, are generally thin and lateritic outcrops are widespread. Perhaps the major problem is remoteness, despite the railway, which was only extended to Ouagadougou in 1954. Until the railway link was completed, much of the trade of north-eastern Upper Volta was carried over Ghanaian roads by the shorter route to Takoradi. There was nothing which Upper Volta could produce which some other territory could not produce more cheaply and in greater abundance nearer the coast. To some extent this should also be true of Niger, but the southern districts of the latter benefit from proximity to the great groundnut markets of Northern Nigeria. Also Upper Volta has tended to receive less interest and less investment. For long it was regarded as a reservoir of labour for neighbouring territories of the French West African Federation. Its main problem was thought to be overpopulation, although some French authorities were less concerned with the problem of surplus labour than with diverting that surplus away from the cocoa plantations of Ghana to those of the Ivory Coast or to the agricultural holdings of the Office du Niger in Mali. Moreover, the Upper Volta is the youngest of the French West African administrative units, and for long was a poor appendage of firstly the former French Soudan and latterly the Ivory Coast. Although high population densities should have made possible the cheaper supplying of modern amenities, the distribution of population hinders this, for even in the very high-density Mossi area it is dispersed. There are few nucleations of any size. Ouagadougou, the capital, has only 70,000 people and Bobo Dioulasso, the only other major town, has 52,000. About half the population are Mossi, who once ruled over most of the present republic from their traditional capitals of Ouahigouya and Ouagadougou. The Mossi resisted the penetration of modern influences and profited from their position on major trade routes between Mali and Songhay on the one hand, and Kong and Ashanti on the other. However, on the northeast, Gourma was invaded by Muslim pastoralists, whilst on the west there have been contacts between the numerous peoples, particularly the Bobo and Lobi, and the peoples of Mali. The political struggle

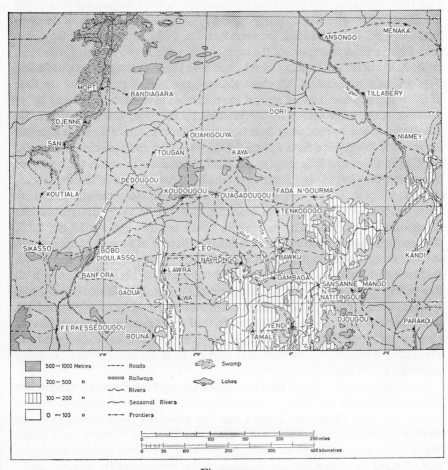

Figure 14.9

over the issue of federalism became a regional struggle between the Bobo and the Mossi of Ouagadougou, the former tending to favour federation with Mali, and the latter a loose association with the Ivory Coast and France. In January 1959 the Upper Volta joined the Mali federation, but left it a few weeks later to join the Conseil de l'Entente. Certainly, although there are important ethnic links with Mali, and there are many Mossi settlers there, most of the economic associations are with the Ivory Coast, which provides the only railway link and port.

However, economic difficulties have created greater problems than regional issues, and led in January 1966 to a military take-over when Lieutenant-Colonel Lamizana became head of state.

Ivory Coast

The Ivory Coast was the last of the former French West African colonies, other than Mauritania with its peculiarly Saharan orientation and its lack of development, to gain independence. Its president, Dr Félix Houphouët-Boigny, was probably the most successful of the overseas deputies to the French Parliament, for he held ministerial rank in several successive French Governments, including the de Gaulle government. He also welcomed the French proposals at the time of the referendum and voted against the federalist movement, supported by 99 per cent of the votes cast in the referendum by the Ivory Coast electorate. He was forced to some extent away from his opposition to federalism, and to a greater degree of independence from France, by the problems and possible adherence of the Upper Volta and Dahomey to the Mali federation. To retain their support he formed the Conseil de l'Entente at which representatives of the four states, the Ivory Coast, Upper Volta, Dahomey and Niger (subsequently joined by Togo) meet twice a year, and over which the chief minister of each state presides in turn for a year. Linked by means of a Customs union and a solidarity fund, the five states have tended to adopt Houphouët-Boigny as their chief spokesman, and the Ivory Coast has provided the chief financial support for the association. In December 1965 it was agreed to institute common nationality between all five member states, but this was soon repudiated by Houphouët-Boigny, who said that within the Ivory Coast 'double nationality' would apply only to Africans of brother countries already established in the Ivory Coast, and who voted in the elections of November 1965. No doubt he feared the political consequences of the arrival of large numbers of migrant workers from the less-developed member countries of the Entente.

The political leadership of the Ivory Coast amongst the Entente is the product not only of Houphouët-Boigny's ability, but of the new state's rapidly-increasing prosperity. Like Ghana the Ivory Coast has benefited from the boom in the tropical perennial crops, cocoa and coffee. For long the overseas trade of the Ivory Coast was hindered by policies favouring European plantations, which were limited in output and distribution, at the expense of the African smallholder, and were limited also by the lack of a suitable port. Once adequate support was given to peasant cultivators, as in Ghana, coffee and cocoa planting expanded enormously, and the completion of the Vridi Canal through the bar enclosing the Ebrié lagoon in 1950 made Abidjan a great port. In 1961 vessels totalling 5·1 million net tons entered the port of Abidjan, compared with a total of just over 10 million tons at the port of Dakar. In addition, Sassandra serves as a minor port for the south-western districts. Abidjan has grown into a great city of 257,500 people, linked with the mainland by its new combined rail and

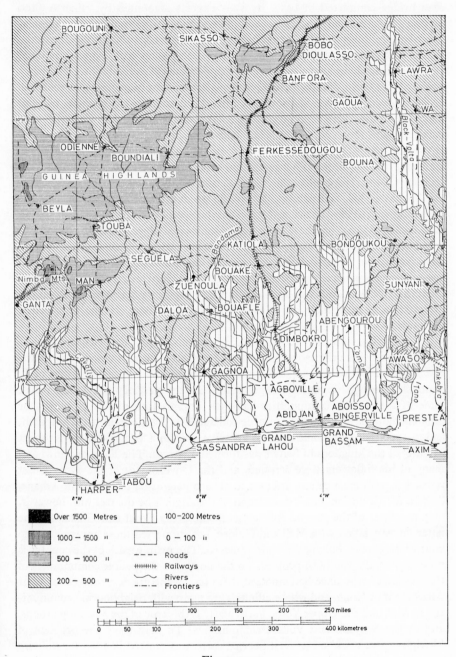

Figure 14.10

road bridge completed in 1957. By 1965 exports amounted by value to £100 million ($280 million) and imports to £85 million ($238 million) for a population of 3·9 millions. Of the imports about one-fifth was in foodstuffs, due to the raising of living standards and increased preoccupation with export cropping. Of the exports about 40 per cent by value came from coffee, and rather less than a quarter from cocoa. Timber provides about 20 per cent of exports and there are 41 sawmills in operation. Although France still dominates the overseas trade of the Ivory Coast, there is an increasing volume of traffic with the United States, particularly in the export of 'robusta' coffee. As in Ghana there is a fear of too great a concentration on a limited range of agricultural products, and attempts are being made to promote a more varied export traffic, and to 'industrialize' the economy. Other crops which are being developed include bananas, rubber, cotton, coconuts, kola, oil palms, tobacco and groundnuts. Electrical capacity has been increased nearly nine times by the building of a hydro-electric power station and dam at Ayamé on the Bia river. Factories, mainly at Abidjan, have been constructed to produce palm oil and margarine, to can fruit and fish and to manufacture soap, matches, textiles, plastics and aluminium sheet. Abidjan also has a motor car assembly plant and two shipyards. Gold mining has declined but the mining of diamonds has been developed, a beginning has been made on the exploitation of manganese ore at Grand Lahou, and there is some prospecting for bauxite.

The adoption of the motto 'Union, discipline and work', suggests the order of the problems which the Government feels are the most important. In the southeast of the Ivory Coast are the Agni, Ashanti and Baoulé peoples, who early established leadership and developed states. To the west of the Bandama river some of the smaller communities had little organization of either political or economic affairs, and had little outside contact. The Agni established a kingdom, and in 1960 there was some attempt to revive it when a 'provisional government in exile' of the kingdom of Sanwi was formed in Accra. The King of Sanwi and many of his followers were arrested, and the Government of the Ivory Coast refused to countenance any attempt to absorb part of its territory into Ghana, despite the Ghanaian ethnic association of the Agni. The quarrel was, however, only one facet of the general split between the Ivory Coast and Ghana, for the latter, in association with Mali and Guinea, has supported those governments to which Houphouët-Boigny was most opposed. The main wealth of the country is produced by the southern peoples. To the north are the poorer communities of the 'savannas' who once had amongst them one of the greatest markets of West Africa, that of Kong, and whose affinities are more with neighbouring communities in Mali and the Upper Volta. Particularly is this true of the Manding groups, and of the Sénoufo and Voltaic communities. To help solve the problem of 'discipline and work' a National Service corps was created in 1961 for military and citizenship training, including labour in diamond fields, palm plantations and rice schemes. The corps thus resembles the Builders Brigade of Ghana. Strong central government has been thought essential, and again the presidential form is preferred, with one-party government. The president may issue regulations, controls the armed forces, negotiates treaties, may appoint or dismiss ministers, and may ask the National Assembly to reconsider a bill, in which case it needs a two-thirds majority to pass. The Government party, the Parti Démocratique de la Côte d'Ivoire, is the creation of Houphouët-Boigny, just as the Convention People's Party of Ghana was Nkrumah's creation.

Nigeria

Nigeria is the most populous state in the whole of Africa, and although at present poor in income and value of export per head of population, has one of the most varied bases for economic development and high economic potential. Nigeria is also peculiar amongst the independent states in that it has a federal structure uniting the four regions of the North, West, Mid-West and East.[10] This federal form of government is especially interesting, for it illustrates, more aptly than any other form of government in West Africa, the regionalization of political issues and struggles in the new states. Perhaps because of this federal structure, Nigeria is one of the very few states of West Africa in which opposition parties have been tolerated, and may even have had some influence on legislation.

Nigeria's regions were the creation in part of struggles for power between rival African communities, in part the work of agents of the British Government and of the Royal Niger Company, and in part the results of modification in the light of later knowledge with regard to ethnic distributions. The boundaries were never satisfactorily delimited, and rarely satisfied ethnic considerations. Some further revision may yet occur.[11] Even before independence there was some call for the creation of new regions to satisfy the needs of large minority groups, notably for: 1) a Mid-West region consisting of the former eastern, mainly Benin, portions of Western Nigeria, and formed in May 1963; 2) a 'C.O.R.' region from Eastern Nigeria, consisting of the Calabar, Ogoja and Rivers Provinces;[12] 3) a Rivers State including the deltaic portions of both Eastern and Western Nigeria; 4) a Middle Belt region of the southern provinces of Northern Nigeria. The earliest attempts at political organization by Nigerians were on a national basis, the first being the Nigerian National Democratic Party formed in 1922, chiefly by Herbert Macaulay. In 1944 the Nigeria Union of Students formed the National Council of Nigeria and the Cameroons, and Herbert Macaulay became its first president and Dr Nnamdi Azikiwe its general secretary. The N.C.N.C. did not, however, satisfy the political aspirations of a number of Yoruba in the Western Region. Members of the Yoruba Tribal Union (Egbe Omo Oduduwa) helped to form a new political party in 1951, the Action Group led by Chief Obafemi Awolowo. In the same year a new political party, the Northern People's Congress, led by Alhaji Sir Ahmadu Bello, was formed in the Northern Region to promote the interests of Northerners. Regionalization was made an essential part of Nigeria's political structure by the Richards Constitution of 1946. Separate Houses of Assembly were created for each of the three

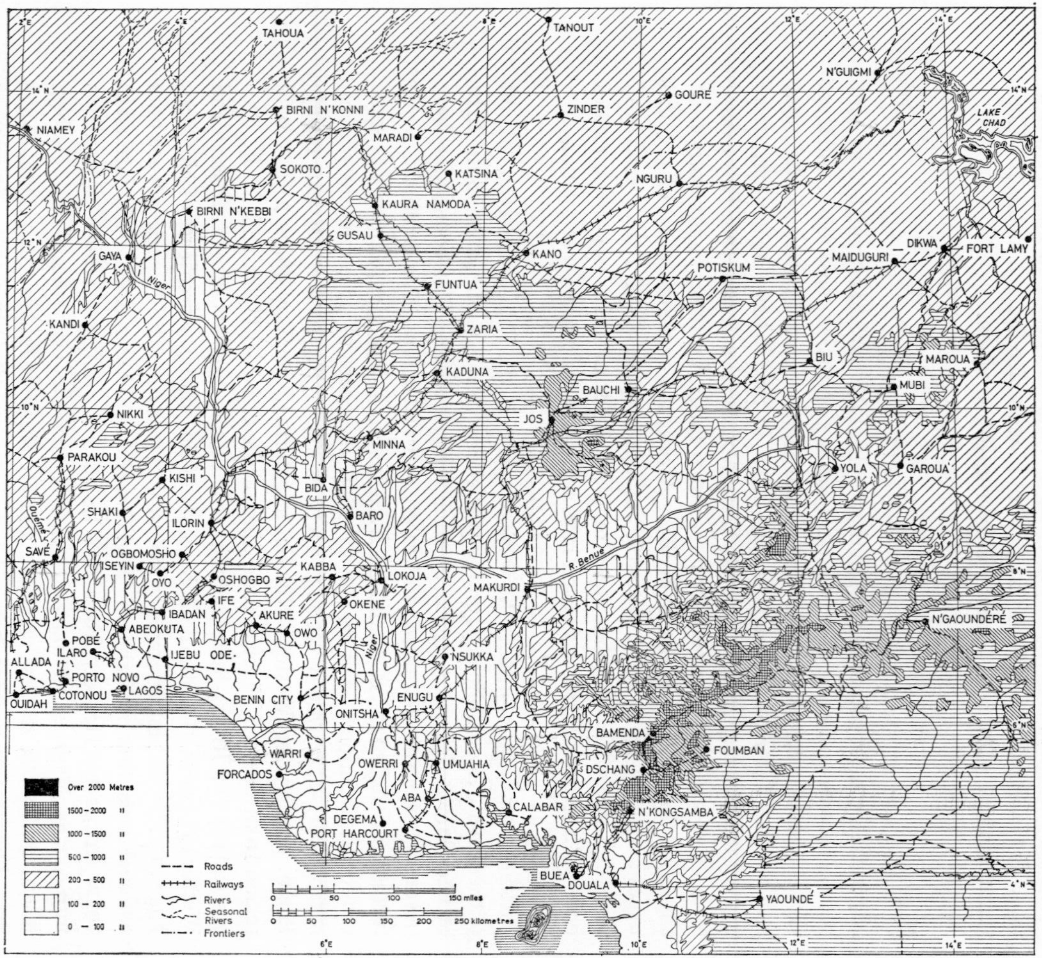
TAHOUA
TANOUT
N'GUIGMI
GOURÉ
ZINDER
BIRNI N'KONNI
NIAMEY
MARADI
LAKE CHAD
SOKOTO
KATSINA
NGURU
BIRNI N'KEBBI
KAURA NAMODA
GUSAU
KANO
GAYA
DIKWA
FORT LAMY
MAIDUGURI
POTISKUM
FUNTUA
KANDI
ZARIA
KADUNA
BIU
MAROUA
BAUCHI
MUBI
NIKKI
JOS
MINNA
PARAKOU
YOLA
GAROUA
KISHI
BIDA
BARO
SHAKI
ILORIN
SAVÉ
OGBOMOSHO
ISEYIN
OYO
KABBA
LOKOJA
OSHOGBO
MAKURDI
R. Benue
IFE
OKENE
IBADAN
AKURE
N'GAOUNDÉRÉ
ABEOKUTA
OWO
POBÉ
ILARO
IJEBU ODE
NSUKKA
ALLADA
PORTO NOVO
OUIDAH
COTONOU
LAGOS
BENIN CITY
ENUGU
ONITSHA
BAMENDA
FOUMBAN
WARRI
OWERRI
UMUAHIA
FORCADOS
DSCHANG
ABA
CALABAR
N'KONGSAMBA
DEGEMA
PORT HARCOURT
BUEA
DOUALA
YAOUNDÉ
Niger
Ouémé
Over 2000 Metres
1500 – 2000 "
1000 – 1500 "
500 – 1000 "
200 – 500 "
100 – 200 "
0 – 100 "
Roads
Railways
Rivers
Seasonal Rivers
Frontiers
0 50 100 150 miles
0 50 100 150 200 250 kilometres
2° E
4° E
6° E
8° E
10° E
12° E
14° E
14° N
12° N
10° N
8° N
6° N
4° N

Figure 14.11

regions, to link the National Authorities with the Legislative Council. A new constitution in 1951 replaced the Legislative Council by a House of Representatives, to which each regional House of Assembly elected unofficial members. In 1954 the Federation of Nigeria was created by the Lyttelton constitution, which gave the regional Governments enhanced responsibilities and made Lagos, formerly an integral part of the Western Region, federal territory. Finally on October 1st, 1960, Nigeria became fully independent with a Federal Government and three Regional Governments: the N.P.C. in the North, the Action Group in the West and the N.C.N.C. in the East. In the Federal elections of December 1959 the N.P.C. gained 142 seats, the N.C.N.C. and its ally, the Northern Elements Progressive Union, 89 seats, and the Action Group and its allies 73 seats. The N.P.C. formed a coalition with the N.C.N.C., and Alhaji Sir Abubakar Tafawa Balewa, the leader of the N.P.C. in the Federal House of Representatives, became the Prime Minister. Thus, in effect, despite early attempts to form national parties, tribal and regional interests prevailed, and the state of the parties roughly paralleled the numbers of the dominant tribal group in each of the regions (1952–3 census):

Hausa and Fulani (Northern Region)	8·5	millions
Ibo (Eastern Region)	4·9	„
Yoruba (Western Region)	4·5	„

The parallel is only very approximate because one must allow for a number of voting 'divergences'. For example, there has been strong Yoruba support for the N.C.N.C. in Ibadan Province, especially in the capital city of the Western Region. Within each region there has been a strong minority consisting mainly, although not entirely, of tribal opposition, which, as described above, has already expressed itself in the demand for the creation of new states. This opposition has frequently given strong support to the majority party of another region. Thus even a party so strongly founded on local sentiment as the Action Group could gain support in Eastern Nigeria from amongst non-Yorubas, and, in consequence, has tended in recent years to become more national and less regional in character. Some of the regional minorities are offshoots of majority tribal units elsewhere. Thus there is a large Yoruba minority in the Ilorin Province of the Northern Region, and a large Ibo minority in the Benin Province of the Mid-Western Region. These minorities in particular can obtain powerful extra-regional support and create major political problems. The recent anti-Ibo riots and mass killings of Ibos in Northern Nigeria were a product of local anti-minority sentiment, which may recur. It may perhaps be surprising that the two southern political parties did not have sufficient common interest to combine together against the N.P.C. until 1964. Immediately after the 1959 election such a coalition was attempted, but it would have meant the sacrifice of N.C.N.C. interests in the Western Region, and in consequence was abandoned.

The Action Group was further weakened not only by the territorial reduction of the Western Region, but by its removal from power in the Region, and by the imprisonment of its leader on a charge of treason. The Region was subsequently governed by the Nigerian National Democratic Party led by Chief Akintola, and linked with the N.P.C. in the Nigerian National Alliance. The N.P.C. repudiated its alliance with the N.C.N.C., which turned at last to the Action Group to join forces, also re-animating its old ally in Northern Nigeria, the N.E.P.U., to form collectively the United Progressive Grand Alliance. Further changes in the situation were the strengthening of a Northern opposition party, the United Middle Belt Congress, and some united trade union opposition in the south which led to a general strike. Because Federal representation depended on regional population totals, successive census figures in the early 1960s were 'adjusted' (see reference [7], Chapter 1, p. 62). The 1965 Federal elections were boycotted in the East and gave surprising results in the West, a situation culminating in the deterioration of law and order in Western Nigeria. In January 1966 members of the Nigerian Army carried out a coup d'état, killing or arresting many of the leading political figures, including Sir Abubakar, the Federal Premier, Chief Akintola, the Premier of Western Nigeria, and Sir Ahmadu Bello. Military governors were appointed in all regions, and a Supreme Military Council headed by General Ironsi was established to administer the new Federal Military Government. General Ironsi claimed that in the new order of things there should be no place for regionalism and tribal consciousness, nor for the subjugation of personal service to personal aggrandizement, nepotism and corruption. Another military coup, in July–August 1966, however, resulted in the assassination of Ironsi and other leaders. The new head of Government, Colonel Gowon, a Tiv, whilst supporting the Federal structure, has been less forthright in condemning regionalism.

Nigeria is not the largest state of West Africa in area, but its 357,000 square miles (1,025,000 sq km) contain the greatest extent of agricultural land, and its 55·6 millions form the largest population of any state of Africa. In 1965 the value of exports was £268 million ($750 million) and of imports £275 million ($770 million), that is overseas trade was worth about twice as much as that of Ghana, but for nearly eight times the population. Each person's share of overseas trade in Nigeria was thus only about a quarter that in Ghana. Again, the national income estimate of £25 ($70) per head for 1956–7 was approximately one-third of that in Ghana. Nigeria's relative poverty is not evenly distributed, however, for the southern regions are more prosperous than the Northern Region. The most valuable exports in 1965 were oil, £68·1 million ($190 million), cocoa, £42·5 million ($119 million), groundnuts, £38 million ($106 million), oil palm produce, £40 million ($112 million), and tin metal, £15 million ($42 million). These exports contributed to the well-being of 29·8 million people in the Northern Region, 12·4 millions in the Eastern Region, 10·3 millions in the Western Region, 2·5 millions in the Mid-West Region, and 0·7 million in Lagos. One may compare budget revenues for 1963–1964.[12]

	Total £'000	Per head
Northern Region	24,363	£0·82 ($2.30)
Western and Mid-Western Regions	22,661	£1·68 ($4.70)
Eastern Region	21,587	£1·74 ($4.87)

On a revenue per head basis the Eastern Region is today the richest of the four major divisions of Nigeria. In 1958–9 it was well below the Western and Mid-Western Regions. Oil and natural gas are mainly responsible for this, and the Western Region has been adversely affected by the dramatic fall in cocoa prices. Mineral developments play an important role in regional finances for, although mineral dues are paid to the federal government, the regional governments receive a return on the earnings, and also enjoy the revenue from local taxation of mineral workers' earnings. However, the Yoruba portion of the Western Region, despite its lack so far of mineral wealth, has not only the entire production of cocoa, the crop which until recently has produced the highest cash return per grower, but is an exporter to the Northern Region of kola and palm oil, and an increasingly important producer of such high-value foodstuffs locally as rice. Moreover, it has the best railway, road and telephone network in Nigeria, and, with its proximity to Lagos, the lowest transport costs to port.

Nigeria's export production would appear to depend heavily on agriculture, although oil has now become the chief overseas currency earner. The export of oil from the Eastern Region began in 1958, and in 1962 some 3·3 million tons were produced. In 1959 oil in important quantities was also discovered in the Mid-Western Region, and exploration is proceeding in several other locations. The main problems are concerned with transport. The chief oil fields, so far exploited, are in or near the delta, with its sand bars at the mouths of the rivers and with its narrow tortuous creeks. Tanker size is therefore very limited until an ocean terminal can be built. Natural gas is being exploited in the Eastern Region and a small export in liquefied form has begun. Small industrial development is proceeding, comprehending a variety of manufactures, including plywood, textiles, cement, asbestos-cement sheet, palm oil, soap, margarine, cigarettes, metal containers, aluminium sheet and utensils, canning and bottling, brewing, engineering, including vehicle and cycle assembly, boat-building, tyre re-treading, paint, pharmaceuticals, and plastics. At Emene near Enugu in the Eastern Region an iron and steel rolling mill has been built, and an aluminium rolling mill at Port Harcourt. At present scrap metal has to be used in the Enugu iron and steel mill, but it is intended eventually to smelt Nigerian ores using Enugu coal converted into coke by a special process. The development plans for 1955–62 provided for a capital expenditure of £339 million ($950 million), of which 78 per cent was provided from internal sources. Of the planned expenditure 30 per cent was on roads and railways, including a bridge over the Niger between Onitsha and Asaba, and a new railway from Kuru, south of Jos, to Maiduguri in Bornu. This line is expected to promote agricultural development in Bauchi and Bornu, but one should note that the existing tarred road from Jos to Maiduguri does not carry a heavy volume of traffic, and may prove a competitor for some commodities. The first National Plan of 1962, intended to accelerate economic growth and increase Nigeria's 'control over her destiny', emphasizes the importance of certain key projects, particularly the Kainji Dam and hydro-electric power scheme on the Niger, the most expensive item (£68 million ($190 million)) of a total anticipated expenditure of £677 million ($1900 million).[13] Other items include the Niger bridge at Onitsha, the second bridge linking Lagos Island with Iddo, new berths at Apapa and Port Harcourt and the modernization of the railways.

Each Region has a Production Development Board to promote new enterprises. Numerous schemes to improve agricultural practice have been promoted. In the Western Region, for example, as part of the 1960-5 development plan, 13 co-operative farm settlements and 5 farm institutes have been established with an initial labour force of 700 selected trainees. Originally each settlement was to be of 50 holdings totalling 1500 acres (600 hectares) and was to expand by stages to 200 holdings totalling 6000 acres (2400 hectares) and supplied with services and amenities held in common. Now sites are to be up to 8000 acres (3200 hectares) with holdings of 20 acres (8 hectares) for tree cultivation and of 70 acres (28 hectares) for field crops. Model villages supplied with tap water have been built. Costs, however, have been high – some £2000 to £3000 ($5600–$8400) per settler, recently reduced to some £1700 ($4760). In the Eastern Region, 5 group farms have been organized by co-operative societies. Nigeria's expansion has received considerable encouragement from the United States which in 1962 provided aid worth about £80 million ($224 million) over 5 years, the largest aid programme at that date for any African country south of the Sahara. There are at present some 180,000 acres of government plantations and ranches in Southern Nigeria, together with some new ranches and agricultural schemes in Northern Nigeria.

Nigeria's greatest economic problem is the development of the southern provinces of the Northern Region – the 'Middle Belt'. Despite early British contact and the use of a river routeway, the Middle Belt has the lowest productivity of export commodities and the lowest incomes of any large portion of Nigeria. Road and railway linking the richer northern and southern high population density regions must therefore cross relatively empty country, with little or no passenger traffic or freight for trains or lorries. Investment in the Middle Belt can bring only small or delayed returns, when there are more promising enterprises for investment elsewhere. Yet, here and there, are some large concentrations of populations, such as the Nupe, and there are local medical, educational and economic problems. With the need to develop the country, and to obtain the best return on investment, Nigeria may well have to concentrate most of her capital resources elsewhere. Yet in the long run some development will have to be undertaken, and the heavy cost of long communications with the northernmost provinces must be borne. The NEDECO scheme for water communication (see pp. 553 and 615) may provide the answer, but must involve great capital outlay.

Nigeria's attainment of independence involved, however, the resolution of the

Cameroons question. Whilst the Northern Cameroons had been administered as a part of the Northern Region, the Southern Cameroons (1961 population: 840,000) had attained separate status in 1954. Previously representatives from the Southern Cameroons had attended the Eastern Region House of Assembly, but their territory was remote geographically, ethnically and economically, without even a satisfactory road link with Nigeria. Moreover, there has been some anti-Ibo feeling in the Southern Cameroons. In 1953 the Cameroons members of the N.C.N.C. left the party, and founded their own organization, the Kamerun National Congress, whose title hearkened back to the German period of occupation. In 1955 the leaders of the ultra-nationalist French Cameroons party, the Union des Populations du Cameroun, fled to Kumba in the British Cameroons, and their policy of re-unification found support also from J. N. Foncha, who created his own party, the Kamerun National Democratic Party. In 1957 the U.P.C. leaders were deported from the British Cameroons which left the K.N.D.P. as the sole protagonists of re-unification. The K.N.C. which formed the Government in 1958 advocated integration with Nigeria after independence, and in the elections of January 1959 was swept out of office, and replaced by the K.N.D.P. In April 1959 the United Nations suggested a plebiscite to decide the political future of the Cameroons. This plebiscite, held on February 11th, 1961, in both Northern and Southern Cameroons, resulted in a vote in favour of joining Nigeria in the North and of joining the Cameroun Republic (formerly French Cameroons) in the South. The former Southern Cameroons are now known as Western Cameroun within the Cameroun Federation.

Mauritania[14]

The Islamic Republic of Mauritania was the last of the French dependencies in West Africa to obtain independence, on November 28th, 1960. In area it is the third largest state of West Africa with 419,000 square miles (1,085,000 sq km), but it is the smallest in population with only one million, and the poorest in overseas trade and probably in national income. Harbour shortage is a serious problem in effecting economic development. Most of Mauritania is Saharan, and settled population exists mainly on the northern bank of the Senegal in the region known as the Chemama, and in the oases and on the pastures of the neighbouring Brakna and Trarza. Except in the extreme south cultivation depends on ground or sub-surface water, and most of the millet consumed in Mauritania comes from the Chemama. The plains of the Trarza and Brakna consist of clay stretches (aftout) and stable dunes (sbar). They are occupied only seasonally by pastoralists and gum collectors. Pastoralism plays a very important part in the economy, with an estimated one million cattle and 5·5 million sheep and goats. Gathering of gum arabic from acacias provided until recently Mauritania's chief export industry. Fibre is also collected from the trees for ropes and nets used by local fishermen. The fishing grounds off the Mauritanian coast are amongst the richest in the world, although little fished by Mauritanians. The surf coast has only one

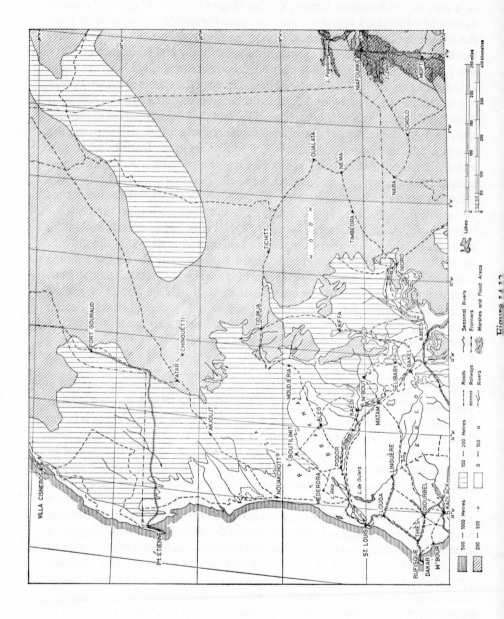

Figure VI.12

suitable anchorage, the Baie du Lévrier, where in 1905 Port Etienne was constructed to provide a safe anchorage for the fishing fleets. At the port fish is both dried and canned, and some fresh fish is flown out by air. The main problem in developing the port has been fresh-water supply. The Senegalese niayes or fresh-water lakes of the coastal regions, are replaced in Mauritania by saline mud flats, the sebkhas remaining from former lagoons. Formerly water had to be obtained by distillation from the sea or by import from France. Today, however, it is brought from Boulanouar, 56 miles (90 km) to the north-east, on the railway to Fort Gouraud. The distribution of water resources in Mauritania has governed population distribution and even affected its political evolution under French control. The uplands of Adrar, Tagant, Assaba and Affollé receive more abundant rainfall, and, wherever ground-water seepage has made possible oases, vast palm groves have been created, such as those of Chinguétti, Ouadane, Atar, Tidjikja, Tichitt, Oulata and Néma. With the major concentrations of population in the Senegal valley, at least during the dry season, and with a problem of water supplies and communications in any location to the north, the French established the former Mauritanian capital at St Louis in Senegal.

Mauritania is the one dominantly non-Negro state of West Africa, for some 800,000 of the population are Moors, for the most part leading a nomadic existence. The state is dominated in its economy not by agriculture, but by pastoralism and gathering, with an estimated 10 million sheep and goats, 1·5 million cattle and 0·5 million camels. The majority of its people are linked ethnically with the peoples of North Africa. The Negro minority, the descendants mainly of former slaves, are engaged chiefly in cultivation. The long-established connections with North Africa, and particularly with Morocco, have led to the claim by the Government of the latter that Mauritania was formerly a part of the Moroccan State known as the Chenguit, and should be returned.

In 1960 budget receipts were £1·5 million ($4·2 million) or approximately £2·4 ($6.70) per head, a high taxation rate for so poor a country, but expenditures were nearly three times receipts. Mauritania so lags behind other West and North African states that a heavy expenditure is essential in order to make the state economically viable. Several small-scale dams have been built to increase irrigation facilities, more watering points have been supplied for livestock, firebreaks have been built and extensive campaigns organized against locusts and the quelea bird or Sudan dioch. Most important of all, however, are the enormous mining developments which promise an economic revolution. Of the 1963–6 Development Plan costing some £40 million ($112 million), one third has been allotted to mining. The two most important mining developments are for iron ore at Fort Gouraud and copper ore at Akjoujt. The Fort Gouraud scheme is much the larger, and will involve a total estimated expenditure of nearly £60 million ($168 million). The deposits are being exploited by a consortium – the Société Anonyme des Mines de Fer de Mauritanie or MIFERMA – of 51 per cent French interests, 20 per cent British, 15 per cent Italian and 5 per cent German. In addition the World Bank has provided a £23·5 million ($66 million) loan.

A mining town to house some 6000 people has been built 15 miles (24 km) east of Fort Gouraud, and the ores are being quarried from deposits comparatively easy to work and totalling some 215 million tons of haematite, averaging 63 per cent iron content, in the Kedia d'Idjill mountains. The deposit is in a massif 18 miles (29 km) long and rising 2000 feet (600 metres) above Fort Gouraud. To export the ores a 419-mile (1085-km) railway, skirting the boundary of Rio de Oro, was constructed to Port Etienne by 1963 – the route is not difficult except near Adrar where a tunnel has been dug through the Choum cliffs and near the Baie du Lévrier where live dunes are crossed. The Spanish Sahara is avoided, partly because of political complications, and partly because its port of Villa Cisneros, although nearer than Port Etienne, would need considerable dredging to accommodate the ore boats. Output is already in excess of 5 million tons of ore a year. At Akjoujt, reserves of some 18 million tons of sulphuretted and oxidized ores of copper, also containing gold, are to be worked by the Société des Mines de Cuivre de Mauritanie or MICUMA (50 per cent French, 25 per cent Mauritanian and 25 per cent private shareholders). The ore export has necessitated the building of a new port 6 miles (10 km) south of Port Etienne, where a pier has been constructed having 44 feet (13 metres) depth of water alongside. The population of Port Etienne was about 1200 in 1958. By 1962 with the development of a railway terminal and mineral wharf it had risen to 10,000.[15]

Other mineral possibilities include iron and copper ores at Legleitat el Khder, 12 miles (19 km) south-east of Akjoujt, iron at Tamagot, 30 miles (48 km) south-west of Akjoujt, copper between Akjoujt and Atar, and tungsten and copper at Tézélé Tarrinkout, 30 miles (48 km) east of Akjoujt. Exploration for oil is taking place in the geological basin of the Senegal river and in the Tindouf and Taoudenni synclines. The salt industry, once the chief mineral enterprise of Mauritania, has now declined with the loss of many of its southern markets to imported refined salt.

Mauritania is a republic. The president, who is elected for five years, determines policy and appoints ministers. The National Assembly is elected for five years, but only legislates on matters which do not fall within the presidential powers of regulation by decree. The governing party consists of a single national movement, the Parti du Peuple Mauritanien, created from a coalition of four parties. In 1957 Nouakchott, near the coast and some 200 miles (320 km) north of the mouth of the Senegal river, was designated the capital city. The choice of site was made partly because of relative coolness near the coast, partly because with the economic developments taking place in the north a southern location had become eccentric, despite the importance of the Chemama, and partly because tradition holds that it was near Nouakchott that the 'ribat' or fortified monastery of Yahya ibn Ibrahim was situated, from which the Almoravid movement began.

Sierra Leone

Sierra Leone attained independence on April 27th, 1961. The majority party is the Sierra Leone People's Party formed from a coalition of two movements, one representing the interests mainly of the former Colony (now the Western Area) and the other the interests of the three Provinces of the interior. Opposition is expressed by the All Peoples' Congress and the Sierra Leone Progressive Independence Movement Alliance, which won 17 out of 56 seats in the 1962 election, but have since lost some members to the Government party.

Sierra Leone was one of the oldest of Britain's African colonies, with the first railway and the first college of higher education in British West Africa. The social and political position of the peoples of the Colony, that is the Freetown Peninsula, was far in advance of that of other British West African peoples by the beginning of this century, and Freetown itself for long provided the chief British naval base in West Africa. Thus Sierra Leone, like its neighbour Liberia, has a longer continuous history of close contact with lands outside Africa than many adjoining territories, and, again like Liberia, the chief factor in this history has been the founding of a settlement for freed slaves. Whereas in Liberia the new colony was soon given independence, in Sierra Leone the colony remained with Britain, providing a base for the anti-slavery vessels which brought fresh recruits to the colony's labour force. Here developed during the 19th century a detribalized community, the 'Creoles', today numbering nearly 100,000 out of a total population of 2·2 millions. Their traditions are as much American and European as they are African, and they have held a privileged position not only in Sierra Leone, but in British West Africa. Because of this privileged position and their fear of being swamped by hinterland voters, the Creole community has tended to oppose the extension of the franchise to the Protectorate or hinterland. This factor has been a major hindrance to the attainment of independence. The emergence of the Creole community meant a lack of accord, as in Liberia, between the interests of the Colony and the interests of the Protectorate. The situation was worsened by the Hut Tax Wars of 1898, in which many Creoles lost their lives. Sir Milton Margai, the first Prime Minister, was by origin a Mende from the Protectorate, but his party gained Creole support, and tried to unite the different major elements. The railway reached the eastern boundary of the Colony in 1899 and Pendembu in 1908, and made the organization of revolt in the hinterland much more difficult.[16] Sierra Leone has extensive mineral resources, and huge areas are available for the propagation of oil palms, cocoa and rubber, and yet her economic development has lagged markedly behind that of either Ghana or Nigeria, and this despite the early building of a railway and the possession of the best deep-water harbour in West Africa. Mineral workings did not begin until 1929, and little was done between the wars to develop the peasant production of export produce (see p. 655).

Minerals provide three-quarters by value of export produce, and of these diamonds are the most important, with an output in 1965 worth some £11·4

million ($32 million). Before the formation of a Government Diamond Office
and marketing organization in 1959, the whole country formed one concession
for the Sierra Leone Selection Trust. This combine was, however, unable to

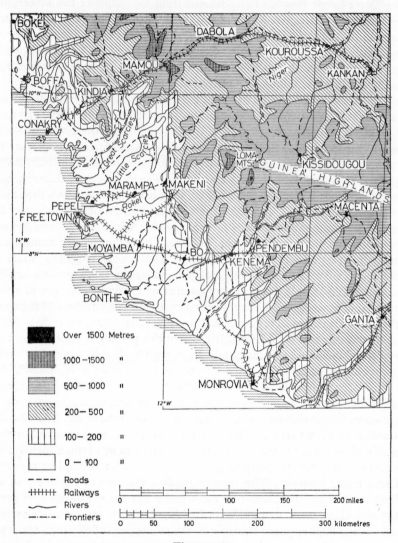

Figure 14.13

prevent illicit digging and the smuggling of diamonds over the border into Liberia
to an estimated value by 1958–9 of some £10 million ($28 million). In 1955 the
Sierra Leone Selection Trust reduced its concession area to 450 square miles
(1165 sq km) in return for £1·6 million compensation. The Government proceeded to license private diggers in the surrendered area. By 1960 the licensed

diggers produced some £10·9 million of diamonds for the legal market, and the
S.L.S.T. produced £4·4 million. The latter pays a much higher proportion of its
earnings in tax than do the licensed diggers, but on the other hand there can be
little doubt that the new policy has produced an increase in output and some
diversion of export away from the illegal market. The iron ore export by private
railway and port at Pepel was worth some £5 million ($14 million), leaving
£4 million of export value amongst the remaining produce: palm kernels,
cocoa, coffee, piassava, chrome ore, kola nuts and ginger. There is also a small
production of gold and platinum and there are possibilities for mining asbestos
and corundum. Minor agricultural exports include groundnuts, benniseed and
copra. The Produce Marketing Board is financing a £2 million project to develop
an oil palm plantation. At Freetown a new fishing base has been built to increase
the tuna catch. There is very little industrial development – chiefly palm oil, rice
and timber milling. The market for manufactured goods is still very small. The
only town of any size is Freetown with 128,000 people in 1963, rather less than
half of whom are Creole. Bo, the next largest town, has only 20,000 people.
Road mileage in 1957 was only 2983 miles (4801 km), with 140 miles (225 km)
of tarred surface to serve an area of 28,000 square miles (72,500 sq km). As with
the governments of other states in West Africa badly in need of capital for development, the Government of Sierra Leone has tended to adopt a policy of accord
with the former metropolitan power, and looks to Britain for financial assistance.
The British Government offered immediately £7·5 million ($21 million) to
assist in anticipated increase in expenditure over the 1961–5 period. On March
21st, 1967, a state of martial law was declared, and a new military government
established, advised by a civilian council.

Gambia

On attaining independence on February 18th, 1965, Gambia became the smallest
state in Africa, both in area and in population. Economically the country is not
viable, and Britain has to contribute to its revenue a sum of nearly £10 ($28) per
head for the period up to June 30th, 1967. Gambia is by no means unproductive.
It was once the richest of Britain's West African possessions, with its export of
groundnuts by its navigable highway extending for vessels of 6 feet (2 metres)
draught some 300 miles (480 km) into the hinterland. Its population of 320,000
plus some 10,000 seasonal immigrants supported in 1964 an export trade worth
nearly £4·3 million ($12 million) and an import trade worth £3·2 million
($9 million). 'Basically, however, it is the small size and relatively very uniform
character of the Gambia, and the separation of the navigable river from its
natural hinterland, that makes economic advance so difficult.'[17] Gambia is
poorly endowed with natural resources and her export trade consists entirely of
groundnuts. With the decline in world oil-seed prices in recent years, the
colony's financial position has been undermined, and the price paid to growers
has been well above sale price in overseas markets. Economic planning hopes to

achieve more efficient groundnut production, greater use of ploughs, and diversification of the economy. The new crops however – cotton, sisal, citrus and tobacco – must all enter highly competitive markets. Gambia has an unfortunate record of failure of development schemes including the Colonial Development Corporation's mechanized rice scheme at Sapu, its poultry and fisheries schemes, the ilmenite quarrying project, and oil drilling.

Gambia and Senegal were joined together in the British colony of Senegambia for 20 years, until the Treaty of Versailles in 1783. Union with Senegal may seem to be the logical solution to Gambia's economic problems, perhaps the only solution for the adequate use of the river and development of its basin, but there are many other problems especially those resulting from changes of import duties, changes in trading links from Britain to the Common Market, and Gambian insistence that the territory could only join a federation. The lower duties in Gambia, compared with those of Senegal, have encouraged the migration of the strange farmers and a local trans-frontier trade. Although the purchase price of groundnuts in Senegal is higher than in Gambia, due to favourable selling conditions in the French market, the prices of goods are higher still, and the franc C.F.A. has been at a discount in Gambia.[18] Yet with the price differential, the Gambian Government must pay its growers more than sale price in the export markets or lose sales in Bathurst and traffic on the river. In November 1960, for example, the price to growers was raised to £27 a ton only by using money which should have gone to development funds. Even so it was still £3 a ton below the price in Senegal.

The remaining colonies

The territories which have not yet attained independence are all small in both area and population. They are significantly all either Spanish or Portuguese, for Spain and Portugal, the two oldest imperial powers, have most consistently pursued a policy of assimilation, and have most effectively prevented or hampered independence movements. However, poor economic development may be the result of backwardness in political development for only a portion of these territories. It is, for example, certainly not true of Fernando Po nor of São Tomé and Príncipe, which all enjoy a considerable overseas trade and, compared with other West African countries, have been well provided with medical and social services.

PORTUGUESE GUINEA

With an area of 14,000 square miles (36,000 sq km) and a population of 565,000 in 1963, Portuguese Guinea is the largest of the colonial territories reamining in West Africa. Its administration, as that of other Portuguese territories in Africa, depends on the ultimate authority of the Overseas Minister advised by the Overseas Council, and the more limited power of the Governor General advised by

the legislative and government councils. The economy is based on peasant cultivation, and depends on the production of swamp rice for local food supplies,
and groundnuts, oil palm produce and copra for export. The groundnut crop is
the chief export and amounts to some 50,000 tons, of which some is crushed
locally and the oil and cake exported. Exports in 1963 were valued at some £2·1
million ($5·9 million) and imports at £5·1 million ($14·3 million). The budget
revenue was less than £3 ($8·40) per head. The economy was a net drain on

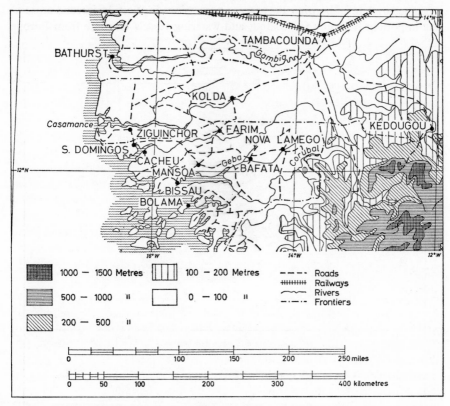

Figure 14.14

Portugal and will remain so with investments of only £1 million in the first
5-year plan (1953–8) and £2½ million in the second. The three rivers, the
Cacheu, Geba and Corubal, provide the main transport routes and there are
only 2000 miles (3200 km) of earth roads. There is no mineral production and
only a very little industrial development. Over 8000 of the population are 'civilized', including whites, those of mixed blood (mainly from the Cape Verde
Islands), Indians and assimilated Africans. Only this 'civilized' population has
full citizenship. Three-quarters of the assimilated population lives in the two
towns of Bissau (22,000), the capital, and Bolama. Independence movements
have developed, the largest of which is the African Independence Party, which

is also the major independence movement in Angola, and which is based partly in Conakry.

CAPE VERDE ISLANDS

Approximately 310 miles (500 km) west of Cape Verde are the Cape Verde Islands, today mostly poverty stricken, but formerly enjoying administrative importance over neighbouring Portuguese possessions in West Africa, and possessing important harbours for coaling and watering vessels en route from Europe

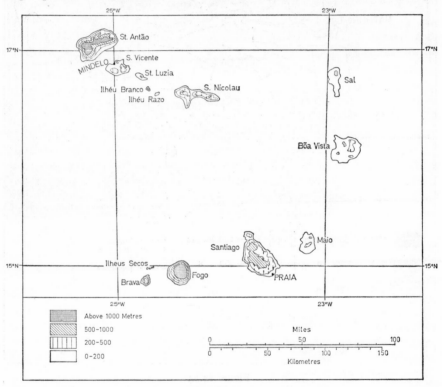

Figure 14.15

for either South America or West Africa. With a population of 202,000 on a total area of 1560 square miles (4040 sq km), the islands are today grossly overcrowded. Moreover, the annual rate of increase is estimated at the remarkably high figure of 3·6 per cent. The overseas trade in 1964 showed a large deficit; exports were worth only £0·3 million ($0·8 million) and imports were £2·5 million ($7 million). The largest and most populous island is Santiago, with its seat of Government for the whole group at Praia. Like the other islands it is, however, extremely dry. The harmattan occasionally makes itself felt and droughts are frequent, in some of the islands for periods of up to three years.

Salt is made from sea water, particularly on Bõa Vista, but by 1958 the traffic had been reduced to only one-third of its total two years before. Coffee, oil-seeds, bananas and tunny are also exported. Porto Grande on São Vicente was once a major coaling port for British steamers, and is still used by some vessels sailing to South America. Little can be grown on São Vicente, however, partly because of exposure to north-east gales, and food must be imported from São Antão, which has only poor landing places. The island of Fogo has been the subject of a study by Ribeiro[19], who has commented on the numerous occurrences of famine and the fluctuations in population totals. Emigration has been chiefly to other islands, to the African coast, and to the United States. A large part of the surface consists of bare lava, scoria and cinders, and most of the springs are on the cliff edges in uninhabitable sites. Irrigation is impossible. The social ideal is emigration to the United States, but most of the population is too poor to afford it.

SÃO TOMÉ AND PRÍNCIPE

The two islands of São Tomé and Príncipe form a province of Portugal overseas, all that remains of formerly more extensive possessions in the Bights of Benin and Biafra, including Fernando Po and Annobon, and the former fort of St John the Baptist at Ouidah in Dahomey. São Tomé and Príncipe, with a total area of only 372 square miles (963 sq km), support a population of 64,000 giving the remarkably high population density of 172 per square mile (66 per sq km). Of the total population, over 55,000 are African, including nearly 30,000 contract labourers, chiefly from Angola and Moçambique, and usually serving four to five years. The remaining Africans are the descendants of freed slaves. This small population produced an overseas trade which in 1964 was worth £2·0 million ($5·6 million) in exports and £1·8 million ($5·0 million) in imports. About three-quarters of exports by value consists of cocoa, which has declined considerably in production since its peak in 1920. As trees, planted in the last century and at the beginning of this century, have gone out of production, difficulty has been experienced in replanting, and there is no suitable new land. In the lowlands cocoa plantations exist side by side with plantings of oil palms, which now account for some 15 per cent of exports. Coconuts on the coasts provide some copra, and on both islands coffee plantations exist above cocoa, whose upper limit is at about 1400 feet (425 metres) above sea-level. Attempts are being made to promote economic recovery and diversify crop resources. Since 1956 studies have been made of the physical features and of 'agricultural aptitudes'.[20] The islands form one of the last preserves not only of colonial government, but of the plantation system controlled by overseas landlords or companies on which the economy is completely dependent.

Ouidah, now part of Dahomey, was a more curious preserve, for it consisted of 11 acres (4½ hectares) of territory forming the site of an old fort in what saw once the greatest slave exporting port of West Africa. In July 1961 the

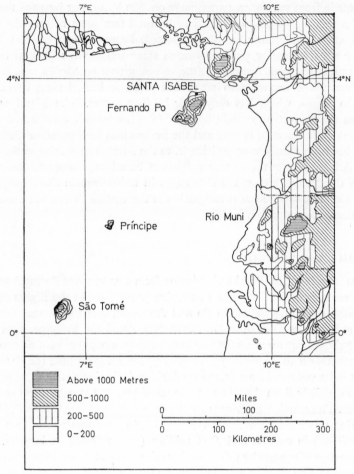

Figure 14.16

government of Dahomey requested its evacuation and its occupants, the 'resident' and his secretary, accordingly set fire to the building.

THE ISLANDS OF SPANISH GUINEA

Spanish Guinea includes Rio Muni together with Corisco and the two Elobeys, or continental Guinea, which is outside the scope of this study, and the islands of Fernando Po and Annobon. Of these Fernando Po, with an area of 779 square miles (2017 sq km) and a 1960 population which may be estimated at some 64,000 is much the largest. Annobon, the next largest island, is only 6½ square miles (17 sq km) and had an estimated 1960 population of only some 1600. Fernando Po has a large immigrant labour force, mainly of young Nigerian males. In 1950 the census showed that there were 23,306 temporary immigrant Africans (today possibly 35,000) who had entered as contract labour to work on the cocoa and coffee plantations. In 1961 after negotiations with the Nigerian Government the wages of contract labourers were more than doubled, and the pass system controlling their movements was abolished. The sedentary African community in 1950 consisted of some 14,700 people, 11,700 of whom were of the island's original Bubi stock, and 3000 of whom were the descendants of former slaves and were known as 'Portos', forming a community similar in character to that of the 'Creoles' of Freetown. The 'Creoles' of Santa Isabel have indeed an origin very similar to those of Freetown, for they are mostly descended from slaves liberated by British warships when Santa Isabel was the British naval base of Port Clarence. In addition there were some 2400 people of European origin, chiefly government officials and plantation managers or owners. Spanish Guinea is an overseas province of Spain, sending representatives to the Spanish Parliament. It has therefore no independent existence. In December 1960 three of the six members from Guinea in the Spanish Cortes were Africans, but these were 'emancipados', i.e. Spanish citizens. Santa Isabel, with a 1960 population of 20,000, is capital of the two provinces of Rio Muni and Fernando Po. It is the centre of island administration and has the chief harbour and airport (improved to accommodate jet aircraft in 1962). Figures for Spanish Guinea as a whole in 1964 showed that the total population of 246,000 maintained an overseas trade worth £11·6 million ($32·5 million) in exports and £5·5 million ($15·4 million) in imports. The budget receipts totalled only about £1·5 million or just over £6 ($16.80) per head. Of the exports cocoa provided the chief item, mainly from Fernando Po, and coffee from the mainland and the two islands provided the next most important item. The third export product was timber from the mainland. The proportions of overseas trade with Spain by value were over 90 per cent of exports and 60 per cent of imports. It has been suggested that without the protected Spanish market cocoa production on Fernando Po would be severely reduced, because it would be unable to compete with the Ghanaian product.[21]

BIBLIOGRAPHICAL NOTES

[1] For a valuable distinction see G. W. Robinson, The Geographic Region: Form and Function, Scottish Geographical Magazine, 69, 1953, pp. 49–58.

[2] See D. Austin, West Africa and the Commonwealth, London, 1957.
Note that in 1965 the Rhodesian crisis resulted in only eight states breaking off diplomatic relations with Britain, whilst not a single country withdrew from the Commonwealth.

[3] For useful political reviews and summaries see K. Post, The New States of West Africa, London, 1964; R. Adloff, West Africa: The French-Speaking Nations, New York, 1964; Smith Hempstone, The New Africa, London, 1961.

[4] G. H. T. Kimble, Tropical Africa, vol. 2, New York, 1960, pp. 194–5.

[5] W. Birmingham and A. G. Ford, Planning and Growth in Rich and Poor Countries, London, 1966.

[6] Manshard notes the separation of Ahafo from Ashanti, with which it was formerly closely linked, by the creation of a Brong-Ahafo region with Sunyani as capital: W. Manshard, Die Stadt Kumasi (Ghana), *Erdkunde*, **15**, 1961, pp. 161–80.

[7] See p. 572. For a detailed study of Ghana's economy see W. Birmingham, I. Neustadt and E. N. Omaboe (eds), *A Study of Contemporary Ghana*, vol. I, The Economy of Ghana, contributors T. Killick, E. N. Omaboe and R. Szereszewski, London, 1966. For a general account of Ghana see: E. A. Boateng, *A Geography of Ghana*, 2nd ed., London, 1966.

[8] Sekou Touré claims to have instituted forced labour, see R. C. Good, Sekou Touré's Guinea, in *Africa Report*, vol. 5, no. 10, October, 1960, p. 5.

[9] The Ewe conference of 1946 which pressed for union was held at Accra.
The problems immediately before independence are discussed in J. S. Coleman, Togoland, *International Conciliation*, No. 509, New York, 1956.

[10] The Southern Cameroons were administered as a federal territory from 1954 to 1961. The Northern Cameroons are administered as a part of the Northern Region. The four regions existed until 1967 when twelve new states were proclaimed by the Federal Government, and the Eastern Region attempted to secede, adopting the name of Biafra Republic. The twelve new states have, therefore, only been enforced for part of the area, and the civil war which broke out between Biafra and the Nigerian Federal Government still continues. In consequence, in order to avoid confusion, all references to Nigeria's regions will refer to the situation prior to 1967.

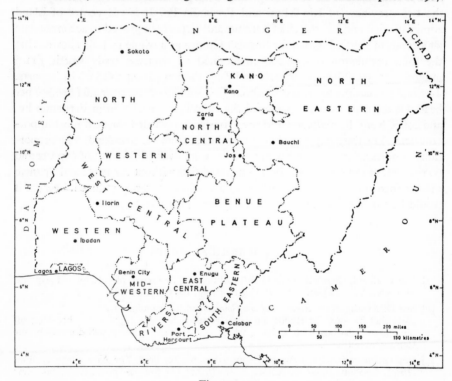

Figure 14.17

[11] See J. R. V. Prescott, Nigeria's Regional Boundary Problems, *Geographical Review*, **49**, 1959, pp. 485–505.

[12] See revealing election map and commentary in J. R. V. Prescott, The Function and Methods of Electoral Geography, *Annals of the Association of American Geographers*, **49**, 1959, pp. 296–304.

[13] *Federation of Nigeria National Development Plan 1962–68*, Federal Ministry of Economic Development, Lagos, 1962.

[14] See R. J. Harrison Church, articles on Mauritania in *West Africa*, October 29, November 5 and November 12, 1960.

[15] R. J. Harrison Church, Port Etienne: a Mauritanian Pioneer Town, *Geographical Journal*, **128**, 1962, pp. 498–504.

[16] H. R. Jarrett, Sierra Leone, *Focus*, American Geographical Society, vol. 8, no. 4, December, 1957.

[17] R. J. Harrison Church, Gambia and Mali, I, The Present Position, *West Africa*, June 25th, 1960.

[18] R. J. Harrison Church, Gambia and Mali, II, Problems and Consequences of Association, *West Africa*, July 2nd, 1960.

[19] O. Ribeiro, A Ilha do Fogo e as Suas Erupções, Lisbôa, Junta de Investigaçóes do Ultramar, Memories, *Serie Geografica I*, 1954.
See also account of above in P. Gourou, Fogo, ou un Géographie de la Pauvreté, *Les Cahiers d'Outre-Mer*, **11**, 1958, pp. 9–24.

[20] H. Lains e Silva, Esboço da Carta de Aptidão Agrícola de São Tomé e Príncipe, *Garcia de Orta*, vol. 6, Lisbon, 1958, pp. 61–86. (Review by R. J. Houk in *Geographical Review*, **50**, 1960, pp. 119–20.)

[21] R. J. Harrison Church, *West Africa*, London, 5th ed., 1966, p. 518.

CHAPTER 15

Conclusion

Of the entire area that is politically West Africa only 0·7 per cent is still (April 1967) colonial, and the population of this small area is rather less than 1·0 per cent of the total. The attainment of independence by almost all the territories concerned brings a re-assessment of their relationships to one another, to other territories within Africa and to territories overseas. Whilst the colonial frontiers have on the whole been preserved, and whilst the economic and political links with the metropolitan countries have for the most part been maintained, independence has brought into power African governments, whose interests are within their own territories, or within Africa rather than without, and in many cases has revived older tribal traditions and given a new significance to regional issues. As discussed in the introduction, the notion of 'West Africa' derived at least in part from the idea of a Guinea coast, that is from its relation to Europe and its development by European commercial interests. Common interests within the hinterland of the Guinea coast led to the formation by the French and British of federations or loose associations of their 'West African' colonies. These federations and associations are now disappearing, and if they are being replaced by any new form of association, that association would appear to be African rather than 'West African'. Pan-Africanism would embrace the continent. In this connection one may note the existence for a while of political accord between the Casablanca group of states on the one hand – the United Arab Republic, Ghana, Guinea, Mali and Morocco together with the Sudan – and the former Monrovia conference group on the other, including most other independent African states.

The physical conditions within neighbouring Equatorial Africa are similar to those within West Africa, or at least the differences are small, much less between the areas hitherto meant by either of these terms, than between either of these areas and 'East', 'Central' or 'Southern' Africa. Admittedly the West African savannas have much in common with the savannas of East and Central Africa, but due to their peculiar relation with the Guinean zone and with North Africa, their development has been quite different. The Guinean zones of West and Equatorial Africa, including the Congo basin, form one huge area of hot, moist lands with a long rainy season, similar vegetation, similar food crops, and not dissimilar African traditions. The ancient states of West Africa were paralleled by those of the Congo basin. There is therefore a good case for the recognition now of a large formal geographical region of 'Western Africa' to include the former West Africa, Equatorial Africa and the Belgian Congo. The notion serves more than an academic exercise for it re-orients thinking about the relationships and development of the newly-independent African states.

The importance of what has been called 'tribalism' in the development of the new states has been perhaps overstressed by outgoing political authorities and underrated by incoming governments. Yet each West African government described has had to face the problem of creating unity, and, because the forces concerned were regional and liable to dismember the new states, has tended either to limit or even suppress the opposition forces. Yet despite these difficulties of creating local unity some governments, such as that of Ghana, appear to have regarded the task of creating even wider unities as not impossible. Others, such as that of Nigeria, significantly the largest unit in terms of population with nearly 59 per cent of the total and itself a federation, have opposed the pan-African idea, and have contended that the difficulties of achieving unity at home are great enough. Thus the late Prime Minister of the Northern Region, Alhaji Sir Ahmadu Bello, Sardauna of Sokoto, whose Northern People's Congress had the largest number of seats in the Federal Parliament, expressed his doubts concerning proposals for larger unions: 'The standard of living of most of our people is too low, our social services are too limited, our agriculture needs developing and industry is only just starting. These are grave and serious problems and in my view we must deal with them before we take on more and unknown problems.' [1] However, even if greater unities are not achieved or are achieved only on a limited scale it has been claimed that many of the political boundaries need revision.[2] There is a good case for local revision to satisfy minority complaints on the lines suggested by Prescott, but large-scale revision would now seem impossible. Only union of the territories concerned could resolve the complaints made by the Ewe and by other groups divided by international frontiers. One may even ask what constitutes an 'unrealistic boundary'? The notion of natural frontiers has been dying for some time. Are ethnic frontiers easier either to establish or define? In any case the so-called tribes are not great immutable unities, but are themselves the product of the dismemberment and re-unification of other social groups. It might be agreed that as social systems they can no longer serve any major useful purpose, and should make way for groupings better suited to modern economic and political realities. When the newly-independent states are seeking to achieve their own extra-tribal loyalty, the re-unification of dismembered tribes ceases to be a practical issue, except where it may be raised for some local political purpose.

Much more importance is attached by the new governments to economic than to social problems. Within West Africa economic problems, like social issues, are markedly regionalized. Economic development has been confined mainly to small, widely-separated areas, mainly coastal in location. The only major interior area of high productivity is Hausaland in Northern Nigeria, with its high population densities and its great production for export of groundnuts and cotton. The other coastal areas of high productivity with correspondingly high incomes are associated also with high population densities: south-eastern and south-western Nigeria, southern Ghana, south-eastern Ivory Coast, and western Senegal. But apart from these great areas of cocoa and oil-seed production, there still remains the contrast between areas of moderate productivity and incomes, and areas of very low productivity. Productivity is at its lowest and is least commercial in character in that zone of lowest population density which extends from west to east across approximately the centre of West Africa. This 'Middle Belt' is nearest the coast in south-western Ivory Coast. Its problems have been described in its Nigerian portions, since Nigeria is the only state with great latitudinal extent, and within which the question of developing the Middle Belt is of major importance. In the other states the problem is important enough, but the Middle Belt in each of them occupies a peripheral position, and except in Upper Volta, does not lie across the main lines of communication. With very low densities of population Middle Belt areas suffer a high degree of tsetse fly infestation, severely limiting the possibilities of developing pastoralism, either in the form of ranching or mixed farming. The all too frequent outcropping of laterite or the occurrence of only thin soil horizons similarly limits agriculture. Existing settlements are scattered, and only in a few locations, as amongst the Nupe, are there extensive areas well developed agriculturally. Health is threatened, particularly by fly-borne diseases such as sleeping sickness and river blindness, which not only present a problem to existing settlement, but limit the creation of new settlement units in order to make use of the 'empty' lands.

Distance has set great limits to West African economic development, and despite the construction of a great network of roads and railways in less than half a century, transport costs are still high compared with those by sea. So long as economic development must depend on exchange with overseas territories, the coastal regions must retain their present advantage, and attract the greater part of the migrant labour forces. Yet this advantage of the coast lands for the production of raw materials, both agricultural and mineral, for export, has in turn proved a disadvantage for the development of new industries, which must face the competition of overseas production. Frequently railway freight rates have favoured export crop production in the interior by a disguised subsidy in the form of a flat rate, whilst imposing differential rates according to distances on imported commodities. Thus a new industry, providing that fuel, resources, labour and market are available, may in some cases have found a more favourable location in the interior. A policy of protection may be necessary in the coastal lands, but it carries with it the danger of an international trade war. However, as the new states develop and as they increase their overseas trade, they must begin to spend an increasing proportion of their capital accumulation and loans on production for the home market, and may need to revise both their freight rates and their communications net. Few states in West Africa today are not concerned to produce whatever they need to import at home wherever possible, in order that a greater proportion of overseas earnings may be spent on items which cannot be produced in Africa. At least West Africa's roads and railways have had the advantage of the existence of comparatively level surfaces inland, and the highest densities of population have tended to locate themselves on the more level lands. River transport has been neglected, partly because of poor physical conditions, and partly because the great waterways mostly penetrate areas of low population density. Improvement schemes such as those suggested by NEDECO may, however, offer the advantage of cheap river transport to develop low population density areas. Only cheap transport could in some cases make such development possible. Thus if any portion of the Middle Belt is more favoured than others for development, it is the Nigerian portion, where the rivers Niger and Benue may yet give the water route into the interior sought by the early explorers, and may also provide cheap power.

From the geographical viewpoint water resources are the most outstanding asset needing development in West Africa, as in many other tropical lands. Where rainfall is heavy for long periods or continuous throughout the year, drainage is needed for improved cultivation, and high soil acidities may be a problem. Elsewhere the marked dry season, frequently long, is the chief limitation to agricultural productivity and practice. In the present condition of much of West Africa's cultivation, the dry season provides a valuable rest period, and the desiccating harmattan, which is normally its accompaniment, provides ideal conditions for the burning hitherto regarded as essential. The greater development of rotations, green manuring, and of planted fallows, and the introduction of manures, composts and artificial fertilizers may, however, change the whole question of balanced use of soils. The lack of winter means not only that certain chemical and bacterial processes take place in the soil throughout the year, but that plant growth may be continuous, providing water is available. More careful use of rain and ground water, and the greater use of sub-surface supplies may therefore lengthen the growing season, to make possible not only more succession cropping or even double cropping, but the cultivation of plants which need longer growing periods. It may also provide the dry season pastures essential for the further development of the schemes for 'mixed farming' so far attempted. Some use has already been made of rivers and sub-surface water, where physical conditions allow, and where overcrowding has created a demand for increased food supplies locally, or where towns provide a good market for garden produce. Food production could be increased, however, to satisfy not only West African demands for both a higher standard of living and the needs of a growing population, but even, where economically possible, to provide an export overseas. Although Asian methods of water conservation are practised in areas orographically, and in many cases geologically, distinct from West Africa, yet it is conceivable that some of those methods, subject to adaptation, may be applied in the West African environment. Hitherto great bodies of running or standing water have offered not so much the advantage of improved cropping as the disadvantage of bad health. But here tropical medicine has much to offer to reduce or even exterminate the fly-borne diseases commonly associated with water. The need for both hydrological and climatological investigation is great. The development of water resources, however, will satisfy not only the needs of agriculture, the basic industry, but the need for greatly increased and purer domestic supplies, the needs of mining and industry, and the needs for power. West Africa's poverty in fossil fuels, except in Nigeria, and except possibly in the few sedimentary basins outside Nigeria, may be offset by the development of hydro-electric power, but the cost of removing the disadvantages of West African river régimes will be high. Even so, with the present high cost of electricity in territories where fuels must be imported, the high capital cost may be easily repaid.

High air temperatures are not so great a problem perhaps as water resources, although the European and North American may normally consider heat as the outstanding feature of tropical lands. The major temperature feature is the occurrence not of very high temperatures, but the non-occurrence of temperature below freezing point, and, over most of West Africa, below 42°F. However, the generally high temperatures have their distinctive effect on soils and on the inhabitants, who must suffer some degree of enervation or desiccation according to relative humidities. Architecture and clothing must be adapted to heat, and the demand for refrigeration and air-conditioning is rapidly increasing. Daily work periods in factories and offices are normally shorter than in the temperate world. The working day begins and ends earlier. There may be a case for a greater proportion of night work, and cheap power will make possible a greatly extended use of air-conditioning. Again, much more research is needed on labour efficiency in relation to temperatures to calculate the gain of lowering temperatures against the costs. Associated with the lack of low temperatures are certain diseases and insect pests unknown in the temperate lands. The distinctive character of such diseases and pests has attracted to them considerable publicity. Without wishing to deny the importance of malaria, yellow fever, sleeping sickness, and other distinctively tropical diseases, one must stress the need for more preventive work for those diseases already known and partly controlled in the temperate world, but which are still responsible for reduced efficiency and many millions of deaths in the tropics, particularly smallpox, meningitis and the deficiency diseases. The tendency to associate climate and disease is traditional and misleading.

Except in the northern portions of West Africa, that is in the Sudanic and Sahelian zones, the soils tend to suffer from the rapid break-down of humus and the leaching associated with the tropical world. The phosphorus content of West African soils is on the whole low, and annual crops are particularly susceptible to applications of soluble phosphate. As there appears to be a good relation between the amount of soluble phosphate available and the length of fallows, more intensive use of West African soils may make particularly heavy demands on artificial sources of phosphorus, whilst in the woody fallow areas any reduction in the supply of wood ash will similarly demand heavier applications of potash. Increasing densities of agricultural population will bring their own peculiar soil problems. Accelerated soil erosion due to heavier use of soils is a serious problem in only a few areas as yet, but the further development of soil conservation services and increased work on soil research in order to make a proper inventory of West African soils would appear essential in a region where dependence on soils is so great. The dangers of 'laterization', a distinctive feature, have almost certainly been overstressed, but more careful use of thin soil horizons, and of soils containing concretionary materials is needed, together with development of work already begun on the development of soils on laterites, or where possible the removal of such concretionary crusts.

Whilst many geographers have properly stressed West Africa's physical problems, they have tended to neglect, particularly in agriculture, some of the economic problems. Soils and water resources are of vital importance, but so is the efficiency of the methods employed by the cultivator, and the size of his market. Local limitations of productivity and earning capacity make possible only a small market for those cultivators who may find the means to increase their output. Hence, in part, the attractions of the enormous overseas market, which, in a few areas at least, has brought an increase of earning capacity, and enlarged local markets. In part the new demands have been met by the commercialization of local food production, but only in part. West Africa, with an agriculture whose efficiency could be greatly improved, and with land still unproductive which could be made to yield, has become a food importer. Whilst those territories with little overseas trade show a high proportion of food imports for expatriate technicians and managers, and a high proportion of beer and spirits imports, there are several territories with extensive overseas trade whose food imports are as much as a quarter of the total, and include large quantities of wheat flour, rice, fish and animal products. In 1962, of Ghana's total import of some £119 million worth of goods, 7 per cent was devoted solely to livestock, wheat flour and sugar. In the same year Senegal spent 7·7 per cent of its import bill on rice alone. Analysis of Nigeria's food, beverages and tobacco bill in 1962 shows that first came imported fish, chiefly Norwegian stockfish at £7·2 million, secondly sugar at £3·2 million, thirdly wheat flour at £3·0 million, and fourthly beer and other fermented cereal beverages at £2·8 million. Other major imports under the same heading included salt, tobacco, milk and milk products. West Africa is becoming an important food importer particularly in terms of value of those protein foodstuffs which the region lacks, but also perhaps surprisingly of cereals and flour. West African agriculture may expect to satisfy eventually the demand for rice, but the recently acquired taste for wheaten bread in southern Nigeria and southern Ghana can only be met by importation. Except in certain overcrowded areas, notably in south-eastern Nigeria, the need for agriculture is not so much increased production per acre, as increased production per man, and traditional methods of cultivation normally show the cultivator's awareness of this. Mechanization has not proved the answer to the development of low population density areas that its sponsors had hoped. Labour costs are still appreciably lower than the running costs of mechanical equipment, and technical skills are at a premium. Moreover, many schemes have been over-ambitious and have lacked essential preliminary ecological investigation. Much increased output may yet come from more efficient use of labour within the existing agricultural system, by planned use of labour time, and the introduction of more efficient tools and perhaps fertilizers, and from the lengthening of the growing season in areas limited by long dry periods, from which at present labour must emigrate every year if it is to be fully occupied. To make such increased output worth while, the market must, however, be enlarged, and the cultivator must be offered a greater variety of commodities to encourage him to earn more in order to buy. In this context the development of some measure of industrialization may be costly, but it may not only provide more commodities for the internal market, but may provide a market in itself for agricultural produce. Some economists have stressed the need for increased food production as the basis of industrial development, but such increased production may prove expensive and may not find a market even where diets are claimed to be unsatisfactory. Improvements in West Africa's agricultural and mining productivity have done much to increase prosperity, but prosperity has now become dependent on the export trade, and in most territories this trade is heavily dependent on only one or two commodities. In some territories such as Senegal, south-eastern Ivory Coast, southern Ghana and south-western Nigeria purchasing power is higher than in many territories of south-east Asia, modern transport and communications networks have been developed, and there is local capital for investment in both agriculture and industry, besides a greater attraction for capital from overseas. Yet there is a need for diversification to offset a dependence on overseas markets, which may suffer either from a slump in prices or competition. Malaya, Indonesia and the Congo are all important competitors. Prices of oil-seeds and vegetable oils have been declining in recent years and the marketing boards have to offer price support. Only the disastrous crop failures of China and the political troubles of the Congo Republic (Kinshasa) helped to raise oil-seed prices in 1961. With the failure of some western schemes, a few of the new governments have turned to the methods of socialized agriculture, and have tried to introduce co-operative farming. The success or failure of these ventures has yet to be seen, but at least the hand labour element is still great, the attempts so far made are not too divorced from traditional practice, and the combination of labour within a larger unit offers the possibility of attaining greater efficiency.

West Africa's population was estimated in 1963 at some 95 millions, a considerable increase on earlier estimates. Censuses hardly bear comparison, yet there is a reasonable body of evidence to suggest that as elsewhere in the tropical world there is an increase of population and that increase may be guessed at about $1\frac{1}{2}$–2 per cent per annum. In the few crowded areas such a rate of increase may prove a great problem, although the probability that it is highest in the towns, which are expanding their demand for labour rapidly, is perhaps some compensation. Over most of West Africa, however, particularly in the savannas and in the Middle Belt, the problems of 'underpopulation' are at least as acute as those of 'overpopulation', and the problem of overcrowding is likely to be localized for some years to come. There is considerable room for improvement in living conditions and medical services before the death rate will be markedly reduced. Urbanism is increasingly rapid, and despite the slums which have already been developed, standards of living and of health are generally higher in the towns. With the greater concentrations of population achieved, the task of supplying people with water, electricity and other services becomes cheaper. There may be space in West Africa, but without more people it may prove too costly in modern terms to use.

Some West African governments may see similar problems to their own in the socialist or communist countries with mainly peasant populations. They may, therefore, consider socialist methods of production more suited to their needs. Yet at the same time they may be willing to promote every means of economic development, encourage local private investment and capital investment from non-socialist countries. France, the United Kingdom and the United States have provided much of the capital investment of West Africa either in the form of gifts or loans. In recent years France has offered more financial aid to West Africa than has Britain, and in many cases with less return, for the problems of economic development in the lower population density areas of the former French West Africa have been great. Ghana and Nigeria particularly have proved on the whole more prosperous, and have attracted by comparison considerable private investment. Much more investment is planned and the speed of economic progress is likely to be increased. This is needful because, despite the advances made, the gap between the living standards of Western Europe and West Africa may well have widened.[3] Western Europe and West Africa have benefited for long by their commercial relation. The terms of that relation may change with new political and economic conditions, but the relation as such is likely to remain for at least several decades.

'For our part, we came to Africa as traders and it is as traders that we shall, in the last resort, remain; for it is our trade that is wanted, and African trade that we need. In this, the inclinations of the two peoples coincide. The future of our missionary endeavour – the spread of the gospel of parliamentary democracy – is, I think, a great deal more dubious. But the parable of the sower warns us to expect only a modicum of fertile ground – as do the words of the poet that there are nine and sixty ways of constructing tribal lays, and every single one of them is right.'[4]

BIBLIOGRAPHICAL NOTES

[1] Address to the Overseas Press Club in New York in July 1960 in *Africa Special Report*, August 1960, vol. 5, No. 8.

[2] The case for boundary revision has been made notably by Harrison Church, who has written of 'unrealistic boundaries' (*West Africa*, 1957, p. 533) and by J. R. V. Prescott, who has presented the regional boundary problems of Nigeria and made proposals towards their solution (Nigeria's Regional Boundary Problems, *Geographical Review*, 49, 1959, pp. 485–505).

[3] United Africa Company, *Statistical and Economic Review*, 23, 1959.

[4] Elspeth Huxley, *Four Guineas*, London, 1954.

A Note on the Statistical Sources

Much of the West African statistical material is based on only the crudest of estimates. There have been few attempts at accurate counting of either population or productivity, and possible margins of error are in consequence considerable. Even some of the so-called censuses are based on samples so small that large errors in the published data are quite probable. Attempts at counting or at estimation vary considerably in method and in depth of treatment from country to country, and, within a given country, from 'census' to 'census'. In consequence it becomes very difficult to assess the relative values of counts purporting to treat the same material in different countries, or to compare one census with another. Possible margins of error may be greater than the differences. In this situation attempts to calculate growth become extremely difficult, and in some cases impossible. Regional comparisons likewise are hard to assess, except perhaps where very big differences are involved. Maps using such data and purporting to show distributions of people, livestock or crop production, merely summarize the statistical guesswork in a convenient areal form. They do no more than hint at probable distributions, and need careful interpretation with the aid of the few detailed field studies available, or of the few more reliable sample counts and surveys such as that at Bongouanou.[1] Many of the problems of mapping with such material have been discussed in the *Oxford Regional Economic Atlas of Africa* and in *Essays on African Population* edited by Barbour and Prothero.[2] We wish merely to comment on the problems peculiar to the data used in this study.

In using statistics for the purpose of areal comparison, the main problems are concerned with the size and consistency of the units used, and the number of years between the earliest and the latest counts or estimates. To obtain figures for the whole of West Africa which refer to only one year is quite impossible. Generally one has to choose between using censuses or sample censuses spread over a fairly long period, say ten years, and using mostly very doubtful estimates, but spread over only two to three years. Generally the smallest statistical units available are the cercles of former French West Africa and the divisions of former British West Africa. These can be very large units in areas of low population density and low unit area productivity as in Mali or Niger, and are frequently quite small in areas of high population density and high unit area productivity as in southern Ghana or southern Nigeria. Analysis is therefore frequently confused by this lack of uniformity in the net which provides many more items at the high density and high productivity end of the range and tends to record greater extremes of high than of low density and productivity.

The population maps (Figs. 1.2 and 1.3) are based on data spread over the ten-year period, 1952–61. Liberia has been omitted because it lacked a published census at the time of writing. The excellent attempts at estimation from air photo analysis[3] have not been ignored. This is simply a small attempt at some kind of consistency amidst the abundance of doubtful material available. For former French West Africa figures by cercles for 1956 were published in the *Annuaire Statistique de l'Afrique Occidentale Française* published in 1957. These figures were mostly estimates for the censuses proper of French West Africa were, unfortunately, never carried out over the entire area. However, there appears to be no better material available in point of accuracy, and there have been few attempts at counting or careful estimation since, and none over the whole of former French territory in a single year. The Nigerian census or rather censuses of 1952–3 provide the earliest data used. More recent attempts at counting have either been suppressed as unreliable or still remain unpublished in a divisional form. [4] The Ghana census of 1960 is undoubtedly the most accurate and carefully compiled of all the counts published, and has the additional advantage of careful mapping of census unit boundaries. The units used were generally much smaller than in any former count, and in consequence the Ghana portion of the map showing population densities by cercles and administrative divisions (Fig. 1.2) may be distinguished immediately by its greater detail. For Sierra Leone unfortunately the 1963 census had not been published at the time of writing, and 1960 estimates had to be used.

The maps of crop and cattle distribution refer almost entirely to the years 1951–4. For Nigeria the 1950–1 sample census of agriculture has been used, and for French West Africa the 1954 estimates available in the *Annuaire Statistique de l'Afrique Occidentale Française* published in 1956. For the remaining territories various estimates referring to the four-year period were used, with the exception of Liberia for which no data were available in any comparable form. Within Nigeria the two portions of Oyo Province (Oyo and Ife Divisions), for which no returns were available in the 1950–1 sample census, have been left blank. Later material was available at the time of writing for certain portions of Nigeria and of former French West Africa, but the advantage of having over-all coverage within a short period seemed to outweigh the advantage of more recent material, more especially as the possibilities of error in the more recent estimates seemed almost as great as in the earlier figures. Moreover, the probable margins of error in figures for agricultural production seemed so great that there appeared to be little to choose between one particular year's data and another. Nigerian counts, for example, generally depended on the distinction first of all of strata or regional divisions with some anticipated uniformity of production or agricultural type. Within each stratum a random sample of $1\frac{1}{2}$ per cent of villages was chosen, and within each village 5 per cent of tax-payers were selected. The 'farms' or holdings of these people were surveyed field by field and sample plots of one-fortieth of an acre were selected within each field as the basis for crop checking and weighing. In an economic atlas, data some twelve to fifteen years old could hardly find a place, but in a text of this kind they can provide useful regional comparison, especially when allied to a description which is concerned more especially with the whole pattern of agricultural change, and in particular with the changes which have taken place since 1945.

BIBLIOGRAPHICAL NOTES

1] J. L. Boutillier, *Bongouanou, Côte d'Ivoire*, Paris, 1960.

[2] P. H. Ady, Clarendon Press and A. H. Hazelwood, *Africa*, Oxford Regional Economic Atlas, Oxford, 1965.
K. M. Barbour and R. M. Prothero (eds), *Essays on African Population*, London, 1961. See also R. M. Prothero, Problems of Population Mapping in an Under-Developed Territory (Northern Nigeria), *Nigerian Geographical Journal*, 3(1), 1960, pp. 1–7; and African Population Maps: Problems and Progress, *Geog. Annaler*, 45(4), 1963.

[3] Particularly outstanding is the attempt to estimate Liberian population by hut counting from aerial photographs. See *Resources and Economic Development of Liberia*, Joint U.S.–Liberian Commission, 1957.

[4] See Reference [7], p. 62. The 1962 Nigerian census recorded 36·5 million.

Index of Maps and Diagrams

Index of Places and Peoples

———◦⟨⟩◦———

An attempt has been made to keep spelling uniform for each name, but this has not always been possible. Not only does spelling vary as between French and English writers, but also in many cases within one language. In general one form has been preferred in this study, but references to the work of other writers inevitably require use of alternative spellings on occasion.

Page numbers in italics indicate identification on a map or diagram.

Subject Index

Numbers in italics refer to maps or diagrams

Beecroft, Consul John, 399
Beer, 118, 166, 562, 571, 573, 729
Beidan, 17
Belime, E., 518, 646
Bella, 19
Bello, Alhaji Sir Ahmadu, 703, 706
Berlin Agreement and Conference, 405, 407, 412, 585
Bevels, 226, 231, 268
Bicycles, 169, 527, 613; assembly, 564
Birni, 360
Bocage, 639
Boli lands, 520, 656, 657
Bore holes, 192, 235, 368, 436, 449–450, 485–486; quadrilateral system, 450, 509–510
Bornhardts, xxii, 226–228, 231, 243, 268, 273, 277, 306, 350
Borrow pits, xx, 164, 362
Botanical gardens, 501–502
Bottling, 561, 562–563, 707
Bouli, 142
Boundary, regional, Cross River, xviii
Bowal, (pl. bowé), 12, 26, 46, 143, 144, 193, 266, 291, see also under GEOLOGY, laterite
Bowen, Rev. T. J., 401
Brass ware, 165
Bread, see under FOOD
Breezes, land and sea, 181–183
Bremen Society, 401
Brewing, 166, 562–563, 689, 707
Brick manufacture, 303, 552
Bridges, 244, 302, 436, 440, 590, 595, 596, 600, 601
British Commonwealth, 673
British Cotton Growing Association (B.C.G.A.), 472, 490, 597
British West Africa, xv, 407–410, 499
Bronze casting, 165
Builders' Brigade, 523, 681
Bullock carts, 596–597
Bunds, 649, 657
Burning, in cultivation, xxvi, 67, 103, 105, 214, 368, 502, 514, 516, 727; of grassland, 141, 145, 148, 210–212, 368, 509; -control in, 635; relation to soils, 213
Bus services, 609, 610, 619
Busije, 367
Buxton, T. F., 399

Caillié, René, 391
Calabash, used as float, 162, 172
Cameroons Development Corp. (C.D.C.), 500
Cameroon Republic, xv, 709
Campbell, Sir Neil, Governor of Sierra Leone, 472

Canals; Asagny, 604; cut by Sonni Ali, 253–254, 353; MacGregor, 452; Vridi, 294, 436, 614, 700; -early attempt to cut, 593
Canning, 561, 562, 689, 702, 707
Canoes, 121, 160, 162, 166, 245, 337, 346, 353, 541, 584, 615; of papyrus, 162
Canyon, submarine, 239, 614
Cape Verde Is., Colony of, 718–719
Capitals, colonial, 405, 430–432
Caravans, 167, 341, 424, see Azalai
Cargo, moisture condensation on, 288–290; trans-shipment, 589
Carriers, see Porterage
Casks, wooden, 169
Caste, 17, 19, 24, 141, 341, 346, 349, 355
Catch-pits, 322
Cattle, see under LIVESTOCK
Causeways, stone, 27
Cave dwellings, see under DWELLINGS
Cayor, kingdom of, 23, 397, 398, 633
Cement, 220, 299, 551, 560, 619, 689, 707
Cereals, wild, 146, 253
Cess pits, 69
Charcoal, 164, 333, 343
Chariots, 169, 170
Chemicals industry, 563, 689
Chiefs, 409–410
Christianity, spread of, 380, 381, 400–402
Cisterns, 410, 434, 449–450
Cities, see TOWNS
Civil Service, 415
Clapperton, Lt. Hugh, 391
Clay, building, 164, 552
CLIMATE
    Change, 176–178, 254–258, 261–262, see Sahara, former southward extension
    Description, 179 ff., 202–205, 258, 261, 264–265, 270–271, 276, 277, 278, 284, 288–290, 292, 294–295
    Relation to disease, 201–208
    Relation to land forms, x, 180, 271, 276, 285–287
    Zoning with altitude, 271, 305, 307
Clinker grinding, 560, 665
Close-farmed zone, around Kano, 118–119, 127, 212, 281, 362–365
Cloth, cotton, 165, 371, 489, 490, 560–561
Coast, drowned, 226, 290
'Coast, The', Guinea Coast, xv, xxi, 384, 724
Coastlands, 288–307
Coffin squadron, 413
Coke, 550, 707
Colonial Development Act, 624
Colonial Development and Welfare Acts, 624
Colonial Rule, direct, 403–412; indirect, 409–410, 412

Author Index

784